IF FOUND, please notify and arrange return to owner. This text is an important study guide for the owner's career and/or exam preparation.

Name: _____

Address: _____

City, State, ZIP: _____

Telephone: (_____) _____ Email: _____

GLEIM Exam Questions and Explanations Series

Auditing & Systems EQE with Test Prep

Business Law/Legal Studies EQE with Test Prep

Federal Tax EQE with Test Prep

Financial Accounting EQE with Test Prep

Cost/Managerial Accounting EQE with Test Prep

GLEIM Review Systems

GLEIM CPA Review System

GLEIM CIA Review System
Updated for the New 3-Part Exam

GLEIM CMA Review System

GLEIM EA Review System

Use the order form provided at the back of this book, or contact us at www.gleim.com or (800) 874-5346.

REVIEWERS AND CONTRIBUTORS

Tatiana Cherniawsky-Walsh graduated from Queens College, City University of New York in 2012 with a Bachelor of Arts degree in Accounting and Information Systems. She is pursuing her Master of Science in Accounting at Queens College, and her goal is to get her CPA license and pursue her career in auditing. Ms. Cherniawsky-Walsh is a member of the Golden Key International Honour Society and a student member of the NYSSCPA. She helped develop the instructor materials to be used in conjunction with this text.

Garrett W. Gleim, B.S., CPA (not in public practice), received a Bachelor of Science degree from The Wharton School at the University of Pennsylvania. Mr. Gleim coordinated the production staff, reviewed the manuscript, and provided production assistance throughout the project.

Grady M. Irwin, J.D., is a graduate of the University of Florida College of Law, and he has taught in the University of Florida College of Business. Mr. Irwin provided substantial editorial assistance throughout the project.

Dr. Steven A. Solieri, CPA, CMA, CIA, CISA, CITP, CFF, CRISC, is an Assistant Professor at Queens College in Flushing, New York, and is a Founding Member in the Firm of Solieri & Solieri, CPAs, PLLC, New Hyde Park, NY, where he currently practices. Dr. Solieri earned his Ph.D. from Binghamton University and holds four Masters from the University of Michigan, Pace University, Kettering University, and Binghamton University. Dr. Solieri helped develop the instructor materials to be used in conjunction with this text.

A PERSONAL THANKS

This manual would not have been possible without the extraordinary effort and dedication of Jacob Brunny, Julie Cutlip, Eileen Nickl, Teresa Soard, Justin Stephenson, Joanne Strong, Elmer Tucker, and Candace Van Doren, who typed the entire manuscript and all revisions, and drafted and laid out the diagrams and illustrations in this book.

The authors also appreciate the production and editorial assistance of Jessica Felkins, Chris Hawley, Katie Larson, Diana Leon, Cary Marcous, Shane Rapp, Drew Sheppard, and Martha Willis.

The authors also appreciate the critical reading assistance of Jared Armenti, Jeffrey Bennett, Ellen Buhl, Ray Busler, Stephanie Garrison, Daniela Guanipa, Alyssa Hagerty, Jack Hahne, Bethany Harris, Elizabeth Ibarra, Binish John, Eric Malinasky, Jerry Mathis, Dustin Wallace, Yuan Wen, Diana Weng, Kenneth Wilbur, and Hailun Zhu.

Finally, we appreciate the encouragement, support, and tolerance of our families throughout this project.

TABLE OF CONTENTS

vi

DETAILED TABLE OF CONTENTS

PREFACE FOR CPA CANDIDATES

The purpose of this Gleim CPA Review study book is to help YOU prepare to pass the 2014 Auditing and Attestation (referred to throughout the rest of this text as Auditing or AUD) section of the CPA examination. Our overriding consideration is to provide an inexpensive, effective, and easy-to-use study program. This book

1. Explains how to optimize your grade by focusing on the Auditing section of the CPA exam.
2. Defines the subject matter tested on the Auditing section of the CPA exam.
3. Outlines all of the subject matter tested on the Auditing section in 20 easy-to-use-and-complete study units.
4. Presents multiple-choice questions from recent CPA examinations to prepare you for questions in future CPA exams. Our answer explanations are presented to the immediate right of each question for your convenience. Use a piece of paper to cover our answer explanations as you study the questions.
5. Presents several task-based simulations in each study unit to acquaint you with simulation task formats. Answer the simulations in your book. The answers and grading instructions follow each simulation.

The outline format, the spacing, and the question and answer formats in this book are designed to facilitate readability, learning, understanding, and success on the CPA exam. Our most successful candidates use the entire Gleim CPA Review System,* which includes books, CPA Test Prep, Audio Review, Gleim Online, Simulation Wizard, Exam Rehearsal, and access to a Personal Counselor; or a group study CPA review program. (Check our website for live courses we recommend.) This review book and all Gleim CPA Review materials are compatible with other CPA review materials and courses that follow the AICPA Content and Skill Specification Outlines (CSOs/SSOs).

To maximize the efficiency and effectiveness of your CPA review program, augment your studying with *How to Pass the CPA Exam: A System for Success*. This booklet has been carefully written and organized to provide important information to assist you in passing the CPA examination.

Thank you for your interest in the Gleim CPA Review materials. We deeply appreciate the thousands of letters and suggestions received from CIA, CMA, EA, RTRP, and CPA candidates during the past 5 decades.

If you use the Gleim materials, we want YOUR feedback immediately after the exam and as soon as you have received your grades. The CPA exam is NONDISCLOSED, and you will sign an attestation including, "I hereby agree that I will maintain the confidentiality of the Uniform CPA Examination. In addition, I agree that I will not divulge the nature or content of any Uniform CPA Examination question or answer under any circumstance . . ." We ask only for information about our materials, i.e., the topics that need to be added, expanded, etc. Our approach has AICPA approval.

Please go to www.gleim.com/feedbackAUD to share your suggestions on how we can improve this edition.

Good Luck on the Exam,

Irvin N. Gleim
William A. Hillison
December 2013

OPTIMIZING YOUR AUDITING SCORE

CBT-e Exam

Gleim Section Title	**Auditing**	Business	Financial	Regulation
AICPA Formal Title	**Auditing & Attestation**	Business Environment & Concepts	Financial Accounting & Reporting	Regulation
Acronym	**AUD**	BEC	FAR	REG
Exam Length	**4 hours**	3 hours	4 hours	3 hours
Testlets:				
Multiple-Choice	**3, 30 questions each**	3, 24 questions each	3, 30 questions each	3, 24 questions each
Simulations	**1 with 7 tasks**	0	1 with 7 tasks	1 with 6 tasks
Written Communication	**0**	1 with 3 scenarios	0	0

The Auditing Standards Board Clarity Project

In an effort to make U.S. GAAS easier to read, understand, and apply, the Auditing Standards Board has redrafted the auditing sections into a new Codification of Statements on Auditing Standards. Under this clarity project, each standard presents the requirement paragraphs separate from an addendum of the application and example material. The new standards also converge as much as possible with the International Auditing Standards. In addition, material has been reorganized and redundancies removed. Standards have been given a new three-digit identification number. Virtually all the standards became effective at one time for audits on or after December 15, 2012.

FOLLOW THESE STEPS TO PASS THE EXAM

1. Read this **Introduction** to familiarize yourself with the content and structure of the Auditing section of the exam. In the following pages, you will find

    a. An **overview of the Auditing section** and what it generally tests, including

        1) The AICPA's Content Specification Outlines (CSOs) for Auditing, cross-referenced with the Gleim study units that contain each topic
        2) The AICPA's Skill Specification Outlines (SSOs) for Auditing
        3) The AICPA's suggested references for Auditing

    b. A detailed plan with **steps to obtain your CPA license**, including

        1) The order in which you should apply, register, and schedule your exam
        2) The studying tactics on which you should focus
        3) How to organize your study schedule to make the most out of each resource in the Gleim CPA Review System (i.e., books, CPA Test Prep, Audio Review, Gleim Online, Simulation Wizard, Exam Rehearsals, etc.)

    c. Tactics for your **actual test day**, including

        1) Time budgeting so you complete each testlet with time to review
        2) Question-answering techniques to obtain every point you can in both the multiple-choice and simulation testlets
        3) An explanation of how to be in control of your CPA exam

2. Scan the Gleim *How to Pass the CPA Exam: A System for Success* booklet and note where to revisit later in your studying process to obtain a deeper understanding of the of the CPA exam.

    a. *How to Pass the CPA Exam: A System for Success* has seven study units:

        Study Unit 1: The CPA Examination: An Overview and Preparation Introduction
        Study Unit 2: AICPA Content Specification Outlines and Skill Specification Outlines
        Study Unit 3: Content Preparation, Test Administration, and Performance Grading
        Study Unit 4: Multiple-Choice Questions
        Study Unit 5: Task-Based Simulations and Written Communications
        Study Unit 6: Preparing to Pass the CPA Exam
        Study Unit 7: How to Take the CPA Exam

    b. If you feel that you need even more details on the test-taking experience, watch our **Free Tutorial** at www.gleim.com/CPAbasics.

        1) This tutorial is best for candidates who have little or no experience with the basic computer skills required for the CPA exam (e.g., copy/paste, search, etc.).

    c. Additionally, the AICPA requires that all candidates review the tutorial and sample tests at www.aicpa.org.

3. Follow the steps outlined on page 11, "How to Study an Auditing Study Unit Using the Gleim CPA Review System." This is the **study plan** that our most successful candidates adhere to. Study until you have reached your **desired proficiency level** (e.g., 75%) for each study unit in Auditing.

    a. As you proceed, be sure to check any **Updates** that may have been released.

        1) Gleim Online, Simulation Wizard, and CPA Test Prep are updated automatically.
        2) Book updates can be viewed at www.gleim.com/CPAupdate, or you can have them emailed to you. The information box in the top right corner of page iv contains details.

      b.   **Review the *How to Pass the CPA Exam: A System for Success* booklet** and become completely comfortable with what will be expected from you on test day.

4.   Shortly before your test date, take an **Exam Rehearsal** (complimentary with the CPA Review System) at www.gleim.com/RehearseCPA.

      a.   The Gleim Exam Rehearsal is designed to exactly emulate the CPA test-taking experience at Prometric.

      b.   This timed, scored exam tests you not only on the content you have studied, but also on the question-answering and time-management techniques you have learned throughout the Gleim study process.

      c.   When you have completed the exam, consult with your Personal Counselor to discuss where you should **focus your review during the final days before your exam** (question-answering techniques, time management, specific content areas, etc.).

5.   **Take and PASS** the Auditing section of the CPA exam!

      a.   When you have completed the exam, please contact Gleim with your **suggestions, comments, and corrections**. We want to know how well we prepared you for your testing experience.

OVERVIEW OF AUDITING

Auditing is scheduled for 4 hours (240 minutes).

AICPA title:	Auditing and Attestation
AICPA acronym:	AUD
Gleim title/acronym:	Auditing/AUD
Question format:	90 multiple-choice questions in three testlets of 30 questions each
	One testlet with seven Task-Based Simulations
Areas covered:	I. (14%) Engagement Acceptance and Understanding the Assignment
	II. (18%) Understanding the Entity and Its Environment (including Internal Control)
	III. (18%) Performing Audit Procedures and Evaluating Evidence
	IV. (18%) Evaluating Audit Findings, Communications, and Reporting
	V. (14%) Accounting and Review Services Engagements
	VI. (18%) Professional Responsibilities

The Auditing and Attestation section tests knowledge and understanding of the following professional standards: Auditing standards promulgated in the United States of America [related to audits of an "Issuer" (a public company), a "Nonissuer" (an entity that is not a public company), governmental entities, not-for-profit entities, and employee benefit plans], standards related to attestation and assurance engagements, and standards for performing accounting and review services.

Candidates are expected to demonstrate an awareness of (1) the International Auditing and Assurance Standards Board (IAASB) and its role in establishing International Standards on Auditing (ISAs), (2) the differences between ISAs and U.S. auditing standards, and (3) the audit requirements under U.S. auditing standards that apply when they perform audit procedures on a U.S. company that supports an audit report based upon the auditing standards of another country, or the ISAs.

This section also tests knowledge of professional responsibilities of certified public accountants, including ethics and independence. Candidates are also expected to demonstrate an awareness of (1) the International Ethics Standards Board for Accountants (IESBA) and its role in establishing requirements of the International Federation of Accountants (IFAC) *Code of Ethics for Professional Accountants* and (2) the independence requirements that apply when they perform audit procedures on a U.S. company that supports an audit report based upon the auditing standards of another country, or the ISAs.

In addition to demonstrating knowledge and understanding of the professional standards, candidates are required to demonstrate the skills required to apply that knowledge in performing auditing and attestation tasks as certified public accountants.

According to the AICPA, candidates will be expected to perform the following inclusive list of tasks to demonstrate such knowledge and skills:

- Demonstrate an awareness and understanding of the process by which standards and professional requirements are established for audit, attestation, and other services performed by CPAs, including the role of standard-setting bodies within the U.S. and those bodies with the authority to promulgate international standards.
- Differentiate between audits, attestation and assurance services, compilations, and reviews.
- Differentiate between the professional standards for issuers and nonissuers.
- Identify situations that might be unethical or a violation of professional standards, perform research and consultations as appropriate, and determine the appropriate action.
- Recognize potentially unethical behavior of clients and determine the impact on the services being performed.
- Demonstrate the importance of identifying and adhering to requirements, rules, and standards that are established by licensing boards within their states, and which may place additional professional requirements specific to their state of practice.
- Appropriately apply professional requirements in practice, and differentiate between unconditional requirements and presumptively mandatory requirements.
- Exercise due care in the performance of work.
- Demonstrate an appropriate level of professional skepticism in the performance of work.
- Maintain independence in mental attitude in all matters relating to the audit.
- Research relevant professional literature.

AICPA CONTENT SPECIFICATION OUTLINES (CSOs) WITH GLEIM CROSS-REFERENCES

In the Uniform CPA Examination Alert newsletter of Spring 2009, when it was first unveiling the new CBT-e exam, the AICPA indicated that the content specification outlines have several purposes, including

1. *Ensure that the testing of entry-level knowledge and skills that are important to the protection of the public interest is consistent across examination administrations*

2. *Determine what kinds of questions should be included on the CPA Examination so that every version of the examination reflects the required distribution and balance of knowledge and skill components*

3. *Provide candidates preparing for the examination with information about the subject matter that is eligible to be tested*

For your convenience, we have reproduced verbatim the AICPA's Auditing CSOs. We also have provided cross-references to the study units and subunits in this book that correspond to the CSOs' coverage. If one entry appears above a list, it applies to all items.

AICPA CONTENT SPECIFICATION OUTLINE

Auditing and Attestation

I. **Engagement Acceptance and Understanding the Assignment (14%)**

   A. Determine Nature and Scope of Engagement - 1.1-1.4

   B. Consider the Firm's Policies and Procedures Pertaining to Client Acceptance and Continuance - 1.5

   C. Communicate with the Predecessor Auditor - 3.1

   D. Establish an Understanding with the Client and Document the Understanding Through an Engagement Letter or Other Written Communication with the Client - 3.1

   E. Consider Other Planning Matters

   1. Consider using the work of other independent auditors - 3.2, 17.1
   2. Determine the extent of the involvement of professionals possessing specialized skills - 3.2, 4.2
   3. Consider the independence, objectivity, and competency of the internal audit function - 4.1

   F. Identify Matters Related to Planning and Prepare Documentation for Communications with Those Charged with Governance - 9.2

II. **Understanding the Entity and Its Environment (including Internal Control) (18%)**

   A. Determine and Document Materiality - 3.2, 3.3

   B. Conduct and Document Risk Assessment Discussions Among Audit Team, Concurrently with Discussion on Susceptibility of the Entity's Financial Statement to Material Misstatement Due to Fraud - 3.3

   C. Consideration of Fraud - 3.6

   1. Identify characteristics of fraud
   2. Document required discussions regarding risk of fraud
   3. Document inquiries of management about fraud
   4. Identify and assess risks that may result in material misstatements due to fraud

   D. Perform and Document Risk Assessment Procedures

   1. Identify, conduct and document appropriate inquiries of management and others within the entity - 3.4

   2. Perform appropriate analytical procedures to understand the entity and identify areas of risk - 3.5

   3. Obtain information to support inquiries through observation and inspection (including reading corporate minutes, etc.) - 3.4

   E. Consider Additional Aspects of the Entity and its Environment, including: Industry, Regulatory and Other External Factors; Strategies and Business Risks; Financial Performance - 3.4

   F. Consider Internal Control

   1. Perform procedures to assess the control environment, including consideration of the COSO framework and identifying entity-level controls - 5.1-5.4

   2. Obtain and document an understanding of business processes and information flows - 5.1-5.4

   3. Determine the effect of information technology on the effectiveness of an entity's internal control - 5.5

   4. Perform risk assessment procedures to evaluate the design and implementation of internal controls relevant to an audit of financial statements - 5.3

   5. Identify key risks associated with general controls in a financial IT environment, including change management, backup/recovery, and network access (e.g., administrative rights) - 5.5, 8.3

   6. Identify key risks associated with application functionality that supports financial transaction cycles, including: application access control (e.g., administrative access rights); controls over interfaces, integrations, and e-commerce; significant algorithms, reports, validation, edit checks, error handling, etc. - 5.5, 6.4, 7.5, 8.3

   7. Assess whether the entity has designed controls to mitigate key risks associated with general controls or application functionality - 5.5

8.   Identify controls relevant to reliable financial reporting and the period-end financial reporting process - SU 6, SU 7

9.   Consider limitations of internal control - 5.1

10.   Consider the effects of service organizations on internal control - 9.4

11.   Consider the risk of management override of internal controls - 3.6

G.   Document an Understanding of the Entity and its Environment, including Each Component of the Entity's Internal Control, in Order to Assess Risks - 5.3, 5.4

H.   Assess and Document the Risk of Material Misstatements - SU 8

1.   Identify and document financial statement assertions and formulate audit objectives including significant financial statement balances, classes of transactions, disclosures, and accounting estimates

2.   Relate the identified risks to relevant assertions and consider whether the risks could result in a material misstatement to the financial statements

3.   Assess and document the risk of material misstatement that relates to both financial statement level and specific assertions

4.   Identify and document conditions and events that may indicate risks of material misstatement

I.   Identify and Document Significant Risks that Require Special Audit Consideration

1.   Significant recent economic, accounting, or other developments - 3.4
2.   Related parties and related party transactions - 4.3
3.   Improper revenue recognition - 3.4, 11.1
4.   Nonroutine or complex transactions - 3.4
5.   Significant accounting estimates - 4.4, 13.2
6.   Illegal acts - 3.7

III.   Performing Audit Procedures and Evaluating Evidence (18%)

A.   Develop Overall Responses to Risks - 8.2

1.   Develop overall responses to risks identified and use the risks of material misstatement to drive the nature, timing, and extent of further audit procedures

2.   Document significant risks identified, related controls evaluated, and overall responses to address assessed risks

3.   Determine and document performance materiality/level(s) of tolerable misstatement

B.   Perform Audit Procedures Responsive to Risks of Material Misstatement; Obtain and Document Evidence to Form a Basis for Conclusions

1.   Design and perform audit procedures whose nature, timing, and extent are responsive to the assessed risk of material misstatement - 10.1

2.   Integrating audits: in an integrated audit of internal control over financial reporting and the financial statements, design and perform testing of controls to accomplish the objectives of both audits simultaneously - 9.3

3.   Design, perform, and document tests of controls to evaluate design effectiveness - 8.1, 9.3, 10.1

4.   Design, perform, and document tests of controls to evaluate operating effectiveness - 8.1, 9.3, 10.1

5.   Perform substantive procedures - SU 11, SU 12, SU 13

6.   Perform audit sampling - SU 15

7.   Perform analytical procedures - 3.5

8.   Confirm balances and/or transactions with third parties - 10.2

9.   Examine inventories and other assets - 12.2, 13.1

10.   Perform other tests of details, balances, and journal entries - SU 11, SU 12, SU 13

11.   Perform computer-assisted audit techniques (CAATs), including data query, extraction, and analysis - 10.4

12. Perform audit procedures on significant accounting estimates - 4.4

13. Auditing fair value measurements and disclosures, including the use of specialists in evaluating estimates - 4.4

14. Perform tests on unusual year-end transactions - SU 11, SU 12, SU 13

15. Audits performed in accordance with International Standards on Auditing (ISAs) or auditing standards of another country: determine if differences exist and whether additional audit procedures are required - Highlighted in each affected SU

16. Evaluate contingencies - 14.1

17. Obtain and evaluate lawyers' letters - 14.1

18. Review subsequent events - 14.2

19. Obtaining and placing reliance on representations from management - 14.3

20. Identify material weaknesses, significant deficiencies, and other control deficiencies - 9.1

IV. **Evaluating Audit Findings, Communications, and Reporting (18%)**

    A. Perform Overall Analytical Procedures - 3.5

    B. Evaluate the Sufficiency and Appropriateness of Audit Evidence and Document Engagement Conclusions - 10.3

    C. Evaluate Whether Audit Documentation is in Accordance with Professional Standards - 10.3

    D. Review the Work Performed by Others, including Specialists and Other Auditors, to Provide Reasonable Assurance that Objectives are Achieved - 4.2, 17.1

    E. Document the Summary of Uncorrected Misstatements and Related Conclusions - 10.3

    F. Evaluate Whether Financial Statements are Free of Material Misstatements - 16.1

    G. Consider the Entity's Ability to Continue as a Going Concern - 14.4, 17.3

    H. Consider Other Information in Documents Containing Audited Financial Statements (e.g., Supplemental Information and Management's Discussion and Analysis) - 18.1-18.7

    I. Retain Audit Documentation as Required by Standards and Regulations - 10.3

    J. Prepare Communications

        1. Reports on audited financial statements - SU 16, SU 17
        2. Reports required by government auditing standards - SU 20
        3. Reports on compliance with laws and regulations - 19.7
        4. Reports on internal control - 9.3
        5. Reports on the processing of transactions by service organizations - 9.4
        6. Reports on agreed-upon procedures - 19.4
        7. Reports on financial forecasts and projections - 19.5
        8. Reports on pro forma financial information - 19.6
        9. Special reports - 18.8-18.11
        10. Reissue reports - 14.2, 17.4
        11. Communicate internal control related matters identified in the audit - 9.1
        12. Communications with those charged with governance - 9.2
        13. Subsequent discovery of facts existing at the date of the auditor's report - 14.2
        14. Consideration after the report date of omitted procedures - 4.5

V. **Accounting and Review Services Engagements (14%)**

    A. Plan the Engagement

        1. Determine nature and scope of engagement - 19.1, 19.2

        2. Decide whether to accept or continue the client and engagement including determining the appropriateness of the engagement to meet the client's needs and consideration of independence standards - 19.1, 19.2

        3. Establish an understanding with the client and document the understanding through an engagement letter or other written communication with the client - 19.1, 19.2

        4. Consider change in engagement - 19.3

        5. Determine if reports are to be used by third parties - 19.1, 19.2

B.   Obtain and Document Evidence to Form a Basis for Conclusions

    1.   Obtain an understanding of the client's operations, business, and industry - 19.1, 19.2

    2.   Obtain knowledge of accounting principles and practices in the industry and the client - 19.1, 19.2

    3.   Perform analytical procedures for review services - 19.2

    4.   Obtain representations from management for review services - 19.2

    5.   Perform other engagement procedures - 19.1, 19.2

    6.   Consider departures from generally accepted accounting principles (GAAP) or other comprehensive basis of accounting (OCBOA) - 19.1, 19.2

    7.   Prepare documentation from evidence gathered - 19.1, 19.2

    8.   Retain documentation as required by standards - 19.1, 19.2

    9.   Review the work performed to provide reasonable assurance that objectives are achieved - 19.1, 19.2

C.   Prepare Communications

    1.   Reports on compilations - 19.1, 19.3
    2.   Reports on reviews - 19.2, 19.3
    3.   Restricted use of reports - 19.1-19.3
    4.   Communicating to management and others - 19.1-19.3
    5.   Subsequent discovery of facts existing at the date of the report - 19.1-19.3
    6.   Consider degree of responsibility for supplementary information - 19.1-19.3

VI.   Professional Responsibilities (18%)

A.   Ethics and Independence

    1.   Code of Professional Conduct (AICPA) - 2.1-2.6

    2.   Requirements related to issuers, including the PCAOB, the SEC and the Sarbanes-Oxley Act of 2002, Titles II and III, Section 303 - 2.7

    3.   Government Accountability Office (GAO) - 20.1

    4.   Department of Labor (DOL) - 2.7

    5.   Code of Ethics for Professional Accountants (IFAC) - 2.7

B.   Other Professional Responsibilities

    1.   A firm's system of quality control - 1.5

    2.   General role, structure, and requirements of the PCAOB (Title I and Title IV of the Sarbanes-Oxley Act of 2002) - 2.7

AICPA SKILL SPECIFICATION OUTLINES (SSOs)

The SSOs identify the skills that will be tested on the CPA exam. The following table explains the skills tested, the weight range assigned to each skill category (approximate percentage of CPA exam that will use skills in the category) in Auditing, the question format that will be used to test the skill in Auditing, and the resources that will be available to the candidates to demonstrate proficiency in each skill.

Skills Category	Weight	Question Format	Resource(s)
Knowledge and Understanding	60%	Multiple-choice questions	Calculator
Application of the Body of Knowledge	40%	Task-based simulations	Authoritative literature, calculator, spreadsheets, etc.
Written Communication*	--	--	--

*The Written Communication category is tested through essays, which are not present in the Auditing section of the CPA exam.

REFERENCES

The AICPA suggests that the following publications will be sources of questions for Auditing. Our outlines and answer explanations are based on these publications and are organized into meaningful, easy-to-use study units to facilitate your exam preparation via the Gleim Knowledge Transfer System.

- AICPA Statements on Auditing Standards and Interpretations
- Public Company Accounting Oversight Board (PCAOB) Standards (SEC-Approved) and Related Rules, PCAOB Staff Questions and Answers, and PCAOB Staff Audit Practice Alerts
- U.S. Government Accountability Office Government Auditing Standards
- Single Audit Act, as amended
- Office of Management and Budget (OMB) Circular A-133
- AICPA Statements on Quality Control Standards
- AICPA Statements on Standards for Accounting and Review Services and Interpretations
- AICPA Statements on Standards for Attestation Engagements and Interpretations
- AICPA Audit and Accounting Guides
- AICPA *Code of Professional Conduct*
- IFAC *Code of Ethics for Professional Accountants*
- Sarbanes-Oxley Act of 2002
- Department of Labor Guidelines and Interpretive Bulletins re: Auditor Independence
- SEC Independence Rules
- Employee Retirement Income Security Act of 1974
- The Committee of Sponsoring Organizations of the Treadway Commission (COSO): Internal Control – Integrated Framework
- Current textbooks on auditing, attestation services, ethics, and independence
- International Standards on Auditing (ISAs)

STEPS TO BECOME A CPA

1. Become knowledgeable about the exam, and decide which section you will take first.
2. Purchase the Gleim CPA Review System to thoroughly prepare for the CPA exam. Commit to our systematic preparation for the exam as described in our review materials, including *How to Pass the CPA Exam: A System for Success.*
3. Communicate with your Personal Counselor to design a study plan that meets your needs. Call (800) 874-5346 or email CPA@gleim.com.
4. Determine the board of accountancy (i.e., state) to which you will apply to sit for the CPA exam.
5. Obtain, complete, and submit your application form, including transcripts, fees, etc., to your State Board or NASBA. You should receive a Notice To Schedule (NTS) from NASBA in 4 to 6 weeks.
    a. Do not apply for a section of the exam until you are ready to take it. An NTS is valid for a specific period established by the boards of accountancy, and you will forfeit any fees you paid for sections not taken.
    b. Remember, the following testing windows are available for test taking: January/February, April/May, July/August, and October/November.
6. Schedule your test with Prometric (online or by calling your local Prometric testing site). Schedule at least 45 days before the date you plan to sit for the exam.
7. Work systematically through the study units in each section of the Gleim CPA Review System (Auditing, Business, Financial, and Regulation).
8. Use Gleim CPA Test Prep: thousands of questions, all updated to current tax law, Accounting Standards Codification, etc. Listen to CPA Audio Review as a supplement.
9. Sit for and PASS the CPA exam while you are in control.

10. Enjoy your career and pursue multiple certifications (CIA, CMA, EA, RTRP, etc.), recommend Gleim to others who are also taking these exams, and stay up-to-date on your continuing professional education with Gleim CPE.

More specifically, you should focus on the following **system for success** on the Auditing section of the CPA exam:

1. **Understand the exam, including its purpose, coverage, preparation, format, administration, grading, and pass rates.**

   a. The better you understand the examination process from beginning to end, the better you will perform.

   b. Study the Gleim *How to Pass the CPA Exam: A System for Success*. Please be sure you have a copy of this useful booklet. (*How to Pass the CPA Exam: A System for Success* is also available as an e-book at www.gleim.com/sfs.)

2. **Learn and understand the subject matter tested.** The AICPA's CSOs and SSOs for the Auditing section are the basis for the study outlines that are presented in each of the 20 study units that make up this book.* You will also learn and understand the Auditing material tested on the CPA exam by answering numerous multiple-choice questions from recent CPA exams. Multiple-choice questions with the answer explanations to the immediate right of each question are a major component of each study unit.

3. **Practice answering actual exam questions to perfect your question-answering techniques.** Answering recent exam questions helps you understand the standards to which you will be held. This motivates you to learn and understand while studying (rather than reading) the outlines in each of the 20 study units.

   a. Question-answering techniques are suggested for multiple-choice questions and task-based simulations in Study Units 4 and 5 of *How to Pass the CPA Exam: A System for Success*.

   b. Our CPA Test Prep contains thousands of additional multiple-choice questions that are not offered in our books. Additionally, CPA Test Prep has many useful features, including documentation of your performance and the ability to simulate the CBT-e exam environment.

   c. Our CPA Gleim Online is a powerful Internet-based program that allows CPA candidates to learn in an interactive environment and provides feedback to candidates to encourage learning. It includes multiple-choice questions and task-based simulations in Prometric's format. Each CPA Gleim Online user has access to a Personal Counselor, who helps organize study plans that work with busy schedules.

   d. Additionally, all candidates are required by the AICPA to review the tutorial and sample tests at www.aicpa.org. According to the AICPA, failure to follow the directions provided in the tutorial and sample tests, including the directions on how to respond, may adversely affect your scores.

4. **Plan and practice exam execution.** Anticipate the exam environment and prepare yourself with a plan: When to arrive? How to dress? What exam supplies to bring? How many questions and what format? Order of answering questions? How much time to spend on each question? Study Unit 7 in *How to Pass the CPA Exam: A System for Success* contains more information on these topics.

   a. Expect the unexpected and adjust! Remember, your sole objective when taking an examination is to maximize your score. You must outperform your peers, and being as comfortable and relaxed as possible gives you an advantage!

5. **Be in control.** Develop confidence and ensure success with a controlled preparation program followed by confident execution during the examination.

---

*Please fill out our online feedback form (www.gleim.com/feedbackAUD) IMMEDIATELY after you take the CPA exam so we can adapt to changes in the exam. Our approach has been approved by the AICPA

PRELIMINARY TESTING: GLEIM CPA DIAGNOSTIC QUIZ

The Gleim CPA Diagnostic Quiz provides a representative sample of 40 multiple-choice questions for each exam section. You should use this tool to determine which section of the exam you will take first and/or how much time you need to devote to studying particular topic areas (i.e., what your strengths and weaknesses are).

When you have completed the quiz, you will be able to access a Review Session, where you can study answer explanations for the correct and incorrect answer choices of the questions you answered incorrectly. You will also have the option to consult with a Personal Counselor in order to better focus your review on any areas in which you have less confidence.

For smartphone users, there is also a Gleim Diagnostic Quiz App for iPhone, iPod Touch, and Android. More information can be found at www.gleim.com/QuizCPA.

Candidates who have already purchased the Gleim CPA Review System should skip the Diagnostic Quiz and immediately begin the steps provided below. These steps incorporate study-unit-specific diagnostic testing.

HOW TO STUDY AN AUDITING STUDY UNIT USING THE GLEIM CPA REVIEW SYSTEM

To ensure that you are using your time effectively, we recommend that you follow the steps listed below when using all of the CPA Review System materials together (books, CPA Test Prep, Audio Review, Gleim Online, and Simulation Wizard).

1. (30 minutes, plus 10 minutes for review) In the CPA Gleim Online course, complete Multiple-Choice Quiz #1 in 30 minutes. It is expected that your scores will be lower on the first quiz in each study unit than on subsequent quizzes.

    a. Immediately following the quiz, you will be prompted to review questions you flagged and/or answered incorrectly. For each question, analyze and understand why you were unsure or answered it incorrectly. This step is an essential learning activity.

2. (30 minutes) Use the online audiovisual presentation for an overview of the study unit. **CPA Audio Review** can be substituted for audiovisual presentations and can be used while driving to work, exercising, etc.

3. (45 minutes) Complete the 30-question online True/False quiz. It is interactive and most effective if used prior to studying the Knowledge Transfer Outline.

4. (60-80 minutes) Study the Knowledge Transfer Outline, particularly the troublesome areas identified from the multiple-choice questions in the Gleim Online course. The Knowledge Transfer Outline can be studied either online or from the books.

5. (30 minutes, plus 10 minutes for review) Complete Multiple-Choice Quiz #2 in the Gleim Online course.

    a. Immediately following the quiz, you will be prompted to review questions you flagged and/or answered incorrectly. For each question, analyze and understand why you were unsure or answered it incorrectly. This step is an essential learning activity.

6. (60 minutes) Complete two 20-question Practice Exams in CPA Test Prep. Review as needed.

7. (90 minutes) Complete and review the simulation section of the Gleim Online course.

8. Continue taking customized Practice Exams in CPA Test Prep until you approach your desired proficiency level, e.g., 75%. Use Study Sessions as needed to get immediate feedback on questions in your problem areas.

9. For additional practice answering simulations, complete all of the task-based simulations in the Gleim Simulation Wizard.

The times mentioned above are recommendations based on prior candidate feedback and how long you will have to answer questions on the actual exam. Each candidate's time spent in any area will vary depending on proficiency and familiarity with the subject matter.

CPA FINAL REVIEW

Final review is the culmination of all your studies and topics and should occur one week prior to when you sit for your exam. All study units in Gleim Online should be completed by this time.

Step 1: Take the CPA Exam Rehearsal under exam conditions at the beginning of your final review stage. The Practice Exam is 4 hours (240 minutes) long and contains three testlets with 30 multiple-choice questions each and one testlet with seven Task-Based Simulations, just like the CPA exam. This will help you identify any weak areas for more practice. Discuss your results with your Personal Counselor for additional guidance.

Step 2: Create Practice Exams in Gleim CPA Test Prep, focusing on your weak areas identified from your Practice Exam. Also, be sure to focus on all the material as a whole to refresh yourself with topics you learned at the beginning of your studies. View your performance chart to make sure you are scoring 75% or higher.

> **The following is a detailed description of Gleim products that will prepare you to pass the CPA exam according to the steps given on the previous page and above (including the Final Review).**

CPA GLEIM ONLINE

CPA Gleim Online is a multi-platform self-study review program delivered via the Internet. It is divided into four courses (one for each section of the CPA exam) and contains AICPA-released multiple-choice questions and task-based simulations in an interface designed to emulate the CPA exam.

CPA Gleim Online contains

- Audiovisual presentations
- Comprehensive review book outlines
- Thousands of multiple-choice and true/false questions
- Hundreds of task-based simulations

CPA Gleim Online provides you with access to a Personal Counselor, a real person who will provide support to ensure your competitive edge. CPA Gleim Online is a great way to get confidence as you prepare with Gleim. This confidence will continue during and after the exam.

GLEIM SIMULATION WIZARD

The Gleim Simulation Wizard for Auditing is a training program that focuses on the Task-Based Simulations that appear in the last testlet of the Auditing section of the CPA exam. This online course provides five Task-Based Simulations per study unit, as well as test-taking tips from Dr. Gleim to help you stay in control.

GLEIM BOOKS

This edition of the CPA Auditing Review book has the following features to make studying easier:

1. **Examples:** Illustrative examples, both hypothetical and those drawn from actual events, are set off in shaded, bordered boxes.

EXAMPLE

If financial statement materiality was set at $50,000, and materiality for the accounts receivable balance was set at $10,000, performance materiality for the audit of accounts receivable might be set at $3,000 to compensate for the possibility of multiple undetected or uncorrected misstatements in accounts receivable.

2. **Backgrounds:** In certain instances, we have provided historical background or supplemental information. This information is intended to illuminate the topic under discussion and is set off in bordered boxes with shaded headings. This material does not need to be memorized for the exam.

Background

Prior to 1984, agencies of the federal government that provided awards to state and local governments audited specific grants, contracts, subsidies, etc. This process often resulted in numerous audits of a recipient by various agencies and a wasteful duplication of effort. In other cases, large amounts of federal awards went unaudited.

---

3. **Gleim Success Tips:** These tips supplement the core exam material by suggesting how certain topics might be presented on the exam or how you should prepare for an issue.

 The AICPA has increased its emphasis on quality control, and you should recognize its importance in your study for the exam. Be familiar with the role of practice monitoring, and make certain that you understand the six elements of the AICPA's Statements on Quality Control Standards. Each element requires the CPA firm to have "policies and procedures" in place to ensure conformance with standards.

---

4. **Memory Aids:** These mnemonic devices are designed to assist you in memorizing important concepts.

   For example, "Controls stop **CRIME**" helps candidates remember the five interrelated components of internal control.

5. **Detailed Table of Contents:** This information at the beginning of the book contains a complete listing of all study units and subunits in the Gleim CPA Auditing Review program. Use this list as a study aid to mark off your progress and to provide jumping-off points for review.

6. **ISA Differences:** When international standards differ significantly from U.S. auditing standards, we note the differences.

ISA Difference

The ISAs contain only one category of professional requirements. The auditor is required to comply with requirements when they are relevant, except in rare circumstances.

---

7. **Auditing Authoritative Pronouncements Cross-References:** This section at the end of the Introduction lists all authoritative pronouncements and cross-references them to the Gleim study unit(s) in which they are discussed.

CPA TEST PREP

CPA Test Prep is an online question bank that offers unlimited Practice Exams to give you unprecedented studying potential.

Twenty-question Practice Exams in CPA Test Prep will help you to focus on your weaker areas. Make it a game: How much can you improve?

Our CPA Test Prep Practice Exams force you to commit to your answer choice before looking at answer explanations; thus, you are preparing under true exam conditions. They also keep track of your time and performance history for each study unit, which is available in either a table or graphical format. Using Cloud technology, your performance data can be synced to any computer or mobile device so you can study anywhere.

STUDYING WITH BOOK AND CPA TEST PREP*

Simplify the exam preparation process by following our suggested steps listed below. DO NOT omit the step in which you diagnose the reasons for answering questions incorrectly; i.e., learn from your mistakes while studying so you avoid making similar mistakes on the CPA exam.

1. Create and complete a 20-question diagnostic Practice Exam before studying any other information.

2. Study the Knowledge Transfer Outline for the corresponding study unit in your Gleim book.

    a. Place special emphasis on the weaker areas that you identified with the initial diagnostic quiz in Step 1.

3. Take two or three 20-question Practice Exams after you have studied the Knowledge Transfer Outline.

4. Immediately following each Exam, you will be prompted to review the questions you flagged and/or answered incorrectly. For each question, analyze and understand why you were unsure or answered it incorrectly. This step is an essential learning activity.

5. Continue this process until you approach a predetermined proficiency level, e.g., 75%+.

6. Modify this process to suit your individual learning process.

    a. Learning from questions you answer incorrectly is very important. Each question you answer incorrectly is an **opportunity** to avoid missing actual test questions on your CPA exam. Thus, you should carefully study the answer explanations provided until you understand why the original answer you chose is wrong as well as why the correct answer indicated is correct. This learning technique is clearly the difference between passing and failing for many CPA candidates.

    b. Also, you **must** determine why you answered questions incorrectly and learn how to avoid the same error in the future. Reasons for missing questions include

        1) Misreading the requirement (stem)
        2) Not understanding what is required
        3) Making a math error
        4) Applying the wrong rule or concept
        5) Being distracted by one or more of the answers
        6) Incorrectly eliminating answers from consideration
        7) Not having any knowledge of the topic tested
        8) Using a poor educated guessing strategy

    c. It is also important to verify that you answered correctly for the right reasons (i.e., read the discussion provided for the correct answers). Otherwise, if the material is tested on the CPA exam in a different manner, you may not answer it correctly.

    d. It is imperative that you complete the predetermined number of study units per week so you can review your progress and realize how attainable a comprehensive CPA review program is when using the Gleim CPA Review System. Remember to meet or beat your schedule to give yourself confidence.

---

*Gleim does not recommend studying for Auditing using only this book and CPA Test Prep. Candidates need to practice the task-based simulations in an exam environment, which means on a computer. Use CPA Gleim Online and CPA Simulation Wizard to become an expert on task-based simulations.

GLEIM AUDIO REVIEWS

Gleim **CPA Audio Reviews** provide an average of 30 minutes of quality review for each study unit. Each review provides an overview of the Knowledge Transfer Outline in the *CPA Review* book. The purpose is to get candidates started so they can relate to the questions they will answer before reading the study outlines in each study unit. The reviews are available via download from our website.

The audios get to the point, as does the entire **Gleim System for Success**. We are working to get you through the CPA exam with minimum time, cost, and frustration. You can listen to four short sample audio reviews on our website at www.gleim.com/accounting/demos.

TIME BUDGETING AND QUESTION-ANSWERING TECHNIQUES FOR AUDITING

Expect three testlets of 30 multiple-choice questions each and one testlet with seven Task-Based Simulations (TBS) on the Auditing section with a 240-minute time allocation. Study Units 4 and 5 in *How to Pass the CPA Exam: A System for Success* contain additional discussion of how to maximize your score on multiple-choice questions and simulations.

MULTIPLE-CHOICE QUESTIONS

1. **Budget your time.** We make this point with emphasis. Just as you would fill up your gas tank prior to reaching empty, so too would you finish your exam before time expires.

   a. Here is our suggested time allocation for Auditing:

	Minutes	Start Time	
Testlet 1 (MC)	45	4 hours	00 minutes
Testlet 2 (MC)	45	3 hours	15 minutes
Testlet 3 (MC)	45	2 hours	30 minutes
Testlet 4 (TBS)	90	1 hour	45 minutes
***Extra time	15	0 hours	15 minutes

   b. Before beginning your first testlet of multiple-choice questions, prepare a Gleim Time Management Sheet as recommended in Study Unit 7 of *How to Pass the CPA Exam: A System for Success*.

   c. As you work through the individual items, monitor your time. In Auditing, we suggest 45 minutes for each testlet of 30 questions. If you answer five items in 7 minutes, you are fine, but if you spend 10 minutes on five items, you need to speed up.

   ***Remember to allocate your budgeted extra time, as needed, to each testlet. Your goal is to answer all of the items and achieve the maximum score possible.

2. **Answer the questions in consecutive order.**

   a. Do **not** agonize over any one item. Stay within your time budget.

   b. Flag for review any questions you are unsure of and return to them later as time allows.

      1) Once you have selected either the Continue or Quit option, you will no longer be able to review or change any answers in the completed testlet.

   c. Never leave a multiple-choice question unanswered. **Make your best educated guess in the time allowed.** Remember that your score is based on the number of correct responses. You will not be penalized for guessing incorrectly.

3.   **For each multiple-choice question,**

    a.   **Try to ignore the answer choices.** Do not allow the answer choices to affect your reading of the question.

        1)   If four answer choices are presented, three of them are incorrect. These choices are called **distractors** for good reason. Often, distractors are written to appear correct at first glance until further analysis.

        2)   In computational items, the distractors are carefully calculated such that they are the result of making common mistakes. Be careful, and double-check your computations if time permits.

    b.   **Read the question** carefully to determine the precise requirement.

        1)   Focusing on what is required enables you to ignore extraneous information, to focus on the relevant facts, and to proceed directly to determining the correct answer.

            a)   Be especially careful to note when the requirement is an **exception**; e.g., "Which of the following is **not** a management assertion?"

    c.   **Determine the correct answer** before looking at the answer choices.

    d.   **Read the answer choices carefully.**

        1)   Even if the first answer appears to be the correct choice, do **not** skip the remaining answer choices. Questions often ask for the "best" of the choices provided. Thus, each choice requires your consideration.

        2)   Treat each answer choice as a true/false question as you analyze it.

    e.   **Click on the best answer.**

        1)   You have a 25% chance of answering the question correctly by guessing blindly; improve your odds with educated guessing.

        2)   For many multiple-choice questions, two answer choices can be eliminated with minimal effort, thereby increasing your educated guess to a 50-50 proposition.

4.   After you have answered all the items in a testlet, consult the question status list at the bottom of each multiple-choice question screen **before** clicking the "Exit" button, which permanently ends the testlet.

    a.   Go back to the flagged questions and finalize your answer choices.

    b.   Verify that all questions have been answered.

5.   **If you don't know the answer,**

    a.   Make an educated guess, which means selecting the best possible answer. First, rule out answers that you think are incorrect. Second, speculate on what the AICPA is looking for and/or the rationale behind the question. Third, select the best answer or guess between equally appealing answers. Your first guess is usually the most intuitive. If you cannot make an educated guess, read the stem and each answer and pick the most intuitive answer. It's just a guess!

    b.   Make sure you accomplish this step within your predetermined time budget per testlet.

TASK-BASED SIMULATIONS

In Auditing, Testlet 4 consists of seven task-based simulations. The following information and toolbar icons are located at the top of the testlet screen.

1. **Exam Section and Testlet Number:** For Auditing, this part of the toolbar will always show Auditing and Attestation as the Exam Section and Testlet 4 of 4 as the Testlet Number.
2. **Time Remaining:** This information box displays to the examinee how long (s)he has remaining in the entire exam. Consistently check the amount of time remaining in order to stay on schedule.
3. **Unsplit:** This icon, when selected, will unsplit the screen between two tabs.
4. **Split Horiz:** This icon, when selected, will split the screen horizontally between two tabs, enabling you to see, for example, both the simulation question and the help tab at the same time.
5. **Split Vertical:** This icon, when selected, will split the screen vertically between two tabs, enabling you to see, for example, both the simulation question and the help tab at the same time.
6. **Spreadsheet:** This icon opens a spreadsheet that operates like most others and is provided as a tool available for complex calculations. You may enter and execute formulas as well as enter text and numbers.
7. **Calculator:** The calculator provided is a basic tool for simple computations. It is similar to calculators used in common software programs.
8. **Exit:** There are three options when you choose this icon.
   - You may choose Review Testlet to return to the beginning of the testlet to review your answers. You will be able to change your answers.
   - You may choose Continue Exam to close the current testlet and go on to the next testlet. Once you have chosen Continue, you may not return to that testlet. For Auditing, the choice to Continue will only be relevant after each multiple-choice testlet, since the simulation is the last testlet.
   - Finally, you may choose Quit Exam, which means either that you have completed the exam or that you chose not to complete it. Your exam will end and you will not be able to return to any testlet. If you chose to quit your exam before you have completed it, there are security measures in place to determine that you are intentionally not completing the exam.
9. **Work Tabs:** A work tab requires the test taker to respond to given information. Each task will have at least one work tab (distinguished by a pencil icon), and each work tab will have specific directions that you must read in order to complete the tab correctly. There are different varieties of work tabs; the one in the toolbar above is just an example. You may encounter work tabs that require you to complete forms, fill in spreadsheets, or select an option from multiple choices.
10. **Information Tabs:** An information tab gives the test taker information to aid in responding to work tabs. Each task will have at least one information tab (the Authoritative Literature, as shown in the example above). If your task has additional information tabs, go through each to familiarize yourself with the task's content.
11. **Help:** This tab, when selected, provides a quick review of certain functions and tool buttons specific to the type of task you are working on. It will also provide directions and general information but will not include information related specifically to the test content.

Task-Based Simulation Grading

Remember, on the real exam, you will need to complete seven different task-based simulations, all of which will count toward your final grade. Your score on all of the tasks together will make up **40%** of your total grade. The other **60%** of your grade will be your total score on the multiple-choice testlets.

IF YOU HAVE QUESTIONS

Content-specific questions about our materials will be answered most rapidly if they are sent to us via the easily accessible feedback forms within the online study components. For inquiries regarding your Review book or Test Prep Software Download, please visit www.gleim.com/questions and complete the on-screen form. Our team of accounting experts will give your correspondence thorough consideration and a prompt response.

Questions regarding the information in this Introduction (study suggestions, studying plans, exam specifics) should be emailed to personalcounselor@gleim.com.

Questions concerning orders, prices, shipments, or payments should be sent via email to customerservice@gleim.com and will be promptly handled by our competent and courteous customer service staff.

For technical support, you may use our automated technical support service at www.gleim.com/support, email us at support@gleim.com, or call us at (800) 874-5346.

HOW TO BE IN CONTROL

Remember, you must be in control to be successful during exam preparation and execution. Perhaps more importantly, control can also contribute greatly to your personal and other professional goals. Control is the process whereby you

1. Develop expectations, standards, budgets, and plans
2. Undertake activity, production, study, and learning
3. Measure the activity, production, output, and knowledge
4. Compare actual activity with expected and budgeted activity
5. Modify the activity, behavior, or study to better achieve the expected or desired outcome
6. Revise expectations and standards in light of actual experience
7. Continue the process or restart the process in the future

Exercising control will ultimately develop the confidence you need to outperform most other CPA candidates and PASS the CPA exam! Obtain our *How to Pass the CPA Exam: A System for Success* booklet for a more detailed discussion of control and other exam tactics.

AICPA's NONDISCLOSURE AGREEMENT

The following is taken verbatim from the Uniform CPA Examination: Candidate Bulletin dated September 2013. It is reproduced here to remind all CPA candidates about the AICPA's strict policy of nondisclosure, which Gleim consistently supports and upholds.

Policy Statement and Agreement Regarding Exam Confidentiality and the Taking of Breaks

I hereby agree that I will maintain the confidentiality of the Uniform CPA Examination. In addition, I agree that I will not:

- *Divulge the nature or content of any Uniform CPA Examination question or answer under any circumstance*
- *Engage in any unauthorized communication during testing*
- *Refer to unauthorized materials or use unauthorized equipment during testing; or*
- *Remove or attempt to remove any Uniform CPA Examination materials, notes, or any other items from the examination room*

I understand and agree that liability for test administration activities, including but not limited to the adequacy or accuracy of test materials and equipment, and the accuracy of scoring and score reporting, will be limited to score correction or test retake at no additional fee. I waive any and all right to all other claims.

I further agree to report to the AICPA any examination question disclosures, or solicitations for disclosure of which I become aware.

I affirm that I have had the opportunity to read the Candidate Bulletin and I agree to all of its terms and conditions.

I understand that breaks are only allowed between testlets. I understand that I will be asked to complete any open testlet before leaving the testing room for a break.

In addition, I understand that failure to comply with this Policy Statement and Agreement may result in invalidation of my grades, disqualification from future examinations, expulsion from the testing facility and possible civil or criminal penalties.

AUDITING AUTHORITATIVE PRONOUNCEMENTS CROSS-REFERENCES

The following listing relates AU-C and other auditing pronouncements to the Gleim study unit(s) in which they are discussed. Note that the subject matter may be covered without specific reference to the pronouncement. Recall that the CPA exam does not test pronouncement numbers or titles.

Section No.	Gleim Study Unit	Statements on Auditing Standards
Preface	1	Principles Underlying an Audit Conducted in Accordance With Generally Accepted Auditing Standards

AU-C 200–299 General Principles and Responsibilities

Section No.	Gleim Study Unit	
200	1, 3	Overall Objectives of the Independent Auditor and the Conduct of an Audit in Accordance With Generally Accepted Auditing Standards
210	3	Terms of Engagement
220	1, 3	Quality Control for an Engagement Conducted in Accordance With Generally Accepted Auditing Standards
230	10	Audit Documentation
240	3	Consideration of Fraud in a Financial Statement Audit
250	3	Consideration of Laws and Regulations in an Audit of Financial Statements
260	9	The Auditor's Communication With Those Charged With Governance
265	9	Communicating Internal Control Related Matters Identified in an Audit

AU-C 300–499 Risk Assessment and Response to Assessed Risk

Section No.	Gleim Study Unit	
300	3	Planning an Audit
315	1, 3, 5, 8	Understanding the Entity and Its Environment and Assessing the Risks of Material Misstatement
320	3	Materiality in Planning and Performing an Audit
330	8, 10	Performing Audit Procedures in Response to Assessed Risks and Evaluating the Audit Evidence Obtained
402	9	Audit Considerations Relating to an Entity Using a Service Organization
450	3	Evaluation of Misstatements Identified During the Audit

AU-C 500–599 Audit Evidence

Section No.	Gleim Study Unit	
500	4, 10-14	Audit Evidence
501	10-14	Audit Evidence—Specific Considerations for Selected Items
505	10, 11	External Confirmations
510	3	Opening Balances—Initial Audit Engagements, Including Reaudit Engagements
520	3	Analytical Procedures
530	15	Audit Sampling
540	4, 13	Auditing Accounting Estimates, Including Fair Value Accounting Estimates, and Related Disclosures
550	4	Related Parties
560	14, 17	Subsequent Events and Subsequently Discovered Facts
570	14, 17	The Auditor's Consideration of an Entity's Ability to Continue as a Going Concern
580	14	Written Representations
585	4	Consideration of Omitted Procedures After the Report Release Date

AU-C 600–699 Using the Work of Others

Section No.	Gleim Study Unit	
600	17	Special Considerations—Audits of Group Financial Statements (Including the Work of Component Auditors)
610	4	The Auditor's Consideration of the Internal Audit Function in an Audit of Financial Statements
620	4	Using the Work of an Auditor's Specialist

AU-C 700–799 Audit Conclusions and Reporting

Section No.	Gleim Study Unit	
700	16, 17	Forming an Opinion and Reporting on Financial Statements
705	16, 17	Modifications to the Opinion in the Independent Auditor's Report
706	17	Emphasis-of-Matter Paragraphs and Other-Matter Paragraphs in the Independent Auditor's Report
708	17	Consistency of Financial Statements
720	18	Other Information in Documents Containing Audited Financial Statements
725	18	Supplementary Information in Relation to the Financial Statements as a Whole
730	18	Required Supplementary Information

AU-C 800–899 Special Considerations

Section No.	Gleim Study Unit	
800	18	Special Considerations—Audits of Financial Statements Prepared in Accordance With Special Purpose Frameworks
805	18	Special Considerations—Audits of Single Financial Statements and Specific Elements, Accounts, or Items of a Financial Statement
806	17	Reporting on Compliance With Aspects of Contractual Agreements or Regulatory Requirements in Connection with Audited Financial Statements
810	18	Engagements to Report on Summary Financial Statements

Section No.	Gleim Study Unit	**Statements on Auditing Standards**

AU-C 900–999 Special Considerations in the United States

905	18	Alert That Restricts the Use of the Auditor's Written Communication
910	18	Financial Statements Prepared in Accordance With a Financial Reporting Framework Generally Accepted in Another Country
915	18	Reports on Application of Requirements of an Applicable Financial Reporting Framework
920	18	Letters for Underwriters and Certain Other Requesting Parties
925	18	Filings With the U.S. Securities and Exchange Commission Under the Securities Act of 1933
930	18	Interim Financial Information
935	20	Compliance Audits

Statements on Standards for Attestation Engagements

AT 20	1	Defining Professional Requirements in SSAEs
AT 50	1	SSAE Hierarchy
AT 101	1	Attest Engagements
AT 201	1, 19	Agreed-Upon Procedures Engagements
AT 301	1, 19	Financial Forecasts and Projections
AT 401	1, 19	Reporting on Pro Forma Financial Information
AT 501	1, 9	An Examination of an Entity's Internal Control over Financial Reporting that is Integrated with an Audit of Its Financial Statements
AT 601	1, 19	Compliance Attestation
AT 701	1	Management's Discussion and Analysis
AT 801	1, 9	Reporting on Controls at a Service Organization

Statements on Standards for Accounting and Review Services

AR 60	19	Framework for Performing and Reporting on Compilation and Review Engagements
AR 80	1, 19	Compilation of Financial Statements
AR 90	1, 19	Review of Financial Statements
AR 110	19	Compilation of Specified Elements, Accounts, or Items of a Financial Statement
AR 120	19	Compilation of Pro Forma Financial Information
AR 200	19	Reporting on Comparative Financial Statements
AR 300	19	Compilation Reports on Financial Statements Included in Certain Prescribed Forms
AR 400	19	Communications Between Predecessor and Successor Accountants
AR 600	19	Reporting on Personal Financial Statements Included in Written Personal Financial Plans

Statements on Quality Control Standards

QC 10	1, 3	A Firm's System of Quality Control

Standards for Performing and Reporting on Peer Reviews

PR 100	1	Standards for Performing and Reporting on Peer Reviews

Other Standards and References

	2	AICPA *Code of Professional Conduct*
	2	Sarbanes-Oxley Act of 2002
	2	Department of Labor: Auditor Independence
	20	*Government Auditing Standards* (Yellow Book)
	2	IFAC *Code of Ethics for Professional Accountants*
	5	The Committee of Sponsoring Organizations (COSO)

Public Company Accounting Oversight Board

AS No. 1	16	References in Auditor's Reports to the Standards of the PCAOB
AS No. 2	N/A	[Superseded by AS No. 5]
AS No. 3	3, 10	Audit Documentation
AS No. 4	9	Reporting on Whether a Previously Reported Material Weakness Continues to Exist
AS No. 5	5, 9, 14	An Audit of Internal Control Over Financial Reporting That is Integrated with an Audit of Financial Statements
AS No. 6	17	Evaluating Consistency of Financial Statements
AS No. 7	1	Engagement Quality Review
AS No. 8	3	Audit Risk
AS No. 9	3	Audit Planning
AS No. 10	3	Supervision of the Audit Engagement
AS No. 11	3	Consideration of Materiality in Planning and Performing an Audit
AS No. 12	3, 5, 8	Identifying and Assessing Risks of Material Misstatement
AS No. 13	8	The Auditor's Responses to the Risks of Material Misstatement
AS No. 14	10	Evaluating Audit Results
AS No. 15	4, 10-14	Audit Evidence
AS No. 16	9	Communications with Audit Committees

STUDY UNIT ONE
ENGAGEMENT RESPONSIBILITIES

(15 pages of outline)

This study unit begins the consideration of engagement planning for attest and audit engagements. Candidates should understand the types of services performed by CPAs. The differences among compilation, review, examination or audit, and agreed-upon procedures engagements are stressed. The list below is an overview:

> **Compilation** – disclaimer of any assurance
> **Review** – limited assurance
> **Examination/audit** – positive assurance or opinion expressed
> **Agreed-upon procedures** – results of procedures but no assurance

The 11 **attestation standards** address many practitioner services. Most are considered in more detail in other study units.

Assurance services also are in this study unit. They are a significant enlargement of the practice of CPAs. An understanding of how these services contrast with others provided by a CPA should be obtained.

Quality control is the final subject in this study unit. The Statements on Quality Control Standards (SQCSs) address the responsibilities of a CPA firm for its accounting and auditing practice. The SQCSs, which are codified in QC Section 10, identify six specific quality control elements. Candidates must learn the elements and what each includes. This topic is receiving more attention from standards setters. For example, the AICPA's clarified SASs contain a greatly expanded treatment of quality control that includes requirements and explanatory material. The clarified statement addresses the auditor's responsibilities for quality control procedures in an audit.

1.1 ATTEST ENGAGEMENTS (AT 101)

1. **Applicable Pronouncements**

   a. The AICPA's **Statements on Standards for Attestation Engagements (SSAEs)** are codified in section AT of the professional standards within the framework of the 11 attestation standards. The AICPA also issues SASs (auditing services), SSARSs (accounting and review services), and SSCSs (consulting services).

   1) **SAS** = Statement on Auditing Standards issued by the Auditing Standards Board (ASB)
   SSARS = Statement on Standards for Accounting and Review Services
   SSCS = Statement on Standards for Consulting Services

   2) The **Sarbanes-Oxley Act of 2002** is federal legislation that has had a dramatic effect on the engagement responsibilities of public accounting firms. This act created the **Public Company Accounting Oversight Board (PCAOB)**. The PCAOB's standards apply to audits of issuers (companies required to file with the SEC) by public accounting firms.

2. **Nature of an Attest Engagement**

   a. In an **attest engagement**, a practitioner is engaged to issue or does issue an **examination**, a **review**, or an **agreed-upon procedures** report on subject matter, or an assertion about the subject matter, that is the **responsibility of another party**.

   b. A **practitioner** is a CPA in **public practice**. Public practice involves performing professional (1) accounting, (2) tax, (3) personal financial planning, and (4) litigation support services for a client.

   c. Because the attestation standards apply **only to attest engagements involving a practitioner**, they apply only to the performance by a CPA in public accounting of professional services that are considered attest services (attest engagements).

      1) However, the SSAEs provide for a compilation of prospective financial statements (AT 301).

   d. Attest services have traditionally been limited to expressing an **opinion on historical financial statements** on the basis of an audit in accordance with U.S. generally accepted auditing standards.

      1) But CPAs increasingly provide assurance on representations other than historical statements and in forms other than an opinion. For example, positive assurance may be provided on financial forecasts based on an **examination**, and limited (negative) assurance may be provided on historical financial statements based on a **review**.

   e. SSAEs cover only attest engagements, not services to which specific standards apply, for example, SASs, SSARSs, and SSCSs.

      1) Other professional services to which the SSAEs specifically do not apply include engagements in which the practitioner (a) advocates a client's position, (b) prepares tax returns or gives tax advice, (c) has the sole function of assisting the client (e.g., to prepare information other than financial statements), or (d) testifies as an expert witness given certain stipulated facts.

   f. Some of the assurance services developed by the AICPA are considered attestation engagements, for example, **WebTrust** and **SysTrust**.

   g. Compilations of prospective financial statements (financial forecasts and projections) are addressed in the SSAEs. These services require a disclaimer of assurance.

3. **Attestation Standards (AT 50)**

   a. The need to provide standards for the growing range of attest services resulted in the issuance of 11 attestation standards.

   b. **General Standards**

      1) *The practitioner must have adequate technical training and proficiency to perform the attestation engagement.*

      2) *The practitioner must have adequate knowledge of the subject matter.*

      3) *The practitioner must have reason to believe that the subject matter is capable of evaluation against criteria that are suitable and available to users.*

         a) Suitable criteria have the attributes of objectivity, measurability, completeness, and relevance.

            i) For example, an engagement to attest to management's representation that "workers recorded an average of 40 hours per week on a project" could be accepted by a CPA. "Recorded" and "40 hours" are measurable and objectively determinable.

ii) However, an engagement to attest that "workers worked very hard on the project" could not be accepted. "Very hard" is not measurable or objectively determinable.

b) Criteria should be available to users in one or more of the following ways:

i) Publicly available

ii) Clearly included in the presentation of the subject matter or in the assertion

iii) Clearly included in the practitioner's report

iv) Well understood by most users (e.g., 40 hours per week)

v) Available only to specified parties (in which case the report should be restricted to those parties)

4) *The practitioner must maintain independence in mental attitude in all matters relating to the engagement.*

5) *The practitioner must exercise due professional care in the planning and performance of the engagement and the preparation of the report.*

c. **Standards of Field Work**

1) *The practitioner must adequately plan the work and must properly supervise any assistants.*

2) *The practitioner must obtain sufficient evidence to provide a reasonable basis for the conclusion that is expressed in the report.*

d. **Standards of Reporting**

1) *The practitioner must identify the subject matter or the assertion being reported on and state the character of the engagement in the report.*

2) *The practitioner must state the practitioner's conclusion about the subject matter or the assertion in relation to the criteria against which the subject matter was evaluated in the report.*

3) *The practitioner must state all of the practitioner's significant reservations about the engagement, the subject matter, and, if applicable, the assertion related thereto in the report.*

4) *The practitioner must state in the report that the report is intended solely for the information and use of the specified parties under the following circumstances:*

a) *When the criteria used to evaluate the subject matter are determined by the practitioner to be appropriate only for a limited number of parties who either participated in their establishment or can be presumed to have an adequate understanding of the criteria*

b) *When the criteria used to evaluate the subject matter are available only to specified parties*

c) *When reporting on subject matter and a written assertion has not been provided by the responsible party*

d) *When the report is on an attest engagement to apply agreed-upon procedures to the subject matter*

e.   The summary below is useful for learning the standards. But memorizing their order is not necessary.

SUMMARY OF THE ATTESTATION STANDARDS		
General Standards	Key Terms	Memory Aids
1. **Training** and proficiency in attestation	**T** = Training	Trisha
2. Knowledge of **subject matter**	**S** = Subject matter	Said
3. Suitable and available **criteria**	**C** = Criteria	Chris
4. **Independence** in mental attitude	**I** = Independence	Is
5. Due **professional care**	**P** = Professional care	Profane
Standards of Field Work		
1. **Planning** and supervision	**P** = Planning and supervision	Please
2. Sufficient **evidence**	**E** = Evidence	Excuse
Standards of Reporting		
1. **Character** of engagement	**C** = Character	Cousin
2. **Conclusion** about the subject matter	**C** = Conclusion	Chris's
3. Significant **reservations**	**R** = Reservations	Rude
4. Any **restrictions** on use	**R** = Restrictions	Remarks

4.   Two **levels of attest assurance** are permitted in general-distribution reports:

a.   **Positive** (high level) assurance should be given in reports that express conclusions on the basis of an **examination**.

b.   **Limited** (moderate level) assurance (sometimes termed negative assurance) should be given in reports that express conclusions on the basis of a **review**.

5.   **Scope Limitations**

a.   The practitioner may report directly on the subject matter. Nevertheless, as part of the attestation procedures for examinations and reviews, the practitioner ordinarily should obtain a **written assertion provided by the responsible party**.

b.   A failure to obtain a written assertion is considered a **scope limitation** when the responsible party is the client.

c.   In addition, a **representation letter** is typically obtained by the practitioner from the responsible party. A failure of the responsible party or client to provide written representations is normally considered a **scope limitation**.

6.   **Attest documentation** (working papers) should be prepared and maintained.

a.   Its form and content will vary with the circumstances and the practitioner's judgment.

b.   The procedures performed, evidence gathered, and the findings reached should be documented.

Stop and review! You have completed the outline for this subunit. Study multiple-choice questions 1 through 4 beginning on page 36.

1.2 OVERALL OBJECTIVES AND CONDUCTING AN AUDIT (AU-C 200 AND AU-C 315)

1.   **Overview**

a.   To make U.S. generally accepted auditing standards (GAAS) easier to read, understand, and apply, the AICPA's Auditing Standards Board (ASB) undertook a clarity project. The result was a redrafting of its standards into a new Codification of Statements on Auditing Standards. Each clarified statement states (1) objectives, (2) definitions (if relevant), (3) requirements, and (4) application and other explanatory material.

    c.   Some assertions overlap categories. Thus, only eight separate assertions are included in the model. If these are known, they can easily be assigned to the three categories of assertions. The following memory aid is helpful for learning the assertions (envision management as a large crocodile emerging from a cave):

        C - Completeness
        A - Accuracy
        V - Valuation and Allocation
        E - Existence

        C - Cutoff
        R - Rights and Obligations
        O - Occurrence
        C - Classification and Understandability

    d.   The PCAOB's AS No. 15, *Audit Evidence*, describes just five assertions to be applied selectively to the financial statement transactions, balances, and disclosures. These are essentially the same as those previously described.

        1)   **Existence or occurrence** -- Assets or liabilities of the company exist at a given date, and recorded transactions have occurred during a given period.

        2)   **Completeness** -- All transactions and accounts that should be presented in the financial statements are so included.

        3)   **Valuation or allocation** -- Asset, liability, equity, revenue, and expense components have been included in the financial statements at appropriate amounts.

        4)   **Rights and obligations** -- The company holds or controls rights to the assets, and liabilities are obligations of the company at a given date.

        5)   **Presentation and disclosure** -- The components of the financial statements are properly classified, described, and disclosed.

    e.   An audit performed by an independent, external auditor provides assurance to external users of the financial statements of the objectivity of the auditor's opinion.

        1)   The auditor may make suggestions about the form or content of the financial statements or draft them based on management's information. However, the auditor's responsibility for the financial statements is confined to the **expression of an opinion**.

    f.   The auditor's report states, "An audit involves performing procedures to obtain audit evidence about the amounts and disclosures in the financial statements. The procedures selected depend on the auditor's judgment, including the assessment of the risks of material misstatement of the financial statements, whether due to fraud or error" (AU-C 700).

4.   **Defining Professional Responsibilities**

    a.   GAAS and the PCAOB standards use the following categories of professional requirements to describe the degree of responsibility imposed on auditors:

        1)   Unconditional responsibility. The auditor must comply with an unconditional requirement whenever it is relevant. The word **must** indicates an unconditional requirement.

        2)   Presumptively mandatory responsibility. The auditor must comply with a presumptively mandatory requirement whenever it is relevant except in rare circumstances. The word **should** indicates a presumptively mandatory requirement.

            a)   When the auditor judges that such a departure is necessary, (s)he should perform alternative audit procedures to achieve the intent of the requirement. A departure is expected to be needed only when a specific required procedure would be ineffective in achieving that intent.

3)   Responsibility to consider. The words "may," "might," "could," or other terms and phrases describe actions and procedures that the auditor should use professional judgment in determining whether to perform.

ISA Difference

The ISAs contain only one category of professional requirements. The auditor is required to comply with requirements when they are relevant, except in rare circumstances.

Stop and review! You have completed the outline for this subunit. Study multiple-choice questions 5 through 8 beginning on page 37.

1.3 ADDITIONAL PROFESSIONAL SERVICES

1.   **Compilations and Reviews (AR 80 and AR 90)**

   a.   The AICPA bylaws designate the Accounting and Review Services Committee as the senior technical committee authorized to issue pronouncements in connection with the unaudited financial statements or other unaudited financial information of a nonissuer (nonpublic entity).

   b.   A **compilation of financial statements** is the presentation in statement form of financial information that is the representation of management. The accountant expresses **no assurance** in a compilation report. It includes a disclaimer. Thus, a compilation is an attest engagement but not an assurance engagement. The accountant need **not** be independent to compile financial statements.

   c.   In a **review** of financial statements, the accountant makes inquiries, applies analytical procedures, and obtains management representations. These procedures provide the accountant with a reasonable basis for expressing **limited assurance** that no material modifications need to be made to the statements for them to be in conformity with the applicable financial reporting framework. Thus, a review is an attest engagement and an assurance engagement. The accountant **must** be independent to review financial statements.

2.   **Agreed-Upon Procedures (AT 201)**

   a.   Attest engagements include reporting on findings based on **agreed-upon procedures** performed on subject matter. The practitioner is engaged by a client to assist specified parties to evaluate the subject matter or an assertion. The report is restricted to the specified parties who have agreed to the specific procedures and taken responsibility for their sufficiency.

   1)   The practitioner provides **neither positive nor limited assurance**.
   2)   The practitioner must be independent.

3.   **Prospective Financial Statements (PFSs) (AT 301)**

   a.   PFSs consist of financial forecasts or projections, including summaries of significant assumptions and accounting policies. An accountant should examine, compile, or apply agreed-upon procedures to PFSs if they are, or reasonably might be, expected to be used by another (third) party. As with other attest services, the practitioner must be independent.

   b.   A **financial forecast** consists of PFSs that present, to the best of the responsible party's knowledge and belief, an entity's expected financial position, results of operations, and cash flows. It is based on the responsible party's assumptions reflecting conditions it expects to exist and the course of action it expects to take.

c. Quality control over the audits of public companies will be evaluated during periodic inspections by the **Public Company Accounting Oversight Board (PCAOB)**. The Center PRP is designed to review and evaluate those portions of a firm's accounting and auditing practice that are not inspected by the PCAOB.

d. Public accounting firms that are without public clients and that are required to maintain a monitoring program should enroll in the AICPA PRP.

2. An audit firm has a responsibility to adopt a system of quality control. Thus, it should establish policies and procedures to provide reasonable assurance that (1) the firm and its personnel comply with professional standards and legal and regulatory requirements, and (2) the firm issues appropriate reports.

   a. Quality control standards apply to the conduct of a firm's practice as a whole. Thus, quality control may affect audits.

   b. Nevertheless, a deficiency in the system of quality control does not necessarily indicate that (1) a specific audit was not performed in accordance with professional, legal, and regulatory requirements, or (2) the auditor's report was inappropriate.

3. **Statements on Quality Control Standards (SQCSs)**

   a. SQCSs, codified as QC Section 10, require that a CPA firm have a system of quality control.

   b. Other professional standards provide guidance on the quality control responsibilities of firm personnel for specific types of engagements. For example, AU-C 220 applies to audits in accordance with GAAS. It establishes requirements at the audit engagement level that are consistent with those in the SQCSs.

   c. SQCSs apply to all CPA firms with regard to their accounting and auditing practice. This practice includes engagements to provide audit, attestation, compilation, review, and other services for which standards have been established by the Auditing Standards Board or the Accounting and Review Services Committee.

      1) A firm is defined broadly to include "a form of organization permitted by law or regulation whose characteristics conform to resolutions of Council of the AICPA that is engaged in the practice of public accounting." This definition includes proprietorships, partnerships, and professional corporations.

   d. The following are the six elements of a system of quality control:

      1) **Leadership responsibilities for quality within the firm (the "tone at the top").** The firm should promote an internal culture recognizing that quality is essential in performing engagements. This requires clear, consistent, and frequent actions and messages from all levels of management that emphasize quality control policies and procedures. Emphasis also should be on (a) performing work that complies with all professional standards and legal/ regulatory requirements and (b) issuing appropriate reports.

      2) **Relevant ethical requirements.** Policies and procedures should be established to provide reasonable assurance that the firm and personnel comply with relevant ethical requirements (e.g., the AICPA *Code of Professional Conduct*).

      3) **Acceptance and continuance of client relationships and specific engagements.** Policies and procedures should be established to provide reasonable assurance that the firm

         a) Has considered the client's integrity and has no information leading to a conclusion that the client lacks integrity;

         b) Has the competence, capabilities, and resources to perform the engagement; and

         c) Can comply with legal/regulatory and ethical requirements.

4) **Human resources.** Policies and procedures should be established to provide reasonable assurance that the firm has sufficient personnel with the capabilities, competence, and commitment to ethical principles to (a) perform engagements in accordance with professional standards and legal requirements and (b) issue appropriate reports.

   a) Matters addressed include recruitment, hiring, determining competencies, assignment of personnel, development of personnel, performance evaluation, compensation, and advancement.

   b) An engagement partner with the appropriate competence, capabilities, and authority should be responsible for each engagement.

5) **Engagement performance.** Policies and procedures should be established to provide reasonable assurance that engagements are consistently performed in accordance with professional standards and legal requirements and that the firm issues appropriate reports.

   a) Matters addressed include responsibilities for consistency of performance, supervision, and review.

6) **Monitoring.** Policies and procedures should be established to provide reasonable assurance that the policies and procedures relating to the system of quality control are relevant, adequate, operating effectively, and complied with in practice. Monitoring is an ongoing process and includes inspection and evaluation of prior engagements.

e. **Administration of a System of Quality Control**

1) Appropriate individuals should be responsible for designing and maintaining policies and procedures.

2) Those policies and procedures should be communicated so as to provide reasonable assurance that they are understood and complied with.

3) Consideration should be given to whether and to what extent policies and procedures must be documented for effective communication.

4) The firm should appropriately document quality control policies and procedures as well as compliance with them.

5) AU-C 220 assigns responsibility for the administration of quality control standards at the engagement level to the engagement partner.

4. **Peer Review**

a. A peer review does not substitute for monitoring, but it is a necessary part of the practice-monitoring requirement for AICPA membership. The applicable pronouncements issued by the AICPA Peer Review Board are the Standards for Performing and Reporting on Peer Reviews (PR 100). They govern peer reviews supervised by state CPA societies of firms enrolled in the AICPA Peer Review Program.

b. The portion of a firm's accounting and auditing practice covered by the peer review standards includes engagements under SASs, SSARSs, SSAEs, Government Auditing Standards, and PCAOB standards (for audits of non-SEC issuers).

c. A **system review** is an on-site review required for a firm that performs the highest level of services. It provides the reviewer with a reasonable basis for expressing an opinion on the firm's system of quality control.

d. An **engagement review** is for a firm not required to have a system review but not qualifying for a report review. It provides the reviewer with a reasonable basis for expressing limited assurance on whether (1) the financial statements or information and the accountant's reports submitted materially conform with professional standards, and (2) the firm's documentation conforms with professional standards.

5. **Sarbanes-Oxley Act of 2002**

   a. Under the federal Sarbanes-Oxley Act of 2002, a registered accounting firm must adopt quality control standards. Many of the provisions of Sarbanes-Oxley relate to improving the quality control of the audit and improving the quality of financial reporting. These standards relate to the audits of public companies.

   b. A **second partner review and approval** is required of audit reports.

   c. The **lead auditor** and the **reviewing partner** must be rotated off the audit every 5 years.

   d. The accounting firm must supervise any **associated person** with respect to auditing or quality control standards.

   e. **Independence rules have been expanded** by prohibiting the auditor from providing a variety of nonaudit services.

   f. The client's CEO and CFO must certify the appropriateness of the **financial statements and disclosures**.

   g. **Penalties** for destroying documents to impede an investigation have been expanded.

   h. Management must **assess the effectiveness of internal control** and issue a report on its effectiveness.

   i. The auditor must **audit internal control** and express an opinion on its effectiveness.

6. **The PCAOB**

   a. According to AS No. 7, *Engagement Quality Review*, an **engagement quality review (EQR)** and concurring approval of issuance are required for each audit of an issuer.

   b. The **objective** of the **reviewer** is to evaluate the significant judgments made and the related conclusions reached.

   c. The reviewer must be an associated person of a registered public accounting firm. The reviewer may be from outside the firm.

      1) The reviewer must have the competence to serve as a partner on the engagement.

      2) The reviewer also must have independence, integrity, and objectivity.

      3) But an engagement partner on either of the two preceding audits ordinarily may not be the reviewer.

   d. The EQR process in an audit evaluates the **significant judgments** made.

      1) This involves discussions with the engagement partner and other team members and reviewing whether the documentation supports the conclusions reached and appropriate responses to significant risks.

   e. The reviewer should evaluate the following:

      1) Significant judgments about planning matters

      2) The assessment of, and responses to, significant risks, including those identified by the reviewer

      3) Corrected and uncorrected identified misstatements and control deficiencies

      4) The audit firm's independence

      5) The engagement completion document and whether unresolved matters are significant

      6) The statements, the internal control report, and the audit report

      7) Other information filed with the SEC

      8) Whether consultations have addressed difficult matters

      9) Whether matters have been communicated to the audit committee, management, and other parties

   f. In an audit, the reviewer may provide **concurring approval of issuance**, and the client may use the report, only if the reviewer is not aware of a significant engagement deficiency.

Stop and review! You have completed the outline for this subunit. Study multiple-choice questions 25 through 34 beginning on page 42.

QUESTIONS
1.1 Attest Engagements (AT 101)

1. Which of the following is a conceptual difference between the attestation standards and generally accepted auditing standards?

A. The attestation standards provide a framework for the attest function beyond historical financial statements.

B. The requirement that the practitioner be independent in mental attitude is omitted from the attestation standards.

C. The attestation standards do not permit an attest engagement to be part of a business acquisition study or a feasibility study.

D. None of the standards of field work in generally accepted auditing standards are included in the attestation standards.

Answer (A) is correct.
REQUIRED: The conceptual difference between the attestation standards and GAAS.
DISCUSSION: Two principal conceptual differences exist between the attestation standards and GAAS. First, the attestation standards provide a framework for the attest function beyond historical financial statements. Second, the attestation standards accommodate the growing number of attest services in which the practitioner expresses assurance below the level that is expressed for the traditional audit (an opinion).
Answer (B) is incorrect. In any attest engagement, the practitioner must be independent in mental attitude. Answer (C) is incorrect. Attestation services may be provided in conjunction with other services provided to clients. Answer (D) is incorrect. The attestation standards and GAAS require that work be adequately planned and that assistants be properly supervised. Both also require sufficient evidence.

2. Which of the following is **not** an attestation standard?

A. Sufficient evidence shall be obtained to provide a reasonable basis for the conclusion that is expressed in the report.

B. The report shall identify the subject matter or the assertion being reported on and state the character of the engagement.

C. The work shall be adequately planned and assistants, if any, shall be properly supervised.

D. A sufficient understanding of internal control shall be obtained to plan the engagement.

Answer (D) is correct.
REQUIRED: The item not an attestation standard.
DISCUSSION: No attestation standard mentions internal control. However, the audit standards state, "The auditor should obtain an understanding of internal control relevant to the audit" (AU-C 315).
Answer (A) is incorrect. The evidentiary requirement is contained in the second attestation standard of field work. Answer (B) is incorrect. The first attestation standard of reporting concerns the character of the engagement. Answer (C) is incorrect. The first attestation standard of field work concerns planning and supervision.

3. In performing an attest engagement, a CPA typically

A. Supplies litigation support services.

B. Assesses the risks of material misstatement.

C. Expresses a conclusion about a written assertion.

D. Provides management consulting advice.

Answer (C) is correct.
REQUIRED: The CPA's usual task in an attestation engagement.
DISCUSSION: When a CPA in the practice of public accounting performs an attest engagement, the engagement is subject to the attestation standards. An attest engagement is one in which a practitioner is engaged to issue or does issue an examination, a review, or an agreed-upon procedures report on subject matter, or an assertion about the subject matter, that is the responsibility of another party. Moreover, according to the second attestation standard of reporting, the report shall state the practitioner's conclusion about the subject matter or the assertion in relation to the criteria against which the subject matter was evaluated. However, the conclusion may refer to that assertion or to the subject matter to which the assertion relates. Furthermore, given one or more material deviations from the criteria, the practitioner should modify the report and ordinarily should express the conclusion directly on the subject matter.
Answer (A) is incorrect. Litigation support services are consulting services. Answer (B) is incorrect. The CPA assesses the risks of material misstatement in an audit but not necessarily in all attest engagements. Furthermore, the assessment may not be at a low level. Answer (D) is incorrect. An attest engagement results in a report on subject matter or on an assertion about the subject matter.

4. Which of the following professional services is considered an attest engagement?

    A. A consulting service engagement to provide computer advice to a client.

    B. An engagement to report on compliance with statutory requirements.

    C. An income tax engagement to prepare federal and state tax returns.

    D. The compilation of financial statements from a client's accounting records.

Answer (B) is correct.

    REQUIRED: The attest service.

    DISCUSSION: Attest services have traditionally been limited to expressing an opinion on historical financial statements on the basis of an audit in accordance with GAAS. But CPAs increasingly provide assurance on representations other than historical statements and in forms other than an opinion. Thus, attest services may extend to engagements related to management's compliance with specified requirements or the effectiveness of internal control over compliance.

    Answer (A) is incorrect. The attestation standards explicitly do not apply to consulting services in which the practitioner provides advice or recommendations to a client. Answer (C) is incorrect. Tax return preparation is not an attest service according to the attestation standards. Answer (D) is incorrect. A compilation of a financial statement is not an attest service according to the attestation standards.

1.2 Overall Objectives and Conducting an Audit (AU-C 200 and AU-C 315)

5. Which of the following statements is true concerning an auditor's responsibilities regarding financial statements?

    A. Making suggestions that are adopted about the form and content of an entity's financial statements impairs an auditor's independence.

    B. An auditor may draft an entity's financial statements based on information from management's accounting system.

    C. The fair presentation of audited financial statements in conformity with GAAP is an implicit part of the auditor's responsibilities.

    D. An auditor's responsibilities for audited financial statements are not confined to the expression of the auditor's opinion.

Answer (B) is correct.

    REQUIRED: The true statement about the auditor's responsibilities for financial statements.

    DISCUSSION: The independent auditor may make suggestions about the form or content of the financial statements or draft them, in whole or in part, based on information from management's accounting system. However, the auditor's responsibility for the financial statements (s)he has audited is confined to the expression of his/her opinion on them.

    Answer (A) is incorrect. Suggestions about the form and content of an entity's financial statements do not impair an auditor's independence as long as management takes responsibility for the financial statements. Answer (C) is incorrect. The presentation of the financial statements in conformity with GAAP is the responsibility of management. Answer (D) is incorrect. The auditor's responsibilities for audited financial statements are confined to the expression of the opinion.

6. Who establishes generally accepted auditing standards?

    A. Auditing Standards Board and the Public Company Accounting Oversight Board.

    B. Financial Accounting Standards Board and the Governmental Accounting Standards Board.

    C. State Boards of Accountancy.

    D. Securities and Exchange Commission.

Answer (A) is correct.

    REQUIRED: The organization that issues generally accepted auditing standards (GAAS).

    DISCUSSION: AICPA Conduct Rule 202, *Compliance with Standards*, requires adherence to standards issued by bodies designated by the AICPA Council. The Auditing Standards Board (ASB) is the body designated to issue auditing standards. They are in the form of Statements on Auditing Standards (SASs). The Public Company Accounting Oversight Board (PCAOB) was created by the Sarbanes-Oxley Act of 2002. It establishes by rule auditing, quality control, ethics, independence, and other standards relating to the preparation of audit reports for issuers. The PCAOB is required to cooperate with the AICPA and other groups in setting auditing standards and may adopt their proposals. Nevertheless, the PCAOB is authorized to amend, modify, repeal, or reject any such standards. A number of auditing standards have been issued to date, the most significant requiring opinions on internal control for public companies.

    Answer (B) is incorrect. The FASB and the GASB issue financial accounting pronouncements and interpretations. Answer (C) is incorrect. Boards of Accountancy in the states and territories regulate the practice of accounting. They typically grant CPA certificates and licenses. Answer (D) is incorrect. The SEC issues Financial Reporting Releases and Accounting and Auditing Enforcement Releases.

7. An auditor observes the mailing of monthly statements to a client's customers and reviews evidence of follow-up on errors reported by the customers. This test of controls most likely is performed to support management's financial statement assertion(s) of

	Classification and Understandability	Existence
A.	Yes	Yes
B.	Yes	No
C.	No	Yes
D.	No	No

Answer (C) is correct.
REQUIRED: The financial statement assertion(s) related to observing the client's follow-up on errors reported on monthly statements.
DISCUSSION: The existence assertion relates to whether the related balance exists at the balance sheet date. Observation of the mailing of monthly statements as well as observing the correction of reported errors provides evidence that controls may be effective in ensuring that client customers are genuine.
Answer (A) is incorrect. The observation of client activities related to customer statements provides little evidence about proper classification and understandability in the financial statements. Answer (B) is incorrect. The procedure provides little evidence about the classification and understandability assertion. Answer (D) is incorrect. The mailing and follow-up procedures provide evidence that controls may be effective in ensuring that client customers are genuine.

8. When a PCAOB auditing standard indicates that an auditor "could" perform a specific procedure, how should the auditor decide whether and how to perform the procedure?

A. By comparing the PCAOB standard with related AICPA auditing standards.

B. By exercising professional judgment in the circumstances.

C. By soliciting input from the issuer's audit committee.

D. By evaluating whether the audit is likely to be subject to inspection by the PCAOB.

Answer (B) is correct.
REQUIRED: The means of deciding whether to perform an audit procedure when a PCAOB standard indicates it "could" be performed.
DISCUSSION: Word such as "must" and "should" indicate unconditional responsibilities and presumptively mandatory responsibilities, respectively. Words such as "might" and "could" indicate that the auditor has a responsibility to consider a matter. Thus, (s)he is expected to use professional judgment.
Answer (A) is incorrect. AICPA auditing standards are not authoritative for audits of issuers to the extent the PCAOB Interim Auditing Standards adopted in April 2003 have been suspended or amended. Answer (C) is incorrect. The auditee should not influence what audit procedures are performed. Answer (D) is incorrect. Whether the audit is likely to be subject to inspection by the PCAOB is irrelevant to the choice of a procedure. The decision should be made on the basis of the facts and circumstances.

1.3   Additional Professional Services

9. North Co., a nonissuer, asked its tax accountant, King, a CPA in public practice, to generate North's interim financial statements on King's personal computer when King prepared North's quarterly tax return. King should not submit these financial statements to North unless, as a minimum, King complies with the provisions of

A. Statements on Standards for Accounting and Review Services.

B. Statements on Standards for Unaudited Financial Services.

C. Statements on Standards for Consulting Services.

D. Statements on Standards for Attestation Engagements.

Answer (A) is correct.
REQUIRED: The standards appropriate for an accountant who generates interim financial statements.
DISCUSSION: The Statements on Standards for Accounting and Review Services apply to compilations and reviews performed by practitioners. The AICPA bylaws designate the Accounting and Review Services Committee as the senior technical committee authorized to issue pronouncements in connection with the unaudited financial statements or other unaudited financial information of a nonissuer.
Answer (B) is incorrect. These standards do not exist. Answer (C) is incorrect. The practitioner is providing compilation services, not consulting services. Answer (D) is incorrect. Statements on Standards for Attestation Engagements are appropriate whenever the practitioner is engaged in providing attestation services. A compilation, however, provides no assurance.

10. Which of the following services, if any, may an accountant who is **not** independent provide?

A. Compilations but **not** reviews.

B. Reviews but **not** compilations.

C. Both compilations and reviews.

D. No services.

Answer (A) is correct.
REQUIRED: The service(s), if any, that may be provided by an accountant who is not independent.
DISCUSSION: Attest services provide assurance and require the accountant to be independent. However, a compilation provides no assurance. Thus, the accountant need not be independent. The report describes the compilation service and disclaims an opinion or any other form of assurance on the financial statements. The accountant also states in the report that (s)he is not independent.

11. Which of the following components is appropriate in a practitioner's report on the results of applying agreed-upon procedures?

A. A list of the procedures performed, as agreed to by the specified parties identified in the report.

B. A statement that management is responsible for expressing an opinion.

C. A title that includes the phrase "independent audit."

D. A statement that the report is unrestricted in its use.

Answer (A) is correct.

REQUIRED: The component appropriate for an agreed-upon procedures report.

DISCUSSION: In an agreed-upon procedures engagement, the practitioner is engaged to report on the results of performing specific procedures agreed upon with specified parties. The report lists the procedures performed and provides the results of those procedures but provides no form of positive or negative assurance.

Answer (B) is incorrect. No opinion is expressed in an agreed-upon procedures report. Answer (C) is incorrect. The report does not refer to an audit. Answer (D) is incorrect. An agreed-upon procedures report should have a statement restricting its use to the specified parties who agreed upon the procedures to be performed.

12. The party responsible for assumptions identified in the preparation of prospective financial statements is usually

A. A third-party lending institution.

B. The client's management.

C. The reporting accountant.

D. The client's independent auditor.

Answer (B) is correct.

REQUIRED: The party usually responsible for assumptions identified in the preparation of prospective financial statements.

DISCUSSION: Management is usually the responsible party, that is, the person(s) responsible for the assumptions underlying prospective financial statements. However, the responsible party may be a party outside the entity, such as a possible acquirer.

13. A financial forecast consists of prospective financial statements that present an entity's expected financial position, results of operations, and cash flows. A forecast

A. Is based on the most conservative estimates.

B. Presents estimates given one or more hypothetical assumptions.

C. Unlike a projection, may contain a range.

D. Is based on assumptions reflecting conditions expected to exist and courses of action expected to be taken.

Answer (D) is correct.

REQUIRED: The true statement about a financial forecast.

DISCUSSION: According to AT 301, a financial forecast consists of prospective financial statements "that present, to the best of the responsible party's knowledge and belief, an entity's expected financial position, results of operations, and cash flows." A forecast is based on "the responsible party's assumptions reflecting conditions it expects to exist and the course of action it expects to take."

Answer (A) is incorrect. The information presented is based on expected (most likely) conditions and courses of action rather than the most conservative estimate. Answer (B) is incorrect. A financial projection (not a forecast) is based on assumptions by the responsible party reflecting expected conditions and courses of action, given one or more hypothetical assumptions (a condition or action not necessarily expected to occur). Answer (C) is incorrect. Both forecasts and projections may be stated either in point estimates or ranges.

14. Which of the following presents what the effects on historical financial data might have been if a consummated transaction had occurred at an earlier date?

A. Prospective financial statements.

B. Pro forma financial information.

C. Interim financial information.

D. A financial projection.

Answer (B) is correct.

REQUIRED: The kind of financial data showing what the effects of a consummated transaction would have been if it had occurred at an earlier date.

DISCUSSION: Pro forma information shows what the significant effects on historical financial information would have been had a consummated or proposed transaction (or event) occurred at an earlier date. Examples of these transactions include a business combination, disposal of a segment, a change in the form or status of an entity, and a change in capitalization.

Answer (A) is incorrect. Prospective financial statements do not cover periods that have completely expired. Hence, they are not historical statements. Answer (C) is incorrect. Interim financial information states actual results. Answer (D) is incorrect. A financial projection is a prospective statement and therefore is not a presentation of historical information.

1.4 Assurance Services

15. Assurance services are best described as

A. Services designed for the improvement of operations, resulting in better outcomes.

B. Independent professional services that improve the quality of information, or its context, for decision makers.

C. The assembly of financial statements based on information and assumptions of a responsible party.

D. Services designed to express an opinion on historical financial statements based on the results of an audit.

Answer (B) is correct.
    REQUIRED: The description of assurance services.
    DISCUSSION: The AICPA defines assurance services as "independent professional services that improve the quality of information, or its context, for decision makers." Assurance services encompass audit and other attestation services but also include nonstandard services. Assurance services do not encompass consulting services.
    Answer (A) is incorrect. Consulting services are services designed for the improvement of operations, resulting in better outcomes. Answer (C) is incorrect. Compilation services are the assembly of financial statements based on information and assumptions of a responsible party. Answer (D) is incorrect. The traditional audit consists of services designed to express an opinion on historical financial statements based on the results of an audit.

16. The objective of assurance services is to

A. Provide more timely information.

B. Enhance decision making.

C. Compare internal information and policies to those of other firms.

D. Improve the firm's outcomes.

Answer (B) is correct.
    REQUIRED: The objective of assurance services.
    DISCUSSION: The main objective of assurance services, as stated by the AICPA, is to provide information that assists in better decision making. Assurance services encompass audit and other attestation services but also include nonstandard services. Assurance services do not encompass consulting services.
    Answer (A) is incorrect. Providing more timely information is not a stated objective. Answer (C) is incorrect. Assurance services do not involve analysis of other companies. Answer (D) is incorrect. Providing information that results in better outcomes is an objective of consulting services.

17. Assurance services differ from consulting services in that they

	Focus on Providing Advice	Involve Monitoring of One Party by Another
A.	Yes	Yes
B.	Yes	No
C.	No	Yes
D.	No	No

Answer (C) is correct.
    REQUIRED: The way(s) in which assurance services differ from consulting services.
    DISCUSSION: Assurance services encompass attestation services but not consulting services. Assurance services differ from consulting services in two ways: (1) They focus on improving information rather than providing advice, and (2) they usually involve situations in which one party wants to monitor another rather than the two-party arrangements common in consulting engagements.

18. The AICPA committee on assurance services has identified a professional service called ElderCare (PrimePlus) services. One fundamental purpose of this assurance service is to assist the elderly and their families by

A. Investing the funds of the elderly person.

B. Reporting whether specified objectives are being met by caregivers.

C. Choosing caregivers.

D. Performing operational audits of healthcare providers.

Answer (B) is correct.
    REQUIRED: The fundamental purpose of ElderCare services.
    DISCUSSION: The AICPA committee on assurance services has developed business plans for a number of assurance services, one of which involves elder care. The fundamental purpose of ElderCare services is to gather evidence and report to concerned parties (e.g., adult children of an elderly parent) as to whether agreed-upon objectives have been met with regard to care delivery, such as medical, household, and financial services. Related services provided directly to the elderly person or to the other concerned parties may include oversight of investment of funds (but not making an investment of funds), assistance in the choice of caregivers, accounting for the elderly person's income and expenses, and arranging for care and services, such as transportation, meal delivery, or placement in a retirement facility.
    Answer (A) is incorrect. The CPA might oversee, but not make, investments. Answer (C) is incorrect. The CPA might help in the choice of caregivers but would not make the decision. Answer (D) is incorrect. An operational audit is far beyond the limits of an ElderCare service.

19. SysTrust is an assurance service designed to

A. Increase the comfort of management and other stakeholders relative to an information system.

B. Provide an opinion on the fairness of an information system's output.

C. Provide the SEC with information used to administer the securities laws.

D. Allow a CPA to provide a consulting service to management relating to their information system.

Answer (A) is correct.
REQUIRED: The purpose of SysTrust.
DISCUSSION: The objective of SysTrust is an attestation report on management's assertion about the reliability of an information system that supports a business or a given activity. The CPA also may report directly on the reliability of the system. This assurance service is designed to increase the stakeholders' comfort relative to the system's satisfaction of the SysTrust principles: online privacy, security, processing integrity, availability, and confidentiality. The practitioner may provide assurance about any or all of these principles.
Answer (B) is incorrect. SysTrust does not directly address the output of a system. Answer (C) is incorrect. The report is not specifically designed for any one user. Answer (D) is incorrect. Assurance services are not classified as consulting services.

20. The AICPA assurance service, called CPA Performance Review, attempts to provide users with

A. A profile of the business risks and the appropriate systems in place to manage those risks.

B. An opinion on whether the financial statements are fairly stated.

C. An evaluation of whether an entity has reliable measures of performance beyond the traditional financial statements.

D. An assessment of management's assertion on internal control and whether the system is meeting the objectives of the organization.

Answer (C) is correct.
REQUIRED: The purpose of CPA Performance Review.
DISCUSSION: CPA Performance Review evaluates whether an entity's performance measurement system contains relevant and reliable measures for assessing the degree to which the entity's goals and objectives are achieved. It attempts to provide a more balanced scorecard than just the traditional financial statements.
Answer (A) is incorrect. Evaluation and reporting on an entity's business risk describes the CPA Risk Advisory assurance service. Answer (B) is incorrect. An opinion on the financial statements describes the purpose of a financial audit. Answer (D) is incorrect. An assessment of management's assertion on internal control is performed in an attestation engagement to report on internal control.

21. Which of the following is a term for an attest engagement in which a CPA assesses a client's commercial Internet site for compliance with principles, such as online privacy, security, and confidentiality?

A. ElectroNet.

B. EDIFACT.

C. TechSafe.

D. WebTrust.

Answer (D) is correct.
REQUIRED: The attest engagement for an Internet site.
DISCUSSION: The WebTrust seal provides assurance about compliance with the principles of online privacy, security, processing integrity, availability, and confidentiality. It is a modular service that allows the practitioner to express an opinion about compliance with individual principles or combinations of principles. Online privacy is the protection of the collection, use, disclosure, and retention of personal information. Security is the protection against unauthorized access to the system (both physical and logical). Processing integrity is the assurance that system processing is complete, accurate, timely, and authorized. Availability is the assertion that the system is available for operation and used as agreed. Confidentiality is the protection of information from being viewed by unauthorized parties.
Answer (A) is incorrect. "ElectroNet" is a nonsense term. Answer (B) is incorrect. EDIFACT (Electronic Data Interchange For Administration Commerce and Transport) is an ISO standard for electronic data interchange (EDI). Answer (C) is incorrect. "TechSafe" is a nonsense term.

22. An entity engaged a CPA to determine whether the client's web sites comply with defined WebTrust principles and criteria. In performing this engagement, the CPA should apply the provisions of

A. Statements on Assurance Standards.

B. Statements on Standards for Attestation Engagements.

C. Statements on Standards for Management Consulting Services.

D. Statements on Auditing Standards.

Answer (B) is correct.
REQUIRED: The pronouncements that apply to WebTrust.
DISCUSSION: An attest engagement involves reporting on subject matter, or an assurance about subject matter, that is the responsibility of another party. When providing WebTrust assurance, the accountant must address written assertions by management. Thus, Statements on Standards for Attestation Engagements are applicable.
Answer (A) is incorrect. The AICPA has not issued specific Statements on Assurance Standards. Answer (C) is incorrect. WebTrust is not considered a management consulting service. Answer (D) is incorrect. Statements on Auditing Standards are applicable to audits of financial statements.

23. A WebTrust engagement on processing integrity requires from client management a

    A. Written assertion.

    B. Set of financial statements.

    C. Third-party verification letter.

    D. Statement about the integrity of top management.

Answer (A) is correct.
    REQUIRED: The requirement of management when a CPA provides the WebTrust service.
    DISCUSSION: WebTrust was developed from the attestation standards and requires a written assertion by management for each principle reported on. When the assertion about a website complies with WebTrust principles, it is granted the CPA WebTrust seal to be displayed on the entity's web page. Consumers may access the examination report and CPA WebTrust principles and criteria through the entity's web page.

24. Under the assurance service WebTrust, the broad principles relating to websites are security, availability, confidentiality, processing integrity, and

    A. Information disclosure.

    B. Website performance.

    C. Online privacy.

    D. Transaction assurance.

Answer (C) is correct.
    REQUIRED: The principle relating to websites under the assurance service WebTrust.
    DISCUSSION: WebTrust provides assurance about compliance with the principles of online privacy, security, processing integrity, availability, and confidentiality. It is a modular service that allows the practitioner to express an opinion and grant the corresponding seal with respect to individual principles or combinations of principles.
    Answer (A) is incorrect. Information disclosure is not included in the list of principles. Answer (B) is incorrect. Website performance is not included in the list of principles. Answer (D) is incorrect. Transaction assurance is not included in the list of principles.

1.5 Quality Control

25. One of a CPA firm's basic objectives is to provide professional services that conform with professional standards. Reasonable assurance of achieving this basic objective is provided through

    A. A system of quality control.

    B. A system of peer review.

    C. Continuing professional education.

    D. Compliance with generally accepted reporting standards.

Answer (A) is correct.
    REQUIRED: The means of reasonably assuring that a CPA firm's services meet professional standards.
    DISCUSSION: A CPA firm must have a system of quality control that ensures that its personnel comply with professional standards applicable to its audit and accounting practice. However, a deficiency in an engagement, by itself, does not necessarily indicate that the firm's system of quality control is not sufficient. GAAS apply to individual engagements, and Statements on Quality Control Standards (SQCSs) apply to the firm's practice as a whole.
    Answer (B) is incorrect. A system of peer review is a necessary part of the practice-monitoring requirement for AICPA membership. Answer (C) is incorrect. Continuing professional education is but one element of quality control. Answer (D) is incorrect. Firms must comply with all pronouncements applicable to the services rendered, not just with the reporting standards.

26. The purpose of establishing quality control policies and procedures for deciding whether to accept or continue a client relationship is to

    A. Monitor the risk factors concerning misstatements arising from the misappropriation of assets.

    B. Provide reasonable assurance that personnel are adequately trained to fulfill their responsibilities.

    C. Minimize the likelihood of associating with clients whose management lacks integrity.

    D. Document objective criteria for the CPA firm's responses to peer review comments.

Answer (C) is correct.
    REQUIRED: The purpose of policies and procedures for accepting or continuing clients.
    DISCUSSION: The procedures pertaining to client acceptance or continuation should provide reasonable assurance that the likelihood of association with a client whose management lacks integrity is minimized. They include consideration of the business reputation of the client's principal owners, key management, related parties, and those charged with governance.
    Answer (A) is incorrect. The engagement performance element of quality control should monitor the risk factors concerning misstatements arising from the misappropriation of assets. Answer (B) is incorrect. The human resources element of quality control should provide reasonable assurance that personnel will be adequately trained to fulfill their responsibilities. Answer (D) is incorrect. Documenting objective criteria for the CPA firm's responses to peer review comments is not an objective for establishing quality control policies or procedures. However, it is a result of the monitoring aspect of a quality control system.

27. Which of the following is an element of a CPA firm's quality control system that should be considered in establishing its quality control policies and procedures?

A. Complying with laws and regulations.

B. Using statistical sampling techniques.

C. Managing human resources.

D. Considering audit risk and materiality.

Answer (C) is correct.
REQUIRED: The element of quality control.
DISCUSSION: The quality control element of human resources requires establishment of policies and procedures to provide reasonable assurance that only qualified persons with the required technical training and proficiency perform the work.
Answer (A) is incorrect. The auditor considers compliance with laws and regulations. However, this consideration is not an element of quality control. Answer (B) is incorrect. An auditing firm may use statistical or nonstatistical sampling techniques in performing audits; a particular sampling technique is not an element of quality control. Answer (D) is incorrect. An auditor must consider audit risk and materiality in performing the audit, but this consideration is not an element of quality control.

28. Which of the following are elements of a CPA firm's quality control that should be considered in establishing its quality control policies and procedures?

	Human Resources	Monitoring	Engagement Performance
A.	Yes	Yes	No
B.	Yes	Yes	Yes
C.	No	Yes	Yes
D.	Yes	No	Yes

Answer (B) is correct.
REQUIRED: The elements that should be considered in establishing quality control policies and procedures.
DISCUSSION: The quality control element of human resources relates to providing reasonable assurance that the firm has sufficient personnel with the necessary capabilities, competence, and commitment to ethics. The quality control element of monitoring relates to providing reasonable assurance that the firm has a quality control system that is relevant, adequate, effective, and complied with. The quality control element of engagement performance relates to providing reasonable assurance that (1) engagements are consistently performed in accordance with applicable requirements and (2) issued reports are appropriate (QC 10).

29. A CPA firm should establish procedures for conducting and supervising work at all organizational levels to provide reasonable assurance that the work performed meets the firm's standards of quality. To achieve this goal, the firm most likely would establish procedures for

A. Evaluating prospective and continuing client relationships.

B. Reviewing documentation of the work performed and reports issued.

C. Requiring personnel to adhere to the applicable independence rules.

D. Maintaining personnel files containing documentation related to the evaluation of personnel.

Answer (B) is correct.
REQUIRED: The procedure necessary to provide reasonable assurance that the work performed meets the firm's standards of quality relating to supervision.
DISCUSSION: The engagement performance element of quality control includes policies and procedures that cover planning, performing, supervising, reviewing, documenting, and communicating the results of each engagement. Objectives of supervision include establishing procedures for (1) planning engagements, (2) maintaining the firm's standards of quality, and (3) reviewing documentation of the work performed and reports issued.
Answer (A) is incorrect. Evaluating client relationships relates to the quality control element of acceptance and continuance of client relationships and specific engagements. Answer (C) is incorrect. Requiring adherence to independence rules relates to the quality control element of relevant ethical requirements. Answer (D) is incorrect. Evaluation of personnel relates to the quality control element of human resources.

30. All of the following are audit quality control requirements contained in the Sarbanes-Oxley Act of 2002 **except**

A. The lead audit partner must rotate off the audit every 5 years.

B. The audit report must be submitted to the Public Company Accounting Oversight Board prior to issuance.

C. The audit report must be reviewed and approved by a second partner.

D. The Public Company Accounting Oversight Board will periodically inspect registered CPA firms.

Answer (B) is correct.
REQUIRED: The quality control issue not addressed in the Sarbanes-Oxley Act.
DISCUSSION: Audit reports must be determined appropriate for issuance by the CPA firm but need not be approved by the PCAOB.

31. The nature and extent of a CPA firm's quality control policies and procedures depend on

	The CPA Firm's Size	The Nature of the CPA Firm's Practice	Cost-Benefit Considerations
A.	Yes	Yes	Yes
B.	Yes	Yes	No
C.	Yes	No	Yes
D.	No	Yes	Yes

Answer (A) is correct.
REQUIRED: The factors affecting a CPA firm's quality control policies and procedures.
DISCUSSION: The nature and extent of a firm's quality control policies and procedures depend on a number of factors, such as the firm's size, the degree of operating autonomy allowed, its human resources policies, the nature of its practice and organization, and appropriate cost-benefit considerations.

32. According to PCAOB quality control standards applying to an audit, the engagement quality reviewer evaluates

A. The documentation.

B. Only the uncorrected misstatements.

C. The audit report but not the internal control report.

D. Only the assessment of risks identified by management.

Answer (A) is correct.
REQUIRED: The subject matter evaluated by the engagement quality reviewer (EQR).
DISCUSSION: The EQR process in an audit evaluates the significant judgments made. This involves discussions with the engagement partner and other team members and reviewing whether the documentation supports the conclusions reached and appropriate responses to significant risks.
Answer (B) is incorrect. The reviewer evaluates corrected and uncorrected identified misstatements and control deficiencies. Answer (C) is incorrect. The reviewer evaluates the statements, the internal control report, and the audit report. Answer (D) is incorrect. The reviewer evaluates the assessment of, and responses to, significant risks, including those identified by the reviewer.

33. According to PCAOB quality control standards applying to audits, the engagement quality reviewer most likely

A. May provide concurring approval of issuance of the report even if (s)he is aware of a significant engagement deficiency.

B. Must be an associated person of a registered public accounting firm.

C. Must have integrity and objectivity but not independence.

D. May be an engagement partner on a prior audit but not the current audit.

Answer (B) is correct.
REQUIRED: The limit on an engagement quality reviewer.
DISCUSSION: The objective of the reviewer is to evaluate the significant judgments made and the related conclusions reached. (S)he must be an associated person of a registered public accounting firm and may be from outside the firm. Moreover, the reviewer must have the competence to serve as a partner on the engagement and have independence, integrity, and objectivity. But an engagement partner on either of the two preceding audits ordinarily may not be the reviewer.
Answer (A) is incorrect. Awareness of a significant engagement deficiency precludes concurring approval of issuance. Answer (C) is incorrect. The reviewer must be independent. Answer (D) is incorrect. An engagement partner on either of the two preceding audits ordinarily is disqualified from reviewing the current audit.

34. The in-charge auditor for an audit of an issuer most likely has a supervisory responsibility to explain to the staff assistants

A. That immaterial fraud is not to be reported to the client's audit committee.

B. How the results of various auditing procedures performed by the assistants should be evaluated.

C. What benefits may be attained by the assistants' adherence to established time budgets.

D. Why certain documents are being transferred from the current file to the permanent file.

Answer (B) is correct.
REQUIRED: The responsibility of the audit supervisor.
DISCUSSION: Assistants should be informed of their responsibilities and the objectives of the work they are to perform. They should be informed about the matters that affect the nature, timing, and extent of procedures, including how the results of tests should be evaluated (AS No. 10).
Answer (A) is incorrect. Immaterial fraud may be reported to those charged with governance, e.g., the audit committee. Answer (C) is incorrect. Discussion of time budgets is not a responsibility under the auditing standards. Answer (D) is incorrect. At the end of the audit, supervisors determine which documents are to be transferred to the permanent file. These decisions need not be justified to staff assistants.

Use the additional questions in Gleim **CPA Test Prep** to create Practice Exams that emulate Prometric!

1.6 PRACTICE TASK-BASED SIMULATIONS

			Time Remaining							
Auditing and Attestation			1 hour - 30 minutes	Unsplit	Split Horiz	Split Vertical	Spreadsheet	Calculator	Exit	
Testlet 4 of 4										

DIRECTIONS

Note: If you believe you have encountered a software malfunction, report it to the test center staff immediately.

Navigation

To navigate from task to task, use the controls at the bottom of the screen. Click on the **Next** button to advance to the next task, or the **Previous** button to go to the previous task. To go directly to any task, click on its number.

If you would like a reminder to revisit a task, or want to indicate that you are finished with it, click on the reminder flag below the task number. To clear the flag, click on it again. Reminder flags are for your use only – they do not contribute to your score.

Tabs

In this part of the examination, you will be asked to complete various tasks. Every task has one or more **Work Tabs**. Some tasks have one or more **Information Tabs**, others may have none. Every task has a **Help** tab.

If a task has **Information Tabs**, you may use the information in them to complete your responses in the **Work Tabs**.

Work tab	Information tab	Help tab

Work Tabs:

- **Work Tabs** are identified with a pencil icon. This is where your responses are expected.
- Each task has one or more **Work Tabs**.
- **Work Tabs** contain directions for completing the task – be sure to read these directions carefully.
- The **Work Tab** name in the example above is for illustration only – yours will differ.
- You must complete all of the **Work Tabs** in each task to receive full credit.

Information Tabs:

- The Authoritative Literature will be provided in all tasks in the AUD, FAR, and REG sections for your reference.
- Your simulation may have one or more additional **Information Tabs**. Like the Authoritative Literature tabs, **Information Tabs** do not have a pencil icon.
- If your task has additional **Information Tabs**, go through each to familiarize yourself with the task content.

Help Tab:

- The **Help Tab** provides assistance with the exam software that is used in this task. For example, if the task is to compose a memorandum, **Help** will provide information about the word processor.

The Toolbar

The toolbar at the top of the screen shows the amount of time remaining for you to complete the tasks. In addition, the following tools are available. Note that only the **Exit** button is displayed when Directions are visible - the others will appear when you begin the tasks.

Click on these buttons to split or unsplit the screen. You can split the screen vertically or horizontally.

Click on this button to display the calculator; click on it again to hide the calculator. To move the calculator, click on the calculator title bar and drag the calculator to the desired location.

Click on this button to use the spreadsheet; click on it again to hide the spreadsheet. To move the spreadsheet, click on the the spreadsheet title bar and drag the spreadsheet to the desired location.

Click on this button to go on to the next part of the examination. You must complete all of the tasks to receive full credit. Once you click on **Exit** and confirm the action, you will NOT be able to return to this testlet.

Select a choice from the list provided to match the type of professional service (i.e., attestation, assurance, and consulting) with the associated characteristic of that professional service. Each choice may be used once, more than once, or not at all.

Characteristic	Answer
1. Independence is not required for this service.	
2. This service results in a written conclusion about subject matter.	
3. This service improves the quality of information, or its context, for decision makers.	
4. This service provides recommendations based on the objectives of the engagement.	
5. This service provides for a level of assurance based on an examination.	

Professional Service
A) Attestation
B) Assurance
C) Consulting

Each statement describes a responsibility of an auditor. Select from the list below the type of responsibility each imposes on the auditor.

Statement	Answer
1. The auditor should document the evidence obtained in the audit.	
2. The auditor must be independent.	
3. The auditor should test management's assertions relating to the financial statements.	
4. The auditor may make suggestions about the form or content of the financial statements.	
5. In some cases, the auditor could apply one audit procedure to test more than one assertion.	
6. The auditor must follow GAAS in an audit of a nonissuer.	
7. The auditor should obtain sufficient appropriate evidence to support the opinion.	

Responsibility Choices
A) Unconditional requirement
B) Presumptively mandatory requirement
C) Requirement to consider

Independence and Assurance	Authoritative Literature	Help

The following are various services that accountants perform. For each type of service, select whether the service provided requires the accountant to be independent (Column A) and select the level of assurance provided (Column B). Each choice may be used once, more than once, or not at all.

Service	Column A	Column B
1. Compilation		
2. Consulting		
3. Review		
4. Audit		
5. Agreed-upon procedures		

Column A	Column B
A) Independence required	A) No assurance provided
B) Independence not required	B) Limited assurance provided
	C) Positive assurance provided
	D) Neither positive nor limited assurance provided, but results of procedures provided

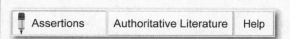

Assertions	Authoritative Literature	Help

Financial statements implicitly or explicitly include management's assertions about the fair presentation of information, that is, about its recognition, measurement, presentation, and disclosure. Select from the list provided the appropriate assertion of a nonissuer's management for each definition. Each assertion may be used once.

Service	Answer
1. Recorded transactions and events actually took place.	
2. Amounts and other data were recorded appropriately.	
3. All assets, liabilities, and equity interests that should have been recorded were recorded.	
4. Financial information is appropriately presented and described, and disclosures are clearly expressed.	
5. Transactions and events were recorded in the proper period.	
6. Assets, liabilities, and equity interest are included at appropriate amounts, and adjustments are appropriately recorded.	
7. The entity owns the assets, and liabilities are its obligations.	
8. Assets, liabilities, and equity interests are bona fide.	

Assertions
A) Valuation and allocation
B) Cutoff
C) Rights and obligations
D) Accuracy
E) Existence
F) Classification and understandability
G) Occurrence
H) Completeness

Unofficial Answers

1. Professional Services (5 Gradable Items)

1.   C) Consulting. Independence is not required to provide consulting services. Independence is required by attestation standards and is included in the definition of assurance services.

2.   A) Attestation. Attestation results in a written conclusion about subject matter or a written assertion of another party. Its objective is to provide reliable information.

3.   B) Assurance. Assurance services provide better information for decision makers, which leads to better decision making.

4.   C) Consulting. Consulting services provide recommendations based on the objectives of the engagement. The goal is to provide better outcomes.

5.   A) Attestation. Attestation services can provide assurance based on an examination, a review, or the results of agreed-upon procedures.

2. Professional Requirements (7 Gradable Items)

1.   B) Presumptively mandatory requirement. The auditor must comply with a presumptively mandatory requirement whenever it is relevant, except in rare circumstances. The word "should" indicates a presumptively mandatory requirement.

2.   A) Unconditional requirement. The auditor must comply with an unconditional requirement whenever it is relevant. The word "must" indicates an unconditional requirement.

3.   B) Presumptively mandatory requirement. The auditor must comply with a presumptively mandatory requirement whenever it is relevant, except in rare circumstances. The word "should" indicates a presumptively mandatory requirement.

4.   C) Requirement to consider. The words "may," "might," "could," or similar terms and phrases describe actions and procedures that the auditor is presumptively required to consider. Whether the action or procedure is performed is a matter of professional judgment.

5.   C) Requirement to consider. The words "may," "might," "could," or similar terms and phrases describe actions and procedures that the auditor is presumptively required to consider. Whether the action or procedure is performed is a matter of professional judgment.

6.   A) Unconditional requirement. The auditor must comply with an unconditional requirement whenever it is relevant. The word "must" indicates an unconditional requirement.

7.   B) Presumptively mandatory requirement. The auditor must comply with a presumptively mandatory requirement whenever it is relevant, except in rare circumstances. The word "should" indicates a presumptively mandatory requirement.

3. Independence and Assurance (10 Gradable Items)

1. <u>Column A: B, Independence not required; Column B: A, No assurance provided.</u> The accountant provides no assurance and is not required to be independent.

2. <u>Column A: B, Independence not required; Column B: A, No assurance provided.</u> The accountant provides no assurance and is not required to be independent.

3. <u>Column A: A, Independence required; Column B: B, Limited assurance provided.</u> The accountant provides limited assurance and is required to be independent.

4. <u>Column A: A, Independence required; Column B: C, Positive assurance provided.</u> The accountant provides assurance and is required to be independent.

5. <u>Column A: A, Independence required; Column B: D, Neither positive nor limited assurance provided, but results of procedures provided.</u> The accountant provides neither positive nor limited assurance and is required to be independent.

4. Assertions (8 Gradable Items)

1. <u>Occurrence.</u> Occurrence relates to the representation that transactions and events actually took place.

2. <u>Accuracy.</u> Accuracy relates to the representation that amounts and other data were recorded appropriately.

3. <u>Completeness.</u> Completeness relates to the representation that all valid transactions were recorded.

4. <u>Classification and understandability.</u> Classification and understandability relates to the representation that items have been properly described and disclosed in the financial statements.

5. <u>Cutoff.</u> Cutoff relates to the representation that transactions and events were recorded in the proper period.

6. <u>Valuation and allocation.</u> Valuation and allocation relates to the representation that balance sheet items are recorded at the properly valued amounts and adjustments to the balances are appropriately determined and recorded.

7. <u>Rights and obligations.</u> The rights and obligations assertion relates to the representation that assets are owned and liabilities are owed.

8. <u>Existence.</u> Existence relates to the representation that balance sheet items are real.

5. Research (1 Gradable Item)

Answer: AU-C 200.25

AU-C Section 200 -- *Overall Objectives of the Independent Auditor and the Conduct of an Audit in Accordance With Generally Accepted Auditing Standards*

Defining Professional Responsibilities in GAAS

.25 GAAS use the following two categories of professional requirements, identified by specific terms, to describe the degree of responsibility it imposes on auditors:

*   Unconditional requirements. The auditor must comply with an unconditional requirement in all cases in which such requirement is relevant. GAAS use the word "must" to indicate an unconditional requirement.

*   Presumptively mandatory requirements. The auditor must comply with a presumptively mandatory requirement in all cases in which such a requirement is relevant except in rare circumstances discussed in paragraph .26. GAAS use the word "should" to indicate a presumptively mandatory requirement.

Gleim Simulation Grading

Task	Correct Responses		Gradable Items		Score per Task
1	____	÷	5	=	____
2	____	÷	7	=	____
3	____	÷	10	=	____
4	____	÷	8	=	____
5 (Research)	____	÷	1	=	____

Total of Scores per Task ____

÷ Total Number of Tasks   5

Total Score ____ %

Use **CPA Gleim Online** and **Simulation Wizard** to practice more task-based simulations in a realistic environment.

STUDY UNIT TWO
PROFESSIONAL RESPONSIBILITIES

(30 pages of outline)

The Auditing and Attestation section of the CPA exam tests the AICPA *Code of Professional Conduct* and other ethics pronouncements, including awareness of the *Code of Ethics for Professional Accountants* of the International Federation of Accountants (IFAC). This review is not a manual or guide but an aid to understanding concepts. The issues related to independence are the most challenging. In that section, the rule or interpretation is given, followed by insights into ethics concepts and examples derived from questions from prior exams.

Focus your attention on the AICPA *Code of Professional Conduct* (Subunits 1 through 6). The material in Subunit 7, "Other Pronouncements on Professional Responsibilities," parallels the *Code* conceptually in most cases. The specific rule or section numbers need not be memorized for any of the material in this study unit. Professional responsibilities constitute 16-20% of this section of the exam.

2.1 CODE OF PROFESSIONAL CONDUCT

1. **Principles and Rules**

    a. The *Code*, which consists of Principles and Rules of Conduct, applies to professional services performed by AICPA **members**.

    b. The Principles provide the framework for the Rules. They are goal-oriented but **nonbinding**.

    c. The following are the Principles:

        1) **Responsibilities.** All members should exercise sensitive professional and moral judgments when carrying out their professional responsibilities.

        2) **The public interest.** All members should act to benefit the public interest, honor the public trust, and demonstrate commitment to professionalism.

            a) The AICPA adopted the ethical standards because a distinguishing mark of a profession is an acceptance of responsibility to the public.

        3) **Integrity.** All members should perform all professional responsibilities with the highest sense of integrity to maintain public confidence.

        4) **Objectivity and independence.** All members should maintain objectivity and be free of conflicts of interest. A member in public practice should be independent in fact (mind) and appearance when providing attestation services.

        NOTE: A member **not** in public practice need not be independent.

        5) **Due care.** All members should follow the profession's technical and ethical standards, strive for improved competence and quality services, and discharge professional responsibility to the best of the member's ability.

            a) All members must adequately plan and supervise any activity for which they are responsible.

6) **Scope and nature of services.** A member in public practice should follow the Principles of the *Code of Professional Conduct* in determining the nature and scope of services. This principle is for members in public practice only.

d. The Rules of Conduct are **mandatory**.

1. Rule 101 – Independence
2. [1]Rule 102 – Integrity and Objectivity
3. [1]Rule 201 – General Standards
4. [1]Rule 202 – Compliance with Standards
5. [1]Rule 203 – Accounting Principles
6. Rule 301 – Confidential Client Information
7. Rule 302 – Contingent Fees
8. [1]Rule 501 – Acts Discreditable
9. Rule 502 – Advertising and Other Forms of Solicitation
10. [2]Rule 503 – Commissions and Referral Fees
11. [1]Rule 505 – Form of Organization and Name

[1] These Rules of Conduct apply to all members.
[2] Conduct Rule 503 applies in part (Referrals) to all members and in part (Commissions) only to members in public practice. The remaining Rules apply only to members in public practice.

2. **Interpretations and Ethics Rulings**

a. AICPA Interpretations provide guidelines for the scope and application of the Rules.
b. Ethics Rulings apply the Rules and Interpretations to **specific facts** to determine whether a violation exists. Many rulings appear in examples in the following subunits.

Stop and review! You have completed the outline for this subunit. Study multiple-choice questions 1 and 2 on page 81.

2.2 INDEPENDENCE

1. **Rule 101 -- Concepts**

a. A member in public practice must be independent when performing professional services (typically auditing and other attestation services) as required by standards-setting bodies.

1) These bodies include, among others, the AICPA, the IFAC, the Securities and Exchange Commission (SEC), the Public Company Accounting Oversight Board (PCAOB), and the Government Accountability Office (GAO).
2) To inspire public confidence, an auditor must not only be independent (intellectually honest) but also recognized as independent (free of any obligation to, or interest in, the client, management, or owners). As defined in the AICPA Conceptual Framework, an auditor must be independent in mind (fact) and independent in appearance, respectively.

b. Independence is impaired if a covered member has certain interests or relationships.
c. A **covered member** includes

1) An individual on the engagement team or who can influence the engagement;
2) A partner or manager who provides nonattest services to a client;
3) A partner in the office where the lead engagement partner primarily practices in relation to the engagement; and
4) The accounting firm, including the firm's employee benefit plans.

2. **Impairment**

   a. Independence **is impaired** if a covered member **has a direct financial interest** in a client.

CONCEPT

The covered member must have no direct ownership of equity, debt securities, or other investments in a client. The restriction also applies to the covered member's immediate family (spouse and dependents). Moreover, the covered member must not (1) have control of a financial interest in the client or (2) own a beneficial interest through an intermediary if the covered member controls the intermediary (trust, estate, etc.).

EXAMPLES

A covered member must not (1) own shares in a mutual fund that is an attest client, (2) participate in a retirement fund or savings plan sponsored by an attest client, (3) own bonds issued by an attest client, or (4) own a prepaid (529) tuition plan administered by an attest client. Even if shares of a client were held in a blind trust for the covered member, independence would be impaired.

An unsolicited financial interest in a client, such as through a gift or inheritance, does not impair independence if disposed of within 30 days.

---

   b. Independence **is impaired** if a covered member **has loans to or from** a client or its officers, directors, or 10% (or greater) owners.

      1) Exceptions. Independence is **not** impaired by

         a) Certain loans from a client financial institution (e.g., bank). These include (1) auto loans and leases collateralized by the auto, (2) loans fully collateralized by the cash surrender value of insurance, (3) loans fully collateralized by cash deposits, and (4) credit cards with a total outstanding balance of $10,000 or less on a current basis by the payment due date.

         b) Certain loans that are considered "grandfathered" because they were in existence before independence rules became more restrictive.

CONCEPT

Loans are considered a direct financial interest. The restriction on loans includes the covered member's immediate family (spouse and dependents).

EXAMPLES

A covered member must not borrow money from an attest client. Also, fees outstanding from an attest client for more than 1 year are considered a loan and would impair independence.

---

   c. Independence **is impaired** if a covered member **has a material indirect financial interest** in a client.

CONCEPT

A covered member (and his or her immediate family) may have some limited financial interests in clients as long as they are not direct and not material to the wealth of the member or the client.

EXAMPLE

A covered member or spouse may own shares in a mutual fund that holds shares of a client as long as the mutual fund investment was not material to the member.

d. In certain circumstances, independence **is impaired** if a covered member **is a trustee of a trust** or **executor of an estate** that has a direct or material indirect financial interest in a client. Independence is impaired if (1) the member can make investment decisions for the trust or estate, (2) the trust or estate holds more than 10% of the ownership interests of a client, or (3) the value of the holding exceeds 10% of the total assets of the trust or estate.

CONCEPT

A covered member must not be in a **position to make decisions** related to a trust or an estate that involves investments or other financial interests in clients.

EXAMPLE

A covered member may be a trustee of a trust that holds shares of a mutual fund that has an investment in a client as long as the amount is not material.

e. Independence **is impaired** if a covered member **has a material joint, closely held investment** with a client.

CONCEPT

A covered member is prohibited from having a material financial relationship with a client that might cause third parties to question the member's objectivity.

EXAMPLES

A covered member must not join with a client to develop and market a product. A covered member also must not own a vacation home jointly with a key officer or principal shareholder of a client.

f. Independence **is impaired** if a firm partner or professional employee **owns more than 5% of a client**.

CONCEPT

This allows some members of a CPA firm, other than covered members, to have some financial interest in clients without affecting the independence of the firm.

EXAMPLES

- A professional employee in the office that conducts an audit, who is not part of the audit team, may own a 5% or less equity interest in a client of the firm.
- However, a partner in that office must not. (S)he is considered a covered member and must have no financial interest in the client.

g. Independence **is impaired** if a firm or one of its partners or professional employees **is associated with the client** as an officer, director, manager, employee, promoter, underwriter, etc.

CONCEPT

The individual or firm must not appear to be acting in the capacity of management or employee of the client. This includes having the responsibility to perform any duties of employees or management.

EXAMPLE

A covered member is a director of an entity. A foundation's sole purpose is to raise funds for the entity. The covered member's independence is impaired with respect to the foundation as well as the entity unless the directorship is clearly honorary.

h. Independence **may be impaired** if a covered member was **formerly employed by or associated with** the client as an officer, director, promoter, underwriter, etc.

CONCEPT

The covered member must disassociate from the client before becoming a covered member. (S)he also must not (1) participate on the engagement team or (2) be able to influence the engagement when his or her former employment/association overlaps the period of the engagement.

EXAMPLE

Disassociation includes, among other things, disposing of direct or material indirect financial interests and ceasing to participate in most employee benefit plans.

i. The covered member's immediate family (spouse or dependents) is subject to Rule 101.

CONCEPT

The financial interests, employment relationships, and other circumstances of immediate family members are attributed to the covered member.

EXAMPLES

An immediate family member may be employed by the client in a non-key position. As a result of such permitted employment, the immediate family member may participate in various employee benefit plans under limited circumstances. For example, the immediate family member must not, among other things, (1) participate on the engagement team or be able to influence the engagement or (2) be involved in investment decisions.

j. As a result of permitted employment, an **immediate family member** of a covered member may participate in a **benefit plan** that is an attest client or is sponsored by an attest client. (However, an exception is described in item k. on the following page.) The plan must be offered to all employees in comparable employment positions, and the immediate family member must not serve in a governance position for the plan or make investment decisions.

1) An immediate family member of a covered member may hold a **direct or material indirect financial interest** in an attest client through participation in a plan if certain conditions are met. For example, the covered member must not be able to influence the attest engagement, and the family member has no other investment option.

CONCEPT

This covers general benefit plans for immediate family members that may create financial interests in clients and affect the covered member.

EXAMPLE

The spouse of a covered member has a non-key position in a client and, along with other employees, is a part of an employee profit sharing plan in a client. Investments in the plan consist solely of the client's securities.

k.   As a result of permitted employment, an **immediate family member** of a covered member may participate in a **share-based compensation arrangement** that results in holding a beneficial financial interest in an attest client. The covered member must not participate on the attest engagement team or be able to influence the attest engagement. Also, the immediate family member must not serve in a governance position for the share-based compensation arrangement.

1)   When the interests are distributed or the immediate family member has the right to dispose of the shares, (s)he must dispose of the shares as soon as practicable. The limit is 30 days after (s)he has the right to dispose of the shares.

CONCEPT

This outline section covers specific stock-based benefit plans for immediate family members that may create financial interests in clients and affect the covered member.

EXAMPLE

The immediate family member may participate in an employee stock ownership plan (ESOP) if the conditions are satisfied.

l.   Independence **is impaired** if an individual participating on the engagement team (or able to exert influence or that is a partner in the lead partner's office) has a **close relative** (sibling, parent, or non-dependent child) who holds **a key position** with the client or certain financial interests.

CONCEPT

If a close relative has a financial interest in the client that (1) the individual knows or has reason to believe is material to the relative or (2) permits the relative to exert significant influence over the client, independence is impaired. Some latitude is permitted in the application of this rule based on the family relationship.

EXAMPLES

- A sibling may be a salesperson for a client but not the CFO or a director.
- A parent may be a production manager (non-key position), but not the CEO or a director.

m.   Independence of the firm **is impaired** if a former partner or professional employee of the firm is **employed by or associated with an attest client** in a key position.

1)   Independence is **not** impaired in this case if the person is no longer associated or active with the CPA firm and any retirement compensation is fixed.

2)   An accounting firm is not independent if a CEO, CFO, controller, or person in an equivalent position for an **issuer** was (a) employed by that firm and (b) participated in any capacity in the audit of that issuer during the year before the beginning of the audit.

CONCEPT

Third parties may believe that the person is in a position to influence the engagement.

EXAMPLE

A retired partner must not become a CFO of a client while performing consulting duties for the CPA firm or having retirement pay contingent on retaining the client.

n. Independence of the firm **may be impaired** if certain **nonattest services** are performed for an attest client.

CONCEPT

The practitioner appears to be an advocate or a decision maker for the attest client when performing certain nonattest services. In these circumstances, (s)he is not independent.

---

1) A member's independence is impaired by assuming **management responsibilities** for an attest client. Before performing nonattest services, the member should determine that the client has agreed to (a) assume all management responsibilities, (b) provide sufficient oversight of the services, (c) evaluate their adequacy and results, and (d) accept responsibility for the results. The following are examples:

   a) Setting policies

   b) Directing employees

   c) Authorizing or executing transactions

   d) Preparing transaction source documents

   e) Having custody of assets

   f) Deciding which member recommendations to implement

   g) Reporting to those in charge of governance on management's behalf

   h) Serving as general counsel, stock transfer or escrow agent, or registrar

   i) Accepting responsibility for (1) a client's project or (2) the preparation and fair presentation of a client's financial statements

   j) Accepting responsibility for designing, implementing, maintaining, or monitoring internal control

---

EXAMPLE

During the period of the professional engagement, a professional employee of a firm engaged in the practice of public accounting served as campaign treasurer of a political candidate. If the campaign organization is a client, independence is impaired.

---

2) Independence **is impaired** by providing to attest clients the following services:

   a) Appraisal, valuation, or actuarial services if they involve a significant degree of uncertainty

   b) Expert witness services

   c) Internal audit services

   d) Tax advocacy services

   e) Recruiting, hiring, terminating, or compensating employees

3) Independence is **not impaired** by providing to attest clients the following services:

   a) Consulting services (if the client is responsible for the decisions)
   b) Tax preparation and compliance services
   c) Business risk advising services
   d) Providing general advice based on audit findings

EXAMPLES

- Internal audit services must not be outsourced to the audit firm, but the audit firm may provide advice on how to improve the internal audit function.
- The auditor may prepare the client's tax return but must not testify as an advocate of the client in a tax case.

4) Independence is **not impaired** for attest engagements of nonissuers by providing bookkeeping, payroll processing, or other conventional recordkeeping functions.

CONCEPT

The AICPA allows practitioners to perform these duties for nonissuers (typically small clients) as long as management functions are not performed. The PCAOB rules do not allow these services to be provided to issuers by their auditors. However, issuers are not likely to request these services. Issuers have their own recordkeeping functions.

EXAMPLE

An auditor of a nonissuer may record transactions in a computer program and generate financial statements but must not provide those services for an issuer.

---

o. Independence **is impaired** by **actual or threatened litigation** by either the CPA or the client.

1) Independence is not impaired when the litigation issue is not related to the work product and is not material, for example, a dispute over billing.

2) Independence is not necessarily impaired when shareholders or others bring a class action suit against both the client and the auditor.

CONCEPT

Legal action creates adverse interests between the parties involved. These interests can affect independence.

EXAMPLES

- The client may allege that the member was negligent, or the member may allege that the client's management committed fraud. In these circumstances, the interests of the client and the CPA are opposed, and independence is impaired.
- However, if a creditor or insurer files a suit that alleges reliance on the audited financial statements of a client, independence is not impaired.

---

p. Independence is **not impaired** if a member holds an **honorary directorship or trusteeship** of a not-for-profit organization that is a client.

1) The position must be clearly honorary, and the member must not be able to vote or participate in board or management decisions.

2) The member must be identified as an honorary director or trustee.

CONCEPT

CPAs may lend their support to charitable organizations without impairing independence. However, they must not have managerial responsibilities.

EXAMPLE

An auditor's name is placed on the letterhead as "Honorary Director" of a not-for-profit charity who is a client. As long as the relationship is purely honorary, the auditor is independent.

---

q. Financial interests in, and other relationships with, entities that are **affiliates** of a financial statement attest client may impair independence. In general, members should apply the independence provisions of the *Code* to the attest client's affiliates. Affiliates may have many different relationships with the client. The following are affiliates of the client:

1) An entity that a client can control

2) An entity that controls the client if the client is material to the entity

3) An entity in which a client has a material direct financial interest that gives the client significant influence over the entity

4) An entity with significant influence over the client in the form of a material direct financial interest

5) A sister entity of a client if the sister entity and the client are material to the entity that controls both

6) A trustee deemed to control a trust client that is not an investment company

7) The sponsor of the plan if the client is a single-employer employee benefit plan

8) Any union or participating employer that has significant influence over a client that is a multiple or multi-employer employee benefit plan

9) An employee benefit plan sponsored by either a client or an entity controlled by the client

10) An investment advisor, general partner, or trustee of an investment company client (fund) who (a) has a material interest in the fund and (b) has significant influence or control over the fund

---

CONCEPT

Various member involvements with affiliates create an indirect interest in an attest client. Thus, some measure of materiality is considered as with other indirect interests. Significant mutual interests of a member and a client may cause an impairment of independence.

EXAMPLE

A member cannot be an investor in, or a director of, an attest client's affiliate.

NOTE: The preceding outline regarding relationships with affiliates of the client is based on Interpretation 101-18 (published November 2011). It is effective on January 1, 2014, but early implementation is allowed. However, (1) Interpretation 101-8, on which the outline below is based, and (2) the related Ethics Rulings have been reestablished by the AICPA. They remain in effect until (1) January 1, 2014, or (2) the adoption of Interpretation 101-18. Accordingly, both Interpretation 101-8 and Interpretation 101-18 are potentially testable until July 1, 2014, when only Interpretation 101-18 will be tested.

Independence **is impaired** if a covered member has certain financial interests in nonclients having **investor or investee relationships** with the client.

1) Any member associated with the statements of the client is considered a covered member.

2) Independence **is impaired** with respect to the client in any of the following circumstances:

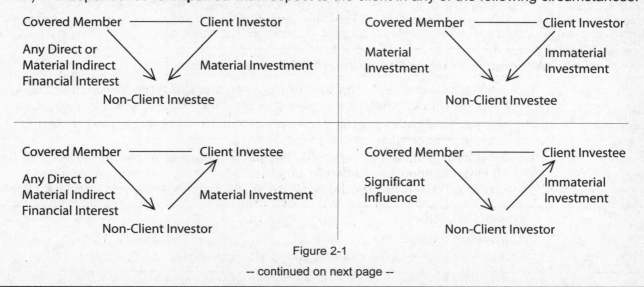

Figure 2-1

-- continued on next page --

-- continued from previous page --

3) Independence **is not impaired** if a member did not, and could not, reasonably know about the relationship.

EXAMPLE

A covered member and an audit client have material investments in a startup entity. The auditor's independence is impaired in relation to the client.

r. An **auditor** of the basic financial statements of a **governmental entity must be independent** of the entity.

1) However, a primary auditor need not be independent in the following circumstances:

   a) With respect to any fund, component unit, or disclosed entity, if the auditor explicitly relies on reports by **other auditors** on such entity

   b) With respect to a disclosed entity, if the reporting entity is **not financially accountable** for it, and the required disclosure does not include financial information

2) Neither the member nor a member of his or her immediate family should occupy a **key position** with the disclosed entity.

3) An auditor who is not auditing the primary government must be independent only of the statements reported on.

   a) Nevertheless, the covered member or a member of his or her immediate family may not occupy a key position with the primary government.

CONCEPT

Governmental financial statements often display combinations of reporting entities. The basic financial statements may include a fund or entity audited by another auditor. Even if the auditor of the basic financial statements is not independent of the fund, it is acceptable to report on the basic financial statements.

EXAMPLE

The reporting entity is a local government. A state authority with a state-approved board provides temporary fiscal oversight. Because it issues bonds and collects revenues on behalf of the local government, it is included in the reporting entity. Moreover, the primary auditor must be independent of the authority although the reporting entity is not financially accountable for it. The disclosures required for the authority consist in part of financial information. However, the primary auditor need not be independent of the authority if (s)he relies on the report of another auditor.

s. **Alternative Practice Structures (APSs)**

1) Independence rules for an APS apply when the traditional CPA firm is closely aligned with another organization that performs other professional services.

2) In an APS, **direct superiors** of covered members are subject to the same independence rules as covered members.

3) In an APS, **indirect superiors** (including a spouse or dependents) may not have a material financial interest in an attest client of the firm that offers attest services. They also should not have significant influence over an attest client.

CONCEPT

Today's business environment has created many alternative practice structures for CPA firms. Regardless of the structure, relationships that create concern about the influence on the attest function are not permitted.

EXAMPLE

A CPA firm becomes a subsidiary of a non-CPA firm that provides nonattest services (tax, consulting, etc.). The owners and employees of the CPA firm become employees of a subsidiary and may offer nonattest services. The original owners create a **new CPA firm** to offer attest services within the structure. The relationship is represented by the following:

Figure 2-2

Majority ownership in the new firm must be held by CPAs. In this case, employees, offices, and equipment are leased from the parent, which also may provide various other services. The CPA firm and any leased or employed persons are potentially **covered members**. Any direct supervisors of activities of the new CPA firm are subject to the independence rules.

    t.   The practitioner must be independent of the party responsible for the subject matter of **restricted-use reports**. The Statements on Standards for Attestation Engagements describe certain engagements resulting in restricted-use reports.

        1)   Restricted-use reports may be issued on (a) agreed-upon procedures, (b) internal control, (c) prospective financial information, (d) compliance, (e) pro forma financial information, and (f) management's discussion and analysis.

CONCEPT

Attest engagements may be performed for many reasons and involve different kinds of clients. Regardless of the nature of the attest service or client, the practitioner must be independent of the party that is responsible for the subject matter of the attest engagement.

EXAMPLE

A bank, in anticipation of making a loan to an entity, engages a practitioner to perform certain agreed-upon procedures on the assets of the entity. The practitioner's report on the agreed-upon procedures must be restricted to the bank's use. The practitioner must be independent of the entity, the party responsible for the subject matter of the procedures.

    u.   Independence will be **impaired** if, during the period of a professional engagement, a member or his or her firm had any **cooperative arrangement** with the client that was material to the member's firm or to the client. A cooperative arrangement exists when a member's firm and a client jointly participate in a business activity.

CONCEPT

The relationship may create a conflict of interest between the member and those users of the auditor's services.

EXAMPLE

Cooperative arrangements with a client include

●   Prime/subcontractor arrangements to provide services or products to a third party
●   Joint ventures to develop or market products or services
●   Distribution or marketing arrangements

v.   To enhance their capabilities to provide professional services, firms frequently join larger groups, such as **membership associations (networks)**, that are separate legal entities otherwise unrelated to their members. Whether a firm is part of a network depends on the nature of shared goals and resources. A network firm is required to be independent of financial statement audit and review clients of the other network firms.

CONCEPT

Firms that are part of larger attest organizations must be aware of the independence requirements and work with other members of the network to achieve independence.

EXAMPLE

ABC Firm is part of a network of five other firms to share audit methodology, audit manuals, technical departments to consult on technical or industry specific issues, training courses, and facilities. It is considered part of the network and is required to be independent of clients of other firms in the network.

---

w.   Partners or professional employees of a firm may seek employment as an **adjunct faculty member** of a client educational institution. Independence is **not impaired**, provided that the partner or professional employee

1)   Does not hold a key position at the educational institution;

2)   Does not participate on the attest engagement team;

3)   Is not an individual in a position to influence the attest engagement team;

4)   Is employed by the educational institution on a part-time and nontenure basis;

5)   Does not participate in any employee benefit plans sponsored by the educational institution, unless participation is required; and

6)   Does not assume any management responsibilities or set policies for the educational institution.

Stop and review! You have completed the outline for this subunit. Study multiple-choice questions 3 through 8 beginning on page 81.

2.3 INTEGRITY AND OBJECTIVITY

1.   **Rule 102 -- Concepts**

a.   A member shall maintain objectivity and integrity, be free of conflicts of interest, not knowingly misrepresent facts, and not subordinate his or her judgment to others when performing professional services.

2.   **Knowing Misrepresentations of Facts**

a.   These include

1)   Knowingly making materially false and misleading entries in financial statements or records,

2)   Failing to make corrections in materially false or misleading statements or records when the member has such authority, or

3)   Signing a document with materially false and misleading information.

EXAMPLE

The use of the CPA designation by a member not in public practice to imply that the member is independent of his or her employer is an intentional misrepresentation. The member should clearly indicate the employment title in any communication in which (s)he uses the CPA designation.

---

3. **Conflicts of Interest**

   a. A conflict of interest may be permitted in certain circumstances if disclosure is made to, and consent is obtained from, the appropriate parties.

      1) However, an independence objection cannot be overcome by disclosure and consent.

EXAMPLES -- Possible Conflicts of Interest

- Performing litigation services for the plaintiff when the defendant is a client
- Providing tax or personal financial planning (PFP) services to both parties to a divorce
- Suggesting that a PFP client invest in a business in which the member has an interest
- Providing tax or PFP services to family members with conflicting interests
- Performing consulting services for a client that is a major competitor of a company in which the member has a significant financial interest, occupies a management position, or exercises influence
- Serving on a board of tax appeals that hears matters involving clients
- Providing services in connection with a real estate purchase from a client
- Referring a tax or PFP client to a service provider that refers clients to the member under an exclusive arrangement
- Referring a client to a service bureau in which the member or a partner in the member's firm has a material interest

---

EXAMPLE

A member is a director of a fund-raising organization that distributes funds to local charities that are clients (with significant relationships with the member). If the significant relationship is disclosed and consent is received from the appropriate parties, performance of services not requiring independence is allowed.

---

4. **Obligations to the Employer's External Accountant**

   a. A member must be candid and not knowingly misrepresent facts or fail to disclose material facts.

5. **Subordination of Member's Judgment**

   a. A member and his or her supervisor or any other person within the member's organization may have differences of opinion. These may relate to the application of accounting principles, auditing standards, other relevant professional standards, or laws or regulations. The result may be a threat to the member's integrity and objectivity.

   b. If the member concludes that the position taken by others is not in compliance but does not result in a material misrepresentation of fact or violation of laws or regulations, the threats are not considered significant. However, the member should discuss the concerns with the supervisor and, if not resolved, with higher levels of management. If still not resolved, the member should consider

      1) Determining whether any additional reporting requirements exist and

      2) Documenting his or her understanding of the issues and the nature of the discussions.

   c. If the member concludes that appropriate action was not taken and a material misrepresentation of fact or violation of laws or regulations exists, the member should consider ending his or her relationship with the member's organization and take appropriate steps to eliminate his or her exposure to subordination of judgment.

EXAMPLES -- Other Issues Related to Integrity and Objectivity

● A member has an obligation to act if a difference of opinion with a supervisor about financial statement presentation would result in a material misstatement.

● A member lacks integrity if (s)he prematurely expresses an opinion on financial statements because of time pressures imposed by the client.

● A member is required to disclose the use of a third-party service provider when offering professional services to a client. If the client objects, the third-party service provider may not be used.

● A member must act with objectivity and integrity when providing educational services, such as teaching and research.

● A member should not accept gifts or entertainment from a client unless acceptance is reasonable in the circumstances. The nature, cost, occasion, frequency, etc., of the gift or entertainment should be considered in the assessment of reasonableness.

● A member should consider the risks to integrity and objectivity when providing services related to client advocacy.

Stop and review! You have completed the outline for this subunit. Study multiple-choice question 9 on page 83.

2.4 PROFESSIONAL STANDARDS

1. **General Standards -- Rule 201**

   a. A member shall comply with the general standards and interpretations issued by designated bodies (the PCAOB and relevant AICPA committees and boards). The following are the general standards:

      1) Undertake only those services that the member can reasonably expect to complete with **professional competence.**

      2) Exercise **due professional care** when performing professional services.

      3) Adequately **plan and supervise** performance of professional services.

      4) Obtain **sufficient relevant data** to provide a reasonable basis for conclusions in relation to any professional service.

      NOTE: The following is a helpful memory aid:

      "Professional competence uses due professional care to plan, supervise, and obtain sufficient relevant data."

   b. The following is an illustration of the general standards:

Figure 2-3

   c. **Professional Competence**

      1) A member should complete professional services according to professional standards and with reasonable care and diligence.

         a) Competence involves technical qualifications and the ability to supervise and evaluate the work. It relates to knowledge of standards, techniques, and technical subject matter and to the ability to exercise sound judgment.

         b) In some cases, **additional research and consultation** is a normal part of performing services. However, if a member cannot gain sufficient competence, (s)he should suggest the engagement of someone competent.

   d. **Due Professional Care**

      1) According to the Principle of Due Care, an auditor should follow professional standards, both technical and ethical. (S)he also should (a) continually improve competence and the quality of services and (b) be diligent in discharging professional responsibilities to the best of his or her ability.

      2) An auditor should be able to exercise **professional judgment** throughout the audit. It is the application of training, knowledge, and experience in the context of professional standards. Thus, it involves making informed decisions about the actions appropriate in a particular audit.

         a) Professional judgments need to be documented. The audit documentation should suffice to allow an experienced auditor, with no connection to the audit, to understand the judgments made in reaching conclusions about significant findings or issues.

      3) An auditor also should exercise **professional skepticism**.

         a) (S)he should have a questioning mind and critically assess audit evidence.

   e. **Consulting Services**

      1) The general standards apply to consulting services.

EXAMPLES

- In a consulting engagement to design and implement an IT application, a member hires a subcontractor to provide additional programming services. The member has a responsibility to ensure that the subcontractor has the professional qualifications and skills needed.
- A member plans to hire a systems analyst as a member of the firm's staff. The member is not required to be able to perform all the services of the systems analyst. But the member must be qualified to supervise and evaluate the specialist's work.

---

2. **Compliance with Standards -- Rule 202**

   a. A member who performs professional services shall comply with standards issued by designated bodies (the PCAOB and relevant AICPA committees and boards).

EXAMPLES

Professional services include the following:

- Audits, reviews, and compilations of financial statements
- Engagements involving special considerations, e.g., special purpose frameworks
- Attestation engagements other than traditional audits and reviews, such as engagements to report on

    ■ Performance of agreed-upon procedures
    ■ Internal control over financial reporting
    ■ Compliance with statutes, regulations, or contracts
    ■ Financial forecasts or projections

- Tax services
- Consulting services
- Valuation services
- Personal financial planning services

3.   **Accounting Principles -- Rule 203**

    a.   **Any material departure** from an accounting principle issued by an AICPA-designated standard setter prevents a member from

        1)   Expressing an **opinion** (or stating affirmatively) that the financial statements (or other financial data) of any entity are presented in conformity with **generally accepted accounting principles (GAAP)**.

        NOTE: GAAP are issued by (1) the Financial Accounting Standards Board (FASB), (2) the Governmental Accounting Standards Board (GASB), and (3) the International Accounting Standards Board (IASB).

            a)   Thus, the member provides positive assurance.

        2)   Stating that (s)he is **not aware** of any **material modifications** that should be made to achieve conformity with GAAP.

            a)   Thus, the member provides limited assurance.

    b.   Rule 203 applies to **all members**, whether or not in public practice, regarding any affirmative statement about conformity with GAAP.

EXAMPLES

Rule 203 applies

- To members who sign client reports provided to regulatory agencies, creditors, or auditors that contain such representations.
- If a member submits financial statements in his or her capacity as an officer, shareholder, partner, director, or employee to a third party, and the communication states that they conform with GAAP.

---

    c.   A departure is **material** if it has a material effect on the **financial statements or data as a whole**.

    d.   However, in some cases, a member may be able to provide assurance about conformity with GAAP despite a material departure.

        1)   To do so, the member must be able to demonstrate that, due to **unusual circumstances**, the financial statements or data would have been **misleading** without a departure from GAAP. The member must describe

            a)   The departure;
            b)   Its approximate effects, if practicable; and
            c)   The reasons compliance with the principle would be misleading.

        2)   Events that may justify departures from established accounting principles are **new legislation** or evolution of a **new form of business transaction**.

        3)   An unusual degree of materiality or conflicting industry practices ordinarily does not justify departures.

Stop and review! You have completed the outline for this subunit. Study multiple-choice questions 10 and 11 on page 83.

2.5 RESPONSIBILITIES TO CLIENTS

1. **Confidential Client Information -- Rule 301**

   a. A member in public practice must not disclose confidential client information without the client's consent. However, this Rule does not affect a CPA's obligations to

      1) Comply with a valid subpoena or summons or with applicable laws and regulations
      2) Discharge his or her professional obligations
      3) Cooperate in an official review of his or her professional practice
      4) Initiate a complaint with or respond to any inquiry made by an appropriate investigative or disciplinary body

---

EXAMPLES

- A member withdrew from an engagement because of fraud on a client's tax return. If contacted by the successor accountant, the member should suggest that the successor obtain permission from the client to reveal the reasons for leaving.
- A member works for a municipality to verify that proper amounts of taxes have been paid by area businesses. The member is prohibited from releasing any confidential information obtained in his or her professional capacity.
- A member reveals a client's name without permission. Disclosure violates Rule 301 if the client is in bankruptcy and the member specializes in bankruptcy cases. Disclosure in this situation constitutes release of confidential information.
- Knowledge and expertise obtained from a prior engagement may be used on behalf of a current client provided that the details of the other engagement are not revealed without permission.

---

   b. **Review of a Member's Practice**

      1) The rule against disclosure of confidential information does not prohibit the review of a member's practice as part of a purchase, sale, or merger of the practice.
      2) However, appropriate precautions (e.g., a written confidentiality agreement) should be taken so that the prospective buyer does not disclose such information.

2. **Contingent Fees -- Rule 302**

   a. A contingent fee is established as part of an agreement under which the amount of the fee is dependent upon the finding or result.

   b. Nevertheless, fees are not considered to be contingent if

      1) They are fixed by public authorities (e.g., courts).
      2) In tax matters, they are based on

         a) The results of judicial proceedings or
         b) The findings of governmental agencies.

   c. A member in public practice must not perform for a contingent fee any professional services for any of the following:

      1) An audit or review of a financial statement
      2) A compilation of a financial statement if

         a) The member might reasonably expect that a third party will use the statement and
         b) The report does not disclose the lack of independence

      3) An examination of prospective financial information (a financial forecast or projection)

    d.   A member in public practice must not prepare the following for a contingent fee:

       1)   An original tax return
       2)   An amended tax return
       3)   A claim for a tax refund

EXAMPLES

- A member's spouse may provide services to the member's attest client for a contingent fee provided the spouse's activities are separate from the member's practice and the member is not significantly involved. However, a conflict of interest may exist.
- A member who provides investment advisory services for an attest client for a percentage of the investment portfolio ordinarily violates Rule 302.
- Providing investment advisory services to the owners, officers, or employees of an attest client for a contingent fee does not violate Rule 302. However, the member should consider the possible conflict of interest and also Rule 301.
- A contingent fee is allowed for representation of a client (1) in an examination by a revenue agent or (2) in connection with obtaining a private letter ruling.
- A contingent fee is not allowed for the preparation of an amended income tax return for a client claiming a refund of taxes because of an inadvertent omission of a proper deduction.
- A contingent fee is allowed for filing an amended tax return claiming a refund based on a tax issue that is the subject of a test case involving a different taxpayer.

Stop and review! You have completed the outline for this subunit. Study multiple-choice questions 12 and 13 on page 84.

2.6 OTHER RESPONSIBILITIES

1.   **Acts Discreditable -- Rule 501**

    a.   A member shall not commit an act that is discreditable to the profession.

EXAMPLES

- A CPA employed by a firm with one or more non-CPA practitioners must obey the Rules of Conduct. If the CPA becomes a partner, (s)he is responsible for compliance with the Rules of Conduct by all associated practitioners.
- A member not in public practice who is controller of a bank may use the CPA title on bank stationery and in paid advertisements.
- A member who is an attorney and a CPA may use a letterhead with both titles on it.

---

    b.   **Response to Requests for Records**

       1)   Client-provided records must be returned after a client request without exception.

          a)   **Client-provided records** are "accounting or other records belonging to the client that were provided to the member by or on behalf of the client."

       2)   **Member's working papers** are the member's property and need not be made available to the client or others unless required by

          a)   Statute,
          b)   Regulation, or
          c)   Contract.

       3)   **Member's work products** are items (e.g., tax returns) that the member was engaged to prepare. They may be withheld if

          a)   Fees are due,
          b)   The work product is incomplete,
          c)   The member is complying with professional standards (e.g., withholding an audit report until issues are resolved), or
          d)   Litigation exists regarding the engagement or the member's work.

4) **Member-prepared records** are records that the member was not specifically engaged to prepare. Without them, the client's financial information is incomplete.

 a) They are not otherwise available to the client.

 b) Examples are (1) journal entries and (2) supporting schedules and documents prepared as part of an engagement.

 c) Member-prepared records related to a completed and issued work product should be provided to the client unless fees are due.

5) The following summarizes the types of records and responsibilities:

Type	Right to Withhold
Client-provided records	None
Member's working papers	Absolute barring legal or contractual exception
Member-prepared records	If fees due
Member's work products	If fees due, work product incomplete, need to comply with standards, or litigation exists

6) Records also should be given to a client who suffered a loss because of an **act of war or natural disaster**. Otherwise, a member who has complied with the requirements for records requests has no further obligation.

7) In response to a request other than for working papers, the member may

 a) Charge a reasonable fee,
 b) Make and retain copies, and
 c) Provide records in any format usable by the client.

8) Compliance with a client's request usually should be within **45 days**.

EXAMPLES

- Individuals associated with a client may be involved in an internal dispute, and each may request records. A member who has provided records to the designated client representative is not obligated to comply with requests for those records by others associated with the client.

- If the relationship of a member who is not an owner of a firm is terminated, (s)he may not take or retain originals or copies from the firm's client files or proprietary information without permission.

---

c. **Discrimination and Harassment**

1) When a court or administrative agency has made a final determination that a member has violated an antidiscrimination law, (s)he is deemed to have committed an act discreditable.

d. **Following the Requirements of Governmental Bodies**

1) A member must follow GAAP and the requirements of governmental bodies when preparing financial statements or other information for entities subject to their jurisdiction.

2) If the member performs attest services, (s)he must follow the requirements of those bodies as well as GAAS.

3) A material departure from the requirements is an act discreditable unless the member discloses the reasons.

e. **Governmental Audits**

1) In a governmental audit, failure to adhere to applicable audit standards, guides, procedures, statutes, rules, and regulations is an act discreditable to the profession unless the report discloses the failure and the reasons for it.

f.   **CPA Examination**

1)   Solicitation or knowing disclosure of CPA examination questions or answers is an act discreditable.

g.   **Negligence**

1)   It is an act discreditable to be responsible for negligently

a)   Making materially false and misleading entries in the financial statements or records,

b)   Failing to correct materially false and misleading statements, or

c)   Signing a document with materially false and misleading information.

h.   **Failure to File a Tax Return or Pay Tax**

1)   Failing to comply with laws regarding (a) timely filing of personal or firm tax returns or (b) timely payment of taxes collected for others is an act discreditable.

i.   **Regulated Entities and Limitation of Liability**

1)   Regulators may prohibit regulated entities from entering into certain kinds of indemnification and limitation of liability agreements in connection with attest services.

2)   Regulators also may prohibit members from providing services under such agreements.

3)   Failing to comply with such prohibitions is an act discreditable.

j.   **Confidential Information Obtained from Employment**

1)   It is an act discreditable to inappropriately disclose or use confidential employer information obtained as a result of employment or volunteer activities.

k.   **False, Misleading, or Deceptive Acts**

1)   A member who (a) promotes or markets his or her professional services or (b) makes claims about his or her experience or qualifications in a false, misleading, or deceptive manner has committed an act discreditable.

2.   **Advertising and Other Forms of Solicitation -- Rule 502**

a.   A member in public practice must not seek to obtain clients by false, misleading, or deceptive advertising or other forms of solicitation.

b.   Solicitation through coercion, overreaching, or harassing conduct is prohibited.

EXAMPLE

The designation "Personal Financial Specialists" may be used on a letterhead only when all partners or shareholders have the AICPA-awarded designation. However, the individual members holding the designation may use it after their names.

---

c.   **False, Misleading, or Deceptive Acts**

1)   Such acts are prohibited because they are against the public interest. These prohibited activities include the following:

a)   Creating false expectations of favorable results

b)   Implying the ability to influence any court, regulatory agency, etc.

c)   Representing that specific services will be performed for a stated fee when it is likely at the time that the fees will be substantially increased and the client is not advised of the possibility

d)   Other representations that would cause a reasonable person to misunderstand or be deceived

    d.   **Obtaining Clients through Third Parties**

        1) Members are permitted to render services to clients of third parties.

        2) If the third party obtained its clients through advertising, the members must determine that all promotional efforts were within the Rules of Conduct.

           a) Members must not do through others what they are prohibited from doing themselves.

3. **Commissions and Referral Fees -- Rule 503**

    a.   **Prohibited commissions** are those received when a **member in public practice**

        1) Recommends or refers

           a) To a client any product or service or
           b) Any product or service to be supplied by a client.

        2) Also performs for the client

           a) An audit,
           b) A review,
           c) A compilation reasonably expected to be used by a third party if the member's lack of independence is not disclosed, or
           d) An examination of prospective financial information (PFI).

    b.   A **permitted commission** must be **disclosed** to any person or entity to whom the member recommends or refers a related product or service.

    c.   **Referral fees** are not considered commissions and are permitted if disclosed to the client. These include

        1) Acceptance of a referral fee for recommending or referring any service of a CPA to anyone and

        2) Payment of a referral fee to **obtain a client**.

EXAMPLES

- A member is permitted to purchase a product and resell it to a client. Any profits collected are not considered a commission because the member had title to the product and assumed the risks of ownership.

- A member may not refer for commissions products to audit clients through distributors and agents when the member is performing any of the services described in Rule 503. A member may not do through others what (s)he cannot do himself or herself. If the services are not being provided by the member, (s)he may refer the products, provided (s)he discloses the commission to the client.

---

4. **Form of Organization and Name -- Rule 505**

    a.   A member may practice public accounting only in a form of organization allowed by law or regulation that conforms with resolutions of the AICPA Council.

    b.   The firm name must not be misleading.

    c.   Names of past owners may be included in the name of the successor firm.

    d.   A firm cannot designate itself as "members of the AICPA" unless all CPA owners are members.

    e.   According to a Council resolution, if a firm **holds itself out as CPAs** or performs audits, reviews, or examination of prospective financial information, it must have certain attributes:

        1) CPAs own a majority of the firm.
        2) A CPA must be responsible for all services.
        3) A non-CPA owner must be active as a member of the firm or its affiliates.
        4) Non-CPA owners cannot hold themselves out as CPAs.

5) A member must not permit a person (s)he controls to do what is prohibited to the member by the *Code*.

    a) The member also may be responsible for the acts of such a person who is an associate in the practice of public accounting.

6) Non-CPA owners are not eligible to be AICPA members unless they meet the requirements for membership.

7) Owners must, at all times, be the beneficial owners of the equity attributed to them. If an owner ceases to be actively engaged as a member of the firm or its affiliates, his or her ownership should be transferred to the firm or other qualified owners within a reasonable time.

f. Members may practice not only in corporations and general partnerships but also in limited liability companies, limited liability partnerships, and other forms permitted by state law.

g. **Ownership of a Separate Business**

1) A member **practicing public accounting** may own an interest in a separate business that performs the services for which standards are established.

2) If the member controls the separate business, the entity and all its owners and employees must comply with the *Code*.

    a) Absent such control, only the member is subject to the *Code*.

h. **Alternative Practice Structures (APSs)**

1) AICPA requirements emphasize that CPAs remain responsible, financially and otherwise, for the attest work performed to protect the public interest.

2) However, in an APS, CPAs may own the majority of financial interests in the attest firm, but substantially all revenues may be paid to another entity for services and the lease of employees, equipment, etc.

3) Nevertheless, given the requirements of state law and the AICPA, if the CPA-owners of the attest firm remain financially responsible under state law, they are deemed to be in compliance with the financial-interests requirement.

i. **Misleading Firm Names**

1) A name is misleading if it contains a representation likely to cause a reasonable person to misunderstand (a) the legal form of the firm, (b) who its owners are, or (c) who its members are. An example is using the term "company" (or "Co.") when the firm is not a corporation.

j. **Common Network Brand in Firm Name**

1) A network is an association of entities that includes one or more public accounting firms. These entities (a) cooperate to enhance the firms' ability to provide services and (b) share at least one of certain specified characteristics (e.g., a common brand name or initials as part of the firm name, common control, profits or costs, or resources).

2) Sharing of a common brand name or initials as part or all of the firm name is not misleading if the firm is a network firm.

EXAMPLES

- A partnership may continue to practice using a partner's name in the firm name after (s)he withdraws. If the firm later merges with another firm, the title of the new firm may include the retired partner's name.
- If a CPA becomes a partner in a firm with one or more non-CPA practitioners, the CPA is responsible for compliance with the *Code* by all of his or her associates.
- A CPA in partnership with non-CPAs may sign the firm name to a report and below it affix his or her name with the CPA designation. However, it must be clear that the partnership does not consist entirely of CPAs.

In addition to testing the AICPA *Code of Professional Conduct*, the CPA exam includes ethics and independence questions based on standards of the Securities and Exchange Commission (SEC), the Public Companies Accounting Oversight Board (PCAOB), the Government Accountability Office (these standards are covered in Study Unit 20), Department of Labor (DOL), and the Sarbanes-Oxley Act of 2002. Candidates also are expected to demonstrate an awareness of the International Ethics Standards Board for Accountants (IESBA) and its role in establishing requirements of the International Federation of Accountants (IFAC) *Code of Ethics for Professional Accountants*.

The material may appear imposing at first. However, it is important to recognize that in most cases the standards for independence from the various standard setters are very similar. Thus, use your knowledge of the AICPA *Code of Professional Conduct* as a foundation for your study. Regarding other ethics issues, you should focus on those not intuitively obvious to you. With a little effort, you should be able to gain considerable confidence in comprehending the ethics requirements.

Stop and review! You have completed the outline for this subunit. Study multiple-choice questions 14 through 17 beginning on page 84.

2.7 OTHER PRONOUNCEMENTS ON PROFESSIONAL RESPONSIBILITIES

1. **Sarbanes-Oxley, PCAOB, and the SEC**

Background

The Sarbanes-Oxley Act of 2002 was a response to numerous financial reporting scandals involving large public companies. It contains provisions relating to corporate governance that impose new responsibilities on publicly held companies and their auditors. The Public Company Accounting Oversight Board (PCAOB) was created by the act. The act applies to issuers of publicly traded securities subject to federal securities laws. The following section addresses ethics requirements of Sarbanes-Oxley, the PCAOB, and the SEC. Most of the independence rules are parallel to the AICPA rules. Thus, the focus is on other issues not addressed in the AICPA *Code of Professional Conduct*.

    a. **Responsibilities and Activities of the PCAOB**

        1) Register public accounting firms

        2) Oversee the audit of public companies (issuers) that are subject to the securities laws

        3) Establish or adopt standards on auditing, quality control, ethics, and independence

        4) Inspect audit firms to

            a) Examine selected audit and review engagements;

            b) Evaluate the system of quality; and

            c) Test audit, supervisory, and quality control procedures.

        5) Conduct investigations and disciplinary proceedings concerning, and impose appropriate sanctions upon, registered public accounting firms and associated persons

    b. **Preapproval of Services**

        1) Audit committees ordinarily must preapprove the services performed by accountants (permissible nonaudit services and all audit, review, and attest engagements).

            a) Approval must be either explicit or in accordance with detailed policies and procedures.

            b) If approval is based on detailed policies and procedures, the audit committee must be informed, and no delegation of its authority to management is allowed.

c. **Disclosure of Fees**

1) An issuer must disclose in its proxy statement or annual filing fees paid to the accountant segregated into four categories:

   a) Audit,
   b) Audit-related,
   c) Tax, and
   d) All other.

2) The disclosure is for the 2 most recent years.

d. **Rotation of Partners**

1) The lead and concurring (reviewing) audit partners must rotate every 5 years, with a 5-year time-out period. Other audit partners must rotate every 7 years, with a 2-year time-out.

e. **Communications with the Audit Committee**

1) The firm must include

   a) All critical accounting policies and practices;
   b) All material alternative accounting policies and practices within GAAP that were discussed with management; and
   c) Other material written communications with management, such as representations and schedules of unadjusted audit differences.

2) These communications must be prior to filing the audit report with the SEC.

3) The firm must, before accepting an initial engagement and at least annually, (a) discuss the potential effects of the relationships that may affect independence and (b) document the discussion.

f. **Prohibited Nonaudit Services**

1) The firm is prohibited from offering certain nonaudit services to its attest clients, including

   a) Appraisal and other valuation services
   b) Designing and implementing financial information systems
   c) Internal auditing or actuarial functions
   d) Management services
   e) Human resource services
   f) Bookkeeping
   g) Legal and expert services not pertaining to the audit
   h) Investment banking or advisory services
   i) Broker-dealer services

2) Preapproved compliance tax engagements and preparation of comfort letters are not prohibited. The preapproval requirement is waived with respect to the provision of acceptable nonaudit services for an issuer if

   a) The aggregate amount of all such nonaudit services provided to the issuer constitutes not more than 5% of the total amount of revenues paid by the issuer to its auditor during the fiscal year,
   b) Such services were not recognized by the issuer at the time of the engagement to be nonaudited services, and
   c) Such services were promptly brought to the attention of the audit committee of the issuer and approved prior to the completion of the audit.

g. **Audit Committees**

1) Each member of the audit committee must be an independent member of the board of directors.

2) The audit committee must be directly responsible for appointing, compensating, and overseeing the work of the auditor. The issuer must provide for adequate compensation for the auditor as determined by the committee.

3) Audit committees must have at least one member designated as a financial expert with relevant experience (e.g., as principal financial or accounting officer, a supervisor of such persons, or as an assessor of the preparation or audit of financial statements). A financial expert must

a) Understand GAAP and financial statements;

b) Be able to assess the general application of GAAP in accounting for estimates, accruals, and reserves;

c) Have experience with financial statements having a breadth and level of complexity comparable to those of the registrant;

d) Understand internal controls and the procedures for financial reporting; and

e) Understand audit committee functions.

4) Audit committees must establish procedures for

a) The receipt, retention, and treatment of complaints received regarding accounting, internal control, or auditing matters and

b) The confidential, anonymous submission of employees' concerns regarding questionable accounting or auditing matters.

h. **PCAOB Interim Independence Standards**

1) The PCAOB adopted AICPA Conduct Rule 101 as well as pronouncements of the now-defunct Independence Standards Board (ISB). It also has issued specific independence rules that apply to registered public accounting firms. However, these are parallel, in most cases, to the AICPA *Code of Professional Conduct*.

i. **Management's Financial Statement Responsibility**

1) The CEO and CFO of a public company must provide a statement to accompany the audit report. This statement certifies the appropriateness of the financial statements and disclosures. However, a violation of this requirement must be knowing and intentional.

j. **Fraud Issues**

1) Sarbanes-Oxley created a new crime for securities fraud that imposes penalties of fines and imprisonment, extends the statute of limitations on securities fraud claims, and makes it a felony to create or destroy documents to impede a federal investigation.

2. **Department of Labor**

a. The DOL requires auditors to be independent for audits of pension funds administered under the Employee Retirement Income Security Act of 1974 (ERISA).

 The AICPA Content Specification Outlines (CSOs) require candidates to "demonstrate an awareness" of the international ethics standards. As with other ethics standards, in most cases these parallel the AICPA *Code of Professional Conduct*. The following summary of the standards is presented at the awareness level.

3.   **IFAC** *Code of Ethics for Professional Accountants*

   a.   Under the auspices of the International Federation of Accountants (IFAC), the **International Ethics Standards Board for Accountants (IESBA)** has issued a *Code of Ethics for Professional Accountants*. This outline addresses fundamental principles followed by standards for accountants in public practice.

   b.   **Fundamental Principles**

   1)   **Integrity.** A professional accountant must be straightforward and honest in all professional and business relationships.

   2)   **Objectivity.** A professional accountant must not allow bias, conflict of interest, or undue influence of others to override professional or business judgments.

   3)   **Professional competence and due care.** A professional accountant must maintain professional knowledge and skill at the level required to ensure that a client or employer receives competent professional services based on current developments in practice, legislation, and techniques. (S)he also must act diligently and in accordance with applicable technical and professional standards.

   4)   **Confidentiality.** A professional accountant must respect the confidentiality of information acquired as a result of professional and business relationships. Thus, (s)he must not disclose any such information to third parties without proper and specific authority, unless a legal or professional right or duty exists to disclose. Moreover, (s)he must not use the information for the personal advantage of the professional accountant or third parties.

   5)   **Professional behavior.** A professional accountant must comply with relevant laws and regulations and avoid any action that discredits the profession.

   c.   **Public Practice**

   1)   **Threats** to compliance with fundamental principles may arise from many circumstances and relationships. Threats may involve the following:

      a)   **Self-interest** (for example, a direct financial interest in the client)

      b)   **Self-review** (for example, reporting on the effectiveness of a financial accounting system after designing it)

      c)   **Advocacy** (for example, advocating on behalf of a client in litigation)

      d)   **Familiarity** (for example, a close or immediate family member of a person on the engagement team is a director of the client)

      e)   **Intimidation** (for example, the client states that it will not give a consulting contract to the firm if it disagrees with a choice of an accounting principle)

   2)   **Safeguards** eliminate or reduce threats to an acceptable level. Safeguards include the following:

      a)   Safeguards created by the profession, legislation, or regulation (for example, education requirements, professional standards, and external review)

      b)   Safeguards in the work environment (for example, firm-wide safeguards, such as leadership that promotes compliance with fundamental principles; engagement-specific safeguards, such as review of the work by an accountant; and safeguards in the client's systems, such as a governance body that appropriately oversees the firm's work)

d. **Section 210 -- Professional Appointment.** Before accepting a new client, a professional accountant must determine whether acceptance would create any threats to compliance with the fundamental principles.

    1) The principle of professional competence and due care imposes an obligation on a professional accountant to provide only those services that (s)he is competent to perform.

        a) When a professional accountant intends to rely on the advice or work of an expert, (s)he determines whether such reliance is warranted by reputation, expertise, etc.

    2) A professional accountant who is asked to replace another must determine whether there are any reasons, professional or otherwise, for not accepting the engagement.

    3) An existing accountant may be prevented by confidentiality from discussing the affairs of a client with a proposed accountant.

    4) A professional accountant will generally need to obtain the client's permission, preferably in writing, to initiate discussion with an existing accountant.

e. **Section 220 -- Conflicts of Interest.** A professional accountant must take reasonable steps to identify circumstances that could pose a conflict of interest.

f. **Section 230 -- Second Opinions.** Providing a second opinion on the application of standards or principles to specific circumstances or transactions on behalf of an entity that is not an existing client may create threats to compliance with the fundamental principles.

g. **Section 240 -- Fees and Other Types of Remuneration.** Fees should not be so low that it may be difficult to perform the engagement in accordance with applicable technical and professional standards for that price.

    1) The client should be aware of the terms of the engagement, the basis on which fees are charged, and which services are covered by the fees.

    2) **Contingent fees** may create a self-interest threat to objectivity depending on factors including

        a) The nature of the engagement,
        b) The range of amounts,
        c) The basis for the fee, and
        d) Whether the result is to be reviewed by an independent third party.

    3) A contingent fee is prohibited by a firm for an audit engagement or for a nonassurance service provided to an audit client.

    4) A professional accountant may receive a **referral fee** or **commission** relating to a client.

        a) A professional accountant also may pay a referral fee to obtain a client.

        b) Examples of safeguards include

            i) Disclosing to the client any such arrangements
            ii) Obtaining advance agreement from the client for commission arrangements in connection with the sale by a third party of goods or services to the client

        c) Purchasing a firm by making payments to individuals formerly owning the firm does not constitute paying commissions or referral fees.

h. **Section 250 -- Marketing Professional Services.** A professional accountant must not bring the profession into disrepute when marketing professional services. (S)he must be honest and truthful and not make exaggerated claims or disparaging references or unsubstantiated comparisons to the work of another.

i.   **Section 260 -- Gifts and Hospitality.** A professional accountant in public practice, or an immediate or close family member, may be offered gifts and hospitality from a client.

   1)   If a reasonable and informed third party would consider them trivial and inconsequential, they may be accepted.

   2)   But if the resulting threats to compliance with fundamental principles cannot be eliminated or reduced to an acceptable level through safeguards, a professional accountant must not accept such an offer.

j.   **Section 270 -- Custody of Client Assets.** A professional accountant must not assume custody of client assets unless permitted by law and in compliance with any additional legal duties imposed on a professional accountant holding such assets.

   1)   A professional accountant entrusted with assets belonging to others must

      a)   Keep them separate from personal or firm assets
      b)   Use them only for the purpose for which they are intended
      c)   Be ready to account for them and any income
      d)   Comply with all relevant laws and regulations

   2)   A professional accountant must make appropriate inquiries about the source of such assets and consider legal and regulatory obligations.

k.   **Section 280 -- Objectivity: All Services.** A professional accountant must determine when providing any professional service whether there are threats to compliance with the fundamental principle of objectivity resulting from having interests in, or relationships with, a client or its directors, officers, or employees.

l.   **Section 290 -- Independence: Audits and Reviews**

   1)   If a firm is a **network firm**, it must be independent of the audit clients of the other firms within the network.

      a)   The judgment as to whether the larger structure is a network is based on all the specific facts and circumstances.

   2)   The professional accountant must **document** conclusions regarding compliance with independence requirements and the substance of any relevant discussions that support those conclusions.

   3)   Independence from the audit client is required during both the **engagement period** and the **period covered by the financial statements**.

   4)   When, as a result of a **merger or acquisition**, an entity becomes a related entity of an audit client, the firm must evaluate interests and relationships with the related entity that could affect its independence and therefore its ability to continue the audit after the merger or acquisition.

   5)   If an **inadvertent violation** occurs, it generally does not compromise independence, provided the firm has appropriate quality control policies and procedures and the violation is corrected promptly.

   6)   In general, the independence rules for **financial interests**, including loans and guarantees, stated by the IFAC Code of Ethics are similar to those of the AICPA.

   7)   A **close business relationship** between a firm, a member of the audit team, or a member of that individual's immediate family and the audit client or its management arises from a commercial relationship or common financial interest and may create self-interest or intimidation threats. Unless any financial interest is immaterial and the business relationship is insignificant, independence is impaired.

      a)   The **purchase of goods and services** from an audit client by the firm, a member of the audit team, or a member of that individual's immediate family does not generally create a threat to independence if the transaction is in the normal course of business and at arm's length.

8) **Family and personal relationships** between a member of the audit team and a director or officer or certain employees (depending on their role) of the audit client may create self-interest, familiarity, or intimidation threats. The existence and significance of any threats will depend on a number of factors, including the individual's responsibilities on the audit team, the role of the family member or other individual within the client, and the closeness of the relationship.

9) Familiarity or intimidation threats may be created if a director or officer of the client, or an employee in a position to exert significant influence over the preparation of the client's accounting records or the financial statements, has been a **member of the audit team or partner of the firm**.

10) The **lending of staff** by a firm to an audit client may create a self-review threat. Such assistance may be given, but only for a short time and only if the firm's personnel do not provide impermissible services or assume management responsibilities.

11) Self-interest, self-review, or familiarity threats may be created if a member of the audit team has **recently served** as a director, officer, or employee of the audit client. This would be the case when, for example, a member of the audit team has to evaluate elements of the financial statements for which the member of the audit team had prepared the accounting records while with the client.

12) **Serving as a director or officer** of an audit client impairs independence.

13) Familiarity and self-interest threats are created by using the same **senior personnel** on an audit engagement over a long period.

14) Firms provide to their audit clients a range of **nonassurance services**. Providing nonassurance services may, however, create threats to the independence of the firm or members of the audit team.

   a) If a firm were to assume **management responsibility** for an audit client, the threats created would be so significant that no safeguards could reduce the threats to an acceptable level.

   b) Providing an audit client with accounting and bookkeeping services, such as preparing accounting records or financial statements, creates a self-review threat when the firm subsequently audits the financial statements.

      i) But accounting and bookkeeping services, which would otherwise not be permitted, may be provided to audit clients in **emergency** or other unusual situations when it is impractical for the audit client to make other arrangements.

15) **Tax return preparation** does not generally create a threat to independence if management takes responsibility for the returns, including any significant judgments made.

   a) **Tax planning or other tax advisory services** may result in a self-review threat if the advice will affect matters to be reflected in the financial statements.

      i) If the effectiveness of the tax advice depends on a material, doubtful accounting treatment or presentation in the financial statements, the self-review threat would be so significant that no safeguards could reduce the threat to an acceptable level.

16) The provision of **internal audit services** to an audit client creates a self-review threat to independence if the firm uses the internal audit work in the course of a subsequent external audit. Performing a significant part of the client's internal audit activities increases the possibility that firm personnel providing internal audit services will assume management responsibility.

17) Providing services to an audit client involving the **design or implementation of IT systems** that (a) form a significant part of the internal control over financial reporting or (b) generate information that is significant to the client's accounting records or financial statements on which the firm will express an opinion creates a self-review threat.

18) **Litigation support services** may include activities such as acting as an expert witness, calculating estimated damages or other amounts that might become receivable or payable, and assisting with document management and retrieval. These services may create a self-review or advocacy threat.

19) Acting in an **advocacy** role for an audit client in resolving a dispute or litigation when the amounts involved are material to the financial statements on which the firm will express an opinion would create advocacy and self-review threats so significant that no safeguards could reduce the threat to an acceptable level.

20) The firm may generally provide such **recruiting services** as reviewing the professional qualifications of a number of applicants and providing advice on their suitability for the post. In addition, the firm may interview candidates and advise on a candidate's competence for financial accounting, administrative, or control positions.

21) Providing **corporate finance services** may create advocacy and self-review threats.

   a) If the effectiveness of corporate finance advice depends on a **material, doubtful accounting treatment or presentation** in the financial statements, the self-review threat would be so significant that no safeguards could reduce the threat to an acceptable level.

22) When the total **fees** from an audit client represent a large proportion of the total fees of the firm expressing the audit opinion (or a partner or office), the dependence on that client and concern about losing the client creates a self-interest or intimidation threat.

   a) A self-interest threat may be created if **overdue fees** remain unpaid for a long time, especially if a significant part is not paid before the issue of the audit report for the following year. Generally, the firm is expected to require payment of such fees before such audit report is issued.

23) A key audit partner must not be **evaluated on or compensated** based on that partner's success in selling nonassurance services to the partner's audit client.

24) Accepting **gifts or hospitality** from an audit client may create self-interest and familiarity threats. If a firm or a member of the audit team accepts gifts or hospitality, unless the value is trivial and inconsequential, the threats created would be so significant that no safeguards could reduce the threats to an acceptable level.

25) When the firm and the client's management are placed in adversarial positions by **actual or threatened litigation**, affecting management's willingness to make complete disclosures, self-interest and intimidation threats are created.

Stop and review! You have completed the outline for this subunit. Study multiple-choice questions 18 through 30 beginning on page 85.

QUESTIONS

2.1 Code of Professional Conduct

1. A CPA who is **not** in public practice is obligated to follow which of the following rules of conduct?

- A. Independence.
- B. Integrity and objectivity.
- C. Contingent fees.
- D. Commissions.

Answer (B) is correct.
    REQUIRED: The applicable rule of conduct applicable to a CPA not in public practice.
    DISCUSSION: Under Conduct Rule 102, *Integrity and Objectivity*, all members must maintain objectivity and integrity, be free of conflicts of interest, not knowingly misrepresent facts, and not subordinate his or her judgment to others when performing professional services.
    Answer (A) is incorrect. Conduct Rule 101, *Independence*, applies only to CPAs in public practice. Answer (C) is incorrect. Conduct Rule 302, *Contingent Fees*, applies only to CPAs in public practice. Answer (D) is incorrect. Conduct Rule 503, *Commissions and Referral Fees*, applies only in part (Referrals) to all members and in part (Commissions) to CPAs in public practice.

2. Under the *Code of Professional Conduct* of the AICPA, which of the following is required to be independent in fact and appearance when discharging professional responsibilities?

- A. A CPA in public practice providing tax and management advisory services.
- B. A CPA in public practice providing auditing and other attestation services.
- C. A CPA not in public practice.
- D. All CPAs.

Answer (B) is correct.
    REQUIRED: The person(s) required to be independent in fact and appearance.
    DISCUSSION: According to the Principles of Professional Conduct, *Article IV – Objectivity and Independence*, "A member in public practice should be independent in fact and appearance when providing audit and other attestation services."
    Answer (A) is incorrect. A CPA in public practice providing tax and management advisory services need not be independent unless attestation services also are performed. Answer (C) is incorrect. A CPA not in public practice need not be independent. Answer (D) is incorrect. All CPAs do not provide attestation services in public practice.

2.2 Independence

3. Under the AICPA's conceptual framework for independence, the member-client relationship is evaluated to determine whether independence in fact and appearance is jeopardized. This is considered

- A. A sufficiency of safeguards approach.
- B. An avoidance approach.
- C. A risk-based approach.
- D. A professional skepticism approach.

Answer (C) is correct.
    REQUIRED: The term associated with the conceptual framework for independence standards.
    DISCUSSION: The risk-based approach evaluates the risk that a CPA is not independent or is perceived by a reasonable and informed third party with knowledge of all relevant information as not independent. That risk must be reduced to an acceptable level to establish independence. Risk is acceptable when threats are acceptable. They may be acceptable because of the types of threats and their potential effect. Moreover, threats may be sufficiently mitigated or eliminated by safeguards. Threats are acceptable when it is not reasonable to expect that they will compromise professional judgment.
    Answer (A) is incorrect. Safeguards are controls that mitigate the risk. Answer (B) is incorrect. The term "avoidance approach" is not meaningful in this context. Answer (D) is incorrect. Members should exercise professional skepticism, but this is not required for members to be independent.

4. The concept of materiality is **least** important to an auditor when considering the

- A. Adequacy of disclosure of a client's illegal act.
- B. Discovery of weaknesses in a client's internal control.
- C. Effects of a direct financial interest in the client on the CPA's independence.
- D. Decision whether to use positive or negative confirmations of accounts receivable.

Answer (C) is correct.
    REQUIRED: The item with respect to which materiality is least important.
    DISCUSSION: Independence is impaired if a CPA has any direct financial interest in a client. Whether this direct financial interest is material is irrelevant. The test of materiality is applied, however, if the financial interest is indirect.
    Answer (A) is incorrect. In considering the effect of an illegal act on the financial statements and its implications for other aspects of the audit, materiality is important. Answer (B) is incorrect. An auditor who is considering internal control in a financial statement audit must make materiality judgments. Answer (D) is incorrect. Materiality is one factor considered when deciding between positive or negative confirmations.

5. Under the ethical standards of the profession, which of the following investments by a CPA in a corporate client is an indirect financial interest?

    A. An investment held in a retirement plan of which the CPA is a trustee.

    B. An investment held in a blind trust.

    C. An investment held through a regulated mutual fund.

    D. An investment held through participation in an investment club.

Answer (C) is correct.
    REQUIRED: The indirect financial interest.
    DISCUSSION: Independence is impaired if, during the period of the professional engagement, a covered member had a direct or material indirect financial interest in the client. Ownership of fund shares is a direct financial interest in the fund. Underlying investments in the fund are indirect interests.
    Answer (A) is incorrect. Participation in a retirement plan constitutes a direct financial interest in the plan. Investments of a plan sponsored by the member's firm are direct interests of the firm. Investments of a plan controlled or supervised by the member (e.g., as a trustee) are the member's direct interests. Otherwise, they are indirect interests of the members. Answer (B) is incorrect. A blind trust and its investments are direct interests of the grantor. The investments will revert to the grantor. Answer (D) is incorrect. One kind of direct financial interest is a financial interest beneficially owned through an intermediary (e.g., and investment club) when the beneficiary has the authority to participate in the intermediary's investment decisions. In an investment club, the members make investment decisions.

6. A violation of the profession's ethical standards most likely would have occurred when a CPA

    A. Expressed an unmodified opinion on the current year's financial statements when fees for the prior year's audit were unpaid.

    B. Recommended a controller's position description with candidate specifications to an audit client.

    C. Purchased a CPA firm's practice of monthly write-ups for a percentage of fees to be received over a 3-year period.

    D. Made arrangements with a financial institution to collect notes issued by a client in payment of fees due for the current year's audit.

Answer (A) is correct.
    REQUIRED: The violation of the ethical standards.
    DISCUSSION: Audit fees that are long past due take on the characteristics of a loan under Conduct Rule 101. Independence is impaired if billed or unbilled fees, or a note arising from the fees, for client services rendered more than 1 year prior to the current year's report date, remain unpaid when the current year's report is issued. However, this ruling does not apply if the client is in bankruptcy. Moreover, long overdue fees do not preclude the CPA from performing services not requiring independence.
    Answer (B) is incorrect. A CPA will not impair independence by recommending job position descriptions. However, the CPA will be in violation if (s)he is responsible for screening candidates or making decisions to hire. Answer (C) is incorrect. No pronouncement prohibits purchase of a bookkeeping firm for a percentage of fees. Answer (D) is incorrect. The AICPA has ruled that this practice does not violate the *Code*.

7. Which of the following situations would **not** impair objectivity, integrity, or independence with respect to an audit client?

    A. An auditor takes the client's audit committee to Las Vegas for the weekend.

    B. An out-of-town client takes the audit engagement team out to dinner at a renowned local restaurant.

    C. An auditor provides client management with box seats for the season at a major league baseball franchise.

    D. A client takes the audit engagement team on a two-day ski trip after the audit team worked for two consecutive weekends.

Answer (B) is correct.
    REQUIRED: The situation not impairing objectivity, integrity, or independence.
    DISCUSSION: Independence is impaired unless the value of the gift or entertainment from the attest client is clearly insignificant to the recipient(s). Objectivity is impaired unless the gift or entertainment is reasonable in the circumstances. Integrity is impaired if the gift or entertainment violates (1) member or client policies or (2) laws or regulations. A restaurant meal is clearly insignificant to the recipient(s), reasonable in the circumstances, and unlikely to violate policies, laws, or regulations.
    Answer (A) is incorrect. Taking the client's audit committee to Las Vegas for the weekend is more than a token gift. Also, the level of individuals involved (the audit committee) creates doubts about objectivity, integrity, or independence. Answer (C) is incorrect. Providing client management with box seats for the season at a major league baseball franchise is more than a token gift. Answer (D) is incorrect. The cost or value of a two-day ski trip is excessive.

8. According to the profession's ethical standards, an auditor is considered independent in which of the following instances?

   A. The auditor is the officially appointed stock transfer agent of a client.

   B. The auditor's checking account, which is fully insured by a federal agency, is held at a client financial institution.

   C. The client sponsors an employee benefit plan in which the auditor participates.

   D. The client is the only tenant in a commercial building owned by the auditor.

Answer (B) is correct.
   REQUIRED: The circumstance in which the CPA is considered independent.
   DISCUSSION: A CPA's independence is not impaired with respect to a financial institution if checking accounts, savings accounts, or certificates of deposit are fully insured. Moreover, uninsured amounts do not impair independence if they are immaterial.
   Answer (A) is incorrect. Serving as a stock transfer or escrow agent, registrar, general counsel, or its equivalent involves performing management functions or making management decisions for the attest client. Answer (C) is incorrect. The auditor's independence is impaired with regard to the plan and its sponsor. Answer (D) is incorrect. Leasing property to a client results in an indirect financial interest in that client.

2.3 Integrity and Objectivity

9. Which of the following acts by a CPA who is **not** in public practice will most likely be considered a violation of the ethical standards of the profession?

   A. Using the CPA designation without disclosing employment status in connection with financial statements issued for external use by the CPA's employer.

   B. A CPA firm indicates on its letterhead that other CPA firms are correspondents rather than members of an association.

   C. A member sells a newsletter bearing his or her name.

   D. Compiling the CPA's employer's financial statements and making reference to the CPA's lack of independence.

Answer (A) is correct.
   REQUIRED: The action violating ethical standards.
   DISCUSSION: A member not in public practice who uses the CPA designation in a manner implying that (s)he is independent of the employer has committed a knowing misrepresentation of fact in violation of Conduct Rule 102.
   Answer (B) is incorrect. CPA firms are not allowed to use a firm name indicating an association. The public may believe a partnership exists when it does not. Answer (C) is incorrect. A member may sell a newsletter bearing his or her name if the member writes it and ensures that those promoting it do not make statements about the author or his or her writings that violate the Conduct Rule on advertising and other forms of solicitation. Answer (D) is incorrect. An accountant may compile a nonissuer's financial statements if (s)he issues the appropriate report. The lack of independence should be disclosed.

2.4 Professional Standards

10. According to the standards of the profession, which of the following activities may be required in exercising due professional care?

	Consulting with Experts	Obtaining Specialty Accreditation
A.	Yes	Yes
B.	Yes	No
C.	No	Yes
D.	No	No

Answer (B) is correct.
   REQUIRED: The activity(ies) that may be required in exercising due care.
   DISCUSSION: A CPA should undertake only those services that (s)he reasonably expects to complete with professional competence and should exercise due professional care in performing those services. Additional research or consultation with others may be necessary to gain sufficient competence to complete a service in accordance with professional standards. However, professional standards do not require specialty accreditation, although many CPAs choose to specialize in specific services.

11. According to the profession's ethical standards, which of the following events may justify a departure from an established accounting principle?

	New Legislation	Evolution of a New Form of Business Transaction
A.	No	Yes
B.	Yes	No
C.	Yes	Yes
D.	No	No

Answer (C) is correct.
   REQUIRED: The event(s), if any, that may justify departure from an established accounting principle.
   DISCUSSION: In general, strict compliance with accounting principles is required. However, Conduct Rule 203 recognizes that, due to unusual circumstances, adhering to GAAP may cause financial statements to be misleading. New legislation and the evolution of a new form of business transaction are events that may justify departure from an established accounting principle.

2.5 Responsibilities to Clients

12. A CPA is permitted to disclose confidential client information without the consent of the client to

I.   Another CPA firm if the information concerns suspected tax return irregularities

II. A state CPA society voluntary peer review board

    A.   I only.

    B.   II only.

    C.   Both I and II.

    D.   Neither I nor II.

Answer (B) is correct.
    REQUIRED: The event(s), if any, that allow disclosure of confidential client data without the client's consent.
    DISCUSSION: Under Conduct Rule 301, *Confidential Client Information*, a CPA may reveal confidential information without the client's permission for a state board- or state society-sponsored peer review. Identifying information revealed to the review team is precluded from disclosure. However, a CPA may not disclose information to another CPA firm without the client's permission or unless pursuant to a valid subpoena.

13. To which of the following parties may a CPA partnership provide its audit documentation, without being lawfully subpoenaed or without the client's consent?

    A.   The IRS.

    B.   The FASB.

    C.   Any surviving partner(s) on the death of a partner.

    D.   A CPA before purchasing a partnership interest in the firm.

Answer (C) is correct.
    REQUIRED: The true statement regarding records in the CPA's possession.
    DISCUSSION: Audit documentation may be disclosed to another partner of the accounting firm without the client's consent because such information has not been communicated to outsiders. A partner of the CPA has a fiduciary obligation to the client not to disclose confidential information without consent.
    Answer (A) is incorrect. The partnership may not provide the IRS with confidential client information without client permission, a subpoena, or a summons. Answer (B) is incorrect. The CPA or his or her firm may not disclose confidential information to the FASB without client consent. Answer (D) is incorrect. A CPA may not provide audit documentation to a prospective purchaser. However, an exception is made for a review of the practice in conjunction with a prospective purchase, sale, or merger.

2.6 Other Responsibilities

14. According to the ethical standards of the profession, which of the following acts is generally prohibited?

    A.   Purchasing a product from a third party and reselling it to a client.

    B.   Writing a financial management newsletter promoted and sold by a publishing company.

    C.   Accepting a commission for recommending a product to an audit client.

    D.   Accepting engagements obtained through the efforts of third parties.

Answer (C) is correct.
    REQUIRED: The prohibited act.
    DISCUSSION: Conduct Rule 503, *Commissions and Referral Fees*, prohibits a member in public practice from recommending any product or service to a client when the firm performs (1) an audit or review of financial statements, (2) a compilation of a financial statement that is reasonably expected to be used by a third party if the report does not disclose the CPA's lack of independence, or (3) an examination of prospective financial information for that client.
    Answer (A) is incorrect. Resale of products to clients is permitted. The profit is not a commission. Answer (B) is incorrect. If the CPA reasonably concludes that the newsletter does not contain false, misleading, or deceptive information, the arrangement is not an ethics violation. Answer (D) is incorrect. Rule 502 permits accepting engagements obtained through the efforts of third parties.

15. Which of the following is required for a CPA firm to designate itself as "Members of the American Institute of Certified Public Accountants" on its letterhead?

    A.   All CPA owners must be members.

    B.   The owners whose names appear in the firm name must be members.

    C.   At least one of the owners must be a member.

    D.   The firm must be a dues-paying member.

Answer (A) is correct.
    REQUIRED: The requirement for a CPA firm to use the designation, "Members of the AICPA."
    DISCUSSION: Conduct Rule 505, *Form of Organization and Name*, states that a firm may not use the quoted designation unless all of its CPA owners are members of the AICPA.
    Answer (B) is incorrect. All CPA owners, not just certain owners, must be AICPA members. Answer (C) is incorrect. All CPA owners must be members. Answer (D) is incorrect. The CPA owners, not the firm, must be members of the AICPA.

16. Which of the following statements is (are) true regarding a CPA employee of a CPA firm taking copies of information contained in client files when the CPA leaves the firm?

I. A CPA leaving a firm may take copies of information contained in client files to assist another firm in serving that client.

II. A CPA leaving a firm may take copies of information contained in client files as a method of gaining technical expertise.

    A. I only.

    B. II only.

    C. Both I and II.

    D. Neither I nor II.

Answer (D) is correct.
    REQUIRED: The act(s), if any, considered discreditable to the profession.
    DISCUSSION: Conduct Rule 501 states that a member shall not commit an act discreditable to the profession. After the relationship of a member who is not an owner of the firm is terminated, the member may not take or retain copies or originals from the firm's client files or proprietary information without permission.

17. According to the ethical standards of the profession, which of the following acts generally is prohibited?

    A. Accepting a contingent fee for representing a client in connection with obtaining a private letter from the Internal Revenue Service.

    B. Retaining client-provided records after the client has demanded their return.

    C. Revealing client tax returns to a prospective purchaser of the CPA's practice.

    D. Issuing a modified report explaining the CPA's failure to follow a governmental regulatory agency's standards when conducting an attest service for a client.

Answer (B) is correct.
    REQUIRED: The act generally prohibited by the profession's ethical standards.
    DISCUSSION: Retention of client-provided records after the client has demanded their return is an act discreditable to the profession. Even if the state in which a member practices grants a lien on certain records, the ethical standard still applies.
    Answer (A) is incorrect. A contingent fee for representing a client in connection with obtaining a private letter ruling from the IRS is permitted. Answer (C) is incorrect. The disclosure of confidential information in the review of a member's professional practice is not prohibited under a purchase, sale, or merger of the practice. However, appropriate precautions (e.g., a written confidentiality agreement) should be taken so that the prospective buyer does not disclose any confidential client information. Answer (D) is incorrect. Failure to substantially follow such requirements is an act discreditable to the profession, unless the member discloses in his or her report that such requirements were not followed and the reasons. Not following such requirements could require the member to modify the report.

2.7 Other Pronouncements on Professional Responsibilities

18. According to SEC independence regulations,

    A. All audit partners must rotate every 5 years.

    B. Preapproval of accountants' services may be in accord with detailed policies and procedures rather than explicit.

    C. The issuer must disclose only those fees paid to the accountant for audit work.

    D. No partner may sell nonaudit services to the client during the audit.

Answer (B) is correct.
    REQUIRED: The true statement about SEC independence regulations.
    DISCUSSION: Audit committees ordinarily must preapprove the services performed by accountants (permissible nonaudit services and all audit, review, and attest engagements). Approval must be either explicit or in accordance with detailed policies and procedures. If approval is based on detailed policies and procedures, the audit committee must be informed, and no delegation of its authority to management is allowed.
    Answer (A) is incorrect. The lead and concurring (reviewing) audit partners must rotate every 5 years, with a 5-year time-out period. Other audit partners must rotate every 7 years, with a 2-year time-out. Answer (C) is incorrect. An issuer must disclose in its proxy statement or annual filing the fees paid to the accountant segregated into four categories: (1) audit, (2) audit-related, (3) tax, and (4) all other. Answer (D) is incorrect. An accountant is not independent if, during the audit and the period of the engagement, any audit partner (excluding specialty partners such as tax partners) earns or receives compensation for selling services (excluding audit, review, or attest services) to the client.

19. According to the PCAOB, an accounting firm's independence is **least** likely to be impaired if the firm

A. Provides a service to the audit client for a contingent fee.

B. Receives a commission from the audit client.

C. Has an audit client that employs a former firm professional.

D. Provides tax services to a person in a financial reporting oversight role at the audit client.

Answer (C) is correct.
    REQUIRED: The circumstances least likely to impair an accounting firm's independence.
    DISCUSSION: Firm independence is impaired by a client's employment of a former firm professional that could adversely affect the audit unless safeguards are established. Pre-change safeguards include removal from the audit of those negotiating with the client, and post-change safeguards include possibly modifying the audit plan.
    Answer (A) is incorrect. A firm is not independent of its client if the firm or any affiliate, during the audit and engagement period, provides any service or product to the client for a contingent fee or a commission, or receives from the client a contingent fee or commission. Answer (B) is incorrect. A firm is not independent of its client if the firm or any affiliate, during the audit and engagement period, provides any service or product to the client for a contingent fee or a commission, or receives from the client a contingent fee or commission. Answer (D) is incorrect. A registered public accounting firm is not independent of its audit client if the firm or any affiliate, during the professional engagement period, provides any tax service to a person in a financial reporting oversight role at the audit client.

20. The IFAC's *Code of Ethics for Professional Accountants* considers threats to compliance with fundamental principles and safeguards that eliminate or reduce them. Threats may involve

A. Self-interest, such as advocacy for a client.

B. Self-review, such as leadership that promotes compliance.

C. Familiarity, such as an immediate relative's service as a director of the client.

D. Intimidation, such as oversight by a governance body.

Answer (C) is correct.
    REQUIRED: The threat to compliance with fundamental principles.
    DISCUSSION: Threats involve self-interest, self-review, familiarity, intimidation, and advocacy. For example, a familiarity threat arises when a close or immediate family member of a person on the engagement team is a director of the client.
    Answer (A) is incorrect. A self-interest threat arises from a direct financial interest in the client. Answer (B) is incorrect. For example, a self-review threat arises when the designer of a financial accounting system reports on its effectiveness. Answer (D) is incorrect. Oversight by a governance body is a safeguard in the client's systems.

21. According to the PCAOB, an accounting firm is most likely to be independent of its audit client if

A. A reasonable investor would conclude that it is not objective and impartial.

B. The firm's audit professional is responsible for internal control over financial reporting.

C. The firm's audit professional implemented the client's internal control over financial reporting.

D. The firm recommended an aggressive tax position to the client that is more likely than not to be legally allowed.

Answer (D) is correct.
    REQUIRED: The circumstances in which an accounting firm is most likely to be independent.
    DISCUSSION: A firm is not independent of its audit client if, during the audit and engagement period, it provides any nonaudit service related to marketing, planning, or expressing an opinion in favor of the tax treatment of aggressive tax-position transactions for the purpose of tax avoidance. However, this Rule does not apply if the tax treatment is at least more likely than not to be allowable under tax law.
    Answer (A) is incorrect. An auditor is not independent if (s)he is not, or a reasonable investor would conclude that (s)he is not, able to be objective and impartial. Answer (B) is incorrect. Guiding principles regarding independence include whether the auditor assumes a management role or audits his or her own work. Thus, an auditor is not independent if, for example, the auditor is responsible for internal control over financial reporting or had designed or implemented it. Answer (C) is incorrect. Designing or implementing internal control over financial reporting impairs independence.

22. According to the IFAC's *Code of Ethics for Professional Accountants* section on professional appointment,

    A. The existing accountant must discuss relevant matters with the proposed accountant.

    B. The fundamental principle of integrity requires the accountant to provide only the services for which (s)he has the needed expertise.

    C. The client must not provide a second opinion to an existing client.

    D. An accountant generally needs the client's permission to communicate with the current accountant.

Answer (D) is correct.
    REQUIRED: The ethical obligation related to professional appointment.
    DISCUSSION: Before accepting a new client, a professional accountant must determine whether acceptance would create any threats to compliance with the fundamental principles. Thus, a professional accountant will generally need to obtain the client's permission, preferably in writing, to initiate discussion with an existing accountant.
    Answer (A) is incorrect. An existing accountant may be prevented by confidentiality from discussing the affairs of a client with a proposed accountant. Answer (B) is incorrect. The principle of professional competence and due care imposes an obligation on a professional accountant to provide only those services that (s)he is competent to perform. Answer (C) is incorrect. Providing a second opinion on the application of standards or principles to specific circumstances or transactions on behalf of an entity not an existing client may create threats to compliance with the fundamental principles.

23. Under the IFAC's *Code of Ethics for Professional Accountants*, independence is **least** likely to be impaired when

    A. The firm charges a client a contingent fee for an audit.

    B. The firm charges an audit client a contingent fee for a nonassurance service.

    C. The firm provides financial services that depend for their effectiveness on a material, doubtful accounting treatment.

    D. The firm's overdue fees from an audit client are a small part of the firm's total fees.

Answer (D) is correct.
    REQUIRED: The least likely impairment of independence.
    DISCUSSION: When the total fees from an audit client represent a large proportion of the total fees of the firm expressing the audit opinion (or a partner or officer), the dependence on that client and concern about losing the client creates a self-interest or intimidation threat. Safeguards include an external quality control review or consulting a third party (e.g., a regulator or a professional accountant) on key audit decisions. A self-interest threat may be created if overdue fees remain unpaid for a long time, especially if a significant part is not paid before the issue of the audit report for the following year. However, a small amount of overdue fees for a short period of time does not likely create a problem.
    Answer (A) is incorrect. A contingent fee charged by a firm in respect of (1) an audit engagement or (2) a nonassurance service provided to an audit client creates a self-interest threat that is so significant that no safeguards could reduce the threat to an acceptable level. Answer (B) is incorrect. A contingent fee charged by a firm in respect of (1) an audit engagement or (2) a nonassurance service provided to an audit client creates a self-interest threat that is so significant that no safeguards could reduce the threat to an acceptable level. Answer (C) is incorrect. If the effectiveness of corporate finance advice depends on a material, doubtful accounting treatment or presentation in the financial statements, the self-review threat would be so significant that no safeguards could reduce the threat to an acceptable level.

24. According to the IFAC's *Code of Ethics for Professional Accountants*,

    A. A contingent fee arrangement may create a self-interest threat.

    B. An auditor may not receive a referral fee.

    C. An auditor may not receive a commission.

    D. Fees may be too high but not too low.

Answer (A) is correct.
    REQUIRED: The true statement on auditor compensation.
    DISCUSSION: Contingent fees may create a self-interest threat to objectivity depending on factors including (1) the nature of the engagement, (2) the range of amounts, (3) the basis for the fee, and (4) whether the result is to be reviewed by an independent third party.
    Answer (B) is incorrect. An accountant may receive or pay a referral fee given adequate safeguards, such as disclosure to the client. Answer (C) is incorrect. An accountant may receive a commission obtaining advance agreement from the client for commission arrangements in connection with the sale by a third party of goods or services to the client. The AICPA *Code* prohibits commissions related to audit and attest clients. Answer (D) is incorrect. Fees should not be so low that it may be difficult to perform the engagement in accordance with applicable technical and professional standards for that price.

25. When Congress passed the Sarbanes-Oxley Act of 2002, it imposed greater regulation on public companies and their auditors and required increased accountability. Which of the following is **not** a provision of the act?

    A. Executives must certify the appropriateness of the financial statements.

    B. The act provides criminal penalties for fraud.

    C. Auditors may not provide specific nonaudit services for their audit clients.

    D. Audit firms must be rotated on a periodic basis.

Answer (D) is correct.
    REQUIRED: The provision not included in the Sarbanes-Oxley Act.
    DISCUSSION: The act requires rotation of the lead audit or coordinating partner and the reviewing partner on audits of public clients every 5 years. However, the act does not require the rotation of audit firms.
    Answer (A) is incorrect. The CEO and CFO of a public company must provide a statement to accompany the audit report. This statement certifies the appropriateness of the financial statements and disclosures. However, a violation of this requirement must be knowing and intentional. Answer (B) is incorrect. The act creates a new crime for securities fraud with penalties of fines and imprisonment, extends the statute of limitations on securities fraud claims, and makes it a felony to create or destroy documents to impede a federal investigation. Answer (C) is incorrect. The act makes it unlawful for a registered public accounting firm to perform certain nonaudit services for audit clients, for example, bookkeeping, systems design, management functions, or any other service the Public Company Accounting Oversight Board (PCAOB) determines by regulation to be impermissible.

26. Under the IFAC's *Code of Ethics for Professional Accountants,*

    A. An accountant, whether or not in public practice, may not accept a gift from a client.

    B. An accountant in public practice may accept an inconsequential gift from a client.

    C. A close relative of an accountant not in public practice may not accept a gift from a client.

    D. An immediate family member of an accountant, whether or not in public practice, may not accept a gift from a client.

Answer (B) is correct.
    REQUIRED: The acceptability of a gift from a client.
    DISCUSSION: A professional accountant in public practice, or an immediate or close family member, may be offered gifts and hospitality from a client. If a reasonable and informed third party would consider them trivial and inconsequential, they may be accepted. But if the resulting threats to compliance with fundamental principles cannot be eliminated or reduced to an acceptable level through safeguards, a professional accountant must not accept such an offer.

27. The Sarbanes-Oxley Act of 2002 has strengthened auditor independence by requiring that management of a public company

    A. Include only independent persons on the board of directors.

    B. Report the nature of disagreements with former auditors.

    C. Select auditors through audit committees.

    D. Hire a different CPA firm from the one that performs the audit to perform the company's tax work.

Answer (C) is correct.
    REQUIRED: The Sarbanes-Oxley requirement that strengthened auditor independence.
    DISCUSSION: The audit committee must hire and pay the external auditors. Such affiliation inhibits management from changing auditors to gain acceptance of a questionable accounting method. Also, a successor auditor must inquire of the predecessor before accepting an engagement.
    Answer (A) is incorrect. The audit committee must include only independent members. Answer (B) is incorrect. Reporting disagreements with auditors is a long-time SEC requirement. Answer (D) is incorrect. The act does not restrict who may perform tax work. Other engagements, such as outsourcing internal auditing or certain consulting services, are limited.

28. Inspections performed by the PCAOB focus on quality control of registered CPA firms that perform audits of public companies (issuers). As required by the Sarbanes-Oxley Act, inspections determine all of the following **except** that

    A. The lead partner of a client is rotated every 5 years.

    B. A second partner review is performed.

    C. Independence is maintained by audit staff.

    D. Only staff with prior experience work on audits.

Answer (D) is correct.
    REQUIRED: The issue not considered in a PCAOB inspection.
    DISCUSSION: Staff members are required to be trained and supervised in accordance with auditing standards. However, there is no requirement that they have prior experience.
    Answer (A) is incorrect. The lead partner must be rotated at least every 5 years. Answer (B) is incorrect. A second partner review is required for each audit engagement of an issuer. Answer (C) is incorrect. Registered firms must have "policies and procedures in place to comply" with applicable independence requirements.

29. According to the Sarbanes-Oxley Act of 2002, which of the following non-audit services can be provided by a registered public accounting firm to the client contemporaneously with the audit when preapproval is granted by audit committee action?

    A.   Internal audit outsourcing services.

    B.   Tax services.

    C.   Actuarial services related to the audit.

    D.   Advice on financial information system design.

Answer (B) is correct.

REQUIRED: The preapproved nonaudit services that can be provided by a registered public accounting firm at the same time as the audit.

DISCUSSION: The Sarbanes-Oxley Act of 2002 prohibits a registered public accounting firm from performing the following nonaudit services for an issuer: (1) bookkeeping or other services related to the accounting records or financial statements of the audit client; (2) design and implementation of financial information systems; (3) appraisal or valuation services, fairness opinions, or contribution-in-kind reports; (4) actuarial services; (5) internal audit outsourcing services; (6) management functions or human resource services; (7) broker or dealer, investment adviser, or investment banking services; (8) legal services and expert services unrelated to the audit; and (9) any other service that the Board determines is impermissible. But a registered public accounting firm may engage in any nonaudit service, including tax services other than those listed, if the activity is approved in advance by the audit committee of the issuer.

Answer (A) is incorrect. Internal audit outsourcing services are prohibited activities. Answer (C) is incorrect. Actuarial services related to the audit are prohibited activities. Answer (D) is incorrect. Advice on financial information system design is a prohibited activity.

30. While performing certain nonaudit services for an insurance company, a professional accountant is asked to recommend the appropriate accounting treatment for a weather hedge transaction. The accountant has worked with financial hedges but has no experience with weather hedges. Which of the following actions by the accountant would be in compliance with the IFAC *Code of Ethics for Professional Accountants*?

    A.   Agree to recommend the appropriate accounting treatment after performing sufficient research on weather hedges.

    B.   Refuse to conduct the research and make a recommendation because of insufficient experience.

    C.   Refuse to conduct the research and make a recommendation because of a conflict of interest.

    D.   Agree with the accounting treatment recommended by the company's hedge fund trader.

Answer (A) is correct.

REQUIRED: The action complying with the IFAC *Code of Ethics for Professional Accountants*.

DISCUSSION: A professional accountant must maintain professional knowledge and skill at the level required to ensure that a client or employer receives competent professional services based on current developments in practice, legislation, and techniques. (S)he also must act diligently and in accordance with applicable technical and professional standards. Accordingly, the principle of professional competence and due care imposes an obligation on a professional accountant to provide only those services that (s)he is competent to perform. Thus, the accountant may perform the service if (s)he can obtain the necessary competence.

Answer (B) is incorrect. The accountant may perform the service if (s)he can obtain the necessary competence. Answer (C) is incorrect. A professional accountant must not allow a conflict of interest to override professional or business judgments. But these circumstances do not include such a threat to compliance with the fundamental principle of objectivity. Answer (D) is incorrect. The accountant must obtain the necessary competence before (s)he can determine whether (s)he agrees with the client's hedge fund trader (who is not an expert in accounting). But the accountant may rely on the advice or work of an external expert with the appropriate expertise, reputation, etc.

Use the additional questions in Gleim **CPA Test Prep** to create Practice Exams that emulate Prometric!

2.8 PRACTICE TASK-BASED SIMULATIONS

Auditing and Attestation Testlet 4 of 4	**Time Remaining** 1 hour - 30 minutes

DIRECTIONS

Note: If you believe you have encountered a software malfunction, report it to the test center staff immediately.

Navigation

To navigate from task to task, use the controls at the bottom of the screen. Click on the **Next** button to advance to the next task, or the **Previous** button to go to the previous task. To go directly to any task, click on its number.

If you would like a reminder to revisit a task, or want to indicate that you are finished with it, click on the reminder flag below the task number. To clear the flag, click on it again. Reminder flags are for your use only – they do not contribute to your score.

Tabs

In this part of the examination, you will be asked to complete various tasks. Every task has one or more **Work Tabs**. Some tasks have one or more **Information Tabs**, others may have none. Every task has a **Help** tab.

If a task has **Information Tabs**, you may use the information in them to complete your responses in the **Work Tabs**.

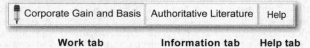

Work tab   Information tab   Help tab

Work Tabs:

- **Work Tabs** are identified with a pencil icon. This is where your responses are expected.
- Each task has one or more **Work Tabs**.
- **Work Tabs** contain directions for completing the task – be sure to read these directions carefully.
- The **Work Tab** name in the example above is for illustration only – yours will differ.
- You must complete all of the **Work Tabs** in each task to receive full credit.

Information Tabs:

- The Authoritative Literature will be provided in all tasks in the AUD, FAR, and REG sections for your reference.
- Your simulation may have one or more additional **Information Tabs**. Like the Authoritative Literature tabs, **Information Tabs** do not have a pencil icon.
- If your task has additional **Information Tabs**, go through each to familiarize yourself with the task content.

Help Tab:

- The **Help Tab** provides assistance with the exam software that is used in this task. For example, if the task is to compose a memorandum, **Help** will provide information about the word processor.

The Toolbar

The toolbar at the top of the screen shows the amount of time remaining for you to complete the tasks. In addition, the following tools are available. Note that only the **Exit** button is displayed when Directions are visible - the others will appear when you begin the tasks.

Click on these buttons to split or unsplit the screen. You can split the screen vertically or horizontally.

Click on this button to display the calculator; click on it again to hide the calculator. To move the calculator, click on the calculator title bar and drag the calculator to the desired location.

Click on this button to use the spreadsheet; click on it again to hide the spreadsheet. To move the spreadsheet, click on the the spreadsheet title bar and drag the spreadsheet to the desired location.

Click on this button to go on to the next part of the examination. You must complete all of the tasks to receive full credit. Once you click on **Exit** and confirm the action, you will NOT be able to return to this testlet.

| Custody of Client Assets | Authoritative Literature | Help |

Under the IFAC Code of Ethics, Section 270, a professional accountant must not assume custody of client assets unless permitted by law and must be in compliance with any additional legal duties imposed on a professional accountant. For each situation, select the applicable requirement regarding an accountant entrusted with client assets (Column A) and whether or not that accountant is in compliance with the requirement (Column B). Each answer choice may be selected once, more than once, or not at all.

Situation	Column A	Column B
1. Job CPAs was given $10,000 of cash from its client to use to pay any regulatory fees required to be paid by the client. Although Job kept the cash in a separate checking account, Job pledged the client's money as security for a loan to obtain a lower interest rate.		
2. Fastidious CPAs was entrusted with the inventory of Larry's Lumberyard for the purposes of testing valuation. While in possession of the inventory, inventory was sold, and Fastidious maintained a record of the inventory sold and any related income.		
3. To cut down on paperwork, Easy CPAs deposited client money entrusted to Easy's checking account but made sure to keep accurate records.		

Requirement	Compliance
A) Keep client assets separate from personal or firm assets	A) In compliance with IFAC requirement
B) Use client assets only for purpose(s) for which they are intended	B) Not in compliance with IFAC requirement
C) Account for client assets and any income	
D) Comply with relevant laws and regulations	

| IFAC Issues | Authoritative Literature | Help |

Threats to compliance with fundamental ethics principles may arise from many circumstances and relationships. Select from the list provided the one example that best matches the threats to an accountant in public practice identified in the IFAC standards. Each selection may be used once, more than once, or not at all.

Threat	Example
1. Self-interest	
2. Self-review	
3. Advocacy	
4. Familiarity	
5. Intimidation	

Choices
A) Testifying for a client
B) Ownership in a client
C) Spouse is on the BOD of a client
D) Client threatens to engage a new auditor over a dispute
E) Client offers inconsequential gift
F) Audit of a client control system designed by the auditor

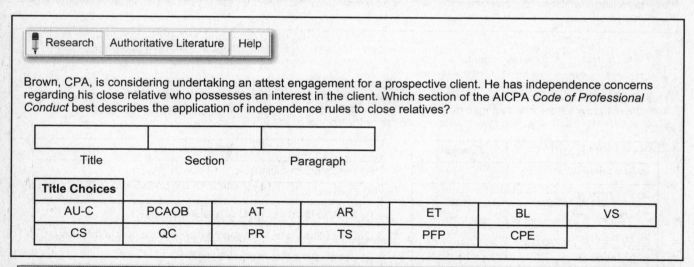

Subordination of Judgment | Authoritative Literature | Help

For each situation below, determine whether or not the member acted appropriately or inappropriately (Column A). If the member acted inappropriately, select what the member should have done (Column B). If the member acted appropriately, select N/A for Column B.

Situation	Column A	Column B
1. Altruistic CPA felt that the position taken by the supervisor was not acceptable even though it complied with GAAP. Altruistic notified the client's regulators of this difference of opinion.		
2. Obedient CPA reasonably believed that the proposed recording of a transaction would result in a material misstatement but did nothing after the supervisor informed Obedient that this was how the client wanted the transaction recorded.		
3. Observant CPA noticed that the client recorded inventory in a way that materially misstated the financial statements. When Observant's supervisor failed to adequately resolve the disagreement, Observant consulted a higher level supervisor.		

Member Action	Suggested Action
A) Appropriate	A) N/A
B) Inappropriate	B) Do nothing
	C) Consult higher level supervisor

⏴ = Reminder   Directions   1 2 **3** 4 5   ◀ Previous   Next ▶

Research | Authoritative Literature | Help

Brown, CPA, is considering undertaking an attest engagement for a prospective client. He has independence concerns regarding his close relative who possesses an interest in the client. Which section of the AICPA *Code of Professional Conduct* best describes the application of independence rules to close relatives?

Title	Section	Paragraph

Title Choices

AU-C	PCAOB	AT	AR	ET	BL	VS
CS	QC	PR	TS	PFP	CPE	

⏴ = Reminder   Directions   1 2 3 **4** 5   ◀ Previous   Next ▶

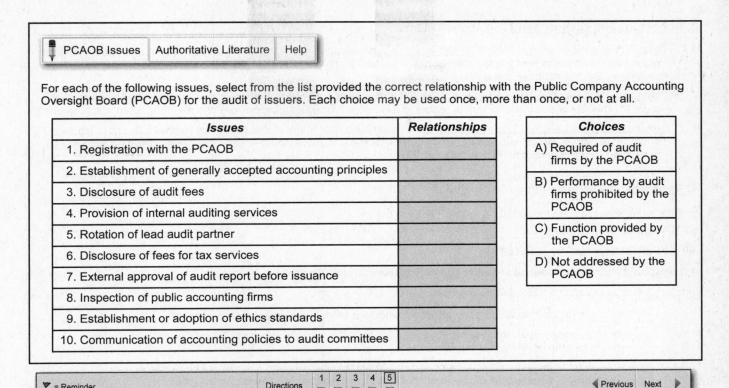

Unofficial Answers

1. Custody of Client Assets (6 Gradable Items)

1. <u>Column A: B) Use client assets only for purpose(s) for which they are intended; Column B: B) Not in compliance with IFAC requirement.</u> Job is required to use client assets only for the purpose for which they are intended. Job is not in compliance with the requirement since it pledged the client's cash when the cash was intended to be used only to pay regulatory fees due by the client.

2. <u>Column A: C) Account for client assets and any income; Column A: A) In compliance with IFAC requirement.</u> Fastidious is required to account for client assets and any income. Fastidious is in compliance with the requirement since it maintained a record of the inventory sold and any related income.

3. <u>Column A: A) Keep client assets separate from personal or firm assets; Column B: B) Not in compliance with IFAC requirement.</u> Easy is required to keep client assets separate from firm assets and is in violation of this requirement even if Easy keeps accurate records.

2. IFAC Issues (5 Gradable Items)

1. <u>B) Ownership in a client.</u> Ownership in a client creates a threat of self-interest.

2. <u>F) Audit of a client control system designed by the auditor.</u> Auditors who evaluate their own designed system create a threat of self-review.

3. <u>A) Testifying for a client.</u> Advocating on behalf of a client in litigation creates a threat of advocacy.

4. <u>C) Spouse is on the BOD of a client.</u> Having a close relative on the board of directors of the client creates a threat of familiarity.

5. <u>D) Client threatens to engage a new auditor over a dispute.</u> Being threatened by a client creates a threat of intimidation.

3. Subordination of Judgment (6 Gradable Items)

1. <u>Column A: B) Inappropriate; Column B: B) Do nothing.</u> If the supervisor's position is an acceptable alternative and does not materially misrepresent the facts, the member should do nothing. By notifying the client's regulators of this disagreement, the member acted inappropriately.

2. <u>Column A: B) Inappropriate; Column B: C) Consult higher level supervisor.</u> If a material misstatement would result, the member should consult the appropriate higher level of supervisor. By doing nothing, the member acted inappropriately.

3. <u>Column A: A) Appropriate; Column B: A) N/A.</u> If a material misstatement would result, the member should consult the appropriate higher level of supervisor. Since a material misstatement would result, Observant acted appropriately by consulting a higher level supervisor on the matter.

4. Research (1 Gradable Item)

Answer: 101.02

ET Section 101 -- *Independence*

.02 101-1 -- Interpretation of Rule 101.

Application of the Independence Rules to Close Relatives

Independence would be considered to be impaired if --

1. An individual participating on the attest engagement team has a close relative who had

    a. A key position with the client, or
    b. A financial interest in the client that

        i)   Was material to the close relative and of which the individual has knowledge or
        ii) Enabled the close relative to exercise significant influence over the client.

2. An individual in a position to influence the attest engagement or any partner in the office in which the lead attest engagement partner primarily practices in connection with the attest engagement has a close relative who had

    a. A key position with the client, or
    b. A financial interest in the client that

        i)   Was material to the close relative and of which the individual or partner has knowledge and
        ii) Enabled the close relative to exercise significant influence over the client.

5. PCAOB Issues (10 Gradable Items)

1. <u>A) Required of audit firms by the PCAOB.</u> The PCAOB registers public accounting firms that audit issuers.

2. <u>D) Not addressed by the PCAOB.</u> The FASB (not the PCAOB) establishes generally accepted accounting principles.

3. <u>A) Required of audit firms by the PCAOB.</u> The PCAOB requires issuers to disclose audit, audit-related, tax, and all other fees paid to their accountants.

4. <u>B) Performance by audit firms prohibited by the PCAOB.</u> Audit firms are prohibited from providing certain internal audit services to their audit clients.

5. <u>A) Required of audit firms by the PCAOB.</u> The PCAOB requires that the lead audit partner be rotated every 5 years.

6. <u>A) Required of audit firms by the PCAOB.</u> The PCAOB requires issuers to disclose audit, audit-related, tax, and all other fees paid to their accountants.

7. <u>D) Not addressed by the PCAOB.</u> The audit report need not be approved by an external party before issuance.

8. <u>C) Function provided by the PCAOB.</u> The PCAOB performs periodic inspections of public accounting firms to evaluate the services that they provide to their clients.

9. <u>C) Function provided by the PCAOB.</u> The PCAOB establishes or adopts standards on auditing, quality control, ethics, and independence.

10. <u>A) Required of audit firms by the PCAOB.</u> The PCAOB requires audit firms to communicate to the audit committee all critical accounting policies and practices used by the client.

Gleim Simulation Grading

Task	Correct Responses		Gradable Items		Score per Task
1	_____	÷	6	=	_____
2	_____	÷	5	=	_____
3	_____	÷	6	=	_____
4 (Research)	_____	÷	1	=	_____
5	_____	÷	10	=	_____

Total of Scores per Task _____

÷ Total Number of Tasks 5

Total Score _____%

Use **CPA Gleim Online** and **Simulation Wizard** to practice more task-based simulations in a realistic environment.

GLEIM® Updates

Keeping your CPA Review materials FRESH

gleim.com/CPAupdate

Updates are available until the next edition is published

STUDY UNIT THREE
PLANNING AND RISK ASSESSMENT

(22 pages of outline)

In general, the recognition and consideration of risks related to an audit have great significance on the CPA exam. The AICPA appears determined to ensure that successful candidates understand the consequences of those risks. Candidates can expect to be tested on the auditor's consideration of audit risk and its components. The interrelationship between risk and materiality is critical.

3.1 PRE-ENGAGEMENT ACCEPTANCE ACTIVITIES (AU-C 210)

1. **Preconditions for an Audit**

    a. Before agreeing to conducting an audit, the auditor should determine that management

        1) Uses an acceptable financial reporting framework (e.g., U.S. GAAP) in the preparation and fair presentation of the financial statements.

        2) Understands its responsibility for the preparation and fair presentation of the financial statements.

        3) Understands its responsibility for the design, implementation, and maintenance of internal control.

        4) Understands its responsibility to provide access to all information and persons deemed necessary for the audit.

2. **Client Acceptance**

    a. Client acceptance includes the continued evaluation of existing clients and the evaluation of new clients. Concluding that management lacks integrity causes the auditor to reject a potential client or to end a relationship with an existing client.

    b. The auditor should communicate with the **predecessor auditor** before final acceptance of the engagement (AU-C 210). The predecessor is expected to respond promptly and, absent unusual circumstances, fully.

    c. The auditor is responsible for initiating the communication.

    d. Conduct Rule 301, *Confidential Client Information*, protects the confidentiality of client information. Hence, both the auditor and his/her predecessor should obtain client permission to have discussions about the integrity of management as well as pertinent audit-related issues.

    e. Inquiries should include

        1) Facts that are relevant to the integrity of management;

        2) Disagreements with management about accounting principles, audit procedures, or other similar matters;

        3) Communications to those charged with governance (e.g., the audit committee) about fraud and noncompliance with laws and regulations;

        4) Communications to management and those charged with governance about significant deficiencies and material weaknesses in internal control; and

        5) The predecessor's understanding as to the reason for the change in auditors.

f.   Certain audit documentation of the auditor's predecessor normally is made available.

g.   The client's refusal to grant permission or the predecessor auditor's failure to respond fully requires the auditor to consider the implications when deciding whether to accept the engagement.

h.   A request by management to change the terms of the engagement should be evaluated by the auditor for reasonableness. If (1) the change is unreasonable and (2) the auditor is not permitted to continue the original engagement, the auditor should withdraw and communicate the circumstances to those charged with governance.

ISA Difference

The ISAs do not require the auditor to communicate with the predecessor auditors in initial or reaudit engagements.

---

3.   **Terms of the Engagement**

a.   The auditor should agree with management or those charged with governance upon the terms. The auditor accepts the engagement only if (1) the preconditions for an audit are present and (2) a common understanding of the terms has been reached.

1)   The preconditions relate to the fundamental responsibilities of management and, if appropriate, those charged with governance. (For a statement of responsibilities, see the sample engagement letter beginning below.)

b.   The terms should be documented in an engagement letter that states the following:

1)   Objective and scope of the audit
2)   Responsibilities of the auditor and management
3)   Inherent limitations of the audit and internal control
4)   The financial reporting framework
5)   The expected form and content of audit reports

c.   An engagement letter should be sent by the CPA to the prospective client on each engagement, audit or otherwise. If the client agrees to the terms by signing a copy of the letter and returning it to the CPA, a contract is formed.

4.   **Sample Engagement Letter**

a.   The following is an example of an audit engagement letter for an audit of general purpose financial statements. This letter is not authoritative and is intended only to be a guide. Its content will vary according to individual requirements and circumstances and is drafted to refer to the audit of financial statements for a single reporting period.

EXAMPLE -- Engagement Letter

SWIFT, MARCH & COMPANY, Certified Public Accountants

January 21, 20XX
Mr. Thomas Thorp, President
Anonymous Company, Inc.
Route 32
Nowhere, New York 10000

Dear Mr. Thorp:

[The objective and scope of the audit]

You have requested that we audit the financial statements of Anonymous Company, Inc., which comprise the balance sheet as of December 31, 20XX and the related statements of income, changes in stockholders' equity, and cash flows for the year then ended as well as the related notes to the financial statements. We are pleased to confirm our acceptance and understanding of this audit engagement by means of this letter. Our audit will be conducted with the objective of our expressing an opinion on the financial statements.

-- Continued on the next page --

EXAMPLE -- Continued

[The responsibilities of the auditor]

We will conduct our audit in accordance with auditing standards generally accepted in the United States of America (GAAS). Those standards require that we plan and perform the audit to obtain reasonable assurance about whether the financial statements are free from material misstatement. An audit involves performing procedures to obtain audit evidence about the amounts and disclosures in the financial statements. The procedures selected depend on the auditor's judgment, including the assessment of the risks of material misstatement of the financial statements, whether due to fraud or error. An audit also includes evaluating the appropriateness of accounting policies used and the reasonableness of significant accounting estimates made by management, as well as evaluating the overall presentation of the financial statements.

Because of the inherent limitations of an audit, together with the inherent limitations of internal control, an unavoidable risk that some material misstatements may not be detected exists, even though the audit is properly planned and performed in accordance with GAAS.

In making our risk assessments, we consider internal control relevant to the entity's preparation and fair presentation of the financial statements in order to design audit procedures that are appropriate in the circumstances but not for the purpose of expressing an opinion on the effectiveness of the entity's internal control. However, we will communicate to you in writing concerning any significant deficiencies or material weaknesses in internal control relevant to the audit of the financial statements that we have identified during the audit.

[The responsibilities of management and identification of the applicable financial reporting framework]

Our audit will be conducted on the basis that management and, when appropriate, those charged with governance acknowledge and understand that they have responsibility

　　a.　*For the preparation and fair presentation of the financial statements in accordance with accounting principles generally accepted in the United States of America;*

　　b.　*For the design, implementation, and maintenance of internal control relevant to the preparation and fair presentation of financial statements that are free from material misstatement, whether due to fraud or error; and*

　　c.　*To provide us with*

　　　　i)　*Access to all information of which management is aware that is relevant to the preparation and fair presentation of the financial statements such as records, documentation, and other matters;*

　　　　ii)　*Additional information that we may request from management for the purpose of the audit; and*

　　　　iii)　*Unrestricted access to persons within the entity from whom we determine it necessary to obtain audit evidence.*

As part of our audit process, we will request from management and, when appropriate, those charged with governance written confirmation concerning representations made to us in connection with the audit.

[Other relevant information]

[Insert other information, such as fee arrangements, billings, assistance to be provided by the client's staff, and other specific terms, as appropriate.]

[Reporting]

[Insert appropriate reference to the expected form and content of the auditor's report. Example follows:]

We will issue a written report upon completion of our audit of Anonymous Company's financial statements. Our report will be addressed to the board of directors of Anonymous Company. We cannot provide assurance that an unmodified opinion will be expressed. Circumstances may arise in which it is necessary for us to modify our opinion, add an emphasis-of-matter or other-matter paragraph(s), or withdraw from the engagement.

We also will issue a written report on [Insert appropriate reference to other auditor's reports expected to be issued.] upon completion of our audit.

Please sign and return the attached copy of this letter to indicate your acknowledgment of, and agreement with, the arrangements for our audit of the financial statements including our respective responsibilities.

SWIFT, MARCH & COMPANY, CPAs

Acknowledged and agreed on behalf of Anonymous Company, Inc., by

_____

[Signed]

[Name and Title]

[Date]

Adapted from AU-C 210

5.   **Representation Letter**

   a.   Management is responsible for adjusting the financial statements to correct material misstatements. Furthermore, the auditor should request that management provide a written representation about whether the effects of any uncorrected misstatements are immaterial, individually or in the aggregate.

      1)   A summary of the uncorrected misstatements should be included in the representation. (See the example management representation letter in Study Unit 14, Subunit 3.)

Stop and review! You have completed the outline for this subunit. Study multiple-choice questions 1 through 5 beginning on page 119.

3.2   PLANNING AN AUDIT (AU-C 220, AU-C 300, AU-C 510, AS NO. 9, AND AS NO. 10)

1.   **Overall Audit Strategy**

   a.   Planning continues throughout the audit. It initially involves developing an overall audit strategy.

   b.   The size and complexity of the entity, the auditor's experience with the entity, and changes in circumstances during the audit affect planning. The following are examples of other matters the auditor should consider in developing the audit strategy:

      1)   Characteristics of the engagement and reporting objectives
      2)   Determination of materiality (See the materiality outline in Subunit 3.3.)
      3)   Areas of high risk of material misstatement
      4)   Involvement of specialists and use of component auditors
      5)   Reliance on controls
      6)   Relevant entity-specific, industry, or financial developments
      7)   Audit resources required
      8)   The results of preliminary engagement activities related to such matters as (a) continuance of the client, (b) compliance with ethical requirements, and (c) the terms of the engagement.

   c.   The engagement partner is responsible for directing, supervising, and performing the audit in accordance with (1) professional standards, (2) legal and regulatory requirements, and (3) firm policies.

2.   **Audit Plans in Accordance with GAAS**

   a.   An audit plan based on the audit strategy must be developed and documented for all audit engagements. It includes the nature, timing, and extent of procedures expected to reduce audit risk to an acceptably low level.

      1)   Thus, the audit plan includes a description of risk assessment procedures.

         a)   **Risk assessment procedures** are performed to obtain an understanding of the entity and its environment, including its internal control, to identify and assess the **risks of material misstatement (RMMs)** at the levels of (1) the financial statements as a whole and (2) relevant assertions.

            i)   The RMM is the combined assessment of **inherent risk** and **control risk**. (See the definitions in Subunit 3.3.)
            ii)   Risk assessment procedures are described in Subunit 3.4.

      2) The plan also includes a description of **further procedures** at the relevant assertion levels for material classes of transactions, account balances, and disclosures. These procedures are to be performed in response to assessed risks and evaluations of audit evidence collected to date.

         a) This element of the plan is based on (1) the decision whether to test the operating effectiveness of controls and (2) the nature, timing, and extent of planned substantive procedures.

      3) The third element of the plan describes any **other procedures** required by GAAS or PCAOB standards.

   b. The overall audit strategy and audit plan are likely to be adjusted as the audit progresses. For example, the auditor may change the nature, timing, and extent of further audit procedures as risk assessments are revised.

   c. The overall audit strategy, the audit plan, and changes in them are documented.

   d. Procedures in planning include the following:

      1) Reviewing prior audit documentation
      2) Discussing audit matters with the CPA firm's personnel
      3) Inquiring about current business developments
      4) Reading the current interim financial statements
      5) Considering the effects of accounting and auditing pronouncements
      6) Coordinating the assistance of entity personnel in data preparation
      7) Determining the involvement, if any, of consultants, specialists, and internal auditors
      8) Establishing the timing of the work
      9) Establishing and coordinating staffing requirements

   e. Planning also involves determining whether and to what extent the services of IT, tax, and other **specialists** will be required. The auditor should have supervisory responsibility for specialists. Moreover, the auditor should have sufficient knowledge to

      1) Communicate their objectives,
      2) Evaluate whether their planned procedures will achieve the objectives, and
      3) Evaluate the results.

3. **Communication**

   a. The auditor should discuss elements of planning with management to facilitate the performance of the audit.

      1) But the communication should not compromise the audit, for example, by making detailed procedures too predictable.

4. **Initial Audits**

   a. The following are examples of additional planning considerations for initial audits:

      1) Performance of quality control procedures, e.g., those related to (a) acceptance and continuance of clients and engagements, (b) assignment of engagement teams, (c) ethical requirements, and (d) performance
      2) Communication with the predecessor auditor
      3) Major issues discussed with management
      4) Planned audit procedures regarding **opening balances** to gain assurance that

         a) Opening balances do not contain misstatements that materially affect the current period's financial statements, and
         b) Accounting policies reflected in the opening balances have been consistently applied in the current period's financial statements.

5.   **Direction and Supervision**

a.   AU-C 220 addresses quality control for an audit. It states that direction involves informing team members about the following:

1)   Their responsibilities, including ethical requirements and planning and performing the audit with professional skepticism
2)   The objectives of the work
3)   The nature of the entity's business
4)   Risks
5)   Potential problems
6)   The specific approach to the engagement

b.   Team members should hold discussions so that questions about the engagement may be raised. Furthermore, teamwork and training facilitate understanding of the objectives of the assigned work.

c.   Supervision includes consideration of the competencies of the team members, such as whether they (1) have enough time for the work, (2) understand the instructions, and (3) carry out the work in accordance with the audit plan.

1)   Supervision also includes (a) tracking engagement progress, (b) addressing significant findings, and (c) modifying the approach if necessary. Moreover, matters may arise that should be considered by qualified team members during the engagement.

d.   According to AU-C 220 and QC 10, differences of opinion (1) within the engagement team, (2) with a consultant, or (3) between the engagement partner and the quality control reviewer should be resolved by following the firm's related policies and procedures.

e.   According to QC 10, a member of the engagement team should be able to document his/her disagreement with the conclusions reached after appropriate consultation. Moreover, (1) conclusions should be documented and implemented, and (2) the report should be released only after resolution of the matter.

f.   The PCAOB's AS No. 3 requires documentation of disagreements among members of the engagement team or with consultants about final conclusions on significant accounting or auditing matters.

6.   Audit team members should be included in the discussion about the susceptibility of the statements to material misstatement due to fraud or error, but especially **fraud**. The discussion aids in understanding the entity and its environment, including its internal control, and the risks it confronts. (See the outline on this topic in Subunit 3.6.)

a.   Moreover, the discussion should emphasize **professional skepticism**.

1)   It is an attitude that includes a questioning mind and critical assessment of audit evidence (AU-C 200).

7.   **Internal Audit Plans**

a.   Internal audit plans differ from those written by the independent external auditor.

1)   The independent external auditor's purpose is to express an opinion on the fairness of the financial statements, i.e., to evaluate the client's financial reporting.

2) However, the internal auditor's work is more comprehensive. According to **The Institute of Internal Auditors**, internal auditing is an independent, objective assurance **and** consulting function that adds value and improves an organization's operations. Internal auditors evaluate and improve the effectiveness of governance, risk management, and control processes. Accordingly, they evaluate risks and the adequacy and effectiveness of controls regarding (a) the reliability and integrity of financial and operational information; (b) the effectiveness and efficiency of operations; (c) the safeguarding of assets; and (d) compliance with laws, regulations, and contracts.

    a) Consequently, the internal auditor's plans are more detailed and cover areas that normally are not considered by the independent auditor.

NOTE: Independence is an organizational attribute of the internal audit activity. Individual internal auditors are employees of the entity and cannot be independent in the same sense as external auditors.

Stop and review! You have completed the outline for this subunit. Study multiple-choice questions 6 through 9 beginning on page 120.

3.3 AUDIT RISK AND MATERIALITY (AU-C 200, AU-C 320, AU-C 450, AS NO. 8, AND AS NO. 11)

The CPA exam can be viewed as your ticket into the profession. The AICPA uses the exam as part of its attempt to ensure that you recognize the risks associated with your new career. Thus, many questions relate to risks that accountants face. Alternatively, few questions relate to the rewards that the profession provides. Study appropriately.

1. Audit risk and materiality are considered in (a) planning and performing the audit, (b) evaluating the results, and (c) forming an opinion on the financial statements. They also are reflected in the auditor's report.

    a. Audit risk is the risk that an auditor expresses an inappropriate opinion on materially misstated financial statements.

2. **Audit Risk**

    a. Audit risk consists of the risks of material misstatement (inherent risk combined with control risk) and detection risk. The RMMs are the entity's risks, and detection risk is the auditor's risk. The components may be assessed in quantitative terms, such as percentages, or in nonquantitative terms.

        1) **Inherent risk** is the susceptibility of an assertion about a class of transaction, account balance, or disclosure to a misstatement that could be material, individually or in the aggregate, before consideration of related controls.

        2) **Control risk** is the risk that internal control will not prevent, or detect and correct, on a timely basis a material misstatement that could occur in an assertion.

        3) **Detection risk** is the risk that the procedures performed by the auditor to reduce audit risk to an acceptably low level will not detect a material misstatement. It is a function of the effectiveness of an audit procedure and its application by the auditor.

            a) Detection risk is the only component of audit risk that can be changed at the auditor's discretion. (Inherent risk and control risk exist independently of the audit and cannot be changed by the auditor.)

            b) The acceptable level of detection risk for a given audit risk is inversely related to the assessed RMMs at the assertion level.

3.   **Materiality**

    a.   Materiality is a matter of professional judgment about whether misstatements could reasonably influence the economic decisions of users as a group, given their common informational needs.

        1)   Users are assumed to be knowledgeable and reasonable economic decision makers with an understanding of financial statements and their limits.

        2)   Materiality judgments are made in light of surrounding circumstances and depend on the size (quantitative considerations) or nature (qualitative considerations) of a misstatement (or both).

            a)   Thus, materiality established when planning the audit is not necessarily an amount below which uncorrected misstatements are always immaterial.

    b.   Materiality is defined for planning purposes at three related levels.

        1)   Materiality at the **financial statement level** as a whole is a monetary amount that results in the misstatement of the financial statements.

        2)   Materiality levels also are set for particular **account balances, classes of transactions, or disclosures**. In specific circumstances, these amounts could influence users.

            a)   Benchmarks often are used as a starting point in determining materiality for the financial statements.

                i)   Examples might include a percentage of client income (e.g., 5%), revenues (e.g., 1%), assets (e.g., 0.5%), or some combination.

        3)   **Performance materiality** is one amount or more set by the auditor at less than the materiality for the statements as a whole. Performance materiality also refers to amounts set at less than materiality for particular classes of transactions, balances, or disclosures.

            a)   Performance materiality is intended to reduce to an appropriately low level the probability that the sum of uncorrected and undetected misstatements exceeds the applicable materiality.

                i)   Accordingly, performance materiality is an adjustment for (a) individually immaterial misstatements and (b) possible undetected misstatements.

EXAMPLE

If financial statement materiality was set at $50,000, and materiality for the accounts receivable balance was set at $10,000, performance materiality for the audit of accounts receivable might be set at $3,000 to compensate for the possibility of multiple undetected or uncorrected misstatements in accounts receivable.

---

    c.   During the audit, the auditor may obtain new information that requires revision of materiality judgments.

        1)   If the revised materiality is lower, the auditor considers whether to revise (a) performance materiality and (b) the nature, timing, and extent of further audit procedures.

    d.   Audit risk and materiality are considered in

        1)   Planning the audit;

        2)   Determining the nature and extent of risk assessment procedures;

        3)   Assessing RMMs;

        4)   Determining the nature, timing, and extent of further audit procedures; and

        5)   Evaluating the effects of any (a) identified misstatements on the audit and (b) uncorrected misstatements on the financial statements and the audit opinion.

            a)   A **misstatement** is the difference between (1) the amount, classification, presentation, or disclosure of a reported item and (2) the amount, etc., required for the item to be presented fairly.

4. **Evaluated Findings**

    a.   When evaluating audit findings, the auditor considers **uncorrected misstatements** and should **accumulate identified misstatements** (unless clearly trivial). To evaluate accumulated misstatements and communicate misstatements to appropriate parties, the auditor may classify them as factual, judgmental, and projected.

        1)   No doubt exists about **factual misstatements**.

        2)   **Judgmental misstatements** result from management's (a) unreasonable accounting estimates or (b) application of inappropriate accounting policies.

        3)   **Projected misstatements** are the auditor's best estimates of the misstatements in populations based on audit samples.

    b.   If accumulated misstatement approaches materiality, a more than acceptable risk may exist that the sum of (1) possible undetected misstatements and (2) accumulated uncorrected misstatements could exceed materiality.

    c.   The auditor should promptly communicate to appropriate management all accumulated misstatements and request their correction.

        1)   The auditor also may request that management

            a)   Examine, based on the auditor's projected misstatement, a transaction class, balance, or disclosure and make an adjustment for the actual misstatement;

            b)   Record an adjustment for factual misstatements; and

            c)   Review the assumptions and methods used to develop a judgmental misstatement.

        2)   Identification of a material misstatement may indicate a significant deficiency or material weakness in internal control that should be communicated to management and those charged with governance.

        3)   Uncorrected misstatements should be communicated to those charged with governance.

5. **Documentation**

    a.   The auditor should document

        1)   The amount of misstatements regarded as clearly trivial,

        2)   All misstatements accumulated,

        3)   Whether accumulated misstatements have been corrected, and

        4)   The basis for the conclusion about whether uncorrected misstatements (individually or aggregated) are material.

Stop and review! You have completed the outline for this subunit. Study multiple-choice questions 10 through 14 beginning on page 121.

3.4 UNDERSTANDING THE ENTITY AND ITS ENVIRONMENT (AU-C 315 AND AS NO. 12)

1. The auditor obtains an understanding of the entity and its environment, including its internal control, to identify and assess the risks of material misstatement of the financial statements, whether due to fraud or error.

   a. The understanding provides a basis for designing and implementing responses to the assessed RMMs.

2. The following are among the other reasons for obtaining the understanding:

   a. Determining materiality for planning the audit and evaluating it during the audit
   b. Considering accounting policies and disclosures
   c. Identifying areas for special audit consideration, e.g., complex financial transactions
   d. Setting expectations for results of analytical procedures
   e. Designing further audit procedures
   f. Evaluating audit evidence, e.g., that related to management's assumptions and representations

3. **Risk Assessment Procedures**

   a. Risk assessment procedures are performed to obtain the understanding. They include (1) inquiries of management and others within the entity, (2) analytical procedures, and (3) observation and inspection.

      1) The auditor also may perform other appropriate procedures, such as inquiring of external parties (e.g., legal counsel) or reviewing externally generated information (e.g., financial publications).

   b. **Inquiries within the entity** may be directed to

      1) Those responsible for financial reporting;
      2) Those charged with governance;
      3) Internal auditors;
      4) Legal counsel;
      5) Marketing, sales, and production managers; and
      6) Others at different levels of authority who may have information about the RMMs.

   c. An **analytical procedures** outline is in the next subunit.

   d. **Observation and inspection** provide support for inquiries and direct evidence about the entity and its environment. Examples are

      1) Observing activities and operations;
      2) Inspecting documents and records;
      3) Reading reports, e.g., internal audit reports, interim statements, quarterly reports, and minutes of board meetings;
      4) Tours of facilities; and
      5) Tracing financial transactions through the information system (a walk-through).

4. **Obtaining the Understanding**

    a.   The understanding of the entity should include the following:

        1)   Industry, regulatory, and other external factors, including the accounting framework

        2)   The nature of the entity, including its operating characteristics

        3)   Ownership and governance structures, especially complex structures such as those that include subsidiaries or multiple locations

        4)   Investments and investment activities, such as acquisitions, divestitures, and capital outlays

        5)   Financing activities

        6)   Selection and application of accounting principles, including any changes

        7)   Objectives and strategies and the related business risks, such as those related to new products, markets, or expansion

        8)   Measurement and review of financial performance as an indication of what the entity considers important

5. Use of **prior-period information** about the entity and its environment (structure, nature of business, controls, and responses to prior misstatements) contributes to the understanding.

    a.   But procedures should be performed to evaluate its current relevance.

6. The auditor specifically assesses the RMM due to **fraud**. (S)he considers this assessment in designing auditing procedures. (See the outline on fraud risks in Subunit 3.6.)

    a.   The audit team members should discuss (1) the susceptibility of the entity's financial statements to material misstatement, whether due to fraud or error, and (2) the application of the financial reporting framework.

        1)   This discussion should be documented.

7. The auditor may consider pertinent information obtained from (a) the auditor's client acceptance (or continuation) procedures, (b) previous engagements for the client, and (c) other sources.

8. **Internal Control**

    a.   The auditor obtains an understanding of relevant internal controls to

        1)   Determine the types of possible misstatements,

        2)   Identify what affects the RMMs, and

        3)   Design further procedures (tests of controls and substantive procedures). (See Study Unit 5 for a full discussion.)

9. **Issuers**

    a.   For an audit of an issuer, the auditor should consider the following:

        1)   Reading public information about the company

        2)   Obtaining information from earnings calls to investors and rating agencies

        3)   Gaining an understanding of compensation for senior management

        4)   Obtaining information about trading activities in the company's securities

        5)   Company performance measures that could create incentives or pressures on management to manipulate the financial information

10. In general, the auditor should consider the likely sources of material misstatement and ask, "What could go wrong?"

Stop and review! You have completed the outline for this subunit. Study multiple-choice questions 15 through 17 beginning on page 123.

3.5 ANALYTICAL PROCEDURES (AU-C 520)

Background

The Auditing Standards Board (ASB) recognized that most audit procedures are fairly narrow in scope. That is, they are directed toward a particular assertion for a specific account. In some cases, auditors have failed because they "missed the forest by focusing on the trees." Analytical procedures, however, are much broader in scope. For example, the auditor might ask "Can the client's reported inventory fit in its current warehouse space?" The ASB decided that analytical procedures should be applied in every audit.

---

1. Analytical procedures are evaluations of financial information made by **a study of plausible relationships among financial and nonfinancial data** using models that range from simple to complex.

2. The basic premise is that plausible relationships among data may reasonably be expected to exist and continue in the absence of known conditions to the contrary. Analytical procedures also include investigating fluctuations or relationships that (1) are inconsistent with other information or (2) differ significantly from expectations. The following exhibit represents the decision process:

Auditor Developed Expectation of Balance or Ratio	⟶	Are These Materially Different?	⟵	Management Reported Balance or Ratio

3. **Timing and Use**

   a. Analytical procedures may be applied not only as risk assessment procedures (analytical procedures used to plan the audit) but also as **substantive procedures**. These are procedures (tests of details and analytical procedures) designed to detect material misstatements at the assertion level. When applying substantive analytical procedures, the auditor should do the following:

      1) Determine their suitability for specific assertions after considering the assessed RMMs and any tests of details.

      2) Evaluate the reliability of data used to develop an expectation of an amount or ratio.

      3) Develop an expectation and determine whether it is sufficiently precise to identify a material misstatement.

      4) Assist in forming an overall conclusion near the end of the audit about whether the statements are consistent with the auditor's understanding of the entity.

4. **Risk Assessment Procedures**

   a. Analytical procedures applied as risk assessment procedures at the beginning of the audit may improve the understanding of the client's business and significant transactions and events since the last audit. They also may identify unusual transactions or events and amounts, ratios, and trends that might indicate matters with audit planning implications.

      1) But when they use highly aggregated data, they provide only broad indications about the RMMs.

5. **Development of Expectations**

   a. The auditor develops expectations or predictions of recorded balances or ratios. The candidate should learn the **five sources of information** used to develop analytical procedures. They are frequently tested on the CPA exam.

1) **Financial Information from Comparable Prior Period(s)**

EXAMPLE

If a client's prior reported sales were $120,000 in Year 1, $130,000 in Year 2, and $140,000 in Year 3, respectively, the auditor is likely to predict Year 4 sales to be approximately $150,000 based on the trend. If management's reported sales are materially different, the auditor increases the assessed RMM and investigates the underlying causes.

---

2) **Anticipated Results**, such as budgets or forecasts prepared by management (or others) prior to the end of the period

---
EXAMPLE

If management prepares a budget at the beginning of the period reporting forecasted cost of sales to be $100,000, the auditor expects cost of sales to approximate $100,000 at year end.

The use of standard costs and variance analysis facilitates the application of analytical procedures in this context.

---

3) **Relationships among Elements of Financial Information**, such as those among the balances on the financial statements

---
EXAMPLE

If the auditor determines that sales increased by 25% for the year, accounts receivable should increase by approximately that amount.

---

4) **Comparable Information from the Client's Industry**

EXAMPLE

If the usual inventory turnover ratio in the industry is 10 times per year, the auditor expects the client's turnover ratio to be approximately 10 times.

---

5) **Relationships between Financial and Relevant Nonfinancial Information**

EXAMPLE

If the number of hours worked increased by 30%, the auditor expects an increase in labor costs of approximately 30%.

---

6. **Substantive Procedures**

   a. The auditor's judgment about expected effectiveness and efficiency in reducing the assessed RMMs to an acceptable level determines the procedures chosen. For some assertions, analytical procedures alone may provide the necessary assurance. The effectiveness and efficiency of analytical procedures depend on the following factors:

      1) **Nature of the assertion.** Analytical procedures may be effective when tests of details may not indicate potential misstatements. For example, they may be effective for testing the completeness assertion.

      2) **Plausibility and predictability of the relationship.** Relationships in stable environments are more predictable than those in unstable environments, and income statement amounts tend to be more predictable than balance sheet amounts.

         a) The reason is that income statement amounts are based on transactions over a period of time, but balance sheet amounts are for a moment in time.

         b) Amounts subject to management discretion may be less predictable.

3) **Availability and reliability of the data used to develop the expectation.** Reliability is affected by the source of the data and the conditions under which they were gathered. For example, data are considered more reliable when

   a) Obtained from independent sources outside the entity,
   b) Obtained from sources inside the entity independent of those responsible for the amount being audited,
   c) Developed under reliable internal control,
   d) Subjected to audit testing in the current or prior years, and
   e) Obtained from a variety of sources.

4) **Precision of the expectation.** As the expectation becomes more precise, significant differences between the expectation and management's reported number are more likely to be caused by misstatements.

   a) Ordinarily, the more detailed the information, the more precise the expectation. For example, monthly data provide more precise expectations than annual data.

b. **Scanning** is a type of analytical procedure using auditor judgment to identify significant or unusual items to test.

7. **Forming an Overall Conclusion**

a. Analytical procedures used to form an overall conclusion ordinarily include reading the financial statements and considering (1) the adequacy of evidence regarding unusual or unexpected balances detected during the audit and (2) such balances or relationships not detected previously.

1) If analytical procedures detect a previously unrecognized RMM, the auditor should revise the assessments of the RMMs and modify the further planned procedures.

8. **Acceptable Differences**

a. The determination that differences between expectations and recorded amounts are acceptable without additional investigation is a function of materiality and the desired degree of assurance. It also considers that the sum of individually insignificant items may be significant.

1) As the assessed risk increases, the amount of acceptable difference decreases.

9. **Investigating Results**

a. Inconsistent fluctuations or relationships or significant differences should result in (1) inquiries of management, (2) corroboration of responses with other audit evidence, and (3) performance of any necessary other procedures. Moreover, the RMMs due to fraud should be considered.

10. **Documentation**

a. When substantive analytical procedures are performed, the auditor should document

1) The expectation,
2) The factors used to develop the expectation,
3) The results of the comparison of the expectation with the recorded amounts or ratios, and
4) Any additional auditing procedures performed to resolve differences and their results.

11. **Ratio Analysis**

a. Auditors apply ratio analysis in all stages of the audit as analytical procedures. An auditor should understand not only how to calculate each ratio but also the potential explanations of changes in a ratio from period to period. Many of the ratios considered here have been tested recently on the CPA exam.

1) **Current ratio**

$$\frac{Current\ assets}{Current\ liabilities}$$

a) Changes in the ratio may be caused by changes in the components of current assets (typically cash, receivables, and inventory) and current liabilities (typically accounts payable and notes payable).

b) If the current ratio is less than 1.0, equal increases in the numerator and denominator increase the ratio, and equal decreases decrease the ratio.

i) However, if the current ratio is more than 1.0, equal increases in the numerator and denominator decrease the ratio, and equal decreases increase the ratio.

2) **Quick (acid-test) ratio**

$$\frac{Current\ assets\ -\ Inventory}{Current\ liabilities}$$

a) Quick assets are convertible to cash quickly. Auditors ordinarily calculate this ratio as current assets minus inventory. Thus, changes in inventory do not affect the quick ratio, but other components of the current ratio do.

3) **Receivables turnover**

$$\frac{Net\ sales}{Average\ net\ receivables}$$

a) Auditors often calculate this ratio using ending net receivables as the denominator because it is the balance being audited. Changes in sales or receivables affect this ratio.

b) In principle, the numerator should be net credit sales, but this amount may not be known.

4) **Days' sales in receivables**

$$\frac{365,\ 360,\ or\ 300}{Receivables\ turnover}$$

a) This ratio has the same components as receivables turnover and is affected by changes in sales or receivables.

b) The number of days in a year may be 365, 360 (a banker's year), or 300 (number of business days).

5) **Inventory turnover**

$$\frac{Cost\ of\ goods\ sold}{Average\ inventory}$$

a) Auditors often calculate this ratio using ending inventory as the denominator because it is the balance being audited. Changes in cost of goods sold or inventory affect this ratio.

b) A high turnover implies that the entity does not hold excessive inventories that are unproductive and lessen its profitability.

c) A high turnover also implies that the inventory is truly marketable and does not contain obsolete goods.

6) **Days' sales in inventory**

$$\frac{365,\ 360,\ or\ 300}{Inventory\ turnover}$$

   a) This ratio has the same components as inventory turnover and is affected by changes in inventory or cost of sales.

   b) The number of days in a year may be 365, 360 (a banker's year), or 300 (number of business days).

7) **Total asset turnover**

$$\frac{Net\ sales}{Total\ assets}$$

   a) This ratio calculates how many times the total assets turn over in sales. It is affected by changes in sales and total assets.

   b) The denominator also may be average total assets.

8) **Debt-to-equity ratio**

$$\frac{Total\ debt}{Total\ equity}$$

   a) This ratio measures how much external parties contribute to assets relative to owners. Shifts in debt or equity affect this ratio.

   b) The ratios of total assets to total equity and total assets to total debt provide similar analysis and conclusions.

9) **Times interest earned**

$$\frac{Net\ income\ +\ Interest\ expense\ +\ Income\ tax\ expense}{Interest\ expense}$$

   a) Times interest earned measures the ability of an entity to pay its interest charges. Taxes are added back to net income because interest is paid before taxes. Interest is added back to net income because it is included in the calculation of net income.

   b) An alternative is to exclude interest from the numerator and to add 1.0 to the quotient once the calculation is made.

   c) Changes in interest and net income may affect this ratio.

   d) If earnings decline sufficiently, no income tax expense will be recognized.

10) **Cost of goods sold ratio**

$$\frac{Cost\ of\ goods\ sold}{Net\ sales}$$

   a) This ratio measures the percentage amount of sales consumed by cost of goods sold. Nonproportional changes in either affect the ratio.

11) **Gross margin percentage**

$$\frac{Net\ sales\ -\ Cost\ of\ goods\ sold}{Net\ sales}$$

   a) The gross margin percentage measures earnings from the sale of products. Nonproportional changes in net sales and cost of goods sold affect the ratio.

12) **Net operating margin percentage**

$$\frac{Operating\ income}{Net\ sales}$$

a) Operating income is calculated before subtracting interest and taxes. Nonproportional changes in either operating income or net sales cause a change in the ratio.

13) **Return on equity**

$$\frac{Net\ income}{Total\ equity}$$

a) This is an overall measure of a rate of return on investment. Changes in net income or changes in equity may affect this ratio.

b) A return on average total equity or on common equity also may be calculated.

Stop and review! You have completed the outline for this subunit. Study multiple-choice questions 18 through 24 beginning on page 124.

3.6 CONSIDERATION OF FRAUD IN A FINANCIAL STATEMENT AUDIT (AU-C 240)

1. **Responsibilities**

    a. Fraud is an "intentional act by one or more individuals among management, those charged with governance, employees, or third parties, involving the use of deception that results in a misstatement in financial statements that are the subject of an audit." The auditor should plan and perform the audit to obtain reasonable assurance about whether the financial statements are free of material misstatement, whether caused by fraud or error.

    b. Those charged with governance (the board and audit committee) and management are primarily responsible for programs and controls that prevent, deter, and detect fraud. They should set the proper tone and maintain a culture of honesty.

        1) Absolute assurance is unattainable because of the characteristics of fraud and the inherent limitations of an audit. Management may override controls in unpredictable ways or alter accounting records. Fraud also may be concealed through collusion, falsifying documentation (including electronic approvals), or withholding evidence.

2. Fraud is intentional. The three conditions ordinarily present when fraud exists include **pressures or incentives** to commit fraud, an **opportunity**, and the capacity to **rationalize** misconduct.

3. The types of fraud relevant to the auditor include misstatements arising from

    a. **Fraudulent financial reporting.** These are intentional misstatements or omissions to deceive users, such as altering accounting records or documents, misrepresenting or omitting significant information, and misapplying accounting principles.

    b. **Misappropriation of assets.** These result from, for example, (1) theft of physical assets, (2) embezzlement (e.g., stealing collections of receivables), (3) an action that causes payment for items not received, or (4) using entity assets for personal reasons.

4. **Professional Skepticism**

   a. Professional skepticism should be maintained in considering the risk of material misstatement due to fraud **(fraud risk)**. An auditor should (1) critically assess evidence, (2) continually question whether fraud has occurred, and (3) not accept unpersuasive evidence solely because management is believed to be honest.

   b. Discussion among the engagement partner and other key engagement team members should emphasize professional skepticism and continual alertness to potential fraud. It may occur before or during information gathering, and communication should be ongoing.

      1) The discussion should include brainstorming about (a) factors that might create the conditions for fraud, (b) how and where the statements might be misstated, (c) how assets might be misappropriated or financial reports fraudulently misstated, (d) how management could conceal fraudulent reporting, and (e) how to respond to fraud risk.

5. **Identifying Fraud Risks**

   a. Obtaining information for identifying fraud risks includes inquiring of (1) management, (2) those charged with governance, (3) the internal auditors, and (4) others. It also involves considering (1) fraud risk factors and (2) the results of analytical procedures performed as risk assessment procedures.

      1) The auditor should apply analytical procedures to **revenue accounts**, e.g., by comparing recorded sales and production capacity to detect fictitious sales.

      2) **Fraud risk factors** are events or conditions indicating possible fraud. The auditor should judge whether they are present and affect the assessment of fraud risks.

      3) Other information may be derived from (a) discussions among audit team members, (b) procedures related to the acceptance and continuance of clients and engagements, (c) reviews of interim statements, and (d) identified inherent risks at the account-balance or class-of-transactions level.

   b. An identifiable risk may exist when all the conditions for fraud have not been observed, especially rationalization. The extent of a condition may by itself create a fraud risk, e.g., pressure to reach an earnings goal.

      1) Fraud risks vary with the entity's size, complexity, ownership, etc.

      2) Fraud risks may relate to specific assertions or to the statements as a whole.

      3) High inherent risk of an assertion about an account balance or transaction class may exist when it is susceptible to management manipulation.

      4) Identifying fraud risks involves considering the type of risk and (a) its significance, (b) likelihood, and (c) pervasiveness.

      5) The auditor should address the risk of **management override** of controls in all audits because of its unpredictability.

      6) The auditor ordinarily should assume the existence of a fraud risk relating to **improper revenue recognition**. The contrary conclusion should be documented in the working papers.

   c. Identified fraud risks are assessed at the statement and assertion levels and treated as significant. This assessment is ongoing after the initial assessment.

      1) To the extent not done previously, the auditor should obtain an understanding of the relevant controls. Also, the auditor should evaluate whether (a) those controls have been suitably designed and implemented and (b) they reduce the risks.

6. **Responses to Fraud Risk**

    a. The responses to the assessment of fraud risks should reflect a critical evaluation of the audit evidence. Responses (1) may have an overall effect on the audit, (2) involve further audit procedures performed in response to assessed fraud risks at the assertion level, or (3) address management override.

    b. One **overall effect** is to assign more experienced personnel, or individuals with special skills, or to increase supervision. A second overall effect is to consider accounting principles, especially those involving subjective measurements and complex transactions, and whether they indicate a **collective bias**. Another overall effect is to make unpredictable choices of audit procedures.

    c. Audit procedures vary with fraud risks and the balances, transactions, and assertions affected. Procedures may (1) provide more reliable evidence or increased corroboration, (2) be performed at year end or throughout the reporting period, or (3) involve larger samples or the use of computer-assisted techniques.

    d. The auditor should further address management override.

        1) Material misstatements may result from inappropriate **journal entries or adjustments**, particularly those made at year end. The auditor should therefore

            a) Understand the financial reporting process and controls

            b) Identify, select, and test entries and adjustments after considering the risk assessments, effectiveness of controls, nature of the reporting process, and audit evidence (electronic or manual)

            c) Choose whether to test entries during the period

            d) Make inquiries about inappropriate or unusual activity

        2) Fraud may result from intentional misstatement of **accounting estimates**. The auditor should perform a retrospective review of estimates in the prior-year statements that are based on sensitive assumptions or significant management judgments.

        3) The auditor should understand **significant unusual transactions**.

7. **Evaluating Audit Evidence**

    a. The assessment of fraud risks should be ongoing because field work may reveal conditions that modify the judgment.

    b. Analytical procedures performed near the end of the audit in forming an overall conclusion or as substantive procedures may detect previously unrecognized fraud risks. These procedures should be applied to revenue through year end. The auditor also should evaluate responses to inquiries about analytical relationships.

    c. At or near the end of field work, the auditor should evaluate earlier assessments of fraud risk. The performance of additional procedures may result. Furthermore, the auditor responsible for the audit should determine that information about fraud risks has been properly communicated to team members.

    d. The auditor should consider whether identified misstatements indicate fraud, with consequent effects on materiality judgments. If the fraud is not material, the auditor still should evaluate the implications for the audit, e.g., the management's representations and integrity.

        1) If management (especially senior management) is involved, the auditor should (a) reevaluate the assessment of fraud risks and its effects on audit procedures and (b) consider the possibility of collusion.

        2) If fraud risk is great, the auditor may consider withdrawing and communicating the reasons to those charged with governance and, possibly, to regulators.

8. **Communications**

   a. Communications about fraud are required given evidence that fraud may exist. Inconsequential fraud should be brought to the attention of the appropriate management. Other fraud should be reported directly to those charged with governance.

   b. In determining a responsibility to report fraud outside the entity, the auditor's legal obligation may, in some circumstances, override the duty of confidentiality.

9. **Documentation**

   a. Documentation of the consideration of fraud should include the following:

      1) Decisions made during the discussions among the engagement team
      2) Identified and assessed risks at the statement and assertion levels
      3) Overall responses, procedures performed, and the connection to assessed risks at the assertion level
      4) Reasons for not identifying improper revenue recognition as a fraud risk
      5) Results of procedures, including those addressing management override
      6) Fraud communications

Stop and review! You have completed the outline for this subunit. Study multiple-choice questions 25 through 30 beginning on page 127.

3.7 CONSIDERATION OF LAWS AND REGULATIONS IN AN AUDIT OF FINANCIAL STATEMENTS (AU-C 250)

Background
The clarified auditing standard AU-C 250, *Consideration of Laws and Regulations in an Audit of Financial Statements*, replaces AU 317, *Illegal Acts by Clients*. Although the auditor's responsibilities have not changed significantly, some terminology has been updated. The standard replaces the phrase "illegal act" with the term "noncompliance." In the prior standard, laws and regulations not expected to have a "direct effect" on the financial statements were described as having a potential "indirect effect." Those are described now as "not having a direct effect."

1. **Noncompliance**

   a. Noncompliance is an intentional or unintentional act or omission by the entity that is contrary to laws or regulations. It includes an act

      1) In the name of the entity or
      2) On its behalf by

         a) Those charged with governance,
         b) Management, or
         c) Employees.

   b. Noncompliance does not include personal misconduct by the client's personnel unrelated to their business activities.

   c. Whether an act constitutes noncompliance is a legal determination normally beyond the auditor's competence.

   d. Noncompliance varies in its relation to the financial statements. The further removed it is from the financial statements, the less likely the auditor is to become aware of or recognize noncompliance.

      1) The auditor should consider laws and regulations recognized as having a **direct effect** on the determination of material amounts and disclosures, such as tax laws.
      2) Examples of laws and regulations less likely to have a direct and material effect include those relating to environmental protection, food and drug administration, securities trading, and antitrust.

2. **Auditor's Responsibilities**

    a. The auditor is responsible for obtaining reasonable assurance that the financial statements as a whole are free from material misstatement, whether caused by fraud or error. Accordingly, the auditor should obtain a general understanding of (1) the legal and regulatory framework applicable to the entity and (2) how it is complying with the framework.

        1) Thus, the auditor's primary responsibility for noncompliance is to obtain sufficient appropriate audit evidence regarding material amounts and disclosures that are determined by laws and regulations generally recognized to have a direct effect on their determination.

    b. **Other laws and regulations** do not have a direct effect. However, compliance with them may be (1) fundamental to the entity's operations or the continuance of its business or (2) necessary to avoid material penalties.

        1) The auditor's responsibility regarding the second category of laws and regulations is to perform specified procedures to identify noncompliance that may materially affect the financial statements.

    c. The auditor must remain alert during the audit to the possibility that other procedures may detect noncompliance or suspected noncompliance.

3. **Audit Procedures**

    a. The auditor should perform the following procedures that may identify noncompliance with **other laws and regulations**:

        1) Inquiring of management and, if appropriate, those charged with governance about whether the entity is in compliance with other laws and regulations

        2) Inspecting correspondence, if any, with the relevant licensing or regulatory authorities

    b. An audit usually does not include audit procedures specifically designed to detect noncompliance that does **not** have direct effects. Because of (1) the inherent limitations of an audit, (2) the possibility of concealment of noncompliance, and (3) the nature of such noncompliance, a properly planned and performed audit may not detect some material misstatements resulting from such noncompliance.

        1) However, an auditor must be aware of the possibility of such noncompliance.

    c. The following **results of normal procedures** should raise questions about the possibility of noncompliance:

        1) Investigations by a governmental or regulatory agency

        2) Unauthorized or improperly recorded transactions

        3) Unexplained payments to consultants, affiliates, employees, or government officials

        4) Unusual payments in cash, purchases of bank checks payable to bearer, or transfers to numbered accounts

        5) Failure to file tax returns or pay governmental fees

        6) Excessive sales commissions on agents' fees

        7) Violations cited in reports by regulators

    d.   If information comes to the auditor's attention indicating **noncompliance or suspected noncompliance**, the auditor should apply appropriate audit procedures. These include the following:

        1)   Obtaining (a) an understanding of the act and the circumstances in which it occurred and (b) further information to evaluate its financial statement effects

        2)   Inquiring of management at a level above those involved or, if appropriate, those charged with governance

        3)   Consulting with the entity's legal counsel or external legal counsel

4.   **Auditor's Response**

    a.   The auditor's response to **detected noncompliance** is to consider the effects on the financial statements and the implications for other aspects of the audit, especially the reliability of management's representations. The auditor should

        1)   Consider the qualitative and quantitative materiality of the noncompliance,

        2)   Consider the adequacy of disclosure, and

        3)   Communicate material problems to those charged with governance.

5.   **Auditor's Opinion**

    a.   If material noncompliance has not been accounted for properly, the auditor should express a qualified or adverse opinion. If unable to collect sufficient appropriate evidence, the auditor usually disclaims an opinion.

    b.   When the auditor concludes that noncompliance has or is likely to have occurred, (s)he should discuss the matter with the appropriate level of management and request that any necessary remedial actions be taken.

    c.   If the alleged noncompliance has a material effect on the financial statements, or the client does not take the necessary remedial action, the auditor should express a qualified or an adverse opinion, depending on the level of materiality, or withdraw from the engagement.

6.   **Disclosure**

    a.   Disclosure of possible noncompliance with laws and regulations to outside parties ordinarily is not the auditor's responsibility and would violate the duty of confidentiality. Any disclosure would be the responsibility of management. However, the auditor may need to

        1)   Comply with certain legal and regulatory requirements;

        2)   Communicate with a successor auditor in accordance with auditing standards;

        3)   Respond to a court order; or

        4)   Report to a funding or other specified agency in accordance with governmental audit requirements, such as those established by the *Single Audit Act*.

ISA Difference

- Several differences between the international standards and the U.S. standards relate to the auditor's responsibilities for fraud detection.
- The ISAs do not require the auditor to document how and when the brainstorming session occurred and the audit team members who participated.
- The ISAs do not require the auditor to perform analytical procedures relating to the revenue accounts through the end of the reporting period.
- The ISAs do not require the auditor to obtain an understanding of the reporting process and controls over journal entries and other adjustments.

Stop and review! You have completed the outline for this subunit. Study multiple-choice questions 31 through 33 on page 129.

QUESTIONS

3.1 Pre-Engagement Acceptance Activities (AU-C 210)

1. Before accepting an audit engagement, an auditor should make specific inquiries of the predecessor auditor regarding the predecessor's

   A. Awareness of the consistency in the application of generally accepted accounting principles between periods.

   B. Evaluation of all matters of continuing accounting significance.

   C. Opinion of any subsequent events occurring since the predecessor's audit report was issued.

   D. Understanding as to the reasons for the change of auditors.

Answer (D) is correct.
   REQUIRED: The inquiries made by an auditor of a predecessor auditor before accepting an engagement.
   DISCUSSION: According to AU-C 210, the auditor should make specific and reasonable inquiries of the predecessor auditor regarding issues bearing upon acceptance of the engagement. The inquiries should include specific questions regarding, among other things, the predecessor's understanding as to the reasons for the change of auditors.
   Answer (A) is incorrect. A specific inquiry about consistency of application of GAAP is not necessary. Answer (B) is incorrect. All matters of continuing accounting significance are not applicable to the auditor's decision to accept the engagement. Answer (C) is incorrect. The predecessor is not responsible for events subsequent to his/her report.

2. The scope and nature of an auditor's contractual obligation to a client is ordinarily set forth in the

   A. Management representation letter.

   B. Scope paragraph of the auditor's report.

   C. Engagement letter.

   D. Introductory paragraph of the auditor's report.

Answer (C) is correct.
   REQUIRED: The form of the contractual agreement with a client.
   DISCUSSION: The terms of the engagement should be documented in an engagement letter that states the (1) objective and scope of the audit, (2) responsibilities of the auditor and management, (3) inherent limitations of the audit and internal control, (4) applicable financial reporting framework, and (5) expected form and content of audit reports. An engagement letter should be sent by the CPA to the prospective client on each engagement, audit or otherwise.
   Answer (A) is incorrect. An auditor obtains a written management representation letter to complement other procedures, but it is not part of the engagement letter. Answer (B) is incorrect. The auditor's report contains an auditor's responsibility section, not a scope paragraph. The engagement letter should state the form and content of audit reports, not audit reports. Answer (D) is incorrect. The introductory paragraph (1) identifies the auditee, (2) states that the financial statements were audited, (3) identifies the title of each statement, and (4) specifies the date or period of each statement.

3. Which of the following would a successor auditor ask the predecessor auditor to provide after accepting an audit engagement?

   A. Disagreements between the predecessor auditor and management about significant accounting policies and principles.

   B. The predecessor auditor's understanding of the reasons for the change of auditors.

   C. Facts known to the predecessor auditor that might bear on the integrity of management.

   D. Matters that may facilitate the evaluation of financial reporting consistency between the current and prior years.

Answer (D) is correct.
   REQUIRED: The information provided by a predecessor auditor after engagement acceptance.
   DISCUSSION: An objective of an initial audit is to obtain sufficient appropriate evidence regarding opening balances. The auditor should determine whether they (1) contain misstatements materially affecting the current statements and (2) reflect appropriate accounting policies consistently applied in the current statements. Relevant audit evidence about these matters may include (1) the most recent audited statements, (2) the predecessor's report on them, (3) the results of inquiry of the predecessor, and (4) a review of the predecessor's audit documentation (AU-C 510).
   Answer (A) is incorrect. Disagreements between the predecessor auditor and management are typically communicated prior to engagement acceptance. Answer (B) is incorrect. The predecessor's understanding of the reasons for the change of auditors is typically communicated prior to engagement acceptance. Answer (C) is incorrect. Facts known to the predecessor bearing on the integrity of management are typically communicated prior to engagement acceptance.

4. Which of the following factors most likely would cause an auditor to decline a new audit engagement?

    A. An inadequate understanding of the entity's internal control.

    B. The close proximity to the end of the entity's fiscal year.

    C. Failure of management to satisfy the preconditions for an audit.

    D. An inability to perform preliminary analytical procedures before assessing control risk.

Answer (C) is correct.
    REQUIRED: The factor most likely to cause an auditor to decline a new audit engagement.
    DISCUSSION: The auditor should agree with management or those charged with governance upon the terms of the engagement. The auditor accepts the engagement only if (1) the preconditions for an audit are present and (2) a common understanding of the terms has been reached. The preconditions are (1) use of an acceptable accounting framework and (2) agreement on the premise of the audit. The premise relates to the fundamental responsibilities of management and, if appropriate, those charged with governance.
    Answer (A) is incorrect. The understanding of the entity's internal control is obtained subsequent to the acceptance of the engagement. Answer (B) is incorrect. Although early appointment is preferable, an independent auditor may accept an engagement near or after the close of the fiscal year. Answer (D) is incorrect. Analytical procedures are performed after the acceptance of the engagement.

5. Hill, CPA, has been retained to audit the financial statements of Monday Co. Monday's predecessor auditor was Post, CPA, who has been notified by Monday that Post's services have been terminated. Under these circumstances, which party should initiate the communications between Hill and Post?

    A. Hill, the auditor.

    B. Post, the predecessor auditor.

    C. Monday's controller or CFO.

    D. The chair of Monday's board of directors.

Answer (A) is correct.
    REQUIRED: The party responsible for initiation of communications between the auditor and the predecessor.
    DISCUSSION: AU-C 210 indicates that the auditor should communicate with the predecessor auditor before accepting the engagement. Initiation of the communication is the responsibility of the auditor. Moreover, the auditor should seek permission from the prospective client to inquire of the predecessor before final engagement acceptance. Thus, the auditor should ask the client to authorize the predecessor to make a full response.
    Answer (B) is incorrect. Post, the predecessor auditor, need not initiate the communication. Answer (C) is incorrect. Monday's controller or CFO need not initiate the communication. Answer (D) is incorrect. The chair of Monday's board of directors need not initiate the communication.

3.2 Planning an Audit (AU-C 220, AU-C 300, AU-C 510, AS No. 9, and AS No. 10)

6. Audit plans should be designed so that

    A. Most of the required procedures can be performed as interim work.

    B. The risks of material misstatement are assessed at a sufficiently low level.

    C. The auditor can make constructive suggestions to management.

    D. The audit evidence gathered supports the auditor's conclusions.

Answer (D) is correct.
    REQUIRED: The use of audit plans.
    DISCUSSION: The auditor is responsible for collecting sufficient appropriate audit evidence to be able to draw reasonable conclusions on which to base the opinion. Audit plans describe the steps involved in that process. Thus, the evidence should support the auditor's conclusions.
    Answer (A) is incorrect. Depending on the assertion, work may be performed at interim dates or in the subsequent events period. Answer (B) is incorrect. The RMMs are assessed based upon the characteristics of the client. Thus, performing more effective procedures may lead to higher assessed RMMs. Answer (C) is incorrect. Suggestions to management are not required in an audit.

7. In developing written audit plans, an auditor should design specific audit procedures that relate primarily to the

    A. Timing of the audit.

    B. Costs and benefits of gathering evidence.

    C. Financial statements as a whole.

    D. Financial statement assertions.

Answer (D) is correct.
    REQUIRED: The item to which specific audit procedures primarily relate.
    DISCUSSION: Most audit work consists of obtaining and evaluating evidence about relevant financial statement assertions. They are management representations embodied in the financial statements that are used by the auditor to consider the types of possible material misstatements.
    Answer (A) is incorrect. Timing is important in developing audit plans, but it is not the primary basis for determining the audit procedures to be performed. Answer (B) is incorrect. The costs and benefits of gathering evidence are important to the auditor but are not the primary basis for determining the audit procedures to be performed. Answer (C) is incorrect. Most audit procedures are performed at the assertion level.

8. During the initial planning phase of an audit, a CPA most likely would

    A. Identify specific internal control activities that are likely to prevent fraud.

    B. Evaluate the reasonableness of the client's accounting estimates.

    C. Discuss the timing of the audit procedures with the client's management.

    D. Inquire of the client's attorney as to whether any unrecorded claims are probable of assertion.

Answer (C) is correct.
    REQUIRED: The activity performed in the initial planning phase of an audit.
    DISCUSSION: The first step in the audit process is the auditor's decision whether to accept a client. After having decided to perform an audit, the auditor enters the initial planning phase. During initial planning, an auditor should, among other things, meet with the client to agree on the type, scope, and timing of certain aspects of the engagement (e.g., observation of inventory).
    Answer (A) is incorrect. Understanding internal control is subsequent to the initial planning phase. Answer (B) is incorrect. Evaluation of estimates occurs during the evidence collection phase of the audit. Answer (D) is incorrect. Communication with attorneys occurs during the evidence collection phase of the audit.

9. The engagement partner responsible for coordinating the field work usually schedules a pre-audit conference with the audit team primarily to

    A. Give guidance to the staff regarding both technical and personnel aspects of the audit.

    B. Discuss staff suggestions concerning the establishment and maintenance of time budgets.

    C. Establish the need for using the work of specialists and internal auditors.

    D. Provide an opportunity to document staff disagreements regarding technical issues.

Answer (A) is correct.
    REQUIRED: The purpose of a pre-audit conference.
    DISCUSSION: A pre-audit conference is useful to provide guidance to the staff regarding such technical issues as the expected use of client personnel and the expectations of the audit team.
    Answer (B) is incorrect. Time budgets are prepared by supervisors based on the estimates of the time necessary to complete the tasks. Answer (C) is incorrect. The determination of the need for specialists and the use of internal auditors is made by supervisors, not the staff. Answer (D) is incorrect. Disagreements regarding technical issues do not normally arise prior to the audit.

3.3 Audit Risk and Materiality (AU-C 200, AU-C 320, AU-C 450, AS No. 8, and AS No. 11)

10. The existence of audit risk is recognized by the statement in the auditor's report that the

    A. Auditor is responsible for expressing an opinion on the financial statements, which are the responsibility of management.

    B. Financial statements are presented fairly, in all material respects, in accordance with GAAP.

    C. Audit includes examining, on a test basis, evidence supporting the amounts and disclosures in the financial statements.

    D. Auditor obtains reasonable assurance about whether the financial statements are free of material misstatement.

Answer (D) is correct.
    REQUIRED: The statement that recognizes the existence of audit risk.
    DISCUSSION: Audit risk is the risk that the auditor expresses an inappropriate audit opinion when the financial statements are materially misstated (AU-C 315). The high, but not absolute, level of assurance that is intended to be obtained by the auditor is described in the auditor's responsibility section of the report. Reasonable assurance means that audit risk is reduced to an acceptably low level.
    Answer (A) is incorrect. The auditor's responsibility is described in the auditor's responsibility section of the report. The responsibility of management is stated in a separate paragraph. Answer (B) is incorrect. Fair presentation does not necessarily imply a reduction in audit risk. In theory, it might imply absolute assurance (elimination of audit risk). Answer (C) is incorrect. Examining all items under audit is not feasible. This limitation is one of many inherent in the audit process. However, this language is not in the report.

11. The acceptable level of detection risk is inversely related to the

   A. Assurance provided by substantive procedures.

   B. Risk of misapplying auditing procedures.

   C. Preliminary judgment about materiality levels.

   D. Risk of failing to discover material misstatements.

Answer (A) is correct.
   REQUIRED: The concept to which acceptable detection risk is inversely related.
   DISCUSSION: For a given audit risk, the acceptable detection risk is inversely related to the assessed risks of material misstatement. As the RMMs increase, the acceptable detection risk decreases, and the auditor requires more persuasive audit evidence. The auditor may (1) change the types of audit procedures and their combination, e.g., confirming the terms of a contract as well as inspecting it; (2) change the timing of substantive procedures, such as from an interim date to year end; or (3) change the extent of testing, such as by using a larger sample (AU-C 330 and AS No. 13).
   Answer (B) is incorrect. Detection risk, not the acceptable level of detection risk, relates directly to the risk of misapplying auditing procedures. As the effectiveness of audit procedures increases, e.g., because of adequate planning, proper assignment of personnel, and supervisory review, the risk of misapplication and detection risk decrease. Answer (C) is incorrect. Preliminary judgments about materiality levels are used by the auditor to determine the acceptable level of audit risk. Materiality and overall audit risk are inversely related. However, detection risk is just one component of audit risk. Answer (D) is incorrect. The lower the acceptable level of detection risk, the greater the required persuasiveness of audit evidence. Given this additional assurance, the risk of failing to detect material misstatements (detection risk) should be decreased. Accordingly, the relationship of acceptable detection risk and the risk of failing to detect material misstatements is direct.

12. Which of the following would an auditor most likely use in determining the auditor's preliminary judgment about materiality for the financial statements as a whole?

   A. The anticipated sample size of the planned substantive procedures.

   B. The entity's year-to-date financial results and position.

   C. The results of the internal control questionnaire.

   D. The contents of the representation letter.

Answer (B) is correct.
   REQUIRED: The factor most likely used in determining the preliminary judgment about materiality for the financial statements as a whole.
   DISCUSSION: The auditor's judgment about materiality for the financial statements as a whole might be based on benchmarks used as starting points. Examples are (1) categories of reported income (profit before tax, total revenue, gross profit, and total expenses), (2) total equity, and (3) net asset value. For profit-oriented entities, pretax profit from continuing operations is often used. The financial data for the benchmark usually includes (1) prior-period information, (2) period-to-date information, (3) budgets, or (4) forecasts. But recognition should be given to the effect of major changes in the entity's circumstances (for example, a significant merger) and relevant changes in the economy as a whole or the industry in which the entity operates (AU-C 320 and AS No. 11).
   Answer (A) is incorrect. The auditor's preliminary judgment about materiality is used to determine the sample sizes for substantive procedures. Sample sizes are calculated during evidence collection. Answer (C) is incorrect. Results of the internal control questionnaire are considered during the assessment of the risk of material misstatement. Answer (D) is incorrect. The contents of the representation letter are determined near the end of the audit.

13. A client decides not to correct misstatements communicated by the auditor that collectively are not material and wants the auditor to issue the report based on the uncorrected numbers. Which of the following statements is correct regarding the financial statement presentation?

A. The financial statements are free from material misstatement, and no disclosure is required in the notes to the financial statements.

B. The financial statements are not in accordance with the applicable financial reporting framework.

C. The financial statements contain uncorrected misstatements that should result in a qualified opinion.

D. The financial statements are free from material misstatement, but disclosure of the proposed adjustments is required in the notes to the financial statements.

Answer (A) is correct.

REQUIRED: The action when a client decides not to correct misstatements communicated by the auditor that collectively are not material.

DISCUSSION: If the uncorrected misstatements are immaterial, by definition the financial statements are free from material misstatement, and an unmodified opinion may be expressed. However, the schedule of uncorrected misstatements must be included in the management representation letter, and management must assert that these uncorrected misstatements are individually and collectively immaterial.

Answer (B) is incorrect. The financial statements are free of material misstatements and are in accordance with the applicable financial reporting framework. Answer (C) is incorrect. An unmodified opinion is warranted. Answer (D) is incorrect. No disclosure in the notes is required.

14. Inherent risk and control risk differ from detection risk in which of the following ways?

A. Inherent risk and control risk are calculated by the client.

B. Inherent risk and control risk exist independently of the audit.

C. Inherent risk and control risk are controlled by the auditor.

D. Inherent risk and control risk exist as a result of the auditor's judgment about materiality.

Answer (B) is correct.

REQUIRED: The way in which inherent risk and control risk differ from detection risk.

DISCUSSION: Audit risk consists of the risks of material misstatement (inherent risk combined with control risk) and detection risk. The RMMs are the entity's risks, and detection risk is the auditor's risk. Detection risk is the risk that the procedures performed by the auditor to reduce audit risk to an acceptably low level will not detect a material misstatement. It is a function of the effectiveness of an audit procedure and its application by the auditor. Detection risk is the only component of audit risk that can be changed at the auditor's discretion. (Inherent risk and control risk exist independently of the audit and cannot be changed by the auditor.)

Answer (A) is incorrect. Inherent risk and control risk (the risk of material misstatement) are assessed by the auditor. Answer (C) is incorrect. Inherent risk and control risk are controlled by the entity. Answer (D) is incorrect. Inherent risk and control risk are the entity's risks. The performance of audit procedures may change the assessment of inherent risk and control risk but not the actual inherent risk and control risk.

3.4 Understanding the Entity and Its Environment (AU-C 315 and AS No. 12)

15. Prior to beginning the field work on a new audit engagement in which a CPA does **not** possess expertise in the industry in which the client operates, the CPA should

A. Reduce audit risk by lowering initial levels of materiality.

B. Design special substantive procedures to compensate for the lack of industry expertise.

C. Engage financial experts familiar with the nature of the industry.

D. Perform risk assessment procedures.

Answer (D) is correct.

REQUIRED: The action taken by an auditor who lacks experience with the client's industry.

DISCUSSION: The auditor should obtain an understanding of the entity and its environment, including its internal control. For this purpose, the auditor performs the following risk assessment procedures: (1) inquiries of management and others within the entity, (2) analytical procedures, and (3) observation and inspection.

Answer (A) is incorrect. The auditor cannot make judgments about materiality levels until (s)he has a sufficient understanding of the entity. Answer (B) is incorrect. The auditor cannot design substantive procedures until (s)he has a sufficient understanding of the entity. Answer (C) is incorrect. The use of experts does not relieve the auditor of the responsibility to obtain an understanding of the entity.

16. To obtain an understanding of a continuing client in planning an audit, an auditor most likely would

    A. Perform tests of details of transactions and balances.

    B. Read internal audit reports.

    C. Read specialized industry journals.

    D. Reevaluate the risks of material misstatement.

Answer (B) is correct.
    REQUIRED: The procedure used to obtain an understanding of a continuing client.
    DISCUSSION: The auditor performs risk assessment procedures to obtain the understanding of the entity and its environment, including its internal control. These include, for example, reading (1) internal audit reports, (2) interim statements, (3) quarterly reports, and (4) minutes of board meetings.
    Answer (A) is incorrect. Tests of details are used to collect sufficient, appropriate audit evidence to support the opinion. Answer (C) is incorrect. Reading specialized industry journals would provide information about the industry, but not necessarily about the specific client. Answer (D) is incorrect. The auditor reevaluates the RMMs after updating the understanding of a continuing client.

17. A CPA wishes to determine how various issuers have complied with the disclosure requirements of a new financial accounting standard. Which of the following information sources would the CPA most likely consult for this information?

    A. AICPA Codification of Statements on Auditing Standards.

    B. AICPA Accounting Trends and Techniques.

    C. PCAOB Inspection Reports.

    D. SEC Statement 10-K Guide.

Answer (B) is correct.
    REQUIRED: The publication most likely consulted for compliance information of a new financial accounting standard.
    DISCUSSION: Practical guidance for conducting accounting and audit engagements can be found in various nonauthoritative publications, such as Accounting Trends and Techniques, which describes current practice regarding corporate financial accounting and disclosure policies. It is a useful source for practitioners in industry and public practice. This annual AICPA publication is based on a survey of the annual financial reports of over 600 public companies.
    Answer (A) is incorrect. The AICPA Codification of Statements on Auditing Standards contains U.S. generally accepted auditing standards (GAAS). Answer (C) is incorrect. Although quality control extends to adherence to GAAP, the PCAOB Inspection Reports do not provide information about prevalent practice regarding compliance with particular disclosure requirements. Answer (D) is incorrect. Consulting the actual Form 10-K filings by public companies, which contain audited financial statements, would be more useful than consulting the guidance information provided by the SEC.

3.5 Analytical Procedures (AU-C 520)

18. A basic premise underlying analytical procedures is that

    A. These procedures cannot replace tests of balances and transactions.

    B. Statistical tests of financial information may lead to the discovery of material misstatements in the financial statements.

    C. The study of financial ratios is an acceptable alternative to the investigation of unusual fluctuations.

    D. Plausible relationships among data may reasonably be expected to exist and continue in the absence of known conditions to the contrary.

Answer (D) is correct.
    REQUIRED: The basic premise underlying analytical procedures.
    DISCUSSION: A basic premise underlying the application of analytical procedures is that plausible relationships among data may reasonably be expected to exist and continue in the absence of known conditions to the contrary. Variability in these relationships can be explained by, for example, unusual events or transactions, business or accounting changes, misstatements, or random fluctuations.
    Answer (A) is incorrect. For some assertions, analytical procedures alone may provide the auditor with the level of assurance (s)he desires. Answer (B) is incorrect. Analytical procedures, such as simple comparisons, do not necessarily require statistical testing. Answer (C) is incorrect. The objective of analytical procedures, such as ratio analysis, is to identify significant differences for evaluation and possible investigation.

19. For all audits of financial statements made in accordance with auditing standards, the use of analytical procedures is required to some extent

	As Risk Assessment Procedures	As Substantive Procedures	To Assist in Forming an Overall Conclusion
A.	Yes	No	Yes
B.	No	Yes	No
C.	No	Yes	Yes
D.	Yes	No	No

Answer (A) is correct.
 REQUIRED: The required use(s), if any, of analytical procedures.
 DISCUSSION: Analytical procedures should be applied as risk assessment procedures to obtain an understanding of the entity and its environment, including internal control, and to assess the risks of material misstatement. They also may, but are not required to, be applied as substantive procedures. These are procedures (tests of details and analytical procedures) designed to detect material misstatements at the assertion level. Moreover, the auditor should perform analytical procedures near the end of the audit to assist in forming an overall conclusion. The purpose is to determine whether the statements are consistent with the auditor's understanding.
 Answer (B) is incorrect. Analytical procedures should be performed as risk assessment procedures and to assist in forming an overall conclusion. The need not be performed as substantive procedures. Answer (C) is incorrect. Analytical procedures should be performed as the risk assessment procedures. They need not be substantive procedures. Answer (D) is incorrect. Analytical procedures should be performed to assist in forming an overall conclusion.

20. Which of the following nonfinancial information would an auditor most likely consider in performing analytical procedures during the planning phase of an audit?

A. Turnover of personnel in the accounting department.

B. Objectivity of audit committee members.

C. Square footage of selling space.

D. Management's plans to repurchase stock.

Answer (C) is correct.
 REQUIRED: The nonfinancial information considered in performing analytical procedures during audit planning.
 DISCUSSION: Although analytical procedures used in planning the audit often use only financial data, sometimes relevant nonfinancial information is considered as well. For example, number of employees, square footage of selling space, volume of goods produced, and similar information may contribute to accomplishing the purpose of the procedures.
 Answer (A) is incorrect. Turnover of personnel in the accounting department is not a measure related to analytical procedures. Answer (B) is incorrect. Objectivity of audit committee members is not a measure related to analytical procedures. Answer (D) is incorrect. Management's plans to repurchase stock is not a measure related to analytical procedures.

21. An auditor's decision either to apply analytical procedures as substantive procedures or to perform tests of transactions and account balances usually is determined by the

A. Availability of data aggregated at a high level.

B. Auditor's determination about whether audit risk can be sufficiently reduced.

C. Timing of tests performed after the balance sheet date.

D. Auditor's familiarity with industry trends.

Answer (B) is correct.
 REQUIRED: The basis for choosing between analytical procedures and tests of details.
 DISCUSSION: For some assertions, analytical procedures alone may suffice to reduce audit risk to an acceptably low level. For example, the auditor's risk assessment may be supported by audit evidence from tests of controls. Substantive analytical procedures generally are more applicable to large transaction volumes that are predictable over time (AU-C 330). The decision is based on the auditor's professional judgment about the expected effectiveness and efficiency of the available procedures.
 Answer (A) is incorrect. Availability of data is among the factors in evaluating whether audit risk can be reduced to an acceptably low level. Answer (C) is incorrect. Timing of tests is among the factors in evaluating whether audit risk can be reduced to an acceptably low level. Answer (D) is incorrect. Familiarity with industry trends is among the factors in evaluating whether audit risk can be reduced to an acceptably low level.

22. Analytical procedures are most appropriate when testing which of the following types of transactions?

    A. Payroll and benefit liabilities.

    B. Acquisitions and disposals of fixed assets.

    C. Operating expense transactions.

    D. Noncurrent debt transactions.

Answer (C) is correct.
    REQUIRED: The most appropriate use of analytical procedures.
    DISCUSSION: Relationships involving income statement accounts tend to be more predictable than relationships involving only balance sheet accounts. Income statement accounts represent transactions over a period of time, but balance sheet accounts represent an amount at a moment in time. Thus, operating expense transactions are likely to be more predictable than balance sheet accounts.
    Answer (A) is incorrect. Payroll and benefit liabilities are balance sheet accounts and not as predictable as, for example, payroll expense. Answer (B) is incorrect. Acquisitions and disposals of fixed assets relate to balance sheet accounts, which are not typically as predictable as income statement accounts. Answer (D) is incorrect. Noncurrent debt transactions relate to balance sheet accounts, which are not typically as predictable as income statement accounts.

23. Analytical procedures performed to assist in forming an overall conclusion suggest that several accounts have unexpected relationships. The results of these procedures most likely indicate that

    A. Misstatements exist in the relevant account balances.

    B. Internal control activities are not operating effectively.

    C. Additional audit procedures are required.

    D. The communication with the audit committee should be revised.

Answer (C) is correct.
    REQUIRED: The implication when analytical procedures applied to form an overall conclusion have unexpected results.
    DISCUSSION: Analytical procedures used to form an overall conclusion ordinarily include reading the financial statements and considering (1) the adequacy of evidence regarding unusual or unexpected balances detected during the audit and (2) such balances or relationships not detected previously. If analytical procedures detect a previously unrecognized risk of material misstatement, the auditor must revise the assessments of the RMMs and modify the further planned procedures. Inconsistent fluctuations or relationships or significant differences should result in (1) inquiries of management, (2) corroboration of responses with other audit evidence, and (3) performance of any necessary other procedures. Moreover, the RMM due to fraud should be considered.
    Answer (A) is incorrect. Analytical procedures can identify unexpected relationships but not their causes. Answer (B) is incorrect. Tests of controls are conducted to determine the effectiveness of their design and operation. Answer (D) is incorrect. Until the auditor determines the cause of the unexpected relationships, the auditor does not know whether the communication with the audit committee should be revised.

24. Analytical procedures used to form an overall audit conclusion generally include

    A. Considering unusual or unexpected account balances that were not previously identified.

    B. Performing tests of transactions to corroborate management's financial statement assertions.

    C. Gathering evidence concerning account balances that have not changed from the prior year.

    D. Retesting controls that appeared to be ineffective during the assessment of control risk.

Answer (A) is correct.
    REQUIRED: The analytical procedures used to form an overall audit conclusion.
    DISCUSSION: Analytical procedures should be applied near the end of the audit. The purpose is to form an overall audit conclusion about whether the statements are consistent with the auditor's understanding of the entity. Procedures ordinarily should include reading the statements and considering (1) the adequacy of evidence regarding previously identified unusual or unexpected balances and (2) unusual or unexpected balances or relationships not previously noted (AU-C 520).
    Answer (B) is incorrect. Analytical procedures are not tests of details. Answer (C) is incorrect. The lack of change from the prior year may not be unusual or unexpected. Answer (D) is incorrect. Analytical procedures are substantive, not tests of controls.

3.6 Consideration of Fraud in a Financial Statement Audit (AU-C 240)

25. Which of the following statements reflects an auditor's responsibility for detecting fraud and errors?

A. An auditor is responsible for detecting employee errors and simple fraud, but not for discovering fraudulent acts involving employee collusion or management override.

B. An auditor should plan the audit to detect errors and fraud that are caused by departures from the applicable financial reporting framework.

C. An auditor is not responsible for detecting fraud unless the application of GAAS would result in such detection.

D. An auditor should design the audit to provide reasonable assurance of detecting fraud and errors that are material to the financial statements.

Answer (D) is correct.
REQUIRED: The statement reflecting the auditor's responsibility for detecting fraud and errors.
DISCUSSION: The auditor has a responsibility to plan and perform the audit to obtain reasonable assurance about whether the financial statements are free of material misstatements, whether caused by fraud or error. Thus, the auditor should (1) identify and assess the risks of material misstatement due to fraud at the financial statement and assertion levels, (2) obtain sufficient appropriate audit evidence regarding those risks through implementing responses, and (3) respond to identified fraud or suspected fraud. Moreover, the consideration of fraud should be logically integrated into the overall audit process in a manner consistent with other pronouncements, e.g., those on (1) planning and supervision, (2) audit risk and materiality, and (3) internal control.

26. Because of the risk of material misstatement due to fraud, an audit of financial statements in accordance with generally accepted auditing standards should be planned and performed with an attitude of

A. Objective judgment.

B. Integrity.

C. Professional skepticism.

D. Impartial conservatism.

Answer (C) is correct.
REQUIRED: The attitude required for planning and performing an audit.
DISCUSSION: The auditor should maintain professional skepticism throughout the audit. Professional skepticism is an "attitude that includes a questioning mind, being alert to conditions that may indicate possible misstatement due to fraud or error, and critical assessment of audit evidence" (AU-C 200).
Answer (A) is incorrect. Although objective judgment is a quality appropriate for practitioners, it is not required to be applied specifically in an audit. Answer (B) is incorrect. Although independent integrity is a quality appropriate for practitioners, it is not required to be applied specifically in an audit. Answer (D) is incorrect. GAAS do not require conservatism.

27. Which of the following statements describes why a properly planned and performed audit may **not** detect a material misstatement due to fraud?

A. Audit procedures that are effective for detecting an error may be ineffective for detecting fraud that is concealed through collusion.

B. An audit is designed to provide reasonable assurance of detecting material errors, but there is no similar responsibility concerning material fraud.

C. The factors considered in assessing the risk of material misstatement indicated an increased risk of intentional misstatements, but only a low risk of errors in the financial statements.

D. The auditor did not consider factors influencing audit risk for account balances that have effects pervasive to the financial statements as a whole.

Answer (A) is correct.
REQUIRED: The reason a properly planned and performed audit may not detect a material fraud.
DISCUSSION: Absolute assurance is unattainable because of the characteristics of fraud and the limitations of audit evidence. Management may override controls in unpredictable ways or alter accounting records, and fraud may be concealed through collusion, falsifying documentation (including electronic approvals), or withholding evidence. Moreover, procedures that effectively detect an error (an unintentional misstatement) may not detect fraud (an intentional act that a perpetrator typically attempts to conceal).
Answer (B) is incorrect. The auditor's responsibility is the same for material misstatements due to fraud or error. Answer (C) is incorrect. A properly planned and performed audit will result in a response to fraud risks that have been identified and assessed. Answer (D) is incorrect. An audit that is properly planned and performed should consider audit risk factors for accounts having pervasive effects on the statements.

28. Which of the following situations represents a risk factor that relates to misstatements arising from misappropriation of assets?

- A. A high turnover of senior management.
- B. A lack of independent checks.
- C. A strained relationship between management and the predecessor auditor.
- D. An inability to generate cash flow from operations.

Answer (B) is correct.
REQUIRED: The risk factor that relates to misstatements arising from misappropriation of assets.
DISCUSSION: Fraud in financial statements results from either fraudulent financial reporting by management or the misappropriation of assets by employees or others. Misappropriation of assets is mitigated by internal controls, including independent checks.
Answer (A) is incorrect. A high turnover of senior management represents a risk factor that relates to fraudulent financial reporting. Answer (C) is incorrect. A strained relationship between management and the predecessor auditor represents a risk factor that relates to fraudulent financial reporting. Answer (D) is incorrect. An inability to generate cash flow from operations represents a risk factor that relates to fraudulent financial reporting.

29. While performing an audit of the financial statements of a company for the year ended December 31, Year 1, the auditor notes that the company's sales increased substantially in December, Year 1, with a corresponding decrease in January, Year 2. In assessing the risk of fraudulent financial reporting or misappropriation of assets, what should be the auditor's initial indication about the potential for fraud in sales revenue?

- A. There is a broad indication of misappropriation of assets.
- B. There is an indication of theft of the entity's assets.
- C. There is an indication of embezzling receipts.
- D. There is a broad indication of financial reporting fraud.

Answer (D) is correct.
REQUIRED: The initial indication about the potential for fraud in sales revenue.
DISCUSSION: The types of fraud relevant to the auditor include misstatements arising from fraudulent financial reporting. These are intentional misstatements or omissions to deceive users, such as altering accounting records or documents, misrepresenting or omitting significant information, and misapplying accounting principles. Fraud also includes misappropriation of assets. These result from, for example, (1) theft of physical assets, (2) embezzlement (e.g., stealing collections of receivables), (3) an action that causes payment for items not received, or (4) using entity assets for personal reasons. The substantial increase in sales revenue at year end followed by a substantial decrease in January is a broad indicator of a failure to apply cut-off procedures, i.e., financial reporting fraud.
Answer (A) is incorrect. The indication of fraud recognition of revenue (fraudulent reporting), not misappropriation of assets. Answer (B) is incorrect. Theft of the entity's assets is a misappropriation of assets, not fraudulent reporting. Answer (C) is incorrect. Embezzling receipts is a misappropriation of assets, not fraudulent reporting.

30. What is the primary objective of the fraud brainstorming session?

- A. Determine audit risk and materiality.
- B. Identify whether analytical procedures should be applied to the revenue accounts.
- C. Assess the potential for material misstatement due to fraud.
- D. Determine whether the planned procedures in the audit plan will satisfy the general audit objectives.

Answer (C) is correct.
REQUIRED: The primary objective of the fraud brainstorming session.
DISCUSSION: The auditor should obtain reasonable assurance about whether the statements are free of material misstatement, whether due to fraud or error. The key members of the engagement team should discuss the potential for material misstatement. The discussion should include an exchange of ideas (brainstorming) about (1) how and where the statements might be susceptible to material misstatement due to fraud ("fraud risk"), (2) how assets might be misappropriated or financial reports fraudulently misstated, (3) how management could conceal fraudulent reporting (including override of controls), (4) how to respond to fraud risk, (5) known factors reflecting pressures/incentives/opportunities to commit fraud or an environment that permits rationalization of fraud, (6) an emphasis on the need to maintain professional skepticism, and (7) consideration of facts indicating manipulation of financial measures (e.g., earnings management).
Answer (A) is incorrect. The auditor should determine audit risk and materiality in every audit. Answer (B) is incorrect. The auditor should apply analytical procedures to the revenue accounts to identify fraud risks in every audit. Based on the assumption that risks of fraud exist in revenue recognition, the auditor evaluates which types of revenue, revenue transactions, or assertions result in these risks. Answer (D) is incorrect. The auditor should determine whether the planned procedures in the audit plan will satisfy the general audit objectives in every audit.

3.7 Consideration of Laws and Regulations in an Audit of Financial Statements (AU-C 250)

31. Which of the following procedures would **least** likely result in the discovery of possible noncompliance with laws and regulations?

- A. Reading the minutes of the board of directors' meetings.
- B. Making inquiries of the client's management.
- C. Performing tests of details of transactions.
- D. Reviewing an internal control questionnaire.

Answer (D) is correct.
    REQUIRED: The procedure least likely to result in the discovery of possible noncompliance with laws and regulations.
    DISCUSSION: Auditors should design the audit to provide reasonable assurance of detecting noncompliance having a material effect on the financial statements. Internal control questionnaires document the auditor's understanding of internal control. Reviewing the responses to the questionnaire may reveal control deficiencies but not noncompliance.
    Answer (A) is incorrect. Reading the minutes of the board of directors' meetings may provide evidence regarding noncompliance. Answer (B) is incorrect. The auditor should inquire of management about the entity's compliance with laws and regulations. Answer (C) is incorrect. Performing tests of details of transactions may provide information regarding noncompliance.

32. If specific information that implies the existence of possible noncompliance with laws and regulations that could have a material effect on the financial statements comes to an auditor's attention, the auditor should next

- A. Apply audit procedures specifically directed to ascertaining whether noncompliance has occurred.
- B. Seek the advice of an informed expert qualified to practice law as to possible contingent liabilities.
- C. Report the matter to an appropriate level of management at least one level above those involved.
- D. Discuss the evidence with the client's audit committee, or others with equivalent authority and responsibility.

Answer (A) is correct.
    REQUIRED: The auditor's responsibility when (s)he becomes aware of noncompliance with laws and regulations having a material effect.
    DISCUSSION: The auditor should apply audit procedures specifically directed to ascertaining whether noncompliance has occurred. When the auditor becomes aware of information concerning possible noncompliance, the auditor should obtain (1) an understanding of the nature of the act and the circumstances in which it occurred and (2) further information to evaluate the effect on the financial statements.
    Answer (B) is incorrect. The auditor need not consult legal counsel until after determining that noncompliance has occurred. Answer (C) is incorrect. Making inquiries of management is just one possible procedure involved in determining whether noncompliance has occurred. Answer (D) is incorrect. The auditor should not discuss the evidence with those charged with governance until after determining that noncompliance has occurred.

33. During the audit of a new client, the auditor determined that management had given illegal bribes to municipal officials during the year under audit and for several prior years. The auditor notified the client's board of directors, but the board decided to take no action because the amounts involved were immaterial to the financial statements. Under these circumstances, the auditor should

- A. Add an explanatory paragraph emphasizing that certain matters, while **not** affecting the unmodified opinion, require disclosure.
- B. Report the illegal bribes to the municipal official at least one level above those persons who received the bribes.
- C. Consider withdrawing from the audit engagement and disassociating from future relationships with the client.
- D. Issue an "except for" qualified opinion or an adverse opinion with a separate paragraph that explains the circumstances.

Answer (C) is correct.
    REQUIRED: The appropriate auditor action.
    DISCUSSION: If the client does not take the remedial action considered necessary by the auditor, the auditor should consider withdrawal from the engagement even when the illegal bribes are not material. The auditor should weigh the effects on the ability to rely on management's representations and the possible results of continued association with the client. The auditor may wish to seek legal advice (AU-C 250).
    Answer (A) is incorrect. The illegal bribes may not require disclosure. However, remedial action would be expected by the auditor. Answer (B) is incorrect. The auditor has no responsibility to report this information to the external organization associated with the bribes. Answer (D) is incorrect. Immaterial items do not affect the fairness of the financial statements. Thus, a modified opinion is unwarranted.

Use the additional questions in Gleim **CPA Test Prep** to create Practice Exams that emulate Prometric!

3.8 PRACTICE TASK-BASED SIMULATIONS

| | Auditing and Attestation | Time Remaining | | | | | | | |
| | Testlet 4 of 4 | 1 hour - 30 minutes | Unsplit | Split Horiz | Split Vertical | Spreadsheet | Calculator | Exit |

DIRECTIONS

Note: If you believe you have encountered a software malfunction, report it to the test center staff immediately.

Navigation

To navigate from task to task, use the controls at the bottom of the screen. Click on the **Next** button to advance to the next task, or the **Previous** button to go to the previous task. To go directly to any task, click on its number.

| ▼ = Reminder | | Directions | 1 2 3 4 5 6 7 ▽ ▽ ▽ ▽ ▽ ▽ ▽ | ◀ Previous   Next ▶ |

If you would like a reminder to revisit a task, or want to indicate that you are finished with it, click on the reminder flag below the task number. To clear the flag, click on it again. Reminder flags are for your use only – they do not contribute to your score.

Tabs

In this part of the examination, you will be asked to complete various tasks. Every task has one or more **Work Tabs**. Some tasks have one or more **Information Tabs**, others may have none. Every task has a **Help** tab.

If a task has **Information Tabs**, you may use the information in them to complete your responses in the **Work Tabs**.

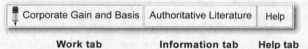

| Corporate Gain and Basis | Authoritative Literature | Help |

Work tab   Information tab   Help tab

Work Tabs:
- **Work Tabs** are identified with a pencil icon. This is where your responses are expected.
- Each task has one or more **Work Tabs**.
- **Work Tabs** contain directions for completing the task – be sure to read these directions carefully.
- The **Work Tab** name in the example above is for illustration only – yours will differ.
- You must complete all of the **Work Tabs** in each task to receive full credit.

Information Tabs:
- The Authoritative Literature will be provided in all tasks in the AUD, FAR, and REG sections for your reference.
- Your simulation may have one or more additional **Information Tabs**. Like the Authoritative Literature tabs, **Information Tabs** do not have a pencil icon.
- If your task has additional **Information Tabs**, go through each to familiarize yourself with the task content.

Help Tab:
- The **Help Tab** provides assistance with the exam software that is used in this task. For example, if the task is to compose a memorandum, **Help** will provide information about the word processor.

The Toolbar

The toolbar at the top of the screen shows the amount of time remaining for you to complete the tasks. In addition, the following tools are available. Note that only the **Exit** button is displayed when Directions are visible - the others will appear when you begin the tasks.

Click on these buttons to split or unsplit the screen. You can split the screen vertically or horizontally.

Click on this button to display the calculator; click on it again to hide the calculator. To move the calculator, click on the calculator title bar and drag the calculator to the desired location.

Click on this button to use the spreadsheet; click on it again to hide the spreadsheet. To move the spreadsheet, click on the the spreadsheet title bar and drag the spreadsheet to the desired location.

Click on this button to go on to the next part of the examination. You must complete all of the tasks to receive full credit. Once you click on **Exit** and confirm the action, you will NOT be able to return to this testlet.

| ▼ = Reminder | | Directions | 1 2 3 4 5 ▽ ▽ ▽ ▽ ▽ | ◀ Previous   Next ▶ |

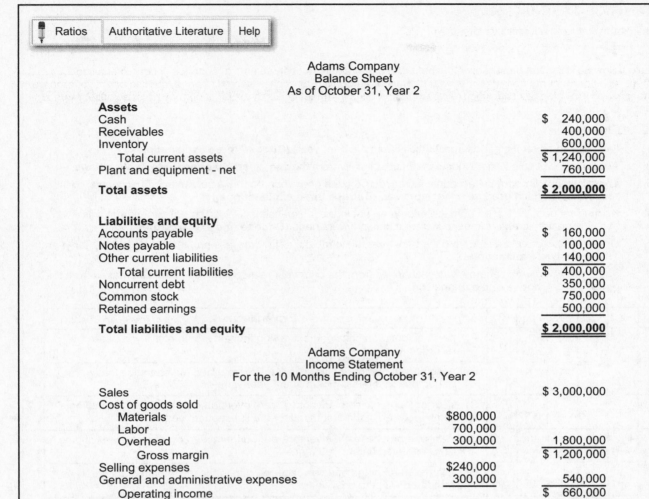

| Ratios | Authoritative Literature | Help |

Adams Company
Balance Sheet
As of October 31, Year 2

Assets
Cash	$ 240,000
Receivables	400,000
Inventory	600,000
Total current assets	$ 1,240,000
Plant and equipment - net	760,000
Total assets	**$ 2,000,000**

Liabilities and equity
Accounts payable	$ 160,000
Notes payable	100,000
Other current liabilities	140,000
Total current liabilities	$ 400,000
Noncurrent debt	350,000
Common stock	750,000
Retained earnings	500,000
Total liabilities and equity	**$ 2,000,000**

Adams Company
Income Statement
For the 10 Months Ending October 31, Year 2

Sales		$ 3,000,000
Cost of goods sold		
Materials	$800,000	
Labor	700,000	
Overhead	300,000	1,800,000
Gross margin		$ 1,200,000
Selling expenses	$240,000	
General and administrative expenses	300,000	540,000
Operating income		$ 660,000
Minus interest expense		40,000
Income before taxes		$ 620,000
Minus federal income taxes		220,000
Net income		**$ 400,000**

Given the year-to-date financial information, calculate the ratios. Enter the appropriate amounts in the shaded cells in the table below. Calculations should be rounded, if necessary, to the same number of places as the prior year's ratios, which are provided for comparative purposes only.

Ratio	Adams Company's Ratios for the 10 Months Ending 10/31/Year 2	Adams Company's Ratios for the 10 Months Ending 10/31/Year 1
1. Current ratio		2.5
2. Quick ratio		1.3
3. Accounts receivable turnover		5.5
4. Inventory turnover		2.5
5. Total asset turnover		1.2
6. Gross margin percentage		35%
7. Net operating margin percentage		25%
8. Times interest earned		10.3
9. Total debt to equity percentage		50%

| Changes in Ratios | Authoritative Literature | Help |

The table below contains the most likely explanation(s) of the auditor's observations of changes in certain financial statement ratios or amounts from the prior year's ratios or amounts. For each observed change, choose one, two, or three explanations (as indicated) by checking the appropriate boxes in the table. Each explanation may be used once, more than once, or not at all.

Observed Changes

1. Inventory turnover increased substantially from the prior year. **(Choose three explanations.)**
2. Accounts receivable turnover increased substantially from the prior year. **(Choose three explanations.)**
3. The allowance for doubtful accounts increased from the prior year, but, as a percentage of accounts receivable, it decreased from the prior year. **(Choose three explanations.)**
4. Noncurrent debt increased from the prior year, but interest expense increased by an amount that was proportionately greater than the increase in noncurrent debt. **(Choose one explanation.)**
5. Operating income increased from the prior year, although the entity was less profitable than in the prior year. **(Choose two explanations.)**
6. The gross margin percentage was unchanged from the prior year, although gross margin increased from the prior year. **(Choose one explanation.)**

1	2	3	4	5	6	*Explanation*
						A) Items shipped on consignment during the last month of the year were recorded as sales.
						B) A significant number of credit memos for returned merchandise that were issued during the last month of the year were not recorded.
						C) Year-end purchases of inventory were overstated by incorrectly including items received in the first month of the subsequent year.
						D) Year-end purchases of inventory were understated by incorrectly excluding items received before year end.
						E) A larger percentage of sales occurred during the last month of the year, as compared with the prior year.
						F) A smaller percentage of sales occurred during the last month of the year, as compared with the prior year.
						G) The same percentage of sales occurred during the last month of the year, as compared with the prior year.
						H) Sales increased by the same percentage as cost of goods sold, as compared with the prior year.
						I) Sales increased by a greater percentage than cost of goods sold increased, as compared with the prior year.
						J) Sales increased by a lower percentage than cost of goods sold increased, as compared with the prior year.
						K) Interest expensed decreased, as compared with the prior year.
						L) The effective income tax rate increased, as compared with the prior year.
						M) The effective income tax rate decreased, as compared with the prior year.
						N) Short-term borrowing was refinanced on a long-term basis at the same interest rate.
						O) Short-term borrowing was refinanced on a long-term basis at lower interest rates.
						P) Short-term borrowing was refinanced on a long-term basis at higher interest rates.

Research | Authoritative Literature | Help

Gary, CPA, is considering undertaking an audit engagement for a prospective nonissuer client. The client has provided the name of the prior auditor, but Gary is unsure whether he must communicate with the auditor. Which section of the generally accepted auditing standards states whether an auditor should communicate with a predecessor auditor before accepting an engagement?

Title	Section	Paragraph

Title Choices

AU-C	PCAOB	AT	AR	ET	BL	VS
CS	QC	PR	TS	PFP	CPE	

= Reminder | Directions | 1 2 [3] 4 5 | ◀ Previous Next ▶

Audit Risk | Authoritative Literature | Help

Bestwood Furniture, Inc., a nonissuer that produces wood furniture, is undergoing a Year 2 audit. The situations in the table below describe changes Bestwood made during Year 2 that may or may not contribute to audit risk. Audit risk is a function of (1) the risks of material misstatement, the components of which are inherent risk and control risk, and (2) detection risk. For each situation, select from the list provided the effect, if any, that the situation has on a specific element of audit risk for the Year 2 audit. A choice may be used once, more than once, or not at all.

Situation	Effect on component of audit risk
1. During Year 2, the company instituted a new procedure whereby the internal audit function distributes payroll checks to employees for selected payroll cycles.	
2. In Year 2, the auditor noted that the company's newly hired purchasing agent was not obtaining competitive bids for all major purchase requisitions.	
3. Early in Year 2, the company extended its existing warranty program on some of its major products in an effort to increase revenue.	
4. At the beginning of Year 2, the company changed insurance carriers for the fire insurance on its building.	
5. During Year 2, the company repaid a floating-interest-rate loan on which it had purchased a derivative as a hedge. The hedge was also sold.	

Choices

A) Decreases control risk
B) Decreases detection risk
C) Decreases inherent risk
D) Increases control risk
E) Increases detection risk
F) Increases inherent risk
G) No effect on audit risk

= Reminder | Directions | 1 2 3 [4] 5 | ◀ Previous Next ▶

Analytical procedures consist of evaluations of financial information made by a study of plausible relationships among both financial and nonfinancial data. They range from simple comparisons to the use of complex models involving many relationships and elements of data. They involve comparisons of recorded amounts, or ratios developed from recorded amounts, to expectations developed by the auditors.

Choose three items from List A that describe the broad purposes of analytical procedures.

Purposes	List A
1.	I) To assist the auditor in planning the nature, timing, and extent of other auditing procedures.
2.	II) As a substantive procedure to obtain audit evidence about particular assertions related to account balances, classes of transactions, or disclosures.
3.	III) To understand relationships between financial and nonfinancial information.
	IV) To test details of account balances and transaction classes.
	V) Near the end of an audit to assist the auditor in forming an overall conclusion on the financial statements.

Choose three items from List B that identify the most likely sources of information from which an auditor develops expectations.

Sources	List B
4.	I) Data aggregated at the lowest level.
5.	II) Gross domestic product and other macroeconomic information.
6.	III) Financial information for comparable prior periods giving consideration to known changes.
	IV) Anticipated results -- for example, budgets, forecasts, and extrapolations.
	V) Company-wide comparisons based on 5-year trend data.
	VI) Information regarding the industry in which the client operates.

Choose three items from List C that identify factors that most likely enhance the reliability of audit evidence.

Reliability Factors	List C
7.	I) Data were obtained from sources within the entity that are responsible for the amounts being audited.
8.	II) Data were developed under a reliable system with adequate controls.
9.	III) Data were not subjected to audit testing in the current or prior year.
	IV) Expectations were developed using data from a variety of sources.
	V) Data were obtained from independent sources outside the entity.

Unofficial Answers

1. Ratios (9 Gradable Items)

1. Current ratio	3.1	($1,240,000 ÷ $400,000)
2. Quick ratio	1.6	[($1,240,000 − $600,000) ÷ $400,000]
3. Accounts receivable turnover	7.5	($3,000,000 ÷ $400,000)
4. Inventory turnover	3.0	($1,800,000 ÷ $600,000)
5. Total asset turnover	1.5	($3,000,000 ÷ $2,000,000)
6. Gross margin percentage	40%	($1,200,000 ÷ $3,000,000)
7. Net operating margin percentage	22%	($660,000 ÷ $3,000,000)
8. Times interest earned	16.5	[($400,000 + $40,000 + $220,000) ÷ $40,000]
9. Total debt to equity percentage	60%	[($400,000 + $350,000) ÷ ($750,000 + $500,000)]

2. Changes in Ratios (13 Gradable Items)

1. A), B), D). Inventory turnover is cost of sales divided by average inventory. Consignment items should still be included in inventory. However, because items shipped on consignment were recorded as sales, the items were removed from inventory. Returned merchandise should increase inventory, but, because the credit memos were not recorded, the inventory was understated. By not including year-end purchases, inventory is also understated. Hence, a lower inventory causes a higher inventory turnover ratio.

2. A), B), E). Accounts receivable turnover is net credit sales divided by average accounts receivable. Goods shipped on consignment are properly included in the consignor's inventory at cost, and sales revenue from such goods should be recognized by the consignor when the merchandise is sold by recording as sales items shipped on consignment but not yet sold.

3. A), B), E). If the allowance for doubtful accounts increased, and allowance for doubtful accounts as a percentage of accounts receivable decreased, accounts receivable must have increased by a greater degree than the allowance decreased. Accounts receivable would have increased if items shipped on consignment were mistakenly recorded as sales, if significant credits for returned goods were not recorded, or if a larger percentage of sales occurred during the month compared with the prior year.

4. P). If short-term debt is refinanced as noncurrent debt at a higher interest rate, noncurrent debt will increase but not as significantly as interest expense will increase. This effect results from applying an increased rate to a greater amount of noncurrent debt.

5. L), P). Operating income minus interest expense and federal income taxes yields net income for the year. If operating income increased from the prior year but net income decreased, interest expense or federal income taxes must have increased. Refinancing short-term debt as noncurrent debt with a higher interest rate or an increase in the effective income tax rate explain this decrease in net income.

6. H). The gross margin percentage is gross margin divided by sales. If it remained constant although gross margin increased, sales also must have increased by the same proportionate amount. Because gross margin is sales minus cost of goods sold, cost of goods sold also must have increased by the same proportionate amount to maintain the relationship between sales and gross margin.

3. Research (1 Gradable Item)

Answer: 210.11

AU-C Section 210 -- *Terms of Engagement*

Initial Audits, Including Reaudit Engagements

.11   Before accepting an engagement for an initial audit, including a reaudit engagement, the auditor should request management to authorize the predecessor auditor to respond fully to the auditor's inquiries regarding matters that will assist the auditor in determining whether to accept the engagement. If management refuses to authorize the predecessor auditor to respond, or limits the response, the auditor should inquire about the reasons and consider the implications of that refusal in deciding whether to accept the engagement.

4. Audit Risk (5 Gradable Items)

1. A) Decreases control risk. Generally, the internal audit function should have no operating responsibilities. However, this may randomly select a period to distribute paychecks as part of its evaluation of internal control. Paychecks should be distributed by someone with no other payroll responsibilities.

2. D) Increases control risk. The deficiency in internal control creates a risk that the purchasing agent may be favoring certain suppliers to gain kickbacks or bribes.

3. F) Increases inherent risk. The extension of the warranty program to increase revenue is a management decision that increases the entity's liability and therefore its inherent risk (the entity's risk before consideration of internal control).

4. G) No effect on audit risk. Changing insurance companies is a normal business decision that would not likely increase risk for the auditor.

5. C) Decreases inherent risk. The termination of complex transactions decreases the inherent risk that material misstatements could exist independent of internal control.

5. Analytical Procedures (9 Gradable Items)*

Purposes

1. I). The audit standards indicate that auditors should apply analytical procedures to assist the auditor in planning the nature, timing, and extent of other auditing procedures.

2. II). The audit standards indicate that auditors may apply analytical procedures as a substantive procedure to obtain audit evidence about particular assertions related to account balances or classes of transactions.

3. V). The audit standards indicate that auditors should apply analytical procedures near the end of the audit to assist the auditor in forming an overall conclusion on the financial statements.

Sources

4. III). The five sources of information to develop expectations include (a) financial information from comparable prior periods; (b) anticipated results, such as budgets or forecasts prepared by management; (c) relationships among data, such as those among the balances on the financial statements; (d) comparable information from the client's industry; and (e) related nonfinancial information.

5. IV). The five sources of information to develop expectations include (a) financial information from comparable prior periods; (b) anticipated results, such as budgets or forecasts prepared by management; (c) relationships among data, such as those among the balances on the financial statements; (d) comparable information from the client's industry; and (e) related nonfinancial information.

6. VI). The five sources of information to develop expectations include (a) financial information from comparable prior periods; (b) anticipated results, such as budgets or forecasts prepared by management; (c) relationships among data, such as those among the balances on the financial statements; (d) comparable information from the client's industry; and (e) related nonfinancial information.

Reliability Factors

7. II). Data are more reliable when developed under reliable internal control.

8. IV). Expectations are more reliable when developed using data from a variety of sources rather than from a single source.

9. V). Data are more reliable when obtained from independent sources outside the entity than from inside the entity.

*Note: Your answers need not be in the same order under each subheading. Give yourself a point for each item chosen correctly regardless of the order in which you entered them.

Gleim Simulation Grading

Task	Correct Responses		Gradable Items		Score per Task
1	_____	÷	9	=	_____
2	_____	÷	13	=	_____
3 (Research)	_____	÷	1	=	_____
4	_____	÷	5	=	_____
5	_____	÷	9	=	_____

Total of Scores per Task _____

÷ Total Number of Tasks _____5

Total Score _____%

Use **CPA Gleim Online** and **Simulation Wizard** to practice more task-based simulations in a realistic environment.

STUDY UNIT FOUR
STRATEGIC PLANNING ISSUES

(12 pages of outline)

This study unit considers issues that are fundamental to planning an audit. Questions about the internal audit function, related parties, and accounting estimates can be expected on the exam. Moreover, most of the issues considered in this study unit have an effect on other facets of the audit, including evidence collection and reporting. We cover the additional matters here to provide comprehensive and coherent coverage.

4.1 USING THE WORK OF INTERNAL AUDITORS (AU-C 610)

1. The independent, external auditor ("the auditor") considers the existence of an internal audit function in determining the nature, timing, and extent of audit procedures.

    a. The auditor must be **independent** of the entity.

2. Internal auditors cannot be independent in the same sense as external auditors because they are employees of the entity.

Background

According to the **International Standards for the Professional Practice of Internal Auditing (ISPELL)** issued by The Institute of Internal Auditors (IIA), internal auditors must be **objective**, and the internal audit activity must be independent. The internal audit activity is independent when it is free from conditions threatening its ability to carry out its responsibilities in an unbiased way.

---

    a. Internal auditors provide analyses, evaluations, assurances, recommendations, and other information to management and those charged with governance.

3. **Understanding the Internal Audit Function**

    a. When obtaining an understanding of internal control, the auditor should obtain an understanding of the internal audit function sufficient to identify activities relevant to audit planning. This function is part of the monitoring component of internal control.

    b. Inquiries should be made about the internal auditors'

        1) Organizational status;
        2) Application of professional standards;
        3) Audit plan, including the nature, timing, and extent of audit work; and
        4) Access to records and limitations on the scope of their work.

    c. Inquiring about the internal audit function's charter, mission statement, or similar directive provides information about its objectives.

    d. Certain internal audit activities may not be relevant to an audit of the financial statements, e.g., evaluating certain management decision-making processes.

    e. Relevant internal audit activities provide the following:

        1) Evidence about the design and effectiveness of internal control relating to the ability to initiate, authorize, record, process, and report financial data consistent with relevant assertions in the financial statements
        2) Direct evidence about potential misstatements of financial data

    f.   The following actions are helpful in assessing the relevance of internal audit activities:

        1)   Considering prior-year audits
        2)   Reviewing how the internal auditors allocate their audit resources
        3)   Reading internal audit reports

    g.   If the auditor concludes that the internal auditors' activities are **not relevant**, (s)he need not further consider the function unless the auditor requests their direct assistance.

        1)   The auditor may conclude that further considering the work of the internal auditors would be **inefficient**, even if some of their activities are relevant.

    h.   The auditor may decide that it is efficient to consider how the internal auditors' work might affect audit procedures. The auditor then should assess the competence and objectivity of the internal auditors in relation to the intended effect of their work on the audit.

4.   **Assessing Competence**

    a.   The auditor considers the following:

        1)   Educational level and professional experience
        2)   Professional certification and continuing education
        3)   Audit policies, programs, and procedures
        4)   Practices regarding assignment of internal auditors
        5)   Supervision and review
        6)   Quality of documentation, reports, and recommendations
        7)   Performance evaluation

5.   **Assessing Objectivity**

    a.   The auditor considers the following:

        1)   The **organizational status** of the chief audit executive (CAE). This assessment includes whether

            a)   The CAE reports to someone with sufficient status to ensure broad audit coverage and adequate consideration of, and action on, findings and recommendations.

            b)   The CAE has direct access and reports regularly to those charged with governance.

            c)   Those charged with governance oversee employment decisions by the CAE.

        2)   Policies to maintain objectivity about the areas audited. These include prohibitions against auditing areas where

            a)   Relatives are employed in important or audit-sensitive positions.
            b)   Internal auditors were recently assigned or are scheduled to be assigned.

6.   Assessing competence and objectivity involves considering information from (a) the auditor's previous experience, (b) discussions with management, and (c) a recent external quality review.

7.   **Effect of the Internal Auditors' Work**

    a.   The internal auditors' work may affect substantive audit procedures and the procedures performed in obtaining the understanding of internal control and assessing risk.

    b.   Because a primary objective of many internal audit functions is to review, assess, and monitor internal control, internal audit procedures may provide useful information.

    c.   Risk assessment at the **financial-statement level** involves an overall assessment of the **risks of material misstatement (RMMs)** and thus may affect the overall audit strategy.

        1)   The internal audit function may affect the overall risk assessment and decisions about audit procedures. For example, the auditor may coordinate work with the internal auditors and reduce the number of locations at which the auditor performs procedures.

    d.   Risk assessment at the **account-balance, class-of-transactions, or disclosure level** involves obtaining and evaluating evidence about relevant assertions. The auditor assesses the RMMs for each relevant assertion and performs tests of controls to support an expectation of the operating effectiveness of controls.

        1)   When testing controls, the auditor may consider the results of internal audit procedures.

    e.   Substantive procedures performed by the internal auditors may provide direct evidence about material misstatements in specific relevant assertions.

    f.   Obtaining sufficient appropriate audit evidence and reporting on the financial statements are solely the responsibilities of the auditor. They cannot be shared with the internal auditors.

        1)   Judgments about (a) assessments of risk, (b) materiality, (c) the sufficiency of tests, (d) the evaluation of estimates, and (e) other matters affecting the report always should be those of the auditor.

    g.   The extent of the effect of the internal auditors' work depends on the materiality of amounts, RMMs for relevant assertions, and the subjectivity involved in evaluating audit evidence.

        1)   For assertions related to material amounts for which the RMMs or the degree of subjectivity is high, the internal auditors' work alone cannot reduce audit risk to an acceptably low level. In these cases, direct tests of assertions by the auditor cannot be eliminated.

        2)   For certain assertions related to less material amounts for which the RMMs or the degree of subjectivity is low, the auditor may decide that (a) audit risk has been reduced to an acceptably low level, and (b) direct testing by the auditor may not be necessary.

8.   **Coordination of Audit Work**

    a.   If the work of the internal auditors is expected to affect the auditor's procedures, it may be efficient for the auditor and the internal auditors to coordinate their work by

        1)   Holding periodic meetings,
        2)   Scheduling audit work,
        3)   Providing access to internal auditors' engagement records (documentation),
        4)   Reviewing audit reports, and
        5)   Discussing possible accounting and auditing issues.

9.   **Evaluating and Testing the Internal Auditors' Work**

    a.   If the work of the internal auditors significantly affects the auditor's work, the auditor should evaluate the quality and effectiveness of the internal auditors' work. Thus, the auditor tests some of that work relevant to significant assertions.

10.   **Using Internal Auditors to Provide Direct Assistance**

    a.   The auditor may request direct assistance from the internal auditors when performing an audit. When direct assistance is provided, the auditor should assess the internal auditors' competence and objectivity and supervise, review, evaluate, and test the work performed by internal auditors to the extent appropriate.

Stop and review! You have completed the outline for this subunit. Study multiple-choice questions 1 through 8 beginning on page 151.

4.2 USING THE WORK OF A SPECIALIST (AU-C 620 AND AU-C 500)

1. **Types of Specialists**

   a. An **auditor's specialist** is an individual or organization possessing expertise in a field other than accounting or auditing. The work in that field is used to assist the auditor in obtaining sufficient appropriate audit evidence.

      1) An auditor's specialist may be either (a) an internal specialist (who is a partner or staff member, including temporary staff, of the auditor's firm or a network firm) or (b) an external specialist.

   b. A **management's specialist** is an individual or organization possessing expertise in a field other than accounting or auditing. The work in that field is used by the entity to assist the entity in preparing the financial statements.

Background

The guidance for using the work of an auditor's specialist (AU-C 620) and a management's specialist (AU-C 500) is provided in two different auditing standards because they serve two different purposes. However, the concern in each case is the consideration of the specialist's objectivity and competence. This emphasis is recognized in the following outline.

---

2. **Auditor's Specialist**

   a. If expertise other than accounting or auditing is necessary to obtain sufficient appropriate audit evidence, the auditor should determine whether to use the work of an auditor's specialist.

      1) However, the auditor has sole responsibility for the audit opinion expressed, and that responsibility is not reduced by the auditor's use of the work of an auditor's specialist.

   b. Examples of a potential specialist's expertise include the following:

      1) Valuation of complex financial instruments and nonfinancial assets and liabilities, such as land and buildings, plant and machinery, jewelry, works of art, and antiques

      2) Actuarial calculations

      3) Estimation of oil and other mineral reserves

      4) Valuation of environmental liabilities and site cleanup costs

      5) Interpretation of contracts, laws, and regulations

      6) Physical characteristics relating to quantity on hand or condition

   c. The auditor should evaluate whether the auditor's specialist has the necessary **competence, capabilities, and objectivity** for the auditor's purposes.

      1) In the case of an auditor's external specialist, the evaluation of objectivity should include inquiry about interests and relationships that may threaten objectivity.

   d. The auditor should obtain an **understanding** of the expertise of the auditor's specialist sufficient to

      1) Determine the nature, scope, and objectives of the work and

      2) Evaluate the adequacy of that work for the auditor's purposes.

   e. The auditor should agree, in writing if appropriate, with the auditor's specialist regarding the arrangements for the services, including objectives, roles, communications, and confidentiality requirements.

     f.   The auditor should evaluate the adequacy of the work of the auditor's specialist, including

        1)   The relevance and reasonableness of the findings and conclusions,

        2)   The understanding of any significant assumptions and methods, and

        3)   The use of source data significant to the work.

     g.   If the auditor determines that the work of the auditor's specialist is not adequate for the auditor's purposes, the auditor should consider (1) performing additional work, (2) requiring additional work by the specialist, or (3) engaging another specialist.

        1)   If the auditor is unable to collect sufficient appropriate evidence, a modified opinion may be necessary.

     h.   The auditor should not refer to the work or findings of the auditor's specialist when expressing an **unmodified opinion**.

        1)   The auditor may refer to the work of an auditor's external specialist if the reference is relevant to understanding a **modified opinion** (e.g., qualified or adverse).

            a)   The report should state that the reference does not reduce the auditor's responsibility.

3.   **Management's Specialist**

     a.   If information to be used as audit evidence has been prepared using the work of a management's specialist, the auditor should

        1)   Evaluate the competence, capabilities, and objectivity of that specialist;

        2)   Obtain an understanding of the work of that specialist; and

        3)   Evaluate the appropriateness of the work as audit evidence for the relevant assertion.

     b.   Matters relevant to evaluating competence, capabilities, and objectivity include whether the work is subject to technical standards or professional requirements.

     c.   The auditor does **not refer** to a management's specialist in an auditor's report.

Stop and review! You have completed the outline for this subunit. Study multiple-choice questions 9 through 12 beginning on page 153.

4.3 RELATED PARTIES (AU-C 550)

Background

Prior auditing standards were based on U.S. GAAP for reporting and disclosing related party transactions in financial statements. Current auditing standards apply to all financial reporting frameworks, including IFRS. However, the auditor's responsibilities and auditing procedures remain the same.

---

1.   **Nature of Related Party Transactions**

     a.   Many related party transactions are in the **normal course of business**. Thus, they may have no higher risks of material misstatement (RMMs) of the financial statements than similar transactions with unrelated parties.

     b.   However, the nature of related party relationships and transactions may cause them to have higher RMMs than transactions with unrelated parties. For example,

        1)   Related parties may operate through an extensive and complex range of relationships and structures,

        2)   Information systems may be ineffective at identifying or summarizing transactions and outstanding balances between an entity and its related parties, and

        3)   Related party transactions may not be conducted under normal market terms and conditions (for example, some related party transactions may be conducted with no exchange of consideration).

2. **Responsibilities of the Auditor**

    a. The auditor should perform audit procedures to identify, assess, and respond to the RMMs arising from the entity's failure to appropriately account for or disclose related party relationships, transactions, or balances.

    b. Because fraud may be more easily committed through related parties, an understanding of the entity's related party relationships and transactions also is relevant to the auditor's evaluation of whether fraud risk factors exist.

    c. **Risk of fraud** is increased and the auditor should act accordingly when

        1) The related party has a dominant influence over the entity.

        2) The related party transactions are outside the normal course of business. The following are examples:

            a) Equity transactions, such as corporate restructurings or acquisitions

            b) Transactions with offshore entities

            c) Leasing if no consideration is exchanged

            d) Sales with large discounts or returns

            e) Transactions with circular arrangements (e.g., a sale with a commitment to repurchase)

            f) Transactions under contracts whose terms are changed

    d. It is ordinarily not feasible to determine (1) whether a transaction would have occurred if the parties were unrelated or (2), given that it did occur, what the terms would have been. However, if management has asserted that the terms of a related party transaction were equivalent to those in an **arm's-length transaction**, the auditor should obtain sufficient appropriate audit evidence about the assertion.

        1) Management is responsible for providing support for the assertion.

        2) If a material assertion is not supported, or the auditor cannot collect sufficient appropriate evidence, the assertion should be removed, or the auditor's report should be modified.

3. **Accounting Considerations**

    a. Because related parties are not independent of each other, financial reporting frameworks establish specific **accounting and disclosure requirements** for related party relationships, transactions, and balances to enable users of the financial statements to understand their nature and actual or potential effects on the financial statements.

    b. Furthermore, the auditor should understand that the substance of a transaction could differ significantly from its form. Financial statements should recognize substance, not legal form.

4. **Audit Procedures**

    a. Given the inherent limitations of an audit, the auditor's ability to detect material misstatements is reduced because

        1) Management may not be aware of all related party relationships and transactions, and

        2) Such relationships may provide a greater opportunity for collusion, concealment, or manipulation by management.

b. Nevertheless, the auditor should perform **risk assessment procedures** to identify RMMs associated with these relationships and transactions. They include specific consideration of the susceptibility of the statements to material misstatement due to fraud or error. The auditor should

   1) Inquire about (a) the identity of related parties, (b) the relationship of the entity with those parties, (c) whether transactions with them have occurred, and (d) the nature and purpose of the transactions.

   2) Obtain an understanding of any **controls** established to (a) account for and disclose related party relationships and transactions and (b) authorize and approve significant transactions and arrangements (1) with related parties or (2) outside the normal course of business.

   3) Be alert for related party relationships and transactions when inspecting records or documents, such as bank confirmations or minutes of meetings of shareholders or those charged with governance.

   4) Transactions that, because of their nature, may indicate the existence of related parties include the following:

      a) Borrowing or lending on an interest-free basis or at a rate of interest significantly above or below market rates prevailing at the time of the transaction

      b) Selling real estate at a price that differs significantly from its appraised value

      c) Exchanging property for similar property in a nonmonetary transaction

      d) Making loans with no scheduled terms for when or how the funds will be repaid

c. The auditor should identify and assess the RMMs associated with related party relationships and transactions and determine whether they are **significant risks**. Significant transactions outside the normal course of business result in significant risks.

   1) The auditor responds by performing further audit procedures to obtain sufficient appropriate evidence about the assessed RMMs.

d. In the absence of contrary evidence, transactions with related parties should not be assumed to be outside the normal course of business. But such transactions may have been motivated solely or largely by any of the following:

   1) Lack of sufficient working capital or credit to continue the business
   2) An overly optimistic earnings forecast
   3) Dependence on one or a few products, customers, or transactions for success
   4) A declining industry with many business failures
   5) Excess capacity
   6) Significant litigation, especially between shareholders and management
   7) Significant obsolescence because the entity is in a high-technology industry

e. **Determining the existence of related parties.** Certain relationships, such as parent-subsidiary or investor-investee, may be clearly evident. Determining the existence of others requires specific audit procedures, which may include the following:

   1) Evaluating the entity's procedures for identifying and properly accounting for related party transactions

   2) Requesting from management the names of all related parties and inquiring whether transactions occurred with them

   3) Reviewing filings with the SEC and other regulatory agencies for the names of related parties and for other businesses in which officers and directors occupy directorship or management positions

4) Determining the names of all pensions and other trusts established for employees and the names of their officers and trustees

5) Reviewing shareholder listings of closely held entities to identify principal shareholders

6) Reviewing prior years' audit documentation for the names of known related parties

7) Inquiring of predecessor or other auditors of related entities concerning their knowledge of existing relationships and the extent of management involvement in material transactions

8) Reviewing material investment transactions during the period to determine whether they have created related parties

f. **Identifying related party transactions.** The following procedures may identify material transactions with known related parties or indicate the existence of previously unknown related parties:

1) Provide personnel performing all segments of the audit with the names of known related parties.

2) Review the minutes of meetings of the board and committees.

3) Review filings with the SEC and other regulatory agencies.

4) Review conflict-of-interest statements obtained by the entity from its management.

5) Review business transacted with major customers, suppliers, borrowers, and lenders for indications of undisclosed relationships.

6) Consider whether unrecognized transactions are occurring, such as receiving or providing accounting, management, or other services at no charge or having a major shareholder absorb entity expenses.

7) Review accounting records for large, unusual, or nonrecurring transactions or balances, especially those near the end of the period.

8) Review confirmations of compensating balance arrangements for indications that balances are or were maintained for or by related parties.

9) Review invoices from law firms.

10) Review confirmations of loans receivable and payable for guarantees.

g. **Examining related party transactions.**

1) After identifying related party transactions, the auditor should become satisfied about their purpose, nature, extent, and effect. The following should be considered:

a) Obtain an understanding of the business purpose of the transaction.

b) Examine invoices, executed copies of agreements, contracts, and other documents.

c) Determine whether the transaction has been approved by those charged with governance.

d) Test for reasonableness the compilation of amounts to be disclosed or considered for disclosure.

e) Arrange for the audits of interentity balances to be performed as of concurrent dates, even if the fiscal years differ, and for the examination of specified, important, and representative related party transactions by the auditors for each of the parties, with appropriate exchange of relevant information.

f) Inspect or confirm and obtain satisfaction concerning the transferability and value of collateral.

    2) To fully understand a particular transaction, the auditor may

        a) Confirm the transaction amount and terms, including guarantees and other significant data, with the other parties.

        b) Inspect evidence in possession of the other parties.

        c) Confirm or discuss significant information with intermediaries, such as banks, guarantors, agents, or attorneys.

        d) Refer to financial publications, trade journals, and credit agencies.

        e) With respect to material uncollected balances, guarantees, and other obligations, obtain information about the financial capability of the other parties from audited financial statements, unaudited financial statements, income tax returns, and reports issued by credit agencies.

Stop and review! You have completed the outline for this subunit. Study multiple-choice questions 13 through 19 beginning on page 154.

4.4 ACCOUNTING ESTIMATES AND FAIR VALUE (AU-C 540)

 The more you study accounting, the more you will realize the importance of estimates. Most significant measurements in financial statements involve estimates. Be sure to understand the importance of estimates and auditors' concerns about them.

1. The **objective** of the auditor is to obtain sufficient appropriate audit evidence about whether accounting estimates, including fair value accounting estimates, are reasonable and related disclosures are adequate.

    a. The auditor performs **risk assessment procedures** to provide a basis for identifying and assessing the risks of material misstatement (RMMs) for accounting estimates.

        1) Thus, the auditor obtains an understanding of the following:

            a) The relevant requirements of the applicable financial reporting framework

            b) How management identifies factors that create a need for estimates

            c) How management makes estimates and the data on which they are based (e.g., methods, models, controls, use of specialists, underlying assumptions, and whether and how the effects of estimation uncertainty are assessed)

        2) The auditor also reviews prior-period estimates to

            a) Understand the reasons for the differences between estimates and outcomes and

            b) Identify intentional or unintentional **management bias**. Bias intended to mislead financial statement users is fraud.

               i) The auditor reviews management's judgments in making estimates to identify indicators of bias. These indicators are not necessarily misstatements.

              ii) Bias at the account level may be hard to detect. Thus, it may be detectable only when (a) groups of estimates, (b) all estimates, or (c) estimates over multiple periods are aggregated.

              iii) If estimation uncertainty was high or amounts have changed significantly, the review may need to be more extensive than the application of analytical procedures.

    b.   In identifying and assessing RMMs, the auditor should evaluate the estimation uncertainty associated with an accounting estimate and whether the risk is significant.

        1)   **Estimation uncertainty** is the susceptibility of an accounting estimate to an inherent lack of precision in its measurement.

2.   An **accounting estimate** approximates a monetary amount in the absence of a precise measurement. This term is used for an amount measured at **fair value** when estimation uncertainty exists and other amounts that require estimation.

    a.   Examples include (1) the allowance for doubtful accounts, (2) inventory obsolescence, (3) warranty obligations, (4) depreciation, (5) outcomes of long-term contracts, and (6) costs of litigation.

    b.   Examples of fair value estimates include (1) complex financial instruments not traded in an active and open market; (2) share-based payments; (3) property or equipment held for disposal; and (4) certain assets or liabilities acquired in a business combination, including goodwill and intangible assets.

3.   **Management** is responsible for making the judgments about accounting estimates.

    a.   These judgments are normally based on subjective as well as objective factors, including knowledge about past and current events and assumptions about future conditions and courses of action.

4.   The auditor should evaluate the **reasonableness** of accounting estimates in the context of the applicable financial reporting framework.

    a.   Even when the estimation process involves competent personnel using relevant and reliable data, **potential bias exists** in the subjective factors, and control may be difficult to establish.

    b.   When planning and performing procedures to evaluate accounting estimates, the auditor should adopt an attitude of **professional skepticism** regarding the subjective and objective factors.

    c.   The auditor should consider whether specialized skills may be necessary to obtain sufficient appropriate evidence.

5.   The RMMs of accounting estimates are related to estimation uncertainty.

    a.   Some accounting estimates involve relatively low estimation uncertainty and may give rise to lower RMMs. Examples include

        1)   Accounting estimates that are not complex

        2)   Accounting estimates that are frequently made and updated because they relate to routine transactions

        3)   Accounting estimates derived from readily available data, such as published interest rate data or exchange-traded prices of securities (referred to as **observable** in the context of a fair value accounting estimate)

        4)   Fair value accounting estimates in which the method of measurement is simple and applied easily to the asset or liability requiring measurement at fair value

        5)   Fair value accounting estimates in which the model used to measure the accounting estimate is well-known or generally accepted, provided that the assumptions or inputs to the model are observable

    b.   Some accounting estimates involve relatively high estimation uncertainty with higher RMMs, particularly when they are based on significant assumptions. Examples include

        1)   Accounting estimates relating to the outcome of litigation

        2)   Fair value accounting estimates for derivative financial instruments not publicly traded

       3) Fair value accounting estimates for which a highly specialized, entity-developed model is used or for which there are assumptions or inputs that cannot be observed in the marketplace

6. **Process for Developing Accounting Estimates**

    a. Management's process of preparing accounting estimates, whether or not documented or formally applied, normally consists of the following:

       1) Determining when estimates are required

       2) Identifying the relevant factors

       3) Accumulating relevant, sufficient, and reliable data

       4) Developing assumptions regarding the most likely circumstances and events with respect to the relevant factors

       5) Determining the estimated amounts based on the assumptions and other relevant factors

       6) Determining that presentation and disclosure conform with the applicable reporting framework

7. **Internal Control Related to Accounting Estimates**

    a. Internal control may reduce the probability of material misstatements of accounting estimates. Specific aspects of internal control relevant to the process of arriving at estimates include the following:

       1) Management communication of the need for proper estimates

       2) Accumulation of relevant, sufficient, and reliable data

       3) Preparation of estimates by qualified personnel

       4) Adequate review and approval by the proper authority of the following:

          a) Sources of relevant factors

          b) Development of assumptions

          c) Reasonableness of assumptions and resulting estimates

       5) Consideration by the proper authority of the need to use the work of specialists

       6) Consideration by the proper authority of changes in methods

       7) Comparison of prior estimates with results to assess the reliability of the process

       8) Consideration by management of whether the resulting estimates are consistent with operational plans

8. **Evaluating Reasonableness**

    a. The auditor's objective is to obtain sufficient appropriate evidence to provide reasonable assurance that

       1) All material accounting estimates have been developed.

       2) Those estimates are reasonable (free from bias).

       3) Presentation and disclosure conform with the applicable reporting framework.

    b. The evaluation concentrates on key factors and assumptions that are

       1) Significant to the estimate,

       2) Sensitive to variations,

       3) Different from historical patterns, and

       4) Subjective and susceptible to misstatement and bias.

    c. The auditor normally also should consider

       1) The entity's experience in making past estimates.

       2) Any changes that may cause factors different from those previously considered to become significant.

       3) The need to obtain written representations from management regarding the key factors and assumptions.

    d.   The auditor should understand, typically through inquiries, how management developed the estimate and then, based on the assessment of risks, use one or more of the following approaches:

        1)   **Review and test the process used by management.** Procedures for this purpose may include the following:

            a)   Identifying any controls over the process that might be useful in the evaluation

            b)   Identifying the sources of data and factors used in forming the assumptions and considering whether they are relevant, reliable, and sufficient in light of information from other audit tests

            c)   Considering whether other key factors or alternative assumptions exist

            d)   Evaluating whether the assumptions are consistent with each other and with relevant data

            e)   Analyzing historical data used to develop assumptions to assess comparability, consistency, and reliability

            f)   Considering whether business or industry changes cause other factors to become significant to the assumptions

            g)   Reviewing documentation of the assumptions and inquiring about plans and objectives that might relate to them

            h)   Using the work of a specialist

            i)   Testing calculations used to translate assumptions and key factors into the estimate

        2)   **Develop an independent expectation of the estimate**, either a point estimate or a range, to corroborate management's estimate by using other key factors or alternative assumptions.

        3)   **Review subsequent events or transactions** occurring after the date of the balance sheet but prior to the date of the auditor's report that are important in identifying and evaluating the reasonableness of accounting estimates, key factors, or assumptions.

Stop and review! You have completed the outline for this subunit. Study multiple-choice questions 20 through 26 beginning on page 157.

4.5 CONSIDERATION OF OMITTED PROCEDURES AFTER THE REPORT RELEASE DATE (AU-C 585)

1.   An auditor may determine, subsequent to the report release date, that (a) auditing procedures considered necessary at the time of the audit were omitted, but (b) nothing indicates that the financial statements are materially misstated.

    a.   However, an auditor has no responsibility to review the work once (s)he has reported.

2.   When the auditor decides that a necessary procedure was omitted, (s)he should assess its importance to his/her current ability to support the previously expressed opinion.

    a.   The results of other procedures applied or audit evidence obtained in a later audit (possibly at an interim date) may compensate for an omitted procedure.

3.   The auditor may determine that the omission impairs his/her current ability to support the opinion. If (s)he believes persons are currently relying, or are likely to rely, on the report, the auditor should promptly apply the omitted procedure or alternative procedures that provide a satisfactory basis for the opinion.

4.   If the auditor is unable to apply the previously omitted procedure or alternative procedures, (s)he may decide to seek legal advice.

Stop and review! You have completed the outline for this subunit. Study multiple-choice questions 27 through 29 beginning on page 159.

QUESTIONS

4.1 Using the Work of Internal Auditors (AU-C 610)

1. In assessing the competence and objectivity of an entity's internal auditor, an independent auditor would **least** likely consider information obtained from

A. Discussions with management personnel.

B. External quality reviews of the internal auditor's activities.

C. Previous experience with the internal auditor.

D. The results of analytical procedures.

Answer (D) is correct.

REQUIRED: The least likely procedure in assessing the competence and objectivity of an entity's internal auditor.

DISCUSSION: Analytical procedures are evaluations of financial information made by a study of plausible relationships among both financial and nonfinancial data, using models that range from simple to complex. They are substantive procedures used by the auditor to gather evidence about the fairness of the financial statements.

Answer (A) is incorrect. Discussion with management is a procedure appropriate for assessing the competence and objectivity of an internal auditor. Answer (B) is incorrect. A quality review is a procedure appropriate for assessing the competence and objectivity of an internal auditor. Answer (C) is incorrect. Consideration of previous experience is a procedure appropriate for assessing the competence and objectivity of an internal auditor.

2. In assessing the competence of an internal auditor, an independent CPA most likely would obtain information about the

A. Quality of the internal auditor's documentation.

B. Organization's commitment to integrity and ethical values.

C. Influence of management on the scope of the internal auditor's duties.

D. Organizational levels to which the internal auditor reports.

Answer (A) is correct.

REQUIRED: The information needed to assess the competence of an internal auditor.

DISCUSSION: In assessing the competence of an internal auditor, the auditor should consider such factors as (1) educational level and professional experience; (2) professional certification and continuing education; (3) audit policies, programs, and procedures; (4) supervision and review of the internal auditor's activities; (5) practices regarding assignments; (6) quality of documentation, reports, and recommendations; and (7) evaluation of the internal auditor's performance.

Answer (B) is incorrect. The organization's commitment to integrity and ethical values relates to objectivity rather than competence. Answer (C) is incorrect. The influence of management on the scope of the internal auditor's duties relates to objectivity rather than competence. Answer (D) is incorrect. The organizational levels to which the internal auditor reports relate to objectivity rather than competence.

3. In assessing the objectivity of internal auditors, an independent auditor should

A. Evaluate the quality control program in effect for the internal auditors.

B. Examine documentary evidence of the work performed by the internal auditors.

C. Test a sample of the transactions and balances that the internal auditors examined.

D. Determine the organizational level to which the internal auditors report.

Answer (D) is correct.

REQUIRED: The procedure performed to assess an internal auditor's objectivity.

DISCUSSION: If the auditor decides that it is efficient to consider how the internal auditors' work may affect the nature, timing, and extent of audit procedures, the competence and objectivity of the internal auditors should be assessed. Assessing objectivity includes obtaining information about (1) organizational status (the level to which the internal auditors report, access to those charged with governance, and whether these individuals oversee employment decisions related to the internal auditors) and (2) policies to maintain internal auditors' objectivity concerning the areas audited (AU-C 610).

Answer (A) is incorrect. Evaluating quality control pertains to competence, not objectivity. Answer (B) is incorrect. Examining internal auditors' engagement records (documentation) pertains to competence, not objectivity. Answer (C) is incorrect. Testing details examined by internal auditors pertains to competence, not objectivity.

4. For which of the following judgments may an independent auditor share responsibility with an entity's internal auditor who is assessed to be both competent and objective?

	Assessment of Inherent Risk	Assessment of Control Risk
A.	Yes	Yes
B.	Yes	No
C.	No	Yes
D.	No	No

Answer (D) is correct.
  REQUIRED: The judgment(s) that an auditor may share with an entity's internal auditor.
  DISCUSSION: The auditor may use the internal auditor to provide direct assistance in the audit as long as the auditor supervises, reviews, evaluates, and tests the work of the internal auditor. However, an internal auditor, regardless of his/her competence and objectivity, should never make judgments about the audit work being conducted. All judgments, including assessments of the risks of material misstatement (inherent and control risk), should be made by the auditor.

5. For which of the following judgments may an independent auditor share responsibility with an entity's internal auditor who is assessed to be both competent and objective?

	Materiality of Misstatements	Evaluation of Accounting Estimates
A.	Yes	No
B.	No	Yes
C.	No	No
D.	Yes	Yes

Answer (C) is correct.
  REQUIRED: The judgment(s) for which an auditor may share responsibility with an internal auditor.
  DISCUSSION: The responsibility to report on financial statements rests solely with the auditor and cannot be shared with internal auditors. Because the auditor has the ultimate responsibility to express an opinion on the financial statements, judgments about (1) assessments of RMMs, (2) materiality of misstatements, (3) sufficiency of tests performed, (4) evaluation of significant accounting estimates, and (5) other matters affecting the auditor's report always should be those of the auditor.

6. During an audit, an internal auditor may provide direct assistance to an independent CPA in

	Obtaining an Understanding of Internal Control	Performing Tests of Controls	Performing Substantive Tests
A.	No	No	No
B.	Yes	No	No
C.	Yes	Yes	No
D.	Yes	Yes	Yes

Answer (D) is correct.
  REQUIRED: The types of direct assistance an internal auditor may provide to an independent CPA.
  DISCUSSION: The auditor may request direct assistance from the internal auditor when performing the audit. Thus, the auditor may appropriately request the internal auditor's assistance in obtaining the understanding of internal control, performing tests of controls, or performing substantive procedures (AU-C 610). The internal auditor may provide assistance in all phases of the audit as long as (1) the internal auditor's competence and objectivity have been tested, and (2) the independent auditor supervises, reviews, evaluates, and tests the work performed by the internal auditor to the extent appropriate.

7. An internal auditor's work would most likely affect the nature, timing, and extent of an independent auditor's auditing procedures when the internal auditor's work relates to assertions about the

A. Existence of contingencies.

B. Valuation of intangible assets.

C. Existence of fixed asset additions.

D. Valuation of related party transactions.

Answer (C) is correct.
  REQUIRED: The assertion most likely affected by the internal auditor's work.
  DISCUSSION: Assertions may relate to material financial statement amounts for which the risks of material misstatement or the degree of subjectivity involved in the evaluation of the audit evidence is high. In these cases, reliance on the internal auditor is less effective. However, certain assertions may relate to less material financial statement amounts for which the risks of material misstatement or the degree of subjectivity involved is low. For example, the auditor may be able to rely on the internal auditor's work regarding assertions about the existence of cash, prepaid assets, and fixed asset additions.
  Answer (A) is incorrect. The auditor is less likely to rely on the internal auditor's work regarding subjective issues such as existence of contingencies. Answer (B) is incorrect. The auditor is less likely to rely on the internal auditor's work regarding subjective issues such as valuation of intangible assets. Answer (D) is incorrect. The auditor is less likely to rely on the internal auditor's work regarding subjective issues such as valuation of related party transactions.

8. Miller Retailing, Inc., maintains a staff of three full-time internal auditors. The independent auditor has found that they are competent and objective. Moreover, the work of the internal auditors is relevant to the audit, and it is efficient to consider how that work may affect the audit. The independent auditor most likely will

A. Nevertheless need to make direct tests of assertions about material financial statement amounts for which the risks of material misstatement are high.

B. Decrease the extent of the tests of controls needed to restrict audit risk to the acceptable level.

C. Increase the extent of the procedures needed to reduce control risk to an acceptable level.

D. Not evaluate and test the work performed by the internal auditors.

Answer (A) is correct.
REQUIRED: The true statement about the effect of the work of the internal auditors.
DISCUSSION: The auditor has the sole reporting responsibility and makes all judgments about matters affecting the report. When amounts are material and the risks of material misstatement are high or the evaluation of the evidence is highly subjective, the consideration of the internal auditors' work cannot alone reduce audit risk to an acceptable level. Thus, direct testing of those assertions by the auditor cannot be eliminated (AU-C 610).
Answer (B) is incorrect. The auditor performs substantive procedures, not tests of controls, to restrict detection risk to the acceptable level. Answer (C) is incorrect. Control risk can be assessed but not restricted by the auditor. Answer (D) is incorrect. The auditor should evaluate the quality and effectiveness of the work of the internal auditors that significantly affects the nature, timing, and extent of the audit procedures.

4.2 Using the Work of a Specialist (AU-C 620 and AU-C 500)

9. An auditor referred to the findings of an auditor's external specialist in the auditor's report. This may be an appropriate reporting practice if the

A. Auditor is not familiar with the professional certification, personal reputation, or particular competence of the specialist.

B. Auditor, as a result of the specialist's findings, adds a paragraph emphasizing a matter regarding the financial statements.

C. Auditor's report contains a qualified opinion.

D. Auditor, as a result of the specialist's findings, decides to indicate a division of responsibility with the specialist for the audit opinion.

Answer (C) is correct.
REQUIRED: The instance in which an auditor may refer to an auditor's specialist's findings.
DISCUSSION: The auditor refers to the work of an auditor's external specialist because it is relevant to a modification of the opinion. In these circumstances, the report should indicate that the reference does not reduce the auditor's responsibility for the opinion. If the auditor's report contains an unmodified opinion, the auditor should not refer to the work of an auditor's specialist (AU-C 620). A modified opinion is a qualified opinion, an adverse opinion, or a disclaimer of opinion (AU-C 705).
Answer (A) is incorrect. The auditor should evaluate the auditor's specialist's competence, capabilities, and objectivity regardless of whether the auditor's report refers to the specialist. Answer (B) is incorrect. An emphasis-of-matter paragraph or an other-matter paragraph may be included in the auditor's report when the opinion is unmodified or modified. Thus, an emphasis-of-matter paragraph is not a basis for referring to a specialist. Answer (D) is incorrect. The auditor has sole responsibility for the audit opinion.

10. Which of the following statements is true about the use of the work of an auditor's specialist?

A. The specialist need not agree to the auditor's use of the specialist's findings.

B. The auditor is required to perform substantive procedures to verify the specialist's assumptions and findings.

C. The auditor must keep client information confidential, but the specialist is not obligated to do so.

D. The auditor should obtain an understanding of the methods and assumptions used by the specialist.

Answer (D) is correct.
REQUIRED: The true statement about the auditor's use of the work of an auditor's specialist.
DISCUSSION: AU-C 620, *Using the Work of an Auditor's Specialist*, states that the auditor should evaluate the adequacy of the work of the auditor's specialist. This process includes (1) obtaining an understanding of any significant assumptions and methods used by the specialist and (2) evaluating the relevance and reasonableness of those assumptions and methods in the circumstances and in relation to the auditor's other findings and conclusions.
Answer (A) is incorrect. The auditor should agree with the specialist, in writing if appropriate, about various matters, such as their roles and responsibilities. These may include consent for the auditor to include details of the specialist's findings or conclusions in the basis for a modified opinion paragraph in the auditor's report. Answer (B) is incorrect. The auditor should understand the assumptions and methods and evaluate their relevance and reasonableness, not verify them. But the auditor may perform corroborative procedures on the specialist's findings and conclusions, e.g., reperformance of calculations and performance of detailed analytical procedures. Answer (C) is incorrect. The auditor should establish an agreement with the specialist to maintain confidentiality.

11. In using the work of an auditor's external specialist, an agreement should exist between the auditor and the specialist as to the nature of the specialist's work. This agreement most likely should include

    A. A statement that the specialist assumes no responsibility to update the specialist's report for future events or circumstances.

    B. The conditions under which a division of responsibility may be necessary.

    C. The applicability of the same confidentiality requirements to the auditor and the specialist.

    D. The auditor's disclaimer as to whether the specialist's findings corroborate the representations in the financial statements.

Answer (C) is correct.
    REQUIRED: The matter covered in the agreement about the work of an auditor's external specialist.
    DISCUSSION: The agreement should be documented and should cover (1) the nature, objectives, and scope of the work; (2) the roles of the auditor and specialist; (3) the nature, timing, and extent of communications between the auditor and specialist; and (4) the need for the specialist to observe confidentiality requirements. The agreement between the auditor and the auditor's external specialist generally is documented in an engagement letter. A matter that should be included is the need for the confidentiality provisions of the relevant ethical requirements that apply to the auditor also to apply to the specialist. For example, a member of the AICPA may use a third-party service provider to render professional services to clients. The member should have a contract with the third-party service provider to maintain the confidentiality of the information (Ethics Ruling). Other requirements may be imposed by law or regulation.
    Answer (A) is incorrect. The agreement need not contain a disclaimer about the specialist's responsibility to update the report. Answer (B) is incorrect. The auditor may not divide responsibility with the specialist. Answer (D) is incorrect. The agreement need not contain a disclaimer about whether the findings corroborate the representations.

12. A management's specialist most likely is useful to

    A. Assist the auditor in collecting sufficient appropriate audit evidence.

    B. Provide the auditor advice on technical accounting issues.

    C. Add credibility to the financial statements.

    D. Assist the client in preparing the financial statements.

Answer (D) is correct.
    REQUIRED: The use of a management's specialist.
    DISCUSSION: A management's specialist is an individual or organization possessing expertise in a field other than accounting or auditing. The work in that field is used by the entity to assist in preparing the financial statements.
    Answer (A) is incorrect. An auditor's specialist may assist the auditor in collecting sufficient appropriate evidence. Answer (B) is incorrect. Both the auditor's specialists and management's specialists provide assistance on matters other than accounting. Answer (C) is incorrect. The auditor adds credibility to the financial statements.

4.3 Related Parties (AU-C 550)

13. When auditing related party transactions, an auditor places primary emphasis on

    A. Confirming the existence of the related parties.

    B. Verifying the valuation of the related party transactions.

    C. Assessing the risks of material misstatement of related party transactions.

    D. Ascertaining the rights and obligations of the related parties.

Answer (C) is correct.
    REQUIRED: The primary concern of the auditor about related party transactions.
    DISCUSSION: The auditor has a responsibility to perform audit procedures to identify, assess, and respond to the risks of material misstatement arising from the entity's failure to appropriately account for or disclose related party relationships, transactions, or balances.

14. An auditor searching for related party transactions should obtain an understanding of each subsidiary's relationship to the total entity because

A. This may permit the audit of interentity account balances to be performed as of concurrent dates.

B. Interentity transactions may have been consummated on terms equivalent to arm's-length transactions.

C. This may reveal whether particular transactions would have taken place if the parties had not been related.

D. The business structure may be deliberately designed to obscure related party transactions.

Answer (D) is correct.
   REQUIRED: The reason for understanding parent-subsidiary relationships when searching for related party transactions.
   DISCUSSION: The nature of related party relationships and transactions may result in greater risks of material misstatement than transactions with unrelated parties. Thus, related parties may operate through a complex set of relationships and structures, with increased complexity of related party transactions. For example, a transaction may involve multiple related parties in a consolidated group. Accordingly, in an audit of group statements, the group engagement team should request each component auditor to communicate with related parties not previously identified by group management or the group engagement team.
   Answer (A) is incorrect. A concurrent audit is not required. Answer (B) is incorrect. The auditor's concern is that related party transactions were not at arm's length. Answer (C) is incorrect. Determining whether a transaction would have occurred and what the terms would have been if the parties were unrelated is not normally an objective of an audit.

15. Which of the following procedures most likely could assist an auditor in identifying related party transactions?

A. Performing tests of controls concerning the segregation of duties.

B. Evaluating the reasonableness of management's accounting estimates.

C. Reviewing confirmations of compensating balance arrangements.

D. Scanning the accounting records for recurring transactions.

Answer (C) is correct.
   REQUIRED: The procedure most likely used to identify related party transactions.
   DISCUSSION: The auditor performs procedures to identify material transactions that may be indicative of previously undetermined relationships. These procedures include reviewing confirmations of compensating balance arrangements for indications that balances are or were maintained for or by related parties (AU-C 550).
   Answer (A) is incorrect. Testing segregation of duties of entity personnel is unlikely to identify related party transactions. Answer (B) is incorrect. Evaluating the reasonableness of accounting estimates has little relevance to related party transactions. The auditor should concentrate on transactions of a kind that tend to be entered into with related parties. Answer (D) is incorrect. Recurring transactions are not by their nature indicative of related party transactions.

16. Which of the following events **least** likely would indicate the existence of related party transactions?

A. Making a loan with **no** scheduled date for the funds to be repaid.

B. Exchanging property for the benefit of a principal shareholder.

C. Borrowing funds at an interest rate significantly below prevailing market rates.

D. Writing off obsolete inventory to net realizable value just before year end.

Answer (D) is correct.
   REQUIRED: The event that least likely indicates the existence of related party transactions.
   DISCUSSION: The following suggest possible related party transactions: (1) exchanging property for similar property in a nonmonetary transaction, (2) borrowing or lending at rates significantly above or below market rates, (3) selling realty at a price materially different from its appraised value, and (4) making loans with no scheduled repayment terms (AU-C 550).

17. Which of the following statements is true about related party transactions?

    A. In the absence of evidence to the contrary, related party transactions should be assumed to be outside the ordinary course of business.

    B. An auditor should determine whether a particular transaction would have occurred if the parties had not been related.

    C. An auditor should substantiate that related party transactions were consummated on terms equivalent to those that prevail in arm's-length transactions.

    D. The auditor should consider whether an identified related party transaction outside the normal course of business is appropriately accounted for and disclosed.

Answer (D) is correct.

    REQUIRED: The true statement about related party transactions.

    DISCUSSION: The auditor should inspect any contracts or agreements to evaluate whether (1) the business purpose (or lack of a business purpose) implies that the transaction's intent was fraudulent, (2) the terms are consistent with management's explanations, and (3) the accounting and disclosure are appropriate. The auditor also should obtain evidence of appropriate authorization and approval.

    Answer (A) is incorrect. In the absence of contrary evidence, related party transactions are assumed to be in the ordinary course of business. Answer (B) is incorrect. Determining whether a particular transaction would have occurred if the parties had not been related is ordinarily not an objective of the audit. Answer (C) is incorrect. The auditor should obtain sufficient appropriate evidence about a management assertion that related party transactions were conducted on terms equivalent to those that prevail in arm's-length transactions. Management is responsible for substantiating the assertion. The auditor evaluates management's support for the assertion.

18. After identifying a significant related party transaction outside the entity's normal course of business, an auditor should

    A. Add an emphasis-of-matter paragraph to the auditor's report to explain the transaction.

    B. Perform analytical procedures to identify similar transactions that were not recorded.

    C. Evaluate the business purpose of the transaction.

    D. Substantiate that the transaction was consummated on terms equivalent to those of an arm's-length transaction.

Answer (C) is correct.

    REQUIRED: The procedure performed after identifying a significant related party transaction outside the entity's normal course of business.

    DISCUSSION: The auditor should inspect any contracts or agreements to evaluate whether (1) the business purpose (or lack of a business purpose) implies that the transaction's intent was fraudulent, (2) the terms are consistent with management's explanations, and (3) the accounting and disclosure are appropriate. The auditor also should obtain evidence of appropriate authorization and approval.

    Answer (A) is incorrect. If (1) the transaction has been properly accounted for and disclosed, and (2) its effects do not prevent fair presentation of the statements, no modification of the opinion is required. But the auditor may wish to add a separate paragraph emphasizing that the entity has had a significant related party transaction (AU-C 706). Answer (B) is incorrect. Analytical procedures are not suitable for identifying particular unrecorded transactions. But the auditor should be alert when inspecting documents or records for indications of unidentified related party relationships or transactions. Answer (D) is incorrect. The auditor normally cannot determine whether a transaction was consummated on terms equivalent to those of an arm's-length transaction. Instead, management is responsible for substantiating the assertion about the transaction. Thus, the auditor should evaluate management's support for the assertion.

19. An auditor most likely modifies the opinion if the entity's financial statements include a note on related party transactions

    A. Disclosing loans to related parties at interest rates significantly below prevailing market rates.

    B. Describing an exchange of real estate for similar property in a nonmonetary related party transaction.

    C. Stating without substantiation that a particular related party transaction occurred on terms equivalent to those that would have prevailed in an arm's-length transaction.

    D. Presenting the dollar volume of related party transactions and the effects of any change from prior periods in the method of establishing terms.

Answer (C) is correct.

    REQUIRED: The note most likely resulting in a modified opinion.

    DISCUSSION: The auditor should obtain sufficient appropriate evidence about a management assertion that related party transactions were conducted on terms equivalent to those that prevail in arm's-length transactions. Management is responsible for substantiating the assertion. The auditor evaluates management's support for the assertion.

4.4 Accounting Estimates and Fair Value (AU-C 540)

20. Which of the following procedures would an auditor ordinarily perform first in evaluating the reasonableness of management's accounting estimates?

- A. Review transactions occurring prior to the date of the auditor's report that indicate variations from expectations.
- B. Compare independent expectations with recorded estimates to assess management's process.
- C. Obtain an understanding of how management developed its estimates.
- D. Analyze historical data used in developing assumptions to determine whether the process is consistent.

Answer (C) is correct.
REQUIRED: The first procedure ordinarily performed in evaluating the reasonableness of accounting estimates.
DISCUSSION: To evaluate reasonableness, the auditor obtains an understanding of the development of the estimates. That understanding is the basis for the approach(es) used to evaluate reasonableness: (1) reviewing and testing the process used, (2) developing an independent estimate to corroborate the estimate, and (3) reviewing events or transactions occurring after the date of the balance sheet but prior to the date of the auditor's report.
Answer (A) is incorrect. The auditor should review transactions only after an understanding of how management developed the estimate is gained. Answer (B) is incorrect. The auditor should compare independent expectations and reported estimates after an understanding of how management developed its estimates is obtained. Answer (D) is incorrect. The auditor should analyze historical data after it is understood how management developed its estimates.

21. In evaluating the reasonableness of an entity's accounting estimates, an auditor normally is concerned about assumptions that are

- A. Susceptible to bias.
- B. Consistent with prior periods.
- C. Insensitive to variations.
- D. Similar to industry guidelines.

Answer (A) is correct.
REQUIRED: The auditor's normal concern about assumptions used in making accounting estimates.
DISCUSSION: In evaluating the reasonableness of an estimate, the auditor normally concentrates on key factors and assumptions that are (1) significant to the accounting estimate, (2) sensitive to variations, (3) deviations from historical patterns, and (4) subjective and susceptible to misstatement and bias.
Answer (B) is incorrect. Assumptions consistent with those of prior periods are of less concern to the auditor. Answer (C) is incorrect. Assumptions insensitive to variations are of less concern to the auditor. Answer (D) is incorrect. Estimates that are similar to industry guidelines are more likely to be reasonable.

22. George Karl, an auditor with extensive experience in the retail industry, is assigned to audit the reasonableness of accounting estimates in the Year 1 financial statements of Haas Company. Haas, which was formed in Year 1, markets fishing lures. Which of the following is the **least** important consideration for Karl's audit of the reasonableness of accounting estimates?

- A. An inexperienced employee at Haas prepared the financial statements and was entirely responsible for the accounting estimates.
- B. Karl has never been involved in an audit of a company that sells fishing lures.
- C. The accounting estimates in the financial statements of Haas Company are based on numerous significant assumptions.
- D. The accounting estimates in the financial statements are susceptible to significant estimation uncertainty.

Answer (B) is correct.
REQUIRED: The least important consideration in an audit of the reasonableness of accounting estimates.
DISCUSSION: The auditor evaluates the reasonableness of estimates. Among the factors considered are (1) the entity's experience in making past estimates, (2) any changes that may cause factors different from those previously considered to become significant, and (3) the need to obtain written representations from management regarding the key factors and assumptions. Karl has extensive experience in the retail industry and therefore most likely has an acceptable level of competence. If necessary, Karl may seek the help of a specialist before conducting the audit.
Answer (A) is incorrect. Preparation of the statements by an inexperienced employee who may not have the competence necessary to formulate accounting estimates suggests the need for additional audit effort. Answer (C) is incorrect. The significant assumptions underlying accounting estimates are crucial to the audit. The auditor should concentrate on the key factors and assumptions that are (1) significant to the estimates, (2) sensitive to variations, (3) deviations from historical patterns, and (4) subjective and susceptible to misstatement and bias. Answer (D) is incorrect. Estimates that are subject to significant estimation uncertainty require additional consideration by the auditor.

23. The auditor's evaluation of the reasonableness of accounting estimates

    A. Should be in the context of individual transactions.

    B. Considers that management bases its judgment on both subjective and objective factors.

    C. Will be unfavorable if the estimates in the financial statements are based on assumptions about future events and transactions.

    D. Should be based on an attitude of conservatism.

Answer (B) is correct.
    REQUIRED: The true statement about the auditor's evaluation of the reasonableness of accounting estimates.
    DISCUSSION: Estimates are based on both subjective and objective factors. Hence, control over estimates may be difficult to establish. Given the potential bias in the subjective factors, the auditor should adopt an attitude of professional skepticism toward both the subjective and objective factors.
    Answer (A) is incorrect. The evaluation should be in the context of the financial statements as a whole. Answer (C) is incorrect. Estimates are often based on assumptions about the future. Answer (D) is incorrect. Estimates should be based on assumptions regarding the most likely circumstances and events. The auditor should evaluate those assumptions with professional skepticism.

24. Auditors should obtain and evaluate sufficient appropriate evidence to support significant accounting estimates. Differences between the estimates best supported by the evidence and those in the financial statements

    A. Are per se unreasonable and should be treated as material misstatements.

    B. May be individually reasonable but collectively indicate possible bias.

    C. May be individually unreasonable, but if they collectively indicate no bias, accumulation of the differences with other identified misstatements is not required.

    D. Should arouse concern only when estimates are based on hypothetical assumptions or subjective factors.

Answer (B) is correct.
    REQUIRED: The true statement about differences between the estimates best supported by the evidence and those in the financial statements.
    DISCUSSION: If the amount in the financial statements is not reasonable, it should be treated as fraud or error and accumulated with other identified misstatements. If the differences between the best estimates and those in the financial statements are individually reasonable but collectively indicate possible bias (for example, when the effect of each difference is to increase income), the auditor should reconsider the estimates as a whole.
    Answer (A) is incorrect. No estimate is considered accurate with certainty. Hence, differences may be reasonable and not considered to be identified material misstatements. Answer (C) is incorrect. An unreasonable difference should be considered an identified misstatement and accumulated. Answer (D) is incorrect. Estimates are based on subjective as well as objective factors.

25. During the audit of fair value estimates and disclosures, the auditor most likely should

    A. Understand the components of internal control but need not specifically obtain an understanding of the entity's process for determining fair value estimates.

    B. Use the understanding of the audited entity's process for determining fair value estimates to assess the risks of material misstatement.

    C. Determine that the entity has measured fair value estimates using discounted cash flows whenever feasible.

    D. Focus primarily on the initial recording of transactions.

Answer (B) is correct.
    REQUIRED: The necessary procedure in an audit of fair value estimates.
    DISCUSSION: To meet its responsibility to make the fair value estimates included in the financial statements, management must adopt financial reporting processes that include (1) adequate internal control, (2) selecting appropriate accounting policies, (3) prescribing estimation processes (e.g., valuation methods, including models), (4) determining data and assumptions, (5) reviewing the circumstances requiring estimation, and (6) making necessary reestimates. The auditor should obtain an understanding of these processes and the relevant controls. It should be sufficient for an effective audit of fair value estimates. The understanding is used to assess the risks of material misstatement. Assessing these risks includes evaluating (1) estimation uncertainty (inherent lack of measurement precision) and (2) determining whether the risks are significant.
    Answer (A) is incorrect. The auditor should obtain an understanding of the entity's process for determining fair value estimates. Answer (C) is incorrect. Accounting standards typically do not require a specific method for measuring fair value. However, use of observable market prices is preferable. In their absence, the measurement is based on the best available information, and the entity's process will be more complex. Answer (D) is incorrect. Measurements also are necessary for changes in fair value subsequent to initial recording, e.g., adjustments at the balance sheet date for holding gains or losses on trading and available-for-sale securities.

26. As part of the audit of fair value estimates and disclosures, an auditor may need to test the entity's significant assumptions. In these circumstances, the auditor should

    A. Verify that the entity has used its own assumptions, not those of marketplace participants.

    B. Obtain sufficient evidence to express an opinion on the assumptions.

    C. Evaluate whether the assumptions individually and as a whole form a reasonable basis for the fair value estimates.

    D. Apply audit effort equally to all assumptions.

Answer (C) is correct.
    REQUIRED: The necessary step in an audit of fair value estimates when the auditor tests significant assumptions.
    DISCUSSION: Observable market prices are not always available for fair value estimates. In this case, the entity uses valuation methods based on the assumptions that the market would employ to estimate fair values, if obtainable without excessive cost. Accordingly, GAAS require the auditor to evaluate whether the significant assumptions form a reasonable basis for the estimates. Because assumptions often are interdependent and must be consistent with each other, the auditor should evaluate them independently and as a whole.
    Answer (A) is incorrect. Valuation methods should be based on the assumptions that participants in the market would use to estimate fair value without undue cost and effort. Answer (B) is incorrect. The procedures applied to the entity's assumptions are required merely to evaluate whether, in the context of the audit of the financial statements as a whole, the assumptions form a reasonable basis for the estimates. Answer (D) is incorrect. The auditor considers the sensitivity of valuations to changes in assumptions. Accordingly, the auditor considers focusing on especially sensitive assumptions.

4.5 Consideration of Omitted Procedures After the Report Release Date (AU-C 585)

27. On February 9, Brown, CPA, expressed an unmodified opinion on the financial statements of Web Co. On October 9, during a peer review of Brown's practice, the reviewer informed Brown that engagement personnel failed to perform a search for subsequent events for the Web engagement. Brown should first

    A. Request Web's permission to perform substantive procedures that would provide a satisfactory basis for the opinion.

    B. Inquire of Web whether persons are currently relying or likely to rely on the financial statements.

    C. Take no additional action because subsequent events have no effect on the financial statements that were reported on.

    D. Assess the importance of the omitted procedures to Brown's present ability to support the opinion.

Answer (D) is correct.
    REQUIRED: The first action taken after a subsequent discovery of an omitted procedure.
    DISCUSSION: The results of other procedures applied or audit evidence obtained in a later audit (possibly at an interim date) may compensate for an omitted procedure. Furthermore, the auditor should assess the importance of the omitted procedure to the support of the audit opinion in relation to the overall engagement and the circumstances of the audit. The auditor determines whether (1) the omission impairs the current ability to support the opinion, and (2) persons are currently relying or are likely to rely on the report. If these conditions exist, the auditor should promptly undertake to apply the omitted procedure or alternative procedures that would provide a satisfactory basis for the opinion (AU-C 585).
    Answer (A) is incorrect. Brown should decide the importance of the omitted procedures before taking action. Answer (B) is incorrect. Brown must first determine whether the omission is important. Answer (C) is incorrect. Subsequent events may require adjustment of, or disclosure in, the financial statements.

28. On March 15, Year 2, Kent, CPA, expressed an unmodified opinion on a client's audited financial statements for the year ended December 31, Year 1. On May 4, Year 2, Kent's internal inspection program disclosed that engagement personnel failed to observe the client's physical inventory. Omission of this procedure impairs Kent's present ability to support the unmodified opinion. If the shareholders are currently relying on the opinion, Kent should first

A. Advise management to disclose to the shareholders that Kent's unmodified opinion should not be relied on.

B. Undertake to apply alternative procedures that would provide a satisfactory basis for the unmodified opinion.

C. Reissue the auditor's report and add an emphasis-of-matter paragraph describing the departure from generally accepted auditing standards.

D. Compensate for the omitted procedure by performing tests of controls to reduce audit risk to an acceptably low level.

Answer (B) is correct.
REQUIRED: The appropriate action when an auditor discovers that a necessary audit procedure was not performed during the previous audit.
DISCUSSION: The auditor determines whether (1) the omission impairs his/her current ability to support the opinion, and (2) persons are currently relying or are likely to rely on the report. If these conditions currently exist, the auditor should promptly undertake to apply the omitted procedure or alternative procedures that would provide a satisfactory basis for the opinion (AU-C 585).
Answer (A) is incorrect. Notification of users is only necessary if the auditor could not become satisfied upon applying the procedure. Answer (C) is incorrect. The auditor has followed GAAS in becoming satisfied with the application of the procedure. Answer (D) is incorrect. Tests of controls do not substitute for required substantive procedures.

29. An auditor is considering whether the omission of the confirmation of investments impairs the auditor's ability to support a previously expressed unmodified opinion. The auditor need **not** perform this omitted procedure if

A. The results of alternative procedures that were performed compensate for the omission.

B. The auditor's assessed level of detection risk is low.

C. The omission is documented in a communication with the audit committee.

D. No individual investment is material to the financial statements taken as a whole.

Answer (A) is correct.
REQUIRED: The circumstance in which the auditor need not confirm investments to support a previously expressed unmodified opinion.
DISCUSSION: The results of other procedures may compensate for the omitted procedure or make its omission less significant. Furthermore, a subsequent audit (e.g., at an interim date) may provide audit evidence to support the previous opinion (AU-C 585).
Answer (B) is incorrect. If the omission impairs the auditor's ability to support the previous opinion, (s)he should promptly perform the omitted procedure or alternative procedures. Answer (C) is incorrect. The auditor should promptly perform the omitted procedure or alternative procedures. Documenting the omission is not a means of obtaining sufficient appropriate audit evidence regarding the assertion about investments. Answer (D) is incorrect. The overall investment balance may be material.

Use the additional questions in Gleim **CPA Test Prep** to create Practice Exams that emulate Prometric!

4.6 PRACTICE TASK-BASED SIMULATIONS

Auditing and Attestation Testlet 4 of 4	Time Remaining 1 hour - 30 minutes	Unsplit Split Horiz Split Vertical Spreadsheet Calculator Exit

DIRECTIONS

Note: If you believe you have encountered a software malfunction, report it to the test center staff immediately.

Navigation

To navigate from task to task, use the controls at the bottom of the screen. Click on the **Next** button to advance to the next task, or the **Previous** button to go to the previous task. To go directly to any task, click on its number.

If you would like a reminder to revisit a task, or want to indicate that you are finished with it, click on the reminder flag below the task number. To clear the flag, click on it again. Reminder flags are for your use only – they do not contribute to your score.

Tabs

In this part of the examination, you will be asked to complete various tasks. Every task has one or more **Work Tabs**. Some tasks have one or more **Information Tabs**, others may have none. Every task has a **Help** tab.

If a task has **Information Tabs**, you may use the information in them to complete your responses in the **Work Tabs**.

Work tab   Information tab   Help tab

Work Tabs:

- **Work Tabs** are identified with a pencil icon. This is where your responses are expected.
- Each task has one or more **Work Tabs**.
- **Work Tabs** contain directions for completing the task – be sure to read these directions carefully.
- The **Work Tab** name in the example above is for illustration only – yours will differ.
- You must complete all of the **Work Tabs** in each task to receive full credit.

Information Tabs:

- The Authoritative Literature will be provided in all tasks in the AUD, FAR, and REG sections for your reference.
- Your simulation may have one or more additional **Information Tabs**. Like the Authoritative Literature tabs, **Information Tabs** do not have a pencil icon.
- If your task has additional **Information Tabs**, go through each to familiarize yourself with the task content.

Help Tab:

- The **Help Tab** provides assistance with the exam software that is used in this task. For example, if the task is to compose a memorandum, **Help** will provide information about the word processor.

The Toolbar

The toolbar at the top of the screen shows the amount of time remaining for you to complete the tasks. In addition, the following tools are available. Note that only the **Exit** button is displayed when Directions are visible - the others will appear when you begin the tasks.

Click on these buttons to split or unsplit the screen. You can split the screen vertically or horizontally.

Click on this button to display the calculator; click on it again to hide the calculator. To move the calculator, click on the calculator title bar and drag the calculator to the desired location.

Click on this button to use the spreadsheet; click on it again to hide the spreadsheet. To move the spreadsheet, click on the the spreadsheet title bar and drag the spreadsheet to the desired location.

Click on this button to go on to the next part of the examination. You must complete all of the tasks to receive full credit. Once you click on **Exit** and confirm the action, you will NOT be able to return to this testlet.

▼ = Reminder   Directions   1 2 3 4 5   ◀ Previous   Next ▶

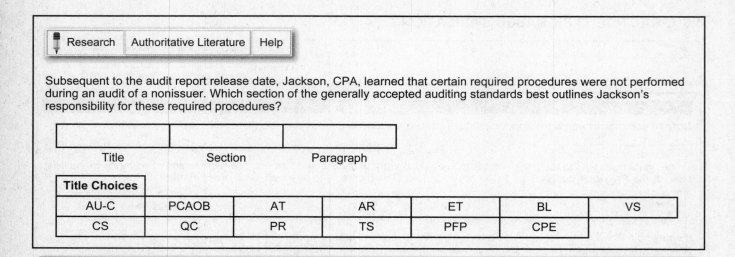

Subsequent to the audit report release date, Jackson, CPA, learned that certain required procedures were not performed during an audit of a nonissuer. Which section of the generally accepted auditing standards best outlines Jackson's responsibility for these required procedures?

Title	Section	Paragraph

Title Choices

AU-C	PCAOB	AT	AR	ET	BL	VS
CS	QC	PR	TS	PFP	CPE	

⏴ = Reminder   Directions | 1 | 2 | 3 | 4 | 5 | ◀ Previous   Next ▶

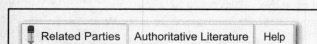 Related Parties   Authoritative Literature   Help

Each of the following describes a possible related party transaction, motive for such a transaction, audit procedure pertinent to related party transactions, or disclosure. Select from the list provided the appropriate choice. Each choice may be used once, more than once, or not at all.

Description	Answer
1. An overly optimistic earnings forecast.	
2. Management asserts, without substantiation, that the transaction was conducted on terms equivalent to those that prevail at arm's length.	
3. Confirm significant information with intermediaries.	
4. Review conflict-of-interest statements obtained by the company for its management.	
5. Making nonmonetary exchanges of similar property.	
6. Interest-free borrowing.	
7. Reviewing shareholder listings of closely held companies.	
8. Excess capacity.	
9. The transaction would have occurred even if the parties were not related.	
10. Determine whether the transaction was approved by the board of directors.	

Choices
A) Transactions indicative of the existence of related parties.
B) Motivation for entering into related party transactions.
C) Specific audit procedure that may uncover related parties.
D) Procedure to gain an understanding of a related party transaction.
E) Appropriate financial statement disclosure by management about related party transactions.
F) Inappropriate financial statement disclosure by management about related party transactions.

⏴ = Reminder   Directions | 1 | 2 | 3 | 4 | 5 | ◀ Previous   Next ▶

Estimates | Authoritative Literature | Help

Auditors and management have responsibilities for accounting estimates. Select from the list provided the most appropriate statement about responsibilities for each item below. Each choice may be used once, more than once, or not at all.

Responsibility Relative to Estimates	Answer		Choices
1. Take action on subjective as well as objective factors, including knowledge about past and current events and assumptions about future conditions and courses of action			A) Auditor's responsibility only
2. Determine that all needed estimates have been developed			B) Management's responsibility only
3. Maintain an attitude of professional skepticism toward both the subjective and objective factors			C) Both management's and auditor's responsibility
4. Review and evaluate the process used			D) Neither management's nor auditor's responsibility
5. Consider whether a bias might exist			
6. Report failures to make optimal estimates to authorities			
7. Maintain internal control over the process of development			
8. Communicate to those charged with governance about significant estimates			

Consideration of Omitted Procedures | Authoritative Literature | Help

An auditor may determine, subsequent to the date of the report, that auditing procedures considered necessary at the time of the audit were omitted. Select from the list provided the action that the auditor should take. Each selection may be used once, more than once, or not at all.

Situation	Answer		Choices
1. Lucky CPAs did not make test counts of inventory before issuing its audit report. However, it has determined that, because of audit evidence obtained from performing other procedures, it can still support the unmodified opinion.			A) Do nothing
2. Forgetful CPAs failed to confirm material accounts receivable for one of its audit clients.			B) Assess the importance of the omitted procedure to the auditor's current ability to support the previously expressed opinion
3. Four months after Post CPAs completed the audit of Harp, Inc., a final resolution regarding a contractual contingency was made. The contingency was properly disclosed in the notes to the financial statements.			
4. During a peer review, Simple CPAs was informed that it failed to determine whether the effects of a material related party transaction was properly disclosed in the notes to the financial statements. Simple believes this will affect its current ability to support its unmodified opinion.			C) Promptly apply the omitted procedure
5. Mal CPAs determined that an omitted procedure will affect its current ability to support its unmodified opinion and that it will be unable to apply the previously omitted procedure.			D) Consult an attorney

| Activities | Authoritative Literature | Help |

The independent external auditor decides that it is efficient to consider how the internal auditors' work might affect the nature, timing, and extent of audit procedures. Thus, the independent auditor should assess both the competence and objectivity of the internal auditors. For each of the following procedures, select from the list provided to show whether it is appropriate for assessing competence, objectivity, both, or neither. Each choice may be used once, more than once, or not at all.

Procedures	Answer
1. Update or obtain information about the supervision and review of internal auditors' work.	
2. Update or obtain information about the policies regarding the employment of relatives of internal auditors in audit-sensitive positions.	
3. Evaluate evidence from a recent external quality review of the internal auditors.	
4. Update or obtain information about the audit plans and procedures used by the internal auditors.	
5. Evaluate the personal financial statements of the internal auditors.	
6. Determine whether the internal auditors have direct access to the board of directors.	
7. Update or obtain information about the professional certification of the internal auditors.	
8. Update or obtain information about the continuing education programs provided to the internal auditors.	
9. Consider information obtained in previous audits about the activities of internal auditors.	
10. Consider whether the internal auditors are well paid.	

Choices
A) The independent auditor should perform this procedure to test the competence and objectivity of the internal auditors.
B) The independent auditor should perform this procedure to test the competence but not the objectivity of the internal auditors.
C) The independent auditor should perform this procedure to test the objectivity but not the competence of the internal auditors.
D) The auditor would not perform this procedure.

Unofficial Answers

1. Research (1 Gradable Item)

Answer: 585.07

AU-C Section 585 -- *Consideration of Omitted Procedures after the Report Release Date*

.07 If the auditor concludes that an omitted procedure of which the auditor has become aware impairs the auditor's present ability to support a previously expressed opinion on the financial statements and the auditor believes that there are users currently relying, or likely to rely, on the previously released report, the auditor should promptly perform the omitted procedure, or alternative procedures, to determine whether there is a satisfactory basis for the auditor's previously expressed opinion. The auditor should include in the audit documentation the procedures performed, in accordance with the provisions of section 230, *Audit Documentation.*

2. Related Parties (10 Gradable Items)

1. B) Motivation for entering into related party transactions. Management may be motivated to enter into related party transactions in order to meet overly optimistic forecasts.

2. F) Inappropriate financial statement disclosure by management about related party transactions. It is inappropriate for management to assert, without substantiation, that a transaction was conducted on terms equivalent to those that prevail at arm's length.

3. D) Procedure to gain an understanding of a related party transaction. Procedures to gain an understanding of a related party transaction would include confirming significant information with intermediaries.

4. C) Specific audit procedure that may uncover related parties. Reviewing conflict-of-interest statements may uncover the existence of related parties.

5. A) Transactions indicative of the existence of related parties. Nonmonetary exchange of similar property is indicative of transactions made with related parties.

6. A) Transactions indicative of the existence of related parties. Interest-free borrowing is indicative of transactions made by related parties.

7. C) Specific audit procedure that may uncover related parties. Reviewing shareholder listings of closely held companies may uncover the existence of related parties.

8. B) Motivation for entering into related party transactions. Attempting to fill excess capacity may motivate management to enter into related party transactions.

9. F) Inappropriate financial statement disclosure by management about related party transactions. It is ordinarily not feasible to determine whether a transaction would have occurred if the parties were not related.

10. D) Procedure to gain an understanding of a related party transaction. Procedures to gain an understanding of a related party transaction would include determining whether the transaction was approved by the board of directors.

3. Estimates (8 Gradable Items)

1. B) Management's responsibility only. It is management's responsibility to take action to make estimates based on their knowledge.

2. C) Both management's and auditor's responsibility. Management should determine that all estimates have been made, and the auditor should collect evidence to support that determination.

3. A) Auditor's responsibility only. The auditor should maintain an attitude of professional skepticism toward both the subjective and objective factors that management has used.

4. A) Auditor's responsibility only. The auditor should review and evaluate the process used by management.

5. A) Auditor's responsibility only. The auditor should consider whether management may have been biased in making estimates.

6. D) Neither management's nor auditor's responsibility. Neither management nor the auditor needs to report to authorities about estimates.

7. B) Management's responsibility only. Management is responsible for establishing and maintaining internal control.

8. A) Auditor's responsibility only. The auditor is responsible to communicate to those with oversight about management's estimates.

4. Consideration of Omitted Procedures (5 Gradable Items)

1. A) Do nothing. If the audit report can still be supported, no further action is required of the auditor.

2. B) Assess the importance of the omitted procedure to the auditor's current ability to support the previously expressed opinion. When the auditor determines that a procedure considered necessary at the time of the audit was omitted, the auditor should assess his/her ability to support the previously expressed opinion regarding the financial statements taken as a whole.

3. A) Do nothing. Because the contingency was adequately stated in the financial statements, the auditor has no obligation to make any further inquiries with respect to the audited financial statements covered by that report.

4. C) Promptly apply the omitted procedure. If the auditor determines that the omission impairs his/her current ability to support the opinion, the auditor should promptly undertake to apply the omitted procedure.

5. D) Consult an attorney. If the auditor is unable to apply the previously omitted procedure or alternative procedures, the auditor should seek legal advice.

5. Activities (10 Gradable Items)

1. B) The independent auditor should perform this procedure to test the competence but not the objectivity of the internal auditors. The supervision and review of internal auditors' work relate to their competence.

2. C) The independent auditor should perform this procedure to test the objectivity but not the competence of the internal auditors. The employment of relatives of internal auditors in audit-sensitive positions relates their objectivity.

3. A) The independent auditor should perform this procedure to test the competence and objectivity of the internal auditors. Evidence from a recent external quality review of the internal auditors provides information about both objectivity and competence.

4. B) The independent auditor should perform this procedure to test the competence but not the objectivity of the internal auditors. Evaluating audit plans and procedures used by the internal auditors provides information about their competence.

5. D) The auditor would not perform this procedure. The personal financial statements of the internal auditors would not be evaluated by the auditor.

6. C) The independent auditor should perform this procedure to test the objectivity but not the competence of the internal auditors. Having direct access to the board of directors by the internal auditors relates to their objectivity.

7. B) The independent auditor should perform this procedure to test the competence but not the objectivity of the internal auditors. The professional certification of the internal auditors relates to their competence.

8. B) The independent auditor should perform this procedure to test the competence but not the objectivity of the internal auditors. The continuing education programs provided to the internal auditors relate to their competence.

9. A) The independent auditor should perform this procedure to test the competence and objectivity of the internal auditors. Information from previous audits about the activities of internal auditors relates to both objectivity and competence.

10. D) The auditor would not perform this procedure. Considering whether the internal auditors are well paid would not be performed by the auditor.

Gleim Simulation Grading

Task	Correct Responses		Gradable Items		Score per Task
1 (Research)	___	÷	1	=	___
2	___	÷	10	=	___
3	___	÷	8	=	___
4	___	÷	5	=	___
5	___	÷	10	=	___

Total of Scores per Task		___
÷ Total Number of Tasks		5
Total Score		___ %

Use **CPA Gleim Online** and **Simulation Wizard** to practice more task-based simulations in a realistic environment.

STUDY UNIT FIVE
INTERNAL CONTROL CONCEPTS
AND INFORMATION TECHNOLOGY

(16 pages of outline)

Concepts related to the client's internal control are tested extensively. AU-C 315, *Understanding the Entity and its Environment and Assessing the Risks of Material Misstatement*, provides the basis for consideration of this topic. Emphasis also is placed on technology in the standards. Accordingly, this study unit contains definitions and concepts of great significance for exam preparation. Many of these were developed in the report of the Committee of Sponsoring Organizations of the Treadway Commission **(the COSO report)** and are reflected in AU-C 315 and other AICPA pronouncements.

Because of the Sarbanes-Oxley Act of 2002, control concepts are crucially important to entities subject to the Securities Exchange Act of 1934. PCAOB AS No. 12, *Identifying and Assessing Risks of Material Misstatement*, requires consideration of internal control in a financial statement audit. Moreover, certain issuers ("accelerated filers" with $75 million in market equity) must include in their annual reports an assessment by management of whether internal control over financial reporting is effective. The auditor is required to attest to the effectiveness of internal control as part of the overall audit. However, PCAOB AS No. 5 requires the auditor merely to express or disclaim an opinion on internal control, not on management's assessment of internal control.

The general concepts described in this study unit are applied specifically in the transaction processing cycles considered in Study Units 6 and 7. CPA candidates should master the material in this study unit before continuing.

5.1 INTRODUCTION TO INTERNAL CONTROL

1. **Objective of the Auditor**

   a. The objective of the auditor is to identify and assess the **risks of material misstatement** (RMMs), whether due to fraud or error, at the financial statement and relevant assertion levels. This objective is achieved through understanding the entity and its environment, including the entity's internal control, to provide a basis for designing and implementing responses to the assessed RMMs.

      1) A relevant assertion has a reasonable possibility of containing a misstatement that could cause a material misstatement(s) of the financial statements. Thus, a relevant assertion has a meaningful bearing on whether the account is fairly stated.

2. **Definition of Internal Control**

   a. Internal control is a process–effected by those charged with governance, management, and other personnel–designed to provide reasonable assurance regarding the achievement of objectives related to the following:

      1) Reliability of financial reporting
      2) Effectiveness and efficiency of operations
      3) Compliance with applicable laws and regulations

3.   **Components of Internal Control**

a.   Auditing standards (and the COSO's internal control framework) define the following five interrelated components (a useful memory aid is "Controls stop **CRIME**," with E representing the control environment):

1)   **Control activities** are the policies and procedures that help ensure that management directives are carried out.

2)   The **risk assessment process** is the entity's identification and analysis of relevant risks.

3)   The **information system**, including related and relevant business processes, supports the identification, capture, and exchange of information in a form and time frame that enable people to carry out their responsibilities.

4)   **Monitoring of controls** assesses the effectiveness of internal control over time.

5)   The **control environment** sets the tone of an organization, influencing the control consciousness of its people.

4.   **Relevant Controls**

a.   The relationship between an entity's objectives and the components is direct. Moreover, internal control is relevant to the whole entity (or any operating unit or business function).

b.   However, an entity generally has controls relating to objectives that are not relevant to an audit and need not be considered, for example, a computerized production scheduling system.

c.   Furthermore, understanding internal control relevant to each operating unit or business function may not be needed to perform an audit.

5.   **Inherent Limitations of Internal Control**

a.   Because of its inherent limitations, internal control can be designed and operated to provide only **reasonable assurance** that the entity's objectives are met.

b.   Human judgment is faulty, and controls may fail because of human error. For example, design changes for an automated order entry system may be faulty because the designers did not understand the system or because programmers did not correctly code the design changes. Errors also may arise when automated reports are misinterpreted by users.

c.   Manual or automated controls can be circumvented by collusion.

d.   Management may inappropriately override internal control.

e.   Custom, culture, the corporate governance system, and an effective control environment are not absolute deterrents to fraud. For example, if the nature of management incentives increases the RMMs, the effectiveness of controls may be reduced.

f.   An inherent limitation of an audit as well as internal control is the need to balance benefit and cost. Although the ability to provide only reasonable assurance is a primary design criterion for internal control, the precise measurement of costs and benefits is not feasible.

1)   However, costs should not exceed the benefits of control. Thus, the cost constraint limits internal control.

Stop and review! You have completed the outline for this subunit. Study multiple-choice questions 1 through 4 beginning on page 183.

5.2 INTERNAL CONTROL COMPONENTS

1. **Control Environment**

   a. This component is the foundation for the other components. It provides discipline and structure and sets the tone of the organization. To understand the control environment, the auditor considers programs and controls addressing **fraud risk** that have been implemented by management and those charged with governance. Their absence or inadequacy may be a material weakness. The evaluation of the design of the control environment includes the following factors:

      1) Communication and enforcement of **integrity and ethical values.** These are essential elements of the control environment and influence the effectiveness of the other components. Standards should be effectively communicated, e.g., by management example. Management also should remove incentives and temptations for dishonest or unethical acts.

      2) **Commitment to competence.** Management must consider the competence levels for particular jobs.

      3) **Participation of those charged with governance** (board of directors, audit committee, etc.). Their independence, experience, and stature are among the qualities that affect the entity's control consciousness.

      4) **Management's philosophy and operating style.** They relate to management's approach to taking and managing business risks. They also relate to management's attitudes and actions toward (a) financial reporting, (b) information processing, (c) accounting functions, and (d) personnel.

      5) **Organizational structure.** Key areas of authority and responsibility and appropriate lines of reporting should be considered. The organizational structure is depicted by an organizational chart. (This chart is presented in Study Unit 6 on page 200.)

      6) **Assignment of authority and responsibility.** This factor concerns how authority over and responsibility for operating activities are assigned and how reporting relationships and authorization hierarchies are established.

      7) **Human resource policies and practices.** These relate to recruitment, orientation, training, evaluation, counseling, promotion, compensation, and remedial action. Training policies should communicate roles, responsibilities, and expected levels of performance and behavior.

2. **Risk Assessment Process**

   a. Relevant risks include events and circumstances that may adversely affect an entity's ability to initiate, authorize, record, process, and report financial data consistent with financial statement assertions. The following factors affecting risk should be considered:

      1) **Changes in operating environment.** A shift in the regulatory or operating environment may require reconsideration of risks.

      2) **New personnel.** New employees may have a different focus on control issues.

      3) **New or revamped information systems.** Automated systems are important to the risk assessment process because they provide timely information for identifying and managing risks. However, significant and rapid changes in information systems themselves may affect risk.

      4) **Rapid growth.** Significant and rapid expansion may strain controls and increase risk.

      5) **New technology.** Integrating new technology into production or information processes may change risk.

      6) **New business models, products, or activities.** Inexperience with respect to new business areas or transactions may change risk.

7) **Corporate restructurings.** Staffing and supervision changes may change risk.

8) **Expanded foreign operations.** Expansion to foreign markets may result in changes in risk, for example, from changes in currency exchange rates.

9) **New accounting pronouncements.** Adoption or changes of principles may affect risk in statement preparation.

10) **Changes in economic conditions.** Economic change can stress an organization.

3. **Control Activities**

a. These are the policies and procedures helping to ensure that management's directives are followed. Whether automated or manual, they have various objectives and are applied at various levels.

1) **Authorization** should ensure that only valid transactions are initiated.

2) **Performance reviews** include comparisons of actual performance with budgets and prior performance.

3) **Information processing** requires checks of accuracy, completeness, and authorization of transactions. These controls include general controls and application controls.

4) **Physical controls** involve the physical security of assets, authorization of access, periodic counts, and reconciliations to create asset accountability.

5) **Segregation of duties** involves the separation of the functions of authorization, recordkeeping, and asset custody. The effect should be to minimize the opportunities for a person to be able to perpetrate and conceal fraud or errors in the normal course of his/her duties.

4. **Information Systems**

a. An information system, including the related and relevant business processes, consists of (1) physical and hardware elements (infrastructure), (2) people, (3) software, (4) data, and (5) manual and automated procedures. It often is used extensively.

b. For financial reporting, the information system (including the accounting system) encompasses automated and manual procedures and records used to initiate, authorize, record, process, and report transactions, events, and conditions and to maintain accountability for assets, liabilities, and equity.

1) Initiation may be automatic through programmed methods. Authorizing is management's approval process. Recording includes identification and capture of relevant information. Processing involves edit and validation, calculation, measurement, valuation, summarization, and reconciliation by manual or automated means. Reporting of financial and other information for use in, for example, the monitoring function, may be in a print or electronic medium.

c. An **information system**

1) Identifies and records all valid transactions,
2) Describes transactions sufficiently for proper classification,
3) Measures transactions,
4) Determines the proper reporting period for transactions, and
5) Presents transactions and related disclosures properly.

d. **Communication** includes providing an understanding to employees about their roles and responsibilities. For example, communication may be through policy manuals, financial reporting manuals, and memoranda. It also may be by electronic and oral means or by management actions.

5.   **Monitoring of Controls**

a.   Monitoring is management's timely assessment of internal control and the taking of corrective action so that controls operate as intended and are modified for changes in conditions. Establishing and maintaining internal control is **management's responsibility**.

b.   The monitoring process involves the following:

1)   Ongoing activities built into normal recurring actions such as supervision, possibly combined with separate evaluations

2)   The actions of internal auditors

3)   Consideration of communications from external parties

c.   Monitoring information may be produced by the information system. Hence, the auditor should obtain sufficient knowledge about major monitoring activities, including the sources of related information and the basis for considering it to be reliable.

Stop and review! You have completed the outline for this subunit. Study multiple-choice questions 5 through 11 beginning on page 184.

5.3 UNDERSTANDING INTERNAL CONTROL

1.   In all audits, the auditor should obtain an understanding of the five components of internal control to identify and assess the RMMs and to design further audit procedures. An understanding is obtained by performing **risk assessment procedures** to evaluate the design of controls relevant to the audit and determine whether they have been implemented.

a.   Implemented at a moment in time differs from operating effectiveness over a period of time.

b.   However, the auditor is not obligated to search for deficiencies in internal control, although (s)he must communicate any significant deficiencies and material weaknesses noted.

2.   The risk assessment should determine whether any identified risks are significant risks, i.e., require special audit consideration. This judgment is made without regard to related controls but should address at least the following factors:

a.   Whether risks of fraud or significant transactions with related parties are involved

b.   Whether the risks relate to significant transactions outside the normal course of business (or that are otherwise unusual) or to significant recent developments

c.   The complexity of the transactions or the subjectivity of the measurements

3.   The understanding should be used to

a.   Identify types of potential misstatements,

b.   Consider factors that affect the RMMs,

c.   Design tests of controls if appropriate, and

d.   Design substantive procedures.

4.   **Accounting Policies**

a.   The auditor should obtain an understanding of the selection and application of accounting policies and consider whether they are appropriate. This understanding includes the following:

1)   Significant and unusual transactions

2)   Significant policies applied when controversial or emerging areas lack guidance or consensus

3)   Changes in policies

4)   Adoption of new reporting standards, laws, and regulations

5.   **Relevant Controls**

a.   Relevant controls ordinarily address the entity's objectives related to the preparation of fairly presented financial statements, including management of RMMs.

1)   But assessing all such controls is not necessary, and the auditor should use professional judgment regarding what should be assessed.

b.   The auditor determines whether a control is relevant by considering factors such as the following:

1)   The control component
2)   The circumstances
3)   Materiality
4)   The size of the entity
5)   The nature of the business, including organizational and ownership characteristics
6)   The diversity and complexity of operations
7)   The nature and complexity of control systems, including the use of service organizations
8)   Legal and regulatory concerns
9)   The significance of the related risk

c.   Controls over the **completeness and accuracy** of information used by the auditor are relevant if the auditor intends to use it.

d.   **Identifying** relevant controls is facilitated by

1)   Previous experience with the entity,
2)   The understanding of the entity and its environment, and
3)   Information gathered during the audit.

e.   Controls over **operations and compliance** may be relevant if they relate to information or data involved in performance of audit procedures.

1)   Examples are controls related to (a) nonfinancial data used in analytical procedures or (b) noncompliance with laws and regulations having a direct effect on the determination of material amounts in the statements.

f.   Controls over **safeguarding of assets** against unauthorized acquisition, use, or disposition may include those relating to financial reporting and operations objectives.

1)   But the auditor's consideration is usually limited to **controls relevant to financial reporting**, such as controls that limit access to the data and programs (e.g., passwords) that process cash payments.

6.   **Design and Implementation**

a.   The **evaluation of design** considers whether a control (alone or with others) can effectively prevent, or detect and correct, material misstatements.

b.   A control has been **implemented** if it exists and the entity is using it.

1)   An auditor may decide not to consider implementation if the design is improper.

a)   An improper design may be a **material weakness** in internal control that the auditor should communicate to management and those charged with governance.

7.   **Risk Assessment Procedures**

a.   Risk assessment procedures performed to obtain evidence about the design and implementation of relevant controls include (1) inquiries, (2) observation of the application of specific controls, (3) inspection of documents and reports, and (4) tracing transactions.

1)   Inquiries alone are not sufficient.

8. **Operating Effectiveness**

   a. Obtaining the understanding is insufficient to test the operating effectiveness of controls, unless they are automated and subject to effective general IT controls (e.g., software acquisition, access, and change controls).

   b. Operating effectiveness is concerned with how and by whom the control (manual or automated) was applied and the consistency of application.

9. **Understanding IT-Based Systems**

   a. IT skills may be required to (1) determine the effect of IT on the audit, (2) understand IT controls, and (3) design and perform tests of IT controls and substantive procedures.

   b. These skills may be obtained from an audit staff member or an outside professional.

      1) Whether a professional is needed depends on such factors as (a) the complexity of systems and IT controls, (b) their use in the business, (c) the extent of data sharing among systems, (d) implementation of new systems or changes in old ones, (e) the involvement in electronic commerce, (f) use of emerging technologies, and (g) audit evidence available only electronically.

      2) An outside professional may make inquiries of the entity's IT personnel, inspect documentation, observe operation of controls, and test IT controls.

      3) The auditor must have sufficient IT expertise to (a) communicate audit objectives, (b) evaluate whether the IT professional's procedures will meet those objectives, and (c) evaluate the results.

   c. The auditor should understand the **information system relevant to financial reporting**, that is, (1) the classes of significant transactions; (2) the automated and manual procedures used to initiate, authorize, record, process, and report transactions; (3) the related accounting records, supporting information, and specific accounts; (4) how the system captures other significant events and conditions; and (5) the financial reporting process, including significant accounting estimates and disclosures.

      1) Thus, the auditor should understand not only the manual procedures but also the IT systems, programs, and controls in the financial reporting process.

10. **Documentation**

   a. Documentation of the understanding is required by GAAS. It includes the following:

      1) Discussions among team members about the susceptibility of the statements to material misstatement and the application of the reporting framework

      2) The understanding of the entity and its environment and each control component, the sources of information, and the risk assessment procedures performed

      3) The assessed RMMs at the financial statement and relevant assertion levels

      4) The significant risks identified and related controls evaluated requiring special audit consideration

   b. The form and extent of documentation are influenced by the nature and complexity of the controls. For example, a complex information system that electronically initiates, authorizes, records, processes, and reports a large volume of transactions requires extensive documentation.

      1) Accordingly, flowcharts, questionnaires, or decision tables may be appropriate for a complex information system, but a memorandum may suffice when little or no use is made of IT or few transactions are processed. In general, the more complex the controls and the more extensive the audit procedures, the more extensive the documentation.

c. **Systems (document) flowcharts** are diagrams of the client's system that track the flow of documents and processing. Advantages are that they provide a visual representation of the system and are flexible in construction. Flowcharts are introduced in Subunit 5.4 and are illustrated in Study Units 6 and 7.

d. **Questionnaires** consist of a series of interrelated questions about internal control policies and procedures. The questions are typically phrased so that a "Yes" indicates a control strength and a "No" indicates a potential weakness. An area is provided next to the responses for the auditor to explain the responses or cross-reference the answer with other working papers.

    1) An advantage of the questionnaire is that it helps identify control issues.

e. A **narrative memorandum** is a written description of the process and flow of documents and of the control points. Its advantage is flexibility. However, following the flow from the narrative may be difficult for a complex system.

f. A **decision table** identifies the contingencies considered in the description of a problem and the appropriate actions to be taken in each case. Decision tables are logic diagrams presented in matrix form. Unlike flowcharts, they do not present the sequence of the actions described.

g. A **checklist** consists of a series of procedures to be performed.

Stop and review! You have completed the outline for this subunit. Study multiple-choice questions 12 through 18 beginning on page 186.

5.4 FLOWCHARTING

Flowcharting is a topic that many CPA candidates try to avoid. However, you should realize that flowcharting is just another auditor's tool. The good news is that it is improbable that you will be required to construct a flowchart. Any questions that you may get will likely require you to interpret a flowchart. Keep an open mind as you begin using the flowcharts in Study Units 6 and 7. Spend enough time to understand the general flow of information and documents. You will likely surprise yourself with the confidence you gain.

1. Flowcharting is a useful tool for systems development as well as for understanding internal control. A flowchart is a pictorial diagram of the definition, analysis, or solution of a problem in which symbols are used to represent operations, data flow, documents, records, etc.

a. The processing is presented sequentially from the point of origin to the distribution of final output.

    1) Processing usually flows from top to bottom and from left to right in the flowchart.

b. A **system flowchart** provides an overall view of the inputs, processes, and outputs of a system.

c. A **program flowchart** represents the specific steps in a computer program and the order in which they will be carried out.

    1) Macro- and microflowcharts describe a program in less or greater detail, respectively.

d. A **document flowchart** depicts the flow of documents through an entity.

    1) Areas of responsibility (e.g., data processing or purchasing) are usually depicted in vertical columns or areas.

2. Flowcharts are used to understand, evaluate, and document client internal control. Many CPA questions address flowcharting itself. Other CPA questions address specific controls, audit procedures, weaknesses, etc., that are related to or are a part of internal control.

3. Commonly used document flowchart symbols include

Starting or ending point or point of interruption

Input or output of a document or report

Computer operation or group of operations

Manual processing operation, e.g., prepare document

Generalized symbol for input or output used when the medium is not specified

Magnetic tape used for input or output

Magnetic disk used for storage

Decision symbol indicating a branch in the flow

Connection between points on the same page

Connection between two pages of the flowchart

Storage (file) that is not immediately accessible by computer

Flow direction of data or processing

Display on a video terminal

Manual input into a terminal or other online device

Adding machine tape (batch control)

Figure 5-1

Stop and review! You have completed the outline for this subunit. Study multiple-choice questions 19 through 22 beginning on page 188.

5.5 INTERNAL CONTROL AND INFORMATION TECHNOLOGY

 The material included in this section overlaps with the Information Systems and Communications category representing 15% to 19% of the Business Environment and Concepts (BEC) section of the exam. We have attempted to include here those issues that are more likely to be tested on the Auditing and Attestation section of the exam. However, if you have studied for BEC, many issues should be familiar. If you have not yet studied for BEC, the following will be a good introduction to that material.

1. The objectives of a business information system are the same regardless of whether it is manual or computer-based. The risks, on the other hand, can be quite different.

   a. **System availability.** The ability to make use of any computer-based system is dependent on the following:

      1) An uninterrupted flow of electricity
      2) Protection of computer hardware from environmental hazards (e.g., fire and water)
      3) Protection of software and data files from unauthorized alteration
      4) Preservation of functioning communications channels among devices

   b. **Volatile transaction trails.** In any computer-based environment, a complete trail useful for audit purposes might exist for only a short time or in only computer-readable form. In online, real-time systems, data are entered directly into the computer, eliminating portions of the audit trail provided by source documents.

   c. **Decreased human involvement.** Because employees who enter transactions may never see the "final results," the potential for detecting errors is reduced. Also, output from a computer system often carries a mystique of infallibility, reducing the incentive of system users to closely examine reports and transaction logs.

   d. **Uniform processing of transactions.** Computer processing uniformly subjects like transactions to the same processing instructions, therefore virtually eliminating clerical error. Thus, it permits consistent application of predefined business rules and the performance of complex calculations in high volume.

      1) However, programming errors (or other similar systematic errors in either the hardware or software) will result in all like transactions being processed incorrectly.

   e. **Unauthorized access.** When accounting records were kept in pen-and-ink format, physical access to them was the only way to carry out an alteration. Once they are computer-based, however, access can be carried out from multiple work stations throughout the organization or from anywhere in the world by determined hackers using the Internet.

      1) Thus, security measures, such as firewalls and user identification-and-password combinations, are vital to maintaining security over data in an automated environment.

   f. **Data vulnerability.** Destruction of hardware devices or units of storage media could have disastrous consequences if they contain the only copies of crucial data files or application programs.

      1) For this reason, it is vital that an organization's computer files be duplicated and stored offsite periodically.

   g. **Reduced segregation of duties.** Many functions once performed by separate individuals may be combined in an automated environment.

EXAMPLE

Receiving cash, issuing a receipt to the payor, preparing the deposit slip, and preparing the journal entry may once have been performed by separate individuals. In a computer-based system, the receipt, deposit slip, and journal entry may be automatically generated by the computer. If the same employee who receives the cash is also responsible for entering the relevant data into the system, the potential for fraud or error is increased.

---

h. **Reduced individual authorization of transactions.** Certain transactions may be initiated automatically by a computer-based system. This is becoming ever more widespread as an increasing number of business processes become automated.

EXAMPLE

An enterprise resource planning system at a manufacturing concern may automatically generate a purchase order when raw materials inventory reaches a certain level. If the company shares an EDI system with the vendor, the purchase order may be sent to the vendor electronically without any human intervention.

---

    1) This reduced level of oversight for individual transactions requires careful coding to ensure that computer programs accurately reflect management's objectives for business processes.

2. **Two Basic Processing Modes of Data**

    a. **Batch processing.** In this mode, transactions are accumulated and submitted to the computer as a single batch. In the early days of computers, this was the only way a job could be processed.

        1) In batch processing, the user cannot influence the process once the job has begun (except to ask that it be aborted completely). (S)he must wait until processing is complete to see whether any transactions in the batch were rejected and not processed.

        2) Despite huge advances in computer technology, this accumulation of transactions for processing on a delayed basis is still widely used. It is very efficient for applications (e.g., payroll) that must process large numbers of routine transactions on a regular schedule.

    b. **Online, real-time processing.** In some systems, having the latest information available at all times is crucial to the proper functioning of the system. An airline reservation system is a common example.

        1) In an online, real-time system, the database is updated immediately upon entry of the transaction by the operator. Such systems are **online transaction processing (OLTP)** systems.

3. The two broad groupings of information systems control activities are **general controls** and **application controls**.

    a. General controls are the umbrella under which the IT function operates. Because they affect the organization's entire processing environment, the auditor should achieve satisfaction about their proper operation before relying on application controls. They commonly include controls over (1) data center and network operations; (2) systems software acquisition, change, and maintenance; (3) access security; and (4) application system acquisition, development, and maintenance.

        1) Controls over data center and network **operations** ensure efficient and effective operations of the computer activity. These include aspects of the control environment and risk assessment.

        2) Controls over **software acquisition, change, and maintenance** ensure that proper software is available for use.

        3) Controls over **access** encompass access to both computer hardware devices themselves (physical access) and to data and programs through the system (logical access).

b.   Application controls are particular to each of the organization's applications. Some features come built-in when applications are acquired from vendors. Software developed by the organization's own programmers must have appropriate controls incorporated in the design. Application controls may be further classified as follows:

1)   **Input controls** provide reasonable assurance that (a) data received for processing have been identified, properly authorized, and converted into machine-sensible form, and (b) data (including data transmitted over communication lines) have not been lost, added to, suppressed, duplicated, or otherwise improperly changed. Input controls also relate to rejection, correction, and resubmission of initially incorrect data.

2)   **Processing controls** provide reasonable assurance that processing has been performed as intended for the particular application. Thus, (a) all transactions should be processed as authorized, (b) no authorized transactions should be omitted, and (c) no unauthorized transactions should be added.

3)   **Output controls** ensure the accuracy of the processing result (such as account listings, reports, files, invoices, or disbursement checks) and the receipt of output by authorized personnel only.

c.   Both categories of controls are discussed in greater detail in the rest of this subunit.

4.   **General Controls -- Controls over Operations**

a.   From an audit perspective, the most significant of these general controls is the assignment of **authority and responsibility**.

1)   **Segregation of duties** is vital because a separation of functions (authorization, recording, and access to assets) may not be feasible in an IT environment. For example, a computer may print checks, record disbursements, and generate information for reconciling the account balance. These activities customarily are segregated in a manual system.

2)   The following are typical jobs within the IT function:

a)   **Database administrators (DBAs)** are responsible for developing and maintaining the organization's databases and for establishing controls to protect their integrity.

b)   **Network technicians** maintain the bridges, hubs, routers, switches, cabling, and other devices that connect the organization's computers. They are also responsible for maintaining the organization's connection to other networks, such as the Internet.

c)   The **webmaster** is responsible for the content of the organization's website. (S)he works closely with programmers and network technicians to ensure that the appropriate content is displayed and that the site is reliably available to users.

d)   **Computer (console) operators** are responsible for the moment-to-moment running of the organization's medium- and large-scale computers, i.e., servers and mainframes.

i)   Computers in this size range, unlike desktop computers, require 24-hour monitoring. Operators respond to messages received from the system by consulting run manuals that detail the steps for processing.

e)   **Librarians** maintain control over and accountability for documentation, programs, and data storage media.

f)   **Systems programmers** maintain and fine-tune the operating systems on the organization's medium- and large-scale computers. The operating system is the core software that performs a computer's basic tasks.

g) A **systems analyst** uses his/her detailed knowledge of the organization's databases and applications programs to determine how an application should be designed to best serve the user's needs.

   i) These duties are often combined with those of programmers. **Applications programmers** design, write, test, and document computer programs according to specifications provided by the end users.

h) **Help desk** personnel log problems reported by users, resolve minor difficulties, and forward more difficult problems to the appropriate person, such as a database administrator or the webmaster. Help desk personnel are often called on to resolve such issues as the crashing of desktop computers or problems with email.

b. **Periodic backup and offsite rotation** of computer files is the most basic part of any disaster recovery/business continuity plan.

   1) A **typical backup routine** involves duplicating all data files and application programs at least once a month. Incremental changes are then backed up and stored in an offsite location periodically, often once a week. (Application files must be backed up in addition to data because programs also are changed.)

   2) The **offsite location** must be temperature- and humidity-controlled and guarded against physical intrusion. Just as important, it must be geographically remote enough from the site of the organization's main operations that it will not be affected by the same natural disaster. Adequate backup files are useless if they are not accessible or have been destroyed.

   3) **Fully protected systems** have generator or battery backup to prevent data destruction and downtime from electrical power disturbances.

   4) **Fault-tolerant computer systems** have additional hardware and software as well as a backup power supply.

   5) **Hot-site and cold-site backup facilities.** A hot site is a fully operational processing facility that is immediately available (e.g., a service bureau). A cold site is a shell facility where the user can quickly install equipment.

c. Protection against Malicious Software (Malware)

   1) **Virus protection.** A virus is a software program that infects another program or a system's primary storage (main memory) by altering its logic. Infection often results in the destruction of data. Once infected, a software program can spread the virus to other software programs. Obtaining software through a shareware network or by downloading from untrustworthy sources is a typical cause of infection. Propagation of viruses through email attachments is also common.

   2) To protect against viruses, three types of controls should be implemented:

      a) **Preventive controls** include (1) establishing a formal security policy, (2) using only clean and certified copies of software, (3) not using shareware software, (4) checking new software with antivirus software, (5) restricting access, and (6) educating users.

      b) **Detective controls** include making file size and date/time stamp comparisons.

      c) **Corrective controls** include ensuring that clean backup is maintained and having a documented plan for recovery from a virus.

   3) **Worms** are viruses that make copies of themselves with either benign or malignant intent. They ordinarily exist as independent programs and use operating system services as their means of replication.

   4) A **Trojan horse** is software that appears to have a legitimate function but performs some destructive or illicit function after it begins to run.

    d.   Network Security

        1)   **Local area networks (LANs)** and **wide area networks (WANs)** are defined by the area over which they provide communications.

        2)   **Intranets and extranets** are defined by who has access. An intranet is a network based on the same technology (connectivity standards and web software) as the Internet, but access is limited to an organization or those with specific authorization. An extranet provides web access for existing customers or specific users rather than the general public.

        3)   The most important control is to install an entity-wide network security system. **User account management** involves installing a system to ensure that

            a)   New accounts are added correctly and assigned only to authorized users.

            b)   Old and unused accounts are removed promptly.

            c)   **Passwords** are changed periodically, and employees are taught how to choose a password that cannot be easily guessed.

        4)   **Internet security.** Connection to the Internet presents security issues.

            a)   A **firewall** separates an internal from an external network (e.g., the Internet) and prevents passage of specific types of traffic. It identifies names, Internet Protocol (IP) addresses, applications, etc., and compares them with programmed access rules.

            b)   Firewall systems ordinarily produce reports on entity-wide Internet use, exception reports for unusual activity patterns, and system penetration-attempt reports. These reports are very helpful to the auditor as a method of continuous monitoring, or logging, of the system.

                i)   Firewalls do not provide adequate protection against viruses. Thus, an entity should include one or more of the virus controls listed in its network security policy.

        5)   **Digital signatures** are a form of **encryption** technology used by businesses to authenticate documents. A plaintext document is sent with an encrypted portion of the same document over the Internet. If the plaintext document is tampered with, the two will not match.

5.   **General Controls -- Controls over Software Acquisition, Change, and Maintenance**

    a.   **Controls over systems software** ensure that operating systems, utilities, and database management systems are acquired and changed only under close supervision and that vendor updates are routinely installed.

    b.   **Controls over application software** ensure that programs used for transaction processing (e.g., payroll and accounts receivable) are cost-effective and stable.

    c.   These **change controls** require proper authorization, testing, and acceptance. All changes should be properly documented.

6.   **General Controls -- Access Controls**

    a.   Access controls prevent improper use or manipulation of data files and programs. They ensure that only those persons with a bona fide purpose and authorization have access.

    b.   Physical security controls protect against unauthorized access to equipment and information.

    c.   **Passwords and ID numbers.** The use of passwords and identification numbers (for example, a PIN used for an ATM) is an effective control in an online system to prevent unauthorized access to files. Lists of authorized persons are maintained online. To avoid unauthorized access, the entity may combine (1) the entry of passwords or identification numbers; (2) a prearranged set of personal questions; and (3) the use of badges, magnetic cards, or optically scanned cards.

d. **Device authorization table.** This control grants access only to those physical devices that should logically need access. For example, because it is illogical for anyone to access the accounts receivable file from a manufacturing terminal, the device authorization table will deny access even when a valid password is used.

e. **System access log.** This log records all uses and attempted uses of the system. The date and time, codes used, mode of access, data involved, and interventions by operators are recorded.

f. **Encryption.** Encoding data before transmission over communication lines makes it more difficult for someone with access to the transmission to understand or modify its contents. Encryption technology converts data into a code. Unauthorized users may still be able to access the data but, without the encryption key, will be unable to decode the information.

g. **Callback.** This feature requires the remote user to call, give identification, hang up, and wait for a call to an authorized number. This control ensures acceptance of data only from authorized modems. However, a call-forwarding device may thwart this control by transferring access from an authorized to an unauthorized number.

h. **Controlled disposal of documents.** One method of enforcing access restrictions is to destroy data when they are no longer in use. Thus, paper documents may be shredded, and magnetic media may be erased.

i. **Biometric technologies.** These are automated methods of establishing an individual's identity using physiological or behavioral traits. These characteristics include fingerprints, retina patterns, hand geometry, signature dynamics, speech, and keystroke dynamics.

j. **Automatic log-off** (disconnection) of inactive data terminals may prevent the viewing of sensitive data on an unattended work station.

k. **Security personnel.** An entity may hire security specialists. For example, (1) developing an information security policy for the entity, (2) commenting on security controls in new applications, and (3) monitoring and investigating unsuccessful access attempts are appropriate duties of the information security officer.

7. **Application Controls -- Input**

a. **Input controls** provide reasonable assurance that data submitted for processing are (1) authorized, (2) complete, and (3) accurate. These controls vary depending on whether input is entered in online or batch mode.

b. **Online input controls** can be used when data are keyed into an input screen.

1) **Preformatting.** The data entry screen mimics a hardcopy document, forcing data entry in all necessary fields.

2) **Edit (field) checks.** The data entry screen prevents certain types of incorrect data from entering the system. For example, the system rejects any attempt to enter numerals in the Name box or letters in the Amount box. Dropdown menus can restrict the user's choices to only valid selections.

3) **Limit (reasonableness) checks.** Certain amounts can be restricted to appropriate ranges, such as hours worked being limited to less than 10 per day or invoices over $100,000 requiring supervisor approval.

4) **Check digits.** An algorithm is applied to any kind of serial identifier to derive a check digit. During data entry, the check digit is recomputed by the system to ensure proper entry.

5) **Closed-loop verification.** Inputs by a user are transmitted to the computer, processed, and displayed back to the user for verification.

c.   **Batch input controls** can be used when data are grouped for processing.

   1)   **Management release.** A batch is not released for processing until a manager reviews and approves it.

   2)   **Record count.** A batch is not released for processing unless the number of records in the batch, as reported by the system, matches the number calculated by the user.

   3)   **Financial total.** A batch is not released for processing unless the sum of the dollar amounts of the individual items as reported by the system matches the amount calculated by the user.

   4)   **Hash total.** The arithmetic sum of a numeric field, which has no meaning by itself, can serve as a check that the same records that should have been processed were processed. An example is the sum of all Social Security numbers.

      a)   This number is much too unwieldy to be calculated by the user. But once it is calculated by the system, it can follow the batch through subsequent stages of processing.

8.   **Application Controls -- Processing**

   a.   Processing controls provide reasonable assurance that (1) all data submitted for processing are processed, and (2) only approved data are processed. These controls are built into the application code by programmers during the systems development process.

   b.   Some processing controls repeat the steps performed by the **input controls**, such as limit checks and batch controls.

   c.   **Validation.** Identifiers are matched against master files to determine existence. For example, any accounts payable transaction in which the vendor number does not match a number on the vendor master file is rejected.

   d.   **Completeness.** Any record with missing data is rejected.

   e.   **Arithmetic controls.** Cross-footing compares an amount with the sum of its components. Zero-balance checking adds the debits and credits in a transaction or batch to ensure that their sum is zero.

   f.   **Sequence check.** Computer effort is expended most efficiently when data are processed in a logical order, such as by customer number. This check ensures the batch is sorted in the proper order before processing begins.

   g.   **Run-to-run control totals.** The controls associated with a given batch are checked after each stage of processing to ensure all transactions have been processed.

   h.   **Key integrity.** A record's key is the group of values in designated fields that uniquely identify the record. No application process should be able to alter the data in these key fields.

9.   **Application Controls -- Output**

   a.   **Output controls** provide assurance that processing was complete and accurate.

   b.   A complete **audit trail** should be generated by each process: batch number, time of submission, time of completion, number of records in batch, total dollars in batch, number of records rejected, total dollars rejected, etc.

   1)   The audit trail is immediately submitted to a **reasonableness check** by the user, who is most qualified to judge the adequacy of processing and the proper treatment of erroneous transactions.

   c.   **Error listings** report all transactions rejected by the system. These should be corrected and resubmitted by the user.

Stop and review! You have completed the outline for this subunit. Study multiple-choice questions 23 through 33 beginning on page 190.

QUESTIONS

5.1 Introduction to Internal Control

1. The primary objective of procedures performed to obtain an understanding of internal control is to provide an auditor with

    A. Knowledge necessary for audit planning.

    B. Evidence to use in assessing inherent risk.

    C. A basis for modifying tests of controls.

    D. An evaluation of the consistency of application of management's policies.

Answer (A) is correct.
    REQUIRED: The objective of procedures performed to obtain an understanding of internal control.
    DISCUSSION: The auditor is required to obtain an understanding of the entity and its environment, including its internal control, to assess the risks of material misstatement of the financial statements, whether due to fraud or error, to provide a basis for responding to the assessed RMMs. The auditor obtains the understanding and assesses the RMMs to plan the audit. The audit plan describes (1) the risk assessment procedures, (2) further audit procedures at the assertion level, and (3) other procedures required by GAAS.
    Answer (B) is incorrect. Inherent risk is independent of internal control. Answer (C) is incorrect. The understanding is obtained to plan all aspects of the audit, not merely tests of controls. Answer (D) is incorrect. Evaluating the consistency of application of management's policies is a test of controls.

2. An auditor uses the knowledge provided by the understanding of internal control and the assessed risks of material misstatement primarily to

    A. Determine whether procedures and records concerning the safeguarding of assets are reliable.

    B. Determine whether the opportunities to allow any person to both perpetrate and conceal fraud are minimized.

    C. Modify the initial assessments of inherent risk and judgments about materiality levels for planning purposes.

    D. Determine the nature, timing, and extent of substantive procedures for financial statement assertions.

Answer (D) is correct.
    REQUIRED: The auditor's purpose in understanding internal control and assessing the risks of material misstatement.
    DISCUSSION: The auditor is required to obtain an understanding of the entity and its environment, including its internal control, to assess the risks of material misstatement of the financial statements, whether due to fraud or error, to provide a basis for responding to the assessed RMMs. Regardless of the assessed RMMs, the auditor performs substantive procedures for all relevant assertions for material classes of transactions, account balances, and disclosures. Moreover, the auditor designs and performs further audit procedures whose nature, timing, and extent respond to the assessed RMMs at the relevant assertion level.
    Answer (A) is incorrect. Knowledge about operating effectiveness need not be obtained as part of the understanding of internal control. Answer (B) is incorrect. Knowledge about operating effectiveness need not be obtained as part of the understanding of internal control. Answer (C) is incorrect. Inherent risk and materiality are independent of internal control.

3. In an audit of financial statements, an auditor's primary consideration regarding an internal control is whether the control

    A. Reflects management's philosophy and operating style.

    B. Affects management's financial statement assertions.

    C. Provides adequate safeguards over access to assets.

    D. Relates to operational objectives.

Answer (B) is correct.
    REQUIRED: The auditor's primary consideration regarding an internal control.
    DISCUSSION: Assertions are management representations embodied in the financial statements. They are used by the auditor to consider the different potential misstatements. A relevant assertion has a reasonable possibility of containing a misstatement that could cause a material misstatement(s) of the financial statements. Thus, a relevant assertion has a meaningful bearing on whether the account is fairly stated. Tests of controls are designed to evaluate the operating effectiveness of controls in preventing, or detecting and correcting, material misstatements at the assertion level. They should be performed when (1) the auditor's assessment of the RMMs at the relevant assertion level includes an expectation of the operating effectiveness of controls, or (2) substantive procedures alone do not provide sufficient appropriate evidence at the relevant assertion level. Thus, the auditor is primarily concerned with whether a control affects relevant financial statement assertions.
    Answer (A) is incorrect. Management's philosophy and operating style is just one factor in one component (the control environment) of internal control. Answer (C) is incorrect. Restricting access to assets is only one of many physical controls, which constitute one element of one component (control activities) of internal control. Answer (D) is incorrect. Many controls relating to operational objectives are not relevant to an audit.

4. Which of the following most likely would **not** be considered an inherent limitation of the potential effectiveness of an entity's internal control?

    A. Incompatible duties.

    B. Management override.

    C. Faulty judgment.

    D. Collusion among employees.

Answer (A) is correct.
    REQUIRED: The item not considered an inherent limitation of internal control.
    DISCUSSION: Internal control has inherent limitations. The performance of incompatible duties, however, is a failure to assign different people the functions of authorization, recording, and asset custody, not an inevitable limitation of internal control. Segregation of duties is a category of control activities.
    Answer (B) is incorrect. Management establishes internal controls. Thus, it can override those controls. Answer (C) is incorrect. Human judgment in decision making may be faulty. Answer (D) is incorrect. Controls, whether manual or automated, may be circumvented by collusion among two or more people.

5.2 Internal Control Components

5. An auditor would most likely be concerned with controls that provide reasonable assurance about the

    A. Efficiency of management's decision-making process.

    B. Appropriate prices the entity should charge for its products.

    C. Decision to make expenditures for certain advertising activities.

    D. Entity's ability to initiate, authorize, record, process, and report financial data.

Answer (D) is correct.
    REQUIRED: The controls about which an auditor is most likely to be concerned.
    DISCUSSION: The information system relevant to financial reporting objectives, which includes the accounting system, consists of the procedures, whether automated or manual, and records established to initiate, authorize, record, process, and report entity transactions (as well as events and conditions) and to maintain accountability for the related assets, liabilities, and equity (AU-C 315).
    Answer (A) is incorrect. The efficiency of certain management decision-making processes is not likely to be relevant to a financial statement audit. Answer (B) is incorrect. Product pricing is not likely to be relevant to a financial statement audit. Answer (C) is incorrect. Decisions about advertising are not likely to be relevant to the auditor's consideration of controls.

6. Which of the following is a management control method that most likely could improve management's ability to supervise company activities effectively?

    A. Monitoring compliance with internal control requirements imposed by regulatory bodies.

    B. Limiting direct access to assets by physical segregation and protective devices.

    C. Establishing budgets and forecasts to identify variances from expectations.

    D. Supporting employees with the resources necessary to discharge their responsibilities.

Answer (C) is correct.
    REQUIRED: The management control method most likely to improve supervision.
    DISCUSSION: The control activities component of internal control includes performance reviews. Performance reviews involve comparison of actual performance with budgets, forecasts, or prior performance. Identifying variances alerts management to the need for investigative and corrective actions. Such actions are necessary for effective supervision.
    Answer (A) is incorrect. Management's supervisory responsibilities extend well beyond internal control requirements imposed by regulatory bodies. Answer (B) is incorrect. Access control pertains to the physical controls factor. Answer (D) is incorrect. Supporting employees concerns the human resource policies and practices factor of the control environment component.

7. Which of the following are considered control environment elements?

	Detection Risk	Commitment to Competence
A.	Yes	Yes
B.	Yes	No
C.	No	Yes
D.	No	No

Answer (C) is correct.
    REQUIRED: The element(s), if any, considered part of the control environment.
    DISCUSSION: Commitment to competence is a control environment element. It relates to the knowledge and skills needed to do the tasks included in a job and management's consideration of required competence levels.

8. Which of the following is **not** a component of internal control?

- A. Control risk.
- B. Monitoring of controls.
- C. Information system.
- D. The control environment.

Answer (A) is correct.
    REQUIRED: The item not a component of internal control.
    DISCUSSION: Control risk is one of the elements in the audit risk model. It is the risk that a material misstatement that could occur in an assertion will not be prevented, or detected and corrected, on a timely basis by the entity's internal control. Hence, control risk is a function of the effectiveness of internal control, not a component.

9. Which of the following factors are included in an entity's control environment?

	Audit Committee Participation	Integrity and Ethical Values	Organizational Structure
A.	Yes	Yes	No
B.	Yes	No	Yes
C.	No	Yes	Yes
D.	Yes	Yes	Yes

Answer (D) is correct.
    REQUIRED: The factors in a control environment.
    DISCUSSION: The control environment is the foundation for all other control components. It provides discipline and structure, sets the tone of the organization, and influences the control consciousness of employees. Its components include (1) participation of those charged with governance, (2) integrity and ethical values, (3) organizational structure, (4) management's philosophy and operating style, (5) assignment of authority and responsibility, (6) human resource policies and practices, and (7) commitment to competence.

10. Proper segregation of duties reduces the opportunities to allow persons to be in positions both to

- A. Journalize entries and prepare financial statements.
- B. Record cash receipts and cash disbursements.
- C. Establish internal control and authorize transactions.
- D. Perpetrate and conceal fraud and error.

Answer (D) is correct.
    REQUIRED: The effects of the segregation of duties.
    DISCUSSION: Segregation of duties is a category of the control activities component of internal control. Segregating responsibilities for authorization, recording, and asset custody reduces an employee's opportunity to perpetrate fraud or error and subsequently conceal it in the normal course of his/her duties.
    Answer (A) is incorrect. Accountants typically journalize entries and prepare financial statements. Answer (B) is incorrect. Accountants may record both cash receipts and cash disbursements as long as they do not have custody of cash. Answer (C) is incorrect. Management establishes internal control and ultimately has the responsibility to authorize transactions.

11. Proper segregation of functional responsibilities to achieve effective internal control calls for separation of the functions of

- A. Authorization, execution, and payment.
- B. Authorization, recording, and custody.
- C. Custody, execution, and reporting.
- D. Authorization, payment, and recording.

Answer (B) is correct.
    REQUIRED: The duties separated to achieve effective internal control.
    DISCUSSION: One person should not be responsible for all phases of a transaction, i.e., for authorization of transactions, recording of transactions, and custodianship of the related assets. These duties should be performed by separate individuals to reduce the opportunities to allow any person to be in a position both to perpetrate and conceal fraud or error in the normal course of his/her duties.
    Answer (A) is incorrect. Payment is a form of execution (operational responsibility). Answer (C) is incorrect. Custody of assets and execution of related transactions are often not segregated. Answer (D) is incorrect. Payments must be recorded when made.

5.3 Understanding Internal Control

12. In obtaining an understanding of internal control in a financial statement audit, an auditor is **not** obligated to

    A. Determine whether the controls have been implemented.

    B. Perform procedures to understand the design of internal control.

    C. Document the understanding of the entity's internal control components.

    D. Search for significant deficiencies in the operation of internal control.

Answer (D) is correct.
    REQUIRED: The step an auditor need not take in obtaining an understanding of internal control.
    DISCUSSION: In all audits, the auditor should obtain an understanding of each of the five components of internal control sufficient to plan the audit. An understanding is obtained by performing risk assessment procedures to evaluate the design of controls relevant to the audit and to determine whether they have been implemented. In addition, the auditor should obtain and document the understanding of the entity's internal control components. However, in an audit, the auditor is not obligated to search for significant deficiencies or material weaknesses (AU-C 265).
    Answer (A) is incorrect. The auditor should determine whether the relevant controls are in operation. Answer (B) is incorrect. The auditor should understand the design of relevant controls. Answer (C) is incorrect. The auditor should document the understanding of each control component.

13. As part of understanding internal control relevant to the audit of a non issuer, an auditor does **not** need to

    A. Consider factors that affect the risks of material misstatement.

    B. Determine whether controls have been implemented.

    C. Identify the risks of material misstatement.

    D. Obtain knowledge about the operating effectiveness of internal control.

Answer (D) is correct.
    REQUIRED: The procedure not required in obtaining the understanding of internal control of a non issuer.
    DISCUSSION: Understanding internal controls relevant to the audit involves evaluating the design of the controls and determining whether they have been implemented. The auditor of a nonissuer need not obtain an understanding about operating effectiveness as part of understanding internal control. However, (1) the auditor's assessment of the risks of material misstatement (RMMs) may include an expectation of the operating effectiveness of controls, or (2) substantive procedures may not provide sufficient appropriate evidence at the relevant assertion level about operating effectiveness. In these circumstances, the auditor should test controls (AU-C 330).
    Answer (A) is incorrect. The auditor performs risk assessment procedures to obtain an understanding of the entity and its environment, including its internal control, to identify and assess the RMMs, whether due to fraud or error, at the financial statement and relevant assertion levels. Answer (B) is incorrect. The understanding of internal control provides assurance that controls have been implemented. Answer (C) is incorrect. The understanding of the entity and its environment, including its internal control, involves identifying and assessing RMMs.

14. An auditor should obtain an understanding of an entity's information system, including

    A. Safeguards used to limit access to computer facilities.

    B. Process used to prepare significant accounting estimates.

    C. Procedures used to ensure the proper supervision of staff.

    D. Programs and controls intended to address the risks of fraud.

Answer (B) is correct.
    REQUIRED: The purpose of obtaining an understanding of an entity's information system.
    DISCUSSION: The auditor should obtain an understanding of the information system, including (1) the classes of significant transactions; (2) the ways those transactions are initiated, authorized, recorded, processed, corrected, transferred to the general ledger, and reported; (3) the accounting records, whether electronic or manual; (4) how significant events and conditions other than transactions are captured; (5) the financial reporting process used to prepare the entity's financial statements, including significant accounting estimates and disclosures; and (6) controls over journal entries (AU-C 315 and AS No. 12).
    Answer (A) is incorrect. Limiting access to computer facilities involves activity outside the information system relevant to financial reporting. Answer (C) is incorrect. Ensuring the proper supervision of staff involves activity outside the information system relevant to financial reporting. Answer (D) is incorrect. Programs and controls intended to address the risks of fraud may be included in any of the components of internal control, not just the information system component (which encompasses the information system relevant to financial reporting).

15. In obtaining an understanding of controls that are relevant to audit planning, an auditor is required to obtain knowledge about the

A. Design of the controls included in the internal control components.

B. Effectiveness of the controls that have been implemented.

C. Consistency with which the controls are currently being applied.

D. Controls related to each principal transaction class and account balance.

Answer (A) is correct.
REQUIRED: The knowledge required in gaining an understanding of internal control.
DISCUSSION: In all audits, the auditor should obtain an understanding of each of the five components of internal control sufficient to plan the audit. An understanding is obtained by performing risk assessment procedures to evaluate the design of controls relevant to the audit and to determine whether they have been implemented (AU-C 315).
Answer (B) is incorrect. The issue of the effectiveness of controls is required to be addressed when the auditor tests controls. Answer (C) is incorrect. The issue of the consistency of application is required to be addressed when the auditor tests controls. Answer (D) is incorrect. Audit planning ordinarily does not require understanding every balance and transaction class or every relevant assertion.

16. When obtaining an understanding of an entity's internal control, an auditor should concentrate on their substance rather than their form because

A. The controls may be operating effectively but may not be documented.

B. Management may establish appropriate controls but not enforce compliance with them.

C. The controls may be so inappropriate that no reliance is expected by the auditor.

D. Management may implement controls whose costs exceed their benefits.

Answer (B) is correct.
REQUIRED: The reason an auditor should concentrate on the substance of controls, not their form.
DISCUSSION: The auditor must concentrate on the substance rather than the form of controls because management may establish appropriate controls but not apply them. Whether controls have been implemented at a moment in time differs from their operating effectiveness over a period of time. Thus, operating effectiveness concerns not merely whether the entity is using controls but also how the controls (manual or automated) are applied, the consistency of their application, and by whom they are applied.
Answer (A) is incorrect. An auditor is concerned with the actual operating effectiveness of controls, not with a lack of evidence about form (documentation). Answer (C) is incorrect. If controls are so inappropriate that the auditor does not expect to rely on them, their substance is irrelevant. Answer (D) is incorrect. When considering internal control in a financial statement audit, the auditor is primarily concerned with the effectiveness of controls, not their cost-benefit relationship.

17. In obtaining an understanding of a manufacturing entity's internal control concerning inventory balances, an auditor most likely would

A. Review the entity's descriptions of inventory policies and procedures.

B. Perform test counts of inventory during the entity's physical count.

C. Analyze inventory turnover statistics to identify slow-moving and obsolete items.

D. Analyze monthly production reports to identify variances and unusual transactions.

Answer (A) is correct.
REQUIRED: The step in obtaining an understanding of an entity's internal control concerning inventory balances.
DISCUSSION: The auditor should obtain an understanding of the internal control components to plan the audit, including knowledge about the design of relevant controls and whether they have been implemented. Reviewing the entity's descriptions of inventory policies and procedures helps the auditor understand their design.
Answer (B) is incorrect. Performing test counts of inventory is a test of details (a substantive procedure). Answer (C) is incorrect. Analysis of inventory turnover statistics is an analytical procedure performed as a substantive procedure. Answer (D) is incorrect. Analysis of monthly production reports to identify variances and unusual transactions is an analytical procedure performed as a substantive procedure.

18. In an audit of financial statements in accordance with generally accepted auditing standards, an auditor should

A. Identify specific controls relevant to management's financial statement assertions.

B. Perform tests of controls to evaluate the effectiveness of the entity's accounting system.

C. Determine whether procedures are suitably designed to prevent, or detect and correct, material misstatement.

D. Document the auditor's understanding of the entity's internal control.

Answer (D) is correct.
REQUIRED: A procedure in an audit of financial statements in accordance with GAAS.
DISCUSSION: The auditor should document (1) the understanding of the entity and its environment and the components of internal control, (2) the sources of information regarding the understanding, and (3) the risk assessment procedures performed. The form and extent of the documentation are influenced by the nature and complexity of the entity's controls (AU-C 315).

5.4 Flowcharting

19. An auditor's flowchart of a client's accounting system is a diagrammatic representation that depicts the auditor's

- A. Assessment of the risks of material misstatement.
- B. Identification of weaknesses in the system.
- C. Assessment of the control environment's effectiveness.
- D. Understanding of the system.

Answer (D) is correct.
   REQUIRED: The purpose of an auditor's flowchart.
   DISCUSSION: The auditor should document (1) the understanding of the entity and its environment and the components of internal control, (2) the sources of information regarding the understanding, and (3) the risk assessment procedures performed. The form and extent of this documentation are influenced by the nature and complexity of the entity's controls (AU-C 315). For example, documentation of the understanding of internal control of a complex information system in which many transactions are electronically initiated, authorized, recorded, processed, or reported may include questionnaires, flowcharts, or decision tables.
   Answer (A) is incorrect. The conclusions about the assessments of the RMMs should be documented. These are professional judgments of the auditor documented in the working papers. Answer (B) is incorrect. The flowchart is a tool to document the auditor's understanding of internal control, but it does not specifically identify weaknesses in the system. Answer (C) is incorrect. The auditor's judgment is the ultimate basis for concluding that controls are effective.

20. The following is a section of a system flowchart for a payroll application:

Symbol X could represent

- A. Erroneous time cards.
- B. An error report.
- C. Batched time cards.
- D. Unclaimed payroll checks.

Answer (B) is correct.
   REQUIRED: The item represented by Symbol X.
   DISCUSSION: Symbol X is a document, that is, hard copy output of the validation routine shown. The time card data, the validated data, and the errors are recorded on magnetic disk after the validation process. Thus, either an error report or the valid time card information is represented by Symbol X.
   Answer (A) is incorrect. Time cards were stored offline before the validation process. Answer (C) is incorrect. Time cards were stored offline before the validation process. Answer (D) is incorrect. No payroll checks are shown.

21. An advantage of using systems flowcharts to document information about internal control instead of using internal control questionnaires is that systems flowcharts

A. Identify internal control deficiencies more prominently.

B. Provide a visual depiction of clients' activities.

C. Indicate whether controls are operating effectively.

D. Reduce the need to observe clients' employees performing routine tasks.

Answer (B) is correct.

REQUIRED: The advantage of systems flowcharts over internal control questionnaires.

DISCUSSION: Systems flowcharts provide a visual representation of a series of sequential processes, that is, of a flow of documents, data, and operations. In many instances, a flowchart is preferable to a questionnaire because a picture is usually more easily comprehended.

Answer (A) is incorrect. A systems flowchart can present the flow of information and documents in a system, but it does not specifically identify the deficiencies. Answer (C) is incorrect. The flowchart does not provide evidence of how effectively controls are actually operating. Answer (D) is incorrect. The flowchart is useful in documenting the understanding of internal control, but it does not reduce the need for observation of employees performing tasks if those tests of controls are deemed necessary.

22. Which of the following symbolic representations indicates that new payroll transactions and the old payroll file have been used to prepare payroll checks, prepare a printed payroll journal, and generate a new payroll file?

A.

B.

C.

D.

Answer (D) is correct.

REQUIRED: The symbolic representation for updating the payroll file and generating checks and a payroll journal.

DISCUSSION: The new payroll transactions and the old payroll file are represented by the magnetic tape symbols. These files are entered into the process function (the rectangle). The output is a new payroll file on magnetic tape and payroll checks and a printed payroll journal represented by the document symbols.

Answer (A) is incorrect. Two magnetically stored payroll files and two offline storage files are produced from a single document form. Answer (B) is incorrect. Two offline storage files and one document are produced (manually) from an offline storage file and a tape file. Answer (C) is incorrect. Two magnetically stored files and a punchcard are produced from the processing of a punchcard and an offline storage file.

5.5 Internal Control and Information Technology

23. Which of the following characteristics distinguishes computer processing from manual processing?

A. Computer processing virtually eliminates the occurrence of computational error normally associated with manual processing.

B. Errors or fraud in computer processing will be detected soon after their occurrence.

C. The potential for systematic error is ordinarily greater in manual processing than in computerized processing.

D. Most computer systems are designed so that transaction trails useful for audit purposes do not exist.

Answer (A) is correct.
 REQUIRED: The feature that distinguishes computer processing from manual processing.
 DISCUSSION: Computer processing uniformly subjects like transactions to the same processing instructions. A computer program defines the processing steps to accomplish a task. Once the program is written and tested appropriately, it will perform the task repetitively and without error. However, if the program contains an error, all transactions will be processed incorrectly.
 Answer (B) is incorrect. When an error does occur, for example, in input, it may not be discovered on a timely basis. Ordinarily, much less human intervention occurs once the transaction is processed. Answer (C) is incorrect. Systematic (repetitive) errors occur in computerized processing if an error exists in the program. Answer (D) is incorrect. Adequately designed systems maintain transaction, console, and error logs that create useful audit trails.

24. In which of the following circumstances would an auditor expect to find that an entity implemented automated controls to reduce risks of misstatement?

A. When errors are difficult to predict.

B. When misstatements are difficult to define.

C. When large, unusual, or nonrecurring transactions require judgment.

D. When transactions are high-volume and recurring.

Answer (D) is correct.
 REQUIRED: The circumstance in which an entity is most likely to implement automated controls.
 DISCUSSION: Automated controls are cost effective when they are applied to high-volume, recurring transactions. For example, credit limit checks on customer orders could be automated to relieve management from evaluating each customer order as it is received.
 Answer (A) is incorrect. When errors are difficult to predict, judgment may be required and it would be less likely that a control could be automated. Answer (B) is incorrect. When misstatements are difficult to define, designing automated controls to prevent, or detect and correct, them also is difficult. Answer (C) is incorrect. When judgment is required, automated controls are less likely to be effective.

25. Which of the following controls most likely could prevent computer personnel from modifying programs to bypass programmed controls?

A. Periodic management review of computer utilization reports and systems documentation.

B. Separation of duties for computer programming and computer operations.

C. Participation of user department personnel in designing and approving new systems.

D. Physical security of computer facilities in limiting access to computer equipment.

Answer (B) is correct.
 REQUIRED: The control necessary to prevent computer personnel from modifying programs to bypass controls.
 DISCUSSION: Programmers and analysts can modify programs, data files, and controls, so they should have no access to programs used to process transactions. Separation of programming and operations is necessary to prevent unauthorized modifications of programs.
 Answer (A) is incorrect. Although periodic management review is appropriate, reports and systems documentation do not prevent, or detect and correct, unauthorized modifications. Answer (C) is incorrect. User participation relates to new systems, not modification of existing systems. Answer (D) is incorrect. Programmers may have access through data communications. Thus, physical security is not sufficient to prevent unauthorized modifications.

26. A client is concerned that a power outage or disaster could impair the computer hardware's ability to function as designed. The client desires off-site backup hardware facilities that are fully configured and ready to operate within several hours. The client most likely should consider a

A. Cold site.

B. Cool site.

C. Warm site.

D. Hot site.

Answer (D) is correct.
 REQUIRED: The type of off-site backup hardware facility that is an available, fully operational processing facility.
 DISCUSSION: A hot site is a service facility that is fully operational and is promptly available in the case of a power outage or disaster.
 Answer (A) is incorrect. A cold site is a shell facility suitable for quick installation of computer equipment. Installing computer equipment requires more time in a cold site than in a hot site. Answer (B) is incorrect. "Cool site" is not a meaningful term in this context. Answer (C) is incorrect. A warm site provides an intermediate level of backup and causes more downtime than a hot site.

27. Which of the following is a computer program that appears to be legitimate but performs some illicit activity when it is run?

A. Hoax virus.
B. Web crawler.
C. Trojan horse.
D. Killer application.

Answer (C) is correct.
REQUIRED: The apparently legitimate computer program that performs an illicit activity.
DISCUSSION: A Trojan horse is a computer program, for example, a game, that appears friendly but that actually contains an application destructive to the computer system.
Answer (A) is incorrect. A hoax virus is a false notice about the existence of a computer virus. It is usually disseminated through use of distribution lists and is sent by email or via an internal network. Answer (B) is incorrect. A web crawler (a spider or bot) is a computer program created to access and read information on websites. The results are included as entries in the index of a search engine. Answer (D) is incorrect. A killer application is one that is so useful that it may justify widespread adoption of a new technology.

28. A client who recently installed a new accounts payable system assigned employees a user identification code (UIC) and a separate password. Each UIC is a person's name, and the individual's password is the same as the UIC. Users are not required to change their passwords at initial log-in nor do passwords ever expire. Which of the following statements does **not** reflect a limitation of the client's computer-access control?

A. Employees can easily guess fellow employees' passwords.
B. Employees are not required to change passwords.
C. Employees can circumvent procedures to segregate duties.
D. Employees are not required to take regular vacations.

Answer (D) is correct.
REQUIRED: The item not a limitation of the client's computer-access control.
DISCUSSION: To be effective, passwords should consist of random letters, symbols, and numbers. They should not contain words or phrases that are easily guessed. Proper user authentication by means of passwords requires procedures to ensure that the valid passwords generated are known only by appropriate individuals. Moreover, passwords should be changed frequently so that the maximum retention period (the period during which they may be compromised) is relatively short. However, a minimum retention period should be required so that users cannot change passwords back to their old, convenient forms. Another weakness in access control is that different passwords are not required to perform different functions, e.g., to obtain access, to read certain files, or to update certain files. Use of separate passwords is a means of segregating duties. However, the password security system is unrelated to the absence of a requirement to take vacations. Nevertheless, such requirement may be appropriate for personnel in a position to embezzle funds.
Answer (A) is incorrect. A control deficiency exists if employees can easily guess fellow employees' passwords. Answer (B) is incorrect. A control deficiency exists if employees are not required to change passwords. Answer (C) is incorrect. A control deficiency exists if employees can circumvent procedures to segregate duties.

29. Which of the following is the most serious password security problem?

A. Users are assigned passwords when accounts are created, but they do not change them.
B. Users have accounts on several systems with different passwords.
C. Users copy their passwords on note paper, which is kept in their wallets.
D. Users select passwords that are not listed in any online dictionary.

Answer (A) is correct.
REQUIRED: The password technique that poses the greatest security problem.
DISCUSSION: Proper user authentication by means of a password requires password-generating procedures to ensure that valid passwords are known only by the proper individuals. If passwords are assigned, users should change passwords frequently so that they are the only persons with access under those identifiers.
Answer (B) is incorrect. No security issue arises when different passwords are used for accounts on different systems. Answer (C) is incorrect. Although any record of a password is potentially a security problem, storing a password online would be a greater problem. Answer (D) is incorrect. A password should not be an item in an online dictionary.

30. An entity has the following invoices in a batch:

Invoice Number	Product	Quantity	Unit Price
201	F10	150	$ 5.00
202	G15	200	10.00
203	H20	250	25.00
204	K35	300	30.00

Which of the following most likely represents a hash total?

A. FGHK80

B. 4

C. 204

D. 810

Answer (D) is correct.

REQUIRED: The example of a hash total.

DISCUSSION: Input controls in batch computer systems are used to determine that no data are lost or added to the batch. Depending on the sophistication of a particular system, control may be accomplished by using record counts, financial totals, or hash totals. The hash total is a control total without a defined meaning, such as the total of employee numbers or invoice numbers, that is used to verify the completeness of data. The hash total of the invoice numbers is 810.

Answer (A) is incorrect. A hash total is ordinarily the sum of a numeric field. Answer (B) is incorrect. The record count is four. Answer (C) is incorrect. The last invoice number is 204.

31. A customer intended to order 100 units of product Z96014 but incorrectly ordered nonexistent product Z96015. Which of the following controls most likely would detect this error?

A. Check digit verification.

B. Record count.

C. Hash total.

D. Redundant data check.

Answer (A) is correct.

REQUIRED: The control that would detect a nonexistent product number.

DISCUSSION: Check digit verification is used to identify incorrect identification numbers. The digit is generated by applying an algorithm to the ID number. During input, the check digit is recomputed by applying the same algorithm to the entered ID number.

Answer (B) is incorrect. A record count is a control total of the number of transactions in a batch. Answer (C) is incorrect. A hash total is a control total that is the sum of a field without a defined meaning. Answer (D) is incorrect. A redundant data check searches for duplicate information in a database.

32. Able Co. uses an online sales order processing system to process its sales transactions. Able's sales data are electronically sorted and subjected to edit checks. A direct output of the edit checks most likely would be a

A. Report of all missing sales invoices.

B. File of all rejected sales transactions.

C. Printout of all user code numbers and passwords.

D. List of all voided shipping documents.

Answer (B) is correct.

REQUIRED: The output of edit checks.

DISCUSSION: Edit checks test transactions prior to processing. Rejected transactions should be recorded in a file for evaluation, correction, and resubmission. Edit checks are applied to the sales transactions to test for completeness, reasonableness, validity, and other related issues prior to acceptance. A report of missing invoices, a printout of all user code numbers and passwords, and a list of all voided shipping documents are unlikely to be direct outputs of the edit routine.

33. One of the major problems in a computer system is that incompatible functions may be performed by the same individual. One compensating control is the use of

A. Echo checks.

B. A check digit system.

C. Computer-generated hash totals.

D. A computer access log.

Answer (D) is correct.

REQUIRED: The control compensating for inadequate segregation of duties in a computer system.

DISCUSSION: A computer (console) access log is a record of computer and software usage usually produced by the operating system. Proper monitoring of the log is a compensating control for the lack of segregation of duties. For example, the log should list operator interventions.

Answer (A) is incorrect. Echo checks are hardware controls used to determine whether the correct message was received by an output device. Answer (B) is incorrect. A check digit system is an input control that tests identification numbers. Answer (C) is incorrect. Hash totals are control totals used to check for losses or inaccuracies arising during data processing or movement.

Use the additional questions in Gleim **CPA Test Prep** to create Practice Exams that emulate Prometric!

5.6 PRACTICE TASK-BASED SIMULATIONS

Auditing and Attestation Testlet 4 of 4	**Time Remaining** 1 hour - 30 minutes

Unsplit · Split Horiz · Split Vertical · Spreadsheet · Calculator · Exit

DIRECTIONS

Note: If you believe you have encountered a software malfunction, report it to the test center staff immediately.

Navigation

To navigate from task to task, use the controls at the bottom of the screen. Click on the **Next** button to advance to the next task, or the **Previous** button to go to the previous task. To go directly to any task, click on its number.

⚑ = Reminder   Directions   1 2 3 4 5 6 7   ◀ Previous   Next ▶

If you would like a reminder to revisit a task, or want to indicate that you are finished with it, click on the reminder flag below the task number. To clear the flag, click on it again. Reminder flags are for your use only – they do not contribute to your score.

Tabs

In this part of the examination, you will be asked to complete various tasks. Every task has one or more **Work Tabs**. Some tasks have one or more **Information Tabs**, others may have none. Every task has a **Help** tab.

If a task has **Information Tabs**, you may use the information in them to complete your responses in the **Work Tabs**.

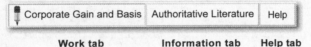

Corporate Gain and Basis	Authoritative Literature	Help
Work tab	Information tab	Help tab

Work Tabs:
- **Work Tabs** are identified with a pencil icon. This is where your responses are expected.
- Each task has one or more **Work Tabs**.
- **Work Tabs** contain directions for completing the task – be sure to read these directions carefully.
- The **Work Tab** name in the example above is for illustration only – yours will differ.
- You must complete all of the **Work Tabs** in each task to receive full credit.

Information Tabs:
- The Authoritative Literature will be provided in all tasks in the AUD, FAR, and REG sections for your reference.
- Your simulation may have one or more additional **Information Tabs**. Like the Authoritative Literature tabs, **Information Tabs** do not have a pencil icon.
- If your task has additional **Information Tabs**, go through each to familiarize yourself with the task content.

Help Tab:
- The **Help Tab** provides assistance with the exam software that is used in this task. For example, if the task is to compose a memorandum, **Help** will provide information about the word processor.

The Toolbar

The toolbar at the top of the screen shows the amount of time remaining for you to complete the tasks. In addition, the following tools are available. Note that only the **Exit** button is displayed when Directions are visible - the others will appear when you begin the tasks.

Unsplit · Split Horiz · Split Vertical

Click on these buttons to split or unsplit the screen. You can split the screen vertically or horizontally.

Calculator

Click on this button to display the calculator; click on it again to hide the calculator. To move the calculator, click on the calculator title bar and drag the calculator to the desired location.

Spreadsheet

Click on this button to use the spreadsheet; click on it again to hide the spreadsheet. To move the spreadsheet, click on the the spreadsheet title bar and drag the spreadsheet to the desired location.

Exit

Click on this button to go on to the next part of the examination. You must complete all of the tasks to receive full credit. Once you click on **Exit** and confirm the action, you will NOT be able to return to this testlet.

⚑ = Reminder   Directions   1 2 3 4 5   ◀ Previous   Next ▶

Internal Control Documentation Methods | Authoritative Literature | Help

An entity may use a variety of methods for documenting internal controls. The same methods may be used by the auditor to document the understanding of the controls in a financial statement audit. Select from the list provided to match the documentation method with the phrase or description with which it is most closely associated. Each choice may be used once, more than once, or not at all.

Phrase or Description	Documentation Method	Choices
1. A written description of a process		A) Flowchart
2. A logic diagram in matrix form		B) Questionnaire
3. A problem and appropriate actions		C) Narrative memorandum
4. Diagram of a series of sequential processes		D) Decision table
5. Visual depiction of the flow of documents		
6. Series of interrelated queries		
7. The most flexible documentation method		
8. Control strength represented by a "Yes"		

Audit Procedures | Authoritative Literature | Help

Select from the list provided to match each audit procedure with the most appropriate statement. Each choice may be used once, more than once, or not at all.

Procedures	Answer	Choices
1. The auditor performs tests of controls.		A) Describes a reason for the auditor to obtain an understanding of the entity and its environment, including its internal control
2. The auditor prepares flowcharts, narratives, questionnaires, or other material.		
3. The auditor considers the factors affecting the risks of material misstatement.		B) Describes what is done when an auditor has an expectation of the operating effectiveness of controls
4. The auditor performs risk assessment procedures to test the operating effectiveness of controls.		
5. The auditor designs substantive procedures.		C) Describes the documentation of the understanding of the entity and its environment, including its internal control, and assessment of the risks of material misstatement
6. The auditor documents the assessed risks of material misstatement and the basis for the assessment.		
7. The auditor documents the significant risks identified.		
8. The auditor considers whether substantive procedures alone provide sufficient appropriate audit evidence at the relevant assertion level.		D) Describes a procedure that is not performed
9. The auditor applies limited substantive procedures to determine whether a control is operating effectively.		
10. The auditor identifies the types of potential misstatement.		

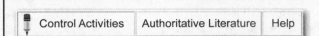

Control Activities | Authoritative Literature | Help

Select from the list provided to match each management action with the appropriate control activity. Each choice may be used once, more than once, or not at all.

Management's Action	Answer		Choices
1. Investigating performance indicators			A) Performance reviews
2. Review of documents and transactions			B) Information processing
3. Safeguarding assets			C) Physical controls
4. Comparing actual performance with budgeted performance			D) Segregation of duties
5. Reconciliation			
6. Dividing authorization of transactions and recordkeeping			
7. Periodic counting of inventory			
8. Design and use of adequate documents and records			

▼ = Reminder | Directions | 1 2 [3] 4 5 | ◀ Previous Next ▶

Backup and Disaster Recovery | Authoritative Literature | Help

Select from the list the appropriate definition of each method of periodic backup or disaster recovery. Each choice may be used once, more than once, or not at all.

Description	Answer		Choices
1. Because Lumberjack, Inc., relies more on human labor than computing power, it duplicates its data files at the end of each month.			A) Cold-site backup facility
2. Magma Partnerships is located in an area near an active volcano. Each time a database file is copied for backup, it is moved and stored in a bank vault in another city.			B) Fully protected system
3. Mercy Hospital relies on access to their medical data at all times. Thus, Mercy has installed a generator to prevent data destruction and downtime from electrical power disturbances.			C) Hot-site backup facility
4. Millennium Edge is a software company that cannot afford even one day of downtime. Accordingly, it invested in a separate location that can be used immediately.			D) Offsite location
5. Century Corner is in the information technology industry. It is planning on investing in a backup facility. Because it does not have enough capital, it can afford only to rent an empty office. Century plans to install the necessary hardware if and when it is needed.			E) Typical backup routine

▼ = Reminder | Directions | 1 2 3 [4] 5 | ◀ Previous Next ▶

Smith, CPA, is auditing a nonissuer client. In order to increase the efficiency of the audit, Smith has asked you to gather information regarding which internal controls he is responsible for obtaining an understanding of. Which section of the generally accepted auditing standards best describes the internal controls that Smith will be responsible for obtaining an understanding of?

Title	Section	Paragraph

Title Choices

AU-C	PCAOB	AT	AR	ET	BL	VS
CS	QC	PR	TS	PFP	CPE	

▼ = Reminder   Directions   1 2 3 4 **5**   ◄ Previous   Next ►

Unofficial Answers

1. Internal Control Documentation Methods (8 Gradable Items)

1. <u>C) Narrative memorandum.</u> A narrative memorandum is a written description of the processing and flow of documents and control points. The advantage of this method is its flexibility.

2. <u>D) Decision table.</u> A decision table identifies the contingencies considered in the description of a problem and the appropriate actions to be taken relative to those contingencies. Decision tables are logic diagrams presented in matrix form.

3. <u>D) Decision table.</u> A decision table identifies the contingencies considered in the description of a problem and the appropriate actions to be taken relative to those contingencies. Decision tables are logic diagrams presented in matrix form.

4. <u>A) Flowchart.</u> A flowchart is a pictorial diagram of a set of sequential processes. It may be a diagram of the documents and processes of a system or of the steps in a computer program.

5. <u>A) Flowchart.</u> A flowchart is a pictorial diagram of a set of sequential processes. It may be a diagram of the documents and processes of a system or of the steps in a computer program.

6. <u>B) Questionnaire.</u> A questionnaire consists of a series of interrelated questions about internal control polices and procedures. The questions are typically phrased so that a "Yes" response indicates a control strength and a "No" indicates a potential weakness.

7. <u>C) Narrative memorandum.</u> A narrative memorandum is a written description of the processing and flow of documents and control points. The advantage of this method is its flexibility.

8. <u>B) Questionnaire.</u> A questionnaire consists of a series of interrelated questions about internal control polices and procedures. The questions are typically phrased so that a "Yes" response indicates a control strength and a "No" indicates a potential weakness.

2. Audit Procedures (10 Gradable Items)

1.   B) Describes what is done when an auditor has an expectation of the operating effectiveness of controls. The auditor tests controls when (a) his/her assessment of the risks of material misstatement is based on an expectation of the operating effectiveness of controls, or (b) substantive procedures alone do not provide sufficient appropriate evidence at the relevant assertion level.

2.   C) Describes the documentation of the understanding of the entity and its environment, including its internal control, and assessment of the risks of material misstatement. Required documentation includes, among other things, the understanding of the entity and its environment, including its internal control. This documentation extends to the five components of internal control and discussions among the members of the engagement team. Also documented are (a) the sources of information, (b) the risk assessment procedures, (c) the assessed risks of material misstatement, and (d) the significant risks identified and related controls evaluated (AU-C 315). Flowcharts, questionnaires, decision tables, checklists, and narratives are among the possible forms of documentation.

3.   A) Describes a reason for the auditor to obtain an understanding of the entity and its environment, including its internal control. The auditor should obtain an understanding of internal control to assess the risks of material misstatement, whether due to fraud or error, and to design further audit procedures. This knowledge should be used to (a) determine the types of potential misstatement, (b) consider factors affecting the risks of material misstatement, (c) design tests of controls (when applicable), and (d) design substantive procedures.

4.   D) Describes a procedure that is not performed. Risk assessment procedures are performed to obtain an understanding of the entity and its environment, including its internal control. Tests of controls evaluate operating effectiveness.

5.   A) Describes a reason for the auditor to obtain an understanding of the entity and its environment, including its internal control. The auditor should obtain an understanding of internal control to assess the risks of material misstatement, whether due to fraud or error, and to design further audit procedures. This knowledge should be used to (a) determine the types of potential misstatement, (b) consider factors affecting the risks of material misstatement, (c) design tests of controls (when applicable), and (d) design substantive procedures.

6.   D) Describes a procedure that is not performed. AU-C 315 does not require the auditor to document the basis for the assessment of the RMMs.

7.   C) Describes the documentation of the understanding of the entity and its environment, including its internal control, and assessment of the risks of material misstatement. The auditor documents the significant risks identified and the related controls evaluated requiring special audit consideration.

8.   B) Describes what is done when an auditor has an expectation of the operating effectiveness of controls. The auditor tests controls when (a) his/her assessment of the risks of material misstatement is based on an expectation of the operating effectiveness of controls, or (b) substantive procedures alone do not provide sufficient appropriate evidence at the relevant assertion level.

9.   D) Describes a procedure that is not performed. The auditor performs substantive procedures to detect material misstatements. The auditor tests controls to determine their operating effectiveness.

10. A) Describes a reason for the auditor to obtain an understanding of the entity and its environment, including its internal control. The auditor should obtain an understanding of internal control to assess the risks of material misstatement, whether due to fraud or error, and to design further audit procedures. This knowledge should be used to (a) determine the types of potential misstatement, (b) consider factors affecting the risks of material misstatement, (c) design tests of controls (when applicable), and (d) design substantive procedures.

3. Control Activities (8 Gradable Items)

1.   A) Performance reviews. These include reviews of actual performance versus budgets and prior performance.

2.   B) Information processing. This requires checks of accuracy, completeness, and authorization of transactions.

3.   C) Physical controls. These involve the safeguarding of assets, records, periodic counts, and reconciliations that creates asset accountability.

4.   A) Performance reviews. These include reviews of actual performance versus budgets and prior performance.

5.   B) Information processing. This requires checks of accuracy, completeness, and authorization of transactions.

6.   D) Segregation of duties. This involves the segregation of the functions of authorization, recordkeeping, and asset custody. The purpose is to minimize the opportunities for a person to be able to perpetrate and conceal errors or fraud in the normal course of his/her duties.

7.   C) Physical controls. These involve the safeguarding of assets, records, periodic counts, and reconciliations to create asset accountability.

8.   B) Information processing. This requires checks of accuracy, completeness, and authorization of transactions.

4. Backup and Disaster Recovery (5 Gradable Items)

1. E) Typical backup routine. In a typical backup routine, all data files and application programs are duplicated at least once a month. Incremental changes are then backed up and taken to the offsite location periodically (e.g., once a week).

2. D) Offsite location. Physical storage of backup files should be geographically remote enough from the site of the organization's main operations that it would not be affected by the same natural disaster. It does the organization no good to have adequate backup files if the files are not accessible or have been destroyed.

3. B) Fully protected system. A fully protected system has a generator or battery backup to prevent data destruction and downtime from electrical power disturbances.

4. C) Hot-site backup facility. A hot site is a fully operational processing facility that is immediately available.

5. A) Cold-site backup facility. A cold site is a shell facility where the user can quickly install equipment.

5. Research (1 Gradable Item)

Answer: 315.13

AU-C Section 315 -- *Understanding the Entity and its Environment and Assessing the Risks of Material Misstatement*

.13 The auditor should obtain an understanding of internal control relevant to the audit. Although most controls relevant to the audit are likely to relate to financial reporting, not all controls that relate to financial reporting are relevant to the audit. It is a matter of the auditor's professional judgment whether a control, individually or in combination with others, is relevant to the audit.

Gleim Simulation Grading

Task	Correct Responses		Gradable Items		Score per Task
1	_____	÷	8	=	_____
2	_____	÷	10	=	_____
3	_____	÷	8	=	_____
4	_____	÷	5	=	_____
5 (Research)	_____	÷	1	=	_____

Total of Scores per Task	_____
÷ Total Number of Tasks	5
Total Score	_____ %

Use **CPA Gleim Online** and **Simulation Wizard** to practice more task-based simulations in a realistic environment.

STUDY UNIT SIX
INTERNAL CONTROL --
SALES-RECEIVABLES-CASH RECEIPTS CYCLE

(10 pages of outline)

A standard approach to understanding internal control as well as designing substantive procedures is to divide the auditee's transactions, balances, and related control activities into groupings of related items. This cycle approach is consistent with how transactions are recorded in journals and ledgers. Among the relevant accounts considered are cash, trade receivables, other receivables, allowance for bad debts, sales, sales returns, and bad debt expense.

Understanding how information and documents flow through a particular cycle enables an auditor to determine what controls have been implemented and whether they are effective in safeguarding assets and preventing, or detecting and correcting, fraud and error. Auditors are required to obtain and document an understanding of internal control relevant to the audit. Thus, a knowledge of flowcharts is important in preparing for the CPA exam.

Some candidates may feel that information presented in flowcharts is difficult to master. The study materials presented here provide the foundation of understanding. They have been kept simple and straightforward. Nevertheless, they provide the information most often tested on the CPA exam. CPA candidates in the past have not been required to prepare flowcharts but have been expected to evaluate them. The narrative should be studied in conjunction with the flowcharts. Candidates should understand and not just memorize the various documents, flows, and control points. Although the basic concepts are derived from a manual system, they can be extended to a computer environment. Subunit 6.4 provides candidates with an understanding of the effect of technology on the sales cycle.

6.1 RESPONSIBILITIES/ORGANIZATIONAL STRUCTURE/FLOWCHARTS

1. **Management's Responsibility**

   a. Management is responsible for the establishment of the controls over the sales-receivables-cash receipts cycle to ensure

      1) Proper acceptance of the customer order
      2) Granting of credit approval in accordance with credit limits
      3) Safeguarding of assets associated with the sale
      4) Timely shipment of goods to customers
      5) Billing for shipments at authorized prices
      6) Accounting for and collection of receivables
      7) The recording, safeguarding, and depositing intact of cash (checks) received

2. **The Auditor's Responsibility**

   a. The auditor is required to obtain an understanding of the entity and its environment, including its internal control, to assess the risks of material misstatement and to design further audit procedures. For this purpose, the auditor performs risk assessment procedures. The plan for further audit procedures reflects (1) the auditor's decision whether to test the operating effectiveness of controls over the sales-receivables-cash receipts cycle and (2) the nature, timing, and extent of substantive procedures.

Organizational Chart

This is a standard organizational chart. To help you visualize the internal control of this typical organization, the following document flowcharts with explanations are presented for your study:

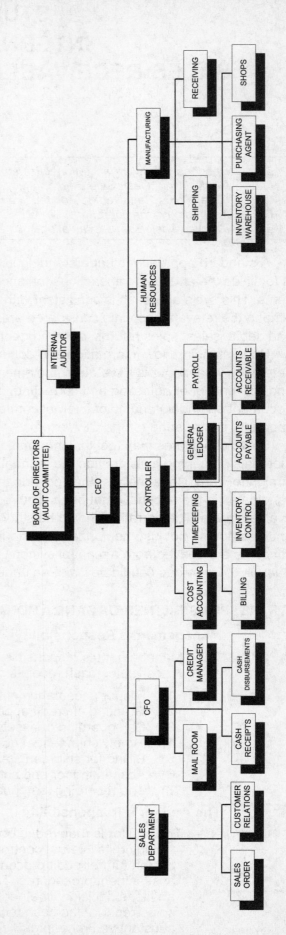

Figure 6-1

3. **Segregation of Duties**

    a. The organizational structure should segregate duties and responsibilities so that an individual is not in the position both to perpetrate and conceal fraud or error. The ideal segregation of duties is

        1) **Authorization** of the transaction

            a) **Specific authorization** may be needed for some transactions, such as unusual credit approvals, but a **general authorization** may suffice for others, such as retail cash sales.

        2) **Recording** of the transaction

        3) **Custody** of the assets (e.g., inventory, receivables, and cash) associated with the transaction

    b. However, **cost-benefit** considerations typically affect the organizational structure, and complete segregation may not be feasible. Compensating controls are likely to be established when the segregation of duties is not maintained. Typical compensating controls may include

        1) More supervision.
        2) Owner involvement in the process.

4. **Responsibilities of Personnel**

    a. The following are the responsibilities of personnel or departments in the sales-receivables-cash receipts cycle:

        1) **Sales** prepares sales orders based on customer orders.

            a) Customer Relations is commonly regarded as a separate operating unit that deals with customers after sales have been made. Thus, it is not involved in the basic transactional functions performed in the sales-receivables-cash receipts cycle.

        2) **Credit Manager** authorizes customer credit and initiates write-off of bad debts. The credit manager should report to the CFO.

        3) **Inventory Warehouse** maintains physical custody of products.

        4) **Inventory Control** maintains records of quantities of products in the Inventory Warehouse.

        5) **Shipping** prepares shipping documents and ships products based on authorized sales orders.

        6) **Billing** prepares customer invoices based on goods shipped.

        7) **Accounts Receivable** maintains the accounts receivable subsidiary ledger.

        8) **Mail Room** receives mail and prepares initial cash receipts records.

        9) **Cash Receipts** safeguards and promptly deposits cash receipts.

        10) **General Ledger** maintains the accounts receivable control account and records sales. Daily summaries of sales are recorded in a sales journal. Totals of details from the sales journal are usually posted monthly to the general ledger.

        11) **Receiving** department prepares receiving reports and handles all receipts of goods or materials, including sales returns.

As you are considering the flowcharts in this and subsequent study units, remember that they are simply examples. Instead of assigning importance to the actual number of documents prepared or the document numbers, you should focus on the control provided by the division of duties and responsibilities and the control processes. Your understanding of the issues will help you answer many more CPA exam questions than just those related to flowcharting.

Sales-Receivables Manual System Flowchart

Figure 6-2

5. **Sales-Receivables Flowchart**

   a. Study the flowchart on the previous page. Understand and visualize the sales-receivables process and controls. Read the following description as needed. Note the control activities implemented and listed in item 7. below.

6. **The Document Flow**

   a. The process begins in the upper left corner of the flowchart marked **START**. (To simplify the presentation, the flowchart does not show the disposition of all documents, for example, by filing or other supplemental procedures.)

      1) The Sales Order department receives a customer order and prepares a multi-part sales order. Copy 2 of the sales order is sent to the Credit Manager.

      2) The Credit Manager performs a credit check and authorizes the order if appropriate. The approval is conveyed to Sales Order, and an acknowledgment (copy 6) is sent to the customer.

      3) Sales Order then releases the remaining copies of the order. Two copies, the invoice copy and accounts receivable copy (copies 4 and 5), are sent to Billing and held awaiting notification of shipment.

      4) A copy (the packing slip copy 3) is sent to Shipping pending arrival of the goods from the Inventory Warehouse.

      5) A copy (the shipping copy 1) is released to the Inventory Warehouse as authorization to release the goods to be sent to the Shipping department.

      6) When the goods and the shipping copy 1 arrive at the Shipping department, the matching packing slip copy 3 is pulled from the file, and shipping documents (e.g., a bill of lading) are prepared. The goods are packed for shipment along with the packing slip copy 3. The shipping copy 1 is marked "shipped" and forwarded to Billing.

      7) Billing pulls the matching invoice and accounts receivable copies (4 and 5). Prices are checked and extended based on the quantities shipped. The invoice (copy 4) is completed and mailed to the customer. The invoice contains a section (a remittance advice) to be returned with the customer check.

      8) Billing prepares a journal entry to be posted by the General Ledger department (credit to sales and debit to the accounts receivable control account).

      9) The accounts receivable copy 5 is forwarded to Accounts Receivable for posting to the individual account in the accounts receivable subsidiary ledger.

      10) The shipping copy 1 is sent to Inventory Control for reduction of quantities for goods shipped.

7. **Control Activities Implemented**

   a. The division of the duties of the transaction is as follows: authorization, recording, and custody of assets.

   b. Routing the sales order copy through the Credit Manager ensures that goods are shipped only to customers who are likely to pay (i.e., properly valued).

   c. Routing the shipping copy through the Inventory Warehouse helps ensure that goods are safeguarded and released only upon proper approval of the order.

   d. Matching of the packing slip copy held by Shipping can ensure that all goods released from the Inventory Warehouse are received by Shipping on a timely basis.

   e. Matching of the copies held by the Billing department can ensure that all goods shipped are invoiced to customers.

   f. Documents are prenumbered to permit detection of unrecorded or unauthorized transactions. For example, sales invoices are prenumbered and accounted for to ensure that all orders are billed.

   g. Periodic reconciliation of the accounts receivable subsidiary ledger with the general ledger can ensure that all invoices are recorded in customers' accounts.

8. **Cash Receipts Flowchart**

    a. Study the flowchart below. Understand and visualize the cash receipts process and controls. Read the following description as needed. Note the control activities implemented and listed in item 10. on the next page.

Cash Receipts Manual System Flowchart

Figure 6-3

9. **The Document Flow**

    a. This flowchart represents the procedures and documents for cash collections from credit customers; cash receipts from cash sales are considered in Subunit 2 of this study unit. (To simplify the presentation, the flowchart does not show the disposition of documents, for example, by filing or other supplemental procedures.) The process begins at **START**.

        1) The Mail Room receives all customer receipts, opens the mail, separates the checks from the remittance advices, and prepares a daily listing of the checks received (the daily remittance list). If no remittance advice is received, the mail clerks prepare one. A copy of the daily remittance list is sent to the Controller.

            a) A remittance advice is part of or a copy of the sales invoice sent to a customer and intended to be returned with the payment. It contains the customer's name, the invoice number, and its amount.

        2) Cash receipts and copy 1 of the daily remittance list are forwarded to Cash Receipts for preparation of the deposit ticket and recording in the cash receipts register.

        3) The receipts are deposited daily by Cash Receipts. The validated (by the bank) deposit ticket is returned to the Controller. The Controller reconciles the validated deposit ticket with the daily remittance list of cash received from the Mail Room.

4) A journal voucher (entry) prepared by Cash Receipts indicating the debit to cash and credit to accounts receivable is sent to the General Ledger.

5) The remittance advices are sent to Accounts Receivable for posting the reductions in accounts receivable to the individual customers' accounts.

10. **Control Activities Implemented**

   a. Two clerks should be present in the Mail Room during the opening and recording of the receipts.

   b. Checks are endorsed "For Deposit Only into Account Number XXXX" immediately upon opening the mail.

   c. All cash is deposited intact daily. This procedure ensures that the cash received and recorded on the daily remittance list can be reconciled with the deposit ticket validated by the bank.

   d. Periodic reconciliation of the accounts receivable subsidiary ledger and the accounts receivable control account in the general ledger establishes agreement of the total amounts posted. However, the reconciliation cannot determine whether an amount was posted to the wrong account in the subsidiary ledger. Moreover, application of such a control will be ineffective if sales were not recorded in the books of original entry, e.g., the sales journal.

   e. Monthly statements are sent to customers to ensure that failure to receive and/or record payments made by customers is detected (not shown on flowchart).

   f. A **lockbox system** (not depicted in the flowchart) can ensure that cash receipts are not abstracted by mail clerks or other employees. This system provides for customer payments to be sent to a post office box and collected directly by the bank.

   1) Hence, a lockbox system prevents lapping. **Lapping** occurs when an employee with access to both the accounts receivable subsidiary ledger and customer payments steals a portion of the receipts without recording them in the customer accounts. To conceal the theft, subsequent receipts are posted to the accounts of customers whose payments were stolen. This process of using new receipts to cover a recent theft must continue indefinitely to avoid detection.

Stop and review! You have completed the outline for this subunit. Study multiple-choice questions 1 through 15 beginning on page 209.

6.2 CONTROLS IN A CASH SALE ENVIRONMENT

1. Cash sales cycles often lack the segregation of duties necessary for the proper framework of control. For example, the sales clerk often

   a. Authorizes the sale (e.g., acceptance of a check),
   b. Records the sale (i.e., enters it on the sales terminal), and
   c. Has custody of the assets related to the sale (i.e., cash and inventory).

2. Compensating controls include

   a. Use of a cash register or sales terminal to record the sale. The terminal makes a permanent record of the event that the clerk cannot erase.

   b. Assignment of one clerk to be responsible for sales recording and cash receipts during a work period. The cash drawer can be reconciled with the record of sales and accountability assigned to the clerk.

   c. Increased supervision. For example, the manager's office may be positioned to observe the clerks' sales recording and cash collection activities.

    d.   Customer audit of the transaction. Displaying the recorded transaction and providing a receipt to the customer provides some assurance that the recording process was accomplished appropriately by the clerk.

    e.   Bonding of employees responsible for handling cash. Because the bonding company investigates employees before providing the bond, some assurance is provided concerning their integrity. Also, the bond provides insurance against losses.

Stop and review! You have completed the outline for this subunit. Study multiple-choice questions 16 and 17 on page 213.

6.3 OTHER SALES-RECEIVABLES RELATED TRANSACTIONS

1.   Sales returns and allowances should have controls to assure proper approval and processing. The key controls include the following:

    a.   Approval by the sales department to return goods

    b.   Receipt of the returned goods by the receiving department and preparation of a receiving report

    c.   The separate approval of the credit memo related to a sales return or allowance, that is, approval by someone not in the sales department

2.   The write-off of bad debts requires strong controls. The key controls include

    a.   Initiation of the write-off by the credit manager and approval by the CFO or other officer. The credit manager will be evaluated, in part, on the amount of bad debts written off and will require significant evidence before initiating a write-off.

    b.   Maintenance of a separate accounting ledger for accounts written off.

Stop and review! You have completed the outline for this subunit. Study multiple-choice questions 18 through 21 on page 214.

6.4 TECHNOLOGY CONSIDERATIONS

1.   Computer processing typically replaces the activities of clerks performing recording functions, e.g., recording sales and accounts receivable, updating the inventory file to reflect goods sold, and recording customer receipts by posting the amounts to the accounts receivable subsidiary file.

2.   Periodic reconciliations (weekly or monthly) of the accounts receivable subsidiary file and general ledgers are usually replaced by daily reconciliations.

3.   Sophisticated systems may replace the paper flow with computer control over authorization of the release of goods for packing and shipping.

    a.   The use of online systems expedites the response to customer orders.

    b.   Batching transactions is useful for processing large volumes of data, especially when the transactions are sorted sequentially. Batch processing is appropriate when an immediate response is not necessary.

4.   Study the flowchart on the next page. Understand and visualize the sales-receivables process and controls in a normative computer environment. Read the following description as needed. Note the control activities implemented and listed in item 6. on page 208.

Sales-Receivables Computer System Flowchart

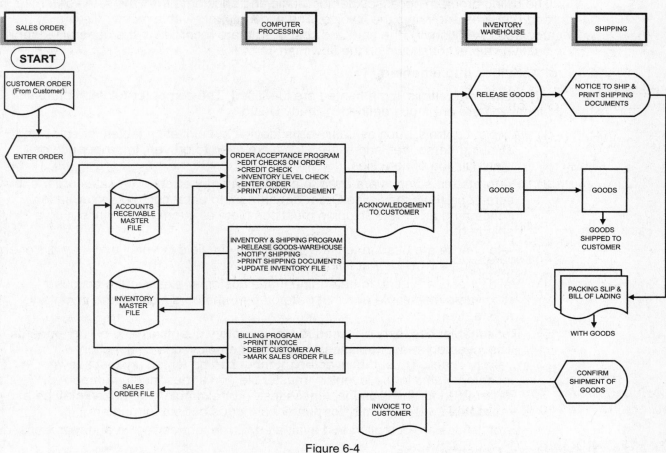

Figure 6-4

5. **The Information Flow**

    a. The sales-receivables computer system flowchart above provides one view of computer processing using online systems. In this case, paper flow is replaced with electronic transmissions, and manual files and ledgers are replaced by computer files. The accounting departments (from the previous flowcharts) of Billing, Inventory Control, and Accounts Receivable are replaced by the Computer Processing department. Furthermore, routine credit decisions are replaced by a computer program.

    b. The Sales Order department receives a customer order (beginning at **START** in the flowchart) and records it into the order acceptance program on a preformatted sales entry screen. Edit checks are used to ensure proper entry. The accounts receivable master file is checked for current customer information and credit limits. Inventory levels are checked for availability from the inventory master file. The accepted order, along with prices determined from the inventory master file, is entered into the sales order master file, and an acknowledgment is printed and sent to the customer.

    c. Information is passed to the inventory and shipping program that sends a release authorization to the Inventory Warehouse via a computer workstation. Inventory levels are formally updated upon release of the goods from the Inventory Warehouse. An electronic shipping authorization is sent to the Shipping department. The communication also generates a packing slip and shipping documents (e.g., a bill of lading) that are printed in the Shipping department.

    d.   Shipping provides the billing program with the information concerning the shipment. The billing program accesses demographic and price data from the sales order file and prepares and prints the invoice. The accounts receivable master file is also updated. (Additionally, the sale and cost of sale are recorded in the general ledger, but this step is not shown on the flowchart.)

6.   **Control Activities Implemented**

    a.   Only the major controls implemented are identified. The computer-related controls identified here are those defined in Study Unit 5.

        1)   Access controls, such as passwords, device authorization tables for sales and shipping personnel, and access logs, are used to prevent improper use or manipulation of data files.

        2)   Preformatted screens are used to avoid data entry errors. The sales order entry screen prompts the Sales Order department to enter complete information concerning an order. Shipping must complete all information concerning a shipment.

        3)   Field checks are used to test the characters in a field to verify that they are of an appropriate type for that field.

        4)   Validity tests are used to determine that a customer exists in the accounts receivable master file and that ordered part numbers exist on the inventory master file.

        5)   Reasonableness tests are used to test inventory quantities and billing amounts. The inventory reasonableness test can be employed in conjunction with a validity check. Thus, the inventory number can be tested against known inventory items in the inventory master file and a reasonable number determined for the reasonableness test. (For example, 100 dozen may be a reasonable order quantity for printer cartridges but not for printers.)

        6)   Error listings are compiled and evaluated. Errors are corrected and reprocessed.

7.   **E-Commerce Considerations**

    a.   The sales-receivables computer flowchart may be used to envision sales processing for a firm using an Internet website. Likely changes include direct entry of the order by the customer, elimination of the sales order department, and payment by credit card. Thus, accounts receivable will not be maintained. Acknowledgment of the order acceptance would be immediately communicated to the customer via an email or other Internet response. However, shipping department procedures and controls would be largely unaltered.

        1)   Additional controls include

            a)   A **firewall** between the customer and internally stored client data

            b)   **Passwords** for authorized or preferred customers

            c)   **Encryption** procedures for transmission of sensitive information

Stop and review! You have completed the outline for this subunit. Study multiple-choice questions 22 through 27 beginning on page 215.

QUESTIONS

6.1 Responsibilities/Organizational Structure/Flowcharts

1. At which point in an ordinary sales transaction of a wholesaling business is a lack of specific authorization of **least** concern to the auditor in the conduct of an audit?

A. Granting of credit.

B. Shipment of goods.

C. Determination of discounts.

D. Selling of goods for cash.

Answer (D) is correct.
REQUIRED: The point in an ordinary sales transaction at which specific authorization is of least concern to an auditor.
DISCUSSION: Selling goods for cash is the consummation of a transaction that is likely to be covered by a general authorization. Thus, the risk of loss arising from lack of specific authorization of cash sales is minimal.
Answer (A) is incorrect. Granting of credit in a sales transaction may require specific authorization, i.e., special consideration before approval by the appropriate person. Answer (B) is incorrect. Shipment of goods in a sales transaction may require specific authorization. Answer (C) is incorrect. Determination of discounts in a sales transaction may require specific authorization.

2. During the consideration of a small business client's internal control, the auditor discovered that the accounts receivable clerk approves credit memos and has access to cash. Which of the following controls would be most effective in offsetting this weakness?

A. The owner reviews errors in billings to customers and postings to the subsidiary ledger.

B. The controller receives the monthly bank statement directly and reconciles the checking accounts.

C. The owner reviews credit memos after they are recorded.

D. The controller reconciles the total of the detail accounts receivable accounts to the amount shown in the ledger.

Answer (C) is correct.
REQUIRED: The most effective control to compensate for an employee's performance of incompatible functions.
DISCUSSION: The clerk can both perpetrate and conceal a fraud in the normal course of his/her duties. The clerk has custody of cash, performs the recordkeeping function for accounts receivable, and authorizes credit memos. Thus, the clerk could conceal a theft of cash collected from customers on account by authorizing sales returns. In a small business, cost-benefit considerations ordinarily preclude establishment of formal control activities. In this situation, effective owner-management involvement may compensate for the absence of certain control activities. Accordingly, the owner should determine that credit memos are genuine.
Answer (A) is incorrect. The clerk could commit a theft without errors in billing and postings to the subsidiary ledger. Answer (B) is incorrect. The bank reconciliation will not detect a theft of cash concealed by improper credit memos. Cash stolen by the clerk would not be recorded. Answer (D) is incorrect. Improper credits to accounts receivable do not cause a discrepancy between the control account and the subsidiary ledger.

3. Which of the following controls most likely would be effective in offsetting the tendency of sales personnel to maximize sales volume at the expense of high bad debt write-offs?

A. Employees responsible for authorizing sales and bad debt write-offs are denied access to cash.

B. Shipping documents and sales invoices are matched by an employee who does not have authority to write off bad debts.

C. Employees involved in the credit-granting function are separated from the sales function.

D. Subsidiary accounts receivable records are reconciled to the control account by an employee independent of the authorization of credit.

Answer (C) is correct.
REQUIRED: The control most effective in offsetting the tendency of sales personnel to maximize sales volume at the expense of high bad debt write-offs.
DISCUSSION: Salespeople should be responsible for generating sales and providing service to customers. For effective control, the credit department should be responsible for monitoring the financial condition of prospective and continuing customers in the credit approval process and should report to the CFO.
Answer (A) is incorrect. Denial of access to cash does not address the problem of the incompatibility of the sales and credit granting functions. Answer (B) is incorrect. Matching of shipping and sales documents does not address the issue. Answer (D) is incorrect. Reconciliation of the subsidiary and general ledgers does not address the issue.

4. An auditor tests an entity's policy of obtaining credit approval before shipping goods to customers in support of management's financial statement assertion of

    A. Valuation.

    B. Completeness.

    C. Occurrence.

    D. Rights and obligations.

Answer (A) is correct.
    REQUIRED: The assertion related to the policy of credit approval before shipping goods to customers.
    DISCUSSION: The proper approval of credit provides assurance that the account receivable is collectible. Thus, it is related to the valuation assertion that balances are reported at appropriate amounts, e.g., accounts receivable at net realizable value.
    Answer (B) is incorrect. The completeness assertion is that all transactions, events, and balances that should have been recorded have been recorded. Answer (C) is incorrect. The occurrence assertion is that recorded transactions and events have occurred and pertain to the entity. Answer (D) is incorrect. Rights and obligations assertions relate to whether assets are rights of the entity and liabilities are obligations of the entity.

5. An auditor is determining whether internal control over the revenue cycle of a wholesaler is operating effectively in minimizing the failure to prepare sales invoices. The auditor most likely will select a sample of transactions from the population represented by the

    A. Sales order file.

    B. Customer order file.

    C. Shipping document file.

    D. Sales invoice file.

Answer (C) is correct.
    REQUIRED: The population sampled to test control over preparation of sales invoices.
    DISCUSSION: The auditor should trace shipping document file copies relating to customer shipments to sales invoices (or possibly to the accounts receivable subsidiary ledger) to determine whether shipments were billed.
    Answer (A) is incorrect. The sales order file may contain orders not yet shipped. Answer (B) is incorrect. The customer order file may contain orders that were not approved and shipped. Answer (D) is incorrect. To test for failure to invoice, the auditor should not sample from a file of invoiced orders. Comparing sales invoices with shipping documents provides evidence of actual shipments and therefore occurrence.

6. Which of the following activities most likely would **not** be an internal control activity designed to reduce the risk of errors in the billing process?

    A. Comparing control totals for shipping documents with corresponding totals for sales invoices.

    B. Using computer programmed controls over the pricing and accuracy of sales invoices.

    C. Matching shipping documents with approved sales orders before invoice preparation.

    D. Reconciling the control totals for sales invoices with the accounts receivable subsidiary ledger.

Answer (D) is correct.
    REQUIRED: The procedure not considered an internal control designed to reduce the risk of errors in the billing process.
    DISCUSSION: The accounts receivable subsidiary ledger contains all receivables outstanding to date. It is not feasible to attempt to reconcile current sales invoices with the accounts receivable subsidiary ledger. However, the accounts receivable subsidiary ledger should be reconciled to the general ledger control account periodically.
    Answer (A) is incorrect. The total amounts shipped should correspond to the sales invoices and can be reconciled on a daily basis. Answer (B) is incorrect. Programmed controls are appropriate in a computerized environment. Answer (C) is incorrect. The preparation of an invoice should depend on the shipment of goods.

7. Which of the following controls most likely would help ensure that all credit sales transactions of an entity are recorded?

    A. The billing department supervisor sends copies of approved sales orders to the credit department for comparison to authorized credit limits and current customer account balances.

    B. The accounting department supervisor independently reconciles the accounts receivable subsidiary ledger to the accounts receivable control account monthly.

    C. The accounting department supervisor controls the mailing of monthly statements to customers and investigates any differences they report.

    D. The billing department supervisor matches prenumbered shipping documents with entries in the sales journal.

Answer (D) is correct.
    REQUIRED: The control to detect unrecorded sales.
    DISCUSSION: The sequential numbering of documents provides a standard control over transactions. The numerical sequence should be accounted for by an independent party. A major objective is to detect unrecorded and unauthorized transactions. Moreover, comparing shipments with the sales journal also will detect unrecorded transactions.
    Answer (A) is incorrect. Credit approval does not ensure that sales have been recorded. Answer (B) is incorrect. The reconciliation will not detect sales that were never recorded. Answer (C) is incorrect. Customers are unlikely to report understatement of their accounts.

8. Refer to the flowchart below.

In a credit sales and cash receipts system flowchart, Symbol X could represent

A. Auditor's test data.

B. Remittance advices.

C. Error reports.

D. Credit authorization forms.

Answer (B) is correct.

REQUIRED: The document in the credit sales and cash receipts flowchart represented by Symbol X.

DISCUSSION: Remittance advices (Symbol X) are sent with sales invoices to customers to be returned with cash payments. Credit memos are internal documents crediting customer accounts for returns or allowances granted. These documents are processed against the master file in the updating run.

Answer (A) is incorrect. Auditor's test data are not part of the client's processing of accounts receivable payments. Answer (C) is incorrect. Error reports are an output of the process. Answer (D) is incorrect. Credit authorization forms are documents approving credit sales. They should be distinguished from credit memos.

9. An auditor would consider a cashier's job description to contain compatible duties if the cashier receives remittances from the mail room and also prepares the

A. Prelist of individual checks.

B. Monthly bank reconciliation.

C. Daily deposit slip.

D. Remittance advices.

Answer (C) is correct.

REQUIRED: The cashier's duty compatible with receiving remittances from the mail room.

DISCUSSION: Preparing the bank deposit slip is a part of the custodial function, which is the primary responsibility of a cashier. The cashier is an assistant to the CFO and thus performs an asset custody function. The preparation of a bank deposit slip is an integral part of the custodial function, along with the depositing of remittances daily at a local bank.

Answer (A) is incorrect. The mail room prepares the prelist of checks as soon as they are received. Answer (B) is incorrect. Someone independent of the custodial function (e.g., the controller) should prepare the monthly bank reconciliation. Answer (D) is incorrect. The mail room prepares remittance advices if one is not received from the customer.

10. Cash receipts from sales on account have been misappropriated. Which of the following acts would conceal this defalcation and be **least** likely to be detected by an auditor?

A. Understating the sales journal.

B. Overstating the accounts receivable control account.

C. Overstating the accounts receivable subsidiary ledger.

D. Understating the cash receipts journal.

Answer (A) is correct.

REQUIRED: The act that conceals misappropriation of cash.

DISCUSSION: Not recording sales on account in the books of original entry is the most effective way to conceal a subsequent theft of cash receipts. The accounts will be incomplete but balanced, and procedures applied to the accounting records will not detect the defalcation.

Answer (B) is incorrect. The discrepancy between the control account and the subsidiary ledger indicates a misstatement. Answer (C) is incorrect. The discrepancy between the control account and the subsidiary ledger indicates a misstatement. Answer (D) is incorrect. Cash receipts will not reconcile with the credits to accounts receivable. If accounts receivable are not credited, confirmation will detect the theft.

11. Upon receipt of customers' checks in the mail room, a responsible employee should prepare a remittance listing that is forwarded to the cashier. A copy of the listing should be sent to the

A. Internal auditor to investigate the listing for unusual transactions.

B. CFO to compare the listing with the monthly bank statement.

C. Accounts receivable bookkeeper to update the subsidiary accounts receivable records.

D. Entity's bank to compare the listing with the cashier's deposit slip.

Answer (C) is correct.
   REQUIRED: The use of a copy of the client's remittance listing.
   DISCUSSION: The individuals with recordkeeping responsibility should not have custody of cash. Hence, they should use either the remittance advices or a listing of the remittances to make entries to the cash and accounts receivable control account and to the subsidiary accounts receivable records. Indeed, having different people make entries in the control account and in the subsidiary records is an effective control.
   Answer (A) is incorrect. The internal auditors should have no ongoing control responsibilities. The investigation of unusual transactions is first conducted in the CFO's department. Answer (B) is incorrect. The monthly bank statement should be reconciled by someone outside of the treasury function. Answer (D) is incorrect. The entity's bank supplies a validated deposit slip based on the deposit for the day. Company management outside the treasury function compares the validated deposit slip with the remittance listing.

12. Which of the following internal controls most likely would reduce the risk of diversion of customer receipts by an entity's employees?

A. A bank lockbox system.

B. Prenumbered remittance advices.

C. Monthly bank reconciliations.

D. Daily deposit of cash receipts.

Answer (A) is correct.
   REQUIRED: The control that reduces the risk of employee misappropriation of cash.
   DISCUSSION: A lockbox system ensures that cash receipts are not stolen by mail clerks or other employees. Customer payments are mailed to a post office box and collected directly by the bank.
   Answer (B) is incorrect. Prenumbering facilitates control over remittance advices, but it would not prevent diversion of cash. Answer (C) is incorrect. A bank reconciliation reconciles the cash in the bank with the amount recorded. However, if cash is not recorded, the reconciliation does not detect its diversion. Answer (D) is incorrect. If the diversion occurs prior to the deposit, timely deposits do not necessarily reduce the risk of diversion.

13. Evidence concerning the proper segregation of duties for receiving and depositing cash receipts ordinarily is obtained by

A. Completing an internal control questionnaire that describes the control activities.

B. Observing the employees who are performing the control activities.

C. Performing substantive procedures to verify the details of the bank balance.

D. Preparing a flowchart of the duties performed and the entity's available personnel.

Answer (B) is correct.
   REQUIRED: The procedure testing segregation of duties for receiving and depositing cash.
   DISCUSSION: Observation is a risk assessment procedure performed to obtain an understanding of the entity and its environment, including its controls. It is also a test of controls. Observation of entity activities and operations supports inquiries of management and provides information about the entity and its environment.
   Answer (A) is incorrect. The questionnaire documents the understanding of the controls, not whether they are operating effectively. Answer (C) is incorrect. Substantive procedures directly address financial statement assertions, not controls. Answer (D) is incorrect. The flowchart documents the understanding of the controls, not whether they are operating effectively.

14. Employers bond employees who handle cash receipts because fidelity bonds reduce the possibility of employing dishonest individuals and

A. Protect employees who make unintentional errors from possible monetary damages resulting from their errors.

B. Deter dishonesty by making employees aware that insurance companies may investigate and prosecute dishonest acts.

C. Facilitate an independent monitoring of the receiving and depositing of cash receipts.

D. Force employees in positions of trust to take periodic vacations and rotate their assigned duties.

Answer (B) is correct.
   REQUIRED: The purpose of bonding employees.
   DISCUSSION: Effective internal control, including human resources practices that stress the hiring of trustworthy people, does not guarantee against losses from embezzlement and other fraudulent acts committed by employees. Accordingly, an employer may obtain a fidelity bond to insure against losses arising from fraud by the covered employees. Prior to issuing this form of insurance, the underwriters investigate the individuals to be covered. Also, employees should be informed that bonding companies are diligent in prosecuting bonded individuals who commit fraud.
   Answer (A) is incorrect. Bonding insures employers against intentional wrongdoing. Answer (C) is incorrect. Bonding is irrelevant to monitoring the receipt and deposit of cash receipts. Answer (D) is incorrect. Bonding is irrelevant to periodic vacations and rotation of duties.

15. Which of the following internal control activities most likely would deter lapping of collections from customers?

A. Independent internal verification of dates of entry in the cash receipts journal with dates of daily cash summaries.

B. Authorization of write-offs of uncollectible accounts by a supervisor independent of credit approval.

C. Separation of duties between receiving cash and posting the accounts receivable ledger.

D. Supervisory comparison of the daily cash summary with the sum of the cash receipts journal entries.

Answer (C) is correct.
REQUIRED: The best protection from lapping of collections from customers.
DISCUSSION: Lapping is the delayed recording of cash receipts to cover a cash shortage. Current receipts are posted to the accounts of customers who paid one or two days previously to avoid complaints (and discovery) when monthly statements are mailed. The best protection is for the customers to send payments directly to the company's depository bank. The next best procedure is to ensure that the accounts receivable clerk has no access to cash received by the mail room. Thus, the duties of receiving cash and posting the accounts receivable ledger are separated.
Answer (A) is incorrect. Lapping delays recording cash receipts so that posting the cash receipts journal and recording in the cash summary occur on the same date and in the same amounts. Answer (B) is incorrect. Lapping involves delayed posting of cash payments, not bad debt write-offs. Moreover, the credit manager should initiate write-offs to be approved by the CFO. Answer (D) is incorrect. Lapping delays recording cash receipts so that posting the cash receipts journal and recording in the cash summary occur on the same date and in the same amounts.

6.2 Controls in a Cash Sale Environment

16. Which of the following procedures would an auditor most likely perform to test controls relating to management's assertion about the completeness of cash receipts for cash sales at a retail outlet?

A. Observe the consistency of the employee's use of cash registers and tapes.

B. Inquire about employee's access to recorded but undeposited cash.

C. Trace the deposits in the cash receipts journal to the cash balance in the general ledger.

D. Compare the cash balance in the general ledger with the bank confirmation request.

Answer (A) is correct.
REQUIRED: The test of controls for the completeness assertion.
DISCUSSION: An assertion about completeness of transactions addresses whether all transactions that should be presented are included in the financial statements. To determine that controls are operating effectively to ensure that all cash receipts are being recorded for cash sales in a retail environment, the auditor may observe the activities of the employees. Controls should provide assurance that employees use cash registers that contain internal functions (e.g., tapes) to record all sales.
Answer (B) is incorrect. Inquiry about employees' access to recorded cash pertains to the existence assertion. Once the sales are recorded, other controls are in place to determine that the existence of cash can be assured. Answer (C) is incorrect. Tracing cash receipts to the ledger is a substantive procedure, not a test of controls. Answer (D) is incorrect. Confirmation of cash with the bank is a substantive procedure, not a test of controls.

17. In a retail cash sales environment, which of the following controls is often absent?

A. Competent personnel.

B. Separation of functions.

C. Supervision.

D. Asset access limited to authorized personnel.

Answer (B) is correct.
REQUIRED: The control often absent in a cash sales environment.
DISCUSSION: In the usual retail cash sales situation, the sales clerk authorizes and records the transactions and takes custody of assets. However, management ordinarily employs other compensating controls to minimize the effects of the failure to separate functions. The cash receipts function is closely supervised, cash registers provide limited access to assets, and an internal recording function maintains control over cash receipts.

6.3 Other Sales-Receivables Related Transactions

18. An auditor noted that the accounts receivable department is separate from other accounting activities. Credit is approved by a separate credit department. Control accounts and subsidiary ledgers are balanced monthly. Similarly, accounts are aged monthly. The accounts receivable manager writes off delinquent accounts after 1 year, or sooner if a bankruptcy or other unusual circumstances are involved. Credit memoranda are prenumbered and must correlate with receiving reports. Which of the following areas could be viewed as an internal control deficiency of the above organization?

   A. Handling of credit memos.

   B. Monthly aging of receivables.

   C. Credit approvals.

   D. Write-offs of delinquent accounts.

Answer (D) is correct.
   REQUIRED: The area viewed as an internal control deficiency of the organization.
   DISCUSSION: The accounts receivable manager has the ability to perpetrate fraud because (s)he performs incompatible functions. Authorization and recording of transactions should be segregated. Thus, someone outside the accounts receivable department should authorize write-offs.
   Answer (A) is incorrect. The procedures regarding credit memoranda are standard controls. Answer (B) is incorrect. Monthly aging is appropriate. Answer (C) is incorrect. Credit approval is an authorization function that is properly segregated from the recordkeeping function.

19. Which of the following most likely would be the result of ineffective internal control in the revenue cycle?

   A. Final authorization of credit memos by personnel in the sales department could permit an employee defalcation scheme.

   B. Fictitious transactions could be recorded, causing an understatement of revenues and an overstatement of receivables.

   C. Fraud in recording transactions in the subsidiary accounts could result in a delay in goods shipped.

   D. Omission of shipping documents could go undetected, causing an understatement of inventory.

Answer (A) is correct.
   REQUIRED: The most likely result of ineffective internal controls in the revenue cycle.
   DISCUSSION: Ineffective controls in the revenue cycle, such as inappropriate segregation of duties and responsibilities, inadequate supervision, or deficient authorization, may result in the ability of employees to perpetrate fraud. Thus, sales personnel should approve sales returns and allowances but not the related credit memos. Moreover, no authorization for the return of goods, defective or otherwise, should be considered complete until the goods are returned as evidenced by a receiving report.
   Answer (B) is incorrect. Recording fictitious sales would overstate revenues. Answer (C) is incorrect. The customers' accounts are not posted until after goods are shipped. Answer (D) is incorrect. If shipping documents are omitted, shipments of goods may not be credited to inventory, thereby overstating the account.

20. Proper authorization of write-offs of uncollectible accounts should be approved in which of the following departments?

   A. Accounts receivable.

   B. Credit.

   C. Accounts payable.

   D. CFO.

Answer (D) is correct.
   REQUIRED: The department authorizing write-offs of applicable accounts.
   DISCUSSION: The write-off of uncollectible accounts requires effective controls. The initiation of the write-off is performed by the credit manager. However, authorization should be by an independent party, typically the CFO. The credit manager is evaluated, in part, on the amount of bad debt written off and should require significant evidence before initiating a write-off.
   Answer (A) is incorrect. Accounts receivable is a recording function and should not authorize transactions. Answer (B) is incorrect. The credit manager should not both initiate and approve the write-off. Answer (C) is incorrect. Accounts payable is a recording function and should not authorize transactions.

21. Sound internal control activities dictate that defective merchandise returned by customers be presented initially to the

   A. Accounts receivable supervisor.

   B. Receiving clerk.

   C. Shipping department supervisor.

   D. Sales clerk.

Answer (B) is correct.
   REQUIRED: The individual to whom customers should return defective merchandise.
   DISCUSSION: For control purposes, all receipts of goods or materials should be handled by the receiving clerk. Receiving reports should be prepared for all items received.
   Answer (A) is incorrect. The accounts receivable supervisor has a recordkeeping function incompatible with access to assets. Answer (C) is incorrect. Shipping and receiving should be segregated. Answer (D) is incorrect. All returns of goods should be handled by an independent receiving function.

6.4 Technology Considerations

22. An online sales order processing system most likely would have an advantage over a batch sales order processing system by

- A. Detecting errors in the data entry process more easily by the use of edit programs.
- B. Enabling shipment of customer orders to be initiated as soon as the orders are received.
- C. Recording more secure backup copies of the database on magnetic tape files.
- D. Maintaining more accurate records of customer accounts and finished goods inventories.

Answer (B) is correct.
    REQUIRED: The advantage of an online system over a batch system.
    DISCUSSION: An online processing system can handle transactions as they are entered because of its direct connection to a computer network. Thus, shipment of customer orders may be initiated instantaneously as they are received. Batch processing is the accumulation and grouping of transactions for processing on a delayed basis.
    Answer (A) is incorrect. Both systems use edit programs. Answer (C) is incorrect. Online systems record information on direct-access memory devices. Answer (D) is incorrect. Online and batch systems provide equivalent accuracy.

23. Mill Co. uses a batch processing method to process its sales transactions. Data on Mill's sales transaction file are electronically sorted by customer number and are subjected to programmed edit checks in preparing its invoices, sales journals, and updated customer account balances. One of the direct outputs of the creation of this file most likely would be a

- A. Report showing exceptions and control totals.
- B. Printout of the updated inventory records.
- C. Report showing overdue accounts receivable.
- D. Printout of the sales price master file.

Answer (A) is correct.
    REQUIRED: The most likely direct output of the creation of a sales transaction file.
    DISCUSSION: Batch processing is useful for processing large volumes of data, especially when sorted in sequential order, for example, by customer number. Editing (validation) of data should produce a cumulative automated error listing that includes not only errors found in the current processing run but also uncorrected errors from earlier runs. Each error should be identified and described, and the date and time of detection should be given. The creation of the file also generates various totals that serve as controls over the accuracy of the processing.
    Answer (B) is incorrect. A batch system is less appropriate for printing records that require up-to-date information. Answer (C) is incorrect. Testing for overdue accounts receivable should be done prior to approving current sales orders. Answer (D) is incorrect. A complete listing of sales prices should not be in a sales transactions file.

24. When evaluating internal control of an entity that processes sales transactions on the Internet, an auditor would be most concerned about the

- A. Lack of sales invoice documents as an audit trail.
- B. Potential for computer disruptions in recording sales.
- C. Inability to establish an integrated test facility.
- D. Frequency of archiving and data retention.

Answer (B) is correct.
    REQUIRED: The greatest concern about Internet controls.
    DISCUSSION: Processing sales on the Internet (often called e-commerce) creates new and additional risks for clients. The client should use effective controls to ensure proper acceptance, processing, and storage of sales transactions. Threats include not only attacks from hackers but also system overload and equipment failure.
    Answer (A) is incorrect. E-commerce sales transactions would not typically result in sales invoice documents. Answer (C) is incorrect. An integrated test facility is just one of many techniques for testing sales processing controls and transactions. Answer (D) is incorrect. Although archival and data retention are disaster recovery concerns, the question relates to controls over sales processing.

25. A CPA is gaining an understanding of the internal controls for a client that sells garden products using an Internet site. Which of the following is **not** likely to be found on the client's organization chart?

- A. The sales order department.
- B. The shipping department.
- C. The warehouse.
- D. Computer processing.

Answer (A) is correct.
    REQUIRED: The department or process not associated with an e-commerce client.
    DISCUSSION: The customer directly communicates the order via the Internet site. Thus, a sales order department is not needed to handle and process the order. Acceptance of the order, collection of payment, and scheduling of products for shipment are largely independent of human involvement.
    Answer (B) is incorrect. The products must be stored and subsequently shipped to the customer. Answer (C) is incorrect. The products must be stored and subsequently shipped to the customer. Answer (D) is incorrect. The order processing procedure is handled primarily by computer, and a computer processing department is likely to be found on the organization chart.

Questions 26 and 27 are based on the following information. A flowchart of a client's revenue cycle appears below.

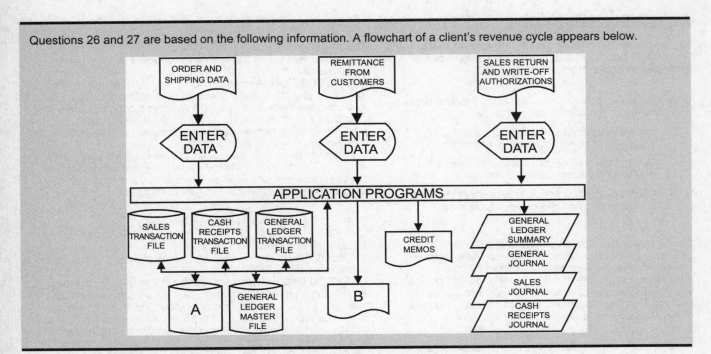

26. Symbol A most likely represents

A. Remittance advice file.

B. Receiving report file.

C. Accounts receivable master file.

D. Cash disbursements transaction file.

Answer (C) is correct.
REQUIRED: The file accessed during the processing of a client's revenue transactions.
DISCUSSION: During the processing of sales orders and remittances from customers, as well as sales returns and write-off authorizations, the accounts receivable master file is accessed and updated. Thus, symbol A represents the accounts receivable master file.
Answer (A) is incorrect. The remittance advice file is represented by the cash receipts transaction file. Answer (B) is incorrect. The receiving report file relates to the purchasing cycle. Answer (D) is incorrect. The cash disbursements transaction file relates to the purchasing cycle.

27. Symbol B most likely represents

A. Customer orders.

B. Receiving reports.

C. Customer checks.

D. Sales invoices.

Answer (D) is correct.
REQUIRED: The document represented by symbol B.
DISCUSSION: One output of the revenue cycle is the generation of sales invoices to be sent to customers.
Answer (A) is incorrect. Customer orders are entered online and not outputted from the system. Answer (B) is incorrect. Receiving reports are generated from the purchasing cycle, not the revenue cycle. Answer (C) is incorrect. Customer checks are represented by remittances from customers and entered online. However, the customer checks are safeguarded and deposited daily into the bank account.

Use the additional questions in Gleim **CPA Test Prep** to create Practice Exams that emulate Prometric!

6.5 PRACTICE TASK-BASED SIMULATIONS

Auditing and Attestation	Time Remaining						
Testlet 4 of 4	1 hour - 30 minutes	Unsplit	Split Horiz	Split Vertical	Spreadsheet	Calculator	Exit

DIRECTIONS

Note: If you believe you have encountered a software malfunction, report it to the test center staff immediately.

Navigation

To navigate from task to task, use the controls at the bottom of the screen. Click on the **Next** button to advance to the next task, or the **Previous** button to go to the previous task. To go directly to any task, click on its number.

▼ = Reminder		Directions	1	2	3	4	5	6	7		◀ Previous	Next ▶

If you would like a reminder to revisit a task, or want to indicate that you are finished with it, click on the reminder flag below the task number. To clear the flag, click on it again. Reminder flags are for your use only – they do not contribute to your score.

Tabs

In this part of the examination, you will be asked to complete various tasks. Every task has one or more **Work Tabs**. Some tasks have one or more **Information Tabs**, others may have none. Every task has a **Help** tab.

If a task has **Information Tabs**, you may use the information in them to complete your responses in the **Work Tabs**.

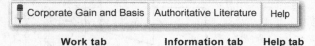

Corporate Gain and Basis	Authoritative Literature	Help
Work tab	Information tab	Help tab

Work Tabs:
- **Work Tabs** are identified with a pencil icon. This is where your responses are expected.
- Each task has one or more **Work Tabs**.
- **Work Tabs** contain directions for completing the task – be sure to read these directions carefully.
- The **Work Tab** name in the example above is for illustration only – yours will differ.
- You must complete all of the **Work Tabs** in each task to receive full credit.

Information Tabs:
- The Authoritative Literature will be provided in all tasks in the AUD, FAR, and REG sections for your reference.
- Your simulation may have one or more additional **Information Tabs**. Like the Authoritative Literature tabs, **Information Tabs** do not have a pencil icon.
- If your task has additional **Information Tabs**, go through each to familiarize yourself with the task content.

Help Tab:
- The **Help Tab** provides assistance with the exam software that is used in this task. For example, if the task is to compose a memorandum, **Help** will provide information about the word processor.

The Toolbar

The toolbar at the top of the screen shows the amount of time remaining for you to complete the tasks. In addition, the following tools are available. Note that only the **Exit** button is displayed when Directions are visible - the others will appear when you begin the tasks.

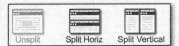

Click on these buttons to split or unsplit the screen. You can split the screen vertically or horizontally.

Click on this button to display the calculator; click on it again to hide the calculator. To move the calculator, click on the calculator title bar and drag the calculator to the desired location.

Click on this button to use the spreadsheet; click on it again to hide the spreadsheet. To move the spreadsheet, click on the the spreadsheet title bar and drag the spreadsheet to the desired location.

Click on this button to go on to the next part of the examination. You must complete all of the tasks to receive full credit. Once you click on **Exit** and confirm the action, you will NOT be able to return to this testlet.

▼ = Reminder		Directions	1	2	3	4	5		◀ Previous	Next ▶

The following flowchart depicts the activities relating to the sales, credit, shipping, billing, and collecting processes used by Newton Hardware, Inc.

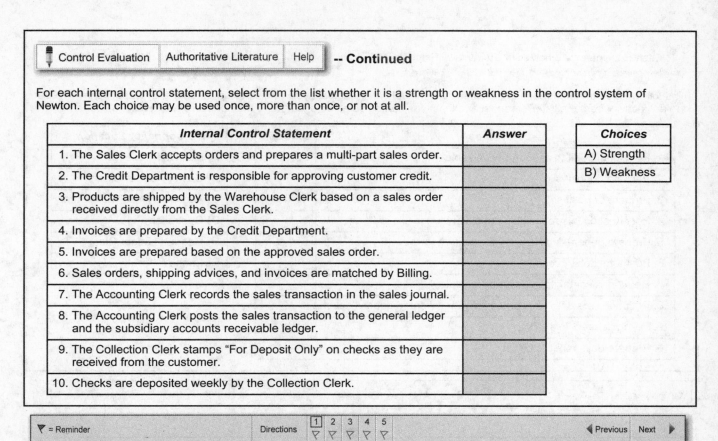

Control Evaluation | Authoritative Literature | Help   **-- Continued**

For each internal control statement, select from the list whether it is a strength or weakness in the control system of Newton. Each choice may be used once, more than once, or not at all.

Internal Control Statement	*Answer*
1. The Sales Clerk accepts orders and prepares a multi-part sales order.	
2. The Credit Department is responsible for approving customer credit.	
3. Products are shipped by the Warehouse Clerk based on a sales order received directly from the Sales Clerk.	
4. Invoices are prepared by the Credit Department.	
5. Invoices are prepared based on the approved sales order.	
6. Sales orders, shipping advices, and invoices are matched by Billing.	
7. The Accounting Clerk records the sales transaction in the sales journal.	
8. The Accounting Clerk posts the sales transaction to the general ledger and the subsidiary accounts receivable ledger.	
9. The Collection Clerk stamps "For Deposit Only" on checks as they are received from the customer.	
10. Checks are deposited weekly by the Collection Clerk.	

Choices
A) Strength
B) Weakness

▼ = Reminder   Directions   [1] 2 3 4 5   ◀ Previous Next ▶

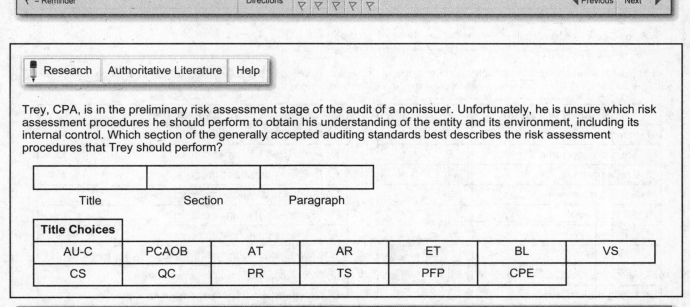

Research | Authoritative Literature | Help

Trey, CPA, is in the preliminary risk assessment stage of the audit of a nonissuer. Unfortunately, he is unsure which risk assessment procedures he should perform to obtain his understanding of the entity and its environment, including its internal control. Which section of the generally accepted auditing standards best describes the risk assessment procedures that Trey should perform?

Title	Section	Paragraph

Title Choices						
AU-C	PCAOB	AT	AR	ET	BL	VS
CS	QC	PR	TS	PFP	CPE	

▼ = Reminder   Directions   1 [2] 3 4 5   ◀ Previous Next ▶

| Cash Receipts | Authoritative Literature | Help |

The following statements relate to activities in a manual cash receipts system. Select the personnel or locations involved in each activity from the list. Personnel and locations can be selected once, more than once, or not at all.

Activities	Answer
1. Post total credit to accounts receivable	
2. Validate deposit slip	
3. Prepare deposit slip	
4. Post to accounts receivable subsidiary ledger	
5. Prepare general ledger entry for cash received	
6. Post total debit to cash	
7. Open mail containing customer receipts	
8. Reconcile the daily remittance list with validated deposit ticket	
9. Take cash receipts to bank	
10. Prepare daily remittance list	

Personnel or Location
A) Mail Room Clerks
B) Cash Receipts Clerk
C) Accounts Receivable Clerk
D) Controller
E) General Ledger Clerk
F) Bank

| Sales-Cycle Responsibilities | Authoritative Literature | Help |

Select from the list provided to match each department or person involved in the sales-receivables-cash receipts cycle with the associated responsibility. Each choice may be used once, more than once, or not at all.

Department or Person	Answer
1. Inventory warehouse	
2. Shipping department	
3. Credit manager	
4. Sales department	
5. General ledger	
6. Cash receipts	
7. Mail room	
8. Accounts receivable clerk	
9. Billing department	

Responsibilities
A) Prepares sales orders
B) Authorizes customer credit
C) Prepares purchase orders to vendors
D) Maintains physical custody of products
E) Prepares shipping documents
F) Prepares customer invoices
G) Maintains accounts receivable subsidiary ledger
H) Receives initial customer receipts
I) Safeguards and deposits cash receipts
J) Maintains the accounts receivable control account

Select from the list provided to match each department or person involved in the sales-receivables-cash receipts cycle with the associated control. Each choice may be used once, more than once, or not at all.

Department or Person	Answer		Controls
1. Inventory warehouse		K)	Safeguards the cash and checks prior to deposit in the bank
2. Shipping department		L)	Releases goods only upon receipt of a valid copy of a sales order
3. Credit manager		M)	Matches copies of documents to ensure that all customers are invoiced
4. Sales department		N)	Checks are immediately endorsed "For Deposit Only" when received
5. General ledger		O)	Only remittance advices are forwarded here for posting to customer accounts
6. Cash receipts		P)	Approved customer orders are required before sales orders are released for processing
7. Mail room		Q)	Goods sent to customers based only on authorized sales orders
8. Accounts receivable clerk		R)	Goods are paid for only when proper documentation is on hand to support a payment
9. Billing department		S)	Investigates potential customers and their likelihood to pay
		T)	Provides the check balance for the sum of the accounts receivable

Unofficial Answers

1. Control Evaluation (10 Gradable Items)

1. <u>A) Strength.</u> The Sales Clerk should accept customer orders and prepare sales orders for internal processing.

2. <u>A) Strength.</u> The Credit department should be responsible for approving customer credit.

3. <u>B) Weakness.</u> Products may be shipped to customers before credit approval. There is no communication between Credit and the Warehouse Clerk.

4. <u>B) Weakness.</u> Invoices should be prepared by the Billing department.

5. <u>B) Weakness.</u> Invoices should be prepared based on the products shipped, not ordered.

6. <u>A) Strength.</u> Matching by the Billing department of the sales orders, shipping advices, and invoices assures that the order was completed and the customer was billed.

7. <u>A) Strength.</u> Recording is an accounting function and should be separate from authorization and custody.

8. <u>B) Weakness.</u> Although posting is an accounting function, ideally the general ledger and subsidiary ledger should be maintained by different individuals. The two records should be reconciled periodically.

9. <u>A) Strength.</u> Stamping "For Deposit Only" (ideally with a bank account number) on checks would help ensure that checks could not be stolen and cashed.

10. <u>B) Weakness.</u> Receipts should be deposited intact daily.

2. Research (1 Gradable Item)

Answer: 315.06

AU-C Section 315 -- *Understanding the Entity and its Environment and Assessing the Risks of Material Misstatement*

Risk Assessment Procedures and Related Activities

.06   The risk assessment procedures should include the following:

      a.   Inquiries of management and others within the entity who, in the auditor's professional judgment, may have information that is likely to assist in identifying risks of material misstatement due to fraud or error

      b.   Analytical procedures

      c.   Observation and inspection

3. Cash Receipts (10 Gradable Items)

1.   <u>E) General Ledger Clerk.</u> The General Ledger Clerk posts the entry received from the Cash Receipts Clerk debiting cash and crediting accounts receivable.

2.   <u>F) Bank.</u> The Bank accepts the receipts and validates the deposit ticket.

3.   <u>B) Cash Receipts Clerk.</u> The Cash Receipts Clerk receives the cash from the Mail Room Clerks and prepares the deposit ticket.

4.   <u>C) Accounts Receivable Clerk.</u> The Accounts Receivable Clerk posts the individual receipts from the remittance list to customers' account.

5.   <u>B) Cash Receipts Clerk.</u> The Cash Receipts Clerk prepares the general journal entry based on the cash receipts and the remittance list.

6.   <u>E) General Ledger Clerk.</u> The General Ledger Clerk posts the entry received from the cash receipts clerk debiting cash and crediting accounts receivable.

7.   <u>A) Mail Room Clerks.</u> The Mail Room Clerks open the mail, endorse checks "For Deposit Only," and prepare the remittance list.

8.   <u>D) Controller.</u> The Controller, who is independent of the cash receipts process, reconciles the daily remittance list and the validated deposit ticket received directly from the bank.

9.   <u>B) Cash Receipts Clerk.</u> The Cash Receipts Clerk is responsible for depositing the receipts in the bank.

10.   <u>A) Mail Room Clerks.</u> The Mail Room Clerks open the mail, endorse checks "For Deposit Only," and prepare the remittance list.

4. Sales-Cycle Responsibilities (9 Gradable Items)

1.   <u>D) Maintains physical custody of products.</u> The inventory warehouse department maintains physical custody of products.

2.   <u>E) Prepares shipping documents.</u> The shipping department prepares shipping documents.

3.   <u>B) Authorizes customer credit.</u> The credit manager authorizes customer credit.

4.   <u>A) Prepares sales orders.</u> The sales department prepares sales orders.

5.   <u>J) Maintains the accounts receivable control account.</u> General ledger personnel maintain the accounts receivable control account.

6.   <u>I) Safeguards and deposits cash receipts.</u> Cash receipts personnel safeguard and deposit cash receipts.

7.   <u>H) Receives initial customer receipts.</u> Mail room personnel receive initial customer receipts.

8.   <u>G) Maintains accounts receivable subsidiary ledger.</u> Accounts receivable personnel maintain the accounts receivable subsidiary ledger.

9.   <u>F) Prepares customer invoices.</u> Billing department personnel prepare customer invoices.

5. Control Responsibilities (9 Gradable Items)

1. L) Releases goods only upon receipt of a valid copy of a sales order. The inventory warehouse releases goods only upon receipt of a valid copy of a sales order.

2. Q) Goods sent to customers based only on authorized sales orders. The shipping department sends goods to customers based only on authorized sales orders.

3. S) Investigates potential customers and their likelihood to pay. The credit manager investigates potential customers and their likelihood to pay.

4. P) Approved customer orders are required before sales orders are released for processing. The sales department approves customer orders before sales orders are released for processing.

5. T) Provides the check balance for the sum of the accounts receivable. General ledger personnel provide the check balance for the sum of the accounts receivable.

6. K) Safeguards the cash and check prior to deposit in the bank. Cash receipts personnel safeguard the cash and checks prior to deposit in the bank.

7. N) Checks are immediately endorsed "For Deposit Only" when received. Mail room personnel ensure that checks are immediately endorsed "For Deposit Only" when received.

8. O) Only remittance advices are forwarded here for posting to customer accounts. The accounts receivable clerk uses only remittance advices for posting to customer accounts.

9. M) Matches copies of documents to ensure that all customers are invoiced. The billing department matches a suspense copy of the sales order with the shipping copy to ensure that all customers are invoiced.

Gleim Simulation Grading

Task	Correct Responses		Gradable Items		Score per Task
1	_____	÷	10	=	_____
2 (Research)	_____	÷	1	=	_____
3	_____	÷	10	=	_____
4	_____	÷	9	=	_____
5	_____	÷	9	=	_____

Total of Scores per Task _____

÷ Total Number of Tasks 5

Total Score _____%

Use **CPA Gleim Online** and **Simulation Wizard** to practice more task-based simulations in a realistic environment.

STUDY UNIT SEVEN
INTERNAL CONTROL --
PURCHASES, PAYROLL, AND OTHER CYCLES

(16 pages of outline)

The initial sections of this study unit describe control concepts in a purchases and payment system. Their focus is on a traditional, manual voucher system that requires each payment to be vouched, or supported, prior to payment. This system has many variations, but the objectives and concepts of control are similar. The manual system presented here has most of the elements that are expected to be tested on future CPA exams.

The computer system described eliminates most of the paper flow from the manual system. However, the objectives of internal control are the same. Only the methods have changed. As always, understanding the concepts rather than attempting to memorize the material is the better approach to learning.

The primary focus of the remainder of this study unit is on payroll. Flowcharts again are used to provide a perspective on the flow of documents and information. The flowcharts are limited to essential points, particularly the payroll computer system flowchart. The narrative should be studied in conjunction with the flowcharts. Candidates should stress obtaining an understanding of the objectives of the controls.

Controls related to other accounts, not previously included in the study units, also are covered at the end of this study unit. Only the major controls are addressed, giving consideration to the questions traditionally asked on the CPA exam.

7.1 PURCHASES RESPONSIBILITIES/ORGANIZATIONAL STRUCTURE/FLOWCHART

1. **Management's Responsibility**

    a. Management is responsible for establishing the controls over the purchases-payables-cash disbursements cycle to ensure the following:

    1) Proper authorization of the purchase
    2) Ordering the proper quality and quantity of goods on a timely basis
    3) Acceptance only of goods that have been ordered
    4) Receipt of proper terms and prices from the vendor
    5) Payment only for those goods and services that were ordered, received, and properly invoiced
    6) Payment on a timely basis (e.g., to take advantage of cash discounts)

2. **The Auditor's Responsibility**

   a. The auditor is required to obtain an understanding of the entity and its environment, including its internal control, to assess the risks of material misstatement and to design further audit procedures. For this purpose, the auditor performs risk assessment procedures. The plan for further audit procedures reflects (1) the auditor's decision whether to test the operating effectiveness of controls over the purchases-payables-cash disbursement cycle and (2) the nature, timing, and extent of substantive procedures.

3. **Organizational Structure**

   a. Although some of the following information was presented in Study Unit 6, it is repeated here for your convenience.

   b. The ideal structure segregates duties and responsibilities as follows:

      1) Authorization of the transaction
      2) Recording of the transaction
      3) Custody over the assets (e.g., inventory and cash disbursements) associated with the transaction

   c. However, cost-benefit considerations may affect the organizational structure, and complete segregation may not be feasible. Compensating controls are likely to be established when the segregation of duties is not maintained. Typical **compensating controls** may include

      1) More supervision or
      2) Owner involvement in the process.

4. **Responsibilities of Personnel**

   a. Responsibilities of personnel and departments in the purchases-payables-cash disbursements cycle include the following:

      1) **Inventory Control** provides authorization for the purchase of goods and performs an accountability function (e.g., Inventory Control is responsible for maintaining perpetual records for inventory quantities and costs).
      2) **Purchasing Agent** issues purchase orders for required goods.
      3) **Receiving** department accepts goods for approved purchases, counts and inspects the goods, and prepares the receiving report.
      4) **Inventory Warehouse** provides physical control over the goods.
      5) **Accounts Payable** (vouchers payable) assembles the proper documentation to support a payment voucher (and disbursement) and records the account payable.
      6) **Cash Disbursements** evaluates the documentation to support a payment voucher and signs and mails the check. This department cancels the documentation to prevent duplicate payment.
      7) **General Ledger** maintains the accounts payable control account and other related general ledger accounts.

5. **The Document Flow**

   a. The organizational chart presented in Study Unit 6, Subunit 1 displays the reporting responsibilities of each function in the flowchart on the next page. To simplify the presentation, the flowchart does not show the disposition, e.g., the filing of documents, or other supplemental procedures. Some text is added to the flowchart to facilitate understanding of the flow. The flowchart begins at the point labeled **START**. Copies of documents are numbered so they may be referenced through the system.

Purchases Manual System Flowchart

Figure 7-1

b.   Inventory Control, based on the pre-established reorder point, initiates a requisition as authorization for the purchase. The quantity authorized is the economic order quantity (EOQ). One copy of the requisition is sent to the Purchasing Agent (copy 2), and another is sent to Accounts Payable (copy 1). Inventory Control maintains a perpetual inventory by recording both reductions for sales of goods to customers and increases for receipts of goods from vendors.

c.   The Purchasing Agent provides additional authorization and determines the appropriate vendor, often through bidding, to supply the appropriate quantity and quality of goods at the optimal price. The purchasing agent then prepares a multi-part (five-part) purchase order. Copies 1 and 2 are sent to the vendor with a request to return one copy as an acknowledgment. Copy 4 of the purchase order (with the quantity omitted—a blind copy) is sent to Receiving as authorization to accept the goods when delivered. Copy 3 is sent to Accounts Payable, matched with the previously received requisition, and filed for subsequent action. Copy 5 is filed in the open purchase order file.

d.   When the goods arrive, Receiving accepts the goods based on the authorization by the Purchasing Agent (the blind copy of the purchase order). Receiving counts and inspects the goods and prepares a receiving report. A copy of the receiving report (copy 1) is sent to Inventory Control and posted to the perpetual inventory records and then sent to Accounts Payable. The copy is then matched with the requisition and purchase order being held, and the three copies are filed for subsequent action. Copy 2 of the receiving report accompanies the goods to the Inventory Warehouse.

   1)   If the goods received are nonconforming, the Shipping department will return them to the vendor and notify the Purchasing Agent so arrangements can be made with the vendor for another shipment. If goods had been previously accepted and an entry had been made, the Purchasing department should send a debit memo to the Accounting department. A debit memo indicates a reduction in the amount owed to a vendor because goods have been returned. The debit memo authorizes the General Ledger to debit the appropriate payable.

e.   The Inventory Warehouse acknowledges receipt and safekeeping of the goods by signing copy 2 of the receiving report. The copy is then forwarded to the Purchasing Agent.

   1)   If goods are produced rather than purchased for resale, the objective of safeguarding assets remains the same. Custody of work-in-process and finished goods should be properly maintained. Accordingly, inventories should be in the custody of a storekeeper, and transfers should be properly documented and recorded to establish accountability.

f.   The Purchasing Agent posts copy 2 of the receiving report to the open purchase order file. This file allows the Purchasing Agent to follow up with vendors concerning delivery times and terms. When a purchase order is filled (i.e., all goods and related invoices are received), it is pulled and filed in the closed purchase order file.

g.   When the invoice is received from the vendor, it is directed to the Purchasing Agent. The terms (e.g., prices and discounts) from the invoice are checked against those from the purchase order (filed in the open purchase order file). The purchasing agent approves the invoice for payment and sends it to Accounts Payable.

h.   Accounts Payable matches the invoice with the related requisition, purchase order, and receiving report, and determines its mathematical accuracy. When all four documents are received and reconciled, a payment voucher, including a check, is prepared (but the check is not signed), and an entry is forwarded to the General Ledger to debit purchases and credit accounts payable. An authorized person should approve the voucher.

  i. The voucher is then filed in a tickler file by due date based on the vendor's terms. For example, if the terms were net 30 days, the voucher would be filed so that it would be pulled just in time for the check to be signed and mailed in accordance with the terms.

  j. On the appropriate due date, the voucher is pulled from the tickler file and sent to Cash Disbursements. Cash Disbursements makes the determination that the documentation supports the voucher and check. If so, the check is signed and mailed to the vendor. At the time the check is signed, the documentation (i.e., payment voucher, approved invoice, requisition, purchase order, and receiving report) is canceled so that it cannot be used to support a duplicate payment.

  k. The check is recorded in the cash disbursements journal, and an entry is forwarded to the General Ledger to debit accounts payable and credit cash.

6. **Controls Implemented**

  a. The segregation of duties for the transaction is as follows: authorization, recording, and custody of assets.

  b. Requisitions, purchase orders, receiving reports, payment vouchers, and checks are prenumbered and accounted for.

  c. Purchases are based only on proper authorizations. Receiving should not accept merchandise unless an approved purchase order is on hand.

  d. Receiving's copy of the purchase order omits the quantity so that employees must count the goods to determine the quantity to record on the receiving report.

  e. The Purchasing Agent compares prices and terms from the vendor invoice with requested and acknowledged terms from the vendor.

  f. Vouchers and the related journal entries are prepared only when goods are received that have been authorized, ordered, and appropriately invoiced.

  g. The tickler file permits timely payments to realize available cash discounts.

  h. Cash Disbursements ascertains that proper support exists for the voucher and check before signing the check.

  i. Two signatures may be required for checks larger than a preset limit.

  j. Cash Disbursements, which reports to the CFO, mails the checks so that no one internal to the entity can gain access to the signed checks.

  k. Cash Disbursements cancels payment documents to prevent their use as support for duplicate vouchers and checks.

  l. Periodic reconciliation of the vouchers in the tickler file with Accounts Payable ensures proper recording in the accounts payable control account.

  m. Periodic counts of inventory, independently reconciled with perpetual records, provide assurance that physical controls over inventory are effective.

    1) Internal verification of inventory is independent if performed by an individual who is not responsible for custody of assets or the authorization and recording of transactions.

  n. Accounts Payable examines the vendor invoice for mathematical errors.

  o. Accounts Payable compares the vendor's invoice with the receiving report, the requisition, and the purchase order to ensure that a valid transaction occurred.

7.   **Other Payment Authorizations**

   a.   This voucher-disbursement system is applicable to virtually all required payments by the entity, not just purchases of inventory as described previously. The following are additional considerations:

      1)   The authorizations may come from other departments based on a budget or policy (e.g., a utility bill might need authorization by the plant manager).

      2)   Accounts Payable would require different document(s) (e.g., a utility bill with the signature of the plant manager) to support the preparation of the payment voucher and check.

      3)   A debit other than purchases (e.g., utilities expense) would be entered on the payment voucher and recorded in the general ledger. Accounts payable would still be credited.

      4)   The use of the tickler file and the functions of Cash Disbursements would not change when other types of payments were made.

Stop and review! You have completed the outline for this subunit. Study multiple-choice questions 1 through 10 beginning on page 241.

7.2 PURCHASES TECHNOLOGY CONSIDERATIONS

1.   Computer Processing ordinarily replaces the activities of clerks performing recording functions (e.g., updating the inventory file to record goods received from vendors and updating the open purchase order file). Computer Processing is not shown on the organizational chart in Study Unit 6, but it is discussed here.

2.   No physical voucher is prepared, the tickler file is maintained by the computer, and no check is prepared until the due date.

3.   Sophisticated systems may replace the internal paper flows with electronic transmissions.

4.   Ordinarily, the manual files and ledgers are replaced by digital files.

5.   **The Information Flow**

   a.   This purchases-payables computer system flowchart depicts one example of an online purchasing system. The accounting departments (refer to Figure 7-1) of Inventory Control and Accounts Payable and the Purchasing Agent's open purchase order file are replaced by Computer Processing. In addition, routine order decisions are replaced by computer programs.

   b.   The shipping of inventory for sales orders and the related reduction of inventory on the inventory master file cause inventory levels to fall below the reorder point (beginning at **START** on the flowchart). As a result, a requisition request is transmitted to the Purchasing Agent. The approved vendor, economic order quantity, costs, and other relevant terms are stored in the inventory master file and provided to the Purchasing Agent. The Purchasing Agent can approve the information or make modifications based on current conditions.

   c.   Once the requisition is approved, the purchase order program prints the purchase order for mailing to the vendor, records it in the open purchase order file, and authorizes Receiving to accept the shipment.

   d.   When the goods arrive, Receiving accepts the shipment and enters the count and other relevant information into the receiving program. This step updates the open purchase order file and the inventory master file. The goods are taken to the Inventory Warehouse.

e. When the invoice arrives, the Purchasing Agent enters the information into the invoice program, which tests the terms against those in the record in the open purchase order file. If the information is complete and the goods have been received, a record is created in the accounts payable master file. Furthermore, the General Ledger is updated for the debit to purchases and the credit to accounts payable. However, this step is not shown.

f. The accounts payable program generates a check when the terms of the purchase require it to do so.

Purchases-Payables Computer System Flowchart

Figure 7-2

6.   **Control Activities Implemented**

a.   The major computer-related controls are identified here. The controls are defined in Study Unit 5.

b.   Access to the programs and data is restricted by password and device authorization tables. For example, Receiving, even with the proper password, can access only the receiving program and can change only the fields in the records affected by the receiving transactions.

c.   Access logs are maintained that automatically record each transaction, the time of the transaction, and the identification of the person who entered the transaction.

d.   Preformatted data entry screens are used to ensure proper input. For example, Receiving's entry screen requires the quantity received to be completed (along with the other data) before the transaction is accepted.

e.   Field checks are used to test the characters in certain fields to verify that they are of an appropriate type for that field (e.g., the quantity field should contain numbers only).

f.   Validity tests are used that ensure the propriety of supplier transactional data prior to accepting the input.

g.   Reasonableness tests are used to test quantities ordered and received to determine if they are within acceptable limits.

Stop and review! You have completed the outline for this subunit. Study multiple-choice question 11 on page 244.

7.3 ELECTRONIC DATA INTERCHANGE (EDI)

1.   EDI is the communication of electronic documents directly from a computer in one entity to a computer in another entity. EDI eliminates the paper documents, both internal and external, that are the traditional basis for many audit procedures.

2.   Advantages include reduction of clerical errors, speed, and the elimination of repetitive clerical tasks. EDI also eliminates document preparation, processing, filing, and mailing costs.

a.   Moreover, an organization that has **reengineered** its procedures and processes to take full advantage of EDI may eliminate even the electronic equivalents of paper documents.

1)   For example, the buyer's **point-of-sale (POS) system** may directly transmit information to the seller, which delivers on a JIT (just-in-time) basis.

b.   Purchase orders, invoices, and receiving reports are replaced with a **long-term contract** establishing

1)   Quantities, prices, and delivery schedules;

2)   Production schedules;

3)   Advance shipment notices;

4)   Evaluated receipts settlements (periodic payment authorizations transmitted to the trading partner); and

5)   Payments by **electronic funds transfer (EFT)**.

a)   EFT is a process based on EDI that transfers money from one account to another by computer.

3. **Audit Procedures**

   a. Accordingly, auditors must seek **new forms of evidence** to support assertions about EDI transactions, whether the evidence exists at the auditee, the trading partner, or a third party (e.g., a value-added network).

      1) Examples of such evidence are

         a) The EDI long-term contract,

         b) An electronic completed production schedule image, and

         c) Internal and external evidence of evaluated receipts settlements sent to the trading partner.

   b. Auditors should evaluate **electronic signatures and reviews** when testing controls.

   c. Auditors may need to consider **other subsystems** when testing a particular system.

      1) Thus, production cycle evidence may be needed to test the expenditure cycle.

   d. Auditing an EDI application requires consideration of the **audit trail**. In addition to the elements listed above, an essential element of an EDI audit trail is an **activity log**.

      1) Because an audit trail allows for the **tracing** of a transaction from initiation to disposition, an activity log provides a key link in the process. Such a log provides information about the

         a) Users who have accessed the system,
         b) Files accessed,
         c) Processing accomplished,
         d) Time of access, and
         e) Amount of time the processing required.

4. **Value-Added Networks (VANs)**

   a. EDI often uses a VAN as a **third-party service provider**, and **controls** provided by the VAN may be critical.

   b. VANs are privately owned telecommunications carriers that sell capacity to outside users.

   c. Among other things, a VAN provides a **mailbox service** permitting EDI messages to be sent, sorted, and held until needed in the recipient's computer system.

      1) **Encryption** of such messages that is performed by physically secure **hardware** is more secure than encryption performed by software.

5. Successful implementation of EDI begins with identifying the work processes and flows that support the entity's objectives.

   a. The initial phase of EDI implementation includes understanding the entity's **mission** and an analysis of its **activities** as part of an integrated solution to its needs.

6. **EDI Terms and Components**

   a. **Standards** focus on procedures to convert written documents into a uniform electronic document-messaging format to facilitate EDI.

   b. **Conventions** are the procedures for arranging **data elements** in specified formats for various accounting transactions, e.g., invoices, materials releases, and advance shipment notices.

      1) To provide standardization and structure for EDI, organizations such as the **American National Standards Institute (ANSI)** have defined virtually every type of business transaction in terms of their fields and information content.

         a) EDI users must **map** their data elements into the standard data fields of each transmission set (e.g., an invoice).

         b) These **transmission sets** facilitate communication between trading partners.

c. **Transmission protocols** are rules on how each envelope or package of information is structured and processed by the communications devices so that messages are kept separate.

7. Telephone or other communication lines and modems are used for communication among computers.

a. **Point-to-point** is the traditional EDI connection. Both parties have fixed computer connections, and the computers are used solely for EDI. The direct connection that is created forces all the computers to be compatible with each other. A point-to-point arrangement is very similar to networks within one company.

b. **Value-added networks** (VAN) are mailbox-type services in which the sender's and receiver's computers are never directly connected to each other. Instead, both parties to the EDI arrangement subscribe to a third-party VAN provider.

   1) Because of the third-party buffer, the VAN users are not required to conform to the same standards, conventions, and protocols.

   2) Also, VANs can store messages, so the parties can batch outgoing and incoming communications.

c. The **Internet** is a means of conducting business directly with a trading partner. It can be used in a more open environment in which one firm transmits documents to another.

   1) This approach is often based on less formal agreements between the trading partners than in EDI and requires the sender to reconfigure documents into the format of the recipient.

Background

XML and XBRL are likely to change the way we communicate information. Currently, data stored in a database are structured. For example, the trial balance in Access has a field for each account, e.g., Cash, with the value stored in the field. When data are taken out of the database, it is difficult to interpret and use without keeping or knowing the structure.

Instead of using a structure, XML and XBRL tag or code each piece of data as it is retrieved from the database so that it can be communicated and then interpreted. For example, the account value may be accessed from the database and tagged as "Cash: $10,000." For now, the CPA exam expects you to understand the uses of XML and XBRL, particularly for financial reporting. Be prepared in the future to gain a much fuller understanding of these languages.

---

8. **XML (extensible markup language)** was developed by an international group of interested organizations as an open standard usable with many programs and platforms. XML codes all information in such a way that a user can determine not only how it should be presented but also what it is.

a. Thus, all computerized data may be **tagged with identifiers**. Unlike HTML, XML uses codes that are extensible, not fixed.

   1) Accordingly, if an industry can agree on a set of codes, software for that industry can be written that incorporates those codes.

9. **XBRL (extensible business reporting language)** for Financial Statements is the specification developed by an AICPA-led group for U.S. commercial and industrial companies that report in accordance with U.S. GAAP.

a. It is a variation of XML that is expected to decrease the costs of generating financial reports, reformulating information for different uses, and sharing business information using electronic media.

b. The SEC requires issuers, unless specifically excluded, to submit and post their financial statements and financial statement schedules on their corporate websites using XBRL. However, the SEC rules do not require assurance on (an audit of) the XBRL files.

Stop and review! You have completed the outline for this subunit. Study multiple-choice questions 12 through 16 beginning on page 244.

7.4 PAYROLL RESPONSIBILITIES/ORGANIZATIONAL STRUCTURE/FLOWCHART

1. **Management's Responsibility**

   a. Management should establish controls to ensure the following:

      1) Proper authorization of the payroll
      2) Appropriate calculation of the payroll
      3) Safeguarding of assets associated with the payment of payroll
      4) Proper distribution of the payroll
      5) Proper accounting for the payroll transactions

2. **The Auditor's Responsibility**

   a. The auditor must obtain an understanding of the entity and its environment, including its internal control, to assess the risks of material misstatement and to design further audit procedures. For this purpose, the auditor performs risk assessment procedures. The plan for further audit procedures reflects (1) the auditor's decision whether to test the operating effectiveness of controls over the payroll cycle and (2) the nature, timing, and extent of substantive procedures.

3. **Organizational Structure**

   a. Although the following information is similar to that in the previous flowchart discussions, it has been repeated for your convenience.

   b. The structure should segregate duties and responsibilities as follows:

      1) Authorization of payroll transactions
      2) Recording of payroll transactions
      3) Custody of the assets (e.g., payroll checks) associated with payroll transactions

   c. Duties and responsibilities for payroll have traditionally been appropriately segregated. However, cost-benefit considerations may affect the organizational structure, and complete segregation may not be feasible. **Compensating controls** are likely to be established when segregation of duties is not maintained. They may include the following:

      1) More supervision
      2) Owner involvement in the payroll process

   d. The following are the responsibilities of organizational subunits in the payroll cycle:

      1) **Human Resources** provides an authorized list of employees and associated pay rates, deductions, and exemptions.
      2) **Payroll** is an accounting function responsible for calculating the payroll (i.e., preparing the payroll register) based on authorizations from Human Resources and the authorized time records from Timekeeping.
      3) **Timekeeping** is an accounting function that oversees the employees' recording of hours on time cards (using the time clock) and that receives and reconciles the job time tickets from Manufacturing.
      4) **Cost Accounting** is an accounting function that accumulates direct materials, direct labor, and overhead costs on job order cost sheets to determine the costs of production.
      5) **Accounts Payable** prepares the payment voucher based on the payroll register prepared by Payroll.
      6) **Cash Disbursements** signs and deposits a check based on the payment voucher into a separate payroll account, prepares individual employee paychecks, and distributes paychecks.

e.   Study the flowchart on the next page. Understand and visualize the payroll process and controls. The organizational chart in Study Unit 6 displays the reporting responsibilities of each function in the flowchart. Read the following description as needed. Note the control activities implemented.

4.   **The Document Flow**

a.   To simplify the presentation, the flowchart does not show the disposition, e.g., the filing of documents, or other supplemental procedures. The process begins at the point labeled **START**.

b.   Human Resources provides authorizations of employees, pay rates, and deductions to Payroll just prior to calculation of the payroll.

c.   Employees punch the time clock with their time cards in Timekeeping before and after each shift.

d.   The shop supervisor assigns employees production-order tasks to be performed, and each employee completes a job time ticket for each task performed. Indirect labor (e.g., down time, cleaning machines, and setup) is also reported on job time tickets. At the end of the shift, the shop supervisor determines that employees have submitted job time tickets to account for all time worked. The job time tickets are then forwarded to Timekeeping.

e.   Timekeeping reconciles the time clock cards with the job time tickets to ensure that employees were present and working. Time clock cards are approved (e.g., initialed) by Timekeeping.

f.   Time clock cards are forwarded to Payroll as authorization of the hours worked. The authorized employees, rates, and deductions from Human Resources, together with the authorized hours from Timekeeping, are used to calculate the payroll for the period. A payroll register is prepared listing each employee, gross pay, all deductions, and net pay. The payroll register is then sent to Accounts Payable.

g.   Accounts Payable uses the payroll register as authorization to prepare a payment voucher and check for the payroll equal to the total of the net pay to employees. (Actually, a number of separate vouchers and checks will be prepared for each required payment generated from the payroll. For example, a check will be prepared with the IRS as payee for withholding taxes, and a check may be prepared with the union as payee for withheld union dues, etc.)

h.   The check, voucher, and supporting documentation will be sent to Cash Disbursements (CFO) for signing. The check for the net payroll drawn on the general cash account is deposited in a separate payroll account. Checks drawn on this special account are prepared for each employee; that is, an imprest payroll checking account is used. The checks are distributed to the employees.

i.   The job time tickets, once used by Timekeeping, are sent to Cost Accounting to charge the work-in-process recorded on job cost sheets for the direct labor used in production. The nonproductive labor is accumulated and reported as overhead incurred (not shown on the flowchart).

j.   The accounting entries are forwarded to the General Ledger (not shown on the flowchart). The entry to record the debit to work-in-process is from Cost Accounting. An entry to credit a payable comes from Accounts Payable. When the check based on the payment voucher is signed, Cash Disbursements forwards the entry to the General Ledger to debit accounts payable and credit cash.

Payroll Manual System Flowchart

Figure 7-3

5.   **Control Activities Implemented**

a.   Human Resources has no functional responsibility other than authorization of employees, pay rates, and deductions.

b.   Supervisors approve (authorize) work performed (executed) by employees.

c.   The Timekeeping reconciliation of the time clock cards and job time tickets ensures that employees are present and working. Punching another person's time clock card would be detected because of the absence of job time tickets.

d.   Payroll accounting calculates pay only. It does not authorize transactions or handle (take custody of) assets.

e.   Cash Disbursements signs the check but does not authorize, prepare, or account for the transaction.

f.   Paychecks are distributed by Cash Disbursements, usually by the paymaster. This individual has no other functions relative to payroll. Supervisors should not distribute paychecks because they have an authorization function.

g.   Unclaimed paychecks are safeguarded by the CFO.

h.   A separate payroll account allows for ease in reconciling bank statements.

Stop and review! You have completed the outline for this subunit. Study multiple-choice questions 17 through 23 beginning on page 245.

7.5 PAYROLL TECHNOLOGY CONSIDERATIONS

1.   Most information may be collected directly by computer.

2.   Physical preparation, handling, and safeguarding of checks can be avoided. Direct deposit into employees' bank accounts is a typical control.

3.   Digital files and data transmission replace the file cabinets and forms.

4.   Several of the accounting clerk's functions are replaced by computer programs. These include some of the duties of Timekeeping and Payroll. Computer Processing is not shown on the organizational chart in Study Unit 6 because it assumes a manual system.

5.   The objectives of control, however, do not change.

6.   The daily processing is immediate because the files are updated as the activities are recorded. However, the calculation of the payroll is normally batch-oriented because checks to employees are prepared periodically (e.g., weekly).

Payroll Computer System Flowchart

Figure 7-4

7. **Payroll Computer System Flowchart**

    a. Study the flowchart on the previous page. Understand and visualize the payroll process and controls in a computer environment. Read the following description as needed. Note the control activities that are implemented.

    b. The payroll computer system flowchart illustrates a system that eliminates virtually all of the paper flow found in the manual system.

    c. Human Resources makes authorized changes in the personnel master file.

    d. As the employee enters the plant, a time clock card record is initiated by passing an ID card through a terminal that contains the timekeeping program.

    e. Production orders, based on the production schedule, are released to the shops via terminal. Shop supervisors assign production employees to the tasks. Prior to beginning, the production employee logs in to the system using his/her ID card. When the production job is complete, the employee logs out, thereby updating the production record. Information is passed to the timekeeping program to be reconciled with the time records and to update the payroll master file.

    f. Periodically (e.g., weekly), information from the payroll master file is matched with wage rate, deduction, and exemption information to calculate the payroll. The checks are printed, and the general ledger is updated (not shown on flowchart).

8. **Control Activities Implemented**

    a. The major computer-related controls are identified here. The controls are defined in Study Unit 5.

    b. Access controls are used, requiring passwords and identification numbers. Only Human Resources has access to the personnel master file and can make changes. Other departments are limited to the changes that can be made to files. Each shop employee is issued an identification card used as input to initiate timekeeping transactions.

    c. Preformatted data entry screens are used for inputs.

    d. Validity checks are made to ensure that an employee record exists on the personnel file before any transactions are accepted.

    e. Time records from Timekeeping are automatically reconciled with the production time logged in the shops.

    f. Reasonableness tests are made when appropriate, e.g., testing at the end of the week to ensure that total hours recorded for an employee are not in excess of 40 hours or the acceptable limit.

    g. Exception reports are printed, identifying all questionable and potentially incorrect transactions. These transactions are investigated, and any corrections are made for reprocessing.

Stop and review! You have completed the outline for this subunit. Study multiple-choice questions 24 and 25 beginning on page 247.

7.6 OTHER CYCLES

1. Other cycles follow the basic pattern of the segregation of duties illustrated in the previous discussions of controls. Flowcharts are not presented for the other cycles discussed here. However, certain basic controls are identified.

2. **Property, Plant, and Equipment Cycle -- Typical Controls**

    a. Formal budgeting process with subsequent variance analysis
    b. Written policies for acquisition and retirement of fixed assets
    c. Written authorizations for acquisition and retirement of fixed assets

        1) Moreover, the same individual should not both approve removal work orders (authorization) and dispose of equipment (asset custody).

    d. Segregation of recordkeeping and accountability (controller) from physical custody (user departments)
    e. Limited physical access to assets when feasible
    f. Periodic reconciliation of subsidiary records and the general ledger control account
    g. Periodic comparisons of physical assets with subsidiary records

3. **Investing Cycle -- Typical Controls**

    a. Written authorizations from the board of directors (or appropriate oversight committee)
    b. Segregation of recordkeeping and accountability (controller) from physical custody (CFO)
    c. Physical safeguards over assets, e.g., a safe-deposit box requiring two signatures to gain admittance
    d. Specific identification of certificate numbers when possible
    e. Periodic reconciliation of subsidiary records and the general ledger control account
    f. Periodic comparisons of physical assets with subsidiary records

4. **Financing Cycle**

    a. The financing cycle concerns obtaining and repaying capital through noncurrent debt and shareholders' equity transactions. These major transactions are authorized by the board of directors or other ultimate authority.

5. **Inventory and Warehousing Cycle**

    a. Transfers of raw materials, finished goods, and costs are subject to cost accounting internal control activities.
    b. The objectives of internal control include safeguarding assets and promoting the reliability of financial reporting. Thus, internal control includes (1) physical controls over storage, (2) assignment of custody to specific individuals, (3) use of prenumbered documents for authorization of transfers, and (4) perpetual inventory records.

        1) For example, requisitions and other documents should have proper authorizations, quantities, descriptions, and dates. Subsidiary ledgers should be independently reconciled with control accounts.

Stop and review! You have completed the outline for this subunit. Study multiple-choice questions 26 through 34 beginning on page 248.

QUESTIONS

7.1 Purchases Responsibilities/Organizational Structure/Flowchart

1. Which of the following controls is most effective in providing assurance that recorded purchases are free of material errors?

A. The receiving department compares the quantity ordered on purchase orders with the quantity received on receiving reports.

B. Vendors' invoices are compared with purchase orders by an employee who is independent of the receiving department.

C. Receiving reports require the signature of the individual who authorized the purchase.

D. Purchase orders, receiving reports, and vendors' invoices are independently matched in preparing vouchers.

Answer (D) is correct.
REQUIRED: The most effective control to provide assurance that recorded purchases are free of material errors.
DISCUSSION: A voucher should not be prepared for payment until the vendor's invoice has been matched against the corresponding purchase order and receiving report (and often the requisition). This procedure provides assurance that a valid transaction has occurred and that the parties have agreed on the terms, such as price and quantity.
Answer (A) is incorrect. The receiving department should receive a blind copy of the purchase order. Answer (B) is incorrect. It is not as comprehensive as the correct answer. Answer (C) is incorrect. The receiving report is prepared by the receiving department.

2. Which of the following describes a weakness in accounts payable procedures?

A. The accounts payable clerk files invoices and supporting documentation after payment.

B. The accounts payable clerk manually verifies arithmetic on the vendor invoice.

C. The accounts payable system compares the receiving report to the vendor invoice.

D. The accounts payable manager issues purchase orders.

Answer (D) is correct.
REQUIRED: The weakness in accounts payable procedures.
DISCUSSION: To maintain a proper segregation of duties, the purchasing agent, not the accounts payable manager, should issue purchase orders. The accounts payable manager performs a recording function. (S)he should not be able to authorize transactions or have custody of assets.
Answer (A) is incorrect. The approved vendor invoice and supporting documentation (requisition, purchase order, and receiving report) are retained by the accounts payable function after the payment voucher (and an unsigned check) is prepared and sent to the cash disbursements function. Answer (B) is incorrect. The purchasing agent approves the invoice for payment and sends it to the accounts payable function. The accounts payable clerk matches the invoice with the related requisition, purchase order, and receiving report and determines its mathematical accuracy. Answer (C) is incorrect. The accounts payable clerk matches the invoice with the related requisition, purchase order, and receiving report and determines its mathematical accuracy.

3. In a well-designed internal control system, the same employee may be permitted to

A. Mail signed checks and also cancel supporting documents.

B. Prepare receiving reports and also approve purchase orders.

C. Approve vouchers for payment and also have access to unused purchase orders.

D. Mail signed checks and also prepare bank reconciliations.

Answer (A) is correct.
REQUIRED: The functions the same employee may be permitted to perform in a well-designed control system.
DISCUSSION: The cash disbursements department has an asset custody function. Consequently, this department is responsible for signing checks after verification of their accuracy by reference to the supporting documents. The supporting documents should then be canceled and the checks mailed. Cancelation prevents the documentation from being used to support duplicate payments. Moreover, having the party who signs the checks place them in the mail reduces the risk that they will be altered or diverted.
Answer (B) is incorrect. The receiving department should not know how many units have been ordered. Answer (C) is incorrect. Accounts is responsible for approving vouchers, and purchasing is the only department with access to the purchase orders. The same employee should not approve the purchase and approve payment. Answer (D) is incorrect. The bank reconciliation is performed by someone with no asset custody function.

4. For effective internal control, the accounts payable department ordinarily should

A. Obliterate the quantity ordered on the receiving department copy of the purchase order.

B. Establish the agreement of the vendor's invoice with the receiving report and purchase order.

C. Stamp, perforate, or otherwise cancel supporting documentation after payment is mailed.

D. Ascertain that each requisition is approved as to price, quantity, and quality by an authorized employee.

Answer (B) is correct.
REQUIRED: The procedure performed by the accounts payable department.
DISCUSSION: The accounts payable department is responsible for matching the vendor's invoice against the corresponding purchase order and receiving report. This procedure provides assurance that a valid transaction has occurred and that the parties have agreed on the terms, such as price and quantity.
Answer (A) is incorrect. The purchasing department is responsible for sending copies of the purchase order to the different departments. Answer (C) is incorrect. The cash disbursements department is responsible for canceling supporting documentation when checks are signed. Answer (D) is incorrect. The purchasing department is responsible for approving each requisition.

5. The authority to accept incoming goods in receiving should be based on a(n)

A. Vendor's invoice.

B. Materials requisition.

C. Bill of lading.

D. Approved purchase order.

Answer (D) is correct.
REQUIRED: The document on which the authority to accept incoming goods in receiving should be based.
DISCUSSION: A receiving department should accept merchandise only if a purchase order or approval granted by the purchasing department is on hand.
Answer (A) is incorrect. The vendor's invoice does not indicate whether purchase of the goods was properly authorized by someone outside the receiving department. Answer (B) is incorrect. Materials requisition does not indicate whether purchase of the goods was properly authorized by someone outside the receiving department. Answer (C) is incorrect. The carrier's bill of lading does not indicate whether purchase of the goods was properly authorized by someone outside the receiving department.

6. In a well-designed internal control system, employees in the same department most likely would approve purchase orders, and also

A. Reconcile the open invoice file.

B. Inspect goods upon receipt.

C. Authorize requisitions of goods.

D. Negotiate terms with vendors.

Answer (D) is correct.
REQUIRED: The task appropriately performed by employees who approve purchase orders.
DISCUSSION: To prevent or detect fraud or error in the performance of assigned responsibilities, duties are often segregated. Approving purchase orders and negotiating terms with vendors are part of the authorization process performed by the purchasing department.
Answer (A) is incorrect. Reconciling the open invoice file is the accounting department's function. Answer (B) is incorrect. Inspection of goods upon receipt is the receiving department's function. Answer (C) is incorrect. Authorization of the requisition is inventory control's function.

7. To provide assurance that each voucher is submitted and paid only once, an auditor most likely would examine a sample of paid vouchers and determine whether each voucher is

A. Supported by a vendor's invoice.

B. Stamped "paid" by the check signer.

C. Prenumbered and accounted for.

D. Approved for authorized purchases.

Answer (B) is correct.
REQUIRED: The observation necessary to determine whether a voucher was paid only once.
DISCUSSION: To provide assurance that voucher documentation is not used to support a duplicate payment, the individual responsible for cash disbursements should examine the voucher and determine the appropriateness of the supporting documents, sign the check, cancel the payment documents, and mail the check to the vendor.
Answer (A) is incorrect. Each voucher should be supported by a vendor's invoice, but if the invoice is not canceled, it may be recycled to support a second voucher. Answer (C) is incorrect. If additional vouchers are prepared and supported with recycled documentation, accounting for the prenumbered vouchers would not ensure that duplicates do not exist. Answer (D) is incorrect. Although vouchers should be approved, unless the documentation is canceled, duplicate payments may be possible.

8. Which of the following situations most likely could lead to an embezzlement scheme?

   A. The accounts receivable bookkeeper receives a list of payments prepared by the cashier and personally makes entries in the customers' accounts receivable subsidiary ledger.

   B. Each vendor invoice is matched with the related purchase order and receiving report by the vouchers payable clerk who personally approves the voucher for payment.

   C. Access to blank checks and signature plates is restricted to the cash disbursements bookkeeper who personally reconciles the monthly bank statement.

   D. Vouchers and supporting documentation are examined and then canceled by the CFO who personally mails the checks to vendors.

Answer (C) is correct.

   REQUIRED: The situation that could most likely lead to embezzlement.

   DISCUSSION: Sufficient segregation of duties should exist to prevent embezzlement (a fraudulent appropriation to one's own use of property entrusted to one's care). The cash disbursements bookkeeper has an asset custody function. (S)he signs checks prepared by the accounts payable function after inspecting the supporting documents. (S)he then cancels those documents and mails the checks. The cash disbursements bookkeeper's access to blank checks and ability to reconcile the monthly bank statement are inappropriate. (S)he can perpetrate and conceal fraud.

   Answer (A) is incorrect. An accounts receivable bookkeeper's responsibility is to record entries into the accounts receivable subsidiary ledger. Answer (B) is incorrect. Vendor invoices should be matched with the related requisition, purchase order, and receiving report by the vouchers payable clerk. (S)he then prepares a payment voucher, including a check. The voucher and unsigned check are then placed in the tickler file. Thus, the vouchers payable bookkeeper may approve vouchers as long as (s)he has no access to any other elements of the transaction, for example, approval of purchase orders. Answer (D) is incorrect. Vouchers and supporting documentation should be examined and canceled by the CFO, a person with responsibility for cash payments, to prevent duplicate payments. It is the CFO's duty to have custody of assets. (S)he should personally mail the checks to vendors.

9. Which of the following events occurring in the year under audit would most likely indicate that internal controls utilized in previous years may be inadequate in the year under audit?

   A. The entity announced that the internal audit function would be eliminated after the balance sheet date.

   B. The audit committee chairperson unexpectedly resigned during the year under audit.

   C. The chief financial officer waived approvals on all checks to one vendor to expedite payment.

   D. The frequency of accounts payable check runs was changed from biweekly to weekly.

Answer (C) is correct.

   REQUIRED: The event indicating that prior-year controls may be currently inadequate.

   DISCUSSION: The CFO's ability to override internal control is a control deficiency. The nature of this action suggests that the CFO may have had this ability in prior years.

   Answer (A) is incorrect. The internal audit function will not be eliminated until the year after the year under audit. Answer (B) is incorrect. The audit committee has not been eliminated or had its functions curtailed. Answer (D) is incorrect. Changing to weekly check runs does not signify that biweekly check runs represent a control deficiency.

10. Which of the following controls most likely would assist in reducing the risks of material misstatement related to the existence or occurrence of manufacturing transactions?

   A. Perpetual inventory records are independently compared with goods on hand.

   B. Forms used for direct materials requisitions are prenumbered and accounted for.

   C. Finished goods are stored in locked limited-access warehouses.

   D. Subsidiary ledgers are periodically reconciled with inventory control accounts.

Answer (A) is correct.

   REQUIRED: The control most likely to reduce the RMMs related to the existence or occurrence assertion.

   DISCUSSION: The recorded accountability for assets should be compared with existing assets at reasonable intervals. If assets are susceptible to loss through fraud or error, the comparison should be made independently. An independent comparison is one made by persons not having responsibility for asset custody or the authorization or recording of transactions.

   Answer (B) is incorrect. Accounting for prenumbered forms relates more to the completeness assertion than the existence or occurrence assertion. This control provides assurance that all transactions were recorded. Answer (C) is incorrect. Although limitation of access is appropriate for safeguarding certain assets, it does not establish accountability, and locking raw materials and work-in-process inventories in limited-access warehouses may not be feasible. Answer (D) is incorrect. Periodic reconciliation of subsidiary ledgers with control accounts is related to the completeness assertion.

7.2 Purchases Technology Considerations

11. In the accounting system of Apogee Company, the quantities counted by the receiving department and entered at a terminal are transmitted to the computer, which immediately transmits the amounts back to the terminal for display on the terminal screen. This display enables the operator to

A. Establish the validity of the account number.

B. Verify that the amount was entered accurately.

C. Verify the authorization of the disbursement.

D. Prevent the overpayment of the account.

Answer (B) is correct.
REQUIRED: The effect of displaying the amounts entered at a terminal.
DISCUSSION: The display of the amounts entered is an input control that permits visual verification of the accuracy of the input by the operator. This is termed closed-loop verification.

7.3 Electronic Data Interchange (EDI)

12. Which of the following statements is correct concerning internal control in an electronic data interchange (EDI) system?

A. Preventive controls generally are more important than detective controls in EDI systems.

B. Control objectives for EDI systems generally are different from the objectives for other information systems.

C. Internal controls in EDI systems rarely permit the risks of material misstatement to be assessed at an acceptably low level.

D. Internal controls related to the segregation of duties generally are the most important controls in EDI systems.

Answer (A) is correct.
REQUIRED: The true statement about EDI controls.
DISCUSSION: In general, preventive controls are more important than detective controls because the benefits typically outweigh the costs. In electronic processing, once a transaction is accepted, the opportunity to apply detective controls is often limited. Thus, preventing fraud or error is important.
Answer (B) is incorrect. The basic control objectives are the same regardless of the nature of the processing: to ensure the integrity of the information and to safeguard the assets. Answer (C) is incorrect. To gather sufficient evidence in a sophisticated computer system, testing controls is often necessary. The RMMs may be assessed at an acceptably low level if relevant controls are identified and tested and if the resulting evidence provides the degree of assurance desired regarding operating effectiveness. Answer (D) is incorrect. The level of segregation of duties achieved in a manual system is usually not feasible in a computer system.

13. Which of the following statements is true concerning the security of messages in an electronic data interchange (EDI) system?

A. When confidentiality of data is the primary risk, message authentication is the preferred control rather than encryption.

B. Encryption performed by physically secure hardware devices is more secure than encryption performed by software.

C. Message authentication in EDI systems performs the same function as separation of duties in other information systems.

D. Security in the transaction phase in EDI systems is not necessary because problems at that level will usually be identified by the service provider.

Answer (B) is correct.
REQUIRED: The true statement about the security of messages in an EDI system.
DISCUSSION: Physically secure hardware for performing encryption is under the direct control of the client. Software is not easily controlled because it is portable. More control is achieved with the hardware approach. However, in the business environment, most encryption applications rely on software.
Answer (A) is incorrect. When confidentiality is a concern, encryption and access controls should be used. Answer (C) is incorrect. Authentication relates to authorization, not security issues. Answer (D) is incorrect. Security in the EDI transaction phase is also an issue. The transmission of information to the service provider, such as a VAN, is subject to a variety of problems, for example, interception or alteration, that may not be detected by the service provider.

14. Many entities use the Internet as a network to transmit electronic data interchange (EDI) transactions. An advantage of using the Internet for electronic commerce rather than a traditional value-added network (VAN) is that the Internet

A. Permits EDI transactions to be sent to trading partners as transactions occur.

B. Automatically batches EDI transactions to multiple trading partners.

C. Possesses superior characteristics regarding disaster recovery.

D. Converts EDI transactions to a standard format without translation software.

Answer (A) is correct.

REQUIRED: The advantage of using the Internet to transmit EDI transactions.

DISCUSSION: VAN services have typically used a proprietary network or a network gatewayed with a specific set of other proprietary networks. A direct Internet connection permits real-time computer-to-computer communication for client-server applications, so transactions can be sent to trading partners as they occur.

Answer (B) is incorrect. The Internet does not automatically batch EDI transactions, although multiple trading partners are possible. Answer (C) is incorrect. The use of the Internet affects the entity's disaster recovery plan. Answer (D) is incorrect. Regardless of the network used to transmit transactions, they first must be translated into a standard format for transmission.

15. Which of the following is usually a benefit of using electronic funds transfer for international cash transactions?

A. Improvement of the audit trail for cash receipts and disbursements.

B. Creation of self-monitoring access controls.

C. Reduction of the frequency of data entry errors.

D. Off-site storage of source documents for cash transactions.

Answer (C) is correct.

REQUIRED: The benefit of using EFT for international cash transactions.

DISCUSSION: The processing and transmission of electronic transactions, such as EFTs, virtually eliminates human interaction. This process not only helps eliminate errors but also allows for the rapid detection and recovery from errors when they do occur.

Answer (A) is incorrect. The audit trail is typically less apparent in an electronic environment than in a manual environment. Answer (B) is incorrect. A key control is management's establishment and monitoring of access controls. Answer (D) is incorrect. Source documents are often eliminated in EFT transactions.

16. Which of the following is an essential element of the audit trail in an electronic data interchange (EDI) system?

A. Disaster recovery plans that ensure proper backup of files.

B. Encrypted hash totals that authenticate messages.

C. Activity logs that indicate failed transactions.

D. Hardware security modules that store sensitive data.

Answer (C) is correct.

REQUIRED: The essential element in an EDI audit trail.

DISCUSSION: Because an audit trail allows for the tracing of a transaction from initiation to its disposition, an activity log provides a key link in the process. Such a log provides information about users who have accessed the system, the files accessed, the processing accomplished, the time of access, and the amount of time the processing required.

Answer (A) is incorrect. Disaster recovery plans are an important control for any system but do not relate to the audit trail. Answer (B) is incorrect. Encrypted hash totals ensure the integrity of the transmission but do not provide for an audit trail. Answer (D) is incorrect. Security of storage is an important control, but it does not relate to the audit trail.

7.4 Payroll Responsibilities/Organizational Structure/Flowchart

17. The purpose of segregating the duties of hiring personnel and distributing payroll checks is to segregate the

A. Authorization of transactions from the custody of related assets.

B. Operational responsibility from the record-keeping responsibility.

C. Human resources function from the controllership function.

D. Administrative controls from the internal accounting controls.

Answer (A) is correct.

REQUIRED: The purpose of segregating the duties of hiring personnel and distributing payroll checks.

DISCUSSION: In principle, the payroll function should be divided into its authorization, recording, and custody functions. Authorization of hiring, wage rates, and deductions is provided by human resources. Authorization of hours worked (executed by employees) is provided by production. Based upon these authorizations, accounting calculates and records the payroll. Based on the calculated amounts, the CFO prepares and distributes payroll checks.

Answer (B) is incorrect. Neither hiring personnel (authorization) nor distributing checks (asset custody) is a recordkeeping activity. Answer (C) is incorrect. Controllership is a recordkeeping activity. Neither the controller nor the human resources department should distribute checks. Answer (D) is incorrect. The professional standards no longer recognize the distinction between administrative controls and internal accounting controls.

18. In determining the effectiveness of an entity's policies and procedures relating to the existence or occurrence assertion for payroll transactions, an auditor most likely would inquire about and

A. Observe the segregation of duties concerning human resources responsibilities and payroll disbursement.

B. Inspect evidence of accounting for prenumbered payroll checks.

C. Recompute the payroll deductions for employee fringe benefits.

D. Verify the preparation of the monthly payroll account bank reconciliation.

Answer (A) is correct.
 REQUIRED: The audit procedure to test controls relating to the existence or occurrence assertion for payroll transactions.
 DISCUSSION: In considering whether transactions actually occurred, the auditor is most concerned about the proper segregation of duties between the human resources department (authorization) and the payroll disbursement (custody function).
 Answer (B) is incorrect. Accounting for prenumbered payroll checks is related to the completeness assertion. Answer (C) is incorrect. Recomputation of the payroll deductions is related to the valuation assertion. Answer (D) is incorrect. The bank reconciliation is related to the completeness and valuation assertions.

19. The sampling unit in a test of controls pertaining to the occurrence of payroll transactions ordinarily is a(n)

A. Time clock card.

B. Employee Form W-2.

C. Employee personnel record.

D. Payroll register entry.

Answer (D) is correct.
 REQUIRED: The evidence required to verify the existence of payroll transactions.
 DISCUSSION: Determining whether payroll transactions occurred is an internal control objective of the human resources and payroll cycle. The payroll register records each payroll transaction for each employee. Thus, an entry in the payroll register is reconciled to time cards to test whether the recorded transaction actually occurred.
 Answer (A) is incorrect. Time clock cards are records of actual hours worked. Using time clock cards as the sampling unit and tracing them to the payroll register tests the completeness assertion. Answer (B) is incorrect. W-2 forms provide withholding and exemption information. Answer (C) is incorrect. Human resources records contain employment data.

20. Which of the following departments most likely would approve changes in pay rates and deductions from employee salaries?

A. Human resources.

B. CFO.

C. Controller.

D. Payroll.

Answer (A) is correct.
 REQUIRED: The department most likely to approve changes in pay rates and deductions.
 DISCUSSION: The human resources department provides the authorization for payroll-related transactions, e.g., hiring, termination, and changes in pay rates and deductions.
 Answer (B) is incorrect. The CFO performs a custody function for payroll-related transactions. Answer (C) is incorrect. The payroll department, which is overseen by the controller, has a recordkeeping function for payroll-related transactions. Answer (D) is incorrect. The payroll department, which is overseen by the controller, has a recordkeeping function for payroll-related transactions.

21. In meeting the control objective of safeguarding of assets, which department should be responsible for

	Distribution of Paychecks	Custody of Unclaimed Paychecks
A.	CFO	CFO
B.	Payroll	CFO
C.	CFO	Payroll
D.	Payroll	Payroll

Answer (A) is correct.
 REQUIRED: The department(s) responsible for the distribution of paychecks and the custody of unclaimed paychecks.
 DISCUSSION: Segregating paycheck preparation from distribution makes it more difficult for fictitious employees to receive payment. In principle, the payroll function should be divided into its authorization, recording, and custody functions. Authorization of hiring, wage rates, and deductions is provided by human resources. Authorization of hours worked is provided by production. Based upon these authorizations, accounting (the payroll department) calculates and records the payroll and prepares checks. The CFO signs and distributes payroll checks. Consistent with its asset custody function, the CFO should distribute paychecks or cash in a manual system (or make electronic funds transfers in a computerized system) so as to prevent payments to fictitious employees. Furthermore, the CFO, not the payroll department, should receive unclaimed paychecks or cash for safeguarding, and incomplete EFTs should not be returned to any of the other functions.

22. Which of the following activities performed by a department supervisor most likely would help in the prevention or detection of a payroll fraud?

A. Distributing paychecks directly to department employees.

B. Setting the pay rate for departmental employees.

C. Hiring employees and authorizing them to be added to payroll.

D. Approving a summary of hours each employee worked during the pay period.

Answer (D) is correct.
REQUIRED: The activity performed by a department supervisor to prevent, or detect and correct, fraud.
DISCUSSION: The department supervisor is in the best position to determine that employees are present and performing the assigned functions.
Answer (A) is incorrect. Supervisors should not have a custody function. The paymaster (CFO's department) should be responsible for distribution of paychecks. Answer (B) is incorrect. Human resources should set the appropriate pay rates based on skills and needs. Answer (C) is incorrect. Human resources should identify and hire the appropriate employees and the payroll department (accounting) should add them to the payroll. Human resources may obtain input from supervisors, but the authorization comes from human resources.

23. Which of the following is a control activity that most likely could help prevent employee payroll fraud?

A. The human resources department promptly sends employee termination notices to the payroll supervisor.

B. Employees who distribute payroll checks forward unclaimed payroll checks to the absent employees' supervisors.

C. Salary rates resulting from new hires are approved by the payroll supervisor.

D. Total hours used for determination of gross pay are calculated by the payroll supervisor.

Answer (A) is correct.
REQUIRED: The control to prevent payroll fraud.
DISCUSSION: The human resources department should forward personnel changes to payroll promptly to ensure that proper authorizations are used to calculate the payroll.
Answer (B) is incorrect. Unclaimed payroll checks should be returned to the treasury department (CFO) for safeguarding, not to supervisors. Answer (C) is incorrect. The human resources department, not the payroll supervisor, approves salary rates. Answer (D) is incorrect. The calculation of batch totals in the payroll department is too late in the payroll process to effectively prevent fraud.

7.5 Payroll Technology Considerations

24. Which of the following activities most likely would detect whether payroll data were altered during processing?

A. Monitoring authorized distribution of data control sheets.

B. Using test data to verify the performance of edit routines.

C. Examining source documents for approval by supervisors.

D. Segregating duties between approval of hardware and software specifications.

Answer (B) is correct.
REQUIRED: The activity most likely to detect alteration of payroll data during processing.
DISCUSSION: The test data approach uses the computer to test the processing logic and controls within the system and the records produced. The auditor prepares a set of dummy transactions specifically designed to test the control activities that management claims to have incorporated into the processing programs. The auditor can expect the controls to be applied to the transactions in the prescribed manner. Thus, the auditor is testing the effectiveness of the controls over the payroll data.
Answer (A) is incorrect. Monitoring authorized distribution of data control sheets detects alteration of data outside the computer, not during processing. Answer (C) is incorrect. Examining source documents for approval by supervisors detects alteration of data outside the computer, not during processing. Answer (D) is incorrect. Segregating duties between hardware and software approval does not affect data during processing.

25. Matthews Corp. has changed from a system of recording time worked on time clock cards to a computerized payroll system in which employees record time in and out with magnetic cards. The computer system automatically updates all payroll records. Because of this change

A. A generalized computer audit program must be used.

B. Part of the audit trail is altered.

C. The potential for payroll-related fraud is diminished.

D. Transactions must be processed in batches.

Answer (B) is correct.
REQUIRED: The effect of computerization of a payroll system.
DISCUSSION: In a manual payroll system, a paper trail of documents would be created to provide audit evidence that controls over each step in processing were operating effectively. One element of a computer system that differentiates it from a manual system is that a transaction trail useful for auditing purposes might exist only for a brief time or only in computer-readable form.
Answer (A) is incorrect. Use of generalized audit software is only one of many ways of auditing through a computer. Answer (C) is incorrect. Conversion to a computer system may actually increase the chance of fraud by eliminating segregation of incompatible functions and other controls. Answer (D) is incorrect. Automatic updating indicates that processing is not in batch mode.

7.6 Other Cycles

26. Which of the following internal control activities most likely justifies reducing the assessment of the risks of material misstatement for plant and equipment acquisitions?

A. Periodic physical inspection of plant and equipment by the internal audit staff.

B. Comparison of current-year plant and equipment account balances with prior-year actual balances.

C. The review of prenumbered purchase orders to detect unrecorded trade-ins.

D. Approval of periodic depreciation entries by a supervisor independent of the accounting department.

Answer (A) is correct.
REQUIRED: The internal control activity that justifies reducing the assessed RMMs.
DISCUSSION: A periodic physical inspection by the internal audit staff is the best activity for verifying the existence of plant and equipment. Direct observation by an independent, competent, and objective internal audit staff helps to reduce the potential for fictitious acquisitions or other fraudulent activities. The result is a lower assessment of the RMMs.
Answer (B) is incorrect. Comparing records of assets may not detect nonexistent assets. Answer (C) is incorrect. Reviewing purchase orders is less effective than direct verification. Answer (D) is incorrect. Depreciation is based on recorded amounts. If they are misstated, depreciation also is misstated.

27. Equipment acquisitions that are misclassified as maintenance expense most likely would be detected by an internal control activity that provides for

A. Segregation of duties for employees in the accounts payable department.

B. Independent verification of invoices for disbursements recorded as equipment acquisitions.

C. Investigation of variances within a formal budgeting system.

D. Authorization by the board of directors of significant equipment acquisitions.

Answer (C) is correct.
REQUIRED: The control activity to detect misclassification of equipment acquisitions as maintenance expense.
DISCUSSION: A formal planning and budgeting system that estimates maintenance expense at a certain level will report a significant variance if capital expenditures are charged to the account. Investigation of the variance is likely to disclose the misclassification.
Answer (A) is incorrect. Accounts payable assembles the required payment documentation but is unlikely to question the classification of the expenditure. Answer (B) is incorrect. Testing the population of recorded equipment acquisitions will not detect items misclassified as maintenance expense. Answer (D) is incorrect. The misclassification would occur subsequent to authorization.

28. Which of the following questions would an auditor most likely include on an internal control questionnaire for notes payable?

A. Are assets that collateralize notes payable critically needed for the entity's continued existence?

B. Are two or more authorized signatures required on checks that repay notes payable?

C. Are the proceeds from notes payable used for the purchase of noncurrent assets?

D. Are direct borrowings on notes payable authorized by the board of directors?

Answer (D) is correct.
REQUIRED: The question most likely included on an internal control questionnaire for notes payable.
DISCUSSION: Control is enhanced when different persons or departments authorize, record, and maintain custody of assets for a class of transactions. Authorization of notes payable transactions is best done by the board of directors.
Answer (A) is incorrect. The importance of specific assets to the entity is an operational matter and not a primary concern of an auditor when (s)he is considering internal control. Answer (B) is incorrect. Questions about the payment function are likely to be on the questionnaire relating to cash disbursements. Answer (C) is incorrect. The use of funds is an operating decision made by management and is not a primary concern of the auditor when considering internal control.

29. Which of the following controls would an entity most likely use in safeguarding against the loss of trading securities?

   A. An independent trust company that has no direct contact with the employees who have record-keeping responsibilities has possession of the securities.

   B. The internal auditor verifies the trading securities in the entity's safe each year on the balance sheet date.

   C. The independent auditor traces all purchases and sales of trading securities through the subsidiary ledgers to the general ledger.

   D. A designated member of the board of directors controls the securities in a bank safe-deposit box.

Answer (A) is correct.
   REQUIRED: The most likely control over trading securities.
   DISCUSSION: Assigning custody of trading securities to a bank or trust company provides the greatest security because such an institution normally has strict controls over assets entrusted to it and access to its vaults.
   Answer (B) is incorrect. Verification of the existence of securities does not prevent their removal between the verification dates, for example, to be used as collateral for unauthorized loans. Answer (C) is incorrect. The independent auditor's procedures are not part of the client's internal control. Answer (D) is incorrect. Access to a safe-deposit box should require the presence of two authorized persons.

30. Which of the following controls would a company most likely use to safeguard marketable securities when an independent trust agent is **not** employed?

   A. The investment committee of the board of directors periodically reviews the investment decisions delegated to the CFO.

   B. Two company officials have joint control of marketable securities, which are kept in a bank safe-deposit box.

   C. The internal auditor and the controller independently trace all purchases and sales of marketable securities from the subsidiary ledgers to the general ledger.

   D. The chairman of the board verifies the marketable securities, which are kept in a bank safe-deposit box, each year on the balance sheet date.

Answer (B) is correct.
   REQUIRED: The control to safeguard marketable securities.
   DISCUSSION: The safeguarding of assets requires physical controls, for example, the use of a safe-deposit box requiring two signatures to gain admittance.
   Answer (A) is incorrect. Proper authorization does not physically safeguard an asset. Answer (C) is incorrect. Independent tracing of purchases and sales to the accounting records ensures proper recording but does not safeguard the asset. Answer (D) is incorrect. Reconciliation once per year is likely to be insufficient to provide adequate control.

31. Which of the following internal control activities would an entity most likely use to assist in satisfying the completeness assertion related to long-term investments?

   A. Senior management verifies that securities in the bank safe-deposit box are registered in the entity's name.

   B. The internal auditor compares the securities in the bank safe-deposit box with recorded investments.

   C. The CFO vouches the acquisition of securities by comparing brokers' advices with canceled checks.

   D. The controller compares the current market prices of recorded investments with the brokers' advices on file.

Answer (B) is correct.
   REQUIRED: The control activity to assist in satisfying the completeness assertion for long-term investments.
   DISCUSSION: The items being tested consist of the assets in the safe-deposit box. This population should be compared with the records of the investments to provide assurance that the balance is complete, that is, contains all long-term investments.
   Answer (A) is incorrect. Verification that securities are registered in the entity's name relates to the rights assertion. Answer (C) is incorrect. Comparing canceled checks with brokers' advices pertains to the rights assertion. Answer (D) is incorrect. Comparing market prices with brokers' advices relates most directly to the valuation assertion.

32. An auditor's tests of controls over the issuance of raw materials to production would most likely include

A. Reconciling raw materials and work-in-process perpetual inventory records to general ledger balances.

B. Inquiring of the custodian about the procedures followed when defective materials are received from vendors.

C. Observing that raw materials are stored in secure areas and that storeroom security is supervised by a responsible individual.

D. Examining materials requisitions and reperforming client controls designed to process and record issuances.

Answer (D) is correct.
REQUIRED: The tests of controls performed with regard to issuance of raw materials.
DISCUSSION: The internal transfer of raw materials is part of the inventory and warehousing cycle, which encompasses the physical flow of goods and the flow of costs. The transfer of raw materials (and costs) is subject to cost accounting internal controls. These include physical controls over storage, assignment of custody to specific individuals, use of prenumbered documents for authorization of transfers, and perpetual inventory records. Thus, prenumbered materials requisitions should be examined for proper authorizations, quantities, descriptions, and dates. Reperformance of relevant control activities is another possible test. For example, subsidiary ledgers and control accounts should be reconciled by an independent party. The auditor should reperform this control.
Answer (A) is incorrect. Reconciling account balances is a substantive test. Answer (B) is incorrect. Tests of controls over issuance of raw materials do not provide evidence about activities followed when defective materials are received. Answer (C) is incorrect. The question concerns issuance, not storage, of raw materials.

33. In obtaining an understanding of a manufacturing entity's internal control concerning inventory balances, an auditor most likely would

A. Analyze the liquidity and turnover ratios of the inventory.

B. Perform analytical procedures designed to identify cost variances.

C. Review the entity's descriptions of inventory policies and procedures.

D. Perform test counts of inventory during the entity's physical count.

Answer (C) is correct.
REQUIRED: The activity for understanding a manufacturer's controls relevant to inventory.
DISCUSSION: The auditor makes inquiries of personnel, observes activities and operations, and reviews an entity's documentation of controls relevant to the management of inventories to obtain an understanding of internal control.
Answer (A) is incorrect. Analytical procedures relate to substantive testing, not the evaluation of controls. Answer (B) is incorrect. Analytical procedures relate to substantive testing, not the evaluation of controls. Answer (D) is incorrect. Test counts relate to substantive testing, not internal controls.

34. Which of the following internal control activities most likely would be used to maintain accurate inventory records?

A. Perpetual inventory records are periodically compared with the current cost of individual inventory items.

B. A just-in-time inventory ordering system keeps inventory levels to a desired minimum.

C. Requisitions, receiving reports, and purchase orders are independently matched before payment is approved.

D. Periodic inventory counts are used to adjust the perpetual inventory records.

Answer (D) is correct.
REQUIRED: The internal control activity most useful in maintaining accurate inventory records.
DISCUSSION: The recorded accountability for assets should be compared with existing assets at reasonable intervals. If assets are susceptible to loss through fraud or error, the comparison should be made independently. Thus, periodic inventory accounts reconciled to the perpetual inventory records provides assurance that the inventory records properly reflect the inventory on hand.
Answer (A) is incorrect. Periodic comparison of inventory records with current cost information may provide assurance that inventories are maintained at lower of cost or market but does not ensure the accuracy of the records. Answer (B) is incorrect. A JIT system may provide assurance that inventory levels are maintained at the desired minimum but does not ensure the accuracy of the records. Answer (C) is incorrect. This control provides assurance that only goods that are authorized and received are paid for but does not assure the accuracy of the inventory records.

Use the additional questions in Gleim **CPA Test Prep** to create Practice Exams that emulate Prometric!

7.7 PRACTICE TASK-BASED SIMULATIONS

| | Auditing and Attestation
Testlet 4 of 4 | Time Remaining
1 hour - 30 minutes | Unsplit | Split Horiz | Split Vertical | Spreadsheet | Calculator | Exit |

DIRECTIONS

Note: If you believe you have encountered a software malfunction, report it to the test center staff immediately.

Navigation

To navigate from task to task, use the controls at the bottom of the screen. Click on the **Next** button to advance to the next task, or the **Previous** button to go to the previous task. To go directly to any task, click on its number.

| ▼ = Reminder | | Directions | 1 2 3 4 5 6 7 | ◀ Previous Next ▶ |

If you would like a reminder to revisit a task, or want to indicate that you are finished with it, click on the reminder flag below the task number. To clear the flag, click on it again. Reminder flags are for your use only – they do not contribute to your score.

Tabs

In this part of the examination, you will be asked to complete various tasks. Every task has one or more **Work Tabs**. Some tasks have one or more **Information Tabs**, others may have none. Every task has a **Help** tab.

If a task has **Information Tabs**, you may use the information in them to complete your responses in the **Work Tabs**.

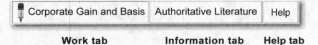

| ✏ Corporate Gain and Basis | Authoritative Literature | Help |

                 Work tab   Information tab   Help tab

Work Tabs:

- **Work Tabs** are identified with a pencil icon. This is where your responses are expected.
- Each task has one or more **Work Tabs**.
- **Work Tabs** contain directions for completing the task – be sure to read these directions carefully.
- The **Work Tab** name in the example above is for illustration only – yours will differ.
- You must complete all of the **Work Tabs** in each task to receive full credit.

Information Tabs:

- The Authoritative Literature will be provided in all tasks in the AUD, FAR, and REG sections for your reference.
- Your simulation may have one or more additional **Information Tabs**. Like the Authoritative Literature tabs, **Information Tabs** do not have a pencil icon.
- If your task has additional **Information Tabs**, go through each to familiarize yourself with the task content.

Help Tab:

- The **Help Tab** provides assistance with the exam software that is used in this task. For example, if the task is to compose a memorandum, **Help** will provide information about the word processor.

The Toolbar

The toolbar at the top of the screen shows the amount of time remaining for you to complete the tasks. In addition, the following tools are available. Note that only the **Exit** button is displayed when Directions are visible - the others will appear when you begin the tasks.

Click on these buttons to split or unsplit the screen. You can split the screen vertically or horizontally.

Click on this button to display the calculator; click on it again to hide the calculator. To move the calculator, click on the calculator title bar and drag the calculator to the desired location.

Click on this button to use the spreadsheet; click on it again to hide the spreadsheet. To move the spreadsheet, click on the the spreadsheet title bar and drag the spreadsheet to the desired location.

Click on this button to go on to the next part of the examination. You must complete all of the tasks to receive full credit. Once you click on **Exit** and confirm the action, you will NOT be able to return to this testlet.

| ▼ = Reminder | | Directions | 1 2 3 4 5 | ◀ Previous Next ▶ |

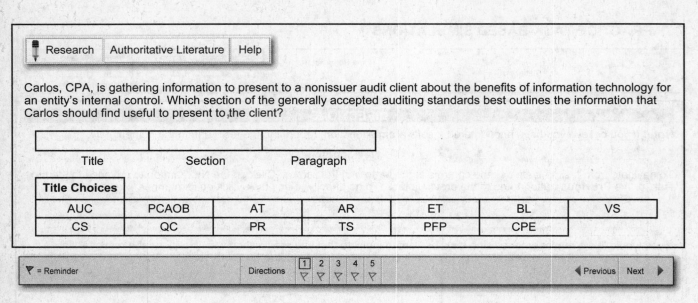

Research | Authoritative Literature | Help

Carlos, CPA, is gathering information to present to a nonissuer audit client about the benefits of information technology for an entity's internal control. Which section of the generally accepted auditing standards best outlines the information that Carlos should find useful to present to the client?

Title	Section	Paragraph

Title Choices

AUC	PCAOB	AT	AR	ET	BL	VS
CS	QC	PR	TS	PFP	CPE	

⛛ = Reminder   Directions   1 2 3 4 5   ◀ Previous Next ▶

Flowchart | Authoritative Literature | Help

Below is a flowchart for the client's current purchasing and cash disbursement transactions.

-- Continued on next page --

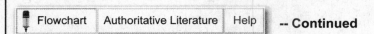

Flowchart | Authoritative Literature | Help   -- **Continued**

Within the flowchart on the previous page are lettered blanks signifying missing information. Select from the list provided the appropriate information for each missing item. Each choice may be used once, more than once, or not at all.

Letter	Answer		Choices
A			1) Purchase order No. 5
B			2) Unpaid voucher file, filed by due date
C			3) Sign checks and cancel voucher package documents
D			4) File by number
E			5) Prepare purchase order
F			6) From Purchasing
G			7) CFO
H			8) Stores
I			9) Receiving report No. 1
J			10) Canceled voucher package
K			11) To purchasing agent
L			12) From Receiving
			13) Prepare receiving report
			14) Prepare and approve voucher
			15) To vendor

▼ = Reminder   Directions   1 [2] 3 4 5   ◄ Previous   Next ►

EDI System | Authoritative Literature | Help

Select from the list provided the most specific and appropriate match for each of the following items. Each choice may be used once, more than once, or not at all.

Item	Answer		Choices
1. Permits timely payments to realize discounts			A) Division of duties
2. Determines that documents support the voucher and check			B) Prenumbering of documents
			C) Purchasing agent
3. Examines vendor invoice for errors			D) Receiving
4. Copy of purchase order omits the quantity			E) Cash disbursements
5. Compares vendor invoice with the receiving reports			F) Accounts payable
6. Cancels payment documents			G) Periodic reconciliation
7. Mails check to avoid improper access			H) Periodic counts
8. Required for checks above a preset limit			I) Dual signatures
9. Assures proper recording in accounts payable control account			J) Tickler file
10. Assures effectiveness of physical controls			K) Proper authorization

▼ = Reminder   Directions   1 2 [3] 4 5   ◄ Previous   Next ►

| Controls Implemented | Authoritative Literature | Help |

Indicate by checking the appropriate box whether management (column M) or the auditor (column A) is responsible for the following payroll activities.

Payroll Activities	M	A
1. Obtain an understanding of internal control over payroll transactions.		
2. Authorize the payroll.		
3. Calculate the proper amount for the payroll.		
4. Safeguard assets associated with the payment of payroll.		
5. Determine that the controls described in the payroll procedures manual have been implemented.		
6. Assess the risks of material misstatement related to payroll.		
7. Distribute the payroll.		
8. Account for the payroll transactions.		

▼ = Reminder   Directions   1   2   3   [4]   5   ◀ Previous   Next ▶

| Payroll | Authoritative Literature | Help |

Indicate by checking the appropriate box the responsibility (authorization, recording, or asset custody) of each organizational subunit below.

Organizational Subunits	Answer
1. Human resources	
2. Payroll	
3. Shops (Supervisor)	
4. Cost accounting	
5. Accounts payable	
6. Cash disbursements	
7. Purchasing agent	
8. Timekeeping	

Choices
A) Authorization
B) Recording
C) Asset custody
D) Not in payroll cycle

▼ = Reminder   Directions   1   2   3   4   [5]   ◀ Previous   Next ▶

Unofficial Answers

1. Research (1 Gradable Item)

Answer: 315.A56

AU-C Section 315 – *Understanding the Entity and its Environment and Assessing the Risks of Material Misstatement*

.A56   Generally, IT benefits an entity's internal control by enabling an entity to

- consistently apply predefined business rules and perform complex calculations in processing large volumes of transactions or data;
- enhance the timeliness, availability, and accuracy of information;
- facilitate the additional analysis of information;
- enhance the ability to monitor the performance of the entity's activities and its policies and procedures;
- reduce the risk that controls will be circumvented; and
- enhance the ability to achieve effective segregation of duties by implementing security controls in applications, databases, and operating systems.

2. Flowchart (12 Gradable Items)

A.   <u>5) Prepare purchase order.</u> The trapezoid symbol represents a manual (offline) activity. The input is the approved purchase requisition, and the output of this process in Purchasing is the purchase order. Accordingly, the activity is "Prepare purchase order."

B.   <u>15) To vendor.</u> Purchase order 1 is sent to the vendor of the goods ordered. All other copies of the purchase order are accounted for. The circle is a connection symbol. Thus, copy 1 of the purchase order goes "To vendor."

C.   <u>13) Prepare receiving report.</u> The goods are received in Receiving, and the output of the manual activity in trapezoid C is the receiving report. Consequently, the activity is "Prepare receiving report."

D.   <u>6) From Purchasing.</u> Circle D in the vouchers payable section of the flowchart represents documents transferred from some other location. Copy 1 of the requisition and copy 5 of the purchase order came from Purchasing where the documents were previously identified. Hence, circle D is "From Purchasing."

E.   <u>12) From Receiving.</u> Circle E in the vouchers payable section represents a document transferred from some other location. Copy 1 of the receiving report came from Receiving. Because circle D reflects the transfer of requisition 1 and purchase order 5, the only unidentified document is the receiving report. Thus, circle E is "From Receiving."

F.   <u>1) Purchase order No. 5.</u> The documents sent from Purchasing to Vouchers Payable are requisition 1 and purchase order 5. Requisition 1 is shown with document F. Document F must therefore be "Purchase order No. 5."

G.   <u>9) Receiving report No. 1.</u> As noted in the answer to question 5, circle E represents "From Receiving." The document sent from Receiving is "Receiving report No. 1."

H.   <u>14) Prepare and approve voucher.</u> The responsibility of Vouchers Payable is to assemble documentation appropriate to support a payment voucher. Once the requisition, purchase order, receiving report, and invoice have been matched, a voucher is created.

I.   <u>2) Unpaid voucher file, filed by due date.</u> The inverted triangle represents a file. The voucher and related supporting documents are filed. The vouchers will be filed by due date, retrieved when due, and sent to the CFO for payment.

J.   <u>7) CFO.</u> Vouchers Payable sends the voucher and related supporting documentation to the CFO (item J on the flowchart) on the due date.

K.   <u>3) Sign checks and cancel voucher package documents.</u> The CFO reviews the documentation in support for the payment. A check is then prepared and signed, and the support for the voucher is canceled so that it cannot be used to support a duplicate payment.

L.   <u>10) Canceled voucher package.</u> Once the check has been mailed, the supporting canceled voucher documentation is filed.

3. EDI System (10 Gradable Items)

1.   J) Tickler file. Vouchers can be filed in a tickler file by due date based on the vendor's terms and pulled from the file for payment on the due date.

2.   E) Cash Disbursements. The Cash Disbursements department should determine that the documentation and voucher support the check before signing and mailing it.

3.   F) Accounts Payable. Accounts Payable should compare the vendor invoice with the purchase order to determine that the terms and prices are correct.

4.   D) Receiving. The Receiving department's copy of the purchase order should omit the quantities ordered to ensure that the Receiving department counts the goods when received.

5.   F) Accounts Payable. Accounts Payable should compare the vendor invoice with the receiving report to determine that the quantity received was the quantity ordered.

6.   E) Cash Disbursements. After signing the check, Cash Disbursements should cancel the voucher and documentation so that they cannot be used to support another payment.

7.   E) Cash Disbursements. After signing the check, Cash Disbursements should maintain control of the payments until they are placed in the mail.

8.   I) Dual signatures. Entities often require large payments to have additional authorization, such as two signatures on one check.

9.   G) Periodic reconciliation. Reconciliation of the general ledger accounts payable account with the accounts payable subsidiary ledger helps ensure proper recording.

10. H) Periodic counts. Physical controls to safeguard inventory can be evaluated by periodic counts of the inventory.

4. Controls Implemented (8 Gradable Items)

1.   A) Auditor. The auditor is responsible for obtaining an understanding of internal control over payroll transactions.

2.   M) Management. Management is responsible for authorizing transactions.

3.   M) Management. Management is responsible for calculating the proper amount for the payroll.

4.   M) Management. Management is responsible for safeguarding the assets associated with the payment of payroll.

5.   A) Auditor. The auditor is responsible for determining that the controls described in the payroll procedures manual have been implemented.

6.   A) Auditor. The auditor is responsible for assessing the risk of material misstatement related to payroll.

7.   M) Management. Management is responsible for distributing the payroll.

8.   M) Management. Management is responsible for accounting for the payroll transactions.

5. Payroll (8 Gradable Items)

1.   A) Authorization. The human resources subunit is responsible for authorization.

2.   B) Recording. The payroll subunit is responsible for recording.

3.   A) Authorization. The shops subunit is responsible for approving job time tickets.

4.   B) Recording. The cost accounting subunit is responsible for recording.

5.   B) Recording. The accounts payable subunit is responsible for recording.

6.   C) Asset custody. The cash disbursements subunit is responsible for asset custody. It signs the check but does not authorize, prepare, or account for the transaction.

7.   D) Not in payroll cycle. The purchasing agent is responsible for acquiring inventory and is not in the payroll cycle.

8.   A) Authorization. Timekeeping reconciles the time clock cards and the job time tickets providing authorization for the time clock cards.

Gleim Simulation Grading

Task	Correct Responses		Gradable Items		Score per Task
1 (Research)	_____	÷	1	=	_____
2	_____	÷	12	=	_____
3	_____	÷	10	=	_____
4	_____	÷	8	=	_____
5	_____	÷	8	=	_____

Total of Scores per Task _____

÷ Total Number of Tasks 5

Total Score _____%

Use **CPA Gleim Online** and **Simulation Wizard** to practice more task-based simulations in a realistic environment.

STUDY UNIT EIGHT
RESPONSES TO ASSESSED RISKS

(13 pages of outline)

To reduce audit risk to an acceptable level, the auditor makes overall responses to the assessed risks of material misstatement at the financial statement level. At the relevant assertion level, the auditor responds by designing and performing further audit procedures (tests of controls and substantive procedures).

If candidates have difficulty understanding the conceptual issues in this study unit, they should review the material in Study Units 5 through 7 before continuing.

8.1 ASSESSING RISKS OF MATERIAL MISSTATEMENT (AU-C 315, AU-C 330, AND AS NO. 12)

1. The risk of material misstatement (RMM) is the combined assessment of inherent risk and control risk.

2. Before designing and performing further audit procedures, the auditor identifies and assesses the RMMs at the financial statement and relevant assertion levels. Thus, while obtaining the understanding of the entity and its environment, the auditor identifies risks and the controls related to those risks that are relevant to the audit. For this purpose, the auditor considers the classes of transactions, balances, and disclosures.

   a. Risks should be related to the threats at the relevant assertion level.
   b. The auditor considers the magnitude of the risks and the likelihood of material misstatement.
   c. As a basis for the risk assessment, the auditor uses audit evidence gathered from performing risk assessment procedures, including that from
      1) Evaluating the design of controls and
      2) Determining whether they have been implemented.
   d. The risk assessment is used to determine the nature, timing, and extent of further audit procedures.
   e. If the risk assessment is based on the expectation that controls are operating effectively at the relevant assertion level, the auditor tests suitably designed controls.
   f. The auditor determines whether the risks relate to
      1) Specific relevant assertions
      2) The statements as a whole
         a) Risks at the statement level may indicate a deficient control environment.
            i) Such a deficiency may affect numerous relevant assertions, and the auditor may need to make an overall response.

g. The auditor identifies controls related to risks and specific relevant assertions.

   1) Some controls may specifically and directly affect an assertion. Others may reduce a risk only indirectly and in conjunction with numerous other controls.

      a) For example, controls over handling of cash receipts directly affect the completeness assertion.

         i) However, a condensed report on merchandise sales is less directly related to the valuation assertion than requiring credit approval by an appropriate manager.

3. **Significant Risks**

   a. As part of the assessment of RMMs, an auditor identifies the risks that require special audit consideration.

   b. The auditor's professional judgment about significance excludes the effect of identified controls.

   c. A risk is more likely to be significant when it involves the following:

      1) A risk of fraud
      2) Recent significant developments (e.g., economic)
      3) A complex transaction
      4) A related party transaction
      5) A high degree of subjectivity or uncertainty in a financial measure, e.g., an accounting estimate
      6) A transaction outside the normal course of business, i.e., a nonroutine (unusual and infrequent) transaction

   d. Significant risks frequently arise from nonroutine transactions and matters requiring significant judgment. But these are less likely to be governed by routine controls.

      1) RMMs related to significant nonroutine transactions may be greater if they result from, among other things, the following:

         a) Increased manual intervention for data processing
         b) Increased management intervention to determine accounting practices
         c) Difficult accounting principles
         d) Transactions with related parties
         e) Transactions for which implementing controls is difficult

      2) RMMs related to significant judgments may be greater if they involve accounting estimates resulting from, among other things, the following:

         a) Accounting principles subject to different interpretations
         b) Subjective or complex judgments
         c) Significant assumptions

   e. The auditor performs substantive procedures that specifically respond to a significant risk.

      1) The auditor also obtains an understanding of the controls relevant to the risk. (S)he then evaluates whether the controls have been suitably designed and implemented.

4. **Insufficiency of Substantive Procedures**

   a. The auditor may be unable to obtain sufficient appropriate audit evidence about some relevant assertions by applying substantive procedures alone.

      1) For example, routine transactions may be highly automated, and audit evidence may not exist in manual form. Thus, tests of controls may be essential.

5. The assessment of RMMs at the relevant assertion level may need to be revised as more audit evidence is gathered.

Stop and review! You have completed the outline for this subunit. Study multiple-choice questions 1 through 4 beginning on page 272.

8.2 AUDITOR'S RESPONSE TO RISKS (AU-C 330 AND AS NO. 13)

1. **Financial Statement Level**

    a. Overall responses apply to the assessed RMMs at the financial statement level. The following are examples of overall responses:

        1) An emphasis on professional skepticism in evidence gathering and evaluation
        2) Increased supervision
        3) Assignment of staff with greater experience or expertise
        4) Greater unpredictability in the choice of further audit procedures
        5) Changing the nature, timing, and extent of audit procedures, such as modifying the nature of a procedure to obtain more persuasive evidence

    b. The assessment of the RMMs depends on the understanding of the control environment.

        1) An effective control environment increases the reliability of internally generated audit evidence.
        2) Responses to deficiencies in the control environment may include, for example,

            a) Seeking more evidence from substantive procedures
            b) Performing more audit procedures at the end of the period
            c) Expanding the engagement's scope to audit more locations

    c. Overall responses relate to the general approach to the audit. Thus,

        1) A substantive audit approach emphasizes substantive procedures
        2) A combined audit approach applies tests of controls and substantive procedures

2. **Relevant Assertion Level**

    a. The nature, timing, and extent of the auditor's further audit procedures should respond to the assessed RMMs at the relevant assertion level.
    b. The further procedures and the assessed RMMs should be clearly connected.
    c. The most important factor in the response is the nature of the procedures.
    d. The design of further audit procedures should consider the following, among other things:

        1) Level of the assessed risk
        2) Likelihood of a material misstatement
        3) Characteristics of the transaction class, balance, or disclosure
        4) Whether the auditor intends to rely on the operating effectiveness of controls

3. **Audit Approach**

    a. The assessment of risks is a basis for choosing the audit approach.
    b. The auditor may decide that the substantive approach is appropriate for specific assertions. Thus, the auditor excludes the effect of controls from the risk assessment. For example, the risk assessment procedures may not identify effective controls for the relevant assertion, or testing controls may be inefficient. In these cases, the auditor does not intend to rely on controls.

        1) The combined approach is appropriate if, for example, the business is conducted without documentation of transactions except through the IT system. In this case, an effective response requires testing of controls.

c. Regardless of the assessment of the RMMs, the auditor should design and perform substantive procedures for all relevant assertions related to each material transaction class, balance, or disclosure.

1) Tests of controls by themselves are insufficient because (a) the assessments of the RMMs are judgments that may not identify all RMMs and (b) internal control has inherent limitations.

2) Analytical procedures applied as substantive procedures also may be insufficient.

4. **Nature of Further Procedures**

a. The nature of further procedures is a function of purpose and type.

1) Purpose – substantive procedures or tests of controls

2) Type – inspection, observation, inquiry, confirmation, recalculation, reperformance, or analytical procedures

b. The choice of audit procedures depends on the following:

1) The relevant assertion

a) For example, a test of controls may be preferable for the completeness assertion about sales.

2) The RMM

a) For a higher RMM, the evidence should be more persuasive. Thus, the auditor increases the quantity of evidence or obtains evidence that is more relevant or reliable. For example, the auditor may seek external confirmation in addition to inspecting internally generated documents and inquiring of management.

3) Reasons for the Assessment of the RMM

a) For example, a lower RMM for a transaction class because of its characteristics (without regard to related controls) may justify performing only substantive analytical procedures.

b) But if a lower RMM is based on the effectiveness of controls, and the design of substantive procedures reflects that RMM, tests of controls should be performed.

5. **Timing of Further Procedures**

a. Timing relates to when a procedure is performed or the date or period of the audit evidence. The greater the RMM, the more likely that tests of controls or substantive procedures will be performed at the end of the period or at unpredictable times.

1) However, earlier performance of procedures may identify significant issues in time to permit their resolution either (a) with the aid of management or (b) by designing an effective audit approach.

b. The timing of procedures is based on considerations such as the following:

1) The relevant period or date
2) Availability of information
3) Nature of the risk
4) The control environment

c. Some procedures are performed only at or after the end of the period, for example, (1) cutoff procedures, (2) comparing financial statement amounts with accounting records, or (3) examining adjustments of the statements.

6. **Extent of Further Procedures**

   a. The extent of a procedure is its quantity, such as the number of sampled items. The extent of a procedure ordinarily increases as the RMMs increase. The auditor's judgment about extent is based on

      1) The desired level of assurance,
      2) The assessed RMM, and
      3) Materiality.

   b. The use of computer-assisted audit techniques (CAATs) may expand the extent of procedures. For example, they may be applied to the whole population of relevant items.

      1) But sampling is often appropriate if statistically sound methods are employed. Study Unit 15 addresses audit sampling.

7. **Tests of Controls**

   a. The auditor tests suitably designed controls at the relevant assertion level in two circumstances:

      1) The risk assessment is based on the expectation that controls are operating with some degree of effectiveness (i.e., the auditor intends to rely on the controls).

         a) The greater the reliance on controls, the more persuasive the evidence of their effectiveness should be.

      2) Substantive procedures are inadequate by themselves to obtain sufficient appropriate evidence.

         a) Tests of controls are necessary for IT processing of routine, high-volume transactions with little manual intervention or hardcopy documentation.

   b. Performing risk assessment procedures to obtain an understanding of the entity and its environment involves, among other things, evaluating the design of controls and determining whether they have been implemented.

      1) Testing controls takes the additional step of obtaining evidence about their operating effectiveness. The evidence addresses such matters as the following:

         a) How controls were applied at relevant times
         b) By whom they were applied
         c) The consistency of their application

   c. The procedures for evaluating design and determining implementation also may serve as tests of operating effectiveness.

      1) For example, if IT general controls are effective, determining that an IT processing control has been implemented also tests effectiveness.

   d. Dual-purpose testing involves performing a test of details and a test of controls on the same transaction. An example is examining an invoice to obtain evidence of (1) the occurrence of a transaction and (2) its approval by a supervisor.

   e. The auditor considers whether the controls to be tested (direct controls) depend upon the effectiveness of indirect controls.

      1) For example, the control group's review of an exception report is a direct control over IT processing supported by indirect controls (general controls and application controls).

8. **Nature of Tests of Controls**

    a. The audit approach may be based primarily on tests of controls. They typically include the following:

        1) Inquiry
        2) Inspection (e.g., of electronic files)
        3) Observation
        4) Reperformance
        5) Recalculation

    b. Inquiry alone is not sufficient to test the operating effectiveness of controls. The auditor should perform other audit procedures in combination with inquiry.

        1) A combination of procedures consisting of inquiry and reperformance, recalculation, or inspection normally provides more assurance than inquiry and observation.

    c. The nature of the control affects the selection of a procedure.

        1) For example, documentation may be inspected.

            a) But in its absence, such as when a control is performed by a computer, inquiry may need to be combined with observation or CAATs.

    d. Misstatements detected by substantive procedures may imply that controls are ineffective.

        1) But nondetection of misstatements is not evidence of effectiveness.

9. **Timing of Tests of Controls**

    a. Timing depends on whether controls are tested at a moment in time or over a period.

        1) For example, a year-end test of controls over property, plant, and equipment may be sufficient.

        2) However, a test at a moment in time of a programmed control over transactions reported in the income statement ordinarily should be combined with other tests. These include procedures to verify consistent operation for the reporting period, e.g., tests of change controls or monitoring controls.

    b. When tests are conducted at an interim period, the auditor should determine procedures to be performed during the remaining period. The auditor considers the following:

        1) Assessed RMMs
        2) Controls tested
        3) The evidence about operating effectiveness
        4) The duration of the remaining period
        5) Any intended reduction of substantive procedures
        6) The control environment
        7) Significant changes in the controls since they were last tested

    c. Procedures should be performed to determine the relevance of audit evidence from prior audits.

        1) For example, the auditor should verify that changes in an effective control have not been made that impair its functioning.

        2) Furthermore, the auditor may not rely on evidence from a prior audit about a control intended to reduce a significant risk.

        3) If the auditor plans to rely on controls that have not changed (other than those related to significant risks), they should be tested at least once every third audit.

            a) At least some controls should be tested every year to provide information about the continuing effectiveness of the control environment.

4) In determining whether to rely on audit evidence from a prior audit, the auditor considers matters such as the following:

   a) The RMMs and extent of reliance on the control
   b) Other elements of internal control (e.g., the control environment)
   c) IT general controls

10. **Extent of Tests of Controls**

    a. The following are considered in determining extent:

       1) Frequency of use of the control
       2) Expected rate of control deviations
       3) Relevance and reliability of needed evidence
       4) Evidence from tests of other controls
       5) Planned reliance on the control
       6) Time during the period for which reliance is sought

    b. Audit sampling should be considered when a control is used frequently.

    c. The extent of tests of controls increases with increases in the following:

       1) Reliance on their operating effectiveness in the assessment of RMMs
       2) The expected deviation rate

          a) But if this rate is high, tests of controls for the specific assertion may not suffice to reduce the audit risk.

11. **Substantive Procedures**

    a. Substantive procedures are performed to detect material misstatements at the relevant assertion level.

    b. The auditor should apply substantive procedures to all relevant assertions about material transaction classes, balances, and disclosures.

    c. Procedures related to the statement closing process include

       1) Examining material entries and other adjustments made in statement preparation.

       2) Reconciling the statements with the accounting records.

    d. Substantive procedures should be performed that respond specifically and with a high degree of reliability to significant risks.

       1) For example, management may have an incentive to recognize revenue prematurely. The specific response may be to (a) seek external confirmation of the terms of sales agreements (e.g., dates, delivery information, and rights of return) and (b) inquire of nonfinancial employees about changes in such agreements.

12. **Nature of Substantive Procedures**

    a. They consist of tests of details (transaction classes, balances, and disclosures) and substantive analytical procedures.

       1) Tests of details normally should be applied to certain assertions about balances, e.g., existence, occurrence, and valuation.

       2) Analytical procedures are most often applied to high-volume, relatively predictable transactions.

          a) Study Unit 3, Subunit 5 has a full outline.

    b. Analytical procedures alone may suffice to reduce audit risk to an acceptable level.

       1) For example, the assessed RMMs may have been reduced by tests of controls.

       2) The best responses in other cases may be to perform (a) tests of details only or (b) a combination of other substantive procedures.

c.   Existence or occurrence assertion. The auditor chooses items from a financial statement amount for testing.

d.   Completeness assertion. The auditor seeks evidence that an item should be and is included in a financial statement amount.

   1)   For example, an auditor may compare cash payments with accounts payable to test for unrecorded liabilities.

e.   The auditor should consider tests of controls over the data used to perform analytical procedures.

   1)   The risk of management override of controls is especially pertinent. It may affect the relationship on which such procedures are based.

      a)   Thus, analytical procedures may not be able to detect certain frauds.

   2)   The auditor also may consider whether the accuracy and completeness of the data have been audited, especially that generated by the entity's information system.

13.   **Timing of Substantive Procedures**

a.   An auditor who performs procedures at an interim date should cover the remaining period.

   1)   For this purpose, the auditor performs

      a)   Further substantive procedures or
      b)   A combination of substantive procedures and tests of controls.

   2)   If neither option suffices, substantive procedures should be performed at the end of the period.

b.   The longer the remaining period, the greater the risk resulting from performing procedures at an interim date. Accordingly, the auditor should consider, among other things, the following:

   1)   Relevant controls, including the control environment
   2)   Availability of information at the end of the remaining period
   3)   Purpose of the procedure
   4)   Assessed RMMs
   5)   Nature of the transaction class or balance and relevant assertions
   6)   Ability to reduce the risk that misstatements at the end of the period will not be detected

c.   Identified RMMs due to fraud. The auditor may decide that substantive procedures should not be performed at an interim date.

d.   Analytical procedures. The auditor may compare interim-date and period-end amounts and perform analytical procedures for the remaining period to identify anomalies.

   1)   The auditor should consider

      a)   The predictability of ending balances
      b)   The entity's procedures for interim-date adjustments and accounting cutoffs
      c)   Whether the information system will produce the information about balances and transactions necessary to an analytical investigation

e.   Detection of misstatements at an interim date may result in modification of risk assessments and planned procedures.

f.   Audit evidence from a prior audit's substantive procedures provide little evidence usable in the current period.

14. **Extent of Substantive Procedures**

    a. The greater the RMMs, the greater the extent of relevant procedures.

        1) The extent of substantive procedures may be reduced if controls are effective.

    b. For tests of details, the extent is usually a function of sampling. See Study Unit 15.

    c. For analytical procedures, the auditor considers the acceptable variation from the expectation.

        1) This variation relates to performance materiality and the desired assurance.

15. **Documentation**

    a. The auditor should document the following:

        1) Overall responses to assessed RMMs at the statement level

        2) Nature, timing, and extent of further audit procedures and their connection with assessed risks at the relevant assertion level

        3) Results of audit procedures

        4) Conclusions if not clear

        5) Conclusions about use of prior-audit evidence with respect to the operating effectiveness of controls

---

Considerable detail has been presented in the previous two subunits. However, do not lose sight of the big picture. In planning the audit, the auditor assesses the risks of material misstatement (RMMs) by performing risk assessment procedures. The RMMs can be assessed at a lower level if controls are operating effectively. Thus, the auditor may perform tests of controls to make this lower assessment. Finally, based on the assessed RMMs, the auditor designs appropriate substantive procedures to identify potential misstatements. Conceptually, this should make sense to you.

Stop and review! You have completed the outline for this subunit. Study multiple-choice questions 5 through 21 beginning on page 273.

8.3 ASSESSING RISK IN A COMPUTER ENVIRONMENT

1. **Similarities**

    a. Assessments of RMMs in a computer environment and in a manual system have many similarities. The candidate should build on these similarities. Most of the terms used here are defined in Study Unit 5.

    b. The **objectives** are the same. The RMMs are assessed by the auditor to help determine the nature, timing, and extent of the substantive procedures and tests of controls appropriate to support the opinion regardless of the nature of the system.

    c. The **concept** is the same. After obtaining an understanding of the entity and its environment, including its internal control, and determining that the controls have been implemented, the auditor considers whether testing the effectiveness of the controls and relying on them is more efficient than forgoing tests of controls. However, the auditee's use of IT requires the auditor to consider whether omitting tests of controls enables him/her to provide the necessary assurance.

        1) The conventional procedure is first to assess the RMMs relative to the control environment (often referred to as the general controls). If the control environment is ineffective, the auditor should not rely on individual controls (application controls).

d.   Many **procedures** are the same. Numerous controls in a computer environment are outside the computer system and can be tested using procedures applicable to a manual system. These procedures include the following:

1)   Inquiries of entity personnel
2)   Inspection of documents, reports, and files
3)   Observation of the application of specific controls
4)   Reperformance by the auditor

e.   Computer controls to which traditional tests of controls apply include those found in the control environment and control activities components of internal control.

f.   **The Control Environment**

1)   **Organizational structure.** The auditor inspects documentation and observes operations demonstrating that the IT function has no custody of assets or transaction authority and is actually

a)   Operating as a service department independently of users and
b)   Reporting to senior-level management.

2)   **Assignment of authority and responsibility.** The auditor inquires and observes whether the following employees are performing functions consistent with their assigned responsibilities (and have no incompatible responsibilities):

a)   Systems analyst
b)   Programmer
c)   Computer (console) operator
d)   Data conversion (key) operator
e)   Librarian
f)   Data control group

g.   **Control Activities**

1)   **Information processing.** The auditor

a)   Observes the backup copies of files and programs to determine that they are safeguarded;
b)   Inspects the written security policy concerning virus protection and observes the existence of available anti-virus software;
c)   Inspects program acquisition and development requests for the proper authorization, assignment of responsibility for design and coding, testing, and acceptance; and
d)   Inspects program documentation to determine whether it is complete and up to date.

2)   The auditor tests **access controls** by

a)   Attempting to sign on to the computer system using various passwords and ID numbers,
b)   Inspecting the system access log for completeness and appropriate use and follow-up (passwords consistent with employees' responsibilities), and
c)   Observing that disposal of sensitive documents and printouts is controlled so that unauthorized persons cannot gain information concerning passwords or ID numbers.

2. **Differences**

    a. Certain controls relating to the input, processing, and output of data are internal to the computer system. They should be tested by procedures that are not traditionally performed in a manual environment. Such techniques have been characterized as auditing around the computer or auditing through the computer.

    b. **Auditing around the computer** is not appropriate when systems are sophisticated or the major controls are included in the computer programs. It may be appropriate for very simple systems that produce appropriate printed outputs.

        1) The auditor manually processes transactions and compares the results with the client's computer-processed results.

        2) Because only a small number of transactions can ordinarily be tested, the effectiveness of the tests of controls must be questioned.

        3) The computer is treated as a black box, and only inputs and outputs are evaluated.

    c. **Auditing through the computer** uses the computer to test the processing logic and controls within the system and the records produced. This approach may be accomplished in several ways, including

        1) Processing test data
        2) Parallel simulation
        3) Creation of an integrated test facility
        4) Programming embedded audit modules

3. **Test Data Approach**

    a. The auditor prepares a set of dummy transactions specifically designed to test the control activities that management claims to have incorporated into the processing programs. The auditor can expect the controls to be applied to the transactions in the prescribed manner. Thus, the auditor is testing the effectiveness of the controls.

EXAMPLE

Management may have represented that the following edit checks were included in the payroll processing program:

1) Field checks for all numeric and alphabetic fields
2) Reasonableness test of hours worked over 40 hours
3) Validity check of employee numbers compared with known employees in the personnel master file
4) Error listings of all transactions that fail a test

The auditor's test transactions include some that should pass the edit checks and be processed and some that should fail the edit checks and be printed on the error listing. Because processing is uniform, only one transaction for each control tested needs to be included.

---

    b. The primary advantage of this method is that it directly tests the controls.

    c. The primary disadvantage is that it tests processing at only one moment in time. That is, the auditor does not have assurance that the program tested is the one used throughout the year to process client transactions.

d.   The following illustrates a test data approach in flowchart form:

Figure 8-1

4. **Parallel Simulation**

   a.   Parallel simulation uses a controlled program to reprocess sets of client transactions and compares the auditor-achieved results with those of the client. The key is for the auditor's program to include the client's edit checks. Thus, the client's results of processing, rejected transactions, and error listing should be the same as the auditor's.

   b.   The auditor's controlled program may be a copy of the client's program that has been tested. An expensive alternative is for the auditor to write a program that includes management's controls. Also, a program may be created from generalized audit software.

   c.   The primary advantage of parallel simulation is that transactions from throughout the period may be reprocessed. The results can then be compared with the client's results to provide assurance that the edit checks (controls) have been applied during the period.

   d.   The primary disadvantages of this method are the cost of obtaining the program and the coordination effort required to obtain transactions to reprocess.

   e.   The following illustrates the parallel simulation method in flowchart form:

Figure 8-2

5.   **Integrated Test Facility Method**

   a.   Using the **integrated test facility (ITF)** method, the auditor creates a dummy record within the client's actual system (e.g., a fictitious employee in the personnel and payroll file). Dummy and actual transactions are processed (e.g., time records for the dummy employee and for actual employees). The auditor can test the edit checks by altering the dummy transactions and evaluating error listings.

   b.   The primary advantage of this method is that it tests the actual program in operation.

   c.   The primary disadvantages are that the method requires considerable coordination, and the dummy transactions must be purged prior to internal and external reporting. Thus, the method is not used extensively by external auditors.

   d.   The following illustrates the ITF method in flowchart form:

Figure 8-3

6.   **Embedded Audit Module**

   a.   An embedded audit module is an integral part of an application system that is designed to identify and report actual transactions and other information that meet criteria having audit significance.

   b.   An advantage is that it permits continuous monitoring of online, real-time systems.

   c.   A disadvantage is that **audit hooks** must be programmed into the operating system and applications programs to permit the use of audit modules.

   d.   Upon completion of the tests of computer controls, the auditor assesses computer control risk and relates it to specific financial statement assertions. This risk assessment is a primary factor in determining the appropriate substantive procedures.

Stop and review! You have completed the outline for this subunit. Study multiple-choice questions 22 through 32 beginning on page 278.

QUESTIONS

8.1 Assessing Risks of Material Misstatement (AU-C 315, AU-C 330, and AS No. 12)

1. The ultimate purpose of understanding the entity and its environment and assessing the risks of material misstatement is to contribute to the auditor's assessment of the risk that

A. Tests of controls may fail to identify procedures relevant to assertions.

B. Material misstatements may exist in the financial statements.

C. Specified controls requiring segregation of duties may be circumvented by collusion.

D. Entity policies may be inappropriately overridden by senior management.

Answer (B) is correct.
   REQUIRED: The purpose of understanding the entity and its environment and assessing the risks of material misstatement.
   DISCUSSION: The auditor's objective is to identify and assess the RMMs, whether due to fraud or error, at the financial statement and relevant assertion levels. This objective is achieved through understanding the entity and its environment, including its internal control. The understanding provides a basis for designing and implementing responses to the assessed RMMs (AU-C 315 and AS No. 12). Moreover, the auditor's overall objectives in an audit include obtaining reasonable assurance about whether the statements as a whole are free from material misstatement (AU-C 200).
   Answer (A) is incorrect. An auditor should obtain an understanding of controls relevant to the audit. Thus, the auditor should evaluate their design and determine whether they have been implemented. The evaluation of design considers whether the controls can effectively prevent, or detect and correct, material misstatements (AU-C 315 and AS No. 12). The auditor then tests relevant controls to obtain sufficient appropriate evidence about their operating effectiveness if (1) the auditor intends to rely on them in determining the nature, timing, and extent of substantive procedures or (2) substantive procedures alone cannot provide sufficient appropriate evidence at the relevant assertion level (AU-C 330 and AS No. 13). Answer (C) is incorrect. Collusion is an inherent limitation of internal control. Answer (D) is incorrect. Inappropriate management override is an inherent limitation of internal control.

2. The risks of material misstatement (RMMs) should be assessed in terms of

A. Specific controls.

B. Types of potential fraud.

C. Financial statement assertions.

D. Control environment factors.

Answer (C) is correct.
   REQUIRED: The approach used in assessing the RMMs.
   DISCUSSION: The auditor's objective is to identify and assess the RMMs, whether due to fraud or error, at the financial statement and relevant assertion levels. This objective is achieved through understanding the entity and its environment, including its internal control. The understanding provides a basis for designing and implementing responses to the assessed RMMs (AU-C 315 and AS No. 12).
   Answer (A) is incorrect. Relevant controls should relate to the identified RMMs, and the RMMs are identified and assessed at the financial statement and relevant assertion levels. Answer (B) is incorrect. The auditor should use information obtained from the understanding to identify types of potential misstatements. Answer (D) is incorrect. The auditor considers the control environment in assessing the RMMs but does not assess risk in terms of control environment factors.

3. The auditor should perform tests of controls when the auditor's assessment of the risks of material misstatement includes an expectation of the operating effectiveness of internal control or when

A. Substantive procedures alone cannot provide sufficient appropriate audit evidence at the relevant assertion level.

B. Tests of details and substantive analytical procedures provide sufficient appropriate audit evidence to support the assertion being evaluated.

C. The auditor is not able to obtain an understanding of internal controls.

D. The owner-manager performs virtually all the functions of internal control.

Answer (A) is correct.
   REQUIRED: The reason to test controls.
   DISCUSSION: For some RMMs, the auditor may determine that it is not feasible to obtain sufficient appropriate audit evidence only from substantive procedures. These RMMs may relate to routine, significant transactions subject to highly automated processing with no documentation except what is recorded in the IT system. In such circumstances, the controls over the RMMs are relevant to the audit. Thus, the auditor should obtain an understanding of, and test, the controls.
   Answer (B) is incorrect. When evidence obtained from substantive procedures is sufficient and appropriate to support an assertion, the auditor need not test controls. Answer (C) is incorrect. The auditor should obtain an understanding of controls relevant to the audit. The understanding includes an evaluation of their design and a determination of whether they have been implemented. Answer (D) is incorrect. In small organizations, when the owner-manager performs many or most control activities, tests of controls ordinarily are not necessary.

4. When assessing the risks of material misstatement at a low level, an auditor is required to document the auditor's

	Understanding of the Entity's Control Environment	Overall Responses to Assessed Risks
A.	Yes	No
B.	No	Yes
C.	Yes	Yes
D.	No	No

Answer (C) is correct.

REQUIRED: The item(s) that should be documented when assessing control risk at a low level.

DISCUSSION: The understanding of the components of internal control, including the control environment, should be documented regardless of the degree of risk (AU-C 315). The overall responses to the assessed risks of material misstatement at the financial statement level also should be documented (AU-C 330).

8.2 Auditor's Response to Risks (AU-C 330 and AS No. 13)

5. Which of the following is a step in an auditor's decision to rely on internal controls?

A. Apply analytical procedures to both financial data and nonfinancial information to detect conditions that may indicate weak controls.

B. Perform tests of details of transactions and account balances to identify potential fraud and error.

C. Identify specific controls that are likely to prevent, or detect and correct, material misstatements and perform tests of controls.

D. Document that the additional audit effort to perform tests of controls exceeds the potential reduction in substantive testing.

Answer (C) is correct.

REQUIRED: The step necessary to rely on internal controls.

DISCUSSION: An auditor should obtain an understanding of controls relevant to the audit. Thus, the auditor should evaluate their design and determine whether they have been implemented. The evaluation of design considers whether the controls can effectively prevent, or detect and correct, material misstatements (AU-C 315 and AS No. 12). The auditor then tests relevant controls to obtain sufficient appropriate evidence about their operating effectiveness if (1) the auditor intends to rely on them in determining the nature, timing, and extent of substantive procedures, or (2) substantive procedures alone cannot provide sufficient appropriate evidence at the relevant assertion level (AU-C 330 and AS No. 13).

Answer (A) is incorrect. Analytical procedures are substantive procedures. The auditor should perform tests of controls to rely on internal controls. Answer (B) is incorrect. Tests of details are substantive procedures. The auditor should perform tests of controls to rely on internal controls. Answer (D) is incorrect. If the effort to perform tests of controls exceeds the potential reduction in substantive testing, the auditor need not rely on controls.

6. An auditor may decide to perform only substantive procedures for certain assertions because the auditor believes

A. Controls are not relevant to the assertions.

B. The entity's control components are interrelated.

C. Sufficient appropriate audit evidence to support the assertions is likely to be available.

D. More emphasis on tests of controls than substantive tests is warranted.

Answer (A) is correct.

REQUIRED: The reason an auditor may decide to perform only substantive procedures.

DISCUSSION: The auditor's risk assessment procedures may not have identified any suitably designed and implemented controls that are relevant to the assertions. Another possibility is that testing of controls may be inefficient. But the auditor needs to be satisfied that performing only substantive procedures will be effective in reducing audit risk to an acceptable level.

Answer (B) is incorrect. The integration of control components may be a valuable consideration in performing tests of controls as well as substantive procedures. Answer (C) is incorrect. The auditor tests controls when sufficient appropriate audit evidence is not provided by substantive procedures. Answer (D) is incorrect. The auditor's decision to perform only substantive procedures is a decision not to perform procedures to obtain evidence about the effectiveness of controls.

7. A nonissuer audit client failed to maintain copies of its procedures manuals and organizational flowcharts. What should the auditor do in an audit of financial statements?

    A. Express a qualified opinion on the basis of a scope limitation.

    B. Document the auditor's understanding of internal control.

    C. Adopt a substantive audit approach.

    D. Restrict the auditor's responsibility to assess the effectiveness of controls in the audit engagement letter.

Answer (C) is correct.
    REQUIRED: The effect on the audit when the client fails to maintain copies of its procedures manuals and organizational flowcharts.
    DISCUSSION: The assessment of risks is a basis for choosing the audit approach. A substantive audit approach is based only on substantive procedures. A combined audit approach applies tests of controls and substantive procedures. For example, the risk assessment procedures may not identify effective controls for the relevant assertion, or testing controls may be inefficient, e.g., because client documentation is not available. The result is that the effect of controls is excluded from the risk assessment. In these cases, if the auditor adopts the substantive audit approach, (s)he needs to be satisfied that it will be effective in reducing audit risk to an acceptable level. For example, the substantive audit approach may not be feasible when the processing of routine transactions is highly automated with little manual intervention. In this case, the combined audit approach is chosen. Moreover, the auditor should design and perform some substantive procedures for all relevant assertions related to each material transaction class, account balance, or disclosure regardless of the assessment of the RMMs or the choice of audit approach.
    Answer (A) is incorrect. The auditor should be able to test the assertions in the financial statements given sufficient appropriate substantive evidence. Answer (B) is incorrect. There would be little understanding to document. Answer (D) is incorrect. The auditor need not assess the effectiveness of internal controls for a nonissuer.

8. Which of the following tests of controls most likely will help assure an auditor that goods shipped are properly billed?

    A. Scan the sales journal for sequential and unusual entries.

    B. Examine shipping documents for matching sales invoices.

    C. Compare the accounts receivable ledger to daily sales summaries.

    D. Inspect unused sales invoices for consecutive prenumbering.

Answer (B) is correct.
    REQUIRED: The test of controls most likely to provide assurance that goods shipped are properly billed.
    DISCUSSION: The proper starting point to determine whether all goods shipped were properly billed is the shipping documents. Tracing the shipping documents to the matching sales invoices provides assurance that controls worked effectively to ensure that all goods shipped were billed.
    Answer (A) is incorrect. Scanning the sales journal provides evidence concerning shipments that were billed but no evidence about unbilled shipments. Answer (C) is incorrect. The accounts receivable ledger represents shipments that were billed. Answer (D) is incorrect. Unbilled shipments do not create gaps in the prenumbered sales invoices.

9. An auditor is **least** likely to test controls that provide for

    A. Approval of the purchase and sale of trading securities.

    B. Classification of revenue and expense transactions by product line.

    C. Separation of the functions of recording disbursements and reconciling the bank account.

    D. Comparison of receiving reports and vendors' invoices with purchase orders.

Answer (B) is correct.
    REQUIRED: The controls that are least likely to be tested.
    DISCUSSION: The auditor is primarily concerned with the fairness of external financial reporting and therefore with controls relevant to a financial statement audit. (S)he is less likely to test controls over records used solely for internal management purposes than those used to prepare financial statements for external distribution. Assertions about the presentation of transactions by product line are not typically made. Thus, the auditor is unlikely to expend significant audit effort in testing such classifications.
    Answer (A) is incorrect. A basic management objective is proper authorization of transactions. Answer (C) is incorrect. A basic management objective is to compare recorded accountability with existing assets at reasonable intervals, such as by reconciling the bank account and the accounting records. Reconciliations should be performed by an independent employee. Answer (D) is incorrect. Comparison of receiving reports, vendors' invoices, and purchase orders is a control over purchasing.

10. After gaining an understanding of a client's computer processing internal control, a financial statement auditor may decide not to test the effectiveness of the computer processing control procedures. Which of the following is **not** a valid reason for choosing to omit tests of controls?

A. The controls duplicate operative controls existing elsewhere in the system.

B. Risk assessment procedures have not identified relevant effective controls.

C. The time and dollar costs of testing exceed the time and dollar savings in substantive testing if the tests of controls show the controls to be effective.

D. The assessment of the risks of material misstatement permits the auditor to rely on the controls.

Answer (D) is correct.
REQUIRED: The invalid reason for omitting tests of controls.
DISCUSSION: Although controls appear to be effective based on the understanding of internal control, the auditor should perform tests of controls when the assessment of the risks of material misstatement at the relevant assertion level includes an expectation of their operating effectiveness. This expectation reflects the auditor's intention to rely on the controls in determining the nature, timing, and extent of substantive procedures.
Answer (A) is incorrect. Compensating controls may appropriately limit the risks of material misstatement. Answer (B) is incorrect. Performing only substantive procedures is appropriate for certain assertions, e.g., when (1) testing controls is inefficient or (2) effective controls relevant to the assertions have not been identified. Answer (C) is incorrect. Difficulty, time, and cost do not justify (1) omitting an audit procedure for which no alternative exists or (2) being satisfied with less than persuasive audit evidence. But users of financial statements expect that the auditor will (1) form an opinion within a reasonable time and (2) balance benefit and cost (AU-C 200).

11. To test the effectiveness of controls, an auditor ordinarily selects from a variety of techniques, including

A. Inquiry and analytical procedures.

B. Reperformance and observation.

C. Comparison and confirmation.

D. Inspection and verification.

Answer (B) is correct.
REQUIRED: The procedures associated with tests of controls.
DISCUSSION: The auditor selects tests of controls from a variety of techniques such as inquiry, observation, inspection, recalculation, and reperformance of a control that pertains to an assertion. No one specific test of controls is always necessary, applicable, or equally effective in every circumstance.
Answer (A) is incorrect. Analytical procedures are more closely associated with substantive procedures. Answer (C) is incorrect. Comparison and confirmation are more closely associated with substantive procedures. Answer (D) is incorrect. Verification is more closely associated with substantive procedures.

12. Which of the following is true related to the auditor's consideration of controls?

A. Misstatements detected by the auditor's substantive procedures should be considered when testing the effectiveness of related controls.

B. The absence of misstatements detected by an auditor's substantive procedures should be considered evidence that controls related to the relevant assertion being tested are effective.

C. A material misstatement detected by the auditor, but not detected by the entity, should be considered a material weakness in internal control.

D. The auditor should consider testing and documenting the efficiency of the entity's controls related to relevant assertions.

Answer (A) is correct.
REQUIRED: The true statement related to the consideration of controls.
DISCUSSION: Misstatements detected by the auditor's substantive procedures should be considered when testing the effectiveness of related controls. The auditor may need to assess the risks of material misstatement at a higher level if fraud or error is detected that should have been detected by the entity's controls.
Answer (B) is incorrect. The absence of misstatements during substantive testing does not normally provide sufficient evidence as to control effectiveness. The samples may not be appropriate for that purpose. Answer (C) is incorrect. A material misstatement detected by the auditor, but not detected by the entity, should be considered a significant deficiency and may be indicative of a material weakness in control. Answer (D) is incorrect. The auditor should test and document the effectiveness, not the efficiency, of the entity's controls related to relevant assertions.

13. An auditor generally tests the segregation of duties related to inventory by

A. Personal inquiry and observation.

B. Test counts and cutoff procedures.

C. Analytical procedures and invoice recomputation.

D. Document inspection and reconciliation.

Answer (A) is correct.
REQUIRED: The audit test of the segregation of duties for inventory.
DISCUSSION: The segregation of duties reduces the opportunity for an individual to perpetrate and conceal fraud or error in the normal course of his/her duties. Authorization of transactions, recording of transactions, and custody of assets should be segregated. The best evidence that controls based on segregation of duties are operating as planned is provided by the auditor's own observation and inquiries.
Answer (B) is incorrect. Test counts and cutoff procedures are substantive procedures, not tests of controls. Answer (C) is incorrect. Analytical procedures and recomputations are substantive procedures, not tests of controls. Answer (D) is incorrect. Although document inspection may be useful as a test of controls, it is not effective to test the segregation of duties.

14. Which of the following procedures concerning accounts receivable is an auditor most likely to perform to obtain evidence in support of the effectiveness of controls?

A. Observing an entity's employee prepare the schedule of past due accounts receivable.

B. Sending confirmation requests to an entity's principal customers to verify the existence of accounts receivable.

C. Inspecting an entity's analysis of accounts receivable for unusual balances.

D. Comparing an entity's uncollectible accounts expense with actual uncollectible accounts receivable.

Answer (A) is correct.
REQUIRED: The procedure used in support of the effectiveness of controls.
DISCUSSION: To test the effectiveness of controls, an auditor performs procedures such as inquiry, observation, inspection, recalculation, and reperformance of a control. Thus, observing an entity's employee prepare the schedule of past due accounts receivable provides evidence of the effectiveness of certain controls over accounts receivable.
Answer (B) is incorrect. Sending confirmation requests to verify the existence of accounts receivable is a test of the details of balances, a substantive procedure. Answer (C) is incorrect. Inspecting an entity's analysis of accounts receivable for unusual balances is a test of the details of balances, a substantive procedure. Answer (D) is incorrect. Comparing uncollectible accounts expense with actual uncollectible accounts receivable is a form of analytical procedure. It is used to determine whether the auditor's expectation is supported by client data.

15. The objective of tests of details of transactions performed as tests of controls is to

A. Monitor the design and use of entity documents such as prenumbered shipping forms.

B. Determine whether internal controls have been implemented.

C. Detect material misstatements in the account balances of the financial statements.

D. Evaluate whether internal controls operated effectively.

Answer (D) is correct.
REQUIRED: The objective of tests of details of transactions performed as tests of controls.
DISCUSSION: The auditor may use tests of details of transactions concurrently as tests of controls (i.e., as dual-purpose tests). As substantive procedures, their objective is to support relevant assertions or detect material misstatements in the financial statements. As tests of controls, their objective is to evaluate whether a control operated effectively.
Answer (A) is incorrect. The client's controls should monitor the use of entity documents. Answer (B) is incorrect. Determination of whether controls have been implemented is made in conjunction with the auditor's understanding of internal control. Answer (C) is incorrect. The objective of substantive procedures is to support relevant assertions or detect material misstatements in the account balances.

16. When an auditor increases the assessment of the risks of material misstatement because certain controls were determined to be ineffective, the auditor will most likely increase the

A. Extent of tests of details.

B. Assessed inherent risk.

C. Extent of tests of controls.

D. Acceptable detection risk.

Answer (A) is correct.
REQUIRED: The effect of an increase in the assessment of the RMMs.
DISCUSSION: An auditor should obtain an understanding of internal control to assess the RMMs. The greater (lower) the assessment of the RMMs, the lower (greater) the acceptable detection risk for a given level of audit risk. In turn, the acceptable audit risk affects substantive testing. For example, as the acceptable audit risk decreases, the auditor changes the nature, timing, or extent of substantive procedures to increase the reliability and relevance of the evidence they provide.
Answer (B) is incorrect. Inherent risk is not affected by the auditor's procedures. Answer (C) is incorrect. Once controls are determined to be ineffective, further tests of controls are unnecessary. Answer (D) is incorrect. The acceptable detection risk for a given level of audit risk decreases when the assessment of the RMMs increases.

17. When numerous property and equipment transactions occur during the year, an auditor who assesses the risks of material misstatement at a low level usually performs

    A. Tests of controls and extensive tests of property and equipment balances at the end of the year.

    B. Analytical procedures for current-year property and equipment transactions.

    C. Tests of controls and limited tests of current-year property and equipment transactions.

    D. Analytical procedures for property and equipment balances at the end of the year.

Answer (C) is correct.
    REQUIRED: The procedures performed when an auditor assesses the RMMs at a low level.
    DISCUSSION: The auditor usually performs tests of controls and substantive procedures (the combined audit approach). The auditor must make decisions about the nature, timing, and extent of substantive procedures that are most responsive to the assessment of the RMMs. These decisions are affected by whether the auditor has tested controls. Thus, the extent of relevant substantive procedures may be reduced when control is found to be effective.
    Answer (A) is incorrect. The extent of substantive procedures may be reduced. Answer (B) is incorrect. When numerous transactions are subject to controls, and the RMMs are low, the auditor may rely on tests of controls. Answer (D) is incorrect. When numerous transactions are subject to effective controls, and the RMMs are low, the auditor may rely on tests of controls.

18. A client maintains perpetual inventory records in both quantities and dollars. If the assessment of the risks of material misstatement is high, an auditor will probably

    A. Apply gross profit tests to ascertain the reasonableness of the physical counts.

    B. Increase the extent of tests of controls relevant to the inventory cycle.

    C. Request the client to schedule the physical inventory count at the end of the year.

    D. Insist that the client perform physical counts of inventory items several times during the year.

Answer (C) is correct.
    REQUIRED: The auditor's action if the assessment of the RMMs for inventory is high.
    DISCUSSION: If the assessment of the RMMs is high, the acceptable detection risk for a given level of audit risk decreases. The auditor should change the nature, timing, or extent of substantive procedures to increase the reliability and relevance of the evidence they provide. Thus, extending work done at an interim date to year end might be inappropriate. Observation of inventory at year end provides more reliable and relevant evidence.
    Answer (A) is incorrect. Comparing the gross profit test results with those of the prior year provides evidence about sales and cost of goods sold but not inventory. Answer (B) is incorrect. If the auditor believes controls are unlikely to be effective, e.g., because the assessment of the RMMs is high, tests of controls may not be performed. However, the auditor needs to be satisfied that performing only substantive procedures will reduce audit risk to an acceptably low level. Answer (D) is incorrect. The risk is that year-end inventory is misstated.

19. An auditor may compensate for a high assessed risk of material misstatement by

    A. Increasing the acceptable level of detection risk.

    B. Eliminating tests of controls.

    C. Decreasing the preliminary judgment about audit risk.

    D. Increasing the extent of substantive analytical procedures.

Answer (D) is correct.
    REQUIRED: The method an auditor may use to compensate for a high assessed risk of material misstatement.
    DISCUSSION: When designing further audit procedures, the auditor obtains more persuasive evidence the higher the risk assessment. Thus, the auditor may increase the quantity of evidence or obtain more relevant or reliable evidence. Furthermore, the extent of audit procedures generally increases as the risks of material misstatement increase. For example, the auditor may increase sample sizes or perform more detailed substantive analytical procedures (AU-C 330).
    Answer (A) is incorrect. The acceptable level of detection risk decreases for a given level of audit risk when the assessed risk of material misstatement increases. Answer (B) is incorrect. The auditor may need to increase the extent of tests of controls or change their nature or timing. Answer (C) is incorrect. The auditor obtains sufficient appropriate audit evidence to reduce audit risk to an acceptably low level. This risk is not necessarily changed because of a high assessed risk of material misstatement.

20. Regardless of the assessed risks of material misstatement, an auditor should perform some

   A. Tests of controls to determine their effectiveness.

   B. Analytical procedures to verify the design of controls.

   C. Substantive procedures to restrict detection risk for significant transaction classes.

   D. Dual-purpose tests to evaluate both the risk of monetary misstatement and preliminary control risk.

Answer (C) is correct.
   REQUIRED: The procedures performed regardless of the assessed risks of material misstatement.
   DISCUSSION: Regardless of the assessed risks of material misstatement (or the effectiveness of the relevant controls), the auditor should design and perform substantive procedures for all relevant assertions related to each material transaction class, account balance, and disclosure.

21. Which of the following explanations best describes why an auditor may decide to reduce tests of details for a particular audit objective?

   A. The audit is being performed soon after the balance sheet date.

   B. Audit staff are experienced in performing the planned procedures.

   C. Analytical procedures have revealed no unusual or unexpected results.

   D. There were many transactions posted to the account during the period.

Answer (C) is correct.
   REQUIRED: The reason to reduce tests of details.
   DISCUSSION: Analytical procedures performed as risk assessment procedures provide a basis for assessing the risks of material misstatement. When those procedures do not identify unusual transactions or events or amounts, ratios, and trends with audit significance, the assessment of the RMMs is lower. The lower assessment may justify reducing tests of details.
   Answer (A) is incorrect. The timing of audit procedures is a response to the assessed RMMs, not part of the assessment. Answer (B) is incorrect. The experience of the audit staff is a response to the RMMs, not part of the assessment. Answer (D) is incorrect. Significant activity in an account typically increases the risks of material misstatement and requires increased tests of details.

8.3 Assessing Risk in a Computer Environment

22. A client maintains a large data center where access is limited to authorized employees. How may an auditor best determine the effectiveness of this control activity?

   A. Inspect the policy manual establishing this control activity.

   B. Ask the chief technology officer about known problems.

   C. Observe whether the data center is monitored.

   D. Obtain a list of current data center employees.

Answer (C) is correct.
   REQUIRED: The best procedure to determine the effectiveness of a control activity.
   DISCUSSION: Physically observing that the data center is being monitored provides direct evidence that the control is in place and is being utilized effectively. The auditor will be able to see, first hand, if the control is preventing unauthorized access.
   Answer (A) is incorrect. Inspecting the policy manual will ensure that a control has been established but will not test the effectiveness of this control. Answer (B) is incorrect. Inquiry will help the auditor understand the control but will not test its effectiveness. Answer (D) is incorrect. Obtaining a list of current employees does not provide evidence of who has been accessing the data center.

23. To obtain evidence that online access controls are properly functioning, an auditor most likely will

   A. Create checkpoints at periodic intervals after live data processing to test for unauthorized use of the system.

   B. Examine the transaction log to discover whether any transactions were lost or entered twice because of a system malfunction.

   C. Enter invalid identification numbers or passwords to ascertain whether the system rejects them.

   D. Vouch a random sample of processed transactions to assure proper authorization.

Answer (C) is correct.
   REQUIRED: The procedure an auditor will most likely use to obtain evidence that user online access controls are functioning as designed.
   DISCUSSION: Employees with access authority to process transactions that change records should not also have asset custody or program modification responsibilities. The auditor should determine that password authority is consistent with other assigned responsibilities. The auditor can directly test whether password controls are working by attempting entry into the system by using invalid identifications and passwords.
   Answer (A) is incorrect. Checkpoints are used as a recovery procedure in batch processing applications. Answer (B) is incorrect. Testing for missing or duplicate transactions will not determine whether online access controls were functioning effectively. Answer (D) is incorrect. Unauthorized transactions may be entered by someone having knowledge of valid passwords, etc.

24. When an accounting application is processed by computer, an auditor **cannot** verify the reliable operation of automated controls by

A. Manually comparing detail transaction files used by an edit program with the program's generated error listings to determine that errors were properly identified by the edit program.

B. Constructing a processing system for accounting applications and processing actual data from throughout the period through both the client's program and the auditor's program.

C. Manually reperforming, as of a moment in time, the processing of input data and comparing the simulated results with the actual results.

D. Periodically submitting auditor-prepared test data to the same computer process and evaluating the results.

Answer (C) is correct.
REQUIRED: The procedure that would not verify the reliable operation of automated controls.
DISCUSSION: This procedure describes what is termed auditing around the computer. The computer is treated as a black box, and only the inputs and outputs are evaluated. Because the actual controls may not be understood or tested, the technique is ordinarily inappropriate if the effectiveness of automated controls is important to the understanding of internal control and the assessment of control risk. Moreover, the auditor is concerned with the reliable operation of the controls throughout the audit period, not at a single moment in time.
Answer (A) is incorrect. A manual comparison of the computer-generated output of an auditor-controlled edit program with the error listings generated by the client's program provides evidence that the client's automated controls were operating as planned. Answer (B) is incorrect. Parallel simulation can be an effective method of testing the reliability of controls. Answer (D) is incorrect. Submitting auditor-prepared test data to the client's computer process is an effective method of assessing the reliability of controls.

25. To obtain evidence that user identification and password controls are functioning as designed, an auditor should

A. Review the online transaction log to ascertain whether employees using passwords have access to data files and computer programs.

B. Examine a sample of password holders and access authority to determine whether they have access authority incompatible with their other responsibilities.

C. Extract a random sample of processed transactions and ensure that transactions are appropriately authorized.

D. Observe the file librarian's activities to discover whether other systems personnel are permitted to operate computer equipment without restriction.

Answer (B) is correct.
REQUIRED: The procedure an auditor should use to obtain evidence that user identification and password controls are functioning as designed.
DISCUSSION: Employees with access authority to process transactions that change records should not also have asset custody or program modification responsibilities. The auditor should determine that password authority is consistent with other assigned responsibilities. In addition, the auditor can directly test whether password controls are working by attempting entry into the system by using invalid identifications and passwords.
Answer (A) is incorrect. Password assignment properly provides employees with access to files and programs. Answer (C) is incorrect. Testing transactions for proper authorization does not ensure that user identification controls were functioning effectively. Answer (D) is incorrect. The file librarian oversees the physical protection of files, programs, and documentation, not the operation of computer equipment.

26. An auditor most likely should test for the presence of unauthorized computer program changes by running a

A. Program with test data.

B. Check digit verification program.

C. Source code comparison program.

D. Program that computes control totals.

Answer (C) is correct.
REQUIRED: The method used to test for the presence of unauthorized computer program changes.
DISCUSSION: The best way to test for unauthorized computer program changes is to examine the program itself. By comparing a program under his/her control with the program used for operations, the auditor can determine whether unauthorized changes have been made.
Answer (A) is incorrect. The test data may not trigger the unauthorized changes. Answer (B) is incorrect. Check digit verification tests the accuracy of data transcription, not programs. Answer (D) is incorrect. Control totals test the reasonableness and accuracy of processing but will not necessarily detect program changes.

27. Which of the following statements is **not** true of the test data approach to testing an accounting system?

A. Test data are processed by the client's computer programs under the auditor's control.

B. The test data need consist of only those valid and invalid conditions that interest the auditor.

C. Only one transaction of each type need be tested.

D. The test data must consist of all possible valid and invalid conditions.

Answer (D) is correct.
   REQUIRED: The false statement about the test data approach.
   DISCUSSION: The test data approach includes preparation of dummy transactions by the auditor. These transactions are processed by the client's computer programs under the auditor's control. The test data consist of one transaction for each valid and invalid condition that interests the auditor. Consequently, the test data need not consist of all possible valid and invalid conditions.
   Answer (A) is incorrect. The test data are processed by the client's computer programs under the control of the auditor. Answer (B) is incorrect. Only those controls deemed important to the auditor need be tested. Answer (C) is incorrect. The computer processes all similar transactions in the same way. Accordingly, only one transaction needs to be tested to determine whether a control is working effectively.

28. An auditor who is testing computer controls in a payroll system will most likely use test data that contain conditions such as

A. Deductions not authorized by employees.

B. Overtime not approved by supervisors.

C. Time tickets with invalid job numbers.

D. Payroll checks with unauthorized signatures.

Answer (C) is correct.
   REQUIRED: The most likely conditions in test data used in a test of computer controls over payroll.
   DISCUSSION: The auditor will most likely test computer controls for detection of time tickets with invalid job numbers. The validity of codes can be determined by the computer system. Testing of approvals, authorizations, and signatures usually require manual procedures.
   Answer (A) is incorrect. Testing of authorizations usually requires manual procedures. Answer (B) is incorrect. Testing of approvals usually requires manual procedures. Answer (D) is incorrect. Testing of signatures usually requires manual procedures.

29. In parallel simulation, actual client data are reprocessed using an auditor software program. An advantage of using parallel simulation, instead of performing tests of controls without a computer, is that

A. The test includes all types of transaction errors and exceptions that may be encountered.

B. The client's computer personnel do not know when the data are being tested.

C. There is no risk of creating potentially material errors in the client's data.

D. The size of the sample can be greatly expanded at relatively little additional cost.

Answer (D) is correct.
   REQUIRED: The advantage of using parallel simulation.
   DISCUSSION: Parallel simulation uses a controlled program to reprocess sets of client transactions and compares those results with those of the client. The primary disadvantages are the initial cost of obtaining the software and the need for coordination with client personnel to gain access to transactions. However, the auditors have the freedom to process transactions (1) at their convenience, (2) using their own equipment, and (3) taking as long as necessary. Thus, the auditors can greatly increase the sample size at relatively little marginal cost.
   Answer (A) is incorrect. Parallel simulation tests for errors and exceptions that occur only as a result of the software being tested. Answer (B) is incorrect. Whether the computer personnel know when the data are tested is not a concern when the test is at the auditor's own facilities. Answer (C) is incorrect. Use of actual data poses some risk of contamination.

30. Which of the following computer-assisted auditing techniques allows fictitious and real transactions to be processed together without the knowledge of client operating personnel?

A. Integrated test facility (ITF).

B. Input controls matrix.

C. Parallel simulation.

D. Data entry monitor.

Answer (A) is correct.
   REQUIRED: The technique that processes fictitious and real transactions without the knowledge of client personnel.
   DISCUSSION: The ITF or minicompany technique is a development of the test data method. It permits dummy transactions to be processed at the same time as live transactions but requires additional programming to ensure that programs will recognize the specially coded test data. The test transactions may be submitted without the computer operators' knowledge.
   Answer (B) is incorrect. Input controls matrix is not a method typically used by auditors to test a client's computer systems. Answer (C) is incorrect. Parallel simulation reprocesses only real, not fictitious, transactions. Answer (D) is incorrect. Data entry monitor is not a method typically used by auditors to test a client's computer systems.

31. An auditor who wishes to capture an entity's data as transactions are processed and continuously test the entity's computerized information system most likely would use which of the following techniques?

    A. Snapshot application.

    B. Embedded audit module.

    C. Integrated data check.

    D. Test data generator.

Answer (B) is correct.

    REQUIRED: The technique that captures an entity's data as transactions are processed and continuously tests the information system.

    DISCUSSION: Continuous monitoring and analysis of transaction processing can be achieved with an embedded audit module. An audit module embedded in the client's software routinely selects and abstracts certain actual transactions and other information with audit significance. They may be tagged and traced through the information system. A disadvantage is that audit hooks must be programmed into the operating system and applications. An alternative is recording in an audit log, i.e., in a file accessible only by the auditor.

32. The following flowchart depicts

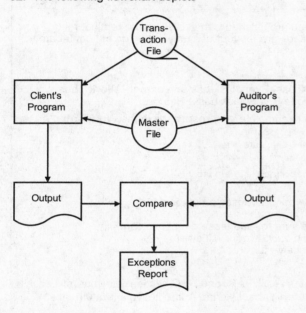

    A. Program code checking.

    B. Parallel simulation.

    C. Integrated test facility.

    D. Test data approach.

Answer (B) is correct.

    REQUIRED: The audit technique depicted by the flowchart.

    DISCUSSION: Parallel simulation is a test of the controls in a client's application program. An auditor-developed program is used to process actual client data and compare the output and the exceptions report with those of the client's application program. If the client's programmed controls are operating effectively, the two sets of results should be reconcilable.

    Answer (A) is incorrect. Program code checking refers to checking the client's application program code to determine if it contains the appropriate controls. Answer (C) is incorrect. An ITF introduces dummy records into the client's files and then processes dummy transactions to update the records. The auditor can test the controls by including various types of transactions to be processed. Answer (D) is incorrect. Using the test data approach, the auditor prepares a set of dummy transactions specifically designed to test the control activities.

Use the additional questions in Gleim **CPA Test Prep** to create Practice Exams that emulate Prometric!

8.4 PRACTICE TASK-BASED SIMULATIONS

DIRECTIONS

Note: If you believe you have encountered a software malfunction, report it to the test center staff immediately.

Navigation

To navigate from task to task, use the controls at the bottom of the screen. Click on the **Next** button to advance to the next task, or the **Previous** button to go to the previous task. To go directly to any task, click on its number.

If you would like a reminder to revisit a task, or want to indicate that you are finished with it, click on the reminder flag below the task number. To clear the flag, click on it again. Reminder flags are for your use only – they do not contribute to your score.

Tabs

In this part of the examination, you will be asked to complete various tasks. Every task has one or more **Work Tabs**. Some tasks have one or more **Information Tabs**, others may have none. Every task has a **Help** tab.

If a task has **Information Tabs**, you may use the information in them to complete your responses in the **Work Tabs**.

| Work tab | Information tab | Help tab |

Work Tabs:
- **Work Tabs** are identified with a pencil icon. This is where your responses are expected.
- Each task has one or more **Work Tabs**.
- **Work Tabs** contain directions for completing the task – be sure to read these directions carefully.
- The **Work Tab** name in the example above is for illustration only – yours will differ.
- You must complete all of the **Work Tabs** in each task to receive full credit.

Information Tabs:
- The Authoritative Literature will be provided in all tasks in the AUD, FAR, and REG sections for your reference.
- Your simulation may have one or more additional **Information Tabs**. Like the Authoritative Literature tabs, **Information Tabs** do not have a pencil icon.
- If your task has additional **Information Tabs**, go through each to familiarize yourself with the task content.

Help Tab:
- The **Help Tab** provides assistance with the exam software that is used in this task. For example, if the task is to compose a memorandum, **Help** will provide information about the word processor.

The Toolbar

The toolbar at the top of the screen shows the amount of time remaining for you to complete the tasks. In addition, the following tools are available. Note that only the **Exit** button is displayed when Directions are visible - the others will appear when you begin the tasks.

   Click on these buttons to split or unsplit the screen. You can split the screen vertically or horizontally.

   Click on this button to display the calculator; click on it again to hide the calculator. To move the calculator, click on the calculator title bar and drag the calculator to the desired location.

   Click on this button to use the spreadsheet; click on it again to hide the spreadsheet. To move the spreadsheet, click on the the spreadsheet title bar and drag the spreadsheet to the desired location.

   Click on this button to go on to the next part of the examination. You must complete all of the tasks to receive full credit. Once you click on **Exit** and confirm the action, you will NOT be able to return to this testlet.

Bond, CPA, is considering the risk of material misstatement (RMM) at the financial statement level for Toxic Waste Disposal (TWD) Company for the year ended December 31, Year 6. TWD is a privately owned entity that contracts with municipal governments to remove environmental wastes. RMM at the financial statement level is influenced by a combination of factors related to management, the industry, and the entity.

Based only on the information in the table, select whether each factor below would most likely increase, decrease, or have no effect on RMM. Each choice may be used once, more than once, or not at all.

Factor	*Answer*
1. This was the first year TWD operated at a profit since Year 2 because the municipalities received increased federal and state funding for environmental purposes.	
2. TWD's board of directors is controlled by Mead, the majority shareholder, who also acts as the chief executive officer.	
3. The internal auditor reports to the controller, and the controller reports to Mead.	
4. The accounting department has experienced a high rate of turnover of key personnel.	
5. TWD's bank has a loan officer who meets regularly with TWD's CEO and controller to monitor TWD's financial performance.	
6. TWD's employees are paid biweekly.	
7. Bond has audited TWD for 5 years.	
8. During Year 6, litigation filed against TWD in Year 1 alleging that TWD discharged pollutants into state waterways was dropped by the state. Loss contingency disclosures that TWD included in prior years' financial statements are being removed for the Year 6 financial statements.	
9. During December Year 6, TWD signed a contract to lease disposal equipment from an entity owned by Mead's parents. This related party transaction is not disclosed in TWD's notes to its Year 6 financial statements.	
10. During December Year 6, TWD increased its casualty insurance coverage on several pieces of sophisticated machinery from historical cost to replacement cost.	

Choices
A) Increase RMM
B) Decrease RMM
C) No Effect

| Computer Environment | Authoritative Literature | Help |

The following are descriptions related to the computer environment. For each one, select from the list provided the term or phrase that best fits the description. Each choice may be used once or not at all.

Description	Answer
1. A methodology that is not appropriate when systems are sophisticated or the major controls are included in the computer programs.	
2. The auditor prepares a set of dummy transactions specifically designed to test the control activities that management claims to have incorporated into the processing programs.	
3. The inappropriate duty assigned to the IT function.	
4. The auditor attempts to sign on to the computer system using various passwords and ID numbers.	
5. Controls that relate to the client's input, processing, and output.	
6. The auditor uses a controlled program to reprocess sets of client transactions and compares the auditor-achieved results with those of the client.	
7. The auditor should test first.	
8. The auditor inspects this to determine whether it is complete and up to date.	
9. A methodology that uses the computer to test the processing logic and controls within the system and the records produced.	
10. May be included in the payroll processing program.	

Term or Phrase

A) Application controls
B) Test data approach
C) Reasonableness test
D) Service department
E) Auditing around the computer
F) Auditing through the computer
G) Parallel simulation
H) Test of access controls
I) Programming
J) General controls
K) Program documentation
L) Asset custody

| Research | Authoritative Literature | Help |

Management informed your firm's engagement partner that a prospective lender made a preliminary request for a CPA's letter regarding the company's solvency. The partner requested that you find guidance, if any, in the AICPA Professional Standards regarding CPA reports on matters relating to solvency.

Research and cite the appropriate attestation standard regarding solvency that answers the question, "May a practitioner provide assurance about matters related to solvency?"

Title	Section	Paragraph

Title Choices						
AU-C	PCAOB	AT	AR	ET	BL	VS
CS	QC	PR	TS	PFP	CPE	

| Analytical Results | Authoritative Literature | Help |

The table below presents some ratios that were considered significant by an auditor in the current and prior year's audits of a client. Select from the list provided the most likely explanation for the analytical results. Each choice may be used once, more than once, or not at all.

Ratio	Year 2	Year 1	Answer
1. Debt to equity	1.99	4.61	
2. Gross profit percentage	38%	41%	
3. Quick	2.00	1.50	
4. Inventory turnover	4.50	3.25	
5. Return on equity	3%	8%	

Explanations
A) Sales decreased compared with the prior year.
B) Cost of goods sold increased during the year at a lower rate than sales increased.
C) Proceeds from the issuance of noncurrent debt were used to pay accounts payable.
D) Capital stock was issued during the year.
E) The entity may have accumulated excess and obsolete inventory.
F) Inventory decreased by more than cost of goods sold decreased for the year.
G) Cost of goods sold decreased by less than sales decreased during the year.

| Evidence | Authoritative Literature | Help |

For each of the [numbers], select from the answer choices the best word(s) to complete the statement. Each choice may be used once, more than once, or not at all.

Statements	Answer
When controls are found to be weak, the [1] assessed level of control risk results in the need for a [2] level of assurance from further audit procedures relative to the fairness of the assertions.	
Evidence about the effectiveness of the operation of controls obtained [3] by the auditor usually provides more assurance than evidence obtained [4].	
A [5] assessment of the risks of material misstatement reduces the audit effort devoted to substantive procedures.	
When various types of evidence support the same conclusion, the degree of assurance provided is usually [6] than when only one type of evidence supports the conclusion.	
When the auditor determines that a specific control may have a significant effect on the assessment of the RMMs, (s)he usually needs to perform testing with a [7] degree of assurance instead of relying on inquiries alone.	
A [8] degree of subjectivity in a financial measure results in more risk for the auditor.	
Some controls [9] affect an assertion, which may make them important for the auditor to test.	
Few tests of controls may be necessary when an auditor intends to place a [10] degree of reliance on controls.	

Choices
A) Lower
B) Higher
C) Directly
D) Indirectly

Unofficial Answers

1. Risk Factors (10 Gradable Items)

1. <u>B) Decrease RMM.</u> Continued losses indicate an increase in risk. However, the turnaround into a profitable organization will likely decrease the risk of material misstatement in the financial statements for the auditor.

2. <u>A) Increase RMM.</u> One set of opportunity risk factors for misstatements arising from fraudulent financial reporting involves ineffective monitoring of management. One such risk factor is domination of management by a single person or small group (in a non-owner managed business) without compensating controls. A compensating control in that circumstance is effective oversight by the board or audit committee of the financial reporting process and internal control.

3. <u>A) Increase RMM.</u> Ideally, the internal auditor should report to the audit committee of the board of directors. If the internal auditor reports to operating management, the risk of material misstatement is increased.

4. <u>A) Increase RMM.</u> When management turnover is high, particularly of senior accounting personnel, the risk of material misstatement is increased.

5. <u>B) Decrease RMM.</u> Oversight by external parties, e.g., a bank loan officer, provides some assurance to the auditor and decreases the risk of material misstatement.

6. <u>C) No effect.</u> Paying employees biweekly likely has little effect on the risk of material misstatement.

7. <u>B) Decrease RMM.</u> A continuing engagement in which the auditor has had experience with management is likely to be less risky than a first-time audit.

8. <u>B) Decrease RMM.</u> The settlement of lawsuits filed against the client likely decreases the risk that the financial statements are misstated.

9. <u>A) Increase RMM.</u> A set of opportunity risk factors for misstatements arising from fraudulent financial reporting involves the nature of the industry or the entity's operations. One such risk factor is the existence of significant related party transactions not in the ordinary course of business or with entities not audited or audited by another firm.

10. <u>C) No effect.</u> The change in insurance coverage for specific assets will not likely change the risk of material misstatement.

2. Computer Environment (10 Gradable Items)

1. <u>E) Auditing around the computer.</u> Auditing around the computer is not appropriate when systems are sophisticated or the major controls are included in the computer programs.

2. <u>B) Test data approach.</u> In the test data approach, the auditor prepares a set of dummy transactions specifically designed to test the control activities that management claims to have incorporated into the processing programs.

3. <u>L) Asset custody.</u> The IT function is primarily recordkeeping and should not be assigned asset custody.

4. <u>H) Test of access controls.</u> In testing access controls, the auditor attempts to sign on to the computer system using various passwords and ID numbers.

5. <u>A) Application controls.</u> Application controls are those that are related to the client's information input, processing, and output.

6. <u>G) Parallel simulation.</u> Parallel simulation is a technique where the auditor uses a controlled program to reprocess sets of client transactions and compares the auditor-achieved results with those of the client.

7. <u>J) General controls.</u> Before testing application controls, the auditor should be satisfied that general controls are designed properly and operating effectively.

8. <u>K) Program documentation.</u> The auditor inspects program documentation to determine whether it is complete and up to date.

9. <u>F) Auditing through the computer.</u> Auditing through the computer is a methodology that uses the computer to test the processing logic and controls within the system and the records produced.

10. <u>C) Reasonableness test.</u> A reasonableness test is an application control that may be included in the payroll processing program.

3. Research (1 Gradable Item)

Answer: AT 9101.25

2. Responding to Requests for Reports on Matters Relating to Solvency

.25   Interpretation—No. For reasons set forth below, a practitioner should not provide any form of assurance, through examination, review, or agreed-upon procedures engagements, that an entity

- is not insolvent at the time the debt is incurred or would not be rendered insolvent thereby.
- does not have unreasonably small capital.
- has the ability to pay its debts as they mature.

In the context of particular transactions other terms are sometimes used or defined by the parties as equivalents of or substitutes for the terms listed above (for example, "fair salable value of assets exceeds liabilities"). These terms, and those matters listed above, are hereinafter referred to as "matters relating to solvency." The prohibition extends to providing assurance concerning all such terms.

4. Analytical Results (5 Gradable Items)

1. D) Capital stock was issued during the year. The debt-to-equity ratio equals total liabilities divided by total equity. It compares the resources provided by creditors with the resources provided by shareholders. The decrease in the debt-to-equity ratio could be explained by the issuance of capital stock.

2. G) Cost of goods sold decreased by less than sales decreased during the year. The gross profit percentage (gross profit margin) equals gross profit (net sales − cost of goods sold) divided by net sales. The smaller gross profit percentage could be explained by a larger cost of goods sold relative to sales.

3. C) Proceeds from the issuance of noncurrent debt were used to pay accounts payable. The quick ratio equals current assets minus inventory, divided by current liabilities. Paying current liabilities with noncurrent debt could explain an increase in the quick ratio.

4. F) Inventory decreased by more than cost of goods sold decreased for the year. Inventory turnover equals cost of goods sold divided by average inventory. A smaller inventory results in a larger turnover.

5. D) Capital stock was issued during the year. Return on equity equals net income divided by total equity. An increase in capital stock reduces the return on equity.

5. Evidence (10 Gradable Items)

1. B) Higher. When controls are found to be weak, the higher assessed level of control risk results in the need for a higher level of assurance from further audit procedures relative to the fairness of the assertions.

2. B) Higher. When controls are found to be weak, the higher assessed level of control risk results in the need for a higher level of assurance from further audit procedures relative to the fairness of the assertions.

3. C) Directly. Evidence about the effectiveness of the operation of controls obtained directly by the auditor usually provides more assurance than evidence obtained indirectly.

4. D) Indirectly. Evidence about the effectiveness of the operation of controls obtained directly by the auditor usually provides more assurance than evidence obtained indirectly.

5. A) Lower. A lower assessment of the risks of material misstatement reduces the audit effort devoted to substantive procedures.

6. B) Higher. When various types of evidence support the same conclusion, the degree of assurance provided is usually higher than when only one type of evidence supports the conclusion.

7. B) Higher. When the auditor determines that a specific control may have a significant effect on the assessment of the RMMs, (s)he usually needs to perform procedures with a higher degree of assurance instead of relying on inquiries alone.

8. B) Higher. A higher degree of subjectivity in a financial measure results in more risk for the auditor.

9. C) Directly. Some controls directly affect an assertion, which may make them important for the auditor to test.

10. A) Lower. Few tests of controls may be necessary when an auditor intends to place a lower degree of reliance on controls.

Gleim Simulation Grading

Task	Correct Responses		Gradable Items		Score per Task
1	_____	÷	10	=	_____
2	_____	÷	10	=	_____
3 (Research)	_____	÷	1	=	_____
4	_____	÷	5	=	_____
5	_____	÷	10	=	_____

Total of Scores per Task   _____

÷   Total Number of Tasks   5

Total Score   _____ %

Use **CPA Gleim Online** and **Simulation Wizard** to practice more task-based simulations in a realistic environment.

STUDY UNIT NINE
INTERNAL CONTROL COMMUNICATIONS AND REPORTS

(18 pages of outline)

This study unit concerns various auditor communications and reports, most involving internal control. During the conduct of an audit, the auditor may observe control deficiencies. If so, the auditor has a responsibility to communicate significant deficiencies and material weaknesses to management and those charged with governance (AU-C 265, *Communicating Internal Control Related Matters Identified in an Audit*). Other issues relating to the conduct of the audit also should be communicated to management and those charged with governance. Some of these issues are closely related to internal control, but others relate to the audit in general (AU-C 260, *The Auditor's Communication with Those Charged with Governance* and AS No. 16, *Communications with Audit Committees*). Public companies (issuers) are required by the Sarbanes-Oxley Act of 2002 to provide a management assessment of the effectiveness of internal control over financial reporting in annual reports. The PCAOB's Auditing Standard No. 5, *An Audit of Internal Control over Financial Reporting That Is Integrated with an Audit of Financial Statements*, provides guidance on the required process and reporting. For example, it requires the auditor to express an opinion, or disclaim an opinion, on internal control, not on management's assessment. For other entities (nonissuers), the CPA may be engaged to provide a report on the effectiveness of an entity's internal control over financial reporting. This service and the reports issued are governed by the AICPA's AT 501, *An Examination of an Entity's Internal Control over Financial Reporting That Is Integrated with an Audit of Its Financial Statements*. The CPA may be either a user or a preparer of a report prepared in accordance with AU-C 402, *Audit Considerations Relating to an Entity Using a Service Organization*, and AT 801, *Reporting on Controls at a Service Organization*. Such a report may affect the user CPA's assessment of a client's risks of material misstatement.

9.1 COMMUNICATING INTERNAL CONTROL RELATED MATTERS IDENTIFIED IN AN AUDIT (AU-C 265)

1. The financial statement auditor is **not** required to perform procedures specifically to identify deficiencies in internal control or to express an opinion on internal control.

2. But, in each audit, the auditor should report **significant deficiencies** and **material weaknesses** in internal control over financial reporting that have been identified.

3. The communication should be **in writing** and directed to **management** and **those charged with governance** (e.g., a board of directors).

4. A **deficiency** in internal control exists when the **design or operation** of a control does not allow management or employees, in the normal course of their assigned functions, to prevent, or detect and correct, misstatements on a timely basis.

5. A **significant deficiency** is a deficiency, or combination of deficiencies, in internal control that is less severe than a material weakness but that merits attention by those charged with governance.

6. A **material weakness** is a deficiency, or combination of deficiencies, in internal control that results in a **reasonable possibility** that a **material misstatement** of the financial statements will not be prevented or timely detected and corrected.

   a. A reasonable possibility means that the likelihood of the event is **more than remote**.

7. **Evaluating Control Deficiencies**

   a. The auditor should evaluate each deficiency to determine whether, individually or in combination, it is a significant deficiency or a material weakness. The **severity of a deficiency** depends on

      1) The magnitude of the potential misstatement and
      2) Whether a reasonable possibility exists that the controls will fail.

   b. Severity does not depend on actual occurrence of a misstatement.

   c. The **magnitude** of a misstatement depends on, among other things,

      1) The financial statement amounts or transactions involved and
      2) The activity in the relevant balance or transaction class.

   d. The maximum **overstatement** ordinarily is the recorded amount, but the **understatement** is unlimited.

      1) The auditor need not quantify the **probability** of misstatement.
      2) A small misstatement often is more likely than a large misstatement.

   e. **Risk factors** may indicate whether a reasonable possibility exists that one or more deficiencies will result in a misstatement. The following are examples of risk factors:

      1) Accounts, transaction classes, disclosures, and assertions involved (e.g., overstatement of revenues and understatement of expenses)
      2) Cause and frequency of exceptions
      3) Susceptibility of the related asset or liability to loss or fraud
      4) Degree of judgment required to determine the amount involved
      5) Relationship of the control with other controls
      6) Interaction among deficiencies
      7) Possible consequences of the deficiency
      8) Importance to financial reporting

   f. Controls may operate individually or in combination, e.g., manual and IT controls over a significant account, disclosure, or assertion. Thus, a deficiency by itself may not be significant.

      1) But a combination of deficiencies affecting a significant account, etc., may increase the RMMs sufficiently to create a deficiency that should be communicated.

   g. **Indicators of material weaknesses** include the following:

      1) Identification of any fraud by senior management
      2) Restatement of financial statements to correct a material misstatement due to fraud or error
      3) Identification by the auditor of a material misstatement that would not have been detected by internal control
      4) Ineffective oversight of financial reporting and internal control by those charged with governance

   h. The auditor considers whether prudent officials, having the same knowledge, would agree with the auditor that one or more deficiencies are **not** a material weakness.

    i.   The following are examples of possible deficiencies, significant deficiencies, or material weaknesses related to **design**:

       1)   Inadequate design of internal control over financial statement preparation
       2)   Inadequate design of controls over a significant account or process
       3)   Inadequate documentation of the components of internal control
       4)   Insufficient control consciousness
       5)   Absent or inadequate segregation of duties or controls
       6)   An ineffective control environment, risk assessment process, or response to significant risks over the safeguarding of assets
       7)   Inadequate design of IT general and application controls
       8)   Employees or management who lack the proper qualifications and training
       9)   Inadequate design of monitoring controls
       10) The absence of an internal process to report deficiencies on a timely basis

    j.   The following are examples of deficiencies, significant deficiencies, or material weaknesses related to **operational failures**:

       1)   Failures in the operation of effectively designed controls over a significant account or process
       2)   Failure of the information and communication component of internal control to provide timely, complete, and accurate information
       3)   Failure of controls designed to safeguard assets
       4)   Failure to perform reconciliations of significant accounts
       5)   Undue bias or lack of objectivity by those responsible for accounting decisions
       6)   Misrepresentation by client personnel to the auditor
       7)   Management override of controls
       8)   Failure of an application control caused by deficient design or operation of an IT general control
       9)   An excessive observed deviation rate in a test of controls

8.   **Communication**

    a.   The auditor should **communicate in writing significant deficiencies** and **material weaknesses** to management and those charged with governance.

       1)   The communication also should describe these conditions and explain their potential effects.

    b.   The communication is best made by the **audit report release date**, but **no later than 60 days** after.

    c.   Communication of **significant and urgent matters** during the audit need not be in writing. But the auditor ultimately should communicate significant deficiencies and material weaknesses in writing even if they have been corrected.

    d.   Management or those charged with governance may explicitly decide, e.g., because of the cost, not to correct significant deficiencies or material weaknesses. However, the auditor should communicate them regardless of such decisions.

       1)   If the communication was made in a prior audit, it should be repeated in the current audit if the condition has not been remedied.

    e.   The auditor should communicate to management other deficiencies that merit attention but are not significant deficiencies or material weaknesses. This communication may be made orally or in writing.

    f.   The **written communication** should

       1)   State that the purpose of the audit was to express an opinion on the financial statements.

2) State that the audit considered internal control to design audit procedures, not to express an opinion, and that the auditor is not expressing an opinion on the effectiveness of internal control.

3) State that the auditor's consideration of internal control was **not** designed to identify all deficiencies that might be significant deficiencies or material weaknesses.

4) Include the definition of a material weakness and, if relevant, the definition of a significant deficiency.

5) Describe significant deficiencies and material weaknesses.

6) Explain the potential effects of each significant deficiency and material weakness.

7) Restrict the use of the communication to (a) management, (b) those charged with governance, and (c) others within the entity (and possibly governmental agencies).

EXAMPLE -- Communications of Significant Deficiencies and Material Weaknesses

To Management and the Board of Directors

In planning and performing our audit of the financial statements of ABC Company (the "Company") as of and for the year ended December 31, Year 1, in accordance with auditing standards generally accepted in the United States of America, we considered the Company's internal control over financial reporting (internal control) as a basis for designing auditing procedures that are appropriate in the circumstances for the purpose of expressing our opinion on the financial statements, but not for the purpose of expressing an opinion on the effectiveness of the Company's internal control. Accordingly, we do not express an opinion on the effectiveness of the Company's internal control.

Our consideration of internal control was for the limited purpose described in the preceding paragraph and was not designed to identify all deficiencies in internal control that might be *[significant deficiencies or material weaknesses]* and therefore, *[significant deficiencies or material weaknesses]* may exist that were not identified. However, as discussed below, we identified certain deficiencies in internal control that we consider to be *[material weaknesses or significant deficiencies]*.

A deficiency in internal control exists when the design or operation of a control does not allow management or employees, in the normal course of performing their assigned functions, to prevent, or detect and correct, misstatements on a timely basis. A material weakness is a deficiency, or a combination of deficiencies, in internal control, such that there is a reasonable possibility that a material misstatement of the entity's financial statements will not be prevented, or detected and corrected, on a timely basis. *[We consider the following deficiencies in the Company's internal control to be material weaknesses:]*

[Describe the material weaknesses that were identified and explain their potential effects.]

[A significant deficiency is a deficiency, or a combination of deficiencies, in internal control, that is less severe than a material weakness, yet important enough to merit attention by those charged with governance. We consider the following deficiencies in the Company's internal control to be significant deficiencies:]

[Describe the significant deficiencies that were identified and explain their potential effects.]

This communication is intended solely for the information and use of management, *[identify the body or individuals charged with governance]*, others within the organization, *[identify any governmental authorities]* and is not intended to be and should not be used by anyone other than these specified parties.

Auditor's signature
Auditor's city and state
Date

---

g. A client may ask the auditor to issue a written communication for the client stating that **no material weaknesses** were identified. A communication similar to the above example is appropriate, with the following paragraph added:

EXAMPLE

Our consideration of internal control was for the limited purpose described in the first paragraph and was not designed to identify all deficiencies in internal control that might be material weaknesses. Given these limitations, during our audit we did not identify any deficiencies in internal control that we consider to be material weaknesses. However, material weaknesses may exist that have not been identified.

    h.   An auditor should **not** issue a written communication stating that **no significant deficiencies** were identified.

    i.   Management may wish to prepare a written response to the auditor's communication. If one is included in the communication document, the auditor should disclaim an opinion on the response.

ISA Difference

The U.S. audit standards require the auditor to communicate significant deficiencies and material weaknesses in internal control. The ISAs do not include or define the term "material weakness."

The U.S. audit standards specifically require the following to be included in the communication, and the ISA standards do not:

●   The definition of "material weakness" and, when relevant, the definition of "significant deficiency."

●   A statement that the auditor is not expressing an opinion on the effectiveness of internal control.

●   An explanation that an audit is not designed to identify all deficiencies in internal control.

●   A statement restricting the use of the communication to specific parties.

Stop and review! You have completed the outline for this subunit. Study multiple-choice questions 1 through 10 beginning on page 307.

9.2 THE AUDITOR'S COMMUNICATION WITH THOSE CHARGED WITH GOVERNANCE (AU-C 260 AND AS NO. 16)

1.   Those charged with governance are responsible for oversight of the entity's strategic direction and accountability, including the **financial reporting process**. The **board of directors** and the **audit committee** are typical governance bodies. In smaller organizations, owners or management may be those charged with governance.

    a.   **Two-way communication** is expected and should provide those charged with governance with information about matters relevant to their responsibilities, including an overview of the audit process and of the auditor's responsibilities.

        1)   It also should allow the auditor to obtain information relevant to the audit.

    b.   Communication may be either **oral or in writing** and should be **documented**.

        1)   The auditor communicates significant findings from the audit in writing when (s)he judges that oral communication is inadequate.

            a)   A written communication should indicate that it is for the **sole use** of those charged with governance.

    c.   Communication should take place on a **timely basis** to enable those charged with governance to meet their responsibilities for oversight of financial reporting (e.g., those relating to planning should take place early in the engagement).

    d.   It may be appropriate for **management** to communicate certain matters to those charged with governance, and the auditor should be satisfied that such communication has occurred.

        1)   Many matters are discussed with management during the audit. But certain discussions may be inappropriate, e.g., those related to management's integrity.

2.   **Matters to be communicated** include (a) the auditor's responsibilities in accordance with GAAS, (b) an overview of the audit, and (c) significant and relevant findings.

3. **Auditor's Responsibilities under GAAS**

    a. The auditor may provide a copy of the **engagement letter** (see Study Unit 3, Subunit 1) to those charged with governance, indicating that, among other things,

        1) The auditor is responsible for forming and expressing an opinion about whether the financial statements are presented fairly.

        2) The audit does not relieve management or those charged with governance of their responsibilities for fair reporting.

4. **Planned Scope and Timing of the Audit**

    a. An **overview** should be provided, but it should in no way compromise the effectiveness of the audit. The auditor should never discuss details of procedures to be used. Issues to be addressed include

        1) How the auditor proposes to address the risks of material misstatement, whether due to fraud or error;

        2) Issues related to internal control and the internal audit function; and

        3) Materiality in planning and performing the audit.

5. **Qualitative Aspects of the Entity's Significant Accounting Practices**

    a. The auditor should inform those charged with governance about the following:

        1) The auditor's views on the entity's significant accounting practices, including policies, estimates, and disclosures

        2) The reasons that the entity should not use a significant accounting practice that is acceptable under the applicable reporting framework

        3) Management's process for making sensitive accounting estimates (including fair value estimates) and the basis for the auditor's conclusions about their reasonableness

        4) Management's selection of, changes in, and application of significant accounting policies

        5) Management's methods used to account for significant, unusual transactions

        6) The effects of significant accounting policies in controversial or emerging areas that lack authoritative guidance or consensus, such as revenue recognition, off-balance-sheet financing, and accounting for equity investments

6. Those charged with governance should be informed of **significant difficulties** encountered in dealing with management, such as delays in providing required information and unnecessary time constraints on the audit. Other significant problems may include unavailability of information and management-imposed restrictions.

7. **Uncorrected misstatements**, other than those not accumulated by the auditor because they are clearly trivial, and their effect on the opinion should be communicated to those charged with governance.

    a. The auditor also should communicate

        1) The effect of uncorrected misstatements from prior periods on the statements as a whole and relevant transaction classes, etc.;

        2) Material, corrected misstatements communicated to management; and

        3) Written representations requested by the auditor.

    b. The auditor may communicate immaterial, corrected misstatements that recur frequently and may indicate a bias in the statements.

    c. The auditor should discuss with those charged with governance the implications of not correcting misstatements.

8.   Management and the auditor may disagree about (a) the application of accounting principles, (b) the basis for accounting estimates, (c) the scope of the audit, (d) disclosures, and (e) the auditor's report.

   a.   The auditor and those charged with governance should discuss any disagreements about matters significant to the statements or the audit report.

9.   When the auditor is aware of consultations between management and other accountants, (s)he should communicate to those charged with governance his/her views about the significant matters involved.

10. The auditor should communicate to those charged with governance discussions with management about significant matters such as (a) business conditions affecting the entity, (b) plans and strategies affecting the RMMs, (c) the initial or recurring retention of the auditors, and (d) the application of accounting principles.

11. Discussions may be appropriate about circumstances or relationships (e.g., financial interests, business or family relationships, or nonaudit services) that, in the auditor's professional judgment,

   a.   May reasonably bear on **independence** and

   b.   Were given significant consideration by the auditor in reaching the conclusion that independence has not been impaired.

12. **Sarbanes-Oxley Act of 2002**

   a.   The act requires the auditor to report the following to those charged with governance:

      1)   All critical accounting policies and practices to be used

      2)   All material alternative treatments of financial information within GAAP discussed with management

      3)   Ramifications of the use of alternative disclosures and treatments

      4)   The treatment preferred by the auditor

ISA Difference

The ISAs do not require the auditor to determine that those charged with governance are informed about the process used by management in formulating particularly sensitive accounting estimates and about the basis for the auditor's conclusion regarding the reasonableness of those estimates.

The ISAs do not require that the auditor communicate (1) material, corrected misstatements that were brought to the attention of management as a result of audit procedures or (2) any disagreements with management.

Stop and review! You have completed the outline for this subunit. Study multiple-choice questions 11 through 18 beginning on page 310.

9.3 REPORTING ON AN ENTITY'S INTERNAL CONTROL (AT 501 AND AS NO. 5)

1. The PCAOB's **Auditing Standard No. 5 (AS No. 5)**, *An Audit of Internal Control over Financial Reporting that is Integrated with an Audit of Financial Statements*, provides guidance on the required process and reporting for **issuers**.

2. AT 501, *An Examination of an Entity's Internal Control over Financial Reporting that is Integrated with an Audit of Its Financial Statements*, describes the service for **nonissuers**. It is consistent with AS No. 5.

   a. The basic differences are that it is **not a required part** of the financial statement audit, and the required reports refer to AICPA standards rather than PCAOB standards.

   b. The outline beginning below covers the **audit** of internal control under AS No. 5, but it also applies to **examinations** under AT 501.

3. A company subject to the reporting requirements of the Securities Exchange Act of 1934 (an issuer) with a market equity value of at least $75 million (an accelerated filer) must include in its annual report **management's assessment** of the design and effectiveness of **internal control over financial reporting**.

   a. The assessment should be performed using suitable **control criteria**, such as *Internal Control – Integrated Framework* published by the Committee of Sponsoring Organizations (COSO) (recall the components of internal control from Study Unit 5, Subunit 1: Controls stop **CRIME**).

      1) The same framework used by management should be used by the auditor.

4. The auditor's objective in an audit of internal control over financial reporting **(audit of internal control)** is to express an opinion on whether the entity maintained, in all material respects, effective internal control over financial reporting **(internal control)** as of the specified date, based on the control criteria. However, internal control is not effective if a material weakness exists.

   a. Accordingly, the auditor must plan and perform the audit to obtain competent evidence (AS No. 5) or sufficient appropriate evidence (AT 501) to obtain **reasonable assurance** about whether **material weaknesses** exist at the date of management's assessment (AS No. 5) or assertion (AT 501).

   b. AS No. 5 applies in an audit of management's assessment of the effectiveness of internal control over financial reporting.

      1) However, the auditor expresses an opinion directly on internal control, not on management's assessment.

         a) If a material weakness exists, the auditor expresses an adverse opinion.

            i) If management's assessment does not include the material weakness, the report is modified to state that the material weakness was not included in the assessment.

   c. Under AT 501, the auditor may express an opinion directly on internal control or on whether management's assertion about internal control is fairly stated.

5. **Integrating the Audits**

   a. The audit of internal control should be integrated with the audit of the financial statements. The integrated audit should achieve the objectives of both.

      1) The auditor should design **tests of controls** to obtain sufficient appropriate evidence to support the auditor's opinion on internal control over financial reporting

         a) At a moment in time (e.g., at year end) and

         b) Taken as a whole (i.e., addressing the effectiveness of selected controls over all relevant assertions).

2) The audit (examination) of internal control typically involves testing controls not tested in a financial statement audit.

6. **Planning the Audit**

   a. The integrated audit should be properly planned, and assistants, if any, should be properly supervised. The auditor should evaluate how the following affect the audit procedures:

      1) Knowledge of internal control obtained during other engagements

      2) Client industry issues, such as financial reporting practices, economic conditions, laws and regulations, and technological changes

      3) Matters related to the business, e.g., operating characteristics, capital structure, and organization

      4) Recent changes in operations or in internal control

      5) Preliminary judgments about materiality, risk, and other factors relating to the determination of material weaknesses

      6) Control deficiencies previously communicated to the audit committee or management

      7) Legal or regulatory matters

      8) The type and extent of available evidence related to the effectiveness of internal control

      9) Preliminary judgments about internal control

      10) Public information relevant to the likelihood of material misstatements and the effectiveness of internal control

      11) The relative complexity of operations

      12) Knowledge about risks obtained from the client acceptance and retention evaluation

7. A direct relationship exists between the degree of risk that a material weakness could exist and the amount of audit attention that should be devoted to that area.

8. The size and complexity of the company, its business processes, and business units may affect the way in which the company achieves many of its **control objectives**. Size and complexity also affect risks and related controls.

   a. Thus, **scaling** is an extension of the risk-based approach.

9. **Addressing the Risk of Fraud**

   a. The auditor should (1) consider the results of the fraud risk assessment and (2) evaluate (a) whether controls sufficiently address the identified risks of material fraud and (b) controls over the risk of management override. The following controls address these risks:

      1) Controls over significant, unusual transactions, particularly those that result in late or unusual journal entries

      2) Controls over journal entries and adjustments made in the period-end financial reporting process

      3) Controls over related party transactions

      4) Controls related to significant management estimates

      5) Controls that mitigate incentives for, and pressures on, management to falsify or inappropriately manage financial results

10. **Using the Work of Others**

    a.   The auditor may use the work performed by, or receive direct assistance from, internal auditors, company personnel, and third parties working under the direction of management or the audit committee that provides evidence about the effectiveness of internal control.

    b.   The auditor should assess the competence and objectivity of the persons whose work the auditor plans to use. The higher the degree of competence and objectivity, the greater use the auditor may make of the work.

11. The same **materiality** considerations apply in the audit of internal control as in planning the audit of the annual financial statements.

12. **Using a Top-Down Approach**

    a.   The auditor begins at the financial statement level by understanding overall risks. (S)he then focuses on **entity-level controls** and works down to significant accounts and disclosures and their relevant assertions. The following are examples of entity-level controls:

        1)   The control environment
        2)   Controls over management override
        3)   Monitoring of the results of operations
        4)   Controls over the period-end financial reporting process
        5)   Monitoring of other controls
        6)   The risk assessment process

    b.   The auditor should evaluate the **control environment** by assessing whether

        1)   Management's philosophy and operating style promote effective internal control.
        2)   Sound integrity and ethical values, particularly of management, are developed and understood.
        3)   The board or audit committee understands and exercises oversight responsibility over financial reporting and internal control.

    c.   The auditor should evaluate the **period-end financial reporting process**, including procedures

        1)   Used to enter transaction totals into the general ledger;
        2)   Related to the selection and application of accounting policies;
        3)   Used to initiate, authorize, record, and process journal entries;
        4)   Used to record recurring and nonrecurring adjustments to the annual and quarterly financial statements; and
        5)   For preparing annual and quarterly financial statements and related disclosures.

13. **Identifying Significant Accounts and Disclosures and Their Relevant Assertions**

    a.   The auditor may use assertions other than those in AS No. 5 if (s)he has tested controls over the pertinent risks. The following are risk factors related to accounts and disclosures:

        1)   Size and composition of the account
        2)   Susceptibility to misstatement due to fraud or error
        3)   Volume of activity, complexity, and homogeneity of the transactions
        4)   Nature of the account or disclosure
        5)   Accounting and reporting complexities
        6)   Exposure to losses in the account
        7)   Possibility of significant contingent liabilities arising from the activities reflected in the account or disclosure
        8)   Existence of related party transactions in the account
        9)   Changes from the prior period or disclosure characteristics

14. **Walkthroughs** (following transactions through the process) frequently are the most effective way of achieving the following objectives:

    a. Understanding the flow of transactions related to relevant assertions

    b. Identifying the points within the company's processes at which a material misstatement, including a misstatement due to fraud, could arise

    c. Identifying the controls that management has implemented to address these potential misstatements

    d. Identifying the controls that management has implemented for the prevention or timely detection of unauthorized acquisition, use, or disposition of assets

15. **Testing Controls**

    a. **Testing Design Effectiveness**

        1) The auditor should determine whether controls, if they are operated as prescribed by persons with the necessary authority and competence to perform them effectively, (a) satisfy the control objectives and (b) can effectively prevent, or detect and correct, fraud or error that could result in material misstatements in the financial statements.

        2) Procedures include (a) inquiry of appropriate personnel, (b) observation of operations, and (c) inspection of relevant documentation. Walkthroughs that include these procedures ordinarily are sufficient to evaluate design effectiveness.

    b. **Testing Operating Effectiveness**

        1) The auditor should determine whether (a) a control is operating as designed and (b) the person performing the control possesses the necessary authority and competence to perform the control effectively.

        2) Procedures the auditor performs to test operating effectiveness include a mix of (a) inquiry of appropriate personnel, (b) observation of operations, (c) inspection of relevant documentation, and (d) reperformance of the control.

    c. **Relationship of Risk to the Evidence to Be Obtained**

        1) More risk requires more testing and more competent evidence.

        2) Generally, a conclusion that a control is not operating effectively can be supported by less evidence than is necessary to support a conclusion that a control is operating effectively.

        3) Different combinations of the **nature, timing, and extent of testing** may provide sufficient evidence.

            a) **Nature** of tests of controls. The following tests are presented in order of the evidence that they ordinarily produce, from least to most: (1) inquiry, (2) observation, (3) inspection of relevant documentation, and (4) reperformance of a control. Inquiry alone does not provide sufficient evidence to support a conclusion about the effectiveness of a control.

            b) **Timing** of tests of controls. Testing controls over a greater period of time provides more evidence of the effectiveness of controls than testing over a shorter period of time. Moreover, testing closer to the date of management's assessment provides more evidence than testing earlier in the year.

            c) **Extent** of tests of controls. The more extensively a control is tested, the greater the evidence obtained from that test.

            d) **Roll-forward procedures.** To roll forward the results of interim work, the auditor should consider (1) the specific controls, their associated risks, and the test results; (2) the sufficiency of evidence obtained at the interim date; (3) the length of the remaining period; and (4) the possibility of changes.

16. **Evaluating Identified Deficiencies**

    a. The auditor should evaluate each deficiency in internal control to determine whether, individually or in combination, they are significant deficiencies or material weaknesses as of the date of management's assessment.

        1) A **deficiency** exists when the design or operation of a control does not allow management or employees, in the normal course of performing their assigned functions, to prevent, or detect and correct, misstatements on a timely basis.

        2) A **significant deficiency** is a deficiency, or a combination of deficiencies, in internal control that is less severe than a material weakness yet important enough to merit attention by those charged with governance.

        3) A **material weakness** is a deficiency, or a combination of deficiencies, in internal control such that a **reasonable possibility** exists that a material misstatement of the entity's financial statements will not be prevented, or detected and corrected, on a timely basis.

The definitions of deficiency, significant deficiency, and material weakness are the same as those used in AU-C 265 (which requires auditor communication with those charged with governance), discussed in Subunit 9.1. Also, these definitions are the same as those used to describe control deficiencies in governmental audits presented in Study Unit 20. Knowing these definitions is important because they are popular topics on the CPA exam.

    b. The auditor is not required to search for deficiencies that, individually or in combination, are **less severe than a material weakness**.

    c. The **severity of a deficiency** does not depend on whether a misstatement actually has occurred but rather on whether a reasonable possibility exists that the controls will fail to prevent, or detect and correct, a misstatement.

17. The following are **indicators of material weaknesses** in internal control:

    a. Identification of fraud, whether or not material, on the part of senior management

    b. Restatement of previously issued financial statements to reflect the correction of a material misstatement

    c. Identification by the auditor of a material misstatement in the current period in circumstances that indicate that the misstatement would not have been detected by internal control

    d. Ineffective oversight by the audit committee of external financial reporting and internal control

18. The auditor should **form an opinion** on the effectiveness of internal control by evaluating evidence obtained from all sources, including (a) the auditor's testing of controls, (b) misstatements detected during the financial statement audit, and (c) any identified control deficiencies.

19. The auditor should obtain **written representations** from management

    a. Acknowledging management's responsibility for establishing and maintaining effective internal control.

    b. Stating that management has performed an evaluation and made an assessment of the effectiveness of the internal control and specifying the control criteria (e.g., the COSO model).

    c. Stating that management did not use the auditor's procedures performed during the audits of internal control or the financial statements as part of the basis for management's assessment of the effectiveness of internal control.

    d. Stating management's conclusion about the effectiveness of internal control based on the control criteria at a specified date.

e.   Stating that management has disclosed to the auditor all deficiencies in internal control identified in its evaluation.

f.   Describing any material fraud and any other fraud involving senior management or management or other employees who have a significant role in internal control.

g.   Stating whether control deficiencies identified and communicated to the audit committee during previous engagements have been resolved.

h.   Stating whether, subsequent to the date being reported on, any changes occurred in internal control or other factors that might significantly affect internal control.

20. **Communicating Certain Matters**

a.   The auditor should communicate, in writing, to management and the audit committee all **material weaknesses** and **significant deficiencies** identified during the audit.

b.   The auditor should communicate to management, in writing, **all deficiencies** in internal control in addition to material weaknesses and significant deficiencies.

c.   The written communication should be made prior to the issuance of the auditor's report.

21. **Reporting on Internal Control**

a.   The report may be a separate report, or it may be combined with the opinion on the financial statements as in the example report.

b.   The auditor should date the audit report no earlier than the date on which the auditor has obtained sufficient competent evidence to support the auditor's opinion. The dates of the report on the financial statements and the report on internal control should be the same.

c.   The auditor's report on an audit of internal control over financial reporting includes the following elements:

1)   A title that includes the word "independent"

2)   A statement that management is responsible for maintaining effective internal control over financial reporting and for assessing the effectiveness of internal control over financial reporting

3)   An identification of management's report on internal control

4)   A statement that the auditor's responsibility is to express an opinion on the company's internal control over financial reporting based on an audit

5)   A definition of internal control over financial reporting

6)   A statement that the audit was conducted in accordance with the standards of the Public Company Accounting Oversight Board (United States) for AS No. 5 audits or AICPA Statements on Standards for Attestation Engagements for AT 501 audits

7)   A statement that the auditor is required to plan and perform the audit to obtain reasonable assurance about whether effective internal control over financial reporting was maintained in all material respects

8)   A statement that an audit includes obtaining an understanding of internal control over financial reporting, assessing the risk that a material weakness exists, testing and evaluating the design and operating effectiveness of internal control based on the assessed risk, and performing such other procedures as the auditor considered necessary in the circumstances

9)   A statement that the auditor believes the audit provides a reasonable basis for the opinion

10) A paragraph stating that, because of inherent limitations, internal control over financial reporting may not prevent, or detect and correct, misstatements and that projections of any evaluation of effectiveness to future periods are subject to the risk that controls may become inadequate because of changes in conditions, or that the degree of compliance with the policies or procedures may deteriorate

11) The auditor's opinion on whether the company maintained, in all material respects, effective internal control over financial reporting as of the specified date, based on the control criteria (For an AT 501 audit, the auditor also may express an opinion on whether management's assertion about the effectiveness of the entity's internal control as of the specified date is fairly stated, in all material respects, based on the control criteria.)

12) The manual or printed signature of the auditor's firm

13) The city and state (or city and country, in the case of non-U.S. auditors) from which the auditor's report has been issued

14) The date of the audit report

22. The auditor should **modify the standard report** on internal control in any of the following circumstances:

   a. A **material weakness** requires an **adverse opinion**.

      1) The report must include the definition of a material weakness.

   b. Elements of management's annual report on internal control are incomplete or improperly presented.

   c. The scope of the engagement is restricted.

   d. The auditor decides to refer to the report of other auditors as the basis, in part, for the auditor's own report.

   e. Other information is contained in management's annual report on internal control.

   f. Management's annual certification under Section 302 of the Sarbanes-Oxley Act is misstated.

23. The PCAOB's **AS No. 4**, *Reporting on Whether a Previously Reported Material Weakness Continues to Exist*, addresses management requests to the auditor to provide a new opinion on whether one or more material weaknesses, which caused an adverse opinion, have been remediated.

   a. The auditor is allowed to reaudit the control based on management's assertion that the deficiency has been corrected and to provide an opinion relative to the control.

   b. Similar standards apply to the new engagement as for the initial reporting engagement on internal control.

Stop and review! You have completed the outline for this subunit. Study multiple-choice questions 19 through 26 beginning on page 312.

9.4 SERVICE ORGANIZATIONS (AU-C 402 AND AT 801)

Background

AT 801, *Reporting on Controls at a Service Organization*, provides guidance for a service auditor's reports on a service organization's internal control. AU-C 402, *Audit Considerations Relating to an Entity Using a Service Organization*, provides guidance to a user auditor when the user entity uses a service organization. An auditor is required to obtain an understanding of controls in all cases and to test controls if they are relied on. These requirements apply whether the relevant controls are the client's or the service provider's. For example, the client may outsource payroll processing, with certain controls over payroll maintained by the service provider. The auditor should consider the controls at the payroll processing service in the audit of the client. The user auditor may directly consider the controls at the service organization or use a service auditor's report to obtain the understanding.

---

1. **Nature of a Service Organization**

    a. A service organization's services and controls are part of the client's information system relevant to financial reporting if they have an effect on

    1) The significant classes of transactions in the user entity's operations;

    2) The systems, both IT and manual, that initiate, authorize, record, process, correct, and report the user entity's transactions;

    3) How the user entity's information system captures significant events and conditions, other than transactions; or

    4) The process used to prepare statements, including significant estimates and disclosures.

    b. If the user auditor is unable to obtain a sufficient understanding of the controls from the user entity, the user auditor should obtain that understanding from one or more of the following procedures:

    1) Obtaining and reading a service auditor's report, if available (This subunit relates to this option.)

    2) Contacting the service organization, through the user entity, to obtain specific information

    3) Performing procedures at the service organization to provide the necessary information about its relevant controls

    4) Using another auditor to perform procedures to provide the necessary information about the relevant controls at the service organization

2. **Definitions**

    a. The **user entity** uses a service organization. The user entity's financial statements are being audited.

    b. The **user auditor** audits and reports on the financial statements of the user entity.

    c. The **service organization** provides services to users that are relevant to their internal control over financial reporting.

    d. The **service auditor** reports on controls at a service organization in one of the following reports:

    1) Report on management's description of a service organization's system and the suitability of the design of controls (a **type 1 report**)

    2) Report on management's description of a service organization's system, the suitability of the design of the controls, and operating effectiveness of controls (a **type 2 report**)

    e. A **subservice organization** is used by another service organization to perform some of the services provided to user entities that are relevant to their internal control over financial reporting.

    f. **Complementary user entity controls** are those that management of the service organization assumes, in the design of its service, will be implemented by user entities to achieve the control objectives.

    g. **Tests of controls** are designed to evaluate the operating effectiveness of controls in achieving the control objectives stated in management's description of the service organization's system.

3. **Objectives of the User Auditor (AU-C 402)**

    a. The user auditor should

    1) Obtain an understanding of the nature and significance of the services provided by the service organization and their effect on the user entity's internal control relevant to the audit. The understanding should be sufficient to identify and assess the risks of material misstatement.

    2) Design and perform audit procedures responsive to those risks.

4. **Understanding a Service Organization's Services and Internal Control**

   a. The user auditor should consider the following:

      1) The nature of the services provided by the service organization and their significance to the user entity, including their effect on the user entity's internal control

      2) The nature and materiality of the transactions processed (or accounts or financial reporting processes affected) by the service organization

      3) The degree of interaction between the service organization and the user entity

      4) The nature of the relationship between the user entity and the service organization, including the relevant contractual terms

5. **Using a Type 1 or Type 2 Report to Support the User Auditor's Understanding**

   a. The user auditor should be satisfied as to

      1) The service auditor's professional competence and independence from the service organization and

      2) The adequacy of the standards under which the report was issued.

   b. If the user auditor plans to use a type 1 or type 2 report, the user auditor should

      1) Evaluate whether the report is appropriate for the user auditor's purposes;

      2) Evaluate the sufficiency and appropriateness of the evidence provided by the report for understanding the user entity's relevant internal control; and

      3) Determine whether complementary user entity controls identified by the service organization are relevant to the RMMs relating to the relevant assertions in the user entity's financial statements and, if so, obtain an understanding of whether the user entity has designed and implemented such controls.

6. **Reliance on Controls**

   a. When the user auditor's risk assessment includes an expectation that controls at the service organization are **operating effectively**, the user auditor should obtain audit evidence about the operating effectiveness of those controls from one or more of the following:

      1) Obtaining and reading a type 2 report
      2) Performing appropriate tests of controls at the service organization
      3) Using another auditor to perform tests of controls at the service organization

7. **Fraud, Noncompliance, and Uncorrected Misstatements**

   a. The user auditor should inquire of management of the user entity about whether the user entity is aware of any (1) fraud, (2) noncompliance with laws and regulations, or (3) uncorrected misstatements at the service organization affecting the financial statements of the user entity.

   b. The user auditor should evaluate how such matters, if any, affect the nature, timing, and extent of the user auditor's further audit procedures, including the effect on the user auditor's conclusions and report.

8. **Reporting by the User Auditor**

   a. The user auditor should express a qualified opinion or disclaim an opinion if (s)he cannot obtain sufficient appropriate audit evidence regarding the services provided by the service organization relevant to the audit of the user entity.

   b. The user auditor should not refer to the work of a service auditor in the user auditor's report containing an unmodified opinion.

   c. If a reference to the work of a service auditor is relevant to understanding a modification of the opinion, the report should indicate that the reference does not reduce the user auditor's responsibility.

9. **Responsibilities of a Service Auditor (AT 801)**

    a. The service auditor should be **independent** of the service organization but not necessarily of each user organization.

    b. As in other audit engagements, the service auditor should consider the following issues and apply the applicable standards or make the appropriate judgments:

        1) Whether to accept a new client or continue with existing clients

        2) Whether to agree to a request for a change in the scope of the engagement

        3) Use of appropriate materiality judgments in planning and performing the audit

        4) Consideration of the cause and nature of any discovered deviations

        5) Whether to use the work of an internal auditor

        6) The need to read other information contained in management's description of the system

        7) Effects of subsequent events after the date of the service auditor's report

        8) The need to document the engagement

    c. The service auditor **should obtain and read management's description** of the service organization's system and should evaluate whether the information is presented fairly. Thus, the service auditor considers whether, among other things,

        1) The control objectives are reasonable.

        2) Controls were implemented.

        3) The major aspects of the service provided are addressed.

        4) The description is sufficiently detailed and complete.

    d. The service auditor should assess whether the controls have been **suitably designed** by determining whether

        1) The risks that threaten the achievement of the control objectives have been identified.

        2) The controls, if operating effectively, mitigate those risks.

    e. For type 1 and type 2 reports, the service auditor should obtain sufficient appropriate evidence to support

        1) The assessment of management's description of the service organization's system and whether those controls described **have been implemented**

        2) The opinion that the controls are **suitably designed**

    f. For type 2 reports, the service auditor also should obtain sufficient appropriate audit evidence to support

        1) The opinion that the controls **operated effectively** throughout the period.

    g. The service auditor should **obtain a representation letter** from management dated as of the date of the service auditor's report.

    h. The service organization may use a subservice organization. The service auditor may test and report on those controls **(inclusive method)** or disclaim an opinion on those controls **(carve-out method)**.

10. **Reports of the Service Auditor**

    a. The service auditor may provide two types of **examination** reports that express opinions.

        1) A **type 1 report** expresses an opinion on the fair presentation of management's description and whether the controls are suitably designed at the specified date.

            a) Suitable design means the controls can attain the control objectives if they operate effectively.

        2)   A **type 2 report** expresses not only the type 1 opinions but also an opinion on whether the controls were operating effectively (meeting the control objectives).

            a)   Type 2 opinions relate to design and effectiveness throughout the period rather than at a specific date.

    b.   **Content of a Service Auditor's Type 1 Report**

        1)   A title that includes the word "independent"

        2)   An addressee

        3)   Identification of management's description of the system

        4)   A reference to management's assertion and a statement of management's responsibility for the controls

        5)   A statement that the service auditor's responsibility is to express an opinion on the fairness of management's description of the system and the suitability of the design of the controls in meeting the objectives

        6)   A statement that the report was conducted in accordance with the AICPA attestation standards

        7)   A statement that the service auditor did not test the effectiveness of the controls

        8)   Statements about the scope of the service auditor's procedures

        9)   A statement about the inherent limitations of controls

        10) An opinion on whether, in all material respects, management's description of the system is fairly stated and whether the controls are suitably designed

        11) A statement restricting the use of the report to management of the service organization, user entities, and auditors of user entities

        12) The date of the report

        13) The name, city, and state of the service auditor

    c.   **Content of a Service Auditor's Type 2 Report**

        1)   The type 2 report includes the same basic information as a type 1 report except it includes an opinion on the operating effectiveness of the controls throughout the specified period. Thus, the statement in a type 1 report that the service auditor did not test the effectiveness of controls is excluded.

    d.   **Modified opinions.** The opinion should be modified if

        1)   Management's description of the service organization's system is not fairly presented,

        2)   The controls are not suitably designed,

        3)   The controls did not operate effectively in the case of a type 2 report, or

        4)   The service auditor was not able to obtain sufficient appropriate evidence.

    e.   If the service auditor becomes aware of (1) fraud, (2) uncorrected errors that are not clearly trivial, or (3) noncompliance with laws and regulations that may affect the user entity, (s)he should determine the effects and whether the information has been communicated to user entities. If not, the service auditor should inform those charged with governance of the service organization. If (s)he is not satisfied with the response, the service auditor may consider obtaining legal advice or withdrawing from the engagement.

Stop and review! You have completed the outline for this subunit. Study multiple-choice questions 27 through 31 beginning on page 314.

QUESTIONS
9.1 Communicating Internal Control Related Matters Identified in an Audit (AU-C 265)

1. An auditor's written communication of internal control related matters identified in an audit would be addressed to "those charged with governance," which would include the

A. Board of directors.

B. Director of internal auditing.

C. Chief financial officer.

D. Chief accounting officer.

Answer (A) is correct.
 REQUIRED: The recipient of the auditor's written communication of internal control related matters identified in an audit.
 DISCUSSION: In many organizations, governance is provided by the board of directors (and its related audit committee). However, the communication may be made to individuals at an equivalent level of authority and responsibility if the organization does not have a board.

2. Which of the following matters would an auditor most likely consider to be a significant deficiency or material weakness to be communicated to those charged with governance?

A. Management's failure to renegotiate unfavorable long-term purchase commitments.

B. Recurring operating losses that may indicate going concern problems.

C. Evidence of a lack of objectivity by those responsible for accounting decisions.

D. Management's current plans to reduce its ownership equity in the entity.

Answer (C) is correct.
 REQUIRED: The significant deficiency or material weakness.
 DISCUSSION: Failures in internal control include deficiencies in internal control design and failures in the operation of internal control. An example of the second type is evidence of undue bias or lack of objectivity by those responsible for accounting decisions (AU-C 265).
 Answer (A) is incorrect. Management's failure to renegotiate unfavorable long-term purchase commitments is not a failure in internal control over financial reporting. Answer (B) is incorrect. Recurring operating losses that may indicate going concern problems are not a failure in internal control over financial reporting. Answer (D) is incorrect. Management's current plans to reduce its ownership equity in the entity are not a failure in internal control over financial reporting.

3. During consideration of internal control in a financial statement audit, an auditor is **not** obligated to

A. Search for significant deficiencies in the operation of internal control.

B. Understand the internal control environment.

C. Determine whether the control activities relevant to audit planning have been implemented.

D. Perform procedures to understand the design of internal control.

Answer (A) is correct.
 REQUIRED: The task not required during the auditor's consideration of the entity and its environment, including its internal control.
 DISCUSSION: The auditor should obtain an understanding of the entity and its environment, including its internal control, and assess the risks of material misstatement. The limited purpose of this consideration does not include the search for significant deficiencies or material weaknesses.
 Answer (B) is incorrect. The auditor should obtain an understanding of the five components of internal control. Answer (C) is incorrect. The understanding includes determining whether relevant controls have been implemented. Answer (D) is incorrect. Obtaining the understanding of controls includes evaluating the design of the relevant controls.

4. Management may already know of the existence of significant deficiencies or material weaknesses in internal control. Which of the following is a true statement about the auditor's communication in this situation?

A. The auditor should communicate these control conditions orally, but need not communicate them in writing.

B. The auditor need not communicate these control conditions if management is already aware of them.

C. The auditor need not communicate these control conditions if they were communicated in prior periods.

D. The auditor should communicate these control conditions in writing regardless of a decision by management and those charged with governance not to remedy them.

Answer (D) is correct.
 REQUIRED: The true statement about communication of significant deficiencies or material weaknesses in internal control.
 DISCUSSION: The auditor's responsibility is to communicate in writing significant deficiencies and material weaknesses regardless of a decision by management and those charged with governance not to remedy them because of cost-benefit considerations or other factors. These should be communicated to management and those charged with governance each period within 60 days after the report release date (AU-C 265).

5. Which of the following issues related to internal control over financial reporting are required to be communicated in writing to management and those charged with governance?

I.   Deficiencies in internal control
II.   Significant deficiencies
III.   Material weaknesses

    A.   I, II, and III.

    B.   II and III only.

    C.   III only.

    D.   None.

Answer (B) is correct.
    REQUIRED: The control issues required to be communicated in writing to management and those charged with governance.
    DISCUSSION: Only those control deficiencies considered to be significant deficiencies or material weaknesses are required to be communicated in writing to management and those charged with governance. (But certain deficiencies should not be reported directly to management.) Other control deficiencies that merit management's attention should be reported to management orally or in writing. A deficiency in internal control exists when the design or operation of a control does not allow management or employees, in the normal course of their assigned functions, to prevent misstatements or detect and correct them on a timely basis. A significant deficiency is a deficiency, or combination of deficiencies, in internal control that is less severe than a material weakness but merits attention by those charged with governance. A material weakness is a deficiency, or combination of deficiencies, in internal control that results in a reasonable possibility that a material misstatement of the financial statements will not be prevented, or detected and corrected, on a timely basis. A reasonable possibility means that the probability of the event is more than remote.
    Answer (A) is incorrect. Control deficiencies that are not significant deficiencies or material weaknesses should be communicated to management orally or in writing if they merit management's attention. Such deficiencies are not required to be reported to those charged with governance. Answer (C) is incorrect. Significant deficiencies should be communicated in writing to management and those charged with governance. Answer (D) is incorrect. Significant deficiencies and material weaknesses should be communicated in writing to management and those charged with governance.

6. Which of the following statements is true about the auditor's communication of a material weakness in internal control?

    A.   A weakness that management refuses to correct should be included in a separate paragraph of the auditor's report on the financial statements.

    B.   The auditor should request management to include a written response in the auditor's communication.

    C.   Suggested corrective action for management's consideration concerning a material weakness need not be communicated to the client.

    D.   The auditor should test the controls that constitute a material weakness before communicating it to the client.

Answer (C) is correct.
    REQUIRED: The true statement about the communication of a material internal control weakness.
    DISCUSSION: Although the auditor should communicate material weaknesses to management and those charged with governance, suggested corrective action need not be communicated.
    Answer (A) is incorrect. A weakness that management refuses to correct is not, by itself, sufficient to require an emphasis-of-matter or other-matter paragraph. Answer (B) is incorrect. In some instances, management may choose to include a written response. The auditor should include a disclaimer of opinion on the response in the communication. Answer (D) is incorrect. The auditor should communicate material weaknesses of which (s)he becomes aware. Testing controls is not a prerequisite of the communication.

7. The development of constructive suggestions to a client for improvements in its internal control is a

    A.   Task addressed by the auditor only during a special engagement.

    B.   Requirement as important as assessing the risks of material misstatement.

    C.   Requirement of the auditor's consideration of internal control.

    D.   Desirable by-product of an audit engagement.

Answer (D) is correct.
    REQUIRED: The true statement about constructive suggestions to a client for improvements in its internal control.
    DISCUSSION: During an audit, the auditor may become aware of matters related to internal control that may be of interest to management and those charged with governance. Those matters meeting the definition of significant deficiencies or material weaknesses in internal control should be communicated in writing. Other deficiencies that merit attention should be communicated to management either orally or in writing. The auditor may make constructive suggestions to the client for improvements in its internal control for the benefit of management or others.
    Answer (A) is incorrect. The auditor should communicate significant deficiencies and material weaknesses in an audit. Answer (B) is incorrect. Constructive suggestions are not necessary, but the auditor should assess the RMMs. Answer (C) is incorrect. Constructive suggestions are not necessary.

8. Under the AICPA's auditing standards, which of the following statements about an auditor's communication of significant control deficiencies is true?

A. A significant control deficiency previously communicated during the prior year's audit that remains uncorrected causes a scope limitation.

B. An auditor should perform tests of controls on significant control deficiencies before communicating them to the client.

C. An auditor's report on significant control deficiencies should include a restriction on the use of the report.

D. An auditor should communicate significant control deficiencies after tests of controls, but before commencing substantive tests.

Answer (C) is correct.
REQUIRED: The true statement about the auditor's communication of significant control deficiencies.
DISCUSSION: A communication of significant control deficiencies should (1) state that the purpose of the audit was to report on the financial statements, not to provide assurance on internal control; (2) give the definition of significant control deficiencies and material weaknesses; and (3) state that the report is intended solely for the information and use of those charged with governance, management, and others within the organization (or specified regulatory agency) and is not intended to be, and should not be, used by anyone other than the specified parties.
Answer (A) is incorrect. Although a significant deficiency previously communicated requires continued communication in the following year, it does not necessarily cause a limitation of the scope of the audit (an inability to obtain sufficient appropriate audit evidence). Answer (B) is incorrect. Tests of controls are performed on internal control, not on significant deficiencies. Answer (D) is incorrect. Significant control deficiencies should be reported no later than 60 days from the report release date. However, they may be communicated orally during the audit if this information is significant or the need for corrective action is urgent.

9. Which of the following statements about an auditor's communication of internal control related matters identified in an audit of a nonissuer is true?

A. The auditor may issue a written report to management and those charged with governance that no significant deficiencies were noted.

B. Significant deficiencies or material weaknesses need not be recommunicated each year if the audit committee has acknowledged its understanding of such deficiencies.

C. Significant deficiencies or material weaknesses may not be communicated in a document that contains suggestions regarding activities that concern other topics such as business strategies or administrative efficiencies.

D. The auditor should communicate significant internal control related matters no later than 60 days after the report release date.

Answer (D) is correct.
REQUIRED: The true statement about an auditor's communication of internal control related matters identified in an audit.
DISCUSSION: Timely communication of significant deficiencies or material weaknesses should be made no later than 60 days after the report release date. But the communication is best made by the report release date. However, early communication may be important because of the significance of the matters noted and the urgency of corrective action.
Answer (A) is incorrect. AU-C 265 prohibits issuance of a report declaring that no significant deficiencies were noted. However, a report can be issued stating that no material weaknesses were detected if it states that material weaknesses may exist and not be identified. Answer (B) is incorrect. Significant deficiencies and material weaknesses that previously were communicated and have not yet been remediated should continue to be communicated. Answer (C) is incorrect. Items beneficial to the client may be communicated even though they are not control related.

10. Which of the following circumstances would be inappropriate for the auditor to communicate to those charged with governance?

A. A material misstatement was noted by the auditor and corrected by management.

B. No significant deficiencies in internal control exist that would affect the financial statements.

C. The auditor is requesting representations regarding the financial statements from management.

D. Management has consulted with other accountants about accounting and auditing matters during the period under audit.

Answer (B) is correct.
REQUIRED: The matter not communicated to those charged with governance.
DISCUSSION: An auditor may issue a written communication stating that no material weaknesses were identified if the auditor complies with the applicable requirements for such communications. But a written communication stating that no significant deficiencies were identified is prohibited. It might be misunderstood or misused (AU-C 265).
Answer (A) is incorrect. Unless all those charged with governance are managers, the auditor should communicate material, corrected misstatements that were brought to management's attention (AU-C 260). Answer (C) is incorrect. Unless all those charged with governance are managers, the auditor should communicate written representations requested by the auditor (AU-C 260). Answer (D) is incorrect. Unless all those charged with governance are managers, the auditor should communicate his/her views on significant accounting and auditing matters about which management consulted other accountants (AU-C 260).

9.2 The Auditor's Communication with Those Charged with Governance (AU-C 260 and AS No. 16)

11. An auditor would **least** likely initiate a discussion with a client's audit committee concerning

A. The methods used to account for significant unusual transactions.

B. The maximum dollar amount of misstatements that could exist without causing the financial statements to be materially misstated.

C. Indications of fraud committed by a corporate officer that were discovered by the auditor.

D. Disagreements with management as to accounting principles that were resolved during the current year's audit.

Answer (B) is correct.
REQUIRED: The item least likely to be discussed with the audit committee.
DISCUSSION: The auditor is responsible for determining the levels of materiality appropriate in the audit of a client's financial statements. Only the general nature of materiality need be discussed.
Answer (A) is incorrect. Methods used to account for significant unusual transactions are communicated to those charged with governance. Answer (C) is incorrect. Fraud is an item communicated to those charged with governance. Answer (D) is incorrect. Disagreements with management are communicated to those charged with governance.

12. Which of the following is true about the auditor's communication with those charged with governance?

A. It should be explained that the auditor is responsible for the fairness of the financial statements.

B. The communication should be a two-way discourse between the auditor and those charged with governance.

C. Specific audit procedures should be described to those charged with governance.

D. The auditor should limit the communication to only those issues required to be communicated.

Answer (B) is correct.
REQUIRED: The true statement about the auditor's communication with those charged with governance.
DISCUSSION: Two-way communication is expected and should provide those charged with governance an overview of the audit process and of the auditor's responsibilities. It should also allow the auditor to obtain information relevant to the audit.
Answer (A) is incorrect. Management is responsible for the fairness of the financial statements. Answer (C) is incorrect. The description of specific audit procedures could compromise the audit. Answer (D) is incorrect. Nothing precludes the auditor from communicating other information to those charged with governance.

13. Which of the following matters should an auditor communicate to those charged with governance?

A. The basis for assessing the risks of material misstatement when the auditor intends to rely on controls.

B. The process used by management in formulating sensitive accounting estimates.

C. The auditor's preliminary judgments about materiality levels.

D. The justification for performing substantive procedures at interim dates.

Answer (B) is correct.
REQUIRED: The communication that should be made to those charged with governance.
DISCUSSION: Certain accounting estimates are particularly sensitive because they are significant to the financial statements, and future events affecting them may differ from current judgments. Those charged with governance should be informed about the process used in formulating sensitive estimates, including fair value estimates, and the basis for the auditor's conclusions about their reasonableness (AU-C 260).
Answer (A) is incorrect. The basis for assessing RMMs need not be communicated to those charged with governance. Answer (C) is incorrect. The preliminary judgments about materiality need not be communicated to those charged with governance. Answer (D) is incorrect. The reasons for interim procedures need not be communicated to those charged with governance.

14. In an audit engagement, should an auditor communicate the following matters to those charged with governance?

	Auditors' Judgments About the Quality of the Client's Accounting Principles	Issues Discussed with Management Prior to the Auditor's Retention
A.	Yes	Yes
B.	Yes	No
C.	No	Yes
D.	No	No

Answer (A) is correct.
REQUIRED: The matter(s), if any, to be communicated to those charged with governance.
DISCUSSION: The matters to be discussed with those charged with governance include the quality of the accounting principles used by management. Management is normally a participant in the discussion. Matters covered may include the auditor's views on the entity's significant accounting practices, e.g., policies, estimates, and disclosures. Furthermore, in any audit engagement, the auditor and those charged with governance should discuss any major issues discussed with management in connection with the initial or recurring retention of the auditors, for example, issues concerning the application of accounting principles and auditing standards.

15. During the planning phase of an audit, an auditor is identifying matters for communication to those charged with governance. The auditor most likely would ask management whether

A. There was significant turnover in the accounting department.

B. It consulted with another CPA firm about installing a new computer system.

C. There were changes in the application of significant accounting policies.

D. It agreed with the auditor's selection of fraud detection procedures.

Answer (C) is correct.
   REQUIRED: The issue relative to communication with those charged with governance.
   DISCUSSION: The auditor should determine that those charged with governance are informed about the initial selection of and changes in significant accounting policies or their application. Moreover, the auditor should discuss the quality of the auditee's accounting principles as applied in its financial reports (AU-C 260).
   Answer (A) is incorrect. The auditor should be concerned about significant turnover in the accounting department in the assessment of risk, but the matter is not likely of sufficient concern to justify disclosure to those charged with governance. Answer (B) is incorrect. The auditor should ask about consultations with other CPAs about accounting and auditing matters, not about the choice of a new computer system. Answer (D) is incorrect. The auditor need not seek approval from management of audit procedures.

16. Which of the following statements is true about an auditor's communication to those charged with governance?

A. Any matters communicated to those charged with governance also should be communicated to the entity's management.

B. The auditor is required to inform those charged with governance about misstatements discovered by the auditor and not subsequently corrected by management.

C. Disagreements with management about the application of accounting principles are required to be communicated in writing to those charged with governance.

D. Issues previously reported to those charged with governance are required to be communicated to the audit committee after each subsequent audit.

Answer (B) is correct.
   REQUIRED: The true statement about an auditor's communication to those charged with governance.
   DISCUSSION: The matters to be communicated to those charged with governance include uncorrected misstatements, other than those not accumulated by the auditor because they are clearly trivial. The auditor communicates uncorrected misstatements and the effect they may have, individually or aggregated, on the opinion. Furthermore, material uncorrected misstatements should be identified individually. Also, the auditor should communicate to those charged with governance the effect of uncorrected misstatements related to prior periods (AU-C 260).
   Answer (A) is incorrect. Certain information should be communicated to those charged with governance, for example, information relating to the integrity of management. Answer (C) is incorrect. Communication with those charged with governance may be oral or written. Answer (D) is incorrect. Communication of recurring matters ordinarily need not be repeated.

17. Which of the following statements is true about an auditor's communication with those charged with governance?

A. This communication is required to occur at the same time as the auditor's report on the financial statements is issued.

B. This communication should include management changes in the application of significant accounting policies.

C. Any significant matter communicated to those charged with governance also should be communicated to management.

D. Audit adjustments proposed by the auditor, whether or not recorded by management, need not be communicated to those charged with governance.

Answer (B) is correct.
   REQUIRED: The true statement about an auditor's communication with those charged with governance.
   DISCUSSION: The auditor should communicate to those charged with governance, among other things, management's selection of and changes in significant accounting policies or their application. The auditor also should determine that those charged with governance are informed about the methods used to account for significant unusual transactions and the effects of significant accounting policies in controversial or emerging areas (AU-C 260).
   Answer (A) is incorrect. The communication should be on a timely basis. Answer (C) is incorrect. The communication is required to be made only to those with oversight authority. Answer (D) is incorrect. Uncorrected misstatements and material corrected misstatements should be communicated to those charged with governance.

18. Which of the following statements is true about an auditor's communication with those charged with governance?

A. This communication should include disagreements with management about audit adjustments, whether or not satisfactorily resolved.

B. If matters are communicated orally, it is necessary to repeat the communication of recurring matters each year.

C. If matters are communicated in writing, the report is required to be distributed to both the audit committee and management.

D. This communication is required to occur after the auditor's report on the financial statements is released.

Answer (A) is correct.
REQUIRED: The true statement about an auditor's communication with those charged with governance.
DISCUSSION: The matters to be discussed with those charged with governance include (1) the auditors' responsibility under GAAS; (2) significant accounting policies; (3) sensitive accounting estimates; (4) uncorrected and material corrected misstatements; (5) the quality of the accounting principles used by management; (6) auditor disagreements with management, whether or not satisfactorily resolved; (7) management's consultations with other accountants; (8) issues discussed with management prior to the auditors' retention; and (9) any serious difficulties the auditors may have had with management during the audit.
Answer (B) is incorrect. The oral or written communication of recurring matters ordinarily need not be repeated. Answer (C) is incorrect. Communications with management are neither required nor precluded. Answer (D) is incorrect. The communication is to be made on a timely basis.

9.3 Reporting on an Entity's Internal Control (AT 501 and AS No. 5)

19. Firms subject to the reporting requirements of the Securities Exchange Act of 1934 are required by the Foreign Corrupt Practices Act of 1977 to maintain satisfactory internal control. Moreover, the Sarbanes-Oxley Act of 2002 requires that annual reports include (1) a statement of management's responsibility for establishing and maintaining adequate internal control and procedures for financial reporting, and (2) management's assessment of their effectiveness. The role of the registered auditor relative to the assessment made by management is to

A. Express an opinion on the assessment.

B. Report clients with unsatisfactory internal control to the SEC.

C. Express an opinion on whether the client is subject to the Securities Exchange Act of 1934.

D. Determine whether management's report is complete and properly presented.

Answer (D) is correct.
REQUIRED: The role of the auditor relative to the assessment by management of internal control.
DISCUSSION: According to PCAOB AS No. 5, the auditor must express (or disclaim) an opinion on the effectiveness of internal control. Moreover, if the auditor determines that elements of management's annual report on internal control over financial reporting are incomplete or improperly presented, the auditor should modify his/her report to describe the reasons for this determination.
Answer (A) is incorrect. According to PCAOB AS No. 5, the auditor must express (or disclaim) an opinion on internal control but not management's assessment. Answer (B) is incorrect. The auditor's report on internal control is issued in conjunction with the audit report on the financial statements. Answer (C) is incorrect. Issuers must report to the SEC, but the auditor need not express an opinion on whether the client is subject to the Securities Exchange Act of 1934.

20. Which of the following best describes a CPA's responsibility to report on an issuer's (public company's) internal control over financial reporting?

A. To examine the effectiveness of its internal control.

B. To identify and communicate control deficiencies to the board of directors.

C. To report on the expected benefits of the entity's internal control.

D. To provide constructive advice to the entity on its internal control.

Answer (A) is correct.
REQUIRED: The best description of an auditor's responsibility to report on an issuer's internal control over financial reporting.
DISCUSSION: The auditor's objective is to express an opinion on whether internal control is effective, in all material respects, based on the control criteria.
Answer (B) is incorrect. Identifying and communicating significant deficiencies and material weaknesses to the board of directors is secondary to the responsibility of expressing an opinion on internal control. Answer (C) is incorrect. The opinion expressed by the CPA should not extend into the future. Answer (D) is incorrect. Consulting engagements do not result in the expression of an opinion.

21. The auditor of an issuer must express an opinion on the effectiveness of internal control. The opinion should be expressed

	As of a Specified Date	For a Specified Period of Time
A.	Yes	Yes
B.	Yes	No
C.	No	Yes
D.	No	No

Answer (B) is correct.

REQUIRED: The applicability of a report on an examination of the effectiveness of internal control.

DISCUSSION: According to PCAOB's AS No. 5, the report states the auditor's opinion on whether the entity maintained, in all material respects, effective internal control over financial reporting as of the specified date based on the control criteria. The date typically is the end of the fiscal period. For a nonissuer, the practitioner may examine the effectiveness of internal control during a period of time (AT 501).

22. An auditor is auditing internal control in conjunction with the audit of financial statements for an issuer. The auditor is considering the appropriate materiality level for planning the audit of internal control. Relative to the materiality level for the audit of the financial statements, materiality levels for the audit of internal control are

A. Larger.

B. Smaller.

C. The same.

D. Cannot determine.

Answer (C) is correct.

REQUIRED: The level of materiality appropriate for planning an audit of internal control.

DISCUSSION: AS No. 5 indicates that the auditor should use the same materiality considerations in the audit of internal control over financial reporting that (s)he would use in planning the audit of annual financial statements.

Answer (A) is incorrect. The materiality levels should be the same. Answer (B) is incorrect. The materiality levels should be the same. Answer (D) is incorrect. The materiality levels for the audit of internal control are based on those for the financial statement audit.

23. In an examination of internal control over financial reporting, which deficiencies in control should be communicated in writing to those charged with governance?

A. All deficiencies.

B. Only material weaknesses.

C. Only significant deficiencies.

D. Both material weaknesses and significant deficiencies.

Answer (D) is correct.

REQUIRED: The deficiencies in control required to be communicated in writing to those charged with governance.

DISCUSSION: The auditor should communicate, in writing, to management and to those charged with governance all material weaknesses and significant deficiencies identified during the audit. The written communication should be made prior to the report release date. The auditor also should communicate to management, in writing, all lesser deficiencies in internal control and inform those charged with governance when such a communication has been made.

Answer (A) is incorrect. Material weaknesses and significant deficiencies should be communicated. Answer (B) is incorrect. Significant deficiencies also should be communicated. Answer (C) is incorrect. Material weaknesses also should be communicated.

24. During the audit of internal controls integrated with the audit of the financial statements, the auditor discovered a material weakness in internal control. The auditor most likely will express a(n)

A. Adverse opinion on internal control.

B. Qualified opinion on internal control.

C. Unmodified opinion on internal control.

D. Disclaimer of opinion on internal control.

Answer (A) is correct.

REQUIRED: The type of opinion expressed because of discovery of a material weakness.

DISCUSSION: Material weaknesses are significant control deficiencies that result in more than a remote chance that a material misstatement will result in the financial statements. A material weakness requires the auditor to express an adverse opinion on the effectiveness of internal control.

Answer (B) is incorrect. A qualified opinion (or disclaimer of opinion) is expressed if there is a scope limitation. Answer (C) is incorrect. An unmodified opinion is not expressed if a material weakness exists. Answer (D) is incorrect. Disclaimer of opinion (or qualified opinion) is expressed if there is a scope limitation.

25. Management of an issuer subject to SEC requirements requests the auditor to report on whether a previously reported material weakness in internal control continues to exist. The request comes 3 months after the annual audited financial statements and report on internal control were released.

A. The audited financial statements and report on internal control have been released, and no report may be issued on subsequent information.

B. The auditor may accept the engagement if (s)he withdraws the original report.

C. The auditor may accept the engagement if management provides a statement that the identified material weakness no longer exists.

D. The auditor may accept the engagement but must wait until the next year's audit to report the remediation of the internal control weakness.

Answer (C) is correct.
REQUIRED: The circumstances in which an auditor of an issuer may report on whether a material weakness still exists.
DISCUSSION: PCAOB AS No. 4 applies to engagements solely to report on whether a previously reported material weakness continues to exist. Such an engagement is voluntary and may be performed as of any reasonable date selected by management. To perform such an engagement, the auditor should receive a written report from management that the identified material weakness no longer exists as of the date specified. The auditor then applies appropriate procedures to assess whether remediation has been accomplished.
Answer (A) is incorrect. The auditor may perform the engagement. Answer (B) is incorrect. The previous reports are not withdrawn. Answer (D) is incorrect. The report may be issued as soon as the auditor has concluded whether the material weakness has been remedied.

26. An auditor is conducting an integrated examination of internal control with the audit of a nonissuer's financial statements. In applying the top-down approach, the auditor first

A. Focuses on entity-level controls and then significant accounts.

B. Communicates material weaknesses and significant deficiencies to those charged with governance.

C. Determines the type of opinion to be expressed.

D. Applies substantive procedures to test financial statement assertions.

Answer (A) is correct.
REQUIRED: The meaning of the top-down approach.
DISCUSSION: The top-down approach to evaluating internal control begins at the financial statement level by understanding overall risks, focusing on entity-level controls, and then working down to significant accounts. Examples of entity-level controls are controls (1) related to the control environment, (2) over management override, (3) to monitor results of operations, (4) over the period-end financial reporting process, and (5) to monitor other controls.
Answer (B) is incorrect. Communication is at the end of the examination, when findings are available. Answer (C) is incorrect. The type of opinion to be expressed cannot be determined until the examination is completed. Answer (D) is incorrect. Substantive procedures are used to test financial statement assertions, not internal controls.

9.4 Service Organizations (AU-C 402 and AT 801)

27. AU-C 402, *Audit Considerations Relating to an Entity Using a Service Organization*, applies to a financial statement audit of an entity that uses services of another organization as part of its information system. For this purpose, the user auditor may need to obtain a service auditor's report. Which of the following is a true statement about a service auditor's report?

A. It provides the user auditor with assurance regarding whether control procedures have been implemented at the user organization.

B. It should include an opinion.

C. If it proves to be inappropriate for the user auditor's purposes, (s)he must personally perform procedures at the service organization.

D. A user auditor need not be concerned about the service auditor's professional competence.

Answer (B) is correct.
REQUIRED: The true statement about a service auditor's report regarding internal control.
DISCUSSION: A service auditor's report should be helpful in providing a sufficient understanding to plan the audit of the user organization. The service auditor's report may express an opinion on the fairness of the description of the controls implemented at the service organization and whether they were suitably designed. If the service auditor also has tested controls, the report may express an opinion on the operating effectiveness of the controls.
Answer (A) is incorrect. A service auditor's report is helpful to the user auditor in obtaining an understanding of internal control at the service organization, but it does not provide assurance regarding conditions at the user organization. Answer (C) is incorrect. Audit procedures at the service organization may be applied by the service auditor at the request of (and under the direction of) the user auditor. Answer (D) is incorrect. The user auditor should be satisfied about the service auditor's independence and professional competence.

28. Lake, CPA, is auditing the financial statements of Gill Co. Gill uses the EDP Service Center, Inc., to process its payroll transactions. EDP's financial statements are audited by Cope, CPA, who recently issued a report on EDP's internal control. Lake is considering Cope's report on EDP's internal control in assessing control risk on the Gill engagement. What is Lake's responsibility concerning making reference to Cope as a basis, in part, for Lake's own unmodified opinion?

   A. Lake may refer to Cope only if Lake is satisfied as to Cope's professional reputation and independence.

   B. Lake may refer to Cope only if Lake relies on Cope's report in restricting the extent of substantive procedures.

   C. Lake may refer to Cope only if Lake's report indicates the division of responsibility.

   D. Lake may not refer to Cope under the circumstances above.

Answer (D) is correct.
   REQUIRED: The reference, if any, in an auditor's report to a service auditor's report on internal control.
   DISCUSSION: The service auditor was not responsible for examining any portion of the user entity's financial statements. Hence, the user auditor should not refer to the service auditor's report as a basis in part for his/her own unmodified opinion on those financial statements. If the user auditor's opinion is modified, the service auditor's work may be referred to if it is relevant to understanding the modification (AU-C 402).
   Answer (A) is incorrect. Although the user auditor should become satisfied about the service auditor's professional competence and consider the service auditor's independence, no reference to the service auditor normally should be made in the user auditor's report. Answer (B) is incorrect. The user auditor should not refer to the service auditor's report even if (s)he uses that report in assessing RMMs and in determining the nature, timing, and extent of further audit procedures. Answer (C) is incorrect. The user auditor should not divide responsibility with the service auditor.

29. Computer Services Company (CSC) processes payroll transactions for schools. Drake, CPA, is engaged to report on CSC's controls implemented as of a specific date. These controls are relevant to the schools' internal control, so Drake's report will be useful in providing the schools' independent auditors with information necessary to plan their audits. Drake's report expressing an opinion on CSC's controls implemented as of a specific date should contain a(n)

   A. Description of the scope and nature of Drake's procedures.

   B. Statement that CSC's management has disclosed to Drake all design deficiencies of which it is aware.

   C. Opinion on the operating effectiveness of CSC's controls.

   D. Paragraph indicating the basis for Drake's assessment of the risks of material misstatement.

Answer (A) is correct.
   REQUIRED: The item in a service auditor's report on controls implemented.
   DISCUSSION: The report expressing an opinion on the description of controls implemented and their design (type 1 report) includes (1) a title that includes the word *independent*; (2) an addressee; (3) identification of management's description of the system; (4) a reference to management's assertion and a statement of management's responsibility for the controls; (5) a statement that the service auditor's responsibility is to express an opinion on the fairness of management's description of the system and the suitability of the design of the controls in meeting the objectives; (6) a statement that the report was conducted in accordance with the AICPA attestation standards; (7) a statement that the service auditor did not test the effectiveness of the controls; (8) statements about the scope of the service auditor's procedures; (9) a statement about the inherent limitations of controls; (10) an opinion on whether, in all material respects, management's description of the system is fairly stated and whether the controls are suitably designed; (11) a statement restricting the use of the report to management of the service organization and user entities; (12) the date of the report; and (13) the name, city, and state of the service auditor.
   Answer (B) is incorrect. The service auditor need not state whether management has disclosed all design deficiencies. Answer (C) is incorrect. A type 1 report does not contain an opinion on operating effectiveness. Answer (D) is incorrect. A type 1 report contains no assessment of RMMs, only an opinion on the description of the controls implemented and their design.

30. Payroll Data Co. (PDC) processes payroll transactions for a retailer. Cook, CPA, is engaged to issue a report on PDC's internal controls implemented as of a specific date. These controls are relevant to the retailer's internal control, so Cook's report may be useful in providing the retailer's independent auditor with information necessary to plan a financial statement audit. Cook's report should

A. Contain a disclaimer of opinion on the operating effectiveness of PDC's controls.

B. State whether PDC's controls were suitably designed to achieve the retailer's objectives.

C. Identify PDC's controls relevant to specific financial statement assertions.

D. Disclose Cook's assessed risks of material misstatement for PDC.

Answer (A) is correct.
  REQUIRED: The components of a service auditor's report.
  DISCUSSION: Service auditors may report (1) on the fairness of management's description of the controls and whether the controls have been implemented and are suitably designed (type 1 report) or (2) additionally on operating effectiveness (type 2 report). The type 1 report should include a disclaimer of opinion related to operating effectiveness of the controls.
  Answer (B) is incorrect. The report should state whether PDC's controls were suitably designed to provide reasonable assurance of achieving the specified control objectives of the service organization. Answer (C) is incorrect. Specific controls relevant to specific financial statement assertions need not be identified in the service auditor's report. Answer (D) is incorrect. The assessed RMMs are not disclosed.

31. Which of the following procedures should a user auditor include in the audit plan to create the most efficient audit when an audit client uses a service organization for several processes?

A. Review the service auditor's type 1 report.

B. Review the service auditor's report and outline the accounting system in a memo to the working papers.

C. Audit the service organization's controls, assess risk, and prepare the audit plan.

D. Audit the service organization's controls to test the work of the service auditor.

Answer (A) is correct.
  REQUIRED: The procedure included in the audit plan of a user auditor if an audit client uses a service organization.
  DISCUSSION: The user auditor should obtain a sufficient understanding of the services provided and their effect on the user entity's internal control relevant to the audit. The understanding should provide a basis for assessing the risks of material misstatement. If a sufficient understanding cannot be obtained from the user entity, the user auditor should obtain it from other procedures. For example, the auditor may obtain and read a type 1 report or a type 2 report. A type 1 report expresses an opinion on (1) the fair presentation of management's description of the service organization's system and (2) whether the controls are suitably designed at the specified date. Suitable design means the controls can attain the control objectives if they operate effectively. A type 2 report expresses not only the type 1 opinions but also an opinion on whether the controls were operating effectively (meeting the control objectives). Type 2 opinions relate to design and effectiveness throughout the period rather than at a specific date (AU-C 402).
  Answer (B) is incorrect. Outlining the service organization's accounting system is inefficient. The auditor's understanding of the services provided addresses only the services and controls relevant to the audit of the user entity's financial statements. Answer (C) is incorrect. Using a type 1 or type 2 report is more efficient than auditing the service organization's controls. Answer (D) is incorrect. Using a type 1 or type 2 report is more efficient than auditing the service organization's controls.

Use the additional questions in Gleim **CPA Test Prep** to create Practice Exams that emulate Prometric!

9.5 PRACTICE TASK-BASED SIMULATIONS

Auditing and Attestation
Testlet 4 of 4

Time Remaining
1 hour - 30 minutes

Unsplit | Split Horiz | Split Vertical | Spreadsheet | Calculator | Exit

DIRECTIONS

Note: If you believe you have encountered a software malfunction, report it to the test center staff immediately.

Navigation

To navigate from task to task, use the controls at the bottom of the screen. Click on the **Next** button to advance to the next task, or the **Previous** button to go to the previous task. To go directly to any task, click on its number.

If you would like a reminder to revisit a task, or want to indicate that you are finished with it, click on the reminder flag below the task number. To clear the flag, click on it again. Reminder flags are for your use only – they do not contribute to your score.

Tabs

In this part of the examination, you will be asked to complete various tasks. Every task has one or more **Work Tabs**. Some tasks have one or more **Information Tabs**, others may have none. Every task has a **Help** tab.

If a task has **Information Tabs**, you may use the information in them to complete your responses in the **Work Tabs**.

Corporate Gain and Basis | Authoritative Literature | Help

Work tab   Information tab   Help tab

Work Tabs:
- **Work Tabs** are identified with a pencil icon. This is where your responses are expected.
- Each task has one or more **Work Tabs**.
- **Work Tabs** contain directions for completing the task – be sure to read these directions carefully.
- The **Work Tab** name in the example above is for illustration only – yours will differ.
- You must complete all of the **Work Tabs** in each task to receive full credit.

Information Tabs:
- The Authoritative Literature will be provided in all tasks in the AUD, FAR, and REG sections for your reference.
- Your simulation may have one or more additional **Information Tabs**. Like the Authoritative Literature tabs, **Information Tabs** do not have a pencil icon.
- If your task has additional **Information Tabs**, go through each to familiarize yourself with the task content.

Help Tab:
- The **Help Tab** provides assistance with the exam software that is used in this task. For example, if the task is to compose a memorandum, **Help** will provide information about the word processor.

The Toolbar

The toolbar at the top of the screen shows the amount of time remaining for you to complete the tasks. In addition, the following tools are available. Note that only the **Exit** button is displayed when Directions are visible - the others will appear when you begin the tasks.

Click on these buttons to split or unsplit the screen. You can split the screen vertically or horizontally.

Click on this button to display the calculator; click on it again to hide the calculator. To move the calculator, click on the calculator title bar and drag the calculator to the desired location.

Click on this button to use the spreadsheet; click on it again to hide the spreadsheet. To move the spreadsheet, click on the the spreadsheet title bar and drag the spreadsheet to the desired location.

Click on this button to go on to the next part of the examination. You must complete all of the tasks to receive full credit. Once you click on **Exit** and confirm the action, you will NOT be able to return to this testlet.

▼ = Reminder   Directions   1 2 3 4 5   ◀ Previous   Next ▶

| Service Auditors | Authoritative Literature | Help |

Arnot, CPA, is considering statements to be included in correspondence to a potential client that has requested a service auditor's report on internal control. For each statement, determine whether it is appropriate for describing a type 1 report (report on management's description of a service organization's system and the suitability of the design of controls), a type 2 report (report on management's description of a service organization's system, the suitability of the design of the controls, and operating effectiveness of controls), both reports, or neither report. Each choice may be used once, more than once, or not at all.

Statements	Answer
1. Our report will have a title with the word "independent."	
2. The report will describe the type of opinion expressed on the financial statements.	
3. The report will include an opinion on whether management's description of the system is fairly stated.	
4. The report will contain a modified opinion if we determine that the controls did not operate effectively.	
5. We will test all phases of controls described in COSO.	
6. Our service auditor's engagement will not include testing the effectiveness of the controls.	
7. The report will include an opinion on the operating effectiveness of controls throughout the specified period.	
8. Our report will include a statement about the inherent limitations of the engagement.	
9. We will update the report periodically after issuance based on information provided by your firm.	
10. We will obtain a management representation letter as part of our engagement procedures.	

Choices
A) Type 1 report
B) Type 2 report
C) Both reports
D) Neither report

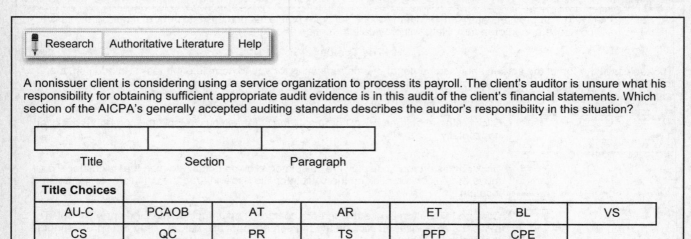

| Research | Authoritative Literature | Help |

A nonissuer client is considering using a service organization to process its payroll. The client's auditor is unsure what his responsibility for obtaining sufficient appropriate audit evidence is in this audit of the client's financial statements. Which section of the AICPA's generally accepted auditing standards describes the auditor's responsibility in this situation?

Title	Section	Paragraph

Title Choices

AU-C	PCAOB	AT	AR	ET	BL	VS
CS	QC	PR	TS	PFP	CPE	

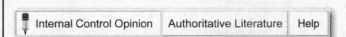

| Internal Control Opinion | Authoritative Literature | Help |

AT 501, *An Examination of an Entity's Internal Control over Financial Reporting that Is Integrated with an Audit of Its Financial Statements*, applies when the service is provided to nonissuers. In accordance with AT 501, a report expressing an unmodified opinion contains certain language. Indicate in the shaded column whether each item should be included in a report.

Report Content	Answer	Choices
1. "We conducted our audits . . . standards of the Public Company Accounting Oversight Board."		A) Included
2. "In our opinion, management's assertion that W Company maintained effective internal control over financial reporting . . ."		B) Excluded
3. "We also have audited, in accordance with auditing standards generally accepted in the United States of America, the *[identify financial statements]* . . ."		
4. "Our examination included . . . testing and evaluating the design but not the operating effectiveness of internal control . . ."		
5. "In our opinion, W Company maintained, in all material respects, effective internal control over financial reporting . . ."		
6. "We have audited W Company's internal control . . . based on generally accepted auditing standards."		
7. "Our responsibility is to express an opinion on management's assertion based on our examination."		
8. "Because of its inherent limitations, internal control over financial reporting may not prevent or detect and correct misstatements."		
9. "Those standards require that we plan and perform the audit to become assured that it is probable that internal control was effective in all material respects."		
10. "An entity's internal control over financial reporting is a process effected by the audit committee, management, and auditors, designed to provide reasonable assurance . . ."		

You have been asked by the audit partner to draft a letter to the client on internal control related matters. You were informed that the written communication regarding significant deficiencies and material weaknesses identified during an audit of financial statements should include certain statements.

For each of the statements below, select from the list provided the appropriate disposition of each statement in regard to the letter to the client on internal control related matters. Each choice may be used once, more than once, or not at all.

Statements	Disposition	Choices
1. State that the purpose of the audit was to express an opinion on the financial statements and to express an opinion on the effectiveness of the entity's internal control over financial reporting.		A) Included
2. Identify, if applicable, items that are considered to be material weaknesses.		B) Excluded
3. State that the auditor is not expressing an opinion on the effectiveness of internal control.		C) Included, but only with client management's approval
4. Include the definition of the term "material weakness," if relevant.		
5. State that the auditor is expressing an unmodified opinion on the effectiveness of internal control.		
6. State that the communication is intended solely for management and external parties.		

▽ = Reminder   Directions   1 2 3 [4] 5   ◀ Previous   Next ▶

Land & Hale, CPAs, are auditing the financial statements of Stone Co., a nonissuer, for the year ended December 31, Year 1. Edwin Land, the engagement supervisor, anticipates expressing an unmodified opinion on May 20, Year 2. Ed Wood, an assistant on the engagement, drafted the auditor's communication of internal control related matters that Land plans to send to Stone's board of directors on May 30, Year 2. Land reviewed Wood's draft and indicated in the *Supervisor's Review Notes* that Wood's draft contained deficiencies.

Independent Auditor's Communication on Internal Control Related Matters

To Management and the Board of Directors:

In planning and performing our audit of the financial statements of Stone Co. as of and for the year ended December 31, Year 1, in accordance with auditing standards generally accepted in the United States of America, we considered Stone Co.'s internal control over financial reporting (internal control) as a basis for designing our auditing procedures for the purpose of expressing our opinion on the financial statements and for the purpose of expressing an opinion on the effectiveness of the Company's internal control.

Our consideration of internal control was for the limited purpose described in the preceding paragraph and can be expected to identify all deficiencies in internal control that might be significant deficiencies or material weaknesses. As discussed below, we identified a deficiency in internal control that we consider to be significant.

A deficiency in internal control exists when the design or operation of a control does not allow the auditors, in the normal course of performing their assigned functions, to prevent, or detect and correct, misstatements on a timely basis. A "significant deficiency" is a deficiency, or a combination of inconsequential deficiencies, in internal control that is less severe than a material weakness, yet important enough to merit attention by those charged with governance.

We consider the following to be a significant deficiency in internal control: failure to safeguard assets, particularly inventory stored at remote locations. The potential effect of this deficiency is that inventory reported on the balance sheet may not exist. An unmodified opinion was expressed on the financial statements.

This communication is intended solely for the information and use of management and the Board of Directors of Stone Co. and is not intended to be and should not be used by anyone other than these specified parties.

Land & Hale, CPAs
Chicago, Illinois
May 30, Year 2

-- Continued on next page --

| Control Deficiencies | Authoritative Literature | Help | -- Continued |

For each item, indicate in the shaded column whether Wood's original draft is correct, Land's modification is correct, or neither Wood's original draft nor Land's modification is correct.

Land's Modifications	Answer
In the first paragraph:	
1. The communication should refer to "our consideration of the internal controls."	
2. The communication should indicate that providing assurance on internal control is not the purpose of the consideration of internal control.	
3. The communication should refer to "conformity with generally accepted accounting principles."	
In the second paragraph:	
4. The communication should use the term "failures" rather than "deficiencies."	
5. The statement "can be expected to identify all deficiencies" should be changed to "can be expected to identify most deficiencies."	
In the third paragraph:	
6. The definition of a control deficiency should be replaced with a definition of internal control.	
7. The phrase "does not allow the auditors" should be replaced with "does not allow the audit committee."	
8. The term "inconsequential" should be changed to "minor."	
9. The communication should define "material weakness."	
In the fourth paragraph:	
10. The report should state that significant deficiencies were identified but should not identify them.	
11. The communication should include the actual effects of noted deficiencies, not the potential effects.	
In the final paragraph:	
12. The restriction on the communication's use is inappropriate because other parties ordinarily would receive the communication.	
13. The communication should refer to an opinion on the financial statements if a modified opinion was expressed.	
14. The communication should indicate that the auditor is not responsible for updating the communication for events or circumstances occurring after the date of the communication.	
Dating the report:	
15. The communication should be dated on the same date as the financial statements.	

Choices

A) Wood's original draft is correct

B) Land's modification is correct

C) Neither Wood's original draft nor Land's modification is correct

Unofficial Answers

1. Service Auditors (10 Gradable Items)

1. <u>Both reports.</u> Both type 1 and type 2 service auditor reports should include a title, e.g., "Independent Service Auditor's Report."

2. <u>Neither report.</u> A service auditor provides a report on internal control, not an opinion on the financial statements.

3. <u>Both reports.</u> Both type 1 and type 2 service auditor reports contain an opinion on whether management's description of the system is fairly stated.

4. <u>Type 2 report.</u> Only a type 2 report reports on testing the effectiveness of the controls.

5. <u>Neither report.</u> Only those aspects of controls related to the financial reporting process are considered by the service auditor. COSO encompasses economy and efficiency controls not related to the fairness of the financial statements.

6. <u>Type 1 report.</u> A type 1 service auditor engagement would include reporting on management's description of the system and the suitability of the design of controls but not on the effectiveness of the controls.

7. <u>Type 2 report.</u> A type 2 service auditor's report includes an opinion on management's description of a service organization's system, the suitability of the design, and operating effectiveness of controls.

8. <u>Both reports.</u> Both type 1 and type 2 reports include a statement about the inherent limitations on testing and reporting on internal controls.

9. <u>Neither report.</u> Service auditors need not follow up on reports unless new information that may affect the report and that was not known to the auditors at the date of the report comes to their attention.

10. <u>Both reports.</u> Service auditors should obtain a representation letter from management dated as of the date of the report.

2. Research (1 Gradable Item)

Answer: 402.01

AU-C Section 402 -- *Audit Considerations Relating to an Entity Using a Service Organization*

.01   This section addresses the user auditor's responsibility for obtaining sufficient appropriate audit evidence in an audit of the financial statements of a user entity that uses one or more service organizations. Specifically, it expands on how the user auditor applies section 315, *Understanding the Entity and Its Environment and Assessing the Risks of Material Misstatement*, and section 330, *Performing Audit Procedures in Response to Assessed Risks and Evaluating the Audit Evidence Obtained*, in obtaining an understanding of the user entity, including internal control relevant to the audit, sufficient to identify and assess the risks of material misstatement and in designing and performing further audit procedures responsive to those risks.

3. Internal Control Opinion (10 Gradable Items)

1. <u>B) Excluded.</u> The AICPA's illustrative report for a nonissuer should state that AICPA standards, not PCAOB standards, were followed.

2. <u>A) Included.</u> The report expresses an opinion on either management's assertion or directly on the effectiveness of internal control.

3. <u>A) Included.</u> The report should refer to the client's financial statements that were audited.

4. <u>B) Excluded.</u> The examination of internal control includes testing both the design and operating effectiveness of internal control.

5. <u>A) Included.</u> The report expresses an opinion on either management's assertion or directly on the effectiveness of internal control.

6. <u>B) Excluded.</u> The report should state that the examination was conducted in accordance with AICPA Statements on Standards for Attestation Engagements.

7. <u>A) Included.</u> The report should state that the auditor's responsibility is to express an opinion on management's assertion about the effectiveness of internal control.

8. <u>A) Included.</u> The report should include a statement about the inherent limitations of internal control over financial reporting.

9. <u>B) Excluded.</u> The report should indicate that the practitioner (auditor) obtained reasonable assurance about the effectiveness of internal control.

10. <u>B) Excluded.</u> Auditors do not participate in the establishment of a client's internal control.

4. Control Communication to Client (6 Gradable Items)

1. <u>B) Excluded.</u> The purpose of the consideration of internal control in a financial statement is to plan the audit.

2. <u>A) Included.</u> The letter should identify any issues that are considered to be material weaknesses.

3. <u>A) Included.</u> The letter should state that the auditor is not expressing an opinion on the effectiveness of internal control

4. <u>A) Included.</u> The letter should include the definition of a material weakness if one is reported.

5. <u>B) Excluded.</u> The consideration of internal control in a financial statement audit provides no assurance on internal control.

6. <u>B) Excluded.</u> The letter should state that the communication is intended solely for management, those charged with governance, others within the organization, and any governance entity to which the auditor must report, not for external parties.

5. Control Deficiencies (15 Gradable Items)

1. <u>A) Wood's original draft is correct.</u> The auditor's written communication should refer to planning and performing our audit.

2. <u>B) Land's modification is correct.</u> The communication should indicate that internal control was considered for the purpose of designing the audit and expressing an opinion on the financial statements but not for expressing an opinion on the effectiveness of internal control.

3. <u>A) Wood's original draft is correct.</u> The communication relates to control deficiencies, not whether the financial statements are in accordance with the applicable reporting framework.

4. <u>A) Wood's original draft is correct.</u> The purpose is to communicate significant deficiencies and material weaknesses. Thus, it is appropriate to refer to control deficiencies in the communication.

5. <u>C) Neither Wood's original draft nor Land's modification is correct.</u> The AICPA's illustrative written communication states that the consideration of internal control "was not designed to identify all deficiencies in internal control that might be significant deficiencies or material weaknesses."

6. <u>A) Wood's original draft is correct.</u> The AICPA's illustrative written communication states the definition of a control deficiency to place significant deficiencies in the correct context.

7. <u>C) Neither Wood's original draft nor Land's modification is correct.</u> The phrase should refer to "management or employees," not to "the auditors" or "the audit committee."

8. <u>C) Neither Wood's original draft nor Land's modification is correct.</u> The definition of significant deficiency does not include the terms "inconsequential" or "minor."

9. <u>B) Land's modification is correct.</u> The communication defines "material weakness" and, if relevant, "significant deficiency."

10. <u>A) Wood's original draft is correct.</u> The specific significant deficiencies should be described in the communication.

11. <u>A) Wood's original draft is correct.</u> The report should include the potential effects of any identified significant deficiencies and material weaknesses.

12. <u>A) Wood's original draft is correct.</u> The communication is intended for use by management, those charged with governance, and others within the organization. If the entity must provide such a communication to a governmental authority, it should specifically refer to that authority. Moreover, it is not intended to be used and should not be used by anyone other than these specified parties.

13. <u>C) Neither Wood's original draft nor Land's modification is correct.</u> The communication does not identify the type of opinion that was expressed on the financial statements.

14. <u>A) Wood's original draft is correct.</u> The communication should not contain a statement about the auditor's responsibility for updating the communication. The auditor has no such obligation.

15. <u>A) Wood's original draft is correct.</u> The communication is best made at the audit report release date, but it should be made no later than 60 days after the audit report release date.

Gleim Simulation Grading

Task	Correct Responses		Gradable Items		Score per Task
1	___	÷	10	=	___
2 (Research)	___	÷	1	=	___
3	___	÷	10	=	___
4	___	÷	6	=	___
5	___	÷	15	=	___

Total of Scores per Task   ___

÷ Total Number of Tasks   5

Total Score   ___ %

Use **CPA Gleim Online** and **Simulation Wizard** to practice more task-based simulations in a realistic environment.

Have something to say?
Tell Gleim what's on your mind!

gleim.com/feedbackAUD

STUDY UNIT TEN
EVIDENCE -- OBJECTIVES AND NATURE

(12 pages of outline)

The auditor should design and perform audit procedures to obtain sufficient appropriate audit evidence. The objective is to be able to draw reasonable conclusions as a basis for the auditor's opinion on whether the financial statements are fairly presented in all material respects. Thus, most audit work involves obtaining and evaluating audit evidence.

Generally accepted auditing standards (GAAS) require the auditor to obtain **reasonable assurance** about whether the statements as a whole are free from material misstatement, whether due to fraud or error. Reasonable assurance is a high but not absolute level of assurance. It is obtained when sufficient appropriate evidence reduces audit risk to an acceptably low level. **Audit risk** is the risk of expressing an inappropriate audit opinion when the statements are materially misstated.

10.1 NATURE, SUFFICIENCY, AND APPROPRIATENESS (AU-C 500 AND AS NO. 15)

 You should recognize that the collection and documentation of evidence are keys to the audit. Be sure to understand these processes and, if necessary, review the role of management assertions that were addressed in Study Unit 1, Subunit 2.

1. **Nature of Audit Evidence**
   a. Audit evidence is all information used by the auditor in arriving at the conclusions on which the audit opinion is based.
   b. **Accounting records** include
      1) Initial entries (manual or electronic).
      2) Supporting records. Examples are (a) checks, (b) electronic funds transfers (EFTs), (c) invoices, (d) contracts, (e) the general and subsidiary ledgers, (f) journal entries, (g) worksheets, (h) spreadsheets, and (i) reconciliations.
   c. **Other information** includes (1) minutes of meetings; (2) confirmations; (3) industry analysts' reports; (4) comparable data about competitors; (5) control manuals; and (6) information obtained by the auditor from inquiries (e.g., management's written representations), observation, and inspection.
   d. The auditor typically relies on persuasive, rather than conclusive, evidence because of the inherent limitations of the audit:
      1) The nature of financial reporting (e.g., use of accounting estimates dependent on forecasts)
      2) The nature of audit procedures (e.g., the possibility of fraud involving collusion or the failure of management to provide all the information requested)
      3) The need to perform the audit (a) within a reasonable period of time and (b) to achieve a balance between benefit and cost
         a) However, the difficulty, time, or cost of obtaining evidence is not a valid reason for (1) omitting an audit procedure for which no alternative exists or (2) being satisfied with evidence that is less than persuasive.

2.   **Assertions**

a.   Management implicitly or explicitly makes assertions about the recognition, measurement, presentation, and disclosure of information in the financial statements. Thus, the auditor should use relevant assertions in sufficient detail to assess the risks of material misstatement (RMMs) and design and perform further audit procedures. Some procedures may relate to more than one assertion. But a combination of procedures may be needed to test a relevant assertion because audit evidence from different sources or of a different nature may be relevant to the same assertion.

b.   The AICPA's and the PCAOB's **assertions models** are in Study Unit 1, Subunit 2.

3.   **Sufficiency and Appropriateness**

a.   Sufficiency is the measure of the **quantity** of evidence.

1)   The greater the assessed RMMs, the more evidence is likely to be required.
2)   The higher the quality of evidence, the less evidence may be required.

b.   Appropriateness is the measure of the **quality** of evidence.

1)   Quality depends on relevance and reliability in supporting the auditor's conclusions. Relevance is the logical connection of information with, or bearing upon, the purpose of the audit procedure and any assertion considered.

2)   The **reliability** of information used as audit evidence is affected by (a) its source, (b) its nature, and (c) how it is obtained. These circumstances include controls over its preparation and maintenance. Evidence is generally more reliable when it is

a)   Obtained from knowledgeable independent sources outside the entity,
b)   Generated internally by the entity under effective internal control,
c)   Obtained directly by the auditor,
d)   In documentary form (in any medium), and
e)   Represented by original documents (rather than photocopies).

4.   **Audit Procedures**

a.   **Risk assessment procedures** are used to obtain an understanding of the entity and its environment, including internal control. Obtaining the understanding permits the auditor to assess the RMMs at the financial statement and relevant assertion levels.

b.   **Further audit procedures** include tests of controls and substantive procedures.

1)   **Tests of controls** test the operating effectiveness of controls in preventing, or detecting and correcting, material misstatements at the relevant assertion level. Study Unit 8 contains the relevant outline. They are required when

a)   The auditor's risk assessment is based on an expectation of the operating effectiveness of controls or

b)   Substantive procedures alone do not provide sufficient appropriate evidence.

2)   **Substantive procedures** are used to detect material misstatements at the relevant assertion level. They include (a) tests of details and (b) substantive analytical procedures.

a)   They should be performed for **all** relevant assertions about each material (1) transaction class, (2) account balance, and (3) disclosure.

    c. The client may rely on a **management's specialist** to prepare information used as audit evidence, e.g., estimates of the fair value of securities (discussed further in Study Unit 4, Subunit 2). A management's specialist is an individual or organization possessing expertise in a field other than accounting or auditing that assists in preparing the financial statements.

        1) The auditor should (a) evaluate the competence, capabilities, and objectivity of such specialists; (b) obtain an understanding of their work relevant to the audit; and (c) evaluate its appropriateness.

5. **Types of Audit Procedures**

    a. The auditor should use the following, singly or in combination, as risk assessment procedures, tests of controls, or substantive procedures:

        1) **Inspection of records or documents** is the examination of records or documents, whether internal or external, in paper, electronic, or other media.

        2) **Inspection of tangible assets** is the physical examination of assets to test existence. For example, it is combined with observation of inventory counts.

        3) **Observation** is looking at a process or procedure being performed.

        4) **Inquiry** seeks financial or nonfinancial information from knowledgeable persons within the entity or outside the entity.

        5) **External confirmation** obtains audit evidence as a direct, written response to the auditor from a third party, e.g., confirmation of account balances or the terms of agreements (discussed further in Subunit 10.2).

        6) **Recalculation** is checking mathematical accuracy.

        7) **Reperformance** is the independent execution of procedures or controls.

        8) **Analytical procedures** are evaluations of financial data made by a study of plausible relationships among both financial and nonfinancial data (further discussed in Study Unit 3, Subunit 5).

            a) **Scanning** is a type of analytical procedure used to review accounting data to identify significant or unusual items for testing.

6. **Electronic Environments**

    a. Some information may exist only in electronic form or only at a certain moment (or period) of time.

        1) For example, transactions in **electronic commerce** may occur solely by exchange of electronic messages.

        2) Moreover, **image processing systems** may convert documents to electronic images with no retention of source documents.

        3) In electronic environments, substantive procedures alone may be insufficient to reduce audit risk to an acceptable level.

    b. The auditor's responses may include the following:

        1) Performing audit procedures using **computer-assisted audit techniques (CAATs)**

        2) Requesting the entity to retain certain information

        3) Performing audit procedures at the moment when information exists

7. **Direction of Testing**

    a. The direction of testing is an important consideration in evaluating certain assertions. The direction of testing for existence (or occurrence) and completeness assertions is illustrated as follows:

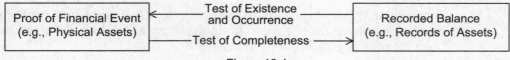

Figure 10-1

    b. In essence, the auditor collects evidence that the economic events of the entity are fairly reflected in the financial statement assertions. The diagram below illustrates (1) how those events flow to the assertions and (2) the direction of testing for the completeness, existence, and occurrence assertions.

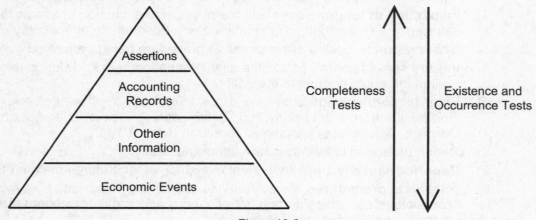

Figure 10-2

    c. For example, to test for completeness that all sales were recorded, an auditor might select a sample of shipping documents (economic event of a sale) and trace them through the recording process to determine that they were included in the sales account. To test that recorded sales occurred, the auditor might select a sample of recorded sales from the sales account and vouch them back through the records to determine that shipments to customers were made.

Stop and review! You have completed the outline for this subunit. Study multiple-choice questions 1 through 9 beginning on page 337.

10.2 EXTERNAL CONFIRMATIONS (AU-C 505)

1. In general, audit evidence is more reliable (and persuasive) when it is (a) obtained from independent sources external to the entity, (b) obtained directly, or (c) in documentary form (paper, electronic, or other medium).

    a. Thus, external confirmations may be more reliable than evidence generated internally by the entity.

2. The auditor is required to consider whether external confirmation procedures should be performed as substantive procedures. External confirmations provide audit evidence as **direct written responses** from a third (confirming) party. They are in documentary form.

    a. An example is providing the auditor with electronic access codes to data held by the confirming party on a secure website.

3. The external confirmation process includes

    a. Determining the information to be confirmed or requested;
    b. Selecting the appropriate confirming parties;
    c. Designing confirmation requests, including determining that they (1) are directed to the appropriate confirming parties and (2) provide for direct responses to the auditor; and
    d. Sending the requests, including follow-up requests when applicable, to the confirming parties.

4. The higher the assessed risks of material misstatement, the more persuasive the audit evidence obtained should be.

    a. For example, the auditor may decide to obtain more evidence directly from third parties by performing external confirmation procedures.

        1) These procedures may provide evidence at the higher level of reliability required for responding to **significant** RMMs, including those due to fraud.

5. External confirmation requests often address assertions about account balances.

    a. **Accounts receivable** are the entity's claims against customers resulting from the sale of goods or services in the normal course of business.

        1) They include the loans of a financial institution.

    b. External confirmation of accounts receivable is required except when

        1) They are immaterial;
        2) Confirmation would be ineffective; or
        3) The assessed RMMs are low, and other substantive procedures address the assessed risks.

    c. An auditor should document the basis for not using external confirmations of accounts receivable when the balance is material.
    d. Confirmation of accounts receivable also is covered in Study Unit 11.

6. External confirmation also may be relevant to other items, such as terms of contracts or other agreements.

    a. External confirmation may provide relevant evidence about, for example,

        1) Bank balances
        2) Inventories held by third parties
        3) Investments held by brokers
        4) Accounts payable and loan balances

    b. External confirmation provides more relevant evidence about the existence assertion than about the recoverability of receivables.

7. **Designing Confirmation Requests**

    a. The following factors affecting the design of the request directly relate to the response rate and the reliability of the evidence obtained:

        1) The assertions addressed
        2) Specific RMMs, including fraud risks
        3) Presentation of the request and method of communication
        4) Management's authorization to confirming parties
        5) Prior experience on the audit
        6) Ability of the confirming parties to confirm or provide the information (e.g., a total balance instead of an invoiced amount)

b.   A **positive confirmation request** asks for a reply in all cases. It may ask the confirming parties to state whether they agree with the information given or to provide information.

   1)   Positive confirmation requests obtain evidence only when responses are received.

   2)   **Blank confirmation requests** are used to reduce the risk that recipients will respond without verifying the information. They omit the amount or other information to be confirmed and ask the confirming parties to fill in the information.

      a)   The disadvantage is a lower response rate because of the additional effort required.

c.   **Negative confirmation requests** ask confirming parties to respond only if they disagree with the stated information.

   1)   Negative confirmation requests are not used as the only substantive procedure addressing an assessed RMM at the assertion level unless

      a)   The assessed RMM is low,

      b)   The auditor has obtained sufficient appropriate evidence about the effectiveness of relevant controls,

      c)   The population consists of many small homogeneous items,

      d)   The expected exception rate is very low, and

      e)   The auditor has no reason to believe that recipients will not consider the requests.

   2)   **Unreturned negative confirmation requests** provide less persuasive evidence than responses to positive confirmation requests.

      a)   An unreturned negative confirmation request provides some evidence of existence because it has not been returned marked *Return to Sender* with an indication that the addressee is unknown. However, it provides no explicit evidence that the intended recipient verified the information.

d.   The auditor may consider information from **prior years' audits** or audits of similar entities when determining the effectiveness and efficiency of using external confirmations.

e.   When designing requests, the auditor should consider the **types of information** to confirm. The nature of the information may directly affect the reliability of the evidence obtained and the response rate.

   1)   Understanding the substance of the client's arrangements and transactions with third parties is fundamental to determining the information to be confirmed. The auditor also should consider the following:

      a)   Requesting confirmation of the terms of unusual agreements or transactions as well as the amounts

      b)   Determining whether oral modifications have been made to agreements

f.   The auditor should direct the confirmation request to the appropriate **confirming party**.

   1)   This party should be knowledgeable about the information, e.g., a bank official with knowledge of specific transactions, assets, or liabilities.

8.   The auditor may need to (a) consider the effects on the assessed RMMs (including the risk of fraud) and (b) perform alternative procedures when

   a.   Responses to confirmation requests are unreliable or

   b.   No response to a confirmation request is made.

9. **Management's Refusal to Allow the Auditor to Perform External Confirmation Procedures**

   a. If management does not allow the auditor to perform confirmation procedures, the auditor should

      1) Inquire about management's reasons for the refusal and seek audit evidence about their validity and reasonableness

      2) Evaluate the implications of management's refusal on the auditor's assessment of the relevant RMMs, including the risk of fraud, and on the nature, timing, and extent of other audit procedures

      3) Perform alternative audit procedures designed to obtain relevant and reliable audit evidence

   b. Management's refusal to allow the auditor to perform external confirmation procedures may be unreasonable, or the auditor may be unable to obtain relevant and reliable audit evidence from alternative audit procedures.

      1) In these cases, the auditor should (a) communicate with those charged with governance and (b) determine the implications for the audit and the opinion.

         a) A management-imposed limitation should result in a disclaimer or withdrawal from the engagement if the possible effects of undetected misstatements are material and pervasive.

10. An **oral response** to a confirmation is not an external confirmation.

    a. But if a direct written response to a positive confirmation is not necessary, the auditor may consider the oral response when determining the alternative procedures to be performed for nonresponses.

11. The auditor may not be able to obtain sufficient appropriate evidence without a written response to a **positive confirmation**. When alternative procedures will not obtain the required evidence, the auditor considers the implications for the audit and the opinion.

12. The auditor should evaluate the evidence provided by external confirmations and alternative procedures to determine whether sufficient appropriate evidence has been obtained. Responses to external confirmation requests may be classified as

    a. Indicating agreement
    b. Unreliable
    c. Nonresponses
    d. Indicating an exception

       1) Exceptions should be investigated because they may be **misstatements**.
       2) If a misstatement is identified, the auditor is required to determine whether it indicates fraud.
       3) Exceptions also may suggest deficiencies in internal control.

Stop and review! You have completed the outline for this subunit. Study multiple-choice questions 10 through 17 beginning on page 339.

10.3 AUDIT DOCUMENTATION (AU-C 230 AND AS NO. 3)

1. Sufficient appropriate audit documentation **(working papers) should** be prepared on a timely basis. Documentation records the work performed (including the nature, timing, extent, and results of audit procedures), the audit evidence obtained, and the conclusions reached. Audit documentation should provide

   a. A sufficient and appropriate record of the basis for the auditor's report
   b. Evidence that the audit was planned and performed in accordance with GAAS and legal and regulatory requirements

2.   The auditor should document

    a.   The characteristics of what was tested
    b.   Who performed the audit work and the date such work was complete
    c.   Who reviewed the audit work and the date and extent of the review

3.   Audit documentation serves **other purposes**, including

    a.   Assisting the audit team to plan and perform the audit
    b.   Assisting new auditors to understand the work performed
    c.   Assisting audit supervisors
    d.   Demonstrating the accountability of the audit team
    e.   Retaining a record of matters of continuing significance to future audits
    f.   Assisting inspectors, peer reviewers, and quality control reviewers
    g.   Assisting a successor auditor

4.   Documentation should be assembled into an **audit file** (physical or electronic). It should enable an experienced auditor to understand the following:

    a.   The procedures performed under GAAS or other requirements
    b.   The results and evidence obtained
    c.   Significant findings or issues, the conclusions drawn, and the judgments made

5.   The **form, content, and extent** of documentation are determined by the following:

    a.   Risks of material misstatement
    b.   Extent of judgment involved in performing the work and evaluating the results
    c.   Nature of the auditing procedures
    d.   Significance of the evidence obtained
    e.   Nature and extent of exceptions identified
    f.   Need to document a conclusion or the basis for a conclusion not readily determinable from other documentation of the work
    g.   Size and complexity of the entity
    h.   Audit methods

6.   **Tickmarks** are used to document work performed and issues uncovered during the field work. A legend should define the tickmarks used on that working paper. For example, the # mark next to the sum of a column of numbers may be defined in the legend as "# -- Footed the column." The same tickmark may be used on different working papers to mean different things as long as it is defined in the legend on that page.

7.   Each page in the working paper should be given a **unique reference number** that identifies its use and location. For example, working paper "C-1" may be for Cash in Bank. These are also used to cross-reference information on other working papers.

8.   **Examples of documentation** include (a) audit plans, (b) analyses, (c) issues memoranda, (d) confirmations, (e) representation letters, (f) abstracts or copies of documents (e.g., copies of contracts), (g) summaries of significant findings or issues (completion memoranda that describe how the identified items were addressed), (h) discussions of significant findings or issues with management or those charged with governance, (i) how the auditor addressed information inconsistent with a significant final conclusion, (j) justification for departing from a presumptively mandatory audit requirement, (k) checklists, and (l) correspondence (including email). Documentation may be on paper or electronic or other media (e.g., tapes, disks, audio, or video).

    a.   A **working trial balance** is ordinarily used to record the year-end ledger balances prior to audit. Reclassifications and adjustments are accumulated on the trial balance to reflect the final audited balances.
    b.   **Lead schedules** are summaries of detailed schedules. For example, a cash lead schedule may summarize findings recorded on the cash in bank, petty cash, and count-of-cash-on-hand detail schedules.

    c.   **Permanent files** are schedules, documents, and records with continuing audit significance for a specific client. These may include, for example, the articles of incorporation, bylaws, and contracts.

    d.   **Current files** include schedules and analyses that relate to the current year under audit. For example, results of substantive procedures, such as confirmations and inventory observation and test counts, are kept in the current files.

ISA Difference

The ISAs do not require the auditor to include copies of significant contracts or agreements in audit documentation.

---

9.   **Significant audit findings or issues** to be documented include the following:

    a.   Matters resulting in significant risks

    b.   Selection, application, and consistency of significant accounting practices, for example,

        1)   Accounting for complex or unusual transactions or
        2)   Treatment of estimates and uncertainties (and any related assumptions)

    c.   Evidence that the financial statements or disclosures may be materially misstated

    d.   Evidence of a need to revise the assessments of RMMs and the responses to them

    e.   Difficulty in applying necessary auditing procedures

    f.   Other findings that could result in modification of the report

---

Background

Rules over the preparation and maintenance of audit documentation were augmented after claims that documents may have been shredded and evidence destroyed in the Enron case.

---

10.   The auditor should complete the assembly of the final audit file within 60 days following the report release date (documentation completion date).

    a.   The auditor should not delete or discard audit documentation after the documentation completion date prior to the end of the retention period.

    b.   The auditor may modify existing documentation or add to the audit file after the documentation completion date. Moreover, (s)he should include the reasons for the change, who made the change, and the date of the change.

11.   **Ownership and Confidentiality**

    a.   Audit documentation is the **property of the auditor**.

    b.   Copies of documentation may be made available to the entity if the validity and independence of the audit are not undermined.

    c.   The auditor should retain audit documentation for a period of time sufficient to meet the needs of his/her practice and to satisfy any applicable legal or regulatory requirements for records retention. The minimum period is **5 years** from the report release date.

    d.   An auditor should take reasonable steps to preserve the **confidentiality** of documented client information, including prevention of unauthorized access.

12. **Sarbanes-Oxley Act of 2002**

   a. The act provides further documentation guidance for registered public accountants. The PCAOB's Auditing Standard No. 3, *Audit Documentation*, which applies to audit engagements and reviews of interim financial information of issuers, reflects these considerations.

   b. Audit documentation must contain sufficient information to enable an **experienced auditor**, having no previous connection with the engagement, to understand the work performed and conclusions reached and to determine who performed and reviewed the work and the relevant dates.

      1) Audit documentation must not only support final conclusions but also must include auditor-identified information about significant findings and issues that is inconsistent with or contradicts the auditor's final conclusions.

   c. The auditor must identify all **significant findings or issues** in an **engagement completion document**, including (1) corrections of misstatements (audit adjustments) that the auditor proposed or should have proposed, (2) significant disagreements among the engagement team, and (3) significant deficiencies or material weaknesses in internal control.

   d. Audit documentation must be retained for **at least 7 years** from the report release date.

   e. A complete and final set of audit documentation should be assembled for retention as of a date **(the documentation completion date)** not more than **45 days** after the report release date.

   f. Audit documentation must **not** be deleted or discarded after the documentation completion date. However, information may be added.

   g. AS No. 3 does not address whether audit documentation is the property of the auditor or the confidentiality of audit documentation.

   NOTE: The PCAOB adopted as interim ethics standards only the AICPA's provisions in its *Code of Professional Conduct* on integrity and objectivity. Thus, Conduct Rule 301, *Confidential Client Information*, is not a PCAOB standard.

13. Still **other documentation standards** may apply, for example, those of the SEC regarding retention of memoranda, communications (sent or received), other documents, and records related to engagements.

Stop and review! You have completed the outline for this subunit. Study multiple-choice questions 18 through 26 beginning on page 341.

10.4 THE COMPUTER AS AN AUDIT TOOL

1. **Computer-Assisted Audit Techniques**

   a. Most auditors use personal computers (PCs) to perform audit functions more efficiently and effectively. For this purpose, auditors must select tasks appropriate for personal computer capabilities and the software for those tasks. The uses of software by the auditor are called computer-assisted audit techniques (CAATs).

   b. **Advantages of CAATs**

      1) The auditor can work independently of the auditee.
      2) The confidentiality of auditor procedures can be maintained.
      3) Audit work does not depend on the availability of auditee personnel.
      4) The auditor has access to records at remote sites.

   c. **Disadvantages of CAATs**

      1) The auditor must have a working understanding of the computer system, e.g., a complicated database system (also may be an advantage).
      2) Supervisory review may be more difficult.

    d. **Audit procedures** include the following:

1) Directly accessing the entity's database (interrogation)
2) Scanning files for certain types of records, items, etc.
3) Building and using predictive models to identify high-risk areas
4) Applying statistical sampling item selection and analysis routines
5) Using input/output routines to provide hard copy and to reformat data (extraction)
6) Preparing financial statements and other reports with spreadsheet routines
7) Illustrating analyses with graphs and other pictorial displays
8) Writing customized audit plans
9) Storing audit plans, routines, and results electronically
10) Implementing other types of audit procedures and analyses electronically
11) Preparing and storing audit documentation
12) Communicating data through networks
13) Using specialized audit software to, among other things, compare source code with object code to detect unauthorized program changes, analyze unexecuted code, or generate test data
14) Embedding code in the entity's programs to routinely extract/select certain transactions or details to be recorded in a file accessible only by the auditor
15) Using expert systems software to automate the knowledge and logic of experts in a certain field to help an auditor with decision making and risk analysis

2. **Generalized Audit Software (GAS)**

    a. GAS is useful for both **tests of controls** and **substantive procedures**. It is software that is written to interface with many different client systems.

    b. GAS may be used to perform **audit tasks** such as the following:

1) Sampling and selecting items (e.g., confirmations)
2) Testing extensions, footings, and calculations
3) Examining records (e.g., accounts receivable for amounts in excess of credit limits)
4) Summarizing and sorting data
5) Performing analytical procedures (e.g., comparing inventory records with transaction details)
6) File access and file reorganization

    c. **Advantages of GAS**

1) It is independent of the client's programs and personnel. Thus, information can be accessed without detailed knowledge of the client's hardware and software.
2) Less computer expertise is needed compared with writing original programs.
3) It can run on a variety of systems.

    d. **Disadvantages of GAS**

1) Some software packages may process only sequential files.
2) Modifications may be necessary for a specific audit.
3) Audit software cannot examine items not in machine-readable form.
4) It has limited application in an online, real-time system.

    e. A discussion of the test data approach, parallel simulation, and integrated test facilities is presented in Study Unit 8, Subunit 3.

f.   The leading GAS software packages are currently Audit Command Language (ACL) and Interactive Data Extraction and Analysis (IDEA) software. These software packages, designed specifically for use in auditing, perform the following **major functions**:

   1)   Aging. An auditor can test the aging of accounts receivable.
   2)   Duplicate identification. Duplicate data can be organized by data field and subsequently identified.
   3)   Exportation. Data can be transferred to other software.
   4)   Extraction. Data can be extracted for exception analysis.
   5)   Gap identification. Gaps in information can be automatically noted.
   6)   Joining and merging. Two separate data files can be joined or merged to combine and match information.
   7)   Sampling. Samples of the data can be prepared and analyzed.
   8)   Sorting. Information can be sorted by any data field.
   9)   Stratification. Large amounts of data can be organized by specific factors, thereby facilitating analysis.
   10) Summarization. Data can be organized to identify patterns.
   11) Total fields. Totals for numeric fields can be quickly and accurately calculated.

3.   **Artificial Intelligence (AI).** AI is computer software designed to perceive, reason, and understand.

   a.   Business applications of AI are called **expert systems**. Expert systems in taxation, financial accounting, managerial accounting, and auditing have long been in use in major CPA firms.

      1)   An expert system is **interactive**. It asks a series of questions and uses knowledge gained from a human expert to analyze answers and make a decision.
      2)   Expert systems allow auditors and accountants to perform their duties in less time and with more uniformity. The result is that different decision makers are more likely to reach the same conclusions given the same set of facts.
      3)   An expert system can be used to (a) choose an audit plan, (b) select a test sample type and size, (c) determine the level of misstatement, (d) perform analytical procedures, and (e) make a judgment based on the findings.

   b.   **Neural networks** are another form of AI. The software learns from experience because it changes its knowledge database when informed of mistakes.

   c.   An expert system imitates a human expert and relies on many programmed rules, but a neural network has a generalized learning capacity.

4.   **Specialized Audit Software**

   a.   Specialized audit software is written to fulfill a specific set of audit tasks. The purposes and users of the software are well defined before the software is written.

   b.   Auditors develop specialized audit software for the following reasons:

      1)   Unavailability of alternative software
      2)   Functional limitations of alternative software
      3)   Efficiency considerations
      4)   Increased understanding of systems
      5)   Opportunity for easy implementation
      6)   Increased auditor independence and prestige

Stop and review! You have completed the outline for this subunit. Study multiple-choice questions 27 through 33 beginning on page 344.

QUESTIONS

10.1 Nature, Sufficiency, and Appropriateness (AU-C 500 and AS No. 15)

1. Which of the following statements about audit evidence is true?

    A. To be appropriate, audit evidence should be either persuasive or relevant but need not be both.

    B. The sufficiency and appropriateness of audit evidence is a matter of professional judgment.

    C. The difficulty and expense of obtaining audit evidence about an account balance is a valid basis for omitting the test.

    D. A client's accounting records can be sufficient audit evidence to support the financial statements.

Answer (B) is correct.
    REQUIRED: The true statement about audit evidence.
    DISCUSSION: The auditor exercises professional judgment when forming a conclusion about whether sufficient appropriate audit evidence has been obtained to reduce audit risk to an acceptably low level. Sufficiency measures the quantity of audit evidence. Appropriateness measures its quality (relevance and reliability). To form this conclusion, the auditor considers all relevant evidence, regardless of whether it corroborates or contradicts the assertions in the statements.
    Answer (A) is incorrect. To be appropriate, audit evidence should be relevant and reliable. Also, because of the inherent limitations of the audit, most audit evidence is persuasive rather than conclusive. Answer (C) is incorrect. Although the cost of obtaining evidence and its usefulness should be rationally related, the matter of difficulty, time, or cost is not in itself a valid basis for (1) omitting a procedure when no alternative exists or (2) being satisfied with less than persuasive evidence. Answer (D) is incorrect. Accounting records should be supported by corroborating information.

2. The objective of tests of details of transactions performed as substantive procedures is to

    A. Comply with generally accepted auditing standards.

    B. Attain assurance about the reliability of the accounting system.

    C. Detect material misstatements at the relevant assertion level.

    D. Evaluate whether management's policies and procedures operated effectively.

Answer (C) is correct.
    REQUIRED: The objective of tests of details.
    DISCUSSION: Substantive procedures are (1) tests of the details of transaction classes, balances, and disclosures and (2) substantive analytical procedures. They are performed to detect material misstatements at the relevant assertion level. The auditor performs substantive procedures as a response to the related assessment of the RMMs (AU-C 330).
    Answer (A) is incorrect. The auditor may use a variety of techniques and is not required to use tests of the details of transactions to comply with GAAS. Answer (B) is incorrect. Tests of controls test the operating effectiveness of internal control. Internally generated audit evidence is generally more reliable when relevant controls are effective. Answer (D) is incorrect. Tests of controls are used to determine whether policies or procedures operated effectively.

3. A retail entity uses electronic data interchange (EDI) in executing and recording most of its purchase transactions. The entity's auditor recognizes that the documentation of the transactions will be retained for only a short period of time. To compensate for this limitation, the auditor most likely would

    A. Increase the sample of EDI transactions to be selected for cutoff tests.

    B. Perform tests several times during the year, rather than only at year end.

    C. Plan to make a 100% count of the entity's inventory at or near year end.

    D. Decrease the assessed risk of material misstatement for the existence or occurrence assertion.

Answer (B) is correct.
    REQUIRED: The auditor's response to limited retention time of documentation supporting EDI transactions.
    DISCUSSION: Accounting records and other evidence may be available only in electronic form. For example, if EDI is used, purchase, shipping, billing, cash receipt, and cash payment transactions often occur by exchange of electronic messages instead of source documents. In an image processing system, documents are scanned and converted into electronic form for storage purposes, and the source documents may not be retained. Thus, electronic evidence may exist at a given moment in time, but it may not be retrievable after a specified period if files are changed and no backups exist. Consequently, the auditor should consider the time during which information is available to determine the nature, timing, and extent of substantive tests and tests of controls. For example, the auditor may change the timing of audit tests by performing them several times during the year instead of only at year end.
    Answer (A) is incorrect. Increasing the sample of transactions does not compensate for the lack of documentation. Answer (C) is incorrect. Inventory is not the only affected balance. Answer (D) is incorrect. The auditor would likely increase the assessed risk of material misstatement for the existence or occurrence assertion in light of this information.

4. In determining whether transactions have been recorded, the direction of the audit testing should begin from the

   A. General ledger balances.

   B. Adjusted trial balance.

   C. Original source documents.

   D. General journal entries.

Answer (C) is correct.
   REQUIRED: The direction of testing to determine whether transactions have been recorded.
   DISCUSSION: Determining whether transactions have been recorded is a test of the completeness assertion. Thus, beginning with the original source documents and tracing the transactions to the appropriate accounting records determines whether they were recorded.

5. Audit evidence can come in different forms with different degrees of persuasiveness. Which of the following is the **least** persuasive type of evidence?

   A. Bank statement obtained from the client.

   B. Test counts of inventory made by the auditor.

   C. Prenumbered purchase order forms.

   D. Correspondence from the client's attorney about litigation.

Answer (C) is correct.
   REQUIRED: The least persuasive type of evidence.
   DISCUSSION: When documentation, such as purchase order forms, is prepared solely by client personnel, its persuasiveness will be less than that prepared by the auditor or an independent party. Ordinarily, the most reliable documentation is created outside the entity and has never been within the client's control.
   Answer (A) is incorrect. Although a bank statement obtained from the client has been within the client's control, it is an externally generated document and is preferable to an internally prepared document. Answer (B) is incorrect. In principle, evidence is more likely to be reliable when it consists of the auditor's direct personal knowledge. Answer (D) is incorrect. Correspondence from the client's attorney about litigation is externally generated and therefore preferable to an internally generated document.

6. Which of the following presumptions is **least** likely to relate to the reliability of audit evidence?

   A. The more effective internal control is, the more assurance it provides about the accounting data and financial statements.

   B. An auditor's opinion is formed within a reasonable time to achieve a balance between benefit and cost.

   C. Evidence obtained from independent sources outside the entity is more reliable than evidence secured solely within the entity.

   D. The auditor's direct personal knowledge obtained through observation and inspection is more persuasive than information obtained indirectly.

Answer (B) is correct.
   REQUIRED: The presumption not relating to the reliability of audit evidence.
   DISCUSSION: Appropriate audit evidence is relevant and reliable. Evidence is usually more reliable when it (1) is obtained from independent sources; (2) is generated internally under effective internal control; (3) is obtained directly by the auditor; (4) is in documentary form, whether paper, electronic, or other medium; and (5) consists of original documents. However, the need for (1) reporting to be timely and (2) maintaining a balance between benefit and cost are inherent limitations of the audit. Thus, for the opinion to be relevant, it must be formed within a reasonable period of time.
   Answer (A) is incorrect. The more effective internal control is, the more assurance it provides about the reliability of the accounting data and financial statements. Answer (C) is incorrect. Evidence obtained from independent sources outside an entity provides greater assurance of reliability than evidence secured solely within the entity. Answer (D) is incorrect. The auditor's direct personal knowledge obtained through physical examination, observation, computation, and inspection is more persuasive than information obtained indirectly.

7. Which statement about audit evidence is **false**?

   A. The auditor is seldom convinced beyond all doubt with respect to all aspects of the statements being audited.

   B. The auditor should not perform a procedure that provides persuasive evidence rather than conclusive evidence.

   C. The auditor evaluates the degree of risk involved in deciding the kind of evidence to gather.

   D. The auditor balances the benefits of the evidence and the cost to obtain it.

Answer (B) is correct.
   REQUIRED: The false statement about audit evidence.
   DISCUSSION: In most cases, evidence that is obtained to enable an auditor to draw reasonable conclusions on which to base the opinion is necessarily persuasive rather than conclusive. The cost of obtaining conclusive evidence may outweigh the benefits. But the difficulty, time, or cost is not in itself a valid reason (1) to omit an audit procedure for which no alternative exists or (2) to be satisfied with less than persuasive evidence (AU-C 200).
   Answer (A) is incorrect. The auditor is seldom persuaded beyond all doubt given the high cost of absolute certainty. Answer (C) is incorrect. The auditor should assess the risks of material misstatement before determining the kind and amount of evidence necessary to form an opinion. Answer (D) is incorrect. A rational relationship should exist between the cost and benefits of evidence.

8. Accounting records alone do not provide sufficient appropriate evidence on which to base an opinion on the financial statements. Thus, the auditor should obtain other information. Which of the following is other information in this context?

A. Worksheets supporting cost allocations.

B. Confirmations of accounts receivable.

C. General and subsidiary ledgers.

D. Journal entries.

Answer (B) is correct.
REQUIRED: The example of other information.
DISCUSSION: Other information includes minutes of meetings; confirmations; and information obtained from inquiry, observation, and inspection. It includes information developed by or available to the auditor that permits valid reasoning (AU-C 500).
Answer (A) is incorrect. Worksheets supporting cost allocations are examples of accounting records. Answer (C) is incorrect. General and subsidiary ledgers are examples of accounting records. Answer (D) is incorrect. Journal entries are examples of accounting records.

9. Each of the following might, by itself, form a valid basis for an auditor to decide to omit a procedure **except** for the

A. Difficulty and cost involved in testing a particular item.

B. Assessment of the risks of material misstatement at a low level.

C. Inherent risk involved.

D. Relationship between the cost of obtaining evidence and its usefulness.

Answer (A) is correct.
REQUIRED: The consideration not a valid reason for omission of an audit procedure.
DISCUSSION: The costs and benefits of obtaining evidence should have a rational relationship. However, the difficulty, time, or cost required to perform a procedure is not in itself a valid reason for its omission if no alternative is available. Such matters also do not justify being satisfied with audit evidence that is less than persuasive (AU-C 500).
Answer (B) is incorrect. The lower the RMMs, the higher the acceptable audit risk and the greater the justification for omitting a substantive procedure. Answer (C) is incorrect. A procedure might be omitted if the susceptibility to material misstatement of an assertion before consideration of related controls is slight. Answer (D) is incorrect. The cost of obtaining evidence and its usefulness should have a rational relationship.

10.2 External Confirmations (AU-C 505)

10. Auditors may use positive or negative forms of confirmation requests. An auditor most likely will use

A. The positive form to confirm all balances regardless of size.

B. The negative form for small balances.

C. A combination of the two forms, with the positive form used for trade balances and the negative form for other balances.

D. The positive form when the assessed risk of material misstatement is acceptably low and the negative form when it is unacceptably high.

Answer (B) is correct.
REQUIRED: The true statement about the use of positive and negative confirmations.
DISCUSSION: Negative confirmation requests may be used to reduce audit risk to an acceptably low level when (1) the assessed risk of material misstatement is low, (2) a large number of small homogeneous balances is involved, (3) a very low exception rate is expected, (4) the auditor has no reason to believe that the recipients of the requests are unlikely to consider them, and (5) the auditor has obtained sufficient appropriate evidence about the effectiveness of relevant controls (AU-C 505). A combination of the two forms is often used.
Answer (A) is incorrect. The negative form is often used, e.g., when many small balances are involved. Answer (C) is incorrect. The nature of the balances does not dictate the form used. Answer (D) is incorrect. The positive form is used when the assessed risk of material misstatement is high.

11. Which of the following statements is correct concerning the use of negative confirmation requests?

A. Unreturned negative confirmation requests rarely provide significant explicit evidence.

B. Negative confirmation requests are effective when audit risk is low.

C. Unreturned negative confirmation requests indicate that alternative procedures are necessary.

D. Negative confirmation requests are effective when understatements of account balances are suspected.

Answer (A) is correct.
REQUIRED: The true statement about negative confirmation requests.
DISCUSSION: Unreturned negative confirmation requests rarely provide significant evidence about assertions other than certain aspects of existence. Additionally, unreturned negative confirmations do not provide explicit evidence that the intended parties received the requests and verified the information provided.
Answer (B) is incorrect. When the acceptable audit risk is low, positive confirmations are more effective. Answer (C) is incorrect. The auditor assumes the account is fairly stated when negative confirmations are not returned, indicating that alternative procedures are not necessary. Answer (D) is incorrect. Positive confirmations are more effective when understatements of account balances are suspected.

12. In which of the following circumstances would the use of the negative form of accounts receivable confirmation most likely be justified?

A. A substantial number of accounts may be in dispute, and the accounts receivable balance arises from sales to a few major customers.

B. A substantial number of accounts may be in dispute, and the accounts receivable balance arises from sales to many customers with small balances.

C. A small number of accounts may be in dispute, and the accounts receivable balance arises from sales to a few major customers.

D. A small number of accounts may be in dispute, and the accounts receivable balance arises from sales to many customers with small balances.

Answer (D) is correct.
REQUIRED: The circumstances in which negative accounts receivable confirmations are most likely justified.
DISCUSSION: Negative confirmation requests may be used to reduce audit risk to an acceptably low level when (1) the assessed risk of material misstatement is low, (2) a large number of small homogeneous balances is involved, (3) a very low exception rate is expected, (4) the auditor has no reason to believe that the recipients of the requests are unlikely to consider them, and (5) the auditor has obtained sufficient appropriate evidence about the effectiveness of relevant controls (AU-C 505).

13. Which of the following strategies most likely could improve the response rate of the confirmation of accounts receivable?

A. Including a list of items or invoices that constitute the account balance.

B. Restricting the selection of accounts to be confirmed to those customers with relatively large balances.

C. Requesting customers to respond to the confirmation requests directly to the auditor by fax or email.

D. Notifying the recipients that second requests will be mailed if they fail to respond in a timely manner.

Answer (A) is correct.
REQUIRED: The strategy most likely to improve confirmation response rates.
DISCUSSION: The auditor should consider what respondents are most readily able to confirm so as to improve the response rate and the competence of the evidence obtained. Thus, some customers may use a voucher system that makes it more convenient to respond to individual invoices rather than the total balance.
Answer (B) is incorrect. Although the auditor will likely focus on the larger balances, this emphasis is not likely to improve the response rate. Answer (C) is incorrect. When responses other than written communications mailed to the auditor (e.g., email or faxes) are received, additional evidence may be required to support their validity, for example, verifying the response by a telephone call to the purported sender. Answer (D) is incorrect. Notifying the recipients that second requests will be mailed if they fail to respond in a timely manner is threatening. It may reduce the response rate.

14. In confirming accounts receivable, an auditor decided to confirm customers' account balances rather than individual invoices. Which of the following most likely will be included with the client's confirmation letter?

A. An auditor-prepared letter explaining that a nonresponse may cause an inference that the account balance is correct.

B. A client-prepared letter reminding the customer that a nonresponse will cause a second request to be sent.

C. An auditor-prepared letter requesting the customer to supply missing and incorrect information directly to the client.

D. A client-prepared statement of account showing the details of the customer's account balance.

Answer (D) is correct.
REQUIRED: The nature of a confirmation request regarding an accounts receivable balance.
DISCUSSION: A confirmation request should contain management's authorization to the confirming party to respond. Also, an external confirmation should be requested by the client because the receiving party has no relationship with the client's auditor. In confirming the customer's account balance, display of the details of the balance will likely help the customer in reconciling the amount and may increase response rates. The auditor, however, will send the request directly to the customer, who will be requested to send the response directly to the auditor.
Answer (A) is incorrect. The request should come from the client. Answer (B) is incorrect. No threats should be included in a confirmation. Answer (C) is incorrect. The response should go directly to the auditor.

15. An auditor decides to use the blank form of accounts receivable confirmation rather than the traditional positive form. The auditor should be aware that the blank form may be **less** efficient because

    A. Subsequent cash receipts need to be verified.

    B. Statistical sampling may not be used.

    C. A higher assessed level of audit risk is required.

    D. More nonresponses are likely to occur.

Answer (D) is correct.
    REQUIRED: The disadvantage of a blank form confirmation request.
    DISCUSSION: The blank form of accounts receivable confirmation requests the recipient to complete the confirmation by providing the balance due to the client. This procedure may require more effort by the recipient and thus limit response rates. Accordingly, the auditor may have to perform alternative procedures.
    Answer (A) is incorrect. Verification of subsequent cash receipts is an alternative procedure performed when the response rate is too low. Answer (B) is incorrect. Statistical sampling may be used with any form of confirmation. Answer (C) is incorrect. Audit risk is a function of the effectiveness, not the efficiency, of an auditing procedure and its application by the auditor. The blank form of positive confirmation tends to reduce audit risk.

16. The confirmation of customers' accounts receivable rarely provides reliable evidence about the completeness assertion because

    A. Many customers merely sign and return the confirmation without verifying its details.

    B. Recipients usually respond only if they disagree with the information on the request.

    C. Customers may not be inclined to report understatement errors in their accounts.

    D. Auditors typically select many accounts with low recorded balances to be confirmed.

Answer (C) is correct.
    REQUIRED: The reason confirmations rarely provide evidence about completeness.
    DISCUSSION: Confirmations do not address all assertions with equal effectiveness. For example, confirmations of accounts receivable do not necessarily provide reliable evidence about the completeness assertion because customers may not report understatements. Also, confirmations may not be designed to provide assurance about information not given in the request forms.
    Answer (A) is incorrect. A customer ordinarily confirms the balance, not its details. Moreover, many confirmation requests do not contemplate a response unless the customer disagrees with the entity's recorded amount. Answer (B) is incorrect. Positive confirmations ask the customer to return the confirmation form whether it is correct or not. Answer (D) is incorrect. Auditors typically select accounts with material balances. The existence assertion is normally tested by confirmation.

17. To reduce the risks associated with accepting email responses to requests for confirmation of accounts receivable, an auditor most likely would

    A. Request the senders to mail the original forms to the auditor.

    B. Examine subsequent cash receipts for the accounts in question.

    C. Consider the email responses to the confirmations to be exceptions.

    D. Mail second requests to the email respondents.

Answer (A) is correct.
    REQUIRED: The most likely method of reducing the risks associated with email responses to confirmation requests.
    DISCUSSION: When responses other than written communications mailed to the auditor (e.g., email or faxes) are received, additional evidence may be required to support their validity. For example, the auditor may wish to verify the sources by calling the purported senders or by having the senders mail the original confirmations directly to the auditor.
    Answer (B) is incorrect. Subsequent collections provide evidence as to valuation once the existence assertion has been tested using confirmations. Answer (C) is incorrect. The responses, if from bona fide debtors, are not exceptions. Answer (D) is incorrect. The respondents should still have the original requests.

10.3 Audit Documentation (AU-C 230 and AS No. 3)

18. Audit documentation

    A. Is the property of the client.

    B. Serves as a substitute for the client's accounting records.

    C. Is unnecessary if the auditor expresses an adverse opinion.

    D. Provides evidence that the audit was performed in accordance with GAAS.

Answer (D) is correct.
    REQUIRED: The true statement about audit documentation.
    DISCUSSION: The objectives of audit documentation are to provide (1) a sufficient and appropriate record of the basis of the auditor's report and (2) evidence that the audit was performed in accordance with GAAS and other requirements. Audit documentation is the record of (1) the audit procedures performed, (2) relevant evidence obtained, and (3) conclusions reached.
    Answer (A) is incorrect. The audit documentation is the property of the auditor. Answer (B) is incorrect. The audit documentation is not a substitute for the client's accounting records. Answer (C) is incorrect. The audit documentation is necessary even if the auditor expresses an adverse opinion.

19. Which of the following factors would **least** likely affect the form, content, and extent of audit documentation?

    A. The risks of material misstatement.

    B. The extent of exceptions identified.

    C. The nature of the auditing procedures.

    D. The medium in which it is recorded and maintained.

Answer (D) is correct.
    REQUIRED: The least likely factor affecting the form, content, and extent of audit documentation.
    DISCUSSION: The medium used to prepare and maintain the audit documentation, e.g., paper or magnetic disk, does not affect its nature and extent. The form, content, and extent of documentation are determined by (1) the risks of material misstatement, (2) the extent of judgment involved in performing the work and evaluating the results, (3) the nature of the auditing procedures, (4) the significance of the evidence obtained, (5) the nature and extent of exceptions identified, (6) the need to document a conclusion or the basis for a conclusion, (7) audit methods, and (8) size and complexity of the entity.

20. An auditor ordinarily uses a working trial balance resembling the financial statements without notes, but containing columns for

    A. Cash flow increases and decreases.

    B. Risk assessments and assertions.

    C. Reclassifications and adjustments.

    D. Reconciliations and tick marks.

Answer (C) is correct.
    REQUIRED: The columns contained on a working trial balance in the audit documentation.
    DISCUSSION: A working trial balance is ordinarily used to record the year-end ledger balances prior to audit in the audit documentation. Reclassifications and adjustments are accumulated on the trial balance to reflect the final audited balances.
    Answer (A) is incorrect. Cash flow increases or decreases are reflected on the client's statement of cash flows. Answer (B) is incorrect. Risk assessments and relevant assertions are determined in the planning stage of the audit and reflected in the audit documentation. Answer (D) is incorrect. The working trial balance has no column for either reconciliations or tick marks.

21. The audit working paper that reflects the major components of an amount reported in the financial statements is the

    A. Interbank transfer schedule.

    B. Carryforward schedule.

    C. Supporting schedule.

    D. Lead schedule.

Answer (D) is correct.
    REQUIRED: The working paper that reflects the major components of a reported amount.
    DISCUSSION: Lead schedules help to eliminate detail from the auditor's working trial balance by classifying and summarizing similar or related items that are contained on the supporting schedules. A lead schedule contains the detailed accounts from the general ledger making up the line item total in the financial statements; e.g., the cash account in the financial statements might consist of petty cash, cash-general, cash-payroll, etc.
    Answer (A) is incorrect. An interbank transfer schedule is a working paper prepared for several days before and after the end of the period to determine that both parts of these transactions are recorded in the same period. Answer (B) is incorrect. A carryforward schedule is a continuing schedule of an account with a balance carried forward for several years. Answer (C) is incorrect. Supporting schedules provide details aggregated in the lead schedule.

22. Although the quantity and content of audit documentation vary with each engagement, an auditor's permanent files most likely include

    A. Schedules that support the current year's adjusting entries.

    B. Prior years' accounts receivable confirmations that were classified as exceptions.

    C. Documentation indicating that the audit work was adequately planned and supervised.

    D. Analyses of capital stock and other owners' equity accounts.

Answer (D) is correct.
    REQUIRED: The component of the permanent section of audit documentation.
    DISCUSSION: The permanent section of audit documentation usually contains copies of important client documents. They may include (1) the articles of incorporation, stock options, contracts, and bylaws; (2) the engagement letter, the contract between the auditor and the client; (3) analyses from previous audits of accounts of special importance to the auditor, such as noncurrent debt, PP&E, and equity; and (4) information concerning internal control, e.g., flowcharts, organization charts, and questionnaires.
    Answer (A) is incorrect. Schedules that support the current year's adjusting entries are not carried forward in the permanent file. They are unlikely to have continuing significance. Answer (B) is incorrect. Prior years' accounts receivable confirmations that were classified as exceptions are not carried forward in the permanent file. They are unlikely to have continuing significance. Answer (C) is incorrect. Documentation indicating that the audit work was adequately planned and supervised is always included in the current files.

23. Which of the following documentation is required for an audit in accordance with PCAOB standards?

A. A flowchart or an internal control questionnaire that evaluates the effectiveness of the entity's internal controls.

B. A list of alternative procedures that were considered but not used in the audit.

C. An indication that the accounting records agree or reconcile with the financial statements.

D. The manner in which management considered trivial errors discovered in the audit.

Answer (C) is correct.
REQUIRED: The audit documentation required by the PCAOB.
DISCUSSION: Audit documentation should (1) demonstrate that the engagement complied with PCAOB standards, (2) support the basis for conclusions about all relevant assertions, and (3) demonstrate that the accounting records agree or reconcile with the financial statements.
Answer (A) is incorrect. Although an auditor must document that a sufficient understanding of internal control has been obtained, a flowchart or questionnaire is not required. Answer (B) is incorrect. Procedures not employed need not be documented. Answer (D) is incorrect. Errors judged as trivial need not be considered by management.

24. The current file of the auditor's audit documentation ordinarily should include

A. A flowchart of the internal control procedures.

B. Organization charts.

C. A copy of the financial statements.

D. Copies of bond and note indentures.

Answer (C) is correct.
REQUIRED: The item included in the current file of the auditor's audit documentation.
DISCUSSION: The current file of the auditor's audit documentation includes all working papers applicable to the current year under audit. A copy of the financial statements must be included in the current file because the amounts included in these statements are the focus of the audit.
Answer (A) is incorrect. A flowchart of the internal control procedures would be included in the permanent file. Answer (B) is incorrect. Organization charts would be included in the permanent file. Answer (D) is incorrect. Copies of bond and note indentures would be included in the permanent file.

25. Which of the following statements concerning audit documentation is **false**?

A. An auditor may support an opinion by other means in addition to audit documentation.

B. The form of audit documentation should be designed to meet the circumstances of a particular engagement.

C. Audit documentation is the property of the client.

D. Audit documentation should show that the auditor has obtained an understanding of internal control.

Answer (C) is correct.
REQUIRED: The false statement about audit documentation.
DISCUSSION: Audit documentation is the property of the auditor. Copies of documentation may be made available to the client if the validity and independence of the audit are not undermined.
Answer (A) is incorrect. Audit documentation supports the auditor's conclusions, but additional means may be used to support an opinion. Answer (B) is incorrect. The form, content, and extent of audit documentation vary with the circumstances. Answer (D) is incorrect. Among other things, the auditor should document the understanding of the components of internal control.

26. Which of the following statements is most accurate regarding sufficient and appropriate documentation?

A. Accounting estimates are **not** considered sufficient and appropriate documentation.

B. Sufficient and appropriate documentation should include evidence that it has been reviewed.

C. If additional evidence is required to document significant findings or issues, the original evidence is **not** considered sufficient and appropriate and therefore should be deleted from the working papers.

D. Audit documentation is the property of the client, and sufficient and appropriate copies should be retained by the auditor for at least 5 years.

Answer (B) is correct.
REQUIRED: The most accurate statement about sufficient and appropriate documentation.
DISCUSSION: On or before the date of the auditor's report, the engagement partner should review the audit documentation and have discussions with the engagement team. The purpose is to be satisfied that sufficient and appropriate evidence supports the conclusions and the report (AU-C 220). The requirement to document (1) who reviewed the audit work and (2) the extent of the review does not require each working paper to bear evidence of review. But it does mean documenting (1) what work was reviewed, (2) who reviewed the work, and (3) when it was reviewed (AU-C 230).
Answer (A) is incorrect. Accounting estimates are part of the financial statements, not audit documentation. However, the auditor should evaluate management's estimates and document the conclusions. Answer (C) is incorrect. Relevant and reliable (appropriate) evidence, although not sufficient by itself, should not be deleted. Answer (D) is incorrect. Audit documentation is the property of the auditor.

10.4 The Computer as an Audit Tool

27. The two requirements crucial to achieving audit efficiency and effectiveness with a personal computer are selecting

A. The appropriate audit tasks for personal computer applications and the appropriate software to perform the selected audit tasks.

B. The appropriate software to perform the selected audit tasks and audit procedures that are generally applicable to several clients in a specific industry.

C. Client data that can be accessed by the auditor's personal computer and audit procedures that are generally applicable to several clients in a specific industry.

D. Audit procedures that are generally applicable to several clients in a specific industry and the appropriate audit tasks for personal computer applications.

Answer (A) is correct.
REQUIRED: The two requirements necessary to achieve audit efficiency and effectiveness using a personal computer.
DISCUSSION: The question relates to using the computer as an audit tool. To use a personal computer for this purpose effectively and efficiently, the auditor must have the appropriate hardware and software.
Answer (B) is incorrect. Selection of standardized procedures for the industry does not relate directly to the efficient and effective use of a personal computer. Answer (C) is incorrect. Access to the client's records and selection of standardized audit procedures pertain more to the use of generalized audit software to perform substantive tests than to using the personal computer as an audit tool. Answer (D) is incorrect. Selection of standardized procedures for the industry does not relate directly to the efficient and effective use of a personal computer.

28. A primary advantage of using generalized audit software packages to audit the financial statements of a client that uses a computer system is that the auditor may

A. Consider increasing the use of substantive tests of transactions in place of analytical procedures.

B. Substantiate the accuracy of data through self-checking digits and hash totals.

C. Reduce the level of required tests of controls to a relatively small amount.

D. Access information stored on computer files while having a limited understanding of the client's hardware and software features.

Answer (D) is correct.
REQUIRED: The advantage of using generalized audit software (GAS).
DISCUSSION: These packages permit the auditor to audit through the computer; e.g., to extract, compare, analyze, and summarize data; and to generate output for use in the audit. Although generalized audit software requires the auditor to provide certain specifications about the client's records, computer equipment, and file formats, a detailed knowledge of the client's system may be unnecessary because the audit package is designed to be used in many environments.
Answer (A) is incorrect. The auditor is required to apply analytical procedures in the planning and overall review phases of the audit. Answer (B) is incorrect. Self-checking digits and hash totals are application controls used by clients. Answer (C) is incorrect. Audit software may permit far more comprehensive tests of controls than a manual audit.

29. An auditor would **least** likely use computer software to

A. Construct parallel simulations.

B. Access data files.

C. Prepare spreadsheets.

D. Assess risk.

Answer (D) is correct.
REQUIRED: The task least likely to be done with computer software.
DISCUSSION: The auditor is required to obtain an understanding of the entity and its environment, including its internal control, and to assess the risk of material misstatement to plan the audit. This assessment is a matter of professional judgment that cannot be accomplished with a computer.
Answer (A) is incorrect. Parallel simulation involves using an auditor's program to reproduce the logic of the client's program. Answer (B) is incorrect. Computer software makes accessing client files much faster and easier. Answer (C) is incorrect. Many audit spreadsheet programs are available.

30. A bank implemented an expert system to help account representatives consolidate the bank's relationships with each customer. The expert system will be used to

A. Calculate balances.

B. Update accounts.

C. Make decisions.

D. Collect loans.

Answer (C) is correct.
REQUIRED: The purpose of an expert system.
DISCUSSION: An expert system relies on a computer's ability to make decisions in a human way. It asks a series of questions and uses knowledge gained from a human expert to analyze answers and make a decision.

31. Which of the following is an engagement attribute for an audit of an entity that processes most of its financial data in electronic form without any paper documentation?

A. Discrete phases of planning, interim, and year-end fieldwork.

B. Increased effort to search for evidence of management fraud.

C. Performance of audit tests on a continuous basis.

D. Increased emphasis on the completeness assertion.

Answer (C) is correct.
   REQUIRED: The engagement attribute for auditing in an electronic environment.
   DISCUSSION: The audit trail for transactions processed in electronic form may be available for only a short period of time. The auditor may conclude that it is necessary to time audit procedures so that they correspond to the availability of the evidence. Thus, audit modules may be embedded in the client's software for this purpose.
   Answer (A) is incorrect. This engagement attribute would be appropriate for any type of client. Answer (B) is incorrect. Processing transactions in electronic form does not inherently increase the risk of management fraud. Answer (D) is incorrect. No inherent additional concern arises about the completeness assertion as a result of processing transactions in electronic form.

32. Using personal computers in auditing may affect the methods used to review the work of staff assistants because

A. Supervisory personnel may not have an understanding of the capabilities and limitations of personal computers.

B. Audit documentation may not contain readily observable details of calculations.

C. The audit standards for supervision may differ.

D. Documenting the supervisory review may require assistance of consulting services personnel.

Answer (B) is correct.
   REQUIRED: The reason using personal computers may affect the review of the work of staff assistants.
   DISCUSSION: With the introduction of computers, accountants have been able to perform fewer manual calculations. Usually, the necessary numbers are entered into computer spreadsheets, and the answer is produced. Thus, the use of computers makes the review of a staff assistant's work different from that needed when the calculations are done manually.
   Answer (A) is incorrect. Supervisors of the audit staff typically have the skills to evaluate the appropriate use of personal computers. Answer (C) is incorrect. The audit standards for supervision are the same whether or not a computer is used. Answer (D) is incorrect. Audit staff typically have skills appropriate for the use of personal computers in documenting the work product of the audit.

33. Specialized audit software

A. Is written to interface with many different client systems.

B. May be written while its purposes and users are being defined.

C. Requires the auditor to have less computer expertise than generalized audit software.

D. May be written in a procedure-oriented language.

Answer (D) is correct.
   REQUIRED: The true statement regarding specialized audit software.
   DISCUSSION: Specialized audit software is written to fulfill a specific set of audit tasks. The purposes and users of the software are well defined before the software is written. Auditors develop specialized audit software for the following reasons:

1. Unavailability of alternative software
2. Functional limitations of alternative software
3. Efficiency considerations
4. Increased understanding of systems
5. Opportunity for easy implementation
6. Increased auditor independence and prestige

   Answer (A) is incorrect. Generalized audit software is written to interface with many different client systems. Answer (B) is incorrect. The purposes and users of this software must be defined before it is written. Answer (C) is incorrect. Generalized audit software purchased "off the shelf" requires less computer expertise than specialized software created by the auditor.

Use the additional questions in Gleim **CPA Test Prep** to create Practice Exams that emulate Prometric!

10.5 PRACTICE TASK-BASED SIMULATIONS

DIRECTIONS

Note: If you believe you have encountered a software malfunction, report it to the test center staff immediately.

Navigation

To navigate from task to task, use the controls at the bottom of the screen. Click on the **Next** button to advance to the next task, or the **Previous** button to go to the previous task. To go directly to any task, click on its number.

If you would like a reminder to revisit a task, or want to indicate that you are finished with it, click on the reminder flag below the task number. To clear the flag, click on it again. Reminder flags are for your use only – they do not contribute to your score.

Tabs

In this part of the examination, you will be asked to complete various tasks. Every task has one or more **Work Tabs**. Some tasks have one or more **Information Tabs**, others may have none. Every task has a **Help** tab.

If a task has **Information Tabs**, you may use the information in them to complete your responses in the **Work Tabs**.

Work Tabs:

- **Work Tabs** are identified with a pencil icon. This is where your responses are expected.
- Each task has one or more **Work Tabs**.
- **Work Tabs** contain directions for completing the task – be sure to read these directions carefully.
- The **Work Tab** name in the example above is for illustration only – yours will differ.
- You must complete all of the **Work Tabs** in each task to receive full credit.

Information Tabs:

- The Authoritative Literature will be provided in all tasks in the AUD, FAR, and REG sections for your reference.
- Your simulation may have one or more additional **Information Tabs**. Like the Authoritative Literature tabs, **Information Tabs** do not have a pencil icon.
- If your task has additional **Information Tabs**, go through each to familiarize yourself with the task content.

Help Tab:

- The **Help Tab** provides assistance with the exam software that is used in this task. For example, if the task is to compose a memorandum, **Help** will provide information about the word processor.

The Toolbar

The toolbar at the top of the screen shows the amount of time remaining for you to complete the tasks. In addition, the following tools are available. Note that only the **Exit** button is displayed when Directions are visible - the others will appear when you begin the tasks.

 Click on these buttons to split or unsplit the screen. You can split the screen vertically or horizontally.

 Click on this button to display the calculator; click on it again to hide the calculator. To move the calculator, click on the calculator title bar and drag the calculator to the desired location.

 Click on this button to use the spreadsheet; click on it again to hide the spreadsheet. To move the spreadsheet, click on the the spreadsheet title bar and drag the spreadsheet to the desired location.

 Click on this button to go on to the next part of the examination. You must complete all of the tasks to receive full credit. Once you click on **Exit** and confirm the action, you will NOT be able to return to this testlet.

For each of the following, select from the list provided the category to which each assertion belongs. Each choice may be used once, more than once, or not at all.

Assertions	Answer
1. All transactions and accounts that should be present in the financial statements are included.	
2. The recorded sales transactions transpired during the current year.	
3. The components of the financial statements are properly described and disclosed.	
4. Assets reported are owned by the entity, and the liabilities are the obligations of the entity as of year end.	
5. All assets, liabilities, revenues, and expenses have been included in the financial statements at the appropriate amounts.	

Choices
A) Rights and obligations
B) Classification and understandability
C) Completeness
D) Occurrence
E) Valuation and allocation

For each of the following items relating to audit evidence, select from the list provided the term with which it is most likely associated. Each term may be used once, more than once, or not at all.

Evidence-Related Item	Answer
1. Test count of inventory	
2. Ownership rights	
3. Payroll register	
4. Control manual	
5. Completeness	
6. Measure of importance	
7. Tracing a purchase into the ledger	
8. Confirmation of an accounts receivable	
9. Occurrence	
10. Minutes of meetings	

Terms
A) Assertion
B) Accounting record
C) Information technology
D) Materiality
E) Test of the details of a balance
F) Other information
G) Test of the details of a transaction

| Documentation Deficiencies | Authoritative Literature | Help |

The following Accounts Receivable – Confirmation Statistics working paper (indexed B-3) was prepared by an audit assistant during the calendar year Year 1 audit of Lewis County Water Co., Inc., a continuing audit client. The engagement supervisor is reviewing the working paper.

Lewis County Water Co., Inc.
ACCOUNTS RECEIVABLE – CONFIRMATION STATISTICS
12/31/Yr 1

			Index	B-3

	Accounts		Dollars	
	Number	Percent	Amount	Percent
Confirmation Requests Positives	54	2.7%	$ 260,000	13.0%
Negatives	140	7.0%	20,000	10.0%
Total sent	194	7.0%	280,000	23.0%
Accounts selected/client asked us not to confirm	6	0.3%		
Total selected for testing	200	10.0%		
Total accounts receivable at 12/31/Yr 1, confirm date	2,000	100.0%	$2,000,000 √ ♦	100.0%
RESULTS				
Replies received through 2/25/Yr 2				
Positives – no exception	44 C	2.2%	180,000	9.0%
Negatives – did not reply or replied "no exception"	120 C	6.0%	16,000	.8%
Total confirmed without exception	164	8.2%	196,000	9.8%
Differences reported and resolved, no adjustment				
Positives	6 Φ	.3%	30,000	1.5%
Negatives	12	.6%	2,000	.1%
Total	18 ‡	.9%	32,000	1.6%
Differences found to be potential adjustments				
Positives	2 CX	.1%	10,000	.5%
Negatives	8 CX	.4%	2,000	.1%
Total – .6% adjustment, immaterial	10	.5%	12,000	.6%
Accounts selected/client asked us not to confirm	6	.3%		

Tickmark Legend
√   Agreed to accounts receivable subsidiary ledger
♦   Agreed to general ledger and lead schedule
Φ   Includes one related party transaction
C   Confirmed without exception, W/P B-4
CX   Confirmed with exception

Overall conclusion – The potential adjustment of $12,000 or .6% is below the materiality threshold. Thus, the accounts receivable balance is fairly stated.

-- Continued on next page --

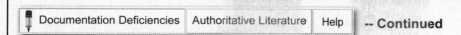

Documentation Deficiencies | Authoritative Literature | Help   -- **Continued**

Indicate which of the below statements about the deficiencies in the working paper that the engagement supervisor should discover are correct and which are incorrect. Assume that the accounts were selected for confirmation on the basis of a sample that was properly planned and documented on working paper B-2.

Statements about Deficiencies	Answer
1. The working paper was not initialed and dated by the audit assistant.	
2. Negative confirmations not returned can be considered to be accounts "confirmed without exception."	
3. All confirmations are accounted for.	
4. There is no documentation of alternate procedures, possible scope limitation, or other working paper reference for the six accounts selected for confirmation that the client asked the auditor not to confirm.	
5. The dollar amount and percent of the six accounts selected for confirmation that the client asked the auditor not to confirm are properly omitted from the "Dollars" columns for the "Total selected for testing."	
6. The "Dollars–Percent" for "Confirmation Requests–Negatives" is correctly calculated at 10%.	
7. There is no indication of follow-up or cross-referencing of the account confirmed–related party transaction.	
8. The tickmark "‡" is used but is not explained in the tickmark legend.	
9. There is no explanation of the 10 differences aggregating $12,000.	
10. The overall conclusion reached is appropriate.	
11. There is no notation that a projection from the sample to the population was made.	
12. There is no reference to second requests.	
13. Cross-referencing is incomplete for the 12 "Differences reported and resolved, no adjustment."	

Choices
A) Correct
B) Incorrect

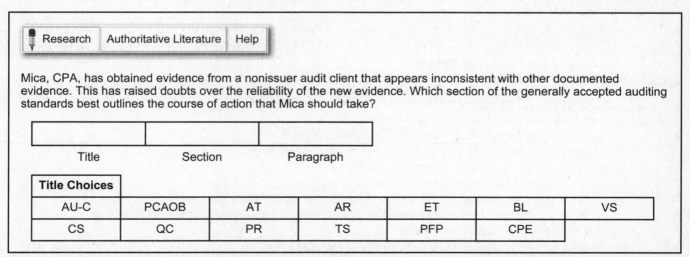

Research | Authoritative Literature | Help

Mica, CPA, has obtained evidence from a nonissuer audit client that appears inconsistent with other documented evidence. This has raised doubts over the reliability of the new evidence. Which section of the generally accepted auditing standards best outlines the course of action that Mica should take?

Title	Section	Paragraph

Title Choices						
AU-C	PCAOB	AT	AR	ET	BL	VS
CS	QC	PR	TS	PFP	CPE	

For each of the situations, the auditor collects evidence that the economic events of the entity are fairly reflected in the financial statement assertions. Indicate by selecting from the choices provided whether the direction of testing will test for completeness or existence and occurrence.

Situation	Answer		Choices
1. The auditor traced shipping documents to the sales journal.			A) Completeness
2. The auditor vouched a sample of recorded payables to purchase orders and approved invoices.			B) Existence and occurrence
3. The auditor checked to ensure that payments of interest and principle conformed with the bank loan.			
4. The auditor matched checks to related payables shortly after year end.			
5. The auditor traced recorded receivables to the bills of lading.			
6. The auditor took a sample of trucks from the motor pool and matched each truck to the subsidiary ledger.			
7. The auditor took a sample from the subsidiary records of recorded trucks and matched each record to the physical truck.			
8. The auditor took a sample of the client's count of inventory and matched it to the inventory records.			

= Reminder   Directions   1 2 3 4 [5]   ◀ Previous   Next ▶

Unofficial Answers

1. Assertions (5 Gradable Items)

1. C) Completeness. The completeness assertion relates to whether the account balance contains all the transactions for the reporting period.

2. D) Occurrence. The occurrence assertion relates to whether the transactions in the statements transpired.

3. B) Classification and understandability. The classification and understandability assertion relates to proper descriptions and classifications in the financial statements, including appropriate notes.

4. A) Rights and obligations. The rights and obligations assertion relates to whether the client has ownership rights to the assets and has obligations for the reported liabilities.

5. E) Valuation and allocation. The valuation and allocation assertion relates to whether the assets, liabilities, and capital accounts are reported in accordance with GAAP and whether proper allocations have been made (e.g., depreciation).

2. Evidence (10 Gradable Items)

1. E) Test of the details of a balance is the term most associated with a test count of inventory.
2. A) Assertion is the term most associated with ownership rights.
3. B) Accounting record is the term most associated with payroll register.
4. F) Other information is the term most associated with a control manual.
5. A) Assertion is the term most associated with completeness.
6. D) Materiality is the term most associated with measure of importance.
7. G) Test of the details of a transaction is the term most associated with tracing a purchase into the ledger.
8. E) Test of the details of a balance is the term most associated with confirmation of an accounts receivable.
9. A) Assertion is the term most associated with occurrence.
10. F) Other information is the term most associated with minutes of meetings.

3. Documentation Deficiencies (13 Gradable Items)

1.   A) Correct. The box in the upper right-hand corner of the working paper would typically contain the initials of the assistant and date the working paper was completed.

2.   B) Incorrect. The unreturned negative confirmations did not necessarily confirm the accounts because there can be other reasons that the confirmations were not returned.

3.   B) Incorrect. There were 200 confirmations selected for testing. The working paper reports: 164 total confirmed without exception, 18 total no adjustment, 10 total with adjustment, and 6 that client requested not to be confirmed. This totals 198, leaving 2 that are not accounted for.

4.   A) Correct. The auditor should perform alternative procedures to determine the existence of those 6 accounts. The conclusions from those procedures should be documented in the working papers.

5.   B) Incorrect. The 6 accounts should be included and, based on alternative procedures, should be used to project the findings to the population.

6.   B) Incorrect. This should be $20,000/$2,000,000, or 1%.

7.   A) Correct. Although the difference in amount is noted as resolved, related party transactions typically require disclosure in the financial statements. This should also be resolved in the working paper.

8.   A) Correct. There is no reference to the tickmark in the tickmark legend.

9.   A) Correct. The $12,000 potential adjustment is based on the sample of 10% of the population dollars. This should be projected to the population, and any issues should be resolved in the working papers.

10.   B) Incorrect. The working paper, as presented, does not appear to support the conclusion that the account is fairly stated. The sample was not projected to the population; thus, the fairness cannot be determined.

11.   A) Correct. The sample should be projected to the population.

12.   A) Correct. It is unlikely that all positive confirmations were returned on the first request. In any case, the auditor should address the issue that either all confirmations were returned based on the first request or second requests were used.

13.   A) Correct. The working paper should describe the issues and how they were resolved or reference another working paper providing the information.

4. Research (1 Gradable Item)

Answer: 500.10

AU-C Section 500 -- *Audit Evidence*

Inconsistency in, or Doubts Over Reliability of, Audit Evidence

.10 If

   a.   audit evidence obtained from one source is inconsistent with that obtained from another or
   b.   the auditor has doubts about the reliability of information to be used as audit evidence,

the auditor should determine what modifications or additions to audit procedures are necessary to resolve the matter and should consider the effect of the matter, if any, on other aspects of the audit.

5. Direction of Testing (8 Gradable Items)

1. <u>A) Completeness.</u> To test for completeness that all sales were recorded, an auditor might select a sample of shipping documents and trace them through the recording process to determine that they were included in the sales account.

2. <u>B) Existence and occurrence.</u> A sample of recorded payables should be reconciled with documentary support (e.g., requisitions, purchase orders, receiving reports and approved invoices) to provide evidence for the existence and occurrence assertions.

3. <u>B) Existence and occurrence.</u> To determine if transactions related to debt occurred, the auditor should ensure that debt transactions are supported by appropriate documentation identifying (a) interest rates, (b) payment dates, (c) collateral, and (d) other items.

4. <u>A) Completeness.</u> Checks should be issued only for recorded payables. Any checks that cannot be matched are likely indications of unrecorded liabilities.

5. <u>B) Existence and occurrence.</u> Because shipment of goods is typically the event creating the sale and receivable, vouching recorded receivables to shipping documents tests for existence.

6. <u>A) Completeness.</u> To test that all trucks were recorded, the auditor would select a sample of trucks and trace them to the records.

7. <u>B) Existence and occurrence.</u> To test that all trucks existed, the auditor would vouch a sample of recorded trucks to the physical trucks.

8. <u>A) Completeness.</u> Although the observation of inventory tests existence, tracing test counts to the inventory records tests completeness.

Gleim Simulation Grading

Task	Correct Responses		Gradable Items		Score per Task
1	_____	÷	5	=	_____
2	_____	÷	10	=	_____
3	_____	÷	13	=	_____
4 (Research)	_____	÷	1	=	_____
5	_____	÷	8	=	_____

	Total of Scores per Task	_____
÷	Total Number of Tasks	5
	Total Score	_____ %

Use **CPA Gleim Online** and **Simulation Wizard** to practice more task-based simulations in a realistic environment.

STUDY UNIT ELEVEN
EVIDENCE -- THE SALES-RECEIVABLES-CASH CYCLE

(9 pages of outline)

The primary purpose of the collection of evidence is to test relevant assertions about the transaction classes, balances, and disclosures in the financial statements. The auditor uses these assertions as a basis for assessing risks of material misstatement (RMMs) and designing and performing further audit procedures. Many audit procedures performed in accordance with the risk assessment are intended to detect overstatement of sales, receivables, and cash. The purpose of this study unit is to develop a comprehensive audit plan for the sales-receivables-cash cycle. This plan includes the customary procedures assuming no unusual risks. Some of the CPA questions that follow the study outlines in this study unit concern special risks that require modification of the audit plan. The candidate should consider those questions and problems and practice the modification of audit plans to address special risks.

The approach to audit plan development described in the outlines may be used in answering CPA exam questions. Application of the AICPA's assertions model (CAVE CROC is the memory aid for the assertions–refer to Study Unit 1, Subunit 2 for additional information) ensures that all assertions are tested. However, other formats for presentation of the steps are acceptable, for example, application of the PCAOB's assertions model also addressed in Study Unit 1, Subunit 2.

11.1 SUBSTANTIVE TESTING OF SALES AND RECEIVABLES

1. **Accounts receivable** are the entity's claims against customers that have arisen from the sale of goods or services in the normal course of business or from a financial institution's loans.

2. **Revenues** result from an entity's ongoing major or central operations, for example, sales of goods or services.

    a. Testing assertions about accounts receivable also results in evidence relevant to the assertions about sales revenues. Thus, testing for the completeness of receivables also tests the completeness of sales. A credit to sales ordinarily is accompanied by a debit to receivables, an entry that is recorded in the sales journal. **Special journals** record a large volume of similar items. Entries not suitable for one of the special journals are recorded in the **general journal**.

    b. **SEC Staff Accounting Bulletin (SAB) 101** provides guidance for the reporting of revenue in financial statements filed with the SEC, including the criteria for revenue recognition. SAB 101 follows current U.S. GAAP but applies them to transactions not addressed in the authoritative literature. In general, three conditions are necessary to recognize revenue: (1) delivery of the product or service, (2) determination of price, and (3) reasonable assurance of collection.

    c. Special sales-related accounts are covered in item 4. of this subunit.

3.   **Testing relevant assertions.** The following is a standard audit plan for sales and receivables that tests relevant assertions (CAVE CROC).

  a.   **Completeness.** Do sales and receivables reflect all recordable transactions for the period?

   1)   Compare (reconcile) the total recorded amounts in the **subsidiary ledger** with the accounts receivable amount recorded in the **general ledger**.

   2)   **Analytical procedures.** Use the appropriate sources of data (e.g., prior experience, budgets prepared by management at the beginning of the period, nonfinancial data, industry information, and interrelationships) to develop expectations to compare with management's presentations. Calculate and compare ratios for the current period, for example, the **accounts receivable turnover ratio** (net credit sales ÷ average accounts receivable), with those of prior periods and industry norms.

   3)   Account for the **numerical sequence** of sales-related documents, such as sales orders, shipping documents, and invoices.

   4)   Compare **shipping documents** with sales invoices and journal entries to test whether the related sales were recorded at the time of sale.

  b.   **Accuracy.** Have transactions and events been recorded appropriately?

   1)   Obtain a **management representation letter** that includes assertions relating to sales and receivables.

   2)   Evaluate management's disclosures about **reportable operating segments** and related information, including products and services, geographic areas, and major customers.

   3)   Compare the general ledger balances with the balances on the financial statements.

  c.   **Valuation and allocation.** Are accounts receivable measured in accordance with the applicable financial reporting framework, e.g., net realizable value (gross accounts receivable − allowance for uncollectible accounts)?

   1)   **Age the accounts receivable.** Classify the receivables by age, and compare percentages within classifications with those of the prior year.

   2)   **Trace subsequent cash receipts.** Cash receipts after the balance sheet date provide the best evidence of collectibility. By the end of the field work, the auditor should be able to judge the likely collections of the outstanding balances and determine whether the allowance for uncollectibles is sufficient to properly measure the year-end balance of receivables.

   3)   Review delinquent customers' **credit ratings**. This procedure provides evidence for assessing collectibility.

  d.   **Existence.** Are the accounts receivable valid assets?

   1)   **Confirm accounts receivable** (also tests the rights and valuation assertions).

    a)   External confirmation of accounts receivable is a generally accepted auditing procedure. Moreover, confirmation at year end provides greater assurance than at an interim date. The auditor confirms accounts receivable unless (1) they are immaterial, (2) confirmation would be ineffective, or (3) RMM based on other procedures is judged to be sufficiently low.

    b)   An oral response to a confirmation request does not meet the definition of an external confirmation.

    c)   An auditor who has not confirmed accounts receivable should **document** how (s)he overcame this presumption.

d) Confirming receivables may detect lapping because the entity's and customer's records of lapped accounts will differ. **Lapping** is the theft of a cash payment from one customer concealed by crediting that customer's account when a second customer makes a payment.

e) Confirmation requests also may detect an **improper cutoff**. The client might have held open the sales journal after year end and improperly recorded sales and receivables for the period under audit rather than for the subsequent period. In this case, responses to confirmations would indicate that amounts owed by debtors at year end are smaller than the recorded amounts.

f) A **negative confirmation** request contains the recorded balance of the receivable. The debtor is requested to respond only if the amount is incorrect. A **positive confirmation** request asks the debtor to respond whether the amount is incorrect or not. The **blank form** of a positive confirmation request asks that the debtor fill out the amount owed to the entity being audited.

g) When customers fail to answer a **second request** for a positive confirmation, the accounts may be in dispute, uncollectible, or fictitious. The auditor should then apply alternative procedures (examination of subsequent cash receipts, shipping documents, and other client documentation of existence) to obtain evidence about the validity of nonresponding accounts.

h) The auditor should be convinced that confirmations received via email, fax, or other electronic media were sent by the debtor and not by an impostor.

ISA Difference

The ISAs do not require the auditor to confirm accounts receivable.

---

2) **Vouch recorded accounts receivable to shipping documents.** Because shipment of goods is typically the event creating the sale and receivable, vouching recorded receivables to shipping documents, such as bills of lading, tests for existence.

e. **Cutoff.** Have transactions been recorded in the proper period?

1) **Sales cutoff test.** Test to determine that a sale and receivable were recorded when title passed to the customer, which often occurs when goods are shipped (i.e., when terms are **FOB shipping point**). Shipping documents are traced to the accounting records for several days prior to and after year end to determine proper recognition in the appropriate period. This test detects inflated sales.

2) **Cash receipts cutoff test.** Test the recording of the receipts of cash and the associated reduction in accounts receivable. Inspection and tracing of the items on the **daily remittance list** for several days prior to and after year end provides evidence of proper recording.

f. **Rights and obligations.** Does the entity have the right to collect receivables?

1) **Inquiries of management.** Consider the motivation and opportunity for factoring or selling the receivables, and inquire of management as to whether such transactions have occurred.

2) **Track cash receipts** to determine that the entity is collecting and depositing the proceeds into bank accounts it controls.

3) Determine whether sales have been made with a **right of return** and what the expected and actual returns are after year end.

g. **Occurrence.** Did sales occur?

    1) **Vouch a sample of recorded sales** to customer orders and shipping documents. Large and unusual sales should be included in the sample selected for testing. This test is useful for detecting overstatements.

h. **Classification and understandability.** Are sales and receivables appropriately described and disclosures fairly and clearly expressed?

    1) **Inspect the income statement** to determine that sales are reported as a revenue, minus returns and allowances. **Inspect the balance sheet** to determine that accounts receivable are presented as a current asset, minus the allowance for uncollectible accounts.

    2) **Evaluate note disclosures** to determine that **accounting policies** are disclosed (e.g., accounts receivable should be presented at net realizable value). **Pledges of accounts receivable** should be disclosed. Any significant sales or receivables transactions with **related parties** also should be disclosed.

4. **Testing Relevant Assertions about Related Accounts**

a. **Sales returns and allowances.** The auditor should test all assertions. But if the risk of material misstatement is low, the primary tests will address the existence and occurrence assertions. Was there a proper authorization for the return of goods, and were those goods actually returned?

    1) The auditor ordinarily tests the **documentation** that supports the return. This procedure determines whether proper **authorization** exists, and the credit to the customer's account was supported by a receiving report representing the return of goods.

b. **Write-off of bad debts.** If the risk of material misstatement is relatively low, the audit plan for accounts receivable described above should provide sufficient appropriate evidence. However, if controls are ineffective, for example, if the accounting function (the accounts receivable bookkeeper) is allowed to approve write-offs, the auditor will perform specific procedures to reduce detection risk to an acceptably low level.

    1) Thus, the auditor might decide to attempt to confirm the receivables previously written off. If the write-offs were legitimate, most requests will be marked *Return to Sender* because the debtors will probably not be in business.

Stop and review! You have completed the outline for this subunit. Study multiple-choice questions 1 through 21 beginning on page 361.

11.2 SUBSTANTIVE TESTING OF CASH

1. **Cash** includes cash on hand, demand accounts, and other asset accounts held in financial institutions.

2. Substantive testing of cash addresses assertions related to the **balance sheet**.

3. **Testing Relevant Assertions**

a. **Completeness.** Does the balance at the end of the accounting period reflect all cash transactions?

    1) For cash **receipts**, trace the **daily remittance list** to the last validated deposit ticket for the period. For cash **disbursements**, determine the **last check written** for the period and trace the effect to the accounting records. Determine that all outstanding checks have been listed on the **bank reconciliation**.

2) Use of **analytical procedures** is not typically as effective for cash as for most other accounts because it is a managed account. However, the auditor may be able to use management's budget, prepared at the beginning of the period, as an expectation with which to compare the year-end balance.

b. **Accuracy.** Has cash been recorded accurately?

1) Compare a sample of daily remittance lists with deposits, journal entries, and ledger postings.

2) Compare the general ledger balances with the balances on the financial statements.

c. **Valuation and allocation.** Is cash valued in accordance with the applicable reporting framework?

1) U.S. currency has low inherent risk relative to this assertion. However, special circumstances, such as holdings of foreign currency, may require additional testing.

d. **Existence.** Does cash exist? Because **inherent risk** is high for cash, most audit procedures are directed toward existence.

1) **Count cash on hand.**

   a) Control all cash and negotiable securities to protect against substitution.
   b) Determine that all received checks are payable to the client.
   c) Determine that all received checks are endorsed "For Deposit Only into Account Number XXXX."

2) **Bank confirmation.** The AICPA *Standard Form to Confirm Account Balance Information with Financial Institutions* is used for specific deposits and loans.

   a) A confirmation request is **authorized by the client**, but it should be **sent by the auditor** to any bank with which the client has had business during the period.
   b) The form confirms the account name and number, interest rate, and balance for deposits.
   c) For **direct liabilities on loans**, the form confirms account number/ description, balance, due date, interest rate, date through which interest is paid, and description of collateral.
   d) To confirm other transactions and written or oral arrangements, such as contingent liabilities, lines of credit, compensating balances, and security agreements, auditors send a **separate letter signed by the client** to an official responsible for the financial institution's relationship with the client.
   e) The standard form (and separate letter) is designed to substantiate only the information that is stated on the confirmation request. Thus, the auditor should be aware that the standard form is **not** intended to elicit evidence about the **completeness assertion**.

      i) Nevertheless, the standard form requests any additional information about other deposit and loan accounts that may have come to the attention of the financial institution.

3) **Bank reconciliation.** Inspect or prepare bank reconciliations for each account.

   a) A bank reconciliation verifies the **agreement** of the bank statements obtained directly from the institution and the amount of cash reported in the financial statements. These amounts should be equal after adjustment for deposits in transit, outstanding checks, bank charges, etc.

STANDARD FORM TO CONFIRM ACCOUNT
BALANCE INFORMATION WITH FINANCIAL INSTITUTIONS

ORIGINAL
To be mailed to accountant

_____
CUSTOMER NAME

Financial
Institution's
Name and
Address

We have provided to our accountants the following information as of

the close of business on _____, 20 _____,
regarding our deposit and loan balances. Please confirm the
accuracy of the information, noting any exceptions to the information
provided. If the balances have been left blank, please complete this
form by furnishing the balance in the appropriate space below.*
Although we do not request or expect you to conduct a
comprehensive, detailed search of your records, if, during the process
of completing this confirmation, additional information about other
deposit and loan accounts we may have with you comes to your
attention, please include such information below. Please use the
enclosed envelope to return the form directly to our accountants.

1.   At the close of business on the date listed above, our records indicated the following deposit balance(s):

ACCOUNT NAME	ACCOUNT NO.	INTEREST RATE	BALANCE*

2.   We were directly liable to the financial institution for loans at the close of business on the date listed above as follows:

ACCOUNT NO./ DESCRIPTION	BALANCE*	DATE DUE	INTEREST RATE	DATE THROUGH WHICH INTEREST IS PAID	DESCRIPTION OF COLLATERAL

_____   _____
(Customer's Authorized Signature)   (Date)

The information presented above by the customer is in agreement with our records. Although we have not conducted a comprehensive, detailed search of our records, no other deposit or loan accounts have come to our attention except as noted below.

_____   _____
(Financial Institution Authorized Signature)   (Date)

_____
(Title)

EXCEPTIONS AND/OR COMMENTS

Please return this form directly to our accountants:

*Ordinarily, balances are intentionally left blank if they are not
available at the time the form is prepared.

Approved 1990 by American Bankers Association, American Institute of Certified Public Accountants, and Bank Administration
Institute. Additional forms available from: AICPA - Order Department, P.O. Box 1003, NY, NY 10108-1003   D451 5951

EXAMPLE OF LETTER TO CONFIRM OTHER FINANCIAL INSTITUTION INFORMATION

[*Date*]
Financial Institution Official
First United Bank
Anytown, USA 00000

Dear Financial Institution Official:

In connection with an audit of the financial statements of [*name of customer*] as of [*balance sheet date*] and for the [*period*] then ended, we have advised our independent auditors of the information listed below, which we believe is a complete and accurate description of our contingent liabilities, including oral and written guarantees, with your financial institution. Although we do not request nor expect you to conduct a comprehensive, detailed search of your records, if during the process of completing this confirmation additional information about other contingent liabilities, including oral and written guarantees, between [*name of customer*] and your financial institution comes to your attention, please include such information below.

Name of Maker	Date of Note	Due Date	Current Balance
Interest Rate	Date Through Which Interest Is Paid	Description of Collateral	Description of Purpose of Note

Information related to oral and written guarantees is as follows:

_____

_____

_____

Please confirm whether the information about contingent liabilities presented above is correct by signing below and returning this directly to our independent auditors [*name and address of CPA firm*].

Sincerely,

[*name of customer*]

_____

By: _____
       (*Authorized Signature*)

Dear CPA Firm:

The above information listing contingent liabilities, including oral and written guarantees, agrees with the records of this financial institution. Although we have not conducted a comprehensive, detailed search of our records, no information about other contingent liabilities, including oral and written guarantees, came to our attention. [Note exceptions below or in an attached letter.]

_____

_____

_____

_____
                                                             (*Name of Financial Institution*)

                                    By: _____   _____
                                              (*Officer and Title*)   (*Date*)

4) **Cutoff bank statement.** This should be requested directly from the bank for the period 7 to 10 days after year end. Use this statement to test reconciling items on the year-end bank reconciliation, e.g., deposits in transit and outstanding checks.

   a) Search for checks written before year end but **not listed as outstanding** on the bank reconciliation. These checks are often evidence of **kiting**, a fraud resulting from an improper recording of a bank transfer.

      i) To cover a shortage of cash (cash is recorded in the accounting records but not in the bank's records), an employee writes a check just prior to year end on the disbursing bank but does not record the disbursement in the accounting records in the current year. Furthermore, the check also does not appear as a disbursement on the year-end statement issued by the disbursing bank because it would not have cleared. However, the receipt is recorded by the receiving bank (at least as a deposit in transit), thereby covering the shortage. In the short term, the cash balance will appear to reconcile.

      ii) To uncover the fraud, the auditor should match the returned checks written prior to year end listed on the cutoff bank statement with the outstanding checks listed on the bank reconciliation for the disbursing bank. Because the kited check was not recorded, it will not be listed as outstanding.

   b) Consider the **number of checks returned** listed on the cutoff bank statement. This procedure may provide evidence of window dressing, that is, trying to improve the **current ratio**. The client may write checks to pay current liabilities but not mail them until the next accounting period.

5) **Schedule of interbank transfers.** Preparing this schedule can help detect errors in transfers but may not be effective to detect kiting if a disbursement has not been recorded. For this procedure to be effective, the auditor should be assured that all transfers have been identified.

6) **Proof of cash.** When internal control over a transaction process is not effective, a proof of cash may be prepared. It provides direct evidence that amounts recorded by the bank (beginning and ending balances, deposits, and disbursements) reconcile with amounts recorded by the entity for a period of time, typically a month.

e. **Cutoff.** Have transactions been recorded in the proper period?

   1) Inspect and trace the daily remittance lists for several days prior to and after year end.

   2) Identify and trace the last check written for the year into the records.

f. **Rights and obligations.** Does the entity have ownership right to the cash?

   1) In most cases, risks related to ownership are low, and few specific procedures are applied. However, confirmations related to the existence assertion provide evidence for the rights and obligations assertion. Inquiries of management are also appropriate.

g. **Occurrence.** Did the cash transactions occur?

   1) **Vouch** a sample of recorded cash receipts to accounts receivable and customer orders.

   2) Vouch a sample of recorded cash disbursements to approved vouchers.

h. **Classification and understandability.** Is cash appropriately described, and are disclosures fairly and clearly expressed?

   1) **Inquire of management about disclosure.** Include references to cash in the management representation letter.

   2) Determine that **restricted cash** (e.g., sinking funds and compensating balances) is reported in the noncurrent asset section of the balance sheet.

   3) **Assess statement of cash flows.**

      a) Determine proper presentation: direct or indirect method.

      b) Reconcile information with income statement and balance sheet presentations.

      c) Examine elements of statement of cash flows classifications: operating activities, investing activities, and financing activities.

   4) Evaluate financial statement note disclosures.

Stop and review! You have completed the outline for this subunit. Study multiple-choice questions 22 through 31 beginning on page 368.

QUESTIONS

11.1 Substantive Testing of Sales and Receivables

1. Which of the following comparisons would be most useful to an auditor in evaluating the results of an entity's operations?

A. Prior-year accounts payable to current-year accounts payable.

B. Prior-year payroll expense to budgeted current-year payroll expense.

C. Current-year revenue to budgeted current-year revenue.

D. Current-year warranty expense to current-year contingent liabilities.

Answer (C) is correct.
  REQUIRED: The best comparison for evaluating the results of operations.
  DISCUSSION: Revenues result from an entity's ongoing major or central operations. These operations reflect numerous activities and affect many accounts. Consequently, comparing current-year revenue with the budgeted current-year revenue provides evidence as to the completeness of revenue. Revenue is a broad measure of the effects of the entity's main activities and is a primary component of the results of operations.
  Answer (A) is incorrect. The change in accounts payable is too narrow a measure to be useful in this evaluation. Answer (B) is incorrect. Payroll expense is too narrow a measure to be useful in this evaluation. Answer (D) is incorrect. The relationship of warranty expense with contingent liabilities is too narrow a measure to be useful in this evaluation.

2. An auditor most likely would limit substantive audit tests of sales transactions when the risks of material misstatement are assessed as low for the existence and occurrence assertions concerning sales transactions and the auditor has already gathered evidence supporting

A. Opening and closing inventory balances.

B. Cash receipts and accounts receivable.

C. Shipping and receiving activities.

D. Cutoffs of sales and purchases.

Answer (B) is correct.
  REQUIRED: The evidence related to the existence and occurrence assertions for sales transactions.
  DISCUSSION: Cash receipts and accounts receivable have a direct relationship with sales. A cash sale results in a debit to cash and a credit to sales. A sale on account results in a debit to accounts receivable and a credit to sales. Thus, evidence related to cash receipts and accounts receivable provides assurances about sales.
  Answer (A) is incorrect. The opening and closing inventory balances do not directly affect the sales transactions. Answer (C) is incorrect. Although shipping activities are related to sales, receiving activities are not. Answer (D) is incorrect. Although cutoffs of sales provide evidence as to sales transactions, cutoffs of purchases do not.

3. If the objective of a test of details is to detect overstatements of sales, the auditor should compare transactions in the

   A. Cash receipts journal with the sales journal.

   B. Sales journal with the cash receipts journal.

   C. Source documents with the accounting records.

   D. Accounting records with the source documents.

Answer (D) is correct.
   REQUIRED: The appropriate test to detect overstatement of sales.
   DISCUSSION: Overstatements of sales likely result from entries with no supporting documentation. The proper direction of testing is to sample entries in the sales account and vouch them to the shipping documents. The source documents represent the valid sales.
   Answer (A) is incorrect. The cash receipts journal and the sales journal are books of original entry, not source documents. Answer (B) is incorrect. The cash receipts journal and the sales journal are books of original entry, not source documents. Answer (C) is incorrect. The proper direction of testing is from the accounting records to the source documents.

4. Tracing shipping documents to prenumbered sales invoices provides evidence that

   A. No duplicate shipments or billings occurred.

   B. Shipments to customers were properly invoiced.

   C. All goods ordered by customers were shipped.

   D. All prenumbered sales invoices were accounted for.

Answer (B) is correct.
   REQUIRED: The evidence provided by tracing shipping documents to prenumbered sales invoices.
   DISCUSSION: The direction of testing to determine that shipments to customers were properly invoiced is from the shipping documents to the sales invoices.
   Answer (A) is incorrect. Tracing a sample of customer orders to the shipping documents provides evidence about duplicate shipments. Answer (C) is incorrect. Tracing sales orders to shipping documents provides evidence that all goods ordered by customers were shipped. Answer (D) is incorrect. Accounting for all the numbered invoices provides assurance that no invoices were lost or misplaced.

5. An auditor most likely would review an entity's periodic accounting for the numerical sequence of shipping documents and invoices to support management's financial statement assertion of

   A. Occurrence.

   B. Rights and obligations.

   C. Valuation and allocation.

   D. Completeness.

Answer (D) is correct.
   REQUIRED: The assertion supported by reviewing the numerical sequence of shipping documents and invoices.
   DISCUSSION: The completeness assertion concerns whether all transactions (or assets, liabilities, and equity interests) that should be recorded are recorded. Testing the numerical sequence of shipping documents and invoices is a means of detecting omitted items.
   Answer (A) is incorrect. The occurrence assertion addresses whether recorded transactions have occurred and pertain to the entity. Answer (B) is incorrect. The rights and obligations assertion concerns whether assets are the rights of the entity and liabilities are obligations at a given date. Answer (C) is incorrect. The valuation and allocation assertion concerns whether assets, liabilities, and equity interests have been included at appropriate amounts.

6. An entity's financial statements were misstated over a period of years because large amounts of revenue were recorded in journal entries that involved debits and credits to an illogical combination of accounts. The auditor could most likely have been alerted to this fraud by

   A. Scanning the general journal for unusual entries.

   B. Performing a revenue cutoff test at year end.

   C. Tracing a sample of journal entries to the general ledger.

   D. Examining documentary evidence of sales returns and allowances recorded after year end.

Answer (A) is correct.
   REQUIRED: The procedure to detect misstatement of revenue as a result of illogical entries.
   DISCUSSION: The general journal is a book of original entry used for transactions not suitable for recording in the special journals (sales, purchases, cash receipts, cash disbursements). Entries involving unusual combinations of accounts are more likely to appear in the general journal than in one of the special journals, which are designed to record large numbers of similar items. For example, credit sales (debit accounts receivable, credit sales) are entered in the sales journal.
   Answer (B) is incorrect. A revenue cutoff is a test of the timing of recognition. Moreover, it applies to transactions at year end only. Answer (C) is incorrect. Tracing journal entries will only test whether recorded transactions were posted to the ledger. Answer (D) is incorrect. This procedure applies to year-end transactions only.

7. Which of the following might be detected by an auditor's review of the client's sales cutoff?

   A. Excessive goods returned for credit.

   B. Unrecorded sales discounts.

   C. Lapping of year-end accounts receivable.

   D. Inflated sales for the year.

Answer (D) is correct.
   REQUIRED: The condition that might be detected by review of the client's sales cutoff.
   DISCUSSION: Sales cutoff tests are designed to detect the client's manipulation of sales. By examining recorded sales for several days before and after the balance sheet date and comparing them with sales invoices and shipping documents, the auditor may detect the recording of a sale in a period other than that in which title passed.
   Answer (A) is incorrect. Sales returns are not examined in the sales cutoff test. Answer (B) is incorrect. Examination of cash receipts would reveal unrecorded discounts. Answer (C) is incorrect. Lapping may be detected by the confirmation of customer balances and tracing amounts received according to duplicate deposit slips to the accounts receivable subsidiary ledger.

8. An audit client sells 15 to 20 units of product annually. A large portion of the annual sales occur in the last month of the fiscal year. Annual sales have not materially changed over the past 5 years. Which of the following approaches would be most effective concerning the timing of audit procedures for revenue?

   A. The auditor should perform analytical procedures at an interim date and discuss any changes in the level of sales with senior management.

   B. The auditor should inspect transactions occurring in the last month of the fiscal year and review the related sale contracts to determine that revenue was posted in the proper period.

   C. The auditor should perform tests of controls at an interim date to obtain audit evidence about the operational effectiveness of internal controls over sales.

   D. The auditor should review period-end compensation to determine if bonuses were paid to meet earnings goals.

Answer (B) is correct.
   REQUIRED: The most effective audit procedure given the timing of revenue.
   DISCUSSION: Tests of the details of transactions at year end are most effective given that total sales consist mostly of a few transactions. Also, because most occur in the last month of the year, the auditor should establish that management made a proper cutoff.
   Answer (A) is incorrect. Because most sales occur at year end, interim analytical procedures are not likely to be effective. Answer (C) is incorrect. Although internal controls are important, given the small number of transactions, substantive procedures are most effective. Answer (D) is incorrect. Firms often pay bonuses as incentives to meet objectives.

9. Which of the following most likely would give the most assurance concerning the valuation assertion about accounts receivable?

   A. Vouching amounts in the subsidiary ledger to details on shipping documents.

   B. Comparing receivable turnover ratios with industry statistics for reasonableness.

   C. Inquiring about receivables pledged under loan agreements.

   D. Assessing the allowance for uncollectible accounts for reasonableness.

Answer (D) is correct.
   REQUIRED: The procedure providing the most assurance about the valuation of accounts receivable.
   DISCUSSION: Assertions about valuation concern whether balance sheet components have been included at appropriate amounts. One such assertion is that trade accounts receivable are stated at net realizable value (gross accounts receivable minus allowance for uncollectible accounts). Hence, assessing the allowance provides assurance about the valuation of the account.
   Answer (A) is incorrect. Vouching amounts in the subsidiary ledger to details on shipping documents provides evidence about the occurrence assertion for transactions. Answer (B) is incorrect. Comparing receivable turnover ratios with industry statistics for reasonableness provides evidence about completeness. Answer (C) is incorrect. Inquiring about receivables pledged under loan agreements pertains to presentation and disclosure assertions.

10. An auditor's purpose in reviewing credit ratings of customers with delinquent accounts receivable most likely is to obtain evidence concerning relevant assertions about

A. Classification and understandability.

B. Existence.

C. Rights and obligations.

D. Valuation and allocation.

Answer (D) is correct.
REQUIRED: The assertion about which evidence is provided by reviewing credit ratings of delinquent customers.
DISCUSSION: Assertions about valuation and allocation concern whether balance sheet components have been included at appropriate amounts. Determining the net realizable value of accounts receivable includes assessing whether the client's allowance for uncollectibility is reasonable. Reviewing the credit ratings of delinquent customers provides evidence for that purpose.
Answer (A) is incorrect. The assertion about classification and understandability concerns whether financial statement components are properly classified, described, and disclosed. Answer (B) is incorrect. The existence assertion concerns whether assets, liabilities, and equity interests exist. Answer (C) is incorrect. The rights and obligations assertion concerns whether assets are the rights of the entity and liabilities are obligations.

11. For the fiscal year ending December 31 of the previous year and for the current year, Justin Co. has net sales of $1,000,000 and $2,000,000; average gross receivables of $100,000 and $300,000; and an allowance for uncollectible accounts receivable of $30,000 and $50,000, respectively. If the accounts receivable turnover and the ratio of allowance for uncollectible accounts receivable to gross accounts receivable are calculated, which of the following best represents the conclusions to be drawn?

A. Accounts receivable turnovers are 10.0 and 6.6, and the ratios of uncollectible accounts receivable to gross accounts receivable are 0.30 and 0.16, respectively. Examine allowance for possible overstatement of the allowance.

B. Accounts receivable turnovers are 10.0 and 6.7, and the ratios of uncollectible accounts receivable to gross accounts receivable are 0.30 and 0.17, respectively. Examine allowance for possible understatement of the allowance.

C. Accounts receivable turnovers are 14.3 and 8.0, and the ratios of uncollectible accounts receivable to gross accounts receivable are 0.42 and 0.20, respectively. Examine allowance for possible overstatement of the allowance.

D. Accounts receivable turnovers are 14.3 and 8.0 and the ratios of uncollectible accounts receivable to gross accounts receivable are 0.42 and 0.20, respectively. Examine allowance for possible understatement of the allowance.

Answer (B) is correct.
REQUIRED: The appropriate conclusions from the accounts receivable turnover and the ratio of the allowance for uncollectible accounts receivable to gross accounts receivable.
DISCUSSION: The accounts receivable turnover equals sales divided by average gross receivables. Thus, it equals 10.0 ($1,000,000 ÷ $100,000) and 6.7 ($2,000,000 ÷ $300,000) for the prior year and current year, respectively. The ratio of allowance for uncollectible accounts receivable to gross accounts receivable is .30 ($30,000 ÷ $100,000) for the prior year and .17 ($50,000 ÷ $300,000) for the current year. The gross accounts receivable tripled in the second year, yet the allowance for uncollectible accounts receivable increased by only 67%. This could be an indication that the allowance for uncollectible accounts receivable is understated.
Answer (A) is incorrect. The gross accounts receivable tripled in the second year, yet the allowance for uncollectible accounts receivable only went up by 67%. This could be an indication that the allowance for uncollectible accounts receivable is understated, not overstated. Answer (C) is incorrect. Net accounts receivable was used to calculate these ratios. Answer (D) is incorrect. Net accounts receivable was used to calculate these ratios.

12. AU-C 505, *External Confirmations*, defines external confirmation as "a direct written response to the auditor from a third party (the confirming party), either in paper form or by electronic or other medium." The assertions for which confirmation of accounts receivable balances provides primary evidence are

A. Completeness and valuation.

B. Valuation and rights and obligations.

C. Rights and obligations and existence.

D. Existence and completeness.

Answer (C) is correct.

REQUIRED: The assertions tested by confirming receivables.

DISCUSSION: Confirmation by means of direct (independent) communication with debtors is the generally accepted auditing procedure for accounts receivable. Properly designed requests may address any assertion in the financial statements, but they are most likely to be effective for the existence and rights and obligations assertions. Thus, confirmation provides evidence that (1) receivables are valid, (2) the client has ownership of the accounts and the right of collection, and (3) the debtor has the obligation to pay.

Answer (A) is incorrect. Confirmation is not effective for the completeness assertion. It is unlikely to detect unrecorded accounts. Answer (B) is incorrect. Confirmation is less effective for the valuation assertion than for the existence and rights and obligations assertions. Answer (D) is incorrect. Confirmation is less effective for the completeness assertion than for the existence and rights and obligations assertions.

13. An auditor confirms a representative number of open accounts receivable as of December 31 and investigates respondents' exceptions and comments. By this procedure, the auditor would be most likely to learn of which of the following?

A. One of the cashiers has been covering a personal embezzlement by lapping.

B. One of the sales clerks has not been preparing charge slips for credit sales to family and friends.

C. One of the computer control clerks has been removing all sales invoices applicable to his account from the data file.

D. The credit manager has misappropriated remittances from customers whose accounts have been written off.

Answer (A) is correct.

REQUIRED: The fraud most likely to be detected by confirming receivables.

DISCUSSION: Lapping is the theft of a cash payment from one customer concealed by crediting that customer's account when a second customer makes a payment. When lapping exists at the balance sheet date, the confirmation of customer balances will probably detect the fraud because the customers' and entity's records of lapped accounts will differ.

Answer (B) is incorrect. If a charge slip has not been prepared, no accounts receivable balance will exist to be confirmed. Answer (C) is incorrect. If a sales invoice is not processed, no account balance will appear in the records. Answer (D) is incorrect. Once the account has been written off, the account is no longer open.

14. An auditor suspects that a client's cashier is misappropriating cash receipts for personal use by lapping customer checks received in the mail. In attempting to uncover this embezzlement scheme, the auditor most likely would compare the

A. Dates checks are deposited per bank statements with the dates remittance credits are recorded.

B. Daily cash summaries with the sums of the cash receipts journal entries.

C. Individual bank deposit slips with the details of the monthly bank statements.

D. Dates uncollectible accounts are authorized to be written off with the dates the write-offs are actually recorded.

Answer (A) is correct.

REQUIRED: The procedure to detect lapping.

DISCUSSION: Lapping involves recording current cash payments on accounts receivable as credits to prior customers' accounts to conceal a theft of cash. Comparing the date that a customer's check was deposited with the date a record was made to reduce the balance determines whether the deposit was made prior to the recording date.

Answer (B) is incorrect. The total cash received and deposited for any one day will reconcile when lapping occurs. Answer (C) is incorrect. The total cash received and deposited for any one day will reconcile when lapping occurs. Answer (D) is incorrect. Lapping does not involve unauthorized write-offs.

15. An auditor who has confirmed accounts receivable may discover that the sales journal was held open past year end if

A. Positive confirmation requests sent to debtors are not returned.

B. Negative confirmation requests sent to debtors are not returned.

C. Most of the returned negative confirmation requests indicate that the debtor owes a larger balance than the amount being confirmed.

D. Most of the returned positive confirmation requests indicate that the debtor owes a smaller balance than the amount being confirmed.

Answer (D) is correct.

REQUIRED: The result of confirmation indicating that the sales journal was held open past year end.

DISCUSSION: When the majority of the returned positive confirmation requests indicate smaller balances at year end than those in the client's records, the client may have held open the sales journal after year end. Thus, the client debited customers' accounts for the period under audit rather than for the subsequent period. The effect is to overstate sales and receivables.

Answer (A) is incorrect. The failure to receive replies to positive confirmation requests may cause the auditor concern about the existence assertion. Answer (B) is incorrect. Nonresponses to negative confirmation requests provide some evidence about the existence assertion. Answer (C) is incorrect. Replies indicating balances larger than those confirmed suggest that the sales journal was closed prior to year end.

16. During the process of confirming receivables as of December 31, Year 1, a positive confirmation was returned indicating the "balance owed as of December 31 was paid on January 9, Year 2." The auditor would most likely

A. Determine whether any changes in the account occurred between January 1 and January 9, Year 2.

B. Determine whether a customary trade discount was taken by the customer.

C. Reconfirm the zero balance as of January 10, Year 2.

D. Verify that the amount was received.

Answer (D) is correct.

REQUIRED: The auditor action when a confirmation response states that the year-end balance was paid.

DISCUSSION: Responses to confirmation requests that involve significant differences are investigated by the auditor. Others are delegated to client employees with a request that explanations be given to the auditor. Such differences often arise because of recent cash payments. In that event, the auditor should trace remittances to verify that stated amounts were received.

Answer (A) is incorrect. The auditor wishes to confirm a year-end balance, not transactions in the subsequent period. Also, the reply does not suggest a discrepancy in the account. Answer (B) is incorrect. The auditor is more concerned with confirming the balance due at year end than with whether a customer took a discount. Answer (C) is incorrect. Reconfirmation is not required.

17. An auditor confirmed accounts receivable as of an interim date, and all confirmations were returned and appeared reasonable. Which of the following additional procedures most likely should be performed at year end?

A. Send confirmation requests for all new customer balances incurred from the interim date to year end.

B. Resend confirmation requests for any significant customer balances remaining at year end.

C. Review supporting documents for new large balances occurring after the interim date, and evaluate any significant changes in balances at year end.

D. Review cash collections subsequent to the interim date and the year end.

Answer (C) is correct.

REQUIRED: The year-end procedure most likely performed after receivables were confirmed at an interim date.

DISCUSSION: If incremental RMMs can be controlled, procedures to cover the remaining period ordinarily include (1) comparing information at the interim date with information at the balance sheet date to identify and investigate unusual amounts (e.g., new large balances) and (2) other analytical procedures or tests of details.

Answer (A) is incorrect. Sampling is normally used in confirming receivables. Answer (B) is incorrect. Second confirmation requests are normally not sent when initial confirmations were returned. Answer (D) is incorrect. Verification of subsequent collections is an alternative procedure used when the response rate to confirmation requests is low.

18. To reduce the risks associated with accepting fax responses to requests for confirmations of accounts receivable, an auditor most likely would

    A. Examine the shipping documents that provide evidence for the existence assertion.

    B. Verify the sources and contents of the faxes in telephone calls to the senders.

    C. Consider the faxes to be nonresponses and evaluate them as unadjusted differences.

    D. Inspect the faxes for forgeries or alterations and consider them to be acceptable if none are noted.

Answer (B) is correct.
    REQUIRED: The procedure to reduce the risk of accepting false confirmations by fax.
    DISCUSSION: Because establishing the source of a fax is often difficult, the auditor should ensure that the confirmations returned by fax are genuine. One way is to verify the sources by following up with telephone calls to the senders.
    Answer (A) is incorrect. The purpose of the confirmation is to test the existence of the receivable by direct communication with the debtor. Answer (C) is incorrect. A fax is considered a valid response if the source can be verified. Answer (D) is incorrect. Faxes may not be signed. Furthermore, the auditor is unlikely to be qualified to recognize forgeries.

19. Cooper, CPA, is auditing the financial statements of a small rural municipality. The receivable balances represent residents' delinquent real estate taxes. Internal control at the municipality is ineffective. To determine the existence of the accounts receivable balances at the balance sheet date, Cooper would most likely

    A. Send positive confirmation requests.

    B. Send negative confirmation requests.

    C. Examine evidence of subsequent cash receipts.

    D. Inspect the internal records such as copies of the tax invoices that were mailed to the residents.

Answer (A) is correct.
    REQUIRED: The best procedure to determine the existence of accounts receivable given ineffective internal control.
    DISCUSSION: The presumption that the auditor will request confirmation of receivables cannot be overcome unless (1) the receivables are not material, (2) external confirmation requests are unlikely to be effective, (3) the assessed risks of material misstatement are low, and (4) other planned substantive procedures apply to the assessed risks. None of these conditions apply. Thus, the auditor should confirm the receivables. However, negative confirmation requests are not used unless the assessed risks of material misstatement are low. Because the municipality's internal control is ineffective, the auditor should send positive confirmation requests.
    Answer (B) is incorrect. Negative confirmation requests do not require a reply if the balance is in agreement. Hence, they decrease the reliability of the evidence. Answer (C) is incorrect. Examining evidence of subsequent cash receipts relates more to the valuation of accounts. Answer (D) is incorrect. Replies to positive confirmation requests constitute independent external evidence that is more persuasive than that derived from inspection of internally generated documents.

20. When an auditor does **not** receive replies to positive requests for year-end accounts receivable confirmations, the auditor most likely would

    A. Inspect the allowance account to verify whether the accounts were subsequently written off.

    B. Increase the assessed risks of material misstatement for the valuation and completeness assertions.

    C. Send the customer a second confirmation request.

    D. Increase the assessed risks of material misstatement for the revenue cycle.

Answer (C) is correct.
    REQUIRED: The auditor action when positive confirmation requests are not returned.
    DISCUSSION: When first requests for positive confirmation are not returned, the auditor should consider second requests. The requests should be authorized by the client and should ask the debtor to respond directly to the auditor.
    Answer (A) is incorrect. It is premature to conclude that the account is uncollectible. Answer (B) is incorrect. The auditor should collect sufficient appropriate evidence to reduce audit risk to an acceptably low level. Answer (D) is incorrect. Increasing the assessed RMMs is premature. The auditor should send second requests or perform alternative procedures.

21. Which of the following procedures would an auditor most likely perform for year-end accounts receivable confirmations when the auditor did **not** receive replies to second requests?

A. Review the cash receipts journal for the month prior to year end.

B. Intensify the study of internal control concerning the revenue cycle.

C. Increase the assessed level of detection risk for the existence assertion.

D. Inspect the shipping records documenting the merchandise sold to the debtors.

Answer (D) is correct.
    REQUIRED: The most appropriate audit procedure when customers fail to reply to second request forms.
    DISCUSSION: When customers fail to answer a second request for a positive confirmation, the accounts may be in dispute, uncollectible, or fictitious. The auditor should then apply alternative procedures (examination of subsequent cash receipts, shipping documents, and other client documentation of existence) to obtain evidence about the validity of nonresponding accounts.
    Answer (A) is incorrect. Previous collections cannot substantiate year-end balances. Answer (B) is incorrect. Nonresponse to a confirmation request is not proof of ineffective controls. Nonresponses do occur and are expected. Answer (C) is incorrect. RMMs are assessed, but detection risk is not. However, the acceptable level of detection risk may be decreased if the assessment of RMMs is increased as a result of nonresponses to confirmation requests.

11.2 Substantive Testing of Cash

22. The best evidence regarding year-end bank balances is documented in the

A. Cutoff bank statement.

B. Bank reconciliations.

C. Interbank transfer schedule.

D. Bank deposit lead schedule.

Answer (B) is correct.
    REQUIRED: The best source of evidence regarding year-end bank balances.
    DISCUSSION: A bank reconciliation verifies the agreement of the bank statements obtained directly from the institution and the amount of cash reported in the financial statements. These amounts should be equal after adjustment for deposits in transit, outstanding checks, bank charges, etc. Thus, a bank reconciliation documents direct (primary) evidence of the year-end bank balance.
    Answer (A) is incorrect. The cutoff bank statement covers a brief period after the end of the period. Answer (C) is incorrect. Only the record of transfer activity between banks is recorded on this schedule. Answer (D) is incorrect. The bank deposit lead schedule contains details supporting the cash amount in the working trial balance, but it is the bank reconciliation that supports the amounts in the lead schedule.

23. Which of the following sets of information does an auditor usually confirm on one form?

A. Accounts payable and purchase commitments.

B. Cash in bank and collateral for loans.

C. Inventory on consignment and contingent liabilities.

D. Accounts receivable and accrued interest receivable.

Answer (B) is correct.
    REQUIRED: The information confirmed on one form.
    DISCUSSION: The AICPA *Standard Form to Confirm Account Balance Information with Financial Institutions* is used by auditors to confirm the deposit balance held by the bank for a client. In addition, this confirmation requests loan information, such as a description of the collateral securing the loan.
    Answer (A) is incorrect. A confirmation of accounts payable balances requests information about purchase commitments. Answer (C) is incorrect. Inventory on consignment is confirmed by a form sent to the consignee holding the inventory, and contingent liabilities are confirmed by a form sent to an official responsible for a financial institution's relationship with the client. Answer (D) is incorrect. A confirmation of accounts receivable does not provide information about interest that is owed to the client.

24. An auditor ordinarily sends a standard confirmation request to all banks with which the client has done business during the year under audit, regardless of the year-end balance. A purpose of this procedure is to

A. Provide the data necessary to prepare a proof of cash.

B. Request that a cutoff bank statement and related checks be sent to the auditor.

C. Detect kiting activities that may otherwise not be discovered.

D. Seek information about other deposit and loan amounts that come to the attention of the institution in the process of completing the confirmation.

Answer (D) is correct.
REQUIRED: The reason confirmations are sent to all banks used by the client.
DISCUSSION: The AICPA *Standard Form to Confirm Account Balance Information with Financial Institutions* is used to confirm specifically listed deposit and loan balances. Nevertheless, the standard confirmation form contains this language: "Although we do not request or expect you to conduct a comprehensive, detailed search of your records, if, during the process of completing this confirmation, additional information about other deposit and loan accounts we may have with you comes to your attention, please include such information below."
Answer (A) is incorrect. The information for a proof of cash is in the month-end bank statement. Answer (B) is incorrect. A cutoff bank statement is for some period subsequent to the balance sheet date. Answer (C) is incorrect. The auditor should compare the returned checks in the cutoff bank statement with those listed as outstanding on the bank reconciliation, as well as prepare a bank transfer schedule for a few days before and after the balance sheet date.

25. The usefulness of the standard bank confirmation request may be limited because the bank employee who completes the form may

A. Not believe that the bank is obligated to verify confidential information to a third party.

B. Sign and return the form without inspecting the accuracy of the client's bank reconciliation.

C. Not have access to the client's cutoff bank statement.

D. Be unaware of all the financial relationships that the bank has with the client.

Answer (D) is correct.
REQUIRED: The reason for the limited usefulness of the standard bank confirmation request.
DISCUSSION: The standard form is designed to substantiate only the information that is stated on the confirmation request. Thus, the auditor should be aware that the standard form is not intended to elicit evidence about the completeness assertion. The individual completing the form may not be aware of all the financial relationships that the bank has with the client.
Answer (A) is incorrect. The client requests the information from the bank, and the bank must provide that information. Answer (B) is incorrect. The bank is not responsible for the accuracy of the client's bank reconciliation. Answer (C) is incorrect. The cutoff bank statement is not necessary to complete the form.

26. An independent auditor asked a client's internal auditor to assist in preparing a standard financial institution confirmation request for a payroll account that had been closed during the year under audit. After the internal auditor prepared the form, the controller signed it and mailed it to the bank. What was the major flaw in this procedure?

A. The internal auditor did not sign the form.

B. The form was mailed by the controller.

C. The form was prepared by the internal auditor.

D. The account was closed, so the balance was zero.

Answer (B) is correct.
REQUIRED: The flaw in the confirmation request to a financial institution regarding a closed payroll account.
DISCUSSION: The AICPA *Standard Form to Confirm Account Balance Information with Financial Institutions* is used for specific deposits and loans. A confirmation is signed (requested) by the client, but it should be sent by the auditor. Thus, the auditor should control confirmation requests and responses. Control means direct communication between the intended recipient and the auditor to minimize possible bias of the results because of interception and alteration of the requests or responses.
Answer (A) is incorrect. The internal auditor need not sign the form. Answer (C) is incorrect. The auditor may request direct assistance from the internal auditors when performing an audit. Answer (D) is incorrect. The auditor must still obtain evidence about the account even though it has been closed.

27. An auditor should test bank transfers for the last part of the audit period and first part of the subsequent period to detect whether

A. The cash receipts journal was held open for a few days after year end.

B. The last checks recorded before year end were actually mailed by year end.

C. Cash balances were overstated because of kiting.

D. Any unusual payments to or receipts from related parties occurred.

Answer (C) is correct.

REQUIRED: The reason for testing bank transfers at year end.

DISCUSSION: Kiting is the recording of a deposit from an interbank transfer in the current period while failing to record the related disbursement until the next period. It is a fraud that exploits the lag (float period) between the deposit of a check in one account and the time it clears the bank on which it is drawn. To detect kiting, the auditor should examine a schedule of bank transfers for a period covering a few days before and after the balance sheet date. For the procedure to be effective, however, the auditor should be assured that all transfers have been identified.

Answer (A) is incorrect. A cutoff bank statement should be examined to determine whether the cash receipts journal was held open for a few days after year end. Answer (B) is incorrect. A cutoff bank statement should be examined to determine whether the last checks recorded before year end were actually mailed by year end. Answer (D) is incorrect. Unusual payments to or receipts from related parties can occur at any time of the year.

Questions 28 and 29 are based on the following information. The following was taken from the bank transfer schedule prepared during the audit of Fox Co.'s financial statements for the year ended December 31, Year 1. Assume all checks are dated and issued on December 30, Year 1.

Check No.	Bank Accounts		Disbursement Date		Receipt Date	
	From	To	Per Books	Per Bank	Per Books	Per Bank
101	National	Federal	Dec. 30	Jan. 4	Dec. 30	Jan. 3
202	County	State	Jan. 3	Jan. 2	Dec. 30	Dec. 31
303	Federal	American	Dec. 31	Jan. 3	Jan. 2	Jan. 2
404	State	Republic	Jan. 2	Jan. 2	Dec. 31	Jan. 2

28. Which of the following checks might indicate kiting?

A. #101 and #303.

B. #202 and #404.

C. #101 and #404.

D. #202 and #303.

Answer (B) is correct.

REQUIRED: The checks that might indicate kiting.

DISCUSSION: Kiting is the recording of a deposit from an interbank transfer in the current period while failing to record the related disbursement until the next period. It is a fraud that exploits the lag (float period) between the deposit of a check in one account and the time it clears the bank on which it is drawn. Checks #202 and #404 may indicate kiting. They were recorded as receipts on the books in the current period. However, they were recorded as disbursements on the books in the next year.

Answer (A) is incorrect. Checks #101 and #303 were recorded as received after year end. Answer (C) is incorrect. Check #101 was recorded as received after year end. Answer (D) is incorrect. Check #303 was recorded as received after year end.

29. Which of the following checks illustrate deposits or transfers in transit at December 31, Year 1?

A. #101 and #202.

B. #101 and #303.

C. #202 and #404.

D. #303 and #404.

Answer (B) is correct.

REQUIRED: The checks indicating deposits or transfers in transit.

DISCUSSION: A deposit or transfer in transit is one recorded in the entity's books as a receipt by the balance sheet date but not recorded as a deposit by the bank until the next period. Check #101 is a deposit or transfer in transit because the check was recorded in the books before the end of the year but not recorded by either bank until January. Check #303 is also a deposit or transfer in transit because the check was deducted from Federal's balance in December but was not added to American's balance until January.

Answer (A) is incorrect. Check #202 was recorded in the books after the balance sheet date. Answer (C) is incorrect. Checks #202 and #404 were recorded in the books after the balance sheet date. Answer (D) is incorrect. Check #404 was recorded in the books after the balance sheet date.

30. Which of the following cash transfers results in a misstatement of cash at December 31, Year 1?

Bank Transfer Schedule

	Disbursement		Receipt	
	Recorded in Books	Paid by Bank	Recorded in Books	Received by Bank
A.	12/31/Yr 1	1/4/Yr 2	12/31/Yr 1	12/31/Yr 1
B.	1/4/Yr 2	1/5/Yr 2	12/31/Yr 1	1/4/Yr 2
C.	12/31/Yr 1	1/5/Yr 2	12/31/Yr 1	1/4/Yr 2
D.	1/4/Yr 2	1/11/Yr 2	1/4/Yr 2	1/4/Yr 2

Answer (B) is correct.
REQUIRED: The interbank cash transfer that indicates an error in cash cutoff.
DISCUSSION: An error in cash cutoff occurs if one half of the transaction is recorded in the current period and one half in the subsequent period. Inspection of the Recorded in Books columns indicates the transfer was recorded as a receipt on 12/31/Yr 1 but not as a disbursement until 1/4/Yr 2. This discrepancy is an error in cutoff called a kite, and it overstates the cash balance.

31. Which of the following procedures would an auditor most likely perform in auditing the statement of cash flows?

A. Compare the amounts included in the statement of cash flows to similar amounts in the prior year's statement of cash flows.

B. Reconcile the cutoff bank statements to verify the accuracy of the year-end bank balances.

C. Vouch all bank transfers for the last week of the year and first week of the subsequent year.

D. Reconcile the amounts included in the statement of cash flows to the other financial statements' balances and amounts.

Answer (D) is correct.
REQUIRED: The procedure useful in auditing the statement of cash flows.
DISCUSSION: The information presented on a statement of cash flows is taken from the income statement and balance sheet. Indeed, a reconciliation of net income and net operating cash flow is required to be presented. Thus, reconciliation of amounts in the statement of cash flows with other financial statements' balances and amounts is an important procedure in the audit of the statement of cash flows.
Answer (A) is incorrect. Analytical procedures for cash are not effective. Cash is a managed account. Answer (B) is incorrect. Reconciling the cutoff bank statements to verify the accuracy of year-end bank balances is an appropriate procedure to audit the cash account but not necessarily the statement of cash flows. Answer (C) is incorrect. Vouching all bank transfers for the last week of the year and the first week of the subsequent year is effective for detecting cutoff misstatements, such as those arising from kiting, but not for auditing the statement of cash flows.

Use the additional questions in Gleim **CPA Test Prep** to create Practice Exams that emulate Prometric!

11.3 PRACTICE TASK-BASED SIMULATIONS

DIRECTIONS

Note: If you believe you have encountered a software malfunction, report it to the test center staff immediately.

Navigation

To navigate from task to task, use the controls at the bottom of the screen. Click on the **Next** button to advance to the next task, or the **Previous** button to go to the previous task. To go directly to any task, click on its number.

If you would like a reminder to revisit a task, or want to indicate that you are finished with it, click on the reminder flag below the task number. To clear the flag, click on it again. Reminder flags are for your use only – they do not contribute to your score.

Tabs

In this part of the examination, you will be asked to complete various tasks. Every task has one or more **Work Tabs**. Some tasks have one or more **Information Tabs**, others may have none. Every task has a **Help** tab.

If a task has **Information Tabs**, you may use the information in them to complete your responses in the **Work Tabs**.

                    Work tab   **Information tab**   **Help tab**

Work Tabs:
- **Work Tabs** are identified with a pencil icon. This is where your responses are expected.
- Each task has one or more **Work Tabs**.
- **Work Tabs** contain directions for completing the task – be sure to read these directions carefully.
- The **Work Tab** name in the example above is for illustration only – yours will differ.
- You must complete all of the **Work Tabs** in each task to receive full credit.

Information Tabs:
- The Authoritative Literature will be provided in all tasks in the AUD, FAR, and REG sections for your reference.
- Your simulation may have one or more additional **Information Tabs**. Like the Authoritative Literature tabs, **Information Tabs** do not have a pencil icon.
- If your task has additional **Information Tabs**, go through each to familiarize yourself with the task content.

Help Tab:
- The **Help Tab** provides assistance with the exam software that is used in this task. For example, if the task is to compose a memorandum, **Help** will provide information about the word processor.

The Toolbar

The toolbar at the top of the screen shows the amount of time remaining for you to complete the tasks. In addition, the following tools are available. Note that only the **Exit** button is displayed when Directions are visible - the others will appear when you begin the tasks.

Click on these buttons to split or unsplit the screen. You can split the screen vertically or horizontally.

Click on this button to display the calculator; click on it again to hide the calculator. To move the calculator, click on the calculator title bar and drag the calculator to the desired location.

Click on this button to use the spreadsheet; click on it again to hide the spreadsheet. To move the spreadsheet, click on the the spreadsheet title bar and drag the spreadsheet to the desired location.

Click on this button to go on to the next part of the examination. You must complete all of the tasks to receive full credit. Once you click on **Exit** and confirm the action, you will NOT be able to return to this testlet.

| | Cutoff | Authoritative Literature | Help |

During the course of the Year 2 audit of the Chester Co., the auditor discovered potential cutoff problems that may or may not require adjusting journal entries. For each of the potential cutoff problems indicated below, complete the required journal entries.

To prepare each entry,

- Select from the list provided the appropriate account name. If no entry is needed, select "No entry required." An account may be used once or not at all for each entry.
- Enter the corresponding debit or credit amount in the appropriate column.
- Round all amounts to the nearest dollar.
- All rows may not be required to complete each entry.

1. The company shipped merchandise held in inventory at $75,000 FOB destination on December 23, Year 2, and recorded the sale and relief of inventory on that date. The customer received the merchandise on December 31, Year 2. The merchandise has a profit margin of 10%. Record the necessary Year 2 adjustments, if any.

Account Name	Debit	Credit

2. The company shipped merchandise held in inventory at $45,000 to a consignee on December 24, Year 2, and recorded the sale and the relief of inventory on that date. The consignee had not sold the merchandise as of January 5, Year 3. The merchandise has a profit margin of 10%. Record the necessary Year 2 adjustments, if any.

Account Name	Debit	Credit

Account Names Choices

- Accounts payable
- Accounts receivable
- Accrued liabilities
- Accumulated depreciation
- Cash
- Cost of goods sold
- Income tax expense
- Interest expense
- Inventory
- Operating expenses
- Other assets
- Other income
- Property and equipment
- Sales
- Stockholders' equity
- No entry required

| Bank Reconciliation | Authoritative Literature | Help |

You are collecting evidence in your audit of a client's cash receipts and cash disbursements. To properly test management's assertions about the balances in the financial statements, you are preparing to perform substantive testing of the cash cycle.

The following is a bank reconciliation prepared by your client, who has a September 30 year end:

General Company
Bank Reconciliation
1st National Bank of U.S. Bank Account
September 30, Year 1

Balance per bank			$28,375
Deposits in transit			
9/29/Year 1		$4,500	
9/30/Year 1		1,525	6,025
			34,400
Outstanding checks			
# 988	8/31/Year 1	2,200	
#1281	9/26/Year 1	675	
#1285	9/27/Year 1	850	
#1289	9/29/Year 1	2,500	
#1292	9/30/Year 1	7,225	(13,450)
			20,950
Customer note collected by bank			(3,000)
Error: Check #1282, written on 9/26/Year 1			
for $270, was erroneously charged by bank			
as $720; bank was notified on 10/2/Year 1			450
Balance per books			$18,400

Assume the following:

- The client prepared the bank reconciliation on 10/2/Year 1.
- The bank reconciliation is mathematically accurate.
- The auditor received a cutoff bank statement dated 10/7/Year 1 directly from the bank on 10/11/Year 1.
- The 9/30/Year 1 deposit in transit, outstanding checks #1281, #1285, #1289, and #1292, and the correction of the error regarding check #1282 appeared on the cutoff bank statement.
- The auditor assessed the risk of material misstatement for cash as high.

-- Continued on next page --

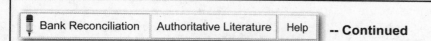

| Bank Reconciliation | Authoritative Literature | Help | -- **Continued** |

Based on the bank reconciliation, select from the list provided one or more procedures (as indicated) for each of the following items that the auditor most likely should perform to gather sufficient, competent, and relevant evidence. Each choice may be used once, more than once, or not at all.

Item	Answer(s)				
1. Balance per bank – **select 2 procedures**					
2. Deposits in transit – **select 5 procedures**					
3. Outstanding checks – **select 5 procedures**					
4. Customer note collected by bank – **select 1 procedure**					
5. Error – **select 2 procedures**					
6. Balance per books – **select 1 procedure**					

Choices
A) Trace to cash receipts journal.
B) Trace to cash disbursements journal.
C) Compare with 9/30/Year 1 general ledger.
D) Confirm directly with bank.
E) Inspect bank credit memo.
F) Inspect bank debit memo.
G) Ascertain reason for unusual delay.
H) Inspect supporting documents for reconciling item not appearing on cutoff statement.
I) Trace items on the bank reconciliation to cutoff statement.
J) Trace items on the cutoff statement to bank reconciliation.

| Research | Authoritative Literature | Help |

Johnson, CPA, is determining whether the accounts receivable balance of a nonissuer client is accurate. He has asked you to evaluate whether external confirmations of accounts receivable balances are necessary for this audit. Which section of the generally accepted auditing standards best describes whether Johnson is required to use external confirmation procedures?

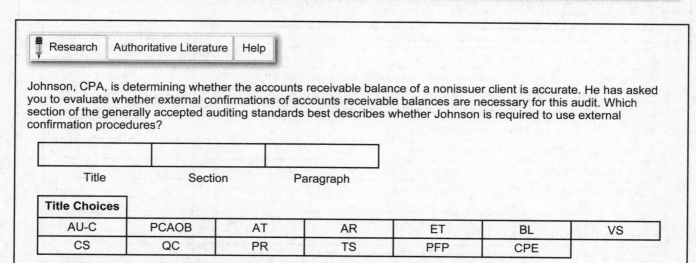

Title	Section	Paragraph

Title Choices						
AU-C	PCAOB	AT	AR	ET	BL	VS
CS	QC	PR	TS	PFP	CPE	

| Audit Procedures and Management Assertions | Authoritative Literature | Help |

Select from the list provided the assertion that is most likely tested by each of the audit procedures. Each choice may be used once, more than once, or not at all.

Audit Procedures	Answer
1. The auditor reviewed delinquent customers' credit ratings.	
2. The auditor confirmed accounts receivable.	
3. The auditor tested sales transactions at year end to determine that they were recorded in the proper period.	
4. The auditor accounted for the numerical sequence of sales orders.	
5. The auditor vouched the recorded accounts receivable to shipping documents.	
6. The auditor determined that accounts receivable was presented on the balance sheet as a current asset.	
7. The auditor aged the accounts receivable.	
8. The auditor inquired of management about the possibility that the receivables had been sold or factored.	
9. The auditor reconciled the total receivables from the subsidiary ledger to the balance in the general ledger.	
10. The auditor determined that a note was included describing any sales to related parties.	

Assertion Choices

A) Completeness

B) Rights and obligations

C) Valuation and allocation

D) Existence

E) Classification and understandability

F) Cutoff

| Bank Confirmation | Authoritative Literature | Help |

For each of the following items, indicate by checking the appropriate box whether the information is typically included on the AICPA *Standard Form to Confirm Account Balance Information with Financial Institutions* (Bank Confirmation) sent by the auditor to all the banks that a client has done business with during the year.

Items of Information	Included	Not Included
1. A place for the signature of the auditor		
2. The following statement: "Please use the enclosed envelope to return the form directly to the auditor."		
3. An area on the form for the bank to list any outstanding checks		
4. An area on the form for a deposit balance to be placed		
5. A place for the signature of the bank official		
6. An area on the form to describe any collateral for loans		
7. A statement on the form that requests the bank to be alert for any fraudulent transactions		
8. The following statement: "Although we do not request or expect you to conduct a comprehensive, detailed search . . ."		
9. An area on the form for the bank to note exceptions or comments		
10. A statement on the form that requests the bank to keep the information confidential		

Unofficial Answers

1. Cutoff (5 Gradable Items)

1. No entry required.

2.

Inventory	$45,000	
Cost of goods sold		$45,000
Sales	$50,000	
Accounts receivable ($45,000 ÷ 0.9 = $50,000)		$50,000

2. Bank Reconciliation (16 Gradable Items)

1. D) Confirm directly with bank, and I) Trace items on the bank reconciliation to cutoff statement. The balance per bank should be confirmed directly with the bank using a "Standard Form to Confirm Account Balance Information with Financial Institutions." Moreover, the cutoff bank statement gives the balance per bank at September 30, Year 1.

2. A) Trace to cash receipts journal, G) Ascertain reason for unusual delay, H) Inspect supporting documents for reconciling item not appearing on cutoff statement, I) Trace items on the bank reconciliation to cutoff statement, and J) Trace items on the cutoff statement to bank reconciliation. Each deposit should be supported by an entry in the cash receipts journal. The 9/29/Year 1 deposit in transit should be investigated to determine the reason for the delay. It should have been reported on the cutoff bank statement. The deposits in transit on the bank reconciliation should be compared with items in the cutoff bank statement to test for their existence. In addition, a test should be performed in the opposite direction. The deposits in transit on the cutoff bank statement should be compared with items in the bank reconciliation to test the completeness of the deposits in transit.

3. B) Trace to cash disbursements journal, G) Ascertain reason for unusual delay, H) Inspect supporting documents for reconciling item not appearing on cutoff statement, I) Trace items on the bank reconciliation to cutoff statement, and J) Trace items on the cutoff statement to bank reconciliation. Each check should be supported by an entry in the cash disbursements journal. Check #988 should be investigated to determine the reason for its delay in clearing and to determine why it did not appear on the cutoff bank statement. Outstanding checks on the bank reconciliation should be compared with the cutoff bank statement to test the existence of the outstanding checks. In addition, a test should be performed in the opposite direction. Outstanding checks on the cutoff bank statement should be compared with the bank reconciliation to test for the completeness of the listed outstanding checks.

4. E) Inspect bank credit memo. The problem involves reconciling the balance per bank to the balance per books. The proceeds of the customer note collected by the bank increased the balance per bank, so the amount of the note must be subtracted to arrive at the balance per books. The amount collected on the note can be verified by inspecting the bank's credit memo. The bank credited the customer's account (a liability to the bank) when it collected the proceeds of the note.

5. E) Inspect bank credit memo, and I) Trace items on the bank reconciliation to cutoff statement. The credit memo issued in October should be inspected and the credit given to the customer for $450 should be compared with the cutoff bank statement.

6. C) Compare to 9/30/Year 1 general ledger. The balance per books should be compared with the 9/30/Year 1 cash balance in the general ledger.

3. Research (1 Gradable Item)

Answer: 330.20

AU-C Section 330 -- *Performing Audit Procedures in Response to Assessed Risks and Evaluating the Audit Evidence*

.20 The auditor should use external confirmation procedures for accounts receivable, except when one or more of the following is applicable:

   a.   The overall account balance is immaterial.

   b.   External confirmation procedures for accounts receivable would be ineffective.

   c.   The auditor's assessed level of risk of material misstatement at the relevant assertion level is low, and the other planned substantive procedures address the assessed risk. In many situations, the use of external confirmation procedures for accounts receivable and the performance of other substantive procedures are necessary to reduce the assessed risk of material misstatement to an acceptably low level.

4. Audit Procedures and Management Assertions (10 Gradable Items)

1. <u>C) Valuation and allocation.</u> Considering delinquent accounts and credit ratings relates to the valuation of accounts receivable.

2. <u>D) Existence.</u> Confirmation is a primary test of existence.

3. <u>F) Cutoff.</u> Evaluating transactions for the recording in the proper accounting period at year end tests cutoff.

4. <u>A) Completeness.</u> Accounting for all documents in a sequence is a test of completeness.

5. <u>D) Existence.</u> Vouching is a primary test of existence.

6. <u>E) Classification and understandability.</u> Considering the presentation of items on the balance sheet is a test of classification.

7. <u>C) Valuation and allocation.</u> Aging of accounts receivable to consider collectibility relates to the valuation assertion.

8. <u>B) Rights and obligations.</u> The possibility of factoring receivables relates to ownership (rights) issues.

9. <u>A) Completeness.</u> Reconciling the subsidiary ledger with the general ledger helps determine if transactions failed to be recorded.

10. <u>E) Classification and understandability.</u> Disclosures in notes to the financial statements relate to the understandability assertion.

5. Bank Confirmation (10 Gradable Items)

1. <u>Not included</u> on confirmation.
2. <u>Included</u> on confirmation.
3. <u>Not included</u> on confirmation.
4. <u>Included</u> on confirmation.
5. <u>Included</u> on confirmation.
6. <u>Included</u> on confirmation.
7. <u>Not included</u> on confirmation.
8. <u>Included</u> on confirmation.
9. <u>Included</u> on confirmation.
10. <u>Not included</u> on confirmation.

Gleim Simulation Grading

Task	Correct Responses		Gradable Items		Score per Task
1	_____	÷	5	=	_____
2	_____	÷	16	=	_____
3 (Research)	_____	÷	1	=	_____
4	_____	÷	10	=	_____
5	_____	÷	10	=	_____

	Total of Scores per Task	_____
÷	Total Number of Tasks	5
	Total Score	_____ %

Use **CPA Gleim Online** and **Simulation Wizard** to practice more task-based simulations in a realistic environment.

STUDY UNIT TWELVE
EVIDENCE --
THE PURCHASES-PAYABLES-INVENTORY CYCLE

(6 pages of outline)

The primary purpose of the collection of evidence is to test relevant assertions about the transaction classes, balances, and disclosures in the financial statements. The auditor uses these assertions as a basis for assessing risks of material misstatement (RMMs) and designing and performing further audit procedures. In general, most testing in the inventory-acquisition process is applied to accounts payable and inventory, with a focus on the likelihood of understatement of accounts payable and overstatement of inventory. Evidence about the debit in the payables transaction (i.e., inventory in a perpetual system and purchases in a periodic system) is gathered when the credit (accounts payable) is tested. The interrelationship is apparent in the opposite direction as well. As the debit is tested, evidence about the credit also is produced. The objective of this study unit is to develop a comprehensive audit plan for the accounts payable and inventory accounts. This plan includes the customary procedures assuming no unusual risks. Some of the questions at the end of this study unit concern special risks that require modification of the audit plan. The candidate should consider those questions and problems and practice the modification of programs to address special risks.

The approach to audit plan development described in the outlines may be used in answering CPA exam questions. Application of the AICPA's assertions model (CAVE CROC is the memory aid for the assertions; see Study Unit 1, Subunit 2) ensures that all assertions are tested. However, other formats for presentation of the procedures are acceptable, for example, application of the PCAOB's assertions model (also addressed in Study Unit 1, Subunit 2).

12.1 SUBSTANTIVE TESTING OF ACCOUNTS PAYABLE AND PURCHASES

1. Testing assertions about accounts payable provides evidence about **purchases** and ultimately **cost of goods sold**. Purchases obviously result in ending inventory, but because inventory is a significant item on the balance sheet, a separate audit plan is typically developed for the account. An audit plan for inventory follows in Subunit 12.2.

    a. Candidates should understand the interrelationship of these accounts and the overlap of the audit procedures.

2. **Accounts payable**, sometimes termed trade payables, represent the most significant current liability of most firms.

3.   **Testing Relevant Assertions.** The following is a standard audit plan for accounts payable and purchases that tests relevant assertions (recall CAVE CROC from Study Unit 1):

   a.   **Completeness.** Do the balances contain all transactions for the period? (This is typically the major detection risk for the auditor in testing payables.)

   1)   **Reconcile** the accounts payable ledger with the general ledger control account. Compare the total recorded amounts in the subsidiary ledger with the amount recorded in the general ledger.

   2)   **Analytical procedures.** The auditor should use appropriate sources of data (e.g., prior-period financial data, budgets prepared by management at the beginning of the period, nonfinancial information, industry data, and interrelationships) to form expectations with which to compare management's presentations. Ratios may be calculated and used (e.g., the **accounts payable turnover ratio**). Unexpected findings should be investigated.

   3)   **Trace subsequent payments** to recorded payables. A primary test is to match the payments (checks) issued after year end with the related payables. Checks should be issued only for recorded payables. Any checks that cannot be matched are likely indications of **unrecorded liabilities**.

   a)   Management may be motivated to delay recording of liabilities to improve the current ratio. However, unrecorded accounts payable must still be paid, and financial statements that fail to report all liabilities at year end are misstated.

   4)   **Search for unvouchered payables.** The accounts payable function prepares and records a voucher (with a debit to purchases and a credit to accounts payable) when all the supporting documentation is assembled. The auditor should search the suspense files for unmatched documents to determine whether relevant documents have been lost, misplaced, or misfiled.

   a)   A **suspense file** contains transactions, the classification and treatment of which are in doubt, for example, because of missing documents.

   b)   For example, a requisition, receiving report, and invoice may be held by the accounts payable department, but no voucher is prepared or entry made if the purchase order has not been matched with the other documents. This situation results in an unrecorded liability.

   b.   **Accuracy.** Have the amounts been recorded appropriately?

   1)   Obtain a management **representation letter** with assertions related to purchases and payables.

   2)   Compare the general ledger balances to the balances on the financial statements.

   c.   **Valuation and allocation.** Are accounts payable measured in accordance with the applicable reporting framework? U.S. GAAP require that debts be stated at the amount necessary to satisfy the obligation.

   1)   Detection risk for this assertion is reduced if the other assertions are tested in accordance with GAAS. The valuation or allocation assertion is interrelated with those for **existence and completeness**.

   d.   **Existence.** Do the recorded accounts payable represent valid liabilities at the balance sheet date?

   1)   **Confirmation** is not a generally accepted auditing procedure because it is not likely to disclose unrecorded payables. Normally, the auditor can become satisfied as to the existence of recorded payables using evidence available directly from the client.

        a)   If confirmation is undertaken, small and zero balances should be sampled as well as larger balances. The auditor should use the **activity in the account** as a basis for selection. That is, if orders are placed with a vendor on a consistent basis, a confirmation should be sent to that vendor regardless of the recorded balance due at year end.

        b)   The **blank form of positive confirmations** should be used. It requests that the balance due be provided by the creditor (e.g., the vendor).

e.   **Cutoff.** Have transactions been recorded in the proper period?

    1)   **Purchases cutoff test.** Determine that all goods for which title has passed to the client at year end are recorded in inventory and accounts payable.

        a)   Goods shipped **FOB shipping point** by the vendor should be recorded in the period of shipment to the client. Thus, receipts for several days after year end should be evaluated to determine whether the goods should be recorded in the current year.

        b)   Goods shipped **FOB destination** by the vendor should be recorded in the period received by the client. Receiving documents are traced to the accounting records by the auditor for several days prior to and after year end to determine proper recognition of inventory and accounts payable.

    2)   **Cash disbursements cutoff test.** Test the recording of cash disbursements and the associated reduction in accounts payable. Inspecting the last check written and tracing it to the accounts payable subsidiary ledger will provide evidence of proper recording.

f.   **Rights and obligations.** Does the balance of accounts payable reflect the liability of this entity? Because the risk is relatively low that management would report liabilities of others, the procedures testing this assertion are not as consequential as those for other assertions.

    1)   **Inquiries.** Obtain management representations about the nature of the recorded payables.

g.   **Occurrence.** Did purchases occur?

    1)   **Vouch recorded payables to documentation.** A sample of recorded payables should be reconciled with documentary support (e.g., requisitions, purchase orders, receiving reports, and approved invoices).

h.   **Classification and understandability.** Are (1) purchases and payables appropriately described and (2) disclosures fairly and clearly expressed?

    1)   **Inspect the financial statements.** Accounts payable should be presented as a current liability on the balance sheet. Purchases should be used in the determination of cost of sales for the income statement.

    2)   **Evaluate note disclosures.** Any unusual significant transactions or events should be described by management in the notes (e.g., significant accounts payable to related parties).

Stop and review! You have completed the outline for this subunit. Study multiple-choice questions 1 through 13 beginning on page 385.

Background

Recent auditing standards emphasize the importance of understanding clients and their businesses. Ironically, this has long been an issue with auditing inventory. Auditors have been frequently fooled by their clients about the amount or measurement of inventory because clients have more knowledge than the auditor. This is particularly true of certain types of inventory, for example, bulk or liquid inventory, high-tech products, or manufactured parts. Current auditing standards require some physical contact (observe and test count) with the inventory in an attempt to mitigate the risks associated with existence of inventory, but auditors still face significant risks.

12.2 SUBSTANTIVE TESTING OF INVENTORY

1. The primary purpose of the collection of evidence for inventory is to test management's assertions about the presentation of the balance and disclosures in the financial statements.

2. **Inventory** consists of the goods held for resale by the client and is presented as a current asset on the balance sheet.

3. **Testing Relevant Assertions.** The following is a standard audit plan that tests relevant assertions (CAVE CROC) about the inventory balance:

    a. **Completeness.** Does the inventory balance contain all inventory owned by the entity at year end?

        1) **Analytical procedures.** The calculation of amounts and ratios and their comparison with expectations can identify unusual findings indicative of misstatements.

            a) The **inventory turnover ratio** (cost of sales ÷ average or ending inventory) should be compared with that of the prior period and industry averages.

            b) **Vertical analysis** (e.g., the percentage of inventory to total assets), using industry information, can identify unusual conditions.

            c) Information from the client's previously prepared **budgets** can provide the basis for expectations.

            d) **Nonfinancial information** (e.g., the volume, in boxes or pounds) may provide expectations about the flow of inventory as well as sales and receivables.

    b. **Accuracy.** Have the amounts been recorded appropriately?

        1) Compare the general ledger balance to the balance on the financial statements.

    c. **Valuation and allocation.** Is inventory recorded at **lower of cost or market**?

        1) **Compare recorded costs with current cost to replace the goods.** Current vendor price lists should be compared with recorded inventory costs to determine that current prices are not less than recorded costs.

        2) **Calculate the turnover ratio.** An applicable analytical procedure is to calculate the inventory turnover ratio for the individual inventory items. Excessive inventory results in small turnover ratios and provides evidence of potentially obsolete items.

        3) **Test costs of manufactured items.** Manufactured goods should be costed to include direct materials, direct labor, and an allocation of overhead. The overhead allocation rate should be tested for reasonableness.

d. **Existence.** Does the inventory exist at a given date?

1) **Observation** of inventories is generally required. The auditor should observe and make test counts but is not responsible for taking inventory.

a) If the entity uses the **periodic inventory method**, test counts should be made at or very close to year end because the counted inventory is used to calculate cost of sales.

b) If the entity uses the **perpetual inventory method**, counts may be made at interim dates if records are well kept. If the RMMs are high, inventory counts should be done at year end.

i) The client may use methods, including **statistical sampling**, that are sufficiently reliable to make an annual count of all items unnecessary. The auditor must be assured these methods are reasonable and statistically valid and have been properly applied. Observations and test counts must still be performed.

c) Observations should encompass all **significant inventory locations**.

i) The auditor should observe and make test counts even if inventory is taken by **management specialists** (i.e., businesses that perform inventory counts as their service).

2) The client's plan for taking inventory should make effective use of, and exercise control over, **prenumbered inventory tags** and **summary sheets**.

a) The plan should include provisions for handling receipts and shipments during the count.

b) Goods not owned by the client, such as goods held on consignment, should be separated.

c) Appropriate instructions and supervision should be given to employees conducting the count.

3) **Performing tests of the count** should include the following:

a) Observing employees following the plan

b) Assuring that all items are tagged

c) Evaluating control over the movement of inventory before, during, and after the count

d) Observing employees making counts and recording amounts on tags

e) Determining that tags and inventory summary sheets are controlled

f) Making test counts, comparing test counts with amounts recorded on the tags and summary sheets, and reconciling amounts with records

g) Being alert for empty boxes, empty squares (i.e., boxes stacked to suggest the block of boxes is solid when the middle does not contain boxes), and inventory defects (e.g., damaged or dirty items)

h) Establishing a cutoff by documenting the last receiving report and shipping document

4) The performance of procedures should be **documented**.

      5) The auditor should confirm or investigate inventories held by **public warehouses** or other third parties.

          a) The auditor ordinarily obtains confirmation by direct communication with the custodian. When a significant portion of current or total assets is held in a public warehouse, the auditor should consider testing the client's procedures by (1) evaluating the warehouser, (2) obtaining an independent accountant's report on the warehouser's internal control, (3) visiting the warehouse and observing physical counts, and (4) investigating the use of warehouse receipts (e.g., whether they are being used for collateral). The auditor should confirm with lenders the details of any pledged receipts.

e. **Cutoff.** Have transactions been recorded in the proper period?

    1) **Purchases and sales cutoff tests**. Test recording of transactions subject to the terms (FOB shipping point or FOB receiving point) of both purchase and sale of inventory.

f. **Rights and obligations.** Does the entity own the inventory reported on the balance sheet?

    1) **Vouch recorded purchases to documentation.** Vouch a sample of recorded inventory items to payment records. Payment vouchers for inventory should have supporting documentation (e.g., requisition, purchase order, receiving report, and vendor invoice) and canceled checks (if payment has been made).

    2) **Consider the industry or client practices for consigned goods.** The nature of the client or industry suggests the possibility of consignment transactions (e.g., the client has held or shipped consigned goods in the past). The auditor should review the client's correspondence, evaluate sales and receivables records, and consider the results of vouching purchases to detect unrecognized consignment activity.

        a) For example, if the client has inappropriately recorded consignment shipments as sales, the auditor most likely will find a pattern of large sales on account and many small, periodic cash receipts for the receivables.

g. **Occurrence.** Did the inventory transactions occur?

    1) Vouch a sample of recorded purchases to documentation.
    2) Vouch a sample of recorded cost of sales to documentation.

h. **Classification and understandability.** Are inventories properly displayed as current assets, and has cost of sales been properly reflected in the income statement? Have adequate disclosures been made concerning inventory measurement, cost flow assumptions, and significant transactions, such as pledging of inventory?

    1) **Read financial statements.** The auditor should read the financial statements to determine that accounts are properly reflected and notes adequately informative.

    2) **Inquire of management.** The auditor should inquire of management about (a) consigned goods, (b) major purchase commitments, (c) pledging of inventory, and (d) other significant transactions or events.

    3) Obtain a **management representation letter** that includes assertions relating to inventory and cost of sales.

Stop and review! You have completed the outline for this subunit. Study multiple-choice questions 14 through 24 beginning on page 389.

QUESTIONS

12.1 Substantive Testing of Accounts Payable and Purchases

1. Which of the following is a substantive procedure that an auditor most likely would perform to verify the existence and valuation assertions about recorded accounts payable?

A. Investigating the open purchase order file to ascertain that prenumbered purchase orders are used and accounted for.

B. Receiving the client's mail, unopened, for a reasonable period of time after year end to search for unrecorded vendor's invoices.

C. Vouching selected entries in the accounts payable subsidiary ledger to purchase orders and receiving reports.

D. Confirming accounts payable balances with known suppliers who have zero balances.

Answer (C) is correct.
  REQUIRED: The substantive procedure for the existence and valuation assertions about recorded accounts payable.
  DISCUSSION: Vouching a sample of recorded accounts payable to purchase orders and receiving reports provides evidence that the obligations exist at a given date. The purchase orders evidence the initiation of the transactions, and the receiving reports indicate that goods were received and that liabilities were thereby incurred. Thus, these documents provide evidence that amounts are owed to others, that the transactions occurred, and that the liabilities have been included at appropriate amounts.
  Answer (A) is incorrect. Ascertaining that prenumbered documents are used and accounted for relates most directly to the completeness assertion. Answer (B) is incorrect. Searching for unrecorded liabilities relates most directly to completeness. Answer (D) is incorrect. Confirming payables with known suppliers having zero balances is a procedure for detecting unrecorded liabilities. Thus, it relates most directly to completeness.

2. To determine whether accounts payable are complete, an auditor performs a test to verify that all merchandise received is recorded. The population of documents for this test consists of all

A. Payment vouchers.

B. Receiving reports.

C. Purchase requisitions.

D. Vendors' invoices.

Answer (B) is correct.
  REQUIRED: The population of documents for a test to verify that all merchandise received is recorded.
  DISCUSSION: The population to be tested consists of receiving reports. An accounts payable record should be available for each receiving report.
  Answer (A) is incorrect. A payment voucher is prepared for each account payable. A payment voucher would not exist for an unrecorded payable. Answer (C) is incorrect. The goods requisitioned may not have been ordered. If ordered, they may not have been received. Hence, a payable may not exist for each requisition. Answer (D) is incorrect. A vendor's invoice does not provide evidence that the goods have been received and a liability incurred. Thus, a payable need not exist for every vendor's invoice.

3. When performing a substantive test of a random sample of cash disbursements, an auditor is supplied with a photocopy of vendor invoices supporting the disbursements for one particular vendor rather than the original invoices. The auditor is told that the vendor's original invoices have been misplaced. What should the auditor do in response to this situation?

A. Increase randomly the number of items in the substantive test to increase the reliance that may be placed on the overall test.

B. Reevaluate the risk of fraud and design alternate tests for the related transactions.

C. Increase testing by agreeing more of the payments to this particular vendor to the photocopies of its invoices.

D. Count the missing original documents as misstatements, and project the total amount of the error based on the size of the population and the dollar amount of the errors.

Answer (B) is correct.
  REQUIRED: The auditor's response to finding a photocopy of an invoice in support of a disbursement.
  DISCUSSION: Several issues should cause the auditor to be suspicious. First, how could the client lose the original? Second, how did the client obtain a photocopy if the original was lost? Finally, and most importantly, photocopies are much less credible given the ease with which they can be altered. Thus, the auditor should reevaluate the risk of fraud.
  Answer (A) is incorrect. The auditor should resolve this issue. The change in audit plan depends on the disposition of this transaction. Answer (C) is incorrect. More tests of this vendor may be in order, but the auditor should insist on obtaining originals of the documents. Answer (D) is incorrect. This may or may not be a misstatement. However, the transaction could be fraudulent with much broader implications.

4. An auditor performs a test to determine whether all merchandise for which the client was billed was received. The population for this test consists of all

A. Merchandise received.

B. Vendors' invoices.

C. Canceled checks.

D. Receiving reports.

Answer (B) is correct.
REQUIRED: The population for a test to determine whether all merchandise for which the client was billed was received.
DISCUSSION: Vendors' invoices are the billing documents received by the client. They describe the items purchased, the amounts due, and the payment terms. The auditor should trace these invoices to the related receiving reports.
Answer (A) is incorrect. Testing merchandise received will not detect merchandise billed but not received. Answer (C) is incorrect. Tracing canceled checks to the related receiving reports tests whether goods paid for, not goods billed, were received. Answer (D) is incorrect. Tracing receiving reports to vendors' invoices tests whether all goods received were billed.

5. In auditing accounts payable, an auditor's procedures most likely will focus primarily on the relevant assertion about

A. Existence.

B. Classification and understandability.

C. Completeness.

D. Valuation and allocation.

Answer (C) is correct.
REQUIRED: The assertion that is the focus of an audit of accounts payable.
DISCUSSION: The primary audit risk for accounts payable is understatement of the liability. Thus, the auditor will most likely focus on the completeness assertion.
Answer (A) is incorrect. The existence assertion concerns whether liabilities exist at a given date. The audit risk for accounts payable is not great for that assertion. Answer (B) is incorrect. The risk of inappropriate classification and understandability on the financial statements is not as great as the risk that some items are not included. Answer (D) is incorrect. The risk that accounts payable are not measured in accordance with the applicable reporting framework is lower than the risk that the balance may not be complete.

6. Which of the following procedures would an auditor most likely perform in searching for unrecorded liabilities?

A. Trace a sample of accounts payable entries recorded just before year end to the unmatched receiving report file.

B. Compare a sample of purchase orders issued just after year end with the year-end accounts payable trial balance.

C. Vouch a sample of cash disbursements recorded just after year end to receiving reports and vendor invoices.

D. Scan the cash disbursements entries recorded just before year end for indications of unusual transactions.

Answer (C) is correct.
REQUIRED: The procedure most likely to detect unrecorded liabilities.
DISCUSSION: The greatest risk in the audit of payables is that unrecorded liabilities exist. Omission of an entry to record a payable is a fraud or error that is more difficult to detect than an inaccurate or false entry. The search for unrecorded payables should include (1) examining cash disbursements made after the balance sheet date and comparing them with the accounts payable trial balance, (2) sending confirmations to vendors with small and zero balances, and (3) reconciling payable balances with vendors' documentation.
Answer (A) is incorrect. Sampling from known accounts payable provides little evidence of unrecorded liabilities. Answer (B) is incorrect. A sample of purchase orders issued after year end is expected to be recorded in the subsequent year, not in the current year. Answer (D) is incorrect. Payments in the current year represent satisfied liabilities, not unrecorded liabilities.

7. An auditor's purpose in reviewing the renewal of a note payable shortly after the balance sheet date most likely is to obtain evidence concerning relevant assertions about

A. Existence.

B. Classification and understandability.

C. Completeness.

D. Valuation and allocation.

Answer (B) is correct.
REQUIRED: The auditor's purpose in reviewing the renewal of a note payable shortly after year end.
DISCUSSION: Events such as the renewal of the note payable do not require adjustment of the financial statements but may require disclosure. Accordingly, the auditor should determine that the renewal had essentially the same terms and conditions as the recorded debt at year end. A significant change may affect the classification of notes payable (e.g., as current or noncurrent), the understandability of the statements, and the required disclosures.

8. Which of the following procedures would an auditor **least** likely perform before the balance sheet date?

    A. Confirmation of accounts payable.

    B. Observation of merchandise inventory.

    C. Assessment of the risks of material misstatement.

    D. Identification of related parties.

Answer (A) is correct.
    REQUIRED: The audit procedure least likely to be performed prior to the balance sheet date.
    DISCUSSION: The most important assertion about accounts payable is completeness, which is best tested at year end. For example, the auditor may examine subsequent cash payments to determine whether the related payables are not recorded. Although confirmation is not a required auditing procedure, it may be useful in detecting unrecorded payables if the auditor's sample includes vendors for which the risk of understatement is high, e.g., regular vendors with zero or low recorded balances.
    Answer (B) is incorrect. Observation of inventory at an interim date is more likely when controls are effective. It is also more likely when the year-end balances of the particular transaction classes or account balances that might be selected for interim examination are reasonably predictable with respect to amount, relative significance, and composition. In these circumstances, substantive analytical procedures performed with regard to the remaining period are more likely to be effective. Answer (C) is incorrect. The auditor may assess risks prior to year end. Answer (D) is incorrect. The auditor may identify related parties prior to year end.

9. When using confirmations to provide evidence about the completeness assertion for accounts payable, the appropriate population most likely is

    A. Vendors with whom the entity has previously done business.

    B. Amounts recorded in the accounts payable subsidiary ledger.

    C. Payees of checks drawn in the month after the year end.

    D. Invoices filed in the entity's open invoice file.

Answer (A) is correct.
    REQUIRED: The appropriate population when confirmations of accounts payable are used to test the completeness assertion.
    DISCUSSION: When sending confirmations for accounts payable, the population of accounts should include small and zero balances as well as large balances. The auditor should use the activity in the account as a gauge for sample selection. That is, if orders are placed with a vendor on a consistent basis, a confirmation should be sent to that vendor regardless of the recorded balance due.
    Answer (B) is incorrect. The auditor, in testing the completeness assertion, is concerned with balances that have not been recorded or invoices that have not been filed. Answer (C) is incorrect. The payees of checks are not an appropriate population for the confirmation process. Payments in the month after year end do not necessarily reflect year-end liabilities. Answer (D) is incorrect. The auditor, in testing the completeness assertion, is concerned with balances that have not been recorded or invoices that have not been filed.

10. An auditor suspects that certain client employees are ordering merchandise for themselves over the Internet without recording the purchase or receipt of the merchandise. When vendors' invoices arrive, one of the employees approves the invoices for payment. After the invoices are paid, the employee destroys the invoices and the related vouchers. In gathering evidence regarding the fraud, the auditor most likely would select items for testing from the file of all

    A. Cash disbursements.

    B. Approved vouchers.

    C. Receiving reports.

    D. Vendors' invoices.

Answer (A) is correct.
    REQUIRED: The file tested to determine whether checks are being issued for unauthorized expenditures.
    DISCUSSION: The best procedure to test whether any checks have been issued without supporting vouchers, purchase orders, and receiving reports is to select an appropriate sample of canceled checks (cash disbursements) and trace them to the related supporting documentation.
    Answer (B) is incorrect. The approved vouchers relating to the fraudulent transactions have been destroyed and therefore could not be chosen for audit. Answer (C) is incorrect. The receipt of the merchandise is not recorded. Answer (D) is incorrect. The vendors' invoices relating to the fraudulent transactions have been destroyed and therefore could not be chosen for audit.

11. Tests designed to detect purchases made before the end of the year that have been recorded in the subsequent year most likely would provide assurance about the relevant assertion regarding

   A. Valuation and allocation.

   B. Existence.

   C. Cutoff.

   D. Classification and understandability.

Answer (C) is correct.
   REQUIRED: The purpose of an audit procedure.
   DISCUSSION: The cutoff assertion is that transactions and events have been recorded in the proper period. To determine that all goods for which title has passed to the client at year end are recorded in inventory and accounts payable, a purchases cutoff test is appropriate.
   Answer (A) is incorrect. The procedure does not directly test the assertion of valuation and allocation. Answer (B) is incorrect. The procedure does not directly test the assertion of existence. Answer (D) is incorrect. The procedure does not directly test the assertion of classification and understandability.

12. An internal control narrative indicates that an approved voucher is required to support every check request for payment of merchandise. Which of the following procedures provides the greatest assurance that this control is operating effectively?

   A. Select and examine vouchers and ascertain that the related canceled checks are dated no later than the vouchers.

   B. Select and examine vouchers and ascertain that the related canceled checks are dated no earlier than the vouchers.

   C. Select and examine canceled checks and ascertain that the related vouchers are dated no earlier than the checks.

   D. Select and examine canceled checks and ascertain that the related vouchers are dated no later than the checks.

Answer (D) is correct.
   REQUIRED: The procedure giving the greatest assurance that approved vouchers support check requests.
   DISCUSSION: Payment vouchers bearing the required approvals should be supported by a properly authorized purchase requisition, a purchase order executing the transaction, a receiving report indicating all goods ordered have been received in good condition, and a vendor invoice confirming the amount owed. To determine that check requests are valid, the appropriate audit procedure is therefore to compare checks and the related vouchers. The direction of testing should be from a sample of checks to the approved vouchers. If the date of a voucher is later than the date of the related check, the inference is that a check was issued without proper support.
   Answer (A) is incorrect. Tracing from vouchers to canceled checks does not give assurance that all checks are supported by approved vouchers. This test will not detect canceled checks unsupported by approved vouchers, although it will permit comparison of the dates of the respective documents. Answer (B) is incorrect. Tracing from vouchers to canceled checks does not give assurance that all checks are supported by approved vouchers. This test will not detect canceled checks unsupported by approved vouchers, although it will permit comparison of the dates of the respective documents. Answer (C) is incorrect. The checks should be dated no earlier than the vouchers. Each voucher should be dated earlier than (or have the same date as) the related check.

13. When performing procedures to test assertions about purchases, an auditor vouches a sample of entries in the voucher register to the supporting documents. Which relevant assertion would this procedure most likely support?

   A. Completeness.

   B. Occurrence.

   C. Valuation and allocation.

   D. Classification.

Answer (B) is correct.
   REQUIRED: The assertion tested by vouching.
   DISCUSSION: A voucher signifies a liability. Its issuance is recorded in the voucher register after comparison of the vendor's invoice with the purchase requisition, purchase order, and receiving report. The direction of testing is an important consideration in addressing the RMMs. Selecting a sample of recorded entries in the voucher register to vouch to the supporting documentation provides evidence that the transactions occurred.
   Answer (A) is incorrect. Sampling recorded transactions to vouch to supporting documents does not test for unrecorded transactions. Answer (C) is incorrect. Sampling recorded transactions provides evidence regarding the amount owed and whether the entry reflects an obligation of the company, but it most directly supports the existence assertion. Answer (D) is incorrect. Sampling recorded transactions provides evidence regarding the amount owed but provides little evidence that the transactions have been recorded in the proper accounts.

12.2 Substantive Testing of Inventory

14. The element of the audit-planning process most likely to be agreed upon with the client before implementation of the audit strategy is the determination of the

A. Evidence to be gathered to provide a sufficient basis for the auditor's opinion.

B. Procedures to be undertaken to discover litigation, claims, and assessments.

C. Pending legal matters to be included in the inquiry of the client's attorney.

D. Timing of inventory observation procedures to be performed.

Answer (D) is correct.
REQUIRED: The element of audit planning most likely agreed upon with the client before implementation.
DISCUSSION: The client is responsible for taking the physical inventory. The auditor is responsible for observing this process and performing test counts. The audit procedures are dependent upon management's plans. Thus, the auditor must coordinate the collection of this evidence with management.
Answer (A) is incorrect. The evidence to be gathered is a matter of professional judgment to be determined solely by the auditor. Answer (B) is incorrect. The procedures performed to discover litigation, claims, and assessments are matters of professional judgment to be determined solely by the auditor. Answer (C) is incorrect. Pending legal matters to be included in the inquiry of the client's attorney are matters of professional judgment to be determined solely by the auditor.

15. When auditing inventories, an auditor would **least** likely verify that

A. All inventory owned by the client is on hand at the time of the count.

B. The client has used proper inventory pricing.

C. The financial statement presentation of inventories is appropriate.

D. Damaged goods and obsolete items have been properly accounted for.

Answer (A) is correct.
REQUIRED: The procedure not performed in an audit of inventories.
DISCUSSION: An auditor does not expect all inventory to which the auditee has title to be on hand at the date of the count. Some purchased goods may still be in transit at that time. Also, some inventory may be on consignment or in public warehouses although properly included in the count.
Answer (B) is incorrect. The auditor should test relevant assertions about valuation of inventory. Answer (C) is incorrect. The auditor should test relevant assertions about presentation in the financial statements. Answer (D) is incorrect. The auditor should test relevant assertions about valuation of inventory.

16. To gain assurance that all inventory items in a client's inventory listing schedule are valid, an auditor most likely would vouch

A. Inventory tags noted during the auditor's observation to items listed in the inventory listing schedule.

B. Inventory tags noted during the auditor's observation to items listed in receiving reports and vendors' invoices.

C. Items listed in the inventory listing schedule to inventory tags and the auditor's recorded count sheets.

D. Items listed in receiving reports and vendors' invoices to the inventory listing schedule.

Answer (C) is correct.
REQUIRED: The step to provide assurance that all inventory items in a client's inventory listing are valid.
DISCUSSION: Validity relates to the existence assertion. To determine that the items exist, the direction of testing should be from the schedule to the inventory tags and ultimately to the auditor's count sheet.
Answer (A) is incorrect. Tracing tags to the inventory listing schedule should provide evidence of completeness. That is, all items counted are included on the listing sheet. Answer (B) is incorrect. Tracing inventory tags to receiving reports and vendors' invoices should provide information useful in determining whether inventory was recorded at cost. Answer (D) is incorrect. Tracing inventory items on receiving reports and vendors' invoices to the inventory listing schedule is not an effective test. Many items received are sold by the inventory date.

17. An auditor selected items for test counts while observing a client's physical inventory. The auditor then traced the test counts to the client's inventory listing. Tracing test counts most likely obtained evidence concerning the relevant assertion about

A. Rights and obligations.

B. Completeness.

C. Existence.

D. Valuation.

Answer (B) is correct.
REQUIRED: The assertion relevant to tracing test counts to the client's inventory listing.
DISCUSSION: Tracing the details of test counts to the final inventory schedule assures the auditor that items in the observed physical inventory are included in the inventory records. The auditor should compare the inventory tag sequence numbers in the final inventory schedule with those in the records of his/her test counts made during the client's physical inventory.
Answer (A) is incorrect. The reconciliation of the test counts with the inventory listing does not provide assurance that the inventory is owned by the client. Answer (C) is incorrect. Although the observation of inventory provides evidence as to existence, specifically tracing test counts to the inventory listing provides evidence of completeness. Answer (D) is incorrect. The valuation assertion is tested by determining whether inventory items are included in inventory at lower of cost or market.

18. While observing a client's annual physical inventory, an auditor recorded test counts for several items and noticed that certain test counts were higher than the recorded quantities in the client's perpetual records. This situation could be the result of the client's failure to record

A. Purchase discounts.

B. Purchase returns.

C. Sales.

D. Sales returns.

Answer (D) is correct.
  REQUIRED: The transaction class not recorded when test counts are greater than recorded quantities.
  DISCUSSION: Failure to record sales returns for goods returned to the physical inventory will result in test counts greater than the quantities reported by the perpetual inventory system.
  Answer (A) is incorrect. Purchase discounts relate to the measurement of inventory, not to the quantity. Answer (B) is incorrect. Failure to record purchase returns results in lower quantities in the physical inventory than in the perpetual records. Answer (C) is incorrect. Failure to record sales results in lower quantities in the physical inventory than in the perpetual records.

19. Which of the following audit procedures probably would provide the most reliable evidence concerning the entity's assertion of rights and obligations related to inventories?

A. Trace test counts noted during the entity's physical count to the entity's summarization of quantities.

B. Inspect agreements to determine whether any inventory is pledged as collateral or subject to any liens.

C. Select the last few shipping advices used before the physical count and determine whether the shipments were recorded as sales.

D. Inspect the open purchase order file for significant commitments that should be considered for disclosure.

Answer (B) is correct.
  REQUIRED: The procedure providing the most reliable evidence of rights and obligations related to inventories.
  DISCUSSION: Testing the assertion of rights and obligations for inventories determines that the entity has legal title or similar rights to the inventories. Typically, the auditor examines paid vendors' invoices, consignment agreements, and contracts.
  Answer (A) is incorrect. Tracing test counts to the summary of quantities tests the assertion of completeness. Answer (C) is incorrect. Examining purchase transactions at year end tests the assertion of cutoff. Answer (D) is incorrect. Determining whether commitments should be disclosed tests the assertions about statement classification and understandability.

20. To measure how effectively an entity employs its resources, an auditor calculates inventory turnover by dividing average inventory into

A. Net sales.

B. Cost of goods sold.

C. Operating income.

D. Gross sales.

Answer (B) is correct.
  REQUIRED: The calculation of the inventory turnover ratio.
  DISCUSSION: Inventory turnover equals cost of goods sold divided by average inventory. It provides a measure of how many times inventory requires replacement.

21. An auditor most likely would analyze inventory turnover rates to obtain evidence concerning relevant assertions about

A. Existence.

B. Rights and obligations.

C. Classification and understandability.

D. Valuation and allocation.

Answer (D) is correct.
  REQUIRED: The assertion about which analysis of inventory turnover rates provides evidence.
  DISCUSSION: Assertions about valuation and allocation address whether (1) assets, liabilities, and equity interests are included in the financial statements at appropriate amounts and (2) resulting adjustments are properly recorded. An examination of inventory turnover pertains to identifying slow-moving, excess, defective, and obsolete items included in inventories. This audit procedure tests the valuation and allocation assertion.
  Answer (A) is incorrect. Analysis of inventory turnover does not test existence. Answer (B) is incorrect. Analysis of inventory turnover does not test whether the entity has rights to the inventory. Answer (C) is incorrect. The classification and understandability assertion concerns whether financial information is properly presented and described and disclosures are clear.

22. An auditor most likely would make inquiries of production and sales personnel concerning possible obsolete or slow-moving inventory to support the relevant assertion about

A. Valuation and allocation.

B. Rights and obligations.

C. Existence.

D. Classification and understandability.

Answer (A) is correct.
REQUIRED: The assertion tested when considering obsolete or slow-moving inventory.
DISCUSSION: The valuation and allocation assertion is directed towards whether inventory is recorded at lower of cost or market. The discovery of slow-moving, excess, defective, or obsolete inventory suggests that the cost of inventory be written down to market.

23. An auditor concluded that no excessive costs for an idle plant were charged to inventory. This conclusion most likely related to the auditor's objective to obtain evidence about the relevant assertions regarding inventory, including presentation and disclosure and

A. Valuation and allocation.

B. Completeness.

C. Occurrence.

D. Rights and obligations.

Answer (A) is correct.
REQUIRED: The assertion related to the conclusion that no excessive costs for an idle plant were inventoried.
DISCUSSION: Inventory should properly include the costs of direct labor, direct materials, and manufacturing overhead. Thus, to be properly measured, an appropriate amount of manufacturing overhead should be charged to inventory. Costs of an idle plant should not be included in manufacturing overhead.

24. Which of the following auditing procedures most likely would provide assurance regarding a manufacturing entity's relevant assertions about inventory valuation?

A. Testing the entity's computation of standard overhead rates.

B. Obtaining confirmation of inventories pledged under loan agreements.

C. Reviewing shipping and receiving cutoff procedures for inventories.

D. Tracing test counts to the entity's inventory listing.

Answer (A) is correct.
REQUIRED: The procedure that provides assurance about a manufacturing entity's inventory measurement.
DISCUSSION: Manufactured goods should be recorded at cost, including direct materials, direct labor, and an allocation of overhead. The overhead allocation rate should be tested for reasonableness.
Answer (B) is incorrect. Obtaining confirmation of inventories pledged under loan agreements tests the assertion of rights and obligations. Answer (C) is incorrect. Reviewing shipping and receiving cutoff procedures tests the assertion of cutoff. Answer (D) is incorrect. Tracing test counts to the inventory listing tests the assertion of completeness.

Use the additional questions in Gleim **CPA Test Prep** to create Practice Exams that emulate Prometric!

12.3 PRACTICE TASK-BASED SIMULATIONS

DIRECTIONS

Note: If you believe you have encountered a software malfunction, report it to the test center staff immediately.

Navigation

To navigate from task to task, use the controls at the bottom of the screen. Click on the **Next** button to advance to the next task, or the **Previous** button to go to the previous task. To go directly to any task, click on its number.

If you would like a reminder to revisit a task, or want to indicate that you are finished with it, click on the reminder flag below the task number. To clear the flag, click on it again. Reminder flags are for your use only -- they do not contribute to your score.

Tabs

In this part of the examination, you will be asked to complete various tasks. Every task has one or more **Work Tabs**. Some tasks have one or more **Information Tabs**, others may have none. Every task has a **Help** tab.

If a task has **Information Tabs**, you may use the information in them to complete your responses in the **Work Tabs**.

Work tab   Information tab   Help tab

Work Tabs:
- **Work Tabs** are identified with a pencil icon. This is where your responses are expected.
- Each task has one or more **Work Tabs**.
- **Work Tabs** contain directions for completing the task -- be sure to read these directions carefully.
- The **Work Tab** name in the example above is for illustration only -- yours will differ.
- You must complete all of the **Work Tabs** in each task to receive full credit.

Information Tabs:
- The Authoritative Literature will be provided in all tasks in the AUD, FAR, and REG sections for your reference.
- Your simulation may have one or more additional **Information Tabs**. Like the Authoritative Literature tabs, **Information Tabs** do not have a pencil icon.
- If your task has additional **Information Tabs**, go through each to familiarize yourself with the task content.

Help Tab:
- The **Help Tab** provides assistance with the exam software that is used in this task. For example, if the task is to compose a memorandum, **Help** will provide information about the word processor.

The Toolbar

The toolbar at the top of the screen shows the amount of time remaining for you to complete the tasks. In addition, the following tools are available. Note that only the **Exit** button is displayed when Directions are visible - the others will appear when you begin the tasks.

Click on these buttons to split or unsplit the screen. You can split the screen vertically or horizontally.

Click on this button to display the calculator; click on it again to hide the calculator. To move the calculator, click on the calculator title bar and drag the calculator to the desired location.

Click on this button to use the spreadsheet; click on it again to hide the spreadsheet. To move the spreadsheet, click on the the spreadsheet title bar and drag the spreadsheet to the desired location.

Click on this button to go on to the next part of the examination. You must complete all of the tasks to receive full credit. Once you click on **Exit** and confirm the action, you will NOT be able to return to this testlet.

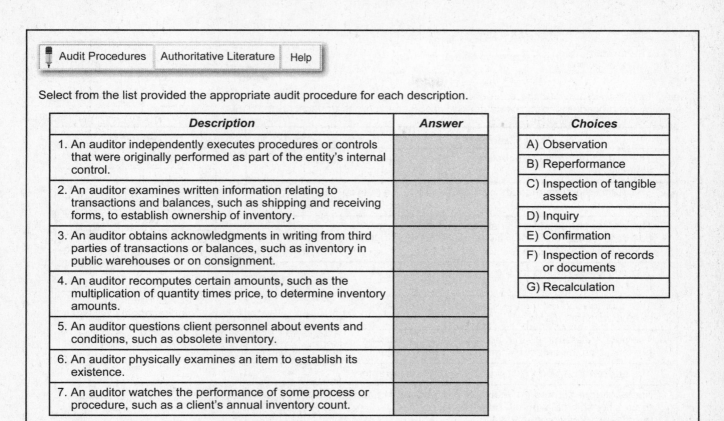

Select from the list provided the appropriate audit procedure for each description.

Description	Answer		Choices
1. An auditor independently executes procedures or controls that were originally performed as part of the entity's internal control.			A) Observation
2. An auditor examines written information relating to transactions and balances, such as shipping and receiving forms, to establish ownership of inventory.			B) Reperformance
3. An auditor obtains acknowledgments in writing from third parties of transactions or balances, such as inventory in public warehouses or on consignment.			C) Inspection of tangible assets
4. An auditor recomputes certain amounts, such as the multiplication of quantity times price, to determine inventory amounts.			D) Inquiry
5. An auditor questions client personnel about events and conditions, such as obsolete inventory.			E) Confirmation
6. An auditor physically examines an item to establish its existence.			F) Inspection of records or documents
7. An auditor watches the performance of some process or procedure, such as a client's annual inventory count.			G) Recalculation

Select from the list provided the appropriate assertions for each audit procedure. Choose the assertion most likely being tested by the procedure. Each choice may be used once, more than once, or not at all.

Audit Procedure	Answer	Choices
1. The auditor determined that pledged inventory was identified.		A) Completeness
2. The auditor confirmed goods held by the client in a public warehouse.		B) Accuracy
3. The auditor performed a test at year end to assure all purchase transactions for the year were included in the proper period.		C) Valuation and allocation
4. The auditor accounted for the numerical sequence of purchase orders.		D) Existence
5. The auditor vouched the transactions to record payables to receiving documents.		E) Cutoff
6. The auditor determined that accounts payable was presented on the balance sheet as a current liability.		F) Rights and obligations
7. The auditor observed the taking of the physical inventory.		G) Occurrence
8. The auditor performed an analytical procedure comparing the relationship of inventory balances with recent purchases, production, and sales.		H) Classification and understandability
9. The auditor obtained representations from management about the amounts included on the financial statements for recorded transactions involving sales and purchases of inventory.		
10. The auditor compared recorded inventory costs with replacement costs.		

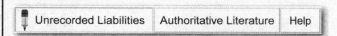

| Unrecorded Liabilities | Authoritative Literature | Help |

In conducting the audit procedures for the search for unrecorded liabilities, the materiality/scope for this area was assessed by the auditors at $6,000. Adjustments are only recorded for items equal to or exceeding materiality.

For the items reflected in the following check register, which are not recorded in the accounts payable subsidiary ledger at December 31, Year 2, determine whether each potential liability is recorded in the proper accounting period and also determine the amount that should be journalized, if any. If no action is required, you must enter $0.

For each of the check numbers in the table below, select from the lists provided (1) whether any action or adjustment is required and (2) the dollar value of the required adjustment. Each selection may be used once, more than once, or not at all.

Check Register

Vendor	Check #	Check Date	Amount	Nature of the Expenses
Water World Distributors, Inc.	1333	1/6/Yr 3	$3,500	Water coolers in office and warehouse delivered 12/31/Yr 2
Daniel Breen, Esquire	1334	1/6/Yr 3	$6,000	Corporate legal services for December Year 2
Telephone Services, Inc.	1335	1/8/Yr 3	$6,500	December Year 2 telephone and computer services
Payroll processing -- Paychecks	1336	1/10/Yr 3	$25,500	Bi-weekly payroll (12/25/Yr 2 - 1/7/Yr 3)
Pitt Ohio Trucking Company	1337	1/10/Yr 3	$45,601	Trucking services 12/4/Yr 2 - 1/3/Yr 3, deliveries made evenly throughout the period
Petty cash	1338	1/17/Yr 3	$2,002	Replenish petty cash box
Smith's Forklift Repairs	1339	1/22/Yr 3	$11,000	Received new fork lift on 12/29/Yr 2, ordered on 12/18/Yr 2
Glenn's Glass Distribution Center	1340	1/23/Yr 3	$12,230	Specialty goods ordered 12/20/Yr 2, delivered 12/31/Yr 2
Payroll processing -- Paychecks	1341	1/24/Yr 3	$25,500	Bi-weekly payroll (1/8/Yr 3 - 1/15/Yr 3)
Daniel Breen, Esquire	1342	2/6/Yr 3	$6,800	Corporate legal services for January Year 3

Check #	Adjustment Needed?	Amount
1. 1333		
2. 1334		
3. 1335		
4. 1336		
5. 1337		
6. 1338		
7. 1339		
8. 1340		
9. 1341		
10. 1342		

List for Adjustment Needed
i) No action required
ii) Adjustment

List for Amount
A) $0
B) $2,002
C) $2,970
D) $3,500
E) $4,413
F) $6,000
G) $6,500
H) $6,800
I) $7,650
J) $9,900
K) $11,000
L) $12,230
M) $12,750
N) $25,500
O) $41,188
P) $45,601

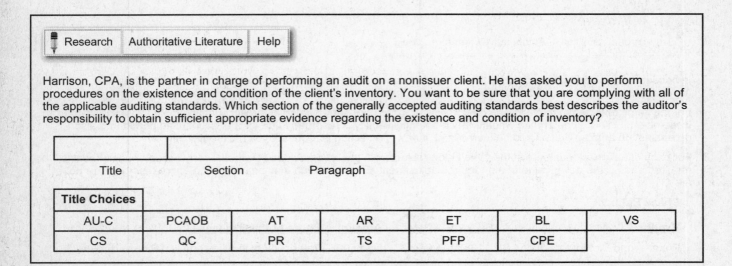

| Research | Authoritative Literature | Help |

Harrison, CPA, is the partner in charge of performing an audit on a nonissuer client. He has asked you to perform procedures on the existence and condition of the client's inventory. You want to be sure that you are complying with all of the applicable auditing standards. Which section of the generally accepted auditing standards best describes the auditor's responsibility to obtain sufficient appropriate evidence regarding the existence and condition of inventory?

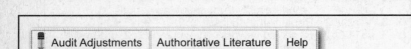

Title	Section	Paragraph

Title Choices

AU-C	PCAOB	AT	AR	ET	BL	VS
CS	QC	PR	TS	PFP	CPE	

▼ = Reminder   Directions   1 2 3 [4] 5   ◀ Previous   Next ▶

| Audit Adjustments | Authoritative Literature | Help |

The year under audit is Year 2.

During the course of the Year 2 audit of the company, the auditor discovered the following situations that may or may not require an adjusting journal entry. Each audit finding is independent of any of the other findings. Select from the list provided the account or accounts included in the adjusting journal entry, if required, to correct the audit finding. Accounts may be used once, more than once, or not at all.

Audit Finding	Adjusting Journal Entry		Accounts
	Dr.	Cr.	A) Cash
1. The bank's confirmation reply regarding the company's line of credit indicated that the December Year 2 interest was unpaid at year end. Accruals for monthly interest expense have been made for 11 months in Year 2 by the company.			B) Accounts receivable
			C) Other current assets
			D) Property and equipment
			E) Accounts payable
			F) Accrued liabilities
2. Employee overtime pay for hours worked before year end, but paid in the following year, was not recorded in Year 2.			G) Common stock
			H) Revenues
3. In the last week of Year 2, the company recorded revenue for services rendered to some clients in Year 3.			I) Allowance for doubtful accounts
			J) Operating expenses
4. During Year 2, a former client sued the company for inappropriate work. Legal counsel has advised that it is "reasonably possible" that the company will be assessed damages. An amount can be estimated.			K) Interest expense
			L) Other income
			M) Accumulated depreciation
5. At the end of Year 2, a major customer filed for bankruptcy.			N) Disclosure but no entry required
			O) No entry or disclosure required

▼ = Reminder   Directions   1 2 3 4 [5]   ◀ Previous   Next ▶

Unofficial Answers

1. Audit Procedures (7 Gradable Items)

1. B) Reperformance. Reperformance is independently executing procedures or controls that were originally performed as part of the entity's internal control.

2. F) Inspection of records or documents. Inspection of records or documents includes the examination of written information.

3. E) Confirmation. Confirmations are communications, in writing, from third parties providing evidence.

4. G) Recalculation. Recalculations are computations of mathematical accuracy.

5. D) Inquiry. Inquiries are questions, typically posed to management and others with information of interest to the auditor.

6. C) Inspection of tangible assets. Inspection of tangible assets includes physically examining an item to establish its existence.

7. A) Observation. Observation means watching activities or procedures. It provides the auditor with direct personal knowledge.

2. Audit Procedures and Relevant Assertions (10 Gradable Items)

1. F) Rights and obligations. This is the assertion being tested when the auditor determines that pledged inventory was identified. Thus, another party has rights in the inventory.

2. D) Existence. This is the assertion being tested when the auditor confirmed goods held by the client in a public warehouse.

3. E) Cutoff. This is the assertion being tested when the auditor performed a purchases test to ensure that all purchase transactions for the year were included in the proper period.

4. A) Completeness. This is the assertion being tested when the auditor accounted for the numerical sequence of purchase orders.

5. G) Occurrence. This is the assertion being tested when the auditor vouched transactions to record payables to receiving documents.

6. H) Classification and understandability. This is the assertion being tested when the auditor determined that accounts payable was presented on the balance sheet as a current liability.

7. D) Existence. This is the assertion being tested when the auditor observed the taking of the physical inventory.

8. A) Completeness. This is the assertion being tested when the auditor performed an analytical procedure comparing the relationship of inventory balances with recent purchases, production, and sales.

9. B) Accuracy. This is the assertion about transactions that is tested when the auditor obtains representations from the client about sales and purchases of inventory.

10. C) Valuation and allocation. This is the assertion being tested when the auditor compared recorded inventory costs with replacement costs.

3. Unrecorded Liabilities (10 Gradable Items)

1. i) No action required; A) $0. Although the purchase is for Year 2, the amount of $3,500 is below the materiality limit.

2. ii) Adjustment; F) $6,000. The services are for Year 2, and the amount is equal to the materiality limit.

3. ii) Adjustment; G) $6,500. The services are for Year 2, and the amount is greater than the materiality limit.

4. ii) Adjustment; M) $12,750. One half of the total amount, which is material, is accrued in Year 2.

5. ii) Adjustment; O) $41,188. The total amount is for 31 days, 28 of which were in December Year 2. Thus, 28/31 × $45,601 is $41,188, which is greater than the materiality limit.

6. i) No action required; A) $0. The amount is below the materiality limit, and there is no indication that the transaction relates to Year 2.

7. ii) Adjustment; K) $11,000. The asset was received in Year 2, and the amount is greater than the materiality limit.

8. ii) Adjustment; L) $12,230. The assets were received in Year 2, and the amount is greater than the materiality limit.

9. i) No action required; A) $0. The services were received in Year 3.

10. i) No action required; A) $0. The services were received in Year 3.

4. Research (1 Gradable Item)

Answer: 501.11

AU-C Section 501 – *Audit Evidence – Specific Considerations for Selected Items*

Inventory

.11   If inventory is material to the financial statements, the auditor should obtain sufficient appropriate audit evidence regarding the existence and condition of inventory by

    a.   attending physical inventory counting, unless impracticable, to

        i)   evaluate management's instructions and procedures for recording and controlling the results of the entity's physical inventory counting,

        ii) observe the performance of management's count procedures,

        iii) inspect the inventory, and

        iv) perform test counts and

    b.   performing audit procedures over the entity's final inventory records to determine whether they accurately reflect actual inventory count results.

5. Audit Adjustments (5 Gradable Items)

1.   K) Interest expense; F) Accrued liabilities. The interest expense accrual for December would require recording.

2.   J) Operating expenses; F) Accrued liabilities. The wages accrued for December would require recording.

3.   H) Revenues; B) Accounts receivable. The revenue recorded, but not earned, for December would be reversed.

4.   N) Disclosure but no entry required; N) Disclosure but no entry required. Since the contingent amount was not "probable," it requires only note disclosure in the financial statements.

5.   I) Allowance for doubtful accounts; B) Accounts receivable. Since it is unlikely that the customer receivable will be collected, it would be written off to allowance for doubtful accounts.

Gleim Simulation Grading

Task	Correct Responses		Gradable Items		Score per Task
1	___	÷	7	=	___
2	___	÷	10	=	___
3	___	÷	10	=	___
4 (Research)	___	÷	1	=	___
5	___	÷	5	=	___

	Total of Scores per Task	___
÷	Total Number of Tasks	5
	Total Score	___ %

Use **CPA Gleim Online** and **Simulation Wizard** to practice more task-based simulations in a realistic environment.

STUDY UNIT THIRTEEN
EVIDENCE --
OTHER ASSETS, LIABILITIES, AND EQUITIES

(10 pages of outline)

The objective of this study unit is to develop comprehensive audit plans for accounts not previously considered. Each plan includes the customary procedures assuming no unusual risks. The candidate also should consider whether audit plans and procedures need to be modified to address special risks.

The approach to audit plan development described in the outlines may be used in answering CPA exam questions. Application of the AICPA's assertions model (CAVE CROC is the memory aid for the assertions, addressed in Study Unit 1, Subunit 2) ensures that all assertions are tested. However, other formats for presentation of the procedures are acceptable, for example, application of the PCAOB's assertions model (also addressed in Study Unit 1, Subunit 2).

13.1 SUBSTANTIVE TESTING OF PROPERTY, PLANT, AND EQUIPMENT

1. **Scope**

    a. The following balances are included in this audit plan:

    1) Buildings, equipment, improvements, and vehicles including associated depreciation expense, repairs and maintenance, and accumulated depreciation

    2) Land

    3) Capital leases and associated amortization expense

2. **Testing Relevant Assertions.** The following is a standard audit plan for property, plant, and equipment that tests relevant assertions (CAVE CROC):

    a. **Completeness.** Are all transactions affecting property, plant, and equipment for the period reflected in the balance?

    1) **Perform analytical procedures.** The five sources of information for analytical procedures (covered in Study Unit 3, Subunit 5) can be used to develop expectations. Typical ratios include rate of return on plant assets and plant assets to total assets.

    2) **Reconcile subsidiary and general ledgers.** The client usually maintains records for individual assets or classes of assets. The subsidiary records, including cost, current depreciation expense, and accumulated depreciation, should reconcile with the general ledger and the amounts to be included on the financial statements.

    a) A schedule of fixed assets is typically prepared from the subsidiary records to be used in testing and is included in the audit documentation.

3)   **Analyze repairs and maintenance.** The auditor should vouch significant debits from the repairs and maintenance expense account to determine whether any should have been capitalized.

a)   Vouching additions to property, plant, and equipment also tests the completeness assertion because debits may have been for non-capital items.

b.   **Accuracy.** Have the amounts for the specific accounts been recorded appropriately?

1)   Include amounts and classifications in the management representation letter.
2)   Compare the general ledger balances with the financial statement balances.

c.   **Valuation and allocation.** Are balances of property, plant, and equipment reported in accordance with the applicable reporting framework [assumed to be U.S. GAAP in this study unit (historical cost – accumulated depreciation)]?

1)   **Inspect records of purchases.** The purchase of fixed assets should result in payments. Vouching the entries to the payment records supports the rights and obligations assertion as well as the valuation assertion.

2)   **Vouch additions and disposals.** These are tests of the details of transactions. In a continuing audit, the prior year's balance of property, plant, and equipment is an audited balance. If the auditor tests the details of the transactions that changed the balance, (s)he has made significant progress in obtaining evidence about the valuation assertion (as well as other assertions such as completeness and existence).

3)   **Test depreciation.** Fixed assets (except certain nondepreciable assets such as land) are usually measured at cost minus accumulated depreciation. The depreciation methods and their application should be tested to determine that they are generally accepted and applied consistently.

d.   **Existence.** Do the assets reflected in property, plant, and equipment exist at the balance sheet date?

1)   **Inspect plant additions.** The focus is on additions to property, plant, and equipment.

a)   The auditor vouches a sample from the recorded asset additions by examining the supporting documents and inspecting the physical assets. Testing in the opposite direction, i.e., by tracing from the supporting documentation to the general ledger, does not provide evidence that recorded assets exist.

b)   Initial audits require inspection of significant assets reflected in the beginning balance as well as additions.

e.   **Cutoff.** Have transactions relating to property, plant, and equipment been recorded in the proper period?

1)   **Test the cutoff.** Additions and disposals near year end should be tested to ensure recording in the proper periods.

f.   **Rights and obligations.** Does the entity have ownership rights in the reported property, plant, and equipment?

1)   **Examine titles and leases.** Certain property (e.g., autos and trucks) should have certificates of title. For leased assets, contracts should allow the auditor to determine whether leases have been properly recorded as either capital or operating leases.

2)   **Inspect insurance policies.** The entity should insure its assets. Vouching the recorded assets to insurance policies supports the rights assertion.

a) When liens are placed on equipment or property, the lienholder often requires that the assets be insured and that the lienholder be named as the beneficiary. Hence, the policy is likely to be held by the lienholder even though the client is required to pay the premiums.

3) **Inspect property tax records.** Many states assess property tax on certain fixed assets. Payment of taxes is evidence that the client has rights in the assets.

g. <u>O</u>ccurrence. Did the transactions relating to property, plant, and equipment occur?

1) The auditor should test the authorization, execution, recording, and custody aspects of a sample of transactions.

h. **<u>C</u>lassification and understandability.** Is the balance of property, plant, and equipment reflected on the balance sheet in the noncurrent section? Are adequate disclosures presented for methods of depreciation, commitments of assets, and capital lease terms?

1) **Read financial statements.** The auditor should determine that property, plant, and equipment is presented as a noncurrent asset. Depreciable assets and land should be reported at cost minus accumulated depreciation and cost, respectively. Notes to the financial statements should describe classes of assets, lease agreements, depreciation methods, and any property mortgaged or used as collateral for loans.

2) **Make inquiries of management about disclosures and other reporting issues.** Significant items should be included in the management representation letter.

Stop and review! You have completed the outline for this subunit. Study multiple-choice questions 1 through 9 beginning on page 409.

13.2 SUBSTANTIVE TESTING OF INVESTMENTS AND DERIVATIVES (AU-C 501 AND AU-C 540)

1. **Scope**

a. The following balances are included in this audit plan:

1) **Noncurrent items.** These include (a) capital stock or other equity interests reported using the fair value or equity methods, (b) bonds and similar debt instruments, (c) loans and advances that are essentially investments, and (d) goodwill.

2) **Current items.** These include trading, held-to-maturity, and available-for-sale securities classified as current.

3) **Derivatives and hedges.** A derivative is an unperformed contract that results in cash flow between two counterparties based on (derived from) the change in some other indicator of value. Hedges are defensive strategies to protect an entity against the risk of adverse price or interest rate movements on certain assets, liabilities, or anticipated transactions.

4) **Revenues** generated from investments.

b. According to U.S. GAAP, the appropriate classification of investments depends on (1) management's **intent** in purchasing and holding the investment, (2) the entity's actual investment activities, and (3) for certain debt securities, the entity's **ability** to hold the investment to maturity. The auditor should obtain an understanding of the process used by management to classify investments before determining the nature, timing, and extent of further audit procedures.

c. AU-C 501, *Audit Evidence -- Specific Consideration for Selected Items*, provides guidance for planning and performing audit procedures to test assertions about investments in securities and derivatives.

2. **Securities Valued Based on Investee Financial Results**

   a. In accordance with AU-C 501, the following procedures should be performed to support the investee's financial results (excluding equity method investments, which are accounted for as components under AU-C 600):

      1) Read the investee's statements and related audit report and determine whether the other auditor's report is satisfactory.

         a) These statements may be unaudited, or the other auditor's report may be unsatisfactory. In this case, apply the procedures to the statements that are appropriate given the investment's materiality to the investor.

      2) Obtain evidence to support (a) an investment carrying amount based on factors not in the investee's statements or (b) fair values materially different from the investee's carrying amounts.

      3) Determine whether the entity has properly considered a **lack of comparability**, resulting from a difference between the dates of the investor's and investee's statements. For example, a significant transaction occurring between those dates may have a material effect on the entity's statements.

   b. The auditor should (1) read interim statements of the investee and (2) make inquiries of investor management to identify **subsequent events and transactions** of the investee that may be material to the investor.

3. **Derivatives and Securities Measured at Fair Value**

   a. The auditor should

      1) Determine whether the applicable reporting framework specifies the method for measuring fair value

      2) Evaluate whether the measurement is consistent with the method

   b. Fair value estimates may be obtained from a third-party source (e.g., a broker-dealer). The auditor should understand the method used by the source to make the estimate and consider the significance of the work of the management's specialist.

      1) If the entity has used a valuation model, the auditor applies AU-C 540, *Auditing Accounting Estimates, including Fair Value Accounting Estimates, and Related Disclosures*.

4. **Impairment Losses**

   a. The auditor

      1) Evaluates management's conclusion about recognition of a loss for a decline in fair value below cost or carrying amount

      2) Obtains support for the amount of the recorded adjustment, including compliance with the reporting framework

5. **Unrealized Appreciation or Depreciation**

   a. The auditor should obtain sufficient appropriate evidence about the unrealized amount of a derivative's fair value that is recognized or disclosed because a hedge is ineffective.

NOTE: This subunit does not apply to investments accounted for using the equity method. For guidance on audits of such investments, see AU-C 600, *Special Considerations -- Audits of Group Financial Statements (Including the Work of Component Auditors)*. This topic is covered in Study Unit 17, Subunit 1.

ISA Difference

The ISAs do not require the auditor to perform specific audit procedures on investments in securities and derivative instruments.

6. **Testing Relevant Assertions.** The following is a standard audit plan for investments that tests relevant assertions (CAVE CROC):

   a. **Completeness.** Are all transactions affecting investments for the period reflected in the balance?

      1) **Perform analytical procedures.** Prior-period amounts held should be compared with current amounts. The expected return on investments held can be compared with actual recorded amounts.

      2) **Reconcile the subsidiary ledger with the control accounts.** The auditor should prepare a schedule from the subsidiary ledger and reconcile the amounts with the balances in the general ledger and financial statements.

      3) **Evaluate contracts and agreements.** The auditor should determine whether all securities, derivatives, and hedges have been identified and reported.

   b. **Accuracy.** Have the balances for specific accounts been recorded appropriately?

      1) **Recalculate interest revenue.** The auditor should determine that interest revenue, based on stated rates for recorded investments, has been properly recorded.

      2) Compare the general ledger balances with the financial statement balances.

   c. **Valuation and allocation.** Are balances reported in accordance with the applicable reporting framework?

      1) **Vouch recorded amounts for trading securities and available-for-sale securities to market quotations if available.** When market quotations are unavailable, the auditor can obtain fair-value estimates from broker-dealers and other third-party sources who derive the fair value of a security by using modeling or a similar technique. The auditor should evaluate the appropriateness of the valuation models and the variables and assumptions used in the model.

      2) **Determine that unrealized gains and losses (changes in fair value) are properly accounted for.** Unrealized gains and losses on trading securities are included in earnings. Unrealized gains and losses on available-for-sale securities are reported in other comprehensive income until realized. (An exception is provided for all or part of the unrealized gain or loss on an available-for-sale security designated as hedged in a fair-value hedge.)

      3) **Vouch recorded costs for held-to-maturity securities to market quotations.** The entity should measure these securities at amortized cost only if it has the positive intent and ability to hold them to maturity. The auditor also should recalculate the premium or discount.

      4) **Determine that transfers between categories of investments are at fair value.**

      5) **Inspect relevant records and documents and make appropriate inquiries about nontemporary declines in fair value.** Individual available-for-sale or held-to-maturity securities may suffer a nontemporary decline in fair value below their cost basis. The securities should be written down to fair value reflecting the new cost basis, and the amount of the write-down should be included in earnings.

      6) **Obtain audited financial statements from the investees if investments are accounted for by the equity method.** The investment accounts should be based on percentage ownership in the investee and reported income or loss of the investee.

      7) **Evaluate goodwill for potential impairments.** If management cannot provide evidence to support the value, it should be written off.

    d.   **Existence.** Do investments reported at the balance sheet date exist?

        1) **Physically inspect and count securities in the client's possession.** Serial numbers should be recorded and compared with the entity's records. Inspection and counting also should be performed when counting other liquid assets (e.g., cash). The client's representative should be available to acknowledge that the securities have been returned intact.

        2) **Confirm securities.** Confirmation requests may be made to the issuer, custodian, counterparty, or broker-dealer for unsettled transactions.

    e.   **Cutoff.** Have transactions relating to investments been recorded in the proper period?

        1) **Test the cutoff.** The auditor should test transactions made near year end to ensure they are reflected in the proper period.

    f.   **Rights and obligations.** Does the entity own the reported investments?

        1) **Trace dividend and interest revenue.** The auditor should determine that revenue has been properly recorded.

    g.   **Occurrence.** Did the transactions relating to investments occur?

        1) **Vouch recorded costs to documentation.** The cost of recorded securities can be established by comparing recorded amounts with broker invoices, canceled checks, and other evidence of purchase.

    h.   **Classification and understandability.** Are balances related to investments reflected on the balance sheet in the current or noncurrent section depending on management expectations?

        1) **Read financial statements.** Determine that individual trading, available-for-sale, and held-to-maturity securities are reported as current or noncurrent as appropriate. Determine whether derivatives, hedges, and other financial instruments are adequately described in the notes to the financial statements.

        2) **Make inquiries of management about intentions to dispose of investments.** Classification often is based on the actions of management. The responses should be documented in the management representation letter. Also, the auditor should consider whether investment activities corroborate or conflict with management's stated intent.

Stop and review! You have completed the outline for this subunit. Study multiple-choice questions 10 through 19 beginning on page 411.

13.3 SUBSTANTIVE TESTING OF NONCURRENT DEBT

    1. **Scope**

        a.   The following balances are included in this audit plan:

            1) Noncurrent notes payable, mortgages payable, and bonds payable
            2) Related interest expense

    2. **Testing Relevant Assertions.** The following is a standard audit plan for noncurrent debt that tests relevant assertions (CAVE CROC):

        a.   **Completeness.** Are all transactions affecting noncurrent debt reflected in the balances for the period?

            1) **Perform analytical procedures.** Prior-period amounts recorded should be compared with current amounts. A key procedure to detect unrecorded debt is to recalculate interest expense based on recorded debt and compare it with recorded interest expense. Significant unexpected interest expense recorded in the general ledger suggests the existence of unrecorded debt. The debt-to-equity ratio, which equals total liabilities divided by total equity, can also be calculated and compared with previous periods.

    2) **Reconcile the subsidiary ledger with the control accounts.** The auditor should prepare a schedule from the subsidiary ledger and reconcile the amounts with the balances in the general ledger and financial statements.

  b. **Accuracy.** Have the balances for specific accounts been recorded appropriately?

    1) **Make inquiries of management.** Questions about the sources and uses of the recorded debt may be addressed to management.

    2) Compare the general ledger balances with financial statement balances.

  c. **Valuation and allocation.** Are balances reported in accordance with GAAP?

    1) **Vouch recorded debt to debt instruments.** Bonds should be recorded at their face amounts, with separate recognition of premium or discount. Debt due in the next year should be reclassified as current (also a classification issue).

    2) **Test amortization.** Recorded debt premium or discount should be recalculated to determine that it is being amortized using appropriate GAAP (the interest method).

  d. **Existence.** Does noncurrent debt reported at the balance sheet date exist?

    1) **Confirm debt.** Debt is confirmed with investment bankers, lenders, and bond trustees. Noncurrent notes payable may be confirmed directly with the holders of the notes. See Study Unit 11, Subunit 2 for the AICPA *Standard Form to Confirm Account Balance Information with Financial Institutions*.

  e. **Cutoff.** Have transactions relating to noncurrent debt been recorded in the proper period?

    1) **Test the cutoff.** Consider transactions near year end.

  f. **Rights and obligations.** Does the entity owe the noncurrent debt?

    1) **Evaluate existing agreements.** The auditor should obtain evidence that the debt is the obligation of the auditee.

    2) **Examine bond trust indentures.** The auditor should obtain evidence that the client is meeting the conditions of the contract and is in compliance with the law. Thus, the client should have obtained an attorney's opinion. The indenture contains information about contractual arrangements with bondholders, such as (a) the face amount of the bonds, (b) interest rates, (c) payment dates, (d) descriptions of collateral, (e) provisions for conversion or retirement, (f) trustee duties, and (g) sinking-fund requirements.

  g. **Occurrence.** Did the transactions relating to noncurrent debt occur?

    1) **Review contracts and agreements.** Debt transactions should be supported by appropriate documentation identifying (a) interest rates, (b) payment dates, (c) collateral, and (d) other terms.

  h. **Classification and understandability.** Are balances properly reflected in the balance sheet, is interest expense properly reported on the income statement, and are adequate disclosures provided?

    1) **Evaluate financial statements.** Determine that noncurrent and current debt are properly classified.

    2) **Inspect disclosures.** Appropriate disclosures should be made about the terms of the debt and collateral securing the debt.

Stop and review! You have completed the outline for this subunit. Study multiple-choice questions 20 and 21 beginning on page 414.

13.4 SUBSTANTIVE TESTING OF EQUITY

1. **Scope**

    a. The following typical balances for a corporation are included in this audit plan:

    1) Common and preferred stock
    2) Additional paid-in capital
    3) Retained earnings
    4) Treasury stock
    5) Accumulated other comprehensive income

2. **Testing Relevant Assertions.** The following is a standard audit plan for equity that tests relevant assertions (CAVE CROC):

    a. **Completeness.** Are all transactions affecting equity included in the balances for the period?

    1) **Perform analytical procedures.** Prior-period amounts recorded should be compared with current amounts.
    2) **Reconcile the subsidiary ledger with the control accounts.** The auditor should prepare a schedule from the subsidiary ledger and reconcile the amounts with the balances in the general ledger and financial statements.

    b. **Accuracy.** Have the balances for the specific accounts been recorded appropriately?

    1) The auditor should inquire of management about the actions, activities, and balances related to equity.
    2) Compare the general ledger balances with the financial statement balances.

    c. **Valuation and allocation.** Are balances reported in accordance with GAAP?

    1) **Trace entries to equity accounts.** The closing entries should be tested to determine that net income has been closed to retained earnings. Any designations (appropriations) of retained earnings should be traced to the related account.
    2) **Test sales of treasury stock.** "Gains" or "losses" on the sale of treasury stock are recognized directly in the equity section of the balance sheet, not in earnings.

    d. **Existence.** Do the shares reported as outstanding or treasury stock exist at the balance sheet date?

    1) **Confirm shares issued and outstanding with the registrar and transfer agent.** The auditor should have direct communication with external parties responsible for contact with the shareholders to request information about the number of shares issued and outstanding and payment of dividends.
    2) **Inspect stock certificates held in treasury.** Treasury stock should be counted.
    3) **Inspect stock certificate book.** If the client keeps its own stock records, the shares outstanding and stubs should be reconciled.

    e. **Cutoff.** Have transactions relating to equity been recorded in the proper period?

    1) The auditor should consider whether transactions near year end have been recognized in the proper period.

    f. **Rights and obligations.** Do equity balances reflect owners' interests?

    1) **Inspect the articles of incorporation and bylaws of the corporation.** These documents provide evidence about the legal status of the shareholders and their relationship(s) to the entity. The auditor should include copies in the working papers.

g. **Occurrence.** Did the transactions relating to equity occur?

1) **Vouch entries to supporting documents.** Documentation should exist for each equity transaction.

h. **Classification and understandability.** Are balances appropriately presented, and are adequate disclosures provided?

1) **Read minutes of meetings of the board of directors.** Authorizations of actions related to equity (e.g., issuances of additional shares, purchases or sales of treasury shares, and declarations of dividends) should be documented in the minutes. Many of these issues have implications for disclosure.

2) **Inspect disclosures about treasury stock.** The auditor should determine the proper use of the method (cost or par value) to report treasury stock.

3) **Search for restrictions.** Restrictions on retained earnings may arise from loans, agreements, or state law. The auditor should determine that disclosure is appropriate.

Stop and review! You have completed the outline for this subunit. Study multiple-choice questions 22 through 24 on page 415.

13.5 SUBSTANTIVE TESTING OF PAYROLL

1. **Scope**

a. The following balances are included in this audit plan:

1) Payroll expense
2) Inventories (for manufacturing firms)
3) Accrued payroll and vacation
4) Payroll tax liability
5) Pension costs and other post-employment benefit (OPEB) costs

b. Payroll processing has traditionally included controls that have allowed the auditor to assess the RMM at a low level and thereby reduce the audit effort devoted to substantive testing. Most entities recognize that the benefits of controls exceed the costs related to the payroll processing system.

1) One key control is a division of duties that includes the establishment of a **separate human resources department**. This control separates authorization from recordkeeping by the payroll department.

2. **Testing Relevant Assertions.** The following is a standard audit plan for payroll and related accounts that tests relevant assertions (CAVE CROC):

a. **Completeness.** Are all transactions affecting payroll reflected in the balances for the period?

1) **Perform analytical procedures.** The auditor should compare current expense with expectations from prior periods and management-prepared budgets from the beginning of the period with actual results. Total hours worked should be used to develop an expectation for total payroll expense. This expectation is compared with recorded expense. Industry percentages for labor-related ratios also should be compared with the client's results.

2) **Reconcile payroll tax expense with payroll tax returns** (income tax, FICA, and unemployment taxes).

b. **Accuracy.** Have the balances for specific accounts been recorded appropriately?

   1) **Make inquiries** of management. Questions include those relating to the reporting and disclosure of contractual arrangements with officers, union contracts, and pension and OPEB agreements.

   2) Compare the general ledger balances with the financial statement balances.

c. **Valuation and allocation.** Are balances reported in accordance with GAAP?

   1) **Trace costs to inventories (for manufacturing firms).** The auditor should determine that they contain direct labor costs.

   2) **Recalculate pension and OPEB costs.** Appropriate amounts should have been recorded and funded based on the appropriate agreements.

d. **Existence.** Do the accounts and balances exist at the balance sheet date?

   1) **Observe the distribution of paychecks.** A surprise observation of the distribution will provide assurance that only bona fide employees are being paid.

e. **Cutoff.** Have transactions relating to payroll been recorded in the proper period?

   1) **Test payroll cutoff.** Amounts to be accrued for the period should be recalculated from the last payroll date to year end. Also, amounts should have been recorded as payroll expense and accrued payroll.

f. **Rights and obligations.** Are the assets (capitalized in inventory), expenses, and payables those of the entity?

   1) **Inspect canceled checks.** These checks indicate payment to employees, government, and others relating to payroll.

g. **Occurrence.** Did the transactions relating to payroll occur?

   1) **Vouch a sample of employee transactions.** These should be sampled from the payroll-related balances and compared with the supporting documentation, including approved time cards, time tickets, and notations in the human resources records. The purpose is to verify that employees worked the number of hours for which they were paid.

h. **Classification and understandability.** Are payroll costs properly reflected as an expense in the income statement (or properly allocated to inventory and cost of sales for manufacturing firms)? Are liabilities properly displayed as current or noncurrent on the balance sheet, and are disclosures presented adequately?

   1) **Read the financial statements and disclosures.** The auditor should determine the appropriate presentation of balances. Disclosures should include a description of accounting policies and pension-related transactions.

You have completed Study Units 11 through 13. They address the auditor's substantive procedures performed in response to the assessment of the risks of material misstatement in the various accounting cycles. You should understand the relationship between management's assertions about the transactions, balances, and disclosures and the auditor's tests of the assertions. If you are having difficulty understanding this relationship or the role of management's assertions, review Study Unit 1, Subunit 2, which defines the assertions and the auditor's responsibility. Even if you have a solid understanding, a refreshed look at that material will likely help you.

Stop and review! You have completed the outline for this subunit. Study multiple-choice questions 25 through 30 beginning on page 416.

QUESTIONS

13.1 Substantive Testing of Property, Plant, and Equipment

1. Which of the following combinations of procedures would an auditor most likely perform to obtain evidence about fixed asset additions?

A. Inspecting documents and physically examining assets.

B. Recomputing calculations and obtaining written management representations.

C. Observing operating activities and comparing balances with prior-period balances.

D. Confirming ownership and corroborating transactions through inquiries of client personnel.

Answer (A) is correct.

REQUIRED: The combination of procedures most likely to obtain evidence about fixed asset additions.

DISCUSSION: The auditor's direct observation of fixed assets is one means of determining whether additions have been made. Tracing to the detailed records determines whether additions have been recorded. Inspection of deeds, lease agreements, insurance policies, invoices, canceled checks, and tax notices may also reveal additions.

Answer (B) is incorrect. Recomputations are based on recorded amounts and will not reveal unrecorded additions. Answer (C) is incorrect. Analytical procedures may not detect additions offset by disposals. Answer (D) is incorrect. The auditor must become aware of additions before confirming ownership or corroborating transactions.

2. In testing plant and equipment balances, an auditor may inspect new additions listed on the analysis of plant and equipment. This procedure is designed to obtain evidence concerning relevant assertions about

	Existence	Classification and Understandability
A.	Yes	Yes
B.	Yes	No
C.	No	Yes
D.	No	No

Answer (B) is correct.

REQUIRED: The relevant assertion(s), if any, tested by inspection of new additions of plant and equipment.

DISCUSSION: Assertions about existence address whether assets or liabilities of the entity exist at a particular date. Assertions about classification and understandability concern whether financial statement components are appropriately presented, described, and disclosed (AU-C 315). Thus, inspection by the auditor provides direct evidence that new plant and equipment assets exist but is irrelevant to the classification and understandability assertions. Reading the financial statements and related notes provides evidence about these assertions.

3. A weakness in internal control over recording retirements of equipment may cause an auditor to

A. Inspect certain items of equipment in the plant and trace those items to the accounting records.

B. Review the subsidiary ledger to ascertain whether depreciation was taken on each item of equipment during the year.

C. Trace additions to the "other assets" account to search for equipment that is still on hand but no longer being used.

D. Select certain items of equipment from the accounting records and locate them in the plant.

Answer (D) is correct.

REQUIRED: The procedure performed as a result of ineffective control over equipment retirements.

DISCUSSION: Failure to record retirements results in overstating equipment in the subsidiary records because the physical assets are not in the entity's possession. Thus, vouching items from the accounting records by locating the physical assets they represent provides evidence of whether retirements are unrecorded.

Answer (A) is incorrect. The test is in the wrong direction to discover the failure to record retirements. Answer (B) is incorrect. Depreciation should not be taken on equipment that is no longer in possession of the entity. Answer (C) is incorrect. Equipment should be in the equipment account, not other assets. Thus, a search of additions to other assets provides no evidence of retirements to equipment.

4. Determining that proper amounts of depreciation are expensed provides assurance about management's assertions of valuation and allocation and

A. Classification and understandability.

B. Completeness.

C. Rights and obligations.

D. Occurrence.

Answer (A) is correct.

REQUIRED: The assertions tested by consideration of the amounts of depreciation that are expensed.

DISCUSSION: The classification and understandability assertion states whether particular components of the financial statements are properly presented, described, and disclosed. For example, if cost of sales includes depreciation, the auditor should determine that this classification is appropriate and that it is properly disclosed.

Answer (B) is incorrect. The completeness assertion addresses whether all transactions, accounts, and disclosures that should be presented are included. Answer (C) is incorrect. The rights and obligations assertion addresses whether assets are rights, and obligations are liabilities, of the entity at a specified time. Answer (D) is incorrect. The occurrence assertion addresses whether recorded transactions and events occurred during the period.

5. In performing a search for unrecorded retirements of fixed assets, an auditor most likely would

A. Inspect the property ledger and the insurance and tax records, and then tour the client's facilities.

B. Tour the client's facilities, and then inspect the property ledger and the insurance and tax records.

C. Analyze the repair and maintenance account, and then tour the client's facilities.

D. Tour the client's facilities, and then analyze the repair and maintenance account.

Answer (A) is correct.
REQUIRED: The step performed in a search for unrecorded retirements of fixed assets.
DISCUSSION: In a search for unrecorded retirements, that is, a test of the completeness assertion, the auditor should first determine from the property ledger what assets are recorded and then tour the facilities to determine whether those assets are physically present. The completeness assertion addresses whether all transactions that should be presented (e.g., retirements) are included in the statements. However, in this case, the completeness assertion is closely related to the existence assertion.
Answer (B) is incorrect. Touring the facilities and then inspecting the property ledger and insurance and tax records tests to determine whether existing assets are recorded. Answer (C) is incorrect. Analyzing the repair and maintenance account provides evidence as to whether capital assets have been inappropriately expensed. Answer (D) is incorrect. Analyzing the repair and maintenance account provides evidence as to whether capital assets have been inappropriately expensed.

6. Which of the following explanations most likely would satisfy an auditor who questions management about significant debits to accumulated depreciation accounts in the current year?

A. Prior years' depreciation expenses were erroneously understated.

B. Current year's depreciation expense was erroneously understated.

C. The estimated remaining useful lives of plant assets were revised upward.

D. Plant assets were retired during the current year.

Answer (D) is correct.
REQUIRED: The satisfactory explanation about significant debits to accumulated depreciation accounts in the current year.
DISCUSSION: If plant assets were retired during the current year, their carrying amount is removed from the accounts. Accordingly, the asset (plant assets) is credited, accumulated depreciation is debited, and any consideration received and gain or loss are recognized.
Answer (A) is incorrect. The correction of an error for the prior period requires restatement of those statements. The effects of the adjustment are not recognized currently. Furthermore, a prior-period restatement of an understatement of depreciation increases the credit balance of accumulated depreciation. Answer (B) is incorrect. The current-year correction of an understatement of depreciation increases the credit balance of accumulated depreciation. Answer (C) is incorrect. A change in estimate is accounted for prospectively. Thus, no previously recognized depreciation is derecognized when the estimated remaining useful lives of plant assets are revised upward.

7. When auditing prepaid insurance, an auditor discovers that the original insurance policy on plant equipment is not available for inspection. The policy's absence most likely indicates the possibility of a(n)

A. Insurance premium due but not recorded.

B. Deficiency in the coinsurance provision.

C. Lien on the plant equipment.

D. Understatement of insurance expense.

Answer (C) is correct.
REQUIRED: The likely reason an insurance policy is not available for inspection.
DISCUSSION: When liens are placed on equipment or property, the lienholder often requires that the assets be insured and that the lienholder be named as the beneficiary. Hence, the policy is likely to be held by the lienholder even though the client is required to pay the premiums.
Answer (A) is incorrect. The premium has been paid and recorded as prepaid insurance. Answer (B) is incorrect. Coinsurance provisions require that the policy holder maintain coverage of a certain percentage of the value of the property (often 80-90%). Answer (D) is incorrect. The issue is not the recording of insurance, but the physical existence of the policy.

8. An auditor analyzes repairs and maintenance accounts primarily to obtain evidence in support of the relevant assertion that all

A. Noncapitalizable expenditures for repairs and maintenance have been recorded in the proper period.

B. Expenditures for property and equipment have been recorded in the proper period.

C. Noncapitalizable expenditures for repairs and maintenance have been properly charged to expense.

D. Expenditures for property and equipment have not been charged to expense.

Answer (D) is correct.
REQUIRED: The reason an auditor analyzes repairs and maintenance expense.
DISCUSSION: The auditor should vouch significant debits from the repairs and maintenance expense account to determine whether any should have been capitalized.
Answer (A) is incorrect. An improper cutoff of repairs and maintenance expenses is not typically a major risk. Answer (B) is incorrect. The repairs and maintenance expense accounts are not the appropriate sources of evidence regarding the cutoff of expenditures for property and equipment. Answer (C) is incorrect. Vouching additions to plant, property, and equipment provides evidence of whether any expense has been inappropriately charged as a capital item.

9. In auditing intangible assets, an auditor most likely would review or recompute amortization and determine whether the amortization period is reasonable in support of the relevant financial statement assertion of

A. Valuation and allocation.

B. Existence.

C. Completeness.

D. Rights and obligations.

Answer (A) is correct.
REQUIRED: The assertion tested in examining intangible assets and recomputing amortization.
DISCUSSION: Amortization is an allocation process that the auditor tests by recomputing the amortization based upon the recorded assets and the useful lives.
Answer (B) is incorrect. The existence assertion is that intangible assets exist. Answer (C) is incorrect. The completeness assertion is that the intangible assets that should be recorded are recorded. Answer (D) is incorrect. The rights and obligations assertion is that the entity controls the rights to the assets.

13.2 Substantive Testing of Investments and Derivatives (AU-C 501 and AU-C 540)

10. Which of the following pairs of accounts would an auditor most likely analyze on the same working paper?

A. Notes receivable and interest income.

B. Accrued interest receivable and accrued interest payable.

C. Notes payable and notes receivable.

D. Interest income and interest expense.

Answer (A) is correct.
REQUIRED: The pairs of accounts that an auditor most likely analyzes on the same working paper.
DISCUSSION: The auditor analyzes information and presents the analysis for related accounts on the same working paper. Notes receivable and interest on them are such related accounts.
Answer (B) is incorrect. Interest receivable and interest payable are independent of one another and are not likely to be analyzed on the same working paper. Answer (C) is incorrect. Notes payable and notes receivable are independent of one another and are not likely to be analyzed on the same working paper. Answer (D) is incorrect. Interest income and interest expense are independent of one another and are not likely to be analyzed on the same working paper.

11. An auditor would most likely verify the interest earned on bond investments by

A. Verifying the receipt and deposit of interest checks.

B. Confirming the bond interest rate with the issuer of the bonds.

C. Recomputing the interest earned on the basis of face amount, interest rate, and period held.

D. Testing internal controls relevant to cash receipts.

Answer (C) is correct.
REQUIRED: The method most likely used to verify bond interest earned.
DISCUSSION: The audit plan for investments includes making an independent computation of revenue (such as dividends and interest). For example, the auditor may use information from bond certificates (interest rates, payment dates, issue date, and face amount) to recalculate bond interest earned. This amount includes uncollected accruals.
Answer (A) is incorrect. Verifying the receipt and deposit of interest checks does not consider accrued interest. Answer (B) is incorrect. Confirming the rate would not, by itself, verify interest earned, which must be recomputed. Answer (D) is incorrect. Verification of interest earned requires substantive testing, not tests of controls.

12. An auditor is testing the reasonableness of dividend income from investments in issuers. The auditor most likely would compute the amount that should have been received and recorded by the client by

    A. Reading the details of the board of directors' meetings.

    B. Confirming the details with the investees' registrars.

    C. Electronically accessing the details of dividend records on the Internet.

    D. Examining the details of the client's most recent cutoff bank statement.

Answer (C) is correct.
    REQUIRED: The procedure for testing dividend income.
    DISCUSSION: Standard investment advisory services publish dividend records for all listed stocks. They show amounts and payment dates for dividend declarations and permit the auditor to independently recompute the client's reported dividend income.
    Answer (A) is incorrect. Reading the details of the board of directors' meetings may provide the auditor with evidence about the significant events of the entity, but not about the reasonableness of dividend income. Answer (B) is incorrect. Evidence about dividend income from investments in issuers can be obtained more efficiently from publicly available sources. Answer (D) is incorrect. Cutoff bank statements provide evidence about the client's deposits and disbursements made shortly after year end, not about investment income.

13. In performing a count of negotiable securities, an auditor records the details of the count on a security count worksheet. What other information is usually included on this worksheet?

    A. An acknowledgment by a client representative that the securities were returned intact.

    B. An analysis of realized gains and losses from the sale of securities during the year.

    C. An evaluation of the client's internal control concerning physical access to the securities.

    D. A description of the client's procedures that prevent the negotiation of securities by just one person.

Answer (A) is correct.
    REQUIRED: The information usually included on a security count worksheet.
    DISCUSSION: A securities count worksheet should include a record of all the significant information from the securities, such as names, amounts, and interest rates. Also, to ensure a clear chain of custody, it should contain an acknowledgment by a client representative that the securities were returned intact when the count was complete.

14. In confirming with an outside agent, such as a financial institution, that the agent is holding investment securities in the client's name, an auditor most likely gathers evidence in support of relevant financial statement assertions about existence or occurrence and

    A. Valuation and allocation.

    B. Rights and obligations.

    C. Completeness.

    D. Classification and understandability.

Answer (B) is correct.
    REQUIRED: The assertion tested by confirming investments to determine whether they are in the client's name.
    DISCUSSION: External confirmations may be designed to test any financial statement assertion (AU-C 505). However, a given confirmation request does not test all assertions equally well. For example, if the issue is whether securities are being held in the client's name by an outside agent, the completeness assertion with regard to the investment account is not adequately addressed by a confirmation request. Other agents may be holding securities for the client. Moreover, the agent may be holding other securities not specified in the request. Thus, the request tends to be most effective for testing the existence (whether the assets exist at a given date) assertion and the rights (whether the client has a specified ownership interest in the assets) assertion.

15. An auditor inspects a client's investment records to determine that any transfers between categories of investments have been properly recorded. The primary purpose of this procedure is to obtain evidence concerning relevant financial statement assertions about

A. Rights and obligations, and existence.

B. Valuation and allocation, and rights and obligations.

C. Existence or occurrence, and classification and understandability.

D. Classification and understandability, and valuation and allocation.

Answer (D) is correct.
REQUIRED: The assertions tested by inspecting reclassification of investments.
DISCUSSION: Assertions about classification and understandability address whether the information is appropriately presented and described and disclosures are clear. For example, U.S. GAAP require that a debt security be reclassified as available for sale if the entity (1) does not have the positive intent and ability to hold it to maturity but (2) does not intend to sell it in the near term. Inspecting the client's records just prior to and just after year end could help the auditor determine whether investment classifications are appropriate. Assertions about valuation address whether reported amounts conform with U.S. GAAP. Classification affects valuation. For example, held-to-maturity securities are measured at cost, and available-for-sale and trading securities are measured at fair value. Thus, inspecting transfers between categories also helps determine whether the investments are recorded at proper amounts.

16. To test the valuation assertion when auditing an investment accounted for by the equity method, an auditor most likely would

A. Inspect the stock certificates evidencing the investment.

B. Examine the audited financial statements of the investee company.

C. Review the broker's advice or canceled check for the investment's acquisition.

D. Obtain market quotations from financial newspapers or periodicals.

Answer (B) is correct.
REQUIRED: The procedure to test the valuation assertion for an equity-based investment.
DISCUSSION: The equity method recognizes undistributed income arising from an investment in an investee. Under the equity method, investor income is recorded as the investee reports income. Consequently, the audited financial statements of the investee provide the auditor with the undistributed income from the investee.
Answer (A) is incorrect. Inspection of stock certificates provides evidence about existence, not valuation. Answer (C) is incorrect. Reviewing the broker's advice or canceled check provides evidence about rights. Answer (D) is incorrect. Equity-based investments are not accounted for at fair value.

17. A client has a large and active investment portfolio that is kept in a bank safe-deposit box. If the auditor is unable to count the securities at the balance sheet date, the auditor most likely will

A. Request the bank to confirm to the auditor the contents of the safe-deposit box at the balance sheet date.

B. Examine supporting evidence for transactions occurring during the year.

C. Count the securities at a subsequent date and confirm with the bank whether securities were added or removed since the balance sheet date.

D. Request the client to have the bank seal the safe-deposit box until the auditor can count the securities at a subsequent date.

Answer (D) is correct.
REQUIRED: The procedure most likely performed when the auditor cannot count securities at the balance sheet date.
DISCUSSION: Securities should be inspected simultaneously with the verification of cash and the count of other liquid assets to prevent transfers among asset categories for the purpose of concealing a shortage. If this procedure is not possible but the securities are kept by a custodian in a bank safe-deposit box, the client may instruct the custodian that no one is to have access to the securities unless in the presence of the auditor. Thus, when the auditor finally inspects the securities, (s)he may conclude that they represent what was on hand at the balance sheet date.
Answer (A) is incorrect. The bank does not have access to the contents of the client's safe-deposit box. Answer (B) is incorrect. Supporting evidence for transactions occurring during the year is not a substitute for inspection of the securities. Answer (C) is incorrect. The bank does not have access to the contents of the client's safe-deposit box.

18. An auditor testing investments would ordinarily use analytical procedures to ascertain the reasonableness of the

A. Existence of unrealized gains or losses.

B. Completeness of recorded investment income.

C. Classification as available-for-sale or trading securities.

D. Valuation of trading securities.

Answer (B) is correct.
    REQUIRED: The use of analytical procedures when an auditor tests investments.
    DISCUSSION: The auditor may develop expectations regarding the completeness assertion for recorded investment income from stocks by using dividend records published by standard investment advisory services to recompute dividends received. Interest income from bond investments can be calculated from interest rates and payment dates noted on the certificates. Income from equity-based investments can be estimated from audited financial statements of the investees. Thus, applying an expected rate of return to the net investment amount may be an effective means of estimating total investment income.
    Answer (A) is incorrect. Unrealized gains or losses are dependent on the fair values of specific securities and cannot be calculated based on plausible relationships among the data. Answer (C) is incorrect. Available-for-sale securities may meet the definition of current assets. Answer (D) is incorrect. Individual trading securities may meet the definition of current assets.

19. Auditors may need to plan and perform auditing procedures for financial statement assertions about derivatives and hedging activities. Which of the following substantive procedures most clearly tests the completeness assertion about derivatives?

A. Assessing the reasonableness of the use of an option-pricing model.

B. Determining whether changes in the fair value of derivatives designated and qualifying as hedging instruments have been reported in earnings or in other comprehensive income.

C. Requesting counterparties to provide information about them, such as whether side agreements have been made.

D. Physically inspecting the derivative contract.

Answer (C) is correct.
    REQUIRED: The substantive procedure that most clearly tests the completeness assertion about derivatives.
    DISCUSSION: An audit of the completeness assertion addresses whether balances and transactions related to derivatives and hedging activities that should be recorded are recorded. A substantive procedure for the completeness assertion about derivatives and hedging activities is a request to the counterparty to a derivative for information about it, for example, whether an agreement exists to repurchase securities sold or whether side agreements have been made.
    Answer (A) is incorrect. Assessing the reasonableness of the use of an option-pricing model tests the valuation assertion. Answer (B) is incorrect. Determining whether changes in the fair value of derivatives designated and qualifying as hedging instruments have been reported in earnings or in other comprehensive income tests the classification and understandability assertion. Answer (D) is incorrect. Physically inspecting the derivative contract tests the existence assertion.

13.3 Substantive Testing of Noncurrent Debt

20. An audit plan for noncurrent debt should include steps that require

A. Examining bond trust indentures.

B. Inspecting the accounts payable subsidiary ledger.

C. Investigating credits to the bond interest income account.

D. Verifying the existence of the bondholders.

Answer (A) is correct.
    REQUIRED: The procedure to be included in the audit plan for noncurrent debt.
    DISCUSSION: The bond trust indenture contains information about contractual arrangements made with bondholders, such as (1) the face amount of the bonds, (2) interest rates, (3) payment dates, (4) descriptions of collateral, (5) provisions for conversion or retirement, (6) trustee duties, and (7) sinking fund requirements. The auditor should examine any bond trust indenture to determine that the client is meeting the conditions of the contract and is in compliance with the law.
    Answer (B) is incorrect. Accounts payable are current liabilities, not noncurrent debt. Answer (C) is incorrect. Credits to bond interest income do not pertain to noncurrent debt (income relates to investments, not debt). Answer (D) is incorrect. The existence of bondholders is implied by the reporting of bonded debt.

21. In auditing for unrecorded noncurrent bonds payable, an auditor most likely will

    A. Perform analytical procedures on the bond premium and discount accounts.

    B. Examine documentation of assets purchased with bond proceeds for liens.

    C. Compare interest expense with the bond payable amount for reasonableness.

    D. Confirm the existence of individual bondholders at year end.

Answer (C) is correct.
    REQUIRED: The appropriate procedure for testing noncurrent bonds payable.
    DISCUSSION: The recorded interest expense should reconcile with the outstanding bonds payable. If interest expense appears excessive relative to the recorded bonds payable, unrecorded noncurrent liabilities may exist.
    Answer (A) is incorrect. Performing analytical procedures on bond premium and discount are not likely to uncover unrecorded payables. Answer (B) is incorrect. The examination of documentation related to asset additions is considered in the audit of assets, not bonds payable. Answer (D) is incorrect. The greatest risk is that the bonds payable balance is not complete.

13.4 Substantive Testing of Equity

22. During an audit of a company's equity accounts, the auditor determines whether restrictions have been imposed on retained earnings resulting from loans, agreements, or state law. This audit procedure most likely is intended to verify relevant assertion about

    A. Existence or occurrence.

    B. Completeness.

    C. Valuation and allocation.

    D. Classification and understandability.

Answer (D) is correct.
    REQUIRED: The assertion that the auditor tests relative to restrictions on retained earnings.
    DISCUSSION: The presentation and disclosure assertions include assertions about classification and understandability. Financial information should be properly presented and disclosed, and disclosures should be clear (AU-C 315 and AS No. 15). Hence, when restrictions have been placed on retained earnings, the auditor should determine that they are properly disclosed in the notes to the financial statements.
    Answer (A) is incorrect. Restrictions on retained earnings have little relevance to the existence or occurrence assertion. Answer (B) is incorrect. Restrictions on retained earnings have little relevance to the completeness assertion. Answer (C) is incorrect. Restrictions on retained earnings have little relevance to the valuation assertion.

23. An auditor usually obtains evidence of a company's equity transactions by reviewing its

    A. Minutes of board of directors meetings.

    B. Transfer agent's records.

    C. Canceled stock certificates.

    D. Treasury stock certificate book.

Answer (A) is correct.
    REQUIRED: The source of evidence about equity transactions.
    DISCUSSION: Equity transactions are typically few in number and large in amount. They require authorization by the board of directors. Thus, an auditor reviews the minutes of the board meetings to identify transactions.
    Answer (B) is incorrect. Although the auditor might confirm certain transactions with the client's transfer agent, the agent's records are not typically made available to the auditor. Answer (C) is incorrect. Canceled stock certificates represent only those shares that were retired. Answer (D) is incorrect. Treasury stock records include only those transactions involving reacquisition and resale of the entity's own stock.

24. When a client's company does not maintain its own stock records, the auditor should obtain written confirmation from the transfer agent and registrar concerning

    A. Restrictions on the payment of dividends.

    B. The number of shares issued and outstanding.

    C. Guarantees of preferred stock liquidation value.

    D. The number of shares subject to agreements to repurchase.

Answer (B) is correct.
    REQUIRED: The information confirmed by the transfer agent and registrar.
    DISCUSSION: The independent stock registrar is a financial institution employed to prevent improper issuances of stock, especially over-issuances. The transfer agent maintains detailed shareholder records and facilitates transfer of shares. Both are independent and reliable sources of evidence concerning total shares issued and outstanding.
    Answer (A) is incorrect. The payment of dividends is confirmed, but dividend restrictions are found in the articles of incorporation, bylaws, and minutes of directors' and shareholders' meetings. Answer (C) is incorrect. Guarantees of preferred stock liquidation value are not made by the transfer agent and registrar. Answer (D) is incorrect. The number of shares subject to agreements to repurchase is not the concern of the transfer agent and registrar.

13.5 Substantive Testing of Payroll

25. An auditor vouched data for a sample of employees in a payroll register to approved clock card data to provide assurance that

A. Payments to employees are computed at authorized rates.

B. Employees work the number of hours for which they are paid.

C. Segregation of duties exists between the preparation and distribution of the payroll.

D. Internal controls relating to unclaimed payroll checks are operating effectively.

Answer (B) is correct.
    REQUIRED: The purpose of vouching payroll register information to approved clock card data.
    DISCUSSION: To test that payroll events actually occurred, an auditor vouches a sample of employee transactions recorded in the payroll-related balances to supporting documentation, including approved time cards, time tickets, and notations in personnel records. The purpose is to verify that employees work the hours for which they are paid.
    Answer (A) is incorrect. The auditor compares the pay rates used in calculating payments to employees with the authorized rates in the personnel files to determine whether they were authorized. Answer (C) is incorrect. The auditor tests segregation of duties by inquiry and observation. Answer (D) is incorrect. The auditor observes the activities of the treasurer to determine whether unclaimed payroll checks were being properly controlled.

26. When the risk of material misstatement is assessed as low for assertions related to payroll, substantive tests of payroll balances most likely would be limited to applying analytical procedures and

A. Observing the distribution of paychecks.

B. Footing and crossfooting the payroll register.

C. Inspecting payroll tax returns.

D. Recalculating payroll accruals.

Answer (D) is correct.
    REQUIRED: The audit procedure for payroll when the RMM is low.
    DISCUSSION: When controls are judged to be effective, the auditor's procedures are typically limited to analytical procedures and testing for completeness and cutoff of the year-end accruals.
    Answer (A) is incorrect. The auditor considers the observation of the distribution of the paychecks if the RMM is high. Answer (B) is incorrect. Effective controls should provide assurance of proper reporting. Analytical procedures also should indicate likely misstatements. Answer (C) is incorrect. Effective controls should provide assurance of proper reporting. Analytical procedures also should indicate likely misstatements.

27. An auditor most likely would perform substantive tests of details on payroll transactions and balances when

A. Cutoff tests indicate a substantial amount of accrued payroll expense.

B. The assessed risk of material misstatement relative to payroll transactions is low.

C. Analytical procedures indicate unusual fluctuations in recurring payroll entries.

D. Accrued payroll expense consists primarily of unpaid commissions.

Answer (C) is correct.
    REQUIRED: The situation in which the auditor most likely will perform tests of details on payroll transactions and balances.
    DISCUSSION: The auditor should evaluate significant unexpected differences revealed by analytical procedures. The first step is to reconsider the methods and factors used in developing the expectations and to make inquiries of management. If a suitable explanation is not received, additional procedures to investigate the differences are necessary.
    Answer (A) is incorrect. A substantial amount of accrued payroll expense is not an abnormal condition. Answer (B) is incorrect. A low assessed RMM may permit the auditor to devote less effort to substantive tests. Answer (D) is incorrect. The existence of unpaid earned commissions provides no indication of a misstatement.

28. In auditing payroll when control risk is assessed as low, an auditor most likely will

A. Verify that checks representing unclaimed wages are mailed.

B. Trace individual employee deductions to entity journal entries.

C. Observe entity employees during a payroll distribution.

D. Compare payroll costs with entity standards or budgets.

Answer (D) is correct.
    REQUIRED: The procedure most likely performed during the audit of payroll.
    DISCUSSION: Comparing payroll costs with budgeted amounts is a standard analytical procedure that is performed in most audits of payroll.
    Answer (A) is incorrect. Checks representing unclaimed wages should be maintained by the CFO until claimed by the appropriate employees. Answer (B) is incorrect. The individual employee deductions do not result in entity journal entries, but cumulative journal entries record the sum of the payroll. Answer (C) is incorrect. Observation of payroll distribution may not be necessary when the RMMs are low.

29. An auditor most likely increases substantive tests of payroll when

    A. Payroll is extensively audited by the state government.

    B. Payroll expense is substantially higher than in the prior year.

    C. Overpayments are discovered in performing tests of details.

    D. Employees complain to management about too much overtime.

Answer (C) is correct.
    REQUIRED: The situation in which the auditor most likely will extend substantive tests of payroll.
    DISCUSSION: During the application of substantive tests, the auditor may decide to extend the tests when unexpected findings (e.g., overpayments) are made. The purpose is to determine the extent of any fraud.
    Answer (A) is incorrect. When payroll is audited by external parties, the auditor may decide to do less testing in the area. Answer (B) is incorrect. Although an analytical procedure in the planning stage might suggest more testing, the question indicates that substantive tests have already begun. Answer (D) is incorrect. Employees' concern about too much overtime is not likely to affect the auditor's testing of the payroll.

30. Which of the following circumstances most likely will cause an auditor to suspect an employee payroll fraud scheme?

    A. There are significant unexplained variances between standard and actual labor cost.

    B. Payroll checks are disbursed by the same employee each payday.

    C. Employee time cards are approved by individual departmental supervisors.

    D. A separate payroll bank account is maintained on an imprest basis.

Answer (A) is correct.
    REQUIRED: The circumstance most likely to cause the auditor to suspect an employee payroll fraud scheme.
    DISCUSSION: Analytical procedures, such as variance analysis, alert the auditor when actual results were not anticipated. Thus, the auditor should consider the possibility that payroll is fraudulently overstated.
    Answer (B) is incorrect. The payroll checks should be disbursed by the paymaster each pay period. Answer (C) is incorrect. Supervisors should approve individual time cards. Answer (D) is incorrect. A separate payroll account using an imprest basis provides additional control over payroll.

Use the additional questions in Gleim **CPA Test Prep** to create Practice Exams that emulate Prometric!

13.6 PRACTICE TASK-BASED SIMULATIONS

| | Auditing and Attestation
Testlet 4 of 4 | Time Remaining
1 hour - 30 minutes | Unsplit | Split Horiz | Split Vertical | Spreadsheet | Calculator | Exit |

DIRECTIONS

Note: If you believe you have encountered a software malfunction, report it to the test center staff immediately.

Navigation

To navigate from task to task, use the controls at the bottom of the screen. Click on the **Next** button to advance to the next task, or the **Previous** button to go to the previous task. To go directly to any task, click on its number.

| ⚑ = Reminder | | Directions | 1 2 3 4 5 6 7 | | Previous   Next ▶ |

If you would like a reminder to revisit a task, or want to indicate that you are finished with it, click on the reminder flag below the task number. To clear the flag, click on it again. Reminder flags are for your use only – they do not contribute to your score.

Tabs

In this part of the examination, you will be asked to complete various tasks. Every task has one or more **Work Tabs**. Some tasks have one or more **Information Tabs**, others may have none. Every task has a **Help** tab.

If a task has **Information Tabs**, you may use the information in them to complete your responses in the **Work Tabs**.

| ✏ Corporate Gain and Basis | Authoritative Literature | Help |

| **Work tab** | **Information tab** | **Help tab** |

Work Tabs:
- **Work Tabs** are identified with a pencil icon. This is where your responses are expected.
- Each task has one or more **Work Tabs**.
- **Work Tabs** contain directions for completing the task – be sure to read these directions carefully.
- The **Work Tab** name in the example above is for illustration only – yours will differ.
- You must complete all of the **Work Tabs** in each task to receive full credit.

Information Tabs:
- The Authoritative Literature will be provided in all tasks in the AUD, FAR, and REG sections for your reference.
- Your simulation may have one or more additional **Information Tabs**. Like the Authoritative Literature tabs, **Information Tabs** do not have a pencil icon.
- If your task has additional **Information Tabs**, go through each to familiarize yourself with the task content.

Help Tab:
- The **Help Tab** provides assistance with the exam software that is used in this task. For example, if the task is to compose a memorandum, **Help** will provide information about the word processor.

The Toolbar

The toolbar at the top of the screen shows the amount of time remaining for you to complete the tasks. In addition, the following tools are available. Note that only the **Exit** button is displayed when Directions are visible - the others will appear when you begin the tasks.

Click on these buttons to split or unsplit the screen. You can split the screen vertically or horizontally.

Click on this button to display the calculator; click on it again to hide the calculator. To move the calculator, click on the calculator title bar and drag the calculator to the desired location.

Click on this button to use the spreadsheet; click on it again to hide the spreadsheet. To move the spreadsheet, click on the the spreadsheet title bar and drag the spreadsheet to the desired location.

Click on this button to go on to the next part of the examination. You must complete all of the tasks to receive full credit. Once you click on **Exit** and confirm the action, you will NOT be able to return to this testlet.

| ⚑ = Reminder | | Directions | 1 2 3 4 5 | | Previous   Next ▶ |

| Relevant Assertions and Substantive Audit Procedures | Authoritative Literature | Help |

Select from the list provided the most likely assertion being tested with each audit procedure in the table below. Each choice may be used once, more than once, or not at all.

Substantive Audit Procedure	Answer
1. The auditor tested the equipment balance by evaluating large debits recorded in repairs and maintenance to determine whether any should have been capitalized.	
2. The auditor tested depreciation related to equipment to determine that it is generally accepted and applied consistently.	
3. The auditor examined titles related to vehicles reported in the equipment account.	
4. The auditor determined that equipment was displayed in the noncurrent asset category on the balance sheet.	
5. The auditor applied an analytical procedure to noncurrent debt by comparing the current year's balance with that of the previous year.	
6. The auditor examined purchase transactions for equipment for several days before and after year end to determine that they were recorded in the proper year.	
7. The auditor reconciled the amounts of debt in the subsidiary ledger with the total in the general ledger account.	
8. The auditor confirmed shares of common stock issued and outstanding with the registrar and transfer agent of the client.	
9. The auditor determined that restrictions on the issuance of dividends were properly described in the financial statement notes.	
10. The auditor determined that the loss associated with the sale of treasury stock was appropriately calculated.	

Relevant Assertion
A) Completeness
B) Accuracy
C) Valuation and allocation
D) Existence
E) Cutoff
F) Rights and obligations
G) Occurrence
H) Classification and understandability

▼ = Reminder Directions 1 2 3 4 5 ◀ Previous Next ▶

| Research | Authoritative Literature | Help |

Wilhelm, CPA, is auditing a nonissuer client with significant investments in derivative securities to be measured and disclosed at fair value. Which section of the generally accepted auditing standards best outlines the auditor's responsibilities for these derivatives?

Title	Section	Paragraph

Title Choices						
AU-C	PCAOB	AT	AR	ET	BL	VS
CS	QC	PR	TS	PFP	CPE	

▼ = Reminder Directions 1 2 3 4 5 ◀ Previous Next ▶

Relevant Assertions | Authoritative Literature | Help

This question has a multiple-choice format that requires you to select the correct response from a drop-down list. Write the answer in the shaded column next to the audit assertion.

Items 1 through 10 represent relevant financial statement assertions for the investments, accounts receivable, and property and equipment accounts. Select from the list provided the substantive audit procedure that primarily addresses each relevant assertion. Select only one procedure for each assertion. Each procedure may be selected only once or not at all.

Relevant Assertions for Investments	Answer
1. Investments are properly presented and described.	
2. Recorded investments represent investments actually owned at the balance sheet date.	
3. Available-for-sale securities are properly measured at fair value at the balance sheet date.	

Substantive Procedures – Investments
A) Trace investment transactions to minutes of the board of directors' meetings to determine that transactions were properly authorized.
B) Obtain positive confirmations as of the balance sheet date of investments held by independent custodians.
C) Determine that any other-than-temporary impairments of the price of investments have been properly recorded.
D) Verify that available-for-sale securities are properly classified as current or noncurrent.

Relevant Assertions for Accounts Receivable	Answer
4. Accounts receivable represent amounts owed to the entity up to the balance sheet date.	
5. The entity has a legal right to all accounts receivable at the balance sheet date.	
6. Accounts receivable are stated at net realizable value.	
7. Accounts receivable are properly presented and described in the financial statements.	

Substantive Procedures – Accounts Receivable
A) Review the aged trial balance for significant past-due accounts.
B) Review the accounts receivable trial balance for amounts due from officers and employees.
C) Perform sales cutoff tests to obtain assurance that sales transactions and corresponding entries for inventories and cost of goods sold are recorded in the same and proper period.
D) Review loan agreements for indications of whether accounts receivable have been factored or pledged.

Relevant Assertions for Property and Equipment	Answer
8. The entity has a legal right to property and equipment acquired during the year.	
9. Recorded property and equipment represent assets that actually exist at the balance sheet date.	
10. Net property and equipment are properly measured at the balance sheet date.	

Substantive Procedures – Property and Equipment
A) Review the provision for depreciation expense and determine that depreciable lives and methods used in the current year are consistent with those used in the prior year.
B) Physically examine all major property and equipment additions.
C) Examine deeds and title insurance certificates.

| Journal Entries | Authoritative Literature | Help |

During the course of the Year 2 audit of King Co., the auditor discovered potential cutoff and valuation problems that may or may not require adjusting journal entries. For each of the potential cutoff and valuation problems indicated below, complete the required journal entries.

To prepare each entry,

- Double-click in the shaded cells in the Account Name column and select from the list provided the appropriate account name. If no entry is needed, select "No entry required." An account may be used once or not at all for each entry.
- Enter the corresponding debit or credit amount in the appropriate column.
- Round all amounts to the nearest dollar.
- All rows may not be required to complete each entry.

1. On January 1, Year 2, the company paid an insurance premium of $36,000 for the three following years. The entire payment was recognized as Year 2 insurance expense. No additional entry was made by the company in relation to this transaction. Record the necessary Year 2 adjustments, if any.

Account Name	Debit	Credit

2. In their response to the letter of audit inquiry for Year 2, the company's legal counsel indicated that a former employee has sued the company for $100,000. Management and counsel believe that a material loss probably will occur when pending litigation is resolved, and the reasonable estimate of the amount of range for the potential loss is $20,000 to $80,000. No amount within that range appears to be a better estimate that any other. No accrual was made in the financial statements regarding this suit. Record the necessary Year 2 adjustments, if any.

Account Name	Debit	Credit

3. On July 1, Year 2, the company received a 5-year loan of $100,000 from the bank. The loan bears a 10% interest that paid annually from July 1, Year 3. Accrued interest payable on the loan were not recorded at year end. Record the necessary Year 2 adjustments, if any.

Account Name	Debit	Credit

Account Names Choices

Account Names Choices
Cash
Cost of goods sold
Income tax expense
Insurance expense
Interest expense
Interest payable
Interest receivable
Inventory
Loss from contingent liability
No entry required
Payroll expense
Prepaid insurance expense
Provision for contingent liability
Shareholders' equity
Trade receivables

| Derivatives, Investments, and Hedges | Authoritative Literature | Help |

During the audit of derivatives, investments, and hedges, a number of misstatements were detected by the auditor. For each misstatement, select from List I the assertion affected by the misstatement. Select from List II the audit procedure that most likely detected the misstatement. Each choice may be used once, more than once, or not at all.

Misstatement	Assertion Affected	Audit Procedure Used to Detect Misstatement
1. A derivative used as a fair value hedge was reported at less than fair value.		
2. A contract for a future delivery of a commodity used as a hedge was not clearly described in the notes to the financial statements.		
3. A contract approved by the board of directors creating and defining a derivative was not recorded in the financial statements.		
4. A cash flow hedge created to protect against an interest rate increase was ineffective and resulted in a loss that was unrecognized in the current year.		
5. A derivative security being reported at year end had been sold by the client's broker earlier in the year.		

List I - Assertion Affected
A) Existence
B) Valuation and allocation
C) Completeness
D) Rights and obligations
E) Classification and understandability

List II - Audit Procedure Used to Detect Misstatement
F) Confirm securities and other assets held by third parties.
G) Review the financial statements and inquire of management about investments and derivatives.
H) Obtain and review minutes of meetings of those charged with governance.
I) Obtain prices at year end from an independent source and compare with recorded amounts.
J) Read and evaluate available contracts for effects on the financial statements.
K) Determine that no contracts or arrangements creating derivatives or hedges have been made with related parties.

Unofficial Answers

1. Relevant Assertions and Substantive Audit Procedures (10 Gradable Items)

1. <u>A) Completeness.</u> Evaluating large debits recorded in repairs and maintenance to determine whether any should have been capitalized tests the completeness assertion for the equipment balance.

2. <u>C) Valuation and allocation.</u> Testing depreciation to determine that the methods are generally accepted and applied consistently relates primarily to the valuation and allocation assertion.

3. <u>F) Rights and obligations.</u> Examining titles related to vehicles reported in the equipment account relates to ownership (rights).

4. <u>H) Classification and understandability.</u> The proper balance sheet presentation of equipment relates primarily to the classification assertion.

5. <u>A) Completeness.</u> Analytical procedures primarily test the completeness assertion.

6. <u>E) Cutoff.</u> Examining purchase transactions for equipment for several days before and after year end to determine that they were recorded in the proper year tests cutoff.

7. <u>A) Completeness.</u> Reconciling the amounts of debt in the subsidiary ledger with the total in the general ledger account is a primary test of completeness.

8. <u>D) Existence.</u> Confirmations primarily test the existence assertion.

9. <u>H) Classification and understandability.</u> Determining that restrictions on the issuance of dividends were properly described in the financial statement notes relates primarily to the assertion of understandability.

10. <u>B) Accuracy.</u> Verifying calculations primarily tests the accuracy assertion.

2. Research (1 Gradable Item)

Answer: 501.06

AU-C Section 501 -- *Audit Evidence -- Spe   siderations for Selected Items*

Investments in Derivative Instruments a   ities Measured or Disclosed at Fair Value

.06   With respect to investments in deriva   ments and securities measured or disclosed at fair value, the auditor should

   a.   determine whether the applicable financial reporting framework specifies the method to be used to determine the fair value of the entity's derivative instruments and investments in securities and

   b.   evaluate whether the determination of fair value is consistent with the specified valuation method.

3. Relevant Assertions (10 Gradable Items)

1.   D) Classification of available-for-sale securities relates to the assertion about proper presentation and description of investments (the classification and understandability assertion).

2.   B) Confirmations are most effective for the existence and rights and obligation assertions.

3.   C) Impairment of investments means that fair value is less than the recorded amount. If available-for-sale securities are subject to an other-than-temporary impairment, their cost basis is written down and the change is included in earnings, not in other comprehensive income. The valuation and allocation assertion about assets is that (a) they are reported at appropriate amounts and (b) adjustments are appropriately recorded.

4.   C) Cutoff tests determine that all transactions occurring during a period are recorded in that period. Thus, they address the cutoff assertion.

5.   D) Pledging receivables as security for a loan or selling receivables means that rights have been conveyed to a creditor or a buyer, respectively. Accordingly, reviewing loan agreements tests the rights and obligations assertion about balances.

6.   A) Aging of receivables analyzes the probability of collection of receivables and is therefore related to the valuation and allocation assertion about balances. Accounts receivable should be reported at net realizable value.

7.   B) Accounts receivable should be presented as a current asset with any significant issues disclosed. One required disclosure is the existence of related party transactions. Thus, material amounts due from officers and employees should be disclosed.

8.   C) Deeds and title insurance provide evidence supporting the rights and obligations assertion about balances.

9.   B) Physical examination of property provides strong evidence supporting the existence assertion about balances. The auditor usually inspects all major additions of property recorded during the period.

10.   A) Property and equipment (except land) should be recorded at cost and depreciated over their useful lives. The auditor reviews depreciation procedures during the testing of the valuation and allocation assertion about balances.

4. Journal Entries (12 Gradable Items)

1.   A cutoff test verifies that transactions have been recorded in the proper period. The amount of $36,000 is an insurance premium for 3 years. Thus, Year 2 insurance expense and prepaid insurance expense are 1/3 and 2/3 of this amount, respectively.

Account Name	Debit	Credit
Prepaid insurance expense	$24,000	
Insurance expense		$24,000

2.   Because the loss is probable and can be reasonably estimated, it should be accrued if the amount is material. If the estimate is stated within a given range and no amount within that range appears to be a better estimate than any other, the minimum of the range should be accrued.

Account Name	Debit	Credit
Loss from contingent liability	$20,000	
Provision for contingent liability		$20,000

3.   Since the loan was received in the middle of the year, the interest on loan is accrued for half of the year and calculated as follows: $5,000 = $100,000 × 10% × 0.5.

Account Name	Debit	Credit
Interest expense	$5,000	
Interest payable		$5,000

5. Derivatives, Investments, and Hedges (10 Gradable Items)

1. B) Valuation and allocation. Derivatives are always accounted for   They should be reported at fair value at year end along with the related item being hedged.

    I) Obtain prices at year end from an independent source and comp   orded amounts. Fair value estimates may be obtained from a third-party source (e.g., a broker-dealer).

2. E) Classification and understandability. Derivatives and hedges sho   quately disclosed in the financial statements.

    G) Review the financial statements and inquire of management abo   ents and derivatives. Classification and required disclosure are often based on the actions of managemer   of management may help determine whether derivatives, hedges, and other financial instruments are   lescribed in the notes to the financial statements.

3. C) Completeness. The auditor should determine that all transaction   ed in the financial statements.

    H) Obtain and review minutes of meetings of those charged with g   he auditor should obtain, read, and follow up on significant issues discussed and approved by those charg   nance, including the board of directors.

4. C) Completeness. The financial statements should reflect all gains   or the period.

    J) Read and evaluate available contracts for effects on the financi   Contracts should be read and evaluated. Derivatives used as hedges should be evaluated with the associ   g hedged to determine the effect on the financial statements.

5. A) Existence. The auditor should determine that reported assets exist at the balance sheet date.

    F) Confirm securities and other assets held by third parties. Confirmation with a broker-dealer should uncover reported securities that do not exist.

Gleim Simulation Grading

Task	Correct Responses		Gradable Items		Score per Task
1	____	÷	10	=	____
2 (Research)	____	÷	1	=	____
3	____	÷	10	=	____
4	____	÷	12	=	____
5	____	÷	10	=	____

Total of Scores per Task	____
÷ Total Number of Tasks	5
Total Score	____ %

Use **CPA Gleim Online** and **Simulation Wizard** to practice more task-based simulations in a realistic environment.

STUDY UNIT FOURTEEN
EVIDENCE -- KEY CONSIDERATIONS

(14 pages of outline)

This study unit presents a number of topics related to the collection of evidence. Of these issues, inquiry of the client's legal counsel, an entity's ability to continue as a going concern, and client representations have been tested most consistently on recent exams. All topics presented here are likely subjects of future multiple-choice questions.

14.1 CONSIDERATION OF LITIGATION, CLAIMS, AND ASSESSMENTS (AU-C 501)

1. Management is responsible for adopting policies and procedures to identify, evaluate, and account for **litigation, claims, and assessments (LCA)**. Accordingly, it is the primary source of information about LCA.

    a. The applicable accounting principles are those relevant to **contingencies** and contingent liabilities.

2. The auditor should **obtain evidence** relevant to the following:

    a. Circumstances indicating an uncertainty as to possible loss from LCA

        1) Under U.S. GAAP, the outcomes of an uncertainty are included in the following probability classifications: (a) remote, (b) reasonably possible, and (c) probable.

            a) This language need not be used by legal counsel to evaluate the outcomes of LCA. However, legal counsel's descriptions are sufficiently clear for the auditor's purposes if they can be used to classify outcomes in the three categories established by U.S. GAAP.

    b. The period in which the underlying cause for legal action occurred

    c. The probability of an unfavorable outcome

    d. The amount or range of potential loss

3. The **auditor's procedures** include the following:

    a. Inquiring about, and discussing with management and in-house legal counsel, the policies and procedures for identifying, evaluating, and accounting for LCA that may result in a risk of material misstatement (RMM).

    b. Obtaining from management a description and evaluation of LCA at period end, and from then to the date the information is provided, including an identification of matters referred to legal counsel.

        1) The auditor also should obtain **written representations** from management that all actual and possible LCA that should be considered in preparing the statements have been (a) disclosed to the auditor and (b) accounted for and disclosed in accordance with the applicable reporting framework.

    c. Examining documents in the entity's possession (e.g., legal expense accounts and invoices from, and correspondence with, external legal counsel).

    d.   Applying related procedures. An audit normally includes procedures undertaken for other purposes that also might produce evidence about LCA. Some examples are the following **risk assessment** procedures performed to obtain an understanding of the entity and its environment:

        1)   Reading minutes of meetings of shareholders, directors, and appropriate committees held during, and subsequent to, the period being audited

        2)   Reading contracts, loan agreements, leases, correspondence from governmental agencies, and similar documents

        3)   Obtaining information about guarantees from bank confirmations

        4)   Inspecting other documents for possible guarantees by the client

4.   If the auditor concludes that no actual or potential LCA exist that indicate RMMs, **no direct communication** with the entity's legal counsel is required. This decision should be documented.

    a.   Otherwise, the auditor should send a letter of inquiry prepared by the entity's management requesting that legal counsel communicate directly with the auditor. Thus, the auditor should request that management authorize legal counsel to discuss relevant matters.

5.   **Communication with Legal Counsel**

    a.   A **letter of inquiry** to external legal counsel is the auditor's primary means of obtaining corroboration of the information provided about material LCA by management. An auditor usually cannot make legal judgments.

        1)   Evidence provided by in-house counsel may corroborate management's information.

    b.   The letter of inquiry includes the following:

        1)   Identification of the entity and its subsidiaries and the date of the audit

        2)   A management list (or a request by management that legal counsel prepare a list) that describes and evaluates **pending** or **threatened** LCA with respect to which legal counsel has performed substantive legal services on behalf of the entity

           a)   For each matter, legal counsel should be requested either to provide the following information or to comment on disagreements with management:

              i)   The nature of the matter, the progress of the case, and the entity's intended action

              ii)   The probability of an unfavorable outcome and an estimate, if possible, of the amount or range of loss

              iii)   Omission of any pending or threatened LCA from management's list

        3)   A management list that describes and evaluates **unasserted** claims and assessments that (a) management considers to be probable and (b) have at least a reasonable possibility of an unfavorable outcome, with respect to which legal counsel has performed substantive legal services on behalf of the entity

           a)   Also included is a request that legal counsel comment on those matters that are the basis for disagreements with management.

        4)   A statement that management understands that legal counsel will advise the client when an unasserted claim or assertion with respect to which (s)he has provided legal services requires the entity to disclose or consider disclosure in accordance with the applicable reporting framework

           a)   The letter of inquiry should request legal counsel to confirm this understanding.

5) A request that legal counsel explain any limitation on, and specify the effective date of, his/her response

c. An example of the text of a letter of inquiry to legal counsel is presented below.

EXAMPLE -- Audit Inquiry Letter to Legal Counsel

In connection with an audit of our financial statements at (balance sheet date) and for the (period) then ended, management of the Company has prepared and furnished to our auditors (name and address of auditors) a description and evaluation of certain contingencies, including those set forth below involving matters with respect to which you have been engaged and to which you have devoted substantive attention on behalf of the Company in the form of legal consultation or representation. These contingencies are regarded by management of the Company as material for this purpose (management may indicate a materiality limit if an understanding has been reached with the auditor). Your response should include matters that existed at (balance sheet date) and during the period from that date to the date of your response.

Pending or Threatened Litigation (Excluding Unasserted Claims)

[Ordinarily, the information would include the following: (1) the nature of the litigation, (2) the progress of the case to date, (3) how management is responding or intends to respond to the litigation (for example, to contest the case vigorously or to seek an out-of-court settlement), and (4) an evaluation of the likelihood of an unfavorable outcome and an estimate, if one can be made, of the amount or range of potential loss.] This letter will serve as our consent for you to furnish our auditor all the information requested herein. Accordingly, please furnish to our auditors such explanation, if any, that you consider necessary to supplement the foregoing information, including an explanation of those matters for which your views may differ from those stated and an identification of the omission of any pending or threatened litigation, claims, and assessments or a statement that the list of such matters is complete.

Unasserted Claims and Assessments (Considered by Management to be Probable of Assertion and That, if Asserted, Would Have at Least a Reasonable Possibility of an Unfavorable Outcome)

[Ordinarily, management's information would include the following: (1) the nature of the matter, (2) how management intends to respond if the claim is asserted, and (3) an evaluation of the likelihood of an unfavorable outcome and an estimate, if one can be made, of the amount or range of potential loss.] Please furnish to our auditors such explanation, if any, that you consider necessary to supplement the foregoing information, including an explanation of those matters for which your views may differ from those stated.

We understand that whenever, in the course of performing legal services for us with respect to a matter recognized to involve an unasserted possible claim or assessment that may call for financial statement disclosure, if you have formed a professional conclusion that we should disclose or consider disclosure concerning such possible claim or assessment, as a matter of professional responsibility to us, you will so advise us and will consult with us concerning the question of such disclosure and the applicable requirements of Accounting Standards Codification (ASC) 450, *Contingencies*. Please specifically confirm to our auditors that our understanding is correct.

Please specifically identify the nature of and reasons for any limitation on your response.

[The auditor may request the client to inquire about additional matters, for example, unpaid or unbilled charges or specified information on certain contractually assumed obligations of the company, such as guarantees of indebtedness of others.]

[The letter should be signed by the client.]

---

6. **Limitations on the Scope of Legal Counsel's Response**

a. Legal counsel may limit the response to matters to which **substantive attention** has been given.

b. Legal counsel's response may be limited to matters considered **individually or collectively material**, for example, when (1) the entity and auditor agree on the limits of materiality for this purpose, and (2) management has communicated the agreement to legal counsel.

   1) These limits are not limits on the audit scope.

c. Legal counsel may not be able to reach a conclusion about the probability of an unfavorable outcome or the amount or range of loss because of **inherent uncertainties**.

7. **Modification of the Opinion**

    a. The opinion in the auditor's report is modified if

        1) Legal counsel refuses to respond appropriately to the letter of inquiry, and the auditor cannot obtain sufficient appropriate evidence by performing alternative procedures, or

        2) Management refuses permission for the auditor to communicate or meet with external legal counsel.

    b. External legal counsel's refusal to provide (orally or in writing) information requested in a letter of inquiry may be a scope limitation sufficient to preclude an unmodified opinion.

        1) However, the need for confidentiality of client communications with legal counsel protects some matters from disclosure even to the auditor.

Stop and review! You have completed the outline for this subunit. Study multiple-choice questions 1 through 9 beginning on page 439.

14.2 SUBSEQUENT EVENTS AND SUBSEQUENTLY DISCOVERED FACTS (AU-C 560)

> The Clarified Standards do not contain the accounting guidance that was previously included in the auditing standards covered in this subunit because it is included in the accounting standards. In the future, the CPA exam is not likely to test accounting for subsequent events in the auditing section, but you should still know the relevant accounting principles. In general, subsequent events that relate to issues that existed at the balance sheet date should be reflected in the balances of the financial statements. Those that occur after the balance sheet date may require disclosure in the financial statements. Several questions at the end of this study unit consider these issues to show the contrast between accounting and auditing concerns.

1. **Definitions**

    a. **Subsequent events** occur between the date of the financial statements and the date of the auditor's report.

    b. **Subsequently discovered facts** become known to the auditor after the date of the auditor's report. Had they been known to the auditor at that date, they might have caused the auditor to revise the auditor's report.

ISA Difference

U.S. auditing standards define subsequent events and subsequently discovered facts separately, but the ISAs include both in the definition of subsequent events. The U.S. standards are more explicit regarding the requirements.

2. The accounting treatment of events that happen after the date of the financial statements depends on whether they provide evidence of conditions that

    a. Existed at the date of the financial statements or

    b. Arose after the date of the financial statements.

3. **Subsequent Events**

    a. The auditor should perform audit procedures designed to obtain sufficient appropriate audit evidence that all subsequent events that require adjustment of, or disclosure in, the financial statements have been identified.

    b. The following procedures should be performed as near as practicable to the report date:

        1) Understanding management's procedures for identifying subsequent events.

        2) Reading the latest subsequent interim financial statements, if any.

        3) Inquiring of management and those charged with governance about the current status of items accounted for using preliminary or inconclusive data.

        4) Inquiring specifically about whether

            a) New commitments, borrowings, or guarantees have been entered into.

            b) Sales or acquisitions of assets have occurred or are planned.

            c) Increases in capital or issuance of debt have occurred, or an agreement to merge or liquidate has been made or is planned.

            d) Any assets have been appropriated by the government or destroyed (for example, by fire or flood).

            e) Any developments regarding contingencies have occurred.

            f) Any unusual accounting adjustments have been made or are contemplated.

            g) Any events have occurred or are likely to occur that affect the appropriateness of accounting policies.

            h) Any events have occurred that are relevant to the measurement of estimates or provisions made in the financial statements.

            i) Any events have occurred that are relevant to the recoverability of assets.

        5) Reading the available **minutes** of meetings of owners, those charged with governance, and management after the date of the statements.

        6) Sending, if appropriate, a letter of inquiry prepared by management to **legal counsel** requesting direct communication about litigation, claims, and assessments.

        7) Obtaining **written representations**, dated as of the date of the auditor's report, from appropriate management stating that adjustments or disclosures have been made for any subsequent events requiring such treatment. This is one of many written representations obtained from the entity. Representations are discussed in Subunit 14.3.

    c. The auditor should determine whether any subsequent events identified have been properly accounted for and disclosed.

4. **Subsequently Discovered Facts That Become Known to the Auditor Before the Report Release Date**

    a. The auditor is not required to perform any audit procedures regarding the financial statements after the date of the auditor's report. However, if a subsequently discovered fact becomes known to the auditor before the report release date, the auditor should

        1) Discuss the matter with management and, if appropriate, those charged with governance.

        2) Determine whether the financial statements need revision and, if so, inquire how management intends to address the matter.

    b. If management revises the financial statements, the auditor should perform the audit procedures necessary on the revision. The auditor also should either

        1) Date the auditor's report as of a later date and extend the audit procedures to the new date of the auditor's report, including obtaining an update of the management representation letter, or

        2)   Include an additional date in the auditor's report on the revised statements that is limited to the revision (that is, dual-date the auditor's report). Dual-dating indicates that the auditor's procedures subsequent to the original date are limited solely to the relevant note to the statements. The auditor also should request written representations from management as of the additional date in the auditor's report about whether

            a)   The previous representations should be modified.

            b)   Any other events have occurred subsequent to the date of the statements.

    c.   If management does not revise the statements that need revision, the auditor should modify the opinion (express a qualified opinion or an adverse opinion).

5.   **Unaudited events** occurring after the date of the auditor's report may be disclosed by management to prevent the statements from being misleading.

    a.   If the event is described in a separate note labeled as **unaudited**, the auditor need not perform procedures on the revision of the statements, and the report date is not changed.

6.   **Subsequently Discovered Facts That Become Known to the Auditor After the Report Release Date**

    a.   If a subsequently discovered fact becomes known to the auditor after the report release date, the auditor should

        1)   Discuss the matter with management and, if appropriate, those charged with governance.

        2)   Determine whether the financial statements need revision and, if so, inquire how management intends to respond.

    b.   Management may revise the financial statements before they have been made available to third parties. In this case, the auditor should apply the appropriate procedures and either extend the date of the audit or dual-date the report for the revision.

    c.   However, the unrevised audited statements may have been made available to third parties. In this case, the auditor should assess whether the steps taken by management were timely and appropriate. The auditor should ensure that anyone who has received the statements is informed of the situation, including that the audited statements are not to be relied upon.

        1)   When revised statements are issued, and the auditor's opinion on the revised statements differs from the opinion the auditor previously expressed, the following matters should be disclosed in an other-matter paragraph:

            a)   The date of the auditor's previous report

            b)   The type of opinion previously expressed

            c)   The substantive reasons for the different opinion

            d)   That the auditor's opinion on the revised statements is different from the auditor's previous opinion

    d.   Management may not take the necessary steps to ensure that anyone who has received the audited statements is informed of the situation. In this case, the auditor should notify management and those charged with governance that the auditor will seek to prevent future reliance on the auditor's report. If, despite such notice, the necessary steps are still not taken, the auditor should take appropriate action to seek to prevent reliance on the auditor's report. Unless the auditor's legal counsel recommends otherwise, the auditor may take the following steps to the extent applicable:

        1)   Notify management and those charged with governance that the auditor's report is not to be relied upon.

2) Notify regulatory agencies having jurisdiction over the entity that the auditor's report is not to be relied upon. This notice should include a request that the agency take appropriate steps to make the necessary disclosure.

3) If feasible, notify anyone known to the auditor to be relying on the statements that the auditor's report is not to be relied upon.

Stop and review! You have completed the outline for this subunit. Study multiple-choice questions 10 through 21 beginning on page 441.

14.3 WRITTEN REPRESENTATIONS (AU-C 580)

1. **Audit Evidence**

   a. The auditor is required to obtain written representations from management. (In this study unit, management includes those charged with governance.)

   b. Written representations confirm certain matters or support other evidence. They complement other procedures but do **not** provide sufficient appropriate evidence or affect other procedures.

   c. Written representations should be in a letter addressed to the auditor.

      1) The auditor should possess this letter before release of the auditor's report.

2. **Specific Representations**

   a. Among other things, written representations are based on the **premise** of the audit. It relates to management's responsibilities for (1) preparing and fairly presenting the financial statements; (2) internal control relevant to the statements; and (3) providing access to (a) information relevant to the statements, (b) other information requested for audit purposes, and (c) persons within the entity.

   b. The auditor should request the following written representations:

      1) Management is responsible for the preparation and fair presentation of the financial statements and for internal control relevant to their preparation.

      2) Management has provided all relevant information and access, and all transactions have been recorded and reflected in the statements.

      3) Management is responsible for internal controls to prevent and detect fraud and has disclosed to the auditor its knowledge of fraud, suspected fraud, and allegations of fraud.

      4) All instances of noncompliance with laws and regulations that should be considered in preparing the statements have been disclosed to the auditor.

      5) Management states whether the effects of uncorrected misstatements are immaterial and that a list is attached to the representation letter.

      6) All known actual or possible litigation and claims that should be considered in preparing the statements have been disclosed to the auditor.

      7) The significant assumptions used to make estimates are reasonable.

      8) Management has disclosed to the auditor the identities of related parties, related party relationships, and related party transactions.

      9) Subsequent events have been disclosed to the auditor, and required adjustments or disclosures have been made.

      10) Management has provided additional written representations (a) required by GAAS or (b) requested by the auditor to support other audit evidence or specific assertions.

3. **Representation Letter**

Background

The example representation letter in the auditing standards is a one-page document. It affirms management's responsibilities to the auditor and for the fairness of the financial statements. In practice, letters are often much longer than the AICPA's example letter. Many CPA firms require management to affirm each key assertion for each major account as well as the other affirmations from the example letter. This should not be too surprising because representation is synonymous with assertion.

---

    a.   The example representation letter on the next page is taken from AU-C 580. Although addressed to the auditor, the letter is drafted by the auditor. It should be signed by management with overall responsibility for financial and operating matters, including preparation and fair presentation of the statements.

    b.   Management's representations may be limited to matters that are considered **material** to the financial statements, either individually or collectively, provided that management and the auditor have reached an understanding on materiality for this purpose. But materiality does not apply to

        1)   Management's responsibility for internal control to prevent or detect fraud or
        2)   Representations not directly related to financial statement amounts.

    c.   The auditor may determine, based on the circumstances, that other matters should be specifically included among the written representations.

    d.   If the auditor reports on **consolidated** statements, the representations obtained from the parent should specify that they pertain to the consolidated statements and, if applicable, to the parent's separate statements.

    e.   The written representations should be

        1)   Addressed to the auditor,
        2)   Dated as of the date of the audit report, and
        3)   Signed by responsible and knowledgeable members of management. The chief executive officer and the chief financial officer usually should sign the representations.

ISA Difference

The U.S. auditing standards require that the management representation letter be dated at the same date as the auditor's report. The ISAs require the date to be as near as practicable to, but no later than, the date of the auditor's report.

---

    f.   The auditor may want to obtain written representations from other individuals, such as the completeness of the minutes of meetings from the person responsible for the minutes.

EXAMPLE -- Management Representation Letter

Date of the Auditor's Report
To Independent Auditor (Named)

This representation letter is provided in connection with your audit of the financial statements of ABC Company, which comprise the balance sheet as of December 31, 20XX, and the related statements of income, changes in stockholders' equity, and cash flows for the year then ended, and the related notes to the financial statements, for the purpose of expressing an opinion on whether the financial statements are presented fairly, in all material respects, in accordance with accounting principles generally accepted in the United States (U.S. GAAP).

Certain representations in this letter are described as being limited to matters that are material. Items are considered material, regardless of size, if they involve an omission or misstatement of accounting information that, in the light of surrounding circumstances, makes it probable that the judgment of a reasonable person relying on the information would be changed or influenced by the omission or misstatement.

Except where otherwise stated below, immaterial matters less than $[insert amount] collectively are not considered to be exceptions that require disclosure for the purpose of the following representations. This amount is not necessarily indicative of amounts that would require adjustment to or disclosure in the financial statements.

Financial Statements

- We have fulfilled our responsibilities, as set out in the terms of the audit engagement dated [insert date], for the preparation and fair presentation of the financial statements in accordance with U.S. GAAP.

- We acknowledge our responsibility for the design, implementation, and maintenance of internal control relevant to the preparation and fair presentation of financial statements that are free from material misstatement, whether due to fraud or error.

- We acknowledge our responsibility for the design, implementation, and maintenance of internal control to prevent and detect fraud.

- Significant assumptions used by us in making accounting estimates, including those measured at fair value, are reasonable.

- Related party relationships and transactions have been appropriately accounted for and disclosed in accordance with the requirements of U.S. GAAP.

- All events subsequent to the date of the financial statements and for which U.S. GAAP requires adjustment or disclosure have been adjusted or disclosed.

- The effects of uncorrected misstatements are immaterial, both individually and in the aggregate, to the financial statements as a whole. A list of the uncorrected misstatements is attached to the representation letter.

- The effects of all known actual or possible litigation and claims have been accounted for and disclosed in accordance with U.S. GAAP.

Information Provided

- We have provided you with:

    o Access to all information of which we are aware that is relevant to the preparation and fair presentation of the financial statements such as records, documentation and other matters;

    o Additional information that you have requested from us for the purpose of the audit; and

    o Unrestricted access to persons within the entity from whom you determined it necessary to obtain audit evidence.

- All transactions have been recorded in the accounting records and are reflected in the financial statements.

- We have disclosed to you the results of our assessment of the risk that the financial statements may be materially misstated as a result of fraud.

- We have [no knowledge of any] [disclosed to you all information that we are aware of regarding] fraud or suspected fraud that affects the entity and involves:

    o Management;
    o Employees who have significant roles in internal control; or
    o Others when the fraud could have a material effect on the financial statements.

- We have [no knowledge of any] [disclosed to you all information that we are aware of regarding] allegations of fraud, or suspected fraud, affecting the entity's financial statements communicated by employees, former employees, analysts, regulators or others.

- We have disclosed to you all known instances of non-compliance or suspected non-compliance with laws and regulations whose effects should be considered when preparing financial statements.

- We [have disclosed to you all known actual or possible] [are not aware of any pending or threatened] litigation, claims, and assessments whose effects should be considered when preparing the financial statements [and we have not consulted legal counsel concerning litigation, claims, or assessments]

- We have disclosed to you the identity of the entity's related parties and all the related party relationships and transactions of which we are aware.

[Include other representations unique to the entity and related to specific accounts and assertions.]

(Name of Chief Executive Officer and Title)   (Name of Chief Financial Officer and Title)

4. **Unreliable or Omitted Representations**

    a. The auditor disclaims an opinion or withdraws from the engagement if

        1) Management does not provide the representations regarding the premise of the audit (**management's responsibilities** for the audit), or

        2) The auditor concludes that such representations are unreliable because of doubts about management's integrity.

    b. Management's refusal to provide other written representations also often precludes an unmodified opinion.

        1) The auditor should consider the effects of the refusal on his/her (a) evaluation of management's integrity and (b) ability to rely on other representations.

        2) Furthermore, failure to provide representations about certain matters (fraud, noncompliance, misstatements, litigation and claims, estimates, related parties, and subsequent events) may cause the auditor to disclaim an opinion or withdraw from the engagement. But circumstances may permit expression of a qualified opinion.

5. **Other Pronouncements**

    a. The PCAOB's AS No. 5 requires that an audit of an **issuer's** internal control over financial reporting be integrated with the financial statement audit. The AICPA's AT 501 provides for the **optional** performance of a similar service for a **nonissuer**. Additional representations required by AS No. 5 include the following:

        1) Management has evaluated internal control, specified the control criteria, and stated its conclusion about the effectiveness of internal control.

        2) Management has disclosed to the auditor all deficiencies in internal control.

        3) Deficiencies identified and communicated to those charged with governance during previous engagements have been resolved, and unresolved deficiencies have been identified.

        4) Management has stated certain changes subsequent to the date reported on. These are changes in factors that might significantly affect internal control over financial reporting.

Stop and review! You have completed the outline for this subunit. Study multiple-choice questions 22 through 29 beginning on page 446.

14.4 AUDITOR'S CONSIDERATION OF AN ENTITY'S ABILITY TO CONTINUE AS A GOING CONCERN (AU-C 570)

1. The auditor should evaluate whether a **substantial doubt** exists about an entity's ability to continue as a going concern for a reasonable period of time.

    a. A reasonable period of time is **1 year** beyond the date of the statements audited (hereafter, the term "substantial doubt" is used when referring to this language).

    b. Continuation as a going concern is assumed in financial reporting, absent significant contrary information. Such information relates to the inability to continue to meet obligations as they become due without, for example, one of the following:

        1) Substantial disposal of assets outside the ordinary course of business
        2) Debt restructuring
        3) Externally forced revisions of operations

    c.   This standard applies to all audits of financial statements except audits of statements prepared on the **liquidation basis**.

        1)   Thus, it applies to audits of financial statements prepared in accordance with a general purpose or a special purpose framework.

2. **Evaluating Whether Substantial Doubt Exists**

    a.   The evaluation is based on relevant conditions and events as of the date of the report.

        1)   Necessary information is obtained by applying the auditing procedures planned and performed to test the assertions in the financial statements.

    b.   The following is the process of evaluation:

        1)   The auditor considers whether the results of normal auditing procedures identify **conditions and events** that, in the aggregate, indicate that substantial doubt could exist (hereafter, "conditions and events").

            a)   Additional information about the conditions and events, as well as evidence supporting information that mitigates the substantial doubt, may need to be gathered.

        2)   If the auditor believes a substantial doubt exists, (s)he should obtain information about **management's plans** to mitigate the effect of such conditions or events and assess the likelihood that the plans will be effective.

        3)   The auditor then determines whether (s)he has a substantial doubt.

            a)   If so, (s)he should

                i)   Consider the adequacy of disclosure about the going concern issue.

                ii)   Include an **emphasis-of-matter** paragraph (immediately after the opinion paragraph) in the audit report. Also, a disclaimer of opinion is possible.

            b)   If not, (s)he should still consider the need for disclosure but need not include an emphasis-of-matter paragraph in the audit report.

    c.   Because of the inherent limitations of an audit, the entity's **failure to continue as a going concern**, even within the year after the date of the statements, does not, in itself, indicate inadequate auditor performance.

        1)   Thus, omission of the reference to substantial doubt provides no assurance of continuation as a going concern.

3. **Audit Procedures**

    a.   Procedures need not be designed solely to identify conditions and events because typical audit procedures should be sufficient. Such procedures may include the following:

        1)   Analytical procedures
        2)   Review of subsequent events
        3)   Review of compliance with debt and loan agreements
        4)   Reading minutes of meetings of shareholders, the board, and committees
        5)   Inquiry of legal counsel about litigation, claims, and assessments
        6)   Confirmation with related and third parties of arrangements for financial support

4. **Conditions and Events**

    a. The significance of conditions and events depends on the circumstances, and some may be significant only in conjunction with others. Such conditions and events include the following:

        1) **Negative trends**, e.g., (a) recurring operating losses, (b) working capital deficiencies, (c) negative cash flows from operations, and (d) adverse key financial ratios

        2) **Financial difficulties**, e.g., (a) default on loans, (b) unpaid dividends, (c) denial of normal trade credit by suppliers, (d) debt restructuring, (e) noncompliance with statutory capital requirements, and (f) the need to seek new financing or to dispose of substantial assets

        3) **Internal matters**, e.g., (a) labor difficulties, (b) substantial dependence on the success of one project, (c) uneconomic long-term commitments, and (d) the need to revise operations significantly

        4) **External matters**, e.g., (a) litigation, legislation, or similar matters jeopardizing operating ability; (b) loss of a key franchise, license, or patent; (c) loss of a principal customer or supplier; and (d) an uninsured or underinsured catastrophe, such as a drought, earthquake, or flood

5. **Written Representations**

    a. If the auditor believes that a substantial doubt exists before considering management's plans, discussed in the next section, (s)he should obtain written representations from management

        1) About its plans to mitigate the adverse effects of conditions or events and the likelihood that those plans can be effectively implemented and

        2) That the statements disclose all the matters of which management is aware that are relevant to the going concern issue, including principal conditions or events and management's plans.

6. **Management's Plans**

    a. Given substantial doubt, the auditor should (1) consider management's plans for responding to the adverse effects of the conditions and events, (2) obtain information about the plans, and (3) consider the likelihood that the adverse effects will be mitigated and the plans can be effectively implemented.

    b. These considerations may include the following:

        1) **Disposing of assets**

            a) Restrictions such as those in loan agreements or interests held by other parties (e.g., mortgages or security interests)

            b) Marketability of the assets to be sold

            c) Direct or indirect effects

        2) **Borrowing money or restructuring debt**

            a) Availability of debt financing, including credit arrangements, such as lines of credit, factoring of receivables, or sale-leasebacks

            b) Arrangements to restructure or subordinate debt or to guarantee loans to the entity

            c) Existing restrictions on borrowing or the sufficiency of available collateral

       3) **Reducing or delaying expenditures**

         a) Feasibility of plans to reduce overhead or administrative expenses, postpone maintenance or R&D, or lease rather than purchase

         b) Direct or indirect effects

       4) **Increasing ownership equity**

         a) Feasibility of such plans, including arrangements to obtain capital

         b) Arrangements to reduce dividends or accelerate cash receipts from affiliates or other investors

  c. The elements of plans that are particularly significant to overcoming the adverse effects should be identified and procedures performed to obtain evidence about them, for example, about the ability to obtain **additional financing**.

  d. **Prospective financial information (PFI)** may be important to management's plans, and the auditor should request such information and consider the adequacy of support for significant underlying **assumptions**.

       1) Special attention should be given to assumptions that are

         a) Material,

         b) Especially sensitive or susceptible to change, and

         c) Inconsistent with historical trends.

       2) The auditor should have knowledge of the entity, its business, and its management. The auditor should

         a) Read the PFI and assumptions.

         b) Compare PFI for prior periods with results and, for the current period, with results to date.

       3) If the effects of certain factors are not reflected in the PFI, the auditor should discuss them with management and, if necessary, request revision.

7. **Financial Statement Effects**

  a. After considering management's plans, the auditor may decide that a substantial doubt exists and should consider the possible effects on the statements and the **adequacy of disclosure.**

  b. Information disclosed may include the following:

       1) The conditions and events on which the substantial doubt is based, their possible effects, and management's evaluation of their significance and of any mitigating factors

       2) Possible discontinuance of operations

       3) Management's plans, including PFI

         a) The information need not meet guidelines for PFI, and the consideration need not go beyond that required by GAAS.

       4) Information about recoverability or classification of recorded assets or the amounts or classification of liabilities

  c. The auditor may decide, primarily because of the consideration of management's plans, that the substantial doubt is mitigated. (S)he then should consider **disclosure** of (1) the principal conditions and events that led to the substantial doubt; (2) their possible effects; and (3) any mitigating factors, including management's plans.

8. **Effects on the Auditor's Report**

    a.   If the auditor has a substantial doubt, the audit report should include an **emphasis-of-matter** paragraph immediately following the opinion paragraph (described more fully in Study Unit 17, Subunit 3). The wording of the auditor's conclusion should include the phrases **substantial doubt** and **going concern**.

    b.   If disclosure is inadequate, the auditor may modify the opinion.

    c.   Also, the auditor is not precluded from **disclaiming** an opinion in cases involving uncertainties.

9. **Documentation**

    a.   If the auditor has a substantial doubt (even if that doubt is mitigated by management actions), the following should be documented in the working papers:

        1)   The conditions or events causing the substantial doubt

        2)   The significant elements of management's plans to overcome the problem considered by the auditor

        3)   The auditing procedures performed and evidence obtained

        4)   The auditor's conclusions about whether the substantial doubt remains, including any effects on the financial statements or disclosures and any effect on the audit report

10. **Communications**

    a.   An auditor who has a substantial doubt should communicate the following to **those charged with governance**:

        1)   Nature of identified conditions and events
        2)   Financial statement effects
        3)   Adequacy of disclosure
        4)   Audit report effects

ISA Difference

The ISAs state that management is responsible for assessing the ability to continue as a going concern. The auditor's responsibility is to evaluate the assessment. AICPA standards require the auditor to evaluate whether the entity is a going concern for a reasonable period not to exceed 1 year beyond the financial statement date, but the ISAs require consideration of going concern issues for **at least**, but not limited to, **1 year**.

Stop and review! You have completed the outline for this subunit. Study multiple-choice questions 30 through 33 beginning on page 448.

QUESTIONS

14.1 Consideration of Litigation, Claims, and Assessments (AU-C 501)

1. The primary source of information to be reported about litigation, claims, and assessments is the

A. Client's legal counsel.

B. Court records.

C. Client's management.

D. Independent auditor.

Answer (C) is correct.

REQUIRED: The primary source of information to be reported about litigation, claims, and assessments.

DISCUSSION: According to AU-C 501, "Management is responsible for adopting policies and procedures to identify, evaluate, and account for litigation, claims, and assessments as a basis for the preparation of financial statements in accordance with the requirements of the applicable financial reporting framework." The auditor should discuss with management its policies and procedures for identifying and evaluating these matters.

Answer (A) is incorrect. The client's legal counsel is the auditor's primary source of evidence to corroborate the information furnished by management. Answer (B) is incorrect. The auditor does not ordinarily examine court records. Answer (D) is incorrect. The auditor collects evidence to support management's assertions about litigation, claims, and assessments.

2. Which of the following procedures would best detect a liability omission by management?

A. Inquiry of senior support staff and recently departed employees.

B. Review and check mathematical accuracy of financial statements.

C. Review articles of incorporation and corporate bylaws.

D. Review purchase contracts and other legal documents.

Answer (D) is correct.

REQUIRED: The procedure to detect a liability omission by management.

DISCUSSION: The auditor's search for unrecorded liabilities should include reading contracts, loan agreements, leases, correspondence from governmental agencies, and any legal documents in the client's possession.

Answer (A) is incorrect. The support staff and departed employees do not likely have knowledge about devious actions of management. Answer (B) is incorrect. The omitted liabilities would not be included in the financial statements. Answer (C) is incorrect. The articles of incorporation and the bylaws will not address litigation or liabilities.

3. Legal counsel's response to an auditor's inquiry about litigation, claims, and assessments may be limited to matters that are considered individually or collectively material to the client's financial statements. Which parties may reach an understanding on the limits of materiality for this purpose that are stated in the letter of inquiry?

A. The auditor and the client's management.

B. The client's audit committee and legal counsel.

C. The client's management and legal counsel.

D. Legal counsel and the auditor.

Answer (A) is correct.

REQUIRED: The parties responsible for setting materiality limits stated in the letter of inquiry about litigation, claims, and assessments.

DISCUSSION: The letter of inquiry is prepared by management and sent by the auditor to the entity's legal counsel. Among other things, the letter requests a statement about the nature of, and reasons for, any limitation on legal counsel's response. Legal counsel may limit the response to matters to which (s)he has given substantive attention in the form of legal consultation or representation. Furthermore, legal counsel's response may be limited to those matters that are considered individually or collectively material to the financial statements, such as when the entity and the auditor have agreed on materiality limits, and management has stated the limits in the letter of inquiry (AU-C 501). NOTE: According to the American Bar Association's statement of policy, the lawyer may wish to reach an understanding with the auditor about the test of materiality. However, the lawyer need not do so if (s)he assumes responsibility for the criteria.

Answer (B) is incorrect. Legal counsel and the audit committee do not draft the letter of inquiry or agree on its terms. Answer (C) is incorrect. Legal counsel may reach an understanding with the auditor about materiality but does not draft the letter of inquiry. Moreover, the auditor ultimately must make materiality judgments relevant to the audit. Answer (D) is incorrect. Legal counsel does not determine the content of the letter of inquiry.

4. If the auditor determines that an inquiry of a client's external legal counsel is necessary, who should make the inquiry?

    A. The auditor.

    B. The stockholders.

    C. Client management.

    D. The auditor's attorney.

Answer (C) is correct.
    REQUIRED: The party(ies) who should make an inquiry of a client's external legal counsel.
    DISCUSSION: A letter of inquiry to a client's legal counsel is the auditor's primary means of corroborating information furnished by management about litigation, claims, and assessments. Evidence obtained from the client's legal department may provide the needed corroboration, but it does not substitute for information that external legal counsel may refuse to furnish. Thus, the auditor should request management to send a letter of inquiry to legal counsel with whom management consulted. Without the client's consent, legal counsel may not respond (AU-C 501).

5. The primary reason an auditor requests letters of inquiry be sent to a client's legal counsel is to provide the auditor with

    A. The probable outcome of asserted claims and pending or threatened litigation.

    B. Corroboration of the information furnished by management about litigation, claims, and assessments.

    C. Legal counsel's opinion of the client's historical experiences in recent similar litigation.

    D. A description and evaluation of litigation, claims, and assessments that existed at the balance sheet date.

Answer (B) is correct.
    REQUIRED: The primary reason that letters of inquiry are sent to a client's legal counsel.
    DISCUSSION: A letter of inquiry to a client's external legal counsel is the auditor's primary means of corroborating information furnished by management about litigation, claims, and assessments. If in-house legal counsel is primarily responsible for the entity's litigation, claims, and assessments, the auditor should send a similar letter of inquiry to in-house legal counsel. But the letter to in-house legal counsel is not a substitute for direct communication with external legal counsel.
    Answer (A) is incorrect. Management provides information about the probable outcome of asserted claims and impending or threatened litigation. Answer (C) is incorrect. The auditor is concerned with current litigation, not recent similar litigation. Answer (D) is incorrect. Management provides a description and evaluation of litigation, claims, and assessments that existed at the balance sheet date. The letter of inquiry corroborates that information.

6. A client is a defendant in a patent infringement lawsuit against a major competitor. Which of the following items would **least** likely be included in legal counsel's response to the auditor's letter of inquiry?

    A. A description of potential litigation in other matters unrelated to the patent infringement lawsuit.

    B. A discussion of case progress and the strategy currently in place by client management to resolve the lawsuit.

    C. An evaluation of the probability of loss and a statement of the amount or range of loss if an unfavorable outcome is reasonably possible.

    D. An evaluation of the ability of the client to continue as a going concern if the verdict is unfavorable and maximum damages are awarded.

Answer (D) is correct.
    REQUIRED: The items least likely included in legal counsel's response to the auditor's letter of inquiry.
    DISCUSSION: An inquiry letter response from the client's legal counsel will normally include information or comment about each pending or threatened litigation, claim, or assessment. Legal counsel should (1) address the progress of the case, (2) describe the action the company plans to take, (3) evaluate the likelihood of an unfavorable outcome, and (4) estimate (if possible) the range of any potential loss. Legal counsel does not have the expertise or appropriate information to make a judgment about the client's ability to continue as a going concern. The auditor normally makes that judgment.
    Answer (A) is incorrect. A description of potential litigation in other matters unrelated to the patent infringement lawsuit is included in legal counsel's response. Answer (B) is incorrect. A discussion of case progress and the strategy currently in place by client management to resolve the lawsuit is included in legal counsel's response. Answer (C) is incorrect. An evaluation of the probability of loss and a statement of the amount or range of loss if an unfavorable outcome is reasonably possible is included in legal counsel's response.

7. The refusal of a client's legal counsel to provide information requested in an inquiry letter generally is considered

    A. Grounds for an adverse opinion.

    B. A limitation on the scope of the audit.

    C. Reason to withdraw from the engagement.

    D. A significant deficiency in internal control.

Answer (B) is correct.
    REQUIRED: The nature of the refusal of a client's legal counsel to provide information requested.
    DISCUSSION: Legal counsel's refusal to furnish the information requested in an inquiry letter either in writing or orally may be a limitation on the scope of the audit sufficient to preclude an unmodified opinion.
    Answer (A) is incorrect. A scope limitation never requires an adverse opinion. Answer (C) is incorrect. The refusal is not immediate grounds for withdrawal from an engagement. The auditor should attempt to become satisfied by alternative means. Answer (D) is incorrect. Consideration of internal control is related to the client, not the client's legal counsel.

8. Which of the following statements about litigation, claims, and assessments extracted from a letter from a client's legal counsel is most likely to cause the auditor to request clarification?

   A. "I believe that the possible liability to the company is nominal in amount."

   B. "I believe that the action can be settled for less than the damages claimed."

   C. "I believe that the plaintiff's case against the company is without merit."

   D. "I believe that the company will be able to defend this action successfully."

Answer (B) is correct.
   REQUIRED: The statement by legal counsel most likely causing an auditor's request for clarification.
   DISCUSSION: The letter of inquiry requests, among other things, that legal counsel evaluate the likelihood of pending or threatened litigation, claims, and assessments. It also requests that legal counsel estimate, if possible, the amount or range of potential loss. Thus, the auditor is concerned about the amount of the expected settlement as well as the likelihood of the outcome. The statement that the action can be settled for less than the damages claimed is an example given in AU-C 501 of an evaluation that is unclear about the likelihood of an unfavorable outcome.
   Answer (A) is incorrect. Legal counsel's statement that the amount of possible liability will not be material states an amount or range of loss. Answer (C) is incorrect. Legal counsel has stated that no liability is expected. Answer (D) is incorrect. Legal counsel has stated that no liability is expected.

9. The scope of an audit is **not** restricted when legal counsel's response to an auditor as a result of a client's letter of inquiry limits the response to

   A. Matters to which the legal counsel has given substantive attention in the form of legal representation.

   B. An evaluation of the likelihood of an unfavorable outcome of the matters disclosed by the entity.

   C. The legal counsel's opinion of the entity's historical experience in recent similar litigation.

   D. The probable outcome of asserted claims and pending or threatened litigation.

Answer (A) is correct.
   REQUIRED: The appropriate limitation on the legal counsel's response to the auditor's inquiry.
   DISCUSSION: Two limitations on an entity's external legal counsel's response are not scope limitations. The response may be limited to matters to which the legal counsel has given substantive attention in the form of legal consultation or representation. Also, the response may be limited to matters that are individually or collectively material, such as when the entity and the auditor have agreed on materiality limits, and management has stated the limits in the letter of inquiry.
   Answer (B) is incorrect. An evaluation of the likelihood of an unfavorable outcome of the matters disclosed by the entity is just one matter covered in a letter of inquiry. Answer (C) is incorrect. A response should be made regarding all material litigation, claims, and assessments to which legal counsel has given substantive attention. Answer (D) is incorrect. The probable outcome of asserted claims and pending or threatened litigation is just one matter covered.

14.2 Subsequent Events and Subsequently Discovered Facts (AU-C 560)

10. Which of the following procedures should an auditor ordinarily perform regarding subsequent events?

   A. Read the latest subsequent interim financial statements.

   B. Send second requests to the client's customers who failed to respond to initial accounts receivable confirmation requests.

   C. Communicate material weaknesses in internal control to the client's audit committee.

   D. Review the cutoff bank statements for several months after the year end.

Answer (A) is correct.
   REQUIRED: The subsequent events procedure.
   DISCUSSION: Subsequent events procedures include (1) reading the latest subsequent interim statements, if any; (2) inquiring of management and those charged with governance about the occurrence of subsequent events and various financial and accounting matters; (3) reading the minutes of meetings of owners, management, and those charged with governance; (4) obtaining a letter of representations from management; (5) inquiring of client's legal counsel; and (6) obtaining an understanding of management's procedures for identifying subsequent events.
   Answer (B) is incorrect. Second confirmation requests do not disclose subsequent events. Answer (C) is incorrect. Communication of material weaknesses is not a subsequent events procedure. Answer (D) is incorrect. Cutoff bank statements are requested from banks 7 to 10 days after year end. They are used to verify the client's bank reconciliations and detect kiting.

11. An auditor should be aware of subsequent events that provide evidence concerning conditions that did not exist at year end but arose after year end. These events may be important to the auditor because they may

    A. Require adjustments to the financial statements as of the year end.

    B. Have been recorded based on preliminary accounting estimates.

    C. Require disclosure to keep the financial statements from being misleading.

    D. Have been recorded based on year-end tests for asset obsolescence.

Answer (C) is correct.
    REQUIRED: The reason the auditor should be aware of subsequent events.
    DISCUSSION: One type of subsequent event provides evidence about conditions that arose after the balance sheet date. This type of event does not require adjustment of amounts in the statements. But the auditor should evaluate these events to determine whether disclosure is necessary for proper understanding of the financial statements.
    Answer (A) is incorrect. Because the event did not relate to conditions that existed at the balance sheet date, the financial statements should not be adjusted. Answer (B) is incorrect. Because the event happened after year end, it would not have been recorded. Answer (D) is incorrect. Because the event happened after year end, it would not have been recorded.

12. Which of the following procedures will an auditor most likely perform to obtain evidence about the occurrence of subsequent events?

    A. Recomputing a sample of large-dollar transactions occurring after year end for arithmetic accuracy.

    B. Investigating changes in equity occurring after year end.

    C. Inquiring of the entity's legal counsel concerning litigation, claims, and assessments arising after year end.

    D. Confirming bank accounts established after year end.

Answer (C) is correct.
    REQUIRED: The auditing procedure for the subsequent events period.
    DISCUSSION: Subsequent events procedures include (1) reading the latest subsequent interim statements, if any; (2) inquiring of management and those charged with governance about the occurrence of subsequent events and various financial and accounting matters; (3) reading the minutes of meetings of owners, management, and those charged with governance; (4) obtaining a letter of representations from management; (5) inquiring of client's legal counsel; and (6) obtaining an understanding of management's procedures for identifying subsequent events.
    Answer (A) is incorrect. Testing the arithmetic accuracy of known events does not obtain evidence about the occurrence of a subsequent event. Answer (B) is incorrect. The auditor should inquire of officers and other executives as to significant changes in equity, but an investigation of such changes is less likely than the inquiry of legal counsel. Answer (D) is incorrect. A bank account established after year end is not an asset that existed at the balance sheet date.

13. Which of the following procedures would an auditor most likely perform in obtaining evidence about subsequent events?

    A. Determine that changes in employee pay rates after year end were properly authorized.

    B. Recompute depreciation charges for plant assets sold after year end.

    C. Inquire about payroll checks that were recorded before year end but cashed after year end.

    D. Investigate changes in noncurrent debt occurring after year end.

Answer (D) is correct.
    REQUIRED: The procedure most likely to be performed in obtaining evidence about subsequent events.
    DISCUSSION: Procedures that should be performed as near as practicable to the report date include investigating any increases in capital or issuance of debt, such as the issue of new shares or bonds.
    Answer (A) is incorrect. Changes in employee pay rates are not typically considered material subsequent events. Answer (B) is incorrect. Depreciation charges for a given period do not change as a result of sale of plant assets in the next period. Answer (C) is incorrect. The times when employee paychecks are cashed are not typically considered material subsequent events.

14. Zero Corp. suffered a loss having a material effect on its financial statements as a result of a customer's bankruptcy that rendered a trade receivable uncollectible. This bankruptcy occurred suddenly because of a natural disaster 10 days after Zero's balance sheet date but 1 month before the issuance of the financial statements and the auditor's report. Under these circumstances, the

	Financial Statements Should Be Adjusted	Event Requires Financial Statement Disclosure, but No Adjustment	Auditor's Report Should Be Modified for a Lack of Consistency
A.	Yes	No	No
B.	Yes	No	Yes
C.	No	Yes	Yes
D.	No	Yes	No

Answer (D) is correct.
REQUIRED: The effect on the financial statements and the auditor's report of a subsequent event.
DISCUSSION: Certain subsequent events may provide evidence about conditions at the date of the balance sheet and require adjustment of the statements in accordance with the applicable financial reporting framework. For example, U.S. GAAP require recognition in the statements of the effects of a subsequent event providing additional evidence about conditions at the balance sheet date, including accounting estimates. Other subsequent events provide evidence about conditions not existing at the date of the balance sheet but arising subsequent to that date. These events may require disclosure but do not require adjustment of financial statement balances. In this case, the financial statements should not be adjusted, but disclosure should be made. The report is unaffected if disclosure is made.

15. Which of the following procedures will an auditor most likely perform to obtain evidence about the occurrence of subsequent events?

A. Confirming a sample of material accounts receivable established after year end.

B. Comparing the financial statements being reported on with those of the prior period.

C. Investigating personnel changes in the accounting department occurring after year end.

D. Inquiring as to whether any unusual adjustments were made after year end.

Answer (D) is correct.
REQUIRED: The subsequent events procedure.
DISCUSSION: Subsequent events procedures include inquiring of management as to whether (1) subsequent events occurred that might affect the statements; (2) new commitments, borrowings, or guarantees were made; (3) sales or acquisitions of assets occurred or were planned; (4) capital increased or debt was issued; (5) developments regarding contingencies occurred; (6) any events occurred (a) casting doubt on the appropriateness of accounting policies or (b) that are relevant to the measurement of estimates or the recovery of assets; (7) any unusual accounting adjustments were made or considered; and (8) changes occurred in the current status of items that were accounted for on the basis of preliminary or inconclusive data.
Answer (A) is incorrect. The auditor confirms receivables before year end. Answer (B) is incorrect. Comparing the financial statements being reported on with those of the prior period is an analytical procedure performed at the beginning of the audit. Answer (C) is incorrect. Personnel changes after year end do not typically relate to the recording of subsequent events.

16. After an audit report containing an unmodified opinion on a nonissuer's financial statements was dated and the financial statements issued, the client decided to sell the shares of a subsidiary that accounts for 30% of its revenue and 25% of its net income. The auditor should

A. Determine whether the information is reliable and, if determined to be reliable, request that revised financial statements be issued.

B. Notify the entity that the auditor's report may no longer be associated with the financial statements.

C. Describe the effects of this subsequently discovered information in a communication with persons known to be relying on the financial statements.

D. Take no action because the auditor has no obligation to make any further inquiries.

Answer (D) is correct.
REQUIRED: The auditor's responsibility after the report date when the client sells shares of its subsidiary.
DISCUSSION: AU-C 560 states, "The auditor is not required to perform any audit procedures regarding the financial statements after the date of the auditor's report."

17. After the date of the report, an auditor has no obligation to make continuing inquiries or perform other procedures concerning the audited financial statements, **unless**

    A. Information, which existed at the report date and may affect the report, comes to the auditor's attention.

    B. The control environment changes after the date of the report.

    C. Information about an event that occurred after the date of the report comes to the auditor's attention.

    D. Final determinations or resolutions are made of contingencies that had been disclosed in the financial statements.

Answer (A) is correct.
    REQUIRED: The basis for the obligation to perform procedures after the report date.
    DISCUSSION: Although the auditor may need to extend subsequent events procedures when issuers make filings under the Securities Act of 1933 (AU-C 925, *Filings with the U.S. Securities and Exchange Commission Under the Securities Act of 1933*), (s)he ordinarily need not apply any procedures after the date of the report. However, facts may be discovered by the auditor after the report release date that, if known at that date, might have caused the auditor to revise the report. In this case, the auditor should (1) discuss the matter with management and (2) determine whether the statements should be revised and, if so, how management intends to address the matter in the statements (AU-C 560).
    Answer (B) is incorrect. Additional audit procedures are ordinarily not necessary prior to reissuing a report. Answer (C) is incorrect. The subsequent event must have occurred prior to the date of the auditor's report (ordinarily, the date of the completion of field work) for the auditor to have additional responsibilities. Answer (D) is incorrect. The auditor has no continuing responsibility to monitor disclosed contingencies.

18. Which of the following events occurring after the date of the report most likely will cause the auditor to make further inquiries about the previously issued financial statements?

    A. A technological development that could affect the entity's future ability to continue as a going concern.

    B. The discovery of information regarding a contingency that existed before the financial statements were issued.

    C. The entity's sale of a subsidiary that accounts for 30% of the entity's consolidated sales.

    D. The final resolution of a lawsuit explained in a separate paragraph of the auditor's report.

Answer (B) is correct.
    REQUIRED: The event occurring after the date of the report most likely resulting in further inquiries.
    DISCUSSION: Facts may be discovered by the auditor after the date of the report that, if known at that date, might have caused the auditor to revise the report. In this case, the auditor should (1) discuss the matter with management and (2) determine whether the statements should be revised and, if so, how management intends to address the matter in the statements (AU-C 560).
    Answer (A) is incorrect. An event occurring after the date of the report need not be considered by the auditor if it would not affect the report. Answer (C) is incorrect. An event occurring after the date of the report need not be considered by the auditor if it would not affect the report. Answer (D) is incorrect. The auditor need not consider final determinations or resolutions of contingencies that were disclosed in the financial statements or that resulted in a modification of the auditor's report.

19. Soon after Boyd's audit report was released, Boyd learned of certain related party transactions that occurred during the year under audit. These transactions were not disclosed in the notes to the financial statements. Boyd should

    A. Plan to audit the transactions during the next engagement.

    B. Recall all copies of the audited financial statements.

    C. Discuss the matter with management.

    D. Ask the client to disclose the transactions in subsequent interim statements.

Answer (C) is correct.
    REQUIRED: The step taken when the auditor discovers previously unknown facts existing at the report date.
    DISCUSSION: The auditor should (1) discuss the matter with management and those charged with governance and (2) determine whether the financial statements need revision and, if so, inquire how management intends to address the matter in the statements (AU-C 560).
    Answer (A) is incorrect. The auditor must take more immediate action. Answer (B) is incorrect. Recall of the audited financial statements is not feasible. However, client revision of the statements and notice to appropriate parties may be necessary. Answer (D) is incorrect. Issuance of revised statements is preferable but only if the auditor has determined that the original statements are affected.

20. On February 25, financial statements were released with an auditor's report expressing an unmodified opinion on the statements for the year ended January 31. On March 2, the CPA learned that on February 11, the entity incurred a material loss on an uncollectible trade receivable as a result of the deteriorating financial condition of the entity's principal customer that led to the customer's bankruptcy. Management then refused to adjust the financial statements for this subsequent event. The CPA determined that the information is reliable and that creditors are currently relying on the financial statements. The CPA's next course of action most likely is to

A. Notify the entity's creditors that the financial statements and the related auditor's report should no longer be relied on.

B. Notify management and those charged with governance that the auditor will seek to prevent future reliance on the auditor's report.

C. Issue revised financial statements and distribute them to each creditor known to be relying on the financial statements.

D. Issue a revised auditor's report and distribute it to each creditor known to be relying on the financial statements.

Answer (B) is correct.
REQUIRED: The actions of an auditor related to an event discovered subsequent to the release of the financial statements.
DISCUSSION: If management does not take the necessary steps to revise the financial statements and ensure that anyone in receipt of the audited financial statements is informed of the situation, the auditor should notify management and those charged with governance that the auditor will seek to prevent future reliance on the auditor's report. If, despite such notice, management or those charged with governance do not take the necessary steps, the auditor should take appropriate action to prevent reliance on the auditor's report (AU-C 560).
Answer (A) is incorrect. Management and those charged with governance should be notified first. Answer (C) is incorrect. The auditor has no authority to revise management's financial statements. Answer (D) is incorrect. The auditor should not revise the report but should notify those relying on the report that it is no longer valid.

21. Wilson, CPA, obtained sufficient appropriate audit evidence on which to base the opinion on Abco's December 31, Year 1, financial statements on March 6, Year 2, the date of the auditor's report. A subsequently discovered fact requiring revision of the Year 1 financial statements occurred on April 10, Year 2, and came to Wilson's attention on April 24, Year 2. If the fact became known prior to the report release date, and the revision is made, Wilson's report ordinarily should be dated

A. March 6, Year 2.

B. April 10, Year 2.

C. April 24, Year 2.

D. Using dual-dating.

Answer (D) is correct.
REQUIRED: The date of the report if the statements are adjusted for a subsequent;y discovered fact.
DISCUSSION: A subsequently discovered fact (1) becomes known to the auditor after the report date and (2) may cause the auditor to revise the report. The report date is no earlier than the date when sufficient appropriate evidence is obtained. If such a fact becomes known to the auditor before the report release date, the auditor should (1) discuss the matter with management and (2) determine whether the statements need revision (adjustment or disclosure). If management revises the statements, the auditor should perform the necessary procedures on the revision. The auditor also (1) dates the report as of a later date or (2) dual-dates the report. Dual-dating indicates that the procedures performed subsequent to the original date are limited to the revision. Unless the auditor extends subsequent events procedures to a new date (one presumably later than April 24, Year 2, the date when the subsequently discovered fact became known), the auditor should dual-date the report.
Answer (A) is incorrect. March 6, Year 2, is the original report date. Answer (B) is incorrect. April 10, Year 2, is inappropriate because the discovery of a fact requiring revision of the report did not occur until later. Answer (C) is incorrect. The new (or additional) date is presumably later than April 24, Year 2, the date when the subsequently discovered fact became known.

14.3 Written Representations (AU-C 580)

22. Which of the following documentation is required for an audit in accordance with generally accepted auditing standards?

- A. An internal control questionnaire.
- B. An organization chart.
- C. A planning memorandum or checklist.
- D. A management representation letter.

Answer (D) is correct.
    REQUIRED: The requirement of an audit made in accordance with GAAS.
    DISCUSSION: AU-C 580 requires that the auditor obtain certain written representations from management. The written representations confirm certain matters (e.g., oral representations) or support other audit evidence. They complement other audit procedures but do not provide sufficient appropriate evidence or affect the other procedures.

23. A purpose of a management representation letter is to reduce

- A. Audit risk to an aggregate level of misstatement that could be considered material.
- B. An auditor's responsibility to detect material misstatements only to the extent that the letter is relied on.
- C. The possibility of a misunderstanding concerning management's responsibility for the financial statements.
- D. The scope of an auditor's procedures concerning related party transactions and subsequent events.

Answer (C) is correct.
    REQUIRED: The purpose of written representations by management.
    DISCUSSION: Management's written representations should be in the form of a representation letter addressed to the auditor. The auditor should have possession of the letter before release of the auditor's report. Among other things, the auditor should request that management provide a written representation that it has met its responsibilities stated in the terms of the audit engagement. These responsibilities include those for (1) the preparation and fair presentation of the statements in accordance with the applicable reporting framework and (2) the design, implementation, and maintenance of the relevant internal control.
    Answer (A) is incorrect. Written representations by management complement but do not affect the procedures necessary to enable an auditor to obtain sufficient appropriate evidence to draw reasonable conclusions on which to base the opinion. Answer (B) is incorrect. Written representations by management do not affect other audit procedures. Answer (D) is incorrect. Written representations by management do not pertain only to related party transactions and subsequent events and do not affect other procedures.

24. Which of the following statements ordinarily is included among the written management representations obtained by the auditor in an audit of a nonissuer?

- A. Management acknowledges that internal control has no material weaknesses.
- B. Sufficient appropriate evidence has been made available to permit the expression of an unmodified opinion.
- C. All transactions have been recorded in the accounting records.
- D. Instances of fraud involving management that exceeded the materiality limits have been acknowledged.

Answer (C) is correct.
    REQUIRED: The statement included among written management representations.
    DISCUSSION: AU-C 580 lists the concerns ordinarily addressed in management representation letters, if applicable. The list includes disclosures about the recording of all transactions.
    Answer (A) is incorrect. Management should acknowledge its responsibility for internal control relevant to financial reporting and fraud. It need not represent that internal control has no material weaknesses. However, an issuer must include an internal control report in its annual report that assesses the effectiveness of internal control and the procedures for financial reporting. Presumably, a representation letter of an issuer will contain the same representation. Answer (B) is incorrect. The auditor judges the sufficiency and appropriateness of evidence. Answer (D) is incorrect. Materiality limits do not apply to representations regarding fraud involving management and employees with significant roles in internal control.

25. To which of the following matters would an auditor **not** apply materiality limits when obtaining specific written management representations?

A. Disclosure of compensating balance arrangements involving restrictions on cash balances.

B. Information concerning related party transactions and related amounts receivable or payable.

C. The absence of errors and unrecorded transactions in the financial statements.

D. Fraud involving employees with significant roles in internal control.

Answer (D) is correct.
REQUIRED: The matter to which an auditor does not apply materiality limits.
DISCUSSION: Management's representations may be limited to matters that are considered individually or collectively material if management and the auditor have reached an understanding about materiality for this purpose. Materiality considerations do not apply to certain representations not directly related to amounts in the financial statements, for example, representations about the premise of the audit (i.e., acknowledgment of responsibility for fair presentation, internal control, and auditor access to information and people). Materiality also does not apply to knowledge of fraud or suspected fraud affecting the entity involving (1) management, (2) employees with significant roles in internal control, or (3) others if the fraud could materially affect the statements (AU-C 580).

26. An auditor finds several misstatements in the financial statements that the client prefers not to correct. The auditor determines that the misstatements are not material in the aggregate. Which of the following actions by the auditor is most appropriate?

A. Document all misstatements accumulated during the audit and the conclusion about whether uncorrected misstatements are material.

B. Document the conclusion that the misstatements do not cause the financial statements to be misstated, but do not accumulate uncorrected misstatements in the audit documentation.

C. Accumulate the uncorrected misstatements in the working papers, but do not document whether they cause the financial statements to be misstated.

D. Do **not** accumulate the uncorrected misstatements in the audit documentation, and do not document a conclusion about whether the uncorrected misstatements cause the financial statements to be misstated.

Answer (A) is correct.
REQUIRED: The most appropriate auditor action for uncorrected misstatements that are not material in the aggregate.
DISCUSSION: The auditor should document (1) the amount below which misstatements are clearly trivial; (2) all misstatements accumulated during the audit and whether they were corrected; and (3) the conclusion about whether uncorrected misstatements are material, individually or aggregated, and the basis for the conclusion (AU-C 450). Furthermore, the representation letter should have an accompanying list of uncorrected misstatements. The letter should include a sentence stating, "The effects of the uncorrected misstatements are immaterial, both individually and in the aggregate, to the financial statements as a whole."

27. Which of the following expressions most likely would be included in a representation letter by management of an issuer?

A. No events have occurred subsequent to the balance sheet date that require adjustment to, or disclosure in, the financial statements.

B. There are no significant deficiencies identified during the prior year's audit of which the audit committee of the board of directors is unaware.

C. We do not intend to provide any information that may be construed to constitute a waiver of the attorney-client privilege.

D. Certain computer files and other required evidence may exist only for a short period of time and only in computer-readable form.

Answer (A) is correct.
REQUIRED: The expression most likely found in a management representation letter.
DISCUSSION: AU-C 580 requires that the auditor obtain certain written representations from management. The written representations confirm certain matters (e.g., oral representations) or support other audit evidence. They complement other audit procedures but do not provide sufficient appropriate evidence or affect the other procedures. Information concerning subsequent events is a common matter covered in the letter (AU-C 580).
Answer (B) is incorrect. The representations from management of an issuer should include whether significant control deficiencies and material weaknesses identified and communicated to those charged with governance during previous engagements have been resolved. The board should be aware of all previous issues. Answer (C) is incorrect. A statement that the client does not intend to provide information that may be interpreted as a waiver of the attorney-client privilege may be made in a communication to the auditor, but it is not a customary element of the representation letter. Answer (D) is incorrect. The statement that certain computer files and other required evidence may exist only for a short period of time and only in computer-readable form is a description of the nature of evidence, not a common management representation.

28. To which of the following matters would materiality limits **not** apply in obtaining written management representations?

A. The availability of minutes of shareholders' and directors' meetings.

B. Losses from purchase commitments at prices in excess of fair value.

C. The disclosure of compensating balance arrangements involving related parties.

D. Reductions of obsolete inventory to net realizable value.

Answer (A) is correct.
REQUIRED: The matter to which materiality limits do not apply when obtaining written management representations.
DISCUSSION: Materiality does not apply to representations not directly related to amounts in the financial statements. The availability of minutes of shareholders' meetings and directors' meetings is independent of amounts in the financial statements. Thus, materiality limits do not apply.

29. Key Co. plans to present comparative financial statements for the years ended December 31, Year 1 and Year 2, respectively. Smith, CPA, audited Key's financial statements for both years and plans to report on the comparative financial statements on May 1, Year 3. Key's current management team was not present until January 1, Year 2. What period of time should be covered by Key's management representation letter?

A. January 1, Year 1, through December 31, Year 2.

B. January 1, Year 1, through May 1, Year 3.

C. January 1, Year 2, through December 31, Year 2.

D. January 1, Year 2, through May 1, Year 3.

Answer (B) is correct.
REQUIRED: The dates to be covered by a management representation letter.
DISCUSSION: The auditor is concerned with events occurring through the date of his/her report that may require adjustment of, or disclosure in, the financial statements. Thus, the representations should be made (1) as of a date no earlier than the date of the auditor's report and (2) for all periods referred to in the report. Moreover, if current management was not present during all periods covered by the auditor's report, the auditor should nevertheless obtain written representations from current management for all such periods (AU-C 580).

14.4 Auditor's Consideration of an Entity's Ability to Continue as a Going Concern (AU-C 570)

30. An auditor has substantial doubt about the entity's ability to continue as a going concern for a reasonable period of time because of negative cash flows and working capital deficiencies. Under these circumstances, the auditor would be most concerned about the

A. Control environment factors that affect the organizational structure.

B. Correlation of detection risk and inherent risk.

C. Effectiveness of the entity's internal control activities.

D. Possible effects on the entity's financial statements.

Answer (D) is correct.
REQUIRED: The auditor's priority given substantial doubt about the entity's ability to continue as a going concern for a reasonable period of time.
DISCUSSION: If an auditor has substantial doubt about the entity's ability to continue as a going concern for a reasonable period of time, (s)he should assess the possible effects on the entity's financial statements, including the adequacy of disclosure of uncertainties related to the going-concern issue. The auditor also should include in the auditor's report an emphasis-of-matter paragraph.
Answer (A) is incorrect. The control environment factors that affect the organizational structure have a lower audit priority than a substantial doubt about the entity's ability to continue as a going concern for a reasonable period of time. Answer (B) is incorrect. The correlation of detection risk and inherent risk is considered in every audit. For a given audit risk, the acceptable detection risk is inversely related to the assessed risks of material misstatement (combined inherent risks and control risks). Answer (C) is incorrect. The auditor sometimes may obtain sufficient appropriate evidence without testing controls.

31. Which of the following auditing procedures most likely would assist an auditor in identifying conditions and events that may indicate substantial doubt about an entity's ability to continue as a going concern?

- A. Inspecting title documents to verify whether any assets are pledged as collateral.
- B. Confirming with third parties the details of arrangements to maintain financial support.
- C. Reconciling the cash balance per books with the cutoff bank statement and the bank confirmation.
- D. Comparing the entity's depreciation and asset capitalization policies to other entities in the industry.

Answer (B) is correct.
REQUIRED: The audit procedure that may identify conditions indicating substantial doubt about an entity's continuation as a going concern.
DISCUSSION: The procedures typically employed to identify going-concern issues include (1) analytical procedures, (2) review of subsequent events, (3) review of compliance with debt and loan agreements, (4) reading minutes of meetings, (5) inquiry of legal counsel, and (6) confirmation with related and third parties of arrangements for financial support.
Answer (A) is incorrect. Searching for pledged assets is related to disclosure issues. Answer (C) is incorrect. Reconciling the cash balance with cutoff bank statements and the bank confirmation tests the existence of cash. Answer (D) is incorrect. This comparison might identify conditions needing additional consideration but would not provide evidence about going-concern issues.

32. Cooper, CPA, believes there is substantial doubt about the ability of Zero Corp. to continue as a going concern for a reasonable period of time. In evaluating Zero's plans for dealing with the adverse effects of future conditions and events, Cooper most likely will consider, as a mitigating factor, Zero's plans to

- A. Discuss with lenders the terms of all debt and loan agreements.
- B. Strengthen internal controls over cash disbursements.
- C. Purchase production facilities currently being leased from a related party.
- D. Postpone expenditures for research and development projects.

Answer (D) is correct.
REQUIRED: The managerial action that will mitigate adverse effects of future conditions and events.
DISCUSSION: Once an auditor has identified conditions and events indicating that substantial doubt exists about an entity's ability to continue as a going concern, the auditor should first obtain written representations and then consider management's plans to mitigate their adverse effects. The auditor should consider plans to dispose of assets, borrow money or restructure debt, reduce or delay expenditures, and increase equity.
Answer (A) is incorrect. Discussion with lenders is not a sufficient action to mitigate the circumstances. Answer (B) is incorrect. Internal control improvements do not increase cash flows or postpone expenditures. Answer (C) is incorrect. The purchase of facilities may worsen the company's problems.

33. When an auditor concludes there is substantial doubt about a continuing audit client's ability to continue as a going concern for a reasonable period of time, the auditor's responsibility is to

- A. Express a qualified or adverse opinion, depending upon materiality, due to the possible effects on the financial statements.
- B. Consider the adequacy of disclosure about the client's possible inability to continue as a going concern.
- C. Report to the client's audit committee that management's accounting estimates may need to be adjusted.
- D. Reissue the prior year's auditor's report and add a separate paragraph that specifically refers to "substantial doubt" and "going concern."

Answer (B) is correct.
REQUIRED: The auditor's action given substantial doubt about a client's ability to continue as a going concern.
DISCUSSION: After considering (1) identified conditions and events in the aggregate that raise going concern issues and (2) management's plans for coping with their adverse effects, the auditor may conclude that a substantial doubt exists about the entity's ability to continue as a going concern for a reasonable period of time. In that case, the auditor should consider the possible effects on the financial statements and the adequacy of disclosure. The auditor also should include an emphasis-of-matter paragraph in the report.
Answer (A) is incorrect. An auditor may still express an unmodified opinion and refer to the going-concern issue in an emphasis-of-matter paragraph. Answer (C) is incorrect. Going-concern considerations are independent of the accounting estimates that may need adjustment. Answer (D) is incorrect. The prior year's audit report should not be changed. The auditor's opinion on the prior year has not been altered.

Use the additional questions in Gleim **CPA Test Prep** to create Practice Exams that emulate Prometric!

14.5 PRACTICE TASK-BASED SIMULATIONS

Auditing and Attestation	Time Remaining		
Testlet 4 of 4	1 hour - 30 minutes		

(Toolbar: Unsplit   Split Horiz   Split Vertical   Spreadsheet   Calculator   Exit)

DIRECTIONS

Note: If you believe you have encountered a software malfunction, report it to the test center staff immediately.

Navigation

To navigate from task to task, use the controls at the bottom of the screen. Click on the **Next** button to advance to the next task, or the **Previous** button to go to the previous task. To go directly to any task, click on its number.

If you would like a reminder to revisit a task, or want to indicate that you are finished with it, click on the reminder flag below the task number. To clear the flag, click on it again. Reminder flags are for your use only – they do not contribute to your score.

Tabs

In this part of the examination, you will be asked to complete various tasks. Every task has one or more **Work Tabs**. Some tasks have one or more **Information Tabs**, others may have none. Every task has a **Help** tab.

If a task has **Information Tabs**, you may use the information in them to complete your responses in the **Work Tabs**.

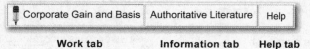

Work tab   Information tab   Help tab

Work Tabs:

- **Work Tabs** are identified with a pencil icon. This is where your responses are expected.
- Each task has one or more **Work Tabs**.
- **Work Tabs** contain directions for completing the task – be sure to read these directions carefully.
- The **Work Tab** name in the example above is for illustration only – yours will differ.
- You must complete all of the **Work Tabs** in each task to receive full credit.

Information Tabs:

- The Authoritative Literature will be provided in all tasks in the AUD, FAR, and REG sections for your reference.
- Your simulation may have one or more additional **Information Tabs**. Like the Authoritative Literature tabs, **Information Tabs** do not have a pencil icon.
- If your task has additional **Information Tabs**, go through each to familiarize yourself with the task content.

Help Tab:

- The **Help Tab** provides assistance with the exam software that is used in this task. For example, if the task is to compose a memorandum, **Help** will provide information about the word processor.

The Toolbar

The toolbar at the top of the screen shows the amount of time remaining for you to complete the tasks. In addition, the following tools are available. Note that only the **Exit** button is displayed when Directions are visible - the others will appear when you begin the tasks.

Click on these buttons to split or unsplit the screen. You can split the screen vertically or horizontally.

Click on this button to display the calculator; click on it again to hide the calculator. To move the calculator, click on the calculator title bar and drag the calculator to the desired location.

Click on this button to use the spreadsheet; click on it again to hide the spreadsheet. To move the spreadsheet, click on the the spreadsheet title bar and drag the spreadsheet to the desired location.

Click on this button to go on to the next part of the examination. You must complete all of the tasks to receive full credit. Once you click on **Exit** and confirm the action, you will NOT be able to return to this testlet.

(Bottom navigation bar: ⚐ = Reminder   Directions   1 2 3 4 5   ◀ Previous   Next ▶)

| Management Representation Letter | Authoritative Literature | Help |

Determine whether each statement should be included, may be included, or should not be included in the management representation letter obtained by the auditor. An answer choice may be used once, more than once, or not at all.

Statement	Answer
1. The entity is not independent with regard to the financial statements.	
2. Management approved all estimates made by the auditor in the financial statements.	
3. Management has provided access to all information relevant to the audit.	
4. All information in the notes to the financial statements is the representation of the auditor.	
5. In response to a request by the auditor, management states that it has no plans that may materially affect the carrying amount of assets or liabilities.	
6. Management has no knowledge of alleged fraud or suspected fraud.	
7. All items included in this letter are assumed to be immaterial.	
8. Related party transactions have been properly disclosed in the financial statements.	
9. All recorded liabilities are the obligations of the entity.	
10. Management has recorded no transactions with a negative effect on earnings.	

Choices
A) Should be included
B) May be included
C) Should not be included

| Going Concern Evaluation | Authoritative Literature | Help |

Select from the list provided the best description of each statement that addresses the auditor's evaluation of whether the entity is a going concern. Each choice may be used once, more than once, or not at all.

Statement	Answer
1. Restructuring existing debt to attain more favorable conditions	
2. Negative trends in earnings	
3. Inquiry of legal counsel	
4. Review of subsequent events	
5. Resolve any substantial doubt	
6. Delay expenditures	
7. Loss of a key patent	
8. Accelerate cash receipts from affiliates	
9. Document findings	
10. Gathering evidence for relevant assertions about going concern	

Choices
A) A procedure performed by the auditor
B) A purpose of the auditor's procedures
C) An expectation of the client
D) A condition or event that will cause the auditor concern
E) A management plan to address adverse effects of conditions or events

Misstatements | Authoritative Literature | Help

The year under audit is Year 2.

During the audit of accounts payable, you detected misstatements previously undetected by the client. All misstatements were related to Year 2. For each of the liability misstatements shown below, select from the lists provided the most appropriate item.

- In Column I, select the audit procedure that was most likely used to detect the misstatement.
- In Column II, select the internal control that most likely could prevent or detect this type of misstatement in the future.

Audit procedures and internal controls may be selected once, more than once, or not at all.

Misstatement	Column I Audit Procedure Used to Detect Misstatement	Column II Internal Control that Could Prevent or Detect Misstatement in the Future
1. An accounts payable clerk misplaces year-end invoices for raw materials that were received on December 21, Year 2, and therefore liabilities were not recorded.		
2. The company tends to be careless in recording payables in the correct period.		
3. The company has the same person approving pay requests and preparing checks.		
4. The company's receiving department misplaces receiving reports for purchases of raw materials at year end, and therefore liabilities were not recorded.		

Column I Selection List

A) From the January Year 3 cash disbursements journal, select payments and match to corresponding invoices.

B) Review the cash disbursements journal for the month of December Year 2.

C) On a surprise basis, review the receiving department's filing system and test check quantities entered on December Year 2 receiving reports to packing slips.

D) Identify open purchase orders and vendors' invoices at December 31, Year 2, and investigate their disposition.

E) Request written confirmation from the accounts payable supervisor that all vendor invoices have been recorded in the accounts payable subsidiary ledger.

F) Investigate unmatched receiving reports dated prior to January 1, Year 3.

G) Compare the balances for selected vendors at the end of Year 2 and Year 1.

H) Determine that credit memos received 10 days after the balance sheet date have been recorded in the proper period.

I) Select an unpaid invoice and ask to be walked through the invoice payment process.

Column II Selection List

A) The purchasing department supervisor forwards a monthly listing of matched purchase orders and receiving reports to the accounts payable supervisor for comparison to a listing of vouched invoices.

B) The accounts payable supervisor reviews a monthly listing of open purchase orders and vendors' invoices for follow-up with the receiving department.

C) Copies of all vendor invoices received during the year are filed in an outside storage facility.

D) All vendor invoices are reviewed for mathematical accuracy.

E) On a daily basis, the receiving department independently counts all merchandise received.

F) All vendor invoices with supporting documentation are canceled when paid.

G) At the end of each month, the purchasing department confirms terms of delivery with selected vendors.

H) Separate the functions of accounts payable and cash disbursements.

I) A clerk is responsible for matching purchase orders with receiving reports and making certain they are included in the proper month.

Litigation, Claims, and Assessments | Authoritative Literature | Help

Determine whether each audit procedure below is likely to be performed when testing for loss contingencies relating to litigation, claims, and assessments.

Audit Procedure	Answer
1. Read minutes of meetings of shareholders, directors, and committees.	
2. Inquire of officials at the courthouse in the county of the client.	
3. Read contracts, loan agreements, leases, and other documents.	
4. Read client correspondence with taxing and other governmental agencies.	
5. Read client correspondence with insurance and bonding companies.	
6. Read legal briefs of all suits filed against competitors of the client.	
7. Read confirmation replies for information about guarantees.	
8. Obtain from management or in-house counsel a description and evaluation of litigation, claims, and assessments.	
9. Obtain representation letters from all staff and professional employees of the client.	
10. Obtain an analysis of professional fee expenses and review supporting invoices for indications of contingencies.	
11. Inquire of SEC officials about reported violations creating claims or assessments.	
12. Request management to prepare for transmittal a letter of inquiry to legal counsel consulted by the entity about litigation, claims, and assessments.	
13. Obtain written representations that the financial statements include proper accruals and disclosures of contingencies.	
14. Obtain written or oral assurance from the audit committee that the financial statements include all accruals and disclosures required by the FASB's guidance applicable to accounting for contingencies.	

Choices
A) Perform
B) Do not perform

Research | Authoritative Literature | Help

Brody, CPA, is auditing a nonissuer client. After evaluating the audit evidence obtained thus far, he believes that there may be doubt regarding the client's ability to continue as a going concern. He has asked you to further investigate this concern. Which section of the generally accepted auditing standards best describes the audit procedures you should perform that may identify conditions and events indicative of substantial doubt regarding the client's ability to continue as a going concern?

Title	Section	Paragraph

Title Choices

AU-C	PCAOB	AT	AR	ET	BL	VS
CS	QC	PR	TS	PFP	CPE	

Unofficial Answers

1. Management Representation Letter (10 Gradable Items)

1.   C) Should not be included. No statement about the client's independence is in the management representation letter.

2.   C) Should not be included. Management, not the auditor, develops the estimates used in the financial statements.

3.   A) Should be included. The letter should include a representation that management has given the auditor (1) access to all information relevant to the preparation and fair presentation of the financial statements of which the entity is aware, (2) additional requested information, and (3) unrestricted access to persons from whom the auditor needs to obtain evidence. The information described presumably includes minutes of all meetings that might affect the audit.

4.   C) Should not be included. All information in the notes to the financial statements is the representation of management.

5.   B) May be included. The letter may include any additional written representations requested by the auditor.

6.   A) Should be included. The letter should state that management has disclosed its knowledge of fraud, suspected fraud, or allegations of fraud, if any.

7.   C) Should not be included. Items included in the letter are assumed to be material.

8.   A) Should be included. The letter should state that (1) the identities of related parties, (2) related party relationships, and (3) related party transactions have been properly disclosed in the financial statements.

9.   B) May be included. The letter may include any additional written representations requested by the auditor.

10.   C) Should not be included. Many recorded transactions, such as expenses, have a negative effect on earnings.

2. Going Concern Evaluation (10 Gradable Items)

1.   E) A management plan to address adverse effects of conditions or events. Restructuring existing debt to attain more favorable conditions is a management plan to address adverse effects of conditions or events.

2.   D) A condition or event that will cause the auditor concern. Negative trends in earnings is a condition that will cause the auditor concern.

3.   A) A procedure performed by the auditor. Inquiry of legal counsel is a procedure performed by the auditor to learn about uncertainties that could lead going-concern issues.

4.   A) A procedure performed by the auditor. A review of subsequent events is a procedure performed by the auditor to learn about going-concern issues.

5.   B) A purpose of auditor's procedures. A purpose of the auditor's procedures is to resolve any substantial doubt about going concern.

6.   E) A management plan to address adverse effects of conditions or events. Delaying expenditures is a management plan to address adverse effects of conditions or events.

7.   D) A condition or event that will cause the auditor concern. The loss of a key patent is an event that will cause the auditor concern.

8.   E) A management plan to address adverse effects of conditions or events. Accelerating cash receipts from affiliates is a management plan to address adverse effects of conditions or events.

9.   A) A procedure performed by the auditor. Documenting findings is a procedure completed by the auditor.

10.   B) A purpose of auditor's procedures. A purpose of the auditor's procedures is to gather evidence for relevant assertions about going concern.

3. Misstatements (8 Gradable Items)

	Column I	Column II
1.	F)	A)
2.	A)	I)
3.	I)	H)
4.	D)	B)

1. <u>F) Investigate unmatched receiving reports dated prior to January 1, Year 3.</u> Receiving reports should be matched with purchase orders and vendor invoices as support for a payment voucher. Investigating unmatched documents would uncover the failure to prepare a voucher.

   <u>A) The purchasing department supervisor forwards a monthly listing of matched purchase orders and receiving reports to the accounts payable supervisor for comparison to a listing of vouched invoices.</u> Comparing an independent listing of matched purchase orders and receiving reports with vouched invoices would detect a lost document in accounts payable.

2. <u>A) From the January Year 3 cash disbursements journal, select payments and match to corresponding invoices.</u> A cutoff test that evaluates transactions recorded at or near year end would detect transactions recorded in the improper period.

   <u>I) A clerk is responsible for matching purchases orders with receiving reports and making certain they are included in the proper month.</u> Having an employee responsible for making certain that transactions are recorded in the proper period would be a control to help ensure proper cutoff.

3. <u>I) Select an unpaid invoice and ask to be walked through the invoice payment process.</u> A walkthrough of the process would allow the auditor to identify weaknesses in the system.

   <u>H) Separate the functions of accounts payable and cash disbursements.</u> Separation of the approval and custody functions is a control to mitigate risks in a payment system.

4. <u>D) Identify open purchase orders and vendors' invoices at December 31, Year 2, and investigate their disposition.</u> To detect missing or lost receiving reports, the auditor should identify open purchase orders and vendors' invoices at December 31, Year 2, and investigate their disposition.

   <u>B) The accounts payable supervisor reviews a monthly listing of open purchase orders and vendors' invoices for follow-up with the receiving department.</u> A useful control would be to have the accounts payable supervisor review a monthly listing of open purchase orders and vendors' invoices for follow-up with the receiving department.

4. Litigation, Claims, and Assessments (14 Gradable Items)

1. <u>A) Perform.</u> Minutes of the meetings of the board of directors, shareholders, and various committees often provide evidence about unusual events giving rise to potential contingencies.

2. <u>B) Do not perform.</u> Inquiring of local officials is not a normal procedure. However, in certain instances, the auditor may need to gather evidence from public records.

3. <u>A) Perform.</u> Contracts, agreements, and leases often contain provisions that create contingent liabilities.

4. <u>A) Perform.</u> Correspondence with governmental agencies should be read and evaluated for numerous reasons (e.g., potential violations of laws or regulations, taxes or fees due, and claims or assessments on property).

5. <u>A) Perform.</u> Insurance companies and bonding agencies often insure clients against potential losses. These losses should be identified and evaluated relative to potential financial reporting requirements.

6. <u>B) Do not perform.</u> Reading all legal briefs for suits filed against the entity's competitors is not feasible or necessary.

7. <u>A) Perform.</u> Confirmations may disclose certain guarantees offered to customers that could result in contingent liabilities.

8. <u>A) Perform.</u> The auditor should obtain from management a description and evaluation of litigation, claims, and assessments that existed at the balance sheet date and from that date to the date the information is provided.

9. <u>B) Do not perform.</u> The auditor is required to obtain written representations from management with overall responsibility for the matters covered in the representations. The auditor would not normally obtain written representations from all client staff.

10. <u>A) Perform.</u> Professional fees (for example, fees paid to external legal counsel) should be evaluated to determine their purpose. Often, the services are in relation to contingencies.

11. <u>B) Do not perform.</u> Normally, the auditor will not inquire of SEC officials. However, written correspondence, available from the client, should be evaluated by the auditor.

12. <u>A) Perform.</u> A letter of inquiry to external legal counsel is the auditor's primary means of obtaining corroboration of the information provided by management about litigation, claims, and assessments.

13. <u>A) Perform.</u> The auditor should obtain written representations that all actual and possible litigation, claims, and assessments that should be considered in preparing the statements have been accounted for and disclosed in accordance with the applicable framework.

14. <u>B) Do not perform.</u> It is management's responsibility, not the audit committee's, to ensure that contingencies are properly accounted for.

5. Research (1 Gradable Item)

Answer: 570.A1

AU-C Section 570 -- *The Auditor's Consideration of an Entity's Ability to Continue as a Going Concern*

Identifying Conditions or Events That Indicate Substantial Doubt Could Exist

.A1   It is not necessary to design audit procedures solely to identify conditions and events that, when considered in the aggregate, indicate there could be substantial doubt about the entity's ability to continue as a going concern for a reasonable period of time. The results of audit procedures designed and performed to identify and assess risk in accordance with section 315, gather audit evidence in response to assessed risks in accordance with section 330, *Performing Audit Procedures in Response to Assessed Risks and Evaluating the Audit Evidence Obtained*, and complete the audit are expected to be sufficient for that purpose. The following are examples of procedures that may identify such conditions or events:

- Analytical procedures
- Review of subsequent events
- Review of compliance with the terms of debt and loan agreements
- Reading of minutes of meetings of stockholders, board of directors, and important committees of the board
- Inquiry of an entity's legal counsel about litigation, claims, and assessments
- Confirmation with related and third parties of the details of arrangements to provide or maintain financial support

Gleim Simulation Grading

Task	Correct Responses		Gradable Items		Score per Task
1	_____	÷	10	=	_____
2	_____	÷	10	=	_____
3	_____	÷	8	=	_____
4	_____	÷	14	=	_____
5 (Research)	_____	÷	1	=	_____

	Total of Scores per Task	_____
÷	Total Number of Tasks	5
	Total Score	_____%

Use **CPA Gleim Online** and **Simulation Wizard** to practice more task-based simulations in a realistic environment.

STUDY UNIT FIFTEEN
EVIDENCE -- SAMPLING

(20 pages of outline)

The first subunit defines terms, describes the purpose of and approach to sampling, and presents the basic concepts traditionally tested on the CPA exam. A study of these fundamentals is an effective way to prepare for most sampling-related questions. However, some comprehensive questions may be asked, including those requiring basic calculations or the consideration of tables.

The remaining three subunits contain study materials related to more extensive questions and simulations. They describe, in more detail, specific sampling methods and provide several examples. Although more comprehensive than the first subunit, they are not intended to be an exhaustive treatment of sampling. These sections are based on concepts that have been tested in the past or are likely to be tested on future CPA exams and are discussed in the AICPA Audit Guide, *Audit Sampling* (2013).

15.1 SAMPLING FUNDAMENTALS (AU-C 530)

No one can accurately predict what will be on the exam you take. However, we can give you some facts to help you make informed decisions about your study strategy. Sampling is included in the CSO's Area III -- Auditing and Attestation: Performing Audit Procedures and Evaluating Evidence. The percentage of total test questions projected to be associated with this area is between 16% and 20%. "Perform audit sampling" is 1 of 24 topics listed. When the exam was disclosed, sampling questions normally accounted for about 3% to 4% of the questions, but occasionally more. Many, if not most, of those questions could have been answered with a solid understanding of the material in Subunit 1. Understand all you can about the exam and your strengths and weaknesses, then decide how much time to invest in studying more specialized sampling topics.

1. **Audit Sampling**

   a. Audit sampling selects and evaluates fewer than 100% of the items in the relevant audited population.

      1) The population is the entire data set (a) from which a sample is selected and (b) about which conclusions are to be drawn.

      2) The auditor expects the sample (items selected) to (a) represent the population and (b) provide a reasonable basis for conclusions about it.

         a) The sample is representative if, subject to sampling risk, conclusions are similar to those drawn if the same procedures were applied to every item in the population.

b.   Sampling may be nonstatistical or statistical.

1)   **Nonstatistical (judgment) sampling** uses the auditor's subjective judgment to determine the sample size (number of items to examine) and sample selection (which items to examine). This subjectivity is not always a weakness. The auditor, based on other audit work, may be able to test the most material and risky transactions and emphasize the types of transactions subject to high risk of material misstatement.

a)   However, nonstatistical sampling does not have both characteristics of statistical sampling. Thus, the auditor cannot (1) project the results to the entire population or (2) obtain sufficient appropriate evidence about the rest of the population without performing other procedures.

2)   **Statistical sampling** (a) **randomly** selects sample items and (b) uses an appropriate statistical method to evaluate the results, including measurement of sampling risk.

a)   Accordingly, statistical sampling provides an objective method of determining sample size and selecting the items to be examined. Unlike nonstatistical sampling, it also provides a means of quantitatively assessing the confidence level and precision.

i)   The **confidence level**, also called the reliability level, is the percentage of times the sample should adequately reflect the population. It is the complement of the applicable sampling risk factor. For a test of controls, if the allowable risk of overreliance is 5%, the auditor's desired confidence level is 95% (100% – 5%). For a test of details, if the risk of incorrect rejection is 5%, the auditor's desired confidence level is 95% (100% – 5%).

ii)   **Precision** (allowance for sampling risk) is a measure of how closely the sample represents the population.

b)   **Random selection** includes (1) simple random sampling; (2) stratified random sampling; (3) probability-weighted, including monetary-unit, sampling; and (4) systematic random sampling.

c)   Statistical sampling helps the auditor design an efficient sample, measure the sufficiency of the evidence obtained, and evaluate the sample results.

d)   Auditors are required to obtain sufficient appropriate evidence. Sufficiency is the measure of the quantity of evidence. Thus, it relates to the design and size of the sample.

i)   Statistical sampling permits the auditor to measure **sampling risk** and, therefore, to design more efficient samples (i.e., the minimum samples necessary to provide sufficient appropriate evidence).

c.   Statistical sampling applies to **tests of controls** (attribute sampling) and **tests of details** (variables sampling).

2.   The auditor must address uncertainties due to sampling (sampling risk) and uncertainties due to factors other than sampling (nonsampling risk).

3.   **Sampling Risk**

a.   Sampling risk is the risk that the auditor's conclusion based on a sample may differ from the conclusion when the same procedure is applied to the entire population. Two types of erroneous conclusions may be drawn:

1)   **Controls** are more effective than they actually are (overreliance), or a **material misstatement** does not exist when in fact it does exist (incorrect acceptance).

a)   This type of error affects audit effectiveness and is more likely to result in an inappropriate opinion.

2) **Controls** are less effective than they actually are (underreliance), or a **material misstatement** exists when in fact it does not exist (incorrect rejection).

    a) This type of error affects audit efficiency and results in more work.

3) The following table is helpful in understanding sampling risk:

	Tests of Controls (Attribute Sampling)	Tests of Details (Variables Sampling)
Audit Efficiency Error	Controls are less effective than they actually are. (Unnecessary audit effort)	A material misstatement exists when in fact it does not exist. (Unnecessary audit effort)
Audit Effectiveness Error	Controls are more effective than they actually are. (Potential audit failure)	A material misstatement does not exist when in fact it does exist. (Potential audit failure)

4. **Nonsampling Risk**

    a. Nonsampling risk is the risk of an erroneous conclusion caused by a factor not related to sampling risk. For example, the auditor may apply inappropriate procedures or misinterpret audit evidence and not recognize misstatements or control deviations.

    b. Adequate **planning** and effective **quality control**, among other things, decrease nonsampling risk.

5. **Sample Design, Size, and Selection**

    a. The auditor considers the purpose of the audit procedure(s) and the characteristics of the population.

        1) The auditor (a) defines the nature of a control deviation or misstatement, (b) chooses the population to be sampled, and (c) determines whether it is complete.

        2) For tests of controls, the auditor assesses the expected deviation rate based on the understanding of internal control. If the rate is unacceptably high, controls ordinarily are not tested.

        3) For tests of details, the auditor assesses the expected misstatement. If the expected misstatement is high, an increased sample size or a 100% audit may be needed.

        4) The characteristics of the population may be appropriate for stratification or value-weighted selection.

    b. **Sample size** is inversely related to the acceptable sampling risk. The following factors determine sample size:

        1) **Tests of controls**

            a) The tolerable rate of deviation in the population

            b) The expected rate of deviation in the population

            c) The desired level of assurance **(complement of risk overreliance)** that the actual rate of deviation is **not** greater than the tolerable rate

                i) The desired assurance (confidence level) may be based on the extent of the reliance on the relevant controls.

            d) The number of individual items (sampling units) in the population (if the population is very small)

2) **Tests of details**

    a) The desired level of assurance **(complement of the risk of incorrect acceptance)** that actual misstatement is **not** greater than tolerable misstatement. The desired level (confidence level) may be based on the following:

        i) Assessed risks of material misstatement

        ii) Evidence provided by other substantive procedures performed on the same assertion

        iii) Tolerable misstatement

        iv) Expected misstatement

        v) If relevant, stratification of the population and the sampling units in each stratum

    NOTE: For tests of details, auditors also consider a measure of **variance** (e.g., the standard deviation). Furthermore, auditors may directly consider the **risk of incorrect rejection**. Computer programs used to calculate sample size commonly require the auditor to enter the risk of incorrect rejection and the desired allowance for risk of incorrect rejection (precision). See the table in Subunit 15.3. It is based on factors used to determine an amount of precision that is appropriate to give the specified protection against incorrect acceptance.

6. If the appropriate procedures or alternative procedures cannot be performed on a sample item, the auditor treats the item as a misstatement or a control deviation.

    a. In some cases, the auditor may select a **replacement item** if (s)he is satisfied that the initially selected item is not a misstatement or a control deviation.

7. The auditor should investigate the causes and evaluate the effects of identified misstatements and control deviations.

    a. The misstatements and control deviations may have a **common feature** (e.g., type of transaction or period of time), and the auditor may wish to examine all items with that feature.

        1) The presence of a common feature also may indicate **fraud** if intentional.

    b. The auditor also evaluates the **qualitative** aspects of misstatements, e.g., whether they are (1) differences in accounting principles or their application or (2) caused by fraud.

        1) Another qualitative aspect is the potential effect on other parts of the audit.

8. The auditor should project the results of sampling to the population.

    a. The projection for tests of details is the **projected misstatement**.

    b. The projection for tests of controls is the **sample deviation rate**.

9. **Evaluation of Results**

    a. The auditor should evaluate the results of sampling, including sampling risk, and whether the results provide a reasonable basis for conclusions about the population.

        1) In the absence of other audit evidence,

            a) An unexpectedly high deviation rate for a test of controls may require higher assessed risks of material misstatement.

            b) An unexpectedly high misstatement amount may indicate that a transaction class or account balance is materially misstated.

                i) The closer projected misstatement is to tolerable misstatement, the more likely that actual misstatement is greater than tolerable misstatement.

        ii)   If expected misstatement used to calculate sample size is less than projected misstatement, it is more likely that sampling risk is unacceptable.

   2)   If sampling does not provide a reasonable basis for conclusions, the auditor may

      a)   Ask management to investigate misstatements and make needed adjustments or

      b)   Perform further audit procedures, for example, increasing sample size.

10.   **Basic Steps in a Statistical Plan**

   a.   **Determine the objectives of the plan.**

      1)   For a test of controls, an example is to conclude that control is reasonably effective.

      2)   For a test of details, an example is to conclude that a balance is not misstated by more than an immaterial amount.

   b.   **Define the population.** This step includes defining the sampling unit (an individual item in the population) and considering the completeness of the population.

      1)   For tests of controls, the period covered is defined.
      2)   For tests of details, individually significant items may be defined.

   c.   **Determine acceptable levels of sampling risk** (e.g., 5% or 10%).
   d.   **Calculate the sample size** using tables or sample-size formulas.

      1)   In some cases, it is efficient to divide the population into subpopulations or strata. The primary objective of **stratification** is to minimize variability. Because the variance within each subpopulation or stratum is lower than in the population as a whole, the auditor may sample a smaller number of items while holding the allowance for sampling risk (precision) and the confidence level constant.

      2)   Stratification also allows the auditor to apply more audit effort to larger elements or more risky parts of the population.

      3)   For example, when auditing sales revenue, an auditor could divide the population into strata of dollar increments. The auditor could test transactions under $500, between $501 and $2,000, and $2,001 and above.

   e.   **Select the sampling approach**, e.g., random number, systematic, or block.

      1)   In **random sampling**, each item in the population has an equal and nonzero probability of selection. Random selection is usually accomplished by generating random numbers from a random number table or computer program and tracing them to associated documents or items in the population.

      2)   **Systematic sampling** begins with selecting a random start and then taking every nth item in the population. The value of n is computed by dividing the population by the number of sampling units. The random start should be in the first interval. Because the sampling method requires only counting in the population, no correspondence between random numbers and the items in the population is necessary as in random number sampling. A systematic sampling plan assumes the items are arranged randomly in the population. If the auditor discovers that this is not true, a random selection method should be used.

EXAMPLE

If the population contains 8,200 items and a sample of 50 is required, every 164th item is selected (8,200 ÷ 50). After a random start in the first interval (1 to 164), every additional 164th item is selected. For example, if the 35th item were the first selected randomly, the next would be the 199th (35 + 164). The next item would be the 363rd (199 + 164). The process would be continued until the 50 items were identified.

3) **Block sampling** (cluster sampling) randomly selects groups of items as the sampling units rather than individual items. An example is the inclusion in the sample of all cash payments for May and September. One possible drawback is that the variability of items within the blocks may not be representative of the variability within the population. The advantage of block sampling is that it avoids the need to assign random numbers to individual items in the population. Instead, blocks (clusters) are randomly selected.

f.   **Take the sample.** The auditor selects the items to be evaluated.

g.   **Evaluate the sample results.** The auditor draws conclusions about the population.

h.   **Document the sampling procedures.** The auditor prepares appropriate working papers.

11. **Overview of Attribute Sampling**

a.   Attribute sampling is used to test the effectiveness of controls (tests of controls).

EXAMPLE

The auditor desires to test the effectiveness of the approval process of purchase orders. (S)he selects a sample of purchase orders from the population of all purchase orders issued during the year and inspects each one in the sample for the required approval.

---

b.   The deviation (failure) rate in the application of the control in the sample is used to project the deviation rate to the whole population.

c.   By specifying a tolerable deviation rate, a preliminary expected deviation rate, and the risk of overreliance, the auditor can determine the appropriate sample size by consulting a table.

12. **Primary Methods of Variables Sampling**

a.   Variables sampling applies to dollar values or other quantities for tests of details. In contrast, attribute sampling tests binary propositions (see Subunit 15.2).

b.   **Mean-per-unit** averages the audit amounts of the sample items and multiplies the average by the number of items in the population to estimate the population amount. An allowance for sampling risk (achieved precision at the desired level of confidence based on the normal distribution) is then calculated.

c.   **Difference estimation** (of population misstatement) (1) determines differences between the audit and recorded amounts of items in the sample, (2) adds the differences, (3) calculates the mean difference, and (4) multiplies the mean by the number of items in the population. An allowance for sampling risk (achieved precision at the desired level of confidence based on the normal distribution) is then calculated.

1)   **Ratio estimation** is similar to difference estimation except that it estimates the population misstatement by multiplying the recorded amount of the population by the ratio of the total audit amount of the sample items to their total recorded amount.

d. **Monetary-unit sampling (MUS)**, also known as probability-proportional-to-size (PPS) or dollar-unit sampling (DUS), uses the dollar or another monetary unit as the sampling unit. MUS is appropriate for testing account balances (typically assets) for overstatement when some items may be far larger than others in the population. In effect, it stratifies the population because the larger account balances have a greater chance of being selected. MUS is most useful if few misstatements are expected.

    1) Also, the method does not require the use of a measure of variance (e.g., standard deviation or expected deviation rate) to determine sample size or interpret the results.

Stop and review! You have completed the outline for this subunit. Study multiple-choice questions 1 through 10 beginning on page 477.

15.2 STATISTICAL SAMPLING IN TESTS OF CONTROLS (ATTRIBUTE SAMPLING)

1. **Attribute sampling** tests binary (yes/no or error/nonerror) questions. It is used to test the effectiveness of controls because it can estimate a rate of occurrence of control deviations in a population.

    a. Attribute sampling requires the existence of evidence indicating performance of the control being tested (e.g., a control indicating that the purchasing agent has signed all purchase orders before sending them to the vendor). It is most helpful for a large population of documentary evidence. In general, the performance of any task that leaves evidence of its execution is suitable for attribute sampling. In such cases, the auditor can form conclusions about the population by examining a sample.

    b. The following are examples of activities subject to controls that may be tested using attribute sampling:

        1) Billing
        2) Voucher processing
        3) Payroll
        4) Inventory pricing

2. **Steps for Testing Controls**

    a. **Define the objectives of the plan.** The auditor should clearly state what is to be accomplished, for example, to determine that the deviation rate from an approval process for a transaction is at an acceptable level.

    b. **Define the population.** The population is the focus of interest. The accountant wants to reach conclusions about all of the items (typically documents) in the population.

        1) The **sampling unit** is the individual item that will be included in the sample. Thus, the population may consist of all the transactions for the fiscal year. The sampling unit is each document representing a transaction and containing the required evidence that a control procedure was performed (e.g., an approval signature).

    c. **Define the deviation conditions.** The characteristic indicative of performance of a control is the attribute of interest, for example, the supervisor's signature of approval on a document. Careful definition of the attribute is important so that deviations (departures) from the control may be determined and the sample items properly evaluated. For example, is it acceptable for another person to sign for the supervisor during vacation periods, and must the signature be in a certain place on the form for it to be considered approved?

d. **Determine the sample size.** Tables ordinarily are used to calculate the appropriate sample size based on the factors below. Tables 1 and 2 below and on the next page are derived from Appendix A of the AICPA Audit Guide, *Audit Sampling* (2013). The sample sizes in the tables are based on the assumption that the population is large.

1) **Allowable risk of overreliance.** This risk has an inverse effect on sample size. The higher the allowable risk, the smaller the sample size. The usual risk specified by auditors is 5% or 10%. The auditor can specify other levels of risk, but the tables most often presented use only these two.

2) **Tolerable deviation rate.** This is the maximum rate of deviations from the prescribed control that the auditor is willing to accept without altering the assessed risk of material misstatement. Deviations increase the likelihood of misstatements in the accounting records but do not always cause misstatements.

    a) If the auditor cannot tolerate any deviations, sampling is inappropriate, and the whole population must be investigated.

3) **Expected population deviation rate.** An estimate of the deviation rate in the current population is necessary to determine the appropriate sample size. This estimate can be based on the prior year's findings or a pilot sample of approximately 30 to 50 items.

    a) The expected rate should be less than the tolerable rate. Otherwise, tests of the control should be omitted, and the auditor should not rely on the effectiveness of the control.

Table 1 -- Sample Sizes for Tests of Controls -- 5% Risk of Overreliance								
Expected Population Deviation Rate	Tolerable Deviation Rate							
	2%	3%	4%	5%	6%	7%	8%	9%	10%
0.00%	149	99	74	59	49	42	36	32	29
.25	236	157	117	93	78	66	58	51	46
.50	313	157	117	93	78	66	58	51	46
.75	386	208	117	93	78	66	58	51	46
1.00	590	257	156	93	78	66	58	51	46
1.25	1,030	303	156	124	78	66	58	51	46
1.50	*	392	192	124	103	66	58	51	46
1.75	*	562	227	153	103	88	77	51	46
2.00	*	846	294	181	127	88	77	68	46
2.25	*	1,466	390	208	127	88	77	68	61
2.50	*	*	513	234	150	109	77	68	61
2.75	*	*	722	286	173	109	95	68	61
3.00	*	*	1,098	361	195	129	95	84	61
3.25	*	*	1,936	458	238	148	112	84	61
3.50	*	*	*	624	280	167	112	84	76
3.75	*	*	*	877	341	185	129	100	76
4.00	*	*	*	1,348	421	221	146	100	89
5.00	*	*	*	*	1,580	478	240	158	116
6.00	*	*	*	*	*	1,832	532	266	179
7.00	*	*	*	*	*	*	*	585	298
8.00	*	*	*	*	*	*	*	*	649

Sample Size	Actual Number of Deviations Found										
	0	1	2	3	4	5	6	7	8	9	10
20	14.0	21.7	28.3	34.4	40.2	45.6	50.8	55.9	60.7	65.4	69.9
25	11.3	17.7	23.2	28.2	33.0	37.6	42.0	46.3	50.4	54.4	58.4
30	9.6	14.9	19.6	23.9	28.0	31.9	35.8	39.4	43.0	46.6	50.0
35	8.3	12.9	17.0	20.7	24.3	27.8	31.1	34.4	37.5	40.6	43.7
40	7.3	11.4	15.0	18.3	21.5	24.6	27.5	30.4	33.3	36.0	38.8
45	6.5	10.2	13.4	16.4	19.2	22.0	24.7	27.3	29.8	32.4	34.8
50	5.9	9.2	12.1	14.8	17.4	19.9	22.4	24.7	27.1	29.4	31.6
55	5.4	8.4	11.1	13.5	15.9	18.2	20.5	22.6	24.8	26.9	28.9
60	4.9	7.7	10.2	12.5	14.7	16.8	18.8	20.8	22.8	24.8	26.7
65	4.6	7.1	9.4	11.5	13.6	15.5	17.5	19.3	21.2	23.0	24.7
70	4.2	6.6	8.8	10.8	12.7	14.5	16.3	18.0	19.7	21.4	23.1
75	4.0	6.2	8.2	10.1	11.8	13.6	15.2	16.9	18.5	20.1	21.6
80	3.7	5.8	7.7	9.5	11.1	12.7	14.3	15.9	17.4	18.9	20.3
90	3.3	5.2	6.9	8.4	9.9	11.4	12.8	14.2	15.5	16.9	18.2
100	3.0	4.7	6.2	7.6	9.0	10.3	11.5	12.8	14.0	15.2	16.4
125	2.4	3.8	5.0	6.1	7.2	8.3	9.3	10.3	11.3	12.3	13.2
150	2.0	3.2	4.2	5.1	6.0	6.9	7.8	8.6	9.5	10.3	11.1
200	1.5	2.4	3.2	3.9	4.6	5.2	5.9	6.5	7.2	7.8	8.4

Table 2 -- Results Evaluation for Tests of Controls -- Upper % Limits at 5% Risk of Overreliance

4) **Population size.** The total number of sampling units in the population should be known. However, the sample size is relatively insensitive to size changes in large populations. For populations over 2,000, a standard table (e.g., Table 1, which assumes a large population) can be used. Use of the standard tables (based on the assumption of large populations) for sampling plans based on a smaller population size is a conservative approach because the sample size will be overstated. Hence, the risk of overreliance is not affected.

   a) A change in the size of the population has a very small effect on the required sample size when the population is large.

EXAMPLE

Assume the risk of overreliance is 5%, the tolerable rate is 6%, the expected population deviation rate is 2.5%, and the population size is over 5,000. Given these data, the sample size determined from Table 1 is 150. This is the intersection of the 6% Tolerable Deviation Rate column and the 2.50% Expected Population Deviation Rate row.

---

e. **Perform the sampling plan.** A random sample should be taken. Each item in the population should have an equal and nonzero chance of being selected. A random number table or a computer program can be used to identify the items to be selected if a correspondence can be established between the random number and the item in the population.

   1) A statistical consideration is whether to use sampling **with** or **without** replacement. The tables are designed for sampling with replacement, which results in a conservative sample size because a slightly larger sample size than necessary will be indicated. However, in practice, auditors normally sample without replacement. No additional evidence is obtained by choosing the same item more than once.

   2) Sampling without replacement means that a population item cannot be selected again after it is selected in the sampling process.

    f.   **Evaluate and document sample results.** The steps include calculating the sample deviation rate and determining the achieved upper deviation limit.

        1) **Sample deviation rate.** The number of deviations observed is divided by the sample size to determine the sample deviation rate. This rate is the best estimate of the population deviation rate. For example, if three deviations were discovered in a sample of 150, the auditor's best estimate of the population deviation rate is 2% (3 ÷ 150). The auditor cannot state with certainty that the sample rate is the population rate because the sample may not be representative of the population. However, (s)he can state at a specified confidence level that the deviation rate is not likely to be greater than a specified upper limit.

        2) **Achieved upper deviation limit.** The achieved upper deviation limit is based on the sample size and the number of deviations discovered. See Table 2 on the previous page. The intersection of the sample size and the number of deviations indicates the achieved upper deviation limit. Accordingly, if the auditor discovers 3 deviations in a sample of 150, (s)he can state at a 95% confidence level (the complement of a 5% risk of overreliance) that the true occurrence rate is not greater than 5.1%.

           a) The difference between the achieved upper deviation limit determined from a standard table and the sample rate is the allowance for sampling risk (achieved precision) and in the example is 3.1% (5.1%-2%).

           b) When the sample deviation rate exceeds the expected population deviation rate, the achieved upper deviation limit will exceed the tolerable rate at the given risk of overreliance. In that case, the sample does not support the planned reliance on the control.

           c) When the sample deviation rate does not exceed the expected population deviation rate, the achieved upper deviation limit will not exceed the tolerable rate at the given risk level. Thus, the sample supports the planned reliance on the control. This is the case in the example. The sample deviation rate (2%) does not exceed the expected population rate (2.5%). Thus, the achieved upper deviation limit (5.1%) does not exceed the tolerable rate (6%).

        3) Each deviation should be analyzed to determine its nature, importance, and probable cause. Obviously, some are much more significant than others. Sampling provides a means of forming a conclusion about the overall population but should not be used as a substitute for good judgment.

3. **Analysis of Results**

    a. The following presentation is a popular method for testing sampling concepts related to tests of controls. It is used to explain how to analyze the information. A variety of questions can be answered based on the analysis.

    b. The table below depicts the possible combinations of the sample results and the true state of the population.

Auditor's Estimate Based on Sample Results	True State of Population	
	Deviation rate is less than tolerable rate.	Deviation rate exceeds tolerable rate.
Deviation rate is less than tolerable rate.	I. Correct	III. Incorrect
Deviation rate exceeds tolerable rate.	II. Incorrect	IV. Correct

   c.   The following definitions and explanations should be understood:

      1)   The true state of the population is the actual rate of deviations in the population.

      2)   If the true deviation rate is less than the tolerable rate, the auditor should have an expectation of the effectiveness of the control tested.

      3)   If the true deviation rate exceeds the tolerable rate, the auditor should not have an expectation of the effectiveness of the control tested.

      4)   The auditor's estimate based on the sample is the auditor's conclusion about the deviation rate in the population based on taking and evaluating a sample.

      5)   Cell I represents a correct decision to have an expectation of the effectiveness of the control tested. The population actually has a deviation rate less than the tolerable rate.

      6)   Cell II represents an incorrect decision not to have an expectation of the effectiveness of the control tested. The population has an acceptable deviation rate. But, because of sampling risk, the sample indicates that the population deviation rate is greater than the tolerable rate. This mistake compels the auditor to expand substantive testing even though the control is effective. Thus, it relates to the efficiency rather than the effectiveness of the audit.

      7)   Cell III represents an incorrect decision (and a critical one) to have an expectation of the effectiveness of the control tested. The population has a greater-than-acceptable deviation rate, but the sample indicates that the deviation rate is less than the tolerable rate. Because the auditor expects the control to have some degree of effectiveness, substantive testing is reduced, and an audit failure could result.

      8)   Cell IV represents a correct decision not to have an expectation of the effectiveness of the control tested. The population has an unacceptable deviation rate, and the sample properly reflects this condition.

   d.   A CPA exam question may take a variety of forms, but the following is representative:

      1)   As a result of tests of a control, the auditor does not have an expectation of the effectiveness of the control and increases substantive testing. This is illustrated by which situation? Answer: Cell II.

Stop and review! You have completed the outline for this subunit. Study multiple-choice questions 11 through 23 beginning on page 479.

15.3 CLASSICAL VARIABLES SAMPLING (MEAN-PER-UNIT)

1.   **Sampling for Tests of Details**

   a.   Sampling for tests of details provides evidence about whether a financial statement assertion about an account balance is materially misstated. For example, the recorded balance of accounts receivable is expected to represent the true balance of the receivables, which is not known (and will never be known without a 100% audit). After taking a sample and drawing a conclusion about the population, the auditor either accepts or rejects the reported number.

   b.   The following are examples:

      1)   Is management's recorded balance of accounts receivable measured at net realizable value?

      2)   Is management's recorded balance of inventory measured at lower of cost or market?

2. **Steps for Mean-per-Unit Sampling**

   a. **Define the objectives of the plan.** The auditor intends to estimate the carrying amount of the population, for example, an accounts receivable balance.

   b. **Define the population and the sampling unit.** This is the balance or class of transactions and the supporting detail under audit.

EXAMPLE

The population consists of 4,000 accounts receivable with a reported carrying amount of $3,500,000. Each customer account is a sampling unit.

The material immediately following is rather technical. However, it is not likely that you will need to know the formula for the sample size. The AICPA Audit Guide, *Audit Sampling* (2013), states, "Because auditors generally use computer programs to assist them in determining sample sizes and evaluating sample results for classical variables sampling applications, it is not essential for auditors to know mathematical formulas to use these methods." However, we present the formula and an example to help you understand the relationship of the factors.

---

   c. **Determine the sample size.** The following is the sample size formula for mean-per-unit variables sampling:

$$n = \left[\frac{C \times S \times N}{A}\right]^2$$

If: n = Sample size

     C = Confidence coefficient or number of standard deviations related to the required confidence level (1 − the risk of incorrect rejection)

     S = Standard deviation of the population (an estimate based on a pilot sample or from the prior year's sample)

     N = Number of items in the population

     A = Allowance for sampling risk. This allowance is a total. In some representations, the allowance (precision) is stated in the denominator on a per-item basis ($A \div N$), and N would not be included in the formula.

    1) The **allowance for sampling risk**, also termed the **precision or confidence interval**, is an interval around the sample statistic that is expected to include the true balance of the population at the specified confidence level. When using classical variables sampling, the allowance for sampling risk is calculated based on the normal distribution.

       a) This allowance is a function of the **tolerable misstatement** determined by the auditor. It is the maximum misstatement that may exist without causing the financial statements to be materially misstated. Tolerable misstatement is an expression of **performance materiality**. This measure of materiality is an amount estimated to reduce the probability that the sum of uncorrected and undetected misstatements exceeds materiality for the statements as a whole. Tolerable misstatement may equal performance materiality or be smaller.

b)   The allowance for sampling risk is established as a function of materiality to control the risk of incorrect acceptance. *C* in the formula is based on the risk of incorrect rejection, but the more important risk to the auditor is that of incorrect acceptance.

   i)   The allowance for sampling risk equals the product of tolerable misstatement and a ratio determined in accordance with Table 3 below. This ratio is based on the allowable risk of incorrect acceptance and the risk of incorrect rejection, both of which are specified by the auditor.

Table 3 -- Ratio of Desired Allowance for Sampling Risk of Incorrect Rejection to Tolerable Misstatement

Risk of Incorrect Acceptance	Risk of Incorrect Rejection (Two Sided)			
	.20	.10	.05	.01
.01	.355	.413	.457	.525
.025	.395	.456	.500	.568
.05	.437	.500	.543	.609
.075	.471	.532	.576	.641
.10	.500	.561	.605	.668
.15	.533	.612	.653	.712
.20	.603	.661	.700	.753
.25	.653	.708	.742	.791
.30	.707	.756	.787	.829
.35	.766	.808	.834	.868
.40	.831	.863	.883	.908
.45	.907	.926	.937	.953
.50	1.000	1.000	1.000	1.000

2)   The confidence coefficient, *C*, is derived from the standard normal distribution and is based on the risk of incorrect rejection.

Risk of Incorrect Rejection	Confidence Level	Confidence Coefficient
20%	80%	1.28
10%	90%	1.64
5%	95%	1.96
1%	99%	2.58

EXAMPLE

The number of sampling units is 4,000, the estimated population standard deviation is $125 based on a pilot sample, and the number of standard deviations related to the desired 90% confidence level (10% risk of incorrect rejection) is 1.64. Assuming tolerable misstatement of $100,000 and a risk of incorrect acceptance of 5%, the desired allowance for sampling risk (precision) can be determined using Table 3. The intersection of the 10% risk of incorrect rejection and 5% risk of incorrect acceptance is .500. The result is a $50,000 allowance for sampling risk ($100,000 tolerable misstatement × .500).

Thus, the sample size is

$$n = \left[\frac{C \times S \times N}{A} \right]^2$$

$$= \left[\frac{1.64 \times \$125 \times 4{,}000}{\$50{,}000} \right]^2$$

$$= 268.96 \text{ or } 269$$

    d.   **Select the sample, execute the plan, and evaluate and document the results.**

1) Randomly select and audit the accounts, e.g., send confirmations.
2) Calculate the average confirmed accounts receivable amount (assume $880).
3) Calculate the sample standard deviation (assume $125).
4) Evaluate the sample results.

    a)   The best estimate of the population balance equals the average accounts receivable amount based on the sample times the number of items in the population. Thus, the amount estimated is determined as follows:

$$\text{Estimated balance} = \text{Average sample amount} \times \text{Items in population}$$
$$= \$880 \times 4{,}000$$
$$= \$3{,}520{,}000$$

    b)   The calculated allowance for sampling risk (achieved precision) is determined by solving the sample size formula for A.

$$A = \frac{C \times S \times N}{\sqrt{n}}$$

$$= \frac{1.64 \times \$125 \times 4{,}000}{\sqrt{269}}$$

$$= \$820{,}000 \div 16.4 = \$50{,}000$$

       i) C, S, and N have the same values used to calculate the original sample size, n. Hence, the allowance for sampling risk, A, will be the same as planned, or $50,000. A will be different only when the standard deviation of the sample, S, differs from the estimate used to calculate n. This difference can result in changes in the levels of risk faced by the auditor, but these issues are beyond the scope of the materials presented here (and are usually not covered on the CPA exam).

    c)   The audit conclusion is that the auditor is 90% confident that the true balance is $3,520,000 plus or minus $50,000, an interval of $3,470,000 to $3,570,000. If the carrying amount is $3,500,000, the auditor cannot reject the hypothesis that it is not materially misstated. Because the carrying amount is within the interval, the auditor accepts it as fair.

Stop and review! You have completed the outline for this subunit. Study multiple-choice questions 24 through 28 beginning on page 483.

15.4 MONETARY-UNIT SAMPLING (MUS)

1. The **monetary-unit-sampling (MUS)** approach to variables sampling is distinct from the classical approach. It is a hybrid method that uses attribute sampling methods to estimate monetary amounts. MUS is based on the Poisson distribution, which is used in attribute sampling to approximate the binomial distribution.

2. MUS uses a monetary unit (e.g., a dollar) as the sampling unit. The classical approach uses items themselves (e.g., invoices, checks, etc.) as the sampling units.

    a. MUS gives each monetary unit in the population an equal chance of selection. As a practical matter, however, the auditor does not examine an individual monetary unit but uses it to identify an entire transaction or balance to audit (termed the logical sampling unit).

    b. MUS is appropriate for account balances that may include only a few overstated items, such as may be expected in inventory and receivables.

        1) MUS is useful only for tests of **overstatements** (e.g., of assets) because a **systematic selection** method is applied (every *n*th monetary unit is selected). Accordingly, the larger the transaction or balance, the more likely it will be selected. This method is inappropriate for testing a population (e.g., liabilities) when understatement is the primary audit consideration.

    c. MUS is used to reach a conclusion regarding the probability of overstating an account balance by a specified monetary amount.

3. **Advantages** of MUS include the following:

    a. The largest items are selected for testing (i.e., the population is stratified).
    b. It is ideal for testing for overstatement.
    c. Small sample sizes may be appropriate, especially when no misstatements are expected.
    d. It is relatively easy to apply, especially if no misstatements are discovered.
    e. The sample size and sample evaluation can be calculated without dependence on the estimated variation (standard deviation) of the population.
    f. The sample selection process may begin even before the complete population is available for testing.

4. **Disadvantages** of MUS include the following:

    a. Items with zero or negative balances have no chance of selection.
    b. It is useful only for detecting overstatement errors.
    c. Sample sizes become relatively large if a significant amount of misstatement is expected.
    d. The calculated allowance for sampling risk tends to be overstated when a significant amount of misstatement is found in the sample.

5. **Steps for MUS**

    a. The steps in MUS are similar to those of other sampling methods:
        1) Determine the objective of the plan.
        2) Define the population and sampling unit.
        3) Determine the sampling interval and sample size.
        4) Select the sample.
        5) Execute the sampling plan.
        6) Evaluate and document the results.

Two examples are provided here, one simple and one more complex. It is probably more important that you understand the uses of MUS, the advantages and disadvantages of MUS, and the steps involved in the process than the illustrations presented here. The formulas and factors are specified; do not be concerned about how they were derived. Try to follow the logic and concepts rather than the details.

6. Simple Example

a. Below is a simple example of the application of MUS. This example is then extended to the case in which overstatement errors are detected.

EXAMPLE -- Simple

The following assumptions apply in an audit of Seminole, Inc.:

- The auditor's objective is to test the assertion that the $900,000 accounts receivable balance is fairly stated. Tolerable misstatement is $35,000.
- The population contains 900,000 sampling units and over 1,000 individual accounts receivable (logical sampling units), all with debit balances.
- The risk of incorrect acceptance specified by the auditor is 5%. Thus, the auditor desires to be 95% confident that the recorded balance is not overstated by more than $35,000.

The **sample size** is determined by the following formula:

$$Sample\ size = Recorded\ amount\ of\ population \div Sampling\ interval$$

The **sampling interval (SI)** is a function of the **risk of incorrect acceptance** and **tolerable misstatement (TM)**. SI is determined by dividing tolerable misstatement by a **confidence factor (CF)** associated with the risk level.

$$SI = TM \div CF$$

The following are CFs taken from Appendix C of the AICPA Audit Guide, *Audit Sampling* (2013):

Risk of Incorrect Acceptance	CF
5%	3.00
10%	2.31
15%	1.90

Because the risk of incorrect acceptance is 5%, the CF is 3.00. Thus, the SI is

$$SI = TM \div CF$$
$$= \$35,000 \div 3.00$$
$$= \$11,667$$

The sample size (n) is

$$n = Recorded\ amount\ of\ population \div SI$$
$$= \$900,000 \div \$11,667$$
$$= 77$$

The auditor uses **systematic sampling** (discussed in the extension of the example that follows) to select 77 dollars (actually 77 account balances) to audit.

If **no misstatements are discovered**, the auditor can form the following conclusion: "I am 95% confident that the recorded accounts receivable balance of $900,000 is not overstated by more than $35,000." The risk is 5% that the account balance is overstated by more than $35,000.

The **allowance for sampling risk** (also known as precision or confidence interval) is $35,000. Because the sample contains no misstatements, the conclusion is that the population has no misstatements. But, because the sample may not be perfectly representative of the population, an allowance for sampling risk must be considered. Thus, the more accurate conclusion is that the auditor is 95% confident that the misstatements are not greater than the allowance for sampling risk.

Given that the allowance for sampling risk is less than or equal to the TM, the objective of the audit test has been met.

7.   **Extended Example**

   a.   The Seminole, Inc., example is extended below and on the next three pages to consider **anticipated misstatements** and to demonstrate the extrapolation of the sample results to the population when misstatements are discovered in the sampling units.

EXAMPLE -- Extended

Objective, population, and sampling unit. In this example, the basic information remains the same. However, the auditor anticipates misstatements (overstatements) in the population to be $10,000 based on the prior audit.

Determining the sampling interval and sample size. When no misstatements are expected, the SI equals TM divided by the CF. However, any anticipated misstatements must be considered in the determination of the SI. Moreover, the **anticipated misstatement (AM)** must be multiplied by an **expansion factor (EF)** appropriate for the risk of incorrect acceptance. The revised SI calculation is given below. The CF is the same as when no overstatements are expected.

$$SI = [TM - (AM \times EF)] \div CF$$

The following are EFs taken from Appendix C of the AICPA Audit Guide, *Audit Sampling* (2013):

Risk of Incorrect Acceptance	EF
5%	1.6
10%	1.5
15%	1.4

Accordingly, the revised SI is

$$
\begin{aligned}
SI &= [TM - (AM \times EF)] \div CF \\
&= [\$35,000 - (\$10,000 \times 1.6)] \div 3.00 \\
&= \$6,333
\end{aligned}
$$

As before, the sample size is calculated as

$$
\begin{aligned}
\text{Sample size} &= \text{Recorded amount of population} \div SI \\
&= \$900,000 \div \$6,333 \\
&= 142
\end{aligned}
$$

The effects of changes in the factors in the sample size formula should be understood. For example, the greater the auditor's allowable risk of incorrect acceptance, the smaller the sample size. Also, the larger the anticipated misstatement, the larger the sample size.

Selecting the sample. The SI is used to select logical sampling units (in this example, accounts receivable) from the population.

A monetary unit (in this example, a dollar) identifies a logical sampling unit. If every 6,333rd cumulative dollar is selected from the population of $900,000, the sample will consist of 142 items. The auditor therefore should start randomly between $1 and $6,333. Given a random start at the 2,733rd cumulative dollar, the sample will include the following:

●   The first dollar selected will be $2,733.
●   The next dollar will be $9,066 ($2,733 + $6,333).
●   The third dollar will be $15,399 ($9,066 + $6,333).
●   The fourth dollar will be $21,732 ($15,399 + $6,333).
●   Each subsequent dollar will equal the prior dollar selected plus $6,333.

-- Continued on next page --

EXAMPLE -- Continued

Table 4 below demonstrates the selection process. When the **cumulative balance** is equal to or greater than the dollar selected, the account is selected because it contains the sampling unit. If an account contains two or more logical sampling units, for example, an account receivable of $15,000, it is selected, but it is given no special consideration. The ultimate sample of logical sampling units may contain fewer items than the calculated n.

Table 4 -- Systematic Selection				
Customer Number	A/R Recorded Amount	Cumulative Balance	Dollar Selected	Recorded Amount of Sample Item
001	$ 2,000	$ 2,000		
002	1,225	3,225	2,733	1,225
003	3,500	6,725		
004	2,500	9,225	9,066	2,500
005	10,000	19,225	15,399	10,000
006	915	20,140		
etc.	etc.	etc.	etc.	etc.
Total	$900,000			

-- Continued on next page --

EXAMPLE -- Continued

Executing the sampling plan. The auditor performs procedures on the sampled items (e.g., confirming the accounts). The auditor identifies **overstatement** errors. (Any **understatement** errors require special consideration, but the issue is beyond the scope of this outline.)

Evaluating and documenting the results. The evaluation process depends on whether any misstatements are found in the sample. The following summarizes that process:

- Project the misstatement from the sample to the population.
- Determine the allowance for sampling risk.

$$Allowance\ for\ sampling\ risk = Basic\ precision\ (BP) + Incremental\ allowance\ (IA)$$

- Calculate the upper misstatement limit (UML).

$$UML = Projected\ misstatement + Allowance\ for\ sampling\ risk$$

If **no overstatement errors** are discovered, the UML equals BP because

- The projected misstatement to the population is $0.
- The allowance for sampling risk equals BP (i.e., the IA is $0).

The calculation for **BP** is

$$BP = SI \times CF$$

Assuming no misstatements are found, BP (and the UML) is

$$BP = \$6,333 \times 3.00$$
$$= \$18,999$$

The conclusion is that the auditor is 95% confident that the balance of accounts receivable is not overstated by more than $18,999. This amount is within the TM of $35,000. Moreover, $18,999 is the allowance for sampling risk.

If **some overstatement errors** are discovered, the evaluation process is more involved but follows that presented above.

Project the sample results to the population if misstatements are discovered. Table 5 below illustrates the projection of misstatements to the population.

Tainting. Because each selected dollar represents a group of dollars (the SI), the percentage of misstatement in the logical sampling unit (the account selected) is the percentage of misstatement in the SI. This is termed tainting. However, if the recorded amount of a logical sampling unit (the account selected) **equals or exceeds** the SI, the projected misstatement is the actual misstatement for the SI, and no tainting is calculated.

For each logical sampling unit with a recorded amount (RA) **less than** the SI, calculate the **tainting percentage**.

$$Tainting\ \% = \frac{(RA - AA)}{RA} \qquad If:\ AA = Audit\ amount$$

$$Projected\ misstatement = SI \times Tainting\ \%$$

Add the individual projected misstatements to determine the projected population misstatement.

Table 5 -- Calculation of Projected Misstatement				
Recorded Amount	Audit Amount	Tainting % = (RA − AA) ÷ RA	SI	Projected Misstatement
$ 1,000	$ 800	20%	$6,333	$ 1,267
10,000	6,000	N/A	N/A	4,000
300	0	100%	6,333	6,333
$11,300	$6,800			$11,600

The first and third projected misstatements equal the tainting percentage times SI because the RA of the logical unit sampled is less than the SI. The second projected misstatement included is the actual misstatement. The RA of the logical unit sampled is greater than the SI. The total projected misstatement to the population is $11,600, but the allowance for sampling risk must be added to derive the UML.

-- Continued on next page --

EXAMPLE -- Continued

Calculate the **allowance for sampling risk** and the UML.

Allowance for sampling risk has two components: BP and IA.

BP is the same as when no misstatements are found (i.e., SI × CF).

IA is based on projected misstatements related to logical sampling units less than SI. (The misstatements related to logical sampling units greater than SI are not considered in the calculation of IA in Table 5 on the previous page.)

Projected misstatements are ranked by size (but only for misstatements related to logical sampling units less than SI). Each projected misstatement is multiplied by a factor that gives greater weights to the larger amounts. The first few factors for the 5% risk of incorrect acceptance, sufficient to calculate the allowance for sampling risk for this example, are presented in Table 6 below. Each factor equals the incremental change in the confidence factor minus one. Given a 5% risk of incorrect acceptance, the confidence factors for 0, 1, 2, and 3 misstatements are 3.00, 4.75, 6.30, and 7.76, respectively.

In this example, two misstatements are related to logical sampling units less than the SI of $6,333.

The ranked projected misstatements are multiplied by the factors from Table 6 and added to determine IA in Table 7.

Table 6 -- Misstatement Factors 5% Risk of Incorrect Acceptance		
Misstatement Number	Change in Confidence Factor	Change in CF – 1.0
1	1.75 (4.75 – 3.00)	.75
2	1.55 (6.30 – 4.75)	.55
3	1.46 (7.76 – 6.30)	.46
etc.	etc.	etc.

Table 7 -- Calculation of the IA		
Ranked Projected Misstatements	Factor	Incremental Allowance
$6,333	.75	$4,750
1,267	.55	697
Total IA (rounded)		$5,447

The allowance for sampling risk is the sum of BP and IA.

$$\text{Allowance for sampling risk} = \$18,999 + \$5,447$$
$$= \$24,446$$

The total projected misstatement (PM) plus the allowance for sampling risk equals the upper misstatement limit (UML).

$$\text{UML} = \text{PM} + \text{Allowance for sampling risk}$$
$$= \$11,600 + \$24,446$$
$$= \$36,046$$

The **auditor's conclusion** is that (s)he is 95% confident that the balance of accounts receivable is not overstated by more than $36,046. However, TM is only $35,000. Thus, the auditor cannot conclude within the acceptable level of risk that the balance is fairly presented. (The auditor would likely require the client to make adjustments downward to the account before presentation on the balance sheet.)

Stop and review! You have completed the outline for this subunit. Study multiple-choice questions 29 through 33 beginning on page 485.

QUESTIONS

15.1 Sampling Fundamentals (AU-C 530)

1. An advantage of statistical over nonstatistical sampling methods in tests of controls is that the statistical methods

   A. Afford greater assurance than a nonstatistical sample of equal size.

   B. Provide an objective basis for quantitatively evaluating sample risks.

   C. Can more easily convert the sample into a dual-purpose test useful for substantive testing.

   D. Eliminate the need to use judgment in determining appropriate sample sizes.

Answer (B) is correct.
   REQUIRED: The advantage of statistical over nonstatistical sampling methods.
   DISCUSSION: The results of statistical (probability) sampling are objective and subject to the laws of probability. Hence, sampling risk can be quantified and controlled, and the degree of reliability desired (the confidence level) can be specified. Sampling risk is the risk that the sample selected does not represent the population.
   Answer (A) is incorrect. A nonstatistical method may permit the auditor to test the most material and risky transactions and therefore may provide equal or greater assurance. However, that assurance cannot be quantified. Answer (C) is incorrect. Statistical sampling provides no advantage for converting to dual-purpose testing. Answer (D) is incorrect. Sample size is subject to judgments about the sampling plan factors.

2. An advantage of statistical sampling over nonstatistical sampling is that statistical sampling helps an auditor to

   A. Minimize the failure to detect errors and fraud.

   B. Eliminate the risk of nonsampling errors.

   C. Reduce the level of audit risk and materiality to a relatively low amount.

   D. Measure the sufficiency of the evidence obtained.

Answer (D) is correct.
   REQUIRED: The advantage of statistical sampling over nonstatistical sampling.
   DISCUSSION: Statistical sampling helps the auditor to design an efficient sample, to measure the sufficiency of the evidence obtained, and to evaluate the sample results. Auditors are required to obtain sufficient appropriate evidence. Sufficiency is the measure of the quantity of evidence. It relates to the design and size of the sample.
   Answer (A) is incorrect. In some circumstances, professional judgment may indicate that nonstatistical methods are preferable to minimize the failure to detect errors and fraud. Answer (B) is incorrect. Statistical sampling is irrelevant to nonsampling errors. Answer (C) is incorrect. Statistical sampling is irrelevant to materiality. Moreover, nonstatistical methods may be used to reduce audit risk.

3. The risk of underreliance is the risk that the sample selected to test controls

   A. Indicates that the controls are less effective than they actually are.

   B. Contains misstatements that could be material to the financial statements when aggregated with misstatements in other account balances or transactions classes.

   C. Contains proportionately fewer deviations from prescribed internal controls than exist in the balance or class as a whole.

   D. Does not support the tolerable misstatement for some or all financial statement assertions.

Answer (A) is correct.
   REQUIRED: The risk of underreliance.
   DISCUSSION: One aspect of sampling risk in performing tests of controls is the risk of underreliance. It is the risk that the sample indicates that the controls are less effective than they actually are.
   Answer (B) is incorrect. Tests of details are directed towards misstatements in assertions. Answer (C) is incorrect. If the sample deviation rate is lower than the population rate, the risk is overreliance. Answer (D) is incorrect. Tests of details are directed toward misstatements in assertions.

4. A principal advantage of statistical methods of attribute sampling over nonstatistical methods is that they provide a scientific basis for planning the

   A. Risk of overreliance.

   B. Tolerable deviation rate.

   C. Expected population deviation rate.

   D. Sample size.

Answer (D) is correct.
   REQUIRED: The item for which statistical methods provide a scientific basis for planning.
   DISCUSSION: Statistical theory permits the auditor to measure sampling risk and to restrict it to an acceptable level. Statistical methods determine the sample size that will accomplish the auditor's objectives.
   Answer (A) is incorrect. The risk of overreliance is the risk of believing a control is effective when it is not. Answer (B) is incorrect. The tolerable deviation rate is a function of the auditor's judgment about the assessed risks and the desired degree of assurance to be provided by the evidence, not of the statistical methods used. Answer (C) is incorrect. The expected population deviation rate prior to sampling is a function of auditor judgment.

5. While performing a test of details during an audit, the auditor determined that the sample results supported the conclusion that the recorded account balance was materially misstated. It was, in fact, not materially misstated. This situation illustrates the risk of

A. Incorrect rejection.

B. Incorrect acceptance.

C. Overreliance.

D. Underreliance.

Answer (A) is correct.
    REQUIRED: The risk of erroneously concluding that a balance is materially misstated.
    DISCUSSION: An auditor is concerned with two aspects of sampling risk in performing substantive tests of details: the risk of incorrect acceptance and the risk of incorrect rejection. The second is the risk that the sample supports the conclusion that the recorded account balance is materially misstated when it is not materially misstated.
    Answer (B) is incorrect. The risk of incorrect acceptance is the risk that an auditor will erroneously conclude that a balance is not materially misstated. Answer (C) is incorrect. The risk of overreliance is an aspect of sampling risk for tests of controls. Answer (D) is incorrect. The risk of underreliance is an aspect of sampling risk for tests of controls.

6. An auditor may decide to increase the risk of incorrect rejection when

A. Increased reliability from the sample is desired.

B. Many differences (audit amount minus recorded amount) are expected.

C. Initial sample results do not support the assessed risk of material misstatement.

D. The cost and effort of selecting additional sample items are low.

Answer (D) is correct.
    REQUIRED: The reason to increase the risk of incorrect rejection.
    DISCUSSION: The risk of incorrect rejection is the risk that the sample supports the conclusion that the recorded account balance is materially misstated when it is not. This risk relates to the efficiency, not the effectiveness, of the audit. Incorrect rejection ordinarily results in the application of additional procedures that finally lead the auditor to the proper conclusion. If the cost and effort of selecting additional sample items are low, a higher risk of incorrect rejection may be acceptable.
    Answer (A) is incorrect. An increase in the desired reliability (confidence level) for a substantive test of details requires a decrease in the risk of incorrect rejection. This risk is the complement of the confidence level for a substantive test of details. Answer (B) is incorrect. If many differences are expected, the account balance is more likely to be materially misstated and incorrect rejection is less likely. Answer (C) is incorrect. The risk of incorrect rejection is associated with substantive testing.

7. In statistical sampling methods used in substantive testing, an auditor most likely would stratify a population into meaningful groups if

A. Monetary-unit sampling (MUS) is used.

B. The population has highly variable recorded amounts.

C. The auditor's estimated tolerable misstatement is extremely small.

D. The standard deviation of recorded amounts is relatively small.

Answer (B) is correct.
    REQUIRED: The condition under which the auditor would stratify a population.
    DISCUSSION: The primary objective of stratification is to reduce the effect of high variability by dividing the population into subpopulations. Reducing the effect of the variance within each subpopulation allows the auditor to sample a smaller number of items while holding precision and the confidence level constant.
    Answer (A) is incorrect. MUS automatically stratifies the population. Answer (C) is incorrect. When the tolerable misstatement is extremely small, the auditor will take relatively large sample sizes. Answer (D) is incorrect. When the standard deviation of recorded amounts is relatively small, the auditor would consider the population in total when selecting samples.

8. The use of the ratio estimation sampling technique is most effective when

A. The calculated audit amounts are approximately proportional to the client's carrying amounts.

B. A relatively small number of differences exist in the population.

C. Estimating populations whose records consist of quantities but not carrying amounts.

D. Large overstatement differences and large understatement differences exist in the population.

Answer (A) is correct.
    REQUIRED: The most effective use of ratio estimation sampling.
    DISCUSSION: Ratio estimation calculates the population misstatement by multiplying the carrying amount of the population by the ratio of the total audit amount of the sample items to their total carrying amount. The precision is determined by considering the variances of the ratios of carrying amount to audited amount. Thus, the more homogeneous the ratios, the smaller the precision.
    Answer (B) is incorrect. The population of differences must be fairly large for ratio estimation to be useful. Answer (C) is incorrect. Each audited amount must have a carrying amount so that a ratio may be calculated. Answer (D) is incorrect. The ratios are important to the process, not the specific amounts of the population.

9. An auditor is performing tests of details of pricing and extensions of perpetual inventory balances consisting of a large number of items. Past experience indicates numerous pricing and extension errors. Which of the following statistical sampling approaches is most appropriate?

A. Unstratified mean-per-unit.

B. Monetary-unit.

C. Stop or go.

D. Ratio or difference estimation.

Answer (D) is correct.
REQUIRED: The appropriate sampling method for tests of details of pricing and extensions of perpetual inventory balances.
DISCUSSION: Difference estimation of population misstatement involves (1) determining the differences between the audit and carrying amounts for items in the sample, (2) adding the differences, (3) calculating the mean difference, and (4) multiplying the mean by the number of items in the population. An allowance for sampling risk also is calculated. Ratio estimation is similar except that it estimates the population misstatement by multiplying the carrying amount of the population by the ratio of the total audit value of the sample items to their total carrying amount. It has been demonstrated that ratio or difference estimation is both reliable and efficient when small misstatements predominate and they are not skewed.
Answer (A) is incorrect. Unstratified mean-per-unit requires sample sizes that may be too large to be cost effective. Answer (B) is incorrect. MUS may result in a larger sample size than a classical variables sampling approach when the estimated misstatement is relatively large. Answer (C) is incorrect. Stop-or-go sampling is an attribute sampling mode. It is appropriate when few deviations are expected. The method is not applicable in these circumstances.

10. Which of the following statements about audit sampling risks is correct for a nonissuer?

A. Nonsampling risk arises from the possibility that, when a substantive test is restricted to a sample, conclusions might be different than if the auditor had tested each item in the population.

B. Nonsampling risk can arise because an auditor failed to recognize misstatements.

C. Sampling risk is derived from the uncertainty in applying audit procedures to specific risks.

D. Sampling risk includes the possibility of selecting audit procedures that are not appropriate to achieve the specific objective.

Answer (B) is correct.
REQUIRED: The true statement about audit sampling risks for a nonissuer.
DISCUSSION: Nonsampling risk is the risk that the auditor may draw an erroneous conclusion for any reason not related to sampling risk. Examples include the use of inappropriate audit procedures or misinterpretation of audit evidence and failure to recognize a misstatement or deviation. Nonsampling risk may be reduced to an acceptable level through such factors as adequate planning and proper conduct of a firm's audit practice in accordance with the quality control standards (AU-C 530).
Answer (A) is incorrect. Sampling risk is the risk that the auditor's conclusion based on a sample may differ from the conclusion if the same audit procedure were applied to every item in the population. Answer (C) is incorrect. Sampling risk results from not performing an audit procedure on every sampling unit in a population. Answer (D) is incorrect. Nonsampling risk includes the use of inappropriate audit procedures.

15.2 Statistical Sampling in Tests of Controls (Attribute Sampling)

11. Which of the following combinations results in a decrease in sample size in an attribute sample?

	Allowable Risk of Overreliance	Tolerable Rate	Expected Population Deviation Rate
A.	Increase	Decrease	Increase
B.	Decrease	Increase	Decrease
C.	Increase	Increase	Decrease
D.	Increase	Increase	Increase

Answer (C) is correct.
REQUIRED: The combination that results in a decrease in size in an attribute sample.
DISCUSSION: To determine the sample size for a test of controls, the auditor considers (1) the tolerable rate of deviations from the control being tested, (2) the expected actual rate of deviations, and (3) the allowable risk of overreliance. An increase in the allowable risk of overreliance, an increase in the tolerable rate, and a decrease in the expected rate each has the effect of reducing the required sample size.

12. In determining the number of documents to select for a test to obtain assurance that all sales returns have been properly authorized, an auditor should consider the tolerable rate of deviation from the control activity. The auditor should also directly consider the

I.   Likely rate of deviations
II. Allowable risk of underreliance

    A. I only.

    B. II only.

    C. Both I and II.

    D. Either I or II.

Answer (A) is correct.
    REQUIRED: The factor(s) in determining sample size.
    DISCUSSION: The factors necessary to determine sample size in an attribute sampling plan for a large population include (1) the tolerable deviation rate, (2) the acceptable risk of overreliance, and (3) the expected deviation rate.

13. In planning a statistical sample for a test of controls, an auditor increased the expected population deviation rate from the prior year's rate because of the results of the prior year's tests of controls and the overall control environment. The auditor most likely would then increase the planned

    A. Tolerable deviation rate.

    B. Allowance for sampling risk.

    C. Risk of overreliance.

    D. Sample size.

Answer (D) is correct.
    REQUIRED: The effect of an increase in the expected population deviation rate.
    DISCUSSION: To determine the sample size for a test of controls, the auditor considers (1) the tolerable rate of deviations, (2) the expected actual rate of deviations, and (3) the allowable risk of overreliance. An increase in the expected rate has the effect of increasing the degree of assurance to be provided by the sample and therefore increasing the planned sample size.
    Answer (A) is incorrect. The tolerable rate is a function of the assessed risk of material misstatement and the degree of assurance sought from the evidence. It does not necessarily increase with the expected population deviation rate. Answer (B) is incorrect. The allowance for sampling risk is the difference between the calculated upper deviation rate and the sample rate. According to standard tables, it increases as the actual number of deviations found increases. Answer (C) is incorrect. The risk of overreliance is specified by the auditor. It does not necessarily increase with the expected rate.

14. Which of the following statements is true concerning statistical sampling in tests of controls?

    A. As the population size increases, the sample size should increase proportionately.

    B. Deviations from specific control activities increase the likelihood of misstatements but do not always cause misstatements.

    C. There is an inverse relationship between the expected population deviation rate and the sample size.

    D. In determining the tolerable deviation rate, an auditor considers detection risk and the sample size.

Answer (B) is correct.
    REQUIRED: The true statement about statistical sampling in tests of controls.
    DISCUSSION: Deviations from a specific control increase the risk of misstatements in the accounting records but do not always result in misstatements. Thus, deviations from a specific control at a given rate ordinarily result in misstatements at the financial statement level at a lower rate.
    Answer (A) is incorrect. As population size increases, the required sample size increases at a decreasing rate. Answer (C) is incorrect. The relationship between the expected population deviation rate and the required sample size is direct. Answer (D) is incorrect. The tolerable rate depends on the planned assessed risk of material misstatement and the assurance to be provided by the evidence in the sample.

15. For which of the following audit tests would an auditor most likely use attribute sampling?

    A. Making an independent estimate of the amount of a LIFO inventory.

    B. Examining invoices in support of the measurement of fixed asset additions.

    C. Selecting accounts receivable for confirmation of account balances.

    D. Inspecting employee time cards for proper approval by supervisors.

Answer (D) is correct.
    REQUIRED: The appropriate use of attribute sampling.
    DISCUSSION: The auditor uses attribute sampling to test the effectiveness of controls. Attribute sampling enables the auditor to estimate the occurrence rate of deviations and to determine its relation to the tolerable deviation rate. Thus, a control, such as proper approval of time cards by supervisors, can be tested for effectiveness using attribute sampling.
    Answer (A) is incorrect. Variables sampling is useful in estimating the amount of inventory. Answer (B) is incorrect. Examining invoices in support of the measurement of fixed asset additions is a substantive test for which variables sampling is appropriate. Answer (C) is incorrect. The selection of accounts receivable for confirmation is a substantive test.

16. An auditor should consider the tolerable rate of deviation when determining the number of check requests to select for a test to obtain assurance that all check requests have been properly authorized. The auditor should also consider

	The Average Dollar Value of the Check Requests	The Allowable Risk of Overreliance
A.	Yes	Yes
B.	Yes	No
C.	No	Yes
D.	No	No

Answer (C) is correct.
REQUIRED: The issue(s), if any, to consider in determining the size of a sample in a test of controls.
DISCUSSION: Tests of controls, such as tests whether check requests have been properly authorized, are binary in nature. The auditor determines whether the control has been applied. Dollar amounts are irrelevant in this form of testing. However, in sampling, the auditor must consider the acceptable risk of overreliance to determine sample size. The auditor also must estimate a population deviation rate.

17. Which of the following statements is true concerning statistical sampling in tests of controls?

A. The population size has little or no effect on determining sample size except for very small populations.

B. The expected population deviation rate has little or no effect on determining sample size except for very small populations.

C. As the population size doubles, the sample size also should double.

D. For a given tolerable rate, a larger sample size should be selected as the expected population deviation rate decreases.

Answer (A) is correct.
REQUIRED: The true statement about statistical sampling.
DISCUSSION: A change in the size of the population has a very small effect on the required sample size when the population is large. Tables are available for smaller population sizes providing appropriate smaller sample sizes.
Answer (B) is incorrect. The expected population deviation rate is a variable in the sample size formula. Answer (C) is incorrect. The population size and the sample size are not proportionate. Answer (D) is incorrect. A lower expected population deviation rate results in a smaller sample size.

18. What is an auditor's evaluation of a statistical sample for attributes when a test of 50 documents results in 3 deviations if the tolerable rate is 7%, the expected population deviation rate is 5%, and the allowance for sampling risk is 2%?

A. Modify the planned assessed risk of material misstatement because the tolerable deviation rate plus the allowance for sampling risk exceeds the expected population deviation rate.

B. Accept the sample results as support for the assessed risk of material misstatement because the sample deviation rate plus the allowance for sampling risk exceeds the tolerable deviation rate.

C. Accept the sample results as support for the assessed risk of material misstatement because the tolerable deviation rate minus the allowance for sampling risk equals the expected population deviation rate.

D. Modify the assessed risk of material misstatement because the sample deviation rate plus the allowance for sampling risk exceeds the tolerable deviation rate.

Answer (D) is correct.
REQUIRED: The evaluation of an attribute sample given the deviations in the sample, sampling risk, tolerable rate, and expected rate.
DISCUSSION: The sample has a 6% (3 ÷ 50) deviation rate. The auditor's achieved upper deviation limit is 8% (6% + the 2% allowance for sampling risk). The allowance for sampling risk may be calculated from a standard table as the difference between the upper deviation limit and the sample rate. However, the allowance is given. Thus, the true deviation rate could be as large as 8% and exceed the tolerable rate. Accordingly, the auditor should revise the assessed risk of material misstatement for the relevant assertions and possibly alter the nature, timing, and extent of substantive procedures.
Answer (A) is incorrect. The precision interval is constructed around the sample rate, not the tolerable deviation rate. Answer (B) is incorrect. A deviation rate that may be as large as 8% is a reason for revising the assessed risk of material misstatement. Answer (C) is incorrect. The sample deviation rate, which is the best estimate of the true rate, must not be ignored.

19. The risk of incorrect acceptance and the risk of overreliance relate to the

A. Effectiveness of the audit.

B. Efficiency of the audit.

C. Preliminary estimates of materiality levels.

D. Tolerable misstatement.

Answer (A) is correct.
   REQUIRED: The true statement about the risks of incorrect acceptance and overreliance.
   DISCUSSION: If a financial statement amount is erroneously accepted as fairly stated based upon a sample, additional audit work and the chances of exposing the mistake will probably be minimal. However, rejection of a fairly stated amount typically results in further audit investigation and ultimately the acceptance of the amount. Similarly, overreliance on a control leads to an unjustified reduction in substantive testing, thereby decreasing the effectiveness of the audit. However, underreliance on a control results in an unneeded increase in substantive testing but most likely does not decrease ultimate audit effectiveness.
   Answer (B) is incorrect. The risks of incorrect acceptance and overreliance relate to effectiveness. Answer (C) is incorrect. Preliminary judgments about materiality are considered when planning a sample for a substantive procedure. The risk of overreliance relates directly to tests of controls. Answer (D) is incorrect. The tolerable misstatement is considered when planning a sample for a substantive procedure. The risk of overreliance relates directly to tests of controls.

Questions 20 and 21 are based on the following information. An auditor desired to test credit approval on 10,000 sales invoices processed during the year. The auditor designed a statistical sample that would provide 1% risk of overreliance (99% confidence) that not more than 7% of the sales invoices lacked approval. The auditor estimated from previous experience that about 2.5% of the sales invoices lacked approval. A sample of 200 invoices was examined, and seven of them were lacking approval. The auditor then determined the achieved upper deviation limit to be 8%.

20. In the evaluation of this sample, the auditor decided to increase the level of the preliminary assessment of the risk of material misstatement because the

A. Tolerable deviation rate (7%) was less than the achieved upper deviation limit (8%).

B. Expected deviation rate (7%) was more than the percentage of deviations in the sample (3.5%).

C. Achieved upper deviation limit (8%) was more than the percentage of deviations in the sample (3.5%).

D. Expected deviation rate (2.5%) was less than the tolerable deviation rate (7%).

Answer (A) is correct.
   REQUIRED: The reason for increasing the preliminary assessment of the risk of material misstatement.
   DISCUSSION: The sample results support the assessment of the risk of material misstatement only if the achieved upper deviation limit is equal to or less than the tolerable deviation rate. The achieved upper deviation limit is a value that may be derived from a standard table based on (1) the actual deviations, (2) the specified risk of overreliance, and (3) the sample size. In this case, it signifies that the auditor is 99% confident that not more than 8% of the invoices lacked approval. Hence, the sample does not support the assessment of the risk of material misstatement.
   Answer (B) is incorrect. The expected deviation rate is 2.5%. Answer (C) is incorrect. By definition, the achieved upper deviation limit equals the sample deviation rate plus an allowance for sampling risk. Answer (D) is incorrect. The expected deviation rate from the sampling plan is not used in the evaluation of the sample.

21. The allowance for sampling risk was

A. 5.5%

B. 4.5%

C. 3.5%

D. 1%

Answer (B) is correct.
   REQUIRED: The allowance for sampling risk.
   DISCUSSION: The allowance for sampling risk equals the achieved upper deviation limit (8%) minus the sample deviation rate (7 ÷ 200 = 3.5%), or 4.5%.

22. The diagram below depicts the auditor's estimated maximum deviation rate compared with the tolerable deviation rate and also depicts the true population deviation rate compared with the tolerable deviation rate.

Auditor's Estimate Based on Sample Results	True State of Population	
	Deviation rate is less than tolerable rate.	Deviation rate exceeds tolerable rate.
Maximum deviation rate is less than tolerable rate.	I. Correct	III. Incorrect
Maximum deviation rate exceeds tolerable rate.	II. Incorrect	IV. Correct

As a result of testing controls, the auditor underrelies on the controls and increases substantive testing. This is illustrated by situation

A. I.

B. II.

C. III.

D. IV.

Answer (B) is correct.

REQUIRED: The situation that involves underreliance.

DISCUSSION: The risk of underreliance (situation II) is one aspect of sampling risk in testing controls. It is the risk that the controls are more effective than indicated by the sample. Like the risk of incorrect rejection in substantive testing, the risk of underreliance relates to the efficiency, not effectiveness, of the audit. It ordinarily leads to application of further audit procedures and ultimate arrival at the correct conclusion.

Answer (A) is incorrect. In situation I, the auditor properly should rely on the controls. Answer (C) is incorrect. In situation III, the sample might lead to overreliance. Answer (D) is incorrect. In situation IV, the auditor properly should not rely on the controls.

23. In addition to evaluating the frequency of deviations in tests of controls, an auditor should also consider certain qualitative aspects of the deviations. The auditor most likely would give broader consideration to the implications of a deviation if it was

A. The only deviation discovered in the sample.

B. Identical to a deviation discovered during the prior year's audit.

C. Caused by an employee's misunderstanding of instructions.

D. Initially concealed by a forged document.

Answer (D) is correct.

REQUIRED: The aspect of a control deviation requiring broader consideration.

DISCUSSION: The discovery of a fraud ordinarily requires broader consideration than the discovery of an error. The discovery of an initially concealed forged document indicates that the integrity of employees may be in doubt.

Answer (A) is incorrect. A single deviation discovered in a sample may not cause major concern. Answer (B) is incorrect. Deviations are often repetitive. Discovery of an identical deviation in a subsequent year is not unusual. Answer (C) is incorrect. A misunderstanding is an error rather than fraud and does not necessarily arouse concern.

15.3 Classical Variables Sampling (Mean-per-Unit)

24. An auditor examining inventory most likely would use variables sampling rather than attributes sampling to

A. Identify whether inventory items are properly priced.

B. Estimate whether the dollar amount of inventory is reasonable.

C. Discover whether misstatements exist in inventory records.

D. Determine whether discounts for inventory are properly recorded.

Answer (B) is correct.

REQUIRED: The purpose of using variables sampling rather than attribute sampling in an audit of inventory.

DISCUSSION: Variables sampling is used by auditors to estimate quantities or dollar amounts in substantive testing. Attribute sampling applies to tests of controls and is used to estimate a deviation rate (occurrence rate) for a population. Thus, an auditor who wants to estimate whether the dollar amount of inventory is reasonable uses variables sampling.

Answer (A) is incorrect. An auditor who wants to determine whether inventory items are properly priced uses attribute sampling, as an item is either properly priced or not. Answer (C) is incorrect. An auditor who wants to discover whether misstatements exist in inventory records uses attribute sampling. Answer (D) is incorrect. An auditor who wants to determine whether discounts for inventory are properly recorded uses attribute sampling, as an item is either properly recorded or not.

25. Which of the following statements is true concerning the auditor's use of statistical sampling?

A. An auditor needs to estimate the dollar amount of the standard deviation of the population to use classical variables sampling.

B. An assumption of monetary-unit sampling is that the underlying accounting population is normally distributed.

C. A classical variables sample needs to be designed with special considerations to include negative balances in the sample.

D. The selection of zero balances usually does not require special sample design considerations when using monetary-unit sampling.

Answer (A) is correct.
REQUIRED: The true statement about statistical sampling.
DISCUSSION: Variables sampling is used to estimate the amount of misstatement in, or the value of, a population. In auditing, this process entails estimating the monetary value of an account balance or other accounting total. The estimated population standard deviation is used in the sample size formula for variables estimation. Hence, it should be stated in dollar terms.
Answer (B) is incorrect. MUS is based on the Poisson distribution, which approximates the binomial distribution, not the normal distribution. Answer (C) is incorrect. Classical variables samples do not require special design considerations for negative balances. Answer (D) is incorrect. MUS is not designed to deal with understatements or negative values without special modifications.

26. When planning a sample for a substantive test of details, an auditor should consider tolerable misstatement for the sample. This consideration should

A. Be related to the auditor's business risk.

B. Not be adjusted for qualitative factors.

C. Be related to preliminary judgments about materiality levels.

D. Not be changed during the audit process.

Answer (C) is correct.
REQUIRED: The true statement about the consideration of tolerable misstatement.
DISCUSSION: When planning a sample for a test of details, the auditor should consider how much monetary misstatement in the related account balance or class of transactions may exist without causing the financial statements to be materially misstated. This maximum misstatement is the tolerable misstatement for the sample. It is used in audit planning to determine the necessary precision and sample size. Tolerable misstatement, combined for the entire audit plan, should not exceed the auditor's preliminary judgments about materiality.
Answer (A) is incorrect. The auditor's business risk is irrelevant. Answer (B) is incorrect. Qualitative factors should be considered, for example, the nature and cause of misstatements and their relationship to other phases of the audit. Answer (D) is incorrect. If sample results suggest that planning assumptions were incorrect, the auditor should take appropriate action.

27. An auditor is determining the sample size for an inventory observation using mean-per-unit estimation, which is a variables sampling plan. To calculate the required sample size, the auditor usually determines the

	Variability in the Dollar Amounts of Inventory Items	Risk of Incorrect Rejection
A.	Yes	Yes
B.	Yes	No
C.	No	Yes
D.	No	No

Answer (A) is correct.
REQUIRED: The factor(s), if any, used to determine a mean-per-unit sample size.
DISCUSSION: Four factors are considered in determining the sample size for mean-per-unit estimation. Those factors include (1) the population size, (2) an estimate of population variation (the standard deviation), (3) the risk of incorrect rejection (its complement is the confidence level), and (4) the tolerable misstatement (the desired allowance for sampling risk is a percentage thereof, and this percentage is a function of the risk of incorrect rejection and the allowable risk of incorrect acceptance).

28. How would an increase in tolerable misstatement and an increase in the risk of material misstatement (RMM) affect the sample size in a substantive test of details?

	Increase in Tolerable Misstatement	Increase in the RMM
A.	Increase sample size	Increase sample size
B.	Increase sample size	Decrease sample size
C.	Decrease sample size	Increase sample size
D.	Decrease sample size	Decrease sample size

Answer (C) is correct.
REQUIRED: The effects of increases in tolerable misstatement and the assessed RMM.
DISCUSSION: An increase in tolerable misstatement or the level of materiality decreases the sample size necessary to collect sufficient appropriate audit evidence. An increase in the RMM increases the assurance to be provided by substantive procedures and therefore the necessary sample size.

15.4 Monetary-Unit Sampling (MUS)

29. Which of the following statements is true concerning monetary-unit sampling (MUS), also known as probability-proportional-to-size sampling?

A. The sampling distribution should approximate the normal distribution.

B. Overstated units have a lower probability of sample selection than units that are understated.

C. The auditor controls the risk of incorrect acceptance by specifying that risk level for the sampling plan.

D. The sampling interval is calculated by dividing the number of physical units in the population by the sample size.

Answer (C) is correct.
REQUIRED: The true statement about MUS.
DISCUSSION: MUS is one technique whereby the auditor can measure and control the risks associated with observing less than 100% of the population. The auditor can quantify and measure the risk of accepting a client's recorded amount as fair when it is materially misstated.
Answer (A) is incorrect. MUS is most closely associated with the Poisson distribution. Answer (B) is incorrect. As the size of the units in the population increases, so does the probability of selection. Answer (D) is incorrect. The sampling interval is calculated by dividing the total dollars, not units, in the population by the sample size. Every n[th] dollar is then selected after a random start.

30. In a monetary-unit sample with a sampling interval of $10,000, an auditor discovered that a selected account receivable with a recorded amount of $5,000 had an audited amount of $4,000. If this were the only misstatement discovered by the auditor, the projected misstatement of this sample is

A. $1,000
B. $2,000
C. $5,000
D. $10,000

Answer (B) is correct.
REQUIRED: The projected misstatement of the monetary-unit sample.
DISCUSSION: MUS is a commonly used method of statistical sampling for tests of details of balances because it provides a simple statistical result expressed in dollars. Given that only one misstatement was detected, the projected misstatement for this sample is the product of the tainting percentage and the sampling interval. The tainting percentage is calculated as the difference between the recorded amount and the audited amount, divided by the recorded amount. In this sample, the tainting percentage is 20% [($5,000 − $4,000) ÷ $5,000]. Multiplying this number by the sampling interval results in a projected misstatement based on the sample of $2,000 ($10,000 × 20%).

31. Which of the following most likely would be an advantage in using classical variables sampling rather than monetary-unit sampling?

A. An estimate of the standard deviation of the population's recorded amounts is not required.

B. The auditor rarely needs the assistance of a computer program to design an efficient sample.

C. Inclusion of zero and negative balances usually does not require special design considerations.

D. Any amount that is individually significant is automatically identified and selected.

Answer (C) is correct.
REQUIRED: The advantage of using classical variables sampling rather than MUS.
DISCUSSION: MUS is most useful if few misstatements are expected, and overstatement is the most likely kind of misstatement. One disadvantage of MUS is that it is designed to detect overstatements. It is not effective for estimating understatements. The smaller the item, the less likely it will be selected in the sample, but the more likely the item is understated.
Answer (A) is incorrect. The sample size formula for estimation of variables includes the standard deviation of the population. Answer (B) is incorrect. A computer program is helpful in many sampling applications. Answer (D) is incorrect. In classical variables sampling, every item has an equal and nonzero probability of selection.

Questions 32 and 33 are based on the following information.

An auditor has been assigned to take a monetary-unit sample of a population of vouchers in the purchasing department. The population has a total recorded amount of $300,000. The auditor believes that a maximum misstatement of $900 is acceptable and would like to have 95% confidence in the results. (The confidence factor at 95% and zero misstatements = 3.00.) Additional information is provided in the opposite column.

Table of First 10 Vouchers in Population

Voucher #	Balance	Cumulative Balance
1	$100	$ 100
2	150	250
3	40	290
4	200	490
5	10	500
6	290	790
7	50	840
8	190	1,030
9	20	1,050
10	180	1,230

32. Given a random start of $50 as the first dollar amount, what is the number of the fourth voucher to be selected, assuming that the sample size will be 1,000?

A. 4

B. 6

C. 7

D. 8

Answer (D) is correct.
REQUIRED: The number of the fourth voucher selected using MUS.
DISCUSSION: The vouchers have a recorded amount of $300,000, and 1,000 items are to be sampled, so every 300th dollar will be chosen. Given a random start of $50, the vouchers containing the 50th, 350th, 650th, and 950th dollars will be selected. The cumulative amount of the first eight vouchers is $1,030. Accordingly, voucher 8 should be the fourth voucher audited because it contains the 950th dollar.
Answer (A) is incorrect. Voucher 4 contains the 350th dollar and should be the second voucher selected. Answer (B) is incorrect. Voucher 6 contains the 650th dollar and should be the third voucher selected. Answer (C) is incorrect. Voucher 7 should not be selected.

33. In examining the sample, one overstatement was detected causing an extension of $270 to the tolerable misstatement. Assuming a sample size of 1,000 and assuming that the maximum dollar amount of overstatement, if no misstatements were found, was established to be $900 before the sampling analysis, what conclusion can the auditor now make from the sampling evidence?

A. (S)he is 95% confident that the dollar amount of overstatement in the population of vouchers is between $900 and $1,170.

B. (S)he is 95% confident that the dollar amount of overstatement in the population of vouchers exceeds $1,170.

C. (S)he is 95% confident that the dollar amount of overstatement in the population of vouchers is less than $1,170.

D. An insufficient number of misstatements were detected to warrant a conclusion.

Answer (C) is correct.
REQUIRED: The conclusion from the audit evidence given an extension of tolerable misstatement.
DISCUSSION: Had the auditor detected no misstatements in the sample, (s)he could have been 95% confident that the dollar amount of overstatement in the balance was less than $900. Given discovery of an overstatement causing an extension to the tolerable misstatement of $270, the auditor can conclude with 95% confidence that the overstatement is less than $1,170 ($900 + $270).
Answer (A) is incorrect. The auditor is 95% confident that the overstatement is less than $1,170. Answer (B) is incorrect. The auditor is 95% confident that the overstatement is less than $1,170. Answer (D) is incorrect. A conclusion is warranted even if no misstatements were found.

Use the additional questions in Gleim **CPA Test Prep** to create Practice Exams that emulate Prometric!

15.5 PRACTICE TASK-BASED SIMULATIONS

| | | Auditing and Attestation
Testlet 4 of 4 | Time Remaining
1 hour - 30 minutes | Unsplit | Split Horiz | Split Vertical | Spreadsheet | Calculator | Exit |

DIRECTIONS

Note: If you believe you have encountered a software malfunction, report it to the test center staff immediately.

Navigation

To navigate from task to task, use the controls at the bottom of the screen. Click on the **Next** button to advance to the next task, or the **Previous** button to go to the previous task. To go directly to any task, click on its number.

| ⚑ = Reminder | | Directions | 1 2 3 4 5 6 7 | | ◀ Previous | Next ▶ |

If you would like a reminder to revisit a task, or want to indicate that you are finished with it, click on the reminder flag below the task number. To clear the flag, click on it again. Reminder flags are for your use only – they do not contribute to your score.

Tabs

In this part of the examination, you will be asked to complete various tasks. Every task has one or more **Work Tabs**. Some tasks have one or more **Information Tabs**, others may have none. Every task has a **Help** tab.

If a task has **Information Tabs**, you may use the information in them to complete your responses in the **Work Tabs**.

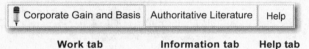

| ✏ Corporate Gain and Basis | Authoritative Literature | Help |

| Work tab | Information tab | Help tab |

Work Tabs:
- **Work Tabs** are identified with a pencil icon. This is where your responses are expected.
- Each task has one or more **Work Tabs**.
- **Work Tabs** contain directions for completing the task – be sure to read these directions carefully.
- The **Work Tab** name in the example above is for illustration only – yours will differ.
- You must complete all of the **Work Tabs** in each task to receive full credit.

Information Tabs:
- The Authoritative Literature will be provided in all tasks in the AUD, FAR, and REG sections for your reference.
- Your simulation may have one or more additional **Information Tabs**. Like the Authoritative Literature tabs, **Information Tabs** do not have a pencil icon.
- If your task has additional **Information Tabs**, go through each to familiarize yourself with the task content.

Help Tab:
- The **Help Tab** provides assistance with the exam software that is used in this task. For example, if the task is to compose a memorandum, **Help** will provide information about the word processor.

The Toolbar

The toolbar at the top of the screen shows the amount of time remaining for you to complete the tasks. In addition, the following tools are available. Note that only the **Exit** button is displayed when Directions are visible - the others will appear when you begin the tasks.

Click on these buttons to split or unsplit the screen. You can split the screen vertically or horizontally.

Click on this button to display the calculator; click on it again to hide the calculator. To move the calculator, click on the calculator title bar and drag the calculator to the desired location.

Click on this button to use the spreadsheet; click on it again to hide the spreadsheet. To move the spreadsheet, click on the the spreadsheet title bar and drag the spreadsheet to the desired location.

Click on this button to go on to the next part of the examination. You must complete all of the tasks to receive full credit. Once you click on **Exit** and confirm the action, you will NOT be able to return to this testlet.

| ⚑ = Reminder | | Directions | 1 2 3 4 5 | | ◀ Previous | Next ▶ |

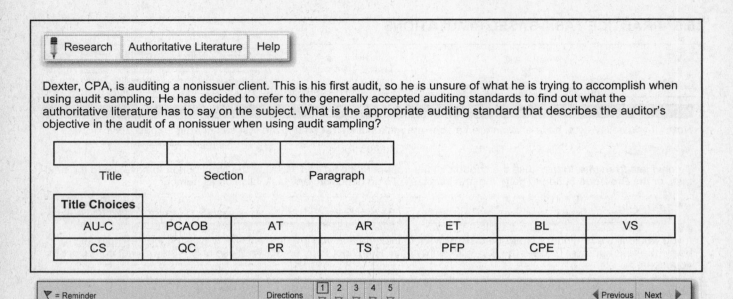

Research | Authoritative Literature | Help

Dexter, CPA, is auditing a nonissuer client. This is his first audit, so he is unsure of what he is trying to accomplish when using audit sampling. He has decided to refer to the generally accepted auditing standards to find out what the authoritative literature has to say on the subject. What is the appropriate auditing standard that describes the auditor's objective in the audit of a nonissuer when using audit sampling?

| Title | Section | Paragraph |

Title Choices

AU-C	PCAOB	AT	AR	ET	BL	VS
CS	QC	PR	TS	PFP	CPE	

▼ = Reminder   Directions   1 2 3 4 5   ◀ Previous   Next ▶

Differences Among Sampling Methods | Authoritative Literature | Help

Select from the list provided the sampling technique that best fits each sampling explanation. Each choice may be used once, more than once, or not at all.

Sampling Explanations	Answer
1. The larger the item in the population, the more likely it will be included in the sample.	
2. Replace(s) the need for the use of judgment by the auditor.	
3. Use(s) the average amount of sampled items to estimate the amount of the population.	
4. Use(s) results from a portion of the population to draw an inference about the total population.	
5. Allow(s) the auditor to measure and control the risk of accepting a materially misstated balance.	
6. Require(s) the auditor to estimate the population standard deviation to determine the appropriate sample size.	
7. Is (are) equally useful for selecting samples and drawing inferences about asset and liability balances.	
8. Eliminate(s) the need for the auditor to consider materiality.	
9. Automatically stratify(ies) the population during sample selection.	
10. Require(s) documentation of results in the working papers.	

Sampling Choices

A) Mean-per-unit (MPU) sampling only

B) Monetary-unit sampling only

C) Both MPU and monetary-unit sampling

D) Neither MPU nor monetary-unit sampling

▼ = Reminder   Directions   1 2 3 4 5   ◀ Previous   Next ▶

MUS Sample Size | Authoritative Literature | Help

Edward Prince, CPA, has decided to use monetary-unit sampling, sometimes called probability-proportional-to-size sampling, in the audit of a client's accounts receivable. Few, if any, overstatements are expected.

Confidence Factors for Misstatements
Risk of Incorrect Acceptance

# of Misstatements	1.00%	5.00%	10.00%	15.00%	20.00%
0	4.61	3.00	2.31	1.90	1.61
1	6.64	4.75	3.89	3.38	3.00
2	8.41	6.30	5.33	4.72	4.28
3	10.05	7.76	6.69	6.02	5.52
4	11.61	9.16	8.00	7.27	6.73

Other information for the current year's audit is outlined below:

Tolerable misstatement	$15,000
Risk of incorrect acceptance	5%
Number of misstatements allowed	0
Recorded amount of accounts receivable	$300,000

Use the current year's audit information to calculate the sampling interval and the sample size. Enter in the table below the proper amounts as given or calculated.

1. Confidence factor	
2. Tolerable misstatement	
3. Sampling interval	
4. Recorded amount	
5. Sample size	

MUS Evaluation | Authoritative Literature | Help

Keith, CPA, used monetary-unit sampling, sometimes called probability-proportional-to-size sampling, in the audit of a client's accounts receivable.

Other information for the current year's audit is outlined below:

Tolerable misstatement	$20,000
Recorded amount of accounts receivable	$200,000

Keith found the three misstatements listed below. Given this information, calculate the total projected misstatement. Enter the appropriate amounts in the shaded cells in the table below.

	Recorded Amount	Audit Amount	Tainting %	Sampling Interval	Projected Misstatement
1st Error	$400	$320	1.	$1,000	4.
2nd Error	$500	$0	2.	$1,000	5.
3rd Error	$3,000	$2,500	3.	$1,000	6.
				Total Projected	7.

| Attribute Sampling | Authoritative Literature | Help |

Carol Baker, CPA, was engaged to audit Mill Company's financial statements for the year ended September 30, Year 1. After obtaining an understanding of Mill's internal control, Baker decided to obtain evidence about the suitability of the design, and the operating effectiveness, of the controls over Mill's shipping and billing functions. During the prior years' audits, Baker used nonstatistical sampling, but for the current year Baker used statistical sampling for tests of controls to eliminate the need for judgment.

Baker assessed the risks of material misstatement based on the expectation that controls were operating effectively. Accordingly, a tolerable rate of deviation or acceptable upper precision limit (UPL) of 20% was established. To estimate the population deviation rate and the achieved UPL, Baker decided to use attribute sampling with a systematic selection approach. The expected population deviation rate was 3% for the 8,000 shipping documents, and Baker deferred consideration of the allowable risk of overreliance until the evaluation of the sample results. Baker used the tolerable deviation rate, the population size, and the expected population deviation rate to determine that a sample size of 100 would be sufficient. When it was subsequently determined that the actual population was about 10,000 shipping documents, Baker did not increase the sample size.

Baker's objective was to determine whether Mill's shipments had been properly billed. Baker took a sample of 100 invoices by selecting the first 25 invoices from the first month of each quarter. Baker then compared the invoices with the corresponding prenumbered shipping documents.

When Baker tested the sample, eight deviations were discovered. Additionally, one shipment that should have been billed at $10,443 was actually billed at $10,434. Baker considered this $9 to be immaterial and did not count it as a deviation.

In evaluating the sample results, Baker made the initial determination that a reliability level of 95% (risk of overreliance of 5%) was desired and, using the appropriate statistical sampling table, determined that for eight observed deviations from a sample size of 100, the achieved UPL was 14%. Baker then calculated the allowance for sampling risk to be 5%, the difference between the actual sample deviation rate (8%) and the expected deviation rate (3%). Baker reasoned that the actual sample deviation rate (8%) plus the allowance for sampling risk (5%) was less than the achieved UPL (14%). Thus, the sample supported the operating effectiveness of the controls.

Indicate whether each listed statement about Baker's procedures is correct or incorrect.

Statements	Answer		Choices
1. Statistical sampling eliminates the need for professional judgment.			A) Correct
2. The tolerable rate of deviation or acceptable upper precision limit (UPL) is acceptable (20%) if Baker plans to rely on internal control.			B) Incorrect
3. Systematic selection is an appropriate sampling method in this attribute sampling application.			
4. The sampling method used is not systematic sampling.			
5. The increase in the population size has little or no effect on sample size.			
6. Baker properly deferred consideration of the allowable risk of overreliance.			
7. The population from which the sample was chosen (invoices) was the wrong population.			
8. The sample selected was randomly selected.			
9. The immaterial difference in the amount of an invoice should have been treated as a deviation.			
10. The allowance for sampling risk was properly calculated.			
11. Baker's reasoning about the decision that the sample supported the effectiveness of the controls was erroneous.			

Unofficial Answers

1. Research (1 Gradable Item)

Answer: 530.04

AU-C Section 530 -- *Audit Sampling*

.04 The objective of the auditor, when using audit sampling, is to provide a reasonable basis for the auditor to draw conclusions about the population from which the sample is selected.

2. Differences Among Sampling Methods (10 Gradable Items)

1. B) Monetary-unit sampling only. In monetary-unit sampling, the probability of selection is related to size of the item.

2. D) Neither MPU nor monetary-unit sampling. Evaluating the appropriateness of evidence is solely a matter of auditing judgment and is not determined by the design and evaluation of an audit sample.

3. A) Mean-per-unit (MPU) sampling only. MPU sampling determines the average amount of sampled items (total audited amount of the sample ÷ number of items in the sample) and then multiplies this average by the number of items in the population to estimate the population amount.

4. C) Both MPU and monetary-unit sampling. Audit sampling is "the selection and evaluation of less than 100% of the population of audit relevance such that the auditor expects the items selected (the sample) to be representative of the population and, thus, to provide a reasonable basis for conclusions about the population."

5. C) Both MPU and monetary-unit sampling. By using statistical theory, the auditor can quantify sampling risk to assist in limiting it to an acceptable level.

6. A) Mean-per-unit (MPU) sampling only. MPU sampling requires the auditor to estimate the population's standard deviation to determine the sample size and evaluate the results. Monetary-unit sampling, however, does not require the use of the population standard deviation.

7. A) Mean-per-unit (MPU) sampling only. Monetary-unit sampling is appropriate only for accounts subject to the risk of overstatement (e.g., assets). Because the focus of liability accounts is ordinarily on the risk of understatement, monetary-unit sampling does not meet the objectives for an audit of liabilities.

8. D) Neither MPU nor monetary-unit sampling. The auditor must quantify the amount considered material for either sampling method. The amount considered material is one of the factors used in calculating the appropriate sample size.

9. B) Monetary-unit sampling only. Because monetary-unit sampling increases the probability of selecting large items, it effectively stratifies the population.

10. C) Both MPU and monetary-unit sampling. All important evidence and conclusions should be documented in the working papers, regardless of what methods are used by the auditor.

3. MUS Sample Size (5 Gradable Items)

1. The risk of incorrect acceptance is 5%, and 0 misstatements are allowed. Thus, the confidence factor is 3.00.

2. The tolerable misstatement is $15,000.

3.
$$\text{Sampling Interval} = \frac{\text{Tolerable Misstatement}}{\text{Confidence Factor}}$$

$$= \frac{\$15,000}{3.00}$$

$$= \$5,000$$

4. The recorded amount is $300,000.

5.
$$\text{Sample Size} = \frac{\text{Recorded Amount}}{\text{Sampling Interval}}$$

$$= \frac{\$300,000}{\$5,000}$$

$$= \underline{60}$$

4. MUS Evaluation (7 Gradable Items)

1. ($400 – $320) ÷ $400 = 20% tainted
2. ($500 – $0) ÷ $500 = 100% tainted
3. The recorded amount is greater than the sampling interval. Thus, the projected misstatement equals the actual misstatement.
4. $1,000 × 20% = $200
5. $1,000 × 100% = $1,000
6. $3,000 – $2,500 = $500
7. $200 + $1,000 + $500 = $1,700

5. Attribute Sampling (11 Gradable Items)

1. B) Incorrect. Regardless of whether the auditor uses statistical or nonstatistical sampling, the use of professional judgment is necessary.

2. B) Incorrect. A tolerable deviation rate of 20% means that it is acceptable to the auditor for the control to fail up to 20% of the time. This is not likely to allow the auditor to rely on the control.

3. A) Correct. Systematic sampling, or taking every nth item after a random start, is an acceptable selection method. Each item in the population has an equal and nonzero chance of selection.

4. A) Correct. Taking the first 25 invoices from the first month of each quarter is block sampling, which is not likely to be random in this case.

5. A) Correct. Changes in the size of large populations have little or no effect on sample size for attribute sampling. Sample size is taken from a table that assumes a large population.

6. B) Incorrect. The desired level of assurance (confidence level) is a factor in determining the sample size for a test of controls. It is the complement of the risk of overreliance.

7. A) Correct. The objective was to determine whether the shipments were properly billed. Thus, the relevant population should consist of shipping documents. The shipping documents are traced to the invoices to determine whether all shipments were properly billed.

8. B) Incorrect. Block sampling typically does not result in a random sample. Each item does not have an equal and nonzero chance of selection.

9. A) Correct. In determining the deviation rate for a control, attribute sampling does not consider the materiality of the deviation, only that one has occurred. However, the auditor should be concerned about the qualitative nature of the deviations as well as the estimation of the deviation rate.

10. B) Incorrect. In evaluating the sample, the achieved allowance for sampling risk is calculated as the upper precision limit (UPL) minus the sample rate. Thus, based on the information given, it should be 14% – 8%, or 6%.

11. A) Correct. The comparison should be made between the tolerable deviation rate of 20% and the UPL of 14%. Although likely not justified given the high tolerable deviation rate, because the UPL was less than the tolerable deviation rate, the auditor should rely on the control.

Gleim Simulation Grading

Task	Correct Responses		Gradable Items		Score per Task
1 (Research)	___	÷	1	=	___
2	___	÷	10	=	___
3	___	÷	5	=	___
4	___	÷	7	=	___
5	___	÷	11	=	___

Total of Scores per Task ___

÷ Total Number of Tasks   5

Total Score   ___%

STUDY UNIT SIXTEEN
REPORTS --
OPINIONS AND DISCLAIMERS

(14 pages of outline)

This study unit presents interrelated reporting issues. Subunit 2 should be studied carefully. Most reporting guidance is based on the auditor's report expressing an unmodified opinion on financial statements. The other subunits of this study unit and all of Study Unit 17 outline the requirements for wording changes in the auditor's report. Special reporting considerations (Study Unit 18), many matters considered in Study Unit 19, and governmental audit reports (Study Unit 20) are variations of the auditor's report.

16.1 THE AUDITOR'S REPORTING RESPONSIBILITY (AU-C 700)

1. **Objectives**

   a. The purpose of an audit is to provide the users of the financial statements with an opinion as to whether the financial statements are presented fairly, in all material respects, in accordance with the applicable financial reporting framework **(the framework)**.

   b. The auditor's objectives are to (1) **form an opinion** on the fairness of the statements based on an evaluation of the audit evidence obtained and (2) clearly express that opinion through a written report (hard copy or electronic) that describes the basis for that opinion.

   c. The framework ordinarily is U.S. generally accepted accounting principles (U.S. GAAP). But another framework may apply, for example, International Financial Reporting Standards (IFRS) issued by the International Accounting Standards Board. IFRS are used in many countries.

2. **Forming an Opinion**

   a. Presented **fairly** means the financial statements as a whole are **free from material misstatement**, whether due to fraud or error.

   1) The auditor should reach a conclusion about whether (s)he has obtained **reasonable assurance** regarding fair presentation.

   2) Reasonable assurance is a high but not absolute standard. It is achieved when the auditor obtains sufficient appropriate evidence that audit risk is acceptably low. Audit risk is the risk of expressing an inappropriate opinion when the statements are materially misstated.

b. The evaluation of fairness should include consideration of the **qualitative aspects** of the entity's accounting practices, including indicators of possible bias in management's judgments. In particular, the auditor should **evaluate** whether, given the requirements of the framework,

1) The statements adequately disclose the significant accounting policies.

2) The accounting policies selected and applied are consistent with the framework and are appropriate.

3) Management's accounting estimates are reasonable.

4) The information in the statements is relevant, reliable, comparable, and understandable.

5) The statements provide adequate disclosures to enable the intended users to understand the effect of material transactions and events.

6) The terminology used, including the title of each statement, is appropriate.

7) The statements adequately refer to or describe the framework.

c. The auditor's evaluation of fair presentation also should consider

1) The overall presentation, structure, and content of the statements.

2) Whether the statements, including the related notes, represent the underlying transactions and events in a manner that achieves fair presentation.

3. **Form of Opinion**

a. The auditor should express an **unmodified opinion** when (s)he concludes that the statements are presented fairly, in all material respects, in accordance with the framework.

Background

Standards prior to the AICPA's Clarified Auditing Standards used the term "unqualified" for a report that expressed assurance that the financial statements were free of material misstatements or on which the auditor had no reservations as to scope. You should expect to encounter the term "unmodified" for this type of audit report, but be aware of the prior terminology.

---

b. If the auditor concludes that the statements are not fairly presented, the auditor should **discuss the matter with management**. Depending on how the matter is resolved, the auditor should determine whether the opinion should be modified.

c. A modified opinion is a qualified opinion, an adverse opinion, or a disclaimer of opinion. The opinion is modified if the auditor

1) Concludes that, based on the audit evidence obtained, the financial statements as a whole **are materially misstated** (qualified or adverse opinion) or

2) Is **unable to obtain sufficient appropriate audit evidence** to conclude that the financial statements as a whole are free from material misstatement (qualified opinion or disclaimer of opinion).

Stop and review! You have completed the outline for this subunit. Study multiple-choice questions 1 through 3 on page 507.

16.2 THE AUDITOR'S REPORT (AU-C 700)

Background

The AICPA's Clarified Auditing Standards change the format of the auditor's report for nonissuers. However, the PCAOB's Interim Auditing Standards continue to use a form for issuers based on prior AICPA standards. The basic difference is that the AICPA's new format uses headings for all the sections of the report other than the introductory paragraph. The basic content of the report is the same based on both AICPA and PCAOB standards. Any specific differences are noted in the subsequent materials presented here.

 We recommend that you memorize the auditor's report. You will not be required to draft a report on the exam, but questions often relate to how the report may change based on audit findings. You should not struggle with the normative language while considering what changes should be made. Having a firm grasp of the report will serve you well.

1. The report for an audit in accordance with GAAS should include the following:

   a. **Title.** The auditor's report should have a title that includes the word **independent** to clearly indicate that it is the report of an independent auditor.

   b. **Addressee.** The auditor's report should be addressed as required by the circumstances of the engagement (this is discussed in further detail in Subunit 16.3).

   c. **Introductory paragraph.** This paragraph should

      1) Identify the entity audited,
      2) State that the financial statements have been audited,
      3) Identify the title of each statement, and
      4) Specify the date or period covered by each statement.

      NOTE: No heading is required for the introductory paragraph. But the other major parts of the report should have appropriate headings or subtitles.

   d. **Management's responsibility for the financial statements.** This paragraph should describe management's responsibility for

      1) Preparation and fair presentation of the statements and
      2) The design, implementation, and maintenance of internal control relevant to their preparation and fair presentation.

   e. **Auditor's responsibility.** This section should

      1) State that the responsibility of the auditor is to express an opinion on the financial statements based on the audit.
      2) State that the audit was conducted in accordance with auditing standards generally accepted in the United States of America. [The PCAOB's AS No. 1, *References in Auditors' Reports to the Standards of the Public Company Accounting Oversight Board*, requires the report on the statements of a client subject to the **Sarbanes-Oxley Act** (an issuer) to refer to "the standards of the Public Company Accounting Oversight Board" rather than to GAAS.]
      3) Explain that those standards require that the auditor plan and perform the audit to obtain reasonable assurance about whether the statements are free from material misstatement.
      4) Describe an audit by stating the following:

         a) An audit involves performing procedures to obtain audit evidence about the amounts and disclosures in the financial statements.

b) The procedures selected depend on the auditor's judgment, including the assessment of the risks of material misstatement of the financial statements, whether due to fraud or error.

c) In making risk assessments, the auditor considers internal control relevant to the entity's preparation and fair presentation of the financial statements. The purpose is to design audit procedures that are appropriate in the circumstances, not to express an opinion on the effectiveness of the entity's internal control. Accordingly, no such opinion is expressed. (If the auditor is also responsible for expressing an opinion on internal control, the caveat is omitted.)

d) An audit also includes evaluating the appropriateness of the accounting policies used, the reasonableness of significant accounting estimates made by management, and the overall presentation of the financial statements.

e) The auditor believes that the audit evidence obtained is sufficient and appropriate to provide a basis for the opinion.

f. **Opinion.** When expressing an unmodified opinion, the auditor should state that the financial statements present fairly, in all material respects, the financial position of the entity as of the balance sheet date and the results of its operations and its cash flows for the period then ended in accordance with the applicable financial reporting framework. (The framework typically is U.S. GAAP.)

g. **Signature of the auditor.** The report should include the manual or printed signature of the auditor's firm.

h. **Auditor's address.** The report should name the city and state where the auditor practices.

i. **Date of the auditor's report.** The report should be dated no earlier than the date on which the auditor has obtained sufficient appropriate audit evidence on which to base the opinion, including evidence that

1) The audit documentation has been reviewed;

2) All of the financial statements, including the related notes, have been prepared; and

3) Management has asserted its responsibility for those statements.

ISA Difference

The ISAs allow the auditor to use the wording "true and fair view" rather than "presented fairly, in all material respects."

The ISAs require the introductory paragraph of the auditor's report to refer to the summary of significant accounting policies and other explanatory information.

The ISAs require the report to state that auditing standards require the auditor to comply with ethical requirements.

---

2. **Separate Statement by Management**

a. The description of management's responsibility for the financial statements in the auditor's report should **not** refer to a separate statement by management about such responsibilities if the statement is included in a document containing the auditor's report.

1) For example, if a section of the annual report describes management's responsibility for internal control, the auditor's report should not refer to that section. The reference may lead users to believe the auditor is providing assurance about the description.

3. **Other Reporting Responsibilities**

    a.   In some cases, the auditor may report on matters in addition to the fair presentation of the statements. For example, for audits conducted under *Government Auditing Standards*, the auditor may be required to report on internal control over financial reporting.

        1)   These other reporting responsibilities are addressed in a separate section of the auditor's report following the opinion paragraph. The section is subtitled **Report on Other Legal and Regulatory Requirements** (if appropriate).

            a)   The form and content vary depending on the nature of the auditor's other reporting responsibilities.

            b)   If this separate section is included, the preceding headings, statements, and explanations should be under the subtitle **Report on the Financial Statements** preceding the introductory paragraph.

4. **Example of an Auditor's Report**

    a.   The following is an auditor's report on consolidated comparative financial statements prepared in accordance with U.S. GAAP. The report expresses an unmodified opinion for all years presented. (If only single-year financial statements are presented, the report is adjusted to refer only to those statements.)

EXAMPLE -- Auditor's Unmodified Report

Independent Auditor's Report

To: <----------- Addressed to the Board of Directors and/or Shareholders

We have audited the accompanying consolidated financial statements of X Company and its subsidiaries, which comprise the consolidated balance sheets as of December 31, 20X1 and 20X0, and the related consolidated statements of income, changes in stockholders' equity, and cash flows for the years then ended, and the related notes to the financial statements.

Management's Responsibility for the Financial Statements

Management is responsible for the preparation and fair presentation of these consolidated financial statements in accordance with accounting principles generally accepted in the United States of America; this includes the design, implementation, and maintenance of internal control relevant to the preparation and fair presentation of consolidated financial statements that are free from material misstatement, whether due to fraud or error.

Auditor's Responsibility

Our responsibility is to express an opinion on these consolidated financial statements based on our audits. We conducted our audits in accordance with auditing standards generally accepted in the United States of America. Those standards require that we plan and perform the audit to obtain reasonable assurance about whether the consolidated financial statements are free from material misstatement.

An audit involves performing procedures to obtain audit evidence about the amounts and disclosures in the consolidated financial statements. The procedures selected depend on the auditor's judgment, including the assessment of the risks of material misstatement of the consolidated financial statements, whether due to fraud or error. In making those risk assessments, the auditor considers internal control relevant to the entity's preparation and fair presentation of the consolidated financial statements in order to design audit procedures that are appropriate in the circumstances, but not for the purpose of expressing an opinion on the effectiveness of the entity's internal control. Accordingly, we express no such opinion. An audit also includes evaluating the appropriateness of accounting policies used and the reasonableness of significant accounting estimates made by management, as well as evaluating the overall presentation of the consolidated financial statements.

We believe that the audit evidence we have obtained is sufficient and appropriate to provide a basis for our audit opinion.

Opinion

In our opinion, the consolidated financial statements referred to above present fairly, in all material respects, the financial position of X Company and its subsidiaries as of December 31, 20X1 and 20X0, and the results of their operations and their cash flows for the years then ended in accordance with accounting principles generally accepted in the United States of America.

Auditor's signature   <----------- May be manual or printed
Auditor's address   <----------- City and state
Date   <----------- No earlier than the date that sufficient appropriate audit evidence was obtained

5. **Overview of Opinions**

   a. An **unmodified opinion** is the conclusion that the financial statements are presented fairly, in all material respects, in accordance with the framework.

   b. A **qualified opinion** is the conclusion that, except for the matter(s) described in the basis for qualified opinion paragraph, the financial statements are presented fairly, in all material respects, in accordance with the framework.

      1) If the auditor has obtained sufficient appropriate audit evidence, misstatements are material but not pervasive.

      2) If the auditor has not obtained sufficient appropriate audit evidence, the possible effects of undetected misstatements are material but not pervasive.

   c. An **adverse opinion** is the conclusion that, because of the significance of the matter(s) described in the basis for adverse opinion paragraph, the financial statements are not presented fairly.

      1) The auditor has obtained sufficient appropriate audit evidence, but the misstatements are material and pervasive.

   d. A **disclaimer of opinion** is the conclusion that, because of the significance of the matter(s) described in the basis for disclaimer of opinion paragraph, the auditor has not been able to obtain sufficient appropriate audit evidence. Accordingly, the auditor does not express an opinion on the financial statements.

      1) The possible effects of undetected misstatements are material and pervasive.

6. The auditor may choose to include, or be required to include, an **emphasis-of-matter** or **other-matter** paragraph in the auditor's report.

   a. The matters addressed do not affect the type of opinion expressed. This is discussed in further detail in Study Unit 17.

7. **Summary of Modified Opinions**

Reason for the Modification	Auditor's Judgment About the Pervasiveness of the Effects or Possible Effects on the Statements	
	Material but Not Pervasive	*Material and Pervasive*
Financial statements are materially misstated	Qualified opinion	Adverse opinion
Inability to obtain sufficient appropriate audit evidence	Qualified opinion	Disclaimer of opinion

   a. **Pervasive effects** on the statements

      1) Are not confined to specific elements, accounts, or items of the statements.

      2) Represent or could represent a substantial proportion of the statements if confined to specific elements, accounts, or items.

      3) Are, with regard to disclosures, fundamental to users' understanding of the statements.

   b. A **misstatement** arises from fraud or error. It is a difference between (1) the amount, classification, presentation, or disclosure of a financial statement item and (2) the amount, etc., required for it to be presented fairly.

Stop and review! You have completed the outline for this subunit. Study multiple-choice questions 4 through 8 beginning on page 508.

16.3 ADDRESSING AND DATING THE REPORT (AU-C 700)

1. The auditor's report should be addressed to those for whom the report is prepared. It may be addressed to the entity whose statements are being audited or to those charged with governance. If the client is an unincorporated entity, the report should be addressed as circumstances dictate, e.g., to the partners or the proprietor.

   a. If an auditor is retained to audit the financial statements of an entity that is **not the client**, the report customarily is addressed to the client and not to those charged with governance. For example, if a bank engages an auditor to audit a loan applicant, the report is addressed to the bank.

2. **The Date of the Auditor's Report**

   a. The date of the audit report is **no earlier than the date on which the auditor has obtained sufficient appropriate evidence** to support the opinion. This date is important because users expect the auditor to perform subsequent events procedures. They are intended to detect events occurring between the date of the statements and the date of the report that materially affect the statements.

      1) The auditor is ordinarily not responsible for making inquiries or carrying out any audit procedures after the date of the report.

   b. When a **subsequent event** disclosed in the financial statements occurs after the date of the report but before the report release date, the auditor may use **dual-dating**. (S)he may use the original date of the report except for the matters affected by the subsequent event, which are assigned the appropriate later date.

      1) In that case, the auditor's responsibility for events after the original date of the report is limited to the specific event.

      2) If the auditor is willing to accept responsibility to the later date and accordingly extends subsequent events procedures to that date, the auditor may choose the later date as the date for the entire report.

   c. Use of the original date by a predecessor auditor in a **reissued report** removes any implication that records, transactions, or events after such date have been audited or reviewed. However, the predecessor auditor should perform the following procedures to determine whether the report is still appropriate: (1) read the statements of the subsequent period, (2) compare the prior statements with the current statements, and (3) obtain written representations from management and the successor auditor about information obtained or events that occurred subsequent to the original date of the report.

      1) An exception exists for filings under the Securities Act of 1933. This exception is covered in AU-C 925 (see Study Unit 18, Subunit 3).

Stop and review! You have completed the outline for this subunit. Study multiple-choice questions 9 through 12 beginning on page 509.

16.4 QUALIFIED OPINIONS (AU-C 705)

1. A qualified opinion should be expressed if the auditor

    a. Has obtained sufficient appropriate audit evidence and concludes that **misstatements**, individually or aggregated, are **material but not pervasive** to the financial statements or

    b. Is **unable** to obtain sufficient appropriate audit evidence but concludes that the possible effects on the financial statements of undetected misstatements, if any, could be **material but not pervasive**.

2. Financial statements may be fairly presented **except for** the effects or possible effects of a certain matter. If the opinion is qualified because of such effects, the auditor should describe the matter(s) resulting in the qualification.

    a. This description is included in a **basis for qualified opinion** paragraph preceding the **opinion** paragraph.

    b. The opinion paragraph should contain qualifying language and refer to the basis for qualified opinion paragraph.

        1) The opinion paragraph should include the words "except for."

        2) "Subject to," "with the foregoing explanation," and similar phrases lack clarity and forcefulness and should **not** be used.

        3) Notes are part of the statements, and language such as "fairly presented when read in conjunction with Note 1" should **not** be used because of the likelihood of misunderstanding.

3. **Inability to Obtain Sufficient Appropriate Evidence**

    a. The inability to obtain sufficient appropriate evidence that is material but not pervasive (also called a scope limitation) may result from the following:

        1) Circumstances not controlled by the entity, such as destruction or government seizure of accounting records.

        2) Circumstances related to the nature or timing of the work, such as not being able to observe inventory due to the late appointment of the auditor or determining that controls are ineffective.

        3) Limitations imposed by management, such as preventing the auditor from (a) observing inventory or (b) confirming receivables.

    b. A **precondition** of the audit is management's agreement to provide the auditor with access to information relevant to preparing and fairly presenting the financial statements.

        1) Management also should agree to provide

            a) Additional information requested for the purpose of the audit and
            b) Unrestricted access to persons having necessary audit evidence.

        2) Accordingly, if a limitation on the scope of the engagement is imposed that will result in a disclaimer of opinion, the auditor should not accept the engagement.

    c. However, the auditor may become aware of a management-imposed scope limitation after accepting the engagement that is likely to result in a qualified opinion or a disclaimer of opinion.

        1) The auditor should request removal of the limitation.

        2) If it is not removed, the auditor should communicate with those charged with governance and determine whether alternative procedures can be performed.

3) If the auditor cannot obtain sufficient appropriate evidence because of the limitation, (s)he should determine whether the possible effects of undetected misstatements could be material and pervasive.

   a) If they are, the auditor should disclaim an opinion or withdraw from the engagement.

d. When a qualified opinion results from an inability to obtain sufficient appropriate evidence, the auditor describes the matter in the basis for qualified opinion paragraph, **not** in a note to the statements.

   1) The description of the audit scope is the responsibility of the auditor, not management.

e. The opinion paragraph should indicate that the qualification pertains to the **possible effects** on the financial statements, not to the scope limitation itself.

   1) The wording ". . . except for the limitation on the scope of the audit . . ." is unacceptable.

   2) The wording ". . . except for the possible effects of the matter described in the basis for qualified opinion paragraph . . ." is appropriate.

f. The following are the effects on the auditor's report when the opinion is qualified due to an inability to obtain sufficient appropriate evidence with possible effects that are material but not pervasive:

   1) The introductory paragraph is unchanged.
   2) The management's responsibility paragraph is unchanged.
   3) The auditor's responsibility section ends with the sentence, "We believe that the audit evidence we have obtained is sufficient and appropriate to provide a basis for our qualified audit opinion."

g. The following are examples of the basis for qualified opinion and opinion paragraphs:

EXAMPLE -- Opinion Qualified for a Material but Not Pervasive Scope Limitation

Basis for Qualified Opinion

ABC Company's investment in XYZ Company, a foreign affiliate acquired during the year and accounted for under the equity method, is carried at $XXX on the balance sheet at December 31, 20X1, and ABC Company's share of XYZ Company's net income of $XXX is included in ABC Company's net income for the year then ended. We were unable to obtain sufficient appropriate audit evidence about the carrying amount of ABC Company's investment in XYZ Company as of December 31, 20X1 and ABC Company's share of XYZ Company's net income for the year then ended because we were denied access to the financial information, management, and the auditors of XYZ Company. Consequently, we were unable to determine whether any adjustments to these amounts were necessary.

Qualified Opinion

In our opinion, except for the possible effects of the matter described in the Basis for Qualified Opinion paragraph, the financial statements referred to above present fairly, in all material respects, the financial position of ABC Company as of December 31, 20X1, and the results of its operations and its cash flows for the year then ended in accordance with accounting principles generally accepted in the United States of America.

---

4. **Material Misstatements**

   a. A material misstatement may result from

      1) Inappropriate selection or application of accounting principles or policies.
      2) Inappropriate presentation of the statements.
      3) Inappropriate or inadequate disclosure. For example, management may (a) not comply with the requirements for a change in accounting policies or (b) not apply those policies consistently from period to period.
      4) Omission of required disclosures, such as when a required statement (e.g., a statement of cash flows) is not reported.

5.   **Misstatement of Specific Amounts**

   a.   If a material misstatement relates to **specific amounts**, the basis for qualified opinion paragraph should describe the financial effects. It also should include a quantification of the effects, if practicable. Practicable means

      1)   Reasonably obtainable from the accounts and records and
      2)   Not putting the auditor in the position of a preparer.

   b.   The auditor is not expected to prepare a basic statement. Moreover, the basis paragraph may be shortened by referring to a note (if any) that contains such information.

   c.   The following are the effects on the auditor's report when the opinion is qualified due to a material but not pervasive misstatement:

      1)   The introductory paragraph is unchanged.
      2)   The management's responsibility paragraph is unchanged.
      3)   The auditor's responsibility section ends with the sentence, "We believe that the audit evidence we have obtained is sufficient and appropriate to provide a reasonable basis for our qualified audit opinion."

   d.   The following are examples of the basis for qualified opinion and opinion paragraphs:

EXAMPLE -- Opinion Qualified for a Material but Not Pervasive Misstatement

Basis for Qualified Opinion

The Company has stated inventories at cost in the accompanying balance sheets. Accounting principles generally accepted in the United States of America require inventories to be stated at the lower of cost or market. If the Company stated inventories at the lower of cost or market, a write down of $XXX and $XXX would have been required as of December 31, 20X1 and 20X0, respectively. Accordingly, cost of sales would have been increased by $XXX and $XXX, and net income, income taxes, and stockholders' equity would have been reduced by $XXX, $XXX, and $XXX, and $XXX, $XXX, and $XXX, as of and for the years ended December 31, 20X1 and 20X0, respectively.

Qualified Opinion

In our opinion, except for the effects of the matter described in the Basis for Qualified Opinion paragraph, the financial statements referred to above present fairly, in all material respects, the financial position of ABC Company as of December 31, 20X1 and 20X0, and the results of its operations and its cash flows for the year then ended in accordance with accounting principles generally accepted in the United States of America.

---

6.   **Misstatement Based on Inadequate Disclosure**

   a.   If a material misstatement relates to narrative disclosures, the auditor includes in the basis paragraph an explanation of the misstatement.

   b.   If information required to be presented or disclosed is omitted, the auditor describes the nature of the information in the basis paragraph. (S)he also includes the information, if practicable, and discusses the omission with those charged with governance. (See the previous discussion of misstatement of specific amounts.)

   c.   The following are the effects on the auditor's report when the opinion is qualified due to inadequate disclosure:

      1)   The introductory paragraph is unchanged.
      2)   The management's responsibility paragraph is unchanged.
      3)   The auditor's responsibility section ends with the sentence, "We believe that the audit evidence we have obtained is sufficient and appropriate to provide a reasonable basis for our qualified audit opinion."

d. The following are examples of the basis for qualified opinion and opinion paragraphs:

EXAMPLE -- Opinion Qualified for Inadequate Disclosure

Basis for Qualified Opinion

The Company's financial statements do not disclose [describe the nature of the omitted information that is not practicable to present in the auditor's report]. In our opinion, disclosure of this information is required by accounting principles generally accepted in the United States of America.

Qualified Opinion

In our opinion, except for the omission of the information described in the Basis for Qualified Opinion paragraph, the financial statements referred to above present fairly, in all material respects, the financial position of ABC Company as of December 31, 20X1 and 20X0, and the results of its operations and its cash flows for the year then ended in accordance with accounting principles generally accepted in the United States of America.

---

7. **Summary of Qualified Opinions**

    a. A qualified opinion is expressed because of

        1) An inability to obtain sufficient appropriate evidence that could result in material but not pervasive undetected misstatements or

        2) Misstatements that are material but not pervasive. Examples of misstatements include the following:

            a) Inappropriate selection of accounting principles
            b) Inappropriate application of accounting principles
            c) Unjustified change in accounting principles
            d) Inadequate disclosure
            e) Failure to provide a basic financial statement, e.g., statement of cash flows

Stop and review! You have completed the outline for this subunit. Study multiple-choice questions 13 through 21 beginning on page 511.

16.5 ADVERSE OPINIONS (AU-C 705)

1. The auditor should express an adverse opinion when, having obtained sufficient appropriate audit evidence, (s)he concludes that **misstatements**, individually or aggregated, are **material and pervasive** to the financial statements.

2. The auditor should include a **basis for adverse opinion** paragraph preceding the opinion paragraph that describes the matter resulting in the modification.

    a. If misstatements relate to specific amounts in the financial statements (including quantitative disclosures), the auditor should include a description and quantification of the financial effects, if practicable. If it is not practicable to quantify the financial effects, the auditor should so state.

3. The opinion should state that, because of the significance of the matter(s) described in the basis for adverse opinion paragraph, the financial statements are **not presented fairly** in accordance with the framework.

4.   **Example of an Adverse Opinion**

    a.   The following are other effects on the auditor's report when an adverse opinion is expressed:

        1)   The introductory paragraph is unchanged.

        2)   The management's responsibility paragraph is unchanged.

        3)   The auditor's responsibility section is changed to state, "We believe that the audit evidence we have obtained is sufficient and appropriate to provide a basis for our adverse audit opinion."

    b.   The following are examples of the basis for adverse opinion and opinion paragraphs:

EXAMPLE -- Adverse Opinion Due to a Material and Pervasive Misstatement

Basis for Adverse Opinion

As described in Note X, the Company has not consolidated the financial statements of subsidiary XYZ Company that it acquired during 20X1 because it has not yet been able to ascertain the fair values of certain of the subsidiary's material assets and liabilities at the acquisition date. This investment is therefore accounted for on a cost basis by the Company. Under accounting principles generally accepted in the United States of America, the subsidiary should have been consolidated because it is controlled by the Company. Had XYZ Company been consolidated, many elements in the accompanying consolidated financial statements would have been materially affected. The effects on the consolidated financial statements of the failure to consolidate have not been determined.

Adverse Opinion

In our opinion, because of the significance of the matter discussed in the Basis for Adverse Opinion paragraph, the consolidated financial statements referred to above do not present fairly the financial position of ABC Company and its subsidiaries as of December 31, 20X1, or the results of their operations or their cash flows for the year then ended.

Stop and review! You have completed the outline for this subunit. Study multiple-choice questions 22 through 24 on page 514.

16.6 DISCLAIMERS OF OPINION (AU-C 705)

1.   The auditor disclaims an opinion due to an **inability to obtain sufficient appropriate audit evidence** when the auditor concludes that the possible effects on the financial statements of undetected misstatements, if any, could be **material and pervasive**. The inability to obtain sufficient appropriate audit evidence may result from the following:

    a.   Circumstances not controlled by the entity, such as destruction or government seizure of accounting records.

    b.   Circumstances related to the nature or timing of the work, such as not being able to observe inventory due to the late appointment of the auditor, determining that controls are ineffective, or not being able to obtain audited financial statements of a long-term investor.

    c.   Limitations imposed by management, such as preventing the auditor from (1) observing inventory or (2) confirming receivables.

2.   The following are the effects on the auditor's report when an opinion is disclaimed:

    a.   The introductory paragraph is changed to state, "We were engaged to audit . . ."

    b.   The management's responsibility paragraph is unchanged.

    c.   Because an audit has not been conducted, the auditor's responsibility section is changed to consist only of (1) a one-sentence description of the auditor's responsibility and (2) a statement that the auditor could not obtain sufficient appropriate audit evidence to express an opinion because of the matters described in the basis for disclaimer of opinion paragraph.

3. The following is an example of a disclaimer of opinion:

EXAMPLE -- Disclaimer of Opinion

Independent Auditor's Report

To: <----------- Addressed to the Board of Directors and/or Shareholders

We were engaged to audit the accompanying financial statements of ABC Company, which comprise the balance sheet as of December 31, 20X1, and the related statements of income, changes in stockholders' equity, and cash flows for the year then ended, and the related notes to the financial statements.

Management's Responsibility for the Financial Statements

Management is responsible for the preparation and fair presentation of these financial statements in accordance with accounting principles generally accepted in the United States of America; this includes the design, implementation, and maintenance of internal control relevant to the preparation and fair presentation of financial statements that are free from material misstatement, whether due to fraud or error.

Auditor's Responsibility

Our responsibility is to express an opinion on these financial statements based on conducting the audit in accordance with auditing standards generally accepted in the United States of America. Because of the matters described in the Basis for Disclaimer of Opinion paragraph, however, we were not able to obtain sufficient appropriate audit evidence to provide a basis for an audit opinion.

Basis for Disclaimer of Opinion

We were not engaged as auditors of the Company until after December 31, 20X1, and, therefore, did not observe the counting of physical inventories at the beginning or end of the year. We were unable to satisfy ourselves by other auditing procedures concerning the inventory held at December 31, 20X1, which is stated in the balance sheet at $XXX. In addition, the introduction of a new computerized accounts receivable system in September 20X1 resulted in numerous misstatements in accounts receivable. As of the date of our audit report, management was still in the process of rectifying the system deficiencies and correcting the misstatements. We were unable to confirm or verify by alternative means accounts receivable included in the balance sheet at a total amount of $XXX at December 31, 20X1. As a result of these matters, we were unable to determine whether any adjustments might have been found necessary in respect of recorded or unrecorded inventories and accounts receivable, and the elements making up the statements of income, changes in stockholders' equity, and cash flows.

Disclaimer of Opinion

Because of the significance of the matters described in the Basis for Disclaimer of Opinion paragraph, we have not been able to obtain sufficient appropriate audit evidence to provide a basis for an audit opinion. Accordingly, we do not express an opinion on these financial statements.

Auditor's signature   <----------- May be manual or printed
Auditor's address   <----------- City and state
Date   <----------- Date disclaimer signed

---

4. **Auditor Not Independent but Required to Report**

   a. An auditor who is not independent may be required by law or regulation to report on the financial statements. The auditor should disclaim an opinion and should specifically state that (s)he is not independent.

      1) The auditor may or may not provide the reasons for the lack of independence. However, if the reasons are provided, the auditor should include all the reasons.

5. **Reporting on a Single Financial Statement**

   a. The auditor may, in appropriate circumstances, express an unmodified opinion on one basic financial statement (e.g., the balance sheet). References in the introductory and opinion paragraphs of the report are made only to the one statement. The other sections of the report are essentially unaffected.

   b. A **piecemeal opinion** is an expression of opinion on a specific element in the financial statements when the auditor has disclaimed an opinion or expressed an adverse opinion on the statements as a whole. This type of assurance is inappropriate because it would contradict the disclaimer or adverse opinion.

6. **Accountant Associated with the Unaudited Financial Statements of an Issuer**

   a. The PCAOB's Interim Auditing Standards consist of GAAS in effect on April 16, 2003, unless amended or superseded by the PCAOB. According to these standards, a disclaimer should be attached to the financial statements of an issuer (public company) when an accountant is associated with those statements and has not audited or reviewed them.

      1) Association means that the accountant has consented to the use of his/her name in a report, document, or written communication containing the statements.

      2) It also may mean that the accountant has submitted financial statements that (s)he prepared or assisted in preparing.

      3) An accountant might become associated by performing consulting services for a nonaudit client, for example, structuring a purchase transaction for a new subsidiary.

   b. The following relate to the disclaimer:

      1) Each page of the financial statements should be marked as **unaudited**.

      2) The accountant has no responsibility to apply any procedures beyond reading the statements for obvious material misstatements. Any procedures that may have been performed should not be described.

      3) If the accountant has reservations regarding fair presentation in accordance with GAAP (e.g., that management has elected to omit substantially all disclosures), (s)he should suggest revision. Failing that, the matter should be disclosed.

      4) The report has no title or salutation.

   c. The following is an example of a disclaimer on unaudited financial statements of an issuer:

EXAMPLE -- Disclaimer of Opinion When Associated with Unaudited Financial Statements of an Issuer

The accompanying balance sheet of X Company as of December 31, Year 1, and the related statements of income, retained earnings, and cash flows for the year then ended were not audited by us and, accordingly, we do not express an opinion on them.

Signature
Date

---

   d. Accountants providing nonaudit services to nonissuers should follow the guidance in *Statements on Standards for Accounting and Review Services* or *Statements on Standards for Attestation Engagements* (this is discussed in further detail in Study Unit 19).

Stop and review! You have completed the outline for this subunit. Study multiple-choice questions 25 through 31 beginning on page 514.

QUESTIONS

16.1 The Auditor's Reporting Responsibility (AU-C 700)

1. The objective of the audit of GAAP-based financial statements is to

A. Make suggestions as to the form or content of the financial statements or to draft them in whole or in part.

B. Express an opinion on the fairness with which the statements present financial position, results of operations, and cash flows in accordance with generally accepted accounting principles.

C. Ensure adoption of sound accounting policies and the establishment and maintenance of internal control.

D. Express an opinion on the accuracy with which the statements present financial position, results of operations, and cash flows in accordance with generally accepted accounting principles.

Answer (B) is correct.
REQUIRED: The objective of an audit.
DISCUSSION: Based on an audit, the auditor expresses an opinion (or a disclaimer of opinion) on the fairness, in all material respects, of the presentation of financial statements, i.e., on whether they will be misleading to users.
Answer (A) is incorrect. The auditor may make suggestions about the statements or help prepare them, but (s)he is responsible only for expressing an opinion as to their fairness. The statements remain the representations of management. Answer (C) is incorrect. Management is responsible for adopting sound accounting policies and establishing and maintaining internal control. Answer (D) is incorrect. The auditor expresses an opinion on the fairness of financial statements, not their accuracy.

2. Which of the following statements best describes the distinction between the auditor's responsibilities and management's responsibilities?

A. Management has responsibility for maintaining and adopting sound accounting policies, and the auditor has responsibility for internal control.

B. Management has responsibility for the basic data underlying financial statements, and the auditor has responsibility for drafting the financial statements.

C. The auditor's responsibility is confined to the audited portion of the financial statements, and management's responsibility is confined to the unaudited portions.

D. The auditor's responsibility is confined to expressing an opinion, but the financial statements remain the responsibility of management.

Answer (D) is correct.
REQUIRED: The statement that best distinguishes between the auditor's and management's responsibilities for audited financial statements.
DISCUSSION: The auditor is responsible for the opinion on financial statements, but management is responsible for the representations made in the financial statements.
Answer (A) is incorrect. Management has responsibility for establishing and maintaining internal control. Answer (B) is incorrect. Management is responsible for preparing the financial statements. Answer (C) is incorrect. The auditor expresses an opinion on the financial statements as a whole, and management is responsible for all the assertions in the financial statements.

3. The evaluation of fairness in determining the appropriate opinion to express should include consideration of the qualitative aspects of the entity's accounting practices, including whether

A. Indicators of possible bias exist in management's judgments.

B. The accounting principles used are the most conservative available.

C. Management and those charged with governance agree with all the standards used in the reporting process.

D. The auditor and management agree with all the standards used in the reporting process.

Answer (A) is correct.
REQUIRED: The auditor's conclusion about a qualitative aspect of the entity's accounting practices.
DISCUSSION: The auditor should be aware of the potential for management bias. For example, management's judgments may indicate a lack of neutrality that results in selective correction of identified misstatements and bias in making accounting estimates.
Answer (B) is incorrect. The accounting principles need to be in accordance with the framework and appropriate, not the most conservative. Answer (C) is incorrect. Fair presentation depends on the qualities of information in the statements, not whether management and those charged with governance agree with all the standards used in the reporting process. Answer (D) is incorrect. Fair presentation depends on the qualities of information in the statements, not whether the auditor and management agree with all the standards used in the reporting process.

16.2 The Auditor's Report (AU-C 700)

4. Which of the following statements is a basic element of the auditor's report for a nonissuer?

A. The disclosures provide reasonable assurance that the financial statements are free of material misstatement.

B. The auditor evaluated management decisions.

C. The procedures used depend on the auditor's judgment.

D. The financial statements are consistent with those of the prior period.

Answer (C) is correct.
   REQUIRED: The statement that is an element of the auditor's report for a nonissuer.
   DISCUSSION: The auditor's responsibility section states, "The procedures selected depend on the auditor's judgment . . ."
   Answer (A) is incorrect. The audit is planned and performed to obtain reasonable assurance about whether the statements are free from material misstatement. Answer (B) is incorrect. The audit addresses the fair presentation of the statements, not the quality of most management decisions. Answer (D) is incorrect. The auditor evaluates the appropriateness (not necessarily the consistency) of the accounting policies used.

5. The existence of audit risk is recognized by the statement in the auditor's report that the auditor

A. Obtains reasonable assurance about whether the financial statements are free of material misstatement.

B. Evaluates the accounting policies used.

C. Realizes some matters, either individually or in the aggregate, are important, while other matters are not important.

D. Is responsible for expressing an opinion on the financial statements.

Answer (A) is correct.
   REQUIRED: The statement in the auditor's report that relates to audit risk.
   DISCUSSION: The existence of audit risk is recognized by the statement in the auditor's report that the auditor obtained reasonable assurance about whether the financial statements are free of material misstatement. Audit risk is the risk that the auditor expresses an inappropriate audit opinion when the financial statements are materially misstated. Audit risk exists because the assurance is not absolute. Reasonable assurance is obtained when the auditor has obtained sufficient appropriate evidence to reduce audit risk to an acceptably low level (AU-C 200).
   Answer (B) is incorrect. The statement about evaluating accounting policies relates to whether the accounting principles selected and applied are consistent with the applicable framework and are appropriate. Answer (C) is incorrect. Materiality is mentioned in the auditor's report, but a statement defining materiality is not. Answer (D) is incorrect. The statement about the responsibilities of the auditor does not pertain to audit risk.

6. An annual shareholders' report includes audited financial statements and contains a management report asserting that the financial statements are the responsibility of management. Is it permissible for the auditor's report to refer to the management report?

A. No, because the reference may lead to the belief that the auditor is providing assurances about management's representations.

B. No, because the auditor has no responsibility to read the other information in a document containing audited financial statements.

C. Yes, provided the reference is included in a separate explanatory paragraph of the auditor's report.

D. Yes, provided the auditor reads the management report and discovers no material misrepresentation of fact.

Answer (A) is correct.
   REQUIRED: The true statement about a reference in the auditor's report to the management report in the annual report.
   DISCUSSION: According to AU-C 700, such a reference in the auditor's report may lead users to the erroneous belief that the auditor is giving assurances about management's representations in the separate statement in the annual report.
   Answer (B) is incorrect. The auditor should read the other information. Answer (C) is incorrect. No reference should be made in the auditor's report. Answer (D) is incorrect. No reference should be made in the auditor's report.

7. When single-year financial statements are presented, an auditor ordinarily expresses an unmodified opinion if the

A. Auditor is unable to obtain audited financial statements supporting the entity's investment in a foreign affiliate.

B. Entity declines to present a statement of cash flows with its balance sheet and related statements of income and retained earnings.

C. Auditor is not independent but judges that an unmodified opinion is appropriate.

D. Prior year's financial statements were audited by another CPA whose report, which expressed an unmodified opinion, is not presented.

Answer (D) is correct.
REQUIRED: The conditions under which an unmodified opinion is expressed.
DISCUSSION: When single-year financial statements are presented, the auditor's reporting responsibility is limited to those statements. If the prior year's financial statements are not presented for comparative purposes, the current-year auditor should not refer to the prior year's statements and the report thereon. Furthermore, the failure to present comparative statements is not a basis for modifying the opinion.
Answer (A) is incorrect. An inability to obtain audited financial statements supporting an entity's material investment in a foreign affiliate is a scope limitation requiring either a qualified opinion or a disclaimer of opinion. Answer (B) is incorrect. If the entity declines to present a statement of cash flows, the auditor should express a qualified opinion. Answer (C) is incorrect. The auditor should not express an opinion if (s)he is not independent.

8. Does an auditor make the following representations explicitly or implicitly in the opinion paragraph when expressing an unmodified opinion?

	Conformity with the Applicable Financial Reporting Framework	Adequacy of Disclosure
A.	Explicitly	Explicitly
B.	Implicitly	Implicitly
C.	Implicitly	Explicitly
D.	Explicitly	Implicitly

Answer (D) is correct.
REQUIRED: The explicit and implicit representations an auditor makes when expressing an unmodified opinion.
DISCUSSION: The opinion paragraph of the auditor's report explicitly states whether the financial statements are in accordance with the applicable financial reporting framework, e.g., U.S. GAAP or IFRS. The adequacy of disclosure is implicit in the auditor's report.
Answer (A) is incorrect. Adequacy of disclosure is implied if the report does not mention disclosure. Answer (B) is incorrect. Presentation in accordance with the applicable financial reporting framework is explicitly stated. Answer (C) is incorrect. Presentation in accordance with the applicable financial reporting framework is explicitly stated, and adequacy of disclosure is implied if the report does not mention disclosure.

16.3 Addressing and Dating the Report (AU-C 700)

9. In May Year 3, an auditor reissues the auditor's report on the Year 1 financial statements at a former client's request. The Year 1 financial statements are to be presented comparatively with subsequent audited statements. They are not restated, and the auditor does not revise the wording of the report. The auditor should

A. Dual-date the reissued report.

B. Use the release date of the reissued report.

C. Use the original report date on the reissued report.

D. Use the current-period auditor's report date on the reissued report.

Answer (C) is correct.
REQUIRED: The date of a reissued report.
DISCUSSION: Use of the original date in a reissued report removes any implication that records, transactions, or events after such date have been audited or reviewed. However, the predecessor auditor should perform the following procedures to determine whether the report is still appropriate: (1) read the statements of the subsequent period, (2) compare the prior statements with the current statements, and (3) obtain written representations from management and the successor auditor about information obtained or events that occurred subsequent to the original date of the report.
Answer (A) is incorrect. The report is dual-dated only if it has been revised since the original reissue date. Answer (B) is incorrect. The release date of the reissued report implies that additional audit procedures have been applied. Answer (D) is incorrect. Use of the current report date implies that the report has been updated for additional audit procedures applied between the original issue date and the current auditor's report date.

10. March, CPA, is engaged by Monday Corp., a client, to audit the financial statements of Wall Corp., a company that is not March's client. Monday expects to present Wall's audited financial statements with March's auditor's report to 1st Federal Bank to obtain financing in Monday's attempt to purchase Wall. In these circumstances, March's auditor's report would usually be addressed to

A. Monday Corp., the client that engaged March.

B. Wall Corp., the entity audited by March.

C. 1st Federal Bank.

D. Both Monday Corp. and 1st Federal Bank.

Answer (A) is correct.
   REQUIRED: The addressee of an auditor's report when the auditee is not the client.
   DISCUSSION: If an auditor is retained to audit the financial statements of an entity that is not his/her client, the report customarily is addressed to the client and not to the board of directors or shareholders of the entity whose financial statements are being audited.

11. An auditor released an audit report that was dual-dated for a subsequently discovered fact occurring after the date of the auditor's report but before issuance of the related financial statements. The auditor's responsibility for events occurring subsequent to the original report date was

A. Limited to the specific event referenced.

B. Limited to include only events occurring before the date of the last subsequent event referenced.

C. Extended to subsequent events occurring through the date of issuance of the related financial statements.

D. Extended to include all events occurring since the original report date.

Answer (A) is correct.
   REQUIRED: The auditor's responsibility for events occurring subsequent to the original report date when the report is dual-dated.
   DISCUSSION: Subsequent to the original report date, the auditor is responsible only for the specific subsequently discovered fact for which the report was dual-dated. (S)he is responsible for other events only up to the original report date.
   Answer (B) is incorrect. After the original report date, the auditor's responsibility extends only to the specified event. Answer (C) is incorrect. The date(s) of the report determines the auditor's responsibility. Answer (D) is incorrect. After the original report date, the auditor's responsibility extends only to the specified subsequent event.

12. On August 13, a CPA dated the audit report on financial statements for the year ended June 30. On August 27, an event came to the CPA's attention that should be disclosed in the notes to the financial statements. The event was properly disclosed by the entity, but the CPA decided not to dual-date the auditor's report and dated the report August 27. Under these circumstances, the CPA was taking responsibility for

A. All subsequent events that occurred through August 27.

B. Only the specific subsequent event disclosed by the entity.

C. All subsequent events that occurred through August 13 and the specific subsequent event disclosed by the entity.

D. Only the subsequent events that occurred through August 13.

Answer (A) is correct.
   REQUIRED: The responsibility assumed by dating the audit report as of the date of a subsequent event requiring disclosure.
   DISCUSSION: Subsequent events are material events or transactions that occur after the balance sheet date but prior to the issuance of the financial statements. They require adjustment or disclosure in the financial statements. If the auditor dates the report August 27, the auditor is assuming responsibility for all subsequent events that occurred through August 27.
   Answer (B) is incorrect. When the report is dual-dated, the auditor's subsequent-events responsibility is for only the specific subsequent event disclosed by the entity. Answer (C) is incorrect. Dating the report August 27 makes the auditor responsible for all subsequent events occurring from June 30th through August 27th. Answer (D) is incorrect. Dating the report August 27 makes the auditor responsible for all subsequent events occurring from June 30th through August 27th.

16.4 Qualified Opinions (AU-C 705)

13. An auditor may express a qualified opinion for which of the following reasons?

	Circumstances Related to the Work	Limitations Imposed by Management
A.	Yes	Yes
B.	Yes	No
C.	No	Yes
D.	No	No

Answer (A) is correct.

REQUIRED: The reasons for which the auditor may express a qualified opinion.

DISCUSSION: An auditor may express a qualified opinion due to an inability to obtain sufficient appropriate audit evidence if the possible effects are material but not pervasive. The inability to obtain sufficient audit evidence (also called a scope limitation) may result from (1) circumstances not controlled by the entity, such as destruction or government seizure of accounting records; (2) circumstances related to the nature or timing of the work, such as not being able to (a) observe inventory due to the late appointment of the auditor, (b) obtain an investee's financial information, or (c) determine that controls are ineffective; or (3) limitations imposed by management, such as preventing the auditor from observing inventory or confirming receivables (AU-C 705).

Answer (B) is incorrect. Limitations imposed by management may require expression of a qualified opinion. Answer (C) is incorrect. Circumstances related to the nature or timing of the work may require expression of a qualified opinion. Answer (D) is incorrect. Circumstances related to the nature or timing of the work and limitations imposed by management may require expression of a qualified opinion.

14. When an issuer refuses to include in its audited financial statements any of the segment disclosures that the auditor believes are required, the auditor should express a(n)

A. Unmodified opinion with an emphasis-of-matter paragraph.

B. Qualified opinion because of inadequate disclosure.

C. Adverse opinion because of a significant uncertainty.

D. Disclaimer of opinion because of the significant scope limitation.

Answer (B) is correct.

REQUIRED: The effect on the report when an issuer refuses to include in its audited financial statements any of the segment disclosures that the auditor believes are required.

DISCUSSION: If the statements are materially misstated because of the omission of required information, the auditor should modify the opinion for inadequate disclosure and describe the information omitted. The auditor also should include this information in the report, if practicable. But the auditor is not expected to prepare segment information. (S)he need not assume the position of a preparer of financial information.

Answer (A) is incorrect. Inadequate disclosure requires an opinion modification if it is material. Answer (C) is incorrect. The issue is disclosure, not uncertainty. Moreover, by itself, an uncertainty does not result in a required report modification. Answer (D) is incorrect. Inadequate disclosure is a misstatement, that is, a difference between the disclosure of the reported item and the disclosure required for the item to be in accordance with the applicable financial reporting framework.

15. In which of the following situations would an auditor ordinarily choose between expressing a qualified opinion and an adverse opinion?

A. The auditor did not observe the entity's physical inventory and is unable to become satisfied about its balance by other auditing procedures.

B. Conditions that cause the auditor to have substantial doubt about the entity's ability to continue as a going concern are inadequately disclosed.

C. There has been a change in accounting principles that has a material effect on the comparability of the entity's financial statements.

D. The auditor is unable to apply necessary procedures concerning an investor's share of an investee's earnings recognized in accordance with the equity method.

Answer (B) is correct.

REQUIRED: The situation ordinarily involving a choice between a qualified opinion and an adverse opinion.

DISCUSSION: When the auditor concludes that there is substantial doubt about an entity's ability to continue as a going concern for a reasonable period of time, (s)he should include an emphasis-of-matter paragraph (following the opinion paragraph) in the auditor's report to describe the uncertainty. By itself, this doubt does not require a modification of the opinion. However, if the entity's disclosures about the issue are inadequate, the misstatement may result in a qualified or an adverse opinion.

Answer (A) is incorrect. A scope limitation requires the auditor to choose between a qualified opinion and a disclaimer of opinion. Answer (C) is incorrect. A justified change in accounting principle requires the auditor to add an emphasis-of-matter paragraph to the report but not to modify the opinion. Answer (D) is incorrect. A scope limitation requires the auditor to choose between a qualified opinion and a disclaimer of opinion.

16. When qualifying an opinion because of an insufficiency of appropriate audit evidence, an auditor should refer to the situation in the

	Auditor's Responsibility Section	Notes to the Financial Statements
A.	Yes	Yes
B.	Yes	No
C.	No	Yes
D.	No	No

Answer (B) is correct.
REQUIRED: The effect on the auditor's report when the opinion is qualified because of an insufficiency of appropriate audit evidence.
DISCUSSION: An auditor may express a qualified opinion due to an inability to obtain sufficient appropriate audit evidence if the possible effects are material but not pervasive. But the notes to the financial statements are unchanged because they were not drafted by the auditor. Moreover, a sentence in the auditor's responsibility section states, "We believe that the audit evidence we have obtained is sufficient and appropriate to provide a basis for our qualified audit opinion."
Answer (A) is incorrect. The notes to the financial statements are unchanged. Answer (C) is incorrect. The notes to the financial statements are unchanged, but the auditor's responsibility section is modified. Answer (D) is incorrect. The auditor's responsibility section is modified.

17. An auditor decides to express a qualified opinion on an entity's financial statements because a major inadequacy in its computerized accounting records prevents the auditor from applying necessary procedures. The opinion paragraph of the auditor's report should state that the qualification pertains to

A. A client-imposed scope limitation.

B. A departure from generally accepted auditing standards.

C. The possible effects on the financial statements.

D. Inadequate disclosure of necessary information.

Answer (C) is correct.
REQUIRED: The wording in the opinion paragraph when the opinion is qualified because of a scope limitation.
DISCUSSION: AU-C 705 states that, when an auditor qualifies his/her opinion because of a scope limitation, the wording in the opinion paragraph should indicate that the qualification pertains to the possible effects on the financial statements and not to the scope limitation itself.
Answer (A) is incorrect. The qualification should not pertain to the scope limitation. Answer (B) is incorrect. The auditor apparently has followed GAAS in the conduct of the audit. Answer (D) is incorrect. Inadequate disclosure is a misstatement, not a lack of sufficient appropriate evidence.

18. In which of the following situations would an auditor ordinarily choose between expressing a qualified opinion and an adverse opinion?

A. The auditor did not observe the entity's physical inventory and is unable to become satisfied as to its balance by other auditing procedures.

B. The financial statements fail to disclose information that is required by the applicable reporting framework.

C. The auditor is asked to report only on the entity's balance sheet and not on the other basic financial statements.

D. Events disclosed in the financial statements cause the auditor to have substantial doubt about the entity's ability to continue as a going concern.

Answer (B) is correct.
REQUIRED: The situation in which an auditor chooses between expressing a qualified opinion and an adverse opinion.
DISCUSSION: Misstatements, including inadequate disclosures, may result in either a qualified or an adverse opinion. The auditor should exercise judgment about materiality by considering such factors as (1) benchmarks for dollar amounts, (2) significance to the statements and the entity, and (3) pervasiveness. If the misstatement is not pervasive, the auditor should express a qualified opinion.
Answer (A) is incorrect. A scope limitation is not a basis for an adverse opinion. Answer (C) is incorrect. A limited reporting engagement may result in the expression of an unmodified opinion. Answer (D) is incorrect. Substantial doubt about the entity's ability to continue as a going concern normally results in the addition of an emphasis-of-matter paragraph to the report.

19. An auditor did not observe a client's taking of beginning physical inventory and was unable to become satisfied about the inventory by means of other auditing procedures. The possible effects are material. Assuming no other scope limitations or reporting problems, the auditor could express an unmodified opinion on the current year's financial statements for

A. The balance sheet only.

B. The income statement only.

C. The income and retained earnings statements only.

D. All of the financial statements.

Answer (A) is correct.
REQUIRED: The financial statement(s) for which the auditor can express an unmodified opinion.
DISCUSSION: The auditor did not observe the counting of physical inventories at the beginning of the year and was not able to become satisfied by performing other procedures on those inventories. Because they enter into the determination of net income and cash flows, the auditor could not determine whether any adjustments were needed with respect to profit and net cash flows from operating activities. Moreover, the possible effects of the inability to obtain sufficient appropriate evidence regarding beginning inventories are material. Thus, the auditor should not express an opinion on the results of operations and cash flows. However, because the balance sheet reports only the ending inventory balance, the auditor can express an unmodified opinion on it alone, assuming (s)he is satisfied with the ending balance.

20. When management does **not** provide reasonable justification for a change in accounting principle, and it presents comparative financial statements, the auditor should express a qualified opinion

A. Only in the year of the accounting principle change.

B. Each year that the financial statements initially reflecting the change are presented.

C. Each year until management changes back to the accounting principle formerly used.

D. Only if the change is to an accounting principle that is not generally accepted.

Answer (B) is correct.
REQUIRED: The year(s) or circumstance in which an unjustified accounting change requires a qualified opinion.
DISCUSSION: If (1) the new principle and the method of accounting for the effect of the change are in accordance with the applicable reporting framework, (2) disclosures are adequate, and (3) the entity has justified that the principle is preferable, the auditor expresses an unmodified opinion. Otherwise, if the change is material, the misstatement results in expression of a qualified or an adverse opinion in the report for the year of change. A basis for modified opinion paragraph is added preceding the opinion paragraph. In the period of the change, the auditor also must add an emphasis-of-matter paragraph following the opinion paragraph to reflect the inconsistency. This paragraph is required in reports on financial statements in the period of change and in subsequent periods until the new principle is applied in all periods presented.

21. An auditor concludes that a client's noncompliance with laws and regulations, which has a material effect on the financial statements, has not been properly accounted for or disclosed. Depending on how pervasive the effect is on the financial statements, the auditor should express either a(n)

A. Adverse opinion or a disclaimer of opinion.

B. Qualified opinion or an adverse opinion.

C. Disclaimer of opinion or an unmodified opinion with a separate explanatory paragraph.

D. Unmodified opinion with a separate emphasis-of-matter paragraph or a qualified opinion.

Answer (B) is correct.
REQUIRED: The opinion(s) expressed when noncompliance has not been properly accounted for or disclosed.
DISCUSSION: When noncompliance with laws and regulations having a material effect on the financial statements has been detected but not properly reported, the auditor should insist upon revision of the financial statements. Failure to revise the statements precludes an unmodified opinion. Depending on the pervasiveness of the misstatement, the auditor should express either a qualified opinion or an adverse opinion.
Answer (A) is incorrect. A disclaimer of opinion is inappropriate. The auditor has concluded that the statements are materially misstated. Answer (C) is incorrect. A disclaimer of opinion is inappropriate. The auditor has concluded that the statements are materially misstated. Answer (D) is incorrect. An unmodified opinion is inappropriate for materially misstated financial statements.

16.5 Adverse Opinions (AU-C 705)

22. An auditor's report includes the following statement: "The financial statements referred to above do not present fairly the financial position, results of operations, or cash flows in conformity with U.S. generally accepted accounting principles." This auditor's report was most likely issued in connection with financial statements that are

A. Inconsistent.

B. Based on prospective financial information.

C. Misleading.

D. Affected by a material uncertainty.

Answer (C) is correct.

REQUIRED: The nature of the financial statements on which the quoted report was issued.

DISCUSSION: The language quoted states an adverse opinion. The essence of an adverse opinion is that the statements reported on, as a whole, are materially and pervasively misstated. If financial statements fail to meet the standards, they are misleading.

Answer (A) is incorrect. An inconsistency, by itself, results in no modification of the opinion paragraph. Answer (B) is incorrect. The accountant's examination report on a financial forecast or projection refers to guidelines for the presentation of a forecast (or projection) established by the AICPA, not to U.S. GAAP (AT 301). Answer (D) is incorrect. A material uncertainty, if properly disclosed, does not require modification of the opinion.

23. When an auditor expresses an adverse opinion, the opinion paragraph should include

A. The effects of the material misstatement.

B. A direct reference to a separate paragraph disclosing the basis for the opinion.

C. The financial effects of the misstatement.

D. A description of the uncertainty or scope limitation that prevents an unmodified opinion.

Answer (B) is correct.

REQUIRED: The matter included in the opinion paragraph when an adverse opinion is expressed.

DISCUSSION: An adverse opinion states that the financial statements are not fairly presented in accordance with the applicable financial reporting framework. When an adverse opinion is expressed, the opinion paragraph should directly refer to a basis for adverse opinion paragraph that discloses the basis for the adverse opinion. This paragraph should precede the opinion paragraph (AU-C 705).

Answer (A) is incorrect. The effects of the material misstatement, if practicable, should be stated in the basis for adverse opinion paragraph. Answer (C) is incorrect. The financial effects of the misstatement should be stated in the basis paragraph. Answer (D) is incorrect. An adverse opinion is not expressed as a result of an uncertainty or scope limitation.

24. In which of the following circumstances would an auditor be most likely to express an adverse opinion?

A. Information comes to the auditor's attention that raises substantial doubt about the entity's ability to continue as a going concern.

B. The chief executive officer refuses the auditor access to minutes of board of directors' meetings.

C. Tests of controls show that the entity's internal control is so poor that it cannot be relied upon.

D. The financial statements are not in conformity with the FASB Codification's guidance regarding the capitalization of leases.

Answer (D) is correct.

REQUIRED: The basis for an adverse opinion.

DISCUSSION: An adverse opinion is expressed when, in the auditor's judgment, the financial statements as a whole are not presented fairly in conformity with GAAP. The FASB Accounting Standards Codification is authoritative with regard to U.S. GAAP.

Answer (A) is incorrect. Substantial doubt about the entity's ability to continue as a going concern requires an emphasis-of-matter paragraph following the opinion paragraph, not an adverse opinion. Answer (B) is incorrect. A client-imposed scope limitation ordinarily results in a disclaimer of opinion. Answer (C) is incorrect. Lack of an expectation of the effectiveness of internal control may affect the nature, timing, and extent of substantive procedures but is not a basis for an adverse opinion. Ineffective internal control does not, by itself, indicate that the financial statements are not fairly presented.

16.6 Disclaimers of Opinion (AU-C 705)

25. Under which of the following circumstances might an auditor disclaim an opinion?

A. The financial statements contain a material misstatement.

B. Material related party transactions are disclosed in the financial statements.

C. There has been a material change between periods in the method of application of accounting principles.

D. The auditor is unable to obtain sufficient appropriate evidence to support management's assertions concerning an uncertainty.

Answer (D) is correct.

REQUIRED: The reason for a disclaimer.

DISCUSSION: Based on the audit evidence that is, or should be, available, the auditor assesses whether the audit evidence is sufficient to support managements' assertions about an uncertainty. When the auditor cannot obtain sufficient appropriate evidence, (s)he expresses a qualified opinion if the possible effects are material but not pervasive. If the possible effects are material and pervasive, (s)he disclaims an opinion.

Answer (A) is incorrect. The auditor should express a qualified or an adverse opinion when the statements contain a material misstatement. Answer (B) is incorrect. It is appropriate to disclose related party transactions. Answer (C) is incorrect. If the auditor concurs in the change, lack of consistency requires only an emphasis-of-matter paragraph.

26. Due to a scope limitation, an auditor disclaimed an opinion on the financial statements as a whole, but the auditor's report included a statement that the current asset portion of the entity's balance sheet was fairly stated. The inclusion of this statement is

A. Not appropriate because it may tend to overshadow the auditor's disclaimer of opinion.

B. Not appropriate because the auditor is prohibited from reporting on only one basic financial statement.

C. Appropriate, provided the auditor's responsibility section adequately describes the scope limitation.

D. Appropriate, provided the statement is in the basis for disclaimer of opinion paragraph preceding the disclaimer of opinion paragraph.

Answer (A) is correct.
REQUIRED: The suitability of a statement in an auditor's disclaimer about whether an element was stated fairly.
DISCUSSION: A piecemeal opinion is an expression of an opinion on a specific element of a financial statement when the auditor has disclaimed an opinion or expressed an adverse opinion on the financial statements as a whole. This type of assurance is inappropriate because it would contradict a disclaimer of opinion or an adverse opinion (AU-C 705).
Answer (B) is incorrect. The auditor may report on one basic financial statement and not on the others. Such a limited reporting engagement is acceptable. Answer (C) is incorrect. A piecemeal opinion is inappropriate in this circumstance. Answer (D) is incorrect. A piecemeal opinion is inappropriate in this circumstance.

27. A CPA concludes that the unaudited financial statements of an issuer on which the CPA is disclaiming an opinion are not in conformity with generally accepted accounting principles (GAAP) because management has failed to capitalize leases. The CPA suggests appropriate revisions to the financial statements, but management refuses to accept the CPA's suggestions. Under these circumstances, the CPA ordinarily would

A. Express limited assurance that no other material modifications should be made to the financial statements.

B. Restrict the distribution of the CPA's report to management and the entity's board of directors.

C. Issue a qualified opinion or adverse opinion depending on the materiality of the departure from GAAP.

D. Describe the nature of the departure from GAAP in the CPA's report and state the effects on the financial statements, if practicable.

Answer (D) is correct.
REQUIRED: The appropriate action when the CPA suggests revisions to the financial statements but management refuses to accept them.
DISCUSSION: PCAOB standards apply to audit engagements involving issuers. Under these standards, an accountant planning to disclaim an opinion may discover a material departure from GAAP. The accountant should disclose the departure in the disclaimer, including its effects if they have been determined by management or by the accountant's procedures.
Answer (A) is incorrect. A disclaimer should provide no assurance. Answer (B) is incorrect. The disclaimer should not be restricted in use. Answer (C) is incorrect. A disclaimer of opinion is necessary when the CPA has not audited the statements.

28. When an independent CPA assists in preparing the financial statements of an issuer but has not audited or reviewed them, the CPA should issue a disclaimer of opinion. In such situations, the CPA has no responsibility to apply any procedures beyond

A. Ascertaining whether the financial statements are in conformity with GAAP.

B. Determining whether management has elected to omit substantially all required disclosures.

C. Documenting that internal control is not being relied on.

D. Reading the financial statements for obvious material misstatements.

Answer (D) is correct.
REQUIRED: The procedure applied by a CPA to an issuer's financial statements that (s)he has assisted in preparing.
DISCUSSION: PCAOB standards apply to audit engagements involving issuers. Under the standards, the accountant has no responsibility to apply any procedures beyond reading the financial statements for obvious material misstatements. Any procedures applied should not be described.
Answer (A) is incorrect. An audit is conducted to determine whether the financial statements are in accordance with the applicable framework. Answer (B) is incorrect. The disclaimer is modified if the accountant concludes on the basis of facts known to him/her that the unaudited financial statements are not in accordance with the applicable framework. Lack of adequate disclosure is a misstatement. Answer (C) is incorrect. The CPA need not consider internal control or assess the risks of material misstatement and has no responsibility for documentation related to these activities.

29. In the first audit of a client, an auditor was not able to gather sufficient appropriate audit evidence about the consistent application of accounting principles between the current and the prior year, as well as the amounts of assets or liabilities at the beginning of the current year. This was due to the client's record retention policies. If the amounts in question could materially affect current operating results, the auditor most likely would

    A. Be unable to express an opinion on the current year's results of operations and cash flows.

    B. Express an adverse opinion on the financial statements because of a client-imposed scope limitation.

    C. Withdraw from the engagement and refuse to be associated with the financial statements.

    D. Specifically state that the financial statements are not comparable to the prior year due to an uncertainty.

Answer (A) is correct.
    REQUIRED: The effect on the report of an inability to obtain sufficient appropriate audit evidence.
    DISCUSSION: According to AU-C 705, in a first audit, the auditor is permitted to (1) express an unmodified opinion on the financial position of the entity and (2) disclaim an opinion on the results of operations and cash flows, if relevant. A disclaimer of opinion is expressed because the auditor is unable to obtain sufficient appropriate audit evidence. This inability may result from (1) circumstances not controlled by the entity, (2) circumstances related to the nature or timing of the auditor's work, or (3) limitations imposed by management.
    Answer (B) is incorrect. A disclaimer of opinion on the income statement and statement of cash flows is appropriate when the audit is not sufficient to permit the formation of an opinion. Answer (C) is incorrect. No ethical or other reason is given to justify withdrawal. Answer (D) is incorrect. Any potential lack of comparability is not due to an uncertainty.

30. If an issuer releases financial statements that purport to present its financial position and results of operations but omits the statement of cash flows, the auditor ordinarily will express a(n)

    A. Disclaimer of opinion.

    B. Qualified opinion.

    C. Review report.

    D. Unmodified opinion with a separate emphasis-of-matter paragraph.

Answer (B) is correct.
    REQUIRED: The opinion expressed when a client fails to present a statement of cash flows.
    DISCUSSION: An entity that reports financial position and results of operations should provide a statement of cash flows. Thus, the omission of the cash flow statement is normally a basis for modifying the opinion. If the statements fail to disclose required information, the auditor should provide the information in the report, if practicable. However, the auditor is not required to prepare a basic financial statement. Accordingly, (s)he should qualify the opinion and explain the reason in a basis for qualified opinion paragraph.
    Answer (A) is incorrect. The question concerns disclosure rather than an inability to obtain sufficient appropriate audit evidence. Answer (C) is incorrect. The engagement is an audit. Answer (D) is incorrect. A material omission of disclosures normally requires modification of the opinion.

31. Morris, CPA, suspects that a pervasive scheme of illegal bribes exists throughout the operations of Worldwide Import-Export, Inc., a new audit client. Morris notified the audit committee and Worldwide's legal counsel, but neither would assist Morris in determining whether the amounts involved were material to the financial statements or whether senior management was involved in the scheme. Under these circumstances, Morris most likely should

    A. Express an unmodified opinion with an other-matter paragraph.

    B. Disclaim an opinion on the financial statements.

    C. Express an adverse opinion on the financial statements.

    D. Issue a special report regarding the illegal bribes.

Answer (B) is correct.
    REQUIRED: The auditor action when (s)he cannot determine the amounts involved in material noncompliance with laws or regulations or the extent of management's involvement.
    DISCUSSION: Bribery is a violation of laws or governmental regulations. If the auditor is precluded by management or those charged with governance (e.g., the audit committee) from obtaining sufficient appropriate evidence to evaluate whether material noncompliance with laws or regulations has (or is likely to have) occurred, the auditor should disclaim an opinion or express a qualified opinion.
    Answer (A) is incorrect. An unmodified opinion is not justified. Answer (C) is incorrect. An adverse opinion is expressed only when the financial statements are not presented fairly. Answer (D) is incorrect. Special reports as defined in AU-C 805 are not issued on such topics.

Use the additional questions in Gleim **CPA Test Prep** to create Practice Exams that emulate Prometric!

16.7 PRACTICE TASK-BASED SIMULATIONS

DIRECTIONS

Note: If you believe you have encountered a software malfunction, report it to the test center staff immediately.

Navigation

To navigate from task to task, use the controls at the bottom of the screen. Click on the **Next** button to advance to the next task, or the **Previous** button to go to the previous task. To go directly to any task, click on its number.

If you would like a reminder to revisit a task, or want to indicate that you are finished with it, click on the reminder flag below the task number. To clear the flag, click on it again. Reminder flags are for your use only – they do not contribute to your score.

Tabs

In this part of the examination, you will be asked to complete various tasks. Every task has one or more **Work Tabs**. Some tasks have one or more **Information Tabs**, others may have none. Every task has a **Help** tab.

If a task has **Information Tabs**, you may use the information in them to complete your responses in the **Work Tabs**.

Corporate Gain and Basis	Authoritative Literature	Help
Work tab	Information tab	Help tab

Work Tabs:
- **Work Tabs** are identified with a pencil icon. This is where your responses are expected.
- Each task has one or more **Work Tabs**.
- **Work Tabs** contain directions for completing the task – be sure to read these directions carefully.
- The **Work Tab** name in the example above is for illustration only – yours will differ.
- You must complete all of the **Work Tabs** in each task to receive full credit.

Information Tabs:
- The Authoritative Literature will be provided in all tasks in the AUD, FAR, and REG sections for your reference.
- Your simulation may have one or more additional **Information Tabs**. Like the Authoritative Literature tabs, **Information Tabs** do not have a pencil icon.
- If your task has additional **Information Tabs**, go through each to familiarize yourself with the task content.

Help Tab:
- The **Help Tab** provides assistance with the exam software that is used in this task. For example, if the task is to compose a memorandum, **Help** will provide information about the word processor.

The Toolbar

The toolbar at the top of the screen shows the amount of time remaining for you to complete the tasks. In addition, the following tools are available. Note that only the **Exit** button is displayed when Directions are visible - the others will appear when you begin the tasks.

Click on these buttons to split or unsplit the screen. You can split the screen vertically or horizontally.

Click on this button to display the calculator; click on it again to hide the calculator. To move the calculator, click on the calculator title bar and drag the calculator to the desired location.

Click on this button to use the spreadsheet; click on it again to hide the spreadsheet. To move the spreadsheet, click on the the spreadsheet title bar and drag the spreadsheet to the desired location.

Click on this button to go on to the next part of the examination. You must complete all of the tasks to receive full credit. Once you click on **Exit** and confirm the action, you will NOT be able to return to this testlet.

Your firm has many clients and many audit reporting obligations. The audits of most clients result in an unmodified report. The following draft represents the report that you contemplate for your nonissuers.

Independent Auditor's Report

To: The Board of Directors

We have (1) the accompanying financial statements of X Company, which comprise the balance sheets as of December 31, 20X1 and 20X0, and the related statements of income, changes in stockholders' equity, and (2) for the years then ended, and the related notes to the financial statements.

Management's Responsibility for the Financial Statements

(3) is responsible for the preparation and fair presentation of these financial statements in accordance with accounting principles generally accepted in the United States of America; this includes the design, implementation, and maintenance of internal control relevant to the preparation and fair presentation of financial statements that are free from material misstatement, whether due to fraud or error.

Auditor's Responsibility

Our responsibility is to express an opinion on these financial statements based on our audits. We conducted our audits in accordance with (4) in the United States of America. Those standards require that we plan and perform the audit to obtain (5) about whether the financial statements are (6) misstatement.

An audit involves performing procedures to obtain audit evidence about the amounts and disclosures in the financial statements. The procedures selected depend on (7), including the assessment of the risks of material misstatement of the financial statements, whether due to fraud or error. In making those risk assessments, the auditor considers internal control relevant to the entity's preparation and fair presentation of the financial statements in order to design audit procedures that are (8) in the circumstances, but not for the purpose of expressing an opinion on the effectiveness of the entity's internal control. Accordingly, we express no such opinion. An audit also includes evaluating the appropriateness of accounting policies used and the reasonableness of significant accounting estimates made by (9), as well as evaluating the overall presentation of the financial statements.

We believe that the audit evidence we have obtained is (10) and appropriate to provide a basis for our audit opinion.

Opinion

In our opinion, the financial statements referred to above present fairly, (11), the financial position of X Company as of December 31, 20X1 and 20X0, and the results of its operations and its cash flows for the years then ended in accordance with (12) generally accepted in the United States of America.

Auditor's signature
Auditor's address
Date

-- Continued on next page --

| Auditor's Report | Authoritative Literature | Help | -- **Continued** |

Each of the rows in the table below corresponds to a number in the Independent Auditor's Report on the previous page. Indicate by checking the appropriate box which word or phrase should be included in the report.

Correct Word or Phrase	A	B
1. A) Examined B) Audited		
2. A) Cash flows B) Sources and uses of funds		
3. A) The auditor B) Management		
4. A) Auditing standards generally accepted B) Accounting principles generally accepted		
5. A) Reasonable assurance B) Absolute assurance		
6. A) Free from B) Free from material		
7. A) Management's expectations B) The auditor's judgment		
8. A) Necessary B) Appropriate		
9. A) Management B) The auditor		
10. A) Reasonable B) Sufficient		
11. A) In all respects B) In all material respects		
12. A) Auditing standards B) Accounting principles		

▽ = Reminder Directions 1 2 3 4 5 ◀ Previous Next ▶

| Opinion Choices | Authoritative Literature | Help |

For each of the conditions represented by the numbers in the table below, select from the list provided the opinion most likely to be expressed by the auditor. Each choice may be used once, more than once, or not at all.

Nature of Matter Giving Rise to the Potential Modification	Auditor's Professional Judgment About the Pervasiveness of the Effects or Possible Effects on the Financial Statements		
	Material but Not Pervasive	Material and Pervasive	Not Material or Pervasive
Financial statements are misstated	(1.)	(2.)	(3.)
Inability to obtain sufficient appropriate audit evidence	(4.)	(5.)	(6.)

Choices
A) Unmodified opinion
B) Qualified opinion
C) Adverse opinion
D) Disclaimer of opinion

▽ = Reminder Directions 1 2 3 4 5 ◀ Previous Next ▶

Types of Opinions	Authoritative Literature	Help

Each of the following is a phrase from a paragraph in an auditor's report. Assume that, except for the information indicated in the phrase, the report would have been a standard audit report. Select from the list provided the most likely report type for each phrase. Each choice may be used once, more than once, or not at all.

Phrase	Answer
1. "In our opinion, except for the omission of the statement of cash flows . . ."	
2. ". . . we have not been able to obtain . . ."	
3. "As discussed in Note 12, the Company changed its method of computing depreciation."	
4. "We are not independent with respect to XYZ company . . ."	
5. ". . . except for the effects of not capitalizing certain lease obligations as discussed in the preceding paragraph . . ."	
6. ". . . based on our audit and the report of other auditors . . ."	
7. ". . . for the year then ended were not audited by us . . ."	
8. ". . . raises substantial doubt about its ability to continue as a going concern."	
9. ". . . presents fairly, in all material respects . . ."	
10. "In our opinion, except for the effects of such adjustments, if any, . . ."	

Choices

A) Unmodified
B) Qualified
C) Adverse
D) Disclaimer

▼ = Reminder   Directions   1 2 [3] 4 5   ◄ Previous   Next ►

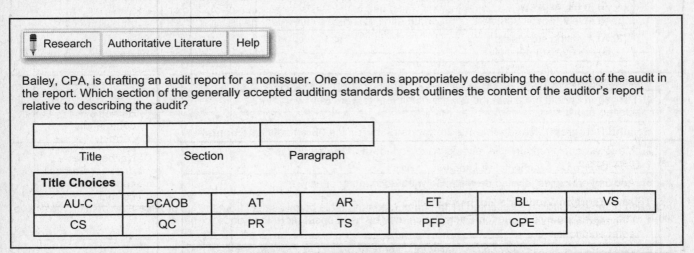

Research	Authoritative Literature	Help

Bailey, CPA, is drafting an audit report for a nonissuer. One concern is appropriately describing the conduct of the audit in the report. Which section of the generally accepted auditing standards best outlines the content of the auditor's report relative to describing the audit?

Title	Section	Paragraph

Title Choices

AU-C	PCAOB	AT	AR	ET	BL	VS
CS	QC	PR	TS	PFP	CPE	

▼ = Reminder   Directions   1 2 3 [4] 5   ◄ Previous   Next ►

| Disclaimers of Opinion | Authoritative Literature | Help |

Allen, a staff member, has drafted a disclaimer for ABC Company that Barnes, a partner, is evaluating. For each of the comments below, indicate whether Allen's draft is correct, Barnes's comment is correct, or neither Allen's draft nor Barnes's comment is correct. A choice may be used once, more than once, or not at all.

Allen's Disclaimer of Opinion Draft

We audited the accompanying financial statements of ABC Company, which comprise the balance sheet as of December 31, 20X1, and the related statements of income, changes in stockholders' equity, and cash flows for the year then ended, and the related notes to the financial statements.

Management's Responsibility for the Financial Statements

Management is responsible for the preparation and fair presentation of these financial statements in accordance with auditing principles generally accepted in the United States of America; this includes the design, implementation, and maintenance of internal control relevant to the preparation and fair presentation of financial statements that are free from material misstatement, whether due to fraud or error.

Auditor's Responsibility

Our responsibility is to express an opinion on management's assertions based on conducting the audit in accordance with auditing standards generally accepted in the United States of America. Because of the matters described in the Basis for Disclaimer of Opinion paragraph, we were not able to obtain sufficient appropriate audit evidence to provide a basis for an audit opinion.

Basis for Disclaimer of Opinion

We were not engaged as auditors of ABC Company until after December 31, 20X1, and, therefore, did not observe the counting of physical inventories at the beginning or end of the year. Also, we were not able to confirm receivables. We were able to satisfy ourselves by other auditing procedures concerning the inventory and receivables held at December 31, 20X1, which is stated in the balance sheet at $XXX and $XXX, respectively. As a result of these matters, we were unable to determine whether any adjustments might have been found necessary in respect to recorded or unrecorded inventories and accounts receivable and the elements making up the statements of income, changes in stockholders' equity, and cash flows.

Disclaimer of Opinion

Because of the significance of the matters described in the Basis for Disclaimer of Opinion paragraph, we have not been able to obtain sufficient appropriate audit evidence to provide a basis for an audit opinion. Accordingly, we express a qualified opinion on these financial statements.

Barnes's Comment	*Answer*
First Paragraph	
1. The report should state that the financial statements were reviewed, not audited.	
Second Paragraph (Management's Responsibility for the Financial Statements)	
2. "Management is responsible" should be replaced with "The auditor is responsible."	
3. "Auditing principles" should be replaced with "accounting principles."	
Third Paragraph (Auditor's Responsibility)	
4. "Management's assertions" should be replaced with "management's representations."	
5. "To obtain sufficient appropriate audit evidence" should be replaced with "to gain confidence sufficient."	
Fourth Paragraph (Basis for Disclaimer of Opinion)	
6. "We were able to satisfy" should be changed to "We were unable to satisfy."	
7. The paragraph should not include the dollar amounts related to the inventories and receivables.	
Fifth Paragraph (Disclaimer of Opinion)	
8. The word "qualified" should be changed to "adverse."	

Choices
A) Allen's draft is correct.
B) Barnes's comment is correct.
C) Neither Allen's draft nor Barnes's comment is correct.

Unofficial Answers

1. Auditor's Report (12 Gradable Items)

1.   B) Audited. The auditor's report uses the term audited.

2.   A) Cash flows. A set of financial statements include a statement of cash flows.

3.   B) Management. The financial statements are the responsibility of management.

4.   A) Auditing standards generally accepted. The audit is conducted in accordance with U.S. GAAS.

5.   A) Reasonable assurance. Reasonable, not absolute, assurance should be obtained by the auditor.

6.   B) Free from material. The financial statements are expected to be free from material misstatement. The auditor need not be concerned with immaterial matters.

7.   B) The auditor's judgment. The procedures are selected by the auditor.

8.   B) Appropriate. The procedures are appropriate in the circumstances.

9.   A) Management. Management is responsible for the estimates and other assertions in the financial statements.

10.   B) Sufficient. The auditor should obtain sufficient appropriate evidence.

11.   B) In all material respects. The opinion that the financial statements are presented fairly is subject to the limitation of materiality.

12.   B) Accounting principles. The financial statements should be in accordance with U.S. GAAP.

2. Opinion Choices (6 Gradable Items)

1.   B) Qualified opinion. If the misstatement is material but not pervasive, the auditor expresses a qualified opinion.

2.   C) Adverse opinion. If the misstatement is material and pervasive, the auditor expresses an adverse opinion.

3.   A) Unmodified opinion. If the misstatement is neither material nor pervasive, the auditor expresses an unmodified opinion.

4.   B) Qualified opinion. If the potential effects on the financial statements of an inability to obtain sufficient appropriate audit evidence is material but not pervasive, the auditor expresses a qualified opinion.

5.   D) Disclaimer of opinion. If the potential effects on the financial statements of an inability to obtain sufficient appropriate audit evidence are material and pervasive, the auditor disclaims an opinion.

6.   A) Unmodified opinion. If the potential effects on the financial statements of an inability to obtain sufficient appropriate audit evidence are neither material nor pervasive, the auditor expresses an unmodified opinion.

3. Types of Opinions (10 Gradable Items)

1.   B) Qualified. A qualified report uses the language "except for" or "with the exception of."

2.   D) Disclaimer. A scope limitation that does not allow the auditor to collect sufficient appropriate evidence results in a disclaimer.

3.   A) Unmodified. Reference to a change in accounting principle is in an emphasis-of-matter paragraph following the paragraph stating an unmodified opinion.

4.   D) Disclaimer. Lack of independence by the auditor results in a disclaimer of opinion.

5.   B) Qualified. A qualified opinion uses the language "except for" or "with the exception of."

6.   A) Unmodified. A reference to other auditors is a division of responsibility that does not affect the opinion on the financial statements.

7.   D) Disclaimer. Financial statements that were not audited require a disclaimer of opinion.

8.   A) Unmodified. Reference to a going concern issue is made in an emphasis-of-matter paragraph following the paragraph stating an unmodified opinion.

9.   A) Unmodified. An unmodified opinion states that the financial statements are presented fairly.

10.   B) Qualified. A qualified report uses the language "except for" or "with the exception of."

4. Research (1 Gradable Item)

Answer: 700.32

AU-C Section 700 -- *Forming an Opinion and Reporting on Financial Statements*

.32 The auditor's report should describe an audit by stating that

    a.   an audit involves performing procedures to obtain audit evidence about the amounts and disclosures in the financial statements.

    b.   the procedures selected depend on the auditor's judgment, including the assessment of the risks of material misstatement of the financial statements, whether due to fraud or error. In making those risk assessments, the auditor considers internal control relevant to the entity's preparation and fair presentation of the financial statements in order to design audit procedures that are appropriate in the circumstances but not for the purpose of expressing an opinion on the effectiveness of the entity's internal control, and accordingly, no such opinion is expressed.

    c.   an audit also includes evaluating the appropriateness of the accounting policies used and the reasonableness of significant accounting estimates made by management, as well as the overall presentation of the financial statements.

In circumstances when the auditor also has a responsibility to express an opinion on the effectiveness of internal control in conjunction with the audit of the financial statements, the auditor should omit the phrase required in paragraph .32b that the auditor's consideration of internal control is not for the purpose of expressing an opinion on the effectiveness of internal control, and accordingly, no such opinion is expressed.

5. Disclaimers of Opinion (8 Gradable Items)

1.   <u>C) Neither Allen's draft nor Barnes's comment is correct.</u> The draft should state "We were engaged to audit . . ."

2.   <u>A) Allen's draft is correct.</u> Management is responsible for the preparation and fair presentation of the financial statements.

3.   <u>B) Barnes's comment is correct.</u> The financial statements are prepared in accordance with U.S. GAAP or an other applicable reporting framework.

4.   <u>C) Neither Allen's draft nor Barnes's comment is correct.</u> The report should state "Our responsibility is to express an opinion on these financial statements based on conducting the audit in accordance with auditing standards generally accepted in the United States of America."

5.   <u>A) Allen's draft is correct.</u> The report should state "Because of the matters described in the Basis for Disclaimer of Opinion paragraph, we were not able to obtain sufficient appropriate audit evidence to provide a basis for an audit opinion."

6.   <u>B) Barnes's comment is correct.</u> The draft should indicate that the auditor was unable to collect sufficient appropriate evidence to express an opinion.

7.   <u>A) Allen's draft is correct.</u> The disclaimer should provide for a measure of the pervasiveness of the lack of sufficient appropriate evidence either in dollar amounts or percentages.

8.   <u>C) Neither Allen's draft nor Barnes's comment is correct.</u> The statement should be "Accordingly, we do not express an opinion on these financial statements."

Gleim Simulation Grading

Task	Correct Responses		Gradable Items		Score per Task
1	____	÷	12	=	____
2	____	÷	6	=	____
3	____	÷	10	=	____
4 (Research)	____	÷	1	=	____
5	____	÷	8	=	____

	Total of Scores per Task	____
÷	Total Number of Tasks	5
	Total Score	____ %

Use **CPA Gleim Online** and **Simulation Wizard** to practice more task-based simulations in a realistic environment.

STUDY UNIT SEVENTEEN
REPORTS -- OTHER MODIFICATIONS

(13 pages of outline)

This study unit covers additional language modifying the auditor's report. These modifications normally do not affect the auditor's opinion on the financial statements. They permit the users of the financial statements and readers of the auditor's report to better understand the responsibility assumed by the auditor. They also provide information about the client's financial statements that the auditor considers important. The following summarizes these modifications:

1.   A group auditor's opinion is based in part on the report of a component auditor -- Modify the auditor's responsibility section and the opinion paragraph.

2.   A material accounting change affects consistency -- Add an emphasis-of-matter paragraph.

3.   Substantial doubt exists about the entity's ability to continue as a going concern -- Add an emphasis-of-matter paragraph.

4.   The auditor changes the opinion for a prior period when reporting on current statements in comparative form -- Add an emphasis-of-matter or other-matter paragraph.

5.   Predecessor auditor's report for a prior period is not presented when reporting on current financial statements in comparative form -- Add an other-matter paragraph.

6.   An auditor needs to draw users' attention by an additional communication -- Add an emphasis-of-matter or other-matter paragraph.

17.1 GROUP AUDITS AND COMPONENT AUDITORS (AU-C 600)

1.   **Nature of Group Audits**

   a.   Generally accepted auditing standards (GAAS) apply to an audit of a group of financial statements. In some cases, part of the group audit is performed by a component auditor that is not part of the group engagement team.

      1)   A **component** is an entity or business activity for which group or component management prepares financial information that is required by the applicable financial reporting framework to be included in the group financial statements.

      2)   A **component auditor** performs work on the financial information that will be used as audit evidence for the group audit.

      3)   A component auditor may be a member of the group engagement partner's firm, a network firm of the group engagement partner's firm, or another autonomous firm.

   b.   The **group engagement partner**

      1)   Is responsible for the group engagement, its performance, and the report on the group statements.

    2)   Is responsible for deciding, individually for each component, either to

        a)   **Assume responsibility** for, and thus be required to be involved in, the work of a component auditor to the extent that work relates to the expression of an opinion on the group financial statements or

        b)   **Not assume responsibility** for, and accordingly refer to, the audit of a component auditor in the auditor's report on the group financial statements.

    3)   Is required to be satisfied that those performing the group audit engagement, including component auditors, collectively possess the **appropriate competence and capabilities**.

    4)   Is responsible for the direction, supervision, and performance of the group audit engagement performed by the engagement team.

    5)   Should determine whether sufficient appropriate audit evidence can reasonably be expected to be obtained regarding the consolidation process (e.g., for investments accounted for under the equity method).

c.   This standard may be applied and adapted as necessary when an auditor involves other auditors in the audit of financial statements that are **not group** financial statements.

    1)   For example, an auditor may involve another auditor to observe the inventory count or inspect physical fixed assets at a remote location.

d.   If the auditor decides to act as the auditor of the group financial statements, the **objectives** are to

    1)   Obtain **sufficient appropriate audit evidence** regarding the financial information of the components and the consolidation process to express an opinion about whether the group statements are prepared, in all material respects, in accordance with the applicable financial reporting framework (typically U.S. GAAP),

    2)   **Communicate** clearly with component auditors, and

    3)   Determine **whether to refer** to the audit of a component auditor in the auditor's report on the group financial statements.

e.   If the auditor concludes it is **not** possible to serve as the group auditor because of restrictions imposed by management, the auditor should

    1)   Not accept a new engagement or
    2)   Withdraw from a continuing engagement.

f.   The group engagement team should establish an overall **group audit strategy** and develop a **group audit plan**. The strategy and plan should be approved by the group engagement partner.

    1)   The team should assess (a) the extent to which it will use the work of component auditors and (b) whether the group audit report will refer to the audit of a component auditor.

    2)   The strategy and plan should recognize that detection risk for the group audit includes the detection risk of component auditors.

g.   The group engagement team should obtain an understanding of the components that is sufficient to

    1)   Confirm or revise its initial identification of components that are likely to be significant.

    2)   Assess the risks of material misstatement of the group financial statements, whether due to fraud or error.

     h. **Materiality** should be established by the group engagement team.

          1) Component materiality should be lower than materiality for the group statements as a whole. The purpose is to reduce the risk that the sum of uncorrected and undetected misstatements in the group statements is greater than materiality for the group statements as a whole.

2. **Reference to a Component Auditor**

     a. The group engagement team should obtain an understanding of the component auditor's professional competence and compliance with ethical requirements (especially independence).

     b. The group auditor's report should **not refer** to the audit of a component auditor unless the following requirements are met:

          1) The component auditor has audited the statements of the component in accordance with GAAS or auditing standards of the PCAOB (if required by law or regulation).

               a) However, the component auditor's report may not have stated that the component audit was in accordance with GAAS or PCAOB standards. In this case, if the group auditor determines that the component auditor performed additional procedures to comply with GAAS, reference may be made to the component auditor. The report should indicate

                    i) The set of standards used by the component auditor and
                    ii) That additional procedures were performed.

          2) The component auditor has issued an auditor's report that is not restricted as to use.

     c. When the group engagement partner decides to refer to the audit of a component auditor, the report on the group statements should clearly indicate that the component was not audited by the group auditor but by the component auditor.

          1) The magnitude of the portion of the statements audited by the component auditor (by dollar amounts or percentages of an appropriate criterion, such as total assets or revenues) should be included.

     d. If certain conditions are met, the group auditor's report may refer to the component auditor even if the reporting frameworks of the component and the group statements differ. Thus, the group auditor's report should disclose   .

          1) The framework used by the component and
          2) That responsibility is taken for evaluating the adjustments needed to convert from one framework to another.

ISA Difference

The ISAs do not permit the auditor's report on group financial statements to refer to a component auditor unless required by law or regulation.

---

3. **No Reference to a Component Auditor**

     a. The group auditor assumes responsibility for the work of the component auditor by not making reference.

     b. When responsibility is assumed, the type of work performed on the financial information of a component depends on whether the component is significant.

          1) A **significant component** is

               a) Of individual financial significance to the group or
               b) Likely to include significant risks of material misstatement (RMMs) of the group statements.

2) When the component has individual financial significance, the group engagement team, or a component auditor on its behalf, audits the financial information, using appropriate component materiality.

    a) When significance depends on RMMs, the response may be (1) an audit of the financial information or one or more balances, transaction classes, or disclosures or (2) the performance of specified audit procedures.

3) When the group auditor assumes responsibility for components that are **not significant**, the group engagement team should perform **analytical procedures** at the group level.

c. In summary, when the auditor of the group financial statements assumes responsibility for the work of a component auditor, the component auditor is not referred to in the report on the group audit. To do so may cause a reader to misinterpret the degree of responsibility being assumed.

4. **Other Issues**

a. A reference in the auditor's report on the group financial statements to a component auditor **is not a qualification** of the opinion. Rather, it is intended to communicate that

1) The auditor of the group financial statements is not assuming responsibility for the work of the component auditor and

2) The component auditor is the source of the audit evidence with respect to those components for which the reference is made.

b. Regardless of whether the component auditor is referred to in the report, the group engagement partner is responsible for the overall group audit opinion.

c. The component auditor's report may include a modified opinion, an emphasis-of-matter paragraph, or an other-matter paragraph that does not affect the report on the group statements. If the component auditor's report is not presented, the group auditor need not refer to those paragraphs in the auditor's report.

1) If the component auditor's report is presented, the group auditor may refer to those paragraphs and their disposition.

d. The group engagement team should communicate its requirements to the component auditor clearly, effectively, and on a timely basis.

1) The group engagement team should communicate to group management (a) fraud and (b) material weaknesses and significant deficiencies in internal control.

    a) It should also request that group management communicate to component management significant matters discovered during the group audit that may affect the component's statements.

e. A component auditor may not meet the independence requirements that are relevant to the group audit. In this case, the group engagement team should obtain sufficient appropriate audit evidence relating to the financial information of the component without (1) referring to the audit of the component auditor in the auditor's report or (2) using that auditor's work.

5. **Report Making Reference**

    a. The following is an example of the two paragraphs from the auditor's report that are changed by the reference to a component auditor.

EXAMPLE

Auditor's Responsibility

Our responsibility is to express an opinion on these consolidated financial statements based on our audits. We did not audit the financial statements of B Company, a wholly-owned subsidiary, which statements reflect total assets constituting 20 percent and 22 percent, respectively, of consolidated total assets at December 31, 20X1 and 20X0, and total revenues constituting 18 percent and 20 percent, respectively, of consolidated total revenues for the years then ended. Those statements were audited by other auditors, whose report has been furnished to us, and our opinion, insofar as it relates to the amounts included for B Company, is based solely on the report of the other auditors. We conducted our audits in accordance with auditing standards generally accepted in the United States of America. Those standards require that we plan and perform the audit to obtain reasonable assurance about whether the consolidated financial statements are free from material misstatement.

[The remainder of the Auditor's Responsibility section is unchanged.]

Opinion

In our opinion, based on our audit and the report of the other auditors, the consolidated financial statements referred to above present fairly, in all material respects, the financial position of ABC Company and its subsidiaries as of December 31, 20X1 and 20X0, and the results of their operations and their cash flows for the years then ended in accordance with accounting principles generally accepted in the United States of America.

Stop and review! You have completed the outline for this subunit. Study multiple-choice questions 1 through 5 beginning on page 537.

17.2 CONSISTENCY OF FINANCIAL STATEMENTS (AU-C 708 AND AS NO. 6)

1. **Evaluation of Consistency**

    a. The auditor should evaluate whether the comparability of the financial statements between or among periods has been materially affected by

        1) A change in accounting principle or

        2) Adjustments to correct a material misstatement in previously issued financial statements.

    b. If the auditor's report does not state otherwise, it implies that comparability between or among periods has not been materially affected by such changes or corrections.

    c. The periods covered in the auditor's evaluation of consistency depend on the periods covered by the auditor's opinion.

        1) For initial audits, the auditor should obtain sufficient appropriate audit evidence about whether the accounting policies reflected in the opening balances have been consistently applied in the current period's financial statements.

        2) When the auditor reports only on the current period, (s)he should evaluate whether the current-period statements are consistent with those of the preceding period, regardless of whether they are presented.

        3) When the auditor's opinion covers two or more periods, (s)he should evaluate consistency between or among such periods.

        4) The auditor also evaluates the consistency of the earliest period covered by the opinion with the period preceding it, if such prior period is presented.

            a) For example, assume that an entity presents comparative statements for 3 years and has a change in auditors. In the current year, the auditor evaluates consistency between the year on which (s)he reports and the immediately preceding year. In the next year, the auditor evaluates consistency between the 2 years on which (s)he reports, and between those years and the earliest year presented.

     5)   The auditor also should evaluate whether the statements for the periods reported on are consistent with previously issued financial statements for the relevant periods.

2.   **Change in Accounting Principle**

    a.   A change in principle is a change from one principle in accordance with the applicable financial reporting framework to another such principle when (1) two or more principles apply or (2) the principle used previously is no longer in accordance with the framework.

    b.   A change in the method of applying a principle also is a change in principle.

    c.   A change from a principle that is not in accordance with the applicable framework to one that is in accordance is a **correction of a misstatement**.

    d.   The applicable framework usually states the method of accounting for the effects of a change in principle and the related disclosures. The auditor should evaluate a change in principle to determine whether

        1)   The new principle and the method of accounting for the effect of the change are in accordance with the applicable framework,

        2)   The disclosures related to the change are adequate, and

        3)   The entity has justified that the alternative principle is preferable.

    e.   The issuance of an accounting pronouncement that (1) requires use of a new principle, (2) interprets an existing principle, (3) expresses a preference for a principle, or (4) rejects a specific principle is **sufficient justification** for a change if it is in accordance with the applicable framework.

    f.   If the criteria stated in 2.d. above are met, and the change in principle is material, the auditor should include an **emphasis-of-matter** paragraph in the report. This paragraph

        1)   Describes the change,

        2)   Refers to the entity's disclosures, and

        3)   Follows the opinion paragraph.

    g.   If the criteria stated in 2.d. are not met, the auditor evaluates whether the change results in a material misstatement. If it does, the opinion should be modified.

    h.   If the change is expected to have a material effect only in later periods, the current-period auditor's report need not recognize the change.

    i.   An emphasis-of-matter paragraph is included in the auditor's report for the period of change and in later periods until the new principle is applied in all periods presented.

    j.   The auditor should evaluate and report on a change in **accounting estimate** that is inseparable from the effect of a related change in principle like other changes in principle.

        1)   An example is a change in a method of depreciation, amortization, or depletion of a long-lived nonfinancial asset.

    k.   A change in the **reporting entity** results in statements that are effectively those of a different entity.

        1)   The auditor should recognize the change by including an emphasis-of-matter paragraph in the report **unless** the change results from a transaction or event.

            a)   A transaction or event is the creation, cessation, or complete or partial purchase or disposition of a subsidiary or other business unit. Thus, **no** emphasis-of-matter paragraph is required.

        2)   Changes in the reporting entity not from a transaction or event include (a) presenting consolidated or combined statements in place of the statements of individual entities, (b) changing the subsidiaries included in consolidated statements, or (c) changing the entities included in combined statements. Thus, an emphasis-of-matter paragraph **is** required.

      l.   If an entity's statements contain an investment accounted for by the equity method, the auditor's evaluation of consistency considers the investee.

           1)   If the investee makes a change in principle that is material to the investor, the auditor's report should include an emphasis-of-matter paragraph.

3.   **Correction of a Material Misstatement in Previously Issued Financial Statements**

     a.   This correction should be recognized in the auditor's report by including an emphasis-of-matter paragraph.

     b.   The paragraph is included only in the period when the statements are restated.

     c.   Certain disclosures are required relating to such misstatements in previously issued statements. If the disclosures are not adequate, the auditor may need to modify the opinion.

     d.   Correction of a material misstatement also includes a change from a principle not in accordance with the applicable framework to one that is.

4.   **Change in Classification**

     a.   Changes in classification, for example, changing "Cash in Bank" to "Cash," in previously issued statements do not require recognition in the auditor's report unless the change is

         1)   The correction of a material misstatement or
         2)   A change in principle.

     b.   For example, certain reclassifications, such as debt from long term to short term or cash flows from operating activities to financing activities, might occur because those items were incorrectly classified. In such situations, the reclassification also is the correction of a misstatement and requires an emphasis-of-matter paragraph.

5.   **Example of Reporting on the Change in Accounting Principle**

     a.   The following is an emphasis-of-matter paragraph that follows an opinion paragraph for a change in principle.

EXAMPLE -- Paragraph Added to Auditor's Report for a Change in Principle

Emphasis of Matter

As discussed in Note X to the financial statements, the Company changed its method of computing depreciation in Year 3. Our opinion is not modified with respect to this matter.

Stop and review! You have completed the outline for this subunit. Study multiple-choice questions 6 through 12 beginning on page 539.

17.3 UNCERTAINTIES AND GOING CONCERN (AU-C 570 AND AU-C 705)

1.   **Uncertainties**

     a.   Conclusive audit evidence about the outcome of uncertainties is not expected to exist at the date of the audit. Accordingly, management is responsible for

         1)   Estimating the effect of future events on the financial statements or
         2)   Determining that a reasonable estimate is not possible and making required disclosures.

     b.   When the auditor is able to conclude that sufficient appropriate audit evidence supports management's assertions about an uncertainty and its presentation and disclosure, an **unmodified** opinion is ordinarily appropriate, with no requirement to add an emphasis-of-matter paragraph.

2.   **Going-Concern Issues**

    a.   If the auditor concludes that substantial doubt exists about an entity's ability to continue as a going concern for a reasonable period (not exceeding 1 year), an **emphasis-of-matter** paragraph should be added following the opinion paragraph.

        1)   The auditor's emphasis-of-matter paragraph should include the terms **substantial doubt** and **going concern**.

        2)   In the emphasis-of-matter paragraph, the auditor should not use conditional language, such as, "If the company is unable to obtain refinancing, there may be substantial doubt about the company's ability to continue as a going concern."

    b.   By itself, the substantial doubt ordinarily does not warrant a modified opinion, but the auditor is not precluded from disclaiming an opinion.

    c.   The following is an example of an emphasis-of-matter paragraph.

EXAMPLE -- Paragraph Added to Auditor's Report Expressing Substantial Doubt about Going Concern

Emphasis of Matter

The accompanying financial statements have been prepared assuming that the Company will continue as a going concern. As discussed in Note X to the financial statements, the Company has suffered recurring losses from operations and has a net capital deficiency that raises substantial doubt about its ability to continue as a going concern. Management's plans in regard to these matters are also described in Note X. The financial statements do not include any adjustments that might result from the outcome of this uncertainty.

---

    d.   If disclosures are inadequate, the misstatement may result in a qualified or an adverse opinion.

    e.   Substantial doubt arising in the current period does not imply that such doubt existed in the prior period and should not affect the report on the prior-period statements.

        1)   If substantial doubt existed at the date of prior-period statements and that doubt has been removed in the current period, the emphasis-of-matter paragraph in the report for the prior period should not be repeated.

Stop and review! You have completed the outline for this subunit. Study multiple-choice questions 13 through 22 beginning on page 541.

17.4 COMPARATIVE FINANCIAL STATEMENTS (AU-C 700)

1.   **General Considerations**

    a.   A continuing auditor should **update** the report for the one or more prior periods presented in comparative form.

        1)   An updated report is not a reissuance of a previous report.

        2)   Updated reports consider information from the audit of the current-period statements and are issued with the report on those statements and dated as of the latest audit.

    b.   The auditor's report

        1)   Should refer to each period for which financial statements are presented and on which an audit opinion is expressed.

        2)   Should not be dated earlier than the date on which the auditor has obtained sufficient appropriate audit evidence on which to support the opinion for the most recent audit.

    c.   If audit firms merge and the new firm becomes the auditor of a former client of one of the merged firms, the new firm may accept responsibility as a continuing auditor.

        1)   The new firm's report may indicate that a merger took place and name the firm that was merged with it.

        2)   If the new firm does not express an opinion on the prior statements, the guidance for the reissuance of reports by a predecessor auditor applies.

      d.   The report applies to individual financial statements, so an auditor may express a qualified or an adverse opinion, disclaim an opinion, or include an emphasis-of-matter or other-matter paragraph for one or more statements for one or more periods while issuing a different report on the other statements.

      e.   During the audit, the auditor **should be alert** for circumstances or events affecting the **prior-period** financial statements presented and should consider their effects when updating the report.

2. **Comparative Information**

      a.   An auditor need not report on comparative information, which consists of condensed statements or summarized prior-period information.

          1)   For example, state and local governmental units and not-for-profit entities often present total-all-funds information rather than information by individual funds.

          2)   If the client requests an opinion on the prior period(s), the auditor should consider whether the information contains sufficient detail for a fair presentation.

          3)   To avoid modification of the report, additional columns or separate detail by fund will usually be needed.

3. **Opinion on Prior-Period Financial Statements Different from the Opinion Previously Issued**

      a.   An auditor may become aware of circumstances or events affecting the statements of a prior period and should consider them when updating the report.

          1)   For example, if the opinion was modified because of a material misstatement and the statements are revised in the current period, the updated report should express an unmodified opinion.

          2)   An emphasis-of-matter or other-matter paragraph should disclose

              a)   All substantive reasons for the different opinion,
              b)   The date of the previous report,
               c)   The type of opinion previously expressed, and
              d)   That the updated opinion differs from the previous opinion.

          3)   The introductory paragraph, management's responsibility paragraph, and auditor's responsibility section are not modified in the updated report.

4. **Report of Predecessor Auditor**

      a.   A predecessor auditor ordinarily can **reissue** the report for a prior period at the request of the former client if (1) satisfactory arrangements are made to perform this service and (2) certain procedures are performed.

      b.   Before reissuing the report, the predecessor auditor should consider whether the report is still appropriate in light of the current form or presentation of the prior-period statements and any subsequent events. The predecessor auditor should

          1)   Read the current-period statements.

          2)   Compare the prior-period statements reported on with those to be presented comparatively.

          3)   Obtain a representation letter from the auditor stating whether the audit revealed matters that might materially affect, or require disclosure in, the statements reported on by the predecessor auditor.

          4)   Obtain a representation letter from management stating whether (a) any new information has caused management to believe that previous representations should be modified, and (b) any events have occurred after the date of the latest prior-period statements reported on by the predecessor auditor that would require adjustment of, or disclosure in, those financial statements.

   c.   Because a predecessor auditor's knowledge of the former client is limited, (s)he should use the **date of the previous report** to avoid implications that (s)he has examined any records, transactions, or events after that date.

      1)   If the report is revised or the statements are restated, the report should be dual-dated with a second date relating to those items changed or revised.

   d.   In certain circumstances, a predecessor auditor's report may not be reissued (e.g., because the CPA is no longer in public practice).

      1)   When the predecessor auditor's report is **not** presented, the auditor's report should include an **other-matter** paragraph that states the following:

         a)   The prior-period statements were audited by a predecessor auditor. (But the auditor should not name the predecessor auditor unless the predecessor's practice was acquired by, or merged with, that of the auditor.)

         b)   The date of the predecessor's report.

         c)   The type of opinion expressed by the predecessor and the reasons for any modification.

         d)   The nature of any emphasis-of-matter or other-matter paragraph in the predecessor's report.

      2)   An auditor's report when the predecessor's report is not reissued includes an other-matter paragraph similar to the example that follows.

EXAMPLE -- Other-Matter Paragraph Added to Auditor's Report to Reference Predecessor's Report

Other Matter

The financial statements of ABC Company as of December 31, Year 1, were audited by other auditors whose report dated March 31, Year 2, expressed an unmodified opinion on those statements.

---

      3)   If the predecessor's report contained an emphasis-of-matter paragraph, the following is an example of an other-matter paragraph.

EXAMPLE -- Other-Matter Paragraph of Auditor's Report to Reference Predecessor's Modified Report

Other Matter

The financial statements of ABC Company as of December 31, Year 1, were audited by other auditors whose report on those statements, dated March 1, Year 2, included an emphasis-of-matter paragraph that described the change in the Company's method of computing depreciation discussed in Note X to the financial statements.

---

      4)   The statements audited by a predecessor auditor whose report is not reissued may have been restated. An auditor who has audited the adjustments includes an other-matter paragraph indicating that a predecessor reported on them before restatement. Also, if the auditor becomes satisfied as to the propriety of the restatement, (s)he also may report on the restatement.

EXAMPLE -- Other-Matter Paragraph of Auditor's Report to Reference Prior Financial Statements that Have Been Restated

Other Matter

(paragraph stating information about the predecessor auditor's report)

As part of our audit of the Year 2 financial statements, we also audited the adjustments described in Note X that were applied to restate the Year 1 financial statements. In our opinion, such adjustments are appropriate and have been properly applied. We were not engaged to audit, review, or apply any procedures to the Year 1 financial statements of the Company other than with respect to the adjustments, and, accordingly, we do not express an opinion or any other form of assurance on the Year 1 financial statements as a whole.

---

5.   **Prior-Period Financial Statements Not Audited**

    a.   Current-period statements may be audited and presented in comparative form with compiled or reviewed financial statements for the prior period. If the report on the prior period is not reissued, the auditor should include an **other-matter paragraph** in the current-period auditor's report that includes the following:

        1)   The service performed in the prior period

        2)   The date of the report on that service

        3)   A description of any material modifications noted in that report

        4)   A statement that the service was less in scope than an audit and does not provide a basis for the expression of an opinion on the financial statements

    b.   If the prior-period financial statements were not audited, reviewed, or compiled, the financial statements should be clearly marked to indicate their status. Moreover, the auditor's report should include an other-matter paragraph to indicate that (1) the auditor has not audited, reviewed, or compiled the prior-period financial statements, and (2) the auditor assumes no responsibility for them.

Stop and review! You have completed the outline for this subunit. Study multiple-choice questions 23 through 28 beginning on page 544.

17.5 EMPHASIS-OF-MATTER AND OTHER-MATTER PARAGRAPHS (AU-C 706)

Background
Prior auditing standards referred to emphasis-of-matter and other-matter paragraphs as simply "explanatory paragraphs." Current PCAOB Interim Auditing Standards maintain the term "explanatory paragraph." The use and content of the paragraph is the same for both the AICPA and the PCAOB report, but the paragraph in the PCAOB audit report for issuers would not be titled.

1.   An **emphasis-of-matter** paragraph is used in the auditor's report to draw users' attention to a matter appropriately presented or disclosed in the financial statements that is of such importance that it is fundamental to users' understanding of the financial statements.

    a.   When the auditor includes an emphasis-of-matter paragraph in the auditor's report, the auditor should do all of the following:

        1)   Include it immediately after the opinion paragraph in the auditor's report

        2)   Use the heading **Emphasis of Matter** or another appropriate heading

        3)   Include in the paragraph a clear reference to the matter being emphasized and to where relevant disclosures that fully describe the matter can be found in the financial statements

        4)   Indicate that the auditor's opinion is not modified with respect to the matter emphasized

    b.   Certain auditing standards require the auditor to include an emphasis-of-matter paragraph. These sections are covered in various study units and include the following:

        1)   AU-C 560, *Subsequent Events and Subsequently Discovered Facts* -- If the auditor's opinion on revised financial statements changes after the original report date, the new report should include either an emphasis-of-matter or other-matter paragraph.

        2)   AU-C 570, *The Auditor's Consideration of an Entity's Ability to Continue as a Going Concern* -- If the auditor has substantial doubt about an entity's ability to continue as a going concern, an emphasis-of-matter paragraph should be included in the report.

    3)   AU-C 708, *Consistency of Financial Statements* -- A material change in principle or the correction of a material misstatement in previously issued statements requires the auditor to include an emphasis-of-matter paragraph in the report.

    4)   AU-C 800, *Special Considerations—Audits of Financial Statements Prepared in Accordance With Special Purpose Frameworks* -- Reports on special purpose financial statements require the auditor to add an emphasis-of-matter paragraph to the report.

  c.   In addition to the required emphasis-of-matter paragraphs, the following are examples of circumstances when the auditor may consider it necessary to include an emphasis-of-matter paragraph:

    1)   An uncertainty relating to the future outcome of unusually important litigation or regulatory action

    2)   A major catastrophe that has had, or continues to have, a significant effect on the entity's financial position

    3)   Significant transactions with related parties

    4)   Unusually important subsequent events

2.   An **other-matter** paragraph is used in the auditor's report to draw users' attention to any matter not presented or disclosed in the financial statements that is relevant to users' understanding of the auditor's audit, responsibilities, or report.

  a.   The paragraph should be titled **Other Matter** or another appropriate heading.

    1)   The auditor normally includes this paragraph immediately after the opinion paragraph and any emphasis-of-matter paragraph.

    2)   However, conditions may warrant placing the other-matter paragraph elsewhere in the auditor's report. For example, the content of the other-matter paragraph may be relevant to the section of the report addressing other legal and regulatory requirements.

  b.   Certain auditing standards require the auditor to include an other-matter paragraph. These sections are covered in various study units and include the following:

    1)   AU-C 560, *Subsequent Events and Subsequently Discovered Facts* -- If the auditor's opinion on revised financial statements changes after the original report date, the new report should include either an emphasis-of-matter or other-matter paragraph.

    2)   AU-C 700, *Forming an Opinion and Reporting on Financial Statements* -- If prior-period financial statements presented in comparative form were (a) audited by a predecessor auditor or (b) reviewed or compiled and the report is not reissued, the auditor should include an other-matter paragraph.

    3)   AU-C 720, *Other Information in Documents Containing Audited Financial Statements* -- Material inconsistencies in the other information presented along with audited financial statements require the auditor to include an other-matter paragraph.

    4)   AU-C 725, *Supplementary Information in Relation to the Financial Statements as a Whole* -- The auditor may report on the supplementary information in an other-matter paragraph or in a separate report.

    5)   AU-C 730, *Required Supplementary Information* -- The auditor reports on the required supplementary information in an other-matter paragraph in the report.

    6)   AU-C 800, *Special Considerations—Audits of Financial Statements Prepared in Accordance With Special Purpose Frameworks* -- If a report on such financial statements restricts the use of the report, it should contain an other-matter paragraph.

7) AU-C 806, *Reporting on Compliance With Aspects of Contractual Agreements or Regulatory Requirements in Connection With Audited Financial Statements* -- If a report on compliance is included in the auditor's report on the financial statements, the compliance report should be presented in an other-matter paragraph.

c. An auditor who expects to include an emphasis-of-matter or other-matter paragraph in the report should communicate with those charged with governance regarding this expectation and the proposed wording of any paragraph.

3. **Summary of Paragraphs that Draw Attention to Certain Matters**

	Emphasis of Matter	Other Matter
Relation to statements	Issue appropriately presented or disclosed in the statements	Issue not presented or disclosed in the statements
Standard for use	Fundamental to users' understanding of the statements	Relevant to users' understanding of the auditor's audit, responsibilities, or report

Stop and review! You have completed the outline for this subunit. Study multiple-choice questions 29 through 33 beginning on page 546.

QUESTIONS

17.1 Group Audits and Component Auditors (AU-C 600)

1. Pell, CPA, is the group engagement partner in the audit of the financial statements of Tech Consolidated, Inc. Smith, CPA, audits one of Tech's subsidiaries. In which situation(s) should Pell refer to Smith's audit?

I. Pell reviews Smith's audit documentation and assumes responsibility for Smith's work but expresses a qualified opinion on Tech's financial statements.

II. Pell is unable to review Smith's audit documentation but reads the financial statements and gains an understanding that Smith has an excellent reputation for professional competence and integrity.

A. I only.

B. II only.

C. Both I and II.

D. Neither I nor II.

Answer (B) is correct.

REQUIRED: The situation, if any, in which a group auditor should refer to a component auditor's audit.

DISCUSSION: Regardless of the decision to make reference, the group engagement team should obtain an understanding of the component auditor's professional competence and compliance with ethical requirements (especially independence). The understanding also addresses (1) the extent of the team's involvement in the component auditor's work, (2) whether (s)he operates under regulatory oversight, and (3) whether the team will be able to obtain information about the consolidation process from the component auditor. Serious concerns about (1) compliance with ethical requirements or (2) lack of competence preclude a reference to the audit of the component auditor. Moreover, the group engagement partner's assumption of responsibility for the component auditor's audit indicates a decision not to refer to the audit of component auditor.

Answer (A) is incorrect. Assumption of responsibility reflects a decision not to refer. Answer (C) is incorrect. Assumption of responsibility reflects a decision not to refer. Answer (D) is incorrect. The component auditor's (1) compliance with ethical requirements and (2) professional competence generally permit a reference.

2. An auditor may issue an unmodified audit report when the

A. Auditor refers to the findings of an auditor's specialist.

B. Financial statements are derived from audited financial statements but contain less detail.

C. Financial statements are prepared on the cash receipts and disbursements basis of accounting chosen by management.

D. Group engagement partner assumes responsibility for the work of a component auditor.

Answer (D) is correct.
  REQUIRED: The situation in which an auditor may issue an unmodified audit report.
  DISCUSSION: If the group engagement partner assumes responsibility for the work of the component auditor, no reference should be made to the component auditor in the report on the group financial statements.
  Answer (A) is incorrect. The auditor does not refer to an auditor's specialist unless (s)he departs from an unmodified opinion. Answer (B) is incorrect. The report on summary financial statements varies in many respects, e.g., it identifies the summary financial statements and the audited financial statements. Answer (C) is incorrect. A modification of the report is appropriate. The cash basis generally is not an acceptable reporting framework.

3. The group engagement partner has identified a significant component of the group that is being audited by a component auditor. The group auditor intends to assume responsibility for the work of the component auditor. Accordingly,

A. A qualified opinion should be expressed on that component.

B. The component auditor should become a member of the group engagement team.

C. The group engagement team should either audit the component directly or have the component auditor audit the information on its behalf.

D. The group engagement team should obtain a representation letter from component management.

Answer (C) is correct.
  REQUIRED: The requirement when a significant component is identified in a group audit with no reference to the component auditor.
  DISCUSSION: A significant component is one that is (1) of individual financial significance to the group or (2) likely to include significant risks of material misstatement of the group financial statements. When the group engagement partner assumes responsibility for the audit of the component, the audit report does not refer to the audit of the component auditor. Thus, the group engagement team should (1) audit the financial information directly or (2) have the component auditor audit the information on its behalf, using appropriate component materiality.
  Answer (A) is incorrect. The opinion is based on the evidence obtained, not on how it is audited. Answer (B) is incorrect. The component auditor may or may not become part of the group engagement team. Answer (D) is incorrect. The communication requested from the component auditor should include exceptions in the written representations that (s)he requested from component management. Thus, the group engagement team's involvement in the work of the component auditor does not necessarily require obtaining a representation letter from component management.

4. In which of the following situations will a group auditor be most likely to refer to a component auditor who audited a subsidiary of the entity?

A. The component auditor performed an audit in accordance with PCAOB standards.

B. The component auditor issued a restricted use report.

C. The financial statements audited by the component auditor are prepared using a financial reporting framework different from that used in the group statements.

D. The component auditor is not independent.

Answer (A) is correct.
  REQUIRED: The situation in which a group auditor is most likely to refer to a component auditor.
  DISCUSSION: The group engagement partner may not refer to the audit of the component auditor unless the component auditor performed an audit in accordance with (1) GAAS or (2), if required by law or regulation, PCAOB auditing standards.
  Answer (B) is incorrect. Reference to the audit of the component auditor is not made unless the component auditor has issued an unrestricted report. Answer (C) is incorrect. When the reporting frameworks differ, no reference is made unless certain conditions are met. Moreover, the group auditor's report should disclose that responsibility is taken for evaluating the adjustments needed to convert from one framework to the other. Answer (D) is incorrect. When the component auditor is not independent, or the group engagement team has serious concerns about other ethical issues or professional competence, no reference is made.

5. The auditor's responsibility section of an auditor's report contains the following: "We did not audit the financial statements of EZ, Inc., a wholly owned subsidiary, which statements reflect total assets and revenues constituting 27% and 29%, respectively, of the related consolidated totals. Those statements were audited by other auditors, whose report has been furnished to us, and our opinion, insofar as it relates to the amounts included for EZ, Inc., is based solely on the report of the other auditors." These sentences

A. Assume no responsibility for the audit of the component auditor.

B. Assume responsibility for the work of a component auditor.

C. Require a departure from an unmodified opinion.

D. Are an improper form of reporting.

Answer (A) is correct.
REQUIRED: The effect of the quoted language.
DISCUSSION: The quoted language is adapted from the auditor's responsibility section in an example of an auditor's report (AU-C 600). It illustrates the reporting by a group auditor who is referring to the audit of a component auditor. The group auditor's report should clearly indicate that the component was not audited by the group auditor. It also should state (1) that the component was audited by the component auditor and (2) the magnitude of the portion audited. However, the ISAs do not permit a reference to a component auditor unless required by law or regulation.
Answer (B) is incorrect. The group auditor does not refer to a component auditor when assuming responsibility for the component auditor's work. Answer (C) is incorrect. An unmodified opinion may be expressed despite a reference to a component auditor. Answer (D) is incorrect. The wording is used as an illustration in AU-C 600.

17.2 Consistency of Financial Statements (AU-C 708 and AS No. 6)

6. The following additional paragraph was included in an auditor's report to indicate a lack of consistency:

"As discussed in note T to the financial statements, the company changed its method of computing depreciation in Year 1."

How should the auditor report on this matter if the auditor concurred with the change?

	Type of Opinion	Location of Additional Paragraph
A.	Unmodified	Before Opinion paragraph
B.	Unmodified	After Opinion paragraph
C.	Qualified	Before Opinion paragraph
D.	Qualified	After Opinion paragraph

Answer (B) is correct.
REQUIRED: The reporting of a lack of consistency.
DISCUSSION: A change in accounting principle meeting certain criteria and having a material effect on the financial statements requires the auditor to refer to the change in an emphasis-of-matter paragraph of the report. This paragraph should follow the opinion paragraph, describe the change, and refer to the entity's disclosure.

7. For which of the following events would an auditor issue a report that omits any reference to a change in accounting principle or correction of a material misstatement?

A. A change in the method of accounting for inventories.

B. A change from an accounting principle that is not in accordance with the applicable reporting framework to one that is.

C. A change in the useful life used to calculate the provision for depreciation expense.

D. Management's lack of reasonable justification for a material change in accounting principle.

Answer (C) is correct.
REQUIRED: The event not requiring a reference to a change in accounting principle or correction of a material misstatement in the auditor's report.
DISCUSSION: A change in estimate is neither a change in accounting principle nor the correction of a material misstatement in previously issued financial statements. Thus, it requires no modification of the opinion or other recognition in the report. However, an exception is a change in estimate that is inseparable from a change in principle. The auditor evaluates and reports on this change as a change in principle.
Answer (A) is incorrect. A change in the method of accounting for inventory, for example, from FIFO to LIFO, is a change in accounting principle. It requires an emphasis-of-matter paragraph in the auditor's report that describes the new accounting guidance. Answer (B) is incorrect. A correction of a material misstatement, e.g., a change from an accounting principle that is not in accordance with the applicable reporting framework to one that is, requires an emphasis-of-matter paragraph that includes a statement that previously issued statements have been restated to correct a material misstatement. Answer (D) is incorrect. Lack of justification for a material change in accounting principle requires the auditor to express a qualified or an adverse opinion. The basis for modification paragraph describes the matter.

8. When an entity changes its method of accounting for income taxes, which has a material effect on comparability, the auditor should refer to the change in an emphasis-of-matter paragraph added to the auditor's report. This paragraph should describe the change and

A. Explain why the change is justified under the applicable reporting framework.

B. Describe the cumulative effect of the change on all periods prior to those presented.

C. State the auditor's explicit concurrence with or opposition to the change.

D. Refer to the financial statement note that discusses the change in detail.

Answer (D) is correct.
REQUIRED: The content of an emphasis-of-matter paragraph added because of a change in an accounting principle.
DISCUSSION: When a change in accounting principle has a material effect on comparability, the auditor should add an emphasis-of-matter paragraph after the opinion paragraph that (1) uses the heading "Emphasis of Matter," (2) describes the change in principle, (3) refers to the entity's disclosure, and (4) indicates that the opinion is not modified with regard to the matter emphasized.
Answer (A) is incorrect. The auditor's concurrence with the change is implicit unless (s)he modifies the opinion. Answer (B) is incorrect. The cumulative effect of a change is described in the financial statements, not the auditor's report. Answer (C) is incorrect. The auditor's concurrence with the change is implicit unless (s)he modifies the opinion.

9. When the auditor concurs with a change in accounting principle that materially affects the comparability of the comparative financial statements, the auditor should

	Concur Explicitly with the Change	Express a Qualified Opinion	Refer to the Change in an Additional Paragraph
A.	No	No	Yes
B.	Yes	No	Yes
C.	Yes	Yes	No
D.	No	Yes	No

Answer (A) is correct.
REQUIRED: The appropriate report when the auditor concurs with a change in accounting principle.
DISCUSSION: A material change in accounting principle raises a consistency issue. Thus, a report with an emphasis-of-matter paragraph is required if the auditor's evaluation concludes that certain criteria have been met: (1) the new principle and the method of accounting for it are in accordance with the applicable framework, (2) related disclosures are appropriate, and (3) the entity has justified that the principle is preferable. The opinion is modified for a material change in principle only if the criteria are not met. Furthermore, the auditor's concurrence is implied by the inclusion of an emphasis-of-matter paragraph. This paragraph is included only if the opinion is not modified with regard to the matter.

10. Digit Co. uses the FIFO method of costing for its international subsidiary's inventory and the LIFO method for its domestic inventory. Under these circumstances, the auditor's report on Digit's financial statements should express an

A. Unmodified opinion.

B. Opinion qualified because of a lack of consistency.

C. Opinion qualified because of a departure from U.S. GAAP.

D. Adverse opinion.

Answer (A) is correct.
REQUIRED: The effect on the report of using different inventory methods for two business segments.
DISCUSSION: A difference between the accounting principles used by two segments of an entity does not raise a consistency issue. The relevant standard essentially concerns the consistent observation of principles in one period in relation to the preceding period. Thus, the use of LIFO for one segment and FIFO for another does not, by itself, affect comparability. Assuming that the use of different methods is appropriate, an unmodified opinion is not precluded, and no emphasis-of-matter paragraph relevant to consistency needs to be added to the report.

11. A nonissuer changed from the straight-line method to the declining-balance method of depreciation for all newly acquired assets. This change has no material effect on the current year's financial statements but is reasonably certain to have a material effect in later years. If the change is disclosed in the notes to the financial statements, the auditor should issue a report with a(n)

A. Qualified opinion.

B. Emphasis-of-matter paragraph.

C. Unmodified opinion.

D. Consistency modification.

Answer (C) is correct.
REQUIRED: The report issued when a change in accounting principle has no current material effect.
DISCUSSION: If a change in accounting principle has no material effect on the current financial statements but is expected to have a material effect in future years, the change should be disclosed by the client if required by the applicable financial reporting framework. But it need not be recognized in the report.
Answer (A) is incorrect. A justified change in accounting principle does not result in an opinion qualified because of the change. Answer (B) is incorrect. If an accounting change has no material effect on the current financial statements, the auditor need not modify the current-period report. Answer (D) is incorrect. If an accounting change has no material effect on the current financial statements but is likely to affect future financial statements, the auditor need not modify the current-period report.

12. When there has been a change in accounting principles but the effect of the change on the comparability of the financial statements is **not** material, the auditor should

    A. Not refer to the change in the auditor's report.

    B. Refer to the note in the financial statements that discusses the change.

    C. Refer to the change in an emphasis-of-matter paragraph.

    D. Explicitly state whether the change conforms with GAAP.

Answer (A) is correct.

    REQUIRED: The effect on the auditor's report of a change in accounting principle that is not material.

    DISCUSSION: An auditor should evaluate whether the comparability of the financial statements has been materially affected by (1) a change in accounting principle or (2) adjustments to correct a material misstatement in previously issued financial statements. If the auditor's report does not state otherwise, it implies that comparability has not been materially affected by such changes or corrections.

    Answer (B) is incorrect. An auditor should not refer to the note in the financial statements that discusses the change. Answer (C) is incorrect. An emphasis-of-matter paragraph is used in the auditor's report to draw users' attention to a matter appropriately presented or disclosed in the financial statements that is of such importance that it is fundamental to users' understanding of the financial statements. An emphasis-of-matter paragraph is used only in certain circumstances. An immaterial change in accounting principle is not one of them. Answer (D) is incorrect. An auditor should not explicitly state whether the change in accounting principle conforms with GAAP.

17.3 Uncertainties and Going Concern (AU-C 570 and AU-C 705)

13. An auditor most likely will express an unmodified opinion and will not add additional language to the report if the auditor

    A. Wishes to emphasize that the entity had significant transactions with related parties.

    B. Concurs with the entity's change in its method of computing depreciation.

    C. Discovers that supplementary information required by FASB has been omitted.

    D. Believes that there is a remote likelihood of a material loss resulting from an uncertainty.

Answer (D) is correct.

    REQUIRED: The condition under which an additional paragraph is not added to the report.

    DISCUSSION: Normally, an uncertainty does not require the auditor to add a paragraph to the report.

    Answer (A) is incorrect. Emphasis of a matter is accomplished with an additional paragraph added to the auditor's report. Answer (B) is incorrect. A change in the depreciation method is a change in estimate inseparable from a change in principle. If material, the change in principle requires an emphasis-of-matter paragraph. Answer (C) is incorrect. AU-C 730 requires the auditor to add an other-matter paragraph when supplementary information that is required by FASB or GASB has been omitted.

14. Management believes, and the auditor is satisfied, that a material loss probably will occur when pending litigation is resolved. Management is unable to make a reasonable estimate of the amount or range of the potential loss but fully discloses the situation in the notes to the financial statements. If management does not make an accrual in the financial statements, the auditor should express a(n)

    A. Qualified opinion due to a scope limitation.

    B. Qualified opinion due to a material misstatement.

    C. Unmodified opinion with an emphasis-of-matter paragraph.

    D. Unmodified opinion with no additional paragraph in the auditor's report.

Answer (D) is correct.

    REQUIRED: The auditor's reporting consideration of a material loss that is probable but not subject to estimation.

    DISCUSSION: If the auditor concludes that sufficient appropriate evidence supports management's assertions about the nature of a matter involving an uncertainty, an unmodified report is ordinarily appropriate.

    Answer (A) is incorrect. Inability to make a reasonable estimate of the potential loss is not a scope limitation. Answer (B) is incorrect. No material misstatement exists, an accrual of the loss contingency is not required in these circumstances, and full disclosure has been made. Thus, no report modification should be made. Answer (C) is incorrect. No basis for including an emphasis-of-matter paragraph to the report is given.

15. Tech Company has disclosed an uncertainty arising from pending litigation. The auditor's decision to express a qualified opinion rather than an unmodified opinion most likely would be determined by the

A. Lack of sufficient appropriate evidence.

B. Inability to estimate the amount of loss.

C. Entity's lack of experience with such litigation.

D. Lack of insurance coverage for possible losses from such litigation.

Answer (A) is correct.
  REQUIRED: The basis for expressing a qualified opinion.
  DISCUSSION: By definition, sufficient appropriate evidence regarding the outcome of an uncertainty cannot be expected to exist at the time of an audit. However, management must analyze existing conditions, including uncertainties, and their financial statement effects. The auditor should therefore determine whether appropriate evidence is sufficient to support these analyses. If, as a result of a scope limitation, sufficient appropriate evidence is not available to the auditor to make this determination, a qualification or disclaimer of opinion is appropriate.

16. When an auditor concludes that substantial doubt exists about an entity's ability to continue as a going concern for a reasonable period of time, the auditor's responsibility is to

A. Prepare prospective financial information to verify whether management's plans can be effectively implemented.

B. Project future conditions and events for a period of time not to exceed 1 year following the date of the financial statements.

C. Express a qualified or adverse opinion, depending on materiality, because of the possible effects on the financial statements.

D. Consider the adequacy of disclosure about the entity's possible inability to continue as a going concern.

Answer (D) is correct.
  REQUIRED: The auditor's responsibility given a substantial doubt about an entity's ability to continue as a going concern.
  DISCUSSION: If the auditor reaches this conclusion after (1) identifying conditions and events that create such doubt and (2) evaluating management's plans to mitigate their effects, (s)he should consider the adequacy of disclosure and include an emphasis-of-matter paragraph (after the opinion paragraph) in the report that includes the words "substantial doubt" and "going concern." If disclosure is inadequate, the material misstatement requires modification of the opinion. By itself, however, the substantial doubt does not require a modified opinion paragraph or a disclaimer of opinion.
  Answer (A) is incorrect. The auditor should consider management's plans but need not prepare prospective financial information. Answer (B) is incorrect. The auditor is not responsible for predicting future conditions or events. Answer (C) is incorrect. The opinion is not modified solely for a going-concern issue.

17. In which of the following circumstances would an auditor most likely add an emphasis-of-matter paragraph to the auditor's report while expressing an unmodified opinion?

A. The auditor is asked to report on the balance sheet but not on the other basic financial statements.

B. There is substantial doubt about the entity's ability to continue as a going concern.

C. Management's estimates of the effects of future events are unreasonable.

D. Certain material transactions cannot be tested because of management's records retention policy.

Answer (B) is correct.
  REQUIRED: The reason for including an emphasis-of-matter paragraph while expressing an unmodified opinion.
  DISCUSSION: If the auditor reaches this conclusion after (1) identifying conditions and events that create such doubt and (2) evaluating management's plans to mitigate their effects, (s)he should consider the adequacy of disclosure and include an emphasis-of-matter paragraph (after the opinion paragraph) in the report. The auditor must use language in the emphasis-of-matter paragraph that includes the words "substantial doubt" and "going concern." By itself, however, the substantial doubt is not a basis for modifying the opinion.
  Answer (A) is incorrect. An auditor may be asked to report on one financial statement. In that event, (s)he may appropriately express an unmodified opinion without adding an additional paragraph. Answer (C) is incorrect. The statements are not fairly presented if material estimates included in them are unreasonable. An unmodified opinion could not then be expressed. Answer (D) is incorrect. A qualification or disclaimer of opinion is appropriate when the scope of the audit is limited.

18. An auditor's report included the following paragraph relative to substantial doubt about a client's ability to continue as a going concern:

"The accompanying financial statements have been prepared assuming that the Company will continue as a going concern. If the Company is not able to renew the contract described in Note X, there may be substantial doubt about the company's ability to continue as a going concern."

Which of the following statements is true?

  A. The paragraph should not refer to a note to the financial statements.

  B. The report should not contain conditional language.

  C. The report should refer to a qualification of the opinion.

  D. The report should not use the phrase "substantial doubt."

Answer (B) is correct.
  REQUIRED: The true statement about a report addressing a client's ability to continue as a going concern.
  DISCUSSION: The report should not contain conditional language. "If the Company is not able to renew the contract . . ." is not permissible language.
  Answer (A) is incorrect. The report may refer to a note that describes the issues. Answer (C) is incorrect. The opinion should not be qualified for a going-concern doubt. Rather, an emphasis-of-matter paragraph should be included in the report. Answer (D) is incorrect. The report should include the phrases "substantial doubt" and "going concern."

19. Green, CPA, concludes that there is substantial doubt about JKL Co.'s ability to continue as a going concern. If JKL's financial statements adequately disclose its financial difficulties, Green's auditor's report should

	Include a Paragraph Following the Opinion Paragraph	Specifically Use the Words "Going Concern"	Specifically Use the Words "Substantial Doubt"
A.	Yes	Yes	Yes
B.	Yes	Yes	No
C.	Yes	No	Yes
D.	No	Yes	Yes

Answer (A) is correct.
  REQUIRED: The effect of a substantial doubt about the going-concern assumption.
  DISCUSSION: An evaluation should be made as to whether substantial doubt exists about the entity's ability to continue as a going concern for a reasonable period of time, not to exceed 1 year beyond the date of the financial statements. If the auditor reaches this conclusion after identifying conditions and events that create such doubt and after evaluating management's plans to reduce their effects, (s)he should consider the possible effects on the statements and the adequacy of disclosure. (S)he also includes an emphasis-of-matter paragraph (after the opinion paragraph) in the report. The auditor should use language in the emphasis-of-matter paragraph that includes the phrases "substantial doubt" and "going concern." Also, the emphasis-of-matter paragraph should not use conditional language in expressing its conclusion about the existence of a substantial doubt. The substantial doubt is not a basis for a qualified or an adverse opinion, but a disclaimer is not precluded in the case of such a material uncertainty.

20. Kane, CPA, concludes that there is substantial doubt about Lima Co.'s ability to continue as a going concern for a reasonable period of time. If Lima's financial statements adequately disclose its financial difficulties, Kane's auditor's report is required to include an emphasis-of-matter paragraph that specifically uses the phrase(s)

	"Possible Discontinuance of Operations"	"Reasonable Period of Time, Not to Exceed One Year"
A.	Yes	Yes
B.	Yes	No
C.	No	Yes
D.	No	No

Answer (D) is correct.
  REQUIRED: The phrase(s), if any, required to be included in a paragraph describing a substantial doubt about a firm's ability to continue as a going concern.
  DISCUSSION: The auditor has a substantial doubt about the firm's ability to continue as a going concern for a reasonable period of time. Accordingly, the auditor should include an emphasis-of-matter paragraph after the opinion paragraph in the report. This paragraph should include the terms "substantial doubt" and "going concern." The specific phrases included in the question are not required.

21. An auditor concludes that there is substantial doubt about an entity's ability to continue as a going concern for a reasonable period of time. If the entity's disclosures concerning this matter are adequate and no other issues prevail, the audit report may include a

	Disclaimer of Opinion	Qualified Opinion
A.	Yes	Yes
B.	No	No
C.	No	Yes
D.	Yes	No

Answer (D) is correct.
   REQUIRED: The nature of the report given a substantial going concern doubt.
   DISCUSSION: By itself, a substantial doubt about an entity's ability to continue as a going concern does not require a modification of the opinion paragraph. Hence, a qualified opinion would be inappropriate. However, nothing precludes the auditor from disclaiming an opinion in these circumstances.

22. Mead, CPA, had substantial doubt about Tech Co.'s ability to continue as a going concern when reporting on Tech's audited financial statements for the year ended June 30, Year 1. That doubt has been removed in Year 2. What is Mead's reporting responsibility if Tech is presenting its financial statements for the year ended June 30, Year 2, on a comparative basis with those of Year 1?

A. The emphasis-of-matter paragraph included in the Year 1 auditor's report should not be repeated.

B. The emphasis-of-matter paragraph included in the Year 1 auditor's report should be repeated in its entirety.

C. A different emphasis-of-matter paragraph describing Mead's reasons for the removal of doubt should be included.

D. A different emphasis-of-matter paragraph describing Tech's plans for financial recovery should be included.

Answer (A) is correct.
   REQUIRED: The effect on an updated report when substantial doubt about the auditee's ability to continue as a going concern has been removed.
   DISCUSSION: The emphasis-of-matter paragraph included in the previous report should not be repeated in subsequent reports if the doubt has been resolved.
   Answer (B) is incorrect. The doubt has been resolved, and the current report should not repeat the emphasis-of-matter paragraph. Answer (C) is incorrect. The reasons for the removal of doubt need not be included. Answer (D) is incorrect. The paragraph should be removed, and a different emphasis-of-matter paragraph describing the plans for financial recovery is not necessary.

17.4 Comparative Financial Statements (AU-C 700)

23. When a predecessor auditor reissues the report on the prior period's financial statements at the request of the former client, the predecessor should

A. Indicate in the introductory paragraph of the reissued report that the financial statements of the subsequent period were audited by another CPA.

B. Obtain a representation letter from the auditor but not from management.

C. Compare the prior period's financial statements that the predecessor reported on with the financial statements to be presented for comparative purposes.

D. Add an additional paragraph to the reissued report stating that the predecessor has not performed additional auditing procedures on the prior period's financial statements.

Answer (C) is correct.
   REQUIRED: The procedure performed by the predecessor auditor before reissuing a report.
   DISCUSSION: The predecessor auditor should perform certain procedures before reissuing a report on prior-period financial statements. (S)he should (1) read the current period's financial statements, (2) compare the prior and current financial statements, (3) obtain a representation letter from the auditor stating whether (s)he has discovered matters having a material effect on (or requiring disclosure in) the statements reported on by the predecessor auditor, and (4) obtain a representation letter from management confirming past representations and stating whether post-balance-sheet events require adjustment of or disclosure in the financial statements.
   Answer (A) is incorrect. The reissued report should not refer to another auditor. Answer (B) is incorrect. The predecessor auditor should obtain a representation letter from the auditor and from management. Answer (D) is incorrect. The report should not be modified unless the auditor's previous conclusions have changed.

24. When reporting on comparative financial statements, an auditor ordinarily should change the previously expressed opinion on the prior year's financial statements if the

A. Prior year's financial statements are restated to correct a material misstatement.

B. Auditor is a predecessor auditor who has been requested by a former client to reissue the previously issued report.

C. Prior year's opinion was unmodified and the opinion on the current year's financial statements is modified due to a change in accounting principle.

D. Reporting entity has changed as a result of the sale of a subsidiary.

Answer (A) is correct.
REQUIRED: The event that causes an auditor to change a previously expressed opinion.
DISCUSSION: If the previous opinion was modified because of a material misstatement, but the prior year's statements were restated to remove the basis for the modification, the updated report should express an unmodified opinion. The auditor's report should include an emphasis-of-matter paragraph that (1) states that the previously issued financial statements have been restated to correct a material misstatement and (2) refers to the entity's disclosure (AU-C 708).
Answer (B) is incorrect. If the predecessor's report is still appropriate, it normally should be reissued without revision. Answer (C) is incorrect. A change in accounting principle in the current period has no effect on the opinion expressed in the prior year. Answer (D) is incorrect. A change in the reporting entity resulting from a transaction or event, for example, a purchase or disposition of a subsidiary, does not require recognition in the auditor's report. Furthermore, such a transaction or event in the current year is not a circumstance that affects the prior period's statements. Thus, it presents no basis for modifying the opinion expressed on those statements.

25. The predecessor auditor, who is satisfied after properly communicating with the current auditor, has reissued a report because the audit client desires comparative financial statements. The predecessor auditor's report should

A. Refer to the report of the current auditor only in the auditor's responsibility section.

B. Refer to the work of the current auditor in the opinion paragraph.

C. Refer to both the work and the report of the current auditor only in the opinion paragraph.

D. Not refer to the report or the work of the current auditor.

Answer (D) is correct.
REQUIRED: The true statement about reference to the current auditor in a reissued report.
DISCUSSION: A predecessor auditor who has been asked to reissue his/her report should (1) read the current-period statements, (2) compare the statements (s)he reported on with other statements to be presented comparatively, (3) obtain a representation letter from the auditor, and (4) obtain a representation letter from management of the former client. However, the reissued report should not refer to the report or work of the auditor.

26. Jewel, CPA, audited Infinite Co.'s prior-year financial statements. These statements are presented with those of the current year for comparative purposes without Jewel's auditor's report, which expressed a qualified opinion. In drafting the current year's auditor's report, the current auditor should

I. Not name Jewel as the predecessor auditor
II. Indicate the type of opinion expressed by Jewel
III. Indicate the reasons for Jewel's qualification

A. I only.

B. I and II only.

C. II and III only.

D. I, II, and III.

Answer (D) is correct.
REQUIRED: The matter(s) included in an auditor's report.
DISCUSSION: The auditor should state in an other-matter paragraph (following the opinion paragraph and any emphasis-of-matter paragraph) (1) that the prior year's financial statements were audited by another auditor, (2) the date of the report, (3) the type of opinion expressed and the reasons for any modification, and (4) the nature of any emphasis-of-matter or other-matter paragraph. Furthermore, the predecessor auditor is not named.

27. In auditing the financial statements of Star Corp., Land discovered information leading Land to believe that Star's prior-year financial statements, which were audited by Tell, require substantial revisions. Under these circumstances, Land should

A. Notify Star's audit committee and shareholders that the prior year's financial statements cannot be relied on.

B. Request Star to reissue the prior year's financial statements with the appropriate revisions.

C. Notify Tell about the information and make inquiries about the integrity of Star's management.

D. Request Star to arrange a meeting among the three parties to resolve the matter.

Answer (D) is correct.
REQUIRED: The auditor's action when financial statements from a prior period require revision.
DISCUSSION: Because the prior year's financial statements appear to require restatement, the auditor should discuss the matter with the predecessor auditor. (S)he should communicate any information that the predecessor auditor may need to meet the responsibilities imposed by AU-C 560, *Subsequent Events and Subsequently Discovered Facts*. A meeting of the three parties should be requested.
Answer (A) is incorrect. The auditor need not notify shareholders. Answer (B) is incorrect. The financial statements should not be revised until the parties have discussed the matter. Answer (C) is incorrect. The auditor should request that the client communicate with the prior auditor.

28. Unaudited financial statements are presented in comparative form with audited financial statements in a document filed with the Securities and Exchange Commission. In accordance with the PCAOB's Interim Auditing Standards, such statements should be

	Marked as "Unaudited"	Withheld until Audited	Referred to in the Auditor's Report
A.	Yes	No	No
B.	Yes	No	Yes
C.	No	Yes	Yes
D.	No	Yes	No

Answer (A) is correct.
REQUIRED: The treatment of unaudited statements presented comparatively with audited statements in a document filed with the SEC.
DISCUSSION: According to the PCAOB's Interim Auditing Standards, when unaudited financial statements are presented in comparative form with audited statements in documents filed with the SEC, such statements should be clearly marked as "unaudited." They should not be referred to in the auditor's report or withheld until audited. NOTE: The source of authoritative guidance is the PCAOB's Interim Auditing Standards, not the clarified SASs published by the AICPA. The Interim Standards apply to services for issuers. They include AICPA auditing standards that existed on April 16, 2003. The relevant guidance at that date was AU 504, Association with Financial Statements (para. .14-.17). The PCAOB has not modified, replaced, or repealed this guidance.

17.5 Emphasis-of-Matter and Other-Matter Paragraphs (AU-C 706)

29. An other-matter paragraph is included in the auditor's report **except** when

A. The opinion on the prior-period statements has changed.

B. Required supplementary information is presented.

C. A predecessor auditor's report is not reissued.

D. The client has materially restated the prior year's comparative financial statements.

Answer (D) is correct.
REQUIRED: The purpose for which an other-matter paragraph is inappropriate.
DISCUSSION: An other-matter paragraph draws attention to a matter not required to be presented or disclosed in the financial statements that is relevant to users' understanding of the auditor's audit, responsibilities, or report. A correction of a material misstatement in previously issued financial statements requires the auditor to include an emphasis-of-matter paragraph. This matter is appropriately presented or disclosed in the financial statements and is fundamental to users' understanding.
Answer (A) is incorrect. An auditor's opinion on prior-period statements reported on in connection with the current audit may have changed. If so, the auditor should make certain disclosures in an emphasis-of-matter or other-matter paragraph. Answer (B) is incorrect. An auditor should include an other-matter paragraph in the auditor's report to refer to the presentation of required supplementary information. Answer (C) is incorrect. The auditor should include an other-matter paragraph in the auditor's report when prior-period statements presented comparatively with the current period's statements were audited by a predecessor auditor whose report is not reissued.

30. An auditor includes an emphasis-of-matter paragraph in an otherwise unmodified report when the entity being reported on had significant transactions with related parties. The inclusion of this paragraph

    A. Is considered a qualification of the opinion.

    B. Violates auditing standards if this information is already disclosed in notes to the financial statements.

    C. Necessitates a revision of the opinion paragraph to include the phrase "with the foregoing explanation."

    D. Is appropriate and would not negate the unmodified opinion.

Answer (D) is correct.
    REQUIRED: The effect of an emphasis-of-matter paragraph in an otherwise unmodified report.
    DISCUSSION: An auditor may emphasize a matter in a separate paragraph and express an unmodified opinion. Matters to be emphasized might include that the entity has had significant related party transactions. Subsequent events and accounting matters affecting comparability (e.g., a change in the reporting entity) are other matters suitable for this treatment.
    Answer (A) is incorrect. Emphasis of a matter is not inconsistent with an unmodified opinion. Answer (B) is incorrect. The auditor may emphasize a matter without violating GAAS or the PCAOB standards. Answer (C) is incorrect. The phrase "with the foregoing explanation" creates doubt as to whether the report was intended to be qualified.

31. In which situation is the auditor most likely **not** to include an emphasis-of-matter paragraph in the auditor's report?

    A. An important audit procedure was performed.

    B. The client suffered a major catastrophe.

    C. Significant transactions with related parties were recorded.

    D. Unusually important subsequent events occurred.

Answer (A) is correct.
    REQUIRED: The situation in which an emphasis-of-matter paragraph is not included in the auditor's report.
    DISCUSSION: An emphasis-of-matter paragraph is not used to describe an audit procedure. It is used to draw attention to a matter appropriately presented or disclosed in the financial statements that is fundamental to users' understanding. The following are examples of circumstances in which the auditor may need to include an emphasis-of-matter paragraph: (1) an uncertainty relating to the future outcome of unusually important litigation or regulatory action; (2) a major catastrophe that has had, or continues to have, a significant effect on the entity's financial position; (3) significant transactions with related parties; and (4) unusually important subsequent events.

32. An emphasis-of-matter paragraph is used in the auditor's report to draw users' attention to

    A. A material misstatement.

    B. A matter that is not presented or disclosed in the financial statements that is relevant to users' understanding of the audit.

    C. A matter that management wishes to highlight.

    D. A matter appropriately presented or disclosed in the financial statements.

Answer (D) is correct.
    REQUIRED: The use of an emphasis-of-matter paragraph.
    DISCUSSION: An emphasis-of-matter paragraph is used in the auditor's report to draw users' attention to a matter appropriately presented or disclosed in the financial statements that is fundamental to users' understanding of the financial statements.
    Answer (A) is incorrect. A material misstatement requires a qualified or adverse opinion. Answer (B) is incorrect. An other-matter paragraph draws attention to a matter not required to be presented or disclosed in the financial statements that is relevant to users' understanding of the auditor's audit, responsibilities, or report. Answer (C) is incorrect. The auditor, not management, determines the content of the auditor's report.

33. A nonissuer's unaudited financial statements for the prior period are presented in comparative form with audited financial statements for the subsequent year. If the prior-period statements were reviewed,

I.   The report on the unaudited financial statements should be reissued.

II. The report on the audited financial statements should include an other-matter paragraph.

    A. I only.

    B. II only.

    C. Neither I nor II.

    D. Either I or II.

Answer (D) is correct.
    REQUIRED: The appropriate reporting when the prior-period's unaudited financial statements of a nonissuer are presented in comparative form with current-period audited financial statements.
    DISCUSSION: A nonissuer's audited statements for the current period may be presented comparatively with the prior period's reviewed or compiled statements. If the prior period's report is not reissued, the auditor's current-period report should include an other-matter paragraph that states (1) the service performed in the prior period, (2) the date of the service, (3) a description of material modifications noted in the report, and (4) that the service was not an audit and did not provide a basis for an opinion (AU-C 700).

17.6 PRACTICE TASK-BASED SIMULATIONS

	Auditing and Attestation	Time Remaining	Unsplit	Split Horiz	Split Vertical	Spreadsheet	Calculator	Exit
	Testlet 4 of 4	1 hour - 30 minutes						

DIRECTIONS

Note: If you believe you have encountered a software malfunction, report it to the test center staff immediately.

Navigation

To navigate from task to task, use the controls at the bottom of the screen. Click on the **Next** button to advance to the next task, or the **Previous** button to go to the previous task. To go directly to any task, click on its number.

If you would like a reminder to revisit a task, or want to indicate that you are finished with it, click on the reminder flag below the task number. To clear the flag, click on it again. Reminder flags are for your use only – they do not contribute to your score.

Tabs

In this part of the examination, you will be asked to complete various tasks. Every task has one or more **Work Tabs**. Some tasks have one or more **Information Tabs**, others may have none. Every task has a **Help** tab.

If a task has **Information Tabs**, you may use the information in them to complete your responses in the **Work Tabs**.

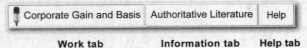

| Work tab | Information tab | Help tab |

Work Tabs:
- **Work Tabs** are identified with a pencil icon. This is where your responses are expected.
- Each task has one or more **Work Tabs**.
- **Work Tabs** contain directions for completing the task – be sure to read these directions carefully.
- The **Work Tab** name in the example above is for illustration only – yours will differ.
- You must complete all of the **Work Tabs** in each task to receive full credit.

Information Tabs:
- The Authoritative Literature will be provided in all tasks in the AUD, FAR, and REG sections for your reference.
- Your simulation may have one or more additional **Information Tabs**. Like the Authoritative Literature tabs, **Information Tabs** do not have a pencil icon.
- If your task has additional **Information Tabs**, go through each to familiarize yourself with the task content.

Help Tab:
- The **Help Tab** provides assistance with the exam software that is used in this task. For example, if the task is to compose a memorandum, **Help** will provide information about the word processor.

The Toolbar

The toolbar at the top of the screen shows the amount of time remaining for you to complete the tasks. In addition, the following tools are available. Note that only the **Exit** button is displayed when Directions are visible - the others will appear when you begin the tasks.

Click on these buttons to split or unsplit the screen. You can split the screen vertically or horizontally.

Click on this button to display the calculator; click on it again to hide the calculator. To move the calculator, click on the calculator title bar and drag the calculator to the desired location.

Click on this button to use the spreadsheet; click on it again to hide the spreadsheet. To move the spreadsheet, click on the the spreadsheet title bar and drag the spreadsheet to the desired location.

Click on this button to go on to the next part of the examination. You must complete all of the tasks to receive full credit. Once you click on **Exit** and confirm the action, you will NOT be able to return to this testlet.

| ▼ = Reminder | | Directions | 1 | 2 | 3 | 4 | 5 | | ◀ Previous | Next ▶ |

For each of the following independent material situations, select from the list provided the appropriate opinion type that will be expressed by the auditor. A choice may be used once, more than once, or not at all.

Situation	Opinion
1. During the current year, the client changed its depreciation method from the straight-line method to the declining-balance method.	
2. During the current year, the client changed its estimate of the building's salvage value from $100,000 to $8,000.	
3. During the current year, the client changed its method of bad debt expense recognition from the allowance method, income statement approach, to the direct write-off method.	
4. During the current year, the client discovered that last year's inventory physical count was incorrect. The client properly corrected the material misstatement in the current year's financial statements.	
5. The client could not refinance its current liabilities, and the auditor concludes that there is a substantial doubt about the client's ability to continue as a going concern for a reasonable period of time. The client's financial statements adequately disclose its financial difficulties.	
6. The auditor discovered a material overstatement of revenues; however, the client failed to correct the misstatement.	
7. The client changed the method for accounting for an expense because of a requirement in a new standard issued by the FASB.	
8. The auditor employed the use of a specialist to help gather evidence relating to pension costs.	

Choices

Choices
A) Qualified or adverse
B) Unmodified
C) Unmodified with an additional paragraph

Going Concern | Authoritative Literature | Help

Lei, a new staff auditor, has drafted the paragraph below, which is intended to be added just before the opinion paragraph to the audit report of JKL Company about going-concern issues. Dale, an experienced auditor, has made comments about the draft. Indicate whether Lei's draft is correct, Dale's comment is correct, or neither Lei's draft nor Dale's comment is correct. A choice may be used once, more than once, or not at all.

Lei's Going-Concern Paragraph

The accompanying financial statements have been prepared assuming that JKL Company will continue as a going concern. As discussed in Note X to the audit report, JKL Company has suffered recurring losses from operations and has a net capital deficiency. If these losses continue, there will be some doubt about its ability to continue as a going concern. Management has plans to deal with these issues. The financial statements do not include any adjustments that might result from the outcome of this uncertainty.

Dale's Comments	Answer
1. The paragraph should be placed after the opinion paragraph of the auditor's report.	
2. Change "Note X to the audit report" to "the management representation letter."	
3. The phrase "If these losses continue" should not be included.	
4. The phrase "some doubt" should be replaced with "substantial doubt."	
5. The phrase "continue as a going concern" should be replaced with the phrase "remain profitable."	
6. No reference to management's plans should be included in the report.	
7. The phrase "include any adjustments that might result" should be replaced with "contain any errors that might result."	
8. The paragraph should include a sentence that management has agreed that there is a going-concern issue.	

Choices

A) Lei's draft is correct.

B) Dale's comment is correct.

C) Neither Lei's draft nor Dale's comment is correct.

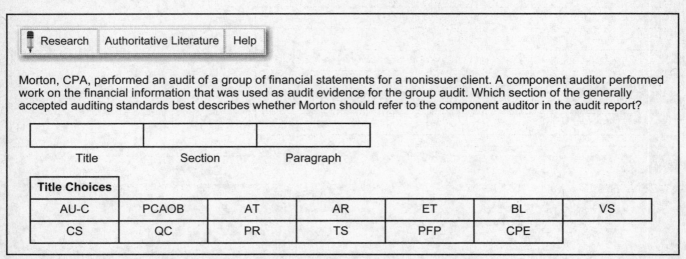

Research | Authoritative Literature | Help

Morton, CPA, performed an audit of a group of financial statements for a nonissuer client. A component auditor performed work on the financial information that was used as audit evidence for the group audit. Which section of the generally accepted auditing standards best describes whether Morton should refer to the component auditor in the audit report?

Title	Section	Paragraph

Title Choices

AU-C	PCAOB	AT	AR	ET	BL	VS
CS	QC	PR	TS	PFP	CPE	

| Accounting Changes | Authoritative Literature | Help |

The auditor should evaluate whether the comparability of the statements has been materially affected by a change in principle or the correction of a material misstatement. Assume that the following changes have a material effect on the financial statements for the current year.

Two answers are required for each of the eight accounting changes.

- In column 1, fill in the letter of the type of change [A) through H)] that best matches each accounting change.
- In column 2, write M) if any modification is required in the auditor's report as it relates to consistency, or write N) if no modification is required.
- Assume that all changes are feasible unless otherwise indicated.
- Each choice may be used once, more than once, or not at all.

1	2	Accounting Changes
		1. A change from the completed-contract method to the percentage-of-completion method of accounting for long-term construction contracts
		2. A change in the estimated useful life of previously recorded fixed assets based on newly acquired information
		3. Correction of a mathematical error in inventory pricing made in the prior period
		4. A change from prime costing to full absorption costing for inventory measurement
		5. A change from presentation of statements of individual companies to presentation of consolidated statements
		6. A change in the method of depreciation
		7. A change to including the employer share of FICA taxes as *Retirement Benefits* on the income statement from including it with *Other Taxes*
		8. A change from the FIFO method of inventory pricing to the LIFO method of inventory pricing when it is impracticable to determine the cumulative effect on the period prior to the period of change

1) Types of Changes
A) Change in accounting estimate
B) Change from one principle in accordance with the applicable framework to another
C) Correction of a misstatement involving a principle
D) Change in reporting entity
E) Change in accounting estimate inseparable from change in principle
F) Change in classification
G) Correction of a misstatement not involving a principle
H) New and different transactions

2) Modification Choices
M) Modification required
N) No modification required

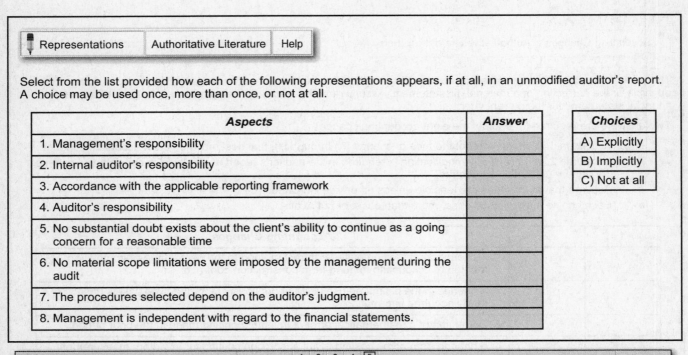

Select from the list provided how each of the following representations appears, if at all, in an unmodified auditor's report. A choice may be used once, more than once, or not at all.

Aspects	Answer	Choices
1. Management's responsibility		A) Explicitly
2. Internal auditor's responsibility		B) Implicitly
3. Accordance with the applicable reporting framework		C) Not at all
4. Auditor's responsibility		
5. No substantial doubt exists about the client's ability to continue as a going concern for a reasonable time		
6. No material scope limitations were imposed by the management during the audit		
7. The procedures selected depend on the auditor's judgment.		
8. Management is independent with regard to the financial statements.		

Unofficial Answers

1. Opinion Types (8 Gradable Items)

1. C) Unmodified with an additional paragraph. A change in the depreciation method is a change in estimate inseparable from a change in principle. The change in principle requires an emphasis-of-matter paragraph describing the change and refers to the entity's disclosure.

2. B) Unmodified. Changes in accounting estimates do not require an additional paragraph.

3. A) Qualified or adverse. The direct write-off method expenses bad debts when they are determined to be uncollectible. This method is not an acceptable accounting principle. Thus, the auditor should express a qualified or an adverse opinion due to a material misstatement.

4. C) Unmodified with an additional paragraph. Correction of a material misstatement requires the auditor to add an emphasis-of-matter paragraph.

5. C) Unmodified with an additional paragraph. If the auditor concludes that substantial doubt exists, an emphasis-of-matter paragraph should be added to the end of the auditor's report.

6. A) Qualified or adverse. Material misstatements, depending on the pervasiveness, require either a qualified or adverse opinion.

7. C) Unmodified with an additional paragraph. A justified change in principle, whether required by FASB or not, results in an unmodified opinion with an emphasis-of-matter paragraph.

8. B) Unmodified. The use of an auditor's specialist does not affect the audit report.

2. Going Concern (8 Gradable Items)

1. <u>B) Dale's comment is correct.</u> The going-concern paragraph should be placed after the opinion paragraph.

2. <u>C) Neither Lei's draft nor Dale's comment is correct.</u> Note X should be referenced to the financial statements. Auditors' reports do not have notes.

3. <u>B) Dale's comment is correct.</u> It is not acceptable to include a contingent statement in a going-concern paragraph.

4. <u>B) Dale's comment is correct.</u> The statement should include the phrase "substantial doubt."

5. <u>A) Lei's draft is correct.</u> The phrase "continue as a going concern" is appropriate to use in the paragraph.

6. <u>C) Neither Lei's draft nor Dale's comment is correct.</u> Management's plans to deal with the issues should be referenced to a note in the financial statements.

7. <u>A) Lei's draft is correct.</u> The phrase "any adjustments that might result" is appropriate to use in the paragraph.

8. <u>A) Lei's draft is correct.</u> There is no comment by management included in the paragraph.

3. Research (1 Gradable Item)

Answer: 600.25

AU-C Section 600 -- *Special Considerations—Audits of Group Financial Statements (Including the Work of Component Auditors)*

.25 Reference to the audit of a component auditor in the auditor's report on the group financial statements should not be made unless

a. the component's financial statements are prepared using the same financial reporting framework as the group financial statements;

b. the component auditor has performed an audit on the financial statements of the component in accordance with GAAS or, when required by law or regulation, with auditing standards promulgated by the Public Company Accounting Oversight Board (PCAOB); and

c. the component auditor has issued an auditor's report that is not restricted as to use.

4. Accounting Changes (16 Gradable Items)

1. <u>1) B) Change from one principle in accordance with the applicable framework to another.</u>
    <u>2) M) Modification required.</u>

2. <u>1) A) Change in accounting estimate.</u>
    <u>2) N) Modification not required.</u>

3. <u>1) G) Correction of a misstatement not involving a principle.</u>
    <u>2) M) Modification required.</u>

4. <u>1) C) Correction of a misstatement in principle.</u>
    <u>2) M) Modification required.</u>

5. <u>1) D) Change in reporting entity.</u>
    <u>2) M) Modification required.</u>

6. <u>1) E) Change in accounting estimate inseparable from change in principle.</u>
    <u>2) M) Modification required.</u>

7. <u>1) F) Change in classification.</u>
    <u>2) N) Modification not required.</u>

8. <u>1) B) Change from one principle in accordance with the applicable framework to another.</u>
    <u>2) M) Modification required.</u>

5. Representations (8 Gradable Items)

1. <u>Explicitly.</u> The management's responsibility paragraph states explicitly, "Management is responsible for the preparation and fair presentation of these consolidated financial statements in accordance with accounting principles generally accepted in the United States of America; this includes the design, implementation, and maintenance of internal control relevant to the preparation and fair presentation of consolidated financial statements that are free from material misstatement, whether due to fraud or error."

2. <u>Not at all.</u> The internal auditor's responsibility neither explicitly nor implicitly appears in the auditor's report.

3. <u>Explicitly.</u> The opinion paragraph of the unmodified auditor's report explicitly states that the financial statements are in accordance with the applicable reporting framework (typically U.S. GAAP).

4. <u>Explicitly.</u> The auditor's responsibility section of the auditor's report explicitly states the auditor's responsibility: "Our responsibility is to express an opinion on these financial statements based on our audit."

5. <u>Implicitly.</u> When an auditor concludes that substantial doubt exists about the client's ability to continue as a going concern for a reasonable period of time, the auditor should include an emphasis-of-matter paragraph in the report. Thus, a client's ability to continue as going concern for a reasonable time is implicit when no emphasis-of-matter paragraph is included.

6. <u>Implicitly.</u> When a material scope limitation is imposed by management, the auditor should qualify or disclaim an opinion. Thus, an unmodified report implicitly states that no material scope limitations were imposed by management during the audit.

7. <u>Explicitly.</u> The report states that "the procedures selected depend on the auditor's judgment, including the assessment of risks of material misstatement, whether due to fraud or error."

8. <u>Not at all.</u> The auditor, not management, is independent.

Gleim Simulation Grading

Task	Correct Responses		Gradable Items		Score per Task
1	___	÷	8	=	___
2	___	÷	8	=	___
3 (Research)	___	÷	1	=	___
4	___	÷	16	=	___
5	___	÷	8	=	___

Total of Scores per Task ___

÷ Total Number of Tasks 5

Total Score ___%

Use **CPA Gleim Online** and **Simulation Wizard** to practice more task-based simulations in a realistic environment.

STUDY UNIT EIGHTEEN
RELATED REPORTING TOPICS

(22 pages of outline)

This study unit addresses miscellaneous reporting issues. Subunit 1 applies the relevant standards to a review of interim (e.g., quarterly) financial information. The procedures and the report are similar to those of a review of annual statements of nonissuers (discussed in Study Unit 19). Subunits 2 and 3 relate to SEC engagements. The next four subunits (4 through 7) apply to information outside the basic financial statements. Subunit 8 addresses the auditor's responsibilities for financial statements prepared for use in other countries. Subunit 9 includes material about the accountant's responsibility when requested to provide an evaluation of, or a conclusion on, how accounting principles will be applied to specific transactions of a particular entity. Subunit 10 relates to audits of statements prepared in accordance with a special purpose framework (e.g., the tax basis or the cash basis). Subunit 11 addresses audits of historical information in the form of single statements or specific elements, accounts, or items. These may be prepared in accordance with a general or special purpose framework.

18.1 INTERIM FINANCIAL INFORMATION (AU-C 930)

1. Interim financial information (IFI) covers a period of (a) less than a full year or (b) the 12 months ending on a date other than fiscal year end.

    a. The IFI may be in the form of a complete set of statements.

        1) The applicable financial reporting framework (**framework**) should be the same one used in the annual statements.

            a) For example, the framework adopted by management may be U.S. GAAP, International Financial Reporting Standards, or a special purpose framework.

    b. The IFI also may be **condensed**.

        1) This IFI should be prepared in accordance with a framework appropriate for condensed IFI. Examples are the interim reporting standards of the FASB, SEC, or IASB.

2. An auditor may review the IFI of an entity if the latest annual statements have been audited by the auditor or a predecessor. Moreover, the auditor

    a. Should be engaged to audit the current-year statements, or

    b. Should have audited the latest annual statements, if the successor auditor's engagement is not yet effective.

    NOTE: "Auditor" is used in this standard because the review of IFI is performed by an auditor of the annual statements.

3. **Objective of a Review**

    a. The objective of a review of IFI is to enable the auditor to state whether (s)he is aware of any material modifications needed for the IFI to be in accordance with the framework (also known as negative assurance).

    b. A review primarily involves performing analytical and inquiry procedures. It does **not** involve (1) testing accounting records and the effectiveness of controls, (2) obtaining corroborating evidence, (3) applying certain other auditing procedures, or (4) becoming aware of all significant matters identified in an audit.

    c. Thus, a review is **not** intended to (1) result in expression of an opinion, (2) provide assurance about internal control, or (3) identify significant deficiencies and material weaknesses in internal control (but these should be communicated to those charged with governance if identified).

4. **Acceptance of Engagement**

    a. Prior to acceptance, the auditor should request that management authorize the predecessor to fully respond to inquiries. (S)he should (1) evaluate the responses or (2) consider the implications if management refuses to authorize the predecessor to respond.

    b. Also prior to engagement acceptance, the auditor should (1) determine that the framework is acceptable and (2) obtain an agreement with management about its responsibilities.

5. **Agreement with Management**

    a. Management is responsible for (1) fair presentation of IFI in accordance with the framework, (2) internal control that provides a reasonable basis for fair presentation, (3) giving the auditor unrestricted access to relevant information and persons within the entity, (4) including the report in any document containing IFI that indicates the IFI has been reviewed by the auditor, (5) providing a representation letter, and (6) adjusting the IFI for material misstatements.

        1) The auditor's responsibility is to comply with applicable GAAS.

    b. The agreement should include (1) the objectives, scope, and limitations of the engagement; (2) the responsibilities of management and the auditor; and (3) identification of the framework.

        1) The agreement should be written, for example, in an **engagement letter**.

6. **Auditor's Understanding of the Entity**

    a. The auditor's understanding of the entity and its environment, including its **internal control**, should be sufficient to (1) identify types of misstatements, (2) consider the likelihood of their occurrence, and (3) select inquiries and analytical procedures.

      b.   This understanding may have been obtained from an audit of the entity's annual statements.

           1)   But internal control over annual reporting may differ from that for interim reporting because accounting principles and practices also may differ. For example, IFI is based on estimated effective income tax rates.

                a)   Nevertheless, the review is **not** intended to provide assurance about internal control or identify control deficiencies.

                b)   However, the auditor cannot complete the review if control deficiencies are so significant that it is not feasible to perform effective review procedures.

      c.   Procedures to obtain the understanding should include

           1)   Reading documentation of the prior audit and of prior reviews. The auditor specifically considers (a) corrected and uncorrected misstatements, (b) identified fraud risks (e.g., of management override), and (c) significant matters of continuing interest (e.g., control weaknesses).

           2)   Reading the recent annual information and prior IFI.

           3)   Considering current audit results.

           4)   Inquiring of management about changes in the business or in internal control.

           5)   Inquiring of the predecessor auditor in an initial review and reviewing his/her documentation, if permitted.

7.   **Analytical Procedures**

      a.   Analytical procedures should be applied to identify unusual relationships and items.

           1)   The auditor's expectations developed in a review are less precise than in an audit, and management responses generally are not corroborated. The reasonableness and consistency of the responses are considered.

      b.   Analytical procedures should include the following:

           1)   Comparing the IFI with comparable information for the preceding interim period, if applicable, and with the corresponding period(s) in the previous year, considering knowledge about changes in the entity's business and specific transactions

           2)   Considering plausible relationships among financial and, if relevant, nonfinancial information

           3)   Comparing recorded amounts or ratios developed from recorded amounts with expectations developed by the auditor by identifying and using relationships that are reasonably expected to exist based on the auditor's understanding of the entity and the industry in which it operates

           4)   Comparing disaggregated revenue data (e.g., monthly revenue of the current interim period with that of comparable prior periods)

8.   **Inquiries and Other Procedures**

      a.   The following inquiries and other procedures are required:

           1)   Reading the minutes of meetings of shareholders, the board, and committees and inquiring about the results of meetings for which minutes are unavailable.

           2)   Obtaining reports of auditors who have reviewed IFI of significant components of the entity or its investees. (If their reports are unissued, inquiries should be made.)

          3)   Inquiring of management about the following:

                a)   Unusual or complex situations
                b)   Significant recent transactions
                c)   Status of uncorrected misstatements
                d)   Knowledge of fraud
                e)   Deficiencies in control
                f)   Significant entries and other adjustments
                g)   Questions arising from application of review procedures
                h)   Events subsequent to the date of the IFI
                i)   Communications from regulators
                j)   Preparation of the IFI in accordance with the framework
                k)   Related parties and related party transactions

          4)   Reconciling the IFI and the accounting records.

          5)   Reading the IFI to consider, based on information coming to the auditor's attention, whether it is in accordance with the framework.

          6)   Reading other information accompanying the IFI.

    b.   Inquiries about **litigation, claims, and assessments** and the entity's ability to continue as a **going concern** ordinarily are not made unless the auditor becomes aware of reasons for such inquiries.

          1)   The auditor extends procedures if (s)he believes that the IFI is not in accordance with the framework. The auditor of the annual statements usually performs the review of the IFI and may be able to coordinate the engagements.

    c.   For all IFI and all periods covered, the auditor should request that management provide **written representations** as of the date of the report. See Study Unit 14, Subunit 3 for an example representation letter that addresses most of the same matters.

9. **Evaluating Results**

    a.   The auditor should **accumulate misstatements** unless they are clearly trivial.

          1)   Misstatements, including inadequate disclosure, are evaluated individually and in the aggregate to determine whether the IFI must be materially modified.

10. **Auditor Communications**

    a.   Possible matters communicated to management and those charged with governance include (1) the inability to issue a report because the review cannot be completed, (2) any material modifications of the IFI that should be made, (3) the auditor's awareness of material fraud or noncompliance with laws and regulations, (4) significant control deficiencies, and (5) certain other matters required to be communicated to those charged with governance.

    b.   Any discussion of the **quality** of the entity's accounting principles as applied to its interim reports is ordinarily limited to the effects of significant events, transactions, and changes in estimates considered in performing the review.

11. **Example Review Report on IFI**

    a.   The review report should be in **writing**.

    b.   The report should accompany the IFI if the entity refers to the auditor's review in a report, document, or written communication.

          1)   If management does not comply with a request to include the review report, the auditor should request that his/her name **not be associated** with the IFI or referred to.

    c.   Each page of the IFI must be clearly marked as unaudited.

d. The auditor modifies the review report for material departures from GAAP or other frameworks. The modification describes the departure and, if feasible, states its effects.

    1) If disclosure is inadequate, the auditor provides the necessary information.

e. If modification of the review report is not sufficient to address the deficiencies in the IFI, the auditor should withdraw from the engagement.

EXAMPLE -- Auditor's Review Report

[Appropriate Addressee]

We have reviewed the accompanying [describe the interim financial information or statements reviewed] of ABC Company and subsidiaries as of September 30, 20X1, and for the three-month and nine-month periods then ended.

Management's Responsibility

The Company's management is responsible for the preparation and fair presentation of the interim financial information in accordance with [identify the applicable financial reporting framework; for example, accounting principles generally accepted in the United States of America]; this responsibility includes the design, implementation, and maintenance of internal control sufficient to provide a reasonable basis for the preparation and fair presentation of interim financial information in accordance with the applicable financial reporting framework.

Auditor's Responsibility

Our responsibility is to conduct our review in accordance with auditing standards generally accepted in the United States of America applicable to reviews of interim financial information. A review of interim financial information consists principally of applying analytical procedures and making inquiries of persons responsible for financial and accounting matters. It is substantially less in scope than an audit conducted in accordance with auditing standards generally accepted in the United States of America, the objective of which is the expression of an opinion regarding the financial information. Accordingly, we do not express such an opinion.

Conclusion

Based on our review, we are not aware of any material modifications that should be made to the accompanying interim financial information for it to be in accordance with [identify the applicable financial reporting framework; for example, accounting principles generally accepted in the United States of America].

Auditor's signature
Auditor's city and state
Date of the auditor's report

Stop and review! You have completed the outline for this subunit. Study multiple-choice questions 1 through 3 on page 577.

18.2 LETTERS FOR UNDERWRITERS AND CERTAIN OTHER REQUESTING PARTIES (AU-C 920)

1. **Comfort Letters**

    a. Independent auditors audit financial statements and schedules contained in registration statements filed with the SEC under the Securities Act of 1933. Because underwriters and others may be liable if a registration statement contains material misstatements or omissions, they seek to establish a defense against liability.

        1) A defense is available under the act if a party demonstrates that a **reasonable investigation** provided reasonable grounds for believing that no material misstatements existed in the securities offering.

        2) A comfort letter issued by an auditor in connection with a securities offering is one of the various ways of demonstrating that a reasonable investigation was made.

            a) However, a comfort letter is not required by law and is not filed with the SEC. Furthermore, GAAS do not require an auditor to accept an engagement to issue a comfort letter.

b.   An auditor may issue a comfort letter in connection with financial statements included in a securities offering **only** to requesting parties. A **requesting party** is a specified party that has negotiated an agreement with the entity.

   1)   An underwriter may be a requesting party. An **underwriter** is a purchaser of an issue of securities for the purpose of public distribution.

   2)   Among the other requesting parties are those who are conducting a review process consistent with the **due diligence** process performed when a securities offering is registered.

   3)   A requesting party should provide either (a) a written attorney's opinion stating that the party has a due diligence defense or (b) a suitable representation letter.

      a)   When a requesting party other than an underwriter requests a comfort letter but does not provide a legal opinion or a representation letter, the auditor should **not** provide negative assurance. However, the comfort letter may describe the procedures that the requesting party asked the auditor to perform.

c.   Because the nature of a reasonable investigation has not been established, only the requesting party can determine what is sufficient. Thus, the assistance provided in a comfort letter is limited.

   1)   Auditors can comment only on matters to which their expertise is relevant, and the procedures permit the expression of, at most, negative assurance.

2.   **Form and Content**

   a.   The letter ordinarily is **dated** on, or shortly after, the date the underwriting agreement is signed. The agreement specifies the cut-off date. Thus, the letter states that the described procedures did **not** cover the period from the cut-off date to the date of the letter.

   b.   The letter should be **addressed** only to the requesting party (or that party and the entity) and should not be given to anyone else.

   c.   The auditor should refer to, but **not repeat**, the report on the audited statements included in the securities offering.

   d.   A typical comfort letter includes a statement about the auditor's **independence**.

   e.   A typical comfort letter expresses, if applicable, an opinion on whether audited statements included in the securities offering **comply as to form,** in all material respects, with the applicable accounting requirements of the 1933 act and the related rules and regulations adopted by the SEC.

   f.   The requesting party may request the auditor to **repeat** in the comfort letter the report on the audited statements. Because of the significance of the date of the auditor's report, the auditor must **not** agree to the request.

      1)   Moreover, the auditor must **not** agree to a request to provide **negative assurance** regarding the audit report.

         a)   Auditors have a statutory responsibility for their opinion as of the effective date of the securities offering. In addition, the significance of negative assurance is unclear, and such assurance might result in misunderstanding.

      2)   But the auditor should discuss the subject matter of any modification of the report.

3.   **Comments on Other Matters**

   a.   The comments on information other than audited statements should describe the procedures performed by the auditor and the criteria specified by the requesting party. The auditor should **not**

      1)   State or imply that (s)he determined the procedures applied to be necessary or sufficient for the requesting party's purposes.

2) Use terms of uncertain meaning (e.g., "check," "test," or "general review") unless the procedures are described.

3) State that nothing else came to the auditor's attention that is of interest to the requesting party.

b. An auditor should obtain an understanding of the entity's **internal control** when commenting on (1) unaudited IFI (including condensed IFI), (2) capsule information, (3) financial forecasts, or (4) subsequent changes.

1) But no comment should be made on internal control.

c. A typical comfort letter includes **negative assurance** on whether, if applicable, **unaudited IFI** included in the registration statement materially complies as to form with the 1933 act and SEC pronouncements.

1) Moreover, negative assurance may be provided on whether any material modifications should be made to the unaudited IFI for them to conform with the applicable framework.

2) But the auditor provides negative assurance on unaudited IFI included in the securities offering only if (s)he has performed a **review** in accordance with GAAS.

d. **Capsule information** is (1) unaudited summarized IFI for periods subsequent to the periods covered by the audited statements or (2) unaudited IFI in the securities offering.

1) The auditor may provide **negative assurance** on whether the capsule information is in accordance with the applicable framework if (a) the auditor has reviewed the underlying statements in accordance with GAAS and (b) the capsule information meets the framework's disclosure requirements.

e. The auditor should not comment on **pro forma financial information** unless (s)he has acquired the appropriate level of knowledge. This topic is covered by AT 401, which is discussed in Study Unit 19, Subunit 6.

f. To apply agreed-upon procedures to a **forecast** and comment on it in a comfort letter, the auditor must perform compilation procedures for a forecast and should attach the report to the comfort letter. Negative assurance on the results of such procedures may **not** be provided. Forecasts are covered by AT 301, which is discussed in Study Unit 19, Subunit 5.

g. Comments on **subsequent changes** ordinarily apply to whether (1) a change has occurred in capital stock, (2) long-term debt has increased, or (3) other specified financial statement items have decreased during the change period (the period subsequent to the latest financial statements included in the registration statement that ends on the cut-off date).

1) The auditor is usually requested to read minutes and make inquiries.

h. A comfort letter should not comment on **tables, statistics, and other financial information** in the securities offering unless the information is (1) expressed in dollars (or percentages derived from such amounts) and obtained from records subject to internal control or (2) derived directly from the accounting records by analysis or computation.

1) Comments should include (a) an identification of the information, (b) a description of the procedures performed, and (c) the findings.

2) The term "presents fairly" should not be used.

3) No comments on the compliance as to form of management's discussion and analysis (MD&A) with SEC rules should be made. Furthermore, no comments should be made on nonfinancial data in MD&A unless the auditor has examined or reviewed the MD&A.

    i.   The **concluding paragraph** of the comfort letter should state that it is solely for the information of the addressees and to assist the requesting parties with regard to the securities offering.

Stop and review! You have completed the outline for this subunit. Study multiple-choice questions 4 through 6 on page 578.

18.3 FILINGS WITH THE SEC UNDER THE SECURITIES ACT OF 1933 (AU-C 925)

1.   **Responsibilities**

    a.   **Management** is responsible for the financial representations contained in documents filed under the federal securities statutes.

    b.   The **auditor's** responsibility is ordinarily similar to that for other types of reporting, but the statutes specify that responsibility in detail.

        1)   For example, the Securities Act of 1933 imposes responsibility for false or misleading statements in an effective registration statement.

        2)   The SEC has a **whistleblower** provision for informants other than the auditor. A whistleblower is a person who provides information to the SEC about a possible violation of securities laws. To be considered for an award, a whistleblower must voluntarily provide the SEC with original information that leads to monetary sanctions in excess of $1 million.

    c.   The independent auditor has a responsibility as an auditing and accounting **expert** when his/her report is included in a registration statement. The 1933 act states that no person is liable

        1)   If (s)he, after **reasonable investigation**, had reasonable grounds to believe that (a) the statements in the registration statement were true, and (b) no material fact required to be stated (or necessary to make the statements not misleading) was omitted.

        2)   If the part of the registration statement for which (s)he had responsibility did **not fairly represent** his/her statement as an expert or was not a fair copy of or extract from his/her report or valuation as an expert.

    d.   The standard of reasonableness is that required of a prudent individual in the management of his/her own property.

    e.   The independent auditor whose report on audited financial statements is included in a registration statement has a statutory responsibility that is determined in light of the circumstances on the **effective date** of the registration statement.

        1)   A report based on a review of unaudited interim financial information is **not deemed to be a report** or **part of the registration statement** for this purpose. The SEC requires that the prospectus contain language to this effect.

        2)   If unaudited annual statements or unaudited interim information does not conform with the applicable framework, the auditor should request revision.

        3)   The SEC requires that registrants obtain reviews of unaudited interim financial information by their independent auditors prior to filing **quarterly reports** in Form 10-Q or Form 10-QSB. But the SEC does not require an entity to include a review report on unaudited interim information in the registration statement if it does not state that the information has been reviewed.

    f.   The independent auditor should be certain that his/her name is not being used in a way indicating his/her responsibility is greater than intended.

2. **Subsequent Events Procedures**

    a.   To sustain the burden of proof that the auditor has made a reasonable investigation, subsequent events procedures should be performed at or shortly before the **effective date of the registration statement**. These procedures are intended to identify events occurring between the date of the report and the effective date of the registration statement that require adjustment of, or disclosure in, the financial statements.

    b.   Following the date of the report, the independent auditor may rely mostly on **inquiries**. The auditor should

        1)   Apply the normal subsequent events procedures.

        2)   Read the prospectus and other pertinent portions of the registration statement.

        3)   Obtain written representations from management about whether (a) previous representations should be modified or (b) any events have occurred that require adjustment of, or disclosure in, the financial statements.

    c.   An auditor may have audited the statements for a prior period included in the registration statement but not those for the most recent period included in the registration statement.

        1)   This **predecessor** auditor is responsible for material subsequent events occurring after the date of the prior-period statements through a date at or shortly before the effective date of the registration statement.

    d.   If the auditor becomes aware of **subsequently discovered facts**, (s)he should consider their effect on the report.

        1)   If this consideration is not satisfactory, e.g., because management does not agree to a necessary revision of the statements, the auditor may need to withhold consent to the inclusion of the report.

Stop and review! You have completed the outline for this subunit. Study multiple-choice questions 7 through 9 on page 579.

Overview of the Reporting Responsibilities Covered in the Next Four Subunits

Subunit	AU-C Section	Type of Information/Example	Auditor's Procedures	Reporting Responsibility
18.4	AU-C 720	**Other**/Quarterly data	Read for consistency with financial statements	Add an other-matter paragraph to audit report only if other information is not consistent with financial statements
18.5	AU-C 730	**Required Supplementary**/Oil and gas reserve information	Apply limited procedures	Add an other-matter paragraph to audit report describing the auditor's responsibility
18.6	AU-C 725	**Supplementary in Relation to Statements**/Schedule of fixed assets	Audit	Refer to and report on fair presentation in audit report
18.7	AU-C 810	**Summary Financial Statements**/ Summary of financial results	Determine whether consistent with audited financial statements	In a separate report, refer to audit report and state opinion about consistency with complete audited financial statements

18.4 OTHER INFORMATION IN DOCUMENTS CONTAINING AUDITED FINANCIAL STATEMENTS (AU-C 720)

1. **Other Information**

    a. Other information is financial or nonfinancial information (other than the financial statements and the auditor's report) that is included in a document containing audited statements and the auditor's report.

        1) An example of such a document is an annual report to owners.
        2) Examples of other information are reports by management on operations, financial summaries, and quarterly data.
        3) Examples of items that are not other information are press releases and analysts' briefings.

    b. "Other information" is a technical term that excludes information required to be included by a designated accounting standards setter.

        1) Thus, required supplementary information (RSI) is not other information. RSI is covered in the next subunit.

2. **Auditor's Objective**

    a. The auditor's responsibility is to respond appropriately when the other information may undermine the credibility of the statements and the auditor's report. However, unless otherwise required for a specific engagement, the opinion on the statements does not cover other information.

        1) Also, the auditor has no responsibility for determining whether it is properly stated.

3. **Material Inconsistencies**

    a. The auditor should read the other information to identify material inconsistencies with the audited statements.

        1) An inconsistency is a conflict with the audited information. It may create doubt regarding the audit conclusions.
        2) The auditor need not refer to the other information in the auditor's report. But (s)he may **disclaim** an opinion on it in an **other-matter** paragraph.

    b. A material inconsistency may be identified **prior** to the report release date that requires revision of the **audited statements**. If management refuses, the auditor should modify the opinion.

    c. A material inconsistency may be identified **prior** to the report release date that requires revision of the **other information**.

        1) If management refuses to revise the other information, the auditor should consult legal counsel.
        2) The auditor also should communicate the matter to those charged with governance and

            a) Include an other-matter paragraph in the auditor's report,
            b) Withhold the auditor's report, or
            c) Withdraw from the engagement.

    d. If a material inconsistency is identified **after** the report release date, and revision is needed, the guidance for subsequent discovery of facts existing at the report date applies.

    NOTE: The outline for subsequently discovered facts is in Study Unit 14, Subunit 2.

4.   **Material Misstatements of Fact**

   a.   A misstatement of fact is other information that is **unrelated** to matters in the audited statements and is incorrectly stated or presented.

   1)   When management refuses to correct a material misstatement of fact, the auditor should notify those charged with governance. (S)he also should take any appropriate further action (e.g., consulting counsel, withholding the report, or withdrawing).

Stop and review! You have completed the outline for this subunit. Study multiple-choice questions 10 and 11 on page 580.

18.5 REQUIRED SUPPLEMENTARY INFORMATION (RSI) (AU-C 730)

1.   RSI is information that the designated accounting standards setter has determined must accompany the basic financial statements.

   a.   Thus, authoritative guidelines for its measurement and presentation have been prescribed.

2.   **Procedures**

   a.   The auditor should perform the following procedures:

   1)   Inquire about

   a)   Whether the RSI is within the guidelines,

   b)   Whether methods of measurement or presentation have changed and the reasons for any change, and

   c)   Any significant assumptions or interpretations.

   2)   Compare the RSI for **consistency** with (a) the basic statements, (b) management's responses to inquiries, and (c) other audit evidence.

   3)   Obtain management's **written representations** relevant to its responsibilities for RSI and compliance with guidelines.

3.   **Reporting**

   a.   The auditor should add an **other-matter** paragraph (following the opinion paragraph and any emphasis-of-matter paragraph) to the auditor's report to refer to RSI. If (1) RSI is not omitted, (2) prescribed guidelines are followed, and (3) required audit procedures are completed, the paragraph should include the following:

   1)   A statement that identifies the RSI and the applicable reporting framework

   2)   A statement that such information, although not part of the basic financial statements, is required to place them in context

   3)   A statement that the auditor has applied certain limited procedures to the RSI in accordance with U.S. GAAS and a description of those procedures

   4)   A statement that the auditor does not express an opinion or provide any assurance on the information and that limited procedures provide insufficient evidence

b. The following is an example of an other-matter paragraph added to the auditor's report:

EXAMPLE -- Other-Matter Paragraph

Other Matter

[Identify the applicable financial reporting framework (for example, accounting principles generally accepted in the United States of America)] require that the [identify the required supplementary information] on page XX be presented to supplement the basic financial statements. Such information, although not a part of the basic financial statements, is required by [identify designated accounting standards setter] who considers it to be an essential part of financial reporting for placing the basic financial statements in an appropriate operational, economic, or historical context. We have applied certain limited procedures to the required supplementary information in accordance with auditing standards generally accepted in the United States of America, which consisted of inquiries of management about the methods of preparing the information and comparing the information for consistency with management's responses to our inquiries, the basic financial statements, and other knowledge we obtained during our audit of the basic financial statements. We do not express an opinion or provide any assurance on the information because the limited procedures do not provide us with sufficient evidence to express an opinion or provide any assurance.

---

c. The paragraph should be revised when

1) Some or all RSI is omitted,
2) Measurement or presentation departs materially from prescribed guidelines or the auditor has unresolved doubts regarding such matters, or
3) The auditor is unable to complete the prescribed procedures.

d. Deficiencies in, or omissions of, RSI do not affect the opinion on the basic financial statements, and the auditor need not present the information if management fails to do so.

Stop and review! You have completed the outline for this subunit. Study multiple-choice questions 12 and 13 beginning on page 580.

18.6 SUPPLEMENTARY INFORMATION IN RELATION TO THE FINANCIAL STATEMENTS AS A WHOLE (AU-C 725)

1. Supplementary information **(SI)** is presented outside the basic statements and is not necessary for the statements to be fairly presented in accordance with the applicable financial reporting framework.

a. Examples include summaries extracted from the financial statements and statistical data.

2. **Conditions for Reporting**

a. An auditor ordinarily does not report on SI but may be engaged to do so.

b. An auditor who is engaged to report on whether SI is fairly stated, in all material respects, in relation to the statements as a whole should determine that certain conditions are satisfied:

1) The SI is derived directly from the underlying records used to prepare the statements and relates to the same period.
2) The financial statements were audited, and the auditor issued a report that did not express an adverse opinion or disclaim an opinion.
3) The SI will accompany the audited statements or be made readily available without further action by the entity (e.g., on the entity's website).

3. **Agreement with Management**

a. Management should understand its responsibilities for

1) Preparing SI in accordance with applicable criteria,
2) Providing written representations, and
3) Including the auditor's report on the SI with the SI and the audited statements.

4. **Procedures**

    a. The following procedures to express an opinion on the SI are performed based on the **materiality level** used for the audit of the statements:

        1) Inquiring about the purpose of, and criteria for, the SI

        2) Determining conformity with the criteria

        3) Understanding methods of preparation

        4) Reconciling SI with underlying records or the statements

        5) Inquiring about significant assumptions or interpretations

        6) Evaluating the appropriateness and completeness of the SI

        7) Obtaining management's written representations about (a) responsibility for, and fairness of, presentation; (b) whether methods of measurement or presentation have changed; (c) assumptions or interpretations; and (d) ready availability of the SI

    b. The auditor need not perform **subsequent events** procedures on the SI.

5. **Reporting**

    a. When the SI and the audited statements are presented together, the auditor reports on the SI in (1) a separate report or (2) an other-matter paragraph following the opinion paragraph and any emphasis-of-matter paragraph. The following is an example of an other-matter paragraph:

EXAMPLE -- Other-Matter Paragraph for Supplementary Information in Relation to the Financial Statements as a Whole

Other Matter

Our audit was conducted for the purpose of forming an opinion on the financial statements as a whole. The *[identify accompanying supplementary information]* is presented for purposes of additional analysis and is not a required part of the financial statements. Such information is the responsibility of management and was derived from and relates directly to the underlying accounting and other records used to prepare the financial statements. The information has been subjected to the auditing procedures applied in the audit of the financial statements and certain additional procedures, including comparing and reconciling such information directly to the underlying accounting and other records used to prepare the financial statements or to the financial statements themselves, and other additional procedures in accordance with auditing standards generally accepted in the United States of America. In our opinion, the information is fairly stated in all material respects in relation to the financial statements as a whole.

---

        1) If the SI and the audited statements are presented separately, a separate report should be issued.

6. The guidance above also applies, with any needed wording changes, when an auditor reports on whether RSI is fairly stated, in all material respects, in relation to the financial statements as a whole.

Stop and review! You have completed the outline for this subunit. Study multiple-choice questions 14 and 15 on page 581.

18.7 ENGAGEMENTS TO REPORT ON SUMMARY FINANCIAL STATEMENTS (AU-C 810)

1. This subunit addresses the auditor's responsibilities when reporting separately on summary financial statements. Such statements consist of historical information derived from financial statements audited in accordance with GAAS by the same auditor.

2. The auditor's objectives include forming an opinion on whether the summary statements are consistent, in all material respects, with the audited statements from which they are derived.

    a. This determination includes evaluating whether the summary statements are prepared in accordance with the criteria applied by management.

    b.   The auditor also should

        1)   Perform procedures necessary to form an opinion and

        2)   Clearly express that opinion through a written report that describes the basis for the opinion.

3.   The auditor should not accept an engagement to report on summary statements unless (s)he has been engaged to audit the statements from which they are derived.

4.   **Procedures**

    a.   The auditor should perform the following procedures:

        1)   Evaluate whether the summary statements (a) adequately disclose their nature and (b) identify the audited statements.

        2)   Evaluate whether the summary statements adequately disclose the applied criteria.

        3)   Determine whether the summary statements agree with, or can be recalculated from, the related information in the audited statements.

        4)   Evaluate whether the summary statements are prepared in accordance with the applied criteria.

        5)   Given the purpose of the summary statements, evaluate whether they (a) contain the necessary information and (b) are at an appropriate level of aggregation so that they are not misleading.

        6)   Request management to provide written representations in the form of a representation letter addressed to the auditor.

    b.   When the summary statements are not accompanied by the audited statements, the auditor should evaluate whether

        1)   They clearly describe where the audited statements are available, and

        2)   The audited statements are readily available to the intended users of the summary statements without further action by the entity, e.g., on a website.

            a)   They are not considered readily available if a request must be made by the user.

5.   **Opinion**

    a.   When an **unmodified** opinion on the summary statements is appropriate, the opinion should state that they are consistent, in all material respects, with the audited statements in accordance with the applied criteria.

        1)   If they are not, and management does not agree to the necessary changes, the auditor should express an **adverse** opinion.

            a)   The opinion paragraph should state that, because of the significance of the matter(s) described in the basis for adverse opinion paragraph, the summary statements are not consistent, in all material respects, with the audited statements.

            b)   A qualified opinion on summary statements is **not** appropriate.

    b.   When the auditor's report on the **audited statements** contains an **adverse** opinion or a **disclaimer** of opinion, the auditor should withdraw from the engagement.

    c.   If the auditor's report on the audited statements contains (1) a qualified opinion, (2) an emphasis-of-matter paragraph, or (3) an other-matter paragraph, the report on the summary statements should so state. Furthermore, it should describe the following:

        1)   The basis for the qualified opinion or additional paragraph in the report on the audited statements

        2)   The effect on the summary financial statements, if any

d. The auditor should **date** the auditor's report on the summary statements no earlier than (1) the date on which the auditor has obtained sufficient appropriate evidence on which to base the opinion and (2) the date of the auditor's report on the audited statements.

6. **Report on Summary Statements**

a. The following are included in the report:

1) A title that includes the word "independent," for example, "Independent Auditor's Report on Summary Financial Statements"

2) Addressee

3) An introductory paragraph that

a) Identifies the summary statements on which the auditor is reporting, including the title of each statement

b) Identifies the audited statements from which the summary statements are derived

c) Refers to the auditor's report on the audited statements, the type of opinion it expresses, and the date of that report

d) Indicates that (1) the summary statements do not contain all the disclosures required by the framework applied in the preparation of the financial statements, and (2) reading the summary statements is not a substitute for reading the audited statements

4) A paragraph describing management's responsibility for the summary statements

5) A section describing the auditor's responsibility for expressing an opinion about whether the summary statements are consistent, in all material respects, with the audited statements based on the procedures required by U.S. GAAS. The procedures primarily involve

a) Comparing the summary statements with the related information in the audited statements from which they are derived and

b) Evaluating whether the summary statements are prepared in accordance with the applied criteria.

6) Opinion

7) Auditor's signature

8) Auditor's city and state

9) Date of the auditor's report

7. **Other Considerations**

a. The auditor should evaluate whether any **unaudited** information presented with the summary statements is clearly differentiated from them.

b. The auditor should read **other information** included in a document containing the summary statements and the related auditor's report to identify material inconsistencies, if any, with the summary statements and the audited statements.

c. The auditor may become aware that the entity plans to state that the auditor has reported on summary statements in a document containing those statements. If the entity does not plan to include the related auditor's report, the auditor should request management to include it.

d. The auditor may learn that the entity plans to make a statement in a document that refers to (1) the auditor and (2) the derivation of the summary statements from the statements audited by the auditor. If the auditor has not reported on the summary statements, (s)he should become satisfied that users are not misled about the auditor's responsibility.

Stop and review! You have completed the outline for this subunit. Study multiple-choice questions 16 through 18 on page 582.

18.8 FINANCIAL STATEMENTS PREPARED IN ACCORDANCE WITH A FINANCIAL REPORTING FRAMEWORK GENERALLY ACCEPTED IN ANOTHER COUNTRY (AU-C 910)

1. An auditor practicing in the U.S. may report on the financial statements of a **U.S. entity** prepared in accordance with a financial reporting framework generally accepted in another country for use outside the U.S.

   a. The auditor should clearly understand the purpose of the statements and obtain written representations from management.

   b. If the statements are for general use and the report form and content of the foreign country will be used, the auditor should consider any additional legal responsibilities.

   c. However, AU-C 910 does not apply to statements prepared in accordance with International Financial Reporting Standards (IFRS) issued by the International Accounting Standards Board (IASB).

      1) The reporting standards (e.g., AU-C 700 and AU-C 705) covered in Study Units 16 and 17 apply because the IASB is an AICPA-designated standards setter.

   d. Because the auditor should understand the entity's selection and application of accounting policies (AU-C 315), (s)he should understand the other accounting principles.

2. **Compliance with Auditing Standards of Another Country**

   a. An auditor engaged to audit financial statements prepared in accordance with a reporting framework generally accepted in another country may be requested to apply the auditing standards of that country or International Standards on Auditing (ISAs). This is acceptable if

      1) The auditor understands those standards.
      2) The auditor uses the guidance in this standard for reporting.

3. **Use Limited to Outside the United States**

   a. If the financial statements and auditor's report are intended for use only outside the United States, the auditor should report using either

      1) A U.S. form of report reflecting that the statements reported on have been prepared in accordance with a reporting framework generally accepted in another country (see Study Unit 16 for the format of the basic U.S. report).

         a) The introductory paragraph should refer to the note to the statements that describes their basis of presentation, including identification of the country of origin of the accounting principles.

      2) The report form and content of the other country (or, if applicable, as set forth in the ISAs).

   b. The auditor expresses an opinion on whether the financial statements are presented fairly in accordance with the framework of the other country.

4. **Use in the United States**

   a. If financial statements prepared in accordance with a reporting framework generally accepted in another country also are intended for use in the United States, the auditor should report using the U.S. form of report. This report includes an emphasis-of-matter paragraph

      1) Identifying the reporting framework used in the preparation of the financial statements,

     2)   Referring to the note in the statements that describes the framework, and

     3)   Indicating that the framework differs from accounting principles generally accepted in the U.S.

   b.   The auditor expresses an opinion on whether the financial statements are presented fairly within the framework of the other country.

Stop and review! You have completed the outline for this subunit. Study multiple-choice questions 19 and 20 on page 583.

18.9 REPORTS ON APPLICATION OF REQUIREMENTS OF AN APPLICABLE FINANCIAL REPORTING FRAMEWORK (AU-C 915)

1.   Management and others may consult with accountants to learn how to apply (a) accounting policies in a financial reporting framework (e.g., U.S. GAAP) to new transactions or (b) new accounting policies in a framework to existing transactions. They also may want to increase their knowledge of specific financial reporting issues.

2.   **Applicability**

   a.   AU-C 915 should be applied by an accountant in public practice (reporting accountant), other than a continuing accountant, who has been requested to issue a **written report** on

     1)   The application of the requirements of a financial reporting framework to a specific transaction (completed or proposed) involving facts or circumstances of a specific entity or

     2)   The type of report that may be issued on a specific entity's statements.

   b.   AU-C 915 also applies to **oral advice** believed to be an important factor in the decisions about accounting principles made by a principal to the transaction.

   c.   AU-C 915 does not apply to

     1)   A continuing accountant's engagement to report on a specific entity's financial statements;

     2)   Assistance in litigation involving accounting matters or related expert testimony;

     3)   Professional advice provided to another public accountant; or

     4)   Position papers, such as (a) newsletters, (b) articles, (c) speeches, or (d) letters for the public record to standards-setting bodies.

   d.   The accountant need not be independent. But if (s)he is not, the report should state the lack of independence.

3.   **Acceptance, Planning, and Performance**

   a.   Before accepting the engagement, the reporting accountant should consider the circumstances in which the report or advice is requested, the purpose, and the intended use.

     1)   An engagement to issue a written report should be accepted only when the transaction involves facts or circumstances of a specific entity, not a hypothetical transaction.

   b.   When planning and performing the engagement, the reporting accountant should

     1)   Obtain an understanding of the form and substance of the transaction(s) or the conditions relevant to the type of report that might be issued

     2)   Review the relevant requirements of the framework (e.g., U.S. GAAP)

     3)   Consult with other professionals or experts, if appropriate

     4)   Consider creditable precedents or analogies

     5)   Consult with the continuing accountant of the entity to determine the available relevant facts, including disputes with management

     c.   The reporting accountant should have an understanding with the requesting party that management

         1)   Acknowledges the reporting accountant's need to consult with the continuing accountant and

         2)   Upon request, will authorize the continuing accountant to respond fully.

4.   **Reporting**

     a.   The addressee of the accountant's written report is the requesting entity. The report should do the following:

         1)   Briefly describe the engagement and state that it was in accordance with AU-C 915.

         2)   Identify the specific entity; describe the transaction(s); state the facts, circumstances, and assumptions; and state the source of the information.

         3)   Describe the appropriate application of the framework (including the country of origin) to the specific transaction or type of report and, if appropriate, the reasons for the conclusion.

         4)   State that the responsibility for proper accounting is with the preparers of the statements, who should consult with their continuing accountant.

         5)   State that any difference in the facts, circumstances, or assumptions may change the report.

         6)   Include a separate paragraph the restricts the use of the report to specified and identified parties.

         7)   If appropriate, state any lack of independence.

Stop and review! You have completed the outline for this subunit. Study multiple-choice questions 21 and 22 on page 584.

18.10 AUDITS OF FINANCIAL STATEMENTS PREPARED IN ACCORDANCE WITH SPECIAL PURPOSE FRAMEWORKS (AU-C 800)

Background
Standards prior to the AICPA's Clarified Auditing Standards used the term "special reports" for the reporting described in the next two study units. They were "special" in the sense that the reports related to other types of reporting objectives.

1.   Auditors can report on the fairness of financial statements prepared in accordance with a special purpose framework.

2.   Special purpose frameworks include the following:

     a.   The **cash basis** is used to record cash receipts and cash payments.

     b.   The **tax basis** is used to file income tax returns.

     c.   The **regulatory basis** is used to comply with the requirements of a regulatory agency.

     d.   The **contractual basis** is used to comply with an agreement between the entity and a third party.

     e.   An **other basis** consisting of a definite set of logical, reasonable criteria that is applied to all material items in the statements.

3.   The cash, tax, regulatory, and other bases of accounting are commonly referred to as **other comprehensive bases of accounting (OCBOA)**.

4. The auditor obtains sufficient appropriate evidence, including evaluation of appropriate disclosures, to judge the fairness of the presentation.

    a. Statements also should be appropriately titled.

        1) For example, "Income Statement" and "Balance Sheet" are not appropriate titles for cash-basis statements. Instead, they may be labeled "Statement of Revenue Collected and Expenses Paid" or "Statement of Assets and Liabilities Arising from Cash Transactions."

    b. Moreover, the statements should include a summary of significant accounting policies and describe how the special purpose framework varies from GAAP.

5. **Auditor's Report**

    a. In addition to the requirements in AU-C 700, the report should

        1) Refer to management's responsibility to determine that the reporting framework is acceptable (if management has a choice).

        2) Describe the purpose of the statements (or refer to a note with that information) if the framework used is

            a) A regulatory or contractual basis or
            b) An other basis, and the use of the report is restricted.

    b. The auditor's report should have a basic format with the following items:

        1) Title -- Independent Auditor's Report

        2) Addressee -- For example, the entity or those charged with governance

        3) Introductory paragraph -- Identification of the entity, statement of the service performed (an audit), title of each financial statement, and the date or period of each statement

        4) Management's responsibility for the financial statements -- Description of responsibilities for preparation and fair presentation in accordance with the applicable framework, including relevant internal control, and for the determination that the framework is acceptable (if management has a choice)

        5) Auditor's responsibility -- Description of responsibilities for (a) expressing an opinion, (b) auditing in accordance with GAAS, (c) obtaining reasonable assurance, (d) assessing risks, (e) considering internal control, and (f) evaluating accounting policies and estimates and the overall presentation

        6) Opinion -- Opinion on fair presentation

        7) Auditor's signature -- Manual or printed

        8) Auditor's city and state -- Location of the auditor

        9) Date -- No earlier than when sufficient appropriate evidence was obtained

6. **Emphasis-of-Matter Paragraph**

    a. Except when regulatory-basis statements are intended for general use, this paragraph (titled "Basis of Accounting") should follow the opinion paragraph. It

        1) Identifies the special purpose framework,
        2) Refers to the note describing the framework, and
        3) States that the framework is not GAAP.

    b. The following is an example of an emphasis-of-matter paragraph included in a report on a cash-basis financial statement:

EXAMPLE -- Emphasis-of-Matter Paragraph

Basis of Accounting

We draw attention to Note X of the financial statements, which describes the basis of accounting. The financial statements are prepared on the cash basis of accounting, which is a basis of accounting other than accounting principles generally accepted in the United States of America. Our opinion is not modified with respect to this matter.

7.   **Other-Matter Paragraph**

   a.   Except when regulatory-basis statements are intended for general use, this paragraph (titled "Restriction on Use") should follow any emphasis-of-matter paragraph. It restricts the use of the report when the special purpose framework is

   1)   A contractual basis of accounting,

   2)   A regulatory basis of accounting, or

   3)   An other basis of accounting (if measurement or disclosure criteria are suitable only for limited users or available only to the specified parties).

   b.   The following is an example of an emphasis-of-matter paragraph and an other-matter paragraph included in a report on a regulatory-basis financial statement not intended for general use:

EXAMPLE -- Emphasis-of-Matter Paragraph and Other-Matter Paragraph

Basis of Accounting

We draw attention to Note X of the financial statements, which describes the basis of accounting. As described in Note X to the financial statements, the financial statements are prepared by ABC City on the basis of the financial reporting provisions of Section Y of Regulation Z of Any State, which is a basis of accounting other than accounting principles generally accepted in the United States of America, to meet the requirements of Any State. Our opinion is not modified with respect to this matter.

Restriction on Use

Our report is intended solely for the information and use of ABC City and Any State and is not intended to be and should not be used by anyone other than these specified parties.

---

8.   **Regulatory Basis (General Use)**

   a.   The auditor's report on regulatory-basis statements intended for general use does not include emphasis-of-matter and other-matter paragraphs.

   1)   The auditor's report includes separate paragraphs expressing an opinion on fair presentation in accordance with (a) GAAP and (b) the special purpose framework, respectively.

   b.   The following is an example:

EXAMPLE

Basis for Adverse Opinion on U.S. Generally Accepted Accounting Principles

As described in Note X of the financial statements, the financial statements are prepared by XYZ City on the basis of the financial reporting provisions of Section Y of Regulation Z of Any State, which is a basis of accounting other than accounting principles generally accepted in the United States of America, to meet the requirements of Any State.

The effects on the financial statements of the variances between the regulatory basis of accounting described in Note X and accounting principles generally accepted in the United States of America, although not reasonably determinable, are presumed to be material.

Adverse Opinion on U.S. Generally Accepted Accounting Principles

In our opinion, because of the significance of the matter discussed in the "Basis for Adverse Opinion on U.S. Generally Accepted Accounting Principles" paragraph, the financial statements referred to above do not present fairly, in accordance with accounting principles generally accepted in the United States of America, the financial position of each fund of XYZ City as of December 31, 20X1, or changes in financial position or cash flows thereof for the year then ended.

Opinion on Regulatory Basis of Accounting

In our opinion, the financial statements referred to above present fairly, in all material respects, the cash and unencumbered cash of each fund of XYZ City as of December 31, 20X1, and their respective cash receipts and disbursements, and budgetary results for the year then ended in accordance with the financial reporting provisions of Section Y of Regulation Z of Any State described in Note X.

Stop and review! You have completed the outline for this subunit. Study multiple-choice questions 23 through 28 beginning on page 584.

18.11 AUDITS OF SINGLE FINANCIAL STATEMENTS AND SPECIFIC ELEMENTS, ACCOUNTS, OR ITEMS OF A FINANCIAL STATEMENT (AU-C 805)

1. The objective of an audit of (a) a single financial statement or (b) a specific element, account, or item of a financial statement is to address the special considerations that are relevant to

   a. Acceptance of the engagement,
   b. Planning and performance of the audit, and
   c. Forming an opinion and reporting.

2. An **element** is defined for the purposes of AU-C 805 as an **element, account, or item** of a financial statement.

3. A single financial statement or a specific element includes the related notes.

   a. The notes ordinarily include a summary of significant accounting policies and other explanatory information.

4. All relevant auditing standards apply for auditing an element or a single financial statement regardless of whether the auditor also audits the entity's complete set of statements.

   a. However, if the auditor did not audit those statements, (s)he should determine whether the audit of a single statement or a specific element in accordance with GAAS is feasible. The auditor also should determine whether (s)he can perform procedures on interrelated items.

5. For an audit of a single statement or a specific element, the auditor should obtain an **understanding** of

   a. The purpose for which the statement or element is prepared,
   b. The intended users, and
   c. Management's steps to ensure proper reporting.

6. In planning and performing the audit of a single statement or a specific element, the auditor should adapt all relevant auditing standards as necessary.

   a. Furthermore, the auditor should perform procedures on **interrelated items** as necessary to meet the objective of the audit. For example, sales and receivables, inventory and payables, and equipment and depreciation are interrelated.

      1) Thus, an auditor of a single statement may be unable to consider that statement in isolation.

7. **Audit of a Specific Element**

   a. The specific element may be, or may be based upon, the entity's **equity** or **net income**. The auditor should perform procedures necessary to obtain sufficient appropriate evidence to permit expression of an opinion on, respectively, (1) financial position and (2) financial position and results of operations.

      1) But the procedures need not address matters related to classification or disclosure that are not relevant to the audit of the specific element.

8. **Materiality**

   a. The auditor should determine materiality for the **single statement** being reported on, not for the complete set of statements.

   b. In an audit of one or more **specific elements**, the auditor should determine materiality for each element reported on, not the aggregate of all elements or the complete set of statements.

9.   **Reporting**

a.   If the auditor of the complete set of statements also audits a single statement or a specific element, (s)he should

    1)   Issue a separate auditor's report and express a separate opinion for each engagement.

    2)   Indicate in the report on a specific element the date of the auditor's report on the complete set of statements and the nature of the opinion expressed on those statements.

ISA Difference

The ISAs do not require the separate opinions to be in separate reports.

---

b.   An audited single statement or an audited specific element ordinarily may be published with the entity's audited complete set of statements. But the presentation of the single statement or the specific element should be sufficiently differentiated from the complete set of statements.

c.   If the auditor's opinion on an entity's complete set of statements is **modified**, the auditor should determine the effect on the auditor's opinion on a single statement or a specific element.

    1)   For example, a modified opinion due to **material misstatement** of the complete set of statements may be relevant to a specific element. In this case, an **adverse opinion** should be expressed on the element.

    2)   A modified opinion on the complete set of statements also may be due to an inability to obtain sufficient appropriate evidence. If this modified opinion is relevant to a specific element, the auditor should disclaim an opinion on the specific element.

d.   The auditor's report on an entity's complete set of statements may include an **emphasis-of-matter** paragraph or an **other-matter** paragraph that is relevant to the audit of the single statement or the specific element.

    1)   In this case, the auditor should include a similar paragraph in the auditor's report on the single statement or the specific element.

e.   An auditor may wish to express (1) an adverse opinion or disclaimer of opinion on the complete set of statements and (2) an unmodified opinion on a specific element. Doing so in the same auditor's report would contradict the adverse opinion or disclaimer and be equivalent to expressing a piecemeal opinion.

    1)   However, in the context of a separate audit of a specific element included in those statements, when the auditor considers it appropriate to express an unmodified opinion on the specific element, the auditor should do so only if

        a)   That opinion is expressed in an auditor's report that is neither published with nor accompanies the auditor's report containing the adverse opinion or disclaimer of opinion.

        b)   The specific element is not a major portion of the entity's complete set of statements or is not, or is not based upon, the entity's equity or net income.

Stop and review! You have completed the outline for this subunit. Study multiple-choice questions 29 through 31 beginning on page 586.

QUESTIONS

18.1 Interim Financial Information (AU-C 930)

1. The objective of a review of interim financial information of an issuer is to provide an auditor with a basis for reporting whether

  A. A reasonable basis exists for expressing an updated opinion regarding the financial statements that were previously audited.

  B. Material modifications should be made to conform with generally accepted accounting principles.

  C. The financial statements are presented fairly in accordance with standards of interim reporting.

  D. The financial statements are presented fairly in accordance with generally accepted accounting principles.

Answer (B) is correct.
  REQUIRED: The objective of a review of interim financial information.
  DISCUSSION: The review provides the auditor with a basis for reporting whether (s)he is aware of material modifications that should be made for such information to conform with the applicable financial reporting framework. This objective differs significantly from that of an audit, which is to provide a basis for expressing an opinion (AU-C 930).
  Answer (A) is incorrect. The review of interim financial information does not provide a basis for expressing an opinion. Answer (C) is incorrect. Reporting on whether the statements are fairly presented is the expression of an opinion. Answer (D) is incorrect. Reporting on whether the statements are fairly presented is the expression of an opinion.

2. Which of the following procedures ordinarily should be applied when an independent auditor conducts a review of interim financial information of an issuer?

  A. Verify changes in key account balances.

  B. Read the minutes of the board of directors' meetings.

  C. Inspect the open purchase order file.

  D. Perform cutoff tests for cash receipts and disbursements.

Answer (B) is correct.
  REQUIRED: The procedure applied in a review of IFI.
  DISCUSSION: A review involves (1) establishing an understanding with the client; (2) obtaining knowledge of the entity's business and controls; (3) performing analytical procedures, making inquiries, and applying other limited procedures; (4) obtaining written representations from management; and (5) evaluating the results of procedures. The specific procedures performed include reading the minutes of meetings of shareholders, the board of directors, and committees of the board of directors and inquiring about the results of meetings for which minutes are unavailable.

3. A modification of the auditor's report on a review of interim financial information is necessitated by which of the following?

  A. A substantial doubt about the entity's ability to continue as a going concern.

  B. Lack of consistency.

  C. Use of another auditor's report.

  D. Inadequate disclosure.

Answer (D) is correct.
  REQUIRED: The reason for modifying a review report on interim financial information.
  DISCUSSION: Modification of the report on a review of IFI is necessary if it is not, in all material respects, in accordance with the applicable reporting framework. If the departure is due to inadequate disclosure, the auditor should, if feasible, include the information in the report. But many circumstances that preclude the issuance of an unmodified report on audited statements do not cause a modification of a review report (AU-C 930).
  Answer (A) is incorrect. AU-C 930 specifically states that a substantial doubt about the entity's ability to continue as a going concern is not a cause for modification if appropriately disclosed. Answer (B) is incorrect. AU-C 930 specifically states that lack of consistency is not a cause for modification if appropriately disclosed. Answer (C) is incorrect. The use of the report of another auditor may result in, but does not require, modification of the report. After considering the guidance in AU-C 600 relating to component auditors, the auditor may be able to assume responsibility for the component auditor's work.

18.2 Letters for Underwriters and Certain Other Requesting Parties (AU-C 920)

4. Which of the following matters is covered in a typical comfort letter?

A. Negative assurance concerning whether the entity's internal control activities operated as designed during the period being audited.

B. An opinion regarding whether the entity complied with laws and regulations under Government Auditing Standards and the Single Audit Act.

C. Positive assurance concerning whether unaudited condensed financial information complied with generally accepted accounting principles.

D. An opinion as to whether the audited financial statements comply in form with the accounting requirements of the SEC.

Answer (D) is correct.
REQUIRED: The item in a typical letter for underwriters.
DISCUSSION: A typical comfort letter expresses an opinion on whether audited financial statements and schedules included in the securities offering comply as to form, in all material respects, with the applicable accounting requirements of the Securities Act of 1933 and the related published rules and regulations. However, the comfort letter does not state or repeat an opinion about the fairness of presentation of the statements.

5. When an auditor issues to an underwriter a comfort letter containing comments on data that have not been audited, the underwriter most likely will receive

A. Positive assurance on supplementary disclosures.

B. Negative assurance on capsule information.

C. A disclaimer on prospective financial statements.

D. A limited opinion on pro forma financial statements.

Answer (B) is correct.
REQUIRED: The most likely assurance, if any, provided in a comfort letter commenting on unaudited data.
DISCUSSION: Capsule information is (1) unaudited summarized interim information for periods subsequent to the periods covered by the audited financial statements or (2) unaudited interim financial information in the securities offering. The auditor may provide negative assurance on whether the capsule information is in accordance with the applicable financial reporting framework. The auditor must review the underlying statements in accordance with GAAS, and the capsule information must meet the framework's disclosure requirements.
Answer (A) is incorrect. A comfort letter does not express positive assurance. Answer (C) is incorrect. Prospective statements do not appear in a registration statement. Answer (D) is incorrect. A limited opinion is not a permissible form of reporting.

6. In a comfort letter, an auditor may provide negative assurance about

A. The absence of any significant deficiencies in internal control.

B. Whether the entity's unaudited interim financial information complies as to form with the accounting requirements of the Securities Act of 1933.

C. The results of procedures performed in compiling the entity's financial forecast.

D. The compliance of the entity's registration statement with the requirements of the Securities Act of 1933.

Answer (B) is correct.
REQUIRED: The negative assurance provided by a comfort letter.
DISCUSSION: A typical comfort letter includes negative assurance on whether the unaudited interim financial information included in the registration statement complies as to form, in all material respects, with the applicable accounting requirements of the Securities Act of 1933 and rules and regulations of the SEC.
Answer (A) is incorrect. The auditor should have knowledge of the client's internal controls but does not comment on them in the comfort letter. Answer (C) is incorrect. Practitioners do not provide limited assurance on forecasts. Answer (D) is incorrect. Auditors can comment only on matters to which their expertise is relevant. Compliance with aspects of the law is beyond that expertise.

18.3 Filings with the SEC under the Securities Act of 1933 (AU-C 925)

7. An independent auditor's report is based on a review of interim financial information. If this report is presented in a registration statement, a prospectus should include a statement clarifying that the

A. Auditor's review report is not a part of the registration statement within the meaning of the Securities Act of 1933.

B. Auditor assumes no responsibility for subsequent events.

C. Auditor's review was performed in accordance with rules and regulations adopted by the Securities and Exchange Commission.

D. Auditor obtained corroborating evidence to determine whether material modifications are needed for such information to be in accordance with GAAP.

Answer (A) is correct.
REQUIRED: The statement in a review report on IFI included in a registration statement.
DISCUSSION: The auditor has reviewed interim information, and his/her report is presented or incorporated by reference in a registration statement. In these circumstances, the SEC requires that a prospectus containing a statement about the auditor's involvement clarify that the report is not a report on, or a part of, the registration statement within the meaning of sections 7 and 11 of the Securities Act of 1933. The prospectus should state that reliance on the report should be restricted given the limited procedures applied and that the auditor is not subject to the liability provisions of section 11.
Answer (B) is incorrect. The registration statement contains audited financial statements. Thus, procedures should be extended from the date of the audit report to the effective date of the filing. Answer (C) is incorrect. The report might state that the independent public accountants have reported that they have applied limited procedures in accordance with professional standards for a review of such information. Answer (D) is incorrect. The auditor makes inquiries and applies analytical procedures to determine whether modifications are needed for financial information to be in accordance with the applicable framework. The auditor does not collect corroborating evidence in a review.

8. A registration statement filed with the SEC contains the reports of two independent auditors on their audits of financial statements for different periods. The predecessor auditor who audited the prior-period financial statements generally should obtain a letter of representation from the

A. Successor independent auditor.

B. Client's audit committee.

C. Principal underwriter.

D. Securities and Exchange Commission.

Answer (A) is correct.
REQUIRED: The party from whom the predecessor auditor should obtain a letter of representation.
DISCUSSION: An auditor who has audited the financial statements for prior periods but not for the most recent period included in a registration statement has a responsibility for material subsequent events affecting the prior-period statements. Thus, the predecessor auditor who audited the prior-period financial statements generally should obtain a letter of representation from the successor auditor.

9. The Securities and Exchange Commission has authority to

A. Prescribe specific auditing procedures to detect fraud concerning inventories and accounts receivable of companies engaged in interstate commerce.

B. Deny lack of privity as a defense in third-party actions for gross negligence against the auditors of issuers.

C. Determine accounting principles for the purpose of financial reporting by companies offering securities to the public.

D. Require a change of auditors of governmental entities after a given period of years as a means of ensuring independence.

Answer (C) is correct.
REQUIRED: The authority of the SEC.
DISCUSSION: The SEC has the authority to regulate the form and content of all financial statements, notes, and schedules filed with the SEC and also the financial reports to shareholders if the company is subject to the Securities Exchange Act of 1934. The SEC has stated that financial statements conforming to FASB standards will be presumed to be in accordance with U.S. GAAP. However, the SEC reserves the right to substitute its principles for those of the accounting profession and to require any additional disclosures it deems necessary. The Sarbanes-Oxley Act of 2002 authorized the SEC to recognize as generally accepted any accounting principles established by a standards-setting body that meets the act's criteria.
Answer (A) is incorrect. The SEC may not prescribe specific auditing procedures. The Public Company Accounting Oversight Board (PCAOB), established by the Sarbanes-Oxley Act, adopts auditing standards related to preparation of audit reports for issuers. Answer (B) is incorrect. The SEC may not deny lack of privity as a defense. Answer (D) is incorrect. The SEC may not require a change of auditors of governmental entities.

18.4   Other Information in Documents Containing Audited Financial Statements (AU-C 720)

10. When audited financial statements are presented in a document containing other information, the auditor

A. Has an obligation to perform auditing procedures to corroborate the other information.

B. Should express a qualified opinion if the other information is materially inconsistent with the statements.

C. Should be aware of whether the other information contains a material misstatement of fact.

D. Has no responsibility for the other information because it is not part of the basic financial statements.

Answer (C) is correct.
REQUIRED: The auditor's responsibility for other information.
DISCUSSION: A misstatement of fact is other information that is unrelated to matters in the audited statements and is incorrectly stated or presented. If material, it may undermine the credibility of the document containing the audited statements. When management refuses to correct a material misstatement of fact, the auditor should notify those charged with governance.
Answer (A) is incorrect. The auditor should read, but need not corroborate, the other information. Answer (B) is incorrect. If the audited information is presented fairly, the opinion should be unmodified. However, if the other information needs revision, the auditor should request that management revise it. If revision is not made, (s)he should communicate the matter to those charged with governance and (1) modify the report to include an other-matter paragraph, (2) withhold use of the report, or (3) withdraw from the engagement. Answer (D) is incorrect. The auditor should read the other information to consider whether it is inconsistent with the audited financial statements.

11. An auditor concludes prior to the release date of the report that a material inconsistency exists in the other information in an annual report to shareholders. The report contains audited financial statements. If the auditor concludes that the financial statements do not require revision, but management refuses to revise or eliminate the material inconsistency, the auditor may

A. Revise the auditor's report to include a separate other-matter paragraph describing the material inconsistency.

B. Express a qualified opinion after discussing the matter with the client's directors.

C. Consider the matter closed because the other information is not in the audited statements.

D. Disclaim an opinion on the financial statements after explaining the material inconsistency in a separate other-matter paragraph.

Answer (A) is correct.
REQUIRED: The auditor's response when management presents other information with a material inconsistency.
DISCUSSION: If the other information contains a material inconsistency that requires revision, and management refuses to make the revision, the auditor should communicate the matter to those charged with governance. The auditor also should (1) revise the report to include an other-matter paragraph, (2) withhold use of the report, or (3) withdraw from the engagement.
Answer (B) is incorrect. The opinion is expressed on the financial statements only. The inconsistency in the other information does not affect that opinion. Answer (C) is incorrect. The auditor may not ignore a material inconsistency in other information. Answer (D) is incorrect. The auditor's decision to disclaim an opinion is not affected by the other information.

18.5   Required Supplementary Information (RSI) (AU-C 730)

12. If management declines to present required supplementary information, the auditor should express a(n)

A. Adverse opinion.

B. Qualified opinion with an additional paragraph.

C. Unmodified opinion without an additional paragraph.

D. Unmodified opinion with an other-matter paragraph.

Answer (D) is correct.
REQUIRED: The effect on the auditor's report of management's failure to disclose RSI.
DISCUSSION: Omission of RSI does not affect the auditor's opinion because such information is not part of the basic financial statements. Instead, the auditor should express an unmodified opinion on the basic financial statements (assuming it is otherwise justified). In the other-matter paragraph, the auditor should (1) state that management omitted the RSI; (2) describe the missing RSI; (3) describe the applicable financial reporting framework that requires the RSI to be presented to supplement the basic statements; (4) identify the designated accounting standards setter; (5) state that the RSI is considered to be essential by the designated accounting standards setter, although it is not a part of the basic financial statements; and (6) state that the audit opinion is unaffected by the omission. The information itself need not be presented by the auditor (AU-C 730).
Answer (A) is incorrect. The auditor should modify the other-matter paragraph but not the opinion. Answer (B) is incorrect. The auditor should not modify the opinion. Answer (C) is incorrect. The report should include an other-matter paragraph.

13. What is an auditor's responsibility for required supplementary information (RSI)?

A. Include a disclaimer on the information only if the auditor is unable to apply limited procedures to it.

B. Add an emphasis-of-matter paragraph to the auditor's report before the opinion paragraph.

C. Apply limited procedures to the information and report its omission or the need for material modifications.

D. Audit the RSI in accordance with applicable auditing standards.

Answer (C) is correct.
REQUIRED: The auditor's responsibility for RSI.
DISCUSSION: RSI differs from other information outside the basic statements because the designated accounting standard setter considers it to be an essential part of financial reporting for placing the basic financial statements in context. The auditor at minimum should apply limited procedures and report on the RSI in an other-matter paragraph that follows the opinion paragraph.
Answer (A) is incorrect. The other-matter paragraph referring to RSI (by definition, not part of the basic statements) contains a disclaimer even if limited procedures are completed. Answer (B) is incorrect. An other-matter paragraph is added after the opinion paragraph. Answer (D) is incorrect. RSI need not be audited.

18.6 Supplementary Information in Relation to the Financial Statements as a Whole (AU-C 725)

14. Investment and property schedules are presented for purposes of additional analysis in a document outside the basic financial statements. The schedules are not required supplementary information. When the auditor is engaged to report on whether the supplementary information is fairly stated in relation to the audited financial statements as a whole, the measurement of materiality is the

A. Same as that used in forming an opinion on the basic financial statements as a whole.

B. Lesser of the individual schedule of investments or schedule of property by itself.

C. Greater of the individual schedule of investments or schedule of property by itself.

D. Combined total of both the individual schedules of investments and property as a whole.

Answer (A) is correct.
REQUIRED: The measure of materiality.
DISCUSSION: When reporting on whether supplementary information is fairly stated in relation to the statements as a whole, the measurement of materiality is the same as that used in forming an opinion on the basic financial statements taken as a whole. Accordingly, the auditor need not apply procedures as extensive as would be necessary to express an opinion on the information by itself.

15. The auditor is engaged to report on whether supplementary information is fairly stated in relation to the audited financial statements as a whole. Which of the following best describes the auditor's responsibility for this information if it is outside the basic financial statements and **not** deemed necessary to their fair presentation?

A. The auditor has no reporting responsibility concerning information accompanying the basic financial statements.

B. The auditor should report on the supplementary information only if the auditor participated in its preparation.

C. The auditor must disclaim an opinion on the information if it is supplementary information required by the applicable financial reporting framework.

D. The auditor should not express an opinion on the supplementary information if (s)he disclaimed an opinion on the financial statements.

Answer (D) is correct.
REQUIRED: The auditor's reporting responsibility.
DISCUSSION: Supplementary information is presented outside the basic statements and is not deemed necessary for their fair presentation in accordance with the applicable financial reporting framework. For example, it includes (1) additional details or explanations of items in or related to the statements, (2) consolidating information, (3) statistical data, and (4) historical summaries. The auditor should not express an opinion on the supplementary information if (s)he expressed an adverse opinion or disclaimed an opinion on the audited financial statements. Moreover, the auditor should have served as the group auditor of those statements.
Answer (A) is incorrect. The auditor was engaged to report on the supplementary information. Answer (B) is incorrect. Management is responsible for preparing the supplementary information. Answer (C) is incorrect. The auditor is not precluded from performing an engagement to express an opinion on RSI. But the opinion on the audited financial statements does not cover RSI, absent a specific requirement in the agreement with the client.

18.7 Engagements to Report on Summary Financial Statements (AU-C 810)

16. An auditor may report on summary financial statements that are derived from audited financial statements only if the auditor

- A. Expresses an unmodified opinion on the audited financial statements from which the summary financial statements are derived.
- B. States whether the information is consistent with the audited financial statements.
- C. Determines that the summary financial statements include all the disclosures necessary for the audited financial statements.
- D. Presents the summary financial statements in comparative form with the prior year's summary financial statements.

Answer (B) is correct.
REQUIRED: The condition for reporting on summary financial statements.
DISCUSSION: Summary financial statements consist of historical information derived from financial statements audited in accordance with GAAS by the same auditor. The auditor should not accept an engagement to report on summary statements unless (s)he has been engaged to audit the statements from which they are derived. The report expresses an opinion on whether the summary statements are consistent, in all material respects, with the audited statements, in accordance with the applied criteria.
Answer (A) is incorrect. The report on the audited financial statements need not be unmodified for summary financial statements to be presented and reported on. Answer (C) is incorrect. The summary financial statements need not contain the disclosures necessary for the audited financial statements. Answer (D) is incorrect. The summary financial statements need not be in comparative format.

17. The report on summary financial statements should indicate that the

- A. Summary financial statements are prepared in conformity with a special purpose framework.
- B. Procedures performed included evaluating whether they are prepared in accordance with the applied criteria.
- C. Summary financial statements are fairly presented in all material respects.
- D. The auditor expresses limited assurance that the financial statements conform with GAAP.

Answer (B) is correct.
REQUIRED: The indication in a report on summary financial statements.
DISCUSSION: The report on the summary statements describes, among other things, the procedures performed. They primarily include (1) comparing the summary statements with the related information in the audited statements and (2) evaluating whether the summary statements are prepared in accordance with the criteria applied by management.
Answer (A) is incorrect. Summary financial statements are prepared on the same basis as the audited financial statements. Answer (C) is incorrect. Summary financial statements are to be presented consistently with the audited financial statements. Answer (D) is incorrect. The auditor expresses an opinion.

18. The auditor should not accept an engagement to report on summary statements **unless**

- A. The auditor has been engaged to audit the financial statements from which the summary statements are derived.
- B. The auditor issued an unmodified report on the statements from which the summary statements are derived.
- C. The auditor takes responsibility for the summary financial statements.
- D. A complete audit can be completed on the summary statements.

Answer (A) is correct.
REQUIRED: The requirement to report on summary financial statements.
DISCUSSION: Summary financial statements consist of historical information derived from financial statements audited in accordance with GAAS by the same auditor. The auditor should not accept an engagement to report on summary statements unless (s)he has been engaged to audit the statements from which they are derived. The report expresses an opinion on whether the summary statements are consistent, in all material respects, with the audited statements, in accordance with the applied criteria.
Answer (B) is incorrect. The auditor may have expressed a qualified opinion on the audited statements or included an emphasis-of-matter or other-matter paragraph in the report. But the auditor should not report on the summary statements if an adverse opinion or disclaimer of opinion has been expressed on the audited statements. Answer (C) is incorrect. Management is responsible for the summary financial statements. Answer (D) is incorrect. An auditor applies procedures to determine whether the summary statements are consistent with the audited statements.

18.8 Financial Statements Prepared in Accordance with a Financial Reporting Framework Generally Accepted in Another Country (AU-C 910)

19. The financial statements of KCP America, a U.S. entity, are prepared for inclusion in the consolidated financial statements of its non-U.S. parent. These financial statements are prepared in accordance with a financial reporting framework generally accepted in the parent's country and are for use only in that country. Which is an appropriate report on the financial statements for KCP America's auditor to issue?

I. A U.S. form of report (unmodified)

II. A U.S. form of report modified to report on the financial reporting framework of the parent's country

III. The report form of the parent's country

   A. I only.

   B. II only.

   C. II and III only.

   D. I, II, and III.

Answer (C) is correct.

REQUIRED: The proper reporting on the financial statements of a U.S. entity prepared for inclusion in the consolidated financial statements of its non-U.S. parent.

DISCUSSION: Financial statements may be prepared in accordance with a financial reporting framework generally accepted in another country. In these circumstances, if the statements are prepared for use only outside the U.S., the auditor may use either a U.S. form of report modified to report on the financial reporting framework of the other country or, if appropriate, the report form of the other country. An unmodified U.S. form of report is inappropriate because of the departures from GAAP contained in statements prepared in accordance with a financial reporting framework generally accepted in the other country.

20. An auditor practicing in the U.S. has been engaged to report on the financial statements of a U.S. entity that have been prepared in accordance with a financial reporting framework generally accepted in another country. The auditor should

   A. Understand the framework.

   B. Be certified by the appropriate auditing or accountancy board of the other country.

   C. Notify management that the auditor is required to disclaim an opinion on the financial statements.

   D. Receive a waiver from the auditor's state board of accountancy to perform the engagement.

Answer (A) is correct.

REQUIRED: The requirement for reporting on financial statements prepared in accordance with a financial reporting framework generally accepted in another country.

DISCUSSION: An auditor practicing in the U.S. may report on financial statements prepared in accordance with a financial reporting framework generally accepted in another country. Such a framework is not one adopted by a standards setter designated by the AICPA Council to establish GAAP (e.g., the FASB for U.S. GAAP and the IASB for IFRS). In these circumstances, because of the requirement to understand the entity's selection and application of accounting policies (AU-C 315), the auditor should obtain an understanding of the framework. The auditor's report should identify the country of origin of the accounting standards used to prepare the statements. It also should identify the auditing standards followed in performing the audit.

Answer (B) is incorrect. The auditor needs to be a CPA in the U.S. Answer (C) is incorrect. The auditor can express an opinion on the fairness of the financial statements. Answer (D) is incorrect. No waiver is required to perform this service.

18.9 Reports on Application of Requirements of an Applicable Financial Reporting Framework (AU-C 915)

21. Blue, CPA, has been asked to report on the application of a financial reporting framework to a specific transaction by an entity that is audited by another CPA. Blue may accept this engagement but should

- A. Consult with the continuing accountant to obtain information relevant to the transaction.
- B. Report the engagement's findings to the entity's audit committee, the continuing accountant, and management.
- C. Disclaim any opinion on the application of the financial reporting framework to the hypothetical transaction.
- D. Be independent of the client.

Answer (A) is correct.
REQUIRED: The responsibility of an accountant who is reporting on the application of a financial reporting framework to a specific transaction if (s)he is not the continuing accountant.
DISCUSSION: The reporting accountant should consult with the continuing accountant to determine the available facts relevant to a professional judgment. The continuing accountant may provide information not otherwise available to the reporting accountant. (S)he should (1) explain to the entity's management the need to consult with the continuing accountant, (2) request permission to do so, and (3) request authorization for the continuing accountant to respond fully.
Answer (B) is incorrect. The accountant's written report should be addressed to the requesting entity. Answer (C) is incorrect. The report should describe (1) the appropriate application of the financial reporting framework to the specific transaction and (2), if appropriate, the reasons for the conclusion, not an opinion or a disclaimer. Also, the engagement may not involve reporting on the application of the financial reporting framework to a hypothetical transaction. Answer (D) is incorrect. The accountant need not be independent. But if (s)he is not, the report should state the lack of independence.

22. In connection with a proposal to obtain a new client, an accountant in public practice is asked to prepare a written report on the requirements of an applicable financial reporting framework to a specific transaction. The accountant's report should include a statement that

- A. Any difference in the facts, circumstances, or assumptions presented may change the report.
- B. The engagement was performed in accordance with Statements on Standards for Consulting Services.
- C. The guidance provided is for general use.
- D. Nothing came to the accountant's attention that caused the accountant to believe that the application of the financial reporting framework to the facts is inappropriate.

Answer (A) is correct.
REQUIRED: The statement in a report on the application of a financial reporting framework to a specific transaction.
DISCUSSION: The accountant's report is addressed to the requesting party. The report should contain (1) a description of the engagement and a statement that it was performed in accordance with AU-C 915; (2) a description of the transaction and identification of the entity; (3) a description of the financial reporting framework applied (including its country of origin), the type of report that may be issued, and the reasons for the conclusion; (4) a statement that the responsibility for proper accounting is with the preparers of the financial statements; (5) statements of the facts, circumstances, and assumptions and their sources; (6) a statement that any difference in the facts, etc., may change the report; (7) an alert restricting the use of the report to specified parties; and (8), if the accountant is not independent, a statement of the lack of independence.
Answer (B) is incorrect. The accountant's report should state that the engagement is conducted in accordance with AU-C 915. Answer (C) is incorrect. The use of the report is restricted to specified parties. Answer (D) is incorrect. The report does not provide for limited assurance.

18.10 Audits of Financial Statements Prepared in Accordance with Special Purpose Frameworks (AU-C 800)

23. An auditor's report on financial statements prepared in accordance with the income tax basis of accounting should include all of the following **except**

- A. Reference to the note to the financial statements that describes the basis of accounting.
- B. A statement that the basis of accounting is other than GAAP.
- C. An opinion as to whether the basis of accounting used is appropriate under the circumstances.
- D. An opinion as to whether the financial statements are presented fairly, in all material respects, in accordance with the basis of accounting used for income tax purposes.

Answer (C) is correct.
REQUIRED: The item not in a report on statements prepared in accordance with a special purpose framework.
DISCUSSION: The auditor's report should include paragraphs or sections that (1) describe the financial statements; (2) state management's responsibility for the financial statements; (3) describe the auditor's responsibilities; (4) express an opinion on fair presentation in accordance with the income tax basis; and (5) identify in an emphasis-of-matter paragraph the basis of accounting, state that the basis is other than GAAP, and refer to the note that describes that basis. The auditor's responsibilities include evaluating the appropriateness of the accounting policies used. They do include expression of an opinion on whether the basis of accounting used is appropriate under the circumstances.

24. When an auditor reports on financial statements prepared on an entity's income tax basis, the auditor's report should

A. Disclaim an opinion on whether the statements were examined in accordance with generally accepted auditing standards.

B. Not express an opinion on whether the statements are presented in conformity with income tax basis.

C. Include an explanation of how the results of operations differ from the cash receipts and disbursements basis of accounting.

D. State that the special purpose framework is a basis of accounting other than GAAP.

Answer (D) is correct.
REQUIRED: The content of a report on financial statements prepared on the income tax basis.
DISCUSSION: An emphasis-of-matter paragraph in an auditor's report on financial statements prepared in accordance with a special purpose framework, e.g., the income tax basis, should (1) state that the statements are prepared in accordance with the applicable framework, (2) refer to the note describing the framework, and (3) state that the special purpose framework is a basis other than GAAP. The special purpose framework may be (1) the tax basis, (2) the cash basis, (3) a regulatory basis, (4) a contractual basis, or (5) a definite set of logical and reasonable criteria applied to all material items in the statements.
Answer (A) is incorrect. The auditor applies GAAS in the engagement. Answer (B) is incorrect. The auditor expresses an opinion on whether the statements are presented in conformity with the income tax basis. Answer (C) is incorrect. A note in the financial statements should describe the special purpose framework, but the report need only refer to that note.

25. Which of the following is a suitable title for a financial statement prepared using a special purpose framework?

A. Statement of operations.

B. Statement of income – regulatory basis.

C. Income statement.

D. Statement of comprehensive income.

Answer (B) is correct.
REQUIRED: The suitable title for a statement prepared using a special purpose framework.
DISCUSSION: Terms such as "balance sheet," "statement of income," or similar unmodified titles are ordinarily understood to apply to statements presented in accordance with GAAP. Consequently, the auditor of statements prepared using a special purpose framework should consider whether the statements are suitably titled. If (s)he believes they are not, the auditor should disclose any reservations in a basis for qualified opinion paragraph and modify the opinion (AU-C 800). For example, a statement prepared on a regulatory basis of accounting may be titled "statement of income – regulatory basis."

26. Delta Life Insurance Co. prepares its financial statements on an accounting basis insurance companies use pursuant to the rules of a state insurance commission. If Wall, CPA, Delta's auditor, discovers that the statements are **not** suitably titled, Wall should

A. Disclose any reservations in a basis for qualified opinion paragraph and qualify the opinion.

B. Apply to the state insurance commission for an advisory opinion.

C. Issue a special statutory-basis report that clearly disclaims any opinion.

D. Explain in the notes to the financial statements the terminology used.

Answer (A) is correct.
REQUIRED: The proper action when statements prepared using a special purpose framework are not suitably titled.
DISCUSSION: Terms such as "balance sheet," "statement of income," or other unmodified titles are ordinarily understood to apply to statements presented in accordance with GAAP. Consequently, the auditor of statements prepared under a special purpose framework should consider whether the statements are suitably titled. If (s)he believes they are not, the auditor should disclose his/her reservations in a basis for qualified opinion paragraph (AU-C 800).
Answer (B) is incorrect. AU-C 800 does not require the auditor to apply to the state insurance commission for an advisory opinion. Answer (C) is incorrect. The opinion should be qualified. Answer (D) is incorrect. The notes are the responsibility of management, not the auditor.

27. Auditors' reports issued in connection with which of the following are **not** considered to be on financial statements based on a special purpose framework?

A. Financial statements prepared in accordance with the cash basis of accounting.

B. Financial statements prepared in accordance with a contractual agreement between the entity and a third party.

C. Financial statements prepared in accordance with the tax basis of accounting.

D. Compiled financial statements prepared in accordance with appraised liquidation values.

Answer (D) is correct.
REQUIRED: The statements not prepared using a special purpose framework.
DISCUSSION: AU-C 800 identifies special purpose frameworks for financial statements as frameworks other than GAAP. They are (1) the cash basis, (2) the tax basis, (3) a regulatory basis, (4) a contractual basis, and (5) a definite set of logical and reasonable criteria applied to all items in the statements. Compiled statements are not audited, and appraised value is not a special purpose framework.

28. Whenever a report filed on a printed form designed by authorities calls upon the independent auditor to make an assertion that the auditor believes is **not** justified, the auditor should

    A. Reword the form.

    B. Submit an unmodified report with explanations.

    C. Submit the form with questionable items clearly omitted.

    D. Withdraw from the engagement.

Answer (A) is correct.
REQUIRED: The auditor's action when asked to make an unjustified assertion in a prescribed form.
DISCUSSION: The auditor may be required by law or regulation to use a specific layout, form, or wording of the auditor's report. For example, printed forms designed by the agencies or other authorities that they will be filed with often prescribe the wording of the auditor's report. Many are unacceptable to auditors because they conflict with GAAS. When a report form calls for an unjustified assertion, an auditor should reword the form. If rewording the form would not (1) be permitted or (2) mitigate the risk that users will misunderstand the report, the auditor should not accept the audit unless required by law or regulation. In this case, the auditor's report should not refer to performing an audit in accordance with GAAS (AU-C 210).
Answer (B) is incorrect. An unmodified report with explanations is not appropriate for a special purpose reporting situation. Answer (C) is incorrect. Omission of questionable items does not meet the auditor's reporting responsibility. These items should be resolved. Answer (D) is incorrect. Withdrawal from the engagement is an extreme measure unnecessary in most circumstances and may not be permitted.

18.11 Audits of Single Financial Statements and Specific Elements, Accounts, or Items of a Financial Statement (AU-C 805)

29. Field is an employee of Gold Enterprises. Thomas Hardy, CPA, is asked to express an opinion on Field's profit participation in Gold's net income. Hardy may accept this engagement only if

    A. Hardy also performs procedures on Gold's financial position and results of operations.

    B. Gold's financial statements are prepared in accordance with GAAP.

    C. Hardy's report is available for use only by Gold's other employees.

    D. Field owns a controlling interest in Gold.

Answer (A) is correct.
REQUIRED: The condition for accepting an engagement to express an opinion on an employee's profit participation in the employer's net income.
DISCUSSION: If the auditor does not audit the complete set of statements, (s)he should determine whether it is feasible to (1) audit the profit participation and (2) perform procedures on interrelated items. If a specified element, account, or item is, or is based upon, an entity's net income or the equivalent, the auditor should perform the procedures needed to express an opinion on financial position and results of operations. The reason is that the profit participation interrelates with balance sheet and income statement accounts.
Answer (B) is incorrect. The financial statements could be based on a special purpose framework. Answer (C) is incorrect. The use of the report may be restricted, or the auditor may issue a general-use report. Answer (D) is incorrect. Whether Field owns a controlling interest in Gold is irrelevant.

30. For reporting purposes, the auditor should consider each of the following types of financial presentation to be a financial statement **except** the statement of

    A. Retained earnings.

    B. Operations by product lines.

    C. Changes in the elements of working capital.

    D. Revenue and expenses.

Answer (C) is correct.
REQUIRED: The presentation not a financial statement.
DISCUSSION: AU-C 805 defines financial statements as a structured representation of historical financial information, including related notes, intended to communicate an entity's economic resources and obligations at a point in time or the changes therein for a period of time in accordance with a financial reporting framework. The related notes ordinarily comprise a summary of significant accounting policies and other explanatory information. AU-C 805 lists various types of financial statements but excludes the statement of changes in working capital.
Answer (A) is incorrect. Statements of retained earnings are financial statements. Answer (B) is incorrect. Statements of operations by product lines are financial statements. Answer (D) is incorrect. Statements of revenue and expenses are financial statements.

31. An auditor may express an opinion on an entity's accounts receivable balance even if the auditor has disclaimed an opinion on the financial statements as a whole, provided that the

    A. Report on the accounts receivable discloses the reason for the disclaimer of opinion on the financial statements.

    B. Distribution of the report on the accounts receivable is restricted to internal use only.

    C. Auditor also reports on the current asset portion of the entity's balance sheet.

    D. Report on the accounts receivable is presented separately from the disclaimer of opinion on the financial statements.

Answer (D) is correct.

REQUIRED: The condition for expressing an opinion on an account balance despite disclaiming an opinion on the financial statements as a whole.

DISCUSSION: An auditor may be requested to express an opinion on one or more specified elements, accounts, or items of a financial statement. However, the auditor may not express such an opinion after disclaiming an opinion on the financial statements if such reporting is tantamount to a piecemeal opinion on the financial statements. Nevertheless, an auditor may be able to express an opinion in these circumstances if a major portion of the financial statements is not involved. For example, an auditor who has disclaimed an opinion on the financial statements may be able to express an opinion on the accounts receivable balance. Moreover, the report should be presented separately.

Answer (A) is incorrect. The report on accounts receivable should disclose the modification of the report on the financial statements if it is considered relevant, but any reasons for the modification need not be described. Answer (B) is incorrect. The report need not be restricted to internal use. Answer (C) is incorrect. A report may be presented on one or more specified elements, accounts, or items of a financial statement.

Use the additional questions in Gleim **CPA Test Prep** to create Practice Exams that emulate Prometric!

18.12 PRACTICE TASK-BASED SIMULATIONS

DIRECTIONS

Note: If you believe you have encountered a software malfunction, report it to the test center staff immediately.

Navigation

To navigate from task to task, use the controls at the bottom of the screen. Click on the **Next** button to advance to the next task, or the **Previous** button to go to the previous task. To go directly to any task, click on its number.

If you would like a reminder to revisit a task, or want to indicate that you are finished with it, click on the reminder flag below the task number. To clear the flag, click on it again. Reminder flags are for your use only – they do not contribute to your score.

Tabs

In this part of the examination, you will be asked to complete various tasks. Every task has one or more **Work Tabs**. Some tasks have one or more **Information Tabs**, others may have none. Every task has a **Help** tab.

If a task has **Information Tabs**, you may use the information in them to complete your responses in the **Work Tabs**.

Work tab   Information tab   Help tab

Work Tabs:

- **Work Tabs** are identified with a pencil icon. This is where your responses are expected.
- Each task has one or more **Work Tabs**.
- **Work Tabs** contain directions for completing the task – be sure to read these directions carefully.
- The **Work Tab** name in the example above is for illustration only – yours will differ.
- You must complete all of the **Work Tabs** in each task to receive full credit.

Information Tabs:

- The Authoritative Literature will be provided in all tasks in the AUD, FAR, and REG sections for your reference.
- Your simulation may have one or more additional **Information Tabs**. Like the Authoritative Literature tabs, **Information Tabs** do not have a pencil icon.
- If your task has additional **Information Tabs**, go through each to familiarize yourself with the task content.

Help Tab:

- The **Help Tab** provides assistance with the exam software that is used in this task. For example, if the task is to compose a memorandum, **Help** will provide information about the word processor.

The Toolbar

The toolbar at the top of the screen shows the amount of time remaining for you to complete the tasks. In addition, the following tools are available. Note that only the **Exit** button is displayed when Directions are visible - the others will appear when you begin the tasks.

Click on these buttons to split or unsplit the screen. You can split the screen vertically or horizontally.

Click on this button to display the calculator; click on it again to hide the calculator. To move the calculator, click on the calculator title bar and drag the calculator to the desired location.

Click on this button to use the spreadsheet; click on it again to hide the spreadsheet. To move the spreadsheet, click on the the spreadsheet title bar and drag the spreadsheet to the desired location.

Click on this button to go on to the next part of the examination. You must complete all of the tasks to receive full credit. Once you click on **Exit** and confirm the action, you will NOT be able to return to this testlet.

Select whether each true statement about an engagement to perform and report on a review of an issuer's interim financial information is true or false.

Statement	Answer	Choices
1. The objective of a review of interim financial information is to express an opinion on whether it conforms with the applicable financial reporting framework.		True
2. A review primarily involves performing analytical procedures and inquiries.		False
3. To perform a review, the annual statements must have been audited.		
4. To perform a review of interim financial information, the auditor should have an understanding of the entity sufficient to identify types of typical misstatements.		
5. To perform a review of interim financial information, the auditor should obtain a letter from the entity's legal counsel concerning litigation, claims, and assessments.		
6. To perform a review of interim financial information, the auditor should obtain a client representation letter.		
7. Significant deficiencies in internal control result in a modified review report.		
8. Each page of the reviewed interim financial information should state "Reviewed by Auditor."		
9. A departure from the applicable financial reporting framework in the financial information may result in a modified review report.		
10. As a result of the review, the auditor should communicate any significant fraud or noncompliance with laws and regulations of which (s)he becomes aware to those charged with governance.		

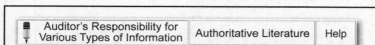

The auditor will encounter various types of information presented by clients. Listed below are four types of information defined in the standards.

- In column (a), select from List 1 an example of each type of information.
- In column (b), select from List 2 an appropriate procedure for each type of information.

Each choice may be used once, more than once, or not at all.

Type of Information	Example of Information (a)	Accountant's Procedures (b)
1. Other information		
2. Required supplementary		
3. Supplementary on which the auditor is engaged to report		
4. Summary		

List 1
A) Oil and gas reserve information
B) Schedule of fixed assets
C) Summary financial statements
D) CEO's letter in the annual report

List 2
E) Audit
F) Apply limited procedures
G) Read for consistency with financial statements
H) Determine whether stated consistently relative to complete financial statements

Research | Authoritative Literature | Help

Weebles & Wobbles Corp. is an international corporation that has operations around the world. In order to conform with its international creditors' obligations, W&W requires a report on its financial statements prepared in accordance with a financial reporting framework generally accepted in a specific country. This report is intended for use only outside the United States. Heidi, CPA, has been engaged by W&W to prepare this report and has decided to research the appropriate auditing standard that outlines the reporting standards applicable in this scenario. Which section of the AICPA's generally accepted auditing standards describes the choice of reports that could be issued in this situation?

Title	Section	Paragraph

Title Choices

AU-C	PCAOB	AT	AR	ET	BL	VS
CS	QC	PR	TS	PFP	CPE	

▼ = Reminder   Directions   1 2 **3** 4 5   ◀ Previous   Next ▶

Summary Financial Statements | Authoritative Literature | Help

A manager is evaluating the audit plan prepared by a staff member for reporting on summary financial statements of a client. Select from the list provided whether the staff member is correct, the manager is correct, or neither is correct.

Staff Member's Procedures	Manager's Evaluation	Answer
1. Be certain our firm has reviewed or audited the financial statements from which the summary statements are derived.	We should be certain we have compiled, reviewed, or audited the related financial statements.	
2. Determine that summary statements identify the audited financial statements.	The summary statements stand alone and need not refer to the audited financial statements.	
3. Compare the summary financial statement balances with the entity's general ledger.	The summary statements should be compared to the related information in the audited financial statements.	
4. Determine that the summary financial statements have been prepared in accordance with accounting standards generally accepted for summary statements.	The summary financial statements should be consistent with the audited statements in accordance with the applied criteria.	
5. Determine whether the level of aggregation is appropriate.	This is management's responsibility and need not be considered.	
6. Form an opinion on whether the summary statements are presented fairly.	A disclaimer should be issued on the summary financial statements.	

Choices
A) The staff member is correct.
B) The manager is correct.
C) Neither is correct.

▼ = Reminder   Directions   1 2 3 **4** 5   ◀ Previous   Next ▶

For each of the following, select from the list provided the appropriate term for each description relating to comments on information other than audited financial statements typically contained in a comfort letter. Each choice may be used once, more than once, or not at all.

Description	Answer		Choices
1. Comments on these statements should be in the form of negative assurance.			A) Financial forecasts
2. The auditors should have this information if they comment on unaudited interim financial information; capsule information; financial forecasts; or changes in capital stock, increases in noncurrent debt, and decreases in selected items.			B) Capsule financial information
3. This information consists of unaudited summarized interim financial information for periods subsequent to periods covered by the audited financial statements or unaudited interim financial information in a securities offering.			C) Pro forma financial information
			D) Subsequent changes
4. The auditors should not comment on this information unless they have acquired the appropriate level of knowledge, such as that obtained from auditing or reviewing the historical statements.			E) Unaudited interim financial information
5. To apply agreed-upon procedures, the auditors should perform compilation procedures on this information and should attach the report to the comfort letter.			F) Management's discussion and analysis
6. Comments that attestations are in accordance with the applicable attestation pronouncement may be made, but no comments on nonfinancial data or the compliance with the forms required by SEC rules should be made.			G) Knowledge of the entity's internal control
7. Comments on these matters ordinarily concern whether a change has occurred in capital stock, noncurrent debt has increased, or other specified financial statement items have increased or decreased during the change period.			

Unofficial Answers

1. Interim Financial Information (10 Gradable Items)

1. <u>False.</u> The objective of a review of IFI is to enable the auditor to provide negative assurance, i.e., to state whether (s)he is aware of any material modifications that should be made for the IFI to conform with the applicable financial reporting framework.

2. <u>True.</u> A review engagement primarily involves the use of inquiries and analytical procedures.

3. <u>True.</u> An auditor may review the IFI of an entity if the latest annual statements have been audited and the auditor is engaged to audit the current-year statements or audited the prior-year statements. Also, the IFI should be prepared using the same applicable financial reporting framework as those statements.

4. <u>True.</u> The auditor's understanding of the entity and its environment, including its internal control, should be sufficient to (a) identify types of misstatements, (b) consider the likelihood of their occurrence, and (c) select inquiries and analytical procedures.

5. <u>False.</u> A review of IFI does not contemplate communication with the client's legal counsel.

6. <u>True.</u> The auditor should obtain written representations from management.

7. <u>False.</u> Significant deficiencies in internal control result in an incomplete review, and no report is issued.

8. <u>False.</u> Each page of the interim financial information should be clearly marked as unaudited.

9.   <u>True.</u> The auditor modifies the review report for material departures from the applicable financial reporting framework, including inadequate disclosure. The modification describes the departure and, if practicable, states its effects or provides the necessary information.

10.   <u>True.</u> Possible communications to management and those charged with governance include (a) the inability to complete the review, (b) the need for material modification of IFI, (c) the auditor's awareness of fraud or noncompliance with laws and regulations, (d) internal-control-related matters, and (e) certain other matters.

2. Auditor's Responsibility for Various Types of Information (8 Gradable Items)

1.   (a) <u>D) CEO's letter in the annual report.</u>
      (b) <u>G) Read for consistency with financial statements.</u>

2.   (a) <u>A) Oil and gas reserve information.</u>
      (b) <u>F) Apply limited procedures.</u>

3.   (a) <u>B) Schedule of fixed assets.</u>
      (b) <u>E) Audit.</u>

4.   (a) <u>C) Summary financial statements.</u>
      (b) <u>H) Determine whether stated consistently relative to complete financial statements.</u>

3. Research (1 Gradable Item)

Answer: 910.12

AU-C Section 910 -- *Financial Statements Prepared in Accordance with a Financial Reporting Framework Generally Accepted in Another Country*

Reporting—Use Only Outside the United States

.12 If the auditor is reporting on financial statements prepared in accordance with a financial reporting framework generally accepted in another country that are intended for use only outside the United States, the auditor should report using either

 a. a U.S. form of report that reflects that the financial statements being reported on have been prepared in accordance with a financial reporting framework generally accepted in another country, including

  i. the elements required by section 700 and

  ii. a statement that refers to the note to the financial statements that describes the basis of presentation of the financial statements on which the auditor is reporting, including identification of the country of origin of the accounting principles, or

 b. the report form and content of the other country (or, if applicable, as set forth in the ISAs), provided that

  i. such a report would be issued by auditors in the other country in similar circumstances,

  ii. the auditor understands and has obtained sufficient appropriate audit evidence to support the statements contained in such a report, and

  iii. the auditor has complied with the reporting standards of that country and identifies the other country in the report.

4. Summary Financial Statements (6 Gradable Items)

1.   <u>C) Neither is correct.</u> The financial statements from which the summary statements are derived should be audited by the auditors.

2.   <u>A) The staff member is correct.</u> The summary financial statements should identify the audited financial statements from which they have been derived.

3.   <u>B) The manager is correct.</u> The summary financial statements should be compared with the related information in the audited financial statements to determine whether the summary financial statements agree with, or can be recalculated from, the related information in the audited financial statements.

4.   <u>B) The manager is correct.</u> The applied criteria are used by management to derive the summary statements from the audited statements. The auditor determines whether the applied criteria are acceptable prior to accepting the engagement.

5.   <u>A) The staff member is correct.</u> The auditor should evaluate whether the summary financial statements contain the information necessary, and are at an appropriate level of aggregation, so that they are not misleading in the circumstances.

6.   <u>C) Neither is correct.</u> The auditor should form an opinion on whether the summary financial statements are consistent, in all material respects, with the audited financial statements from which they have been derived.

5. Comfort Letters (7 Gradable Items)

1. <u>E) Unaudited interim financial information.</u> Comments in the comfort letter about unaudited interim financial information appearing in the securities offering always should be in the form of negative assurance.

2. <u>G) Knowledge of the client's internal control.</u> The auditors should have knowledge of the entity's internal control if they comment on (a) unaudited interim financial information; (b) capsule information; (c) financial forecasts; or (d) changes in capital stock, increases in noncurrent debt, and decreases in selected items. However, they do not comment on internal control.

3. <u>B) Capsule financial information.</u> Capsule information is unaudited summarized interim information for subsequent periods used to supplement the audited financial statements or unaudited interim financial information in a securities offering.

4. <u>C) Pro forma financial information.</u> The auditors should not comment on pro forma financial information unless they have acquired the appropriate level of knowledge of the accounting and financial reporting practices of the entity, e.g., by auditing or reviewing the historical statements.

5. <u>A) Financial forecasts.</u> To apply agreed-upon procedures to a financial forecast and comment on it in a comfort letter, the auditors should perform compilation procedures and attach the report to the comfort letter. Negative assurance on the results of the procedures may not be provided.

6. <u>F) Management's discussion and analysis.</u> Comments that attestations are in accordance with AT 701, *Management's Discussion and Analysis*, may be made. No comments on the compliance of the MD&A with the forms required by SEC rules should be made. Furthermore, no comments should be made on nonfinancial data in the MD&A.

7. <u>D) Subsequent changes.</u> Comments on subsequent changes ordinarily concern whether a change has occurred in capital stock, noncurrent debt has increased, or other specified financial statement items have decreased during the change period (the period subsequent to the latest financial statements included in the securities offering and ending on the cutoff date to which procedures relate).

Gleim Simulation Grading

Task	Correct Responses		Gradable Items		Score per Task
1	_____	÷	10	=	_____
2	_____	÷	8	=	_____
3 (Research)	_____	÷	1	=	_____
4	_____	÷	6	=	_____
5	_____	÷	7	=	_____

Total of Scores per Task _____

÷ Total Number of Tasks   5

Total Score _____%

Use **CPA Gleim Online** and **Simulation Wizard** to practice more task-based simulations in a realistic environment.

594

STUDY UNIT NINETEEN
REVIEW, COMPILATION, AND ATTESTATION ENGAGEMENTS

(25 pages of outline)

Review and compilation services are provided in conjunction with the dissemination of financial statements. These services are not as comprehensive as an audit, which provides positive assurance that financial statements are presented fairly in accordance with GAAP (or other comprehensive basis of accounting). Those performed with respect to unaudited financial statements, except for reviews of interim financial information subject to AU-C 930, are governed by Statements on Standards for Accounting and Review Services (SSARSs), which are codified as AR 60, 80, 90, etc. AR 80 and AR 90 are the basic pronouncements on compilations and reviews and are outlined in the first two subunits.

Regardless of the service provided, the CPA should establish an **understanding with the entity**, preferably in writing, describing the nature and limitations of the services to be performed and the report to be issued. The understanding also should provide that the engagement is not intended to detect errors, fraud, or noncompliance with laws and regulations (illegal acts). The CPA must be **independent** to perform a review but need not be independent to perform a compilation.

Subunits 4 through 7 cover specific **Statements on Standards for Attestation Engagements**. These standards relate to services that practitioners provide beyond those on traditional historical financial statements. AT 501 is not included here, as it relates to examining internal control for a nonissuer and is covered in Study Unit 9. Additionally, AT 101, *Attest Engagements*, the general standard on attestation engagements, is addressed in Study Unit 1. You should do a quick review of these study units while you consider the topics in these subunits.

19.1 COMPILATION (AR 80)

1. A compilation is a service performed to assist management in presenting financial information in the form of financial statements **without undertaking to obtain or provide any assurance**. Thus, an accountant need not be independent to perform a compilation.

    a. AR 80 states that, although a compilation is not an assurance engagement, it is an attest engagement.

    NOTE: The SSAEs apply to compilations of prospective financial statements.

2. A compilation differs significantly from a review or an audit of financial statements, which require independence.

Compilation	Review	Audit
No Assurance	Limited Assurance	Positive Assurance
Independence Not Required	Independence Required	Independence Required

    a. A compilation does not contemplate performing inquiries, analytical procedures, or other procedures performed in a review.

b. Additionally, a compilation does not involve (1) obtaining an understanding of the entity's internal control; (2) assessing fraud risk; (3) testing accounting records by obtaining sufficient appropriate audit evidence through inspection, observation, and confirmation; or (4) examining source documents.

c. Compilations are typically performed for nonissuers.

3. The accountant should establish an **understanding** with management regarding the services to be performed for compilation engagements and should document the understanding through a written communication with management (e.g., an **engagement letter**).

4. **Understanding of the Entity and Industry**

a. The accountant should have an understanding of the industry in which the client operates, including the accounting principles and practices generally used. This understanding should be sufficient to enable the accountant to compile financial statements that are appropriate in form for an entity operating in that industry.

1) Lack of knowledge **does not prevent the accountant from accepting a compilation engagement** for an entity in an industry with which the accountant has no previous experience. It does, however, place upon the accountant a responsibility to obtain the required level of knowledge.

b. The accountant should obtain knowledge about the client, including an understanding of the client's business and accounting principles and practices used by the client.

1) The accountant should obtain an understanding of the accounting principles and practices used by the client in **measuring, recognizing, recording, and disclosing** all significant accounts and disclosures in the financial statements.

5. **Compilation Procedures**

a. **Reading the financial statements.** Before submission of the statements to the client or others, the accountant **should read the financial statements** and consider whether such financial statements appear to be appropriate in form and free from obvious material errors.

b. **Other compilation procedures.** The accountant is **not required to make inquiries or perform other procedures** to verify, corroborate, or review information supplied by the entity. However, the accountant may have made inquiries or performed other procedures.

1) The results of such inquiries or procedures, knowledge gained from prior engagements, or the financial statements on their face may cause the accountant to become aware that information supplied by the entity is **incorrect, incomplete, or otherwise unsatisfactory** or that fraud or a noncompliance with laws and regulations may have occurred.

a) The accountant should request that management consider the effect of these matters on the financial statements and communicate the results of such consideration to the accountant.

b) If the entity refuses to provide additional or revised information, the accountant should **withdraw** from the engagement.

6. **Documentation**

a. The accountant should prepare documentation (working papers) in connection with each compilation engagement to include

1) The **engagement letter** documenting the understanding with the client

2) Any **findings or issues** that, in the accountant's judgment, are significant

3) Communications, whether oral or written, to the appropriate level of management regarding **fraud or illegal acts** that come to the accountant's attention

7. **Standard Compilation Report**

> The Auditing and Attestation part of the CPA exam allocates 12% – 16% to review and compilation topics. Many questions relate to the standard review report and the modifications that are required under various conditions. We recommend that you study the standard report to understand its components and wording and the use of each paragraph. Once the standard report is mastered, modifications to the report should be more easily understood.

a. The accountant's objective in reporting on the financial statements is to prevent misinterpretation of the degree of responsibility the accountant is assuming when his or her name is associated with the financial statements.

b. The standard compilation report contains three paragraphs.

EXAMPLE

Accountant's Compilation Report

To the Owners of XYZ Company:

I (we) have compiled the accompanying balance sheet of XYZ Company as of December 31, 20XX, and the related statements of income, retained earnings, and cash flows for the year then ended. I (we) have not audited or reviewed the accompanying financial statements and, accordingly, do not express an opinion or provide any assurance about whether the financial statements are in accordance with accounting principles generally accepted in the United States of America.

Management (owners) is (are) responsible for the preparation and fair presentation of the financial statements in accordance with accounting principles generally accepted in the United States of America and for designing, implementing, and maintaining internal control relevant to the preparation and fair presentation of the financial statements.

My (our) responsibility is to conduct the compilation in accordance with Statements on Standards for Accounting and Review Services issued by the American Institute of Certified Public Accountants. The objective of a compilation is to assist management in presenting financial information in the form of financial statements without undertaking to obtain or provide any assurance that there are no material modifications that should be made to the financial statements.

Signature of accounting firm or accountant   <---------- May be manual, stamped, electronic, or typed
Date   <---------- Date of completion of review procedures

---

c. The accountant may indicate that (s)he is independent in the title, if applicable. In that case, the title would be "Independent Accountant's Compilation Report."

d. Each page of the financial statements should include the statement "See accountant's compilation report."

e. Financial statements prepared in accordance with an other comprehensive basis of accounting (OCBOA) are not appropriate in form unless they include

1) A description of the OCBOA, including a summary of significant accounting policies and a description of the primary differences from generally accepted accounting principles (GAAP). The effects of the differences need not be quantified.

2) Informative disclosures similar to those required by GAAP.

8. **Reporting on Financial Statements That Omit Substantially All Disclosures**

a. The accountant may compile financial statements that omit substantially all the disclosures required by an applicable reporting framework if the omission is not, to his or her knowledge, done to mislead those who might reasonably be expected to use such statements.

b. When reporting on statements that omit substantially all disclosures, the accountant should include a paragraph stating that

1) Management has elected to omit substantially all disclosures,

2) The omitted disclosures (and statement of cash flows, if applicable) might influence the user's conclusions, and

3) The statements are not designed for those who are not informed about such matters.

    c.   When the entity wishes to include disclosures about only a few matters in the form of notes to the financial statements, such disclosures should be labeled "Selected Information – Substantially All Disclosures Required by Accepted Accounting Principles Generally Accepted in the United States of America Are Not Included."

9.   **Reporting When the Accountant Is Not Independent**

    a.   When the accountant is issuing a report on a compilation of financial statements for an entity from which (s)he is not independent, the accountant's **report should be modified**. The accountant should indicate his or her lack of independence in a **final paragraph** of the accountant's compilation report.

        1)   For example, such a disclosure might be

> I am (We are) not independent with respect to XYZ Company.

    b.   The accountant **may disclose the reason(s)** that his or her independence is impaired. For example, such a disclosure might be

> I am (We are) not independent with respect to XYZ Company as of and for the year ended December 31, 20XX, because I (a member of the engagement team) had a direct financial interest in XYZ Company.

        1)   If the accountant elects to disclose a description about the reasons his or her independence is impaired, the accountant should ensure that **all reasons** are included in the description.

10.   When the compiled financial statements are not expected to be used by a third party, the accountant **is not required to issue a compilation report**. The accountant should include a reference on each page of the financial statements restricting their use, such as "Restricted for management's use only," or "Solely for the information and use by the management of [name of entity] and not intended to be and should not be used by any other party."

11.   The accountant may **emphasize a matter** in the compilation report. Such explanatory information should be presented in a **separate paragraph** of the accountant's report.

    a.   Emphasis paragraphs are **never required**; they may be added solely at the accountant's discretion.

    b.   Examples of matters that the accountant may wish to emphasize are

        1)   Uncertainties
        2)   That the entity is a component of a larger business enterprise
        3)   That the entity has had significant transactions with related parties
        4)   Unusually important subsequent events
        5)   Accounting matters, other than those involving a change or changes in accounting principles, affecting the comparability of the financial statements with those of the preceding period

    c.   Because an emphasis-of-matter paragraph should not be used in lieu of management disclosures, the accountant should not include an emphasis paragraph in a compilation report on financial statements that omit substantially all disclosures unless the matter is disclosed in the financial statements.

12. **Departures from GAAP or Other Applicable Financial Reporting Framework**

   a.   If the accountant concludes that modification of the standard report is appropriate because of a departure from GAAP, the departure should be **disclosed in a separate paragraph** of the report, including disclosure of the effects of the departure on the financial statements if such effects have been determined by management or are known as the result of the accountant's procedures.

      1)   The accountant is not required to determine the effects of a departure if management has not done so, provided that the accountant states in the report that such determination has not been made.

EXAMPLE -- Language to Modify Report for a Departure from GAAP

During our compilation, I (we) did become aware of a departure (certain departures) from accounting principles generally accepted in the United States of America that is (are) described in the following paragraph:

As disclosed in Note X to the financial statements, accounting principles generally accepted in the United States of America require that land be stated at cost. Management has informed me (us) that the company has stated its land at appraised value and that, if accounting principles generally accepted in the United States of America had been followed, the land account and stockholders' equity would have been decreased by $500,000.

---

   b.   If the accountant believes that modification of the standard report is not adequate to indicate the deficiencies in the financial statements as a whole, the accountant should **withdraw** from the compilation engagement and provide no further services with respect to those financial statements.

      1)   There is **no adverse** compilation report.
      2)   The accountant may wish to consult with his or her legal counsel upon withdrawal.

13. **General-Use and Restricted-Use Reports**

   a.   The term **general use** applies to accountants' reports that are not restricted to specified parties. Accountants' reports on financial statements prepared in conformity with an applicable financial reporting framework ordinarily are not restricted regarding use. However, nothing in this section precludes the accountant from restricting the use of any report.

   b.   The term **restricted use** applies to accountants' reports intended only for one or more specified third parties.

      1)   The need for restriction on the use of a report may result from a number of circumstances, including, but not limited to, the purpose of the report and the potential for the report to be misunderstood when taken out of the context in which it was intended to be used.

   c.   The accountant should restrict the use of a report when the subject matter of the report or the presentation being reported on is based on measurement or disclosure criteria contained in contractual agreements or regulatory provisions that are not in conformity with an applicable financial reporting framework.

   d.   If the accountant issues a single combined report covering both (1) subject matter or presentations that require a restriction on use to specified parties and (2) subject matter or presentations that ordinarily do not require such a restriction, the use of such a single combined report **should be restricted** to the specified parties.

   e.   The accountant should consider informing the client that restricted-use reports are not intended for distribution to nonspecified parties, regardless of whether they are included in a document containing a separate general-use report.

   f.   An accountant's restricted-use report should contain a **separate paragraph at the end of the report** that states the restriction.

14. **An Entity's Ability to Continue as a Going Concern**

   a. During the performance of compilation procedures, evidence or information may come to the accountant's attention indicating that an uncertainty may exist about the entity's ability to continue as a going concern for a reasonable period of time, not to exceed 1 year beyond the date of the financial statements being compiled (referred to as a **reasonable period of time**). In those circumstances, the accountant should request that management consider the possible effects of the going concern uncertainty on the financial statements, including the need for related disclosure.

   b. After management communicates to the accountant the results of its consideration of the possible effects on the financial statements, the accountant should consider the reasonableness of management's conclusions, including the adequacy of the related disclosures, if applicable.

   c. If the accountant determines that management's conclusions are unreasonable or the disclosure of the uncertainty regarding the entity's ability to continue as a going concern is not adequate, a deviation from GAAP (or other framework) has occurred, and (s)he should follow the guidance in item 12. on the previous page.

   d. The accountant may emphasize an uncertainty about an entity's ability to continue as a going concern, provided that the uncertainty is disclosed in the financial statements.

15. **Subsequent Events**

   a. If the accountant learns of subsequent events that could affect the financial statements, (s)he should request that management consider the possible effects, including the adequacy of any related disclosure, if applicable.

   b. If the accountant determines that the subsequent event is not adequately accounted for in the financial statements or disclosed in the notes, (s)he should follow the guidance in item 12. on the previous page.

16. **Subsequent Discovery of Facts Existing at the Date of the Report**

   a. After the date of the accountant's compilation report, the accountant has no obligation to perform other compilation procedures with respect to the financial statements unless new information comes to his or her attention. However, when the accountant becomes aware of information that relates to financial statements previously reported on by him or her, but that **was not known** to the accountant at the date of the report (and that is of such a nature and from such a source that the accountant would have investigated it had it come to his or her attention during the course of the compilation), the accountant should, as soon as practicable, undertake to determine whether the information is reliable and whether the facts existed at the date of the report.

   b. The accountant should **discuss the matter** with his or her client at whatever management levels the accountant deems appropriate and request cooperation in whatever investigation may be necessary. In addition to management, the accountant may deem it appropriate to discuss the matter with those charged with governance.

   c. When the accountant has concluded that action should be taken to prevent further use of the accountant's report or the financial statements, the accountant should advise his or her client to make appropriate disclosure of the newly discovered facts and their impact on the financial statements to persons who are known to be currently using or who are likely to use the financial statements.

   d. If the client refuses to make the suitable disclosures, the accountant should notify the appropriate personnel at the highest levels within the entity, such as the manager (owner) or those charged with governance, of such refusal and of the fact that, in the absence of disclosure by the client, the accountant should take steps to prevent further use of the financial statements and the accountant's report.

17. When the basic financial statements are accompanied by information presented for **supplementary** analysis purposes, the accountant should clearly indicate the degree of responsibility, if any, (s)he is taking with respect to such information.

18. **Fraud and Noncompliance with Laws and Regulations**

   a. When evidence or information comes to the accountant's attention during the performance of compilation procedures that **fraud or a noncompliance with laws and regulations** may have occurred, that matter should be brought to the attention of the **appropriate level of management**. The accountant need not report matters regarding noncompliance with laws and regulations that are clearly inconsequential.

   b. The communication may be oral or written. If the communication is oral, the accountant should document it.

   c. When matters regarding fraud or noncompliance with laws and regulations involve an owner of the business, the accountant should consider **resigning** from the engagement.

   d. The disclosure of any evidence or information that comes to the accountant's attention during the performance of compilation procedures that fraud or noncompliance with laws and regulations may have occurred to parties other than the client's senior management (or those charged with governance, if applicable) ordinarily **is not part of the accountant's responsibility** and, ordinarily, would be precluded by the accountant's ethical or legal obligations of confidentiality. However, the accountant should recognize that in the following circumstances, a duty to disclose to parties outside of the entity may exist:

      1) To comply with certain legal and regulatory requirements

      2) To a successor accountant when the successor decides to communicate with the predecessor accountant in accordance with AR 400, Communications Between Predecessor and Successor Accountants, regarding acceptance of an engagement to compile or review the financial statements of a nonissuer

      3) In response to a subpoena

   e. Because potential conflicts between the accountant's ethical and legal obligations for confidentiality of client matters may be complex, the accountant may wish to consult with legal counsel before discussing matters with parties outside the client.

Stop and review! You have completed the outline for this subunit. Study multiple-choice questions 1 through 6 beginning on page 620.

19.2 REVIEW (AR 90)

1. The **objective** of a review is to express **limited assurance** that no material modifications should be made to the statements for them to conform with the applicable financial reporting framework (typically GAAP, but may be an other comprehensive basis of accounting, or OCBOA). A review is significantly less in scope than an audit. (See table in item 2. in Subunit 19.1.)

   a. AR 90 typically relates to a review of annual financial statements of nonissuers.

   b. Reviews of interim (e.g., quarterly) financial statements for issuers follow AU-C 930. (See Study Unit 18, Subunit 1.)

   c. The accountant cannot perform a review if his or her independence is impaired for any reason.

2.   A review ordinarily does not involve (a) obtaining an understanding of the entity's internal control; (b) assessing fraud risk; (c) testing accounting records by obtaining sufficient appropriate audit evidence through inspection, observation, confirmation, or the examination of source documents (for example, canceled checks or bank images); or (d) performing other procedures ordinarily performed in an audit. Accordingly, in a review, the accountant does not obtain assurance that (s)he will become aware of all significant matters that would be disclosed in an audit. Thus, a review provides only limited assurance.

3.   The accountant should establish an **understanding** with management regarding the services to be performed for review engagements and should document the understanding through a written communication with management (e.g., an **engagement letter**).

4.   **Nature of Review Evidence**

   a.   Procedures should be designed to accumulate review evidence that will provide a **reasonable basis** for obtaining **limited assurance** that there are no material modifications that should be made to the financial statements in order for the statements to be in conformity with the applicable financial reporting framework (e.g., GAAP).

   b.   Review evidence obtained through the performance of **analytical procedures** and **inquiry** will ordinarily provide the accountant with a reasonable basis for obtaining limited assurance. However, the accountant should perform **additional procedures** if the accountant determines that such procedures are necessary to obtain limited assurance that the financial statements do not need modification.

   c.   The accountant should obtain **written representations** from management.

5.   **Understanding of the Entity and Industry**

   a.   The accountant should have an understanding of the industry in which the client operates, including the accounting principles and practices generally used in the industry, sufficient to determine the specific nature, timing, and extent of review procedures to be performed.

   b.   The requirement that the accountant have a level of knowledge of the industry in which the entity operates **does not prevent the accountant from accepting a review engagement** for an entity in an industry with which the accountant has no previous experience. However, the accountant has a responsibility to obtain the required level of knowledge through additional research and study.

   c.   The accountant should obtain knowledge about the client sufficient to assist the accountant with determining the specific nature, timing, and extent of review procedures to be performed. That knowledge should include the following:

      1)   An understanding of the client's business
      2)   An understanding of the accounting principles and practices used by the client

   d.   The accountant's understanding of an **entity's business** is ordinarily obtained through experience with the entity or its industry and inquiry of the entity's personnel.

   e.   The accountant may obtain an understanding of the **accounting policies and procedures** used by management through inquiry, the review of client-prepared documents, or experience with the client.

6.   **Designing and Performing Review Procedures**

   a.   The accountant should design and perform **analytical procedures** and make **inquiries** and perform other procedures based on

      1)   His or her understanding of the industry,
      2)   His or her knowledge of the client, and
      3)   The risk of unknowingly failing to modify the report on materially misstated financial statements.

b.   The accountant should focus these procedures on those areas where (s)he believes the risks of misstatements are increased.

7.   **Analytical Procedures**

a.   **Analytical procedures** involve comparisons of expectations developed by the accountant to the client's recorded amounts or ratios. The accountant develops such expectations by identifying and using **plausible relationships** that are reasonably expected to exist based on the accountant's understanding of the industry in which the client operates and knowledge of the client. Following are five sources of information for developing expectations:

1)   Financial information for **comparable prior period(s)**, giving consideration to known changes

2)   **Anticipated results**, for example, budgets or forecasts

3)   **Relationships** among elements of financial information within the period

4)   Information regarding the **industry** in which the client operates

5)   Relationships of financial information with relevant **nonfinancial information**

b.   Analytical procedures may be performed at the **financial statement level** or at the **detailed account level**. Those at the financial statement level typically provide evidence of the "big picture." For example, the accountant may question whether the size of the warehouse is sufficient to hold the entire reported inventory. Alternatively, detailed information, for example, a month-to-month comparison of the prior year's receivable with the current year's, provides evidence of potential account balance misstatement.

c.   If analytical procedures identify fluctuations or relationships that are inconsistent with other relevant information or that **differ from expected values** by a significant amount, the accountant should investigate these differences first by questioning management and then by performing other procedures as necessary in the circumstances.

8.   **Inquiries and Other Review Procedures**

a.   The accountant should consider

1)   **Inquiring** of members of management who have responsibility for financial and accounting matters concerning

a)   Whether the financial statements have been prepared in conformity with the applicable financial reporting framework (e.g., U.S. GAAP)

b)   The entity's accounting principles and practices and the methods followed in applying them

c)   The entity's procedures for recording, classifying, and summarizing transactions and accumulating information for disclosure in the financial statements

d)   Unusual or complex situations that may have an effect on the financial statements

e)   Significant transactions occurring or recognized near the end of the reporting period

f)   The status of uncorrected misstatements identified during the previous engagement

g)   Questions that have arisen in the course of applying the review procedures

        h)   Events subsequent to the date of the financial statements that could have a material effect on the financial statements

        i)   Their knowledge of any fraud or suspected fraud affecting the entity involving management or others

        j)   Significant journal entries and other adjustments

        k)   Communications from regulatory agencies

        l)   Actions taken at meetings of shareholders, the board of directors, committees of the board of directors, or comparable meetings that may affect the financial statements

    2)   **Reading** the financial statements to consider, on the basis of information coming to the accountant's attention, whether the financial statements appear to conform with the applicable financial reporting framework

    3)   **Obtaining reports** from other accountants, if any, who have been engaged to audit or review the financial statements of significant components of the reporting entity, its subsidiaries, and other investees

  b.   The accountant ordinarily **is not required to corroborate management's** responses with other evidence; however, the accountant should consider the reasonableness and consistency of management's responses in light of the results of other review procedures and the accountant's knowledge of the client's business and the industry in which it operates.

9.   **Incorrect, Incomplete, or Otherwise Unsatisfactory Information**

  a.   During the performance of review procedures, the accountant may become aware that information coming to his or her attention is incorrect, incomplete, or otherwise unsatisfactory. In such instances, the accountant should request that management consider the effect of these matters on the financial statements and communicate the results of its consideration to the accountant.

    1)   If the accountant believes the financial statements may be materially misstated, the accountant should **perform additional procedures** deemed necessary to obtain limited assurance that no material modifications should be made to the financial statements in order for the statements to be in conformity with the applicable financial reporting framework.

    2)   If the accountant concludes that the financial statements are materially misstated, the accountant should modify the report, as discussed in item 17. of this subunit.

  b.   The accountant may perform reconciliations, confirmations, tests of details, or other procedures to gain the evidence to provide limited assurance. AR 90, however, does not specifically identify required additional procedures but expects the accountant to use appropriate judgment.

10.   **Written representations are required** from management **(a management representations letter)** for all financial statements and periods covered by the accountant's review report.

  a.   If current management was not present during all periods covered by the accountant's report, the accountant should nevertheless obtain written representations from current management for all such periods.

  b.   The specific written representations obtained by the accountant will depend on the circumstances of the engagement and the nature and basis of presentation of the financial statements.

c. Because the accountant is concerned with events occurring through the date of the report that may require adjustment to or disclosure in the financial statements, management's representations set forth in the management representation letter should be made as of the **date of the accountant's review report.**

d. The letter should be signed by those members of management whom the accountant believes are responsible for and knowledgeable about (directly or through others in the organization) the matters covered in the representation letter. Normally, the **chief executive officer** and **chief financial officer** or others with equivalent positions in the entity should sign the representation letter.

11. **Documentation in a Review Engagement**

a. The accountant **should prepare documentation** (working papers) in sufficient detail to provide a clear understanding of the work performed (including the nature, timing, extent, and results of review procedures performed), the review evidence obtained and its source, and the conclusions reached.

b. Documentation

1) Provides the principal support for the representation in the accountant's review report that the accountant performed the review in accordance with SSARS

2) Provides the principal support for the conclusion that the accountant is not aware of any material modifications that should be made to the financial statements in order for them to be in conformity with the applicable financial reporting framework

c. The form, content, and extent of documentation depend on the circumstances of the engagement, the methodology and tools used, and the accountant's professional judgment. The accountant's documentation should include

1) The engagement letter

2) The analytical procedures performed

3) The significant matters covered in the accountant's inquiry procedures and the responses thereto

4) Any findings or issues that, in the accountant's judgment, are significant (for example, the results of review procedures that indicate the financial statements could be materially misstated, including actions taken to address such findings, and the basis for the final conclusions reached)

5) Significant unusual matters that the accountant considered during the performance of the review procedures, including their disposition

6) Communications, whether oral or written, to the appropriate level of management regarding fraud or illegal acts that come to the accountant's attention

7) The management representation letter

12. **Standard Report**

a. The accountant's objective in reporting on the financial statements is **to prevent misinterpretation of the degree of responsibility** the accountant is assuming when his or her name is associated with the financial statements.

b. When the accountant has **no reservations** providing limited assurance on the financial statements, (s)he issues a standard report.

c. **Each page** of the financial statements reviewed by the accountant should include a reference, such as "**See Independent Accountant's Review Report.**"

d.   The following is an example of the standard review report. We recommend that you study the report to understand its components as well as the general wording and use of each paragraph.

EXAMPLE

Independent Accountant's Review Report

To the Owners of XYZ Company:

I (We) have reviewed the accompanying balance sheet of XYZ Company as of December 31, 20XX, and the related statements of income, retained earnings, and cash flows for the year then ended. A review includes primarily applying analytical procedures to management's (owners') financial data and making inquiries of company management (owners). A review is substantially less in scope than an audit, the objective of which is the expression of an opinion regarding the financial statements as a whole. Accordingly, I (we) do not express such an opinion.

Management (owners) is (are) responsible for the preparation and fair presentation of the financial statements in accordance with accounting principles generally accepted in the United States of America and for designing, implementing, and maintaining internal control relevant to the preparation and fair presentation of the financial statements.

My (our) responsibility is to conduct the review in accordance with Statements on Standards for Accounting and Review Services issued by the American Institute of Certified Public Accountants. Those standards require me (us) to perform procedures to obtain limited assurance that there are no material modifications that should be made to the financial statements. I (We) believe that the results of my (our) procedures provide a reasonable basis for my (our) report.

Based on my (our) review, I am (we are) not aware of any material modifications that should be made to the accompanying financial statements in order for them to be in conformity with accounting principles generally accepted in the United States of America.

Signature of accounting firm or accountant   <---------- May be manual, stamped, electronic, or typed
Date   <---------- Date of completion of the review procedures

---

13. When the accountant is unable to perform the inquiry and analytical procedures (s)he considers necessary or the client does not provide the accountant with a representation letter, the review will be incomplete.

a.   An incomplete review does not provide an adequate basis for issuing a review report. In such a situation, the accountant should consider the effect on the engagement and report.

b.   A typical response would be to withdraw from the engagement.

c.   The accountant may wish to consult with his or her legal counsel in those circumstances.

14. The accountant may be asked to issue a review report on one financial statement, such as a balance sheet, and not on other related financial statements, such as the statements of income, changes in shareholder equity, and cash flows. The accountant may do so if the scope of his or her inquiry and analytical procedures has not been restricted.

15. Financial statements prepared in accordance with an OCBOA are not considered appropriate in form unless the financial statements include

a.   A description of the OCBOA, including a summary of significant accounting policies and a description of the primary differences from GAAP. The effects of the differences need not be quantified.

b.   Informative disclosures similar to those required by GAAP.

16. The accountant may **emphasize a matter** disclosed in the financial statements.

a.   Such explanatory information should be presented in a **separate paragraph** of the accountant's report.

b.   Emphasis paragraphs are never required; they may be added solely at the accountant's discretion.

    c.   The following are examples of matters that the accountant may wish to emphasize:

       1)   Uncertainties

       2)   That the entity is a component of a larger business enterprise

       3)   That the entity has had significant transactions with related parties

       4)   Unusually important subsequent events

       5)   Accounting matters, other than those involving a change or changes in accounting principles, affecting the comparability of the financial statements with those of the preceding period

17. **Departures from the Applicable Financial Reporting Framework**

    a.   An accountant who is engaged to review financial statements may become aware of a departure from the applicable financial reporting framework (e.g., failure to follow GAAP or include adequate disclosure) that is material to the financial statements.

       1)   If the financial statements are not revised, the accountant should **consider whether modification of the standard report is adequate** to disclose the departure.

       2)   If the accountant concludes that modification of the standard report is appropriate, an **"except for" modification** should be included with the departure disclosed in a separate paragraph of the report, including disclosure of the effects of the departure on the financial statements if such effects have been determined by management or are known as the result of the accountant's procedures.

       3)   The accountant is not required to determine the effects of a departure if management has not done so, provided that the accountant states in the report that such determination has not been made.

       4)   The following is an example of the modification of the conclusion paragraph with the additional explanatory paragraph:

EXAMPLE -- **Language to Modify Review Report for a Departure from GAAP**

Based on my (our) review, **with the exception of the matter(s) described in the following paragraph(s)**, I am (we are) not aware of any material modifications that should be made to the accompanying financial statements in order for them to be in conformity with accounting principles generally accepted in the United States of America.

As disclosed in note X to the financial statements, accounting principles generally accepted in the United States of America require that inventory cost consist of material, labor, and overhead. Management has informed me (us) that the inventory of finished goods and work in process is stated in the accompanying financial statements at material and labor cost only, and that the effects of this departure from accounting principles generally accepted in the United States of America on financial position, results of operations, and cash flows have not been determined.

---

    b.   If the accountant believes that modification of the standard report is not adequate to indicate the deficiencies in the financial statements as a whole, the accountant should **withdraw** from the review engagement and provide no further services with respect to those financial statements. The accountant may wish to consult with his or her legal counsel in those circumstances.

18. **General-Use and Restricted-Use Reports**

    a.   The term **general use** applies to accountants' reports that are not restricted to specified parties.

       1)   Accountants' reports on financial statements prepared in conformity with an applicable financial reporting framework **ordinarily are not restricted** regarding use.

       2)   However, nothing in this section precludes the accountant from restricting the use of any report.

  b. The term **restricted use** applies to accountants' reports intended only for one or more specified third parties.

      1) The need for restriction on the use of a report may result from a number of circumstances, including, but not limited to, the purpose of the report and the potential for the report to be misunderstood when taken out of the context in which it was intended to be used.

  c. The accountant should restrict the use of a report when the subject matter of the accountant's report or the presentation being reported on is based on measurement or disclosure criteria contained in contractual agreements or regulatory provisions that are not in conformity with an applicable financial reporting framework.

19. **An Entity's Ability to Continue as a Going Concern**

  a. During the performance of review procedures, evidence or information may come to the accountant's attention indicating an uncertainty about the entity's ability to **continue as a going concern** for a reasonable period of time (not to exceed 1 year beyond the date of the financial statements being reviewed).

      1) In those circumstances, the accountant should request that **management consider the possible effects** of the going concern uncertainty on the financial statements, including the need for related disclosure.

      2) After management communicates to the accountant the results of its consideration of the possible effects on the financial statements, the accountant should consider the reasonableness of management's conclusions, including the adequacy of the related disclosures, if applicable.

      3) If the accountant determines that management's conclusions are **unreasonable** or the disclosure of the uncertainty regarding the entity's ability to continue as a going concern is **not adequate**, (s)he should determine if modification of the standard report (include an "except for" with a separate paragraph) is appropriate to convey the departure.

      4) If the accountant believes that modification of the standard report is not adequate to indicate the deficiencies in the financial statements as a whole, the accountant should **withdraw** from the review engagement. The accountant may wish to consult with his or her legal counsel in those circumstances.

  b. The accountant may emphasize an uncertainty about an entity's ability to continue as a going concern, provided that the uncertainty is disclosed in the financial statements.

20. **Subsequent Events**

  a. The accountant may identify evidence or information about a subsequent event that has a material effect on the reviewed financial statements.

      1) The accountant should request that management consider the possible effects on the financial statements, including the adequacy of any related disclosure, if applicable.

      2) If the accountant determines that the subsequent event is not adequately accounted for in the financial statements or disclosed in the notes, the accountant should determine whether (a) a modified report is appropriate, or (b) the accountant should withdraw from the engagement.

  b. The accountant may emphasize a subsequent event, provided that the event is disclosed in the financial statements.

21. **Subsequent Discovery of Facts Existing at the Date of the Report**

   a. After the date of the accountant's review report, the accountant has **no obligation to perform other review procedures** with respect to the financial statements unless **new information** comes to his or her attention. However, when the accountant becomes aware of information that relates to financial statements previously reported on by him or her but that **was not known** to the accountant at the date of the report (and that is of such a nature and from such a source that (s)he would have investigated it had it come to his or her attention during the course of the review), the accountant should, as soon as practicable, undertake to determine whether the information is reliable and whether the facts existed at the date of the report.

      1) The accountant should discuss the matter with his or her client at whatever management or governance levels the accountant deems appropriate and request cooperation in whatever investigation may be necessary.

   b. The accountant should **perform the additional procedures** deemed necessary to obtain limited assurance that no material modifications should be made to the financial statements in order for the statements to be in conformity with the applicable financial reporting framework.

   c. When the accountant has concluded that action should be taken to prevent further use of the report or the financial statements, (s)he should advise the client to make appropriate disclosure of the newly discovered facts and their impact on the financial statements to persons who are known to be currently using or who are likely to use the financial statements. When the client undertakes to make appropriate disclosure, the method used and the disclosure made will depend on the circumstances but should be made as expeditiously as possible.

   d. If the **client refuses** to make the appropriate disclosures (this is expected to be a rare event) the accountant should notify the appropriate personnel at the highest levels within the entity, such as the manager (owner) or those charged with governance, of such refusal and of the fact that, in the absence of disclosure by the client, the accountant should take steps to prevent further use of the financial statements and the accountant's report.

22. **Supplementary Information**

   a. When the basic financial statements are accompanied by information presented for supplementary analysis purposes, the accountant should clearly indicate the degree of responsibility, if any, (s)he is taking with respect to such information.

   b. When the accountant has reviewed the basic financial statements, an explanation should be included in the review report or in a separate report on the other data.

   c. The report should state that the review has been made for the purpose of expressing a conclusion that there are no material modifications that should be made to the financial statements in order for them to be in conformity with the applicable financial reporting framework.

23. **Fraud and Noncompliance with Laws and Regulations**

   a. When evidence or information comes to the accountant's attention during the performance of review procedures that **fraud or noncompliance with laws and regulations** may have occurred, that matter should be brought to the attention of the appropriate level of management.

      1) The accountant need not report matters regarding noncompliance with laws and regulations that are clearly **inconsequential**.

      2) When matters regarding fraud or noncompliance with laws and regulations involve senior management, the accountant should report the matter to an individual or group at a higher level within the entity, such as the manager (owner) or those charged with governance.

b. The communication may **be oral or written**. If the communication is oral, the accountant **should document** it.

c. When matters regarding fraud or noncompliance with laws and regulations involve an owner of the business, the accountant should consider **resigning** from the engagement. Additionally, the accountant should consider consulting with his or her legal counsel whenever any evidence or information comes to his or her attention during the performance of review procedures that fraud or noncompliance with laws and regulations may have occurred, unless such noncompliance is clearly inconsequential.

d. The disclosure of any evidence or information that comes to the accountant's attention during the performance of review procedures that fraud or noncompliance with laws and regulations may have occurred to parties other than the client's senior management (or those charged with governance, if applicable) ordinarily is not part of the accountant's responsibility and, ordinarily, would be precluded by the accountant's ethical or legal obligations of confidentiality. The accountant should recognize, however, that in the following circumstances, a duty to disclose to parties outside of the entity may exist:

1) To comply with certain legal and regulatory requirements

2) To a successor accountant when the successor decides to communicate with the predecessor accountant regarding acceptance of an engagement to compile or review the financial statements of a nonissuer

3) In response to a subpoena

e. Because potential conflicts between the accountant's ethical and legal obligations for confidentiality of client matters may be complex, the accountant may wish to consult with legal counsel before discussing fraud or illegal matters with parties outside the client.

Stop and review! You have completed the outline for this subunit. Study multiple-choice questions 7 through 16 beginning on page 622.

 Before you move on to the additional considerations for compilation and review, make sure you have given the basics sufficient consideration. To reiterate, the AICPA Content Specification Outlines indicate that 12% to 16% of the auditing exam will be based on accounting and review services. This is a considerable percentage given the relatively small amount of material. We have provided a number of task-based simulations on this topic to help you assess your knowledge.

19.3 OTHER CONSIDERATIONS FOR COMPILATIONS AND REVIEWS

1. **Change in the Engagement**

a. An accountant may be asked to change the engagement from a higher level of service (**audit** or review) to a lower level of service (**review or compilation**).

b. The request may result from (1) a change in circumstances affecting the entity's requirements; (2) a misunderstanding as to the nature of one of the services; or (3) a scope restriction, whether imposed by the client or circumstances.

c. Before an accountant engaged to perform a **higher level** of service agrees to change to a **lower level**, the following should be considered:

1) The reason for the entity's request, particularly the implications of a scope restriction, whether imposed by the entity or by circumstances

2) The additional effort and cost required to complete the original engagement

d. A **change in circumstances** that affects the entity's requirement for the service or a misunderstanding about the **nature of a service** is ordinarily a reasonable basis for requesting a change in the engagement.

e. In considering the implications of a **scope restriction**, the accountant should evaluate the possibility that the information affected may be incorrect, incomplete, or otherwise unsatisfactory.

   1) But, if an accountant engaged to perform an audit has been prohibited by the entity from contacting the entity's legal counsel, (s)he ordinarily is precluded from issuing a review or compilation report.

   2) If the entity in an **audit or review** engagement that has been changed to a **review or compilation** does not provide a signed representation letter, the accountant is not permitted to issue a review report and ordinarily is precluded from issuing a compilation report.

f. If the **cost to complete** the higher level of service is insignificant, the accountant should consider the propriety of accepting a change.

g. If the accountant (1) concludes that the change is reasonably justified and (2) compiles with the standards applicable to the changed engagement, the accountant may issue the appropriate compilation of review report.

h. The **report on the changed engagement** should **not** mention the following:

   1) The original engagement
   2) Any auditing or review procedures performed
   3) Scope limitations that led to the changed engagement

2. **Consideration of Fraud and Noncompliance with Laws and Regulations**

a. Neither a compilation nor a review requires the accountant to perform procedures specifically directed toward the detection of fraud or noncompliance with laws and regulations.

b. However, if fraud or noncompliance with laws and regulations is suspected, the accountant should communicate the matter (unless it is clearly inconsequential) to an appropriate level of management.

3. **AR 110,** *Compilation of Specified Elements, Accounts, or Items of a Financial Statement*

a. An accountant may assist management to compile one or more specified elements, accounts, or items of a financial statement and submit those to a third party.

   1) An accountant, in certain cases, may do so without the issuing of a compilation report.

   2) However, if the accountant has been engaged to report on such compiled specified elements, accounts, or items of a financial statement, a compilation report should be issued.

b. An engagement to report on one or more compiled specified elements, accounts, or items of a financial statement may be a separate engagement or in conjunction with a compilation, review, or audit of financial statements.

c. The accountant should follow the guidelines for compiling and reporting on compiled financial statements.

4. **AR 120,** *Compilation of Pro Forma Financial Information*

a. An accountant may assist management to compile pro forma financial statements and submit those to a third party.

   1) An accountant, in certain cases, may do so without issuing a compilation report.

   2) However, if the accountant has been engaged to report on such compiled pro forma financial statements, a compilation report should be issued.

b.   The accountant may agree to compile pro forma financial information only if the document that contains the pro forma financial information includes (or incorporates by reference) the historical financial statements of the entity on which the pro forma financial information is based.

c.   The accountant should follow the guidelines for compiling and reporting on compiled financial statements.

5.   **AR 200,** *Reporting on Comparative Financial Statements*

a.   Much of the guidance on reporting on comparative statements given in AU-C 700, *Forming an Opinion and Reporting on Financial Statements*, also applies.

b.   A continuing accountant who performs the **same or higher level of service** for the current period should update his or her report for the prior period.

1)   A continuing accountant who performs a **lower level of service** should either include a separate paragraph describing the responsibility assumed for the financial statements of the prior period or reissue the previous report.

c.   Compiled financial statements that **omit substantially all of the disclosures** required by GAAP are not comparable with financial statements that include such disclosures. Accordingly, the accountant ordinarily should not issue a report on comparative financial statements when statements for one or more, but not all, of the periods presented omit substantially all of the disclosures required by GAAP.

d.   Before **reissuing** a compilation or review report, a predecessor accountant should consider whether the report is still appropriate. The predecessor should (1) read the current financial statements and successor's report, (2) compare the prior-period financial statements with the current statements, and (3) obtain a representation letter from the successor.

6.   **AR 300,** *Compilation Reports on Financial Statements Included in Certain Prescribed Forms*

a.   An alternative form of the standard compilation report is used when a prescribed form or related instructions depart from GAAP by (1) specifying a **measurement principle** not in conformity with GAAP or **(2) not requiring disclosures** in accordance with GAAP.

b.   The presumption is that the information required in a prescribed form suffices to meet the **needs of the body** that designed or adopted the form.

c.   In the standard report on statements included in such a form, the accountant should indicate that (1) the statements are in a prescribed form, and (2) **they may differ** from those presented in accordance with GAAP. But (s)he need not describe the differences in the report.

7.   **AR 400,** *Communications Between Predecessor and Successor Accountants*

a.   The successor **may decide to communicate** with the predecessor before accepting a review or compilation engagement.

1)   In an audit, the communication is required.

b.   The predecessor is required to **respond promptly and fully** on the basis of known facts.

c.   Both accountants, however, must have the entity's **specific consent** to disclose confidential information.

d.   Most other provisions of AU-C 210, *Terms of Engagement* (which is discussed in Study Unit 3), apply to these communications.

e.   A successor who believes the statements reported on by the predecessor **may require revision** must request that the client communicate this information to the predecessor.

8. **AR 600,** *Reporting on Personal Financial Statements Included in Written Personal Financial Plans*

    a. An accountant may submit a written personal financial plan containing unaudited personal financial statements to a client without complying with the requirements of AR 80 if the accountant

        1) Has a documented understanding with the client about its use,
        2) Has no reason to believe that the financial statements will be used to obtain credit or for any purpose other than the financial plan, and
        3) Issues a report describing the engagement.

Stop and review! You have completed the outline for this subunit. Study multiple-choice questions 17 through 21 beginning on page 625.

19.4 ENGAGEMENTS TO APPLY AGREED-UPON PROCEDURES (AT 201)

1. **Nature of the Engagement**

    a. An agreed-upon procedures engagement is one in which a practitioner is engaged by a client to issue a report of findings based on specific procedures performed on subject matter.
    b. **Specified parties** assume responsibility for the **sufficiency** of the procedures.
    c. The **report** is in the form of **procedures and findings**, and neither an opinion nor negative assurance should be provided.
    d. The **general, field work, and reporting standards** for attestation engagements apply (discussed in Study Unit 1). However, a written assertion is generally not required in an agreed-upon procedures engagement unless specifically required by another attest standard.

2. **Procedures**

    a. **Appropriate procedures** include

        1) Inspection of specified documents for attributes
        2) Confirmation of specific information with third parties
        3) Comparison of documents or schedules with certain attributes
        4) Performance of mathematical computations or sampling

    b. **Inappropriate procedures** include

        1) Mere reading of the work performed by others to describe their findings
        2) Evaluating the competency or objectivity of another party
        3) Obtaining an understanding about a particular subject
        4) General review, checking, or any other overly subjective procedure
        5) Interpreting documents outside the scope of the practitioner's expertise

3. The practitioner may perform an engagement provided that

    a. (S)he is **independent**.
    b. A specified party is responsible for the **subject matter** (or the client has a reasonable basis for providing a written assertion, if required).
    c. The specified parties agree with the practitioner about the **procedures** to be performed.
    d. The specified parties are responsible for the **sufficiency** of the procedures.
    e. Procedures are expected to result in reasonably consistent **findings**.
    f. **Criteria** to be used in the determination of findings are agreed upon.
    g. Reasonably consistent subject matter **measurement** can be expected.
    h. **Evidence** providing a reasonable basis for findings can be collected.
    i. An agreement exists on **materiality** limits for reporting when applicable.
    j. **Use** of the report is restricted to specified parties.

614   SU 19: Review, Compilation, and Attestation Engagements

4. To ensure that specified parties take **responsibility for the sufficiency of the procedures**, the practitioner should do one or more of the following:

    a. Communicate directly with, and obtain affirmative acknowledgment from, the parties
    b. Distribute the engagement letter to the specified parties
    c. Distribute a draft of the anticipated report to the specified parties
    d. Consider written requirements of the specified parties
    e. Discuss procedures with appropriate representatives of the specified parties
    f. Review contracts with or correspondence from the specified parties

5. Attestation **documentation** (working papers) should be prepared.

EXAMPLE -- Report on Agreed-Upon Procedures

Independent Accountant's Report on Applying Agreed-Upon Procedures

To the Audit Committee and Managements of ABC, Inc., and XYZ Fund:

We have performed the procedures enumerated below, which were agreed to by the audit committees and managements of ABC, Inc., and XYZ Fund, solely to assist you in evaluating the accompanying Statement of Investment Performance Statistics of XYZ Fund (prepared in accordance with the criteria specified therein) for the year ended December 31, Year 1. XYZ Fund's management is responsible for the statement of investment performance statistics. This agreed-upon procedures engagement was conducted in accordance with attestation standards established by the American Institute of Certified Public Accountants. The sufficiency of these procedures is solely the responsibility of those parties specified in this report. Consequently, we make no representation regarding the sufficiency of the procedures described below, either for the purpose for which this report has been requested or for any other purpose.

[Include paragraphs to enumerate procedures and findings.]

We were not engaged to and did not conduct an examination, the objective of which would be the expression of an opinion on the accompanying Statement of Investment Performance Statistics of XYZ Fund. Accordingly, we do not express such an opinion. Had we performed additional procedures, other matters might have come to our attention that would have been reported to you.

This report is intended solely for the information and use of the audit committees and managements of ABC, Inc., and XYZ Fund and is not intended to be and should not be used by anyone other than these specified parties.

Signature
Date

Stop and review! You have completed the outline for this subunit. Study multiple-choice questions 22 through 24 beginning on page 627.

19.5 FINANCIAL FORECASTS AND PROJECTIONS (AT 301)

1. **Prospective Financial Statements (PFSs)**

    a. PFSs consist of financial forecasts or projections, including summaries of significant assumptions and accounting policies. An accountant must examine, compile, or apply agreed-upon procedures to PFSs if they are, or reasonably might be, expected to be used by another (third) party and if the practitioner

        1) Submits to the client or others PFSs that (s)he has assembled or assisted in assembling
        2) Reports on PFSs

    b. The accountant must be independent to report on an examination or agreed-upon procedures for PFSs. An accountant need not be independent to compile PFSs.

        1) However, the compilation report should be modified to include a separate paragraph disclosing the lack of independence.
        2) Additionally, the accountant is not precluded from disclosing the reason(s) that independence is impaired.

2. A **financial forecast** consists of PFSs that present, to the best of the responsible party's knowledge and belief, an entity's expected financial position, results of operations, and cash flows.

   a. It is based on the **responsible party's assumptions** reflecting conditions it expects to exist and the course of action it expects to take.

      1) The responsible party is usually management of the entity, but it may be a party outside the entity, such as a potential acquirer.

   b. It may be expressed in specific monetary amounts as a range or as a single point estimate of forecasted results. For a range, the responsible party selects key assumptions to form an interval within which it reasonably expects, to the best of its knowledge and belief, the item or items subject to the assumptions to actually fall.

3. A **financial projection** differs from a forecast. A projection is based on the responsible party's assumptions reflecting conditions it expects would exist and the course of action it expects would be taken, given one or more **hypothetical assumptions**. A projection is sometimes prepared to present one or more hypothetical courses of action for evaluation, as in response to a question such as, "What would happen if . . .?" A projection may be expressed as a point estimate or a range.

4. PFSs are for **general use** if they are for use by persons with whom the responsible party is not negotiating directly, e.g., in an offering statement of the party's securities. Only a forecast is appropriate for general use. All other presentations are for limited use.

   a. General use PFSs should portray expected results to the best of the responsible party's knowledge and belief.

5. **Limited use** of PFSs means use by the responsible party and those with whom that party is negotiating directly. Examples are use in a submission to a regulatory body or in negotiations for a bank loan. These third parties can communicate directly with the responsible party.

   a. Consequently, any type of PFSs that would be useful in the circumstances would be appropriate for limited use.

   b. A projection is appropriate only for limited use. The reason is that the presentation of a projection is based on one or more hypothetical assumptions.

      1) PFSs are appropriate for general use only if they portray, to the best of the responsible party's knowledge and belief, the expected results. A hypothetical assumption is a condition or course of action that is not necessarily expected to occur.

6. **Examinations**

   a. An examination evaluates the preparation of the statements, the support underlying the assumptions, and the presentation of the statements for conformity with AICPA guidelines.

   b. It also involves issuance of a report stating the practitioner's opinion on whether the PFSs conform with AICPA guidelines and whether the assumptions provide a reasonable basis for (1) the forecast or (2) the projection given hypothetical assumptions.

   c. If assumptions that appear to be significant at the time are not disclosed in the presentation, including the summary of assumptions, the practitioner should express an adverse opinion. Moreover, a practitioner should not examine a presentation that omits all such disclosures.

7. **Compilations**

   a. A compilation of PFSs, such as a financial forecast, involves (1) assembling, to the extent necessary, the statements based on the responsible party's assumptions; (2) performing required compilation procedures; and (3) issuing a compilation report.

    b.   The procedures include reading the statements and considering whether they meet AICPA presentation guidelines and determining that the statements are not obviously inappropriate.

        1)   Other procedures consist of inquiries, testing the mathematical accuracy of the computations, and obtaining written representations. However, these procedures are not required.

        2)   If the accountant inquired or performed procedures before and became aware of incorrect or unsatisfactory information, (s)he should request revised information from the entity. If the entity refuses to provide revised information, the accountant should **withdraw from the engagement**.

    c.   The standard report states that a compilation is limited in scope and does not enable the practitioner to express an opinion or any other form of assurance on the PFSs or the assumptions.

        1)   It adds that a compilation does **not include evaluation of the support** for the assumptions underlying the PFSs.

        2)   A report on a projection also should include a separate paragraph that limits the use of the presentation.

8.   **Agreed-Upon Procedures**

    a.   A practitioner may accept an engagement to apply **agreed-upon procedures** to PFSs.

    b.   The engagement may be accepted if the practitioner is **independent** and

        1)   The specified parties agree to the procedures and take responsibility for their sufficiency.

        2)   Report use is limited to specified parties.

        3)   The statements include a summary of significant assumptions.

    c.   The report should state that the practitioner did not perform an examination and that other matters might have come to his or her attention if additional procedures had been performed.

        1)   It should also **disclaim an opinion** on conformity with AICPA presentation guidelines, etc.

        2)   The report lists the procedures performed and the related findings. It does not provide positive or limited assurance.

9.   **Review**

    a.   The standard does not provide for the **review** form of engagement with regard to PFSs. Thus, it does not provide for the expression of limited assurance on them.

Stop and review! You have completed the outline for this subunit. Study multiple-choice questions 25 through 32 beginning on page 628.

19.6 REPORTING ON PRO FORMA FINANCIAL INFORMATION (AT 401)

1.   Pro forma financial information (PFFI) shows "what the significant effects on historical financial information would have been had a consummated or proposed transaction (or event) occurred at an earlier date." Examples of these transactions include (a) a business combination, (b) disposal of a segment, (c) change in the form or status of an entity, and (d) a change in capitalization.

2.   An accountant may **examine or review** PFFI if three conditions are met:

    a.   The document containing the PFFI includes or incorporates by reference the complete historical statements for the most recent year available. Moreover, if the PFFI is for an interim period, the document also should include the interim historical information for that period.

    b. If the PFFI has been examined, the historical financial statements on which it is based have been audited. If the PFFI has been reviewed, the historical financial statements have been audited or reviewed.

    c. The reporting accountant is appropriately knowledgeable about the accounting and financial reporting practices of each significant part of the combined entity.

3. A compilation of the historical statements provides no assurance. Accordingly, it would not provide a basis for the accountant to examine or review the PFFI.

4. The report on an examination should include an opinion (unmodified, qualified, or adverse). It addresses whether (a) management's assumptions provide a reasonable basis for the significant effects attributable to the transaction or event, (b) the pro forma adjustments give appropriate effect to the assumptions, and (c) the pro forma column reflects the proper application of those adjustments to the historical data.

    a. Scope limitations, reservations about the assumptions or the presentation (including inadequate disclosure), and other matters may lead to modification of the opinion or a disclaimer.

5. An issuer that discloses a material non-GAAP financial measure (a **pro forma release**) also must disclose the most directly comparable GAAP measure (SEC Regulation G).

Stop and review! You have completed the outline for this subunit. Study multiple-choice questions 33 and 34 on page 630.

19.7 COMPLIANCE ATTESTATION (AT 601)

1. A practitioner may be asked to provide assurance about the entity's **compliance with specified requirements** (laws, regulations, rules, contracts, or grants). The engagement also may be directed toward the responsible party's **written assertion about compliance**. For example, management might make the assertion: "Z Company complied with the restrictive covenants in paragraph 20 of its Loan Agreement with Y Bank dated January 1, Year 1, as of and for the 3 months ended March 31, Year 1."

    a. The practitioner also may be asked to provide this type of assurance concerning the **effectiveness of internal control over compliance** with laws, regulations, etc.

2. The standard provides guidance for engagements related to reporting on compliance with requirements that are either **financial or nonfinancial**.

    a. The **general, field work, and reporting attestation standards** (AT 50) are applicable to this type of engagement.

    b. A compliance attestation does **not** provide a legal determination of an entity's compliance.

3. **Scope of Services**

    a. A practitioner may perform **agreed-upon procedures** or an **examination**. However, a practitioner should **not** perform a compliance attestation **review** service.

    b. In an **agreed-upon procedures engagement**, the subject matter (or an assertion about it) consists of (1) compliance with specified requirements, (2) the effectiveness of internal control over compliance, or (3) both.

        1) The users of the report decide the procedures to be performed by the practitioner and take responsibility for those procedures.

        2) The practitioner has **no obligation to perform other procedures**. However, if noncompliance comes to the practitioner's attention by other means, such information should be included in the report.

        3) The practitioner's report should be in the form of procedures and findings but should **not provide negative assurance** about whether an entity is in compliance or whether the responsible party's assertion is fairly stated.

4) The **report**

a) Has a **title** that includes the word **independent**
b) Describes the **nature and scope** of the service
c) **Limits use** to specified parties
d) Is **signed** by the practitioner
e) Is **dated** as of the completion of the agreed-upon procedures

c. In an **examination** engagement, the subject matter (or an assertion about it) consists of compliance with specified requirements.

1) The practitioner gathers evidence to support an opinion on whether an entity is in compliance, in all material respects, based on specified criteria.
2) The practitioner also may examine the **effectiveness** (or the responsible party's assertion about the effectiveness) **of the entity's internal control over compliance**.

4. **Conditions for Engagement Performance**

a. For an **agreed-upon procedures engagement**, the responsible party should

1) Accept responsibility for the entity's compliance with specified requirements and the effectiveness of the entity's internal control over compliance.
2) Evaluate such compliance or effectiveness.

b. For an **examination of the entity's compliance with specified requirements**, sufficient evidence should exist or be capable of development to support management's evaluation. Furthermore, the **responsible party** should

1) Satisfy the condition in item 4.a.1) above.
2) Evaluate compliance with specified requirements.

c. To perform a compliance attestation engagement, the practitioner should obtain from the responsible party a **written assertion about compliance**.

5. **Examination Engagement**

a. The purpose is to **express an opinion** on whether an entity is in compliance (or on whether the responsible party's assertion about such compliance is fairly stated), in all material respects, based on the specified criteria. To express an opinion, the practitioner must gather sufficient evidence to **reduce attestation risk** to an acceptably low level. Attestation risk is similar to the audit risk concept used in Statements on Auditing Standards.

b. The practitioner seeks to obtain **reasonable, not absolute, assurance** of compliance.

c. Based on the extent to which (s)he wishes to restrict attestation risk and the assessments of inherent risk and control risk, the practitioner determines the **acceptable level of detection risk**. This level will determine the nature, timing, and extent of the necessary compliance tests.

d. The consideration of **materiality** differs from that in an audit of financial statements in accordance with GAAS. The following should be considered:

1) The nature of the compliance requirements, which may not be quantifiable in monetary terms
2) The nature and frequency of noncompliance identified, with appropriate consideration of sampling risk
3) Qualitative considerations, including the needs and expectations of users

6. **Performing an Examination Engagement**

    a. The practitioner should use **due care** and exercise **professional skepticism** to achieve reasonable assurance that material noncompliance will be detected. The following summarizes the practitioner's **procedures and considerations** in an examination engagement:

        1) Obtain an **understanding** of the specified compliance requirements.
        2) **Plan** the engagement, including the potential use of specialists and internal auditors.
        3) Obtain an **understanding** of the relevant portions of **internal control** over compliance to plan the engagement and to assess control risk. If control risk is to be assessed at a low level, tests of controls must be performed.
        4) Perform **procedures** to provide reasonable assurance of detecting material noncompliance, including obtaining a **written representation letter** from the responsible party.
        5) Consider **subsequent events**. (The requirement is similar to that established by AU-C 560, *Subsequent Events and Subsequently Discovered Facts*, for a financial statement audit.)
        6) Form an **opinion**.

    b. The practitioner's report on an examination should contain **introductory, scope, and opinion paragraphs**.

EXAMPLE -- Standard Report on Compliance with Specified Requirements Based on an Examination

Independent Accountant's Report

To: <------------ Addressed to Board of Directors or Shareholders

We have examined *[name of entity]*'s compliance with *[list of specified compliance requirements]* during the *[period]* ended *[date]*. Management is responsible for *[name of entity]*'s compliance with those requirements. Our responsibility is to express an opinion on *[name of entity]*'s compliance based on our examination.

Our examination was conducted in accordance with attestation standards established by the American Institute of Certified Public Accountants and, accordingly, included examining, on a test basis, evidence about *[name of entity]*'s compliance with those requirements and performing such other procedures as we considered necessary in the circumstances. We believe that our examination provides a reasonable basis for our opinion. Our examination does not provide a legal determination on *[name of entity]*'s compliance with specific requirements.

In our opinion, *[name of entity]* complied, in all material respects, with the aforementioned requirements for the year ended December 31, Year 1.

Signature   <------------ May be signed, typed, or printed
Date   <------------ Date completed examination

---

7. **Report Modifications**

    a. **Material noncompliance.** When an examination discloses noncompliance with specified requirements that the practitioner believes have a material effect on the entity's compliance, the report should be modified. Depending on materiality, the practitioner should express either a **qualified** (except for) or an **adverse opinion** on compliance. An **explanatory paragraph** (before the opinion paragraph) should be added to the report.

    b. **Scope limitations.** The practitioner should qualify or disclaim an opinion depending on materiality (e.g., if management refuses to provide a written representation letter).

    c. **Report based, in part, on the report of another practitioner.** The practitioner should either refer to the other practitioner or issue the standard report (see the general guidance provided by AU-C 600, *Special Considerations – Audits of Group Financial Statements (Including the Work of Component Auditors)*).

Stop and review! You have completed the outline for this subunit. Study multiple-choice questions 35 and 36 on page 631.

QUESTIONS

19.1 Compilation (AR 80)

1. Statements on Standards for Accounting and Review Services (SSARSs) require an accountant to report when the accountant has

A. Typed client-prepared financial statements, without modification, as an accommodation to the client.

B. Provided a client with a financial statement format that does not include monetary amounts, to be used by the client in preparing financial statements.

C. Proposed correcting journal entries to be recorded by the client that change client-prepared financial statements.

D. Prepared, through the use of computer software, financial statements to be used by third parties.

Answer (D) is correct.
REQUIRED: The situation in which an accountant must issue a report.
DISCUSSION: The accountant should not consent to the use of his/her name in association with unaudited financial statements of a nonissuer to be used by third parties unless (1) the auditor has compiled or reviewed the financial statements in compliance with SSARSs, or (2) the financial statements are accompanied by an indication that the accountant has not compiled or reviewed the statements and that the accountant assumes no responsibility for them (i.e., issue a disclaimer).
Answer (A) is incorrect. Typing or reproducing client-prepared financial statements, without modification, as an accommodation to a client does not constitute a submission of financial statements. Answer (B) is incorrect. Without monetary amounts, the presentation is not a financial statement. Answer (C) is incorrect. Journal entries are not a financial statement.

2. An accountant should not compile unaudited financial statements for management of a nonissuer unless, at a minimum, the accountant

A. Assists in adjusting the books of account and preparing the trial balance.

B. Types or reproduces the financial statements.

C. Complies with the Statements on Standards for Accounting and Review Services.

D. Applies analytical procedures to the financial statements.

Answer (C) is correct.
REQUIRED: The action required of an accountant who compiles unaudited financial statements for management of a nonissuer.
DISCUSSION: The accountant should not compile unaudited financial statements of a nonissuer to the client or others unless, as a minimum, (s)he complies with the standards set forth in AR 80 applicable to compilation engagements.
Answer (A) is incorrect. Assisting in adjusting the books of account and preparing the trial balance is not a compilation service. Answer (B) is incorrect. Typing or reproducing client-prepared financial statements, without modification, is not a compilation service. Answer (D) is incorrect. Application of analytical procedures is not required by the standards for compilations.

3. When engaged to compile the financial statements of a nonissuer, an accountant should possess a level of knowledge of the entity's accounting principles and practices. This most likely will include obtaining a general understanding of the

A. Stated qualifications of the entity's accounting personnel.

B. Design of the entity's internal controls that have been implemented.

C. Risk factors relating to misstatements arising from illegal acts.

D. Internal control awareness of the entity's senior management.

Answer (A) is correct.
REQUIRED: The knowledge acquired to perform a compilation.
DISCUSSION: To perform a compilation, the accountant should possess an understanding of the nature of the entity's business, its accounting records, the qualifications of its accounting personnel, and the content and accounting basis of the financial statements.
Answer (B) is incorrect. The consideration of internal control is not necessary to perform compilation services. Answer (C) is incorrect. No assessment of risk or application of auditing procedures is required in a compilation. Answer (D) is incorrect. The consideration of internal control is not necessary to perform compilation services.

4. Compiled financial statements of a nonissuer intended for third-party use should be accompanied by a report stating that

A. The scope of the accountant's procedures has not been restricted in testing the financial information that is the representation of management.

B. The accountant assessed the accounting principles used and significant estimates made by management.

C. The accountant does not express an opinion or any other form of assurance on the financial statements.

D. A compilation consists principally of inquiries of entity personnel and analytical procedures applied to financial data.

Answer (C) is correct.
   REQUIRED: The language included in a compilation report.
   DISCUSSION: A compilation report contains a disclaimer stating that the accountant has not audited or reviewed the financial statements and does not express an opinion or any other form of assurance on them.
   Answer (A) is incorrect. A compilation does not entail testing the financial information. Answer (B) is incorrect. A financial statement audit, not a compilation, involves assessing the accounting principles used and the estimates made by management. Answer (D) is incorrect. A review, not a compilation, consists principally of inquiries and analytical procedures.

5. When an accountant attaches a compilation report to a nonissuer's financial statements that omit substantially all disclosures required by GAAP, the accountant should indicate in the compilation report that the financial statements are

A. Not designed for those who are uninformed about the omitted disclosures.

B. Prepared in conformity with a comprehensive basis of accounting other than GAAP.

C. Not compiled in accordance with Statements on Standards for Accounting and Review Services.

D. Special-purpose financial statements that are not comparable to those of prior periods.

Answer (A) is correct.
   REQUIRED: The statement in a report on a compilation omitting substantially all GAAP disclosures.
   DISCUSSION: When disclosures are omitted, a paragraph is added to the standard compilation report stating that management has elected to omit substantially all disclosures required by GAAP and that, if the omissions were included, they might influence the users' conclusions.
   Answer (B) is incorrect. The basis of accounting is not at issue. Answer (C) is incorrect. A compilation in accordance with SSARSs is not inconsistent with omission of GAAP disclosures. Answer (D) is incorrect. Financial statements that omit disclosures are not special-purpose.

6. Miller, CPA, is engaged to compile the financial statements of Web Co., a nonissuer, in conformity with the income tax basis of accounting. If Web's financial statements do **not** disclose the basis of accounting used, Miller should

A. Disclose the basis of accounting in the accountant's compilation report.

B. Clearly label each page "Distribution Restricted--Material Modifications Required."

C. Issue a special report describing the effect of the incomplete presentation.

D. Withdraw from the engagement and provide no further services to Web.

Answer (A) is correct.
   REQUIRED: The effect on a compilation report of failure to disclose the basis of accounting used.
   DISCUSSION: Although the accountant is expected to perform no procedures, if (s)he is aware of misapplications of GAAP or the absence of required disclosures, (s)he should disclose that information in the compilation report.
   Answer (B) is incorrect. Each page of the financial statements should contain the statement, "See Accountant's Compilation Report." Answer (C) is incorrect. A special report is issued in conjunction with an audit. Answer (D) is incorrect. The accountant need not withdraw from the engagement.

19.2 Review (AR 90)

7. Which of the following should be the first step in reviewing the financial statements of a nonissuer?

A. Comparing the financial statements with statements for comparable prior periods and with anticipated results.

B. Completing a series of inquiries concerning the entity's procedures for recording, classifying, and summarizing transactions.

C. Obtaining a general understanding of the entity's organization, its operating characteristics, and its products or services.

D. Applying analytical procedures designed to identify relationships and individual items that appear to be unusual.

Answer (C) is correct.
REQUIRED: The first step in reviewing the financial statements of a nonissuer.
DISCUSSION: In a review, the auditor expresses limited assurance concerning the financial statements. In performing the review, the auditor should first obtain an understanding of the entity and the entity's industry. This will provide a foundation for completing the review.
Answer (A) is incorrect. Comparing the financial statement with statements for comparable prior periods and with anticipated results is an analytical procedure, which is performed after obtaining an understanding of the business. Answer (B) is incorrect. Completing a series of inquiries concerning the entity's procedures for recording, classifying, and summarizing transactions is performed after obtaining an understanding of the entity's business. Answer (D) is incorrect. Applying analytical procedures designed to identify relationships and individual items that appear to be unusual is done after obtaining an understanding of the business.

8. Which of the following procedures should an accountant perform during an engagement to review the financial statements of a nonissuer?

A. Communicating control deficiencies discovered during the assessment of control risk.

B. Obtaining a client representation letter from members of management.

C. Sending bank confirmation letters to the entity's financial institutions.

D. Examining cash disbursements in the subsequent period for unrecorded liabilities.

Answer (B) is correct.
REQUIRED: The procedure performed in a review.
DISCUSSION: A review primarily consists of inquiries, analytical procedures, and management representations. In addition, the accountant must obtain a sufficient knowledge of the accounting principles and practices of the entity's industry and an understanding of the entity's business. The representations from management should encompass all statements and periods to be covered by the report. The representation letter should be signed by the current managers (usually the CEO and CFO or the equivalent) responsible for, and knowledgeable about, the matters covered (AR 90).
Answer (A) is incorrect. Significant deficiencies and material weaknesses must be communicated in an audit, not a review. Answer (C) is incorrect. Confirmations to financial institutions are normally sent in an audit, not a review. Answer (D) is incorrect. Tests of details, e.g., tests of subsequent payments, are performed in an audit, not a review.

9. Which of the following inquiry or analytical procedures ordinarily are performed in an engagement to review a nonissuer's financial statements?

A. Analytical procedures designed to test the accounting records by obtaining corroborating evidence.

B. Inquiries concerning unusual or complex situations that may have an effect on the financial statements.

C. Analytical procedures designed to test relevant assertions regarding continued existence.

D. Inquiries of the entity's legal counsel concerning contingent liabilities.

Answer (B) is correct.
REQUIRED: The inquiries or analytical procedures ordinarily performed during a review.
DISCUSSION: These procedures include inquiries to members of management with responsibility for financial and accounting matters that concern, among other things, unusual or complex situations that may affect the financial statements.
Answer (A) is incorrect. A review does not contemplate gathering corroborating evidence. Answer (C) is incorrect. A review does not contemplate the application of procedures concerning assertions regarding continued existence. Answer (D) is incorrect. AR 90 does not require that inquiries be made of the entity's legal counsel.

10. Financial statements of a nonissuer that have been reviewed by an accountant should be accompanied by a report stating that a review

A. Provides only limited assurance that the financial statements are fairly presented.

B. Includes examining, on a test basis, information that is the representation of management.

C. Includes primarily applying analytical procedures to management's financial data and making inquiries of company management.

D. Does not contemplate obtaining corroborating evidential matter or applying certain other procedures ordinarily performed during an audit.

Answer (C) is correct.
    REQUIRED: The statement included in the review report.
    DISCUSSION: The first paragraph of the review report contains a sentence stating, "A review includes primarily applying analytical procedures to management's financial data and making inquiries of company management."
    Answer (A) is incorrect. The report states that the accountant is not aware of material modifications that should be made to the financial statements for them to be in conformity with GAAP. Answer (B) is incorrect. A review engagement does not include examining information that is the representation of management. Answer (D) is incorrect. The report does not contain an explicit description of the difference between an audit and a review.

11. Financial statements of a nonissuer that have been reviewed by an accountant should be accompanied by a report stating that

A. The scope of the inquiry and analytical procedures performed by the accountant has not been restricted.

B. All information included in the financial statements is the representation of the management of the entity.

C. A review includes examining, on a test basis, evidence supporting the amounts and disclosures in the financial statements.

D. A review is greater in scope than a compilation, the objective of which is to present financial statements that are free of material misstatements.

Answer (B) is correct.
    REQUIRED: The true statement included in an accountant's report based upon a review.
    DISCUSSION: According to AR 90, the second paragraph of the standard report should state, "Management is responsible for the preparation and fair presentation of the financial statements in accordance with accounting principles generally accepted in the United States of America and for designing, implementing, and maintaining internal control relevant to the preparation and fair presentation of the financial statements."
    Answer (A) is incorrect. The report does not need to state that the scope of the inquiry and analytical procedures performed by the accountant has not been restricted. Answer (C) is incorrect. An audit, not a review, includes examining, on a test basis, evidence supporting the amounts and disclosures in the financial statements. Answer (D) is incorrect. The standard review report does not mention a compilation.

12. An accountant's standard report on a review of the financial statements of a nonissuer should state that the accountant

A. Does not express an opinion or any form of limited assurance on the financial statements.

B. Is not aware of any material modifications that should be made to the financial statements for them to conform with GAAP.

C. Obtained reasonable assurance about whether the financial statements are free of material misstatement.

D. Examined evidence, on a test basis, supporting the amounts and disclosures in the financial statements.

Answer (B) is correct.
    REQUIRED: The statement in a review report.
    DISCUSSION: The review report states, "Based on my review, I am not aware of any material modifications that should be made to the accompanying financial statements in order for them to be in conformity with accounting principles generally accepted in the United States of America" (AR 90).
    Answer (A) is incorrect. A review provides limited assurance. Answer (C) is incorrect. An audit provides reasonable assurance about whether the financial statements are free of material misstatement. Answer (D) is incorrect. An audit involves gathering sufficient appropriate evidence to support the amounts and disclosures in the financial statements.

13. During an engagement to review the financial statements of a nonissuer, an accountant becomes aware that several leases that should be capitalized are not capitalized. The accountant considers these leases to be material to the financial statements. The accountant decides to modify the standard review report because management will not capitalize the leases. Under these circumstances, the accountant should

A. Express an adverse opinion because of the departure from GAAP.

B. Express no assurance of any kind on the entity's financial statements.

C. Emphasize that the financial statements are for limited use only.

D. Disclose the departure from GAAP in a separate paragraph of the accountant's report.

Answer (D) is correct.
   REQUIRED: The modification of a review report for a departure from GAAP.
   DISCUSSION: When a departure from GAAP precludes an unmodified review report, and modification of the standard report is sufficient to disclose the departure, the accountant should add an additional paragraph to the report disclosing the departure, including its effects on the financial statements if they have been determined by management or are known as the result of the accountant's procedures.
   Answer (A) is incorrect. Unless an audit has been conducted, an opinion may not be expressed. If modification of the report is not adequate to indicate the deficiencies, the auditor should withdraw from the engagement. Answer (B) is incorrect. The accountant provides limited assurance in a review report. Answer (C) is incorrect. A review report need not be limited in distribution.

14. Each page of a nonissuer's financial statements reviewed by an accountant should include the following reference:

A. See Accountant's Review Report.

B. Reviewed, No Accountant's Assurance Expressed.

C. See Accompanying Accountant's Notes.

D. Reviewed, No Material Modifications Required.

Answer (A) is correct.
   REQUIRED: The reference on each page of a nonissuer's financial statements reviewed by an accountant.
   DISCUSSION: Each page should include a reference such as "See Accountant's Review Report" (AR 90).
   Answer (B) is incorrect. A review report ordinarily expresses limited assurance. Answer (C) is incorrect. Notes are part of the financial statements, not the accountant's report. Answer (D) is incorrect. The review report states that the accountant is not aware of any modifications that should be made other than those indicated in the report.

15. Moore, CPA, has been asked to issue a review report on the balance sheet of Dover Co., a nonissuer. Moore will not be reporting on Dover's statements of income, retained earnings, and cash flows. Moore may issue the review report provided the

A. Balance sheet is presented in a prescribed form of an industry trade association.

B. Scope of the inquiry and analytical procedures has not been restricted.

C. Balance sheet is not to be used to obtain credit or distributed to creditors.

D. Specialized accounting principles and practices of Dover's industry are disclosed.

Answer (B) is correct.
   REQUIRED: The condition under which an accountant may issue a review report on a single financial statement.
   DISCUSSION: An accountant may issue a report on one or more of the financial statements and not on the others. This form of reporting is not considered a limitation on scope but a limited reporting engagement. However, the accountant must not be restricted in the procedures to be applied, which, in a review, consist primarily of inquiries and analytical procedures.
   Answer (A) is incorrect. The decision is independent of whether the balance sheet is to be presented in a prescribed form. Answer (C) is incorrect. A reviewed financial statement may be used for any appropriate purpose. Answer (D) is incorrect. A review report may be issued on a comprehensive basis of accounting other than GAAP. The specialized principles, however, need not be disclosed.

16. An entity engaged an accountant to review its financial statements in accordance with *Statements on Standards for Accounting and Review Services.* The accountant determined that the entity maintained its accounts on a comprehensive basis of accounting other than generally accepted accounting principles (GAAP). In this situation, the accountant most likely would have taken which of the following actions?

A. Withdrawn from the engagement because the entity has **not** been following GAAP.

B. Advised management to make the adjustments necessary for the account balances to conform with GAAP.

C. Modified the review report to reflect the fact that the financial statements were presented on another comprehensive basis of accounting.

D. Requested that management justify the use of the other comprehensive basis of accounting in the management representation letter.

Answer (C) is correct.

REQUIRED: The response by an accountant who reviews statements prepared using a special purpose framework.

DISCUSSION: A review report states that the accountant is not aware of any material modifications that should be made to the statements for them to be in accordance with the applicable reporting framework, e.g., GAAP. The framework should be acceptable (1) given the nature of the entity and the purpose of the statements or (2) required by law or regulation. A special purpose framework (also called an other comprehensive basis of accounting, or OCBOA) may be used if the statements include a description of the framework, including a summary of significant accounting policies and a description of the primary differences from GAAP. The effects of the differences need not be quantified. The statements also should include informative disclosures similar to those required by GAAP. Thus, the review report is modified accordingly.

Answer (A) is incorrect. The statements may be prepared using an applicable reporting framework, including a special purpose framework (OCBOA). Use of a special purpose framework is not a basis for withdrawing from the engagement. Answer (B) is incorrect. The statements may be prepared using a framework other than GAAP. Answer (D) is incorrect. Management's written representations include an acknowledgment of its responsibility to prepare and fairly present statements in accordance with the applicable framework. But management does not have to justify use of a special purpose framework.

19.3 Other Considerations for Compilations and Reviews

17. Clark, CPA, compiled and properly reported on the financial statements of Green Co., a nonissuer, for the year ended March 31, Year 1. These financial statements omitted substantially all disclosures required by GAAP. Green asked Clark to compile the statements for the year ended March 31, Year 2, and to include all GAAP disclosures for the Year 2 statements only, but otherwise present both years' financial statements in comparative form. What is Clark's responsibility concerning the proposed engagement? Clark may

A. Not report on the comparative financial statements because the Year 1 statements are not comparable with the Year 2 statements that include the GAAP disclosures.

B. Report on the comparative financial statements, provided the Year 1 statements do not contain any obvious material misstatements.

C. Report on the comparative financial statements, provided an explanatory paragraph is added to Clark's report on the comparative financial statements.

D. Report on the comparative financial statements, provided Clark updates the report on the Year 1 statements that do not include the GAAP disclosures.

Answer (A) is correct.

REQUIRED: The accountant's responsibility when compiled financial statements are presented comparatively but the earlier year's statements omit most disclosures required by GAAP.

DISCUSSION: Compiled financial statements that omit substantially all of the disclosures required by GAAP are not comparable with financial statements that include such disclosures. Accordingly, the accountant ordinarily should not issue a report on comparative financial statements when statements for one or more, but not all, of the periods presented omit substantially all of the disclosures required by GAAP (AR 200).

Answer (B) is incorrect. The statements are not considered comparable and should not be reported on. Answer (C) is incorrect. No report should be issued. The statements are not comparable. Answer (D) is incorrect. The statements are not considered comparable and should not be reported on.

18. Gole, CPA, is engaged to review the Year 2 financial statements of North Co., a nonissuer. Previously, Gole audited North's Year 1 financial statements and expressed an unmodified opinion. Gole decides to include a separate paragraph in the Year 2 review report because North plans to present comparative financial statements for Year 2 and Year 1. This separate paragraph should indicate that

A. The Year 2 review report is intended solely for the information of management and the board of directors.

B. The Year 1 auditor's report may no longer be relied on.

C. No auditing procedures were performed after the date of the Year 1 auditor's report.

D. There are justifiable reasons for changing the level of service from an audit to a review.

Answer (C) is correct.
　　REQUIRED: The reference in a separate paragraph in a review report when comparative statements are presented and an audit was performed in the previous year.
　　DISCUSSION: A continuing accountant who performs a lower level of service should include a separate paragraph describing the responsibility assumed for the financial statements of the prior period or reissue the previous report. The paragraph included in the review report should indicate that no auditing procedures were performed after the date of the original auditor's report.
　　Answer (A) is incorrect. A review report may be distributed to any user. Answer (B) is incorrect. The previous auditor's report may still be relied upon. Answer (D) is incorrect. No mention of the reasons for the change of service should be made in the review report.

19. Before reissuing a compilation report on the financial statements of a nonissuer for the prior year, the predecessor accountant is required to

A. Make inquiries about actions taken at meetings of the board of directors during the current year.

B. Verify that the reissued report will not be used to obtain credit from a financial institution.

C. Review the successor accountant's working papers for matters affecting the prior year.

D. Compare the prior year's financial statements with those of the current year.

Answer (D) is correct.
　　REQUIRED: The procedure necessary before reissuing a compilation report.
　　DISCUSSION: Before reissuing a report, the predecessor should consider whether the report is still appropriate. The predecessor should read the current financial statement, compare the prior financial statements with the current financial statements, and obtain a letter from the successor requesting any information that might affect the prior financial statements.
　　Answer (A) is incorrect. Making inquiries about actions taken at BOD meetings is not required to reissue the report. Answer (B) is incorrect. Determining the use of the report is not required to reissue the report. Answer (C) is incorrect. Reviewing the successor accountant's working papers is not required to reissue the report.

20. Kell engaged March, CPA, to submit to Kell a written personal financial plan containing unaudited personal financial statements. March anticipates omitting certain disclosures required by GAAP because the engagement's sole purpose is to assist Kell in developing a personal financial plan. For March to be exempt from complying with the requirements of AR 80, *Compilation of Financial Statements*, Kell is required to agree that the

A. Financial statements will not be presented in comparative form with those of the prior period.

B. Omitted disclosures required by GAAP are not material.

C. Financial statements will not be disclosed to a non-CPA financial planner.

D. Financial statements will not be used to obtain credit.

Answer (D) is correct.
　　REQUIRED: The circumstances under which an accountant may depart from the requirements of AR 80.
　　DISCUSSION: AR 600, *Reporting on Personal Financial Statements Included in Written Personal Financial Plans*, states that an accountant may submit a written personal financial plan containing unaudited personal financial statements to a client without complying with the requirements of AR 80 if the accountant (1) has an understanding with the client about its use and (2) has no reason to believe that the financial statements will be used to obtain credit or for any other purpose except developing the financial plan.
　　Answer (A) is incorrect. The financial statements may be presented in comparative form. Answer (B) is incorrect. The exemption is appropriate regardless of the disclosures and their materiality level. Answer (C) is incorrect. The financial plan is likely to be used by the client and potentially a financial planner.

21. An accountant who has reviewed statements that did not omit the disclosures required by U.S. GAAP may subsequently be requested to compile and report on statements for the same period that do omit substantially all of those disclosures when they are presented in comparative financial statements. In these circumstances, the accountant may report on the comparative compiled financial statements that omit such disclosures if (s)he

A. Does not mention the omissions.

B. Does not mention the prior report.

C. Includes in the report an additional paragraph indicating the nature of the previous service rendered.

D. States in the report that (s)he is not aware of any material modifications that should be made for the financial statements to be in conformity with U.S. GAAP.

Answer (C) is correct.
REQUIRED: The basis for reporting on comparative compiled statements that omit disclosures required by U.S. GAAP that appeared in previously reviewed statements.
DISCUSSION: The accountant may report on the comparative compiled statements that omit these disclosures if the compilation report includes the date of the previous report and a paragraph that explains the prior service provided (AR 200).
Answer (A) is incorrect. The compilation report must mention the omission of the disclosures. Answer (B) is incorrect. The prior report based upon another accounting service should be referred to and its date given. Answer (D) is incorrect. Limited assurance is provided in a report on a review of financial statements, not a compilation.

19.4 Engagements to Apply Agreed-Upon Procedures (AT 201)

22. Negative assurance may be expressed when a practitioner is requested to apply agreed-upon procedures to specified

	Elements of a Financial Statement	Accounts of a Financial Statement
A.	Yes	Yes
B.	Yes	No
C.	No	No
D.	No	Yes

Answer (C) is correct.
REQUIRED: The report in which negative assurance may be expressed.
DISCUSSION: The practitioner does not express an opinion or negative assurance. Instead, the practitioner's report on agreed-upon procedures should be in the form of procedures and findings.

23. A practitioner may accept an agreed-upon procedures engagement to calculate the rate of return on a specified investment and verify that the percentage agrees with the percentage in an identified schedule provided that

A. The practitioner's report does not enumerate the procedures performed.

B. The practitioner accepts responsibility for the sufficiency of the procedures.

C. Use of the practitioner's report is restricted.

D. The practitioner is also the entity's continuing auditor.

Answer (C) is correct.
REQUIRED: The condition of an engagement to apply agreed-upon procedures.
DISCUSSION: An independent practitioner may accept such an engagement if (1) the specified parties agree to the procedures and take responsibility for their sufficiency, (2) the subject matter is subject to reasonably consistent measurement, (3) evidence is expected to exist providing a reasonable basis for the findings, (4) the use of the report is restricted, and (5) other conditions are met. The report should state that it is intended solely for the information and use of the specified parties and is not intended to be used and should not be used by anyone other than these specified parties.
Answer (A) is incorrect. The procedures performed must be enumerated. Answer (B) is incorrect. The client or specified parties take responsibility for the sufficiency of the procedures. Answer (D) is incorrect. The practitioner need not be a continuing auditor.

24. Which of the following should a practitioner perform as part of an engagement for agreed-upon procedures in accordance with *Statements on Standards for Attestation Engagements*?

A. Issue a report on findings based on specified procedures performed.

B. Assess whether the procedures meet the needs of the parties.

C. Express negative assurance on findings of work performed.

D. Report the differences between agreed-upon and audit procedures.

Answer (A) is correct.

REQUIRED: The action by a practitioner who performs agreed-upon procedures in accordance with SSAE.

DISCUSSION: An agreed-upon procedures engagement is one in which a practitioner is engaged by a client to issue a report of findings based on specific procedures performed on subject matter.

Answer (B) is incorrect. Specified parties assume responsibility for the sufficiency of the procedures. Answer (C) is incorrect. The report is in the form of procedures and findings, and neither an opinion nor negative assurance should be provided. Answer (D) is incorrect. In an engagement to apply agreed-upon procedures, the practitioner does not perform an audit and therefore cannot report the differences between agreed-upon and audit procedures.

19.5 Financial Forecasts and Projections (AT 301)

25. An examination of a financial forecast is a professional service that involves

A. Compiling or assembling a financial forecast that is based on management's assumptions.

B. Restricting the use of the practitioner's report to management and the board of directors.

C. Assuming responsibility to update management on key events for 1 year after the report's date.

D. Evaluating the preparation of a financial forecast and the support underlying management's assumptions.

Answer (D) is correct.

REQUIRED: The accountant's responsibility in an examination of a financial forecast.

DISCUSSION: An examination of a financial forecast entails evaluating the preparation of the statements, the support underlying the assumptions, and the presentation of the statements for conformity with AICPA guidelines (AT 301).

Answer (A) is incorrect. An examination of a financial forecast involves providing assurance on the representations of management. Answer (B) is incorrect. An examination of a financial forecast need not be limited in its distribution. Answer (C) is incorrect. The practitioner need not assume responsibility to update management on key events after the issuance of the report.

26. Given one or more hypothetical assumptions, a responsible party may prepare, to the best of its knowledge and belief, an entity's expected financial position, results of operations, and cash flows. Such prospective financial statements are known as

A. Pro forma financial statements.

B. Financial projections.

C. Partial presentations.

D. Financial forecasts.

Answer (B) is correct.

REQUIRED: The prospective statements based on one or more hypothetical assumptions.

DISCUSSION: Prospective statements include forecasts and projections. The difference between a forecast and a projection is that only the latter is based on one or more hypothetical assumptions, which are conditions or actions not necessarily expected to occur.

Answer (A) is incorrect. Pro forma statements are essentially historical, not prospective, statements. Answer (C) is incorrect. Partial presentations are not prospective statements. They do not meet the minimum presentation guidelines. Answer (D) is incorrect. Forecasts are based on assumptions about conditions the responsible party expects to exist and the course of action it expects to take.

27. Which of the following statements concerning prospective financial statements is true?

A. Only a financial forecast would normally be appropriate for limited use.

B. Only a financial projection would normally be appropriate for general use.

C. Any type of prospective financial statements would normally be appropriate for limited use.

D. Any type of prospective financial statements would normally be appropriate for general use.

Answer (C) is correct.

REQUIRED: The true statement about prospective financial statements.

DISCUSSION: Limited use of prospective financial statements means use by the responsible party and those with whom that party is negotiating directly, e.g., in a submission to a regulatory body or in negotiations for a bank loan. These third parties are in a position to communicate directly with the responsible party. Consequently, AT 100 states, "Any type of prospective financial statements that would be useful in the circumstances would be appropriate for limited use."

28. Accepting an engagement to examine an entity's financial projection most likely would be appropriate if the projection were to be distributed to

A. All employees who work for the entity.

B. Potential shareholders who request a prospectus or a registration statement.

C. A bank with which the entity is negotiating for a loan.

D. All shareholders of record as of the report date.

Answer (C) is correct.
REQUIRED: The situation in which acceptance of an engagement to examine a projection is appropriate.
DISCUSSION: A projection is based on one or more hypothetical assumptions and, therefore, should be considered for limited use only. Limited use of prospective financial statements means use by the responsible party and those with whom that party is negotiating directly. Examples of appropriate use include negotiations for a bank loan and submission to a regulatory body. A projection is inappropriate for distribution to those who will not be negotiating directly with the responsible party.

29. A practitioner's compilation report on a financial forecast should include a statement that

A. The forecast should be read only in conjunction with the audited historical financial statements.

B. The practitioner expresses only limited assurance on the forecasted statements and their assumptions.

C. There will usually be differences between the forecasted and actual results.

D. The hypothetical assumptions used in the forecast are reasonable in the circumstances.

Answer (C) is correct.
REQUIRED: The statement included in a practitioner's compilation report on a financial forecast.
DISCUSSION: The compilation report states that a compilation is limited in scope and does not enable the practitioner to express an opinion or any other form of assurance. It adds that there will usually be differences between the forecasted and actual results.
Answer (A) is incorrect. A forecast may stand alone. Answer (B) is incorrect. A compilation provides no assurance. Answer (D) is incorrect. A financial projection, not a financial forecast, contains hypothetical assumptions.

30. A practitioner has been engaged to apply agreed-upon procedures in accordance with *Statements on Standards for Attestation Engagements* (SSAE) to prospective financial statements. Which of the following conditions must be met for the practitioner to perform the engagement?

A. The prospective financial statement includes a summary of significant accounting policies.

B. The practitioner takes responsibility for the sufficiency of the agreed-upon procedures.

C. The practitioner and specified parties agree upon the procedures to be performed by the practitioner.

D. The practitioner reports on the criteria to be used in the determination of findings.

Answer (C) is correct.
REQUIRED: The condition to be met to perform agreed-upon procedures.
DISCUSSION: The following conditions should be met to accept an engagement: (1) The specified parties have participated in determining its nature and scope, and they take responsibility for the adequacy of the procedures; (2) report use is restricted to those parties; and (3) the statements include a summary of significant assumptions.
Answer (A) is incorrect. A summary of significant accounting policies is not required. Answer (B) is incorrect. The specified parties take responsibility for the adequacy of the procedures performed. Answer (D) is incorrect. The practitioner does not report on the criteria to be used in the determination of findings. Rather, the practitioner reports on the findings themselves. (S)he must believe the subject matter to be capable of reasonably consistent evaluation against suitable available criteria.

31. When an accountant compiles a financial forecast, the accountant's report should include a(n)

A. Explanation of the differences between a financial forecast and a financial projection.

B. Caveat that the prospective results of the financial forecast may not be achieved.

C. Statement that the accountant's responsibility to update the report is limited to 1 year.

D. Disclaimer of opinion on the reliability of the entity's internal controls.

Answer (B) is correct.
REQUIRED: The statement included in an accountant's compilation report on a financial forecast.
DISCUSSION: The standard report states that a compilation is limited in scope and does not enable the accountant to express an opinion or any other form of assurance. It adds that there will usually be differences between the forecasted and actual results (AT 301).
Answer (A) is incorrect. The standard report does not define a forecast, a projection, or their differences. Answer (C) is incorrect. The practitioner's update responsibility is limited to the date of the report. Answer (D) is incorrect. A compilation engagement does not involve consideration of internal control.

32. Which of the following procedures should an accountant perform during an engagement to compile prospective financial statements?

A. Test the entity's internal controls to determine if adequate controls exist so that financial projections can be reasonably achieved.

B. Make inquiries prior to the date of the report about possible future transactions that may impact the forecast once the report is issued.

C. Make inquiries about the accounting principles used in the preparation of the prospective financial statements.

D. Compare the prospective financial statements with the entity's historical results for the prior year.

Answer (C) is correct.
REQUIRED: The procedure applied during a compilation of prospective financial statements.
DISCUSSION: A compilation provides no assurance on the prospective financial statements or on the underlying assumptions. Thus, the accountant need not assess risk or apply substantive procedures during a compilation. But the accountant should determine the accounting principles to be used in the preparation of the statements.
Answer (A) is incorrect. The accountant need not gain an understanding of internal control or assess the control risk during a compilation. Answer (B) is incorrect. The accountant need not consider future events prior to the issuance of the report. Answer (D) is incorrect. The accountant need not apply analytical procedures during a compilation of prospective financial statements.

19.6 Reporting on Pro Forma Financial Information (AT 401)

33. An accountant has been engaged to examine pro forma adjustments that show the effects on previously audited historical financial statements due to a proposed disposition of a significant portion of an entity's business. Other than the procedures previously applied to the historical financial statements, the accountant is required to

	Reevaluate the entity's internal control over financial reporting	Determine that the computations of the pro forma adjustments are mathematically correct
A.	Yes	Yes
B.	Yes	No
C.	No	Yes
D.	No	No

Answer (C) is correct.
REQUIRED: The procedure(s), if any, applied in an examination of pro forma financial statements.
DISCUSSION: In an examination of pro forma financial statements, the practitioner's additional procedures include (1) understanding the underlying transaction or event; (2) discussing the assumptions about the transaction or event with management; (3) evaluating whether adjustments are included for all significant effects; (4) gathering sufficient evidence to support the adjustments; (5) evaluating whether the assumptions are sufficiently, clearly, and comprehensively presented; (6) determining that computations are correct and that the pro forma column properly reflects their application to the historical statements; (7) obtaining written management representations; and (8) evaluating the pro forma information to determine whether certain matters (the transaction or event, assumptions, adjustments, and uncertainties) have been properly described and the sources of the historical information have been properly identified. Moreover, in a business combination, the practitioner must obtain a sufficient understanding of each part of the combined entity. However, no evaluation of internal control beyond that done in the engagement is performed with respect to the historical statements.

34. A practitioner's report on a review of pro forma financial information should include a

A. Statement that the entity's internal control was not relied on in the review.

B. Disclaimer of opinion on the financial statements from which the pro forma financial information is derived.

C. Caveat that it is uncertain whether the transaction or event reflected in the pro forma financial information will ever occur.

D. Reference to the financial statements from which the historical financial information is derived.

Answer (D) is correct.
REQUIRED: The statement that should be included in a review of pro forma financial information.
DISCUSSION: A practitioner's report on pro forma information should include (1) an identification of the pro forma information, (2) a reference to the financial statements from which the historical financial information is derived and a statement as to whether such financial statements were audited or reviewed, (3) a statement that the review was made in accordance with standards established by the AICPA, (4) a caveat that a review is substantially less in scope than an examination and that no opinion is expressed, (5) a separate paragraph explaining the objective of pro forma financial information and its limitations, and (6) the practitioner's conclusion providing limited assurance.
Answer (A) is incorrect. The report should not mention internal control. Answer (B) is incorrect. The practitioner should disclaim an opinion on the pro forma financial information. Answer (C) is incorrect. The transaction may already have occurred.

SU 19: Review, Compilation, and Attestation Engagements

19.7 Compliance Attestation (AT 601)

35. A practitioner's report on agreed-upon procedures related to an entity's compliance with specified requirements should contain

A. A statement of restrictions on the use of the report.

B. An opinion about whether management complied with the specified requirements.

C. Negative assurance that control risk has not been assessed.

D. An acknowledgment of responsibility for the sufficiency of the procedures.

Answer (A) is correct.
  REQUIRED: The statement in a report on a compliance attestation engagement to apply agreed-upon procedures.
  DISCUSSION: The fourth attestation standard of reporting indicates that a report should be restricted to specified parties "when the report is on an attest engagement to apply agreed-upon procedures to the subject matter."
  Answer (B) is incorrect. The report on agreed-upon procedures should be in the form of a summary of procedures and findings, not in the form of an opinion. Answer (C) is incorrect. Negative assurance about whether an entity is in compliance or whether management's assertion is fairly stated is not permitted in reports on applying agreed-upon procedures. Answer (D) is incorrect. The parties who agreed to the procedures are responsible for their sufficiency.

36. Mill, CPA, was engaged by a group of royalty recipients to apply agreed-upon procedures to financial data supplied by Modern Co. regarding Modern's written assertion about its compliance with contractual requirements to pay royalties. Mill's report on these agreed-upon procedures should contain a(n)

A. Disclaimer of opinion about the fair presentation of Modern's financial statements.

B. List of the procedures performed (or reference thereto) and Mill's findings.

C. Opinion about the effectiveness of Modern's internal control activities concerning royalty payments.

D. Acknowledgment that the sufficiency of the procedures is solely Mill's responsibility.

Answer (B) is correct.
  REQUIRED: The statement in a report on a compliance attestation engagement to apply agreed-upon procedures.
  DISCUSSION: The practitioner's report should be in the form of procedures and findings but should not provide negative assurance about whether the entity is in compliance or whether the responsible party's assertion is fairly stated (AT 201).
  Answer (A) is incorrect. The report should not contain a disclaimer of opinion on the fair presentation of Modern's financial statements. However, it should contain a paragraph stating that the independent accountant was not engaged to and did not perform an examination of the financial data regarding the written assertion about compliance with contractual requirements to pay royalties. It also should state that (1) the objective of an examination would have been an expression of opinion on compliance with the specified requirements, and (2) no such opinion is expressed. Answer (C) is incorrect. An agreed-upon procedures engagement typically results in a summary of findings, not an opinion. Answer (D) is incorrect. The specified parties who agreed to the procedures are responsible for their sufficiency.

Use the additional questions in Gleim **CPA Test Prep** to create Practice Exams that emulate Prometric!

19.8 PRACTICE TASK-BASED SIMULATIONS

DIRECTIONS

Note: If you believe you have encountered a software malfunction, report it to the test center staff immediately.

Navigation

To navigate from task to task, use the controls at the bottom of the screen. Click on the **Next** button to advance to the next task, or the **Previous** button to go to the previous task. To go directly to any task, click on its number.

If you would like a reminder to revisit a task, or want to indicate that you are finished with it, click on the reminder flag below the task number. To clear the flag, click on it again. Reminder flags are for your use only – they do not contribute to your score.

Tabs

In this part of the examination, you will be asked to complete various tasks. Every task has one or more **Work Tabs**. Some tasks have one or more **Information Tabs**, others may have none. Every task has a **Help** tab.

If a task has **Information Tabs**, you may use the information in them to complete your responses in the **Work Tabs**.

Work tab   Information tab   Help tab

Work Tabs:
- **Work Tabs** are identified with a pencil icon. This is where your responses are expected.
- Each task has one or more **Work Tabs**.
- **Work Tabs** contain directions for completing the task – be sure to read these directions carefully.
- The **Work Tab** name in the example above is for illustration only – yours will differ.
- You must complete all of the **Work Tabs** in each task to receive full credit.

Information Tabs:
- The Authoritative Literature will be provided in all tasks in the AUD, FAR, and REG sections for your reference.
- Your simulation may have one or more additional **Information Tabs**. Like the Authoritative Literature tabs, **Information Tabs** do not have a pencil icon.
- If your task has additional **Information Tabs**, go through each to familiarize yourself with the task content.

Help Tab:
- The **Help Tab** provides assistance with the exam software that is used in this task. For example, if the task is to compose a memorandum, **Help** will provide information about the word processor.

The Toolbar

The toolbar at the top of the screen shows the amount of time remaining for you to complete the tasks. In addition, the following tools are available. Note that only the **Exit** button is displayed when Directions are visible - the others will appear when you begin the tasks.

Click on these buttons to split or unsplit the screen. You can split the screen vertically or horizontally.

Click on this button to display the calculator; click on it again to hide the calculator. To move the calculator, click on the calculator title bar and drag the calculator to the desired location.

Click on this button to use the spreadsheet; click on it again to hide the spreadsheet. To move the spreadsheet, click on the the spreadsheet title bar and drag the spreadsheet to the desired location.

Click on this button to go on to the next part of the examination. You must complete all of the tasks to receive full credit. Once you click on **Exit** and confirm the action, you will NOT be able to return to this testlet.

The following draft of a review engagement report has been submitted by a staff member to the manager for review. The table below contains the comments by the manager about the draft. Indicate by selecting from the list provided whether the original draft is correct, the audit manager's comment is correct, or neither is correct.

We have reviewed the accompanying balance sheet of ABC Company as of December 31, Year 1, and the related statements of income, retained earnings, and cash flows for the year then ended. A review includes primarily making inquiries of company management. A review is substantially less in scope than an audit, the objective of which is the expression of an opinion regarding the financial statements as a whole. Accordingly, we do not express such an opinion.

Management is responsible for the preparation and fair presentation of the financial statements in accordance with accounting principles generally accepted in the United States of America and for designing, implementing, and maintaining internal control relevant to the preparation and fair presentation of the financial statements.

Our responsibility is to conduct the review in accordance with Statements on Standards for Accounting and Review Services issued by the Auditing Standards Board. Those standards require us to perform procedures to obtain limited assurance that there are no material modifications that should be made to the financial statements. We believe that the results of our procedures provide a reasonable basis for our report.

Based on our examination, we are not aware of any material modifications that should be made to the accompanying financial statements in order for them to be in conformity with accounting principles generally accepted in the United States of America.

Manager's Comments	Answer	Choices
1. The report should not refer to the statement of cash flows because a nonissuer does not prepare this statement.		A) The original draft is correct.
2. The second sentence in the first paragraph also should refer to analytical procedures.		B) The manager's comment is correct.
3. The third sentence in the first paragraph should state that the review is "substantially greater in scope . . ."		C) Neither the original draft nor the manager's comment is correct.
4. The last sentence in the first paragraph should be deleted.		
5. The second paragraph should state that the CPA is responsible for the preparation of the fair presentation of the financial statements.		
6. The first sentence in the third paragraph should state that the accounting and review standards are established by the federal government.		
7. The fourth paragraph should state, "Based on our study . . ." rather than "Based on our examination . . ."		
8. The fourth paragraph should state, "conformity with auditing principles" rather than "conformity with accounting principles."		

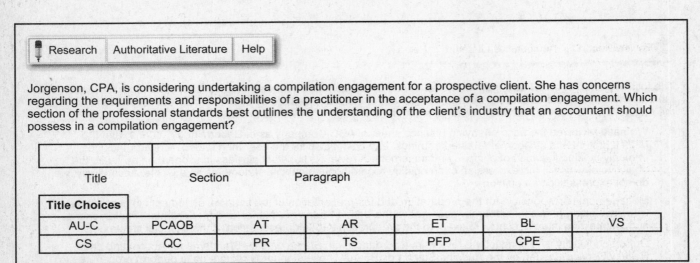

Research   Authoritative Literature   Help

Jorgenson, CPA, is considering undertaking a compilation engagement for a prospective client. She has concerns regarding the requirements and responsibilities of a practitioner in the acceptance of a compilation engagement. Which section of the professional standards best outlines the understanding of the client's industry that an accountant should possess in a compilation engagement?

Title	Section	Paragraph

Title Choices

AU-C	PCAOB	AT	AR	ET	BL	VS
CS	QC	PR	TS	PFP	CPE	

▼ = Reminder   Directions   1 [2] 3 4 5   ◄ Previous   Next ►

Review Report II   Authoritative Literature   Help

Jordan & Stone, CPAs, audited the financial statements of Tech Co., a nonissuer, for the year ended December 31, Year 1, and expressed an unmodified opinion. For the year ended December 31, Year 2, Tech issued comparative financial statements. Jordan & Stone reviewed Tech's Year 2 financial statements and Kent, an assistant on the engagement, drafted the accountants' review report below. Land, the engagement supervisor, decided not to reissue the prior year's auditor's report.

Land reviewed Kent's draft presented below and indicated in the *Supervisor's Noted Deficiencies* below that there were 13 deficiencies in Kent's draft.

> We have reviewed and audited the accompanying balance sheets of Tech Co. as of December 31, Year 1 and Year 2, and the related statements of income, retained earnings, and cash flows for the years then ended. A review is substantially less in scope than an audit, the objective of which is the expression of an opinion regarding the financial statements as a whole. Accordingly, we do not express such an opinion.
>
> Management is responsible for the preparation and full presentation of the financial statements in accordance with accounting principles generally accepted in the United States of America and for designing, implementing, and maintaining internal control relevant to the preparation and fair presentation of the financial statements.
>
> Our responsibility is to conduct the review in accordance with Statements on Standards for Accounting and Review Services issued by the American Institute of Certified Public Accountants. Those standards require us to perform procedures to obtain significant assurance that there are no material modifications that should be made to the financial statements. We believe that the results of our procedures provide a reasonable basis for our report.
>
> Based on our study, we are not aware of any material modifications that should be made to the accompanying financial statements in order for them to be in conformity with accounting principles generally accepted in the United States of America. Because of inherent limitations in a review engagement, this report is intended for the information of management and should not be used for any other purpose.
>
> The financial statements for the year ended December 31, Year 1, were audited by us, and our report was dated March 2, Year 2. We have no responsibility for updating that report for events and circumstances occurring after that date.
>
> Jordan and Stone, CPAs
> March 1, Year 3

For each noted deficiency, indicate whether Kent's draft is correct, Land's noted deficiency is correct, or neither Kent's draft nor Land's noted deficiency is correct. Each item in the answer list may be used once, more than once, or not at all.

-- Continued on next page --

| Review Report II | Authoritative Literature | Help | -- Continued |

Supervisor's Noted Deficiencies	*Answer*
1. The reference to the prior year's audited financial statements should be in a separate paragraph.	
2. All the current-year basic financial statements are **not** properly identified in the first (introductory) paragraph.	
3. A statement should be included in the first paragraph stating that a review includes primarily applying analytical procedures to management's financial data and making inquiries of company management.	
4. In the second paragraph, "full presentation" should be replaced with "accurate presentation."	
5. The reference should be to the PCAOB, not the American Institute of Certified Public Accountants in the third paragraph.	
6. The phrase "to obtain significant assurance" in the third paragraph should be replaced with "to obtain limited assurance."	
7. The last sentence in the third paragraph that begins, "We believe that the results . . ." should be deleted.	
8. The fourth paragraph should begin, "Based on our evidence . . ."	
9. There should be **no** restriction on the distribution of the accountant's review report in the fourth paragraph.	
10. The reference should be "material misstatements," not to "material modifications" in the fourth paragraph.	
11. There should be an indication of the type of opinion expressed on the prior year's audited financial statements in a separate paragraph.	
12. There should be an indication that **no** auditing procedures were performed after the date of the report on the prior year's financial statements in a separate paragraph.	
13. There should be **no** reference to "updating that report for events and circumstances occurring after that date" in the fourth (separate) paragraph.	

Choices
A) Kent's draft is correct.
B) Land's noted deficiency is correct.
C) Neither Kent's draft nor Land's noted deficiency is correct.

Reviews and Compilations | Authoritative Literature | Help

Items 1 through 15 state unrelated procedures that an accountant may consider performing in separate engagements to review the financial statements of a nonissuer (a review) and to compile the financial statements of a nonissuer (a compilation). Indicate whether or not each procedure is contemplated for a review and a compilation. Make two selections for each item.

Procedure	Review A) or B)	Compilation C) or D)
1. The accountant establishes an understanding with the entity regarding the nature and limitations of the services to be performed.		
2. The accountant makes inquiries of management.		
3. The accountant, as the entity's successor accountant, communicates with the predecessor accountant to obtain access to the predecessor's working papers.		
4. The accountant obtains a level of knowledge of the accounting principles and practices of the entity's industry.		
5. The accountant assesses fraud risk.		
6. The accountant performs analytical procedures designed to identify relationships that appear to be unusual.		
7. The accountant obtains an understanding of internal control.		
8. The accountant sends a letter of inquiry to the entity's legal counsel to corroborate the information furnished by management concerning litigation.		
9. The accountant obtains written representations from management of the entity.		
10. The accountant compares recorded amounts with expectations.		
11. The accountant communicates to the entity's senior management illegal employee acts discovered by the accountant that are clearly inconsequential.		
12. The accountant makes inquiries about events subsequent to the date of the financial statements that would have a material effect on the financial statements.		
13. The accountant modifies the accountant's report for a change in accounting principles that is adequately disclosed.		
14. The accountant submits a hard copy of the financial statements and accountant's report when the financial statements and accountant's report are submitted on a computer disk.		
15. The accountant performs specific procedures to evaluate whether substantial doubt exists about the entity's ability to continue as a going concern.		

Review Choices
A) Procedure is contemplated.
B) Procedure is not contemplated.

Compilation Choices
C) Procedure is contemplated.
D) Procedure is not contemplated.

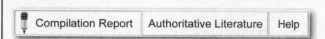

| Compilation Report | Authoritative Literature | Help |

The following report was drafted on October 25, Year 1, by Major, CPA, at the completion of the engagement to compile the financial statements of Ajax Company for the year ended September 30, Year 1. Ajax is a nonpublic entity in which Major's child has a material direct financial interest. Ajax decided to omit substantially all of the disclosures required by GAAP because the financial statements will be for management's use only. The statement of cash flows was also omitted because management does not believe it to be a useful financial statement.

Select from the list provided to indicate which sentences in Major's report on the compiled financial statements contain a deficiency.

To the Board of Directors of Ajax Company:	*Answer*
1. I have compiled the accompanying financial statements of Ajax Company as of September 30, Year 1, and for the year then ended.	
2. I have not audited or reviewed the accompanying financial statements.	
3. Management is responsible for the preparation and fair presentation of the financial statements in accordance with accounting principles generally accepted in the United States of America and for designing, implementing, and maintaining internal control relevant to the preparation and fair presentation of the financial statements.	
4. My responsibility is to conduct the compilation in accordance with accepted standards issued by the American Institute of Certified Public Accountants.	
5. The objective of a compilation is to assist management in presenting financial information in the form of financial statements without undertaking to obtain or provide any assurance that there are no material modifications that should be made to the financial statements.	
6. Management has elected to omit substantially all of the disclosures (and the statement of cash flows) required by generally accepted accounting principles.	
7. If the omitted disclosures and statements were included in the financial statements, they might influence the user's conclusions about the company's financial position, results of operations, and cash flows.	
8. I am not independent with respect to Ajax Company.	
9. This lack of independence is due to my child's ownership of a material direct financial interest in Ajax Company.	
10. This report is intended solely for the information and use of the Board of Directors and management of Ajax Company and should not be used for any other purpose.	

Major, CPA
October 25, Year 1

Choices
Deficient
Not deficient

Unofficial Answers

1. Review Report I (8 Gradable Items)

1. A) The original draft is correct. A nonissuer is required to present a statement of cash flows, and the review report should refer to the statement.

2. B) The manager's comment is correct. A review includes inquiries of company personnel and analytical procedures applied to financial data.

3. A) The original draft is correct. A review is less in scope as an audit.

4. A) The original draft is correct. A disclaimer is required.

5. A) The original draft is correct. Management is responsible for fair presentation.

6. C) Neither the original draft nor the manager's comment is correct. The report should state that the SSARSs are issued by the American Institute of Certified Public Accountants.

7. C) Neither the original draft nor the manager's comment is correct. The paragraph should begin, "Based on our review . . ."

8. A) The original draft is correct. The financial statements should be in conformity with GAAP.

2. Research (1 Gradable Item)

Answer: AR 80.06

AR 80 -- *Compilation of Financial Statements*

Understanding of the Industry

.06   The accountant should possess an understanding of the industry in which the client operates, including the accounting principles and practices generally used in the industry, sufficient to enable the accountant to compile financial statements that are appropriate in form for an entity operating in that industry.

3. Review Report II (13 Gradable Items)

1. B) Land's noted deficiency is correct. A continuing accountant who performs a lower level of service should either include a separate paragraph describing the responsibility assumed for the financial statements of the prior period or reissue the previous report.

2. A) Kent's draft is correct. The basic financial statements are properly identified in the introductory paragraph.

3. B) Land's noted deficiency is correct. The first paragraph describes, in general, the procedures performed in review.

4. C) Neither Kent's draft nor Land's noted deficiency is correct. The phase included in the report should be "fair presentation."

5. A) Kent's draft is correct. The identification of the standards should reference the American Institute of Certified Public Accountants.

6. B) Land's noted deficiency is correct. A review provides limited assurance.

7. A) Kent's draft is correct. The statement, "We believe that the results of our procedures provide a reasonable basis for our report." should be included.

8. C) Neither Kent's draft nor Land's noted deficiency is correct. The fourth paragraph should begin, "Based on our review . . ."

9. B) Land's noted deficiency is correct. A review report is not limited on use or distribution.

10. A) Kent's draft is correct. The report refers to "material modifications" to the financial statements.

11. B) Land's noted deficiency is correct. The opinion expressed on the audited financial statements should be described in a separate paragraph.

12. B) Land's noted deficiency is correct. The paragraph describing the prior year's audit should indicate that no auditing procedures were performed after the audit report date.

13. B) Land's noted deficiency is correct. There is no reference to updating in the standard review report.

4. Reviews and Compilations (15 Gradable Items)

1. <u>A) Procedure is contemplated; C) Procedure is contemplated.</u> According to both AR 90 and AR 80, an accountant should establish with the entity an understanding regarding the nature and limitation of the services to be performed.

2. <u>A) Procedure is contemplated; D) Procedure is not contemplated.</u> When performing a review, an accountant should make inquiries of management and, when deemed appropriate, other company personnel. When performing a compilation, the accountant is not required to make inquiries.

3. <u>B) Procedure is not contemplated; D) Procedure is not contemplated.</u> "A successor accountant is not required to communicate with a predecessor accountant in connection with acceptance of a compilation or review engagement, but (s)he may decide to do so" (AR 400).

4. <u>A) Procedure is contemplated; C) Procedure is contemplated.</u> The accountant should have a level of knowledge of the accounting principles and practices of the entity's industry and an understanding of the entity's business to provide the accountant, through inquiries and analytical procedures, with the reasonable basis for limited assurance sought in a review. The accountant should have a level of knowledge of the accounting principles and practices of the entity's industry to enable the accountant to compile statements that are appropriate in form for an entity in that industry.

5. <u>B) Procedure is not contemplated; D) Procedure is not contemplated.</u> Auditors, not accountants performing review engagements or compilation services, assess fraud risk.

6. <u>A) Procedure is contemplated; D) Procedure is not contemplated.</u> In performing review services, an accountant is required to apply analytical procedures to the financial statements, make inquiries of management, and obtain representations from management. In a compilation engagement, an accountant prepares the financial statements of an entity. No assurance is provided; therefore, no analytical procedures are required.

7. <u>B) Procedure is not contemplated; D) Procedure is not contemplated.</u> An auditor should obtain an understanding of internal control. Neither a compilation nor a review contemplates that the accountant will obtain an understanding of internal control.

8. <u>B) Procedure is not contemplated; D) Procedure is not contemplated.</u> During a review engagement, an accountant is required to obtain written representations from management but not to obtain corroborating evidence. Compilation services do not contemplate performing procedures performed in a review, for example, inquiries about information provided by the entity.

9. <u>A) Procedure is contemplated; D) Procedure is not contemplated.</u> When performing a review of an entity's financial statements, the accountant should obtain written representations from responsible and knowledgeable members of management (e.g., the CEO or the CFO, or the equivalent). However, compilation services do not contemplate performing procedures performed in a review, for example, obtaining written representations from management.

10. <u>A) Procedure is contemplated; D) Procedure is not contemplated.</u> When reviewing an entity's financial statements, the accountant should perform analytical procedures, which include comparing recorded amounts or ratios with expectations developed by the accountant. Compilation services do not contemplate performing procedures performed in a review, for example, applying analytical procedures.

11. <u>B) Procedure is not contemplated; D) Procedure is not contemplated.</u> The accountant should establish an understanding with the entity, in writing, regarding the services to be performed. The understanding should provide that the accountant will inform the appropriate level of management of any illegal acts that come to his or her attention, unless they are clearly inconsequential.

12. <u>A) Procedure is contemplated; D) Procedure is not contemplated.</u> When performing a review, an accountant should make inquiries of management and, when deemed appropriate, other company personnel. When performing a compilation, the accountant is not required to make inquiries.

13. <u>B) Procedure is not contemplated; D) Procedure is not contemplated.</u> Given proper disclosure, inconsistencies in the application of accounting principles do not normally result in modification of the standard report.

14. <u>B) Procedure is not contemplated; D) Procedure is not contemplated.</u> The form of the financial statements is not important. For example, the copy may be on a computer disk, fax, or other medium.

15. <u>B) Procedure is not contemplated; D) Procedure is not contemplated.</u> In providing compilation and review services, the accountant provides no positive assurance about the financial statements taken as a whole. Hence, these services do not contemplate assessing the entity's ability to continue as a going concern.

5. Compilation Report (10 Gradable Items)

1. <u>Deficient.</u> The report should identify the financial statements that were compiled.

2. <u>Deficient.</u> The report should state that "I have not audited or reviewed the accompanying financial statements and, accordingly, do not express an opinion or provide any assurance about whether the financial statements are in accordance with accounting principles generally accepted in the United States of America."

3. <u>Not deficient.</u> Management's responsibility should be stated in the report.

4. <u>Deficient.</u> The compilation should be conducted in accordance with Statements on Standards for Accounting and Review Services.

5. <u>Not deficient.</u> The objective of a compilation should be stated in the report.

6. <u>Not deficient.</u> It is appropriate to state that management has elected to omit the notes and the statement of cash flows.

7. <u>Not deficient.</u> It is appropriate to state that the disclosures, if made, could influence the financial statement users.

8. <u>Not deficient.</u> It is appropriate in a compilation report to indicate lack of independence.

9. <u>Not deficient.</u> It is appropriate to note the reason for lack of independence in a compilation report.

10. <u>Deficient.</u> The accountant need not limit the use of the report.

Gleim Simulation Grading

Task	Correct Responses		Gradable Items		Score per Task
1	_____	÷	8	=	_____
2 (Research)	_____	÷	1	=	_____
3	_____	÷	13	=	_____
4	_____	÷	15	=	_____
5	_____	÷	10	=	_____

	Total of Scores per Task	_____
÷	Total Number of Tasks	5
	Total Score	_____%

Use CPA Gleim Online and Simulation Wizard to practice more task-based simulations in a realistic environment.

STUDY UNIT TWENTY
GOVERNMENTAL AUDITS

(11 pages of outline)

The first subunit addresses *Government Auditing Standards*, the publication of the **Government Accountability Office (GAO)** that is fundamental to governmental auditing and is the basis for most of the related questions on recent CPA exams. Subunit 2 is based on an AICPA auditing standard and relates to opinions on whether an organization complies with applicable laws and regulations. The final subunit describes additional standards for audits of organizations that receive federal awards. The trend has been to increase the coverage of governmental auditing, so expect some questions on this material.

20.1 GOVERNMENT AUDITING STANDARDS

1. The GAO establishes **generally accepted government auditing standards (GAGAS).** They are published in *Government Auditing Standards* (the Yellow Book).

   a. GAGAS pertain to auditors' professional qualifications and the quality of their work, the performance of field work, and the characteristics of meaningful reporting.

   b. *Government Auditing Standards* apply to engagements involving federal government entities, programs, activities, and functions. GAGAS also apply in audits of state and local governments and not-for-profit entities that receive federal awards. Moreover, contract terms or state and local laws may require the use of GAGAS.

2. **Audits and Attestation Engagements**

   a. **Financial Audits**

      1) GAGAS incorporate by reference the AICPA's Statements on Auditing Standards (codified with the identifier AU-C).

      2) **Financial statement audits.** These audits are primarily concerned with whether financial statements are presented fairly, in all material respects, with an applicable financial reporting framework (typically GAAP).

         a) GAGAS require related reporting on (1) internal control and (2) compliance with provisions of laws, regulations, contracts, and grant agreements.

         b) The auditor conducting a governmental audit accepts a **greater scope** and assumes **more responsibility** than in an audit of a business entity.

      3) **Other types.** These engagements provide for different levels of assurance and involve various scopes of work. They include the following:

         a) Opinions on single financial statements, specified elements, accounts, or items of a financial statement

         b) Issuing letters for underwriters and certain other requesting parties

         c) Auditing compliance with requirements relating to government programs

b. **Attestation Engagements**

    1) These engagements cover a broad range of financial or nonfinancial objectives. They involve examining, reviewing, or performing agreed-upon procedures on a subject matter or an assertion about a subject matter that is the responsibility of another party. GAGAS incorporate by reference the AICPA's *Statements on Standards for Attestation Engagements*. The following are examples of attestation engagements on which reports may be issued:

        a) Internal control over financial reporting

        b) Compliance with requirements of specified laws, regulations, rules, contracts, or grants

        c) The effectiveness of internal control over compliance with specified laws, regulations, rules, contracts, or grants

        d) Management's discussion and analysis (MD&A)

        e) Prospective financial or performance information

        f) Accuracy and reliability of performance measures

        g) Quantity, condition, or valuation of assets

        h) Allowability and reasonableness of proposed contract amounts based on detailed costs

        i) Whether incurred final contract costs are supported by required evidence and comply with the contract terms

c. **Performance Audits**

    1) These audits address many objectives, including assessing

        a) Program effectiveness and results,
        b) Economy and efficiency,
        c) Internal control, and
        d) Compliance with legal requirements.

    2) They also may provide prospective analysis, guidance, or summary information.

    3) GAGAS do not incorporate any other standards for performance audits.

3. **Additional Standards**

a. The following are some of the more significant standards in addition to those incorporated by reference:

b. **Independence.**

    1) Audit organizations and auditors must be independent in both mind and appearance.

    2) The standards develop a conceptual framework for independence similar to the AICPA's that requires auditors to

        a) Identify threats to independence;

        b) Evaluate the significance of the threats identified, both individually and in the aggregate; and

        c) Apply safeguards as necessary to eliminate the threats or reduce them to an acceptable level.

c. **Continuing Professional Education.** Auditors who are involved in planning, directing, or reporting on GAGAS audits are required to acquire 80 hours of continuing education in related topics every 2 years. At least 24 hours of CPE should directly relate to governmental auditing.

d. **Quality Control and Assurance.** Each audit organization performing audits or attestation engagements in accordance with GAGAS must establish a system of quality control that is designed to provide the audit organization with reasonable assurance that the organization and its personnel comply with professional standards and applicable legal and regulatory requirements. The organization is required to have an external **peer review** at least once every **3 years**.

e. **Auditor Communication.** In addition to the AICPA requirements for auditor communication, auditors should communicate pertinent information that, in the auditors' professional judgment, needs to be communicated to individuals contracting for or requesting the audit and to cognizant legislative committees when auditors perform the audit pursuant to a law or regulation.

f. **Previous Audits and Attestation Engagements.** Auditors should evaluate whether the audited entity has taken appropriate corrective action to address findings and recommendations from previous engagements that could have a material effect on the financial statements or other financial data significant to the audit objectives.

g. **Developing Elements of a Finding.** When auditors identify findings, they should plan and perform procedures to develop the elements of the findings that are relevant and necessary to achieve the audit objectives. The elements needed for a finding depend on the objectives of the audit but include the following:

   1) **Criteria.** The required or desired state (e.g., law or contract) or expectation with respect to the program or operation.

   2) **Condition.** The situation that exists.

   3) **Cause.** The reason or explanation for the condition.

   4) **Effect or potential effect.** A clear, logical link to establish the impact or potential impact of the difference between the situation that exists (condition) and the required or desired state (criteria).

h. **Compliance with GAGAS.** The auditor's report should state that the audit was performed in accordance with GAGAS.

i. **Reporting on Internal Control and Compliance with Laws, Regulations, Contracts, and Grant Agreements**

   1) The report (or separate reports) on financial statements should describe the scope of the auditor's testing of internal control over financial reporting and compliance with laws and regulations and grant or contract provisions. The report should state whether the tests provided sufficient, appropriate evidence to support opinions on internal control and on compliance.

   2) Auditors should report all of the following:

      a) Significant deficiencies and material weaknesses in internal control

      b) Instances of fraud and noncompliance with provisions of laws or regulations that have a material effect on the audit and any other instances that warrant the attention of those charged with governance

      c) Noncompliance with provisions of contracts or grant agreements that has a material effect on the audit

      d) Abuse that has a material effect on the audit

j. **Reporting Views of Responsible Officials.** If the auditors' report discloses (1) deficiencies in internal control; (2) fraud; (3) noncompliance with provisions of laws, regulations, contracts, or grant agreements; or (4) abuse, auditors should obtain and report the views of responsible officials of the audited entity concerning the findings, conclusions, and recommendations as well as any planned corrective actions.

      k.   **Reporting Confidential or Sensitive Information.** If certain pertinent information is prohibited from public disclosure or is excluded from a report due to the confidential or sensitive nature of the information, auditors should disclose in the report that certain information has been omitted.

      l.   **Distributing Reports.** Audit organizations in government entities should distribute audit reports to (1) those charged with governance, (2) the appropriate officials of the audited entity, and (3) the appropriate oversight bodies or organizations requiring or arranging for the audits.

   4.   **Examples of Reports**

EXAMPLE -- Auditor's Unmodified Report on General-Purpose Financial Statements

Independent Auditor's Report

To: <---------- Oversight Body

Report on the Financial Statements

We have audited the accompanying general-purpose financial statements of the City of Example, Any State, as of and for the year ended June 30, 20X1.

Management's Responsibility for the Financial Statements

Management is responsible for the preparation and fair presentation of these financial statements in accordance with accounting principles generally accepted in the United States of America; this includes the design, implementation, and maintenance of internal control relevant to the preparation and fair presentation of financial statements that are free from material misstatement, whether due to fraud or error.

Auditor's Responsibility

Our responsibility is to express opinions on these financial statements based on our audit. We conducted our audit in accordance with auditing standards generally accepted in the United States of America and the standards applicable to financial audits contained in *Government Auditing Standards*, issued by the Comptroller General of the United States. Those standards require that we plan and perform the audit to obtain reasonable assurance about whether the financial statements are free from material misstatement.

An audit involves performing procedures to obtain audit evidence about the amounts and disclosures in the financial statements. The procedures selected depend on the auditor's judgment, including the assessment of the risks of material misstatement of the financial statements, whether due to fraud or error. In making those risk assessments, the auditor considers internal control relevant to the entity's preparation and fair presentation of the financial statements in order to design audit procedures that are appropriate in the circumstances, but not for the purpose of expressing an opinion on the effectiveness of the entity's internal control. Accordingly, we express no such opinion. An audit also includes evaluating the appropriateness of accounting policies used and the reasonableness of significant accounting estimates made by management, as well as evaluating the overall presentation of the financial statements.

We believe that the audit evidence we have obtained is sufficient and appropriate to provide a basis for our audit opinion.

Opinion

In our opinion, the financial statements referred to above present fairly, in all material respects, financial position of the City of Example, Any State, as of June 30, 20X1, and the results of its operations and cash flows of its proprietary fund types and trust funds for the year then ended in accordance with accounting principles generally accepted in the United States of America.

Other Reporting Required by Government Auditing Standards

In accordance with *Government Auditing Standards*, we have also issued our report dated [date of report] on our consideration of the City of Example's internal control over financial reporting and on our tests of its compliance with certain provisions of laws, regulations, contracts, and grant agreements and other matters. The purpose of that report is to describe the scope of our testing of internal control over financial reporting and compliance and the results of that testing, and not to provide an opinion on internal control over financial reporting or on compliance. That report is an integral part of an audit performed in accordance with *Government Auditing Standards* in considering the City of Example's internal control over financial reporting and compliance.

Signature   <---------- May be signed, typed, or printed
Location   <---------- Auditor's city and state
Date   <---------- No earlier than the date on which the auditor has obtained sufficient appropriate evidence

---

EXAMPLE -- **Auditor's Standard Combined Report on Internal Control and Compliance with Laws and Regulations (No Significant Weaknesses, Material Weaknesses, or Material Noncompliance)**

Independent Auditor's Report

To: <---------- Oversight Body

We have audited, in accordance with the auditing standards generally accepted in the United States of America and the standards applicable to financial audits contained in *Government Auditing Standards* issued by the Comptroller General of the United States, the general-purpose financial statements of Example Entity, as of and for the year ended June 30, 20X1, and have issued our report thereon dated August 15, 20X1.

Internal Control over Financial Reporting

In planning and performing our audit of the financial statements, we considered Example Entity's internal control over financial reporting (internal control) to determine the audit procedures that are appropriate in the circumstances for the purpose of expressing our opinion on the financial statements, but not for the purpose of expressing an opinion on the effectiveness of Example Entity's internal control. Accordingly, we do not express an opinion on the effectiveness of Example Entity's internal control.

A deficiency in internal control exists when the design or operation of a control does not allow management or employees, in the normal course of performing their assigned functions, to prevent, or detect and correct, misstatements on a timely basis. A material weakness is a deficiency, or a combination of deficiencies, in internal control, such that there is a reasonable possibility that a material misstatement of the entity's financial statements will not be prevented, or detected and corrected on a timely basis. A significant deficiency is a deficiency, or a combination of deficiencies, in internal control that is less severe than a material weakness, yet important enough to merit attention by those charged with governance.

Our consideration of internal control was for the limited purpose described in the first paragraph of this section and was not designed to identify all deficiencies in internal control that might be material weaknesses or significant deficiencies. Given these limitations, during our audit we did not identify any deficiencies in internal control that we consider to be material weaknesses. However, material weaknesses may exist that have not been identified.

Compliance

As part of obtaining reasonable assurance about whether Example Entity's financial statements are free from material misstatement, we performed tests of its compliance with certain provisions of laws, regulations, contracts, and grant agreements, noncompliance with which could have a direct and material effect on the determination of financial statement amounts. However, providing an opinion on compliance with those provisions was not an objective of our audit, and accordingly, we do not express such an opinion. The results of our tests disclosed no instances of noncompliance or other matters that are required to be reported under *Government Auditing Standards*.

Purpose of this Report

The purpose of this report is solely to describe the scope of our testing of internal control and compliance and the results of that testing, and not to provide an opinion on the effectiveness of the entity's internal control or on compliance. This report is an integral part of an audit performed in accordance with *Government Auditing Standards* in considering the entity's internal control and compliance. Accordingly, this communication is not suitable for any other purpose.

Signature   <---------- May be signed, typed, or printed
Location   <---------- Auditor's city and state
Date   <---------- No earlier than the date on which the auditor has obtained sufficient appropriate evidence

Stop and review! You have completed the outline for this subunit. Study multiple-choice questions 1 through 19 beginning on page 651.

20.2 COMPLIANCE AUDITS (AU-C 935)

1. A compliance audit is a program-specific or organization-wide audit of compliance with requirements (laws, rules, regulations, contracts, or grants) that apply to government programs.

    a. It normally is performed with a **financial statement audit**.

2. **Scope**

    a. This guidance applies when an auditor performs a compliance audit in accordance with

        1) GAAS,
        2) Financial audit standards in *Government Auditing Standards*, and
        3) A **governmental audit requirement (GAR)** that requires an opinion on compliance.

    b. This guidance does **not** apply to an attestation engagement, including an examination of internal control over compliance. (AT 601 applies.)

3. **Management's Responsibilities**

    a. Identifying the entity's government programs and understanding and complying with the compliance requirements
    b. Establishing and maintaining effective controls over compliance
    c. Evaluating and monitoring compliance
    d. Taking necessary corrective action

4. **Audit Objectives**

    a. Obtain sufficient appropriate evidence to form an opinion and report at the level specified in the GAR on whether the entity complied, in all material respects, with the compliance requirements.
    b. Identify audit and reporting requirements in the GAR that supplement GAAS and *Government Auditing Standards* and perform and report on the related procedures.

5. The auditor, based on professional judgment, adapts AU-C sections for a **financial statement audit** for use in a compliance audit. But some do not apply, for example, AU-C 708, *Consistency of Financial Statements*.

6. **Materiality** levels, generally for a government program as a whole, are based on the GAR.

7. **Programs and Applicable Compliance Requirements (ACRs)**

    a. Based on the GAR, the auditor determines which government programs and ACRs identified by management to test.

8. **The Audit Process**

    a. An audit of compliance typically includes the following steps:

        1) Performing risk assessment procedures
        2) Assessing the risks of material noncompliance
        3) Performing further audit procedures in response to assessed risks
        4) Addressing supplementary audit requirements in the GAR
        5) Obtaining written management representations
        6) Performing subsequent events procedures
        7) Evaluating evidence and forming an opinion
        8) Reporting on compliance
        9) Documenting the audit

9. **Risk Assessment Procedures**

    a. The auditor should obtain a sufficient **understanding** of the ACRs and the entity's **internal control** over compliance to plan the audit.

b.   The auditor should **inquire** of management about whether findings and recommendations in reports or other communications resulting from previous audits or other monitoring relate to compliance.

10.   Based on the results of the risk assessment procedures, the auditor should assess the **risks of material noncompliance**, whether due to fraud or error, for each ACR.

11.   **Further Audit Procedures in Response to Assessed Risks**

a.   If the auditor identifies risks that have a **pervasive** effect on compliance, the auditor should develop an **overall response** to such risks.

1)   For example, the auditor may use more experienced staff or increase supervision.

b.   The audit should detect intentional and unintentional noncompliance. However, the auditor can obtain only **reasonable assurance** because of

1)   Performance of sampling procedures;
2)   Use of professional judgment;
3)   Availability of persuasive, not conclusive, evidence; and
4)   The inherent limitations of internal control, including the potential for collusion of entity employees.

c.   The auditor should perform further audit procedures, including **tests of details** (possibly including tests of transactions), to obtain sufficient appropriate evidence of compliance with each ACR.

1)   Risk assessment procedures, tests of controls, and analytical procedures alone are not sufficient to address the risks of material noncompliance.
2)   Furthermore, the use of analytical procedures as substantive procedures is generally less effective in a compliance audit than in a financial statement audit.

d.   **Tests of controls** should be performed if

1)   The auditor's risk assessment includes an expectation of operating effectiveness of controls related to the ACRs,
2)   Substantive procedures alone do not provide sufficient appropriate evidence, or
3)   Tests of controls over compliance are required by the GAR.

12.   **Supplementary Audit Requirements**

a.   The auditor should determine whether audit requirements are specified in the GAR that supplement GAAS and *Government Auditing Standards* and perform the related procedures.

13.   **Written Management Representations**

a.   The auditor should request written representations specific to the entity and the GAR. (These representations are parallel to those for a financial statement audit and are not repeated here.) Generally, those representations should include the following:

1)   Acknowledgment of management's responsibility for compliance
2)   Acknowledgment of management's responsibility for controls over compliance
3)   Declarations that all evidence has been made available and all instances of noncompliance have been provided to the auditor

14.   **Subsequent Events**

a.   The auditor should perform audit procedures **up to the date of the auditor's report** to obtain sufficient appropriate evidence that all subsequent events related to compliance have been identified.

b.   Audit procedures include (1) considering the risk assessment and examples of noncompliance during the subsequent period and (2) inquiring of management.

15. **Evaluating Evidence and Forming an Opinion**

    a.   The auditor should evaluate the sufficiency and appropriateness of the audit evidence obtained and form an opinion (at the level stated by the GAR) on whether the entity complied, in all material respects, with the ACRs.

    b.   The auditor evaluates (1) **questioned costs**, (2) **likely questioned costs**, and (3) other material noncompliance.

16. **Reporting on Compliance**

    a.   The auditor may issue a separate report on compliance, or it may be included with a report on internal control over compliance required by the GAR.

    b.   Given **material noncompliance** with ACRs or a **restriction on the scope** of the audit, the auditor should **modify the opinion** in accordance with AU-C 705.

    c.   Even without a GAR to report on internal control, the auditor should communicate to management and those charged with governance the identified **significant deficiencies** and **material weaknesses** in internal control over compliance.

        1)   A material weakness in internal control over compliance is a deficiency, or combination of deficiencies, in internal control over compliance that results in a reasonable possibility that material noncompliance with a compliance requirement will not be prevented, or detected and corrected, on a timely basis.

        2)   A significant deficiency in internal control over compliance is a deficiency, or a combination of deficiencies, in internal control over compliance that is less severe than a material weakness, yet merits attention by those charged with governance.

    d.   The following is an example of a separate unmodified report:

EXAMPLE -- Auditor's Report on Compliance

Independent Auditor's Report

To: <---------- Oversight Body

Compliance

We have audited Example Entity's compliance with the *[identify the applicable compliance requirements or refer to the document that describes the applicable compliance requirements]* applicable to Example Entity's *[identify the government program(s) audited or refer to a separate schedule that identifies the program(s)]* for the year ended June 30, 20X1.

Management's Responsibility

Compliance with the requirements referred to above is the responsibility of Example Entity's management.

Auditor's Responsibility

Our responsibility is to express an opinion on Example Entity's compliance based on our audit. We conducted our audit of compliance in accordance with auditing standards generally accepted in the United States of America; the standards applicable to financial audits contained in *Government Auditing Standards* issued by the Comptroller General of the United States; and *[insert the name of the governmental audit requirement or program-specific audit guide]*. Those standards and *[insert the name of the governmental audit requirement or program-specific audit guide]* require that we plan and perform the audit to obtain reasonable assurance about whether noncompliance with the compliance requirements referred to above that could have a material effect on *[identify the government program(s) audited or refer to a separate schedule that identifies the program(s)]* occurred. An audit includes examining, on a test basis, evidence about Example Entity's compliance with those requirements and performing such other procedures as we considered necessary in the circumstances. We believe that our audit provides a reasonable basis for our opinion. Our audit does not provide a legal determination of Example Entity's compliance with those requirements.

Opinion

In our opinion, Example Entity complied, in all material respects, with the compliance requirements referred to above that are applicable to *[identify the government program(s) audited]* for the year ended June 30, 20X1.

Signature   <---------- May be signed, typed, or printed
Location   <---------- Auditor's city and state
Date   <---------- No earlier than the date on which the auditor has obtained sufficient appropriate evidence

17. **Documenting the Audit**

    a. The following should be documented by the auditor:

        1) Risk assessment procedures performed, including those related to understanding internal control over compliance

        2) Materiality levels and how they were determined

        3) Responses to the assessed risks of material noncompliance

        4) Procedures to test compliance with ACRs and their results, including tests of controls

        5) Compliance with supplementary GARs

Stop and review! You have completed the outline for this subunit. Study multiple-choice questions 20 through 23 beginning on page 658.

20.3 FEDERAL AUDIT REQUIREMENTS AND THE SINGLE AUDIT ACT

Background
Prior to 1984, agencies of the federal government that provided awards to state and local governments audited specific grants, contracts, subsidies, etc. This process often resulted in numerous audits of a recipient by various agencies and a wasteful duplication of effort. In other cases, large amounts of federal awards went unaudited.

1. In 1984, Congress passed the Single Audit Act (amended in 1996), which requires one (a single) audit or a program-specific audit of a nonfederal entity that expends $500,000 of federal awards.

    a. A **single audit** is required if the entity expends federal awards under more than one federal program. The single audit covers the operations of the entire entity or, at the option of the entity, may include a **series of audits** of the organizational subunits that expended or administered federal awards.

    b. Each **federal agency** must monitor the use of awards provided by the agency. Moreover, each **nonfederal agency** must be assigned a single federal agency to assess the quality of audits and provide technical assistance.

    c. **Reporting packages** are delivered to a federal clearinghouse. These packages include financial statements, audit reports, a schedule of expenditures of federal awards, and a corrective action plan.

    d. The **Office of Management and Budget (OMB)** prescribes policies and procedures for the single audit. Those policies and procedures are issued in **OMB Circulars** and **compliance supplements.**

    e. The audit focus is greater for **major programs**, which are selected on the basis of **risk-based criteria** subject to certain limitations based on dollar expenditures.

2. According to the Single Audit Act, the auditor must conduct the audit in accordance with GAGAS. The **scope of the audit** extends to

    a. Expressing or disclaiming an opinion on whether the **financial statements** are presented fairly, in all material respects, in conformity with GAAP. (This requirement includes reporting on **compliance** with laws and regulations and **internal control** for expenditures not covered explicitly below and on the following page.)

    b. Expressing or disclaiming an opinion on whether the **schedule of expenditures of federal awards** is presented fairly, in all material respects, in relation to the financial statements taken as a whole.

    c.   Performing procedures to obtain an **understanding of internal control** sufficient to plan the audit to support a low assessed level of control risk for **major programs**, planning **tests of controls** to support that assessment for the assertions relevant to compliance requirements for each major program, and performing **tests of controls**. (Planning and performing tests are not required if the controls are likely to be ineffective.)

        1)   The **report on internal control** related to the financial statements and major programs should describe the scope of testing and the results of tests and, if applicable, should refer to the **schedule of findings and questioned costs**.

        2)   **Control deficiencies** that are individually or cumulatively material should be identified.

    d.   Expressing or disclaiming **an opinion** on whether the **auditee has complied** with laws, regulations, and the provisions of contracts or grants that may have a direct and material effect on each major program.

    e.   Following up.

    f.   Reporting a schedule of findings and questioned costs.

3.   Compliance requirements applicable to awards made by many federal programs are covered in the **Compliance Supplement** (over 1,500 pages) to OMB Circular A-133, *Audits of States, Local Governments, and Non-Profit Organizations.* Its focus is on compliance requirements that could have a direct and material effect on a major program.

    a.   This supplement lists and describes the **types of compliance requirements** and related **audit objectives and procedures** that should be considered in every audit to which it relates. It also discusses objectives, procedures, and compliance requirements that are specific to **each federal program** included.

4.   Auditee **management** is responsible for **identifying federal awards** and the **related programs** and preparing a schedule of the expenditures of federal awards. The auditee also is responsible for (a) maintaining control over federal programs; (b) complying with laws, regulations, and the provisions of contracts and grants; (c) preparing financial statements; (d) ensuring that required audits are performed and submitted when due; and (e) following up and taking corrective action.

    a.   The auditee must submit to the **designated clearinghouse** a data collection form providing information about the auditee, its federal programs, and the results of the audit. Furthermore, the auditee must submit a **reporting package** that includes (1) financial statements, (2) a summary schedule of audit findings, (3) the auditor's reports, and (4) the corrective action plan.

5.   The auditor uses a **risk-based approach** in determining which federal programs are major programs. The criteria considered are (a) current and prior audit experience, (b) oversight by federal agencies and pass-through entities, (c) inherent risk, and (d) amounts of federal awards expended.

    a.   A federal agency or pass-through entity may request that the auditee have a program audited as a **major program**.

    b.   The auditor applies technical rules to determine which programs require audit focus. But, in general, at least 50% of the federal award dollars are required to be audited for compliance.

6. The **schedule of audit findings and questioned costs** includes any instances of (a) **known questioned costs** greater than $10,000 or (b) known questioned costs when likely questioned costs exceed $10,000 for compliance requirements for a major program.

   a. Moreover, **likely questioned costs** (a projection) must be considered when evaluating the effects of questioned costs on the audit opinion.

   b. Known questioned costs greater than $10,000 for a **nonmajor program** also should be included.

   c. **Audit findings** should be sufficiently detailed to permit the auditee to prepare a corrective action plan and to take such action.

7. For the purpose of **reporting an audit finding**, the auditor's determination of whether a **deficiency in internal control** is material or whether an **instance of noncompliance** is material is in relation to a **type of compliance requirement** for a major program or an **audit objective** identified in the OMB Circular A-133 Compliance Supplement.

   a. In contrast, materiality is considered in relation to the **financial statements** in an audit under GAAS.

8. Under the Single Audit Act, a federal agency or the U.S. Comptroller General may, upon request, obtain access to the auditor's **working papers** to (a) provide information for a quality review, (b) resolve audit findings, or (c) carry out oversight responsibilities. Access includes the right to obtain copies.

Stop and review! You have completed the outline for this subunit. Study multiple-choice questions 24 through 30 beginning on page 659.

QUESTIONS

20.1 Government Auditing Standards

1. Which of the following bodies issues standards for audits of recipients of federal awards?

A. Governmental Accounting Standards Board.

B. Financial Accounting Standards Board.

C. Government Accountability Office.

D. Governmental Auditing Standards Board.

Answer (C) is correct.

   REQUIRED: The body that sets standards for audits of federal awards recipients.

   DISCUSSION: The federal agency concerned with accounting and auditing standards for U.S. government programs and services is the Government Accountability Office. The GAO issues generally accepted government auditing standards.

   Answer (A) is incorrect. The GASB promulgates standards for financial accounting and reporting by state and local governments. Answer (B) is incorrect. The FASB issues standards for financial accounting and reporting by nongovernmental entities. Answer (D) is incorrect. There is no Governmental Auditing Standards Board. The committee of the GAO that issues government auditing standards is the Advisory Council on *Government Auditing Standards*.

2. An auditor was engaged to conduct a performance audit of a governmental entity in accordance with *Government Auditing Standards*. These standards do **not** require the auditor to report

A. The audit objectives and the audit scope and methodology.

B. All significant instances of noncompliance and instances of abuse.

C. The views of the audited program's responsible officials concerning the auditor's findings.

D. A concurrent opinion on the financial statements taken as a whole.

Answer (D) is correct.

   REQUIRED: The action not required of an auditor engaged in a performance audit of a governmental entity in accordance with *Government Auditing Standards*.

   DISCUSSION: Performance audits relate to assessing (1) program effectiveness and results; (2) economy and efficiency; (3) internal control; (4) compliance with legal requirements; or (5) providing prospective analysis, guidance, or summary information. There is no requirement that a financial audit be conducted simultaneously or concurrently with a performance audit.

3. *Government Auditing Standards* relates to which of the services provided to government entities, programs, activities, and functions?

	Financial Audits	Nonaudit Services	Performance Audits
A.	Yes	Yes	No
B.	Yes	No	Yes
C.	Yes	Yes	Yes
D.	No	No	Yes

Answer (B) is correct.
    REQUIRED: The scope of *Government Auditing Standards.*
    DISCUSSION: *Government Auditing Standards* relates to financial audits and attestation engagements. Moreover, it relates to performance audits of (1) government entities, programs, activities, and functions and (2) government assistance administered by contractors, not-for-profit entities, and other nongovernmental activities. Although GAGAS are not applicable to nonaudit services, they state independence standards and describe the impact of nonaudit services on auditor independence.

4. An objective of a performance audit is to determine whether an entity's

A. Performance information is presented fairly.

B. Operational information is in accordance with generally accepted government auditing standards.

C. Financial statements present fairly the results of operations.

D. Specific operating units are functioning economically and efficiently.

Answer (D) is correct.
    REQUIRED: The objective of a performance audit.
    DISCUSSION: Performance audits include economy and efficiency audits. The objectives of these audits are to determine (1) whether the entity is acquiring, protecting, and using its resources economically and efficiently; (2) the causes of any inefficiencies; and (3) whether the entity has complied with laws and regulations concerning matters of economy and efficiency.
    Answer (A) is incorrect. Reporting on the fairness of performance information is the subject of attestation engagements. Answer (B) is incorrect. The conduct of the audit and the audit report, not operational information, should be in accordance with *Government Auditing Standards.* Answer (C) is incorrect. Determining whether financial statements present fairly the results of operations is an objective of a financial statement audit.

5. Which of the following is a documentation requirement that an auditor should follow in a financial statement audit in accordance with *Government Auditing Standards*?

A. The audit documentation should contain copies of documents examined.

B. The audit documentation should contain sufficient information to permit another auditor to ascertain the evidence that supports audit conclusions and judgments.

C. Audit documentation should be considered the personal property of the auditor and should not be shared.

D. The audit documentation should contain a caveat that all instances of material errors and fraud may not be identified.

Answer (B) is correct.
    REQUIRED: The documentation requirement under *Government Auditing Standards.*
    DISCUSSION: *Government Auditing Standards* incorporate AICPA auditing standards, which state that audit documentation should contain sufficient information to enable an experienced auditor having no previous connection with the audit to ascertain from them the evidence that supports the auditor's significant conclusions and judgments.
    Answer (A) is incorrect. The audit documentation should document the work performed to support significant conclusions and judgments, including descriptions of transactions and records examined that would enable an experienced auditor to examine the same items. However, the auditors are not required to include copies of documents examined or to list detailed information from those documents. Answer (C) is incorrect. Governmental auditors should share their work product to avoid duplication of audit effort. Answer (D) is incorrect. This type of warning is appropriate for the auditor's report, but it need not be stated in the audit documentation.

6. When engaged to audit a governmental entity in accordance with *Government Auditing Standards*, an auditor prepares a written report on internal control over financial reporting

A. In all financial audits, regardless of circumstances.

B. Only when the auditor has noted significant deficiencies.

C. Only when requested by the governmental entity being audited.

D. Only when requested by the federal government funding agency.

Answer (A) is correct.
    REQUIRED: The true statement about reporting on internal control.
    DISCUSSION: *Government Auditing Standards* imposes more stringent reporting requirements than GAAS. For example, it mandates a written report on internal control over financial reporting in every audit. Furthermore, issuers must report on internal control. In contrast, GAAS require communication only if significant deficiencies or material weaknesses have been observed.
    Answer (B) is incorrect. GAAS, not *Government Auditing Standards*, require communication only if significant deficiencies or material weaknesses have been observed. Answer (C) is incorrect. A written report should be prepared in all audits, regardless of circumstances. Answer (D) is incorrect. A written report should be prepared in all audits, regardless of circumstances.

7. In performing a financial statement audit in accordance with *Government Auditing Standards*, auditors are required to report on the entity's compliance with laws and regulations. This report should

    A. Describe the scope of the auditor's testing of compliance.

    B. Describe the laws and regulations that the entity must comply with.

    C. Express an opinion on overall compliance with laws and regulations.

    D. Indicate that the auditors do not possess legal skills and cannot make legal judgments.

Answer (A) is correct.
    REQUIRED: The content of a report on compliance with laws and regulations.
    DISCUSSION: According to *Government Auditing Standards*, the report should describe the scope of the auditor's testing of compliance with laws and regulations and internal control over financial reporting. Thus, the report states whether (1) tests provided sufficient evidence to support an opinion on compliance or internal control over financial reporting and (2) such opinions are provided.
    Answer (B) is incorrect. The report need not identify the applicable laws and regulations. Answer (C) is incorrect. The report should identify material instances of noncompliance but need not express an opinion on overall compliance. The report may express an opinion, however, if the scope of the work is sufficient. Answer (D) is incorrect. Auditors are required to provide a report on compliance. However, the auditors should take care not to imply that they have made a determination of illegality.

8. Which of the following statements is a standard applicable to financial statement audits in accordance with *Government Auditing Standards* (the Yellow Book)?

    A. An auditor should report on the scope of the auditor's testing of compliance with laws and regulations.

    B. An auditor should assess whether the entity has reportable measures of economy and efficiency that are valid and reliable.

    C. An auditor should report recommendations for actions to correct problems and improve operations.

    D. An auditor should determine the extent to which the entity's programs achieve the desired results.

Answer (A) is correct.
    REQUIRED: The scope of an audit under *Government Auditing Standards*.
    DISCUSSION: According to additional government standards for financial statement audits, the report on the financial statements should either (1) describe the scope of the auditor's testing of compliance with laws and regulations and internal controls over financial reporting and present the results of those tests or (2) refer to separate report(s) containing that information. If the scope of the work performed is sufficient, an opinion on internal control and compliance can be expressed. In presenting the results of those tests, auditors should report (1) significant deficiencies and material weaknesses in internal control; (2) instances of fraud and noncompliance with provisions of laws or regulations that have a material effect on the audit and any other instances that warrant the attention of those charged with governance; (3) noncompliance with provisions of contracts or grant agreements that has a material effect on the audit; and (4) abuse that has a material effect on the audit. In some circumstances, auditors should report fraud and noncompliance directly to parties external to the audited entity.
    Answer (B) is incorrect. Economy and efficiency are subjects of performance audits rather than financial audits. Answer (C) is incorrect. Advice may be provided on the correction of problems and the improvement of operations, but the auditor is not required to provide a report. Answer (D) is incorrect. Achievement of desired results is a subject of performance audits rather than financial audits.

9. In a financial statement audit in accordance with *Government Auditing Standards*, an auditor should report on the auditor's tests of the entity's compliance with applicable laws and regulations. Thus, the audit should be designed to provide

    A. Positive assurance that the internal controls tested by the auditor are operating as prescribed.

    B. Reasonable assurance of detecting misstatements that are material to the financial statements.

    C. Negative assurance that significant deficiencies in internal control communicated during the audit do not prevent the auditor from expressing an opinion.

    D. Limited assurance that internal control designed by management will prevent or detect errors, fraud, and noncompliance.

Answer (B) is correct.
    REQUIRED: The design of the audit that satisfies the requirement to report on compliance.
    DISCUSSION: According to *Government Auditing Standards* for financial audits, the auditor should test compliance with applicable laws and regulations. As part of the process, the auditor should design the audit to provide reasonable assurance of detecting errors, fraud, and noncompliance that could have a direct and material effect on the financial statements. The auditor should also be aware of other noncompliance having indirect and material effects.
    Answer (A) is incorrect. The auditor is not required to provide positive assurance on internal control (but may if the scope of testing is sufficient) under *Government Auditing Standards*. The report on compliance (which may be presented separately) should state the scope of the testing and present the results. Answer (C) is incorrect. Auditors identify significant deficiencies but need not provide assurance in the report. Answer (D) is incorrect. Auditors are not required to provide limited assurance on internal control matters. They are, however, required to obtain a sufficient understanding of internal control.

654   SU 20: Governmental Audits

10. Which of the following statements is a standard applicable to financial statement audits in accordance with *Government Auditing Standards* (the Yellow Book)?

   A. An auditor should report on the scope of the auditor's testing of internal controls.

   B. An auditor should report all instances of fraud, noncompliance with laws and regulations, violations of provisions of contracts or grant agreements, and abuse.

   C. An auditor should report the views of the public about the auditor's findings.

   D. Internal control activities designed to detect or prevent fraud should be reported to the inspector general.

Answer (A) is correct.
   REQUIRED: The standard for financial statement audits under *Government Auditing Standards*.
   DISCUSSION: According to *Government Auditing Standards* for financial statement audits, the report on the financial statements should describe (in the same report or a separate report) the scope of the auditor's testing of (1) compliance with laws and regulations and grant or contract provisions and (2) internal control over financial reporting. Auditors also should state whether the tests provided sufficient appropriate evidence to support opinions on internal control and compliance. The auditors should report (1) significant deficiencies and material weaknesses in internal control; (2) instances of fraud and noncompliance with provisions of laws or regulations that have a material effect on the audit and any other instances that warrant the attention of those charged with governance; (3) noncompliance with provisions of contracts or grant agreements that has a material effect on the audit; and (4) abuse that has a material effect on the audit. In some circumstances, auditors should report fraud, noncompliance, or abuse directly to parties external to the audited entity.
   Answer (B) is incorrect. Auditors should use their professional judgment in determining whether and how to communicate to the audited entity clearly inconsequential instances of (1) fraud, (2) noncompliance with laws and regulations, (3) violations of provisions of contracts or grant agreements, or (4) abuse. Answer (C) is incorrect. The views of the public need not be reported. However, the auditor's report may disclose (1) deficiencies in internal control, (2) fraud, (3) noncompliance with laws and regulations, (4) violations of provisions of contracts or grant agreements, or (5) abuse. Auditors then should obtain and report the views of responsible officials concerning the findings, conclusions, and recommendations, as well as planned corrective actions. Answer (D) is incorrect. The auditor is not required to comment on the design of the controls to the inspector general.

11. In auditing a not-for-profit entity that receives governmental awards, the auditor has a responsibility to

   A. Issue a separate report that describes the expected benefits and related costs of the auditor's suggested changes to the entity's internal control.

   B. Assess whether management has identified laws and regulations that have a direct and material effect on the entity's financial statements.

   C. Notify the governmental agency providing the awards that the audit is not designed to provide any assurance of detecting errors and fraud.

   D. Express an opinion concerning the entity's continued eligibility for the governmental awards.

Answer (B) is correct.
   REQUIRED: The responsibility of an auditor of a not-for-profit entity that receives governmental awards.
   DISCUSSION: Management is responsible for ensuring compliance with laws and regulations. The auditor's responsibility is to understand the possible effects of laws and regulations having direct and material effects on the financial statements and to assess whether management has identified such laws and regulations.
   Answer (A) is incorrect. The auditor need not identify the relative costs and benefits related to the client's internal control. However, the auditor must communicate significant deficiencies and material weaknesses. Answer (C) is incorrect. The audit should be designed to provide reasonable assurance of detecting material fraud. Answer (D) is incorrect. The report should express an opinion on the financial statements and present the results of tests of compliance and of internal control over financial reporting. But it does not express an opinion on continued eligibility.

12. In reporting on compliance with laws and regulations during a financial statement audit in accordance with *Government Auditing Standards*, an auditor should include in the auditor's report

    A. A statement of assurance that all controls over fraud and compliance were tested.

    B. Material instances of fraud and noncompliance that were discovered.

    C. The materiality criteria used by the auditor in considering whether instances of noncompliance were significant.

    D. An opinion on whether compliance with laws and regulations affected the entity's goals and objectives.

Answer (B) is correct.
    REQUIRED: The issues included in an auditor's report in accordance with *Government Auditing Standards*.
    DISCUSSION: An auditor's report, in accordance with *Government Auditing Standards*, should present (1) significant deficiencies and material weaknesses in internal control; (2) instances of fraud and noncompliance with provisions of laws or regulations that have a material effect on the audit and any other instances that warrant the attention of those charged with governance; (3) noncompliance with provisions of contracts or grant agreements that has a material effect on the audit; and (4) abuse that has a material effect on the audit.
    Answer (A) is incorrect. No assurance need be provided that all controls over fraud and compliance were tested. Answer (C) is incorrect. The materiality criteria need not be reported. Answer (D) is incorrect. No opinion need be expressed.

13. Reporting on internal control under *Government Auditing Standards* differs from reporting under generally accepted auditing standards in that *Government Auditing Standards* requires a

    A. Written report describing the entity's internal control activities specifically designed to prevent fraud and noncompliance.

    B. Written report included with the audit report on financial statements describing significant deficiencies and material weaknesses in internal control.

    C. Statement of negative assurance that the internal control activities not tested have an immaterial effect on the entity's financial statements.

    D. Statement of positive assurance that internal control activities designed to detect material errors and fraud were tested.

Answer (B) is correct.
    REQUIRED: The difference between *Government Auditing Standards* and GAAS regarding reports on internal control.
    DISCUSSION: According to *Government Auditing Standards*, the report on the financial statements or a separate report should present any significant deficiencies and material weaknesses in internal control. However, the report need not provide any assurance on internal control design or effectiveness.
    Answer (A) is incorrect. *Government Auditing Standards* does not require the auditor to list internal control activities specifically designed to prevent fraud or noncompliance. Answer (C) is incorrect. The auditor is not required to provide a statement of positive or negative assurance regarding internal control. However, positive assurance in the form of an opinion may be provided if the scope of the work is sufficient. Answer (D) is incorrect. The auditor is not required to provide a statement of positive or negative assurance regarding internal control. However, positive assurance in the form of an opinion may be provided if the scope of the work is sufficient.

14. An auditor most likely will be responsible for communicating significant deficiencies in the design of internal controls

    A. To a court-appointed creditors' committee when the client is operating under Chapter 11 of the Federal Bankruptcy Code.

    B. To shareholders with significant influence (more than 20% equity ownership) when the deficiencies are deemed to be material weaknesses.

    C. To the Securities and Exchange Commission when the client is a publicly held entity.

    D. To specific legislative and regulatory bodies when reporting under *Government Auditing Standards*.

Answer (D) is correct.
    REQUIRED: The circumstance in which an auditor is likely responsible for communicating significant deficiencies in internal control.
    DISCUSSION: An auditor is required to include significant deficiencies and material weaknesses in internal control over financial reporting in a report prepared under *Government Auditing Standards*. The report is required to be distributed to those charged with governance, to the appropriate officials of the audited entity, and to the appropriate oversight bodies or organizations requiring or arranging for the audits.
    Answer (A) is incorrect. Management is responsible for providing audited financial statements to a creditors' committee. Answer (B) is incorrect. The auditor's report is included with the audited financial statements in the annual report, a document that is available to all shareholders. Answer (C) is incorrect. The opinion on internal control of an issuer discloses material weaknesses but not significant deficiencies.

15. When auditing an entity's financial statements in accordance with *Government Auditing Standards* (the Yellow Book), an auditor is required to report on

I. Positive aspects of the program applicable to audit objectives

II. The scope of the auditor's testing of internal controls

    A. I only.

    B. II only.

    C. Both I and II.

    D. Neither I nor II.

Answer (B) is correct.
    REQUIRED: The true statement(s), if any, about reporting under *Government Auditing Standards*.
    DISCUSSION: *Government Auditing Standards* imposes more stringent reporting requirements than GAAS. Under GAGAS, the report on the financial statements should describe (in the same report or a separate report) the scope of the auditor's testing of (1) compliance with laws and regulations and grant or contract provisions and (2) internal control over financial reporting. Auditors also should state whether the tests provided sufficient appropriate evidence to support opinions on internal control and compliance. The auditors should report (1) significant deficiencies and material weaknesses in internal control; (2) instances of fraud and noncompliance with provisions of laws or regulations that have a material effect on the audit and any other instances that warrant the attention of those charged with governance; (3) noncompliance with provisions of contracts or grant agreements that has a material effect on the audit; and (4) abuse that has a material effect on the audit. In some circumstances, auditors should report fraud, noncompliance, or abuse directly to parties external to the audited entity. The report on internal control should identify significant deficiencies and material weaknesses but need not provide any assurance on internal control design or effectiveness. Accomplishments of the program, especially those management improvements in one area that may be applicable elsewhere, should be reported in a performance audit, not a financial audit, if they relate to audit objectives.

16. According to the general standards in *Government Auditing Standards*,

    A. An audit organization performing audits under GAGAS must have an external peer review every 5 years.

    B. The audit organization, but not the auditor, may provide any nonaudit services.

    C. Performing nonaudit services creates an inherent impairment of independence.

    D. An audit organization must be free of the appearance of an impairment to independence.

Answer (D) is correct.
    REQUIRED: The true statement about the requirements under *Government Auditing Standards*.
    DISCUSSION: Auditors must be independent in mind and appearance.
    Answer (A) is incorrect. The entity must have an external peer review at least once every 3 years. Answer (B) is incorrect. The audit organization should not (1) provide nonaudit services that involve performing management functions or making management decisions or (2) audit its work or provide nonaudit services that are significant or material to the subject matter of audits. Answer (C) is incorrect. Performing nonaudit services may create an impairment of independence under certain conditions.

17. When auditing an entity's financial statements in accordance with *Government Auditing Standards* (the Yellow Book), an auditor is required to report on

I. Recommendations for actions to improve operations

II. The scope of the auditor's tests of compliance with laws and regulations

    A. I only.

    B. II only.

    C. Both I and II.

    D. Neither I nor II.

Answer (B) is correct.
    REQUIRED: The true statement(s), if any, about reporting under *Government Auditing Standards*.
    DISCUSSION: *Government Auditing Standards* imposes more stringent reporting requirements than GAAS. Under GAGAS, the report on the financial statements should describe (in the same report or a separate report) the scope of the auditor's testing of (1) compliance with laws and regulations and grant or contract provisions and (2) internal control over financial reporting. Auditors also should state whether the tests provided sufficient appropriate evidence to support opinions on internal control and compliance. The auditors should report (1) significant deficiencies and material weaknesses in internal control; (2) instances of fraud and noncompliance with provisions of laws or regulations that have a material effect on the audit and any other instances that warrant the attention of those charged with governance; (3) noncompliance with provisions of contracts or grant agreements that has a material effect on the audit; and (4) abuse that has a material effect on the audit. In some circumstances, auditors should report fraud, noncompliance, or abuse directly to parties external to the audited entity. Auditors should report recommendations for actions to correct problems and to improve operations in a performance audit, not in a financial audit.

18. In reporting under *Government Auditing Standards*, an auditor most likely would be required to report a falsification of accounting records directly to a federal inspector general when the falsification is

   A. Discovered after the auditor's report has been made available to the federal inspector general and to the public.

   B. Reported by the auditor to the audit committee as a significant deficiency in internal control.

   C. Voluntarily disclosed to the auditor by low-level personnel as a result of the auditor's inquiries.

   D. Communicated by the auditor to the auditee and the auditee fails to make a required report of the matter.

Answer (D) is correct.

REQUIRED: The time when an auditor is required to report externally under *Government Auditing Standards*.

DISCUSSION: Under *Government Auditing Standards*, auditors should report fraud, noncompliance, and abuse directly to parties outside the auditee (for example, to a federal inspector general or a state attorney general) in two circumstances. These requirements are in addition to any legal requirements for direct reporting. First, if auditors have communicated such fraud, noncompliance, or abuse to the auditee and (s)he fails to report them, the auditors should communicate their awareness of that failure to the auditee's governing body. If the auditee does not make the required report as soon as practicable after the auditor's communication with its governing body, the auditors should report the fraud, noncompliance, or abuse directly to the external party specified in the law or regulation. Second, management is responsible for taking timely and appropriate steps to remedy fraud, noncompliance, or abuse that auditors report to it. When fraud, noncompliance, or abuse involves assistance received directly or indirectly from a government agency, auditors may have a duty to report it directly if management fails to take remedial steps. If auditors conclude that such failure is likely to cause them to depart from the standard report or resign from the audit, they should communicate that conclusion to the auditee's governing body. Then, if the auditee does not report the fraud, noncompliance, or abuse as soon as practicable to the entity that provided the government assistance, the auditors should report directly to that entity.

19. Financial audits of certain governmental entities are required to be performed in accordance with generally accepted government auditing standards (GAGAS) as issued in *Government Auditing Standards*. These standards do **not** require, as part of an auditor's report, the inclusion of

   A. A statement as to whether the tests performed provide sufficient appropriate evidence to support an opinion on internal control over financial reporting.

   B. The significant deficiencies, with identification of material weaknesses.

   C. Sampling methods used to test the controls designed to detect fraud whether or not material fraud is found.

   D. A description of the scope of testing of internal control over financial reporting.

Answer (C) is correct.

REQUIRED: The item not required by GAGAS to be identified in an audit report.

DISCUSSION: The Government Accountability Office (GAO) issues *Government Auditing Standards* (the Yellow Book). GAGAS apply to financial audits, attestation engagements, and performance audits. GAGAS for financial audits incorporate by reference the AICPA's Statements on Auditing Standards (SAS) and also state requirements. However, they do not require that the report identify specific sampling techniques used to test the controls. Nevertheless, when presenting material fraud, auditors might consider the report contents standards for performance audits that pertain to, among other things, methodology. Thus, if sampling significantly supports the findings, the auditor might describe the sample design and state why it was chosen.

Answer (A) is incorrect. Auditors should state whether tests provided sufficient appropriate evidence to support opinions on internal control over financial reporting and compliance with laws, regulations, contracts, or grant agreements. Answer (B) is incorrect. Auditors should communicate in writing on a timely basis significant deficiencies and material weaknesses identified during the audit. They are included in the GAGAS report on internal control over financial reporting. Answer (D) is incorrect. The report on the financial statements should describe the scope of testing of (1) compliance with laws, regulations, contracts, or grant agreements and (2) internal control over financial reporting. It should present the findings or refer to separate reports containing that information.

20.2 Compliance Audits (AU-C 935)

20. In a compliance audit, the auditor's primary objective is to

A. Determine that all instances of noncompliance are discovered and reported.

B. Test and express an opinion on internal control over compliance.

C. Obtain sufficient appropriate evidence to form an opinion on compliance.

D. Provide management with recommendations for improvement over compliance.

Answer (C) is correct.

    REQUIRED: The auditor's primary objective in a compliance audit.

    DISCUSSION: The auditor's objective in a compliance audit is to obtain sufficient appropriate evidence to form an opinion and report at the level specified in the governmental audit requirement on whether the entity complied, in all material respects, with the applicable compliance requirements.

    Answer (A) is incorrect. Only instances of material noncompliance need be reported on. Answer (B) is incorrect. Although the auditor considers internal control in planning the audit, no opinion is required. Answer (D) is incorrect. An audit of compliance does not require the auditor to provide recommendations for improvement over compliance.

21. In an audit of an entity's compliance with applicable compliance requirements, an auditor obtains written representations from management acknowledging

A. Its responsibilities for compliance, including disclosure of noncompliance.

B. Implementation of controls designed to detect all noncompliance.

C. Expression of positive assurance to the auditor that the entity complied with all applicable compliance requirements.

D. Employment of internal auditors who can report their findings, opinions, and conclusions objectively.

Answer (A) is correct.

    REQUIRED: The representations obtained from management in a compliance audit.

    DISCUSSION: The auditor obtains written representations from management about its responsibilities for (1) understanding and complying with the compliance requirements and (2) establishing and maintaining controls that provide reasonable assurance that the entity administers government programs in accordance with the compliance requirements. Among other things, the auditor also requests representations that management has disclosed all known noncompliance with the applicable compliance requirements, including that subsequent to the period covered by the auditor's report.

    Answer (B) is incorrect. Management should disclose all known noncompliance. Given the inherent limitations of internal control, it cannot be expected to prevent or detect all noncompliance. Answer (C) is incorrect. In a compliance audit, management does not express an opinion that it has complied with all applicable compliance requirements. Answer (D) is incorrect. The entity will decide whether to employ internal auditors.

22. A material weakness in internal control over compliance arises when

A. At a minimum, a deficiency is important enough to merit attention by those charged with governance.

B. A reasonable possibility exists that material noncompliance will not be prevented or timely detected and corrected.

C. A risk of material noncompliance exists prior to the audit.

D. The design or operation of a control does not allow management or employees to detect noncompliance in the normal course of their duties.

Answer (B) is correct.

    REQUIRED: The definition of a material weakness.

    DISCUSSION: A material weakness in internal control over compliance is a deficiency, or combination of deficiencies, in internal control over compliance that results in a reasonable possibility that material noncompliance with a compliance requirement will not be prevented, or detected and corrected, on a timely basis.

    Answer (A) is incorrect. A significant deficiency in internal control over compliance is a deficiency, or a combination of deficiencies, in internal control over compliance that is less severe than a material weakness yet merits attention by those charged with governance. Answer (C) is incorrect. The risk of material noncompliance prior to the audit is the combination of the inherent risk of noncompliance and the control risk of noncompliance. Answer (D) is incorrect. A deficiency in internal control over compliance exists when the design or operation of a control over compliance does not allow management or employees, in the normal course of performing their assigned functions, to prevent, or detect and correct, noncompliance on a timely basis.

23. When an auditor is performing a compliance audit and identifies pervasive risks of material noncompliance, the auditor should

    A. Withdraw from the engagement.

    B. Develop an overall response to such risks.

    C. Perform additional analytical procedures.

    D. Issue a disclaimer of opinion.

Answer (B) is correct.
    REQUIRED: The auditor's response to pervasive risks of noncompliance.
    DISCUSSION: The auditor should develop an overall response to such risks. For example, the auditor may use more experienced staff or increase supervision.
    Answer (A) is incorrect. The auditor need not withdraw from the engagement and should attempt to mitigate risks by developing an overall response to such risks. Answer (C) is incorrect. The use of analytical procedures to gather substantive evidence in a compliance audit is generally less effective in a compliance audit than it is in a financial statement audit. Answer (D) is incorrect. The auditor should attempt to mitigate risks by developing an overall response to such risks.

20.3 Federal Audit Requirements and the Single Audit Act

24. In an audit of compliance with requirements governing awards under major federal programs performed in accordance with the Single Audit Act, the auditor's consideration of materiality differs from materiality under generally accepted auditing standards. Under the Single Audit Act, materiality for the purpose of reporting an audit finding is

    A. Calculated in relation to the financial statements taken as a whole.

    B. Determined in relation to a type of compliance requirement for a major program.

    C. Decided in conjunction with the auditor's risk assessment.

    D. Ignored, because all account balances, regardless of size, are fully tested.

Answer (B) is correct.
    REQUIRED: The materiality determination under the Single Audit Act.
    DISCUSSION: Under the Single Audit Act, the emphasis of the audit effort is on major programs related to federal awards administered by nonfederal entities. According to OMB Circular A-133 issued pursuant to the Single Audit Act, the schedule of findings and questioned costs includes instances of material noncompliance with laws, regulations, contracts, or grant agreements related to a major program. The auditor's determination of whether a noncompliance is material for the purpose of reporting an audit finding is in relation to a type of compliance requirement for a major program or an audit objective identified in the OMB Circular A-133 Compliance Supplement. Examples of types of compliance requirements include (1) activities allowed or unallowed; (2) allowable costs/cost principles; (3) cash management; (4) eligibility; (5) matching, level of effort, and earmarking; and (6) reporting.
    Answer (A) is incorrect. In a for-profit financial statement audit, materiality is related to the financial statements as a whole. Answer (C) is incorrect. Risk assessment is performed in planning the audit, but once the auditor makes a finding, the decision to report it is contingent on the materiality to the major program. Answer (D) is incorrect. Materiality should be considered in determining the appropriate tests to be applied.

25. Wolf is auditing an entity's compliance with requirements governing a major federal program in accordance with the Single Audit Act. Wolf detected noncompliance with requirements that have a material effect on the program. Wolf's report on compliance should express

    A. No assurance on the compliance tests.

    B. Reasonable assurance on the compliance tests.

    C. A qualified or adverse opinion.

    D. An adverse opinion or a disclaimer of opinion.

Answer (C) is correct.
    REQUIRED: The assurance about compliance given noncompliance with material requirements.
    DISCUSSION: Under the Single Audit Act, the auditor should express an opinion on compliance with requirements having a direct and material effect on a major federal program or state that an opinion cannot be expressed. When the compliance audit detects noncompliance with those requirements that the auditor believes have a direct and material effect on the program, the auditor should express a qualified or adverse opinion. The auditor should state the basis for such an opinion in the report.
    Answer (A) is incorrect. The auditor should express an opinion on compliance. Answer (B) is incorrect. The auditor's report should state that the audit was planned and performed to provide reasonable assurance about whether material noncompliance occurred. Answer (D) is incorrect. A disclaimer is not appropriate when the auditor has detected material noncompliance.

26. Although the scope of audits of recipients of federal awards in accordance with federal audit regulations varies, audits under the Single Audit Act generally have which of the following elements in common?

A. The auditor is to determine whether the federal financial assistance has been administered in accordance with applicable laws and regulations.

B. The materiality levels are lower and are determined by the government entities that provided the federal awards to the recipient.

C. The auditor should obtain written management representations that the recipient's internal auditors will report their findings objectively, without fear of political repercussion.

D. The auditor is required to express both positive and negative assurance that fraudulent acts that could have a material effect on the recipient's financial statements are disclosed to the inspector general.

Answer (A) is correct.
REQUIRED: The common element in federal audit regulations.
DISCUSSION: According to the Single Audit Act, the scope of federal audits may vary, but the auditor should

1. Determine whether the financial statements are presented fairly, in all material respects, in conformity with GAAP.

2. Determine whether the schedule of expenditures of federal awards is presented fairly, in all material respects, in relation to the financial statements as a whole.

3. With respect to controls over compliance, obtain an understanding of those controls, assess control risk, and perform tests of controls unless the controls are ineffective.

4. Determine whether the nonfederal entity has complied with the provisions of laws, regulations, and contracts or grants that have a direct and material effect on each major program.

5. Report audit findings in a schedule of findings and questioned costs.

Answer (B) is incorrect. Materiality is determined by the auditor in relation to a type of compliance requirement for a major program or an audit objective identified in the OMB Circular A-133 Compliance Supplement. Answer (C) is incorrect. Although the auditor should obtain written management representations, no specific requirements concerning the entity's internal auditors are stipulated. Answer (D) is incorrect. The auditor is required to report fraudulent acts but not to provide positive or negative assurance about them.

27. An auditor is auditing a nonfederal entity's administration of a federal award pursuant to a major program under the Single Audit Act. The auditor is required to

	Obtain Evidence Related to Compliance	Express an Opinion on Compliance
A.	Yes	Yes
B.	Yes	No
C.	No	Yes
D.	No	No

Answer (A) is correct.
REQUIRED: The auditor's responsibility in a compliance audit.
DISCUSSION: After an audit of a nonfederal entity that expends federal awards, the audit report on compliance should include an opinion or a disclaimer of opinion as to whether the auditee complied with the applicable compliance requirements, that is, with laws, regulations, rules, and the provisions of contracts or grants. This report also should describe identified noncompliance or refer to an accompanying schedule of noncompliance.

28. When performing an audit of a city that is subject to the requirements of the federal Single Audit Act, an auditor should adhere to

A. Governmental Accounting Standards Board General Standards.

B. Governmental Finance Officers Association Governmental Accounting, Auditing, and Financial Reporting Principles.

C. *Government Auditing Standards*.

D. Securities and Exchange Commission Regulation S-X.

Answer (C) is correct.
REQUIRED: The standards for an audit of a city that is subject to the requirements of the federal Single Audit Act.
DISCUSSION: The Single Audit Act establishes audit requirements for recipients of federal awards administered by nonfederal entities. The act requires that audits of such entities be in accordance with *Government Auditing Standards* issued by the GAO. OMB Circular A-133 and related GAAS also apply. The act and the circular state certain requirements that exceed those of the GAO's Standards.
Answer (A) is incorrect. The GASB establishes accounting standards, not auditing standards. Answer (B) is incorrect. The Governmental Finance Officers Association does not establish auditing standards. Answer (D) is incorrect. The SEC does not establish auditing standards for cities.

29. A CPA has performed an examination of the general-purpose financial statements of Big City. The examination scope included the additional requirements of the Single Audit Act. When reporting on Big City's internal control over the administration of federal awards, the CPA should

   A. Communicate all control deficiencies related to all federal awards.

   B. Express an opinion on the systems used to administer awards under major federal programs and express negative assurance on the systems used to administer awards under nonmajor federal programs.

   C. Communicate significant deficiencies and material weaknesses that are material in relation to a type of compliance requirement for the federal program.

   D. Express negative assurance on the systems used to administer awards under major federal programs and express no opinion on the systems used to administer awards under nonmajor federal programs.

Answer (C) is correct.

REQUIRED: The requirement of a report on internal controls used in administering awards under a federal program.

DISCUSSION: Under the Single Audit Act, the auditor's determination of whether a deficiency in internal control is a significant deficiency or material weakness is in relation to a type of compliance requirement for a major program or an audit objective identified in the OMB Circular A-133 Compliance Supplement. The auditor also should identify all significant deficiencies and weaknesses.

Answer (A) is incorrect. Only significant deficiencies and material weaknesses need be communicated. Answer (B) is incorrect. Although an auditor conducting a single audit is required to report on controls that relate to the systems used to administer awards under federal programs, the auditor is not required to provide assurance. Answer (D) is incorrect. Auditors are required to express an opinion (or disclaim an opinion) as to whether the auditee complied with laws, regulations, and the provisions of contracts or grant agreements that could have a direct and material effect on each major program.

30. Under the Single Audit Act, the auditor should report on compliance with laws, regulations, and the provisions of contracts or grant agreements, noncompliance with which could have a material effect on the financial statements. This report should also express or disclaim an opinion on whether the auditee complied with laws, etc., that could have a direct and material effect on each major program. In accordance with the act and OMB Circular A-133, which contains policies, procedures, and guidelines to implement the act, the auditor

   A. Is not responsible for identifying major federal programs.

   B. Should apply a concept of materiality in the audit of major federal programs that is similar to that in an audit under GAAS.

   C. Should determine whether the recipient has engaged in activities to which particular types of compliance requirements apply.

   D. Is required to restrict control risk and assess inherent and detection risk.

Answer (C) is correct.

REQUIRED: The true statement about compliance auditing of major federal financial assistance programs.

DISCUSSION: OMB Circular A-133 and the related Compliance Supplement list the types of compliance requirements, e.g., activities allowed or unallowed; allowable costs/cost principles; cash management; eligibility; matching, level of effort, and earmarking; and reporting. The data collection form submitted by the auditee should include, for each federal program, a yes or no statement as to whether there are audit findings for each of the types of compliance requirements and the total of any questioned costs.

Answer (A) is incorrect. The auditor determines whether a federal program is major. The auditor uses a risk-based approach that considers current and prior audit experience, oversight by federal agencies and pass-through entities, and the inherent risk of the program. Most large programs (Type A), except those determined to be low risk, and smaller programs (Type B, i.e., non-Type A programs that meet one of two quantitative thresholds) determined to be high risk are audited as major programs. A federal agency or pass-through entity may also request that a program be audited as a major program. Answer (B) is incorrect. Under the act, the materiality of an instance of noncompliance is in relation to a type of compliance requirement for a major program or an audit objective identified in the OMB Circular A-133 Compliance Supplement. Answer (D) is incorrect. The auditor assesses inherent and control risk and restricts detection risk.

Use the additional questions in Gleim **CPA Test Prep** to create Practice Exams that emulate Prometric!

20.4 PRACTICE TASK-BASED SIMULATIONS

| Auditing and Attestation
Testlet 4 of 4 | Time Remaining
1 hour - 30 minutes | Unsplit | Split Horiz | Split Vertical | Spreadsheet | Calculator | Exit |

DIRECTIONS

Note: If you believe you have encountered a software malfunction, report it to the test center staff immediately.

Navigation

To navigate from task to task, use the controls at the bottom of the screen. Click on the **Next** button to advance to the next task, or the **Previous** button to go to the previous task. To go directly to any task, click on its number.

If you would like a reminder to revisit a task, or want to indicate that you are finished with it, click on the reminder flag below the task number. To clear the flag, click on it again. Reminder flags are for your use only – they do not contribute to your score.

Tabs

In this part of the examination, you will be asked to complete various tasks. Every task has one or more **Work Tabs**. Some tasks have one or more **Information Tabs**, others may have none. Every task has a **Help** tab.

If a task has **Information Tabs**, you may use the information in them to complete your responses in the **Work Tabs**.

                Work tab   **Information tab**   **Help tab**

Work Tabs:
- **Work Tabs** are identified with a pencil icon. This is where your responses are expected.
- Each task has one or more **Work Tabs**.
- **Work Tabs** contain directions for completing the task – be sure to read these directions carefully.
- The **Work Tab** name in the example above is for illustration only – yours will differ.
- You must complete all of the **Work Tabs** in each task to receive full credit.

Information Tabs:
- The Authoritative Literature will be provided in all tasks in the AUD, FAR, and REG sections for your reference.
- Your simulation may have one or more additional **Information Tabs**. Like the Authoritative Literature tabs, **Information Tabs** do not have a pencil icon.
- If your task has additional **Information Tabs**, go through each to familiarize yourself with the task content.

Help Tab:
- The **Help Tab** provides assistance with the exam software that is used in this task. For example, if the task is to compose a memorandum, **Help** will provide information about the word processor.

The Toolbar

The toolbar at the top of the screen shows the amount of time remaining for you to complete the tasks. In addition, the following tools are available. Note that only the **Exit** button is displayed when Directions are visible - the others will appear when you begin the tasks.

Click on these buttons to split or unsplit the screen. You can split the screen vertically or horizontally.

Click on this button to display the calculator; click on it again to hide the calculator. To move the calculator, click on the calculator title bar and drag the calculator to the desired location.

Click on this button to use the spreadsheet; click on it again to hide the spreadsheet. To move the spreadsheet, click on the the spreadsheet title bar and drag the spreadsheet to the desired location.

Click on this button to go on to the next part of the examination. You must complete all of the tasks to receive full credit. Once you click on **Exit** and confirm the action, you will NOT be able to return to this testlet.

| ▼ = Reminder | | Directions | 1 ▽ | 2 ▽ | 3 ▽ | 4 ▽ | 5 ▽ | | ◀ Previous | Next ▶ |

GAAS Versus GAS | Authoritative Literature | Help

Government Auditing Standards (GAS) incorporates the AICPA auditing standards (GAAS). However, in some cases, there are differences. Select from the list provided whether each issue is required by both GAAS and GAS, neither GAAS nor GAS, GAS only, or GAAS only.

Issue	Answer	Choices
1. The auditor is required to issue a report on compliance with laws and regulations.		A) Required by both GAAS and GAS
2. The auditor must be independent in mind and appearance.		B) Required by neither GAAS nor GAS
3. Audit organizations are required to establish a system of quality control.		C) Required by GAS only
4. The auditor should request personal financial statements from members of management.		D) Required by GAAS only
5. The auditor should state that the audit was performed in accordance with GAAS.		
6. The auditor should report the views of responsible officials.		
7. The auditor should modify the opinion when material misstatements persist in the financial statements.		
8. The auditor should state that the audit was performed in accordance with GAS.		

⌘ = Reminder   Directions   1 2 3 4 5   ◀ Previous   Next ▶

Competence and Quality Control | Authoritative Literature | Help

Each of the following statements relate to governmental auditing standards and the requirement of auditors to be competent and maintain quality control. Insert the appropriate word or phrase into each statement from the answer list. A word or phrase may be used once, more than once, or not at all.

Statement	Answer	Choices
1. Audit organizations and auditors must be [1] both in mind and appearance.		A) Continuing education
2. Governmental auditors are required to acquire 80 hours of [2] every 2 years.		B) Responsible officials
		C) Other auditors
3. A governmental audit organization must have a [3] every 3 years.		D) Peer review
4. Auditors should eliminate threats to assure that they can be [4].		E) GAGAS
5. Auditors should evaluate whether clients have taken [5] based on findings of previous audits.		F) Independent
6. Auditors should state in their report that the audit was performed in accordance with [6].		G) Governmental auditing
7. If the audit report discloses fraud or noncompliance, the auditor should obtain the views of [7] of the audited entity.		H) Corrective action
8. At least 24 hours of continuing education each cycle should pertain directly to [8].		

⌘ = Reminder   Directions   1 2 3 4 5   ◀ Previous   Next ▶

| Government Auditing Standards | Authoritative Literature | Help |

The auditor's separate report on compliance with laws and regulations was drafted by a staff accountant of Hall & Hall at the completion of the financial statement audit. This audit was in accordance with generally accepted government auditing standards (GAGAS). The report contained the following seven statements. It was submitted to the engagement partner who reviewed matters thoroughly and properly concluded that no material instances of noncompliance were identified.

For each of the following seven statements, indicate by selecting from the list provided whether it is an appropriate element of a report on compliance with laws and regulations under GAGAS and, if it is inappropriate, the reason.

Statements	Answers	Choices
1. A statement that the audit was conducted in accordance with GAAS and with *Government Auditing Standards* issued by the Comptroller General of the United States.		A) Appropriate B) Inappropriate because a governmental audit should not refer to GAAS C) Inappropriate because *Government Auditing Standards* is not issued by the U.S. Comptroller General
2. A statement that the auditor's procedures included tests of compliance.		A) Appropriate B) Inappropriate because the auditor's procedures should not include tests of compliance C) Inappropriate because a statement on the auditor's procedures should not be included within the report on compliance
3. A statement that the purpose of the report is to describe the scope of testing compliance and the results of testing.		A) Appropriate B) Inappropriate because the purpose is to lend credibility to management's assertions relative to compliance C) Inappropriate because the purpose is to provide the auditor's assessment of management's decisions as to compliance
4. A statement that the standards require the auditor to plan and to perform the audit to detect all instances of noncompliance with applicable laws and regulations.		A) Appropriate B) Inappropriate because the auditor is required to plan and perform the audit to provide reasonable assurance of detecting all instances of noncompliance having a direct effect on the financial statements, not all instances of noncompliance C) Inappropriate because the auditor is required to plan and perform the audit to detect instances of noncompliance having a direct and material effect on the financial statements, not all instances of noncompliance
5. A statement that the auditor's objective was to provide an opinion on compliance with the provisions of laws and regulations equivalent to that to be expressed on the financial statements.		A) Appropriate B) Inappropriate because expressing an opinion is a lower level of reporting than the positive and negative assurance required by *Government Auditing Standards* C) Inappropriate because the report does not express an opinion

-- Continued on next page --

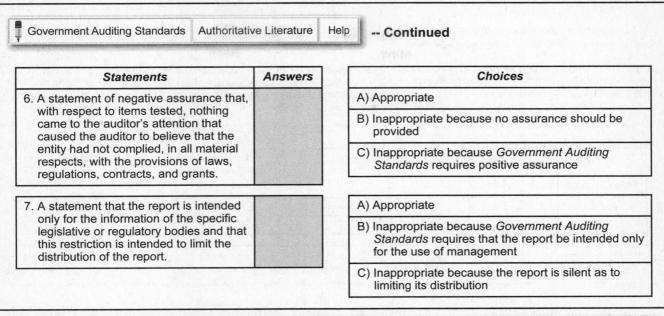

| Government Auditing Standards | Authoritative Literature | Help | -- **Continued** |

Statements	Answers	Choices
6. A statement of negative assurance that, with respect to items tested, nothing came to the auditor's attention that caused the auditor to believe that the entity had not complied, in all material respects, with the provisions of laws, regulations, contracts, and grants.		A) Appropriate B) Inappropriate because no assurance should be provided C) Inappropriate because *Government Auditing Standards* requires positive assurance
7. A statement that the report is intended only for the information of the specific legislative or regulatory bodies and that this restriction is intended to limit the distribution of the report.		A) Appropriate B) Inappropriate because *Government Auditing Standards* requires that the report be intended only for the use of management C) Inappropriate because the report is silent as to limiting its distribution

| ▼ = Reminder | | Directions | 1 ▽ | 2 ▽ | 3 ▽ | 4 ▽ | 5 ▽ | | ◀ Previous | Next ▶ |

| Compliance Issues | Authoritative Literature | Help |

Select whether each statement below represents potential responsibilities of the auditor, the management of Toxic Waste Disposal Co., or neither. Each choice may be used once, more than once, or not at all.

Description	Answer	Choices
1. Ensure compliance with laws and regulations.		A) Auditor
2. Consider laws and regulations to plan and perform the audit.		B) Management
3. Determine whether applicable laws and regulations are fair.		C) Neither management nor the auditor
4. Identify the risks that have a pervasive effect on compliance.		
5. Obtain written representations about laws and regulations.		
6. Review minutes of meetings for evidence concerning compliance with laws and regulations.		
7. Identify laws and regulations requiring compliance.		
8. Suggest new regulations to authorities.		
9. Establish internal controls pertaining to compliance with laws and regulations.		
10. Provide positive assurance that no laws or regulations have been violated by employees.		

| ▼ = Reminder | | Directions | 1 ▽ | 2 ▽ | 3 ▽ | 4 ▽ | 5 ▽ | | ◀ Previous | Next ▶ |

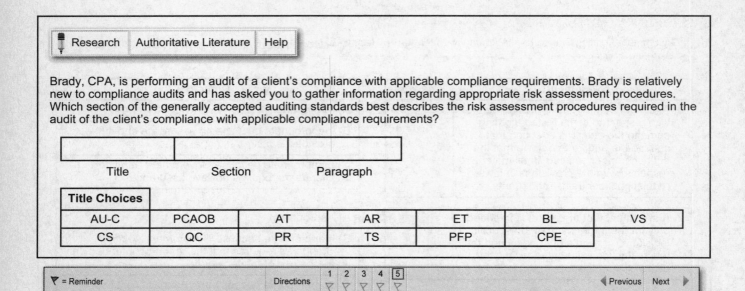

| Research | Authoritative Literature | Help |

Brady, CPA, is performing an audit of a client's compliance with applicable compliance requirements. Brady is relatively new to compliance audits and has asked you to gather information regarding appropriate risk assessment procedures. Which section of the generally accepted auditing standards best describes the risk assessment procedures required in the audit of the client's compliance with applicable compliance requirements?

Title   Section   Paragraph

Title Choices

AU-C	PCAOB	AT	AR	ET	BL	VS
CS	QC	PR	TS	PFP	CPE	

= Reminder   Directions   1 2 3 4 5   ◀ Previous   Next ▶

Unofficial Answers

1. GAAS Versus GAS (8 Gradable Items)

1. <u>C) Required by GAS only.</u> Governmental auditors are required to issue reports on internal control and compliance with laws and regulations.

2. <u>A) Required by both GAAS and GAS.</u> Both GAAS and GAS require auditors to be independent in mind and appearance.

3. <u>A) Required by both GAAS and GAS.</u> Both GAAS and GAS require audit organizations to have a system of quality control.

4. <u>B) Required by neither GAAS nor GAS.</u> Neither GAAS nor GAS require auditors to request personal financial statements from members of management.

5. <u>A) Required by both GAAS and GAS.</u> Under GAAS and GAS, the auditor would state that the audit was conducted in accordance with GAAS. Governmental auditors would also state that the audit was conducted in accordance with GAS.

6. <u>C) Required by GAS only.</u> GAS requires the auditor to report the views of responsible officials when reporting instances of fraud, noncompliance, and abuse.

7. <u>B) Required by neither GAAS nor GAS.</u> Both GAAS and GAS require the audit report to be modified for material misstatements in the financial statements.

8. <u>C) Required by GAS only.</u> GAS requires the auditor to state in the report that the audit was conducted in accordance with GAAS and GAS.

2. Competence and Quality Control (8 Gradable Items)

1. <u>F) Independent.</u> Audit organizations must be independent both in mind and appearance.

2. <u>A) Continuing education.</u> Governmental auditors are required to acquire 80 hours of continuing education in related topics every two years.

3. <u>D) Peer review.</u> A governmental audit organization must have a peer review every 3 years.

4. <u>F) Independent.</u> The conceptual framework indicates that auditors should identify, evaluate, and eliminate threats to independence.

5. <u>H) Corrective action.</u> Auditors should evaluate whether clients have taken corrective action based on findings of previous audits.

6. <u>E) GAGAS.</u> Auditors should state in their report that the audit was performed in accordance with GAGAS.

7. <u>B) Responsible officials.</u> If the audit report discloses fraud or noncompliance, the auditor should obtain the views of responsible officials of the audited entity.

8. <u>G) Governmental auditing.</u> At least 24 hours of continuing education each cycle should pertain directly to governmental auditing.

3. Government Auditing Standards (7 Gradable Items)

1. <u>A) Appropriate.</u> The report should indicate that the audit was conducted in accordance with both GAAS and *Government Auditing Standards*.

2. <u>A) Appropriate.</u> The report should state that the auditor has performed tests of compliance with provisions of certain laws, regulations, contracts, and grant agreements.

3. <u>A) Appropriate.</u> The report states that the purpose is to describe the scope of testing and the results of testing.

4. <u>C) Inappropriate because the auditor is required to plan and perform the audit to detect instances of noncompliance having a direct and material effect on the financial statements, not all instances of noncompliance.</u> The report should state that those standards require that we plan and perform the audit to obtain reasonable assurance about whether the financial statements are free of material misstatement.

5. <u>C) Inappropriate because the report does not express an opinion.</u> The report should describe the scope of testing of compliance with laws and regulations and present the results of those tests, including fraud and material noncompliance. It need not express an opinion.

6. <u>B) Inappropriate because no assurance should be provided.</u> No assurance on compliance, either positive or negative, need be expressed under *Government Auditing Standards*.

7. <u>C) Inappropriate because the report is silent as to limiting its distribution.</u> The report states that it is not intended for use by uninformed parties, but it does not limit the distribution of the report.

4. Compliance Issues (10 Gradable Items)

1. <u>B) Management.</u> It is management's responsibility to ensure compliance with laws and regulations.

2. <u>A) Auditor.</u> The auditor should consider those laws and regulations that have a direct and material effect on the financial statements in planning the audit.

3. <u>C) Neither management nor the auditor.</u> It is neither management's nor the auditor's responsibility to judge whether laws or regulations are fair.

4. <u>A) Auditor.</u> The auditor should identify the risks of pervasive noncompliance.

5. <u>A) Auditor.</u> The auditor should obtain written representations from management concerning laws and regulations.

6. <u>A) Auditor.</u> The auditor should read minutes of committee meetings relating to laws and regulations.

7. <u>B) Management.</u> It is management's responsibility to identify laws and regulations applicable to the organization.

8. <u>C) Neither management nor the auditor.</u> It is neither management's nor the auditor's responsibility to suggest new laws or regulations.

9. <u>B) Management.</u> It is management's responsibility to establish internal controls pertaining to compliance with laws and regulations.

10. <u>C) Neither management nor the auditor.</u> It is neither management's nor the auditor's responsibility to provide positive or negative assurance that no laws or regulations have been violated by employees.

5. Research (1 Gradable Item)

Answer: 935.16

AU-C Section 935 -- *Compliance Audits*

.16 In performing risk assessment procedures, the auditor should inquire of management about whether there are findings and recommendations in reports or other written communications resulting from previous audits, attestation engagements, and internal or external monitoring that directly relate to the objectives of the compliance audit. The auditor should gain an understanding of management's response to findings and recommendations that could have a material effect on the entity's compliance with the applicable compliance requirements (for example, taking corrective action). The auditor should use this information to assess risk and determine the nature, timing, and extent of the audit procedures for the compliance audit, including determining the extent to which testing the implementation of any corrective action is applicable to the audit objectives.

Gleim Simulation Grading

Task	Correct Responses		Gradable Items		Score per Task
1	___	÷	8	=	___
2	___	÷	8	=	___
3	___	÷	7	=	___
4	___	÷	10	=	___
1 (Research)	___	÷	1	=	___

	Total of Scores per Task	___
÷	Total Number of Tasks	5
	Total Score	___ %

Use **CPA Gleim Online** and **Simulation Wizard** to practice more task-based simulations in a realistic environment.

INDEX

GLEIM® - Experts in Accounting Education

CPA

GLEIM CPA REVIEW SYSTEM

Includes: Gleim Online, Review Books, CPA Test Prep, Simulation Wizard, Audio Review, Exam Rehearsal™, *How to Pass the CPA Exam: A System for Success* booklet, plus bonus Book Bag.

Also available by exam section (does not include Book Bag).

$989.95 x _____ = $_____

CMA

GLEIM CMA REVIEW SYSTEM

Includes: Gleim Online, Review Books, CMA Test Prep, Essay Wizard, Audio Review, Exam Rehearsal™, *How to Pass the CMA Exam: A System for Success* booklet, plus bonus Book Bag.

Also available by exam part (does not include Book Bag).

$739.95 x _____ = $_____

CIA

GLEIM CIA REVIEW SYSTEM (New 3-Part Exam)*

Includes: Gleim Online, Review Books, CIA Test Prep, Audio Review, Exam Rehearsal™, *How to Pass the CIA Exam: A System for Success* booklet, plus bonus Book Bag.

Also available by exam part (does not include Book Bag).
*The 4-Part format will remain available through the end of 2013.

$724.95 x _____ = $_____

EA

GLEIM EA REVIEW SYSTEM

Includes: Gleim Online, Review Books, EA Test Prep, Audio Review, Exam Rehearsal™, *EA Review: A System for Success* booklet, plus bonus Book Bag.

Also available by exam part (does not include Book Bag).

$629.95 x _____ = $_____

RTRP

GLEIM RTRP REVIEW SYSTEM*

Includes: Gleim Online, Question Bank Online, Exam Rehearsal™, 15 hours of CE.

*At the time of this printing, the RTRP exam is not currently being offered as a result of a court decision. An appeal has been filed, and may result in the reinstatement of this exam requirement. In the meantime, this course is still available for educational purposes.

$189.95 x _____ = $_____

EQE

"THE GLEIM EQE SERIES" EXAM QUESTIONS AND EXPLANATIONS

Includes: 5 Books and EQE Test Prep.

Also available by part.

$124.95 x _____ = $_____

CPE

GLEIM ONLINE CPE

Try a FREE 4-hour course at gleim.com/cpe
- Easy-to-Complete
- Informative
- Effective

Contact
GLEIM® PUBLICATIONS
for further assistance:

gleim.com
800.874.5346
sales@gleim.com

SUBTOTAL $_____

Complete your order on the next page

GLEIM PUBLICATIONS, INC.

P. O. Box 12848   Gainesville, FL 32604

TOLL FREE:	800.874.5346
LOCAL:	352.375.0772
FAX:	352.375.6940
INTERNET:	gleim.com
EMAIL:	sales@gleim.com

Customer service is available (Eastern Time):

8:00 a.m. - 7:00 p.m., Mon. - Fri.

9:00 a.m. - 2:00 p.m., Saturday

Please have your credit card ready, or save time by ordering online!

SUBTOTAL (from previous page) $ _____

Add applicable sales tax for shipments within Florida. _____

Shipping (nonrefundable) 14.00

TOTAL $ _____

Email us for prices/instructions on shipments outside the 48 contiguous states, or simply order online.

NAME (please print) _____

ADDRESS _____ Apt. _____
(street address required for UPS/Federal Express)

CITY _____ STATE _____ ZIP _____

____ MC/VISA/DISC/AMEX ____ Check/M.O. Daytime Telephone _(____)____

Credit Card No. _____ - _____ - _____ - _____

Exp. ____/____ Signature _____
Month / Year

Email address _____

1. We process and ship orders daily, within one business day over 98.8% of the time. Call by 3:00 pm for same day service.

2. Gleim Publications, Inc. guarantees the immediate refund of all resalable texts, unopened and un-downloaded Test Prep Software, and unopened and un-downloaded audios returned within 30 days of purchase. Accounting and Academic online Test Prep and other online courses may be canceled within 30 days of purchase if no more than the first study unit or lesson has been accessed. In addition, Online CPE courses may be canceled within 30 days of adding the course to your Personal Transcript if the Outline has not yet been accessed. Accounting Exam Rehearsals and Practice Exams may be canceled within 30 days of purchase if they have not been started. Aviation Test Prep Online may be canceled within 30 days of purchase if no more than the first study unit has been accessed. Other Aviation online courses may be canceled within 30 days of purchase if no more than two study units have been accessed. This policy applies only to products that are purchased directly from Gleim Publications, Inc. No refunds will be provided on opened or downloaded Test Prep Software or audios, partial returns of package sets, or shipping and handling charges. Any freight charges incurred for returned or refused packages will be the purchaser's responsibility. For more information regarding the Gleim Return Policy, please contact our offices at (800) 874-5346.

3. Please PHOTOCOPY this order form for others.

4. No CODs. Orders from individuals must be prepaid

Subject to change without notice. 11/13

For updates and other important information, visit our website.

GLEIM
KNOWLEDGE
TRANSFER
SYSTEMS®

gleim.com